Street by Street

LIVERPOOL

BIRKENHEAD, BOOTLE, RUNCORN, ST HELENS, WARRINGTON, WIDNES

Bebington, Crosby, Formby, Heswall, Hoylake, Kirkby, Maghull, Neston, Prescot, Wallasey, West Kirby

GAZETTEER SYMBOL KEY

- ☎ - telephone number
- ✆ - telephone booking service
- @ - email address
- web address
- fax number
- map page number and grid reference

1st edition published July 2008

Published by AA Publishing (a trading name of Automobile Association Developments Limited, whose registered office is Fanum House, Basing View, Basingstoke, Hampshire RG21 4EA. Registered number 1878835).

Cartography produced by the Mapping Services Department of The Automobile Association. (A03534)

A CIP Catalogue record for this book is available from the British Library.

Design and management for listings section by ey communications Ltd. (www.eysite.com). Editorial services by Pam Stagg

Listings data provided by Global DataPoint Limited, London

Printed by Oriental Press in Dubai

The Automobile Association would like to thank the following photographers, companies and picture libraries for their assistance in the preparation of this book.

Abbreviations for the picture credits are as follows: (t) top; (b) bottom; (l) left; (r) right; (AA) AA World Travel Library.
Front Cover AA/S Day;
3 (t) AA/S Day; 3 (c) AA; 3 (b) AA/S Day

Every effort has been made to trace the copyright holders, and we apologise in advance for any accidental errors. We would be happy to apply the corrections in the following edition of this publication.

Ref: ML47y

Opposite page
Top and centre: The Royal Liver Building with the famous Royal Liver Birds perched on the towers
Bottom: Rowing past Albert Dock

Liverpool...

Liverpool, European Capital of Culture 2008, gazes out across the River Mersey to the sea as it has done for centuries, its grand architecture – the Royal Liver Building, the Cunard Building and the Port of Liverpool Building – a reminder of the days when it was a great port. Albert Dock, built in 1864, has been sensitively restored to become the city's recreational centrepiece, this is where you'll find Tate Liverpool, The Beatles Story and The Merseyside Maritime Museum, along with trendy stores, art shops and gallery outlets and stylish bars and restaurants.

Liverpool has some of the largest big-name high street stores in the country. Church Street in the heart of the city, the Cavern Walks shopping complex, the Met Quarter, Bold Street, St John's Shopping Centre and Clayton Square are just some of the options. Liverpool ONE, a new shopping and leisure district in the heart of the city centre, is due to open from Spring 2008. To help you make the most of your leisure time in Liverpool we have provided a useful gazetteer covering a range of attractions from outstanding museums and art galleries, to cinemas and grand theatres featuring everything from opera to live music and classical ballet. Bars, ranging from traditional public houses to the latest designer-chic cafes and cabaret venues, all contribute to Liverpool's lively night scene.

Entries are listed alphabetically (ignoring The) under each category heading. The map reference at the end of each entry denotes the map page number in the mapping section and the grid square in which the street/road is to be found, not the individual establishments. We have given the street name, town/city name, post code, telephone and fax numbers and, where possible, email

Please note: the entries in the following listings section were provided by a third party and are not in any way recommended or endorsed by the AA.

TOURIST ATTRACTIONS

Albert Dock

Situated in the largest group of Grade I listed buildings in the UK, the Albert Dock houses many award-winning visitor attractions including Tate Liverpool, the famous Beatles Story, Merseyside Maritime Museum and the new International Slavery Museum. You can join a number of fascinating Liverpool tours, including the creepy Shiverpool Ghost Tour or a city and water tour on the YellowDuckmarine. There is also a selection of bars and restaurants.

Albert Dock, Liverpool, Merseyside L3 4AF
☎ 0151 708 7334
www.albertdock.com
0151 708 0929
Page 6-B7

The Beatles Story

Established in 1990, The Beatles Story provides an experience that helps to create a fully rounded understanding of the great 60s band. It is divided into 18 separate features, and charts the success of the group from their early days in Hamburg right through to the eventual break-up of the band and their subsequent solo careers.

Britannia Vaults, Albert Dock, Liverpool, Merseyside L3 4AD
☎ 0151 7091 963
@ info@beatlesstory.com
www.beatlesstory.com
0151 7080 039
Page 6-B7

Birkenhead Priory and St Marys Tower

This Benedictine Monastery was established in around 1150. First restored over a century ago the site continues to develop with museum displays, concert space and a chapel. Visitors can climb the tower of the parish church, now also a memorial to those who lost their lives aboard the submarine *Thetis*, and experience the views up, down and across the Mersey to Liverpool.

Priory Street, Birkenhead, Merseyside CH41 5JH
☎ 0151 666 1249
www.wirral.gov.uk
Page 3-J5

Black Bear Park

Black Bear Park is a linear park that provides links across the Latchford, Stockton Heath and Westy areas of the town. A once busy canal route, the park has now been transformed into a wildlife haven. Plants and animals have been gradually encouraged on to the site by a programme of tree and wild flower planting and the creation of habitats such as the excavation of the pond.

Loushers Lane, Latchford, Warrington, Cheshire WA1
☎ 01925 232184
www.warrington.gov.uk/Leisureandculture/Parksandopenspaces/parks/
Page 130-B1

Cross Keys House

This contemporary building is home to a spectacular and daring piece of public art.

37–41 Moorfields, Liverpool, Merseyside L2 2BL
Page 6-D3

Croxteth Hall and Country Park

Croxteth Hall and Country Park is at the heart of a country estate covering hundreds of square miles and was the ancestral home of the Molyneux family, the Earls of Sefton. Attractions include the Historic Hall, Croxteth Home Farm and the Victorian Garden and a 500-acre country park.

Croxteth Hall Lane, Liverpool, Merseyside L12 0HB
☎ 0151 233 6910
@ croxtethcountrypark@liverpool.gov.uk
www.croxteth.co.uk
0151 228 2817
Page 42-D5

Gulliver's Warrington

Gulliver's Warrington is nestled within a park setting, where much of the fantasy is created by towering trees and a lake. Attractions include tumbling and juggling fun of Circus World, high noon in Western World and walk with dinosaurs in the prehistoric Lost World.

Old Hall, Warrington, Cheshire WA5 9YZ
☎ 01925 444888
@ info_world@gulliversfun.co.uk
www.gulliversfun.co.uk
Page 83-E4

Knowsley Safari Park

Knowsley Safari Park was opened in 1971 by the 18th Earl of Derby and features around 30 species of mammals roaming in 500 acres. Birds, reptiles and invertebrates can also be seen.

Knowsley Safari Park, Prescot, Merseyside L34 4AN
☎ 0151 430 9009
@ safari.park@knowsley.com
www.knowsley.com/safari
0151 426 3677
Page 59-F1

Leasowe Lighthouse

Leasowe Lighthouse stands 101-feet tall on Leasowe Common in Wirral and was one of four lights on the North Wirral Foreshore, used to guide ships into the entrance to the Rock Channel and the port of Liverpool. The Lighthouse features guided tours, special events and a visitor centre with displays about Leasowe Lighthouse and the surroundings.

Leasowe Common, Moreton, Wirral, Merseyside CH46 4TA
☎ 0151 678 5488
@ info@leasowelighthouse.co.uk
www.leasowelighthouse.co.uk
Page 66-A2

National Trust: 20 Forthlin Road

Twenty Forthlin Road is a 1950s terraced house, where the Beatles met, rehearsed and wrote many of their earliest songs. Displays include contemporary photographs by Michael McCartney and early Beatles memorabilia while an audio tour features contributions from both Michael and Sir Paul McCartney.

20 Forthlin Road, Allerton, Liverpool, Merseyside L24 1YP
☎ 0870 900 0256
@ 20forthlinroad@nationaltrust.org.uk
www.nationaltrust.org.uk
Page 119-G2

National Trust: Formby

A stretch of coastline set between the sea and Formby town offers miles of walks through the woods and dunes. The site features long sandy beaches and pine woods, home to the red squirrel.

Victoria Road, Freshfield, Formby, Liverpool, Merseyside L37 1LJ

☎ 01704 878591
@ formby@nationaltrust.org.uk
www.nationaltrust.org.uk
01704 835378
Page 16-A1

National Trust: Mendips

John Lennon lived at Mendips with his Aunt Mimi and Uncle George. The house gives an insight into the life and times of John Lennon as a boy through photographs, documents and other memorabilia. It was at this house that some of the earliest Beatles' hits were first composed.

Mendips, Woolton, Liverpool, Merseyside L24 1YP

☎ 0870 900 0256
www.nationaltrust.org.uk/
Page 120-B1

National Trust: Speke Hall, Garden and Estate

The Speke Hall was built in 1530 and features the Great Hall and priest hole from Tudor times along with the Oak Parlour and smaller rooms with William Morris wallpapers. The restored garden has spring bulbs, a rose garden, summer border and stream garden as well as woodland walks.

The Walk, Liverpool, Merseyside L24 1XD

☎ 0151 427 7231
@ spekehall@nationaltrust.org.uk
www.nationaltrust.org.uk/
0151 427 9860
Page 141-F4

National Wildflower Centre

National Wildflower Centre is set in a Victorian park and features seasonal wildflower demonstration areas, a working garden nursery, children's play area, exhibitions and interactive information about wildflowers.

Court Hey Park, Roby Road, Liverpool, Merseyside L16 3NA

☎ 0151 738 1913
@ info@nwc.org.uk
www.nwc.org.uk
Page 74-B4

Orford Park

Orford Park covers 18 acres and offers a wide network of footpaths, picnic benches and a children's play area.

Alder Lane, Orford, Warrington, Cheshire WA2 8AG

☎ 01925 658098
@ rangers@warrington.gov.uk
www.warrington.gov.uk/Leisureandculture/Parksandopenspaces/parks/Orford_Park.aspx
Page 84-A5

Pier Head

Pier Head offers river cruises ranging from a Beatles Cruise and Glam Rock Cruise to a Christmas Cruise and Wildlife Discovery Cruise.

Mersey Ferries, Georges Parade, Liverpool, Merseyside L3 1DP

☎ 0151 227 2660
www.merseyferries.co.uk
0151 236 2298
Page 6-B5

The Port Sunlight Heritage Centre

Port Sunlight is a 19th-century garden village in Wirral and features a museum, an art gallery, garden centre, church, theatre and landscaped gardens.

95 Greendale Road, Port Sunlight, Wirral, Merseyside CH62 4XE

☎ 0151 644 6466
@ info@portsunlightvillage.com
www.portsunlightvillage.com
0151 645 8973
Page 138-B1

Sankey Valley Park

The Sankey Valley Park features woodlands, grasslands and water bodies supporting an array of wildlife. The central section of the park is family orientated with a children's playground, a maze and lawned areas with facilities for birdwatching, angling, cycling and walking.

Bewsey Old Hall, Bewsey Farm Close, Old Hall, Warrington, Merseyside WA5 5PB

☎ 01925 571836
@ rangers@warrington.gov.uk
www.warrington.gov.uk/Leisureandculture/Parksandopenspaces/parks/Sankey_Valley_Park.aspx
Page 49-E1

Sefton Park Palm House

Sefton Park in Liverpool is arguably the best known and most loved park by locals. The magnificent 200-acre park looks like a natural landscape rather than a manmade park. Among the park's many features are a boating lake, replica statues of Eros and Peter Pan and a cafe. The Palm House, a popular visitor attraction, showcases plants from around the world.

Aigburth, Liverpool, Merseyside L17 1AP

☎ 0151 233 2008, 0151 726 2415
@ info@palmhouse.org.uk
www.palmhouse.org.uk
Page 82-D5

Shore Road Pumping Station (The Birkenhead Packet)

The pumping station houses the *Giant Grasshopper* engine and portrays the story of the building and surroundings through an interactive video presentation.

Shore Road, Woodside, Birkenhead, Merseyside CH41 6DN

☎ 0151 650 1182
www.wirral.gov.uk
Page 3-H3

Spaceport

Take a virtual journey through space and time at Spaceport, an amazing space-themed attraction. Get hands-on with interactive exhibits and learn all about space and space travel.

Victoria Place, Wallasey, Merseyside CH44 6QY

☎ 0151 330 1333
@ info@spaceport.org.uk
www.spaceport.org.uk
Page 69-G3

Stadt Moers Park

Pottery Lane, Whiston, Merseyside L35 3RG

L35 3RG
Page 76-C3

Sudley House

Sudley House has within its walls the collection of paintings by Gainsborough, Reynolds, Landseer and Turner.

Mossley Hill Road, Aigburth, Liverpool, Merseyside L18 8BX

☎ 0151 724 3245, 0151 207 0001
www.liverpoolmuseum.org.uk
Page 118-D1

Vale Park

Vale Park, New Brighton, Wallasey, Merseyside CH45 1LZ

☎ 0151 647 2366
www.wirral.gov.uk
Page 52-A3

Walton Hall Gardens

Walton Hall Gardens were built in 1830s and designed by Edmund Sharpe of Lancaster, who later became famous for Gothic revival architecture. The park is home to woodland birds, tree creepers, woodpeckers, bats, foxes, owls, squirrels and weasels. Facilities at the park include spacious lawns, picnic areas, a play area, children's zoo and heritage centre.

Walton Lea Road, Higher Walton, Warrington, Cheshire WA4 6SN

☎ 01925 601617
✆ 01925 263797
@ waltonhall@warrington.gov.uk
www.warrington.gov.uk/Leisureandculture/
Page 129-G5

Wigg Island Community Park and Visitor Centre

A park and nature reserve with a large variety of birdlife, insects and wild flowers.

Astmoor Road, Runcorn, Cheshire WA7 1DA

☎ 01928 568 219
www2.halton.gov.uk/nature/
Page 9-H3

Woolston Park

Woolston Park covers 56 acres and was officially opened in 1977. It was created from neglected farmland to provide a refuge for people and wildlife among the rapidly expanding local community. The park features a wildfowl pond besides an array of willow trees.

Ranger Centre, Woolston, Warrington, Cheshire WA1 4LN

☎ 01925 824398
@ rangers@warrington.gov.uk
www.warrington.gov.uk/Leisureandculture/Parksandopenspaces/
Page 85-F5

The World of Glass

The visitor centre offers an insight into the world of glass blowing through live demonstrations and displays. There is also a special effects show that takes visitors on a journey through time and space.

Chalon Way East, St Helens, Merseyside WA10 1BX

☎ 0870 011 4466
@ info@worldofglass.com
www.worldofglass.com
01744 616966
Page 11-H6

MUSEUMS

Artreach

Unit B24, Brunswick Small Business Centre, Brunswick Business Park, Liverpool, Merseyside L3 4BD

☎ 0151 708 7620
Page 93-H4

Catalyst

Catalyst is a science centre (and museum) solely devoted to chemistry and how the products of chemistry are used in every day life – from medicines to Meccano. The museum displays are about the 'chemistry industry' and its role in our lives, past present and future.

Mersey Road, Widnes, Cheshire WA8 0DF

☎ 015 1420 1121
@ info@catalyst.org.uk
www.catalyst.org.uk
0151 495 2030
Page 146-A1

Cube Liverpool

Launched in November 1998, the museum is committed to the investigation, discussion and advancement of design quality within the built environment.

The Tea Factory, 82 Wood Street, Liverpool, Merseyside L1 4DQ

☎ 01612 375525
@ info@cube.org.uk
www.cube.org.uk
Page 7-F5

HM Customs and Excise National Museum

The museum holds the national collection of the Department of Customs and Excise. It displays the tools of the job, prints, paintings and photographs relating to the work of the department and offers an insight into the world of smuggling, prohibited goods and concealment.

Albert Dock, Liverpool, Merseyside L3 4AQ

☎ 0151 478 4499
www.liverpoolmuseums.org.uk/customs
Page 6-B6

International Slavery Museum

Based in the Merseyside Maritime Museum at Liverpool's Albert Dock, the museum explores both the historical and contemporary aspects of slavery. The museum addresses the many legacies of the slave trade and tells stories of bravery and rebellion among the enslaved people.

Albert Dock, Liverpool, Merseyside L3 4AQ

☎ 0151 478 4499
www.liverpoolmuseums.org.uk/ism
Page 6-B6

Liverpool Football Club Museum and Tour Centre

The museum features two film shows – the first is in a recreation of the standing Kop and tells the story of the 'Kopites', the other is a cinema showing *One Night in May*, the wonderful documentary about that night in Istanbul, May 2005, when Liverpool won the Champions League trophy. The stadium tour takes visitors behind the scenes at Anfield, visiting the dressing rooms, down the tunnel to the sound of the crowd, a chance to touch the famous 'This Is Anfield' sign and sit in the team dug-out.

Anfield Road, Liverpool, Merseyside L4 0TH

☎ 0151 260 6677
www.liverpoolfc.tv/club/tour.htm
Page 54-C3

Merseyside Maritime Museum

The museum narrates the maritime history of Liverpool. The exhibits offer an insight into shipwrecks, the slave trade and maritime wonders over the centuries.

Albert Dock, Liverpool, Merseyside L3 4AQ
☎ 0151 478 4499
www.liverpoolmuseums.org.uk/maritime
Page 6-B6

National Conservation Centre

The Conservation Centre exhibits everything from Roman sculptures, Cold War artefacts and spacesuits, through displays and interactive activities.

Whitechapel, Liverpool, Merseyside L1 6HZ
☎ 015 1478 4999
www.liverpoolmuseums.org.uk/conservation
Page 6-E3

North West Museum of Road Transport

The museum houses the North West Museum of Transport Limited's collection of vehicles. It can trace its roots back over 30 years, when a group of enthusiasts from the St Helens area got together to raise funds to preserve an ex-St Helens trolleybus which was still running in Bradford.

The Old Bus Depot, Hall Street, St Helens, Merseyside WA10 1DU
☎ 01744 451681
@ general@hallstreetdepot.info
www.hallstreetdepot.info
Page 11-J4

Norton Priory Museum and Gardens

Discover the intriguing displays in the atmospheric, prize-winning museum. Find out about the lives of the priory canons, and see examples of the work of medieval craftspeople. Explore the displays which recall the 400 years when Norton Priory was home to the Brooke family.

Tudor Road, Manor Park, Runcorn, Cheshire WA7 1SX
☎ 01928 569895
@ info@nortonpriory.org
www.nortonpriory.org
Page 147-H3

Prescot Museum

Prescot Museum located in a Georgian town house, which was once the site of the local cockerel fighting pit. Prescot has always been famous for its clock and watch making industry and became known as a 'town of little workshops', due to the different parts of the watches being made in workshops attached to houses throughout the town. The museum reflects this legacy through its permanent local history displays. It also explores other local industries, such as pottery manufacture, cable making and mining.

34 Church Street, Prescot, Merseyside L34 3LA
☎ 0151 430 7787
@ prescot.museum@knowsley.gov.uk
www.knowsley.gov.uk/leisure/museums_galleries/prescot_museum.html
Page 59-G4

Rocky's

75, Argyle Street, Birkenhead, Merseyside CH41 6AB
☎ 0151 647 5063
Page 3-G4

Smithy Heritage Centre

Village Hall, Kiln Lane, Eccleston, St Helens, Merseyside WA10 4RA
☎ 07979 066148
Page 47-E2

University of Liverpool, The Garstang Museum of Archaeology

The museum collection contains classical and prehistoric material, most of these being the personal collections of Professors Bosanquet and Droop and Mr R W Hutchinson. There is also a selection of coins from the Barnard and Chevasse collections as well as a photographic archive along with excavations field note books, correspondence and drawings.

14 Abercromby Square, Liverpool, Merseyside L69 3BX
☎ 0151 794 2467
@ hosace@liv.ac.uk
www.liv.ac.uk/sace/facilities/museum.htm
Fax 0151 794 2226
Page 7-K5

University of Liverpool, Museum of Dentistry

The museum contains many early dental artefacts, early documents such as apprentice indentures, research and teaching material connected with famous figures in the history of dentistry such as Cryer, Gottlieb and Gysi, as well as material of a more modern nature. There is also a collection of early textbooks on dentistry and a large collection of dental instruments and furniture.

Edwards Building, School of Dental Surgery, Pembroke Place, Liverpool, Merseyside L3 5PS
☎ 0151 706 2000
www.liv.ac.uk
Page 7-J3

Warrington Museum and Art Gallery

The museum and art gallery's social history collection consists of over 50,000 objects and covers all material relating to Warrington's history from post-medieval period right up to the present day. Collections relate to the municipal, domestic, working life and the leisure conditions of Warrington's inhabitants.

Bold Street, Warrington, Cheshire WA1 1JG
☎ 01925 442733
@ museum@warrington.gov.uk
museum.warrington.gov.uk
Fax 01925 443257
Page 12-C6

Western Approaches

Western Approaches is a reconstructed museum of original World War II war rooms which brings history to life. The main operations room, the Admiral's office, teleprinter station and also a reconstructed educational centre, with an Anderson Shelter and bombed-out room are the main attractions.

1–3 Rumford Street, Liverpool, Merseyside L2 3SZ
☎ 0151 227 2008
www.liverpoolwarmuseum.co.uk
Page 6-C3

Williamson Art Gallery and Museum

Williamson Art Gallery and Museum was opened in December 1928 and it houses the majority of Birkenhead's collection of artistic masterpieces in a series of varied and well proportioned galleries. On permanent display are Victorian oil paintings, English watercolours, Liverpool Porcelain and Della Robbia pottery along with

a range of collections from local history and ship models to fine decorative arts.

Slatey Road, Birkenhead, Merseyside CH43 4UE
☎ 0151 652 4177
@ williamsonartgallery@wirral.gov.uk
www.wirral.gov.uk/
Page 2-A7

Wirral Museum

The building is a combination of Scottish granite and local sandstone and was designed by local architect, Charles Ellison in 1882. Among the artefacts on display is a model of the Woodside area. Additional exhibits include the Wirral Silver and Mayoral collections, and a collection of Della Robbia pottery.

Hamilton Square, Birkenhead, Merseyside CH41 5BR
☎ 0151 666 4010
@ wirralmuseum@wirral.gov.uk
www.wirral.gov.uk/
Page 3-H4

Wirral Transport Museum

Wirral Transport Museum shows a selection of vintage buses representing a variety of local operators over a number of years. There is also a display of cars and motorcycles and a 1930s garage scene. The 26-foot model railway layout is always the centre of attaction.

1 Taylor Street, Birkenhead, Merseyside CH41 1BG
☎ 0151 666 2756
@ info@wirraltransportmuseum.org
www.wirraltransportmuseum.org
Fax 0151 666 3965
Page 3-H2

Woodside Visitor Centre

Wirral Museum Office, Woodside, Birkenhead, Merseyside CH41 6DU
☎ 0151 647 6780
www.visitliverpool.com
Page 3-J3

World Museum Liverpool

The museum has collections on archaeology, ethnology, natural and physical sciences as well as a planetarium.

William Brown Street, Liverpool, Merseyside L3 8EN
☎ 0151 478 4399, 0151 478 4393
www.liverpoolmuseums.org.uk/wml
Page 7-F2

ART GALLERIES AND VISUAL ARTS

A Foundation

The gallery is housed in three former industrial buildings and now serves as three seperate spaces: The Coach Shed, The Furnace and The Blade Factory.

67 Greenland Street, Liverpool, Merseyside L1 0BY
☎ 0151 706 0600
@ press@afoundation.org.uk
www.greenlandstreet.org.uk
Page 93-H1

Almiro Gallery

A family run gallery with a focus on photography and contemporary art.

45 Mersey View, Waterloo, Liverpool, Merseyside L22 6QA
☎ 0845 230 0043
@ info@almirogallery.com
www.almirogallery.com
Page 28-D2

Blackthorn Gallery

Opened in 1997, this contemporary art collection can be viewed by appointment only.

1st Floor, 6 Grange Road West, Charing Cross, Birkenhead, Merseyside CH41 4DA
☎ 01516 490099
@ info@theblackthorn.com
www.blackthorn-online.co.uk
Page 2-B5

Bridewell Studios

The Bridewell Studios building has been run by local, national and international artists since 1976 and regular exhibitions are held by painters, sculptors, printmakers, fashion designers, furniture makers, ceramicists, textile artists, photographers and multimedia artists.

Prescot Street, Liverpool, Merseyside L7 8UE
☎ 0151 263 6730
@ info@bridewellstudios.co.uk
www.bridewellstudios.co.uk
Page 7-K2

The Cornerstone Gallery

The gallery is set on the Liverpool Hope University campus and seeks to assist and promote new artists.

Hope at Everton, Haigh Street, Liverpool, Merseyside L3 8QB
☎ 0151 291 3997
@ thecornerstonegallery@hope.ac.uk
www.hope.ac.uk/cornerstonegallery
Fax 0151 291 3191
Page 7-J1

EggSpace

EggSpace is a popular meeting place at the heart of Liverpool's culture. It boasts one of the most panoramic views of the city and is a unique fusion of an independent gallery space and cafe, with a relaxed and bohemian atmosphere.

2nd Floor, 16–18 Newington, Liverpool, Merseyside L1 4ED
☎ 07915 075503, 07837 219312, 07811 059702
@ info@eggspace.org
www.eggspace.org
Page 7-G5

Huyton Gallery and Library

The gallery provides opportunities for professional and non-professional artists to exhibit their work through open exhibitions. It also offers a diverse educational programme linked to the exhibitions in the form of workshops, residencies, outreach work and collaborative projects.

Huyton Library, Civic Way, Huyton, Merseyside L36 9GD
☎ 0151 443 5642, 0151 443 3734
@ huyton.library.dlcs@knowsley.gov.uk
www.knowsley.gov.uk/leisure/museums_galleries/
Page 75-G3

Kirkby Gallery

Newtown Gardens, Kirkby Merseyside L32 8RR
☎ 0151 443 5619
www.knowsley.gov.uk
Page 33-H2

Kitchen Gallery

The Kitchen Gallery started in 2003 as an exhibition space attached to the studios of two artists, Sarah Nicholson and Stanislaw Jan Krakiewicz. In April 2007 they successfully applied for

Arts Council support for a group exhibition entitled You Are Here, celebrating the creativity of the area.

Norton Priory Museum and Gardens, Runcorn, Cheshire WA7 1SX

☎ 0151 733 5986
@ info@kitchengallery.uk.com
www.kitchengallery.uk.com
Page 147-H3

Lady Lever Art Gallery

The Lady Lever Art Gallery holds collections of fine and decorative arts. It was founded in 1922 by William Hesketh Lever, the first Lord Leverhulme, in memory of his wife. The gallery displays works collected by Leverhulme throughout his life. British 18th- and 19th-century painting, 18th-century furniture and outstanding collections of Wedgwood and Chinese porcelain are among the treasures on show.

Lower Road, Port Sunlight Village, Wirral, Merseyside CH62 5EQ

☎ 0151 478 4136
www.liverpoolmuseums.org.uk/ladylever
Page 116-B5

Novas CUC North West

Set in the heart of the emerging Independent Arts Quarter of Liverpool, the Novas Contemporary Urban Centre North West holds a gallery, restaurant, theatre and a workspace for artists.

41–51 Greenland Street, Liverpool, Merseyside L1 0BS

☎ 0151 706 6900
www.novasscarman.org/contemporary-urban-centres/north-west
Page 93-H1

The Open Eye Gallery

A venue for private functions, receptions and corporate events. Against the backdrop of contemporary photography exhibitions, the gallery offers a unique atmosphere for a formal or informal event. Open Eye Gallery supports, promotes and exhibits photography from the UK and beyond.

28–32 Wood Street, Liverpool, Merseyside L1 4AQ

☎ 0151 709 9460
@ info@openeye.org.uk
www.openeye.org.uk
Page 7-F5

The People's Centre

Former Merseyside Trade Union was founded in the late 1970s to provide facilities and services to all members of the local community.

50–54 Mount Pleasant, Liverpool, Merseyside L3 5SD

☎ 0151 709 3995
www.thepeoplescentre.com/
Fax 0151-708-8862
Page 7-G5

Static Gallery

Static is an art organisation based in Liverpool, UK. Its aim is to increase the production of cultural activity and to build the critical infrastructures that support this nationally and internationally. The development and distribution of ideas, communication with an audience and the growth of a critical sphere are processes that interest most people involved in visual culture. Static hopes to contribute to these areas through a range of deliberately varied, and even conflicting, activities.

23 Roscoe Lane, Liverpool, Merseyside L1 9JD

☎ 0151 707 1703
@ mail@static-ops.org
www.static-ops.org
Page 7-G6

Tate Liverpool

The galleries display selections from the Tate Collection. This comprises the National Collection of British Art from the year 1500 to the present day and also international modern art.

Albert Dock, Liverpool, Merseyside L3 4BB

☎ 0151 702 7400
@ visiting.liverpool@tate.org.uk
www.tate.org.uk/liverpool
Fax 0151 702 7401
Page 6-B7

The University of Liverpool Art Gallery

The art gallery houses permanent displays of fine and decorative art from the University's collections. Elements of these displays are changed on a regular basis and a number of temporary exhibitions are held throughout the year. The University of Liverpool Art Gallery and Collections exist to promote and display art for the education and enjoyment of members of the University and the public, and ensure the care and conservation of this aspect of the University's inheritance.

3 Abercromby Square, Liverpool, Merseyside L69 7WY

☎ 0151 794 2348
@ artgall@liv.ac.uk
www.liv.ac.uk/artgall
Fax 0151 794 2343
Page 7-K5

View Two Gallery

The View Two Gallery is a performance space exhibiting work of art, sculpture, paintings, prints and photography.

23 Mathew Street, Liverpool, Merseyside L2 6RE

☎ 0151 236 9444
@ info@viewtwogallery.co.uk
www.viewtwogallery.co.uk
Fax 0151 236 9555
Page 6-D4

Walker Art Gallery

For over 120 years the gallery has held one of the finest collections of fine and decorative art in Europe. The huge displays cover Renaissance masters to contemporary stars.

William Brown Street, Liverpool, Merseyside L3 8EL

☎ 0151 478 4199
www.liverpoolmuseums.org.uk/walker
Page 7-F2

Warrington Museum and Art Gallery

The museum and art gallery's social history collection consists of over 50,000 objects and covers all material relating to Warrington's history from post-medieval period right up to the present day. Collections relate to the municipal, domestic, working life and the leisure conditions of Warrington's inhabitants.

Bold Street, Warrington, Cheshire WA1 1JG

☎ 01925 442733
@ museum@warrington.gov.uk
museum.warrington.gov.uk
Fax 01925 443257
Page 12-C6

ART CENTRES

Bluecoat Arts Centre

Its unique Queen Anne style architecture, cobbled front courtyard and secret garden place it among the top visitor attractions in the region. This Grade I listed building is an architectural gem and, at almost 290 years old, is the oldest building in the city centre.

School Lane, Liverpool, Merseyside L1 3BX
☎ 0151 709 5297
@ admin@bluecoatartscentre.com
www.bluecoatartscentre.com
Page 6-E5

The Brindley Arts Centre

The Brindley is Halton's brand new, purpose-built theatre and arts centre.

High Street, Runcorn, Cheshire WA7 1BG
☎ 0151424 2061
✆ 0151 907 8360
@ thebrindley@halton.gov.uk
www.thebrindley.org.uk
Page 8-E4

FACT

FACT, the Foundation for Art & Creative Technology is the UKs leading organisation for the commissioning and presentation of film, video and new media art forms.

88 Wood Street, Liverpool, Merseyside L1 4DQ
☎ 0151 707 4450
✆ 0870 758 3217
@ info@fact.co.uk
www.fact.co.uk
Page 7-G6

Liverpool Lighthouse

The Liverpool Lighthouse boasts a spacious auditorium (King's Hall) and offers many other conference rooms, rehearsal space and dance workshops. This former cinema is ideal for music events, performances, presentations and conferences.

Oakfield Road, Anfield, Liverpool, Merseyside L4 0UF
☎ 0151 4762342
@ info@liverpoollighthouse.com
www.liverpoollighthouse.com
Page 54-C4

Pacific Road

Pacific Road is a centre for events and conferences both on a local and national level.

Pacific Road, Birkenhead, Merseyside CH41 1LJ
☎ 0151 666 2756
✆ 0151 647 0752
@ pacificroad@wirral.gov.uk
www.pacificroad.co.uk
Fax 0151 649 0161
Page 3-H2

Pyramid & Parr Hall

Pyramid and Parr Hall, Warrington's Centre for the Arts, is a prime spot for arts and entertainment.

Cultural Quarter, Palmyra Square South, Warrington, Cheshire WA1 1BL
☎ 01925 442345
@ pyramid@warrington.gov.uk
www.pyramid.org.uk
Fax 01925 442888
Page 12-C6

DANCE AND PERFORMING ARTS

Liverpool Olympia

One of Liverpool's largest concert venues with interior decor modelled on the Moscow Kirov Ballet.

West Derby Road, Liverpool, Merseyside L6 9BY
☎ 0151 263 6633
www.liverpoololympia.com/
Page 71-H2

Royal Court Theatre

The theatre hosts a wide variety of shows including plays, ballet, musical events and comedy.

1 Roe Street, Liverpool, Merseyside L1 1HL
☎ 0870 787 1866
www.royalcourtliverpool.co.uk
Page 7-F3

Theatre Royal

The theatre provides a wide variety of entertainment from top-class comedians to musical shows.

Corporation Street, St Helens, Merseyside WA10 1LQ
☎ 01744 756000
www.sthelenstheatreroyal.co.uk
Page 11-H5

Wired Aerial Space

Theatre specialising in theatre-based aerial dance work.

The Higher Space, 10 Cotton Street, Liverpool, Merseyside L3 7DY
☎ 07855 840822
@ info@wiredaerialtheatre.com
www.wiredaerialtheatre.com/
Page 70-B1

LIVE MUSIC VENUES

Alma De Cuba

St Peters Church, Seel Street, Liverpool, Merseyside L1 4AZ
☎ 0151 702 7394
Page 7-F6

Bar Hannah

The bar hosts weekly open mic nights and a stage for live bands.

2 Leece Street, Liverpool, Merseyside L1 2TR
☎ 0151 708 5959
✆ 07710 111197
@ general@barhannah.co.uk
www.barhannah.co.uk
Page 7-G6

Barfly Liverpool

90 Seel Street, Liverpool, Merseyside L1 4BH
☎ 0870 9070999
@ liverpool.info@barflyclub.com
www.barflyclub.com
Page 7-F6

Blundell Street

57 Blundell Street, Liverpool, Merseyside L1 0AJ
☎ 0151 709 5779
www.blundellstreet.com
Page 93-H1

Carling Academy Liverpool

11–13 Hotham Street, Liverpool, Merseyside L3 5UF
☎ 01517 073200
@ boxoffice@liverpool-academy.co.uk
www.liverpool-academy.co.uk
Fax 01417 073201
Page 7-G3

The Cavern Club

It's difficult to dispute claims that this is the most famous club in the world. The Beatles famously played here before they knew worldwide fame, and it remains high on everyone's list of things-to-do while visiting Liverpool.

10 Mathew Street, Liverpool, Merseyside L2 6RE
☎ 0151 236 1964
@ info@cavernclub.org
www.cavernclub.org
Page 6-D4

The Head Of Steam, Liverpool

A family run bar, restaurant and entertainment venue.

7 Lime Street, Liverpool, Merseyside L1 1RJ
☎ 0151 707 9559
@ liverpool@theheadofsteam.co.uk
www.headofsteam.co.uk
0151 707 0550
Page 7-F3

Hotel California

A live music venue situated in Wirral, showcasing tribute bands and club nights.

2 New Chester Road, Tranmere, Wirral, Merseyside CH41 9AY
☎ 0151 666 1668
@ thehotelcalifornia@hotmail.co.uk
www.thehotelcalifornia.co.uk
0151 647 1939
Page 3-H6

Hoylake Chapel

Station Road, Hoylake, Merseyside CH47 4AA
☎ 0151 632 6084
@ mail@hoylakechapel.org.uk
www.hoylakechapel.org.uk
Page 87-F2

Liverpool Aintree Pavilion Arena

The brand new 4,500-capacity Aintree Pavilion Arena is host to many events, including the Liverpool Summer Pops.

Aintree Racecourse, Ormskirk Road, Liverpool, Merseyside L9 5AS
☎ 0151 523 2600
✆ 0151 233 3007
0151 522 2920
Page 31-G3

Liverpool Echo Arena

Liverpool Echo Arena is a state of the art 10,000-plus seater arena. A versatile space that is the perfect venue for concerts, comedy, family entertainment and sport. Situated in the beautiful location of the Kings Dock on the River Mersey, it offers visitors a unique experience in one of the UKs most vibrant cities.

16 Monarchs Quay, Liverpool, Merseyside L3 4FP
☎ 0151 703 7230
✆ 0844 8000 400
www.accliverpool.co.uk
Page 93-G1

Liverpool Olympia

One of Liverpool's largest concert venues with interior decor modelled on the Moscow Kirov Ballet.

West Derby Road, Liverpool, Merseyside L6 9BY
☎ 0151 263 6633
www.liverpoololympia.com/
Page 71-H2

MV Fitzcarraldo

This ex-Norwegian ferry hosts various events including plays, live music, comedy and cabaret.

Canning Dock, 08 Place, Liverpool, Merseyside L1 6DZ
☎ 0161 736 8964
@ info@walktheplank.co.uk
www.walktheplank.co.uk/wtp/
Page 6-C5

The Magnet

45 Hardman Street, Liverpool, Merseyside L1 9AS
☎ 0151 709 6969
www.myspace.com/magnetliverpool
Page 7-H6

Metro Eating Room and Bar

Metro provides live music and food in the heart of Liverpool. Jazz, blues and modern rock can be heard most nights.

5–9 Fowlers Building, Victoria Street, Liverpool, Merseyside L2 5QA
☎ 0151 236 2200
@ info@metro-liverpool.com
www.metro-liverpool.com
0151 236 2266
Page 6-D4

The New Picket

61 Jordan Street, Liverpool, Merseyside L1 0BW
☎ 0151 708 6789
✆ 0151 708 6789
Page 93-H1

The Pilgrim

34 Pilgrim Street, Liverpool, Merseyside L1 9HB
☎ 0151 709 2302
Page 7-H7

Royal Court Theatre

The theatre hosts a wide variety of shows including plays, ballets, musical events and comedy.

1 Roe Street, Liverpool, Merseyside L1 1HL
☎ 0870 787 1866
www.royalcourtliverpool.co.uk
Page 7-F3

Royal Liverpool Philharmonic Hall

This superb art deco Grade II listed building, home of the Royal Liverpool Philharmonic Orchestra, is one of the UKs top arts and entertainment venues.

36 Hope Street, Liverpool, Merseyside L1 9BP
☎ 0151 210 2895
✆ 0151 709 3789
@ customerservice@liverpoolphil.com
www.liverpoolphil.com
0151 210 2902
Page 7-J6

Stadt Moers Park

Pottery Lane, Whiston, Merseyside L35 3RG
✆ L35 3RG
Page 76-C3

The Supper Club

63 Blundell Street, Liverpool, Merseyside L1 0JA
☎ 0151 709 5779
www.supperclubliverpool.com
Page 93-H1

Theatre Royal

The theatre provides a wide variety of entertainment from top-class comedians to musical shows.

Corporation Street, St Helens, Merseyside WA10 1LQ
☎ 01744 756000
www.sthelenstheatreroyal.co.uk
Page 11-H5

University of Liverpool: Mountford Hall, Stanley Theatre and JB's

Student's play area hosting music, comedy and other entertainment events.

160 Mount Pleasant, Liverpool, Merseyside L69 7BR
☎ 0151 794 6868
@ ents@liv.ac.uk
www.lgos.org
Page 7-K5

WA1 Venue Bar

All types of alternative music throughout the week, from hard rock and emo, to indie, britpop and motown.

The White Hart, 56 Sankey Street, Warrington, Cheshire WA1 1SB
☎ 01925 638776
www.wa1venuebar.com
Page 12-B5

Warrington Rhythm 'n' Blues Club

Warrington Town FC, Loushers Lane, Warrington Cheshire WA4 2RS
☎ 01925 488009
@ info@wrbcblues.co.uk
www.wrbcblues.co.uk
Page 130-C1

Zanzibar Club

43 Seel Street, Liverpool, Merseyside L1 4AZ
☎ 0151 707 0633
@ info@thezanzibarclub.com
www.thezanzibarclub.com
Page 7-F6

COMEDY CLUBS AND VENUES

Baby Blue

Baby Blue has regular nights featuring DJs playing classic funk, R'n'B and disco, and also hosts comedy nights every Friday and Saturday.

Edward Pavilion, Albert Dock, Liverpool, Merseyside L3 4AF
☎ 0151 702 5831
www.blue-venue.co.uk
Page 6-C6

Liverpool Echo Arena

Liverpool Echo Arena is a state of the art 10,000-plus seater arena. This versatile space is the perfect venue for concerts, comedy, family entertainment and sport. Situated in the beautiful location of the Kings Dock on the River Mersey, it offers visitors a unique experience in one of the UKs most vibrant cities.

16 Monarchs Quay, Liverpool, Merseyside L3 4FP
☎ 0151 703 7230
✆ 0844 8000 400
www.accliverpool.co.uk
Page 93-G1

Liverpool Olympia

One of Liverpool's largest concert venues with interior decor modelled on the Moscow Kirov Ballet.

West Derby Road, Liverpool, Merseyside L6 9BY
☎ 0151 263 6633
www.liverpoololympia.com/
Page 71-H2

MV Fitzcarraldo

This ex-Norwegian ferry hosts various events including plays, live music, comedy and cabaret.

Canning Dock, 08 Place, Liverpool, Merseyside L1 6DZ
☎ 0161 736 8964
@ info@walktheplank.co.uk
www.walktheplank.co.uk/wtp/
Page 6-C5

Prohibition Bar, Liverpool

1a Bold Street, Liverpool, Merseyside L1 4DJ
☎ 0151 707 2333
@ liverpool@prohibition.uk.com
www.prohibition.uk.com
Fax 0151 707 3782
Page 7-F5

Royal Court Theatre

One of Liverpool's best-known venues for theatre, music and comedy.

1 Roe Street, Liverpool, Merseyside L1 1HL
☎ 0870 787 1866
www.royalcourtliverpool.co.uk
Page 7-F3

Theatre Royal

The theatre provides a wide variety of entertainment from top-class comedians to musical shows.

Corporation Street, St Helens, Merseyside WA10 1LQ
☎ 01744 756000
www.sthelenstheatreroyal.co.uk
Page 11-H5

CLASSICAL MUSIC VENUES

Liverpool Cathedral

Liverpool Cathedral was started in 1904 but inaugurated in 1978, to Giles Gilbert Scott's design; its tower can be seen from north Wales. The cathedral occupies a total area of 9,600 square metres and was built mainly of sandstone quarried from the Liverpool suburb of Woolton. Events held throughout the year include a programme of organ recitals.

6 Cathedral Close, St James Mount, Liverpool, Merseyside L1 7AZ
☎ 0151 709 6271
@ neil.holland@liverpoolcathedral.org.uk
www.liverpoolcathedral.org.uk
Page 94-A1

Liverpool Metropolitan Cathedral

Designed by Sir Edwin Lutyens in 1930, the Cathedral is barrelled with vaulted ceilings and dark brick work and contrasting grey granite. The cathdral hosts concerts and music events.

Cathedral House, Mount Pleasant, Liverpool, Merseyside L3 5TQ
☎ 0151 708 7283
@ enquiries@metcathedral.org.uk
www.liverpoolmetrocathedral.org.uk
Page 7-J5

Royal Liverpool Philharmonic Hall

This superb art deco Grade II listed building, home of the Royal Liverpool Philharmonic Orchestra, is one of the UKs top arts and entertainment venues.

36 Hope Street, Liverpool, Merseyside L1 9BP
☎ 0151 210 2895
✆ 0151 709 3789
@ customerservice@liverpoolphil.com
www.liverpoolphil.com
Fax 0151 210 2902
Page 7-J6

St Saviour's

The foundation stone of the present building was laid by Miss Catherine King on 26th March 1889 and the church was consecrated on Ascension day 1892. The church hosts services, choirs and organ recitals alongside music events.

Bidston Road, Oxton, Merseyside CH43 2JZ
☎ 0151 653 3366
@ oxtonstsaviour@btinternet.com
www.oxtonstsaviour.co.uk
Fax 0151 653 7251
Page 91-G4

CINEMAS

CineWorld Runcorn

Trident Park, Halton Lea, Runcorn, Cheshire WA7 2FQ
☎ 08712 208000
www.cineworld.co.uk
Page 156-B2

Cineworld Liverpool

Edge Lane Retail Park, Liverpool, Merseyside L13 1EW
☎ 0870 777 2775
✆ 08712 002000
www.cineworld.co.uk
Page 72-D3

Cineworld St Helens

Chalon Way West, St Helens, Merseyside WA10 1BF
☎ 01744 697800, 08712 208000
www.cineworld.co.uk
Page 11-G6

Odeon Allerton

Allerton Road, Liverpool, Merseyside L18 5HU
☎ 08712 244007
www.odeon.co.uk
Page 96-B3

Odeon Bromborough

Croft Retail and Leisure Park, Welton Road, Bromborough, Merseyside CH62 3PN
☎ 08712 244007
www.odeon.co.uk
Page 138-D3

Odeon Liverpool London Road

London Road, Liverpool, Merseyside L3 5NF
☎ 08712 244007
www.odeon.co.uk
Page 7-G3

Odeon Liverpool Switch Island

Dunnings Bridge Road, Netherton, Bootle, Merseyside L30 6TQ
☎ 08712 244007
www.odeon.co.uk
Page 31-F1

Odeon Warrington

100 Westbrook Centre, Westbrook Crescent, Cromwell Avenue, Warrington, Cheshire WA5 8UD
☎ 08712 244007
www.odeon.co.uk
Page 82-B4

Picturehouse at FACT

88 Wood Street, Liverpool, Merseyside L1 4DQ
☎ 0870 758 3217
@ liverpool@picturehouses.co.uk
www.picturehouses.co.uk
Page 7-G6

Plaza Community Cinema

13 Crosby Road North, Waterloo, Liverpool, Merseyside L22 0LD
☎ 0151 474 4076
@ manager@plazacinema.org.uk
www.plazacinema.org.uk
Fax 0151 474 1187
Page 29-F3

Royal Liverpool Philharmonic Hall

36 Hope Street, Liverpool, Merseyside L1 9BP
☎ 0151 210 2895
✆ 0151 709 3789
@ customerservice@liverpoolphil.com
www.liverpoolphil.com
Fax 0151 210 2902
Page 7-J6

Showcase Cinema, Liverpool

340 East Lancashire Road, Norris Green, Liverpool, Merseyside L11 9YJ
☎ 08712 201000
✆ 08712 201000
www.showcasecinemas.co.uk
Page 42-A3

Vue Birkenhead

Conway Park, Europa Boulevard, Birkenhead, Merseyside CH41 4PE
☎ 08712 240240
@ guestservices@myvue.com
www.myvue.com
Page 3-F4

Woolton Picture House

Mason Street, Woolton, Liverpool, Merseyside L25 5JH
☎ 0151 428 3737
www.picturehousewoolton.co.uk
Page 120-C1

THEATRES

The Citadel

Live theatre, comedy, dance and fine art along with a traditional music programme.

Waterloo Street, St Helens, Merseyside WA10 1PX
☎ 01744 735436
✆ 01744 735436
@ info@citadel.org.uk
www.citadel.org.uk
Fax 01744 762309
Page 11-G5

Gladstone Theatre

Run by The Gladstone Theatre Trust, a voluntary organisation, the theatre presents both professional and amateur shows.

Greendale Road, Port Sunlight, Merseyside CH62 4XB
☎ 0151 643 8757
@ enquire@gladstone.uk.com
www.gladstone.uk.com/
Page 138-B2

The Liverpool Academy of Arts Actors Studio

36 Seel Street, Liverpool, Merseyside L1 4BE
☎ 0151 709 9034
www.laaas.com/
Page 7-F6

Liverpool Echo Arena

Liverpool Echo Arena is a state of the art 10,000-plus seater arena. This versatile space is the perfect venue for concerts, comedy, family entertainment and sport. Situated in the beautiful location of the Kings Dock on the River Mersey, it offers visitors a unique experience in one of the UKs most vibrant cities.

16 Monarchs Quay, Liverpool, Merseyside L3 4FP
☎ 0151 703 7230
✆ 0844 8000 400
www.accliverpool.co.uk
Page 93-G1

Liverpool Empire Theatre

The theatre hosts touring productions, musicals and concerts.

Lime Street, Liverpool, Merseyside L1 1JE
☎ 0870 606 3536
www.getlive.co.uk/liverpool
Page 7-F3

Liverpool Everyman

Founded in 1964 in the appropriately named Hope Hall, the Everyman has been a producing theatre and the cornerstone of its programme is the living writer.

13 Hope Street, Liverpool, Merseyside L1 9BH
☎ 0151 708 3700
✆ 0151 709 4776
@ info@everymanplayhouse.com
www.everymanplayhouse.com
Fax 0151 708 3701
Page 7-J5

Liverpool Olympia

One of Liverpool's largest concert venues with interior decor modelled on the Moscow Kirov Ballet.

West Derby Road, Liverpool, Merseyside L6 9BY
☎ 0151 263 6633
www.liverpoololympia.com/
Page 71-H2

Liverpool Playhouse

The Playhouse is predominantly a producing theatre. Here, the emphasis is on creative interpretations of great plays. More stately than the Everyman, yet intimate in its own way, the Playhouse is the Liverpool home of classic drama, from ancient to modern, presented with the highest production values.

Williamson Square, Liverpool, Merseyside L1 1EL
@ info@everymanplayhouse.com
www.everymanplayhouse.com/
Page 6-E4

MV Fitzcarraldo

This ex-Norwegian ferry hosts various events including plays, live music, comedy and cabaret.

Canning Dock, 08 Place, Liverpool, Merseyside L1 6DZ
☎ 0161 736 8964
@ info@walktheplank.co.uk
www.walktheplank.co.uk/wtp/
Page 6-C5

Royal Court Theatre

One of Liverpool's best-known venues for theatre, music and comedy

1 Roe Street, Liverpool, Merseyside L1 1HL
✆ 0870 787 1866
www.royalcourtliverpool.co.uk
Page 7-F3

Stadt Moers Park

Pottery Lane, Whiston, Merseyside L35 3RG
☎ L35 3RG
Page 76-C3

Theatre Royal

The theatre provides a wide variety of entertainment from top-class comedians to musical shows.

Corporation Street, St Helens, Merseyside WA10 1LQ
☎ 01744 756000
www.sthelenstheatreroyal.co.uk
Page 11-H5

Unity Theatre

Unity Theatre recently won the Best Performing Venue award at the Mersey Partnership Tourism Awards and has a reputation for staging innovative work in a friendly atmosphere.

1 Hope Place, Liverpool, Merseyside L1 9BG
☎ 0151 709 6502
✆ 0151 709 4988
@ tickets@unitytheatre.co.uk
www.unitytheatreliverpool.co.uk
Fax 0151 709 7182
Page 7-H6

Valley Community Theatre

Childwall Vally Road, Liverpool, Merseyside L27 3YA
☎ 0151 488 0364
@ info@valleytheatre.co.uk
www.valleytheatre.co.uk
Fax 0151 488 1510
Page 98-B3

BARS AND PUBS

Alma De Cuba

St Peters Church, Seel Street, Liverpool, Merseyside L1 4AZ
☎ 0151 702 7394
Page 7-F6

Baa Fleet Street

Baa Bar was opened in a converted warehouse Liverpool City Centre, the first Baa Bar opened in April 1991. Thirteen years on, the original is formally established at the heart of Liverpool nightlife.

43–45 Fleet Street, Liverpool, Merseyside L1 4AN
☎ 0151 708 8673
@ fleetstreet@baabar.co.uk
www.baabar.co.uk
Fax 0151 709 6824
Page 7-F5

Bar Fresa

Colquitt Street, Liverpool, Merseyside L1 4DE
☎ 0151 706 0070
@ cultureclub@djmase.co.uk
Page 7-G6

Brannigans

15–17 Friars Gate, Warrington, Cheshire WA1 2RR
☎ 01925 642510
www.brannigansbars.com
Fax 01925 642 515
Page 12-D6

Bumper

Bumper is one of Liverpool's coolest free clubs, offering live music and DJs every night. Its a venue, club and bar in one, located within the heart of Liverpool's student quarter.

14–18 Hardman Street, Liverpool, Merseyside L1 4RR
☎ 0151 707 9902
www.bumperliverpool.co.uk
Page 7-H6

The Cavern Pub

Opened in August 1994, The Cavern Pub is opposite the Cavern Club and commemorates the fact that between 1957 and 1973 many of the greats of rock, pop, soul, R'n'B and jazz played on the Cavern Club's stage.

8 –10 Mathew Street, Liverpool, Merseyside L2 6RE
☎ 0151 236 9091
www.cavern-liverpool.co.uk/cavern_pub_ents.htm
Fax 0151 236 8081
Page 6-D4

Chicago Rock Cafe, Warrington

Chicago Rock Cafe offers a blend of eating, drinking and entertainment. The music played is the 'greatest classic hits of all time', catering for a wide variety of tastes and age groups, ranging from 1957 to 1995.

St Austins Lane, Warrington, Cheshire WA1 1HG
☎ 01925 415118
@ chicago-rock-cafe-warrington@3d-entertainmentgroup.com
www.chicago-rock-cafe.co.uk
Fax 01925 444947
Page 12-D6

Elude Bar & Restaurant

15 Porter Street, Liverpool, Merseyside L3 7BL
☎ 0151 227 3882
www.eludeliverpool.com
Page 70-B1

Folk at the Prospect

A friendly club which meets on Monday nights at the Prospect Inn. There is usually a guest every month.

70 Weston Road, Runcorn, Weston, Cheshire WA7 4LD
☎ 01928 561280
@ roger@folkattheprospect.co.uk
www.folkattheprospect.co.uk
Page 154-C2

High Society

64 Duke Street, Liverpool, Merseyside L1 5AA
☎ 0151 7073575
@ info@societyuk.com
www.societyuk.com
Page 6-F6

The Living Room, Liverpool
Bar and restaurant that also holds music events.

15 Victoria Street, Liverpool, Merseyside L2 5QS
☎ 0151 236 1999
@ liverpool@thelivingroom.co.uk
www.thelivingroom.co.uk
0870 442 2536
Page 6-D4

Modo
1 Concert Square, Liverpool, Merseyside L1 4NR
☎ 0151 709 8832
@ info@modoliverpool.co.uk
www.modoliverpool.co.uk
Page 7-F5

The Monro
92 Duke Street, Liverpool, Merseyside L1 5AG
☎ 0151 709 1638
Page 7-F6

Nation
Wolstenholme Square, Liverpool, Merseyside L1 4JJ
☎ 0151 709 9172
Page 7-F6

Old Tavern Club
16–18 Magazine Lane, Wallasey, Merseyside CH45 5AD
☎ 0151 639 6015
Page 51-H3

Revolution Bar
Plush, comfortable and distinctively stylish, Revolution St Peters Square is the latest vodka-infused addition to Liverpool's bustling bar scene. Situated in the Tea Factory building the vodka bar and kitchen is nestled amid the up-and-coming Ropewalks and East Village areas of the city. It offers a new dimension to this popular area of Liverpool with a stylish bar on the ground floor and large club room in the basement featuring the stunning 'slate bar'.

St Peters Square, Fleet Street, Liverpool, Merseyside L1 4DQ
☎ 0151 709 8462
www.revolution-bars.co.uk
0151 709 6663
Page 7-F5

Revolution Bar, Liverpool Cavern Quarter
2 Temple Court, Liverpool, Merseyside L2 6PY
☎ 0151 236 0905
www.revolution-bars.co.uk
0151 236 0905
Page 6-D4

Revolution Bar, Liverpool Wood Street
The Revolution on Wood Street has long been a favourite for Liverpool's vodka loving locals and students alike. Fresh, spacious and particularly funky in appearance it offers a different but equally special experience seven days of the week. Lounge by day and party by night to choice sounds and sumptuous sights.

18–22 Wood Street, Liverpool, Merseyside L1 4AQ
☎ 0151 707 1933
@ liverpool@revolution-bars.co.uk
www.revolution-bars.co.uk
0151 707 0094
Page 7-F5

Stamps Wine Bar
4 Crown Buildings, Coronation Road, Crosby, Liverpool, Merseyside L23 5SR
☎ 0151 286 2662
www.stampsbar.co.uk
Page 21-E5

The Swan Hotel
Holm Lane, Prenton, Merseyside CH43 2HP
☎ 0151 609 4311
Page 114-B1

Top Of The Town
110 Albert Road, Widnes, Cheshire WA8 6LG
☎ 0151 420 7477
Page 15-F2

The World
52 Church Street, Warrington, Cheshire WA1 2SY
☎ 01925 241104
Page 13-F4

NIGHTCLUBS

Baby Blue
Baby Blue has regular nights featuring DJs playing classic funk, R'n'B and disco, and also hosts comedy nights every Friday and Saturday.

Edward Pavilion, Albert Dock, Liverpool, Merseyside L3 4AF
☎ 0151 702 5831
www.blue-venue.co.uk
Page 6-C6

Barsswabe
Unit 1, Concert Square, Liverpool, Merseyside L1 4NR
☎ 0151 709 2437
Page 7-F5

Bumper
Bumper is one of Liverpool's coolest free clubs, offering live music and DJs every night. Its a venue, club and bar in one, located within the heart of Liverpool's student quarter.

14–18 Hardman Street, Liverpool, Merseyside L1 4RR
☎ 0151 707 9902
www.bumperliverpool.co.uk
Page 7-H6

Korova Bar
Korova is Liverpool's most creative venue. Korova boasts live music seven nights a week and has taken on a hub-status for a thriving Liverpool music scene. The venue has built a reputation for nurturing new and undiscovered talent, as well as attracting some of the finest established acts from around the world.

39 Fleet Street, Liverpool, Merseyside L1 4AR
☎ 0151 709 7097
@ info@korova-liverpool.com
www.korova-liverpool.com
Page 7-F5

The Krazyhouse
The Krazyhouse has three independant floors and offers a variety of rock, alternative and dance nights featuring a wide range of events and DJs.

16 Wood Street, Liverpool, Merseyside L1 4AQ
☎ 0151 708 5016
@ info@thekrazyhouse.co.uk
www.thekrazyhouse.co.uk
0151 709 3273
Page 7-F5

The Lemon Lounge
21 Berry Street, Liverpool, Merseyside L1 9DF
☎ 0151 709 5055, 0117 4336372
Page 7-G6

Mood Nightclub

18–20 Fleet Street,
Liverpool, Merseyside
L1 4AN

☎ 0151 709 8181
www.moodbars.com
0151 702 6539
Page 7-F5

RJ's Nightclub

Marine Promenade, Wallasey,
Merseyside CH45 2JT

☎ 0151 639 1552
@ info@rjsnightclub.com
www.rjsnightclub.com
Page 51-H1

Synergy

Bridgefoot, Warrington,
Cheshire WA1 2SN

☎ 01925 414801
www.synergysuperclub.com
01925 231117
Page 106-D4

WA1 Venue Bar

All types of alternative music throughout the week, from hard rock and emo, to indie, britpop and motown.

The White Hart, 56 Sankey
Street, Warrington,
Cheshire WA1 1SB

☎ 01925 638776
www.wa1venuebar.com
Page 12-B5

Zanzibar Club

43 Seel Street, Liverpool,
Merseyside L1 4AZ

☎ 0151 707 0633
@ info@thezanzibarclub.com
www.thezanzibarclub.com
Page 7-F6

SPECIAL EVENTS' VENUES

Albert Dock

Situated in the largest group of Grade I listed buildings in the UK, the Albert Dock houses many award-winning visitor attractions including Tate Liverpool, the famous Beatles Story, Merseyside Maritime Museum and the new International Slavery Museum. You can join a number of fascinating Liverpool tours, including the creepy Shiverpool Ghost Tour or a city and water tour on the YellowDuckmarine. Events and activities held throughout the year.

Albert Dock, Liverpool,
Merseyside L3 4AF

☎ 0151 708 7334
www.albertdock.com/index.php
0151 708 0929
Page 6-B7

Anfield Stadium

Home to Liverpool Football Club, Anfield is descended on weekly by thousands of football fans. Concert venue.

Anfield Road, Liverpool,
Merseyside L4 0TH

☎ 0151 260 6677
@ www.liverpoolfc.tv/
Page 54-C3

BBC Screen, Liverpool

Clayton Square, Liverpool,
Merseyside L1 1QR

Page 7-F4

Bootle Town Hall

Originally opened in 1882, Bootle Town Hall is a Grade II listed building. It was designed by John Johnson, in the Renaissance style after a public competition. Hosts concerts and events.

Oriel Road, Bootle, Sefton,
Merseyside L20 7AE

☎ 01704 540011
✆ 0151 934 4422
www.sefton.gov.uk/default.aspx?Page=4626
Page 4-D6

Crosby Civic Hall

Crosby Road North, Crosby
Merseyside L22 0LQ

☎ 01704 540011,
0151 934 2141
@ marketing@seftonarts.co.uk
www.seftonarts.co.uk
Page 29-F3

Liverpool Echo Arena

Liverpool Echo Arena is a state of the art 10,000 plus seater arena. A versatile space that is the perfect venue for concerts, comedy, family entertainment and sport. Situated in the beautiful location of the Kings Dock on the River Mersey, it offers visitors a unique experience in one of the UKs most vibrant cities.

16 Monarchs Quay,
Liverpool, Merseyside L3 4FP

☎ 0151 703 7230
✆ 0844 8000 400
www.accliverpool.co.uk
Page 93-G1

Liverpool Olympia

One of Liverpool's largest concert venues with interior decor modelled on the Moscow Kirov Ballet.

West Derby Road, Liverpool,
Merseyside L6 9BY

☎ 0151 263 6633
www.liverpoololympia.com/
Page 71-H2

Liverpool Town Hall

Flagship building in the heart of the city dating from 1754. Offering a range of events including art exhibitions, concerts and hired events.

High Street, Liverpool,
Merseyside L2 3SW

☎ 0151 225 5530
@ town.hall@liverpool.gov.uk
www.civichalls.liverpool.gov.uk/townhall/index.asp
0151 225 5544
Page 6-C3

Sefton Park Palm House

The Grade II listed Victorian Palm House, set in the leafy surroundings of Sefton Park, offers an elegant and unique backdrop for arts and entertainment events.

Aigburth, Liverpool,
Merseyside L17 1AP

☎ 0151 233 2008,
0151 726 2415
@ info@palmhouse.org.uk
www.palmhouse.org.uk
Page 95-F4

St George's Hall

The hall houses chandeliers, stained glass windows, barrel vaulted ceiling and the Willis Organ. A wide range of concerts, cultural and community events are held here.

William Brown Street,
Liverpool, Merseyside L1 1JJ

☎ 0151 225 6909
✆ 0151 233 2008
@ town.hall@liverpool.gov.uk / events@liverpool08.com
www.liverpool08.com
0151 225 5544
Page 7-F3

University of Liverpool

The University of Liverpool was one of the first civic universities. Founded in 1881 with the establishment of University College Liverpool, the College opened in 1882 with 45 students on Brownlow Hill. Events include exhibitions, music and public lectures.

University of Liverpool,
Liverpool, Merseyside
L69 3BX

☎ 0151 794 2000
www.liv.ac.uk
0151 708 6502
Page 7-J3

Street by Street

LIVERPOOL

BIRKENHEAD, BOOTLE, RUNCORN, ST HELENS, WARRINGTON, WIDNES

Bebington, Crosby, Formby, Heswall, Hoylake, Kirkby, Maghull, Neston, Prescot, Wallasey, West Kirby

Key to map pages ii-iii

Key to map symbols iv-1

Enlarged map pages 2-15

Main map pages 16-159

Index – towns & villages 160

Index – streets 161-193

Index – featured places 193-198

Acknowledgements 198

National Grid references are shown on the map frame of each page.
Red figures denote the 100 km square and blue figures the 1 km square.
Example, page 94: Brewery 335 389

The reference can also be written using the National Grid two-letter prefix shown on this page, where 3 and 3 are replaced by SJ to give SJ3589.

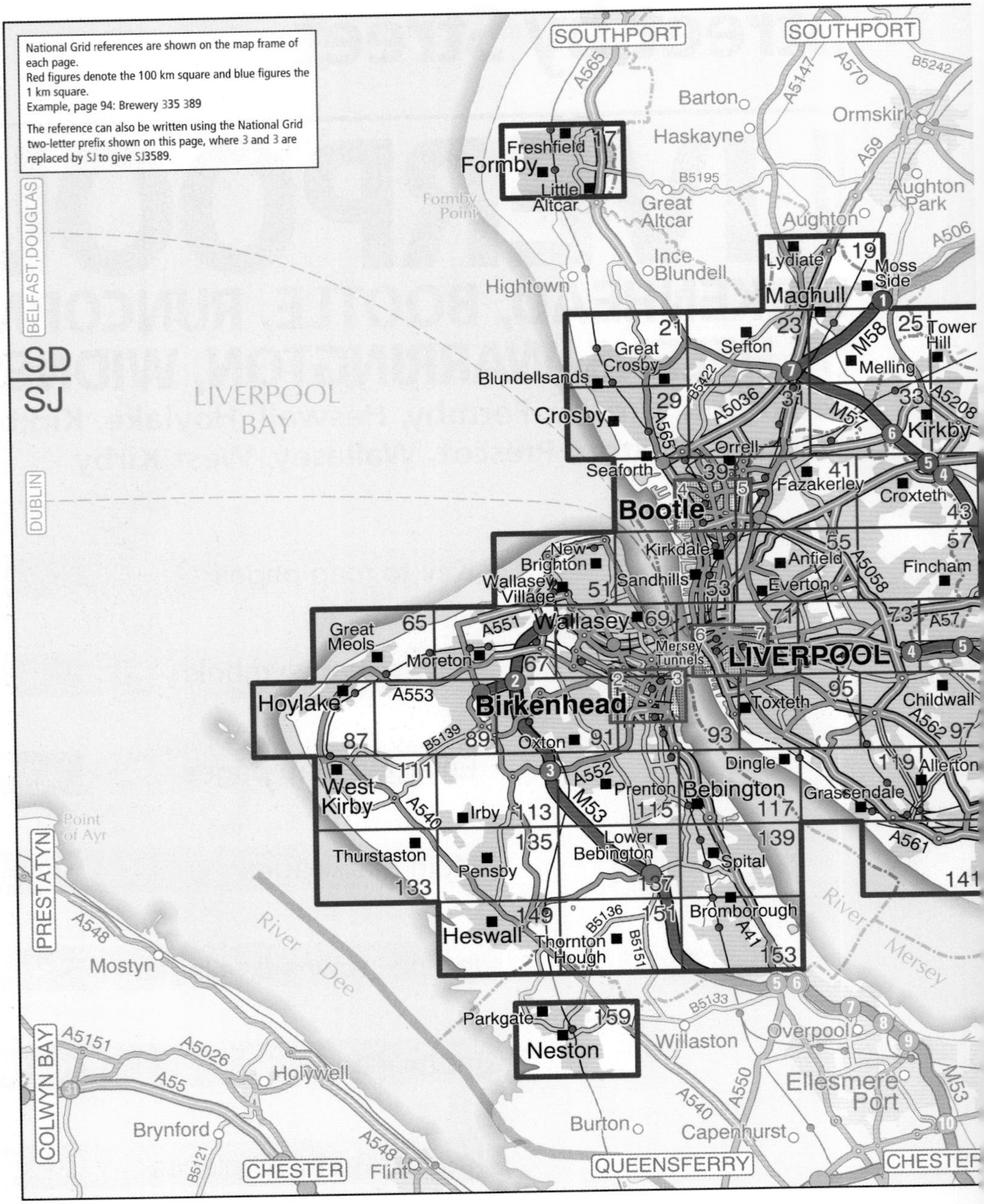

Scale of enlarged map pages 1:10,000

6.3 inches to 1 mile

0 — 1/4 — miles — 1/2 — 3/4 — 1

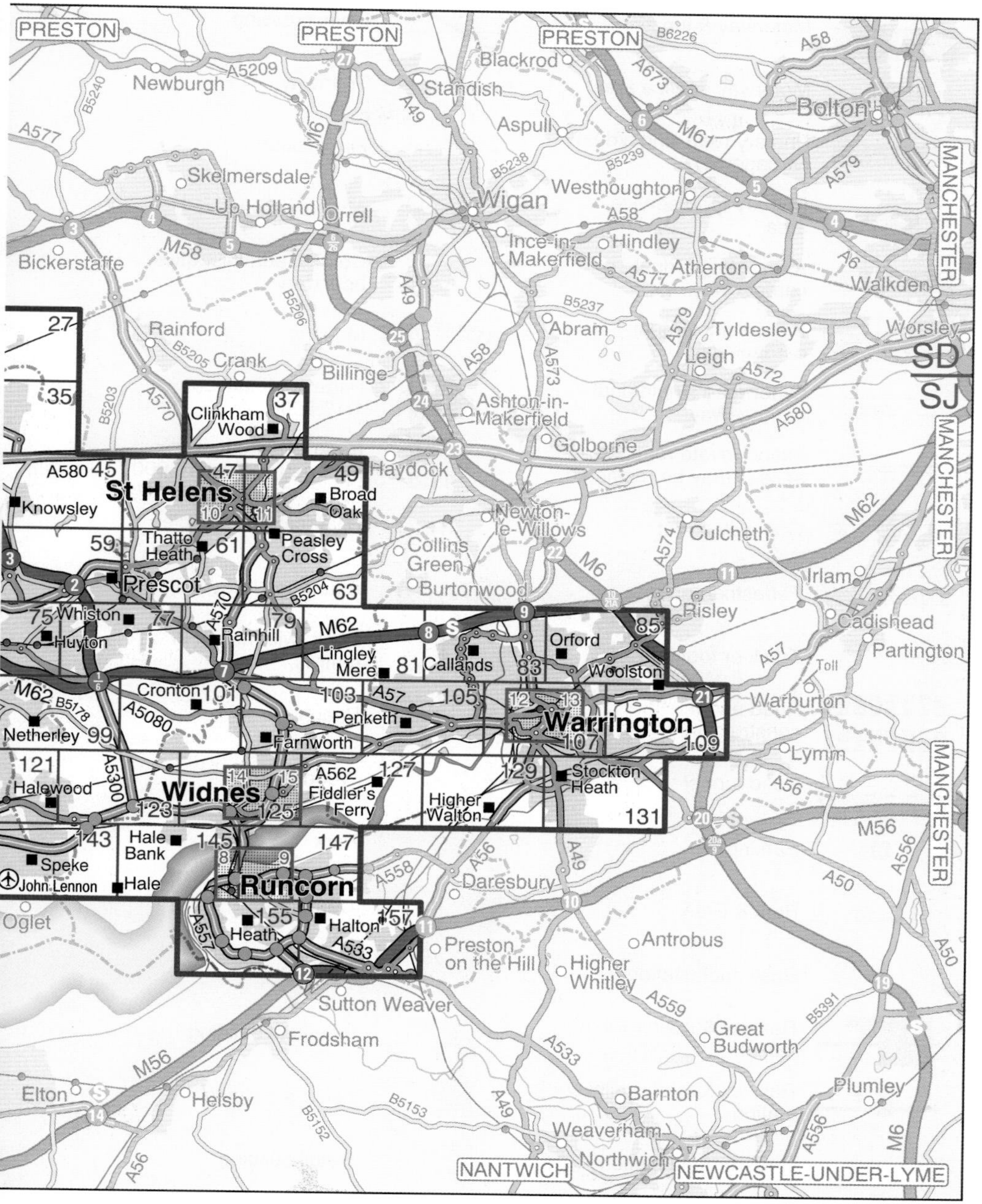

4.2 inches to 1 mile

Scale of main map pages 1:15,000

0 1/4 miles 1/2 3/4 1

0 1/4 1/2 kilometres 3/4

- Junction 9 — Motorway & junction
- Services — Motorway service area
- Primary road single/dual carriageway
- Services — Primary road service area
- A road single/dual carriageway
- B road single/dual carriageway
- Other road single/dual carriageway
- Minor/private road, access may be restricted
- One-way street
- Pedestrian area
- Track or footpath
- Road under construction
- Road tunnel
- P — Parking
- P+ — Park & Ride
- Bus/coach station
- Railway & main railway station
- Railway & minor railway station
- Underground station
- Light railway & station
- Preserved private railway

- LC — Level crossing
- Tramway
- Ferry route
- Airport runway
- County, administrative boundary
- Mounds
- 17 — Page continuation 1:17,500
- 3 — Page continuation to enlarged scale 1:10,000
- River/canal, lake, pier
- Aqueduct, lock, weir
- 465 Winter Hill — Peak (with height in metres)
- Beach
- Woodland
- Park
- Cemetery
- Built-up area
- Industrial building
- Leisure building
- Retail building
- Other building
- IKEA — IKEA store

	City wall
A&E	Hospital with 24-hour A&E department
PO	Post Office
	Public library
i	Tourist Information Centre
i	Seasonal Tourist Information Centre
	Petrol station, 24 hour Major suppliers only
	Church/chapel
	Public toilets
	Toilet with disabled facilities
PH	Public house AA recommended
	Restaurant AA inspected
Madeira Hotel	Hotel AA inspected
	Theatre or performing arts centre
	Cinema
	Golf course
	Camping AA inspected
	Caravan site AA inspected
	Camping & caravan site AA inspected
	Theme park
	Abbey, cathedral or priory

	Castle
	Historic house or building
Wakehurst Place (NT)	National Trust property
M	Museum or art gallery
	Roman antiquity
	Ancient site, battlefield or monument
	Industrial interest
	Garden
	Garden Centre Garden Centre Association Member
	Garden Centre Wyevale Garden Centre
	Arboretum
	Farm or animal centre
	Zoological or wildlife collection
	Bird collection
	Nature reserve
	Aquarium
V	Visitor or heritage centre
	Country park
	Cave
	Windmill
	Distillery, brewery or vineyard

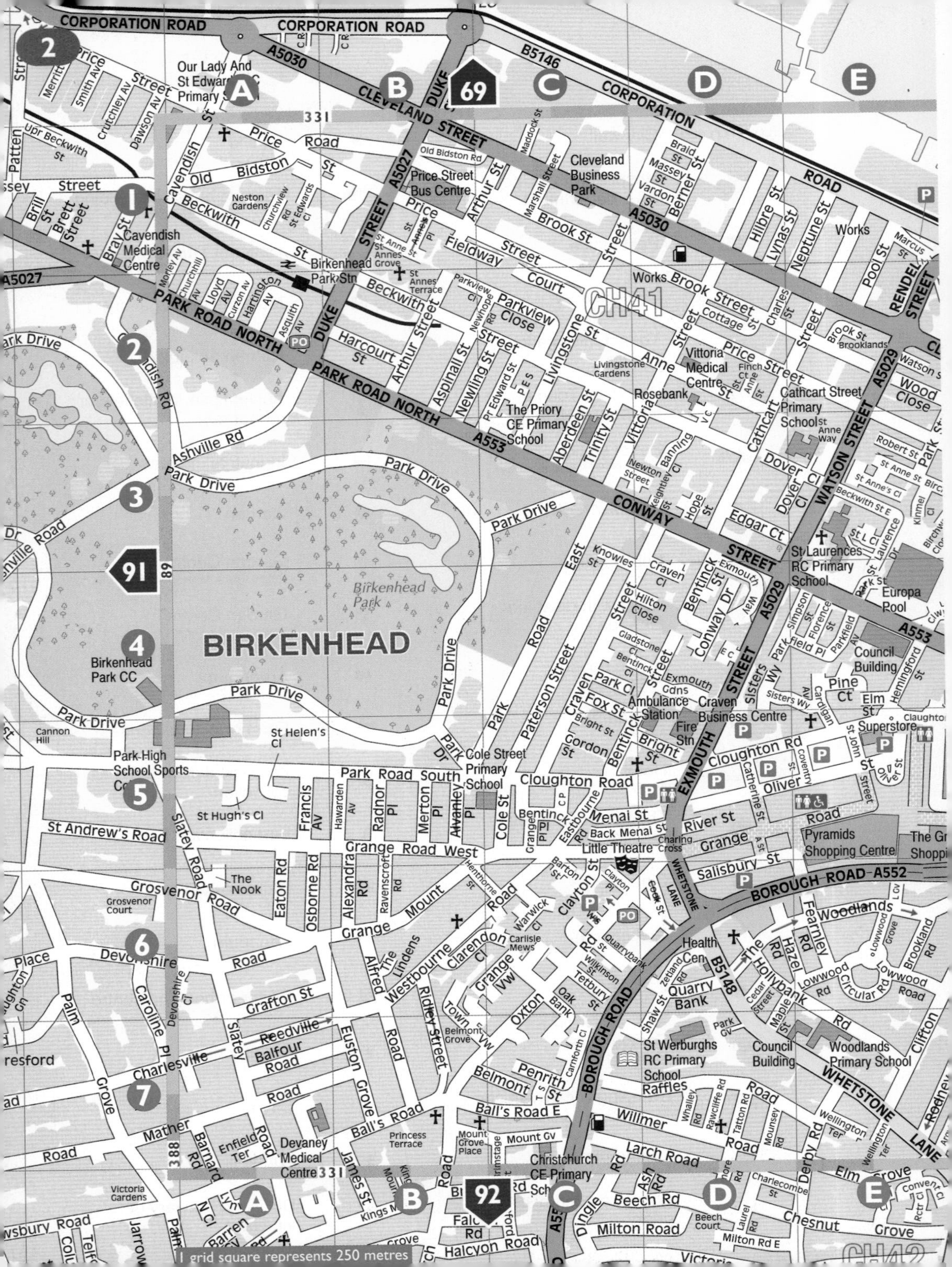

CORPORATION ROAD
CORPORATION ROAD
2
A B C D E
69
B5146
CORPORATION
ROAD
A5030
CLEVELAND STREET
DUKE
Our Lady And St Edwards RC Primary School
Price Street
Merritt
Smith Av
Crutchley Av
Dawson Av
Upr Beckwith St
Patten
Street
Brill St
Brett Street
Bray St
Cavendish
Cavendish Medical Centre
Price Road
Old Bidston
Old Bidston Rd
Neston Gardens
Churchview Rd
St Edwards Cl
Price Street Bus Centre
A5027
STREET
Arthur St
Maddock St
Marshall Street
Cleveland Business Park
Braid St
Massey St
Vardon St
Berner St
Beckwith St
Price St
Annes Pl
St Anne St
St Annes Grove
Fieldway
Street
Brook St
Street
Hilbre St
Lynas St
Neptune St
Works
Marcus St
Pool St
RENDEL STREET
Birkenhead Park Stn
St Annes Terrace
Beckwith Street
Court
Works
Brook Street
Cottage St
Charles St
Brook St
Brooklands
CH41
A5027
Morley Av
Churchhill Av
Lloyd Av
Curzon Av
Hartington Av
Asquith Av
PO
PARK ROAD NORTH
Harcourt St
Arthur Street
Parkview Cl
Newhope Cl
Parkview Close
Aspinall St
Street
Newling St
Pr Edward St
Livingstone St
Livingstone Gardens
Anne St
Vittoria Medical Centre
Finch Ct
Anne St
Price Street
Street
Watson St
Wood Close
A5029
WATSON STREET
Cathcart Street Primary School
St Anne Way
Rosebank
Cathcart
The Priory CE Primary School
Aberdeen St
Trinity St
Vittoria St
PARK ROAD NORTH
A553
Cavendish Rd
Ashville Rd
Park Drive
Park Drive
Park Drive
Birkenhead Park
BIRKENHEAD
91
89
Newton Street
Banning Cl
Keightley St
Hope St
Edgar Ct
Dover Cl
Dover Cl
Robert St
Park
St Anne St
St Anne's Cl
Beckwith St E
St Laurences RC Primary School
Laurence Cl
Kinmel Cl
Europa Pool
CONWAY STREET
A553
Knowles St
Craven Cl
Hilton Close
East Road
Street
Bentinck St
Exmouth Way
Conway Dr
Simpson St
Florence St
Field Pl
Parkfield Av
Park St
Council Building
Hemingford St
Gladstone Cl
Bentinck Cl
Exmouth Gdns
Park Cl
Fox St
Bright St
Gordon St
Bentinck St
Bright St
Craven
Paterson Street
Park Road
Park Drive
Park Dr
Ambulance Station
Fire Stn
Craven Business Centre
Sisters Wy
Sisters Wy
Cardigan Av
Pine Ct
Elm St
Claughton
Superstore
St John St
Oliver St
EXMOUTH STREET
Birkenhead Park CC
Park Drive
Cannon Hill
Park High School Sports Centre
St Helen's Cl
St Hugh's Cl
Park Road South
Cole Street Primary School
Cloughton Road
Claughton Rd
Catherine St
Coventry St
Oliver Street
Francis Av
Hawarden Av
Radnor Pl
Merton Pl
Alvanley Pl
Cole St
CP
Bentinck Pl
Eastbourne Rd
Menai St
Back Menai St
River St
Road
Pyramids Shopping Centre
Grange Pl
Charing Cross
Little Theatre
Grange Rd
A St
St Andrew's Road
Slatey Road
Grange Road West
Barton St
Clayton St
Clayton Pl
WHETSTONE LANE
Salisbury St
BOROUGH ROAD A552
The Nook
Eaton Rd
Osborne Rd
Alexandra Rd
Ravenscroft Rd
Henthorne St
Cook St
PO
Grosvenor Road
Grosvenor Court
Grange Mount
Road
Warwick Cl
Carlisle Mews
Quarrybank
Woodlands
Fearnley Rd
Lowwood Gr
Brookland Rd
Health Cen
Hazel Rd
Hollybank Rd
6
Devonshire Road
Place
Grafton St
Devonshire Cl
Caroline Pl
The Lindens
Alfred Rd
Westbourne Rd
Clarendon Cl
Grange Vw
Tetbury St
Wilkinson St
Zetland Rd
Quarry Bank
B5148
Cedar Street
Maple St
Lowwood Rd
Circular Rd
Lowwood Road
Palm Grove
Slatey Rd
Reedville
Balfour Road
Charlesville
resford
Euston Grove
Road
Ridley Street
Town Vw
Oxton Rd
Oak St
Bank
Camforth Cl
BOROUGH ROAD
Shaw St
Park Gv
St Werburghs RC Primary School
Council Building
Woodlands Primary School
Clifton
WHETSTONE LANE
Belmont Grove
Belmont
Penrith St
Raffles Road
Whalley Rd
Rawcliffe Rd
Tatton Rd
Mounsey Rd
Derby Rd
Wellington Ter
Wellington Ter
7
Road
Mather Road
Barnard Rd
Enfield Ter
Devaney Medical Centre
Ball's Road
Princess Terrace
Mount Grove Place
Ball's Road E
Mount Gv
Willmer Road
Larch Road
Elm Grove
Convent Cl
Rctr Cl
388
331
331
Christchurch CE Primary School
Ash Rd
Charlecombe St
Victoria Gardens
James St
Kings Mount
92
Falcon Rd
Beech Rd
Beech Court
Laurel Rd
Chesnut Grove
Dingle Rd
Milton Road
Milton Rd E
Halcyon Road
Victoria
1 grid square represents 250 metres
CH42

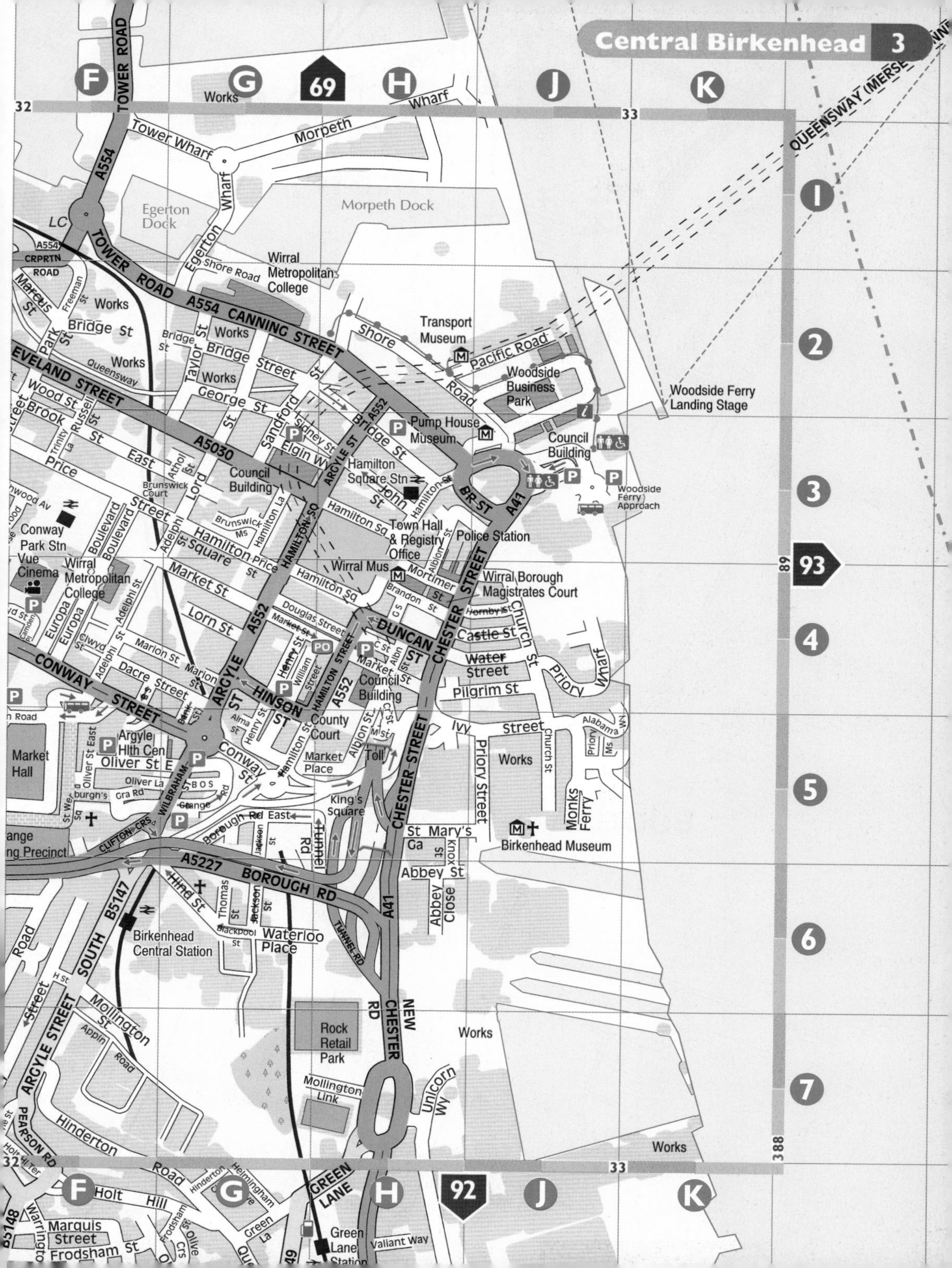
F
G
69
H
J
K
32
33
89
388
93
92
1
2
3
4
5
6
7
TOWER ROAD
A554
Works
Wharf
Tower Wharf
Morpeth
Morpeth Dock
Egerton Dock
Egerton Wharf
LC
CRPRTN ROAD
QUEENSWAY (MERSEY TUNNEL)
Shore Road
Wirral Metropolitan College
TOWER ROAD A554 CANNING STREET
Marcus St
Freeman St
Park St
Bridge St
Taylor St
Bridge Street
Queensway
CLEVELAND STREET
Wood St
Brook St
Russell St
Trinity La
Price St
East
A5030
George St
Sandford St
Sidney St
Elgin Wy
Shore Road
Transport Museum
Pacific Road
Woodside Business Park
Woodside Ferry Landing Stage
Pump House Museum
Council Building
Hamilton Square Stn
John St
Hamilton St
Bridge St
ARGYLE ST
A552
BR ST
A41
Woodside Ferry Approach
Conway Park Stn
Vue Cinema
Wirral Metropolitan College
Brunswick Court
Atholl St
Lord St
Brunswick Ms
Hamilton La
HAMILTON SQ
Hamilton Sq
Town Hall & Registry Office
Police Station
Albion St
Boulevard
Adelphi St
Hamilton Square
Price St
Market St
Hamilton Sq
Wirral Mus
Mortimer St
CHESTER STREET
Wirral Borough Magistrates Court
Brandon St
Europa Blvd
Camden Pl
Lorn St
Douglas Street
Market St
DUNCAN ST
Hornby St
Castle St
Church St
Clwyd St
Marion St
Henry St
William St
HAMILTON STREET
PO
Market St
Albn St
Council Building
Water Street
Priory Wharf
Pilgrim St
CONWAY STREET
Dacre Street
HINSON ST
A552
Bank St
Alma St
Henry St
Hamilton St
County Court
Albion St
Cross St
Ivy Street
Alabama Wy
Priory Ms
Road
Market Hall
Argyle Hlth Cen
Oliver St East
Oliver St E
Oliver La
WILBRAHAM ST
Conway St
Market Place
Toll
Priory Street
Works
Church St
Monks Ferry
Grange Rd
Clifton Crs
Borough Rd East
Tunnel Rd
King's Square
CHESTER STREET
St Mary's Ga
Knox St
Birkenhead Museum
Grange Shopping Precinct
A5227 BOROUGH RD
Hind St
Thomas St
Jackson St
Abbey St
Abbey Close
B5147
SOUTH
Birkenhead Central Station
Blackpool St
Waterloo Place
TUNNEL RD
A41
NEW CHESTER RD
Road
Street
H St
Mollington St
Appin Road
ARGYLE STREET
Rock Retail Park
Works
Mollington Link
Unicorn Wy
PEARSON RD
Hinderton Road
Holt Hill
Holt Ter
Hinderton
Helmingham
GREEN LANE
Green La
Green Lane Station
Valiant Way
B5148
Warrington
Marquis Street
Frodsham St
Frodsham
St Olive
Works

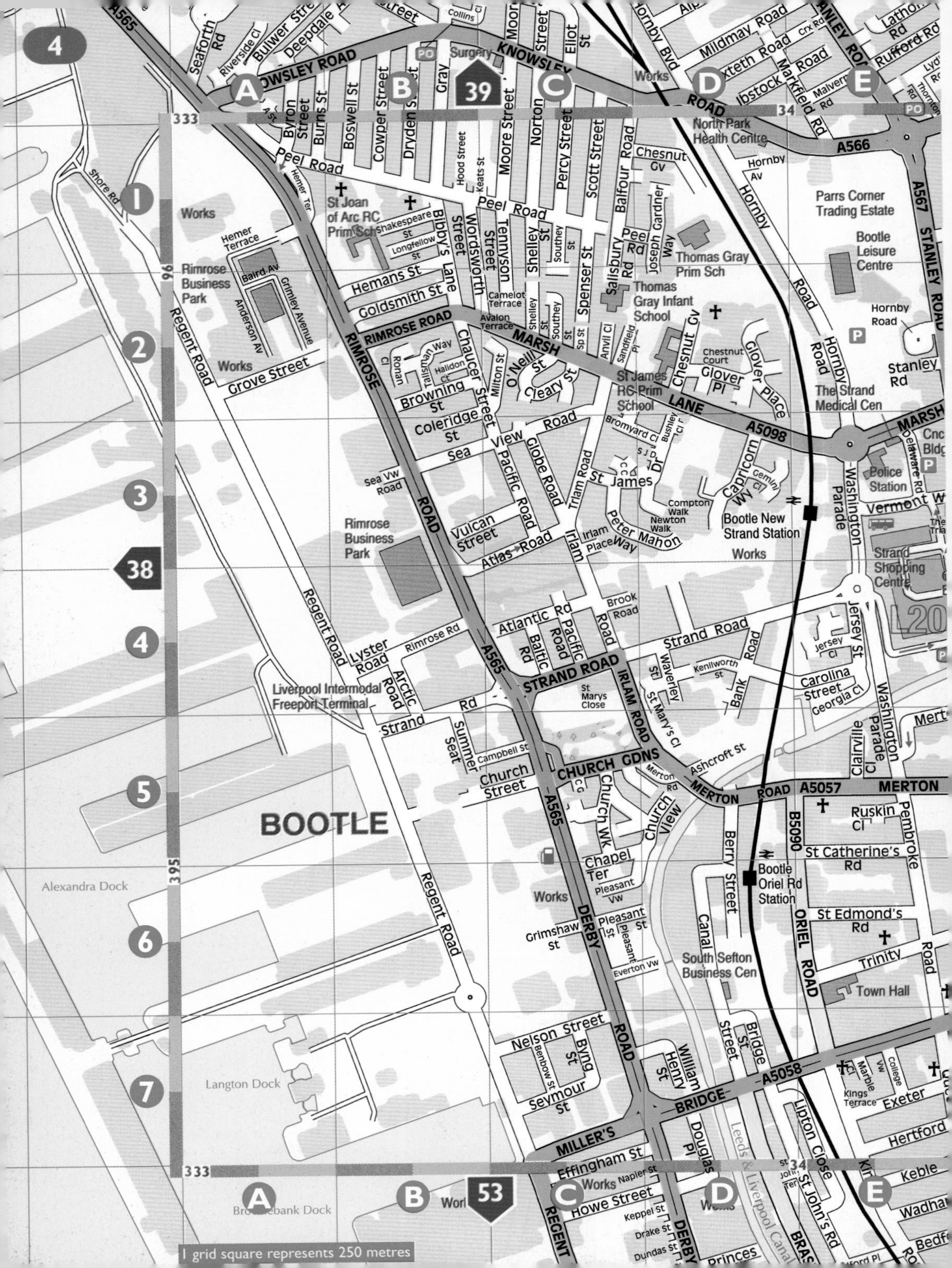
4
39
38
53
A
B
C
D
E
1
2
3
4
5
6
7
333
334
395
396
BOOTLE
KNOWSLEY ROAD
RIMROSE ROAD
MARSH LANE
STRAND ROAD
DERBY ROAD
MERTON ROAD
ORIEL ROAD
STANLEY ROAD
BRIDGE ROAD
MILLER'S BRIDGE
CHURCH GDNS
IRLAM ROAD
A565
A566
A567
A5098
A5057
A5058
B5090
L20
Regent Road
Peel Road
Grove Street
Sea View Road
Church Street
Nelson Street
Atlantic Rd
Strand Road
Washington Parade
Hornby Road
Hornby Bvd
Mildmay Road
Rufford Rd
Chesnut Gv
Balfour Road
Scott Street
Percy Street
Norton St
Moore Street
Dryden Street
Cowper Street
Boswell St
Burns St
Byron Street
Seaforth Rd
Bulwer Street
Deepdale
Riverside Cl
Shore Rd
Hemer Terrace
Baird Av
Grimley Avenue
Anderson Av
Shakespeare St
Longfellow St
Hemans St
Goldsmith St
Bibby's Lane
Wordsworth Street
Tennyson Street
Shelley St
Southey St
Spenser St
Salisbury Rd
Joseph Gardner Way
Chaucer Street
Milton St
O'Neill St
Cleary St
Browning St
Coleridge St
Pacific Road
Globe Road
Vulcan Street
Atlas Road
Irlam Place
Peter Mahon Way
St James Dr
Capricorn Wy
Glover Place
Lyster Road
Arctic Road
Summer Seat
Campbell St
Church Wk
Church View
Chapel Ter
Pleasant Vw
Pleasant St
Grimshaw St
Everton Vw
Byng St
Seymour St
William Henry St
Bridge St
Canal Street
Berry Street
Lipton Close
St John's Rd
Effingham St
Howe Street
Keppel St
Drake St
Dundas St
Douglas Pl
Carolina Street
Georgia Cl
Jersey St
Ruskin Cl
Pembroke Road
St Catherine's Rd
St Edmond's Rd
Trinity Road
Exeter
Hertford
Keble
Works
Surgery
PO
North Park Health Centre
Parrs Corner Trading Estate
Bootle Leisure Centre
Thomas Gray Prim Sch
Thomas Gray Infant School
St Joan of Arc RC Prim Sch
St James RC Prim School
Rimrose Business Park
Bootle New Strand Station
Bootle Oriel Rd Station
The Strand Medical Cen
Police Station
Strand Shopping Centre
South Sefton Business Cen
Town Hall
Liverpool Intermodal Freeport Terminal
Alexandra Dock
Langton Dock
Brocklebank Dock
Leeds & Liverpool Canal
1 grid square represents 250 metres

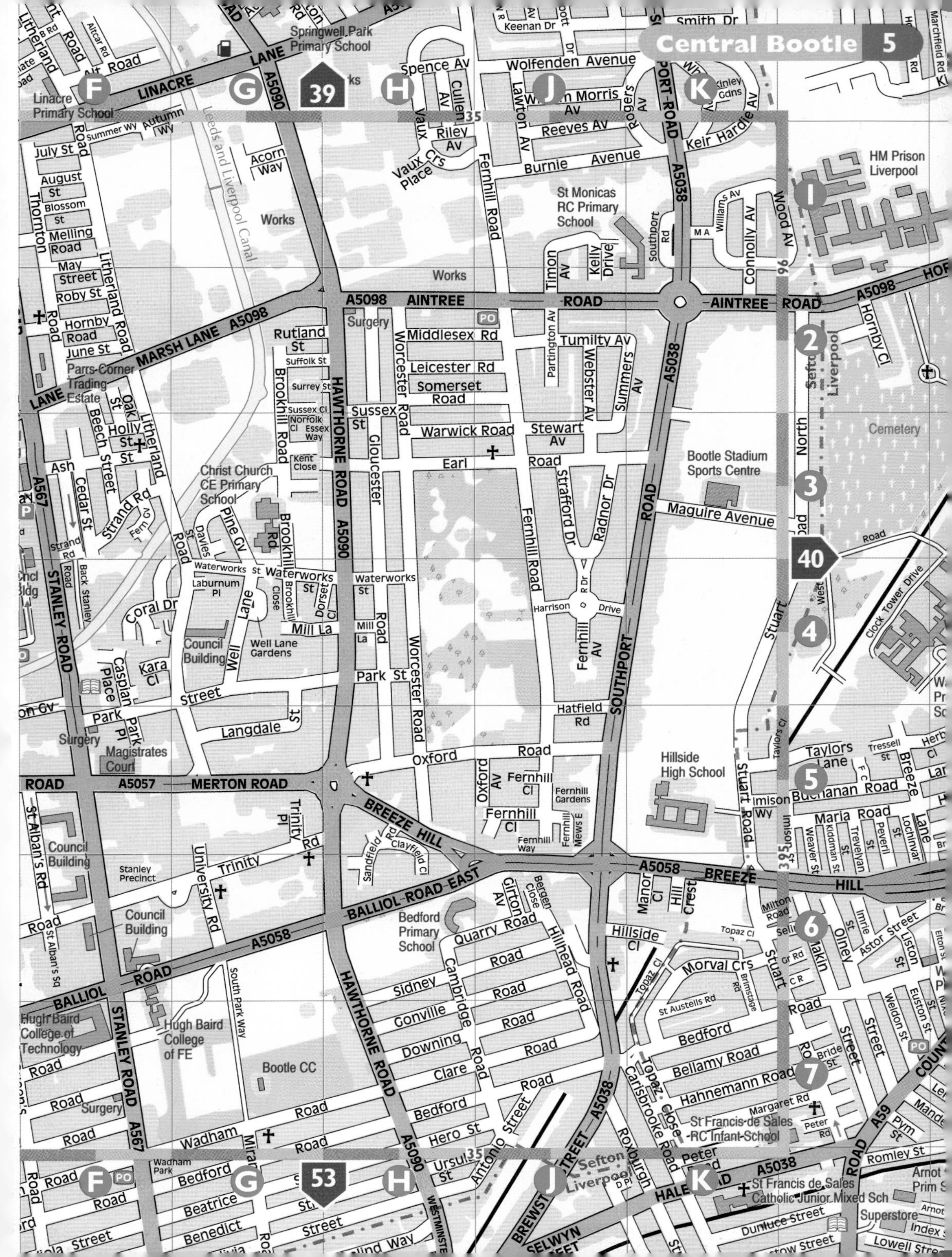
Springwell Park Primary School
Linacre Primary School
LINACRE LANE
A5090
39
35
Spence Av
Wolfenden Avenue
Keenan Dr
Smith Dr
William Morris Av
Reeves Av
Burnie Avenue
Keir Hardie Av
Kinley Gdns
Cullen Av
Vaux Av
Riley Av
Vaux Crs
Place
Lawton Av
Rogers Av
Fernhill Road
SOUTHPORT ROAD
A5038
HM Prison Liverpool
Altcar Rd
Alt Road
Litherland Road
Summer Wy
Autumn Wy
July St
August St
Blossom St
Melling Road
May Street
Roby St
Hornby Road
June St
Thornton Road
Leeds and Liverpool Canal
Acorn Way
Works
St Monicas RC Primary School
Timon Av
Kelly Drive
Southport Rd
Williams Av
Connolly Av
Wood Av
A5098
AINTREE ROAD
MARSH LANE
LANE
Parts Corner Trading Estate
Rutland St
Suffolk St
Surrey St
Sussex Cl
Norfolk Cl
Essex Way
Kent Close
Surgery
PO
Middlesex Rd
Leicester Rd
Somerset Road
Sussex St
Warwick Road
Earl Road
Partington Av
Tumilty Av
Webster Av
Summers Av
Stewart Av
Hornby Cl
North Sefton
Liverpool
Cemetery
Bootle Stadium Sports Centre
Maguire Avenue
40
Road
West
Clock Tower Drive
Oak St
Holly St
Beech Street
Ash St
Cedar St
Strand Rd
Fern Gv
Litherland
Christ Church CE Primary School
Pine Gv
Davies St
Brookhill Road
Brookhill Rd
HAWTHORNE ROAD
Gloucester
Worcester Road
Strafford Dr
Radnor Dr
Fernhill Road
A567
STANLEY ROAD
Strand Rd
Back Stanley Road
Cncl Bldg
Waterworks St
Laburnum Pl
Brookhill Close
Dorset Cl
Coral Dr
Well Lane
Well Lane Gardens
Mill La
Council Building
Kara Cl
Caspian Place
Street
Park Pl
Park St
Mill Road
Harrison Drive
R Dr
Fernhill Av
Stuart Road
Hatfield Rd
Hillside High School
Taylors Cl
Taylors Lane
Tressell St
Herbert Cl
Langdale St
Surgery
Magistrates Court
Oxford Road
Oxford Av
Fernhill Cl
Fernhill Gardens
Fernhill Mews E
Fernhill Way
A5057
MERTON ROAD
BREEZE HILL
A5058
Imison Way
Buchanan Road
Maria Road
Breeze Lane
Lochinvar St
Weaver St
Kiddman St
Trevelyan St
Peveril St
St Alban's Rd
Council Building
Trinity Pl
Trinity Rd
Sandfield Rd
Clayfield Cl
Stanley Precinct
University Rd
BALLIOL ROAD EAST
Girton Av
Bergen Close
Manor Cl
Hill Crest
Milton Road
Bedford Primary School
Quarry Road
Hillhead Road
Hillside Cl
Topaz Cl
Morval Crs
Brimstage Rd
Olney St
Imrie St
Astor Street
Liston St
Elton St
Council Building
BALLIOL ROAD
Sidney Road
Cambridge Road
Gonville Road
Downing Road
Clare Road
Bedford Road
Hero St
St Austells Rd
Bedford Road
Bellamy Road
Hahnemann Road
Margaret Rd
Bride St
Weldon St
Euston St
Hugh Baird College of Technology
Hugh Baird College of FE
South Park Way
Bootle CC
Surgery
Wadham Road
Antonio Street
Ursula St
Carisbrooke Road
Topaz Close
Roxburgh
St Francis de Sales RC Infant School
Peter Rd
Pym St
A59
COUNTY ROAD
Romley St
Wadham Park
53
Bedford Road
Beatrice Street
Benedict Street
Westminster
BREWSTER STREET
Sefton Liverpool
D Pl
HALE ROAD
A5038
St Francis de Sales Catholic Junior Mixed Sch
Superstore
Arnot Prim S
Dunluce Street
Lowell Street
SELWYN
F
G
H
J
K
I
2
3
4
5
6
7

L3
LIVERPOOL
70
93
334
91
390
A
B
C
D
E
1
2
3
4
5
6
7
KINGSWAY
QUEENSWAY (MERSEY TUNNEL)
Chadwick Court Industrial Centre
Superstore
Retail Park
Carruthers St
Blackstock Street
Pumpfields Road
Liverpool Community College
Business Centre
Paul Street
Eaton Street
Gascoyne Street
Naylor
Vauxhall Road
Freemasons Row
Phillips Street
LEEDS STREET
A5053
A5036
GREAT HOWARD STREET
King Edward Industrial Estate
Galton St
Paisley St
Roberts St
Greenock St
King Edward Ind Est
Addison Street
Addison Wy
Mazenod Court
Midghall St
Marlborough St
Marybone
Holy Cross Catholic Primary School
Adlington Street
Pickop St
Lace St
Fontenoy St
Works
Highfield St
Westmorland Dr
Westmorland Pl
Princes Gdns
Cockspur St
Pall Mall
Back Leeds St
Radisson SAS Hotel
Old Leeds St
East Street
Rigby St
Earle St
St Paul's Sq
Old Hall Street
Brook St
Gibraltar Row
William Jessop Wy
BATH STREET
KING EDWARD ST
Princes Dock
Princes Parade
Newspaper Office
Edmund St
Bixteth Street
Union St
Ormond St
GT CROSSHALL
A5046
LJMU
Hatton Garden Ind Est
Council Building
Hatton Gdn
Johnson St
North St
Trueman
Primrose Hl
Cheapside
Cunliffe St
Vernon St
Co Fire HQ
Mag Court
Police Stn
CHURCHILL WAY
Travelodge
TITHEBARN ST
Moorfields
Hale St
Premier Travel Inn
Moorfields Station
Council Building
CROSSHALL ST
A57
Old Haymarket
Preston St
Cncl Bldg
Conservation Centre
WHITECHAPEL
Isle of Man Ferry Terminal
NEW QUAY
QUEENSWAY (MERSEY TUNNEL)
Council Building
Thistle Hotel
Rumford Place
Crowne Plaza Hotel
CHAPEL STREET
Cabinet War Rooms
Exchange St E
High Street
Town Hall
DALE ST
Coll
Stanley St
Princes St
Temple La
VICTORIA ST
Council Buildings
Dawson St
Met Quarter (under development)
Williamson Square
George's Dock
GEORGE'S DOCK GATES
Old Church Yd
Covent Gdn
Rumford St
Tower Gdns
WATER ST
Cncl Bldg
Lower Castle St
Swt St
Union Ct
COOK ST
Mathew St
Cavern Club
Harrington Street
Button Street
Williamson St
St Nicholas Pl
Titanic Memorial
Royal Liver Building
Water St
Cunard Building
SAE Institute
Drury La
Brunswick St
Castle St
PO
HM Coroners Court
Lord St
Lord Street
Church Street
Tarleton Street
Basnett
Canada Bvd
THE STRAND
Moor St
Royal Coll of Nursing
JAMES ST
Derby Square
James Street Stn
Cable St
Paradise Street Bus Station
School La
Police Station
Mersey Ferries
Georges Pierhead
Georges Dockway
Pier Head
Mann Island
Red Cross St
STRAND STREET
Queen Elizabeth II Law Courts
Trans Pennine Trail
BBC North & BBC Radio Merseyside
Manesty's La
Peter's La
College Lane
Hanover St
War Memorial
Port of Liverpool Building
Museum of Liverpool (due to open 2010)
Canning Dock
National Discovery Park
Fire Station
A562
CANNING PL
A5041
PARADISE ST
Campbell St
Gradwell Street
Seddon St
Argyle St
York St
HM Customs & Excise National Museum
Hartley Quay
Granada TV
Merseyside Maritime Museum & International Slavery Museum
Fingerprints of Elvis
Albert Dock
Salthouse Dock
Salthouse Quay
Merseyside Police HQ
LIVER ST
PARK LANE
Lakeland Cl
Surrey St
Gilbert
Tate Gallery
Albert Dock Village
The Beatles Story
Premier Travel Inn
Street
Gower
Hotel Ibis
Pownall Sq
Carpenters Rw
Upr Pownall St
Shaws Alley
Grayson St
Cornhill
Hurst St
Tabley St
Sparling Street
Wapping Basin
WAPPING
Wapping Quay
YHA
Kings Dock St
Kings Dock
1 grid square represents 250 metres

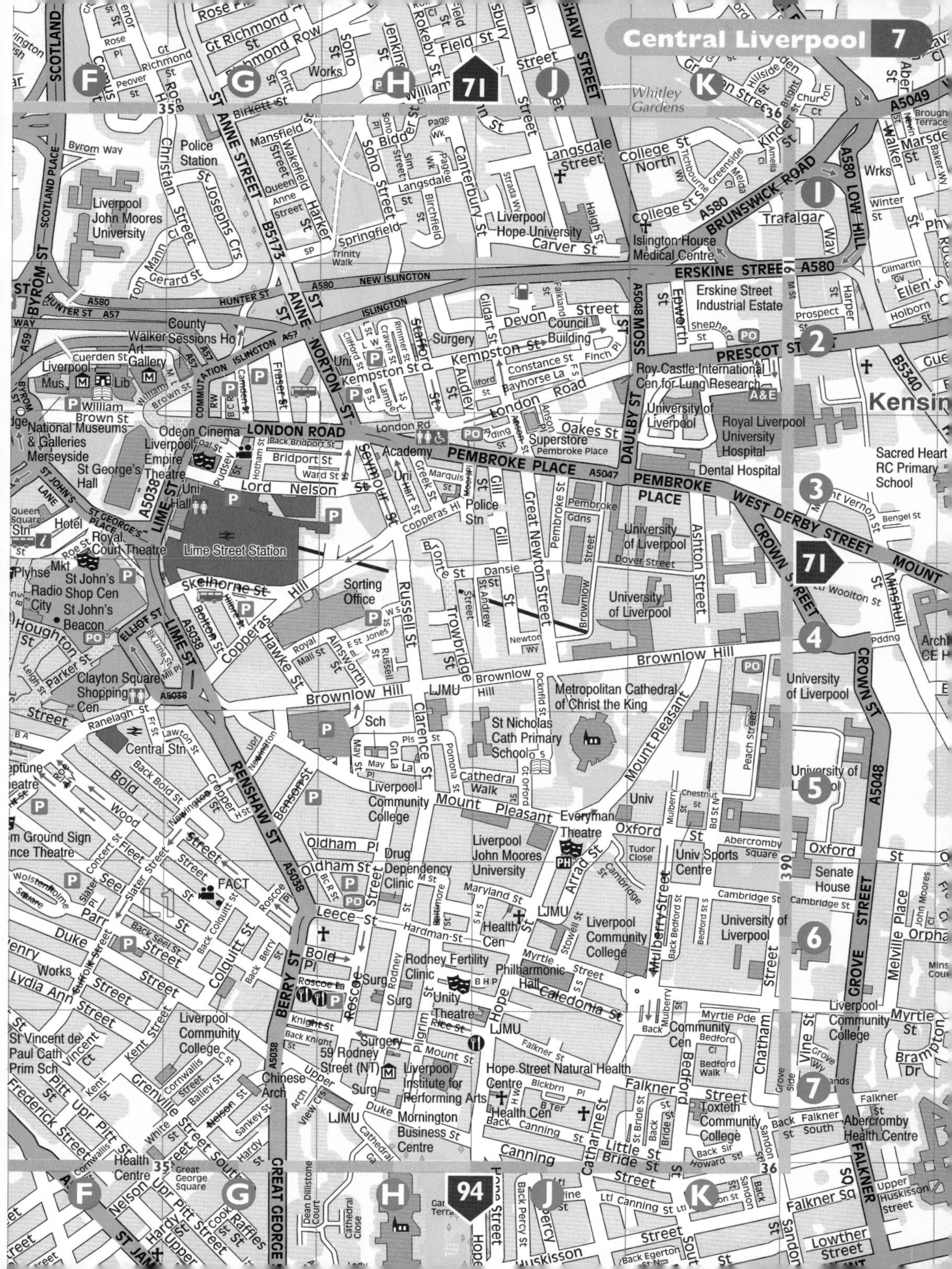
F
G
H
J
K
71
35
36
Whitley Gardens
Scotland Place
Byrom St
Byrom Way
Police Station
Christian Street
St Josephs Crs
Anne Street
B5173
Mansfield St
Soho Street
Bidder St
Canterbury St
Langsdale Street
College St North
Brunswick Road
A580
Low Hill
Trafalgar Way
Liverpool John Moores University
Liverpool Hope University
Carver St
Islington House Medical Centre
Tom Mann Cl
Gerard St
Springfield
Trinity Walk
New Islington
Hunter St
A57
Erskine Street
Erskine Street Industrial Estate
Prescot St
County Sessions Ho
Walker Art Gallery
Liverpool Mus
Lib
Commutation
Islington
Norton St
Stafford St
Kempston St
Devon Street
Council Building
Moss St
A5048
Epworth St
Roy Castle International Cen for Lung Research
A&E
Kensington
William Brown St
National Museums & Galleries Merseyside
Odeon Cinema
London Road
London Rd
Pembroke Place
A5047
Daulby St
University of Liverpool
Royal Liverpool University Hospital
Dental Hospital
Sacred Heart RC Primary School
St George's Hall
Liverpool Empire Theatre
Lime St
A5038
Lord Nelson St
Uni Hall
Lime Street Station
Seymour St
Academy
Police Stn
Great Newton Street
Pembroke Gdns
West Derby Street
Crown Street
Mount Vernon St
Bengel St
St John's Lane
Queen Square
Hotel Royal Court Theatre
Mkt
Plyhse
Radio City
St John's Shop Cen
St John's Beacon
Houghton St
Elliot St
Skelhorne St
Copperas Hill
Sorting Office
Russell St
Trowbridge St
Brownlow Hill
Ashton Street
Dover Street
Minshull St
Ltl Woolton St
Clayton Square Shopping Cen
Parker St
Ranelagh St
Central Stn
Renshaw St
Royal Mail St
Hawke St
Ainsworth St
LJMU
Clarence St
Metropolitan Cathedral of Christ the King
St Nicholas Cath Primary School
Mount Pleasant
Peach Street
University of Liverpool
Crown St
Bold St
Wood St
Cropper St
Benson St
Cathedral Walk
Liverpool Community College
Everyman Theatre
Oxford St
Abercromby Square
Univ Sports Centre
Senate House
Tudor Close
Oldham St
Drug Dependency Clinic
Concert St
Seel St
Slater Street
FACT
Colquitt St
Roscoe St
Parr St
Duke Street
Berry St
Leece St
Hardman St
Hope St
Maryland St
Health Cen
Liverpool Community College
Mulberry Street
Cambridge St
Grove Street
Melville Place
Rodney Fertility Clinic
Philharmonic Hall
Caledonia St
Myrtle Street
Chatham Street
Liverpool Community College
Surg
Unity Theatre
Rice St
Pilgrim St
Mount St
Falkner St
Community Cen
Bedford Walk
Vine St
Brampton Dr
Kent Street
St Vincent de Paul Cath Prim Sch
Pitt Upr Pitt St
Frederick Street
Grenville Street
Chinese Arch
59 Rodney Street (NT)
Liverpool Institute for Performing Arts
Hope Street Natural Health Centre
Mornington Business Centre
Canning St
Catharine St
Little St Bride St
Toxteth Community College
Abercromby Health Centre
Falkner St
Health Centre
Great George Square
Great George St
St James
Nelson St
Upr Pitt Street
Raffles St
Cathedral Close
Dean Dillistone Court
94
Falkner Sq
Upper Huskisson Street
Lowther Street
Ltl Canning St
Huskisson St
Back Percy St
Sandon St
Grove St
A5048
390

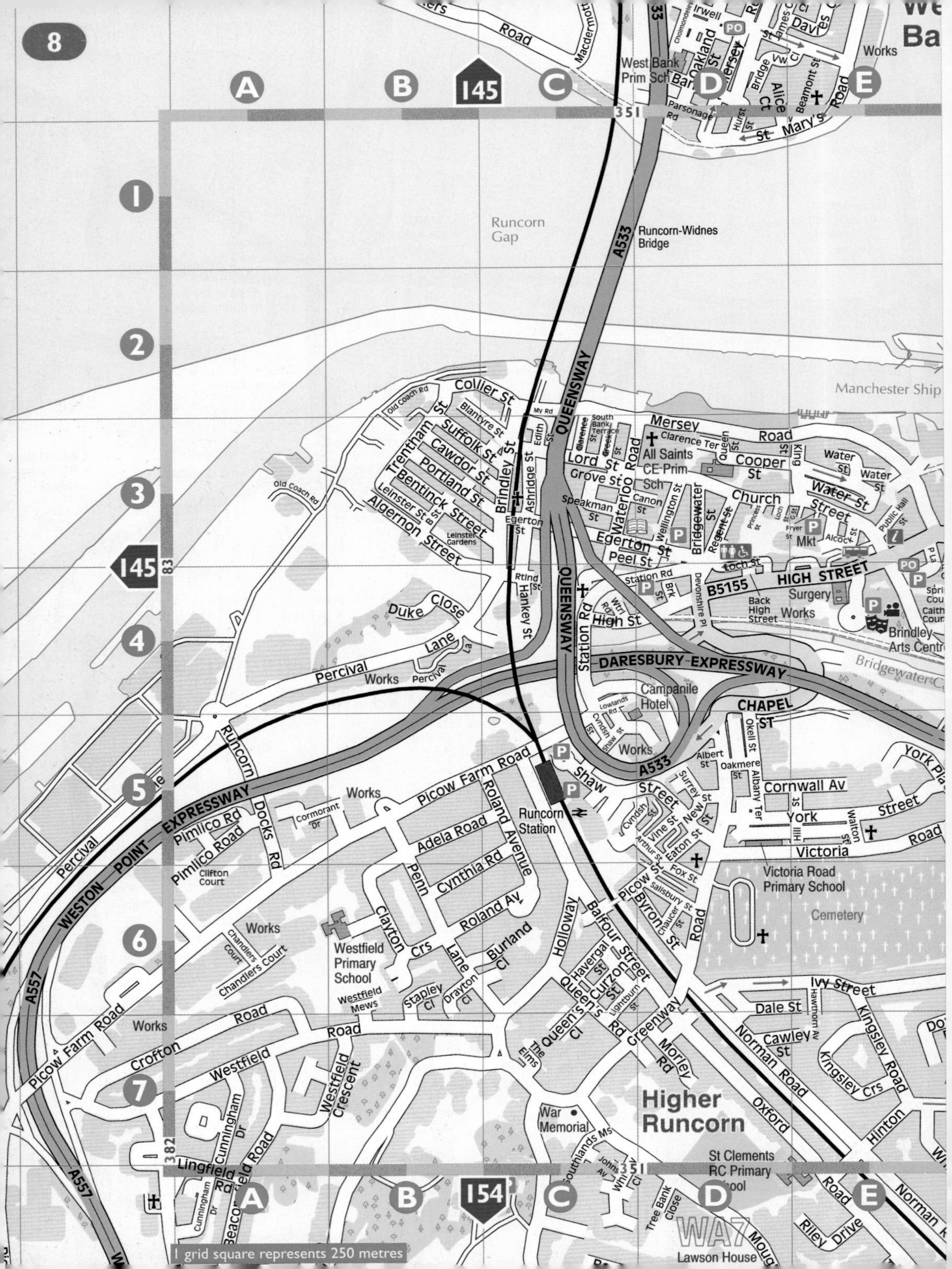
145
A
B
C
D
E
1
2
3
4
5
6
7
351
382
83
154
Road
Macdermott
Irwell
PO
Oakland St
Mersey
West Bank Prim Sch
Parsonage Rd
Hurst St
Alice Ct
Bridge Vw
James Cl
Davies
Beamont St
Road
St Mary's
Works
Runcorn Gap
A533
Runcorn-Widnes Bridge
QUEENSWAY
Manchester Ship
Collier St
Old Coach Rd
Blantyre St
Trentham St
Suffolk St
Cawdor St
Portland St
Bentinck Street
Leinster St
Algernon Street
Leinster Gardens
Brindley St
Ashridge St
Egerton St
Edith St
My Rd
South Bank Terrace
Mersey Road
Clarence Ter
All Saints CE Prim Sch
Lord St
Grove St
Waterloo Road
Speakman St
Canon St
Wellington St
Bridgewater St
Regent St
Cooper St
King St
Queen St
Church Street
Water St
Water Street
Princess St
Loch St
Fryer St
Mkt
Alcock St
Public Hall St
Egerton St
Peel St
Loch St
Station Rd
Brk St
Devonshire Pl
B5155
HIGH STREET
Surgery
Back High Street
Works
Brindley Arts Centre
Bridgewater Canal
Old Coach Rd
Duke Close
Percival Lane
Works
Percival La
Rtlnd St
Hankey St
High St
Station Rd
DARESBURY EXPRESSWAY
Campanile Hotel
Lowlands Rd
Cvndsh St
Shaw St
Works
CHAPEL ST
Albert St
Oakmere St
Okell St
Albany Ter
A533
Shaw Street
Runcorn
Percival
WESTON POINT EXPRESSWAY
Pimlico Rd
Pimlico Road
Docks Rd
Cormorant Dr
Works
Picow Farm Road
Roland Avenue
Adela Road
Penn Lane
Cynthia Rd
Roland Av
Clifton Court
Runcorn Station
Surrey St
New St
Vine St
Eaton St
Arthur St
Fox St
Picow St
Salisbury St
Byron St
Chaucer St
Cornwall Av
York Place
York Street
Hill St
Walton St
Victoria Road
Victoria Road Primary School
Cemetery
Works
Chandlers Court
Chandlers Court
Westfield Primary School
Clayton Crs
Lane
Burland Cl
Holloway
Balfour Street
Havergal St
Curzon St
Queen's Rd
Road
A557
Westfield Mews
Stapley Cl
Drayton Cl
Lightburn St
Greenway
Ivy Street
Dale St
Hawthorn Av
Kingsley Road
Cawley St
Kingsley Crs
Picow Farm Road
Works
Crofton Road
Road
Westfield
Westfield Crescent
Queen's Cl
The Elms
Morley Rd
Norman Road
Oxford Road
Higher Runcorn
Hinton
War Memorial
Cunningham Dr
Southlands Ms
Johns Av
Whitby Cl
St Clements RC Primary School
Lingfield Rd
Beaconsfield Road
Cunningham Dr
Tree Bank Close
WA7
Lawson House
Riley Drive
Norman Road
1 grid square represents 250 metres

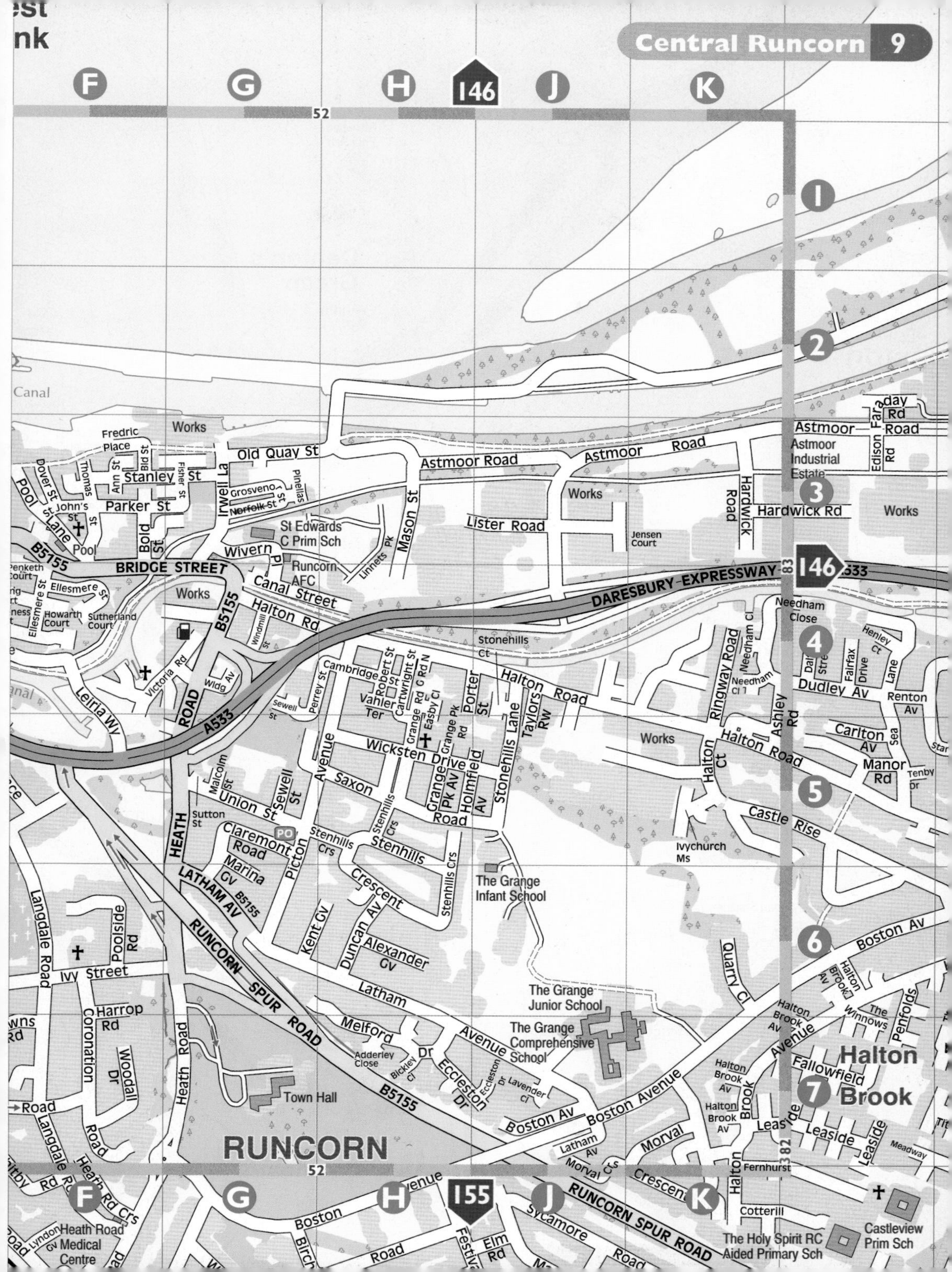
F
G
H
146
J
K
52
1
2
3
4
5
6
7
Canal
Works
Fredric Place
Old Quay St
Astmoor Road
Astmoor Road
Astmoor Road
Astmoor Industrial Estate
Faraday Rd
Edison Rd
Dover St
Thomas St
Ann St
Bld St
Stanley St
Fisher St
Irwell La
Grosvenor St
Pinellas
Norfolk St
Parker St
Pool Lane
St John's
Bold St
Mason St
Hardwick Road
Hardwick Rd
Lister Road
Jensen Court
St Edwards C Prim Sch
Linnets Pk
Wivern Pl
Runcorn AFC
B5155
BRIDGE STREET
Penketh Court
Ellesmere St
Howarth Court
Sutherland Court
Canal Street
Halton Rd
Windmill St
DARESBURY EXPRESSWAY
A533
Needham Close
Henley Ct
Stonehills Ct
Cambridge St
Robert St
Cartwright St
Grange Rd N
Halton Road
Ringway Road
Needham Cl
Fairfax Drive
Lane
Dudley Av
Renton Av
Victoria Rd
Wldg Av
Sewell St
Perrey St
Vahler Ter
Easby Cl
Grange Pk Rd
Porter St
Taylors Rw
Ashley Rd
Leiria Wy
ROAD
Works
Halton Ct
Halton Road
Carlton Av
Manor Rd
Tenby Dr
Wicksten Drive
Malcolm St
Union St
Avenue
Saxon
Grange Pk Av
Holmfield Av
Stonehills Lane
Grange Road
Castle Rise
Sutton St
PO
Claremont Road
Picton
Stenhills Crs
Stenhills
Ivychurch Ms
HEATH
Marina Gv
LATHAM AV
B5155
Crescent
Stenhills Crs
The Grange Infant School
Langdale Road
Poolside Rd
Kent Gv
Duncan Av
Alexander Gv
Quarry Cl
Boston Av
RUNCORN SPUR ROAD
Ivy Street
Latham
Halton Brook Av
The Grange Junior School
Harrop Rd
Coronation Road
Woodall Dr
Heath Road
Melford
Adderley Close
Bickley Cl
Dr
Avenue
The Grange Comprehensive School
Halton Brook Av
Halton Brook Avenue
The Winnows
Penfolds
Halton Brook
Fallowfield
Eccleston Dr
Lavender Cl
Town Hall
Boston Avenue
Boston Av
Leaside
Meadway
RUNCORN
Latham Av
Morval
Morval Cres
Crescent
382
Fernhurst
Langdale Road
Heath Rd Crs
Boston
Avenue
155
RUNCORN SPUR ROAD
Cotterill
Sycamore
Heath Road Medical Centre
Lyndon Gv
Road
Elm Rd
Festival
Road
The Holy Spirit RC Aided Primary Sch
Castleview Prim Sch

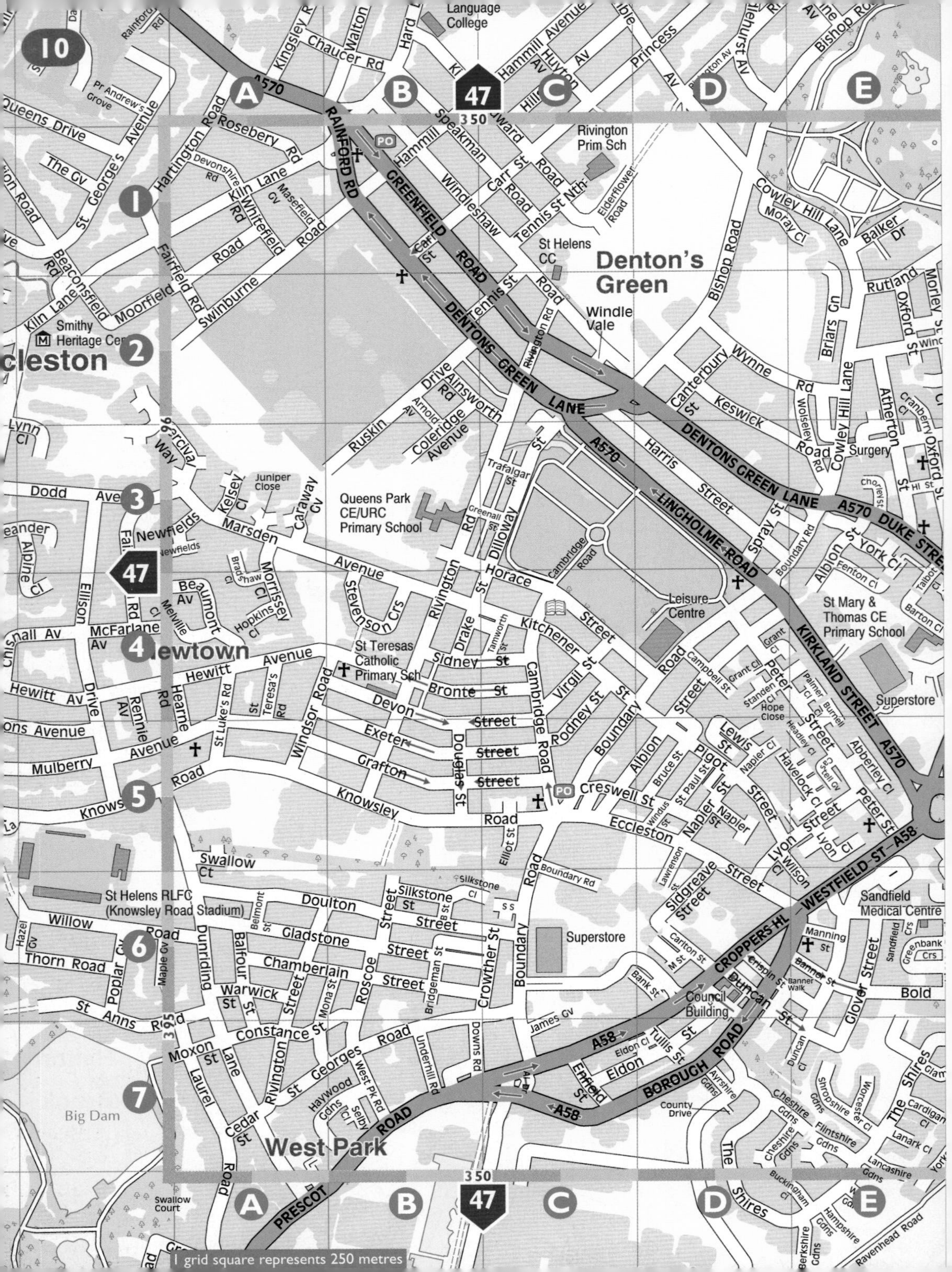

10
47
A
B
C
D
E
1
2
3
4
5
6
7
350
395
Language College
Chaucer Rd
Walton
Kingsley Rd
Rainford Rd
Hammill Avenue
Huyton Av
Hill
Princess Av
Ilchurst Av
Bishop Rd
Pr Andrew's Grove
Queens Drive
St George's Avenue
The Gv
Hartington Road
Rosebery Rd
Devonshire Rd
Kiln Lane
Whitefield Rd
Masefield Gv
Road
Fairfield Rd
Swinburne
Moorfield
Beaconsfield
Kiln Lane
Smithy Heritage Cen
cleston
A570
RAINFORD RD
GREENFIELD ROAD
DENTONS GREEN LANE
PO
Hammill
Speakman
Windleshaw
Carr St
Carr St
Road
Tennis St Nth
Tennis St
Rivington Prim Sch
Elderflower Road
St Helens CC
Denton's Green
Bishop Road
Cowley Hill Lane
Moray Cl
Balker Dr
Rutland
Oxford St
Morley St
Windle Vale
Rivington Rd
Canterbury
Wynne
Rd
Keswick
Briars Gn
Cowley Hill Lane
Wolseley Road
Atherton St
Cranberry Cl
Surgery
Oxford St
Drive
Ainsworth Rd
Arnold Av
Ruskin
Coleridge Avenue
LANE
Harris Street
DENTONS GREEN LANE
A570 DUKE STREET
Lynn Cl
Percival Way
Trafalgar St
Juniper Close
Kelsey Cl
Caraway Gv
Dodd Ave
Queens Park CE/URC Primary School
Greenall St
Dilloway
Rd
LINGHOLME ROAD
Spray St
Boundary Rd
Chorley St
Hl St
Eleander
Alpine Cl
Newfields
Newfields
Marsden
Avenue
Bradshaw
Morrissey Cl
Cambridge Road
Albion St
York Cl
Fenton Cl
Talbot Cl
Ellison
Beaumont Av
Melville Cl
Hopkins Cl
Stevenson Crs
Rivington
Horace St
Leisure Centre
Street
Road
KIRKLAND STREET
St Mary & Thomas CE Primary School
Barton Cl
McFarlane Av
Chisnall Av
Newtown
Drake
Tamworth St
Kitchener
Grant Cl
Campbell St
Grant Cl
St Teresas Catholic Primary Sch
Sidney St
Virgil St
Peter St
Palmer Cl
Burnell Cl
Standen Cl
Hope Close
Superstore
Hewitt Avenue
Hewitt Av
Drive
Rennie Av
Hearne Rd
St Luke's Rd
Teresa's St
Rd
Windsor Road
Bronte St
Cambridge Road
Rodney St
Boundary St
Street
Devon Street
Exeter Street
Grafton Street
Douglas St
Lewis St
Headley Cl
Abberley Cl
A570
ons Avenue
Avenue
Mulberry
Road
Knowsley Road
Creswell St
Albion
Bruce St
St Paul St
Pigot St
Napier Cl
Havelock Cl
Westell Cl
Peter St
Road
Elliot St
Eccleston Street
Windus St
Napier St
Napier St
Lyon Cl
Lyon Cl
Wilson Cl
WESTFIELD ST A58
Swallow Ct
Boundary Road
Boundary Rd
Lawrenson St
Sidgreave Street
Silkstone Cl
Silkstone St
Doulton Street
B St
St Helens RLFC (Knowsley Road Stadium)
Sandfield Medical Centre
Willow Road
Belmont St
Gladstone Street
Hazel Gv
Thorn Road
Poplar Gv
Maple Gv
Dunriding
Balfour St
Chamberlain Street
Bridgeman St
Crowther St
Boundary
Superstore
Carlton St
M St
CROPPERS HL
Crispin St
Manning St
Banner St
Banner Walk
Sandfield Crs
Greenbank Crs
Glover Street
Bold
Warwick St
Street
Mona St
Roscoe
Street
Bank St
Council Building
Duncan St
Duncan Cl
St Anns Road
Constance St
Road
James Gv
A58
Eldon Cl
Tullis St
Moxon St
Lane
Laurel
Rivington
St Georges
Underhill Rd
Downs Rd
Eldon St
Enfield St
BOROUGH ROAD
Ayrshire Gdns
Cheshire Gdns
Shropshire Gdns
Worcester Cl
The Shires
Glam
Big Dam
Cedar St
Haywood Gdns
Selby Cl
West Pk Rd
ROAD
A58
County Drive
Flintshire Gdns
Cardigan Cl
Lanark Cl
West Park
Road
Lancashire Gdns
York
Swallow Court
PRESCOT
The Shires
Buckingham Cl
Hampshire Gdns
Berkshire Gdns
Ravenhead Road
1 grid square represents 250 metres

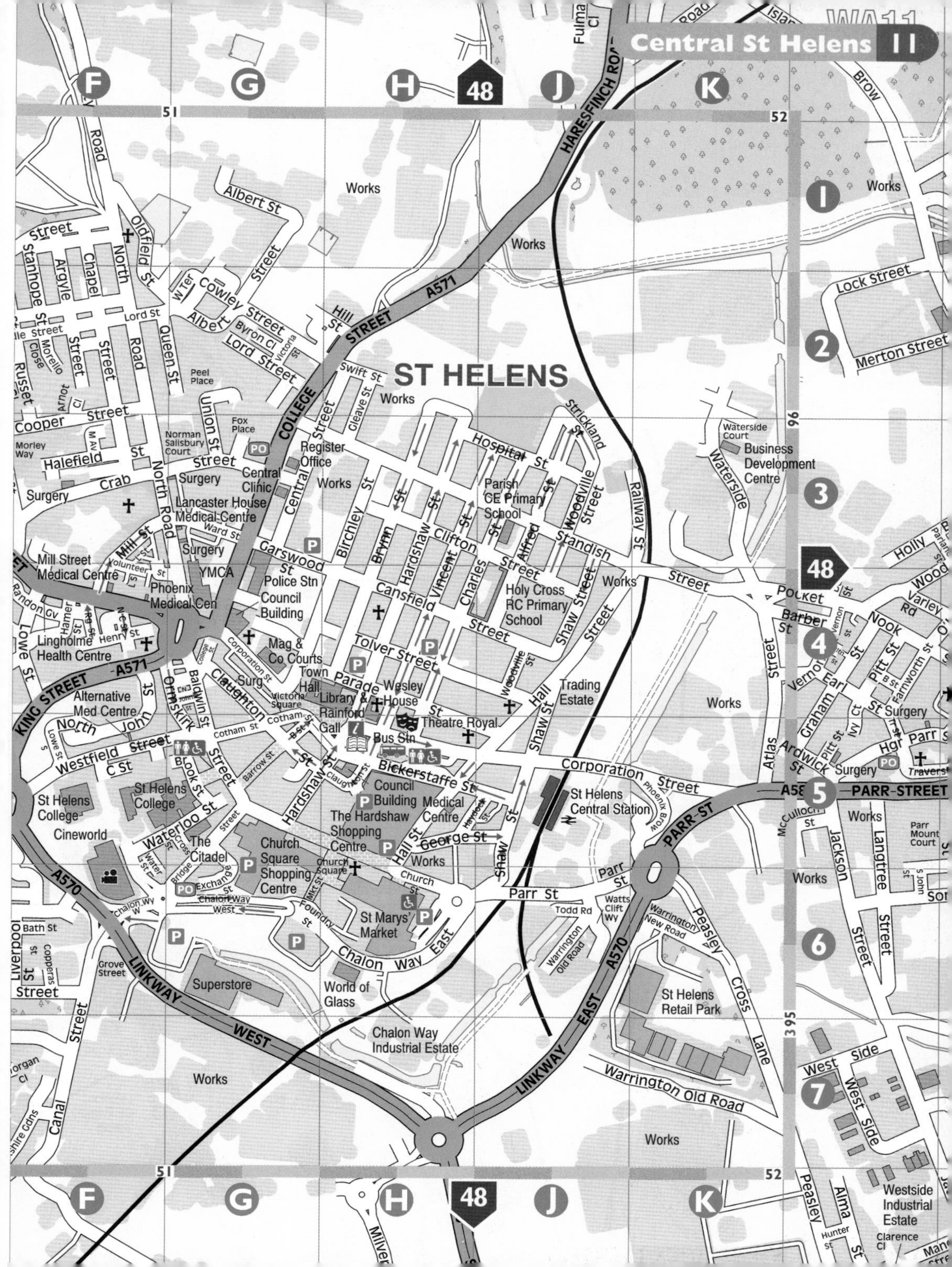
ST HELENS
F
G
H
48
J
K
51
52
96
395
I
2
3
4
5
6
7
HARESFINCH ROAD
A571
COLLEGE STREET
KING STREET
LINKWAY WEST
LINKWAY EAST
A570
PARR ST
PARR STREET
Albert St
Works
Oldfield St
North Road
Street
Stanhope St
Argyle Street
Chapel Street
Cowley Street
W Ter
Albert
Byron Cl
Victoria St
Lord Street
Lord St
Morello Close
Russet
Arnot Cl
Queen St
Peel Place
Hill St
Swift St
Gleave St
Cooper Street
Union St
Fox Place
Norman Salisbury Court
Morley Way
Halefield St
M Av
Crab Street
Surgery
Central Clinic
Register Office
Central Street
Lancaster House Medical Centre
Ward St
Mill St
Mill Street Medical Centre
Volunteer St
YMCA
Phoenix Medical Cen
Police Stn
Council Building
Garswood St
Birchley St
Bryn St
Hardshaw St
Vincent St
Clifton St
Charles St
Hospital St
Strickland St
Parish CE Primary School
Alfred St
Woodville Street
Standish Street
Cansfield Street
Holy Cross RC Primary School
Shaw Street
Railway St
Lingholme Health Centre
Henry St
Lowe St
Hamer St
Randon Gv
Mag & Co Courts
Corporation St
Tolver Street
Town Hall
Parade St
Wesley House
Library & Rainford Gall
Victoria Square
Theatre Royal
Bus Stn
Trading Estate
Hall St
Shaw St
Alternative Med Centre
North John St
Ormskirk Street
Baldwin St
Claughton St
Cotham St
Westfield Street
C St
Brook St
Barrow St
Bickerstaffe St
Corporation Street
St Helens Central Station
Phoenix Brow
St Helens College
Waterloo St
Cineworld
The Citadel
Water St
Bridge St
Exchange St
Church Square Shopping Centre
The Hardshaw Shopping Centre
Council Building
Medical Centre
Haydock St
George St
Church St
Parr St
Chalon Way W
Chalon Way West
Foundry St
St Marys' Market
Chalon Way East
Todd Rd
Watts Clift Wy
Warrington Old Road
Warrington New Road
Bath St
Liverpool St
Copperas St
Street
Grove Street
Superstore
World of Glass
Chalon Way Industrial Estate
St Helens Retail Park
Peasley Cross Lane
Warrington Old Road
Canal Street
Morgan Cl
Works
Waterside Court
Business Development Centre
Waterside
Lock Street
Merton Street
Brow
Pocket Nook Street
Holly
Varley Rd
Barber St
Vernon St
Pitt St
Farnworth St
Earl St
Graham St
Ivy Ct
Atlas Street
Ardwick St
Surgery
PO
McCulloch St
Jackson Street
Langtree Street
Parr Mount Court
Westside
West Side
Westside Industrial Estate
Peasley
Alma
Hunter St
Clarence Cl
Fulmar Cl
Road

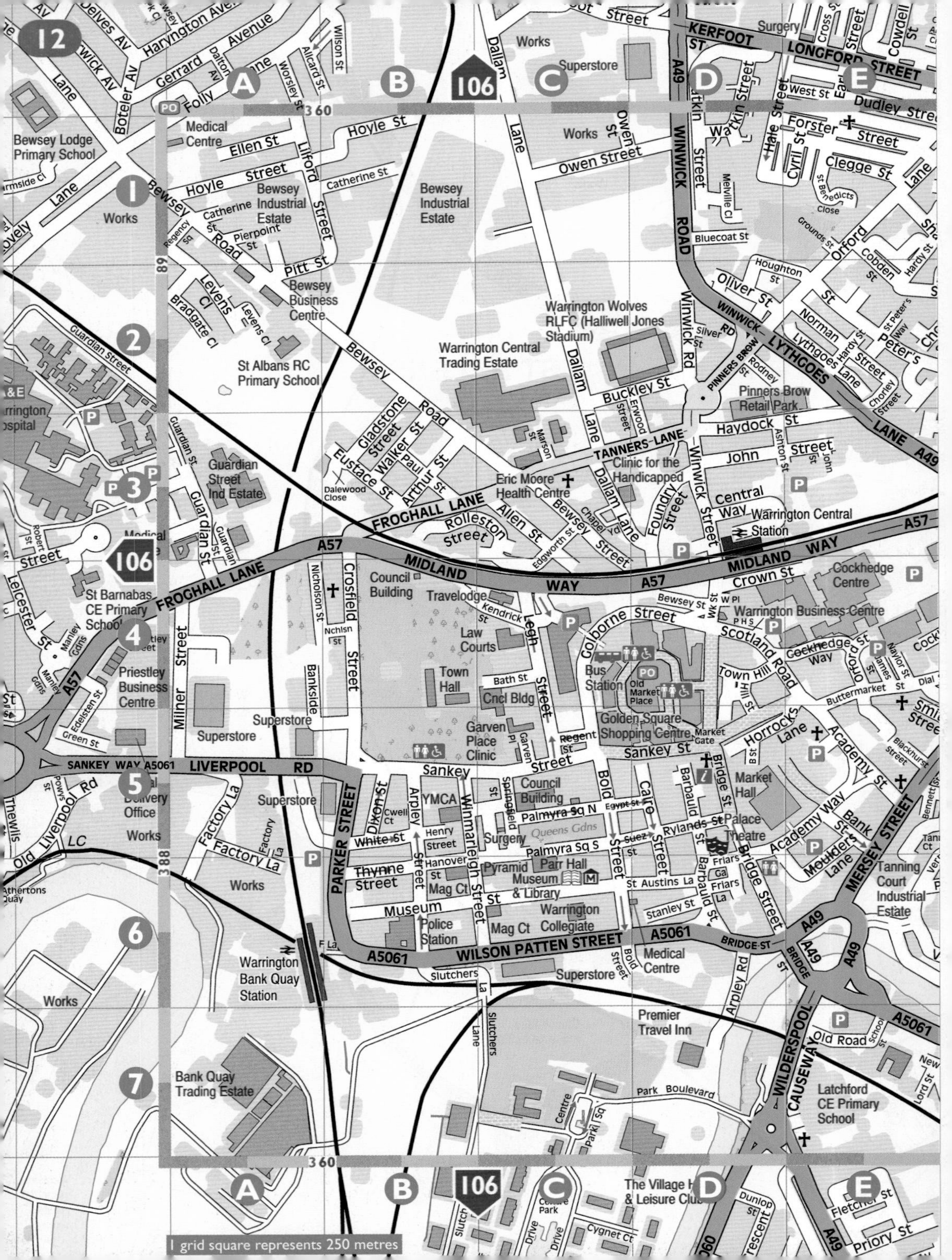

12
106
A
B
C
D
E
1
2
3
4
5
6
7
360
388
89
Delves Av
Harrington Avenue
Gerrard Avenue
Folly Lane
Dalton Av
Worsley St
Allcard St
Wilson St
Boteler Av
Lane
Bewsey Lodge Primary School
Works
Lovely Lane
Medical Centre
Ellen St
Hoyle Street
Lilford Street
Catherine St
Bewsey Industrial Estate
Pierpoint St
Regency Sq
Bewsey Road
Pitt St
Bewsey Business Centre
Levens Cl
Bradgate Cl
St Albans RC Primary School
Guardian Street
A&E
Warrington Hospital
Guardian St
Guardian Street Ind Estate
Medical Centre
Robert St
Leicester St
St Barnabas CE Primary School
Manley Gdns
Priestley Business Centre
Edelsten St
Green St
FROGHALL LANE
A57
Milner Street
Superstore
SANKEY WAY A5061
LIVERPOOL RD
Old Liverpool Rd
Powys St
Thewlis St
Delivery Office
Works
Factory La
LC
Athertons Quay
Warrington Bank Quay Station
Bank Quay Trading Estate
Superstore
Bankside
Nicholson St
Nchlsn St
Crosfield Street
PARKER STREET
Dalham Lane
Superstore
Owen St
Owen Street
Bewsey Industrial Estate
Warrington Wolves RLFC (Halliwell Jones Stadium)
Warrington Central Trading Estate
Gladstone Street
Walker St
Paul St
Eustace St
Arthur St
Dalewood Close
FROGHALL LANE
Rolleston Street
Allen St
Eric Moore Health Centre
Bewsey Street
Edgworth St
Chapel Yd
Marson St
Buckley St
Erwood St
Street
TANNERS LANE
Clinic for the Handicapped
Foundry Street
MIDLAND WAY
A57
Council Building
Travelodge
Kendrick St
Law Courts
Town Hall
Bath St
Cncl Bldg
Garven Place Clinic
Garven Pl
Legh Street
Colborne Street
Bus Station
PO
Old Market Place
Golden Square Shopping Centre
Regent St
Sankey St
Sankey Street
Dixon St
Cwell Ct
Arpley Street
YMCA
Winmarleigh Street
Henry Street
Springfield St
Council Building
Palmyra Sq N
Queens Gdns
Palmyra Sq S
Surgery
White St
Hanover St
Thynne Street
Pyramid
Parr Hall
Museum & Library
Mag Ct
Museum St
Police Station
Warrington Collegiate
Mag Ct
Bold Street
Egypt St
Suez St
Cairo Street
St Austins La
WILSON PATTEN STREET
A5061
F La
Slutchers La
Superstore
Medical Centre
Stanley St
Barbauld St
Premier Travel Inn
Slutchers Lane
Park Boulevard
Centre Park
Park Sq
The Village Hotel & Leisure Club
Kerfoot St
KERFOOT STREET
Surgery
Cross St
LONGFORD STREET
Cowdell St
A49
WINWICK ROAD
Watkin Street
West St
Earl St
Dudley Street
Hale Street
Forster Street
Cyril St
Clegge St
St Benedicts Close
Melville Cl
Bluecoat St
Grounds St
Orford
Cobden St
Hardy St
Houghton St
Oliver St
Orford St
Winwick Rd
WINWICK RD
Silver St
LYTHGOES LANE
Norman Street
Lythgoes Lane
Hardy St
St Peter's Way
Peter's
Rodney St
PINNERS BROW
Pinners Brow Retail Park
Chorley Street
Haydock St
Ashton St
John Street
John St
Central Way
Warrington Central Station
Winwick Street
MIDLAND WAY
Crown St
Cockhedge Centre
Bewsey St
Wk St
W Pl
P H S
Warrington Business Centre
Scotland Road
Cockhedge Way
Town Hill
Hill St
Naylor St
James St
Orford St
Buttermarket St
Dial St
Smith Street
Horrocks Lane
B St
Market Gate
Bridge St
Market Hall
Academy St
Blackhurst Street
Bennett St
Barbauld St
Rylands St
Palace Theatre
Academy Way
Bank St
Friars Ga
Friars La
Bridge Street
Moulders Lane
MERSEY STREET
Tanning Court Industrial Estate
BRIDGE ST
BRIDGE
A49
A5061
Arpley Rd
WILDERSPOOL CAUSEWAY
Old Road
School St
Latchford CE Primary School
New St
Lord St
Dunlop St
Crescent
Fletcher St
Priory St
Cygnet Ct
Drive
1 grid square represents 250 metres

Beamont Junior School
Quebec Road
Synge St
Amelia St
Orford
Wilkins
Garner St
Dorothea
Adam St
Roome St
Cabul Close
Cabul Cl
Benedict's Primary School
107
Primary School
Steel
Oakwood Av
Pinewood
Elmwood Av
Connaught Av
Grantham Av
Queens Avenue
Egerton Avenue
KING EDWARD ST
MARSH HOUSE LANE
Dickenson Street
PO
Leonard St
Forshaw Street
Back Forshaw St
Laira St
Works
A574
Godfrey Street
Elaine Street
Hazel St
Marsh St
PADGATE LANE
Cornwall St
Fife Road
Beresford St
Elliott Av
Alexandra St
Clarence St
Firth Bvd
Rylands Drive
Monks Pl
Winifred St
Street
Battersby Lane
Buckton St
Matthews St
Fothergill St
Surgery
MANCHESTER ROAD
Bibby Avenue
Peacock Avenue
A50
Hume Street
Cranville St
Algernon
Willis Street
Ford St
Arnold Street
Claude St
A57
Stephen Street
Cemetery
St Peter's Way
Harrison Cl
Thorneycroft Dr
St Elphin Fairfield CE Primary Sch
Robson St
Clinic
Glazebrook Street
Wood St
Helsby Street
Salisbury Street
Council Building
Sidings Ct
Dalton Bank
Fairfield St
Morley St
Whalley St
Oxford Ct
SCHOOL BROW
Hpwd St
Grey St
St Elphins Park
Mote Hl Ct
Tilley St
BRICK ST
FENNEL ST
Crossley St
High St
School Brow
P
Surgery
College Close
107
Superstore
Superstore
Fleming Ind Estate
Orchard St
General St
Eldon St
Church Street
St Katherine's Way
Farrell Street
Holmsfield Road
Farrell Street
Victoria St
St Elphins Cl
WA1
Howley Quay Industrial Estate
Egerton St
Gibson St
Pinders Farm Dr
Works
Holywell Dr
Ellesmere St
Dutton St
A49
Church Street Industrial Estate
Napier St
Mason Street
Villars Street
Navigation St
Howley Lane
Works
Howley Lane
Hall Street
Wellington Street
Lord Nelson Street
Nora St
Cleeves Cl
Parr St
Howley
River Mersey
KINGSWAY
STH
Parr Street
Percival St
Fairclough Av
Harbord St
Riverside Cl
Riverside Close
Works
Moorside
Riverside Retail Park
Sutton Street
Victoria Park Arena
Stringer Crescent
Chantler Av
Parkdale Industrial Estate
Wharf Street
Wharf Street
Victoria Park
Avenue
Plinston Av
WARRINGTON
Westy
Griffiths
KNUTSFORD ROAD
New Road
Kent Street
York St
Peartree
Miller St
Barry St
Grove St
Slater Street
Clifton St
Enville St
Marbury Street
Oxford Street
Carol St
A5061
Crange
Rook Road
Manor Industrial Estate
Hewitt St
Cumberland St
Florence St
KNUTSFORD ROAD
Palatine Industrial Estate
Hawthorn Grove
Brook Pl
Lower Wash Lane
Raddon Place
A5061
62
388
389
F
G
H
J
K
1
2
3
4
5
6
7

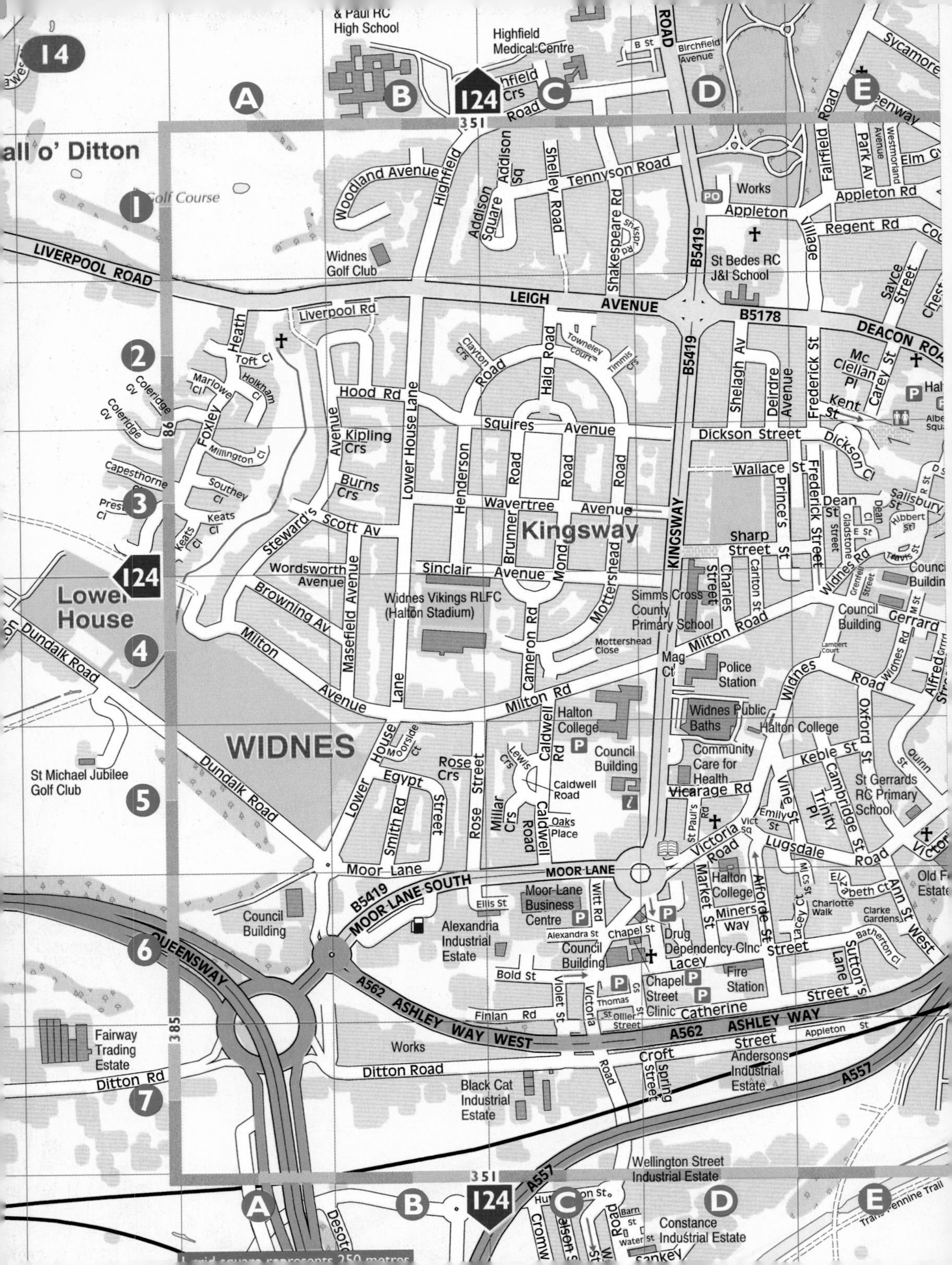
14
& Paul RC High School
Highfield Medical Centre
Highfield Crs
Highfield Road
124
351
A B C D E
1 2 3 4 5 6 7
ROAD
B St
Birchfield Avenue
Sycamore
Greenway
Hall o' Ditton
Golf Course
Widnes Golf Club
LIVERPOOL ROAD
Liverpool Rd
Woodland Avenue
Addison Square
Addison Sq
Shelley Road
Tennyson Road
Shakespeare Rd
Shkspr Rd
B5419
PO
Works
Appleton
Appleton Village
Fairfield Road
Park Av
Westmorland Avenue
Elm Gv
Appleton Rd
Regent Rd
St Bedes RC J&I School
Sayce Street
Chester
LEIGH AVENUE
B5178
DEACON ROAD
Heath
Toft Cl
Holkham Cl
Marlowe Cl
Coleridge Gv
Foxley
Millington Cl
Capesthorne Cl
Southey Cl
Preston Cl
Keats Cl
Clayton Crs
Clayton Road
Haig Road
Towneley Court
Timmis Crs
Shelagh Av
Deirdre Avenue
Frederick St
Mc Clellan Pl
Carey St
Kent St
Hood Rd
Kipling Crs
Avenue
Lower House Lane
Squires Avenue
Dickson Street
Dickson Cl
Burns Crs
Henderson Road
Wallace St
Prince's St
Frederick Street
Dean St
Salisbury
Wavertree Avenue
Kingsway
KINGSWAY
Steward's
Scott Av
Brunner Road
Mond Road
Mottershead Road
Sharp Street
Gladstone Street
E St
Hibbert St
Travis St
Widnes Rd
Wordsworth Avenue
Sinclair Avenue
Masefield Avenue
Browning Av
Widnes Vikings RLFC (Halton Stadium)
Lower House
Dundalk Road
Milton Avenue
Cameron Rd
Mottershead Close
Simms Cross County Primary School
Charles Street
Carlton St
Grenfell Street
Council Building
Gerrard
M St
Milton Road
Mag Ct
Police Station
Lambert Court
Widnes Road
Alfred St
Oxford St
Milton Rd
Caldwell Rd
Halton College
Widnes Public Baths
Moorside Ct
WIDNES
Lower House Lane
Egypt Street
Rose Crs
Rose Street
Lewis Crs
Caldwell Road
Council Building
Community Care for Health
Keble St
Quinn St
Cambridge St
Trinity Pl
St Gerrards RC Primary School
St Michael Jubilee Golf Club
Smith Rd
Millar Crs
Oaks Place
Vicarage Rd
St Paul's Rd
Vict Sq
Victoria Road
Emily St
Vine St
Lugsdale Road
Victoria
Moor Lane
MOOR LANE
Market St
Alforde St
Mi Cs St
Elizabeth Ct
Old Fort Estate
B5419 MOOR LANE SOUTH
Ellis St
Moor Lane Business Centre
Witt Rd
Halton College
Miners Way
Lacey Ct
Charlotte Walk
Clarke Gardens
Ann St West
Council Building
Alexandria Industrial Estate
Alexandra St
Chapel St
Drug Dependency Clnc
Lacey Street
Batherton Cl
Sutton's Lane
QUEENSWAY
Council Building
Bold St
Violet St
Victoria
Chapel Street Clinic
Fire Station
Street
Thomas St
Ollier Street
Catherine Street
A562 ASHLEY WAY WEST
A562 ASHLEY WAY
Finlan Rd
385
Fairway Trading Estate
Works
Appleton St
Ditton Rd
Ditton Road
Road
Croft Street
Spring Street
Andersons Industrial Estate
A557
Black Cat Industrial Estate
Wellington Street Industrial Estate
Hutchinson St
Cromwell
Barn St
Water St
Constance Industrial Estate
Desoto
Sankey
Trans Pennine Trail
1 grid square represents 250 metres

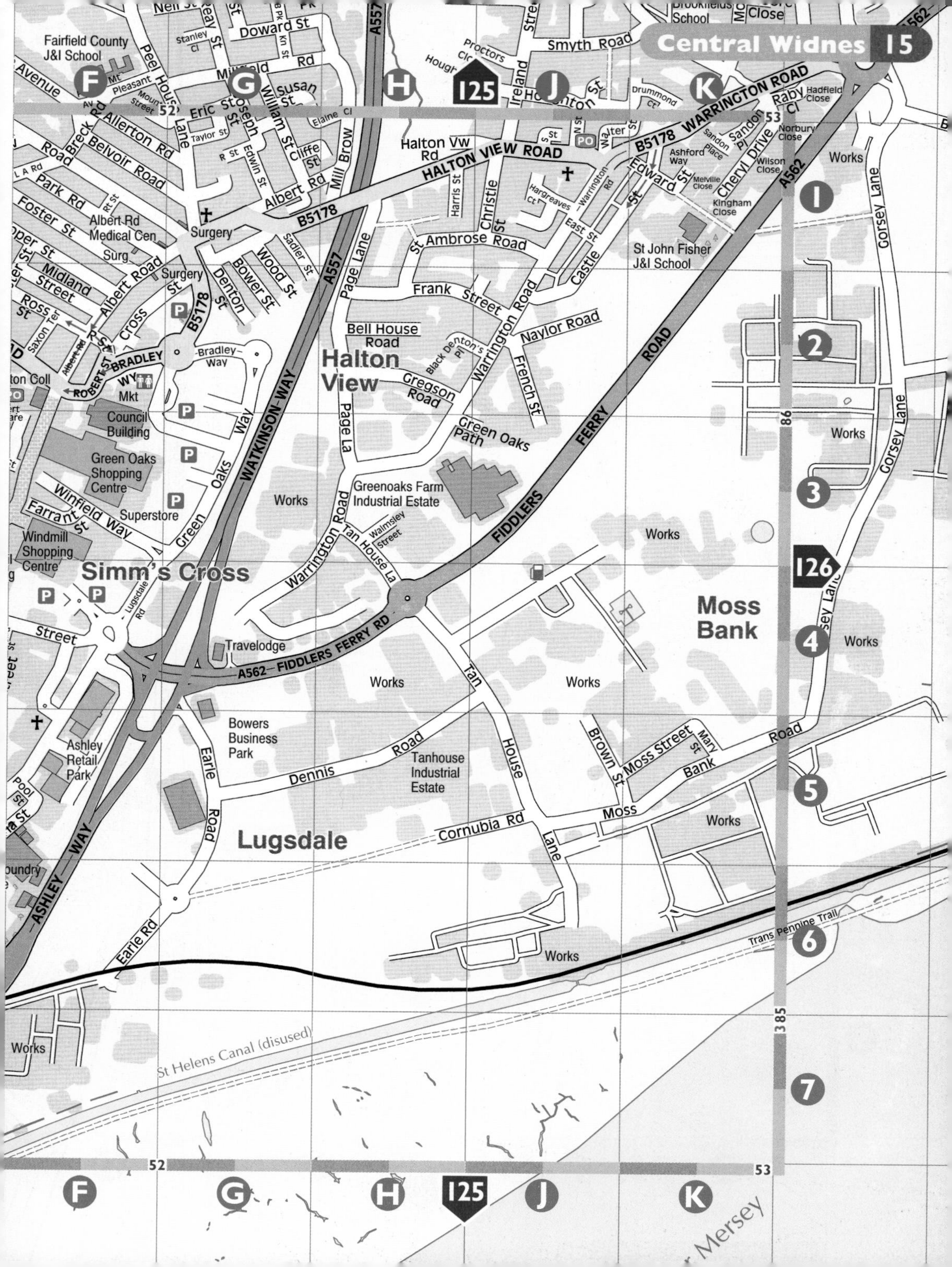

Fairfield County J&I School
Doward St
Stanley Cl
Smyth Road
Proctors Cl
Brookfields School
Close
Mt Pleasant Av
Mount Street
Avenue
Millfield Rd
Peel House Lane
Susan St
Eric St
Joseph St
William St
Elaine Cl
Houghton St
Drummond Ct
Hadfield Close
Raby Cl
WARRINGTON ROAD
B5178
Norbury Close
Allerton Rd
Breck Rd
Belvoir Road
Taylor St
R St
Edwin St
Cliffe St
Mill Brow
Halton Vw Rd
HALTON VIEW ROAD
PO
Walter St
Sandon Place
Sandon Pl
Ashford Way
Cheryl Drive
Wilson Close
Melville Close
Edward St
Works
L A Rd
Park Rd
Foster St
Rt St
Albert Rd Medical Cen
Surg
Surgery
Albert Rd
B5178
Harris St
Christie St
Hargreaves Ct
Warrington Rd
East St
Kingham Close
A562
St John Fisher J&I School
St Ambrose Road
Sadler St
Wood St
Bower St
Denton St
Castle St
Gorsey Lane
Midland Street
Ross St
Albert Road
Cross St
B5178
A557
Page Lane
Frank Street
Warrington Road
Naylor Road
Saxon Ter
Albert Rd
R St
Robert St
BRADLEY WY
Bradley Way
Bell House Road
Black Denton's Pl
Halton View
Gregson Road
French St
FIDDLERS FERRY ROAD
Halton Coll
Mkt
Council Building
WATKINSON WAY
Page La
Green Oaks Path
Green Oaks Shopping Centre
Oaks Way
Works
Greenoaks Farm Industrial Estate
Winfield Way
Farrant St
Superstore
Green
Warrington Road
Tan House La
Walmsley Street
Works
Windmill Shopping Centre
Simm's Cross
Lugsdale Rd
Moss Bank
Street
Travelodge
A562 FIDDLERS FERRY RD
Works
Tan House Lane
Works
Works
Bowers Business Park
Earle Road
Dennis Road
Tanhouse Industrial Estate
Brown St
Moss Street
Mary St
Moss Bank Road
Ashley Retail Park
Pool St
Cornubia Rd
Moss Lane
Works
Lugsdale
ASHLEY WAY
Foundry
Earle Rd
Trans Pennine Trail
Works
Works
St Helens Canal (disused)
Mersey
52
53
86
385
F
G
H
J
K
1
2
3
4
5
6
7
125
126

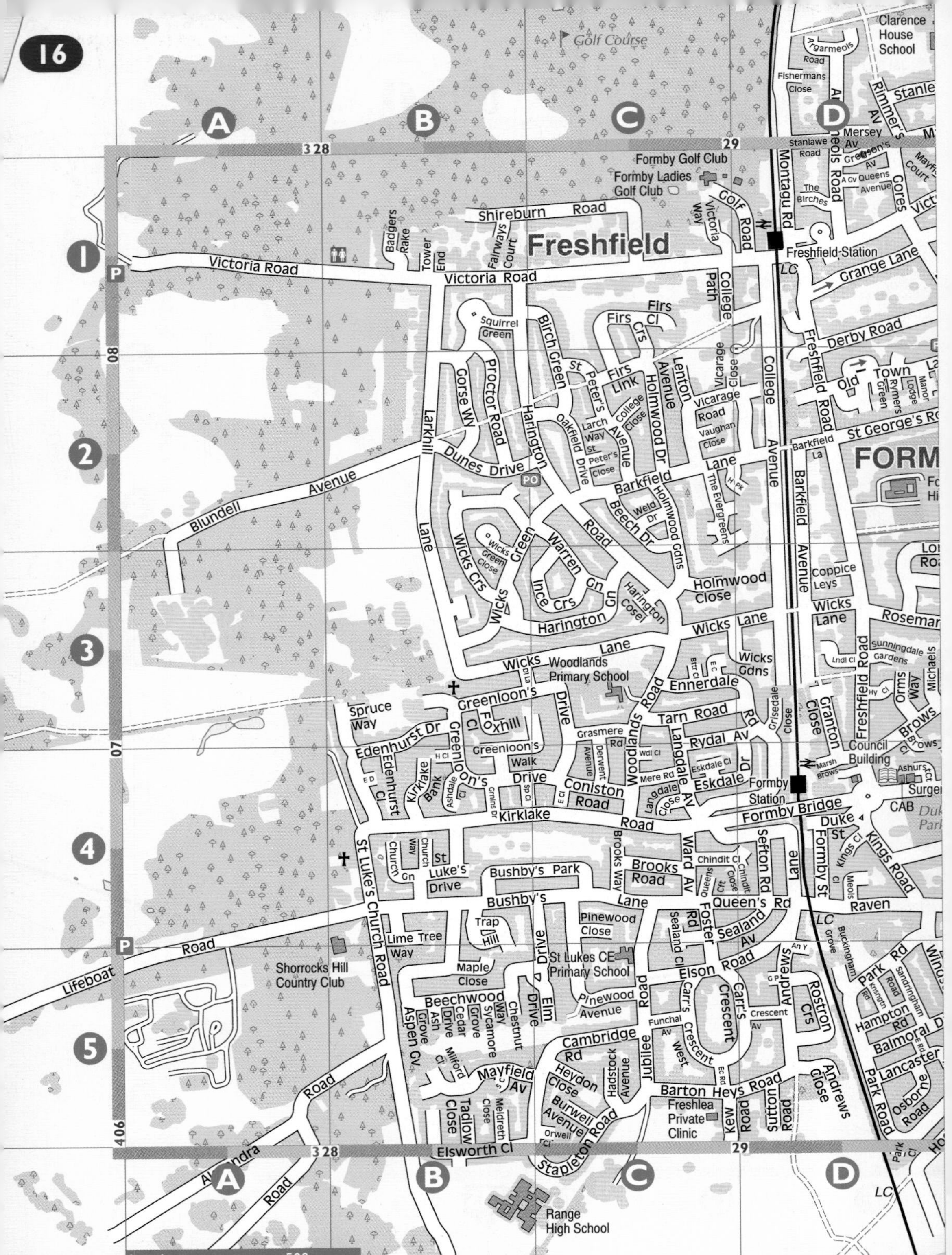
Golf Course
Clarence House School
Argarmeols Road
Fishermans Close
Rimmer's Av
Stanlawe Road
Mersey Av
Gregson's Av
Queens Avenue
A Gv
Mayfield Court
The Birches
Formby Golf Club
Formby Ladies Golf Club
Shireburn Road
Golf Road
Victoria Way
Montagu Rd
Freshfield
Freshfield Station
LC
Grange Lane
Victoria Road
Badgers Rake
Tower End
Fairways Court
College Path
Firs Cl
Firs Crs
Squirrel Green
Derby Road
Birch Green
St Peter's
Firs Link
Holmwood Avenue
Lenton Avenue
Vicarage Close
College Avenue
Freshfield Road
Old Town
Rymers Green
Manor Lodge
Gorse Wy
Proctor Road
Harington
Oakfield Drive
Larch Way
College Close
Holmwood Dr
Vicarage Road
Vaughan Close
St George's Ro
Barkfield La
Larkhill Lane
Dunes Drive
St Peter's Close
PO
Barkfield Lane
The Evergreens
H Pk
Barkfield Avenue
FORM
Blundell Avenue
Beech Dr
Weld Dr
Holmwood Gdns
Road
Wicks Green Close
Wicks Crs
Wicks Green
Warren
Ince Crs
Gn
Harington Cosei
Holmwood Close
Coppice Leys
Wicks Lane
Rosemar
Harington Gn
Wicks Lane
Lndl Cl
Sunningdale Gardens
Wicks Gdns
Woodlands Primary School
Dl La
Bltr Cl
E C
Ennerdale
Greenloon's
Spruce Way
Foxhill Cl
Drive
Woodlands Road
Tarn Road
Rd
Grisedale Close
Granton Close
Freshfield Road
Hy Cl
Orms Way
Michaels
Brows
Edenhurst Dr
Grasmere Rd
Rydal Av
Greenloon's Walk
H Cl
Avenue
Derwent
Wdl Cl
Langdale
Eskdale Cl
Council Building
Marsh Brows
Brows Cl
Ashurst Ct
Kirklake Bank
Edenhurst Cl
E D
Ashdale Cl
Greenloon's Drive
Grnlns Dr
Sp Cl
E Cl
Coniston Road
Mere Rd
Eskdale Dr
Formby Station
Surgery
CAB
Duke Park
Langdale Close
Langdale Av
Kirklake Road
Formby Bridge
Duke St
Kings Cl
Kings Road
Formby St
St Luke's Church Road
Church Gn
Church Way
St Luke's Drive
Brooks Way
Brooks Road
Ward Av
Chindit Cl
Queens Cft
Chindit Close
Sefton Rd
Lane
Meols Cl
Bushby's Park
Bushby's Lane
Queen's Rd
Raven
Trap Hill
Drive
Pinewood Close
Sealand Cl
Foster Rd
Sealand Av
LC
Grove
Buckingham
Park Rd
Lime Tree Way
Lifeboat Road
Shorrocks Hill Country Club
Maple Close
St Lukes CE Primary School
Elson Road
An Y
Andrews
Rostron Crs
Sandringham Road
Knsngtn Rd
Hampton Rd
Beechwood Drive
Ash Grove
Aspen Gv
Cedar Drive
Sycamore Grove
Way
Chestnut
Elm Drive
Pinewood Avenue
Road
Carr's Crescent
G P
Crescent Av
Balmoral Dr
E Rd
Funchal Av
West Crescent
Lancaster
Cambridge Rd
Milford Cl
Mayfield Av
S C
Heydon Close
Hadstock Avenue
Jubilee Road
Ec Rd
Barton Heys Road
Andrews Close
Park Road
Osborne Road
Tadlow Close
Meldreth Close
Burwell Avenue
Orwell Cl
Freshlea Private Clinic
Kew Road
Sutton Road
Road
Alexandra Road
Elsworth Cl
Stapleton Road
Park Cl
Range High School
A
B
C
D
1
2
3
4
5
328
29
08
07
406
P

1 grid square represents 500 metres

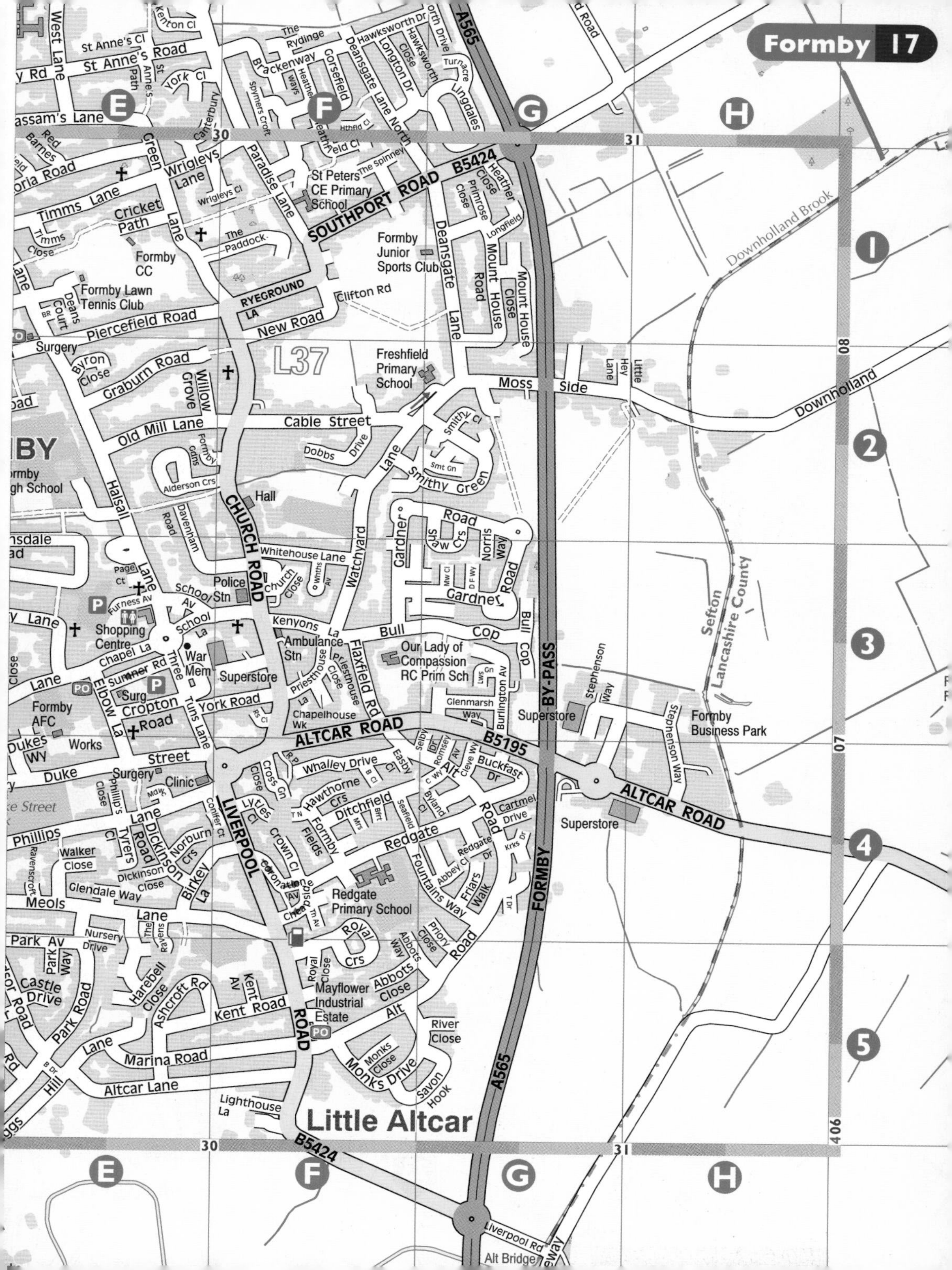

West Lane
Kenton Cl
St Anne's Cl
St Anne's Road
St Anne's Path
York Cl
Canterbury
Bassam's Lane
The Rydinge
Brackenway
Heatherways
Gorsefield
Deansgate Lane North
Longton Dr
Hawksworth Dr
Hawksworth Close
North Drive
Turnacre
Lingdales
Spymers Croft
Hthfld Cl
A565
Red Barnes
Green Lane
Wrigleys Lane
Wrigleys Cl
Paradise Lane
The Spinney
St Peters CE Primary School
SOUTHPORT ROAD B5424
Primrose Close
Heather Close
Longfield
Timms Lane
Timms Close
Cricket Path
The Paddock
Formby CC
Formby Junior Sports Club
Deansgate Lane
Mount House Road
Mount House Close
Mount House
Downholland Brook
Formby Lawn Tennis Club
Deans Court
RYEGROUND LA
Clifton Rd
Piercefield Road
New Road
Surgery
Byron Close
Graburn Road
Willow Grove
L37
Freshfield Primary School
Moss Side
Hey Lane
Little
Downholland
Old Mill Lane
Cable Street
Smithy Cl
Dobbs Drive
Lane
Smt Gn
Smithy Green
Formby Gdns
Alderson Crs
Formby High School
Hall
CHURCH ROAD
Davenham Road
Road
Shaw Crs
Norris Way
Gardner Road
Whitehouse Lane
Watchyard
Church Close
Page Ct
Police Stn
School Av
Furness Av
Shopping Centre
School La
Kenyons La
Bull Cop
Ambulance Stn
Our Lady of Compassion RC Prim Sch
Sefton
Lancashire County
Chapel La
War Mem
Superstore
Priesthouse Close
Flaxfield Rd
Burlington Av
BY-PASS
Stephenson Way
Formby Business Park
Sumner Rd
Three Tuns Lane
Surg
Cropton Road
York Road
Chapelhouse Wk
Glenmarsh Way
Formby AFC
Elbow La
ALTCAR ROAD
B5195
Dukes Wy
Works
Duke Street
Surgery
Clinic
Whalley Drive
Easby Cl
Romsey Av
Cleve Wy
Buckfast Dr
Alt Rd
Phillip's Close
Cross Gn
Hawthorne Crs
Ditchfield
Bylands Cl
Cartmel Drive
Superstore
Conifer Ct
Lytles Cl
Seafield
Redgate
LIVERPOOL
Phillips Lane
Tyrers Cl
Dickinson Road
Norburn Crs
Crown Cl
Formby Fields
Fountains Way
Abbey Cl
Redgate Dr
Friars Walk
FORMBY
Walker Close
Ravenscroft
Dickinson Close
Birkey La
Coronation Av
Redgate Primary School
Glendale Way
Meols Lane
Nursery Drive
The Ravens
Royal Crs
Abbots Way
Priory Close
Park Av
Park Way
Castle Drive
Harebell Close
Ashcroft Rd
Kent Av
Royal Close
Abbots Close
Park Road
Kent Road
Mayflower Industrial Estate
River Close
Lane
Marina Road
ROAD
Alt
Monks Close
Monks Drive
Savon Hook
A565
Hill
Altcar Lane
Lighthouse La
Little Altcar
B5424
Liverpool Rd
Alt Bridge
E
F
G
H
1
2
3
4
5
30
31
08
07
406

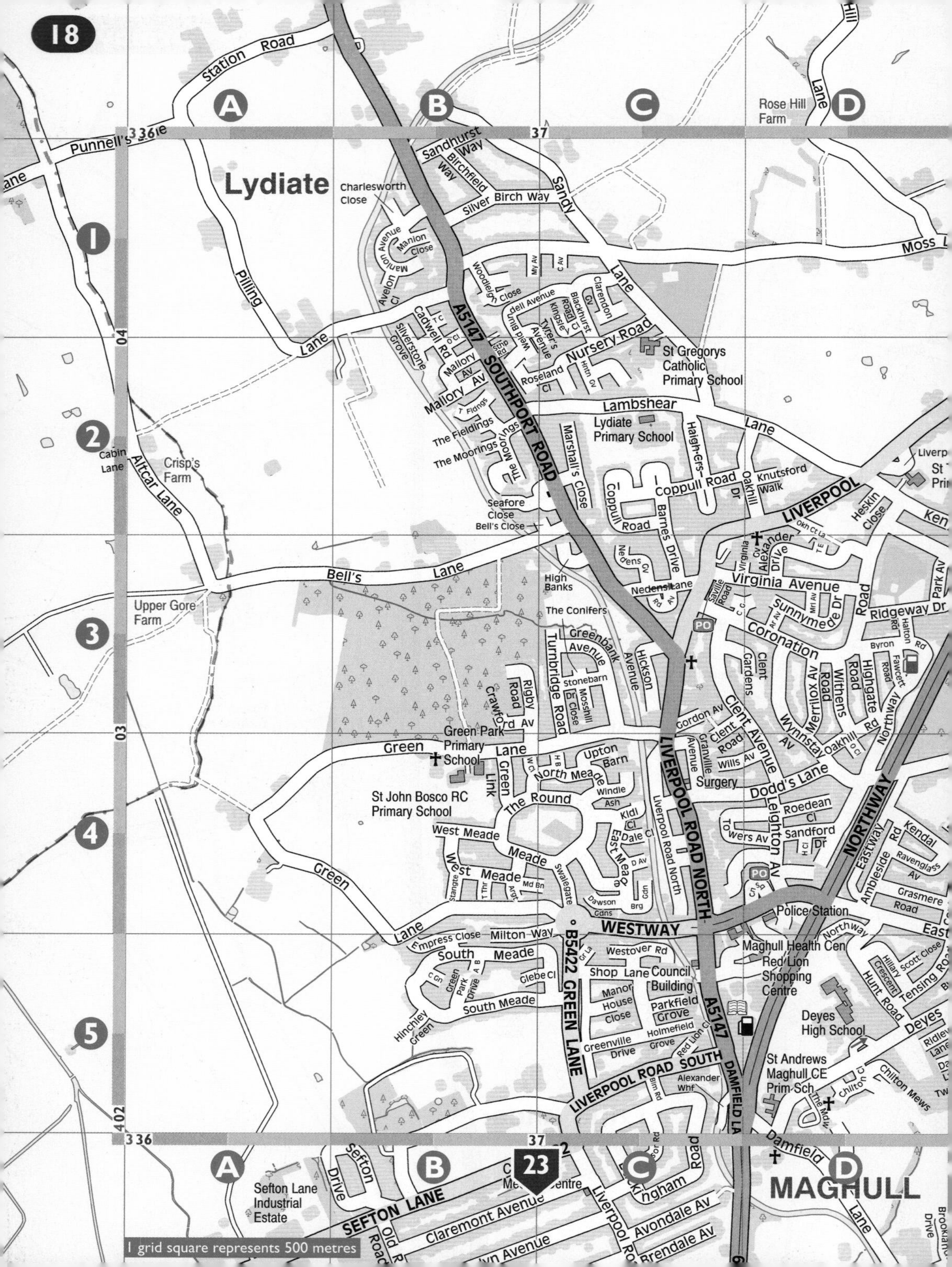
Lydiate
Station Road
Punnell's Lane
Pilling Lane
Charlesworth Close
Manion Avenue
Manion Close
Avelon Cl
Sandhurst Way
Birchfield Way
Silver Birch Way
Sandy Lane
Moss Lane
Rose Hill Farm
A5147 SOUTHPORT ROAD
Woodleigh Close
Cadwell Rd
Silverstone Grove
Mallory Av
Clarendon Gv
Blackhurst Road
Nursery Road
St Gregorys Catholic Primary School
Roseland Cl
Lambshear Lane
Lydiate Primary School
The Fieldings
The Moorings
Marshall's Close
Haigh Crs
Coppull Road
Oakhill Dr
Knutsford Walk
LIVERPOOL
Barnes Drive
Seafore Close
Bell's Close
Cabin Lane
Altcar Lane
Crisp's Farm
Bell's Lane
Upper Gore Farm
High Banks
Nedens Gv
Nedens Lane
Alexander Drive
Virginia Avenue
Saville Road
Sunnymede Dr
Ridgeway Dr
Park Av
Heskin Close
Coronation Road
Byron
Halton Rd
Fawcett Road
Highgate Road
Withens Road
Merrilox Av
Northway
The Conifers
Greenbank Avenue
Turnbridge Road
Hickson Avenue
Stonebarn Dr
Mosshill Close
Rigby Road
Crawford Av
Clent Gardens
Clent Avenue
Clent Road
Gordon Av
Granville Avenue
Wills Av
Wynnstay Av
Oakhill Rd
Green Park Primary School
Green Lane
Green Link
Upton Barn
North Meade
Windle Ash
Kidl Cl
Dale Cl
The Round
St John Bosco RC Primary School
West Meade
Meade
East Meade
Swalegate
Dawson Gdns
Liverpool Road North
LIVERPOOL ROAD NORTH
Surgery
Dodd's Lane
Roedean Cl
Sandford Dr
Leighton Av
Towers Av
NORTHWAY
Kendal
Eastway
Ambleside Rd
Ravenglass Av
Grasmere Road
Police Station
WESTWAY
Milton Way
Empress Close
South Meade
Glebe Cl
Green Park Drive
Hinchley Green
B5422 GREEN LANE
Westover Rd
Shop Lane
Council Building
Manor House Close
Parkfield Grove
Greenville Drive
Holmefield Grove
Red Lion Cl
A5147
Maghull Health Cen
Red Lion Shopping Centre
Hillary Crescent
Scott Close
Tensing Road
Hunt Road
Deyes High School
Deyes Lane
St Andrews Maghull CE Prim Sch
Chilton Cl
Chilton Mews
The Mdw
LIVERPOOL ROAD SOUTH
Alexander Whf
DAMFIELD LA
Damfield Lane
Sefton Drive
Sefton Lane Industrial Estate
SEFTON LANE
Claremont Avenue
Liverpool Road
Buckingham Road
Avondale Av
Brendale Av
MAGHULL
Old Road
Brookland Drive
A
B
C
D
1
2
3
4
5
336
37
04
03
402
23
1 grid square represents 500 metres

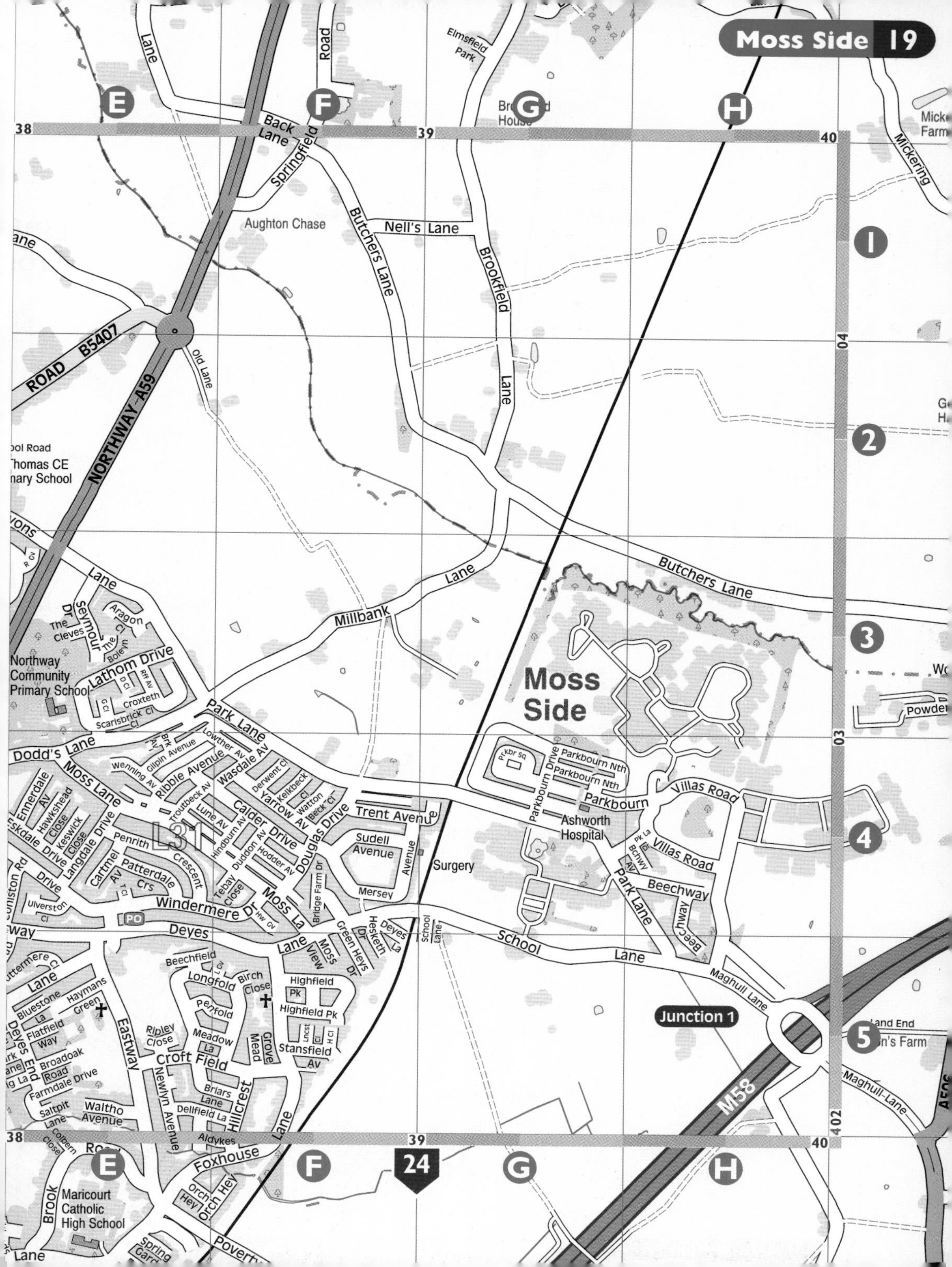
Elmsfield Park
Road
Lane
Back Lane
Springfield
Aughton Chase
Butchers Lane
Nell's Lane
Brookfield Lane
ROAD B5407
NORTHWAY A59
Old Lane
Thomas CE
nary School
Millbank Lane
Butchers Lane
Moss Side
Northway Community Primary School
Lathom Drive
Seymour Dr
The Cleves
Aragon Cl
The Boleyn
Croxteth
Scarisbrick Cl
Park Lane
Dodd's Lane
Moss Lane
Gilpin Avenue
Lowther Av
Wenning Av
Ribble Avenue
Wasdale Av
Derwent Cl
Kelkbeck Cl
Watton Cl
Beck Cl
Yarrow Av
Douglas Drive
Trent Avenue
Sudell Avenue
Avenue
Surgery
Calder Drive
Troutbeck Av
Lune Av
Hindburn Av
Duddon Av
Hodder Av
Ennerdale Av
Hawkshead Close
Keswick Close
Eskdale Drive
Langdale Drive
Penrith Crescent
L31
Cartmel Av
Patterdale Crs
Tebay Close
Moss La
Bridge Farm Dr
Mersey
Ulverston Cl
Windermere Dr
PO
Deyes
Lane
View
Moss
Green Heys Dr
Hesketh Dr
Deyes La
School Lane
School Lane
Parkbourn Drive
Parkbourn Nth
Parkbourn Nth
Parkbourn
Kbr Sq
Ashworth Hospital
Villas Road
Villas Road
Beechway
Beechway
Park Lane
Maghull Lane
Junction 1
Beechfield
Longfold
Birch Close
Penfold
Highfield Pk
Highfield Pk
Ripley Close
Meadow La
Grove Mead
Stansfield Av
Eastway
Croft Field
Hillcrest
Newlyn Avenue
Briars Lane
Dellfield La
Aldykes
Foxhouse Lane
Lane
Bluestone La
Haymans Green
Flatfield Way
Broadoak Road
Farmdale Drive
Deyes End
Saltpit Lane
Waltho Avenue
Colbern Close
Maricourt Catholic High School
Brook
Orch Hey
Orch Hey
Spring Gard
Poverty
Lane
M58
Maghull Lane
Land End
n's Farm
Powder
Mickering
Micke Farm
Brookfield House
24
E
F
G
H
1
2
3
4
5
38
39
40
04
03
402

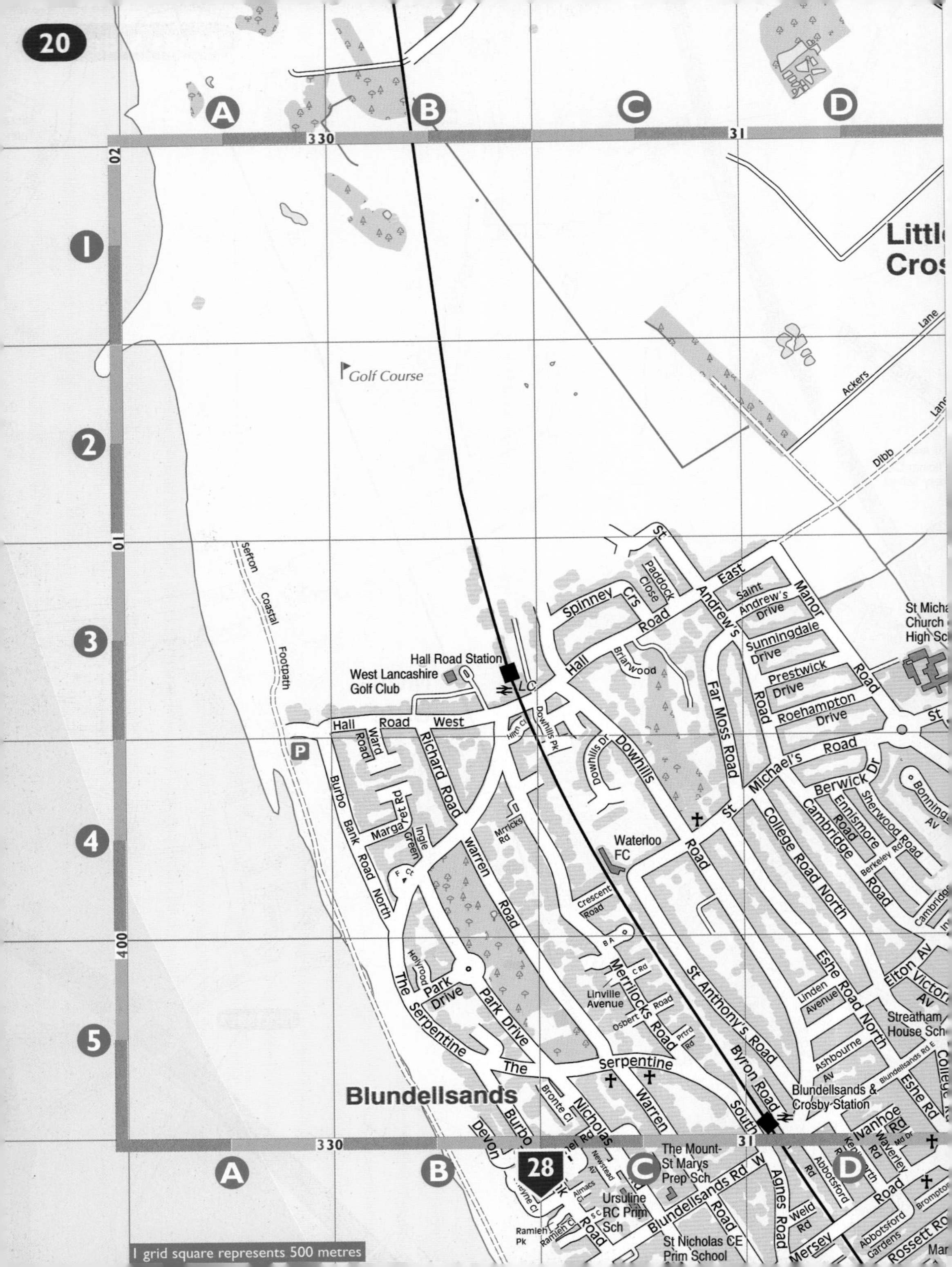

A
B
C
D
330
31
02
1
2
3
4
5
01
400
Little
Cros
Golf Course
Ackers
Lane
Dibb
Sefton
Coastal
Footpath
St
Paddock
Close
East
Saint
Andrew's
Drive
Manor
Spinney
Crs
Road
Hall
Andrew's
Sunningdale
Drive
Prestwick
Drive
Road
Roehampton
Drive
St Michael's
Church
High Sc
Hall Road Station
West Lancashire
Golf Club
Briarwood
Far Moss Road
Road
Hall
Road
West
Ward
Road
Richard Road
Hilton Cl
Dowhills Pk
Dowhills Dr
Dowhills
St Michael's
Road
Berwick Dr
P
Burbo
Bank
Road
North
Margaret Rd
Ingle
Green
Warren
Road
Mrricks
Rd
Waterloo
FC
St
Road
College Road North
Cambridge
Road
Ennismore
Road
Sherwood
Rd
Berkeley Rd
Bonning
Av
Cambridge
Crescent
Road
F Ct
BA
Holyrood
Park
Drive
The
Serpentine
Park Drive
Merrilocks
C Rd
Linville
Avenue
Osbert
Road
Road
Prtrd
Rd
St Anthony's Road
Eshe
Road North
Linden
Avenue
Elton Av
Victoria
Av
Streatham
House Sch
Ashbourne
Av
Blundellsands Rd E
College
Eshe Rd
The
Serpentine
Warren
Bronte Cl
Nicholas
Burbo
Devon
South
Byron Road
Blundellsands &
Crosby Station
Ivanhoe
Rd
Waverley
Rd
Kenilworth
Rd
Blundellsands
28
Newstead
Av
Almacs
Cl
Ramleh
Pk
Ramleh Cl
Road
Ursuline
RC Prim
Sch
The Mount-
St Marys
Prep Sch
Blundellsands Rd W
Road
Agnes Road
Weld
Rd
Rd
Abbotsford
Road
Brompton
Abbotsford
Gardens
Rossett Ro
Mersey
St Nicholas CE
Prim School
Mar
1 grid square represents 500 metres

E
F
G
H
32
33
02
01
400
I
2
3
4
5
22
29
Park
Wrak Farm
Delph Road
Ackers La
St Marys RC Primary School
INCE LANE
A565
Long Lane
Back Lane
B5193
LITTLE CROSBY ROAD
Ince Road
Park Dr
Southport Road
Woodland View
Sefton Dr
Brenda Crescent
Virgin's Lane
Brook Road
Chilwd
Holgate Pk
Rd
QUARRY ROAD
GREEN LAN
Holy Family Catholic High School
Hartdale Road
Westbo
Halifax Cr
Edge Lane
Phillips Crs
Coles Crs
T Crs
PO
Thornfield Road
Ronaldsway
White Meadow Drive
Michael's Road
Boundary Drive
Woodend Avenue
Longfield Av
Crosby High School
Northern CC
Elm Avenue
Chestnut Avenue
Sycamore Av
Beech Avenue
LANE
Edgemoor
Larchfield Rd
Amaury Road
St William Road
Manor Drive
Kaigh Avenue
Ilford Avenue
Manor Avenue
Willow Way
Oaklands Avenue
Halsall Cl
Avenue
L23
Park Av
Poplar Av
Meribel Cl
Moret Cl
Link Av
Corsefield Av
Fern Hey
St William of York RC Primary Sch
Sherwood Av
Fairways
Valewood Primary School
Road
Miller Avenue
Primary School
Mayfair Av
De Villiers
Moorland Av
Esplen Avenue
Moor Coppice
Chesterfield Road
Millcroft
Greenway
Rosemoor Drive
Moorfield Rd
Cranfield Road
Drive
Hey Rd
Seven Acre Rd
Scape La
A565
MOOR
Windmill Av
Chetwood Avenue
Brentwood Avenue
Moor Cl
Maunders Ct
Elmwood Av
Surgery
Richmond Rd
Moor La
Cambridge Av
Moor Drive
The Byway
Highfield Grove
Chesterfield High School Sports College
Rimrose Valley Road
Kings Rd
Victoria Rd W
ISLINGTON
Church Rd
THE BY-PASS
Rd
Old Farm Rd
Tithebarn Rd
Moorside
Close
Forefield Road
Hillcrest Road
Lupton Drive
Newborough Avenue
Vermont Av
Kilnyard Rd
Vermont Rd
Great Crosby
Ascot Pk
Asc Pk
Moorside Road
Alexandra Road
York Av
Princes Av
Vale Rd
St Luke's Rd
York Rd
Lune St
Queens Rd
Enfield Av
The Precincts
The
Great Crosby RC Primary School
Orchard Dl
Forefield Junior School
Lyndhurst Road
Bellair Av
Chester Cl
Valley
Merchant Taylors School for Girls
Regent Rd
Coronation
Claremont Rd
Sacred Heart Catholic College
Fairfield
Rosedale Av
Seafield Av
Northern
Sefton View
Trevor Drive
Forefield Infant School
Preston Wy
Hillary Drive
Jamieson Av
Atherton House School
Shrt Rd
Everest Rd
Fairholme Rd
LIVERPOOL ROAD
Avenue
Hill St
Brownmr Cl
Lane
Windle Av
Redgate Av
Carrfield Av
Rimrose
Kimberley Dr
Prestfield Rd
Sharples Crs
Eden N
Eden Dr S
PO
Warwick
Earl's Cl
Drive
TCl
The Close
Merchant Taylors Junior School for Girls
Surgery
Musker Street
Industrial Estate
Road
Hazel Gv
Wineva Gdns
Wylva Av
Brownmoor
Vogan Avenue
Nazeby Av
Woodville Av
Kingswood Drive
Road
Endbutt
Staley Av
Kershaw Avenue
Desmond Gv

Long Lane
A
B
C
D
Lunt Road
334
35
02
Wrakes Farm
L29
Lunt
Wingfield Close
Lane
Longdale
Lunt Road
Back Lane
Holgate
Rothwells Lane
Holgate Pk
Rd
Park Dr
Woodland View
Sefton Dr
Brenda Crescent
Road
Brook Road
QUARRY ROAD
01
GREEN LANE
Thornton Crematorium
Thornton
Cemetery
A5207
LYDIATE
LANE
Hartdale Road
Water Street
Moorlands Rd
Lydiate La
Northwich Cl
Westbourne Avenue
Lydiate Park
Hedgecroft
Halifax Crs
Edge Lane
Thornfield Road
PO
21
Whinfield Rd
Phillips Cl
Coles Crs
Thornton Primary Sch
Elmsfield Rd
Heather Wy
Masefield Rd
Blakefield Rd
Stanny Field Drive
Newfield Cl
Lane
Bretlands Rd
Green Croft
Tanhouse Road
Larchfield Rd
Radburn Cl
Amaury Road
St William Road
Edge Lane
Humphreys Hey
Runnells Lane
Edgemoor
Link Av
Gorsefield Av
Fern Hey
St William of York RC Primary School
Special School
Lower Hey Rd
Seven Acre Rd
Coney Crs
Drummond Road
Moorfield Rd
Cranfield Road
Drive
B5422
BRICKWALL LANE
Old Rectory Green
Netherton
A5207
BUCKLEY HL LANE
Harrocks Cl
Stanton Cl
Gt Hey
End Park
Hgr End Pk
Stonyfield
Grange Primary Sch
Waterside
Stonyfield
Red Lomes
Mill Ct
Granams Cft
Whalley Ct
Almond's Turn
Buckley Hill
Harrops Croft
Patten's Cl
Eden
Fleetwood's Lane
Glover's La
St Augustine's Wy
St Monica's Dr
Ambrose
St Aidan's Way
Marian Way
St Benet's Way
Sarah's Croft
April Rise
Heathers Cft
Chesterfield High School Sports College
Rimrose Valley Road
Road
Chester Cl
Valley Cl
Valley Road
Hillary Drive
Preston Wy
Jamieson Av
Redgate Av
Carrfield Av
Rimrose
Windle Av
400
5
Bowland Drive
Pendle Drive
St Mark's
Dale
Acre
Drive
Harp's Cft
30
Council Building
Birch Hey
St Christopher's Av
Swift's Cl
St Leonard's Cl
St Nicholas'
Swifts Lane
St Bernard's Drive
Netherton Moss Primary School
L30
Northumberland Way
EDGE LANE
1 grid square represents 500 metres

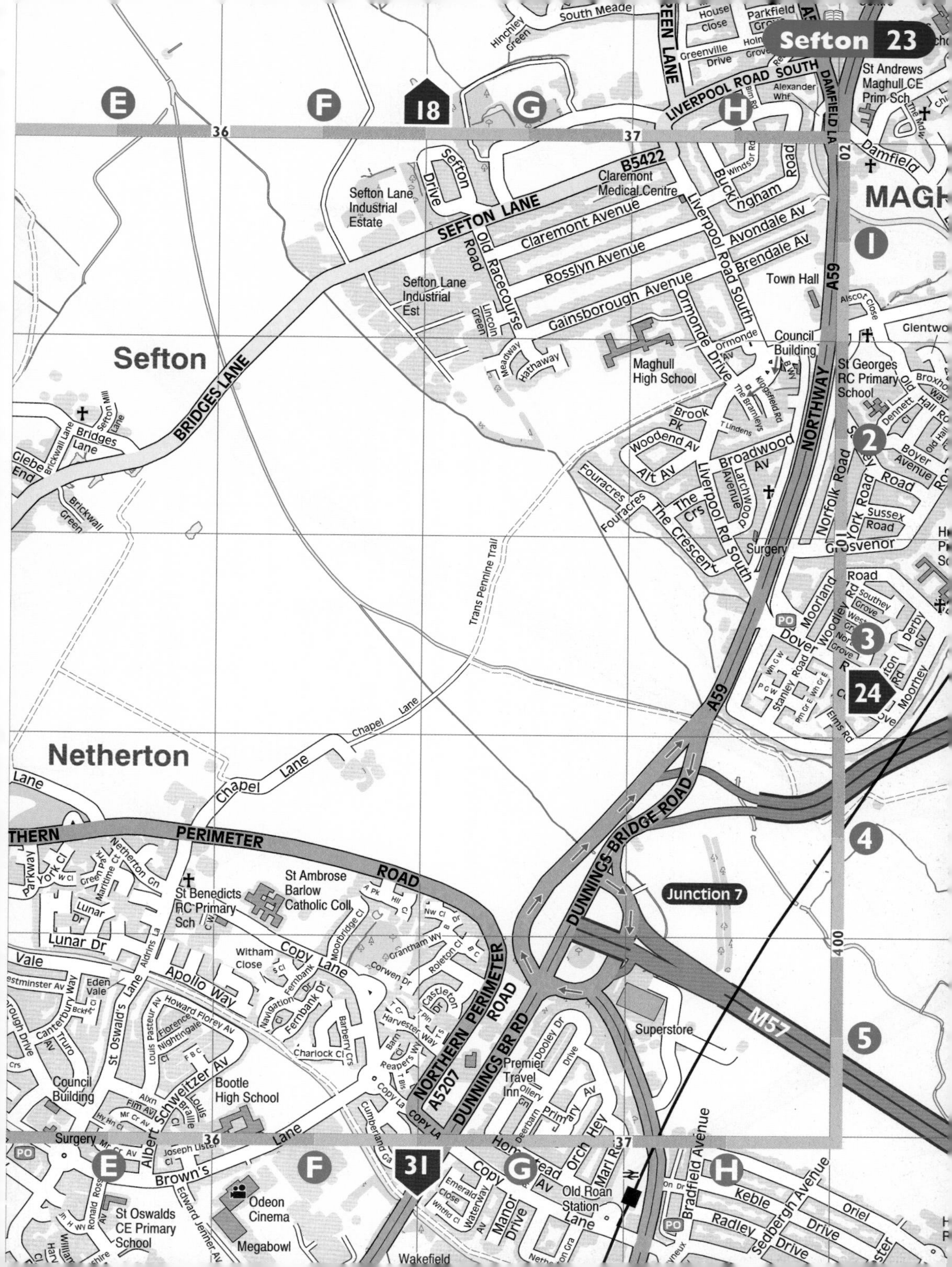
South Meade
Hinchley Green
House Close
Parkfield Grove
Greenville Drive
Holme Grove
LIVERPOOL ROAD SOUTH
Alexander Whf
DAMFIELD LA
St Andrews Maghull CE Prim Sch
Damfield
MAGH
E
F
18
G
H
36
37
B5422
Sefton Drive
Claremont Medical Centre
Windsor Rd
Road
Buckingham
Sefton Lane Industrial Estate
SEFTON LANE
Claremont Avenue
Avondale Av
Old Road
Rosslyn Avenue
Brendale Av
Liverpool Road South
I
Sefton Lane Industrial Est
Racecourse
Gainsborough Avenue
Ormonde Drive
Town Hall
A59
Lincoln Green
Alscot Close
Glentwo
Council Building
Ormonde Av
Meadway
Hathaway
Sefton
Maghull High School
Kingsfield Rd
The Bramleys
St Georges RC Primary School
Old Hall Rd
Broxholme Way
NORTHWAY
BRIDGES LANE
Sefton Mill Lane
Bridges Lane
Brickwall Lane
Glebe End
Brook Pk
T Lindens
Woodend Av
Broadwood Av
Dennett Cl
2
Boyer Avenue
Alt Av
Norfolk Road
Road
Fouracres
Larchwood Avenue
The Crs
York Road
Brickwall Green
The Crescent
Liverpool Rd South
Sussex Road
Surgery
Grosvenor
Trans Pennine Trail
Road
Moorland
Southey Grove
PO
Dover
Woodley Rd
3
Derby Gv
Stanley Road
24
Moorney
Elms Rd
A59
Chapel Lane
Netherton
Chapel Lane
Lane
NORTHERN PERIMETER ROAD
DUNNINGS BRIDGE ROAD
4
Parkway
York Cl
Netherton Gn
St Ambrose Barlow Catholic Coll
Junction 7
St Benedicts RC Primary Sch
Lunar Dr
Copy Lane
Moorbridge Cl
Grantham Wy
Roleton Cl
Vale
Witham Close
Apollo Way
Corwen Dr
Westminster Av
Eden Vale
Canterbury Way
St Oswald's Lane
Aldrins La
Fernbank Dr
Castleton Dr
NORTHERN PERIMETER ROAD
Howard Florey Av
Navigation Cl
Superstore
M57
5
Truro Av
Louis Pasteur Av
Florence Nightingale Cl
Harvester Way
Barberry Crs
Charlock Cl
Reapers Wy
Dooley Dr
Drive
Council Building
Albert Schweitzer Av
Bootle High School
Louis Braille Cl
A5207
DUNNINGS BR RD
Premier Travel Inn
Ollery Gn
Deerbarn
Primary Av
Orch Hey
Bradfield Avenue
Copy La
Cumberland Ga
Surgery
36
Lane
37
Marl Rd
Joseph Lister Cl
E
F
31
G
H
Brown's
Homestead Av
Sedbergh Avenue
Keble Drive
Oriel Drive
Ronald Ross Av
Odeon Cinema
Copy
Emerald Close
Waterway Av
Manor Drive
Old Roan Station
Radley Drive
St Oswalds CE Primary School
Edward Jenner Av
Lane
Megabowl
PO
Wakefield

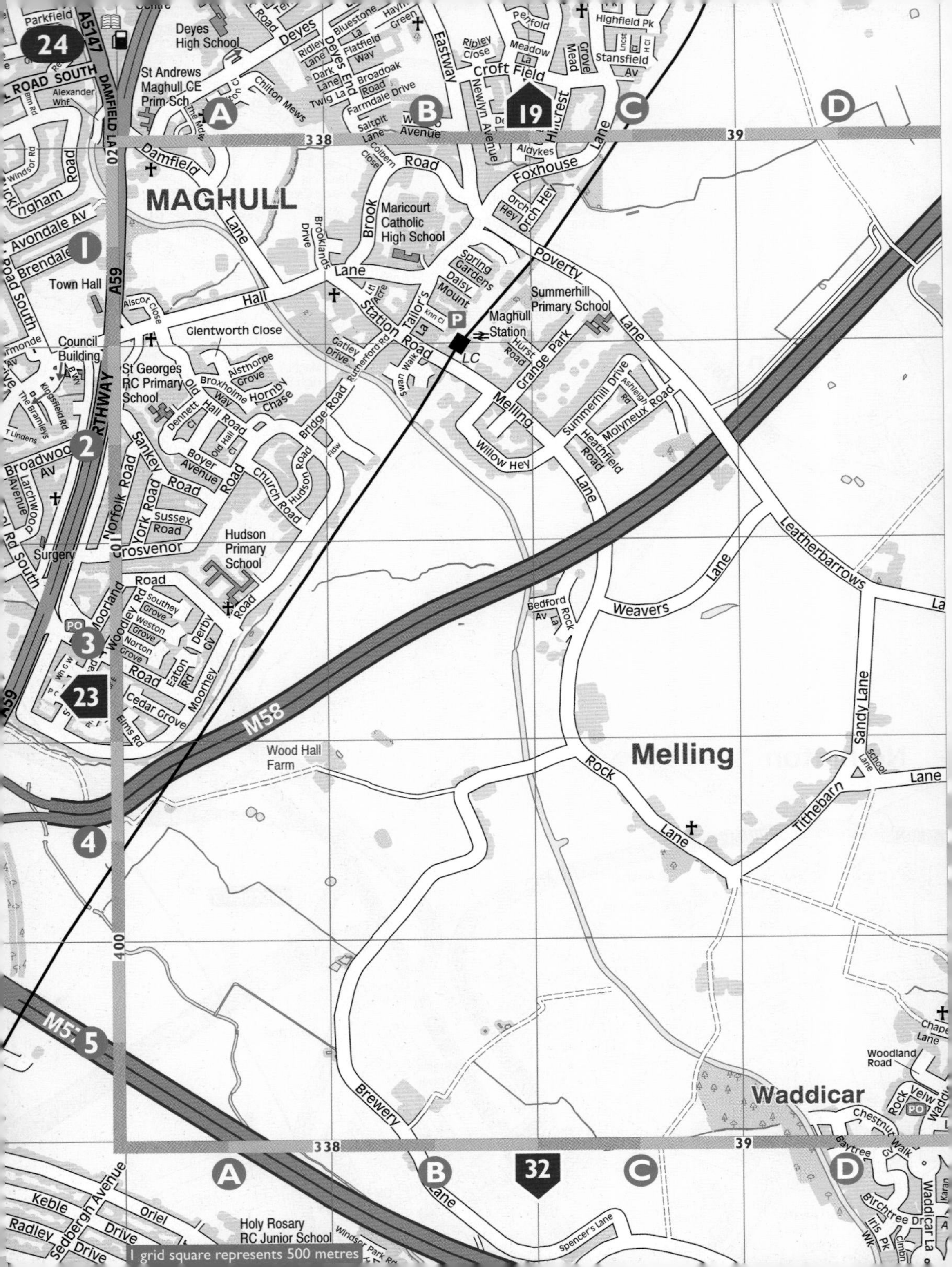
24
19
23
32
A
B
C
D
1
2
3
4
5
338
39
020
401
400
MAGHULL
Melling
Waddicar
Deyes High School
St Andrews Maghull CE Prim Sch
Maricourt Catholic High School
Summerhill Primary School
Maghull Station
St Georges RC Primary School
Hudson Primary School
Town Hall
Council Building
Surgery
Wood Hall Farm
Holy Rosary RC Junior School
A5147
A59
M58
M57
Damfield Lane
Hall Lane
Station Road
Brook Lane
Poverty Lane
Foxhouse Lane
Melling Lane
Leatherbarrows Lane
Weavers Lane
Rock Lane
Tithebarn Lane
Sandy Lane
School Lane
Brewery Lane
Bridge Road
Church Road
Hudson Road
Moorland Road
Sankey Road
Norfolk Road
York Road
Sussex Road
Grosvenor Road
Cedar Grove
Moorhey Road
Eaton Rd
Derby Gv
Woodley Rd
Southey Grove
Weston Grove
Norton Grove
Elms Rd
Boyer Avenue
Hall Road
Old Hall Cl
Dennett Cl
Broxholme Way
Hornby Chase
Alsthorpe Grove
Glentworth Close
Alscot Close
Gatley Drive
Rutherford Rd
Swan Walk
Tailor's La
Daisy Mount
Spring Gardens
Grange Park
Hurst Road
Summerhill Drive
Ashleigh Rd
Molyneux Road
Heathfield Road
Willow Hey
Orch Hey
Bedford Av
Rock La
Colbern Close
Brooklands Drive
Lt Acre
Deyes Lane
Eastway
Croft Field
Hillcrest
Newlyn Avenue
Aldykes
Stansfield Av
Highfield Pk
Penfold
Meadow La
Mead Grove
Ripley Close
Chilton Mews
Twig La
Farmdale Drive
Broadoak Road
Saltpit Lane
Flatfield Way
Bluestone La
Ridley Lane
Dark Lane
Deyes End
Avondale Av
Brendale
Broadwood Av
Larchwood Avenue
Windsor Rd
Kingsfield Rd
The Bramleys
Alexander Whf
Parkfield
Chapel Lane
Woodland Road
Chestnut Walk
Baytree Gv
Birchtree Dr
Waddicar La
Rock View
Keble Drive
Oriel Drive
Radley Drive
Sedbergh Avenue
Spencer's Lane
Windsor Park Rd
1 grid square represents 500 metres

Junction 1
Land End
Lyon's Farm
Maghull Lane
A506
Whitegates Farm
Spurrier's Lane
Moss Nook Lane
Giddygate Lane
Moorfield House
PRESCOT ROAD
Melling Mount
Sefton
Knowlsey
Prescot Road
Angers Lane
Lane
Waddicar Lane
Melling House
BANK LANE
Tern Close
Deva Close
Swallow Close
Linnet Way
Saxon Way
Kingfisher Close
Turner Gv
Lowry Cl
Beattock Cl
Kelso Cl
Knightsbridge Wk
Atlanta Ct
Vermont Cl
Lexington Wy
Washington Dr
Trevlot Close
Dumfries Way
Galston Cl
Melrose Road
Moorfoot Way
Ancrum Rd
Hawick Close
Jedburgh Drive
Ettrick Cl
Lauder Cl
Perth Cl
Bathgate Way
Bridle Way
Stockton Crs
Yoxall Dr
Chadwick Wy
Capilin Cl
Elwood Cl
Penda Dr
Hobart Dr
Horton Cl
Kerr Cl
Saxon Way
Redwood
Gibson Cl
Curran Way
Campbell Crs
Riesling Dr
Aster Dr
Clem Wy
Salvia Way
Shevington's Lane
Steeple View
Fairhaven
Ivory Dr
Ebony Way
Chesterfield Drive
Ascot Drive
Tudor View
St Pauls Close
Grantham Rd
Shaftsbury Av
Conifer Cl
Sapphire Dr
Domingo Drive
Ravenscroft Primary School
Hawkeswater Cl
Ennerdale Cl
Windermere Dr
Rydal Cl
Drwnt Cl
Ambleside Dr
Kendal Rd
Windermere Drive
Bassenthwaite Av
Seathwaite Crescent
Grsmr Close
Buttermere Close
Boyes Brow
Redmoor Crs
Stretford Cl
Ashburn Avenue
Heathfield Dr
Apollo Cres
Redbrow Wy
Fallowfield
Riversdale Cl
Headbolt Lane
Langton Rd
Lidgate Cl
Highsted Gv
Critchley Wy
Eastcroft
Knowsley Prim Sup
Overdale Primary Sch
Appleton Rd
Fern Cl
Brampton Cl
Millbeck Cl
St Kevin's Drive
Bluebell
Highwood Court
Badby Wood
Whttlwd Ct
Everdon Wood
Roughwood Drive
Kenne
County Road
A506
Stiles Rd
Serenade Rd
Hall Lane
Cheviot Wy
Saxon Way
Whitebeam Close
Douglas
Shevington's Lane
Saints Peter & Paul Catholic Sch
Moorfield
Tower
Hall
Malvern Close
Pennine Way
Archers Fold
Rainbow Drive
Marc Av
Beldale Park
Mount Close
North Mount Road
Clover's Brow
Mount Crs
Chiltern Drive
Cleveland Close
Mill Lane
North Park Road
Park Cl
Mount Rd
Surgery
Peach
Melling Primary School
Dunlop Dr
Wheeler Dr
Liddell Av
Station Rd
Stuart Rd
Halton Wd
Granborne Chase
Park Rd
Sefton Close
Sefton Drive
South Park Road
Deerbolt
Kirkby Station
Rowan Drive
Laburnum Crs
Alder Crescent
Elm Road
Willow Avenue
Hazel Av
Partridge Rd
Beech Av
Melling Drive
Church Way
COUNTY ROAD
26
33
40
41
400
01
02
E
F
G
H
1
2
3
4
5
PO

Outlet Lane
A
B
C
D
342
43
02
01
400
1
2
3
4
5
25
34
Hall Lane
Moss Lane
Grayson's Farm
Stopgate Lane
Simonswood Industrial Park
Tern Close
Deva Close
Swallow Close
Saxon
Penda Dr
Elwood Cl
Hobart Dr
Stiles Rd
Serenade Rd
Cheviot Wy
Hall Lane
Way
Douglas Wy
Weaver Avenue
Severn Road
Dee Close
Eden Cl
Calder Cl
Whitebeam Close
Filbert Close
Kerr Cl
Dekker Rd
Lewis Wk
Shevington's Lane
PO
Greenham Avenue
Meadowside
Moorfield
Pingwood Lane
Carl's Way
Winmoss Drive
Steeple View
Fairhaven
Saints Peter & Paul Catholic Sch
Tower Hill Health Centre
Tower Hill
Chesterfield Drive
Loughlin Drive
Brompton Av
Anders Dr
Freckleton Dr
Dorchester Dr
Crofters La
Alvina La
Cherry Vw
Headbolt Lane
Ravenscroft Primary School
Stretford Cl
Lidgate Cl
Langton Road
Sumner Gv
Hllnghrst Rd
Highsted Gv
Eastcroft
Eastcroft Park CP School
Critchley Wy
Fwd Gdns
Kworth Cl
Fallowfield
Riversdale Cl
Langton Rd
Lane
Bramcote Walk
Bramcote Road
Knowsley Northern Prim Support Cen
Chadwell Rd
Lapford Crescent
Pentland Road
Shacklady Road
Roughwood Drive
Overdale Primary School
Warrenhouse Road
Trecastle Rd
Dale Lane
Appleton Rd
Millbeck Cl
Brampton Cl
Bluebell Ct
St Kevin's Drive
Whttlwd Ct
Highwood Court
Badby Wood
Kng Ct
Brook Hey Drive
Devcroft Avenue
Kenbury Road
Gillsecroft Avenue
Jarrett Road
Watts Close
Changford Road
Wingate Road
Wingate Medical Centre
Everdon Wood
Roughwood Drive
Elwood Avenue
Quernmore Road
St Marie RC Prim Sch
Bigdale Medical Cen
Quarry
COUNTY ROAD
Melling Drive
Northwood
Marl Road
No Bus Ce

1 grid square represents 500 metres

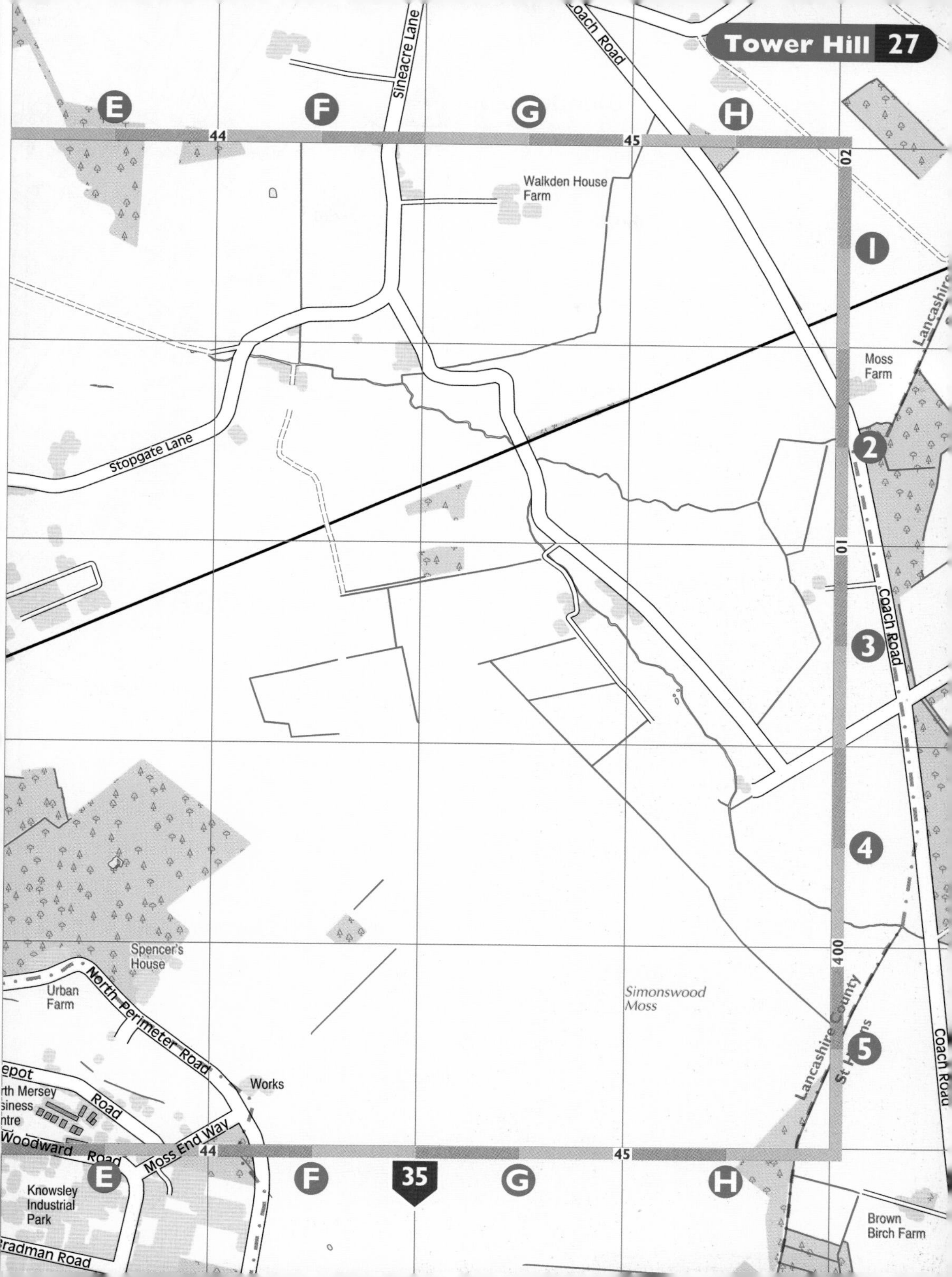
Coach Road
Sineacre Lane
E
F
G
H
44
45
02
Walkden House Farm
I
Moss Farm
Lancashire
2
Stopgate Lane
10
Coach Road
3
4
Spencer's House
Urban Farm
North Perimeter Road
400
Simonswood Moss
Lancashire County
St Helens
5
Coach Road
Works
epot
rth Mersey
siness
ntre
Road
Woodward Road
Moss End Way
Knowsley Industrial Park
Bradman Road
35
Brown Birch Farm

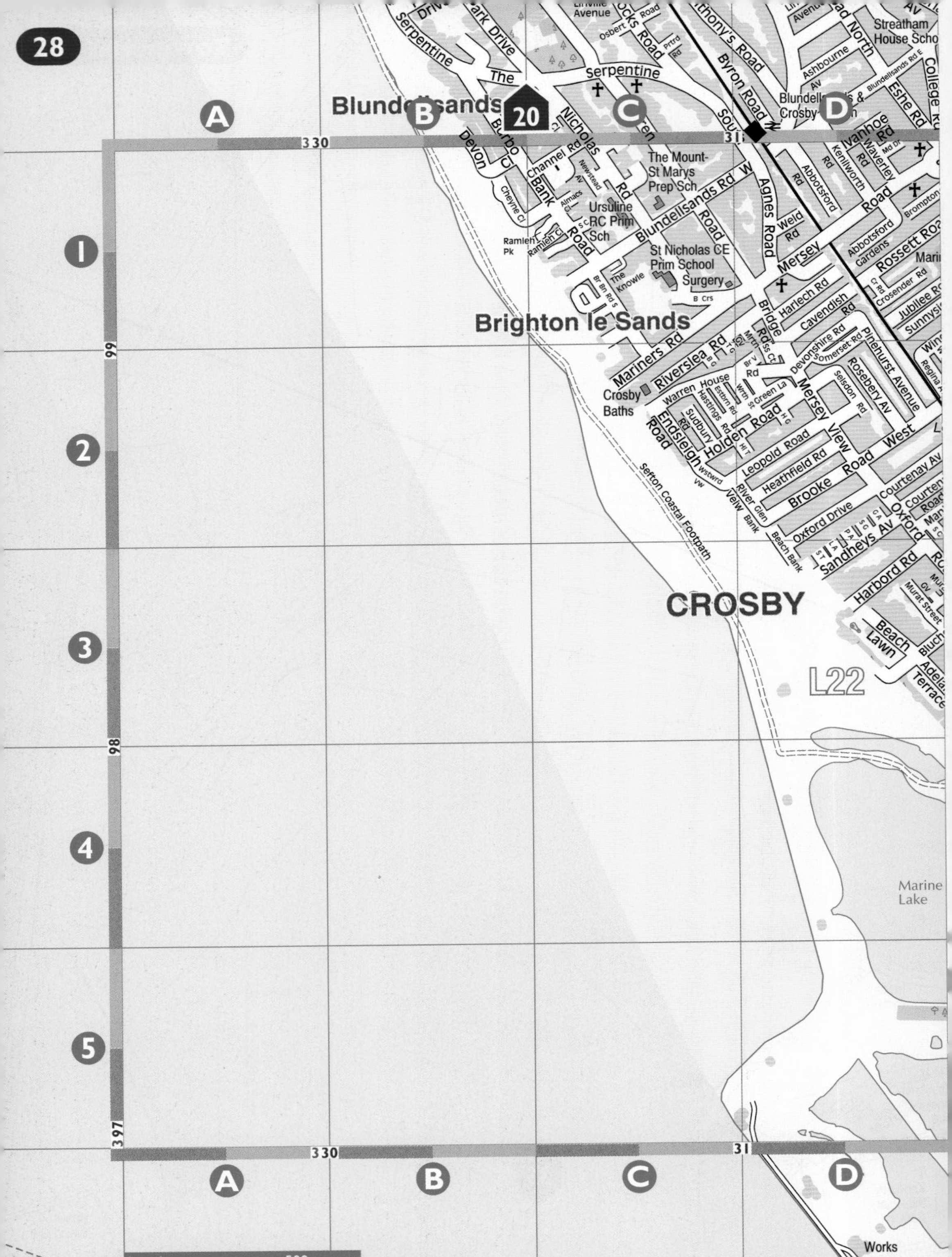
Blundellsands
Brighton le Sands
CROSBY
L22
Marine Lake
Works
Sefton Coastal Footpath
20
A
B
C
D
1
2
3
4
5
330
31
99
98
397
The Serpentine
Serpentine
Nicholas Road
Burbo Cl
Devon
Channel Rd
Newstead Av
Cheyne Cl
Bank
Almacs Cl
Ramleh Pk
Ramleh Cl
The Mount-St Marys Prep Sch
Ursuline RC Prim Sch
Blundellsands Rd W
Blundellsands Road
St Nicholas CE Prim School
Surgery
The Knowle
Agnes Road
Byron Road
Weld Rd
Abbotsford Rd
Kenilworth Rd
Ivanhoe Rd
Waverley
Mersey Road
Abbotsford Gardens
Rossett Road
Crosender Rd
Jubilee
Streatham House School
Ashbourne Av
Blundellsands & Crosby Station
Esher Rd
College
Harlech Rd
Cavendish Rd
Mariners Rd
Riverslea Rd
Bridge Rd
Devonshire Rd
Somerset Rd
Pinehurst Avenue
Rosebery Av
Selsdon Rd
Crosby Baths
Warren House
Hastings Rd
Green La
Mersey View
Endsleigh Road
Sudbury Rd
Holden Road
Leopold Road
Heathfield Rd
Brooke Road West
Courtenay Av
River Glen
Oxford Drive
Oxford Road
Sandheys Av
Beach Bank
Harbord Rd
Murat Street
Beach Lawn
Adelaide Terrace
1 grid square represents 500 metres

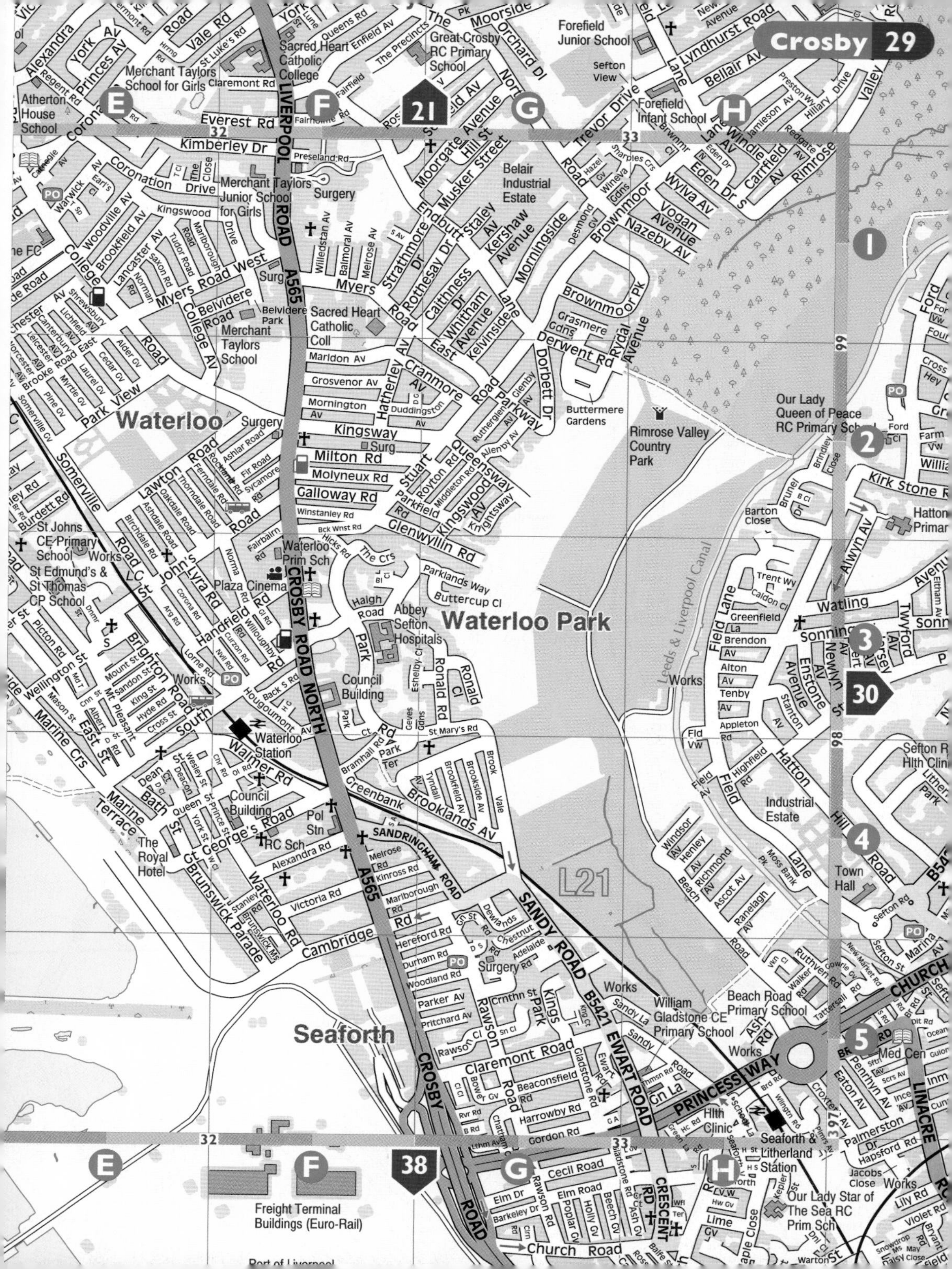
Waterloo
Waterloo Park
Seaforth
Rimrose Valley Country Park
Leeds & Liverpool Canal
L21
LIVERPOOL ROAD
A565
CROSBY ROAD NORTH
CROSBY ROAD
SANDY ROAD
B5421
EWART ROAD
PRINCESS WAY
SANDRINGHAM ROAD
LINACRE
CHURCH
Merchant Taylors School for Girls
Merchant Taylors Junior School for Girls
Merchant Taylors School
Sacred Heart Catholic College
Sacred Heart Catholic Coll
Great Crosby RC Primary School
Forefield Junior School
Forefield Infant School
Atherton House School
Belair Industrial Estate
St Johns CE Primary School
St Edmund's & St Thomas CP School
Waterloo Prim Sch
Plaza Cinema
Abbey Sefton Hospitals
Council Building
Waterloo Station
Pol Stn
RC Sch
The Royal Hotel
Our Lady Queen of Peace RC Primary School
Buttermere Gardens
Industrial Estate
Town Hall
Beach Road Primary School
William Gladstone CE Primary School
Seaforth & Litherland Station
Hlth Clinic
Our Lady Star of The Sea RC Prim Sch
Freight Terminal Buildings (Euro-Rail)
Port of Liverpool
Surgery
Works
21
30
38
32
33
E
F
G
H
I
2
3
4
5

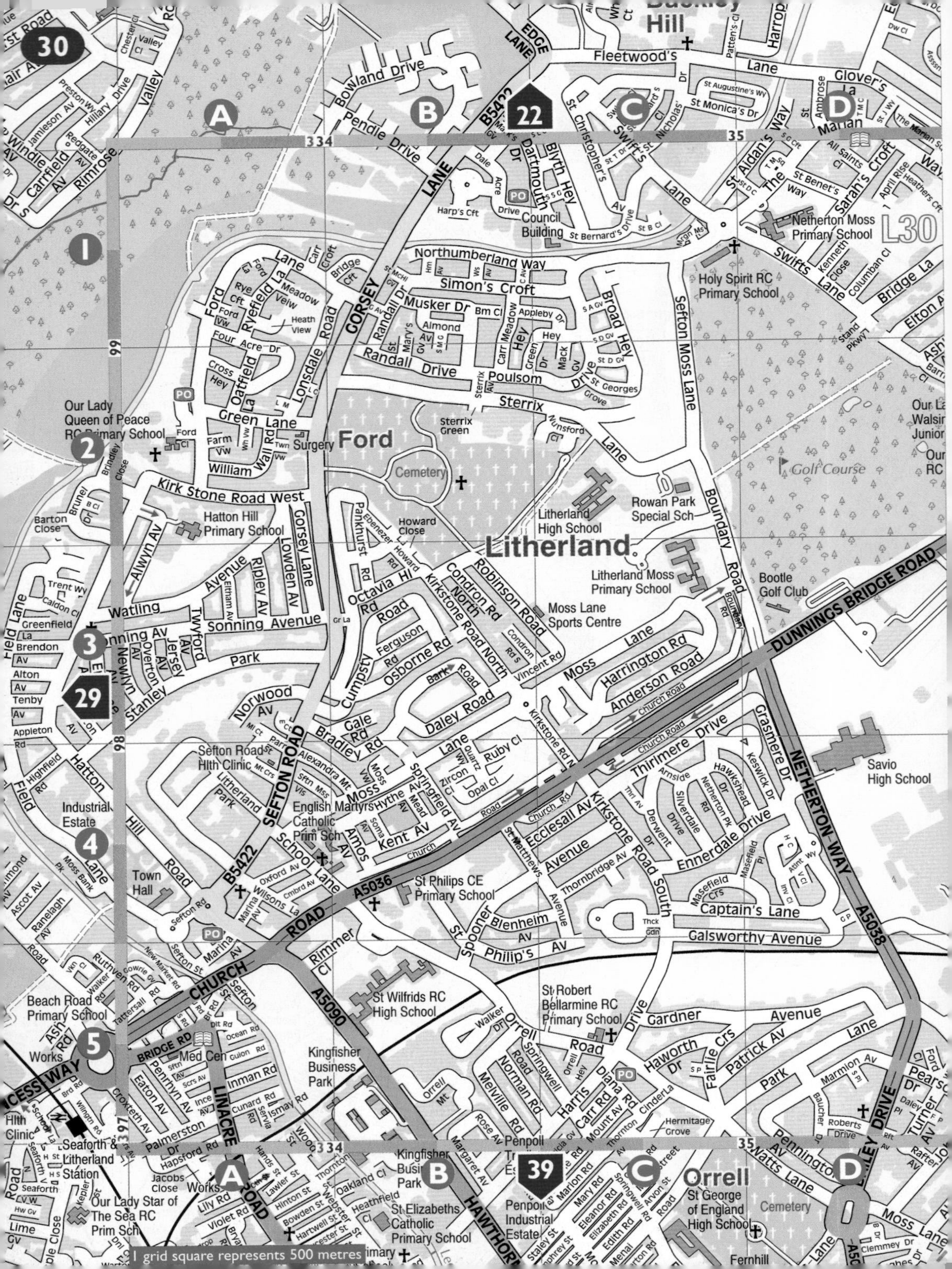
30
22
29
39
A
B
C
D
1
2
3
4
5
334
35
99
98
397
L30
Buckley Hill
Fleetwood's Lane
Glover's La
Bowland Drive
Pendle Drive
Edge Lane
B5422
Gorsey Lane
Dartmouth Dr
Blyth Hey
St Christopher's Av
Swifts Lane
St Monica's Dr
St Augustine's Wy
St Aidan's Way
Marian Way
All Saints Cl
Sarah's Croft
St Benet's Way
April Rise
Netherton Moss Primary School
Holy Spirit RC Primary School
Swifts Lane
Kenneth Close
Columban Cl
Bridge La
Elton Av
Harp's Cft
Council Building
St Bernard's Drive
Northumberland Way
Simon's Croft
Musker Dr
Bm Cl
Appleby Dr
Broad Hey
Sefton Moss Lane
Almond Av
Randall Dr
Randall Drive
Carr Meadow Hey
Green Dr
Mack Gv
Poulsom Drive
St Georges Grove
Sterrix
Sterrix Lane
Sterrix Green
Nunsford Cl
Ford
Ford Lane
Rye Cft
Ryefield La
Meadow Veiw
Heath View
Lonsdale Road
Four Acre Dr
Cross Hey
Oatfield La
Green Lane
Farm Vw
William Wall Rd
Surgery
Our Lady Queen of Peace RC Primary School
Ford Cl
Brindley Close
Brunel Dr
Barton Close
Kirk Stone Road West
Hatton Hill Primary School
Gorsey Lane
Lowden Av
Ripley Av
Alwyn Av
Watling Avenue
Sonning Avenue
Sonning Av
Twyford Av
Jersey Av
Overton Av
Newlyn Av
Park
Stanley
Trent Wy
Caldon Cl
Greenfield La
Field Lane
Brendon Av
Alton Av
Tenby Av
Appleton Rd
Cemetery
Howard Close
Pankhurst Rd
Ebenezer Rd
Howard Rd
Octavia Hl
Kirkstone Road North
Condron Rd
Robinson Road
Litherland
Litherland High School
Rowan Park Special Sch
Boundary Road
Litherland Moss Primary School
Moss Lane Sports Centre
Bootle Golf Club
Golf Course
Dunnings Bridge Road
Ferguson Rd
Osborne Rd
Cumpsty Rd
Bark Road
Vincent Rd
Moss Lane
Harrington Rd
Anderson Road
Church Road
Daley Road
Norwood Av
Gale Rd
Bradley Rd
Sefton Road
Sefton Road Hlth Clinic
Alexandra Mt
Litherland Park
Moss Lane
Springfield Av
Quartz Wy
Ruby Cl
Zircon Cl
Opal Cl
Kirkstone Rd N
Thirlmere Drive
Grasmere Dr
Keswick Dr
Hawkshead Dr
Netherton Pk
Arnside
Silverdale Drive
Derwent Dr
Ennerdale Drive
Netherton Way
Savio High School
English Martyrs Catholic Prim Sch
Hythe Av
Mead Av
Kent Av
Amos Av
Ecclesall Av
Kirkstone Road South
Thornbridge Av
St Matthews Avenue
Masefield Crs
Captain's Lane
Galsworthy Avenue
A5038
A5036
Industrial Estate
Hatton Hill Road
Highfield Rd
Field Rd
Moss Bank Pk
Ascot Av
Ranelagh Av
Town Hall
School Lane
Oxford Av
Wilsons La
St Philips CE Primary School
Church Road
Rimmer Cl
Spooner St
Blenheim Av
St Philip's Av
Sefton Rd
Marina Av
Sefton St
Ruthven Rd
Gowrie Gv
Tattersall Rd
Beach Road Primary School
Ash Rd
Works
Bridge Rd
Med Cen
Ocean Rd
Penrhyn Av
Eaton Av
Inman Rd
Linacre Road
Cunard Rd
Ismay Rd
A5090
St Wilfrids RC High School
Kingfisher Business Park
Walker Dr
Orrell Road
Orrell Mt
Springwell Road
Norman Rd
Melville Rd
St Robert Bellarmine RC Primary School
Gardner Avenue
Haworth Dr
Fairlie Crs
Patrick Av
Park Lane
Marmion Av
Harris Dr
Carr Rd
Diana Rd
Mount Av
Cinder La
Hermitage Grove
Roberts Drive
Pennington Av
Watts Lane
Rose Av
Penpoll
Princess Way
Croxteth Av
Palmerston Dr
Hapsford Rd
Seaforth & Litherland Station
Hlth Clinic
Seaforth
Jacobs Close
Works
Lily Rd
Violet Rd
Lawler St
Hinton St
Bowden St
Hartwell St
Oakland Cl
Heathfield
Kingfisher Busin Park
St Elizabeths Catholic Primary School
Margaret Av
Hawthorne
Penpoll Industrial Estate
Marion Rd
Mary Rd
Eleanor Rd
Elizabeth Rd
Edith Rd
Arvon St
Orrell
St George of England High School
Cemetery
Moss Lane
Fernhill
Our Lady Star of The Sea RC Prim Sch
Lime Gv
1 grid square represents 500 metres

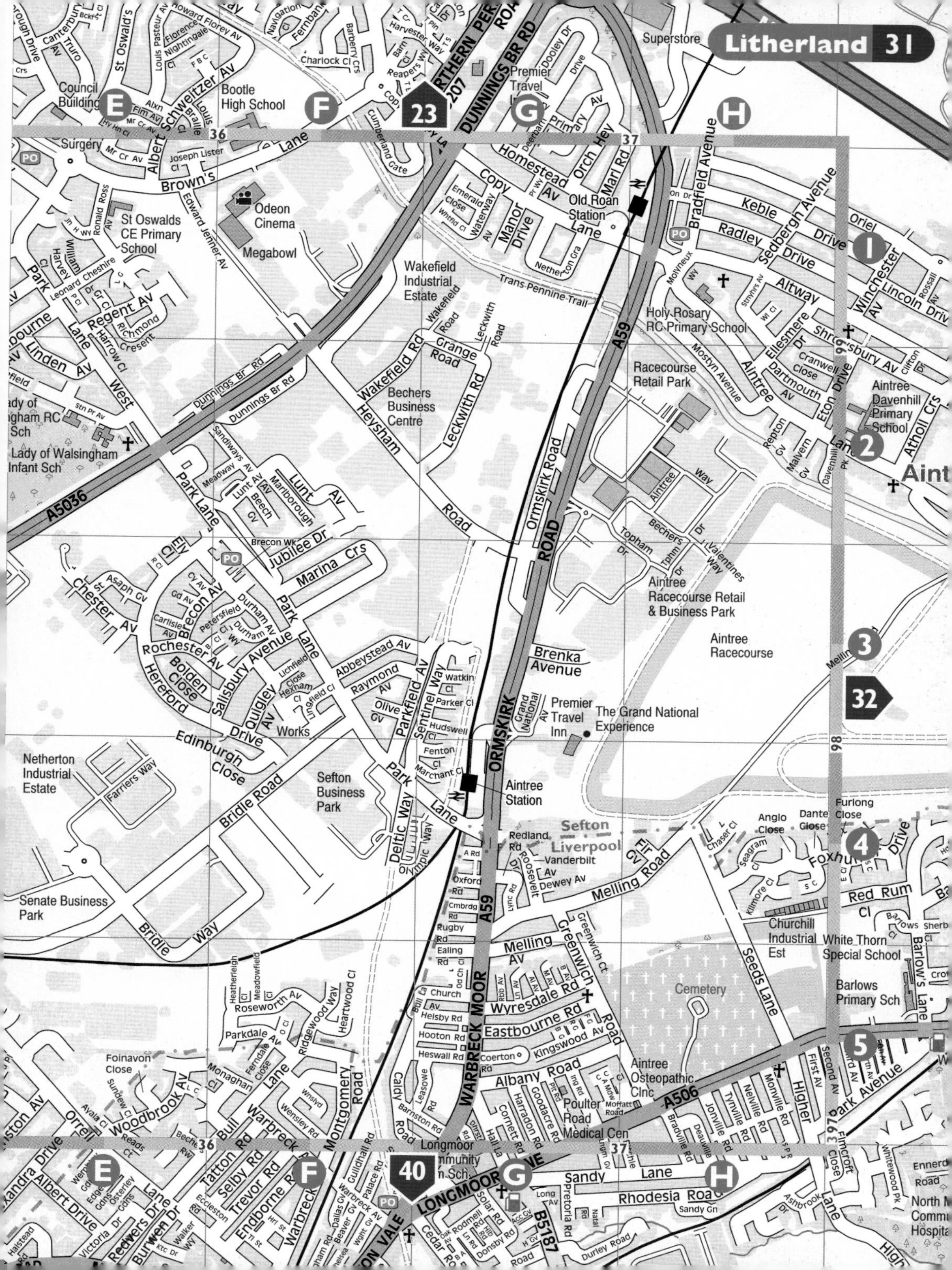
Superstore
Council Building
Bootle High School
Premier Travel Inn
Surgery
Joseph Lister Cl
Brown's Lane
Odeon Cinema
Megabowl
St Oswalds CE Primary School
Old Roan Station
Homestead Av
Orch Hey
Marl Rd
Copy Lane
Manor Drive
Bradfield Avenue
Keble
Radley Drive
Sedbergh Avenue
Oriel Drive
Winchester Av
Lincoln Drive
Altway
Wakefield Industrial Estate
Trans Pennine Trail
Holy Rosary RC Primary School
A59
A5036
Dunnings Br Rd
Regent Av
Linden Av
Richmond Cresent
West Lane
Park Lane
Wakefield Rd
Grange Road
Leckwith Rd
Becher Business Centre
Heysham Road
Racecourse Retail Park
Aintree Davenhill Primary School
Lady of Walsingham RC Sch
Lady of Walsingham Infant Sch
Ormskirk Road
Aintree Way
Becher Dr
Topham Dr
Valentines Way
Aintree Racecourse Retail & Business Park
Aintree Racecourse
Jubilee Dr
Marina Crs
Brecon Av
Chester Av
Rochester Av
Salisbury Avenue
Hereford Drive
Edinburgh Close
Brenka Avenue
Premier Travel Inn
The Grand National Experience
Netherton Industrial Estate
Farriers Way
Bridle Road
Sefton Business Park
Deltic Way
Aintree Station
Sefton
Liverpool
Melling Road
Senate Business Park
Bridle Way
Furlong Close
Dante Close
Anglo Close
Foxhunter Drive
Red Rum Cl
Churchill Industrial Est
White Thorn Special School
Barlows Primary Sch
Barlow's Lane
Seeds Lane
Cemetery
Melling Av
Greenwich Road
Wyresdale Rd
Eastbourne Rd
Kingswood Av
Albany Road
Warbreck Moor
Aintree Osteopathic Clnc
Poulter Road Medical Cen
A506
Higher Lane
Park Avenue
Roseworth Av
Parkdale Av
Foinavon Close
Woodbrook Av
Orrell Lane
Warbreck Av
Montgomery Road
Longmoor Community Sch
Longmoor Lane
Sandy Lane
Rhodesia Road
B5187
North Mersey Community Hospital
Albert Drive
36
37
23
40
32
E F G H
1 2 3 4 5

32
A
B
C
D
24
338
39
Brewery Lane
Waddicar
Chapel Lane
Woodland Road
Rock Veiw
Chestnut Walk
Baytree Gv
Birchtree Dr
Iris Pk
Waddicar La
Spencer's Lane
Ledsons Gv
Works
Canal Veiw
Satinwood Crs
Cypress
Hickory Gv
M57
Keble
Oriel
Radley
Sedbergh Avenue
Drive
Altway
Winchester Av
Lincoln Drive
Rossall Av
Oriel Drive
Oriel Cl
Holy Rosary RC Junior School
Windsor Park Rd
Haydock Pk Rd
Sandown Pk Rd
Kempton Pk Rd
Tonbridge Dr
Denstone Av
Haileybury Av
Martland Av
Lowther Av
Sandhurst Dr
Stowe Av
Ellesmere Dr
Shrewsbury Av
Clifton Dr
Cranwell Close
Dartmouth Av
Aintree Av
Eton Drive
Aintree Davenhill Primary School
Atholl Crs
Harrow Drive
Wrekin Dr
North Av
Bull Bridge Lane
Canterbury Cl
Taunton
Lancing Drive
Greenside Av
Charterhouse Dr
Uppingham Av
Felsted Dr
Rydal Cl
Drive
Rugby Dr
Repton Gv
Davenhill Pk
Lane
Aintree
Sefton Dr
Bisdl Av
School Lane
Wango Lane
Valley Cl
Valentine Grove
Cheltenham Cl
Exeter Close
Epsom Close
Beaumont Dr
Oakham Dr
Monmouth Dr
Downside Dr
Wango Lane
Leeds & Liverpool Canal
River Alt
Sefton
Knowsley
Valentines Way
Aintree Racecourse
Melling Road
31
98
Lytham Cl
Rufford Cl
Ainsdale Cl
Sherwood's Lane
Redbridge High School
Watergate North Primary School
Meadow Bank Special School
Twigden Cl
Leagate
Liverpool
Knowsley
Aintree Lane
Furlong Close
Anglo Close
Dante Close
Chaser Cl
Seagram Cl
Foxhunter Drive
Barlow's Lane
Works Dr
Pavilion
Red Rum Cl
Kilmore Cl
Signal Works Road
Rycroft Rd
Wortley Rd
Adlam Road
Fazakerley Sports Centre
Haven Rd
L10
Churchill Industrial Est
White Thorn Special School
Barlows Sherburn Cl
Barlow's Lane
Lane
West Orch
East Orch
Garden
Croft La
LC
Fazakerley High School
Greenhaven Close
Seeds Lane
Barlows Primary Sch
Fazakerley Stn
Adlam Road
Kinross Rd
LONGMOOR
LANE
A506
PO
Formosa Dr
Elmham Crs
Drake Wy
Longmoor La
Edgemoor Dr
Moor Lane
Copple House La
Ronaldsway
Dereham Crs
Formosa Drive
Mond Rd
Drake Crescent
Ferrey Road
Copple House Centre
Greystone Rd
Moss Pits Lane
Swainson Rd
Holy Name RC Primary School
Meres Rd
Third Av
Lakes Road
University Hospital Aintree
Works
Fifth Av
Fourth Av
Sefton Road
Tenth Av
Ninth Av
Broadway
Woodlands Rd
Karonga Way
Fazakerley Primary Sch
Formosa Way
Drake Road
Grieve Rd
Gribble Road
Edna Av
Grace Av
Karonga Road
Montrovia Crs
Hawksmoor Road
Lower Lane
5
Higher Lane
First Av
Second Av
Third Av
Frth Av
Park Avenue
Monville Rd
Melville Rd
Tynville Rd
Jonville Rd
397
Elmcroft Close
Whitewood Pk
Aintree
Enderdale
South Road
Edge Hill Enterprise Training Centre
Second Avenue
First Avenue
A&E
Broadway
41
Ladysmith Rd
Mandalay Crescent
Delagoa Rd
Falcon
Blueberry Flds
North Mersey Community Hospital
Edge Hill Enterprises
Ashbrook Dr
University
1
2
3
4
1 grid square represents 500 metres

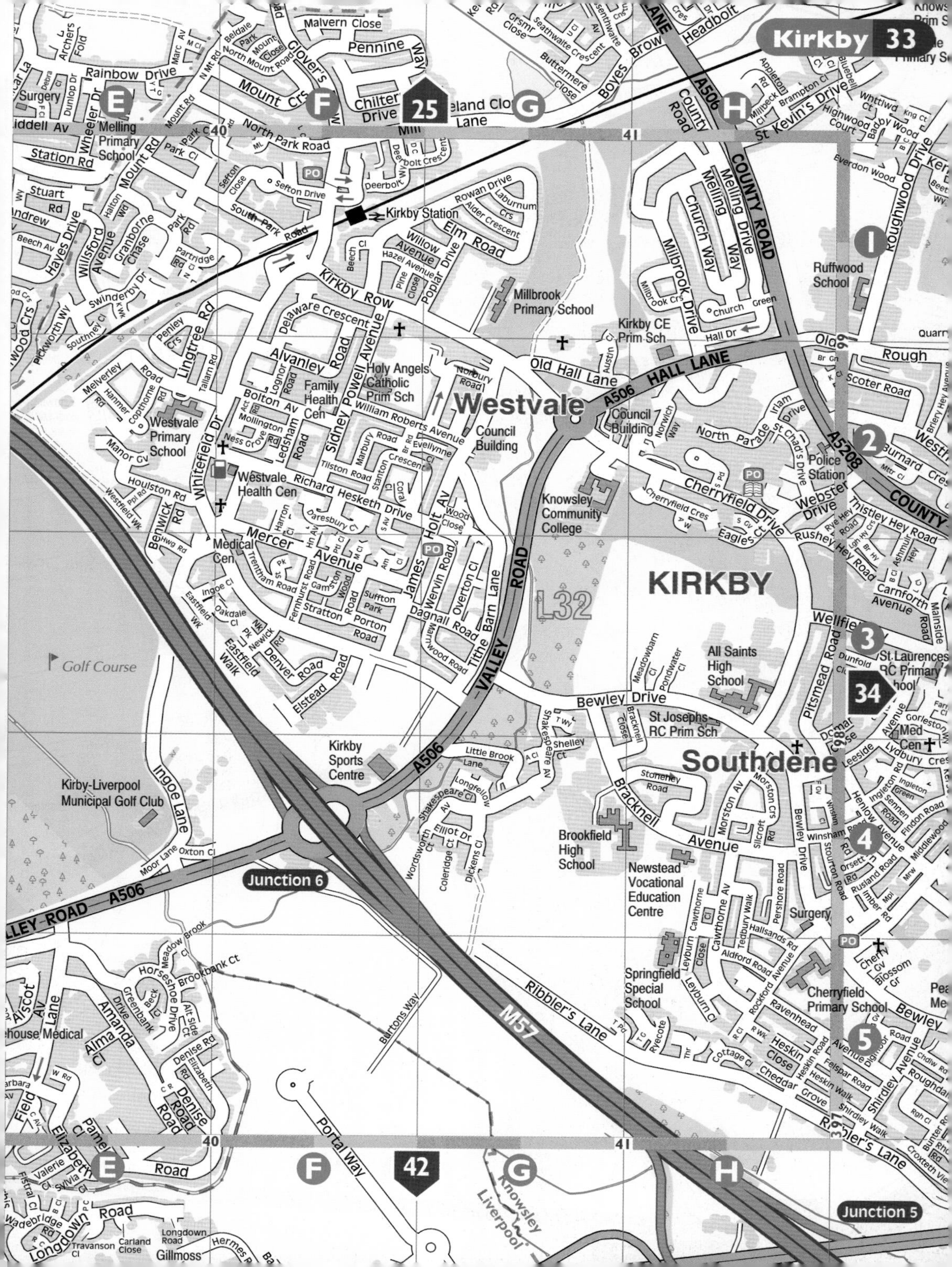
Malvern Close
Pennine Way
Rainbow Drive
Archers Fold
Surgery
Dunlop Dr
Wheeler Dr
Melling Primary School
Liddell Av
Station Rd
Mount Rd
North Mount Road
Mount Crs
Glover's
Chiltern Drive
25
Mill Lane
Boyes Brow
Headbolt Lane
Seathwaite Crescent
Buttermere Close
County Road
A506
St Kevin's Drive
Appleton Rd
Brampton Cl
Bluebell
Highwood Court
Roughwood Drive
Everdon Wood
North Park Road
Park Cl
Sefton Close
Sefton Drive
South Park Road
Deerbolt Crescent
PO
Kirkby Station
Rowan Drive
Laburnum Crs
Alder Crescent
Willow Avenue
Elm Road
Hazel Avenue
Beech Cl
Pine Close
Poplar Drive
Stuart Rd
Andrew
Hayes Drive
Beech Av
Willsford Avenue
Cranborne Chase
Halton Wd
Park Rd
Partridge Rd
Swinderby Dr
Pickworth Wy
Southney Cl
Penley Crs
Lingtree Rd
Tallarn Rd
Kirkby Row
Delaware Crescent
Alvanley Road
Lognor Road
Sidney Powell Avenue
Holy Angels Catholic Prim Sch
Family Health Cen
Millbrook Primary School
Melling Drive
Church Way
Millbrook Drive
Millbrook Crs
Church Green
Hall Dr
Kirkby CE Prim Sch
Old Hall Lane
Austin Cl
Hall Lane
Old Rough
Quarry
Scoter Road
Norbury Road
Westvale
Council Building
North Parade
Irlam Drive
St Chad's Drive
Norwich Way
A5208
Police Station
Burnard Cres
County Road
Melverley Road
Hanmer Rd
Copthorne Rd
Westvale Primary School
Manor Gv
Bolton Av
Mollington Rd
Ness Grove
Ledsham Road
William Roberts Avenue
Marbury Road
Evellynne Cl
Tilston Road
Stanton Crescent
Coral Cl
Richard Hesketh Drive
Holt Av
Wood Close
Whitefield Dr
Westvale Health Cen
Houlston Rd
Westfield Wk
Benwick Rd
Hwg Rd
Medical Cen
Mercer Avenue
Daresbury Cl
Harrison Cl
Trentham Road
Fernhurst Road
Gamston Wood
Suffton Park
Porton Road
Stratton Road
James
Wervin Road
Overton Cl
Dagnall Road
Marrwood Road
Tithe Barn Lane
Valley Road
Knowsley Community College
Cherryfield Drive
Cherryfield Cres
Eagles Ct
Webster Drive
Thistley Hey Road
Rushey Hey Road
Rye Hey Road
Ashmuir Hey
Carnforth Avenue
Mainside Road
KIRKBY
L32
Ingoe Cl
Eastfield Wk
Oakdale Cl
Newick Rd
Denver Road
Elstead Road
Eastfield Walk
Golf Course
Wellfield
Pitsmead Road
Dunfold Cl
St Laurences RC Primary School
34
All Saints High School
Meadowbarn Cl
Pondwater Cl
Bewley Drive
Shakespeare Av
Shelley Ct
Bracknell Close
St Josephs RC Prim Sch
Southdene
Med Cen
Gorleston Wy
Leeside
Lydbury Cres
Kirkby Sports Centre
A506
Little Brook Lane
Longfellow
Shakespeare Cl
Elliot Dr
Stoneney Road
Bracknell Avenue
Morston Av
Morston Crs
Silcroft Rd
Ingleton Rd
Ingleton Green
Sennen Road
Henlow Avenue
Findon Road
Winsham Rd
Kirby-Liverpool Municipal Golf Club
Ingoe Lane
Wordsworth Ct
Coleridge Ct
Dickens Cl
Brookfield High School
Newstead Vocational Education Centre
Pershore Road
Surgery
Stourton Road
Orsett Rd
Rusland Road
Middlewood
Moor Lane
Oxton Cl
Junction 6
Valley Road
A506
Meadow Brook Cl
Brookbank Ct
Horseshoe Drive
Greenbank Drive
Beck Cl
Alt Side Ct
Ascot Av
Lane
Amanda Road
Alma Cl
Medical
Denise Rd
Elizabeth Rd
Denise Road
Burtons Way
Ribbler's Lane
M57
Cawthorne Av
Tedbury Walk
Hallsands Rd
Leyburn Close
Aldford Road
Rockford Avenue
Springfield Special School
Ryecote
Ravenhead Avenue
Cherryfield Primary School
Cherry Gv
Blossom Gr
Bewley
Heskin Close
Heskin Road
Heskin Walk
Felspar Road
Cheddar Grove
Cottage Cl
Shirdley Avenue
Shirdley Walk
Roughdale
Ribbler's Lane
Croxteth View
Pamela Cl
Elizabeth Road
Valerie
Sylvia
Portal Way
42
Knowsley Liverpool
Junction 5
Wadebridge Rd
Longdown Road
Travanson Cl
Carland Close
Longdown Road
Gillmoss
Hermes
E
F
G
H
I
2
3
4
5
40
41

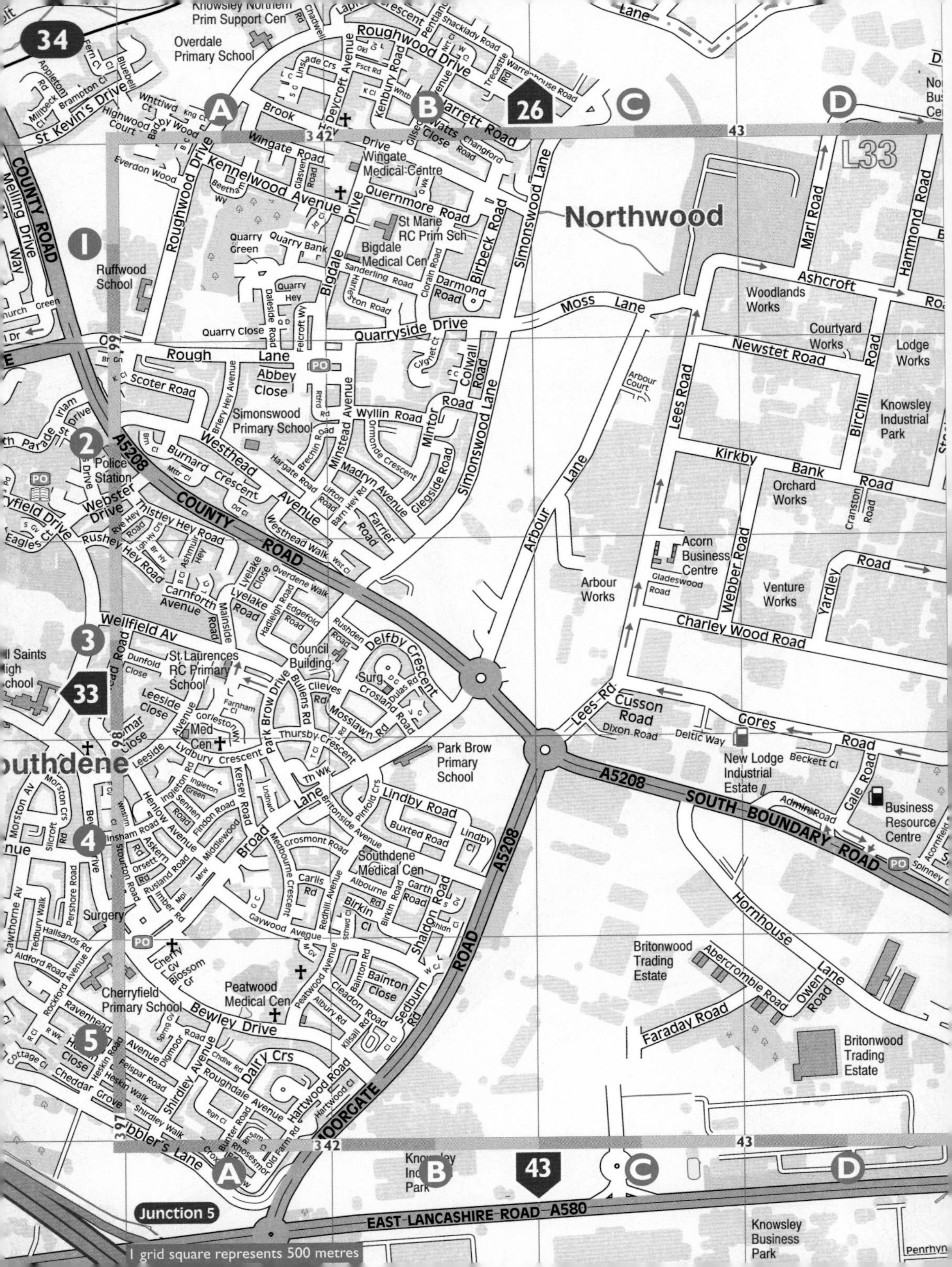
34
26
33
43
A
B
C
D
1
2
3
4
5
342
43
397
398
399
L33
Northwood
Knowsley Northern Prim Support Cen
Overdale Primary School
Roughwood Drive
Shacklady Road
Warrenhouse Road
Pentland
Deycroft Avenue
Kenbury Road
Linslade Crs
Brook
Jarrett Road
Watts Close
Changford Road
Trecastle Rd
St Kevin's Drive
Bluebell Cl
Fern Cl
Appleton Rd
Brampton Cl
Millbeck Cl
Whitlwd Ct
Highwood Court
Badby Wood
Wingate Road
Wingate Medical Centre
Everdon Wood
Kennelwood Avenue
Roughwood Drive
Glasven Road
Quernmore Road
St Marie RC Prim Sch
Bigdale Drive
Bigdale Medical Cen
Quarry Green
Quarry Bank
Quarry Hey
Quarry Close
Daleside Road
Sanderling Road
Harleston Road
Clorain Road
Darmond Road
Birbeck Road
Simonswood Lane
Moss Lane
Quarryside Drive
Felcroft Wy
Rough Lane
Abbey Close
PO
Cygnet Ct
Colwall Road
Minton Road
Wyllin Road
Minstead Avenue
Ormonde Crescent
Simonswood Primary School
Scoter Road
Brierly Hey Avenue
Brechin Road
Westhead Avenue
Burnard Crescent
Hargate Road
Madryn Avenue
Glegside Road
Lifton Road
Barn Hey Rd
Farrier Road
Westhead Walk
COUNTY ROAD
A5208
Ruffwood School
Melling Drive
Police Station
Webster Drive
Cherryfield Drive
Eagles Ct
Rushey Hey Road
Thistley Hey Road
Ashmuir Hey
Carnforth Avenue
Lyelake Close
Lyelake Road
Overdene Walk
Mainside Road
Hadleigh Road
Edgefold Road
Wellfield Av
Dunfold Close
St.Laurences RC Primary School
Council Building
Rushden Road
Delfby Crescent
Surg
Dulas Rd
Crosland Road
Bullens Rd
Clieves Rd
Mosslawn Rd
Park Brow Drive
Park Brow Primary School
Leeside Close
Lydbury Crescent
Thursby Crescent
Med Cen
Corleston Wy
Farnham Cl
Southdene
Ingleton Rd
Ingleton Green
Kersey Road
Sennen Road
Henlow Avenue
Findon Road
Middlewood
Lane
Broad
Britonside Avenue
Pinfold Crs
Lindby Road
Lindby Cl
Buxted Road
Grosmont Road
Medbourne Crescent
Southdene Medical Cen
Carlis Rd
Redhill Avenue
Albourne Road
Birkin Road
Birkin Cl
Garth Road
Shaldon Road
Gaywood Avenue
Askern Rd
Orsett Rd
Rusland Road
Imber Rd
Stourton Road
Winsham Road
Morston Av
Morston Crs
Slicroft
Pershore Road
Surgery
Hallsands Rd
Tedbury Walk
Cawthorne Av
Alford Road
Rockford Avenue
Cherryfield Primary School
Cherry Blossom Gr
Peatwood Medical Cen
Bewley Drive
Peatwood Avenue
Albury Rd
Cleadon Road
Bainton Close
Kilsall Rd
Sedburn Rd
Ravenhead Avenue
Heskin Road
Heskin Close
Cheddar Grove
Cottage Cl
Felspar Road
Heskin Walk
Shirdley Walk
Shirdley Avenue
Roughdale Avenue
Dairy Crs
Hartwood Road
Hartwood Cl
Digmoor Road
Bunter Road
Rhosesmor
Old Farm Rd
Cobbler's Lane
MOORGATE ROAD
Arbour Lane
Arbour Court
Arbour Works
Lees Road
Lees Rd
Woodlands Works
Ashcroft Road
Courtyard Works
Newstet Road
Birchill Road
Lodge Works
Knowsley Industrial Park
Marl Road
Hammond Road
Kirkby Bank Road
Orchard Works
Cranston Road
Acorn Business Centre
Gladeswood Road
Webber Road
Venture Works
Yardley Road
Charley Wood Road
Cusson Road
Dixon Road
Deltic Way
Gores Road
Beckett Cl
New Lodge Industrial Estate
Gale Road
Admin Road
Business Resource Centre
SOUTH BOUNDARY ROAD
Spinney Cl
Acornfield
Hornhouse Lane
Owen Road
Britonwood Trading Estate
Abercrombie Road
Faraday Road
Knowsley Ind Park
Junction 5
EAST LANCASHIRE ROAD A580
Knowsley Business Park
Penrhyn
1 grid square represents 500 metres

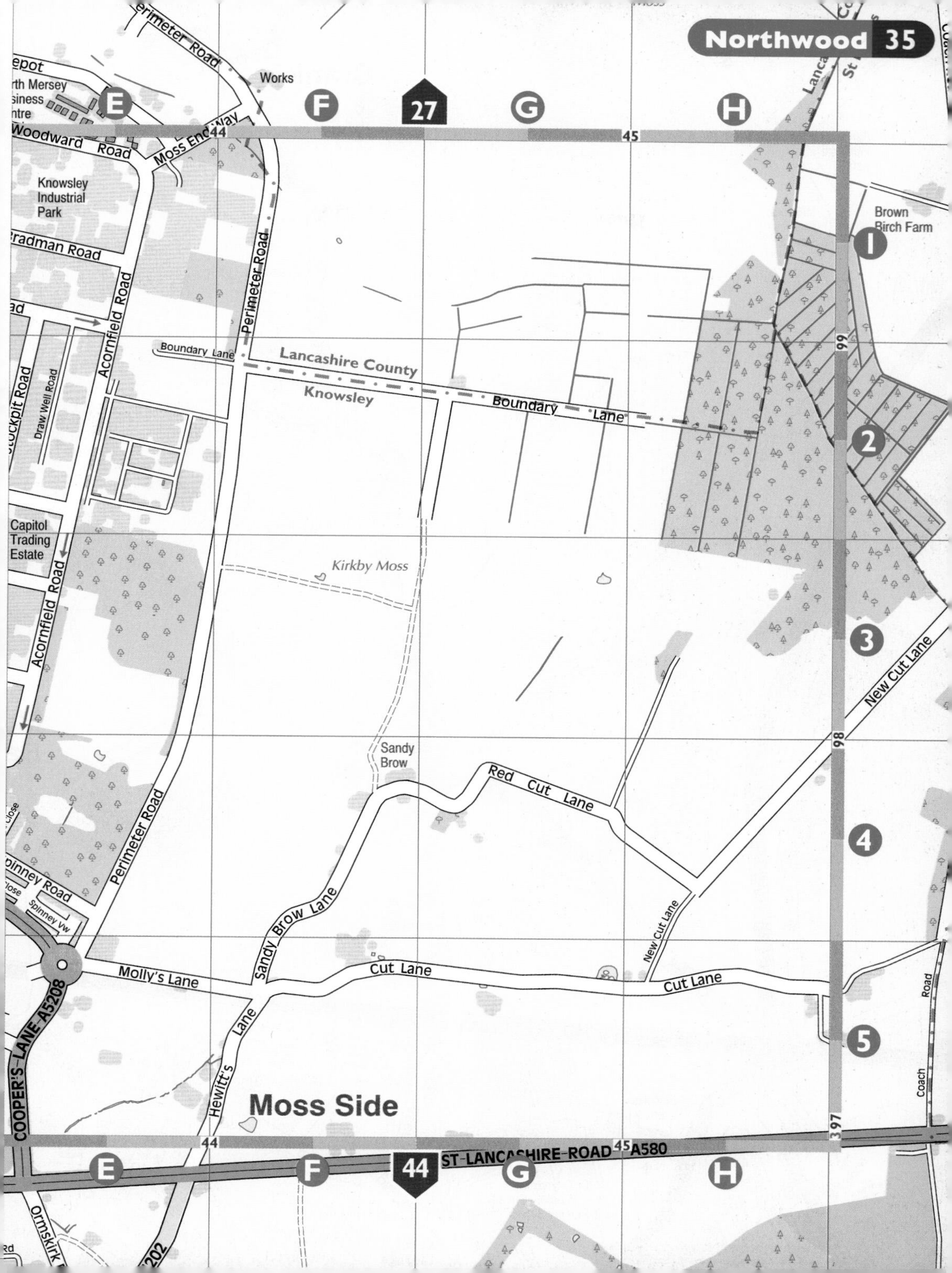
Perimeter Road
Works
E
F
27
G
H
North Mersey Business Centre
Woodward Road
Moss End Way
44
45
Knowsley Industrial Park
Brown Birch Farm
1
Bradman Road
Acornfield Road
Perimeter Road
Boundary Lane
Lancashire County
Knowsley
Boundary Lane
Cockpit Road
Draw Well Road
2
99
Capitol Trading Estate
Kirkby Moss
Acornfield Road
3
New Cut Lane
98
Sandy Brow
Red Cut Lane
Perimeter Road
4
Spinney Road
Spinney Vw
Sandy Brow Lane
New Cut Lane
Molly's Lane
Cut Lane
Cut Lane
Road
5
Coach
Hewitt's Lane
Moss Side
COOPER'S LANE A5208
397
44
45
EAST LANCASHIRE ROAD A580
E
F
44
G
H
Ormskirk
A5202

36
Hazel Business Park
Mill Lane
Close
Crank
B5201
Highfield Drive
Chapel View
Alder
CRANK HILL
LANE B5
A
B
C
D
Rainford Industrial Estate
Millbrook Business Centre
WA11
1
2
3
4
5
49
50
99
98
97
CRANK ROAD
Fairfield Gdns
Fairfield Hospital
Rainford Hall
Hill Top House
Hilltop Road
Berrington's Lane
Rainford Brook
Longwood Close
Inglewood Road
St Helens Rd
St Helens Road
RAINFORD ROAD A570
Sandy La
Sandy Lane
B5201
Woodside Avenue
Birch Tree Avenue
Windle Hall
A580 EAST-LANCASHIRE ROAD
Furness Av
Windle Hall Lane
Wyresdale Av
Cartmel Av
Whalley Av
Drive
Priory Gardens
City Road
Seddon St
Friar St
Birch Av
City Gardens
Birch Gdns
St Helens Crematorium
Borough Cemetery
Abbey Road
B H Cl
Windle Farm
Windle Grove
The Nook
Portreath Way
Padstow Drive
BLEAK HILL ROAD
Stuart Road
RAINFORD ROAD
Malt House Court
St Thomas of Canterbury Catholic Primary School
47
Gamble
Princess Avenue
Martin Av
Rivington
Windlehurst Community Primary Sch
Windle City
Works
Eaton Road
Cowley Language
Pentire Av
Fistral Drive
Mawes
PO
1 grid square represents 500 metres

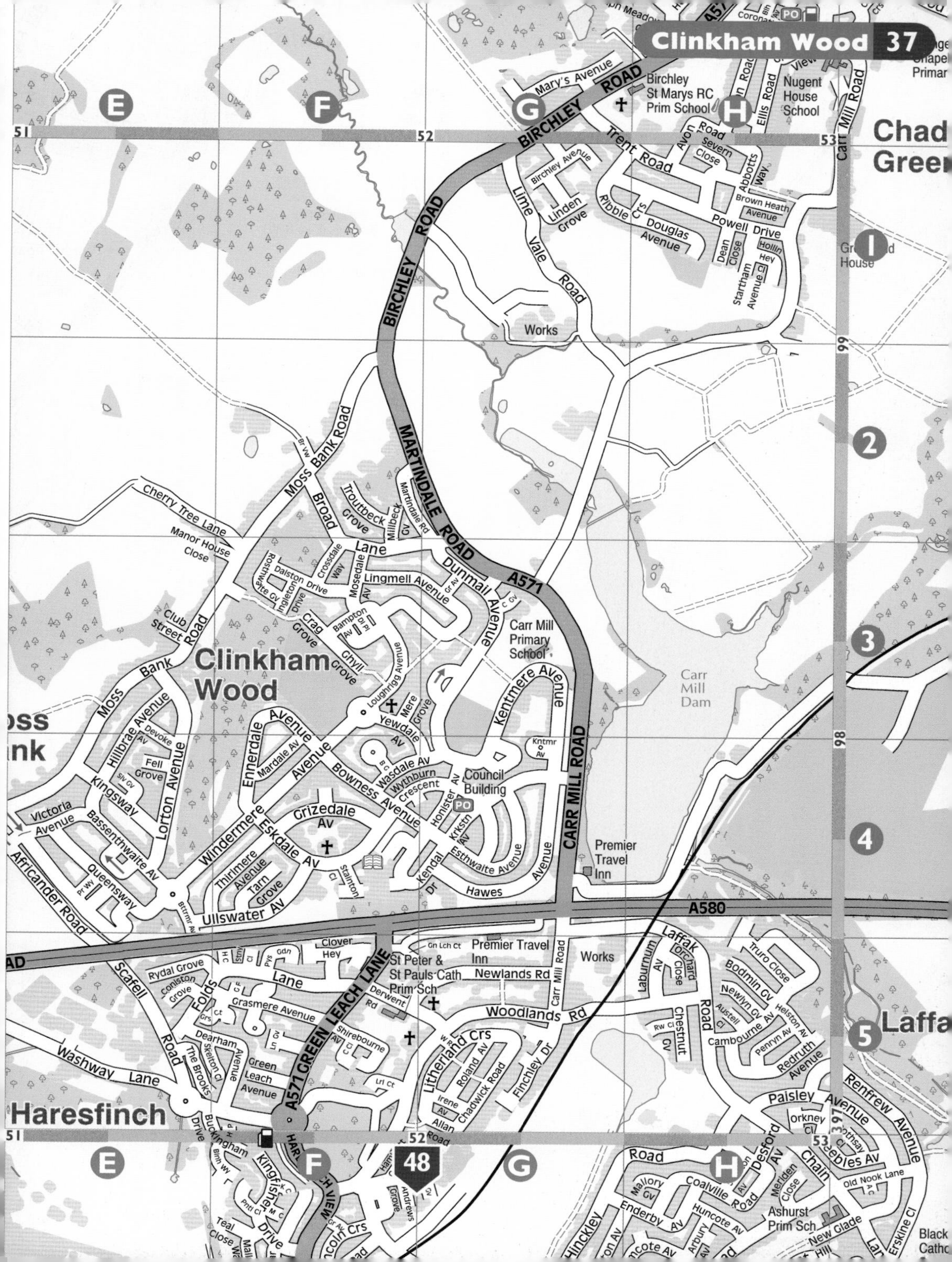
E
F
G
H
I
51
52
53
Mary's Avenue
BIRCHLEY ROAD
Birchley St Marys RC Prim School
Nugent House School
Ellis Road
Carr Mill Road
Chadwell Green
Trent Road
Avon Road
Severn Close
Abbotts Way
Birchley Avenue
Linden Grove
Lime Vale Road
Ribble Crs
Douglas Avenue
Brown Heath Avenue
Powell Drive
Dean Close
Hollin Hey
Startham Avenue Cl
Works
99
2
3
4
5
98
Moss Bank Road
Broad Lane
MARTINDALE ROAD
A571
Cherry Tree Lane
Manor House Close
Troutbeck Grove
Millbeck Gv
Martindale Rd
Crossdale Way
Rosthwaite Gv
Dalston Drive
Ingleton Drive
Mosedale Av
Lingmell Avenue
Dunmail Avenue
Club Street
Road
Crag Grove
Bampton Av
Ghyll Grove
Carr Mill Primary School
Carr Mill Dam
Clinkham Wood
Loughrigg Avenue
Mere Grove
Yewdale Av
Kentmere Avenue
Moss Bank
Hillbrae Avenue
Devoke Av
Fell Grove
Lorton Avenue
Kingsway
Ennerdale Avenue
Mardale Av
Avenue
Bowness Avenue
Wasdale Av
Wythburn Crescent
Honister Av
Council Building
Kntmr Av
CARR MILL ROAD
Victoria Avenue
Bassenthwaite Av
Windermere
Grizedale Av
Eskdale Av
Krkstn Av
Esthwaite Avenue
Premier Travel Inn
Africander Road
Queensway
Thirlmere Avenue
Tarn Grove
Stainton Cl
Kendal Dr
Hawes Avenue
Ullswater Av
A580
Laffak
Scafell Road
Clover Hey
Gn Lch Ct
Premier Travel Inn
Rydal Grove
Coniston Grove
Lane
St Peter & St Pauls Cath Prim Sch
Newlands Rd
Carr Mill Road
Works
Laburnum Av
Orchard Close
Truro Close
Bodmin Gv
Newlyn Gv
Folds
A571 GREEN LEACH LANE
Derwent Rd
Grasmere Avenue
Woodlands Rd
Chestnut Gv
Road
Austell Cl
Helston Av
Camborne Av
Penryn Av
Laffak
Redruth Avenue
Dearham Avenue
Skelton Cl
Shirebourne Av
Litherland Crs
Roland Av
Chadwick Road
Finchley Dr
Washway Lane
The Brooks
Green Leach Avenue
Lrl Ct
Irene Av
Allan Road
Paisley Avenue
Renfrew Avenue
Orkney Cl
Haresfinch
Buckingham Drive
Kingfisher
Drive
HARESFINCH VIEW
48
Andrews Grove
Road
Desford Av
Chain
Peebles Av
Mallory Gv
Coalville Road
Enderby Av
Huncote Av
Meriden Close
Ashurst Prim Sch
Old Nook Lane
New Glade
Erskine Cl
Teal Close
Hinckley
Black Cathc

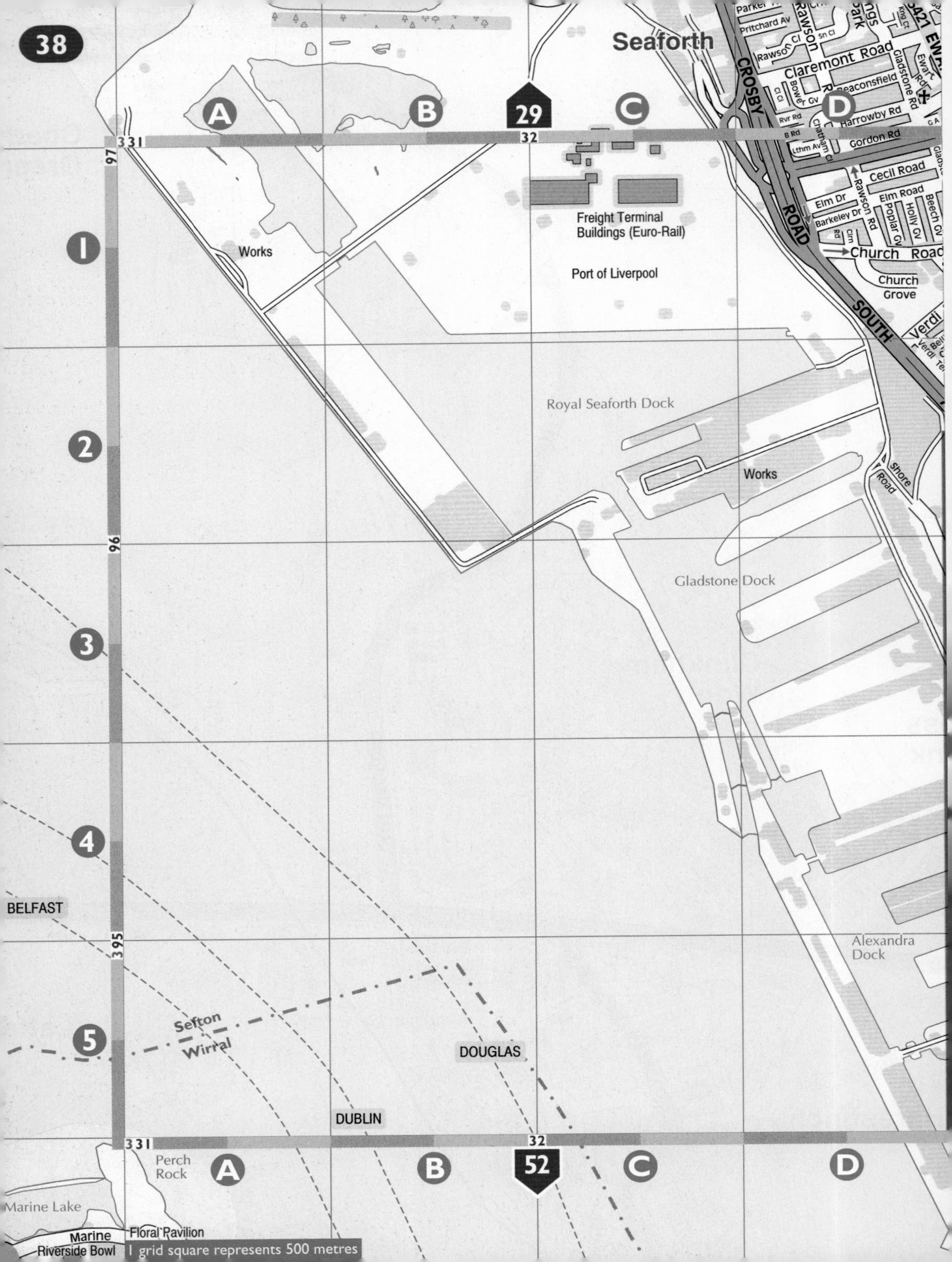
Seaforth
29
52
A
B
C
D
1
2
3
4
5
331
32
97
96
395
Pritchard Av
Rawson
Rawson Cl
Claremont Road
Gladstone Rd
Beaconsfield
Harrowby Rd
CROSBY
ROAD
SOUTH
Gordon Rd
Cecil Road
Elm Dr
Elm Road
Rawson Rd
Barkeley Dr
Poplar Gv
Holly Gv
Beech Gv
Chatham Cl
Church Road
Church Grove
Verdi
Freight Terminal Buildings (Euro-Rail)
Port of Liverpool
Works
Royal Seaforth Dock
Works
Shore Road
Gladstone Dock
Alexandra Dock
BELFAST
Sefton
Wirral
DOUGLAS
DUBLIN
Perch Rock
Marine Lake
Floral Pavilion
Marine
Riverside Bowl
1 grid square represents 500 metres

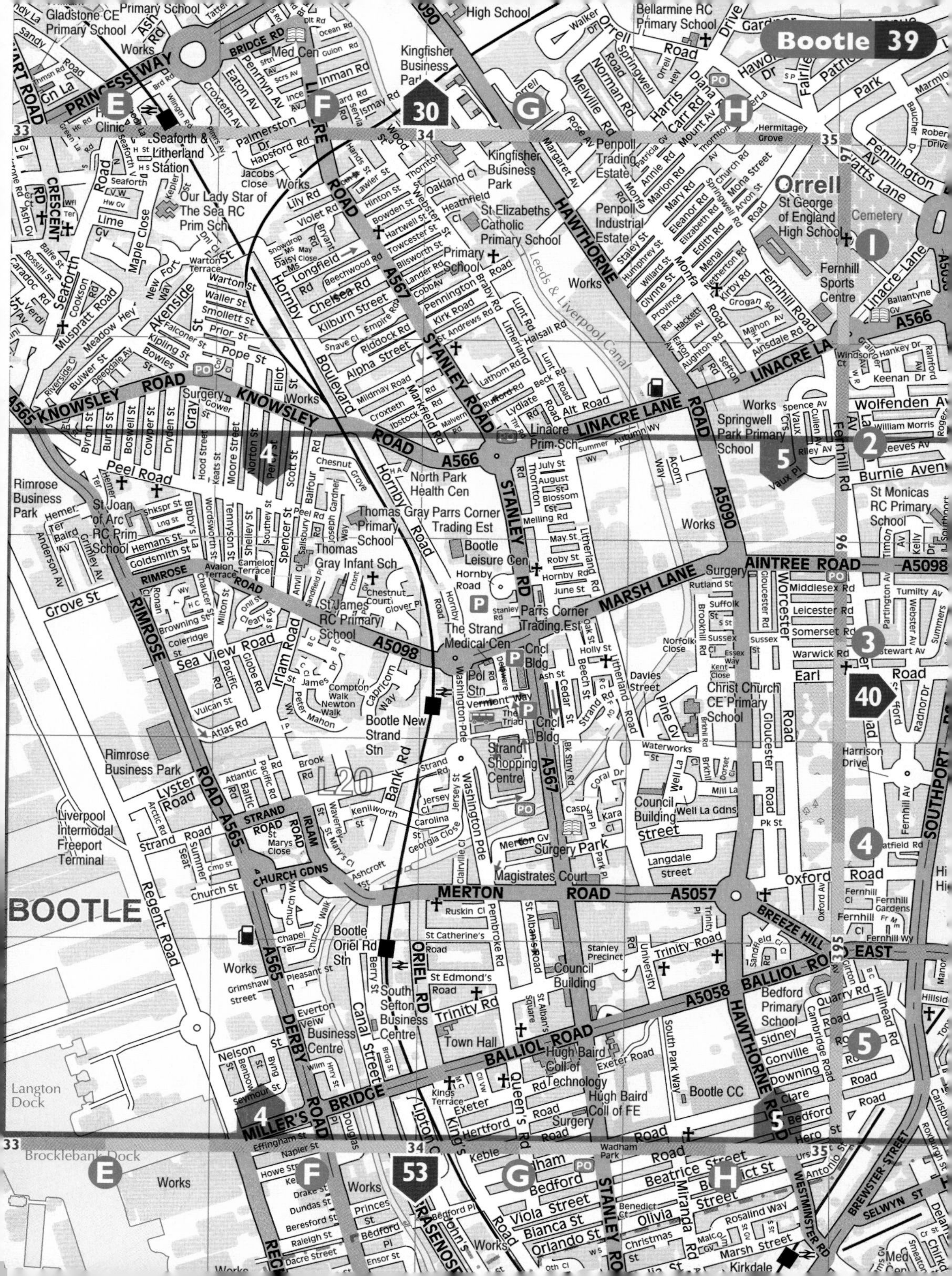
Gladstone CE Primary School
Princess Way
Bridge Rd
Med Cen
Inman Rd
Kingfisher Business Park
30
High School
Bellarmine RC Primary School
Orrell Road
Clinic
Seaforth & Litherland Station
Palmerston Dr
Hapsford Rd
Jacobs Close
Works
Kingfisher Business Park
Penpoll Trading Estate
Penpoll Industrial Estate
Hermitage Grove
Orrell
St George of England High School
Cemetery
Our Lady Star of The Sea RC Prim Sch
Lily Rd
Violet Rd
Longfield Rd
Chelsea Rd
Kilburn Street
St Elizabeths Catholic Primary School
Primary School
Leeds & Liverpool Canal
Hawthorne
Fernhill Sports Centre
Linacre Lane
A566
Seaforth
Musspratt Road
Akenside
Knowsley Road
Pope St
Alpha Street
Stanley Road
A567
Linacre Lane
Alt Road
Springwell Park Primary School
Wolfenden Av
Burnie Avenue
St Monicas RC Primary School
Rimrose Business Park
Peel Road
St Joan of Arc RC Prim School
Hornby Boulevard
North Park Health Cen
Thomas Gray Parrs Corner Primary School
Trading Est
Thomas Gray Infant Sch
Bootle Leisure Cen
Hornby Road
Parrs Corner Trading Est
Marsh Lane
Aintree Road
A5098
Works
A5090
Rimrose Road
Grove St
St James RC Primary School
Sea View Road
The Strand Medical Cen
Pol Stn
Cncl Bldg
Christ Church CE Primary School
Davies Street
Earl Road
40
Bootle New Strand Stn
Strand Shopping Centre
Atlas Rd
Rimrose Business Park
L20
Lyster Road
Liverpool Intermodal Freeport Terminal
Strand Road
Bank Rd
Washington Pde
Council Building Street
Well La Gdns
Langdale Street
Surgery Park
Magistrates Court
Merton Road
A5057
Oxford Road
Southport Road
Fernhill Gardens
BOOTLE
Regent Road
Church Gdns
Church St
Bootle Oriel Rd Stn
Oriel Rd
South Sefton Business Centre
Trinity Rd
Town Hall
Council Building
Stanley Precinct
Trinity Road
Breeze Hill
Balliol Road
A5058
Bedford Primary School
Everton Veiw Business Centre
Canal Street
Balliol Road
Hugh Baird Coll of Technology
Hugh Baird Coll of FE
Exeter Road
South Park Way
Bootle CC
Langton Dock
Miller's Bridge
Derby Road
A565
Brocklebank Dock
Works
Effingham St
Napier St
53
Keble
Bedford
Viola Street
Bianca St
Orlando St
Beatrice Street
Olivia
Marsh Street
Kirkdale
Westminster Rd
Brewster Street
Selwyn St
Stanley Rd

40
31
5
39
54
A
B
C
D
1
2
3
4
5
335
36
Orrell
Walton
Patrick Av
Fairlie Crs
Park Lane
Marmion Av
Pearson Dr
Turner Av
Johnston Av
Woodbrook Av
Monaghan Cl
Warbreck Av
Montgomery Road
Helsby Rd
Hooton Rd
Heswall Rd
Eastbourne Rd
Kingswood Av
Albany Road
Warbreck Moor
Longmoor Lane
Longmoor Community Prim Sch
Poulter Road Medical Centre
Pennington Av
Watts Lane
Bailey Drive
St George of England High School
Cemetery
Fernhill Sports Centre
Linacre Lane
Moss Lane
Alexandra Drive
Albert Drive
Victoria Dr
Redvers Dr
Burwen Dr
Tatton Rd
Selby Rd
Trevor Rd
Endborne Rd
Warbreck Rd
Walton Vale
Cedar Road
Blessed Sacrament RC Infant School
Blessed Sacrament RC Junior School
Northfield Road
Moss La
Surgery
Orrell Park Stn
Orrell La
A566
A5038
A59
B5187
Linacre La
Chatsworth
Devonfield Road
Kingfield Road
Archbishop Beck Catholic High School Sports Coll
Chapel Av
St John's Av
Works
Hartley Avenue
Hartley Trading Estate
Wolfenden Av
Springwell Park Primary School
Fernhill Rd
Burnie Avenue
HM Prison Liverpool
Lynwood Rd
Rice Lane J&I Schools
Rice Lane
Rice-La Stn
Aintree Industrial Estate
Trans Pennine Trail
St Monicas RC Primary School
Southport Road
Hornby Road
A5098
Aintree Road
Evered Avenue
Walton Pk
Walton Station
Sefton Road
Sefton North
Yew Tree Road
Rawcliffe Road
Grey Road
Fazakerley Close
Cemetery
Liverpool
Bootle Stadium Sports Centre
Maguire Av
Worcester Rd
Gloucester Road
Fernhill Road
Stafford Rd
Radnor Dr
Harrison Drive
Walton Hospital
Walton Progressive School
Clock Tower Drive
Dunnys Sports Club
Superstore
Hebrew Cemetery
Cavendish Drive
Cavendish Dr
Northcote Primary School
Barbrook Way
Lavender Way
Lobelia Av
Freesia Av
Honeysuckle Drive
Blackbrook Close
Hollingworth Close
Oxford Road
Hillside High School
Stuart Rd
Taylors La
Buchanan Rd
Lancaster St
Helena St
York St
Queens Drive Family Health Clinic
Breeze Hill
Balliol Road East
Hawthorne Road
Bedford Primary School
Cambridge Road
Walton Park Gardens
Moor Lane
Alsop High School
Walton Medical Cen
County Road
Walton Village
Well Brow Road
Haggerston Rd
Lusitania Rd
Saxonia Rd
Woolhope Rd
Walton Sports Centre
Queens Drive
Cranehurst Road
Courthope Road
Stanley Pk Av North
St Francis De Sales RC Infant School
Westminster Rd
Brewster Street
Selwyn St
Romley St
Walton Hall Village Medical Cen
A580
Dyson St
Lowell St
Lind St
Bodmin Rd
Lilly Green
Cherry La
Drive
1 grid square represents 500 metres

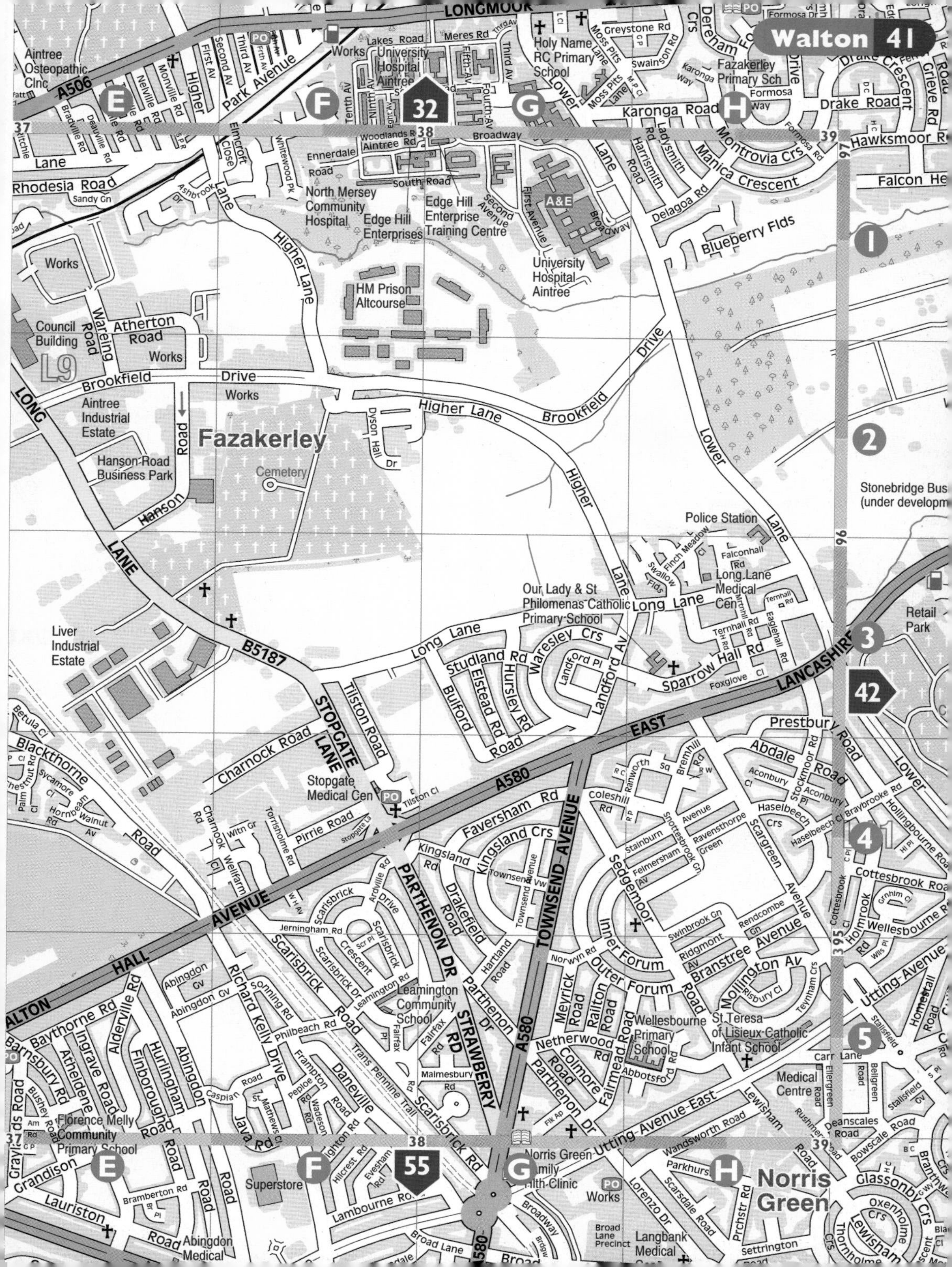

LONGMOOR
A506
Aintree Osteopathic Clnc
Higher Lane
First Av
Second Av
Third Av
Park Avenue
Works
Lakes Road
University Hospital Aintree
Meres Rd
Tenth Av
Ninth Av
Fifth Av
Fourth Av
Third Av
32
Holy Name RC Primary School
Greystone Rd
Moss Pits Lane
Dereham Crs
Fazakerley Primary Sch
Karonga Road
Formosa Rd
Formosa Way
Drake Crescent
Drake Road
Grieve Rd
Hawksmoor Rd
Nelville Rd
Monville Rd
Bradville Rd
Deauville Rd
Elmcroft Close
Whitewood Pk
Woodlands Rd
Aintree Rd
Broadway
Ennerdale Road
South Road
North Mersey Community Hospital
Edge Hill Enterprises
Edge Hill Enterprise Training Centre
Second Avenue
First Avenue
A&E
Lane
Harrismith Rd
Ladysmith Rd
Montrovia Crs
Manica Crescent
Delagoa Rd
Falcon Hey
Rhodesia Road
Sandy Gn
Ashbrook Dr
Higher Lane
University Hospital Aintree
Blueberry Flds
Works
HM Prison Altcourse
Council Building
Wareing Road
Atherton Road
Works
L9
Brookfield Drive
Works
LONG
Aintree Industrial Estate
Road
Higher Lane
Brookfield Drive
Dyson Hall Dr
Fazakerley
Cemetery
Hanson Road Business Park
Hanson
Higher Lane
Lower Lane
Stonebridge Bus (under developm
Police Station
Finch Meadow Cl
Swallow Flds
Falconhall Rd
Long Lane Medical Cen
Our Lady & St Philomenas Catholic Primary School
Long Lane
Ternhall Rd
Eaglehall Rd
Retail Park
LANE
Liver Industrial Estate
Long Lane
Waresley Crs
Landford Pl
Landford Av
Sparrow Hall Rd
Foxglove Cl
LANCASHIRE
B5187
Studland Rd
Elstead Rd
Hursley Rd
Bulford Road
42
STOPGATE LANE
Tilston Road
EAST
Prestbury Road
Abdale Road
Stockmoor Rd
Lower
Betula Cl
Blackthorne
Sycamore Cl
Hornbeam Rd
Walnut Av
Charnock Road
Stopgate Medical Cen
Tilston Cl
A580
Ranworth Sq
Bremhill Rd
Coleshill Rd
Aconbury Cl
Braybrooke Rd
Hollingbourne Road
Haselbeech Crs
Faversham Rd
Avenue
Snottesbrook Gn
Ravensthorpe Green
Scargreen Avenue
Road
Pirrie Road
Torrisholme Rd
Charnock Rd
Wellfarm Cl
Kingsland Crs
Kingsland Rd
Drakefield Road
Townsend Avenue
TOWNSEND AVENUE
Stainburn
Felmersham Av
Seddemoor
Cottesbrook Road
Holmrook Rd
Wellesbourne Rd
AVENUE
PARTHENON DR
Scarisbrick Drive
Ardville Rd
Jerningham Rd
Scarisbrick Crescent
Hartland Road
Inner Forum
Outer Forum
Swinbrook Gn
Rendcombe Gn
Ridgmont Av
Branstree Avenue
Mollington Av
Risbury Cl
Teynham Crs
Utting Avenue
Homestall Road
HALL
Abingdon Gv
Richard Kelly Drive
Sonning Rd
Scarisbrick Road
Leamington Rd
Leamington Community School
STRAWBERRY RD
Parthenon Dr
Norwyn Rd
Meyrick Road
Railton Road
Wellesbourne Primary School
St Teresa of Lisieux Catholic Infant School
ALTON
Baythorne Rd
Alderville Rd
Ingrave Road
Atheldene
Hurlingham Road
Finborough Road
Abingdon Road
Philbeach Rd
Fairfax Rd
Malmesbury Rd
Netherwood Rd
Colmore Road
Fairmead Road
Abbotsford Rd
Carr Lane
Bellgreen Road
Ellergreen Road
Stallisfield Gv
Barnsbury Rd
Bushey Road
Caspian Road
Java Rd
Frampton Rd
Daneville Road
Trans Pennine Trail
Scarisbrick Rd
Medical Centre
Lewisham Road
Utting Avenue East
Deanscales Road
Bowscale Road
Florence Melly Community Primary School
Grandison
Superstore
Hilcrest Rd
Evesham Rd
55
Norris Green Family Hlth Clinic
Wandsworth Road
Parkhurst
Norris Green
Glassonby Crs
Oxenholme Crs
Lauriston Road
Bramberton Rd
Lambourne Rd
Broadway
Lorenzo Dr
Scarsdale Road
Works
Broad Lane Precinct
Langbank Medical
Settrington
Lewisham
Thornholme
Abingdon Medical
Broad Lane
A580

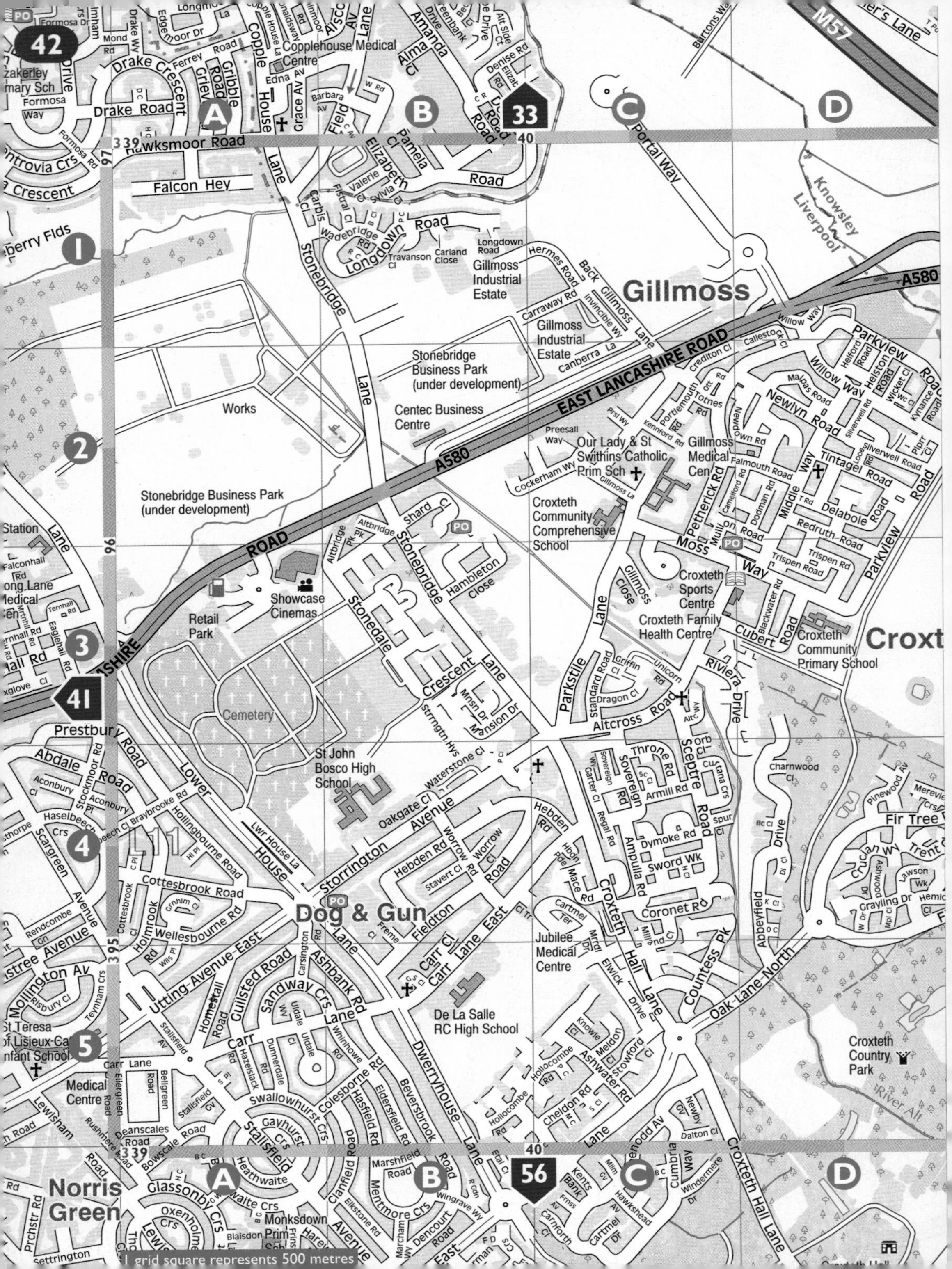

42
33
41
56
A
B
C
D
1
2
3
4
5
M57
A580
EAST LANCASHIRE ROAD
ROAD
Gillmoss
Croxt
Dog & Gun
Norris Green
Drake Crescent
Drake Road
Formosa Way
Hawksmoor Road
Falcon Hey
Copplehouse Medical Centre
Alma Cl
Amanda Road
Portal Way
Knowsley
Liverpool
Stonebridge Lane
Longdown Road
Wadebridge Rd
Travanson Cl
Carland Close
Gillmoss Industrial Estate
Hermes Road
Back Gillmoss Lane
Carraway Rd
Canberra La
Stonebridge Business Park (under development)
Centec Business Centre
Works
Showcase Cinemas
Retail Park
Cemetery
Stonedale Crescent
Hambleton Close
Shard Cl
Altbridge Pk
St John Bosco High School
Storrington Avenue
Oakgate Cl
Waterstone Cl
Lower House Lane
Lwr House La
Our Lady & St Swithins Catholic Prim Sch
Croxteth Community Comprehensive School
Gillmoss Medical Cen
Gillmoss Close
Parkstile Lane
Croxteth Sports Centre
Croxteth Family Health Centre
Croxteth Community Primary School
Cubert Road
Riviera Drive
Altcross Road
Dragon Cl
Griffin Cl
Unicorn Rd
Sceptre Road
Sovereign Rd
Throne Rd
Armill Rd
Dymoke Rd
Sword Wk
Coronet Rd
Croxteth Hall Lane
Countess Pk
Oak Lane North
Abbeyfield Drive
Charnwood Cl
Croxteth Country Park
River Alt
Parkview Road
Willow Way
Newlyn Road
Tintagel Road
Delabole Road
Redruth Road
Trispen Road
Moss Way
Petherick Rd
Falmouth Road
Prestbury Road
Abdale Road
Stockmoor Rd
Cottesbrook Road
Hollingbourne Road
Wellesbourne Rd
Holmrook Rd
Utting Avenue East
Guilsted Road
Sandway Crs
Ashbank Rd
Carr Lane
Carr Lane East
Fieldton Road
Worrow Road
Hebden Rd
Jubilee Medical Centre
De La Salle RC High School
Dwerryhouse Lane
Beversbrook Road
Eldersfield Rd
Hasfield Rd
Colesborne Rd
Swallowhurst Crs
Gayhurst Crs
Stalisfield Avenue
Heathwaite Crs
Glassonby Crs
Monksdown Prim Sch
Mentmore Crs
Marshfield Road
Wingrave Wy
Dencourt Road
Cheldon Rd
Ashwater Rd
Meldon Cl
Stowford Cl
Hollocombe Rd
Kents Bank
Hawkshead Av
Cartmel Dr
Carnforth
Cumbria Way
Windermere Dr
Dalton Cl
Lewisham Road
Medical Centre
St Teresa of Lisieux Cath Infant School
Mollington Av
Scargreen Avenue
Fir Tree
Crucian Wy
Grayling Dr
Pinewood Av
1 grid square represents 500 metres

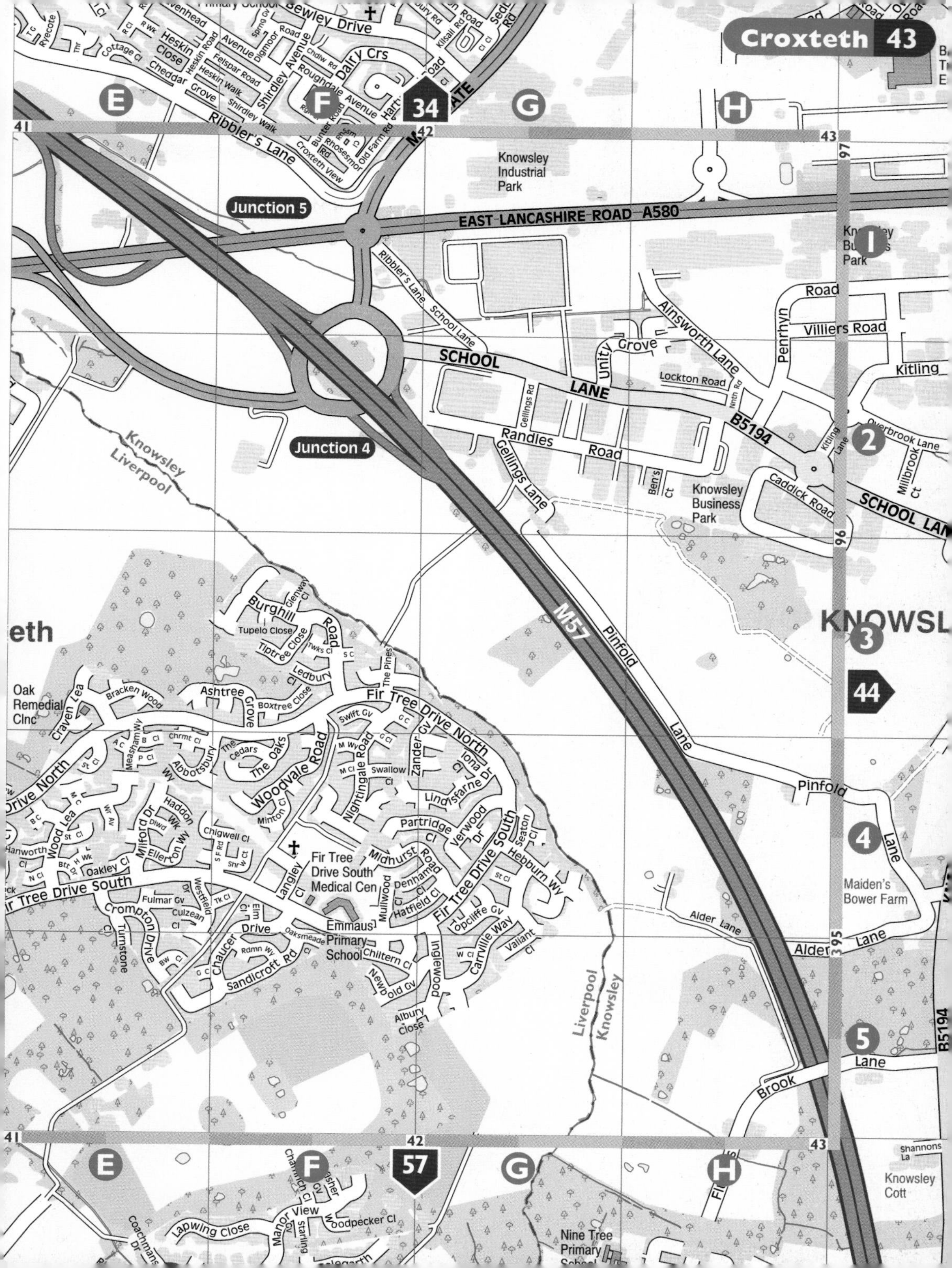

Bewley Drive
Heskin Road
Heskin Close
Cheddar Grove
Cottage Cl
Felspar Road
Heskin Walk
Shirdley Avenue
Shirdley Walk
Digmoor Road
Dairy Crs
Roughdale Avenue
Bunter Road
Rhosesmor Rd
Old Farm Rd
Croxteth View
Ribbler's Lane
34
Junction 5
Knowsley Industrial Park
EAST LANCASHIRE ROAD A580
Ribbler's Lane
School Lane
SCHOOL LANE
Unity Grove
Ainsworth Lane
Lockton Road
Gellings Rd
Randles Road
Gellings Lane
Ben's Ct
B5194
Knowsley Business Park
Penrhyn Road
Villiers Road
Kitling
Kitling Lane
Overbrook Lane
Millbrook Ct
Caddick Road
SCHOOL LANE
Junction 4
Knowsley
Liverpool
M57
Pinfold Lane
KNOWSL
44
Burghill Road
Tupelo Close
Tiptree Close
Ledbury Cl
The Pines
Ashtree Grove
Boxtree Close
Bracken Wood
Craven Lea
Oak Remedial Clnc
Fir Tree Drive North
Swift Gv
Zander Gv
Iona Cl
Abbotsbury Wy
The Cedars
The Oaks
Woodvale Road
Nightingale Road
Swallow Cl
Lindisfarne Dr
Haddon Wk
Milford Dr
Ellerton Wy
Chigwell Cl
Minton Cl
Partridge Cl
Verwood Dr
Midhurst Road
Fir Tree Drive South
Seaton Cl
Hebburn Wy
Wood Lea
Oakley Cl
Fir Tree Drive South Medical Cen
Langley Cl
Denham Cl
Hatfield Cl
Mullwood
Fulmar Gv
Culzean Cl
Crompton Drive
Turnstone
Westfield
Elm Drive
Emmaus Primary School
Chiltern Cl
Topcliffe Gv
Carville Way
Vallant Cl
Chaucer
Sandicroft Rd
Newbold Gv
Inglewood
Albury Close
Liverpool
Knowsley
Alder Lane
Pinfold Lane
Maiden's Bower Farm
Alder Lane
Brook Lane
B5194
57
Lapwing Close
Manor View
Woodpecker Cl
Coachmans Dr
Nine Tree Primary School
Shannons La
Knowsley Cott

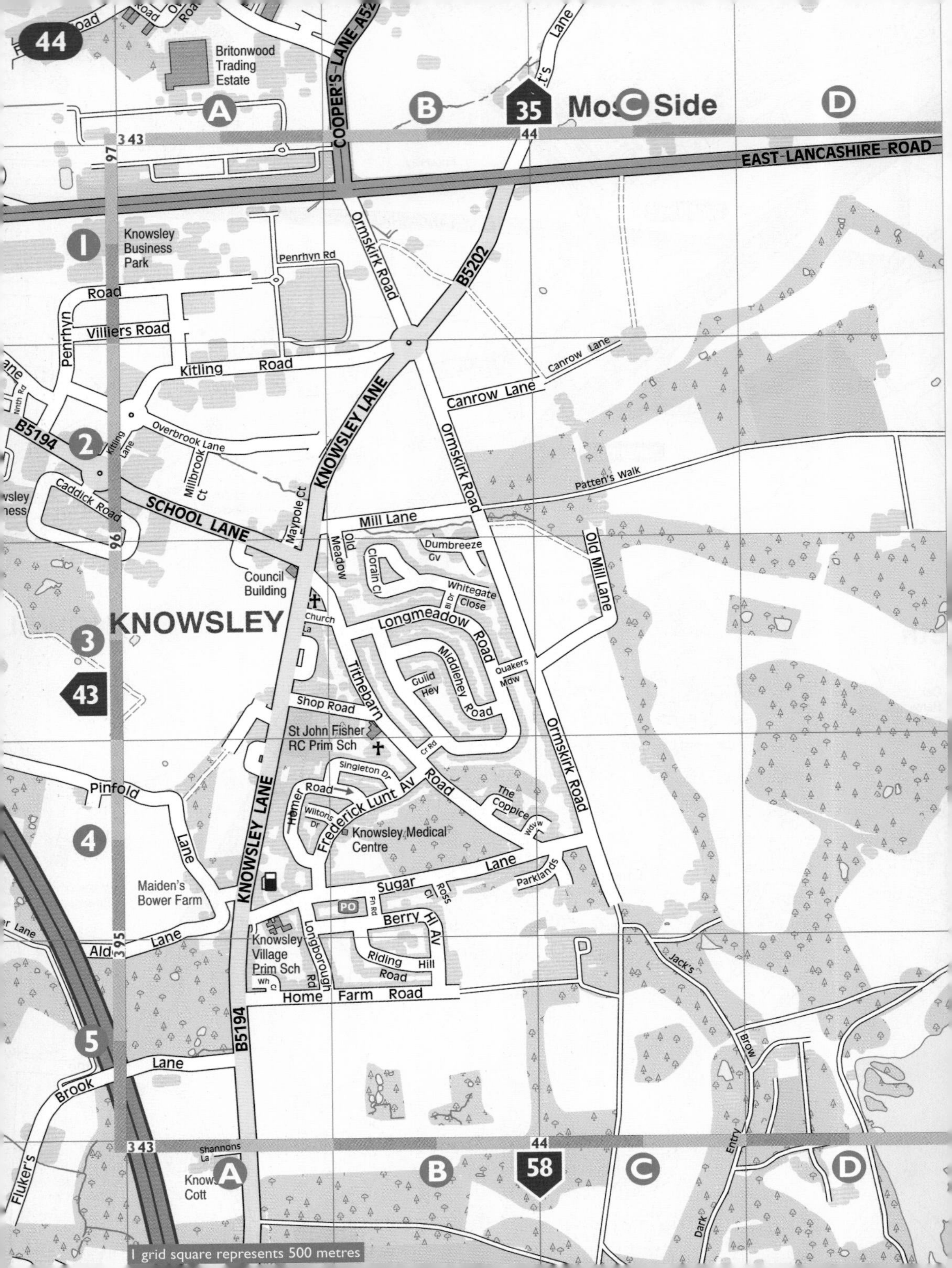

44
Britonwood Trading Estate
COOPER'S LANE A5
A
B
35
Moss Side
C
D
343
44
97
EAST LANCASHIRE ROAD
1
Knowsley Business Park
Penrhyn Rd
Ormskirk Road
B5202
Road
Penrhyn
Villiers Road
Kitling Road
Canrow Lane
KNOWSLEY LANE
B5194
2
Kitling Lane
Overbrook Lane
Millbrook Ct
Ormskirk Road
Patten's Walk
Caddick Road
SCHOOL LANE
Maypole Ct
Mill Lane
Old Meadow
Dumbreeze Gv
Clorain Cl
Old Mill Lane
96
Council Building
Whitegate Close
Bl Dr
KNOWSLEY
Church La
Longmeadow Road
3
Middlehey Road
Guild Hey
Quakers Mdw
43
Tithebarn
Shop Road
St John Fisher RC Prim Sch
Cr Rd
Singleton Dr
Pinfold
Homer Road
Frederick Lunt Av
Road
The Coppice
Wdvw
Wiltons Dr
Ormskirk Road
4
Lane
KNOWSLEY LANE
Knowsley Medical Centre
Lane
Parklands
Maiden's Bower Farm
Sugar
Ross Cl
PO
Fr Rd
Berry Hl Av
Lane
Ald
395
Lane
Knowsley Village Prim Sch
Longborough Rd
Riding Hill Road
Jack's
Wh Cl
Home Farm Road
B5194
5
Lane
Brook
Brow
343
44
Shannons La
A
B
58
C
D
Entry
Fluker's
Knows
Cott
Dark
1 grid square represents 500 metres

A580
Coach
Patten's Walk
CATCHDALE MOSS LANE
B5203
Clay Lane
St Helens
Knowsley
Knowsley Park
White Man's Dam
Knowsley Safari Pa
L34
46
59
E
F
G
H
1
2
3
4
5
45
47
97
96
395

A580
EAST LANCASHIRE ROAD
A580
A
B
C
D
Windle Farm
Sadler's
347
48
97
96
395
1
2
3
4
5
45
60
Houghton's Lane
B5203
Catchdale Moss
CATCHDALE MOSS LANE
Green Lane
Green Lane
Eccleston
Ecclesfield Road
Nicholl Road
Carmelite Crescent
Sandfield Road
Oaktree Road
Walmesley Road
Osborne Road
Barrowfield Road
Pike House Road
The Close
Lester Drive
Springfield Lane
Cecil Drive
Acacia Grove
Brooklands Road
Broadway
Eccleston Medical Centre
PO
Selkirk Drive
Melrose Av
Gunning Close
Gunning Avenue
Davy Close
Ansdell Drive
Daresbury Road
Crockett's Wk
Pike Pl
Clarke's Crescent
MILLBROOK LANE
Washbrook Cl
B5201
Brook
The Nook
Portreath Way
Way
Lynton
Pentire Av
Fistral Drive
Calderhurst Drive
Windlebrook Crescent
Lnk
St Mawes Way
Blea Prim
Villiers Crs
Villiers Crs
Richmond Close
Laurel Drive
St Julie RC Primary School
Howard's Lane
Sp Cl
T Clst
Fiveways
Pikes Br Fold
CHAPEL LANE
Hawthorn Drive
Sycamore Cl
Ln Wy
Holly Cl
Mill Brow
Long Meadow
Millers Fold
Mosslands
Poplar Av
Griffin Cl
The Spires
Whitefriars
Mill Wd Av
Bobbies Lane
Stanwood Close
Council Building
Orith Av
Knowles House Av
Higham Avenue
Summerfield Avenue
Gillars Gn Dr
Brook House Gv
Seddon Close
CHURCH LANE
Millfields
Millfields
Ledbury Close
Brentwood Close
The Avenue
Orch Hey
Eccleston Mere Prim Sch
Saleswood Avenue
Pinfold
Mere Hey
Spinney Gn
Forest Mdw
Drive
Trapwood Cl
Norley Dr
Prestbury Drive
Gawsworth Close
K C
Bw Cl
Holme
Clay Lane
B5203 GILLAR'S LANE
Gillar's Green
LANE
BURROW'S
Eccleston Mere
Carmel College
Te
1 grid square represents 500 metres

EAST LANCASHIRE ROAD
A580
St Helens Crematorium
Borough Cemetery
36
Furness Av
Windle Hall
Wyresdale Av
Cartmel Av
Whalley Av
Drive
Priory Gardens
City Road
Washway
Haresfi
E
F
G
H
I
1
2
3
4
5
49
50
51
97
Malt House Court
St Thomas of Canterbury Catholic Primary School
RAINFORD ROAD
A570
Stuart Road
Rutherford Road
Lawrence Road
Sackville Road
Hamilton Road
Queens Drive
Coronation Road
St George's Avenue
Fair Way
The Grove
Regal Drive
Sidmouth Close
Kiln Lane
Beaconsfield Rd
Fairfield Rd
Moorfield Road
Swinburne Road
Smithy Heritage Centre
Eaton Road
Chaucer Road
Kingsley Road
Walton Road
Hard Lane
Cowley Language College
Speakman Road
King Edward Rd
Hammill Avenue
Huyton Av
Hillside Avenue
Gamble Road
Hard Lane
Windlehurst Community Primary Sch
Princess Avenue
Martin Av
Windlehurst Av
Rivington Av
Pine
Bishop Road
Birch Av
City Gardens
Windle City
Works
PO
10
Rivington Prim Sch
Carr St
Tennis St N
Elderflower Rd
DENTONS GREEN LANE
GREENFIELD ROAD
Windleshaw Road
St Helens CC
Denton's Green
Wynne Road
Moray Cl
Balker Dr
Rutland St
Oldfield St
Albert Street
Cowley St
Lord St
A571
Briars Gn
Windle Street
North Road
Queen St
B5196
Peel Place
Fox Place
Ruskin Drive
Coleridge Avenue
Rivington Road
Queens Park CE/URC Prim Sch
LINGHOLME ROAD
DENTONS GREEN LANE
Keswick Rd
Harris Street
Cowley Hill Lane
Surg
Cooper St
Surgery
Crab
Central Street
Register Office
Central Clinic
DUKE STREET
Dodd Avenue
Hey Road
A10
De La Salle School
Oleander Dr
Alpine
Ellison
Fairclough Rd
Marsden Av
Beaumont Av
McFarlane Av
Chisnall Av
Newtown
St Teresas Catholic Prim Sch
Horace St
Kitchener St
Cambridge Rd
Leisure Centre
KIRKLAND STREET
Prim Sch
A570
Surgery
YMCA
Police Stn
Cncl Bldg
Mag & Co Cts
Town Hall
48
KING ST
Henry St
Superstore
Surgery
North John Street
Westfield St
Barrow St
Ackers La
Peet Av
Gibbons Av
Avenue
Mulberry
Road
Knowsley
Windsor Rd
Rivington Rd
Devon St
Exeter St
Grafton St
Douglas St
Boundary St
Creswell St
Eccleston St
Lyon St
Peter Street
St Helens College
Cineworld
Waterloo St
Palatine Arcade
Church Square
Hardshaw Centre
Old Eccleston La
St Helens RLFC Knowsley Road Stadium
Swallow Ct
Works
Hazel Grove
Willow Road
Thorn Rd
Doulton St
Gladstone St
Chamberlain St
Silkstone St
Boundary Road
Superstore
CROPPERS HILL
WESTFIELD ST
LINKWAY WEST
Sandfield Medical Centre
Bath St
Bold Street
Glover Street
Chalon Way West
Superstore
395
St Anns Road
Balfour St
Dunriding Lane
Poplar Gv
Rivington St
Mona St
St Georges Rd
Bridgeman
Crowther Street
James Gv
Duncan St
Council Bldg
Canal Street
Works
Eldon St
BOROUGH RD
A58
Big Dam
Moxon St
Laurel Road
Cedar St
Haywood Gdns
Cheshire Gdns
Shires
Lancs Gdns
Wilts Gdns
Yorkshire Gdn
Swallow Court
PRESCOT ROAD
West Park
Alexandra Drive
Works
Road
Burtonhead Rd
Golf Course
Grosvenor Rd
Regents Rd
Kings Rd
Lincoln Rd
Queens Rd
Norfolk Rd
Ravenhead
61
Grange Park Golf Club
Stafford Road
Roby Street
French St
Factory Row
Ravenhead Road
Works
Sutton Heath Road
Bar

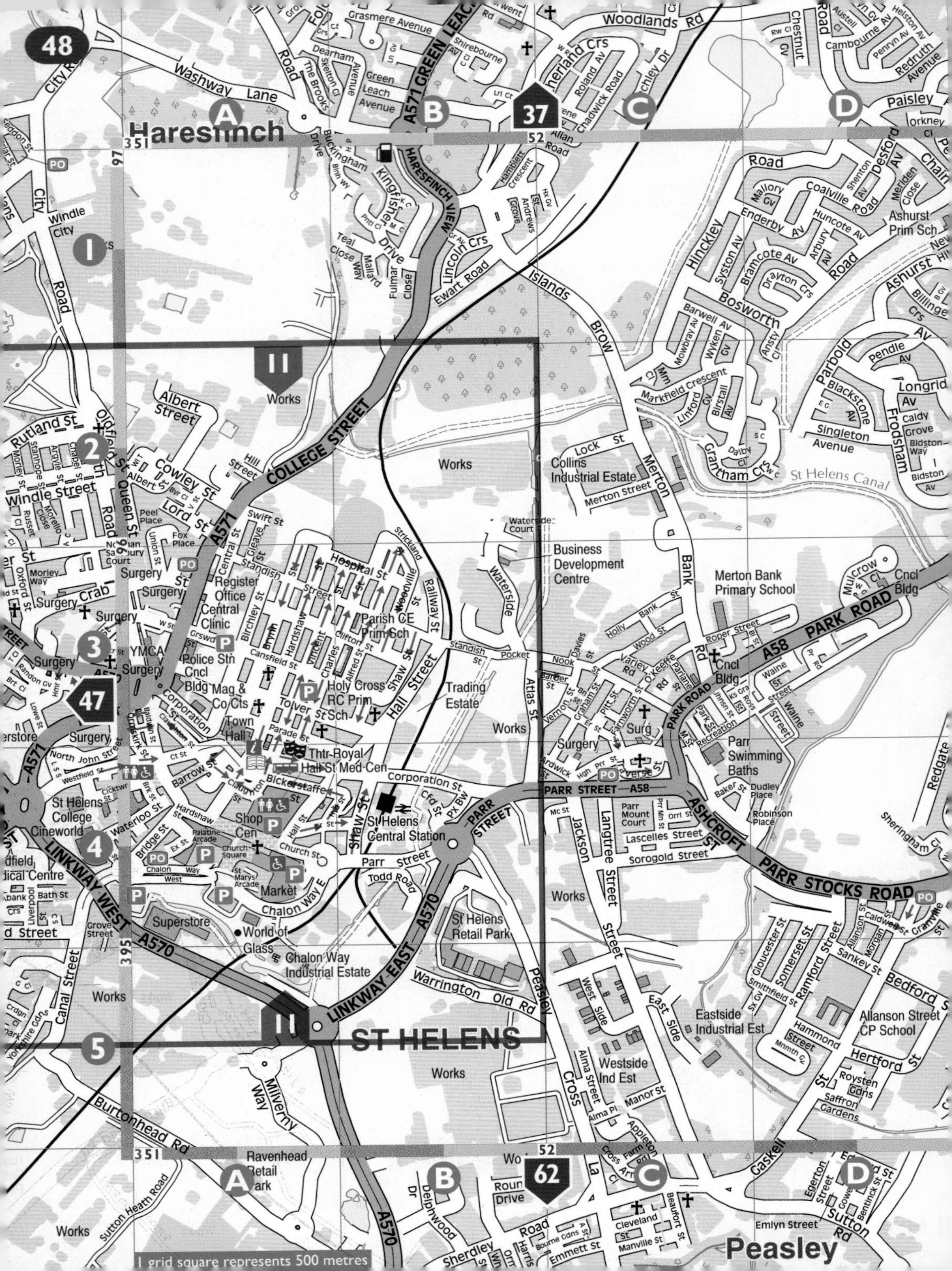
48
37
47
62
Haresfinch
ST HELENS
Peasley
Washway Lane
Grasmere Avenue
Woodlands Rd
A571 GREEN LEACH
HARESFINCH VIEW
Kingfisher Drive
Lincoln Crs
Ewart Road
Islands Brow
Chadwick Road
Roland Av
Allan Road
Hamblett Crescent
St Andrews Grove
Bosworth Road
Hinckley Road
Coalville Road
Enderby Av
Bramcote Av
Syston Av
Drayton Crs
Barwell Av
Markfield Crescent
Grantham Crs
Ashurst Prim Sch
Ashurst
Pendle Av
Parbold Av
Longrid Av
Singleton Avenue
Frodsham
Blackstone Av
St Helens Canal
Merton Bank Rd
Merton Bank Primary School
Collins Industrial Estate
Merton Street
Lock St
Business Development Centre
Waterside Court
Waterside
Works
Albert Street
COLLEGE STREET
A571
Cowley St
Lord St
Hill Street
Rutland St
Windle Street
Windle City
City Road
Oldfield St
Queen St
Peel Place
Fox Place
Surgery
Register Office
Central Clinic
Police Stn
Cncl Bldg
Mag & Co Cts
YMCA
Town Hall
Hospital St
Parish CE Prim Sch
Holy Cross RC Prim Sch
Railway St
Hall Street
Shaw St
Trading Estate
Standish St
Pocket Nook
Atlas St
Corporation St
Parade St
Thtr Royal
Hall St Med Cen
Bickerstaffe St
Barrow St
North John Street
Westfield St
St Helens College
Cineworld
Waterloo St
Bridge St
Shop Cen
Church St
Church Square
St Marys Arcade
Market
Chalon Way West
Chalon Way E
Superstore
World of Glass
Chalon Way Industrial Estate
St Helens Central Station
Parr Street
Todd Road
LINKWAY WEST
LINKWAY EAST
A570
St Helens Retail Park
Warrington Old Rd
Peasley Cross
PARR STREET A58
PARK ROAD A58
Cncl Bldg
Parr Swimming Baths
Dudley Place
Robinson Place
Lascelles Street
Sorogold Street
ASHCROFT ST
PARR STOCKS ROAD
Jackson St
Langtree Street
Parr Mount Court
Westside Ind Est
East Side
Eastside Industrial Est
Allanson Street CP School
Hammond Street
Hertford St
Bedford St
Sankey St
Ramford Street
Somerset St
Gloucester St
Royston Gdns
Saffron Gardens
Gaskell
Egerton Street
Sutton Rd
Emlyn Street
Cleveland St
Manville St
Emmett St
Sherdley Road
Delphwood Dr
Ravenhead Retail Park
Sutton Heath Road
Burtonhead Rd
Milverny Way
Canal Street
Grove Street
Redgate
Mulcrow
Sheringham Cl
Alma Street
Manor St
Appleton
1 grid square represents 500 metres

St Helens 49
Laffak
Blackbrook
Broad Oak
Derbyshire Hill
Parr
Moss Nook
63
Renfrew Avenue
Old Nook Lane
Erskine Cl
Link Av
Lane
Drive
Blackbrook St Marys Catholic Primary School
St Catherines Centre for Girls
Council Building
STANLEY BANK WAY
A58
BLACKBROOK ROAD
Whiteside Av
Dearnley Av
O'Sullivan Crs
Callon Av
St Augustine of Canterbury RC High School
Boardmans
VICARAGE ROAD
VICARAGE RD
St Bk Rd
A599
CLIPSLEY LANE
Vicarage Dr
Brookside Way
Brookside View
Clipsley Crs
Maple Av
Regent Av
Grosvenor Rd
Avondale
Teesdale Road
Wyedale Road
Gardiner Av
O'Connell Close
Juddfield St
Sumner Street
Cumberland Crs
Lenfield Drive
W End Gv
End
West
Old
Street
Park Av
Park
Ebnzr St
Richard Evans Comm Prim Sch
Lloyd St
Whint Road
Fosters Road
William Road
Holly Rd
Rowan Close
Folds Road
Sankey Road
The Close
Burrows Avenue
Redwood
Laurel Road
Chestnut Avenue
Sycmr Av
Morris Close
Littler Road
Roberts Av
Avenue
Whittle
Silver Av
Harty Road
Wedge Av
Troon Close
Gleneagles Dr
Carnoustie Grove
Tobermory Close
Ledger Rd
Canniswood Rd
Edward St
Harrison Drive
Cemetery
Haweswater Avenue
Loweswater Crescent
Road
Legh
Arnside Av
Faircrough Crescent
Legh Vale Primary School
White House Cl
Windermere Road
Wagon Lane
Central Drive
Leyland Grove
Caunce Av
Whiteside Road
Hay High Sch
Cooper Lane
Quayle Close
Works
Moorfoot Road Industrial Estate
Delta Road
Murphy Grove
O'Brien Grove
Seath Avenue
Richards Gv
Bramwell St
Archer Gv
Charnwood St
McCormack Av
Kerr Grove
Rimmer Grove
BROAD OAK ROAD
Fry St
A572
Moorfoot Road
Mendip Gv
Malvern Road
Chiltern Road
Southport St
Mersey St
Weaver Grove
Sky Lark Rl
NEWTON ROAD
Havannah Lane
Winter Grove
PENNINE
CHANCERY LANE
Evelyn Av
Simms Av
Castle Av
Stocks Av
Lansbury Av
Lansbury Bridge School
Pennine Drive
Stretton Avenue
Cheviot Avenue
Pennine Cl
Sidlaw Av
Pentland Avenue
Drive
Maternity & Child Welfare Clinic
Derbyshire Hill
Cotswold Gv
Provident St
Brunswick St
Broad Oak Prim Sch
Holy Spirit Prim Sch
Mount Pleasant Avenue
Moore Av
McMinnis Av
Luther Gv
Avenue
Fleet Lane Industrial Estate
Fleet Lane
Cromdale Gv
Blackdown Grove
Ashtons Green
Swan Avenue
Cherry Tree Dr
Cherry Tree Dr
Price Gv
Hignett Av
Rudd Avenue
Reynolds Avenue
Waring
Neville Av
Winston Av
Sexton Avenue
Inman Av
Parr Industrial Estate
Bromilow Rd
Waterland Lane
Merelands Wy
Pool End
Downland Way
Brookland Lane
Concourse Wy
Fleet Lane
Croft End
Meadow Lane
Ferrys Lane
Pond Wk
Brookway
Lane
Brook End
Downway Lane
Weymouth Av
Portland Way
St Cuthberts Catholic High Sch
Works
E
F
G
H
I
2
3
4
5
53
54
55
96
395

A
B
C
D
1
2
3
4
5
3 27
28
94
93
3 92
King's Pde
KING'S
HARRISON DR
P
Bayview
Drive
Byswtr Gdns
Wallasey
Golf Club
Nwpr Av
Wallasey Grove
Road Stn
Wallasey
Village
Golf Course
Mockbeggar Wharf
BAYSWATER RD
A554
Stanley Av
Hillam Road
Barmouth Rd
Bangor Rd
Asbury
Rd
Beaumaris
Rd
Bayswater
Rd
Green
Kinross
Northcote Rd
Keble
Dr
Greenleas
School
Greenleas Cl
Redcar
Road
Saltburn Rd
Greenleas Road
St Nicholas' Rd
Malvern Rd
Wyndhm Rd
Northcote Rd
Brdtt Rd
Green Lane
P
Golf Course
New
Solar
School
Chorlton Gv
Moorcroft Rd
Southcroft Rd
Longacre Cl
Southbourne
Wal
RFC
Cross
Lane
Works
Ashville
FC
Leasowe
Golf Club
Leasowe
A551
LEASOWE ROAD
Meadowside
Leasowes
Frobisher
Raleigh Rd
Shacklet
Our Lady
RC Primary School
Heyes
Dr
67
A554
1 grid square represents 500 metres

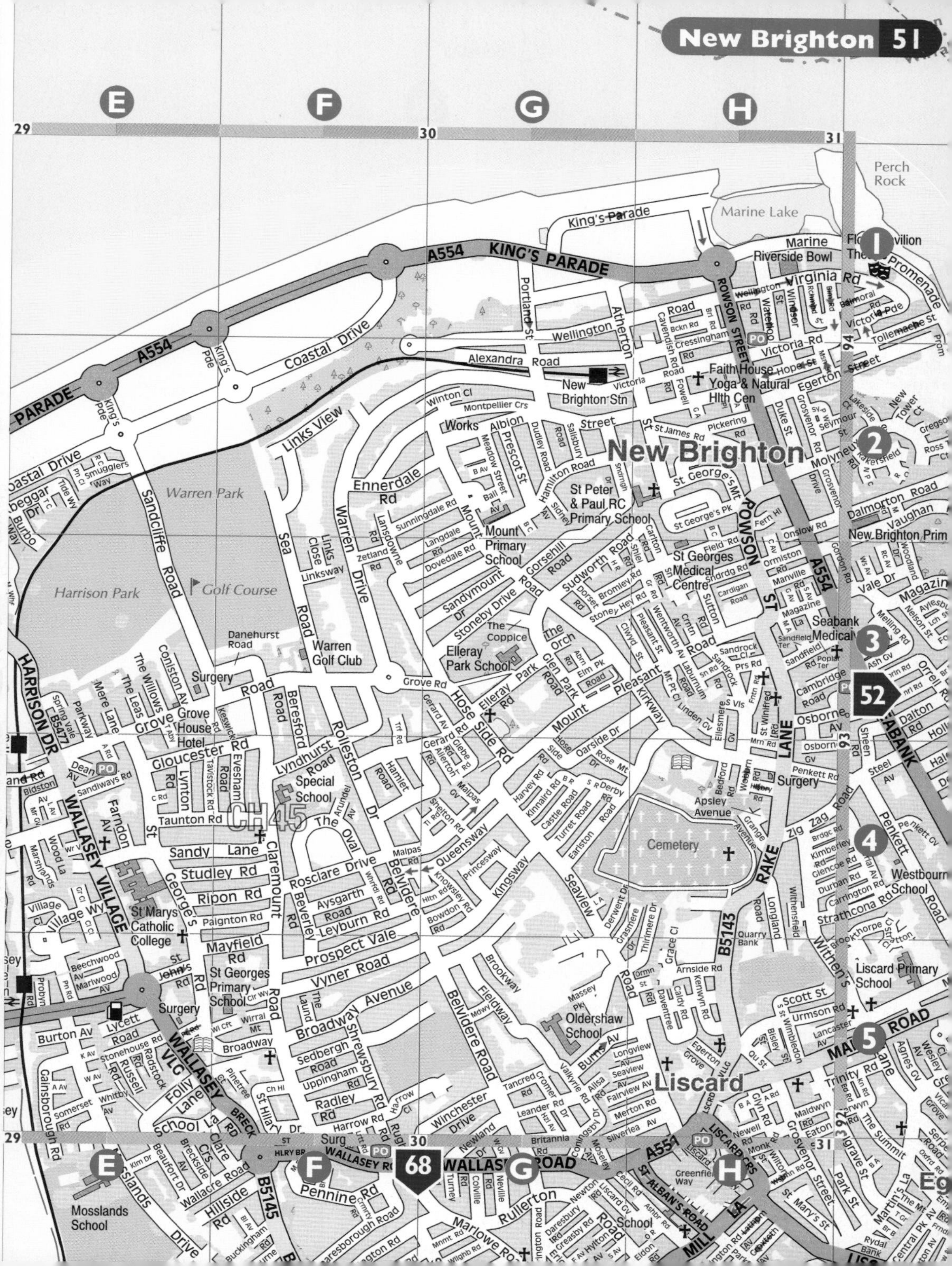
E
F
G
H
29
30
31
Perch Rock
Marine Lake
King's Parade
A554 KING'S PARADE
A554
PARADE
Coastal Drive
Marine
Riverside Bowl
Floral Pavilion Theatre
Promenade
Virginia Rd
Victoria Pde
Tollemache St
Wellington Road
Cavendish Rd
Cressingham
Victoria Rd
Alexandra Road
New Brighton Stn
Faith House Yoga & Natural Hlth Cen
Hope St
Egerton Street
Portland St
Atherton St
ROWSON STREET
Links View
Winton Cl
Montpellier Crs
Works
Albion Street
Prescot St
Dudley Road
Salisbury
St James Rd
Pickering Rd
New Brighton
Molyneux
Dalmorton Road
Vaughan
New Brighton Prim
Smugglers Way
Tide Wy
Burbo Way
Warren Park
Sandcliffe Road
Sea Road
Harrison Park
Golf Course
Links Close
Linksway
Warren Drive
Ennerdale Rd
Lansdowne Rd
Zetland Rd
Sunningdale Rd
Langdale Rd
Dovedale Rd
Mount Rd
Mount Primary School
Meadow Street
Hamilton Road
St Peter & Paul RC Primary School
St George's Mt
St George's Pk
Field Rd
ROWSON ST
A554
Gorsehill Road
Sudworth Road
St Georges Medical Centre
Sandymount Dr
Stoneby Drive
The Coppice
Elleray Park School
Warren Golf Club
Danehurst Road
Surgery
Grove Rd
Grove Road
Grove House Hotel
Coniston Av
The Willows
The Leas
Mere Lane
Parkway
Spring Vale
B5477
HARRISON DR
Beresford Road
Rolleston Dr
Lyndhurst Road
Special School
Hose Side Rd
Elleray Park Rd
Glen Park Road
The Orch
Pleasant Street
Mount Pleasant Road
Kirkway
Sandrock Rd
Seabank Medical
Cambridge Road
Osborne Av
52
SEABANK
Dalton Rd
Gloucester Rd
Lynton Rd
Evesham Road
Tavistock Rd
Dean Av
Sandiways Rd
PO
Bidston Av
Farndon Av
WALLASEY VILLAGE
Taunton Rd
CH45
The Oval
Arundel Av
Hamlet Road
Malpas Gv
Queensway
Oarside Dr
Rose Mt
Derby Rd
Cemetery
Apsley Avenue
Grange Avenue
Surgery
Penkett Rd
Zig Zag Road
RAKE LANE
Sandy Lane
Studley Rd
Ripon Rd
Claremount Road
Rosclare Drive
Aysgarth Road
Leyburn Rd
Beverley Rd
Belvidere Rd
Princesway
Kingsway
Seaview
Derwent Dr
Grasmere Dr
Thirlmere Dr
Grace Cl
Quarry Bank
Longland Road
Withensfield
Withen's
Westbourne School
Strathcona Rd
Carrington Rd
Durban Rd
Glencoe Rd
Kimberley Rd
Village Wy
St Marys Catholic College
George's Rd
Paignton Rd
Mayfield Rd
St Georges Primary School
Prospect Vale
Vyner Road
Broadway Avenue
Brookway
Fieldway
Belvidere Road
Oldershaw School
B5143
Arnside Rd
Caldy Rd
Daventree Rd
Kenwyn Rd
Liscard Primary School
Scott St
Urmson Rd
MANOR ROAD
Beechwood Av
Marlwood Av
Surgery
Lycett Road
Burton Av
Stonehouse Rd
Radstock Rd
Russell Rd
Broadway
Wirral Mt
WALLASEY VLG
Folly Lane
Gainsborough Rd
Somerset Rd
Whitby Av
Sedbergh Road
Shrewsbury Rd
Uppingham Rd
Radley Rd
Harrow Rd
Winchester Drive
Tancred Rd
Cromer Dr
Leander Rd
Burns Av
Longview Av
Seaview Av
Fairview Av
Merton Rd
Liscard
Egerton Grove
Trinity Rd
The Summit
School La
Clare Crs
Brecksid Av
BRECK RD
Beaufort Dr
Wallacre Road
Hillside Rd
B5145
Mosslands School
Pennine Rd
WALLASEY RD
68
WALLASEY ROAD
Newland Dr
Britannia Rd
Coningsby Dr
Silverlea Av
A551
ST ALBAN'S ROAD
LISCARD CRS
Greenfield Way
Grosvenor Street
Park St
St Mary's St
MILL LA
Rullerton Road
Marlowe Rd
School
Liscard Gv
Cecil Rd
Martin's La
Eg

Sefton
Wirral
DOUGLAS
DUBLIN
38
A
B
C
D
331
32
Perch Rock
Marine Lake
1
Floral Pavilion Theatre
Riverside Bowl
Promenade
Virginia Rd
Wellington Rd
Waterloo Rd
Windsor St
Balmoral Rd
Victoria Pde
Tollemache St
Tower Prom
Victoria Rd
Hope St
Egerton Street
94
Seymour St
Lakeside Ct
New Tower Ct
Gregson Ct
Ross Tower Ct
2
Molyneux Drive
Rakersfield
Duke St
Grosvenor Drive
Dalmorton Road
Vaughan Road
Kirkland Rd
Fern Hl
Onslow Rd
New Brighton Prim Sch
POWSON ST
A554
Ormiston Rd
Manville Rd
Gordon Rd
Woodland Dr
Vale Dr
Magazine Lane
Aylesbury Rd
Nelson St
Fort St
Sefton
Liverpool
3
Seabank Medical Cen
Birch Gv
Ash Gv
Melling Rd
Magazine Brow
Magazines Promenade
Sandrock Cl
51
PO
Orrell Rd
Dalton Rd
Holland Road
Haydock Rd
Beach Gv
SEABANK ROAD
St Winifred
LANE
Osborne Av
93
Sheen Rd
Steel Av
Hale Road
Denton Drive
Hertford Drive
Radnor Drive
Elgin Drive
Lincoln Drive
Caithness Drive
Penkett Rd
Surgery
Zig Zag Road
Penkett Road
Penkett Gv
4
Grange Avenue
RAKE
Kimberley Rd
Glencoe Rd
Imperial Av
Durban Rd
Carrington Rd
Strathcona Rd
Westbourne School
Warwick Dr
Kg George Dr
Egremont Promenade
Webster Av
Cunard Avenue
Royden Av
Ismay Dr
Cliff Dr
B5143
Longland Road
Withensfield
Quarry Bank
Brookthorpe Cl
Withen's
Liscard Primary School
Manor Lane
B5142
Maddock Rd
Promenade
Scott St
Urmson Rd
Lancaster Av
5
MANOR ROAD
Stringhey Road
Poole Rd
Blenheim Rd
Trafalgar Av
St Lucia Rd
St Bride's Rd
St Elmo Rd
St Vincent Rd
Kinglake Rd
Trinity Rd
Lane
Agnes Gv
Wesley Av
Brook St
Greenwood Lane
Ivor Rd
Exeter Rd
Vicarage Grove
Upr Rice
Ivor Road
Trafalgar Road
Rice Hey Road
Lea Road
Charlotte Rd
Rudgrave Sq
KING STREET
Glyn Rd
Maldwyn
Berwyn
Newell Rd
Monk Rd
Grosvenor Street
392
331
Beaulave St
The Summit
Serpentine Road
Rice Lane
Chestnut Av
Wright Street
Tobin St
69
WALLASEY
Egremont
Rice La
Med Cen
Union St
Guildford St
Crescent
Park St
St Mary's St
Martin's La
Empress Rd
LISCARD CRS
1 grid square represents 500 metres

Langton Dock
Brocklebank Dock
Canada Dock
Huskisson Dock
Nelson Dock
Stanley Dock
Trafalgar Dock
Sandon Industrial Estate
Sandhills
Kirkdale
Vauxhall
Regent Road
A5036
Derby Road
A565
Great Howard Street
Millers Bridge
Balliol Road
Stanley Road
A567
Commercial Road
A5038
Melrose Road
Westminster Rd
Bankhall Street
A5056
Bankfield Street
Sandhills Lane
A5055
Boundary Street
A5054
Blackstone Street
Scotland Road
A59
Kirkdale Road
Brasenose Road
B5318
Bank Hall Station
Sandhills Station
Kirkdale Station
Sandhills Business Park
Wellington Employment Park (under development)
Police Stn
Liverpool Community College
Stanley Med Cen
Hugh Baird Coll of Technology
Hugh Baird Coll of FE
Town Hall
Bootle CC
Kirkdale St Lawrence CE Primary Sch
St Johns Primary School
Taylor Street Ind Est
Everton Park Sports Cen
Great Homer St Medical Centre
St Anthony's Shopping Centre
Superstore
Works
Vauxhall Road
Silvester Street
Blenheim Street
Latimer Street
Lambeth Road
Orwell Road
Fountains Road
Owen Rd
Rumney Rd W
Juniper St
Belltower Rd
Errington Street
Grundy Street
Walter St
Lightbody Street
Houlgrave Rd
Dickson Street
Cotton Street
Regent Street
Burlington St
Marsh Street
Viola Street
Bedford Road
Wadham Road
Beatrice Street
Benedict St
Olivia Street
Orlando St
Bianca St
Celia St
Kingsway Industrial
E
F
G
H
1
2
3
4
5
33
34
35
39
54
70

54
40
53
71
A
B
C
D
1
2
3
4
5
335
36
93
94
392
Kirkdale
Kirkdale Station
Melrose Road
Westminster Road
Hale Road
Selwyn St
Brewster Street
County Road
Walton Road
Walton Lane
Kirkdale Road
Scotland Road
A59
A567
A580
A5089
A5050
Walton Breck Road
Breck Road
Oakfield Road
Priory Road
Netherfield Road North
St Domingo Road
Heyworth Street
Robson Street
Everton Valley
Queens Drive
Stanley Park
Anfield
Anfield Cemetery
Anfield Crematorium
L4
L5
Everton FC (Goodison Park)
Goodison Rd
Spellow Lane
Liverpool FC (Anfield)
Liverpool FC Museum
Vernon Sangster Sports Centre
Anfield Community Comprehensive School
Gwladys Street Community Primary School
Walton Medical Cen
Alsop High School
Walton Hall Village Medical Cen
St Francis De-Sales RC Infant School
Langham Street Industrial Est
Westminster Road Swimming Pool
Bousfield Health Cen
Notre Dame Catholic Coll
Hope Valley Community Primary School
Breckfield Primary School
Temple of Praise
All Saints Catholic Primary School
Anfield Medical Centre
Liverpool Community College
Stanley Med Cen
Everton Park Sports Cen
Netherfield Family Hlth Clinic
Great Homer Street Medical Centre
St Anthony's Shopping Centre
The Beacon CE Primary School
Breckfield Community Comprehensive Sch
Campion Catholic High School
Whitefield Prim Sch
Prince Edwin Centre
Everton
St Johns Primary School
St Lawrence CE Primary Sch
Council Building
Taylor Street Ind Est
Belmont Road
Boundary Lane
Great Homer Street
1 grid square represents 500 metres

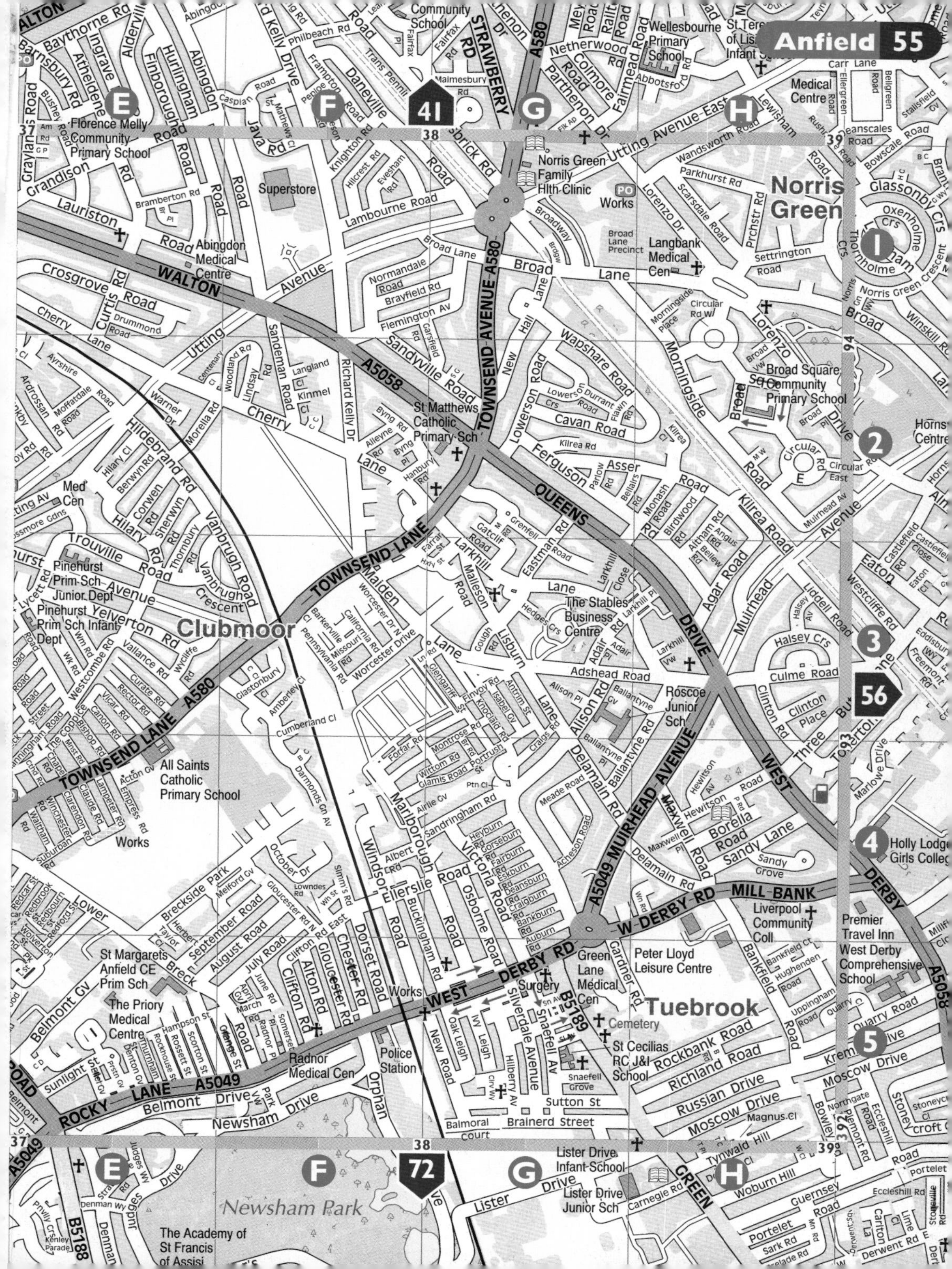
Norris Green
Clubmoor
Tuebrook
Newsham Park
WALTON
QUEENS DRIVE
WEST DERBY RD
W DERBY RD MILL BANK
ROCKY LANE A5049
TOWNSEND LANE A580
TOWNSEND AVENUE A580
A5058
A5049 MUIRHEAD AVENUE
B5189
B5188
STRAWBERRY RD
Utting Avenue East
Broad Lane
Cherry Lane
Utting Avenue
Lower Breck Road
Green Lane
Lister Drive
Newsham Drive
Belmont Drive
Florence Melly Community Primary School
Superstore
Abingdon Medical Centre
Norris Green Family Hlth Clinic
Works
Broad Lane Precinct
Langbank Medical Cen
Broad Square Community Primary School
St Matthews Catholic Primary Sch
Pinehurst Prim Sch Junior Dept
Pinehurst Prim Sch Infant Dept
The Stables Business Centre
Roscoe Junior Sch
All Saints Catholic Primary School
Liverpool Community Coll
Premier Travel Inn
West Derby Comprehensive School
Holly Lodge Girls Colleg
Peter Lloyd Leisure Centre
Green Lane Medical Cen
Surgery
Cemetery
St Cecilias RC J&I School
St Margarets Anfield CE Prim Sch
The Priory Medical Centre
Radnor Medical Cen
Police Station
Lister Drive Infant School
Lister Drive Junior Sch
The Academy of St Francis of Assisi
Wellesbourne Primary School
Medical Centre
Med Cen
Hornsby Centre
41
56
72
E
F
G
H
1
2
3
4
5
37
38
39

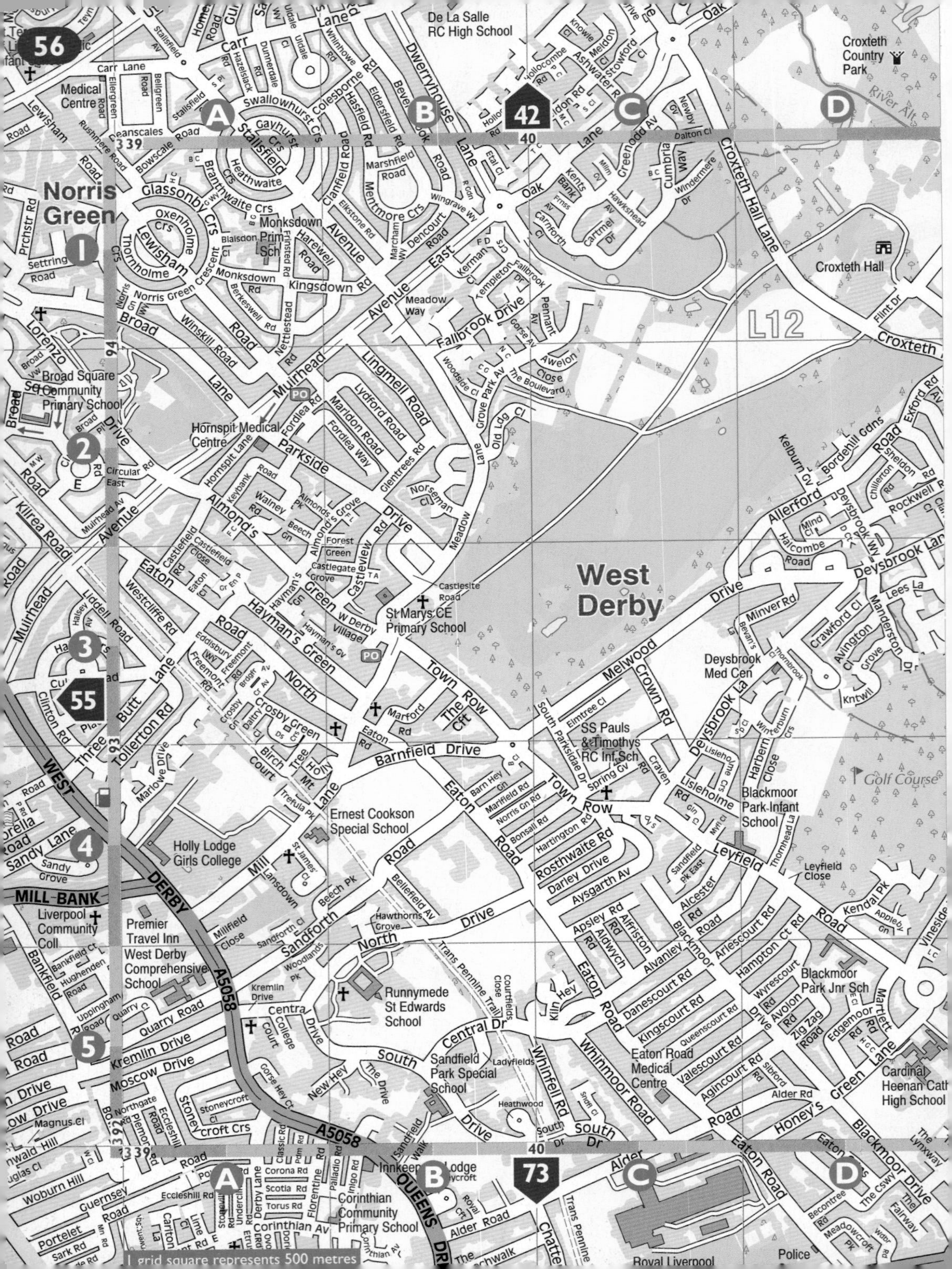

56
42
55
73
A
B
C
D
1
2
3
4
5
40
339
94
93
392
Norris Green
West Derby
L12
Croxteth Country Park
River Alt
Croxteth Hall
Croxteth Hall Lane
De La Salle RC High School
Medical Centre
Monksdown Prim Sch
Meadow Way
Broad Square Community Primary School
Hornspit Medical Centre
St Marys CE Primary School
West Derby Village
SS Pauls & Timothys RC Inf Sch
Deysbrook Med Cen
Blackmoor Park Infant School
Golf Course
Ernest Cookson Special School
Holly Lodge Girls College
Liverpool Community Coll
Premier Travel Inn
West Derby Comprehensive School
Runnymede St Edwards School
Sandfield Park Special School
Eaton Road Medical Centre
Blackmoor Park Jnr Sch
Cardinal Heenan Cath High School
Corinthian Community Primary School
Innkeeper's Lodge
Royal Liverpool
Police
MILL BANK
WEST DERBY
A5058
QUEENS DRIVE
Trans Pennine Trail
Carr Lane
Stalisfield Av
Swallowhurst Crs
Gayhurst Crs
Dwerryhouse Lane
Colesborne Rd
Oak Lane
Ashwater Rd
Stowford Cl
Meldon Cl
Knowle Cl
Bowscale Road
Deanscales Road
Lewisham Road
Rushmere Road
Ellergreen Road
Belgreen Road
Glassonby Crs
Branthwaite Crs
Heathwaite Crs
Clanfield Road
Marshfield Road
Mentmore Crs
Greenodd Av
Cumbria Way
Windermere Dr
Hawkshead Av
Cartmel Dr
Carnforth Cl
Kents Bank
Oxenholme Crs
Thornholme Crs
Monksdown Rd
Kingsdown Rd
Harewell Road
Dencourt Road
Wingrave Wy
Muirhead Avenue East
Fallbrook Drive
Templeton Crs
Pennant Av
Awelon Close
The Boulevard
Grove Park Av
Woodside Cl
Norris Green Crescent
Broad Lane
Winskill Road
Nettlestead Rd
Settring Road
Lorenzo Drive
Circular Rd East
Muirhead Avenue
Kilrea Road
Lingmell Road
Lydford Road
Maridon Road
Fordlea Way
Glentrees Rd
Parkside Drive
Meadow Lane
Old Ldg Cl
Norseman Cl
Almond's Green
Almond's Grove
Castleview Rd
Castlesite Road
Hayman's Green
Eaton Road North
Town Row
Barnfield Drive
Marford Rd
The Croft
Melwood Drive
Crown Rd
Deysbrook Lane
Deysbrook Wy
Allerford Road
Bordehill Gdns
Exford Rd
Halcombe Road
Minver Rd
Crawford Cl
Manderston Dr
Avington Cl
Kntwll Grove
Lisleholme Crs
Harbern Close
Winterburn Crs
Thornbrook
Thornhead La
Leyfield Road
Leyfield Close
Kendal Pk
Appleby Gn
Vineside
Spring Gv
Craven Rd
South Parkside Dr
Elmtree Cl
Barn Hey Gn
Marlfield Rd
Norris Gn Rd
Bonsall Rd
Hartington Rd
Rosthwaite Rd
Darley Drive
Aysgarth Av
Alcester Rd
Blackmoor Road
Arlescourt Rd
Hampton Ct Rd
Apsley Rd
Alfriston Rd
Aldwych Rd
Alvanley
Danescourt Rd
Kingscourt Rd
Queenscourt Rd
Valescourt Rd
Agincourt Rd
Wyrescourt
Avalon Rd
Zig Zag Road
Edgemoor Rd
Martlett Rd
Honey's Green Lane
Alder Rd
Blackmoor Drive
The Lynxway
The Fairway
Eaton Road
Whinmoor Road
Whinfell Rd
South Dr
Central Dr
Courtfields Close
Kiln Hey
Heathwood
Ladyfields
Sandfield Walk
North Drive
Sandforth Road
Beech Pk
Bellefield Av
Hawthorns Grove
Woodlands Pk
Kremlin Drive
Central Drive
College Court
Quarry Road
Moscow Drive
Stoneycroft Crs
Gorse Hey Ct
New Hey
The Drive
Mill Lane
Lansdown
St James' Cl
Birch Tree Court
Holly Mt
Trefula Pk
Crosby Green
Freemont Rd
Eddisbury Wy
Westcliffe Rd
Eaton Cl
Castlefield Close
Tollerton Rd
Three Butts Lane
Liddell Road
Halsey Av
Clinton Rd
Marlowe Drive
Sandy Lane
Sandy Grove
Bankfield Road
Uppingham Road
Quarry Cl
Millfield Close
Northgate Road
Plemont Road
Eccleshill Road
Magnus Cl
Woburn Hill
Guernsey Road
Portelet Road
Sark Rd
Corona Rd
Scotia Rd
Torus Rd
Corinthian Av
Derby Lane
Florentine Rd
Palladio Rd
Inigo Rd
Classic Rd
Alder Road
Royal Cft
Becontree Rd
Meadowcroft Pk
The Cswy
Chatte...
1 grid square represents 500 metres

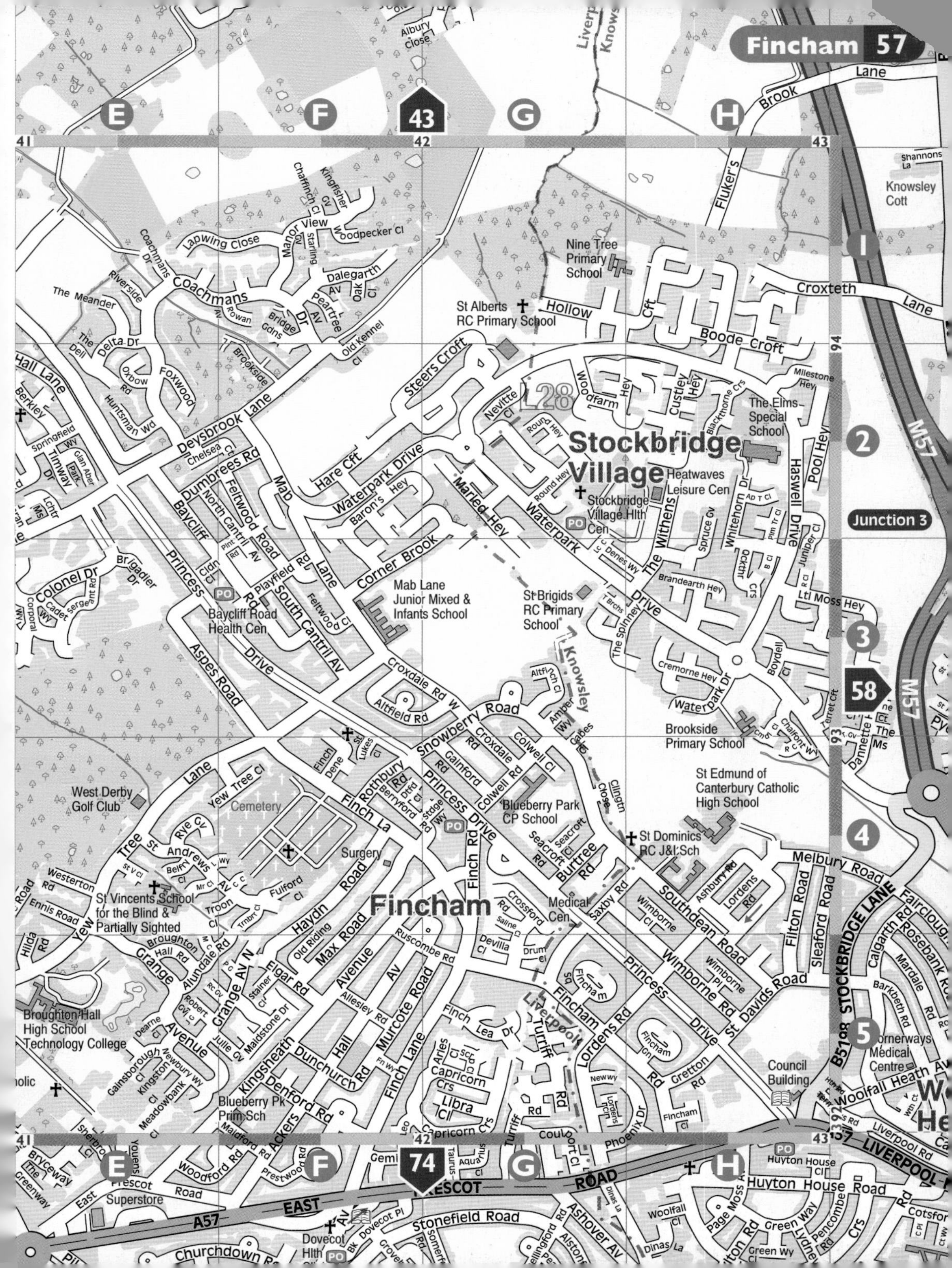

43
E
F
G
H
41
42
43
Brook
Lane
Shannons La
Knowsley Cott
Fluker's
Chaffinch Cl
Kingfisher Gv
Manor View
Lapwing Close
Woodpecker Cl
Starling Gv
Coachmans Dr
Coachmans
Dalegarth Av
Oak Cl
Peartree Av
Bridge Gdns
Rowan Av
Riverside
The Meander
The Delta Dr
The Dell
Old Kennel Cl
Brookside
Oxbow Rd
Foxwood
Huntsman Wd
Hall Lane
Berkley
Springfield Wy
Timway Dr
Glan Aber Park
Deysbrook Lane
Chelsea Ct
Dumbrees Rd
Feltwood Road
North Cantril Av
Baycliff
Princess
Playfield Rd
South Cantril Av
Feltwood Cl
Mab Lane
Brigadier Dr
Colonel Dr
Sergeant Rd
Cadet Wy
Corporal Wy
Baycliff Road Health Cen
PO
Aspes Road
Drive
Steers Croft
Hare Cft
Waterpark Drive
Baron's Hey
Corner Brook
Marled Hey
Mab Lane Junior Mixed & Infants School
Nine Tree Primary School
St Alberts RC Primary School
Hollow
Cft
Boode Croft
Croxteth
Lane
L28
Nevitte Cl
Round Hey
Woodfarm
Hey
Custley Hey
Blackthorne Crs
Milestone Hey
The Elms Special School
Stockbridge Village
Heatwaves Leisure Cen
Stockbridge Village Hlth Cen
Waterpark
Drive
Denes Wy
The Withens
Spruce Gv
Whitehorn Dr
Haswell Drive
Pool Hey
Juniper Cl
M57
Junction 3
Brandearth Hey
Ltl Moss Hey
St Brigids RC Primary School
The Spinney
Knowsley
Cremorne Hey
Waterpark Dr
Boydell Cl
58
Brookside Primary School
Chalfont W
St Edmund of Canterbury Catholic High School
Croxdale Rd W
Altfield Rd
Snowberry Road
Croxdale Rd
Gainford Rd
Colwell Cl
Colwell Rd
Amber Wy
Finch Dene
St Lukes Cl
Rothbury Rd
Berryford Rd
Princess Drive
Finch Rd
Blueberry Park CP School
Seacroft Rd
Seacroft Cl
Burtree Rd
St Dominics RC J&I Sch
Close
Lane
Yew Tree Cl
Cemetery
West Derby Golf Club
Finch La
Rye Gv
St Andrews
Surgery
Fulford Cl
Troon Cl
Westerton Rd
Ennis Road
St Vincents School for the Blind & Partially Sighted
Tree
Yew
Haydn
Road
Fincham
Crossford Rd
Medical Cen
Saxby Rd
Wimborne Cl
Southdean Road
Ashbury Rd
Lordens Rd
Melbury Road
Filton Road
Sleaford Road
STOCKBRIDGE LANE
Calgarth Rd
Rosebank
Mardale Rd
Barkbeth Rd
5
Cornerways Medical Centre
Woolfall Heath Av
Old Riding
Max Road
Avenue
Ruscombe Rd
Devilla Cl
Drum Cl
Fincham Sq
Princess
Wimborne Rd
Wimborne Pl
St Davids Road
Broughton Hall Rd
Grange
Alundale Rd
Grange Av N
Elgar Rd
Allesley Rd
Av
Murcote Road
Finch Lea Dr
Liverpool
Turriff
Fincham
Lordens Rd
Fincham Gn
Drive
Broughton Hall High School Technology College
Robert Gv
Avenue
Julie Gv
Maidstone Dr
Kingsheath
Dunchurch Rd
Hall
Finch Lane
Aries Cl
Capricorn Crs
Libra Cl
Rd
New Wy
Lordens Cl
Gretton Rd
Council Building
Gainsborough Rd
Kingston Cl
Newbury Wy
Meadowbank Cl
Denford Rd
Blueberry Pk Prim Sch
Ackers
Maidford Rd
Capricorn Crs
Coulport Cl
Phoenix Dr
Fincham Cl
Liverpool Rd
LIVERPOOL
B5198
Bryceway
The Greenway
Youens
Woodford Rd
Prestwood Rd
Prescot
Road
Superstore
East
A57
EAST
PRESCOT
ROAD
74
Dinas La
Huyton House Cl
Huyton House Road
Woolfall Cl
Page Moss
Green Way
Green Wy
Pencombe
Crs
Cotsford
Stonefield Road
Ashover Av
Dovecot Pl
Dovecot Hlth
Churchdown R

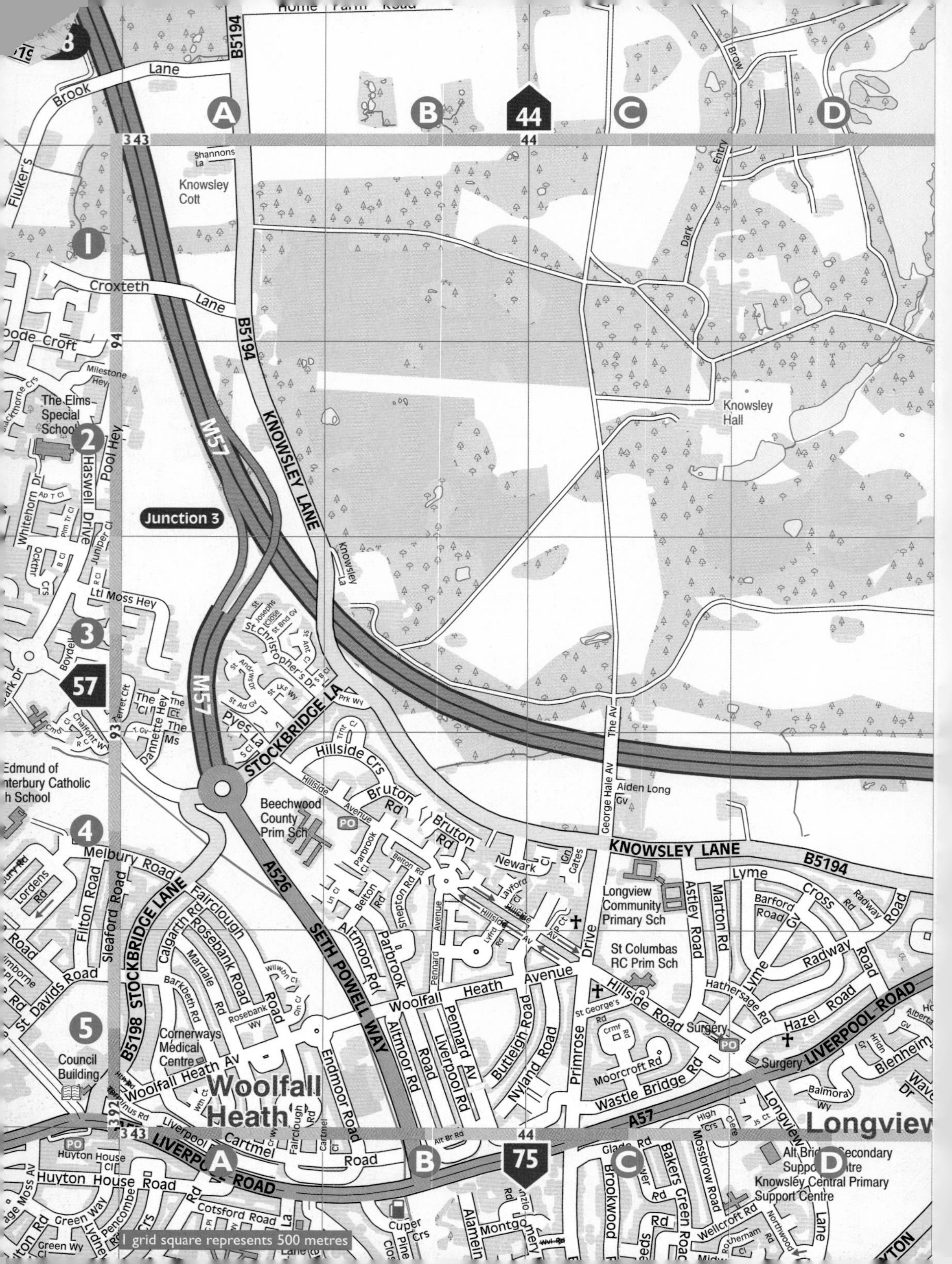

Home Farm Road
B5194
Brook Lane
A
B
44
C
D
3 43
44
Shannons La
Knowsley Cott
Flukers
Brow
Entry
Dark
1
Croxteth Lane
B5194
Goode Croft
94
Milestone Hey
The Elms Special School
2
Haswell Drive
Pool Hey
Whitehorn Dr
M57
KNOWSLEY LANE
Knowsley Hall
Junction 3
Juniper Cl
Knowsley La
Ltl Moss Hey
3
Boydell
57
St Josephs Close
St Christopher's Dr
St Bnd Gv
St Ant Cl
Prk Wy
M57
STOCKBRIDGE LA
The Cl
Dannette Hey
The Ct
The Ms
Chalfont Wy
93
Pyes La
Hillside Crs
Trnt Cl
Hillside Avenue
Bruton Rd
Bruton Rd
The Av
George Hale Av
Aiden Long Gv
Edmund of Canterbury Catholic High School
Beechwood County Prim Sch
PO
4
Melbury Road
KNOWSLEY LANE
B5194
Lordens Rd
Filton Road
Sleaford Road
STOCKBRIDGE LANE
A526
Parbrook Cl
Belton Rd
Newark Cl
Cn Gates
Longview Community Primary Sch
Astley Road
Marton Rd
Lyme Cross
Barford Road
Radway Road
Fairclough
Calgarth Rd
Rosebank Road
Mardale Rd
SETH POWELL WAY
Altmoor Rd
Shepton Rd
Avenue
Layford Cl
Hillside Av
Lytro Rd
Drive
St Columbas RC Prim Sch
Lyme Gv
Radway
Road
Road
Hathersage Rd
Hazel Road
LIVERPOOL ROAD
Wimborne
St Davids Road
Barkbeth Rd
Parbrook
Pennard
Woolfall Heath Avenue
Hillside Road
Surgery
PO
5
Council Building
B5198
Cornerways Medical Centre
Rosebank Wy
Road
Altmoor Road
Liverpool Rd
Pennard Av
Butleigh Road
Nyland Road
Primrose
St George's Rd
Crmf Rd
Moorcroft Rd
Wastle Bridge Rd
Surgery
Blenheim
Balmoral Wy
Longview
Woolfall Heath Av
Woolfall Heath
Endmoor Road
Fairclough Rd
Cartmel Cl
A57
High Crs
3 92
3 43
44
Liverpool Rd
Cartmel Road
Alt Br Rd
75
Glade Rd
Brookwood
Bakers Green Road
Mossbrow Road
Longview Lane
Alt Bridge Secondary Support Centre
Knowsley Central Primary Support Centre
PO
Huyton House Cl
Huyton House Road
LIVERPOOL ROAD
A
B
C
D
Green Way
Lydney
Pencombe
Cotsford Road
Cuper Crs
Pine
Alamein
Montgomery
Wellcroft Rd
Rotherham
Northwood
Green Wy
1 grid square represents 500 metres

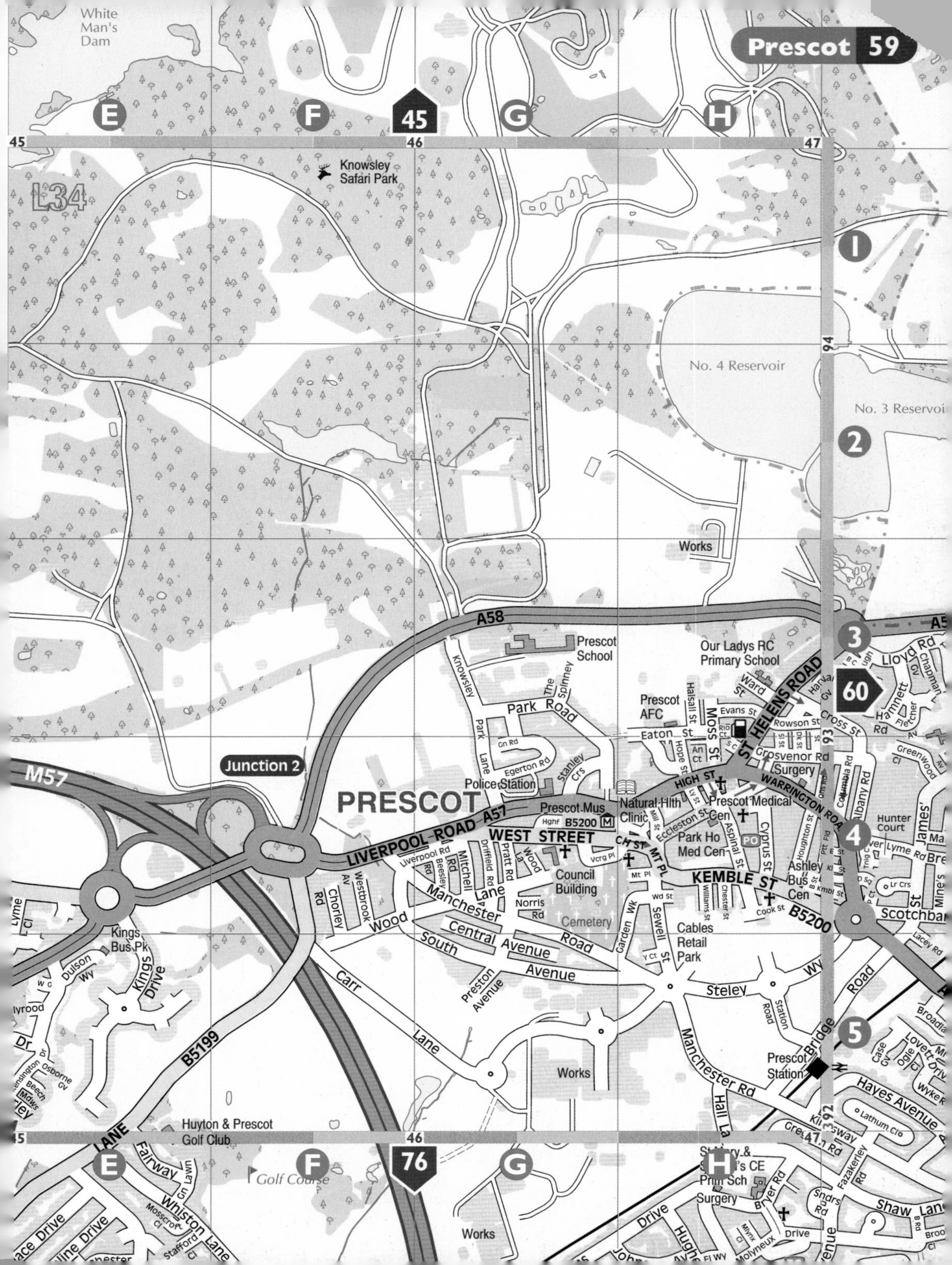
White Man's Dam
Knowsley Safari Park
L34
45
46
47
E
F
G
H
No. 4 Reservoir
No. 3 Reservoi
Works
A58
Prescot School
Our Ladys RC Primary School
Prescot AFC
Park Road
Knowsley
The Spinney
Junction 2
M57
PRESCOT
Police Station
Egerton Rd
Stanley Crs
Eaton St
Moss St
Halsall St
ST HELENS ROAD
HIGH ST
WARRINGTON ROAD
Prescot Medical Cen
Natural Hlth Clinic
Prescot Mus
B5200
LIVERPOOL ROAD A57
WEST STREET
Council Building
Cemetery
Park Ho Med Cen
KEMBLE ST
Cables Retail Park
Manchester Road
Central Avenue
South Avenue
Carr Lane
Steley Wy
Station Road
Bridge Road
Prescot Station
Manchester Rd
Hall La
Kings Bus Pk
Kings Drive
Dulson Wy
B5199
LANE
Huyton & Prescot Golf Club
Golf Course
Fairway
Whiston Lane
Works
Lloyd Rd
Cross St
Grosvenor Rd
Surgery
Albany Rd
Hunter Court
Lyme Rd
Scotchbar
Ashley Bus Cen
Hayes Avenue
Lovett Drive
Kingsway
Shaw Lane
Fazakerley Rd
St Mary & St Paul's CE Prim Sch
Surgery
Boyer Rd
Drive
1
2
3
4
5
93
94
60
76

Eccleston Mere
BURROW'S
A
B
46
C
D
347
48
1
2
3
4
5
94
93
392
No. 4 Reservoir
No. 3 Reservoir
B5201
Carmel College
West Park RFC
ROAD
Eccleston
Gdns
Seddon Rd
Grange Dr
Eccleston Gdns
Hill School Road
Broom Rd
A58 PRESCOT
Standring Gdn
Willoughby Drive
Grange Park
Seascale Av
PO
Lowther Crs
Patterdale Drive
Cumberland Av
Portico
Works
Penrith Rd
Lonsdale Av
Grebe Av
Oriole Cl
Tern Wy
Scholes Lane
Valencia Gv
St Helens Rd
SAINT HELENS ROAD
A58
New Rd
Fern Gdns
Park Avenue
West Close
Central Av
Eccleston Park
Elm Grove
Albany Av
Forest Cl
The Woodlands
The Paddock
Ingleholme Gdns
East Cl
Orchard Cl
Holme Cl
Lane
Heath Cl
Forest Grove
Surgery
Gorsey Croft
Fairholme Av
Eccleston Park Station
Golf Course
Hilary Close
Eccleston Lane Ends Primary School
Lloyd Rd
Chapman Gv
Hammett Rd
Fletcher Av
Evelyn Prim Sch
ST. JAMES' RD
OLD LANE
Beech Av
Broom Cl
Tree Cl
Portico
Plum Cl
B5201
Our Ladys RC Primary School
59
Evans St
Rowson St
Moss St
Cross St
Grosvenor Rd
Surgery
WARRINGTON ROAD
Prescot Medical Cen
Greenwood Cl
Evelyn Av
Road
Hawthorn Rd
Laurel Rd
Alder Road
Derwent Av
Rydal Av
Grasmere Av
Coniston Av
Alder Cl
Columbia Rd
Albany Rd
Hunter Court
James' St
Maryville Rd
Prescot Primary School
Aspinall St
Cyprus St
Houghton St
Ashley Bus Cen
Oliver Lyme Rd
Bretherton Rd
Mine's Av
Sutherland Rd
KEMBLE ST
B5200
Cook St
Scotchbarn Lane
Sinclair Cl
Grays Av
Vining Road
Ford Road
Mcvinnie Rd
Sundale Av
PORTICO LA
Honeybourne Dr
Litchborough Grove
Chater Cl
Watling Way
Eccleston Park Golf Club
Wedgewood Gdns
Lacey Rd
Prescot Leisure Centre
BICC Athletic Club
St Edmund Arrowsmith Catholic High School
TWO BUTT LANE
Steley Wy
Station Road
Bridge Road
A57 WARRINGTON ROAD
Sinclair Av
Gilbert Road
Edward Rd
B5201
Drive
Myers Av
Gilleney Gv
Foster Cl
Tarlton Cl
Croston Av
Amanda Road
Prescot Station
Broadlands
Lovett Drive
Ogle Cl
Case Gv
Mn Gv
Wyke Rd
Hayes Avenue
Grove
Maple Gv
Poplar Gv
Rufford Ct
Warrington Rd
Time Pk
Fire Station Road
Sandstone Gv
DELPH LANE
Blundell Rd
Holt
Road
Lane
Longton Lane
Sandhurst Road
St Winifred Rd
Longton Lane Community Primary School
Chester Rd
Hall La
Gregson Rd
Lathum Cl
Ash Gv
Willow Cl
Windsor Rd
Cable Rd
Brook St
PRSCT RD
77
Longview
St Mary & St Paul's CE Prim Sch
Surgery
Fazakerley Rd
Snders Rd
Shaw Lane
Beechwood
Birch Gv
Crossfield Rd
Whiston Hospital
A&E
Council
Ruth Evans Court
Honiston Av
Horwood Av
Brancker Av
Norcliffe Rd
Second
Molyneux Drive
St Lukes RC Primary
Martin Av
Ivy Av
1 grid square represents 500 metres

Big Dam
Swallow Court
Cedar St
Golf Course
PRESCOT ROAD
A58
West Park
47
Works
Ravenhead
Burtonhead Rd
Grosvenor Rd
Regents Rd
Kings Rd
Queens Rd
Lincoln Rd
Norfolk Rd
Dorset Rd
Henley Ct
Rochester Gdns
Alexandra
Stafford Road
Grange Park Golf Club
Toll Bar
Roby Street
French St
Owen St
Owen Cl
West Street
Fidler St
Whittle Street
Lemon Tree Wk
Royal Gv
Factory Row
Ravenhead Road
Works
Sutton Heath Road
Ravenhead Nature Park
Eccleston Road
Mitchell Rd
Oliver Road
Gra Pk Rd
LUCSMORE LA
Leslie Road
Broadway
Hartley Gv
Lonie Gv
Dickens Rd
Southey Rd
Bewsey St
Bates Crs
Formby Rd
Cairo St
Crossley Road
St John St
B5413
Elm Road
Sutton Heath Rd
Springfield Road
Upland Close
Thackray Rd
Council Building
Thatto Heath
Elmfield Close
The Caravan Pk
Sherdley Road
LINKWAY
Broadway Community High Sch
Lacey St
Fir St
Millom Grove
Thatto Heath Stn
THATTO HEATH ROAD
Police Stn
The Bowry Health Cen
Thatto Heath Community Prim Sch
Heathfield Av
Mayfield Avenue
Canberra Avenue
Adelaide Av
Perth Av
Forshaw Av
Oppenheim Av
Dennis Av
Austin Av
Matthews Gv
Howard St
Hayes St
Main Av
Scholes Lane
Nut St
Heath St
Carnarvon St
Cairn Ct
Balmer St
Hobart St
Brisbane St
Dunedin St
Dorothy Street
Elephant Lane
PO
Parliament St
Nursery Rd
Tasman Gv
Queensland Av
Freemantle Avenue
Kimberley Av
Harlow Cl
Hempstead Cl
Brown Edge
St Austins RC Prim Sch
South St
Birchfield St
Radley St
Kilburn Gv
Elephant Lane
Darwin Gv
Coral Av
Heath Rd
Road
Peterlee Close
Hatfield Cl
Forrester Av
Covett Rd
Florence St
Emily St
Nutgrove Methodist Prim Sch
Norton Gv
Beresford St
Clare Cl
Dawn Cl
Poynter St
Sutton Heath
Sutton Heath
Stevenage Cl
Sherdley
SAINT HELENS
62
Golf Course
Foxwood
Reservoir St
Gertrude St
NUTGROVE ROAD
Edge Street
Billingham Rd
Nutgrove Hall Drive
Auckland Rd
Consett Rd
Wingate Av
Whitebeam Gdns
Wedgewood Gdns
Churchill Gdns
Bexhill Gdns
Heatherleigh Gdns
Hedworth Gdns
Seaton
Easington Rd
Thornaby Gv
Tyne Cl
Hartland Gdns
Stockton Gv
Walsham Gdns
Hg Gdns
Breydon Gdns
Helgham Gdns
Martham Gdns
Welwyn Cl
A570
B5204
Drake Gardens
Mallard Gardens
Swan Gardens
Wood Vale
Marylebone Av
ELTON HEAD
Nut Grove
Tbly Grdns
Stratton Dr
ELTON HEAD ROAD
St John Vianney RC Prim Sch
Lea Green
Lowfield Lane
ROAD
Martlew Day Hospital
B5204
Nottingham Cl
Ellerslie Avenue
Brookfield Av
Field Wy
Gardeners Wy
RAINHILL
Lowfield Industrial Estate
Lea Green Road
Elderswood Rd
Francis
Stapleton Av
Vincent Rd
Ellaby Rd
Ansdell Villas Rd
B5413
78
Green Road
Lea Green
49
50
51
94
93
392
E
F
G
H
1
2
3
4
5

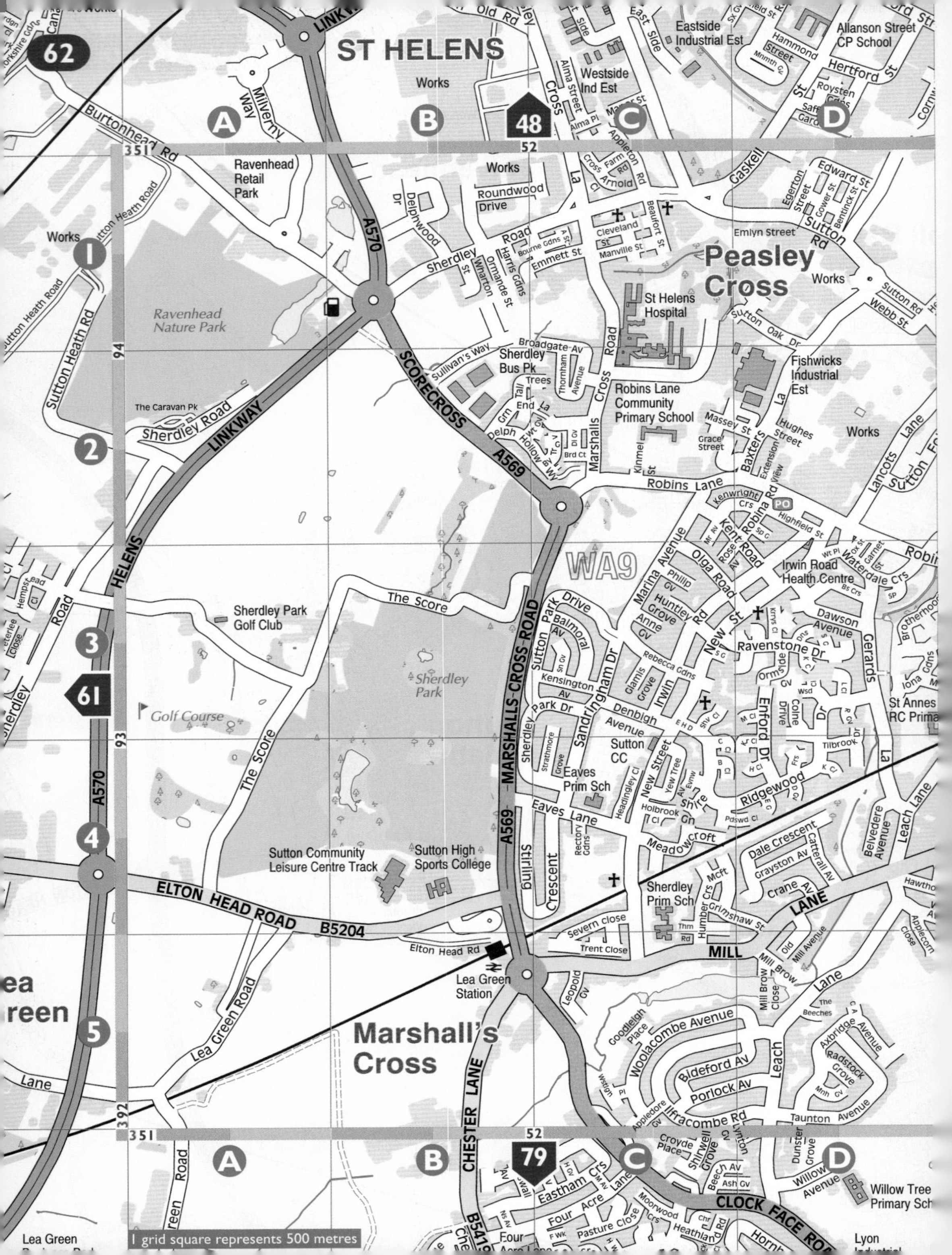

62
ST HELENS
Works
48
Eastside Industrial Est
Allanson Street CP School
Westside Ind Est
Hammond Street
Hertford St
Burtonhead Rd
Milverny Way
Alma Street
Cross
Appleton Rd
Ravenhead Retail Park
Works
Roundwood Drive
Delphwood Dr
Sutton Heath Road
Works
Sherdley Road
Bourne Gdns
Emmett St
Cleveland St
Manville St
Beaufort St
Emlyn Street
Peasley Cross
Sutton Rd
Works
Gaskell
Edward St
Egerton Street
Gower St
Bentinck St
Harris Gdns
Ormande St
Wharton St
Ravenhead Nature Park
St Helens Hospital
Sutton Oak Dr
Webb St
A570
Broadgate Av
Sherdley Bus Pk
Sullivan's Way
Thornham Avenue
Marshalls Cross Road
Robins Lane Community Primary School
Fishwicks Industrial Est
SCORECROSS
A569
Tall Trees
End La
Delph Hollow
The Caravan Pk
Sherdley Road
LINKWAY
Massey St
Grace Street
Baxters
Hughes Street
Works
Kinmel St
Robins Lane
Lancots Lane
Sutton
Kenwright Crs
Robina Rd
PO
Highfield St
HELENS
Marina Avenue
Kent Road
Olga Road
Rose Av
WA9
Irwin Road Health Centre
Waterdale Crs
Philip Gv
Huntley Grove
Anne Gv
New St
The Score
Sherdley Park Golf Club
Sutton Park Drive
Balmoral Av
Dawson Avenue
Ravenstone Dr
Gerards
Brotherhood
MARSHALLS-CROSS-ROAD
Rebecca Gdns
Glamis Grove
Irwin
Kensington Av
Sandringham Dr
Sherdley Park
Golf Course
61
Sherdley Park Dr
Denbigh Avenue
Enford Dr
Colne Drive
Iona Gdns
St Annes RC Prima
Sutton CC
Strathmore Grove
Eaves Prim Sch
New Street
Yew Tree Av
Tilbrook
The Score
Ridgewood
Eaves Lane
Headingley Cl
Holbrook Cl
Shire Gn
Meadowcroft
Belvedere Avenue
Leach Lane
Sutton Community Leisure Centre Track
Sutton High Sports College
Stirling Crescent
Rectory Gdns
Dale Crescent
Grayston Av
Catterall Av
Hawthorn
ELTON HEAD ROAD
B5204
Sherdley Prim Sch
Humber Crs
Grimshaw St
Crane Av
LANE
Applecom Close
Severn close
Trent Close
Elton Head Rd
MILL
Mill Brow
Old Mill Avenue
Lea Green Station
Leopold Gv
Mill Brow Close
Lane
The Beeches
Lea Green
Lea Green Road
Marshall's Cross
Goodleigh Place
Woolacombe Avenue
Axbridge Avenue
Radstock Grove
Bideford Av
Leach
Lane
CHESTER LANE
Porlock Av
Appledore Gv
Ilfracombe Rd
Taunton Avenue
79
Croyde Place
Shirwell Grove
Lynton Gv
Dunster Grove
Willow Avenue
Willow Tree Primary Sch
Eastham Crs
Beech Av
Ash Gv
Lane
Four Acre
Moorwood Crs
Pasture Close
Heathland Rd
CLOCK FACE RO
B5419
Lyon Industrial
Lea Green
1 grid square represents 500 metres
A
B
C
D
351
52
94
93
392
1
2
3
4
5

Parr
Parr Industrial Estate
Moss Nook
Sutton
Sutton Leach
Waterland Lane
Fleet Lane
Brookland Lane
Berrys Lane
Brookway Lane
Weymouth Av
St Cuthberts Catholic High Sch
Works
Nook Lane
Watery La
Worsley Brow
Sutton Oak CE Primary Sch
Carnegie Crescent
Hoghton Rd
Cecil Street
Frederick St
Percy St
Hoghton Road
Telford Dr
Ellamsbridge Road
Edgeworth St
Fisher St
Ellen St
Junction La
Herbert St
Leonard St
Station Road
Rainbow Medical Cen
Smith St
St Helens Junction Station
St Helens AFC
Threadneedle Ct
Cotton Ter
Sutton Moss Rd
Helena Road
Normans Road
Lionel St
Penlake La
Walter Grove
Hills Moss Road
BOLD ROAD
TRAVERS' ENTRY
B5204
The Pastures
Japonica Gdns
Dahlia Cl
Daffodil Gdns
Evergreen Rd
Andromeda Wy
Petunia Cl
Marigold Way
Iberis Gdns
Anemone Wy
Crocus Gdns
Lotus Gdns
Begonia Gdns
Jasmine Gdns
Columbine Wy
Celandine Wy
Orchid Wy
Samphire
Bold Business Centre
Bold
Bold Industrial Park
Neills Road
Douglas Avenue
Rosehill Av
Gorse
Joy Lane
REGINALD ROAD
Brindley Road
Reginald Road Industrial Park
Penlake Industrial Estate
Carole Close
Monastery Rd
Abbotsfield Road Industrial Park
Abbotsfield Road
Abbotsfield Farm
Works
49
80
53
54
55
94
93
392

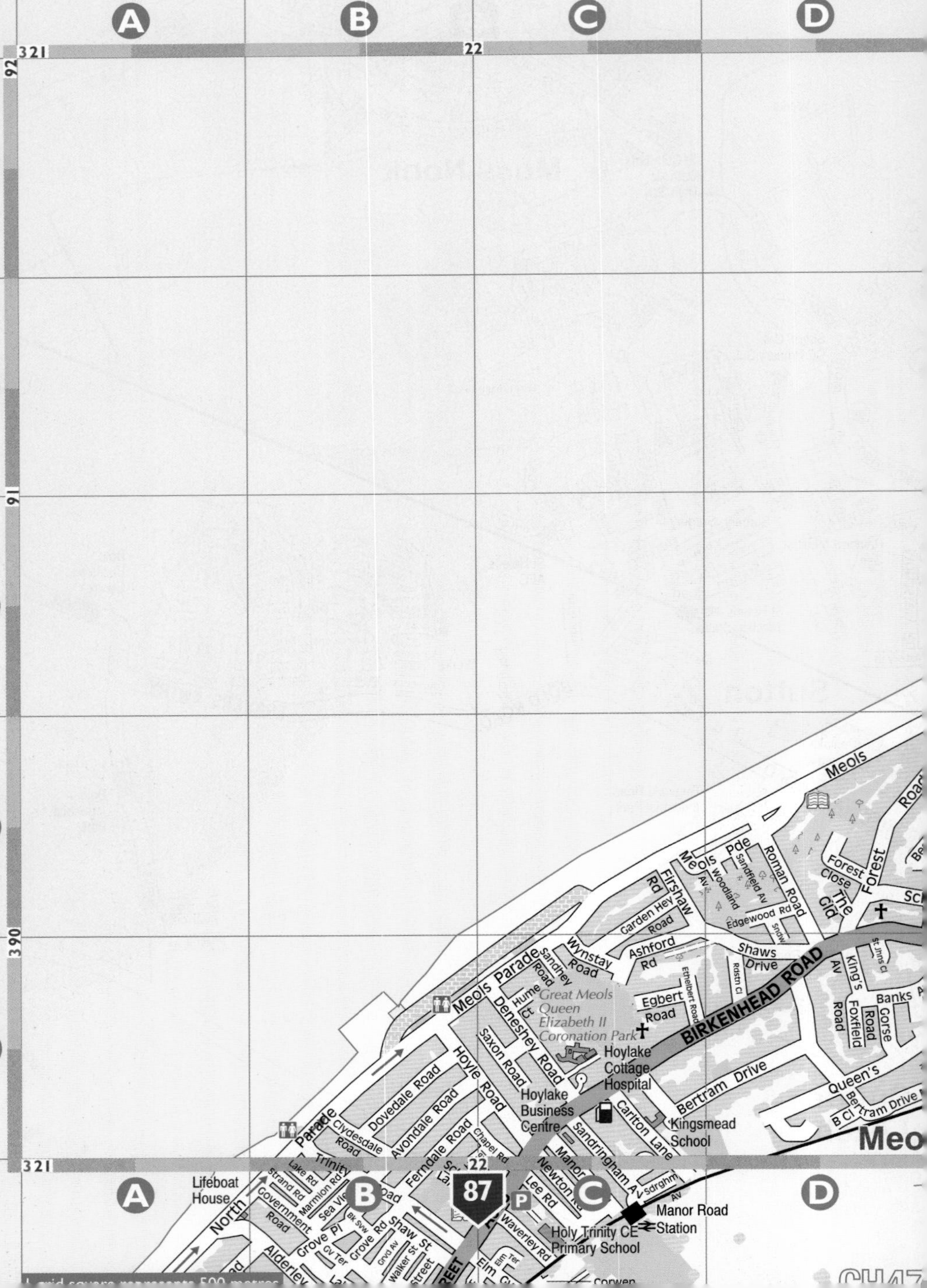

A
B
C
D
321
22
92
91
390
1
2
3
4
5
Meols
Meols Pde
Meols Av
Woodland
Sandfield Av
Roman Road
Forest Close
Forest
The Grd
Firshaw Rd
Garden Hey Road
Edgewood Rd
Wynstay Road
Ashford Rd
Shaws Drive
Sandhey Road
Meols Parade
Hume Ct
Great Meols Queen Elizabeth II Coronation Park
Egbert Road
Ethelbert Road
Rostn Cl
BIRKENHEAD ROAD
King's Av
St Jhns Cl
Banks
Foxfield Road
Corse Road
Queen's
Bertram Drive
B Cl
Meo
Deneshey Road
Saxon Road
Hoyle Road
Hoylake Cottage Hospital
Hoylake Business Centre
Carlton Lane
Kingsmead School
Sandringham Av
Sdrghm Av
Manor Rd
Newton Rd
Lee Rd
Waverley Rd
Holy Trinity CE Primary School
Manor Road Station
Elm Ter
Corwen
Dovedale Road
Avondale Road
Ferndale Road
Chapel Rd
Clydesdale Road
Parade
Trinity Road
Lake Rd
Strand Rd
Marmion Rd
Sea View
Bk Svw
Shaw St
Grove Rd
Grove Pl
Gv Ter
Grvd Av
Walker St
Government Road
North
Alderley
Lifeboat House
87
CH47
1 grid square represents 500 metres

E
F
G
H
23
24
25
92
91
390
I
2
3
4
5
66
88
Dove Point
Parkfields
Parkfield House
Park Lane
Great Meols
Ling Farm
Parade
Newlyn Road
Newlyn Cl
Elwyn Rd
Dovepoint Rd
Bennet's Lane
Guffitts Cl
Guffitt's Rake
Great Meols Prim Sch
Centurion Cl
Centurion Drive
Barnfield Cl
Road
Flowermead Cl
Park Av
Ashley
Lyndhurst
Cranborne Rd
Celtic Rd
Mumfords
Pool Lane
Greenwood
Park Way
Cleveley Rd
Derwent Rd
Station Ap
PO
Meols Station
A553
Avenue
Leighton Av
Mannington Cl
Glenham Cl
Rycroft Road
Birch Road
LC
Carr Lane
Works
Tern Way
Curlew
Millhouse Lane
Millhouse Cl
Ash Cl
Desford Cl
Bradgate Cl
Foxton Cl
Oakham Drive
Belfry Cl
St Austell Cl
Earlswood
Westry Cl
Lapworth Cl
Huxley Cl
Kinnerton Cl
Rosewood Dr
Alnwick Dr
Rothbury Cl
Wastdale
Mallard Wy
Town
Linear Park
Bermuda Road
Smillie Av
Hardie
Wooler
Berwick Cl
Otterburn Close
Rake Hey
Carr House La
Cardus Cl
Carr Gate
Crrw Cl
Tarbot Hey
Garrick Avenue
Broster
HOYLAKE ROAD
Barn Hey Crs
Sherwood Road
Shrwd Gv
A553
Fornalls Green Lane
The Ridgeway
Fieldway
Acres
Carr Farm
Thornley Rd
Amberley Av
The Paddock
Brnsfld Cl

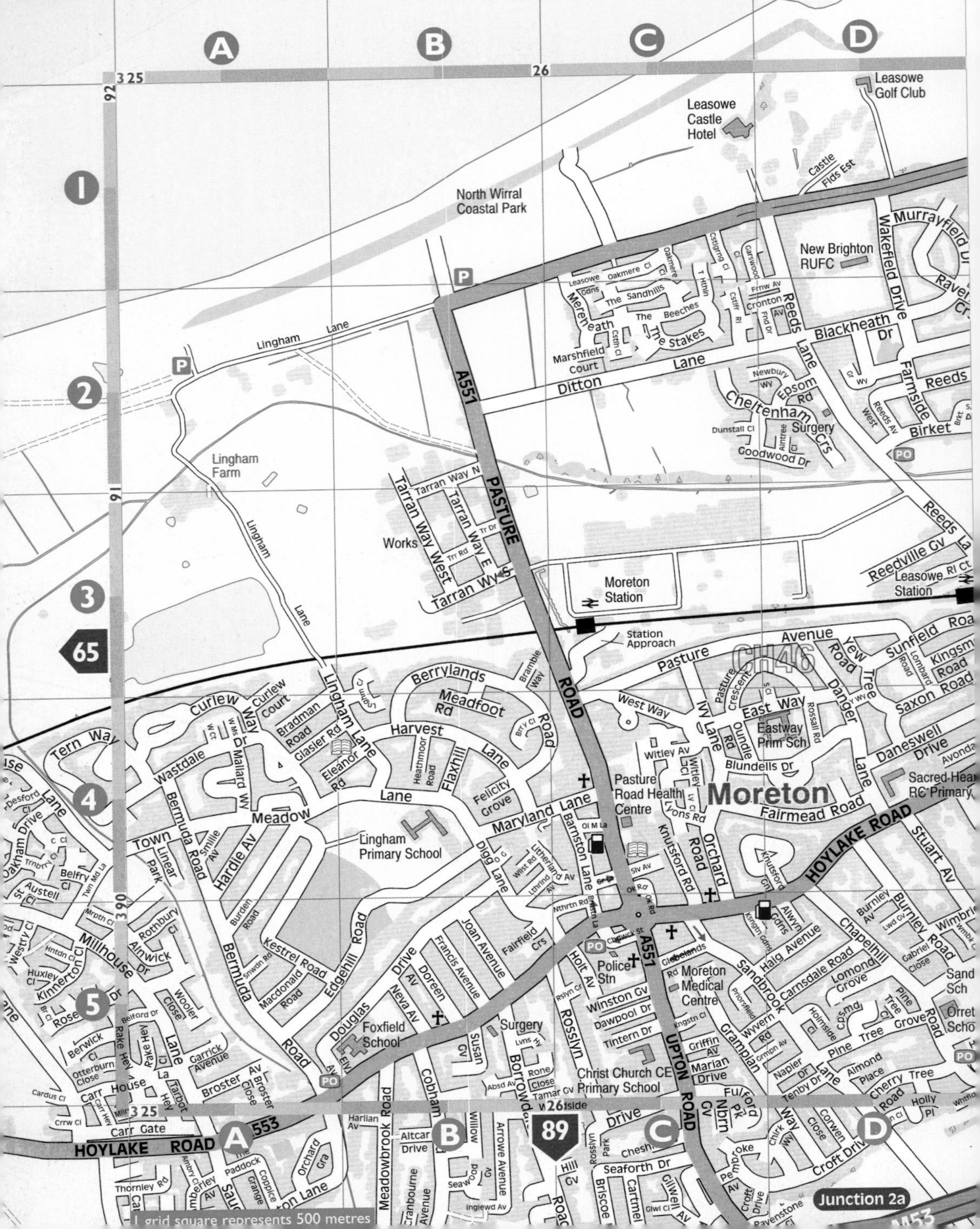
A
B
C
D
325
26
92
91
390
1
2
3
4
5
65
89
Leasowe Golf Club
Leasowe Castle Hotel
Castle
Fids Est
North Wirral Coastal Park
New Brighton RUFC
Wakefield Drive
Murrayfield Dr
Ravel Crs
Lingham Lane
Leasowe Gdns
Oakmere Cl
Oakmere Cl
Cstlgrng Cl
Garswood Cl
The Sandhills
The Beeches
The Stakes
Mereheath
Marshfield Court
Frmw Av
Cronton Av
Fnd Dr
Cstlr Rl
Reeds Lane
Blackheath Dr
Ditton Lane
Newbury Wy
Epsom Rd
Cheltenham Crs
Surgery
Dunstall Cl
Aintree Cl
Goodwood Dr
Farmside
Reeds Av West
Reeds
Birket
PO
A551
PASTURE ROAD
Lingham Farm
Tarran Way N
Tarran Way West
Tarran Way E
Tarran Wy S
Trr Dr
Trr Rd
Works
Lingham Lane
Moreton Station
Station Approach
Reeds La
Reedville Gv
Leasowe Station
Rl Ct
Pasture Avenue
CH46
Yew Tree Road
Sunfield Road
Lombard Road
Kingsmead Road
Saxon Road
Danger Lane
Berrylands
Bramble Way
Meadfoot Rd
Brry Cl
Curlew Way
Curlew Court
Bradman Road
Glasier Rd
Eleanor Rd
Harvest Lane
Heathmoor Road
Flaxhill
Tern Way
Wastdale Dr
Mallard Wy
W Ct
W Ms
West Way
Pasture Crescent
East Way
Eastway Prim Sch
Rossall Rd
Oundle Rd
Ivy Lane
Witley Av
Witley Cl
Blundells Dr
Daneswell Drive
Avondale
Sacred Heart RC Primary
Felicity Grove
Maryland Lane
Pasture Road Health Centre
Moreton
Fairmead Road
HOYLAKE ROAD
Lyons Rd
Ol M La
Meadow Lane
Town Linear Park
Bermuda Road
Smillie Av
Hardie Av
Lingham Primary School
Digg Lane
Litherland Av
Lthrlnd Av
Wllst Rd
Barnston Lane
Slv Av
Knutsford Rd
Orchard Road
Knutsford Grn
Stuart Av
Oakham Drive
Belfry Cl
Austell Cl
Twn Md La
Trnbry
Desford Cl
Lane
Westry Cl
Mrpth Cl
Millhouse Dr
Hntdn Cl
Huxley Cl
Kinnerton Cl
Alnwick Dr
Rothbury Cl
Burden Road
Bermuda Road
Kestrel Road
Macdonald Road
Snwdn Rd
Edgehill Road
Joan Avenue
Fairfield Crs
Nthrtn Rd
Ok Rd
Chadwick St
Glebelands Rd
Knsgtn Gdns
Alwyn Gdns
Burnley Av
Burnley Road
Lwd Gv
Wimbrick
Chapelhill Road
Gabriel Close
Sand Sch
Haig Avenue
Carnsdale Road
Lomond Grove
Pine Tree Grove
Holmside Cl
Cpsmd
Orret Scho
Sandbrook Lane
Priorsfield
Wyvern Rd
Grampian Way
Grmpn Av
Napier Dr
Tenby Dr
Almond Place
Cherry Tree Road
Holly Pl
Whitfld
Police Stn
Moreton Medical Centre
Holt Av
Rslyn Cr
Rosslyn Drive
Winston Gv
Dawpool Dr
Tintern Dr
Kngstn Cl
Griffin Av
Marian Drive
Christ Church CE Primary School
UPTON ROAD
Fulford Pk
Nbrn Gv
Douglas Drive
Neva Av
Doreen Av
Francis Avenue
Foxfield School
Elvl Av
Surgery
Susan Gv
Lyns Hy
Borrowdale
Rone Close
Absd Av
Tamar Gv
Rose Cl
Belford Dr
Berwick Cl
Rake Hey
Lane
Wooler Close
Garrick Avenue
Otterburn Close
Carr House La
Tarbot Hey
Broster Av
Broster Close
Cardus Cl
Carr Hey
Crrw Cl
Carr Gate
HOYLAKE ROAD
A553
Milner
Harlian Av
Meadowbrook Road
Altcar Drive
Cobham
Willow
Arrowe Avenue
Seawood Gv
Cranbourne Avenue
Inglewd Av
Hill Gv
Rosslyn
Park
Drive
Cheshire
Seaforth Dr
Briscoe
Cartmel
Gilwell Av
Glwl Cl
Pembroke Av
Croft Drive
Chirk Wy
Corwen Close
Croft Drive
Ravenstone
Junction 2a
Thornley Rd
Amberley Av
Ambry Cl
Paddock
Grange
Coppice
Orchard Gra
Saughall
Lane
1 grid square represents 500 metres

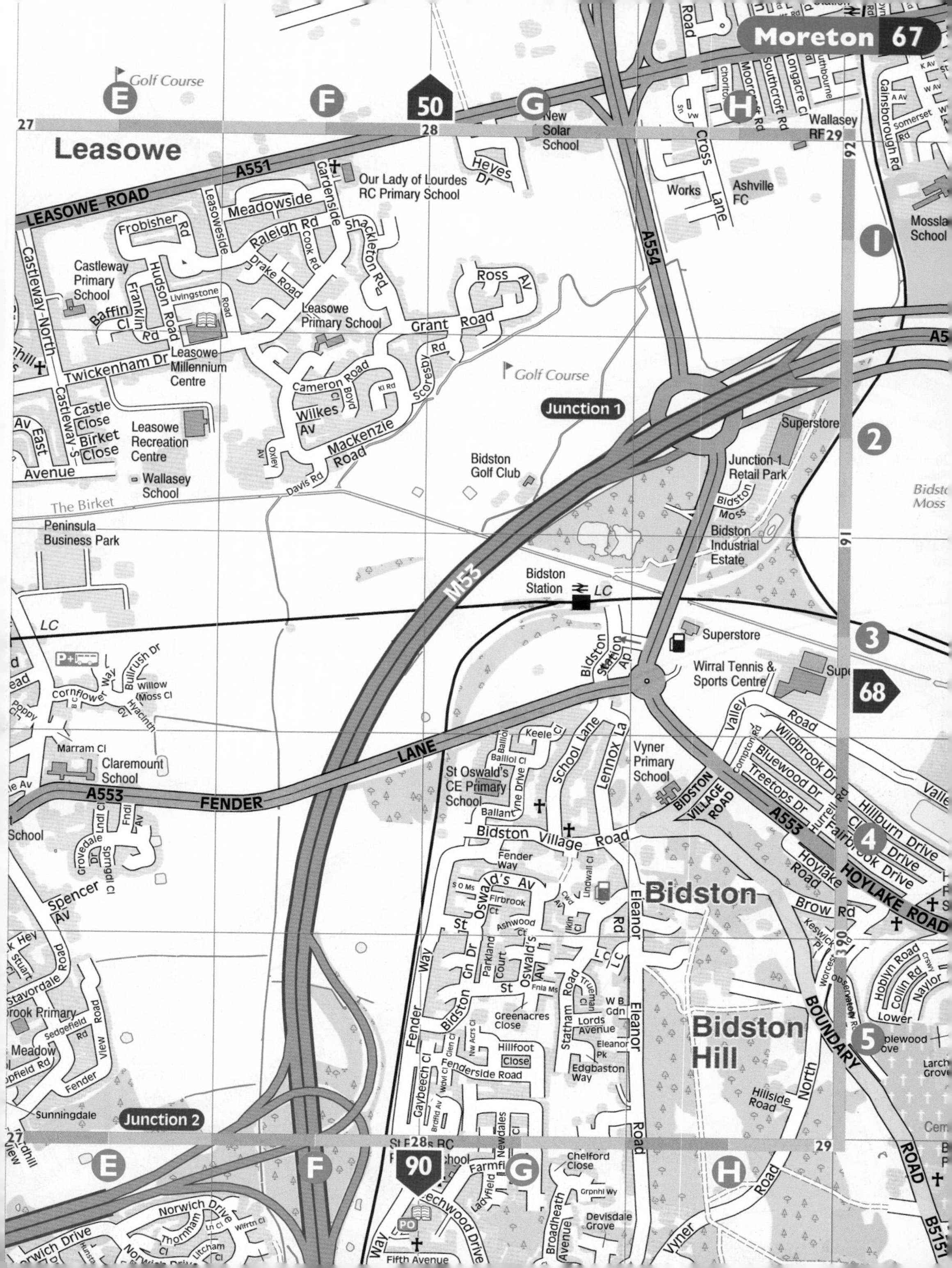
Leasowe
Golf Course
Moreton 67
50
28
29
27
New Solar School
Wallasey RF
Heyes Dr
Cross Lane
Works
Ashville FC
A554
Mossla School
A551
LEASOWE ROAD
Leasoweside
Gardenside
Our Lady of Lourdes RC Primary School
Meadowside
Frobisher Rd
Raleigh Rd
Shackleton Rd
Cook Rd
Drake Road
Castleway North
Castleway Primary School
Hudson Road
Franklin Rd
Baffin Cl
Livingstone Road
Leasowe Primary School
Ross Av
Grant Road
Twickenham Dr
Leasowe Millennium Centre
Scoresby Rd
Cameron Road
Boyd Cl
Kl Rd
Wilkes Av
Oxley Av
Mackenzie Road
Davis Rd
Castle Close
Birket Close
Castleway S
East Av
Avenue
Leasowe Recreation Centre
Wallasey School
Golf Course
Junction 1
Bidston Golf Club
Superstore
Junction 1 Retail Park
Bidston Moss
Bidston Industrial Estate
The Birket
Peninsula Business Park
M53
Bidston Station
LC
Superstore
Bidston Station Ap
Wirral Tennis & Sports Centre
68
Bullrush Dr
Cornflower Way
Willow Moss Cl
Hyacinth Gv
Poppy Cl
Marram Cl
Claremount School
A553
FENDER LANE
Keele Cl
Balliol Cl
School Lane
Lennox La
Vyner Primary School
St Oswald's CE Primary School
Ballantyne Drive
BIDSTON VILLAGE ROAD
Valley Road
Wildbrook Dr
Bluewood Dr
Treetops Dr
Compton Rd
Hurrell Rd
Hillburn Drive
Fairbrook Drive
Hoylake Road
HOYLAKE ROAD
Bidston Village Road
Fender Way
St Oswald's Av
Firbrook Ct
Ashwood Ct
Lindwall Cl
Bidston
Eleanor Rd
Brow Rd
Keswick Pl
Grovedale Rd
Lndl Cl
Fndl Av
Sprngdl Cl
School
Spencer Av
Stavordale Road
Parkland Court
St Oswald's Av
Statham Road
Trueman Cl
Bidston Gn Dr
Greenacres Close
Lords Avenue
Bidston Hill
BOUNDARY ROAD
North Road
Observatory Rd
Hoblyn Road
Collin Rd
Naylor
Lower
Hillside Road
Hillfoot Close
Fenderside Road
Edgbaston Way
Eleanor Pk
Gaybeech Cl
Sedgefield Rd
Fender View Road
Meadow
Sunningdale
Junction 2
E
F
G
H
I
2
3
4
5
90
Chelford Close
Farmfield
Newdales Cl
Ladyfield
Broadheath Avenue
Devisdale Grove
Grpnhl Wy
Vyner Road
Norwich Drive
Thornham Cl
Litcham Cl
Fifth Avenue
Beechwood Drive
PO
B5151

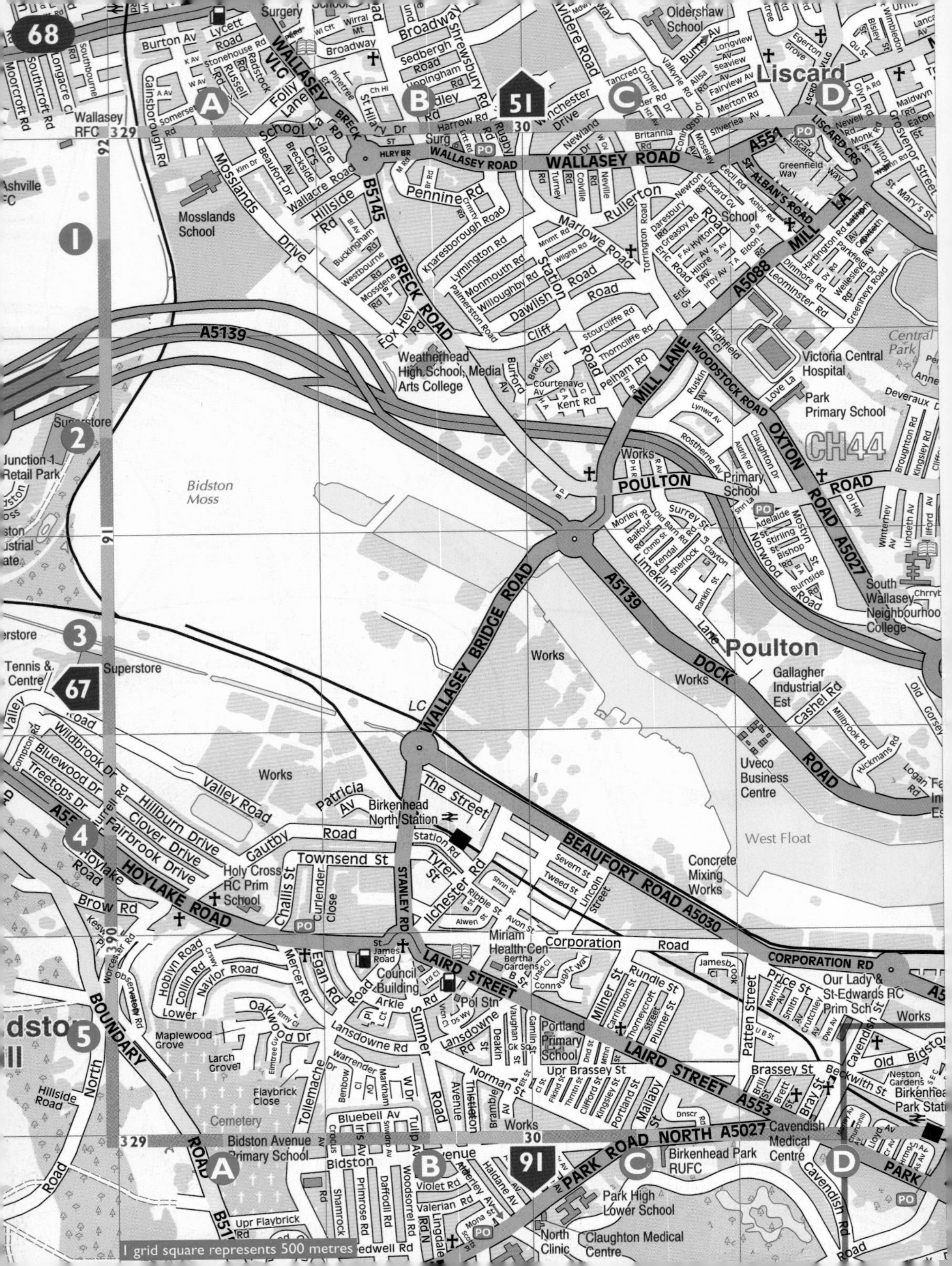
68
51
67
91
Liscard
Poulton
CH44
Bidston Moss
West Float
Central Park
Wallasey RFC
Ashville FC
Mosslands School
Oldershaw School
Weatherhead High School, Media Arts College
Victoria Central Hospital
Park Primary School
South Wallasey Neighbourhood College
Gallagher Industrial Est
Uveco Business Centre
Concrete Mixing Works
Works
Superstore
Junction 1 Retail Park
Tennis & Centre
Birkenhead North Station
Holy Cross RC Prim School
Miriam Health Cen
Bertha Gardens
Council Building
Pol Stn
Portland Primary School
Our Lady & St Edwards RC Prim Sch
Cavendish Medical Centre
Birkenhead Park RUFC
Park High Lower School
North Clinic
Claughton Medical Centre
Bidston Avenue Primary School
Cemetery
Surgery
Surg
PO
A5139
A551
A5088
A5027
A5030
A553
B5145
WALLASEY ROAD
WALLASEY VLG
BRECK RD
BRECK ROAD
MILL LANE
MILL LA
WOODSTOCK ROAD
OXTON ROAD
POULTON ROAD
WALLASEY BRIDGE ROAD
DOCK ROAD
BEAUFORT ROAD A5030
CORPORATION RD
Corporation Road
LAIRD STREET
HOYLAKE ROAD
BOUNDARY ROAD
PARK ROAD NORTH A5027
STANLEY RD
LISCARD CRS
ST ALBAN'S ROAD
Valley Road
Gautby Road
Hillburn Drive
Clover Drive
Fairbrook Drive
Townsend St
Limekiln Lane
Station Road
Marlowe Road
Rullerton Road
Pennine Rd
Mosslands Drive
Dawlish Road
Cliff Road
Broadway
Winchester Drive
Lansdowne Rd
Sumner Road
Bidston
Upr Flaybrick Rd
Upr Brassey St
Brassey St
Cavendish Rd
Old Bidston
1 grid square represents 500 metres
329
390
30
91
92

WALLASEY
Egremont
Seacombe
52
70
92
2
3
E
F
G
H
1
2
3
4
5
32
33
92
91
390
MANOR ROAD
Lane
Greenwood
Stringhey Road
Trafalgar Rd
St Lucia Rd
St Bride's Rd
Promenade
King Street
Kinglake Rd
St Vincent Rd
Wright Street
Tobin St
Rice Lane
Rice Hey Road
Lea Road
Charlotte Rd
Serpentine Road
The Summit
Martin's La
Central Pk Av
Empress Rd
Hawarden Avenue
Rosebery Av
Crescent Rd
Water St
Guildford St
Med Cen
Union St
Church Street
Church Cl
Church Lane
Egremont Prim Sch
Falkland Road
Clarendon Road
Littledale Road
Buchanan Road
Bell Road
Rappart Road
Kenilworth Rd
Brougham Road
Albemarle Rd
Edith Rd
Florence Rd
Harcourt St
Elmswood Rd
Riversdale Rd
Sandon Rd
Harrowby Rd
Seacombe Promenade
Town Hall
Council Offices
Riverview Rd
Guinea Gap Baths & Recreation Centre
Riverside Primary School
A554
BRIGHTON STREET
LISCARD ROAD
A551
Raymond Road
Parkside
Rivington Rd
Alverstone Rd
Lumley Rd
Withington Rd
Silverbeech Rd
Sherwood Rd
Ladywood Rd
Lonsboro Rd
Canterbury Rd
Hampstead Road
Barrington Road
Birnam Rd
Northbrook Rd
Walsingham Rd
Hartismere Rd
Walsingham Court
MAINWARING RD
Liscard Rd
Deveraux Dr
Erskine Rd
Surgery
School
B5145
BOROUGH ROAD
Demesne St
East Park Court
North Park Court
South Park Court
Priory Rd
Lowry Bank
Borough Way
Ferry Vw Rd
Fell St
Ferryside
Seacombe Vw
Kgn Dr
Victoria Place
KINGSWAY
Seacombe Ferry Terminal
DOUGLAS
DUBLIN
BELFAST
DUBLIN
Liverpool
Wirral
Halstead Rd
Brentwood St
Eastcroft Road
Greencroft Rd
Hillcroft Road
Mercroft Av
Lyncroft Rd
Rycroft Road
Ashville Rd
York Av
May Av
York Rd
Clarence Rd
Naples Rd
Oakdale Rd
Milton Rd
Shakespeare Rd
Lucerne Rd
Geneva Rd
WHEATLAND LANE
Primary School
Wickham Cl
Hatherley St
Stanley St
Belle Vue Rd
Luke St
Peter St
Gorse Crs
Beechcroft Rd
Gorsedale Road
Kingsway Primary School
KINGSWAY (TUNNEL)
Toll
St Paul's Rd
Matthew St
CHURCH RD
Vernon Av
Palermo
Palatine Rd
Percy Rd
Hawthorne Gv
Bridle Rd
St Pauls Av
Bridle Av
New Street
Council Building
New Way Business Centre
Oakdale Av
Wheatland Business Park
Wheatland La
BIRKENHEAD ROAD
GORSEY LA
Wirral Business Centre
SMM Business Park
Oakdale Rd
Citrine Rd
Westfield Road
Sovereign Wy
DOCK ROAD
KELVIN ROAD
Alfred Road
Corbyn St
Montrose Av
Works
East Street
Scotts Quays
Kings Whf
Kelvinside
Kelvin Park
Historic Warships
DUKE STREET
A5027
East Float
Twelve Quays Ferry Terminal
LC
CORPORATION ROAD
DUKE ST
Maddock St
Price Street Business Centre
Arthur St
Brd St
Berner St
Vdn St
Hilbre St
Lynas St
Neptune St
B5146
CH41
Cleveland Business Park
Brook Street
CLEVELAND STREET
Fieldway
Fieldway Ct
Parkview
Vittoria Medical Centre
Cottage St
Pool St
Freeman St
TOWER ROAD
Tower Wharf
Morpeth Wharf
Egerton Dock
Egerton Whf
Morpeth Dock
QUEENSWAY (MERSEY TUNNEL)
Wirral Metropolitan College
CANNING STREET
Woodside Business Park
Pacific Rd
Hamilton Square Stn
Pump Ho Mus
Cncl Bldg
Woodside Ferry Landing Stage
Harcourt St
Arthur Street
Aspinall St
Newling St
Pr Edward
Livingstone Street
Livingstone Gdns
The Priory CE Primary School
Rosebank
Price Street
Finch Court
Brooklands
St Anne Way
Prim Sch
Vittoria Court
Wood St
Bridge St
Taylor St
George St
Lord St
Sandford St
Sidney St
Brook St
ROAD
NORTH

LIVERPOOL
Vauxhall
Nelson Dock
Trafalgar Dock
Princes Dock
George's Dock
Albert Dock
Wapping Basin
Kings Dock
REGENT RD
Walter St
Works
Stanley Dock
Bentinck St
Denbigh St
Lightbody Street
Houlgrave Rd
Canalside Grove
Hopwood St
Ashfield St
Herm Road
Silvester St
Lyle St
Bangor St
Benledi St
Boston St
St Brigids Crescent
Colin Dr
Francine Cl
SCOTLAND ROAD
Saltney Street
Dublin Street
Dickson Street
Cotton Street
Carlton Street
Regent Street
Porter Street
Vulcan Street
Vandries Street
Oil Street
Sherwood St
Maddrell St
Clegg St
Stone St
Upr William St
Whitley St
Sprainger St
Ltl Howard St
A565
GREAT HOWARD STREET
Love Lane
Eldonian Way
Elaine Norris Sports Cen
Blenheim Street
Tatlock St
Titchfield St
Vescock St
Limekiln Lane
Limekiln Court
Health Cen
Raymond Place
Mile End
Steinberg Ct
Fleming Ct
Portland Gardens
Green St
Burlington St
Burlington Street
O'Connell Rd
Eldon St
Bond St
Bevington St
Summer Seat
Kings Industrial Park
The Trinity RC Prim Sch
Chisenhale Street
Council Building
Superstore
Retail Park
Chadwick Court Industrial Cen
Carruthers St
Ford Street
Blackstock Street
Pumpfields Rd
College
Paul Street
Oriel Street
Naylor Street
Atlantic Point Village
Vauxhall Business Centre
Eaton St
Gascoyn St
Phillips St
Freemasons Rw
Pall Mall
Vauxhall Rd
Leeds Street
A5053
Ind Est
Holy Cross Catholic Prim Sch
Liverpool John Moores University
Central Library
(TUNNEL)
KINGSWAY
Liverpool Wirral
King Edward Industrial Estate
King Edward Industrial Est
DOUGLAS
DUBLIN
BELFAST
DUBLIN
BATH ST A5036
Princes Parade
William Jessop Way
Isle of Man Ferry Terminal
Crowne Plaza Hotel
St Nicholas Place
Titanic Memorial
Royal Liver Bldg
Cunard Building
Mersey Ferries
Pier Head
War Meml
NEW QUAY
THE STRAND
CHAPEL ST
WATER ST
Town Hall
Cabinet War Rooms
Newspaper Office
Cncl Bldg
TITHEBARN ST
DALE ST
Moorfields Station
Co Fire HQ
Hatton Gdn
CT CROSSHALL ST
Police Stn
LJMU
Travelodge
St George's Hall
Mkt
St Johns Shopping Cen
St John's Beacon
Radio City
Med Cen
HM Coroners Court
Cavern Club
Mathew St
Lord St
Derby Square
James Street Stn
JAMES ST
Queen Elizabeth II Law Courts
BBC Radio
Police Station
Central Stn
SAE Institute
Mann Island
Port of Liverpool Building
Museum of Liverpool (due to open 2010)
HM Customs & Excise Nat Museum
Merseyside Maritime Museum & International Slavery Museum
Fingerprints of Elvis
Tate Gallery
Albert Dock Village
The Beatles Story
Premier Travel Inn
Granada TV
National Discovery Park
Fire Stn
A5041
CANNING PL
Merseyside Police HQ
STRAND STREET
STRAND ST
LIVER ST
PARADISE ST
Duke St
Hotel Ibis
YHA
PARK LANE
WAPPING A562
Upr Frederick St
Prim Sch
Coll
QUEENSWAY (MERSEY TUNNEL)
Woodside Business Park
Pacific Rd
Pump Ho Mus
Cncl Bldg
Woodside Ferry Landing Stage
Wapping Quay
Waterfront Business Area
Parliament St
N Waterfront Bus Area
Queens Wharf
Kings Dock St
Jamaica Street
A561
Health Cen
L3
A
B
C
D
1
2
3
4
5
53
6
69
93
333
34
92
91
390
1 grid square represents 500 metres

Clinic
Conway St
CE Primary School
Comprehensive Sch
Great Homer Street Medical Centre
St Anthony's Shopping Cen
Hamilton Road
Cochrane Street
NORTH
HEYWORTH
BRECK
ROAD
Richmond Ter
Everton
54
Prince Edwin Adult Centre
Roscommon St
Campion Catholic High School
NETHERFIELD RD STH
Everton Terrace
A580
STREET
Tavy Rd
Queens Road
Whitefield Prim Sch
Boundary Lane
White Rock St
Conwy Drive
Cardigan Wy
A5049
ROCKY
B5188 SHEIL ROAD
Denman
Spencer Street
Margaret St
Shakespeare
Kilshaw Street
Hygeia Street
WEST DERBY ROAD
Edwin Street
Prince
Everton Brow
Faith Primary School
Rose Pl
Richmond Row
Halgh Street
SHAW STREET
Eastbourne Way
Cresswell St Hlth Clinic
EVERTON ROAD
Mill Road
Caird St
Primary School
Boaler
Council Building
Boaler Street Industrial Est
New Park Primary Sch
Farnworth St
William Henry St
Whitley Gardens
Gregson Street
Brougham Terrace
Hutchinson
Upr Baker St
Works
Molyneux Road
ST ANNE STREET
B5173
Langsdale St
University
College St N
Medical Cen
BRUNSWICK ROAD
Carver Street
Trafalgar Way
Erskine Street Industrial Estate
Phythian
Police Sta
Kensington Medical Cen
Med Cen
County Sessions Ho
ISLINGTON
Surgery
Cncl Bldg
MOSS ST
PRESCOT STREET
KENSINGTON A57
Hebrew Cem
LONDON ROAD
Superstore
Academy
London Rd
Roy Castle International Cen for Lung Research
Royal Liverpool University Hospital
University of Liverpool
A&E
HALL LANE
Albany Road
Empress Road
Adelaide Road
Jubilee Drive
Kensington CP J&I Schools
Cotswold Street
Fell Street
Ling Street
PEMBROKE PLACE
DAULBY ST
Sacred Heart RC Primary School
Kensington
72
A5047
Lime Street Station
Sorting Office
Russell St
Gt Newton St
Gill St
University of Liverpool
WEST DERBY ST
MOUNT VERNON
NORTH VIEW A5047
Edge La Medical Cen
EDGE LANE
Royston Street
IRVINE ST
Gladstone Road
DURNING ROAD
Health Cen
LIME ST
Brownlow Hill
LJMU Primary School
Metropolitan Cathedral of Christ the King
Archbishop Blanch CE High School
Smithdown Lane
Highgate St
WAVERTREE ROAD
RENSHAW
A5038
Mount Pleasant
YMCA
Everyman Thtr
University of Liverpool Sports Cen
CROWN ST
A5048
Works
Chatham Place
Police Stn
Harbord St
A5089
Wavertree Retail Park
Shop Centre
Oxford Street
Grinfield St
Works
Edge Hill
School
Edge Hill Station
Clinic
Health Cen
Liverpool John Moores University
Cambridge St
University of Liverpool
Liverpool Community College
Orphan St
Cardwell St
Primary School
BERRY ST
Community College
Philharmonic Hall
GROVE ST
Myrtle St
Liverpool Community College
Longstone Walk
Angela St
TUNNEL ROAD
Spekeland
Chinese Arch
Natural Hlth Cen
Community Cen
Abercromby Health Centre
Falkner St
Works
Tideswell Cl
Prim Sch
Health Cen
Toxteth Community College
Harding St
Med Cen
Earle
LJMU
Canning St
Liverpool Womens Hospital
Charles Wooton Cen of FE
Liverpool Anglican Cathedral
Huskisson Street
94
A562
Princes Special School
Newstead Abbey
GT GEORGE ST
Lady Chapel Close
Egerton Street
STREET
Beaumont St
Elimu Academy
PARLIAMENT
Hampton St
Selborne Street
Grierson St

72
55
71
95
A
B
C
D
1
2
3
4
5
337
38
390
92
16
L6
L7
L13
L15
Tuebrook
The Priory Medical Centre
Radnor Medical Cen
Police Station
Cemetery
St Cecilias RC J&I School
Rockbank Road
Richland Road
Russian Drive
Moscow Drive
Magnus Cl
Rock Lane
A5049
Belmont Drive
Newsham Dr
Orphan
New Road
Oak Leigh
Ivy Leigh
Snaefell Av
Snaefell Grove
Sutton St
Brainerd Street
Balmoral Court
Belmont Road
Back Belmont Rd
Sunlight St
Hampson St
Rossett St
Scorton St
Grange St
Gwent Cl
Lincoln Close
Cardigan Wy
Conwy Drive
Jade Rd
Derby Road
Primary School
Boaler St
Lister Drive Infant School
Lister Drive Junior Sch
Lister Drive
Carnegie Rd
Green Lane
Tynwald Hill
Douglas Cl
Woburn Hill
Guernsey Rd
Portelet Rd
Sark Rd
Brelade Rd
Derwent Rd
Cheadle Av
Etna St
Newsham Park
The Academy of St Francis of Assisi
Gardner's Drive
Gardner's Dr
Council Building
Fairfield Medical Cen
Strathmore Rd
Denman Wy
Denman Dr
B5188 Sheil Road
Kenley Parade
Pendine Cl
Carstairs Road
Hampstead Road
Marcot Rd
Hendon Rd
Callander Rd
Elstree Rd
Prospect Vale
Fairfield Crs
Newton Road
Huntly Road
Radstock Road
Swiss Road
Geneva Rd
Malvern Rd
Maiden Rd
Mallow Rd
Maxton Rd
Manton Rd
Channell Rd
Ridley Rd
Bigham Rd
Med Cen
Ottley St
Kelso Rd
Parton St
Hinton St
Onslow Road
Rufford Road
Balmoral Road
Whitland Road
Whitcroft Road
Grove Road
Works
Surgery
Prescot Drive
Prescot Road
A57
Council Building
St Cuthberts RC Primary School
Church Road
Ennismore Road
Gidlow Road
Herrick Street
Ronald Street
Maskell Road
Fairfield
University
Laurel Business Cen
Laurel Road
Lister Crs
Lister Road
Lockerby Road
Lilley Road
Rawlins Street
Holland Street
Freehold Street
Stanley Street
Lorne Street
Fairfield Street
Lindale Rd
Middleton Rd
Cheviot Rd
Edge Grove
Lomond Rd
Grampian Rd
Selkirk Rd
Abergele Rd
Colwyn Rd
Pensarn Rd
Rhuddlan Cl
Ardleigh Rd
Hebrew Cem
Gilead St
Hawkins St
Grantham St
Holt Road
Deane Road
Beech Street
Holly Road
Botanic Pl
Birchfield Rd
Phoenix Primary School
St Sebastians Primary School
Edge Lane
A5047
Edge Lane Retail Park
Thistlewood Road
Tattersall Wy
Milton Rd
Montrose Wy
Cineworld Liverpool
Edge Lane Retail Park
Ling Street
Toft St
Kensington J&I Schools
Wimpole St
Stamford St
Cliff St
Wrenbury Street
Botanic Grove
Botanic Road
Durning Road
Works
Botanic Estate
Wavertree Technology Park
Dryden Road
Binns Road Industrial Estate
Binns Road
Binns Way
Crawford Way
Virgin Cinemas
Hollywood Superbowl
Pighue Lane
Newton Ct
Faraday Rd
Tapton Way
Rutherford Cl
Wavertree Avenue
Rathbone Road
Health Cen
Crosfield Rd
Arnside Rd
Hawthorne Grove
Plimsoll St
Milroy St
Nuttall St
Wavertree Park
Wavertree Boulevard
Wavertree Bvd S
Wavertree Road
Police Stn
Harbord St
Chandos St
B5178
Wavertree Retail Park
Combermere Street
Enterprise Wy
Stephenson Way
Bonchurch Drive
Shanklin Rd
Sandown Rd
Ventnor Rd
Edge Hill
Edge Hill Station
A5089
Tunnel Road
Uxbridge St
Chatsworth Dr
Works
Alexandra Rd
Bridge Rd
Spofforth Road
Alfred St
Cambridge St
Cecil St
Kempton Rd
Picton Road
Larkfield Vw
Tiverton St
Taunton St
Hey Gn Rd
Stevenson St
Comm Prim Sch
Long Lane
Sunningdale Rd
Wavertree CC
Northdale Rd
Westdale Rd
Southdale Rd
Eastdale Rd
Sandown Lane
Olive Lane
Orford St
Spekeland Road
Cadogan St
Cardigan St
Ashfield
Ash Grove
Bishopgate St
Macdonald St
Methuen St
Strathcona Road
Surgery
Broxton St
Prim Sch
Abney Cl
Tideswell Cl
Rokesmith Av
Hawdon Ct
Earle Rd Med Ctr
Earle Road
Galloway St
School
Med Cen
Works
High St
Wellington Road
Newstead Abbey
Elimu Academy
Grierson St
Smithdown Road
Mulliner St
Tunstall St
Garrick St
Webster Road
Cranborne Road
Salisbury Road
Alderson Road
Tabley Rd
Callow Rd
Lawrence Road
Plumer St
Whitman St
Rexmore
Wavertree CE Prim Sch
Pearson
Wavertree Athletics Centre
1 grid square represents 500 metres

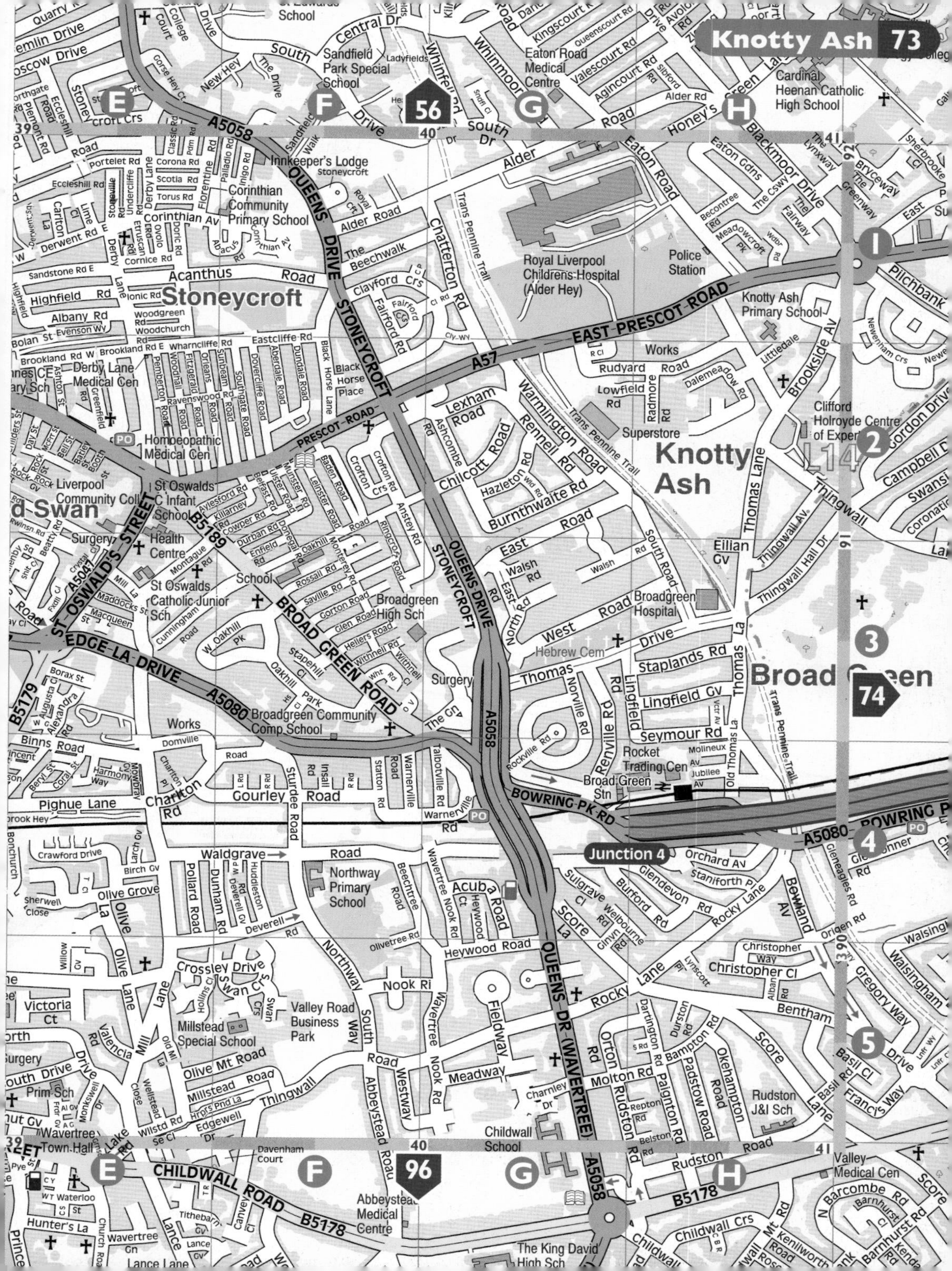
Stoneycroft
Knotty Ash
Broad Green
Swan
A5058
QUEENS DRIVE STONEYCROFT
EAST PRESCOT ROAD
A57
PRESCOT ROAD
EDGE LA DRIVE
A5080
BROAD GREEN ROAD
B5189
ST OSWALD'S STREET
A5047
BOWRING PK RD
QUEENS DR (WAVERTREE)
CHILDWALL ROAD
B5178
B5179
Junction 4
Royal Liverpool Childrens Hospital (Alder Hey)
Police Station
Knotty Ash Primary School
Cardinal Heenan Catholic High School
Eaton Road Medical Centre
Sandfield Park Special School
Innkeeper's Lodge Stoneycroft
Corinthian Community Primary School
Derby Lane Medical Cen
Homoeopathic Medical Cen
Liverpool Community Coll
St Oswalds C Infant School
Health Centre
St Oswalds Catholic Junior Sch
Broadgreen High Sch
Broadgreen Community Comp School
Broadgreen Hospital
Hebrew Cem
Rocket Trading Cen
Broad Green Stn
Superstore
Works
Northway Primary School
Valley Road Business Park
Millstead Special School
Rudston J&I Sch
Childwall School
Valley Medical Cen
Abbeystead Medical Centre
The King David High Sch
Wavertree Town Hall
Clifford Holroyde Centre of Exper
Trans Pennine Trail
Alder Road
Eaton Road
Acanthus Road
Thomas Lane
Thingwall
Rocky Lane
Score Lane
Mill Lane
Olive Lane
Heywood Road
Gourley Road
Pighue Lane
Sturdee Road
Rudston Road
56
74
96
E
F
G
H
1
2
3
4
5
39
40
41

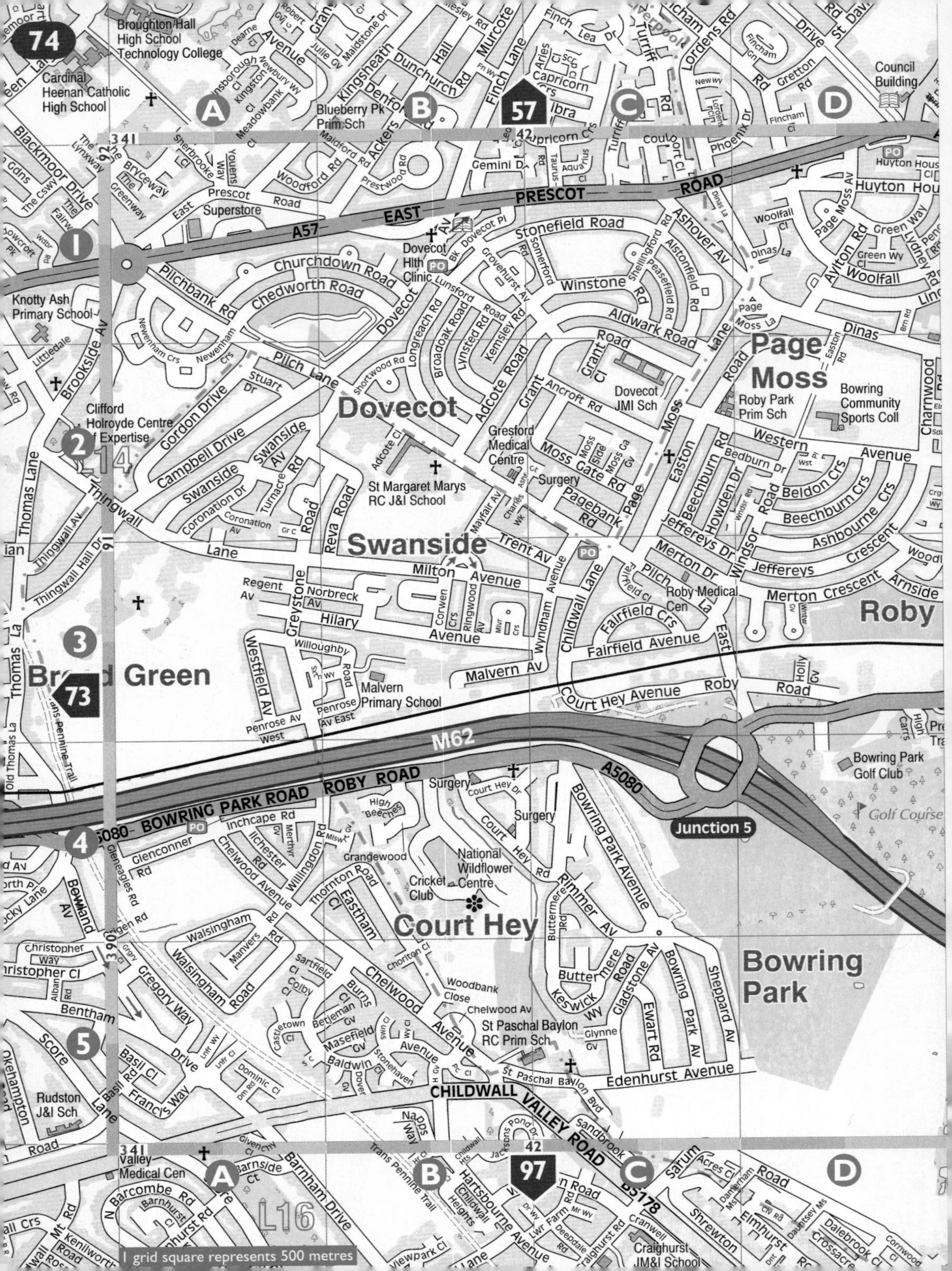
74
57
73
97
A
B
C
D
1
2
3
4
5
341
342
390
391
392
Broughton Hall High School Technology College
Cardinal Heenan Catholic High School
Blueberry Pk Prim Sch
Council Building
Knotty Ash Primary School
Clifford Holroyde Centre of Expertise
L14
Dovecot
Dovecot Hlth Clinic
Page Moss
Roby Park Prim Sch
Bowring Community Sports Coll
Dovecot JMI Sch
Gresford Medical Centre
Surgery
St Margaret Marys RC J&I School
Swanside
Roby Medical Cen
Roby
Broad Green
Malvern Primary School
Bowring Park Golf Club
Golf Course
Junction 5
National Wildflower Centre
Cricket Club
Court Hey
Bowring Park
St Paschal Baylon RC Prim Sch
Rudston J&I Sch
Valley Medical Cen
L16
Craighurst JM&I School
EAST PRESCOT ROAD
A57
M62
A5080
BOWRING PARK ROAD
ROBY ROAD
CHILDWALL VALLEY ROAD
B5178
Trans Pennine Trail
Superstore
Pilch Lane
Thingwall Lane
Thomas Lane
Childwall Lane
Page Moss Lane
Moss Lane
Bowring Park Avenue
Court Hey Avenue
Edenhurst Avenue
Chelwood Avenue
Score Lane
Western Avenue
Jeffereys Crescent
Merton Crescent
Fairfield Avenue
Milton Avenue
Hilary Avenue
Churchdown Road
Chedworth Road
Stonefield Road
Aldwark Road
Winstone Rd
Adcote Road
Gordon Drive
Campbell Drive
Reva Road
Walsingham Road
Gregory Way
Francis Way
Barnham Drive
Hartsbourne Avenue
1 grid square represents 500 metres

Woolfall Heath
HUYTON-WITH-ROBY
Huyton
Longview
Huyton Park
L36
58
76
98
E
F
G
H
1
2
3
4
5
43
44
45
92
91
390
Cornerways Medical Centre
Woolfall Heath Av
Liverpool Road
A57
B5198
Endmoor Road
Cartmel
Altmoor Rd
Pennard Av
Liverpool Rd
Butleigh Road
Primrose
Moorcroft Rd
Bridge Rd
Surgery
Alt Bridge Secondary Support Centre
Knowsley Central Primary Support Centre
Glade Rd
Brookwood Road
Bakers Green Road
Mossbrow Road
Wellcroft Rd
Midway Road
Paxton Rd
Adswood Rd
Alt Road
The Garth
St Mathew's Cl
Huyton Lane
Cotsford Road
Park View
Park View Primary School
Twig Lane Clnc
St Aloysius RC Primary School
Dinas Lane Medical Centre
Centwood Rd
Kingsway
Crownway
Cuper Crs
Pine Close
Montgomery Rd
Alamein Road
Tobruk Rd
Ironside Rd
Arnhem Road
Derna
Salerno
Rome Cl
Malta Cl
Drive
Blue Bell Lane
Reeds Rd
Slim Rd
St Joseph's RC Primary School
St Aidans RC Prim Sch
St Thomas Becket School
Jacqueline Drive
Lancaster Rd
Wallace Av
Longview Lane
Longview Dr
Coral Av
Crosswood Crs
White Ldg Av
Normandy Rd
Oran Wy
Cassino Road
Gort Rd
St Michaels Ct
The Av
Capper Gv
Rupert Road
Huyton with Roby CE Prim Sch
Stanley Road
ARCHWAY ROAD
B5199
Lathom Road Health Cen
Knowsley Magistrates Court
Police Stn
Lathom Rd
Huyton Church Rd
Knowsley Hey School
Attlee Road
Hardie
Lansbury
Forest Dr
Stanhope Dr
Hawthorn Road
Knowsley Community College (Roby Campus)
Council Building
Larch Road
Briar Dr
Knowsley Comm Coll
Poplar Bank
Derby Rd
Victoria Road
Hey Rd
Seel Road
St Gabriels
Church Road
Bridge Rd
Roby Station
Olive Grove
Grinton Crescent
Fernbank Av
Ellison Grove
Huyton Station
Huyton Hey Rd
Hey Rd
Sawpit La
Derby St
ROBY ROAD
A5080
Station Rd
Anderton Ter
Eaton Cl
Roby Mt Av
Ashdale
Blacklow Brow
The Orch
St Mary's St
Graham's Rd
Agnes Road
Wilson Road
Wilson Bus Centre
Boxwood Cl
Wynwood Pk
Lawton Rd
Huyton Leisure Centre
Waterside Park
Carr Lane
Council Building
The Rooley
Wilton Rd
Harrison Hey
The Pk
The Park
Greenhill Pl
Rydal Rd
Oakwood Dr
St Agnes RC Primary School
Muirfield Rd
Newbury Cl
Blacklow Brow Prim Sch
TARBOCK ROAD
Talbot Ct
College Flds
St Anne's Rd
St Mark's Rd
St John's Road
Sylvester Primary School
Byron
Shelley
Keats Gn
Interchange Motorway Est
Twickenham Crs
Twickenham Drive
St Annes RC Prim Sch
Marina Crs
Ruskin Wy
Cedar Crs
Charlwood Av
Surgery
Belfield Crs
Crossvale Rd
Glendevon Rd
Birch Rd
Oak Cottage Medical Cen
Beech Rd
Manor Farm Rd
Surgery
Manor Farm Medical Cen
Browning Cl
Wordsworth Way
Cowper Wy
Kipling Av
Acacia Avenue
Oak Rd
Pine Tree Rd
Chestnut Av
Lilac Gv
Cypress Rd
Rowan Gv
Oak Road
Yew Tree Rd
Laburnum Av
Laurel Gv
Pear Tree Rd
Cherry Tree Road
Sycamore Rd
Linden Dr
Ash Crs
Wokingham Gv
Field's End
Greenfield Dr
Deepfield Dr
Oakfield Drive
Meadow Drive
Fieldway
Alder Av
Elizabeth Rd
Boundary Road
Tarbock Rd
Manley Rd
Wantage Vw
Old Dover Rd
Oulton Lane
Silverstone Dr
Willow Av
Silverdale
M62
The Chase
Huyton Brook
Biglands Dr
Cornel Wy
Mallow Wy
Rickman Wy
Camplor
A5080
Wheat Hill Rd
Wheathill Farm
Lakeside School
Hope School
Naylor's
Drive
Holt Lane
The Childwall
Bardley
Hawke
Oakworth
Richmond Way

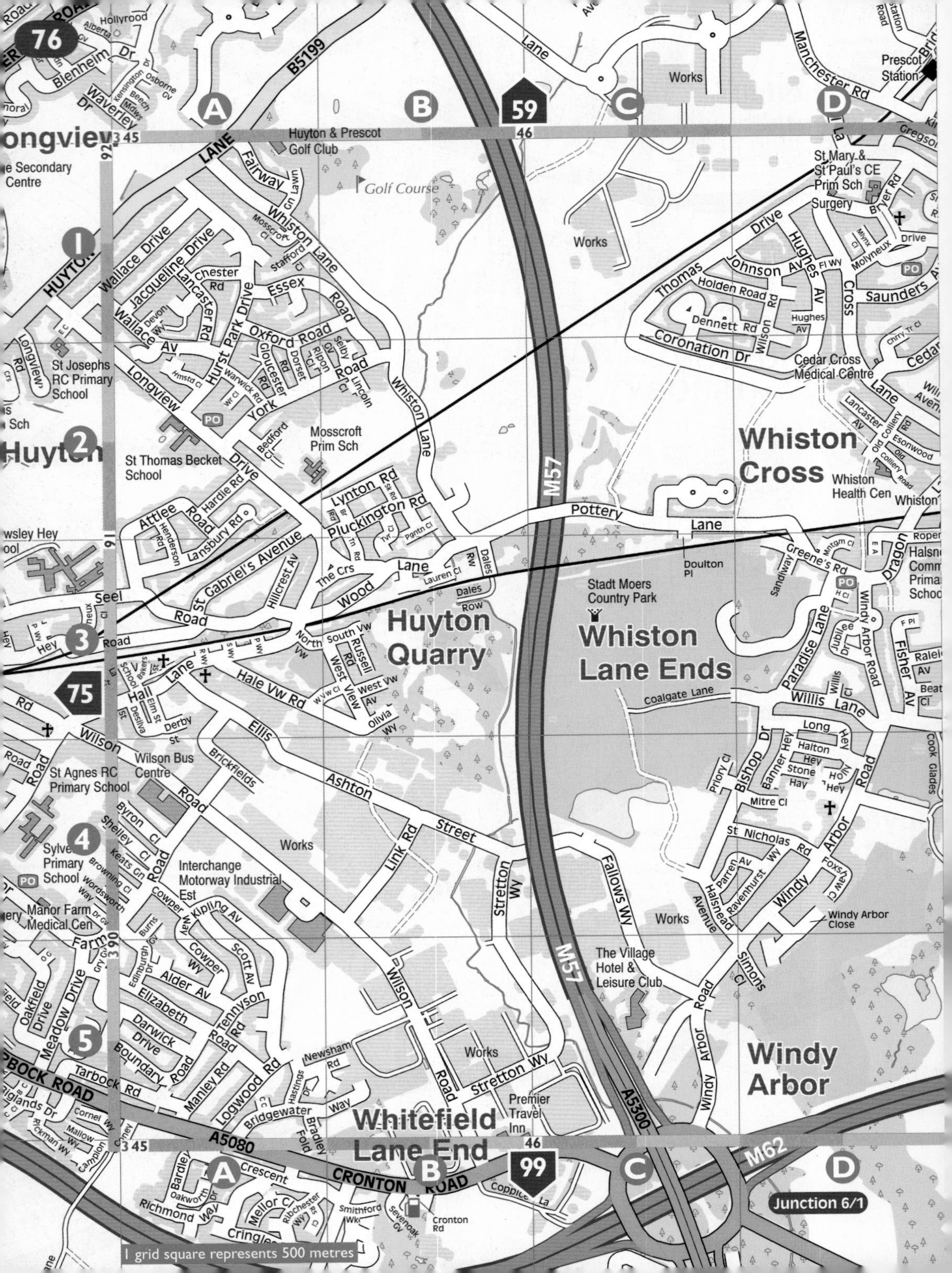

76
59
75
99
A
B
C
D
1
2
3
4
5
345
46
392
391
390
Hollyrood
Alberta Gv
Blenheim Dr
Kensington Dr
Osborne Gv
Beech Mdws
Waverley Dr
B5199
Longview
Secondary Centre
Huyton & Prescot Golf Club
Golf Course
Lane
Works
Manchester Rd
Prescot Station
Gregson
St Mary & St Paul's CE Prim Sch
Surgery
Bryer Rd
Molyneux Drive
Saunders Av
Cedar Cross Medical Centre
Whiston Cross
Whiston Health Cen
LANE
HUYTON
Fairway
Gn Lawn
Mosscroft Cl
Whiston Lane
Stafford Cl
Wallace Drive
Jacqueline Drive
Lancaster Rd
Chester Rd
Essex Road
Hurst Park Drive
Oxford Road
Gloucester Rd
Dorset Rd
Selby Gv
Ripon Cl
Lincoln Cl
Road
Devon Wy
Wallace Av
Hmstd Cl
Warwick Rd
Wr Cl
York
Longview Drive
PO
Bedford Cl
Mosscroft Prim Sch
St Joseph's RC Primary School
Sch
Huyton
St Thomas Becket School
Hardie Rd
Attlee Road
Henderson Rd
Lansbury Rd
St Gabriel's Avenue
Hillcrest Av
Lynton Rd
Pluckington Rd
Pgntn Cl
Tyr Cl
The Crs
Wood Lane
Lauren Cl
Dales Row
Dales Rw
Huyton Quarry
North Vw
South Vw
Russell Rd
West View
West Vw Av
Olivia Wy
Hale Vw Rd
Seel Road
Hey Road
Hall Lane
School
Elm St
Derby St
Ellis
Ashton Street
Wilson Road
Wilson Bus Centre
Brickfields
St Agnes RC Primary School
Byron Cl
Shelley Cl
Keats Gn
Browning Cl
Wordsworth Way
Sylvester Primary School
Manor Farm Medical Cen
Farm
Interchange Motorway Industrial Est
Works
Link Rd
Cowper Wy
Kipling Av
Scott Av
Burns
Edinburgh Dr
Alder Av
Elizabeth Road
Tennyson Rd
Darwick Drive
Boundary Road
Oakfield Drive
Meadow Drive
Tarbock Rd
TARBOCK ROAD
Manley Rd
Logwood Rd
Newsham Rd
Hastings Dr
Bridgewater Way
Bradley Fold
Whitefield Lane End
Premier Travel Inn
Stretton Wy
A5080
CRONTON ROAD
Crescent
Bardley
Oakworth Dr
Richmond Way
Mellor Cl
Ribchester Wy
Cringle
Smithford Wk
Sevenoak Gv
Cronton Rd
Coppice La
M57
Pottery Lane
Doulton Pl
Stadt Moers Country Park
Whiston Lane Ends
Coalgate Lane
Fallows Wy
The Village Hotel & Leisure Club
A5300
M62
Junction 6/1
Windy Arbor
Windy Arbor Road
Windy Arbor Close
Simons Cl
Halsnead Avenue
Ravenhurst Wy
Parren Av
St Nicholas Rd
Mitre Cl
Bishop Dr
Priory Cl
Banner Hey
Halton Hey
Stone Hey
Long Hey
Willis Lane
Paradise Lane
Jubilee Dr
Greene's Rd
Sandiway
Dragon
Halsnead Community Primary School
Fisher Av
Thomas Drive
Johnson Av
Holden Road
Dennett Rd
Wilson Rd
Hughes Av
Cross
Coronation Dr
Lancaster Av
Old Colliery Rd
Esonwood
Whiston
Cook Glades
1 grid square represents 500 metres

Holt
Whiston
Warrington Road
Shaw Lane
Hayes Avenue
Lovett Drive
Ash Grove
Maple Gv
Poplar Gv
Windsor Rd
Cable Rd
Brook St
Cook St
Gilbert Road
Edward Rd
Sinclair
Club
Broadlands
Time Pk
Fire Station Road
Sandstone
Dennis Lane
Myers Av
Foster
Gilleney
Butt
Lane
Tarlton Cl
Croston Av
Amanda Road
Longton Lane
Sandhurst Road
St Winifred Rd
Longton Community Primary School
Ellerslie Avenue
Brookfield Av
Stapleton Road
Rainhill
Dorgan Cl
Francis
Stapleton Av
Vincent Rd
St Ann Pl
B5413
Warburton Hey
Park Av
Rainhill Station
Station Rd
Council
Ruth Evans Court
Whiston Hospital
A&E
PO
Longview
Holt
Martin Av
Brancker Av
Honiston Av
Horwood
Chatsworth Road
Norcliffe Rd
Batey Av
Millom Av
Second Av
First Av
Ivy Farm Rd
Longton Med Cen
Heskin Cl
Ivy Av
Ryder Cl
Burton Av
Burton Cl
Cartmel Dr
Arnside Av
Kendal Drive
Renwick Av
Warrington Rd
St Lukes RC Primary School
Brookside Cl
Youatt Av
Birch Cl
Hazel Av
Dragon Lane
Chestnut Cl
Cedar Cl
Pine Cl
Maple Cl
Lunt Av
Oak Cl
Oak Road
Dryden Cl
Milton Cl
Burns Cl
Milton
Harptree Cl
Pinnington Rd
Weyman Av
The Crs
Keats Av
Byron Av
Scott Av
Huyton Av
Avenue
Whiston Willis Primary School
Walpole Av
Works
Stoney Lane
Amb Stn
Higher Side Community Comprehensive School
Cumber Lane
Hemmingsway
Gidswr Fld
Kirkman Fold
Kendricks Fold
Fairclough Rd
Works
Dee Road
Trent Cl
Trent Road
Severn Rd
Derwent Cl
Weaver Av
Calder Drive
Stour Av
Ribble Av
Swale Av
Rainhill Clinic
School
Lowther Drive
Craven Rd
Eden Cl
Christopher Cl
Marian Dr
Heyes Mt
Old Lane
Saint
St Ann
Mill Lane
Station
Driveway
Grovewood Gdns
Stanwood Gdns
Fellwood Gv
Caldywood Dr
Copperwood Dr
Heywood Gdns
Haslemere
Lyneham
Selborne
Kingsnorth
Dursley
Martock
Driveway
Berrywood Dr
Manorwood Drive
Parkwood Rd
St Leos RC Prim Sch
Southmead Comm Prim Sch
Sherwood Dr
Crftwd Gv
Langbar
Exeley
Skeffington
Domville
Rudgate
Pennywood Drive
Nelson Avenue
Lickers Lane
Blundell's Lane
Cemetery
Blundells Hill Golf Club
Cronton La
L35
Golf Course
Prince's House
Fox's Bank Lane
Main
N Front
Lake Vw
East Front
Main Front
Orchard Cl
Old Orch
Orchard Gdns
Old Hall Dr
S Front
Cronton Lane
M62
St Helens
Knowsley
Hall La
Entry
Higher Shaw Farm
Shaw
60
78
100
47
48
49
390
91
92
E
F
G
H
1
2
3
4
5

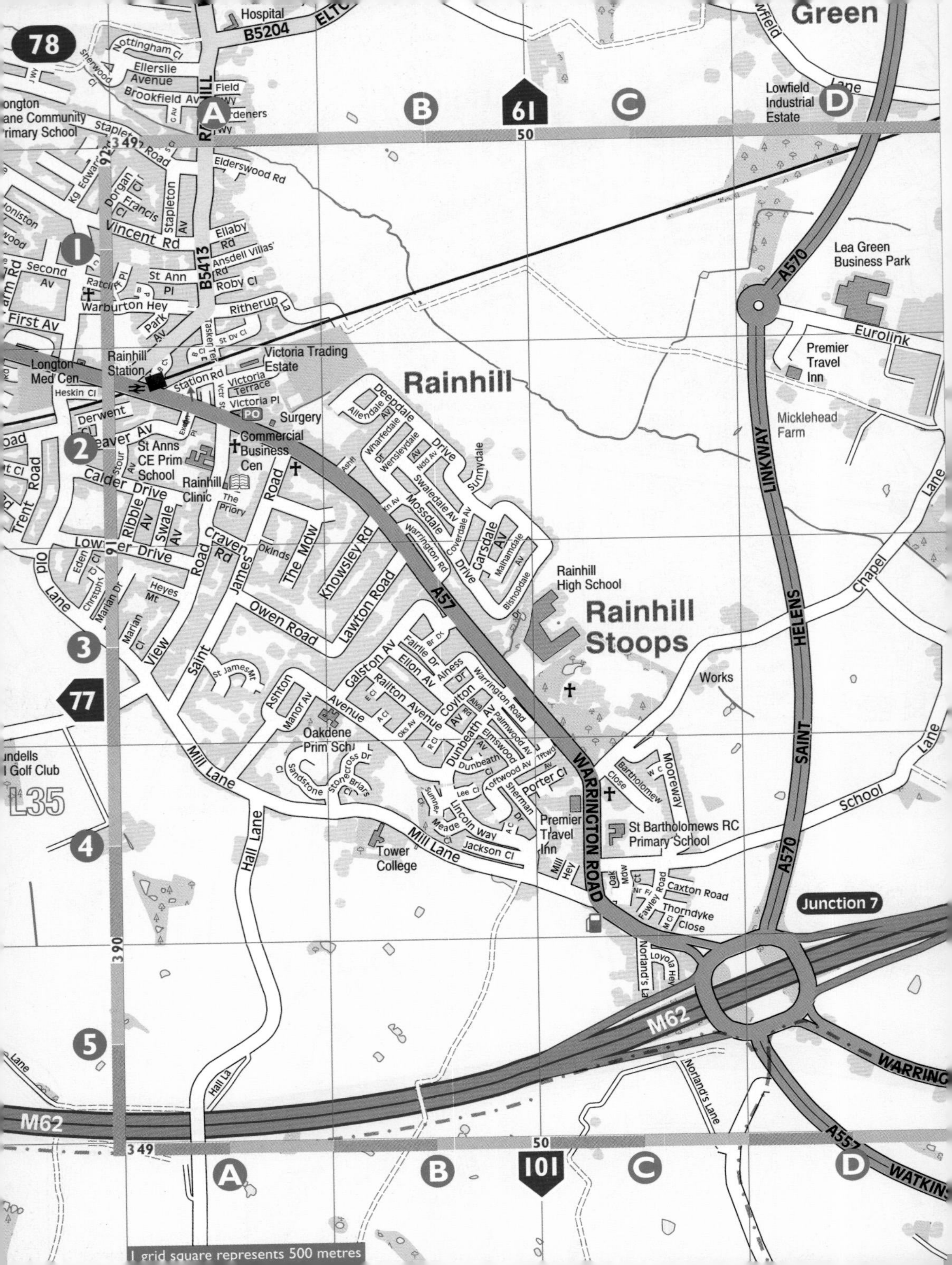
78
61
77
101
A
B
C
D
1
2
3
4
5
50
349
390
Green
Hospital
B5204
Nottingham Cl
Ellerslie Avenue
Brookfield Av
Sherwood Cl
Field Wy
Gardeners Wy
Longton Lane Community Primary School
Stapleton Road
Elderswood Rd
Lowfield Industrial Estate
Lowfield Lane
Kg Edward
Dorgan Cl
Francis Cl
Stapleton Av
Vincent Rd
Ellaby Rd
Ansdell Villas Rd
Roby Cl
St Ann Pl
Second Av
First Av
Warburton Hey
Park Av
Ritherup La
B5413
Rainhill Station
Longton Med Cen
Heskin Cl
Victoria Trading Estate
Station Rd
Victoria Terrace
Victoria Pl
PO
Surgery
Rainhill
Derwent Cl
Beaver Av
St Anns CE Prim School
Commercial Business Cen
Rainhill Clinic
The Priory
Calder Drive
Ribble Av
Swale Av
Trent Road
Lower Drive
Craven Rd
Road
Oklnds
The Mdw
Knowsley Rd
Lawton Road
Allendale Av
Deepdale Drive
Wharfedale Dr
Wensleydale Av
Swaledale Av
Mossdale Drive
Coverdale Av
Sunnydale
Carsdale Av
Malhamdale Av
Bishopdale Dr
Warrington Rd
A57
Eden Cl
Marian Dr
Marian Cl
Heyes Mt
View
Lane
Old
James
Saint
Owen Road
St James Mt
Ashton Avenue
Manor Av
Galston Av
Fairlie Dr
Ellon Av
Alness Dr
Railton Avenue
Coylton Av
Warrington Road
Dunbeath Av
Dunbeath Cl
Elmswood
Palmwood Av
Toftwood Av
Porter Cl
Sherman Dr
Oakdene Prim Sch
Sandstone
Stonecross Dr
Briars Cl
Mill Lane
Hall Lane
Sumner Cl
Lee Cl
Lincoln Way
Meade Cl
Jackson Cl
Tower College
Premier Travel Inn
Mill Hey
WARRINGTON ROAD
Rainhill High School
Rainhill Stoops
Works
Bartholomew Close
Mooreway
St Bartholomews RC Primary School
Caxton Road
Fawley Road
Thorndyke Close
Norland's La
Loyola Hey
Lea Green Business Park
Eurolink
Premier Travel Inn
Micklehead Farm
LINKWAY
A570
SAINT HELENS
Chapel Lane
School Lane
Junction 7
M62
WARRING
A557
WATKINS
Norland's Lane
Hall La
Rundells Golf Club
L35
Lane
1 grid square represents 500 metres

Marshall's Cross
Sutton Leach
Clock Face
Sutton Manor
62
80
102
E
F
G
H
E
F
G
H
2
3
4
5
51
52
53
92
91
390
CHESTER LANE
B5419
Chester Lane
CLOCK FACE ROAD
A569
Lea Green Road
Lea Green Road
Woolacombe Avenue
Goodleigh Place
Bideford Av
Porlock Av
Leach
Ilfracombe Rd
Appledore Gv
Taunton Avenue
Radstock Grove
Dunster Grove
Croyde Place
Shirwell Grove
Lynton
Beech Av
Ash Gv
Willow Tree Avenue
Willow Tree Primary School
Lyon Industrial Estate
Prenton Av
Heswall Av
Eastham Crs
Four Acre Lane
Four Acre Lane Shop Cen
Surgery
Pasture Close
Moorwood Crs
Heathland Rd
Hornby Crs
Dunsop Crs
Ashdown Crs
Avenue
Burnage
Wray Av
Avenue
Crawford Cl
Crawford St
Wilbraham St
Balniel Street
James Street
Farndon Avenue
Kelsall Av
Alf Av
Budworth Avenue
Tarvin Close
Walker Av
Parkside Avenue
Hazelwood Close
Walkers Lane
Tressel Drive
Orwell Close
Burns Rd
Kipling Grove
Cannon St
Hammersley Av
Bentley St
Pollitt Crs
Pendlebury St
Jersey St
Street
Agnes Lane
Lever St
Bodden St
St Theresas Prim.Sch
Gartons
Field Road
Paddock Grove
Farm Road
Farm Rd
Cranshaw Avenue
Finch Close
Abbots Hall Avenue
Eccles Grove
Sweet Brier Ct
Bridge Road
Lane
Scotts Avenue
Shakespeare Road
Forest Road
Delamere Av
Bowland Av
Epping Av
Chandlers Wy
Sutton Manor Community Primary School
Tennyson St
Shelley St
Milton St
Bell Lane
M62
Finger House Lane
Union Bank Lane
Union Bank Farm
Tibbs Cross Lane
A569
JUBITS LANE
B5419
Old Brook Hall
ON ROAD
A57
Wilmere House
WARRINGTON ROAD
Bridge Farm
PO
PO

Sutton Leach
Abbotsfield
Abbotsfield Farm
63
A
B
C
D
353
54
92
Willow Tree Primary School
1
Lyon Industrial Estate
Gorsey Lane
Hall Lane
Home Farm
Crawford Cl
Crawford St
Wilbraham St
Lindsay St
James Street
Balniel Street
A569
PO
Field Road
Paddock Grove
Farm Rd
2
Clock Face Country Park
Eccles Grove
Finch Close
Avenue
Sweet Brier Ct
Bridge Road
Joy Lane
3
79
M62
House Lane
4
Tibbs Cross Lane
Crow's Nest Farm
390
5
Whittle Brook
Bold Heath
103
Mersey Valley Golf & Country Club
Golf Course
School La
CLOCK FACE RD
TON ROAD

1 grid square represents 500 metres

Joy Lane
St Helens
Warrington
E
F
G
H
55
56
57
92
Clay Lane
House
Tan
Lane
I
Joy Lane
Farm
Joy Lane
Burtonwood Rd
Wright's
Limekiln Lane
Lane
2
Junction 8
M62
91
Burtonwood Road
Kir
3
82
Orion Boulevard
4
Omega Bvd
Omega Bvd
Whittle Avenue
Tenbury
Matlock Cl
Harrogate Cl
390
Matlock Close
Tunbridge Cl
Leamington Cl
Malvern Cl
Lingley
Mere
Lingley Mere
Business
Park
5
Malvern Close
Loxley
Chiltrn
Montgomery Cl
Lingley Green Avenue
Lingley Green Av
Lonsdale Cl
Stockdale Dr
Billington Cl
B Cl
Lane
Mm Cl
Wensleydale Cl
Rockford Gdns
Great
Sankey
104
Sankey Med
Centre
Stockdale Dr
Thorntondale Drive
Farndale Cl
Airedale Cl
Bishopdale Cl
Boston Bvd
Bembridge Cl
Godshill Cl
Freshwater Cl
Whitwell
Park
Foreland Cl
Lingley Green Avenue
Hall
Community
Prim School
Hall
Blue Ridge Cl
Thorntondale Dr
Woodale Cl
Bransdale Cl
Gordale Cl
Widdale Cl
Barbondale Cl
Cotterdale
Road
Kingsdale Rd
Whittle Brook

Brook Head Farm
House Lane
Tan
Burtonwood Rd
Lane
Junction 2
Burtonwood Service Area
IKEA
Gemini
Taurus Park
Superstore
Superstore
Superstore
Europa Boulevard
Charon Way
Butts Gn
Archers Gn Rd
Kingswood
Falconers Green
Kingswood Road
Easter Court
Europa Bvd
International Business Centre
CROMWELL AVENUE
Callands
Goldcliffe Cl
Welshpool Cl
Holyhead Cl
Newbridge Cl
Penmark Close
Callands Road
Ridgeborne Close
Cardigan Cl
Carmarthen Cl
Pendine Close
Lydbury Cl
Burtonwood Road
Tourney Green
Westbrook Crescent
Webster Ct
Delta Crs
Castle Green
Carina Pk
Heralds Green
Kingswood
Road
Coppice Green
Westbrook Way
Westbrook Way
Westbrook Crs
St Philip Westbrook CE Prim Sch
Westbrook Medical Cen
Superstore
A574
Willoughby Cl
Raleigh Cl
Grant Close
Westbrook Centre
Westbrook Crs
Ward Close
Westbrook
Nares Close
Ladywood Rd
Purdy Cl
Beecroft Cl
Whittle Avenue
Harrogate Cl
Matlock Cl
Tenbury Cl
Blackshaw Dr
Barford Close
Garwood Close
Garwood Close
Cartier Cl
Sankey Court
Matlock Close
Harrogate
Leamington Cl
Tunbridge Cl
Malvern Cl
Woodhall Cl
Burtonwood Road
Bristow Close
Bicknell Close
Shipton Close
Vincent Close
Twenty Acre Road
Tasman Cl
A574 CROMWELL AV
Shackleton Close
New Hall
Mawson Cl
Malvern Close
Loxley Cl
Buxton Cl
Houston Gdns
The Lees
Tensing Cl
WA5
Montgomery Cl
Morton Cl
California Cl
Franklin Cl
Ellesworth Cl
Westbrook Old Hall Primary School
Palmer Crs
Hudson Cl
Wensleydale Cl
Portland Rd
Rockford Gdns
Atlanta Gdns
Boston
Virginia Gdns
Nevada Cl
Washington Dr
Twenty Acre Road
Old Hall Rd
PO
Kingsdale Road
Airedale Cl
Bishopdale Cl
Kingsdale Rd
Cotterdale
Boston
McKinley St
Jefferson Drive
Olympia Pl
New Hmpshr Cl
Carolina Rd
Arizona Crs
Colorado Cl
Washington Drive
Gregory Cl
Florida Cl
Dakota Dr
Vermont Cl
Cavendish Cl
Lander Cl
Denver Dr
RAF Burtonwood
357
58
92
91
390
A
B
C
D
1
2
3
4
5

81

105

1 grid square represents 500 metres

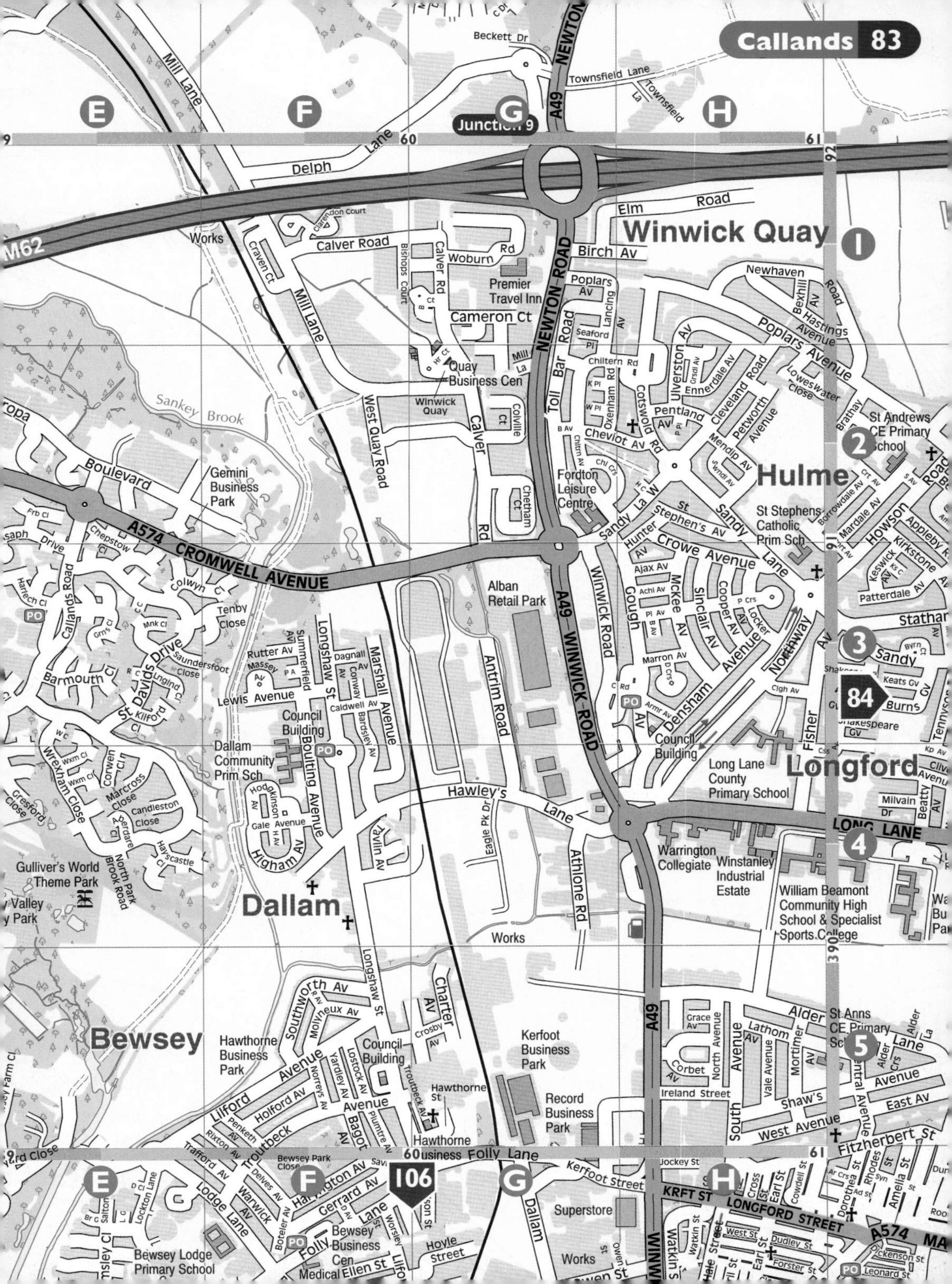

Beckett Dr
NEWTON
Townsfield Lane
Townsfield La
Mill Lane
E
F
G
H
Junction 9
60
61
92
Delph Lane
M62
Elm Road
Winwick Quay
I
Clarendon Court
Works
Calver Road
Woburn Rd
Craven Ct
Bishops Court
Calver Rd
Birch Av
Premier Travel Inn
Poplars Av
Lancing Av
Newhaven Road
Cameron Ct
NEWTON ROAD
A49
Toll Bar Road
Seaford Pl
Mill La
Quay Business Cen
Winwick Quay
Chiltern Rd
Ulverston Av
Ennerdale Av
Cleveland Road
Bexhill Av
Hastings Avenue
Poplars Avenue
Loweswater Close
Oxenham Rd
Cotswold Rd
Pentland Av
Petworth Avenue
Sankey Brook
West Quay Road
Colville Ct
Calver Rd
Cheviot Av
Mendip Av
Brathay
St Andrews CE Primary School
2
Hulme
Boulevard
Gemini Business Park
Chetham Ct
Fordton Leisure Centre
Sandy La
Sandy Lane
St Stephen's Av
St Stephens Catholic Prim Sch
Borrowdale Av
Mardale Av
Howson Road
Appleby Rd
Kirkstone Av
Keswick Av
Patterdale Av
A574 CROMWELL AVENUE
Chepstow Cl
Drive
Callands Road
Harlech Cl
PO
Colwyn Cl
Tenby Close
Alban Retail Park
Hunter Av
Crowe Avenue
Ajax Av
Gough Av
McKee Av
Sinclair Av
Cooper Av
Locker Av
Northway
Statham
3
Sandy
Keats Gv
84
Burns Gv
Shakespeare Gv
Longsdaw St
Summerfield Av
Dagnall Av
Marshall Avenue
Rutter Av
Massey Av
Conway Av
Antrim Road
Winwick Road
A49 WINWICK ROAD
Marron Av
Densham Avenue
Barmouth Cl
St Davids Drive
Saundersfoot Close
Lewis Avenue
Caldwell Av
Bardsley Av
Kilford Cl
Council Building
Fisher Av
Tennyson
Dallam Community Prim Sch
Boulting Avenue
Long Lane County Primary School
Longford
Wrexham Close
Corwen Cl
Marcross Close
Candleston Close
Hodgkinson Av
Gale Avenue
Hawley's Lane
Eagle Pk Dr
Milvain Dr
Beatty Av
Gresford Close
Aberdare Cl
Haverscastle Cl
Higham Av
Tavlin Av
Athlone Rd
LONG LANE
4
Warrington Collegiate
Winstanley Industrial Estate
William Beamont Community High School & Specialist Sports College
Gulliver's World Theme Park
North Park Brook Road
Dallam
Works
390
Southworth Av
Longshaw St
Charter Av
Molyneux Av
Crosby Av
Bewsey
Hawthorne Business Park
Council Building
Kerfoot Business Park
A49
Grace Av
North Avenue
Lathom Av
Alder Lane
St Anns CE Primary School
5
Alder Crs
Corbet Av
Vale Avenue
Mortimer Av
Central Avenue
Avenue
East Av
Lilford Avenue
Holford Av
Norreys Av
Yardley Av
Lostock Av
Troutbeck Av
Hawthorne St
Ireland Street
South Avenue
Shaw's Avenue
West Avenue
Fitzherbert St
Penketh Av
Troutbeck
Bagot Av
Plumtree Av
Record Business Park
Rixton Av
Trafford Av
Bewsey Park Close
Hawthorne Business
Folly Lane
Jockey St
Kerfoot Street
KRFT ST
LONGFORD STREET
A574
Cross St
Earl St
Cowdell St
Rhodes St
Amelia St
Dorothea St
Harrington Av
Gerrard Av
106
Dallam
Superstore
Warwick Av
Delves Av
Lodge Lane
Lockton Lane
Salton
Boteler Av
Folly Lane
Bewsey Business Cen
Worsley
Hoyle Street
Watkin St
West St
Dudley St
Forster St
Dickenson St
Leonard St
Bewsey Lodge Primary School
Medical
Ellen St
Works
Owen St

M62
Midhops Farm
Houghton Green
Peel Hall
WA2
Hulme
Longford
Orford
Blackbrook
Padgate
Bruche
Newhaven Road
Hastings Avenue
Poplars Avenue
Cleveland Road
Petworth Avenue
Loweswater Close
St Andrews CE Primary School
St Stephens Catholic Prim Sch
Windermere Av
Ullswater Av
Buttermere Av
Thrlm Av
Bentham Av
Howson Road
Appleby Rd
Kirkstone Av
Honister Av
Keswick Av
Patterdale Av
Bowness Av
Statham Avenue
Sandy Lane
Morgan Av
Small Crs
Small Av
Festival Av
Hughes Av
Festival Crs
Shakespeare Gv
Keats Gv
Walpole Gv
Burns Gv
Tennyson Dr
Dryden Pl
St Margarets CE Prim Sch
Long Lane County Primary School
Clive Avenue
Milvain Dr
Beatty Av
Marina Dr
LONG LANE A50
Winstanley Industrial Estate
William Beamont Community High School & Specialist Sports College
Warrington Business Park
Longfield Road
Capesthorne Road
Neville Av
Park Road
Birtles Road
Bruce Av
Warren Rd
Burton Rd
ORFORD GREEN
Poplars Av
Harding Av
Martin Av
Boyle Av
Derek Avenue
Brook Acre Primary School
Merewood Close
Linnet Cl
Osprey Cl
Teal Cl
Grasmere Av
Quail Cl
Mallard Cl
Avocet Cl
Canberra Square
Meteor Crs
Greenwood Crs
Fairbrother Crs
Whitby Av
Capesthorne Cl
Tyne Cl
Trossach Cl
Merrick Cl
Pennine Rd
Dunlin Cl
Dovedale Cl
Mill Farm Close
Foxfield Close
Morven
Darley Av
Ballater Drive
Radley Lane
Mill Lane
Blackbrook Avenue
Enfield Park Road
Cinnamon Lane North
Dundee Cl
Kinross Cl
Solway Cl
Gairloch Cl
Kilsyth Cl
Montrose Cl
Perth Cl
Cables Cl
Delafield Close
Welsby Cl
Cinnamon Brow CE Prim Sch
St Bridgets Catholic Primary School
Orange Gv
Avery Cl
Viscount Rd
Harrier Rd
Westland Dr
Handley Dr
Blenheim Cl
Waddington Cl
Valiant Cl
Vulcan Cl
Insall Rd
Council Building
Padgate Community High School
Gosport Cl
Rudloe Ct
Valley Court
Hilden Catfoss Cl
Bawtry Court
BIRCHWOOD WAY A574
Hallows Av
Tomlinson Av
Lyndale Avenue
Smith Drive
Smith Crs
Halsall Av
Ashbrook Crs
Roscoe Av
Malcolm Av
Hallfields Road
Brian Av
Withers Avenue
Stapleton Av
Norris St
Arena Gdns
Venns Rd
ORFORD ROAD A50
Alder Lane
St Anns CE Primary School
Central Avenue
East Av
West Avenue
Shaw's Avenue
South Avenue
North Avenue
Vale Avenue
Fitzherbert St
Beamont Junior School
Quebec Rd
St Benedicts RC Primary School
Oakland St
Connaught Av
Grosvenor Av
Derby Drive
Grantham Av
Queens
Brownhill Drive
Delery Drive
Eric Avenue
Davenham
Padgate Lane
Jubilee Av
Lawn Av
Bruche Drive
Bruche Avenue
Devonshire Road
Westover Road
Belgrave Avenue
St Oswalds RC Prim Sch
Beechwood Av
Sheerwater Cl
Birch Grove
Fir Grove
LONGFORD STREET
A574 MARSH
PADGATE LANE
KING
Works
Surgery
Cross St
Earl St
Cowdell St
Dorothea St
Rhodes St
Amelia St
Roome St
O'Leary St
Cabul Cl
West St
Dudley St
Forster St
Leonard St
Godfrey St
83
107
1 grid square represents 500 metres

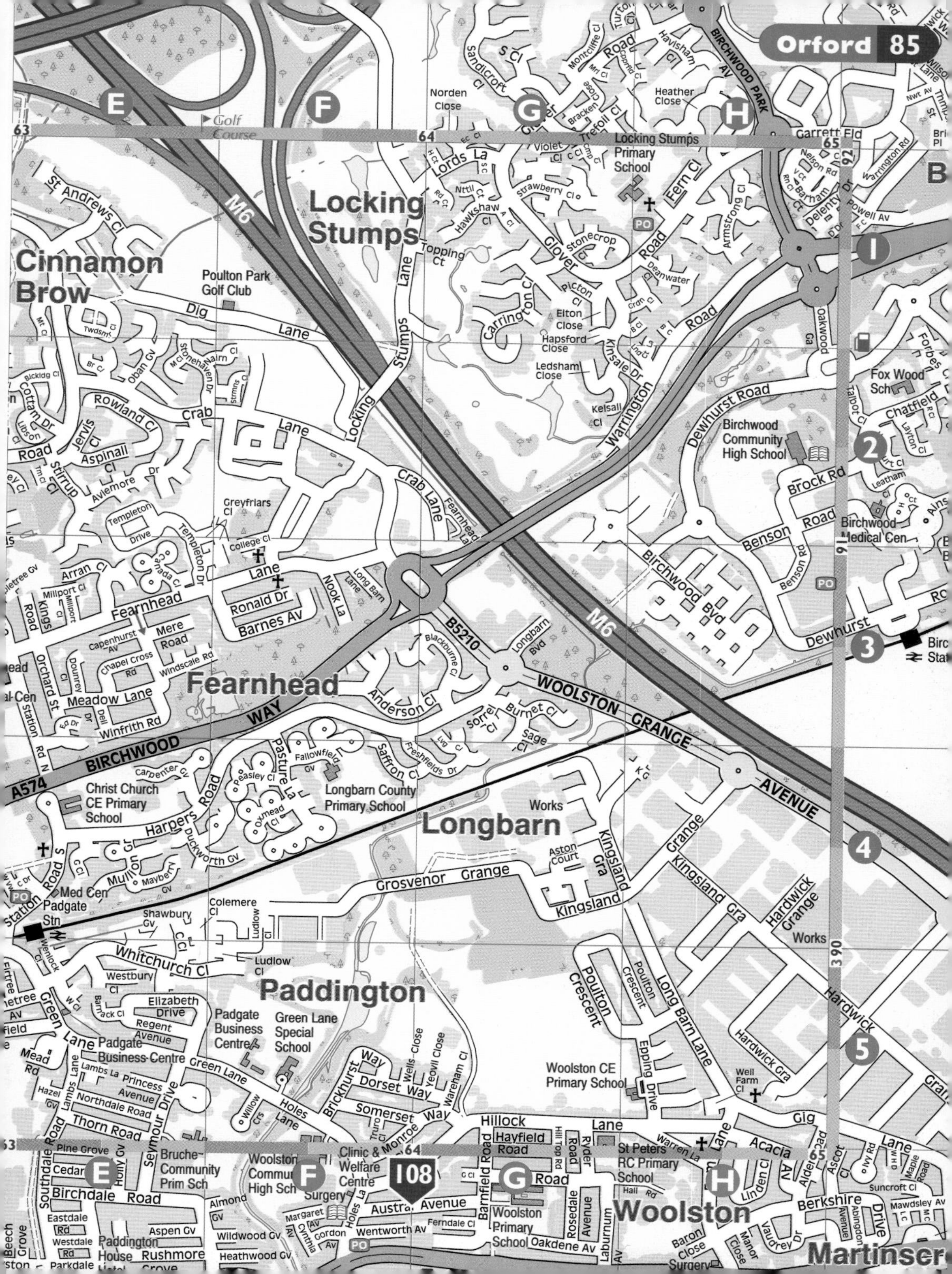
Locking Stumps
Cinnamon Brow
Fearnhead
Longbarn
Paddington
Woolston
Martinscroft
M6
A574
BIRCHWOOD WAY
B5210
WOOLSTON GRANGE AVENUE
BIRCHWOOD PARK AV
Poulton Park Golf Club
Golf Course
Locking Stumps Primary School
Birchwood Community High School
Fox Wood Sch
Birchwood Medical Cen
Christ Church CE Primary School
Longbarn County Primary School
Padgate Business Centre
Green Lane Special School
Woolston CE Primary School
St Peters RC Primary School
Woolston Primary School
Woolston Community High Sch
Bruche Community Prim Sch
Clinic & Welfare Centre
Surgery
Padgate Stn
Med Cen
Works
Paddington House
Dig Lane
Crab Lane
Locking Stumps Lane
Warrington Road
Dewhurst Road
Benson Road
Brock Rd
Birchwood Bvd
Fearnhead Lane
Ronald Dr
Barnes Av
Nook La
Long Barn Lane
Grosvenor Grange
Kingsland Grange
Hardwick Grange
Poulton Crescent
Long Barn Lane
Hillock Lane
Green Lane
Holes Lane
Princess Avenue
Northdale Road
Thorn Road
Birchdale Road
Austral Avenue
Berkshire Drive
Acacia Av
Gig Lane
Whitchurch Cl
Elizabeth Drive
Regent Avenue
Seymour Drive
Harpers Road
Pasture La
Meadow Lane
Winfrith Rd
Orchard St
Station Rd
Mere Road
Anderson Cl
Saffron Cl
Freshfields Dr
Mullion Gr
Duckworth Gv
Carrington Cl
Glover Road
Kinsale Dr
Oakwood Ga
Chatfield
Powell Av
Garrett Fld
108
63
64
65
390
91
92
E
F
G
H
I
B
2
3
4
5

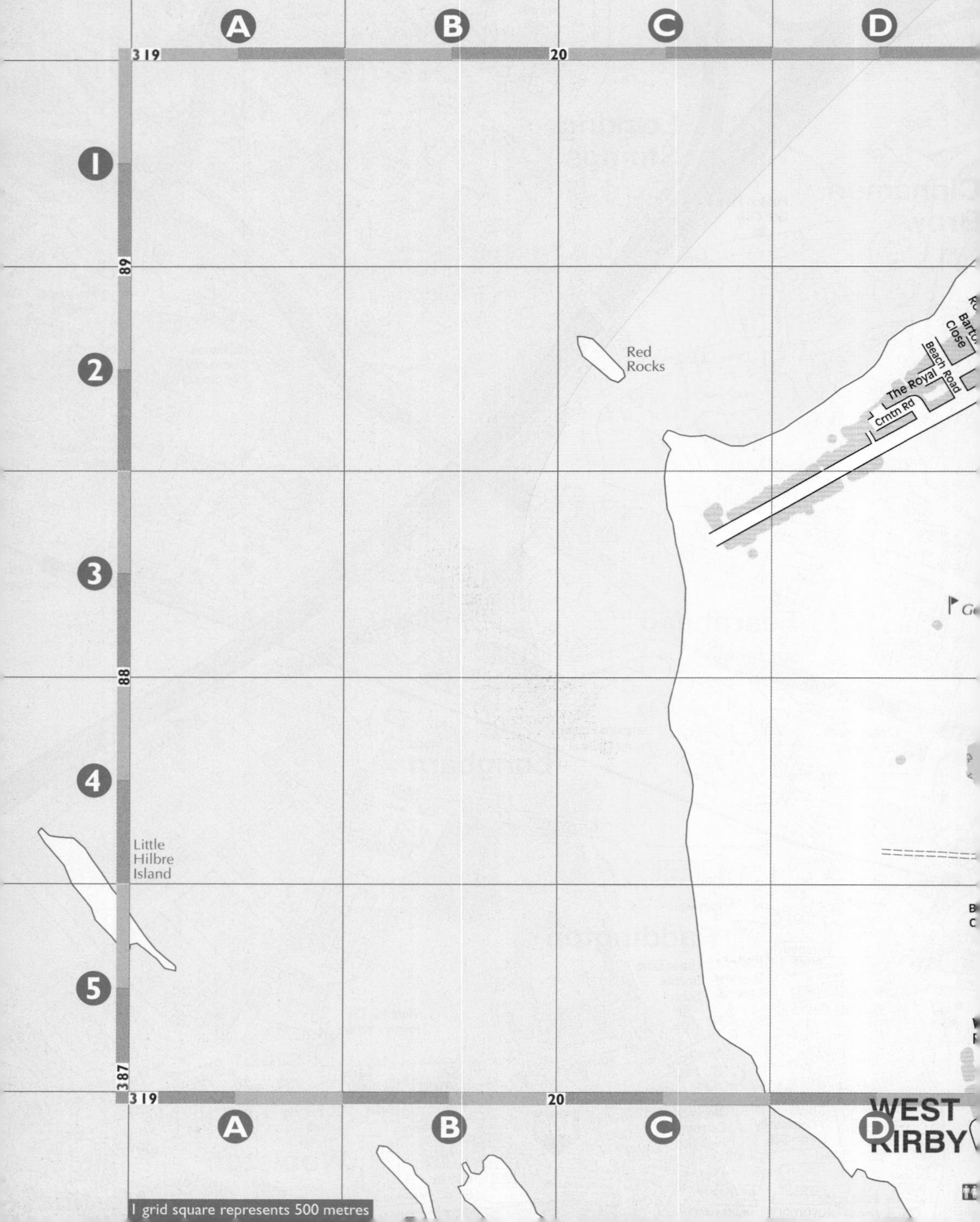
A
B
C
D
319
20
1
2
3
4
5
89
88
387
Red Rocks
Barton Close
Beach Road
The Royal
Crntn Rd
Little Hilbre Island
WEST KIRBY
1 grid square represents 500 metres

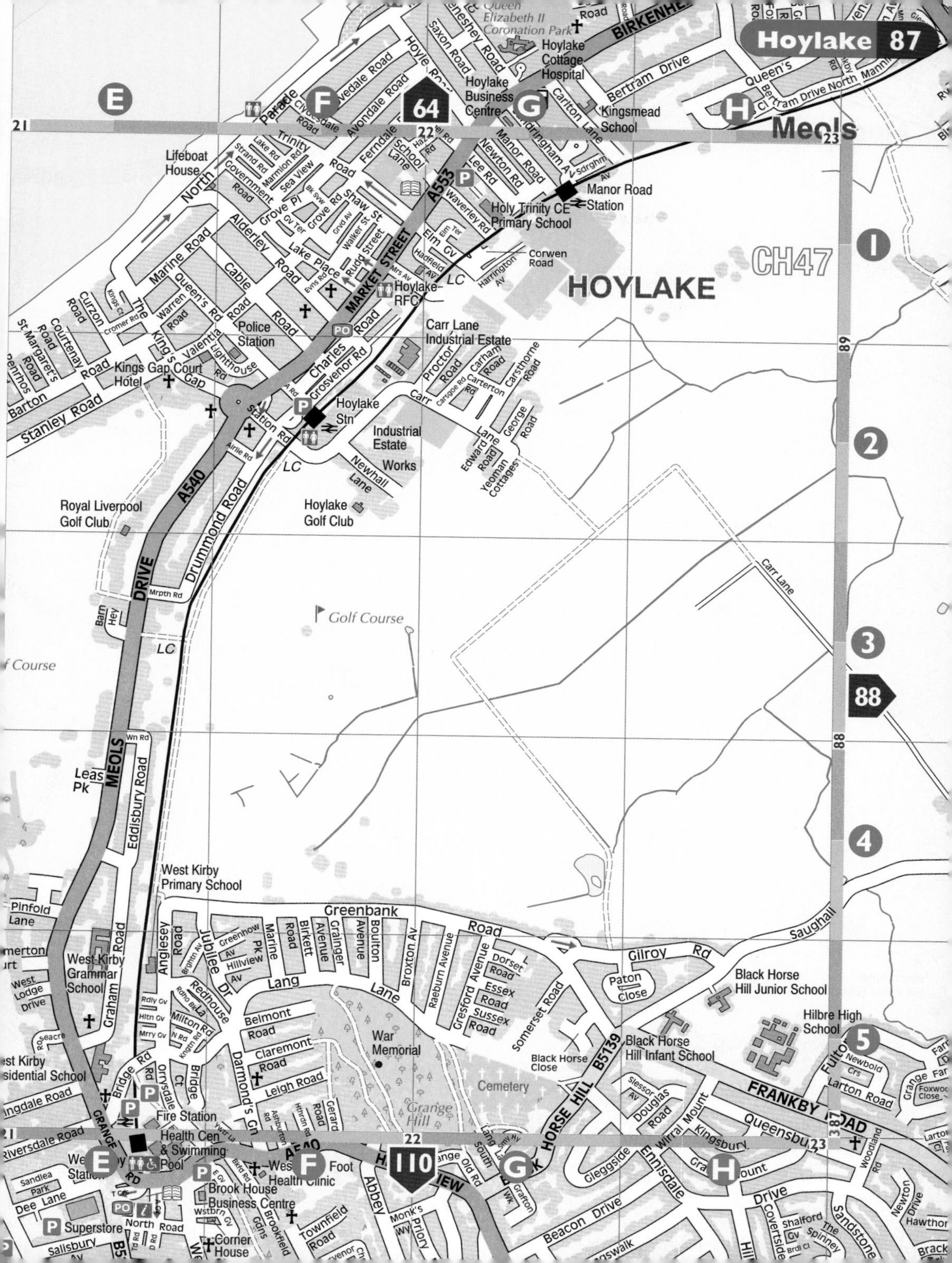
HOYLAKE
CH47
Meols
Queen Elizabeth II Coronation Park
Hoylake Cottage Hospital
Hoylake Business Centre
Kingsmead School
Manor Road Station
Holy Trinity CE Primary School
Corwen Road
Hoylake RFC
Carr Lane Industrial Estate
Police Station
Kings Gap Court Hotel
Lifeboat House
Hoylake Stn
Industrial Estate
Works
Hoylake Golf Club
Royal Liverpool Golf Club
Golf Course
West Kirby Primary School
West Kirby Grammar School
Black Horse Hill Junior School
Black Horse Hill Infant School
Hilbre High School
War Memorial
Cemetery
Grange Hill
Fire Station
Health Cen & Swimming Pool
West Kirby Health Clinic
Brook House Business Centre
Superstore
Corner House
Leas Pk
Birkenhead Road
Bertram Drive
Bertram Drive North
Queen's Road
Hoyle Road
Saxon Road
Market Street
A553
A540
Meols Drive
Drummond Road
Stanley Road
Barton Road
Marine Road
North Parade
Alderley Road
Cable Road
Grosvenor Rd
Station Rd
Carr Lane
Newhall Lane
Proctor Road
Carham Road
Carsthorne Road
George Road
Edward Road
Yeoman Cottages
Greenbank Road
Lang Lane
Gilroy Rd
Saughall
Eddisbury Road
Graham Road
Anglesey Road
Jubilee Dr
Belmont Road
Claremont Road
Leigh Road
Black Horse Hill B5139
Frankby Road
Larton Road
Queensbury
Ennisdale
Beacon Drive
Grange Road
Riversdale Road
Dee Lane
Salisbury Av
North Road
Abbey
Priory
Sandstone
Newton Drive
Woodland Rd
Fulton
Newbold Crs
64
88
110
E F G H
1 2 3 4 5
21 22 23
89 88 387

88
Meols Station
Meols
Queen's
Bertram Drive North
B Cl
Mannington Cl
Leighton Av
Frankby Rd
Pycroft Road
Birch Road
A
B
C
D
65
24
323
Barn Hey Crs
Sherwood Road
Shrwd Gv
BIRKENHEAD ROAD
A553
HOYLAKE
Kinnerton
Rosewood Dr
Berwick Cl
Otterburn Close
Cardus Cl
Carr
Crrw Cl
Lane
CH47
Fornalls Green Lane
The Ridgeway
Fieldway
Acres Road
Bispham Drive
Carr Farm
89
Heron Road
Saughall Massie
Barnacre Lane
2
Carr Lane
3
87
88
Oldfield Manor Farm
Oldfield Lane
Three Lanes End
Saughall Massie Road
Pump Lane
Greasby Brook
4
Massie Road
Saughall
China Farm Lane
Ashdale Park
Stanmore Park
Abingdon
Cranwell Rd
Halton
Martlesham Crs
Frankby Cl
Black Horse Hill Junior School
Hilbre High School
5
Fulton Av
Newbold Crs
Farndon Drive
Grange Farm Crs
Foxwood Close
Fairfield Dr
Larton Road
FRANKBY ROAD
Queensbury
387
323
Springfield Avenue
The Stackfield
Ballard Road
Meadow Rd
Larton
Lartonwood Cl
Larton Farm Cl
Woodland Rd
Newton Drive
Hawthorn Dr
Chantrell Rd
Frankby Stiles
111
Frankby
Newton
Drive
Shalford Gv
The Nook
Lombardy Avenue
Whitebeam Walk

1 grid square represents 500 metres

Upton
Greasby
Arrowe Hill
Junction 2a
M53
A553
A551
A5027
B5139
MORETON ROAD
UPTON ROAD
UPTON BY-PASS
ARROWE PK ROAD
ARROWE PARK ROAD
OLD GREASBY ROAD
GREASBY ROAD
FRANKBY ROAD
Foxfield School
Surgery
Police Stn
Moreton Medical Centre
Christ Church Primary School
Orrets Meadow School
Hayfield School
Overchurch J&I School
St Josephs RC Primary School
Upton Hall School FCJ
Upton CC
Premier Travel Inn
Superstore
Police Station
Brookdale Primary School
Greasby Health Cen
Wirral Business Park
Greasby Infant School
Our Lady of Pity
Arrowe Brook
Arrowe Brook Road
Saughall Road
Acton Lane
Meadowbrook Road
Cobham Road
Borrowdale Road
Overchurch Road
Kingfisher Way
Birch Avenue
Elm Avenue
Beech Avenue
Oak Avenue
Raby Drive
Burrell Drive
Childwall Av
Seaforth Dr
Croft Drive
Royden Road
Warwick Road
The Woodlands
Saughall Massie Lane
Girtrell Road
Woodpecker Close
Brookside Crs
Cortsway
Broadway
Greenway
Kirkway
Eastway
Westway
Wood Lane
Summertrees Av
Bromsgrove Rd
Hambledon Drive
Stapleton Av
Circular Drive
Escolme Drive
Dingwall Drive
Lloyd Drive
Arrowe Road
Hall Dr
Brookdale Avenue South
Norwich Drive
Manor Drive
Church Road
Upland Rd
Doncaster Drive
Frankby Gv
Wallingford Rd
66
26
27
25
90
112
387
CH49
E
F
G
H
I
2
3
4
5

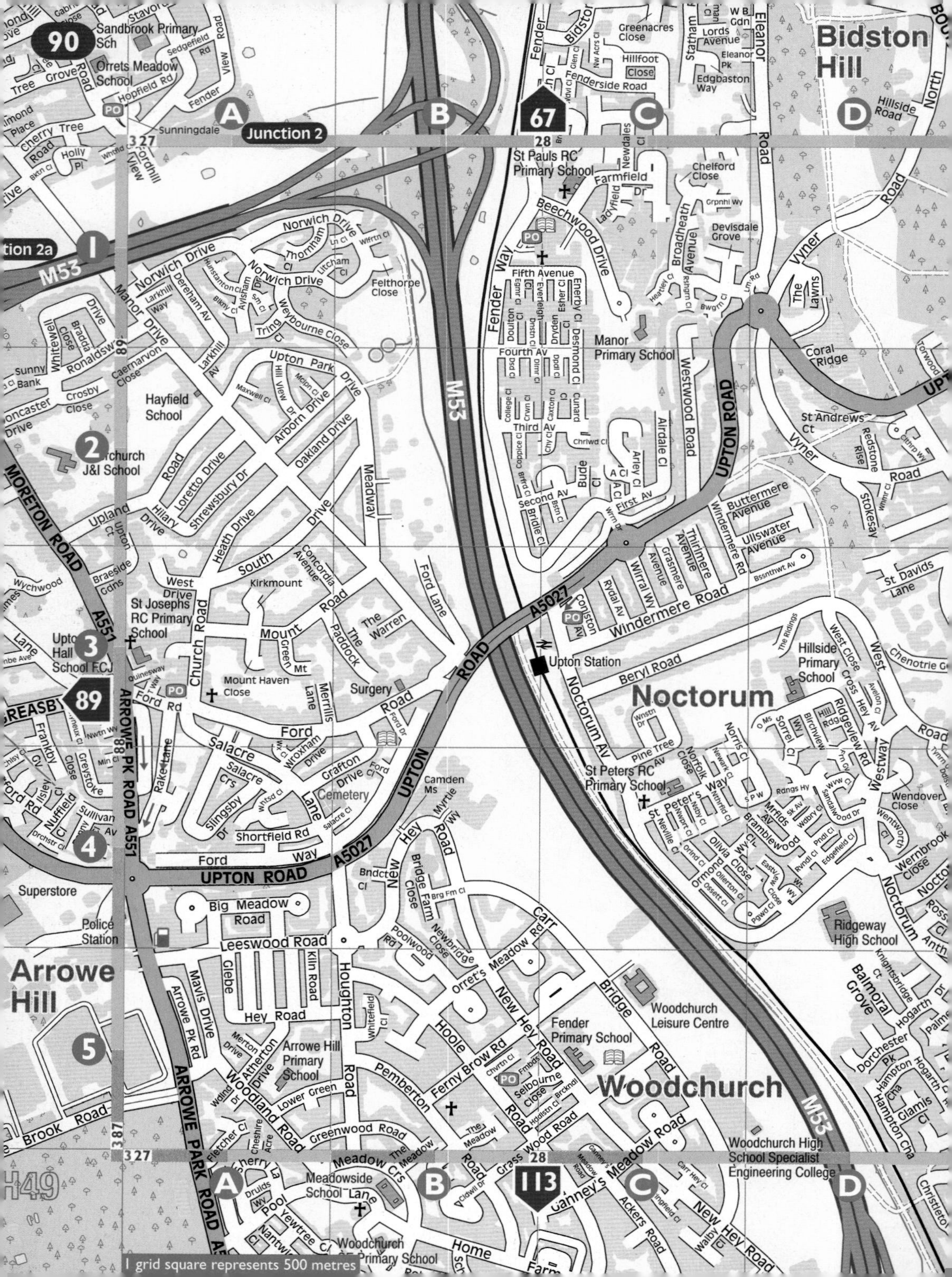
90
Sandbrook Primary Sch
Orrets Meadow School
Hopfield Rd
Sedgefield Rd
View Road
Fender
Tree Grove
Road
Place
Cherry Tree Road
Holly Pl
Sunningdale
Junction 2
Fordhill View
A
B
C
D
67
Fender
Bidston
Greenacres Close
Hillfoot Close
Fenderside Road
Statham
Lords Avenue
Eleanor Pk
Edgbaston Way
Eleanor Road
Bidston Hill
Hillside Road
North
327
28
St Pauls RC Primary School
Newdales Cl
Farmfield Dr
Ladyfield
Chelford Close
Broadheath Avenue
Devisdale Grove
Beechwood Drive
Fender Way
PO
Fifth Avenue
Manor Primary School
Westwood Road
UPTON ROAD
Vyner Road
The Lawns
Coral Ridge
St Andrews Ct
Redstone Rise
Stokesay
Junction 2a
M53
Norwich Drive
Thornham Cl
Litcham Cl
Felthorpe Close
Weybourne Close
Tring Cl
Dereham Av
Manor Drive
Larkhill Way
Larkhill Av
Whitewell Drive
Bradda Close
Ronaldsway
Sunny Bank
Caernarvon Close
Crosby Close
Doncaster Drive
Hayfield School
Upton Park Drive
Hill View Dr
Arborn Drive
Oakland Drive
Meadway
Fourth Av
Third Av
Second Av
First Av
Desmond Cl
Cunard
Airdale Cl
Arnley Cl
Bude Cl
Bridle Cl
2
Woodchurch J&I School
MORETON ROAD
Loretto Drive
Shrewsbury Dr
Hilary Drive
Heath Drive
South Drive
Upland
Upton Ct
Road
Buttermere Avenue
Ullswater Avenue
Windermere Rd
Thirlmere Avenue
Grasmere
Wirral Wy
Avenue
Rydal Av
Coniston Av
Windermere Road
St Davids Lane
Wychwood
Braeside Gdns
West Drive
Kirkmount
Concordia Avenue
Ford Lane
A5027
A551
St Josephs RC Primary School
Church Road
Mount Road
Mount Green
The Paddock
The Warren
Upton Hall School FCJ
3
89
GREASBY
Ford Rd
Quineswav
Mount Haven Close
Merrills Lane
Surgery
ROAD
Upton Station
Noctorum Av
Beryl Road
The Ridings
Hillside Primary School
West Close
Cross Hey Av
West
Chenotrie Gdns
Noctorum
Ford Road
Frankby
Greystoke
Nuffield Cl
Sullivan
Salacre Lane
Salacre Crs
Wroxham Drive
Grafton Drive
Ford Dr
UPTON
Camden Ms
Myrtle Wy
Cemetery
Pine Tree Av
Norfolk Close
St Peters RC Primary School
St Peter's Way
Norris Cl
Ridgeview Rd
Westway
Wendover Close
Wentworth Cl
Sorrel Cl
Birchview
Slingsby Dr
Shortfield Rd
Rake Lane
ARROWE PK ROAD A551
Ford Way
UPTON ROAD
New Hey Road
Bridge Farm Close
Bramblewood
Olivia Close
Ormond Wy
Wernbrook Close
Noctorum
4
Superstore
Police Station
Big Meadow Road
Leeswood Road
Poolwood Rd
Newbridge Close
Carr
Orret's Meadow Rd
Ridgeway High School
Noctorum Ave
Knightsbridge Ct
Balmoral Grove
Arrowe Hill
Glebe
Mavis Drive
Kiln Road
Hey Road
Houghton Road
Whitefield Cl
Hoole
New Hey Road
Bridge Road
Woodchurch Leisure Centre
Fender Primary School
Hogarth Dr
Dorchester Pk
Hampton Cha
Glamis Cl
5
Arrowe Pk Rd
Merton Drive
Atherton Drive
Arrowe Hill Primary School
Pemberton Road
Ferny Brow Rd
Selbourne Close
Woodchurch
M53
Brook Road
Woodland Road
Lower Green
Greenwood Road
The Meadow
Grass Wood Road
Ganney's Meadow Road
Woodchurch High School Specialist Engineering College
387
ARROWE PARK ROAD
Fletcher Cl
Cherry La
Meadow Crs
113
CH49
Meadowside School Lane
Druids Wy
Pool
Yewtree Cl
Woodchurch CE Primary School
Home Farm
Ackers Road
New Hey Road
Christleton
1 grid square represents 500 metres

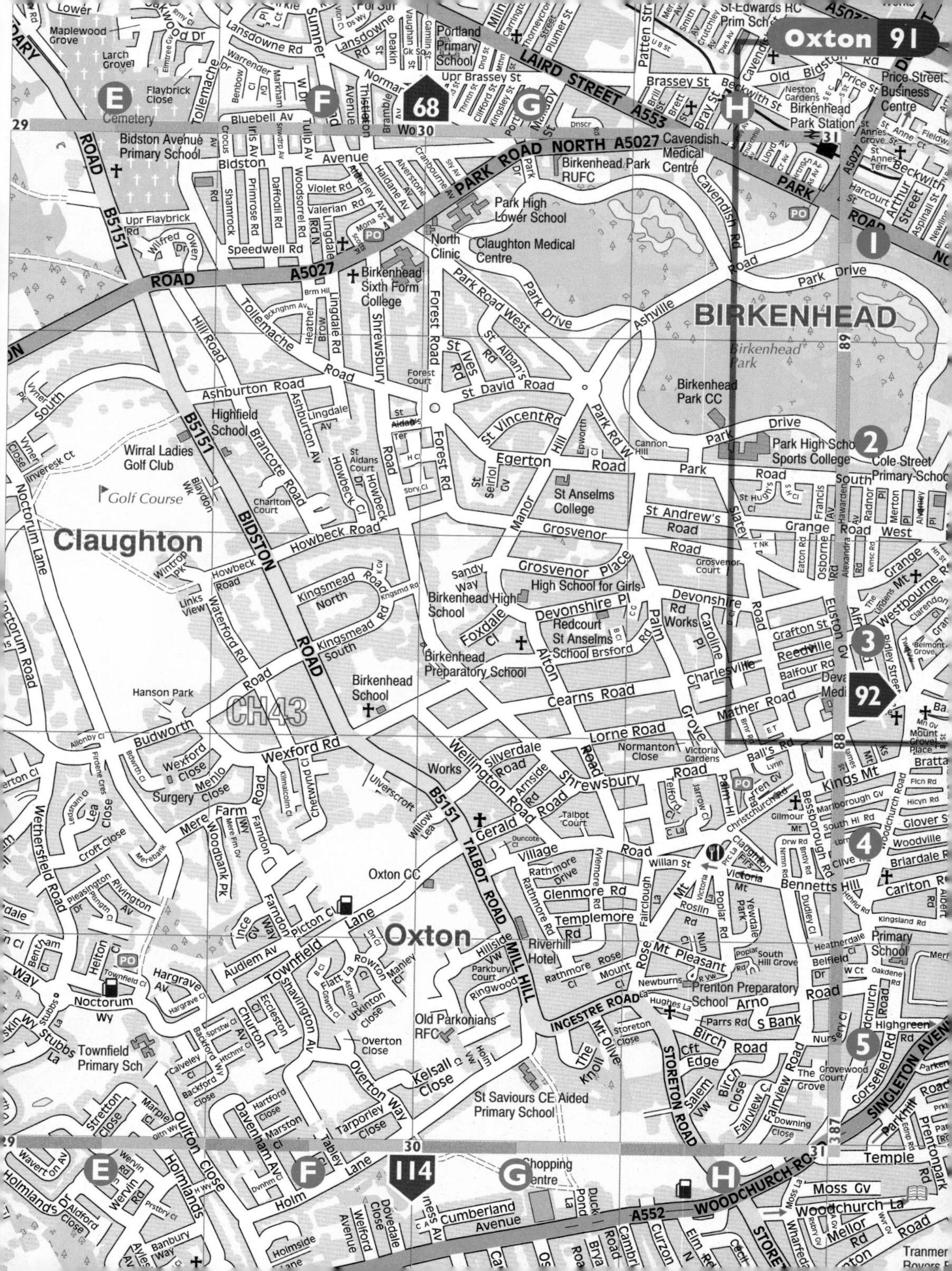

BIRKENHEAD
Birkenhead Park
Claughton
Oxton
CH43
68
92
114
E
F
G
H
I
2
3
4
5
29
30
31
88
89
387
LAIRD STREET A553
PARK ROAD NORTH A5027
A5027
ROAD
B5151
BIDSTON ROAD
TALBOT ROAD
MILL HILL
STORETON ROAD
INGESTRE ROAD
SINGLETON AVENUE
A552 WOODCHURCH RD
Maplewood Grove
Larch Grove
Cemetery
Flaybrick Close
Tollemache
Lansdowne Rd
Sumner
Portland Primary School
Upr Brassey St
Brassey St
Beckwith St
Birkenhead Park Station
Price Street Business Centre
Neston Gardens
St Anne St
Cavendish Medical Centre
Birkenhead Park RUFC
Bidston Avenue Primary School
Bluebell Av
Tulip Av
Iris Av
Crocus Av
Avenue
Bidston
Shamrock Rd
Primrose Rd
Daffodil Rd
Woodsorrel Rd
Violet Rd
Valerian Rd
Lingdale
Haldane Av
Alverstone Av
Cranbourne Av
Mona St
Upr Flaybrick Rd
Wilfred Dr
Owen
Speedwell Rd
Park High Lower School
North Clinic
Claughton Medical Centre
Birkenhead Sixth Form College
Park Road West
Park Drive
Ashville Road
Cavendish Rd
Harcourt St
Arthur Street
Tollemache Road
Hill Road
Heather
Lingdale Rd
Shrewsbury Road
Forest Road
St Ives Rd
St Alban's Rd
Forest Court
St David Road
St Vincent Rd
Park Rd W
Epworth Cl
Ashburton Road
Ashburton Av
Lingdale Av
Highfield School
Brancote Road
Wirral Ladies Golf Club
Golf Course
Inveresk Ct
Vyner Close
South
Noctorum Lane
Noctorum Road
St Aidans Ter
St Aidans Court
Howbeck Dr
Howbeck Cl
Howbeck Road
Forest Rd
Egerton Road
St Seiriol Gv
Manor Hill
Cannon Hill
Birkenhead Park CC
Park Drive
Park Road South
Park High School Sports College
Cole Street Primary School
St Anselms College
St Andrew's Road
Grosvenor Road
Grosvenor Court
Grosvenor Place
Slatey Road
Grange Road West
Eaton Rd
Osborne Av
Francis Av
Radnor Pl
Merton Pl
Hawarden Av
Alexandra Rd
Charlton Court
Blaydon Wk
Wintrop Pk
Howbeck Road
Links View
Waterford Rd
Kingsmead Road North
Kingsmead Rd
Kingsmead Road South
Sandy Way
Birkenhead High School
High School for Girls
Devonshire Pl
Devonshire Rd
Works
Caroline Pl
Palm Grove
Foxdale Cl
Redcourt St Anselms School
Alton Road
Birkenhead Preparatory School
Birkenhead School
Hanson Park
Road
Cearns Road
Charlesville
Grafton St
Reedville
Balfour Rd
Mather Road
Euston Gv
Westbourne Rd
Grange Mt
Budworth
Wexford Close
Wexford Rd
Surgery
Menlo Close
Mere Farm Road
Farndon Way
Woodbank Pk
Wethersfield Road
Lea Close
Croft Close
Pleasington Dr
Rivington Av
Ulverscroft
Willow Lea
Works
Wellington Road
Silverdale Road
Arnside Rd
Road
Shrewsbury Road
Lorne Road
Normanton Close
Victoria Gardens
Ball's Road
Kings Mt
Bessborough Rd
Marlborough Gv
South Hl Rd
Woodchurch Road
Glover St
Woodville
Briardale Rd
Carlton Rd
Kingsland Rd
Gerald Rd
Village Road
Talbot Court
Rathmore Drive
Kylemore Rd
Glenmore Rd
Templemore Rd
Fairclough La
Willan St
Victoria Mt
Claughton Firs
Christchurch Rd
Bennetts Hill
Clive Rd
Dudley Cl
Oxton CC
Picton Cl
Lane
Ince Gv
Riverhill Hotel
Hillside Vw
Parkbury Court
Ringwood
Rathmore Cl
Mount Rose
Rose Mt
Mt Pleasant
Roslin Rd
Poplar Rd
Yewdale Park
South Hill Grove
Heatherdale Cl
Primary School
Belfield Dr
Oakdene Rd
Prenton Preparatory School
Newburns La
Hughes La
Arno Rd
Parrs Rd
S Bank
Birch Road
Cft Edge
Highgreen Rd
Gorsefield Rd
Audlem Av
Townfield Lane
Rowton Cl
Flatt La
Manley Cl
Shavington Av
Utkinton Close
Noctorum Wy
Helton Cl
Hargrave Av
Stubbs La
Townfield Primary Sch
Eccleston Cl
Churton Av
Overton Close
Old Parkonians RFC
Overton Way
Kelsall Close
Holm Vw
The Knoll
Mt Olive
Storeton Close
Salem Vw
Birch Close
Fairview Road
Fairview Cl
Downing Close
The Grove
Grovewood Court
Nursery Cl
St Saviours CE Aided Primary School
Tarporley Close
Marston Close
Hartford Close
Davenham Av
Stretton Close
Marple Cl
Oulton Close
Calveley Cl
Backford Close
Tabley Lane
Holm Lane
Holmlands
Waverton Av
Wervin Rd
Alford
Holmlands Dr
Banbury Way
Holmside
Welford Avenue
Dovedale Close
Cumberland Avenue
Shopping Centre
Duck Pond La
Curzon
Elm Rd
Moss Gv
Woodchurch La
Mellor Rd
Temple Rd
Prentonpark Rd
Tranmere Rovers FC

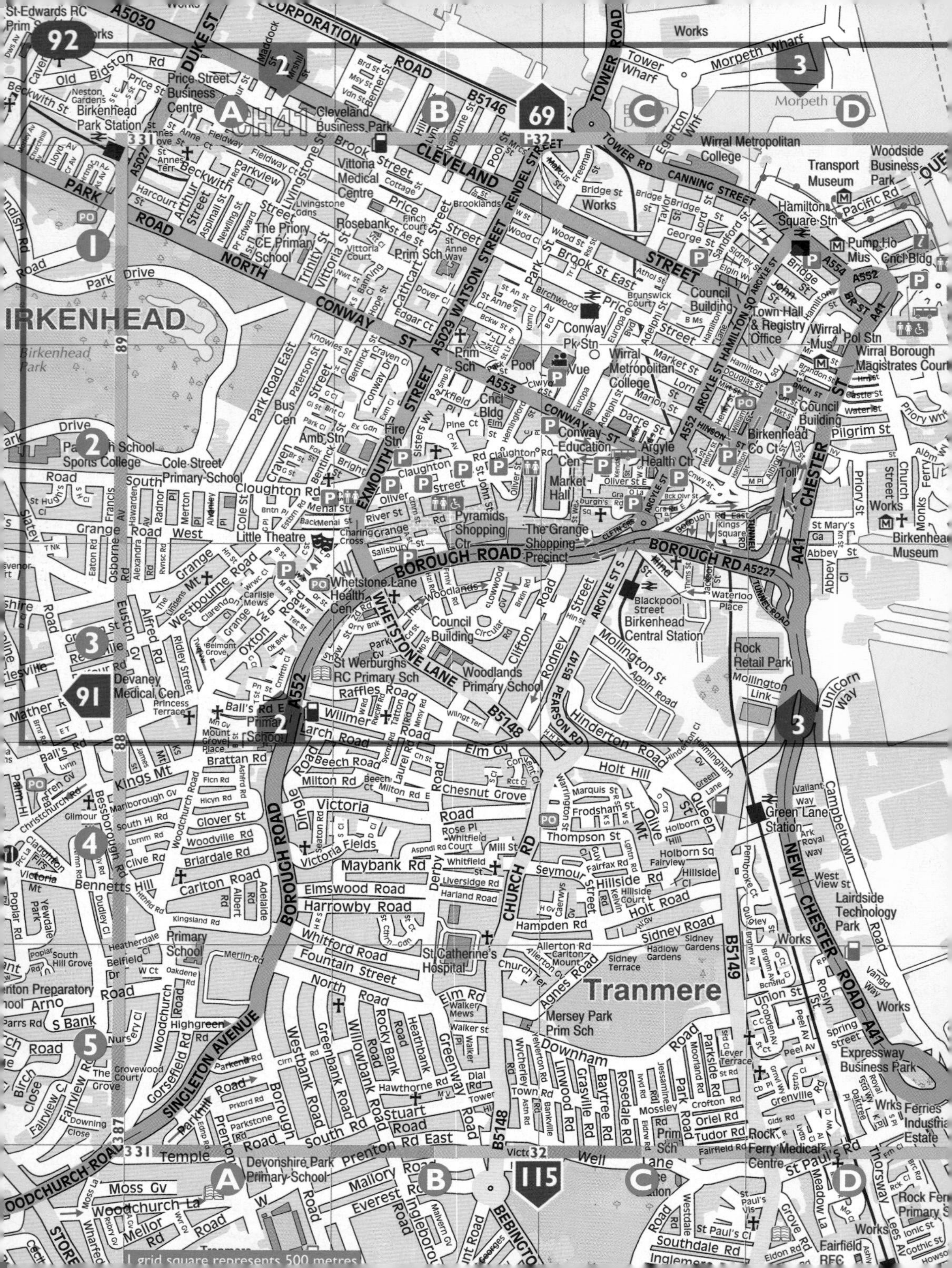

92
A5030
CORPORATION ROAD
DUKE ST
Works
TOWER ROAD
Tower Wharf
Morpeth Wharf
Morpeth Dock
2
3
69
A
B
C
D
CH41
Price Street Business Centre
Cleveland Business Park
Birkenhead Park Station
B5146
CLEVELAND STREET
RENDEL STREET
TOWER RD
CANNING STREET
Wirral Metropolitan College
Woodside Business Park
Transport Museum
Pacific Rd
Hamilton Square Stn
Pump Ho Mus
Cncl Bldg
PARK ROAD NORTH
CONWAY ST
BIRKENHEAD
Birkenhead Park
Park Drive
The Priory CE Primary School
Vittoria Medical Centre
Livingstone St
Rosebank
Prim Sch
WATSON STREET
A5029
Brook St East
Price Street
Conway Pk Stn
Wirral Metropolitan College
Council Building
Town Hall & Registry Office
HAMILTON SQ
ARGYLE ST
Wirral Mus
Pol Stn
Wirral Borough Magistrates Court
Bus Cen
Park Road East
EXMOUTH STREET
A553
Cncl Bldg
Pool
Vue
CONWAY ST
Conway St Education Cen
Argyle Health Ctr
Market Hall
Birkenhead Co Ct
CHESTER ST
Pilgrim St
Council Building
Priory St
Church Street
Works
Birkenhead Museum
Park High School Sports College
Cole Street Primary School
Amb Stn
Fire Stn
Cloughton Rd
Oliver St
Pyramids Shopping Ctr
The Grange Shopping Precinct
Little Theatre
Grange Road West
BOROUGH ROAD
BOROUGH RD A5227
Kings Square
TUNNEL ROAD
A41
Whetstone Lane Health Cen
WHETSTONE LANE
Council Building
Blackpool Street
Birkenhead Central Station
Waterloo Place
Rock Retail Park
Mollington Link
Unicorn Way
Mollington St
Appin Road
Rodney Street
B5147
PEARSON RD
Clifton Road
Westbourne Road
Oxton
St Werburghs RC Primary Sch
Woodlands Primary School
91
Devaney Medical Cen
Princess Terrace
Ball's Rd E Primary School
A552
Raffles Road
Willmer Road
Larch Road
B5148
Hinderton Road
Holt Hill
Kings Mt
Brattan Rd
Beech Road
Milton Rd
Chesnut Grove
Victoria Road
Victoria Fields
Maybank Rd
Elmswood Road
Harrowby Road
Whitford Road
Fountain Street
St Catherine's Hospital
CHURCH RD
Frodsham St
Thompson St
Green Lane Station
Queen St
Holborn Sq
Hillside Rd
Holt Road
Sidney Road
Hampden Rd
Allerton Rd
Agnes Road
Tranmere
Mersey Park Prim Sch
Downham Road
B5149
NEW CHESTER ROAD
Campbeltown Road
Lairdside Technology Park
Works
Expressway Business Park
Wrks
Ferries Industrial Estate
Bessborough Rd
Bennetts Hill
Carlton Road
Woodville Rd
Glover St
Kingsland Rd
Primary School
Merlin Rd
South Hill Grove
Belfield Dr
Highgreen Rd
Woodchurch Road
S Bank
Arno Road
Birch Close
Fairview Rd
The Grove
Grovewood Court
Gorsefield Rd
BOROUGH ROAD
SINGLETON AVENUE
Westbank Road
Greenbank Road
Willowbank Road
Rocky Bank Road
Heathbank Road
Greenway Road
Hawthorne Rd
Stuart Road
South Rd
Prenton Rd East
Elm Rd
Walker St
Dial Rd
Tower Rd
Wycherley Rd
Linwood Rd
Grasville Rd
Baytree Rd
Rosedale Rd
Park Road
Parkside Rd
Crofton Rd
Oriel Rd
Tudor Rd
Rock Ferry Medical Centre
Prim Sch
St Paul's Rd
Thorsway
Rock Ferry Primary S
B5148
1
2
3
4
5
88
89
331
332
387
WOODCHURCH ROAD
Temple Rd
Devonshire Park Primary School
Prenton Rd
115
Moss Gv
Woodchurch La
Mallory Rd
Everest Rd
Ingleborough Rd
BEBINGTON
Well Lane
Westdale Rd
St Paul's Cl
Southdale Rd
Grove Rd
Meadow La
Lees Av
Works
Eldon Rd
Fairfield Rd
Mellor Rd
1 grid square represents 500 metres

Birkenhead 93
International Slavery Museum
Fingerprints of Elvis
Tate Gallery
Albert Dock Village
The Beatles Story
Albert Dock
70
Premier Travel Inn
Wapping Basin
Police HQ
Hotel Ibis
YHA
Wapping Quay
Kings Dock
Waterfront Business Area
Parliament St N Waterfront Bus Area
Campanile Hotel
Queens Dock Business Centre
VAT House & HM Customs & Excise
Queens Dock
Kings Parade
Queens Wharf
Mariners Wharf
Liverpool Marina
Coburg Wharf
Hill Street Business Centre
Navigation Wharf
Quebec Quay
South Ferry Quay
Small Business Centre
Travelodge
Brunswick Business Park
Brunswick Wy
Atlantic Way
Summers Road
Tower Street
Harrison Wy
Sefton Street
Harrington Rd
STRAND
WAPPING A562
CHALONER ST
PARK LANE
PARLIAMENT ST A562
ST JAMES ST
A561
A5036
SEFTON STREET
A5038 GT GEORGE ST
Hill Street
Hill Street Bus Cen
Warwick Street
Northumberland Street
Grafton St
Mann St
Beaufort St
Caryl St
Jamaica Street
Flint St
Greenland St
New Bird St
Jordan St
Brick St
Kings Dock St
Blundell Street
Kitchen Street
Bridgewater St
Watkinson St
Sparling St
Cornhill
Upr Frederick St
Gilbert St
Kent St
Grenville St
Cornwallis St
Bailey St
Chinese Arch
Great George Square
Health Cen
Nelson St
Cookson St
Raffles St
Bus Area
Brewery
Stanhope Street
Fisher St
Brindley St
Gore St
Tox
Woodside Ferry Landing Stage
Woodside Ferry Approach
Priory Mews
Works
Oil Terminal
Mersey Road
Ebenezer St
Bedford Rd
Bedford East Rd
Russell Rd
Rock
KINGSWAY (MERSEY TUNNEL)
The Sloyne
Liverpool
Wirral
E F G H I
1 2 3 4 5
33 34 35
387 388 389
94
116

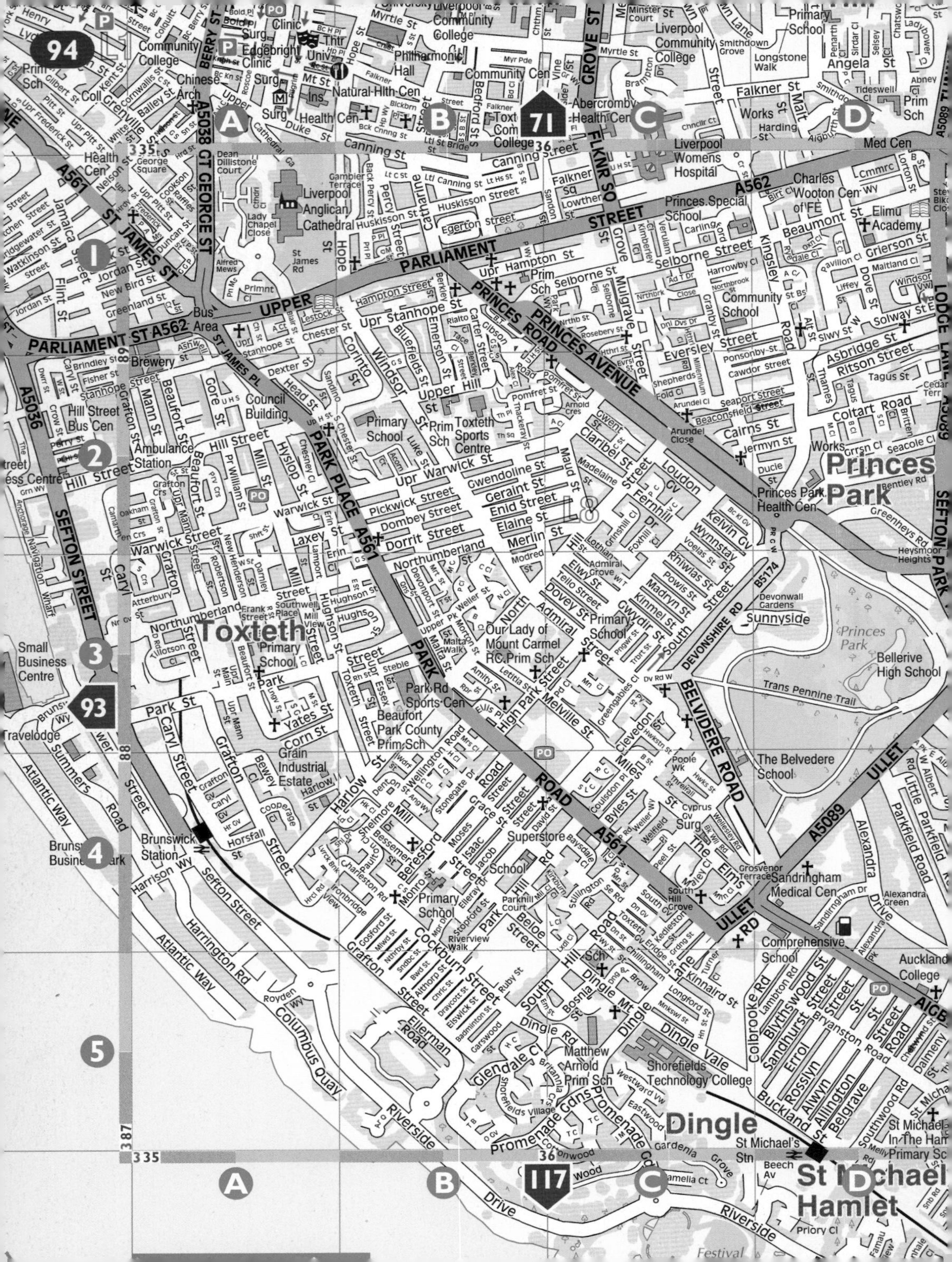
94
93
71
117
A
B
C
D
1
2
3
4
5
335
36
387
88
Liverpool Community College
Philharmonic Hall
Community Cen
Natural Hlth Cen
Health Cen
Edgebright Clinic
Chinese Arch
Community College
Liverpool Community College
Abercromby Health Cen
Liverpool Womens Hospital
Med Cen
Charles Wooton Cen of FE
Elimu Academy
Princes Special School
Community School
Liverpool Anglican Cathedral
Lady Chapel Close
St James Rd
Dean Dillistone Court
St George Square
Gambier Terrace
Canning St
Catharine Street
Huskisson Street
Falkner Sq
Lowther St
Grove Street
FLKNR SQ
GROVE ST
BERRY ST
A5038 GT GEORGE ST
UPPER PARLIAMENT STREET A562
PARLIAMENT ST A562
ST JAMES ST
A561
Jamaica Street
Jordan St
New Bird St
Greenland St
Flint St
Bus Area
Brewery
Hill Street Bus Cen
Ambulance Station
Council Building
Primary School
Upper Hill St
Prim Sch
Toxteth Sports Centre
PRINCES ROAD
PRINCES AVENUE
Selborne Street
Mulgrave Street
Kingsley Road
Granby St
Eversley Street
Beaumont St
Grierson St
Asbridge St
Ritson Street
Coltart Road
Cairns St
Jermyn St
Princes Park
Princes Park Health Cen
LODGE LANE
SEFTON PARK
A5089
A5036
SEFTON STREET
Hill Street
Warwick Street
Grafton Street
Caryl St
Mill St
Northumberland Street
Toxteth
Small Business Centre
Travelodge
Brunswick Business Park
Brunswick Station
Atlantic Way
Summers Road
Harrington Rd
Sefton Street
Park St
Caryl Street
Grafton Street
Horsfall Street
Grain Industrial Estate
Beaufort Park County Prim Sch
Park Rd Sports Cen
PARK PLACE
PARK ROAD
Upr Warwick St
Pickwick Street
Dombey Street
Dorrit Street
Windsor St
Corinto St
Gwendoline St
Geraint St
Enid Street
Elaine St
Merlin St
L8
Admiral Street
Our Lady of Mount Carmel RC Prim Sch
High Park Street
Melville St
Loudon Gv
Kelvin Gv
Wynnstay St
Devonwall Gardens
Sunnyside
Princes Park
Bellerive High School
Trans Pennine Trail
DEVONSHIRE RD
B5174
BELVIDERE ROAD
The Belvedere School
ULLET RD
A5089
Little Parkfield Rd
Parkfield Road
Alexandra Drive
Alexandra Green
Sandringham Medical Cen
Grosvenor Terrace
Comprehensive School
Auckland College
Colbrooke Rd
Blythswood St
Sandhurst St
Errol St
Rosslyn St
Alwyn St
Allington St
Belgrave Rd
Bryanston Road
Southwood Rd
Dalmeny
Superstore
School
Primary School
Riverview Walk
Grafton Street
Cockburn Street
Ellerman Road
Columbus Quay
Riverside Drive
Glendale Cl
Dingle Rd
Dingle Vale
Dingle Mt
Matthew Arnold Prim Sch
Shorefields Technology College
Shorefields Village
Promenade Gdns
Dingle
Gardenia Grove
St Michael's Stn
St Michael's Hamlet
St Michael's In The Hamlet Primary Sc
Priory Cl
Festival
Beech Av
Camelia Ct
Buckland St
Kinnaird St
Longford St
Park Rd
Wellington Road
Stonegate Dr
Harlow St
Beresford St
Moses St
Isaac St
Jacob St
Royden Wy

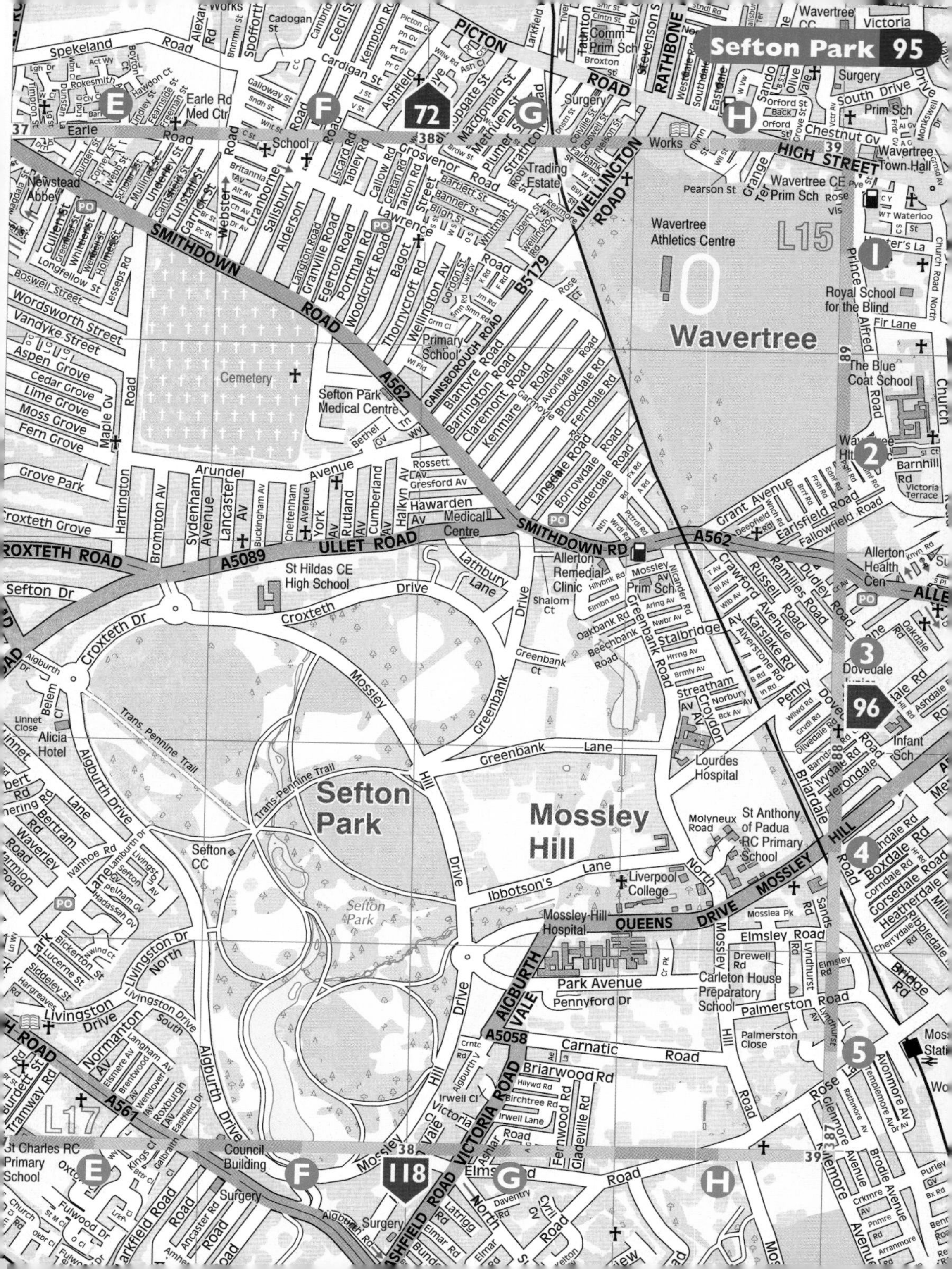
Spekeland Road
Cadogan St
Cardigan St
PICTON ROAD
RATHBONE ROAD
Comm Prim Sch
Wavertree CC
Victoria
Surgery
South Drive
Prim Sch
Earle Rd Med Ctr
Earle Road
School
Grosvenor Road
Trading Estate
Works
Chestnut Gv
HIGH STREET
Wavertree Town Hall
Wavertree CE Prim Sch
Newstead Abbey
SMITHDOWN ROAD
A562
Pearson St
WELLINGTON ROAD
Wavertree Athletics Centre
L15
Cemetery
Primary School
GAINSBOROUGH ROAD
B5179
Royal School for the Blind
Fir Lane
Wavertree
The Blue Coat School
Church Road North
Sefton Park Medical Centre
Wordsworth Street
Vandyke Street
Aspen Grove
Cedar Grove
Lime Grove
Moss Grove
Fern Grove
Maple Gv
Grove Park
Arundel Avenue
Hawarden Av
Medical Centre
Croxteth Grove
CROXTETH ROAD
A5089
ULLET ROAD
SMITHDOWN RD
Grant Avenue
Earlsfield Road
Fallowfield Road
Allerton Health Cen
St Hildas CE High School
Lathbury Lane
Allerton Remedial Clinic
Mossley Prim Sch
Shalom Ct
Croxteth Drive
Croxteth Dr
Greenbank Road
Stalbridge Av
Dovedale
Linnet Close
Alicia Hotel
Trans Pennine Trail
Greenbank Lane
Lourdes Hospital
Sefton Park
Mossley Hill
St Anthony of Padua RC Primary School
Molyneux Road
Sefton CC
Ibbotson's Lane
Liverpool College
Mossley Hill Hospital
QUEENS DRIVE MOSSLEY HILL
Elmsley Road
Carleton House Preparatory School
Park Avenue
Pennyford Dr
Palmerston Road
Palmerston Close
Livingston Drive
AIGBURTH VALE
A5058
Carnatic Road
Briarwood Rd
VICTORIA ROAD
L17
A561
St Charles RC Primary School
Council Building
Surgery
Aigburth Drive
72
96
118
37
38
39
E
F
G
H
I
2
3
4
5

96
73
95
119
89
88
40
339
387
A
B
C
D
1
2
3
4
5
L15
L18
Calderstones
HIGH STREET
CHILDWALL ROAD
B5178
QUEENS DR (WAVERTREE)
A5058
QUEENS DR
MOSSLEY HL
ALLERTON ROAD
MENLOVE AV
HILL
A562
BEECH LANE
MATHER AVENUE
B5180
ALLERTON ROAD
Wavertree CC
Victoria Ct
Valley Road Business Park
Millstead Special School
Olive Mt Road
Millstead Road
Thingwall
Abbeystead Road
Meadway
Childwall School
Rudston Road
Rudston J&I Sch
Wavertree Town Hall
Wavertree CE Prim Sch
Davenham Court
Abbeystead Medical Centre
The King David High Sch
King David Primary School
Royal School for the Blind
Lance Lane Medical Centre
The Blue Coat School
Mosspits J&I School
Wavertree Hlth Clinic
Rutherford Medical Centre
Allerton Health Cen
Dunbabin Road
Dudlow Lane
Menlove Gardens W
Menlove Gdns South
Menlove Gdns N
Our Ladys Bishop Eton RC Primary School
Liverpool Institute of HE
Education Deanery
Liverpool Hope University College
Childwall CE Prim Sch
Woolton Road
Cinder La
Primrose Road
Gwydrin Rd
Beechenhurst School
Dovedale Junior School
Infant Sch
Odeon Cinema
Police Stn
Calderstones School
Calderstones Road
Druids Cross Rd
Council Building
St Anthony of Padua RC Prim School
Carleton House Preparatory School
Mossley Hill Station
Works
Storrsdale Medical Cen
Ballantrae Road
Burnham Road
Pitville Avenue
Rose Lane
Elmsley Road
Palmerston Road
Garthdale Road
Harthill Road
Allerton Beeches
1 grid square represents 500 metres

Childwall
Belle Vale
Gateacre
L16
St Paschal Baylon RC Prim Sch
Craighurst JM&I School
Childwall Valley Prim Sch
Ashfield Special School
Belle Vale Health Centre
Our Lady of the Assumption Primary School
Belle Vale Shopping Centre
Belle Vale Swimming Po
Gateacre Community Comprehensive School
St Francis Xaviers College
Abbots Lea Special School
Harold Magnay Special Sch
Lower Lee Special Sch
Palmerston Special Sch
Garden Centre
Woolton J&I School
Mount Park Court
Bishop Martin CE Prim Sch
Picture House
Woolton House Medical Cen
Village Medical Cen
Valley Medical Cen
Trans Pennine Trail
Liverpool Loop Line
B5178
B5171
Menlove Avenue
Acrefield Road
Gateacre Brow
Belle Vale Road
Woolton Road
Woolton Hill Road
Childwall Lane
Childwall Abbey Rd
Well Lane
Gateacre Park Drive
Hartsbourne Avenue
Beaconsfield Road
Quarry Street
Church Road
Hunts Cross Avenue
Kings Drive
Halewood Road
Speke Rd
Edenhurst Avenue
Score Lane
Barnham Drive
Countisbury Drive
Gipsy Lane
74
98
120
41
42
43
E
F
G
H
I
2
3
4
5

M62
75
A
B
C
D
343
44
Oak Road
Willow Av
Laurel Gv
Pear Tree Rd
Cherry Tree
Field's End
Silverdale Cl
TARBOCK ROAD
Meadow Drive
The Chase
Huyton Brook
Mallow Wy
Campion
Cornel Wy
Rickman Wy
Wheat Hill Rd
Naylor's Road
Lakeside School
Wheathill Farm
Hope School
Holt Lane
The Childwall Golf Club
Golf Course
Coney Lane
Knowsley
Liverpool
Dalebrook Cl
Cornwood Cl
Madeira Drive
Genoa Cl
Eccles Dr
Dorchester Park
Naylorsfield Drive
St Cyrils Cl
School Cl
Farmview
Barnstream Cl
Silverbrook
Fourways Cl
Southbrook Rd
Waterford Rd
Brinton Cl
Naylor's Road
Woodgate
Handel Rd
Fulshaw Cl
Calderwood Pk
Caldway Drive
Wheathill Industrial Estate
Holt Lane
Belle Vale Health Centre
Our Lady of the Assumption Primary School
Hedgefield Road
B5178
Abbeyvale Dr
Stapleford Road
Belle Vale Shopping Centre
Belle Vale Swimming Pool
Hartsbourne Av
Belle Vale
B5171
Police Station
Runton Rd
Westbrook Rd
Paveley Bank
Tuffins Corner
Chalnhurst Cl
Rushlake Dr
Garden Ldg Gv
Crabtree Cl
Dignum Md
Linden Rd
Lydieth Lea
Clematis Rd
Sullington Dr
Damson Rd
Bamboo Cl
Evergreen
Caldway Drive
Pengallo Hey
Laurus Cl
Roseside Drive
NETHERLEY R
St Gregorys RC JM&I Sch
Vancouver Rd
Winnipeg Dr
Montreal Rd
Michigan Cl
Netherley Health Cen
Crispin Rd
PO
Russet Cl
Middlemass Hey
Works
Herdman Cl
Besford Road
Wambo Lane
Oakwood
97
Lenton Rd
Bardon Cl
Churchfield Rd
Lulworth Rd
Cadnam Rd
Lee Hall Rd
Drive
BELLE VALE ROAD
Belle Vue Rd
Station Road
Jones Farm Rd
Marsham Rd
Park Avenue
Woodlee Rd
Dinaro Cl
Widmore Rd
Lee Park
Ringway
Beechill Cl
Fordcombe Rd
Kings
Lee Park Golf Club
Netherley Sports Centre
Gateside Cl
Brownbill Bank
The Norman Pannell School
CALDWAY DRIVE
B5178
Glebe Hey
Blue Jay Cl
Fulmar Cl
Brittarge Brow
Wheatear Cl
Dunlin Cl
Peckmill Gn
Falcon Crescent
Wood Lane
Fern Cl
Parkview Drive
Netherley
L27
Cross Farm Primary School
Lingford Cl
Sharwood Rd
Gladsville Rd
Washington Rd
Victoria Falls Rd
Tothale Turn
Lee Vale Road
Martland Road
Winfrith Rd
Golf Course
Gateacre
Kilester Rd
Elm House Ms
Halewood Cl
The Nook
Cherry V
Orient Drive
Cross Avenue
Halewood
Ribble Rd
Roxborough Wk
Chevasse Wk
Hadfield Gv
Woolton J&I School
Lane
Whitney Road
Garway
Edenhall Drive
Reigate Cl
Merrivale Rd
Liverpool
Knowsley
North End La
Gerrard's Lane
Lane
387
121
Works
Banbury Av
Ruislip Cl
Lydiate Lane
The Cobbles
Clover Av
Firethorne Rd
Tinsley Close
Foxhill Lane
Woodvale Rd
Halewood Dr
Hunts
1 grid square represents 500 metres

Windy Arbor
Whitefield Lane End
Tarbock Green
Works
Stretton Wy
Newsham Rd
Bridgewater Way
A5080
CRONTON ROAD
Coppice La
M62
Junction 6/1
Cronton Rd
Sevenoak Gv
Smithford Wk
Crescent
Hawke Gn
Bardley
Oakworth Dr
Richmond Way
Mellor Cl
Ribchester Wy
Cringles Drive
Elizabeth
Tennyson Rd
Darwick Drive
Boundary Road
Manley Rd
Road
Wood Rd
Rd
Hastings Dr
Bradley Fold
Windy Arbor
Whitefield Lane
Lane
Whitefield
Ox Lane
Dacre's Bridge Lane
KNOWSLEY EXPRESSWAY
A5300
B5178
ROAD
Tarbock Hall Farm
Water Lane Farm
Water Lane
Water L
NETHERLEY ROAD
Winster Drive
Egremont Lawn
Appleby Lawn
Selside Wk
Mardale Lawn
Honister Cl
Scafell Lawn
Winster Drive
Greensbridge Lane
Green's Bridge Farm
Fox Farm
Cross Hillocks Farm
E F G H
I 2 3 4 5
45 46 47
89 88 387
76
100
122

100
77
99
123
St Helens
Knowsley
Cronton Lane
Higher Shaw Farm
Shaw Entry
Fox's Bank Lane
Penny Lane
A5080
CRONTON ROAD
Bridge Lane
Works
Tue Lane
Cront
Prescot Road
Water Lane
Water Lane F
Alder Lane
Lodge Lane
Stockswell Road
Cross Hillocks Lane
Cross Hillocks
Redbourne Dr
Columbine Cl
Cherrysutton
Darley Cl
Blaii
All Saints Upton Prim Sc
Northern La
Brookdale
Innis
Surgery
Bechers
Danescroft
Downside
PO
Upton Medical Centre
St Basil RC Primary School
Brandon
Hough Green Rd
Avon
Aire
Alt
Eversl
Edendale
Arley Dr
Arley Drive
Foxcote
Crizedale
Arden
347
48
387
88
89
1 grid square represents 500 metres

M62
78
WARRINGTON ROAD
A557
WATKINSON WAY
WILMERE LANE
Norland's Lane
Hall Lane
Hall La
Town End
The Ridgeway
Cronton CE Primary School
Holy Family RC Primary School
Brook Cl
C P Cl
Hall Lane
The Rbt
Mill Lane
Iver Cl
Woburn Dr
Hampton Dr
Malton Cl
Lambourn Av
Kenley Av
Smithy Lane
Smithy Forge Cl
Wheatfield Road
Houghton Cft
Nickleford Hall Drive
Norland's Pk
Lindisfarne Ct
The Hillcrest Hotel
A5080 CRONTON LANE
CRONTON RD
PO
Widnes & Runcorn Sixth Form College
Chapel Lane
Sandy Lane
Stratton Park
Tynwald Crs
Cowanway
Hill View
Baileys Cl
Monica Dr
Lunts
102
Coronation
Buckingham
BIRCHFIELD ROAD
Clarence Av
Stone Cross Dr
Pex Hill Ct
Linacre La
Fox Bank Cl
Fox Bank Ct
Alderwood Ct
Bellflower Cl
Upton Rocks Av
Chetwood Dr
Vixen Gv
Upton Lane
Tuson Dr
Linden Wy
Julian Way
Ingham Rd
Upton Bridle Path
Bembridge Cl
Whitstable Pk
Rock La
Sandringham Rd
Windsor Rd
Balmoral Road
New Barnet
Campsey Ash
Lofthouse Ga
Higher Ashton
Lessingham Rd
Newbury Cl
Farnworth
Widnes Crematorium
Fillmore Gv
Rushmore Dr
Telford Cl
Old Upton La
Kennington Park
Cleadon Wy
Harton Cl
Chilwell Cl
Upton Grange
Preece Cl
Upton Gra
Meadow
Lanark Gdns
Falkirk Av
Upton Rocks
Dinnington Ct
Holborn Ct
Wallsend Ct
Cornforth Wy
McKinley Wy
Jefferson Gdns
Widnes Station
Victoria Av
Chedworth Dr
Oxton Cl
Cross Gv
Aylsham Cl
Croston Cl
Haddon Dr
Burnsall Dr
Lea
Clanfield Av
Mortlake Cl
Tiverton Cl
Porthcawl Cl
Astley Cl
Naughton Lea
Ash Priors
Parklands
Ravenfield Dr
Rainbow Cl
Blackbrook Cl
Gainford Cl
Ellerton Cl
Great Ashfield
Prescot Rd
Prescot Road
Cornerhouse La
Rock Lane
Regency Park
Heathfield Pk
Bridgend Cl
Queensbury Wy
Roscommon Wy
Galway Av
Portrush Cl
Deepdale
Simonside
Whernside
Fulbeck
Arley Dr
Gleadmere
Atterbury
Poleacre Dr
Rockfield Cl
Woodstock Gv
Prescot
Crs
Ormond Cl
124
WA8
Wade Deacon High School
Saints Peter
Tabley
E
F
G
H
1
2
3
4
5
49
50
51
89
88
87

102
WARRINGTON ROAD
A57
CUBITS LANE
Old Brook
79
A
B
C
D
351
52
Wilmere House
WATKINSON WAY
WARRINGTON ROAD
A57
Bridge Farm
Halton
St Helens
1
89
Nickleford Hall Drive
2
Lindisfarne Ct
WILMERE LANE
A557
WATKINSON WAY
Cranshaw Lane
Twyford
Lane
Hillcrest
LANE
LUNTS
HEATH
ROAD
Mill Lane
Mill
Green
Mill Green Farm
PO
Tynwald Crs
Hill View
3
Baileys Cl
Hartland Cl
Elworth Av
Monica Dr
Farndale
Dr
Gleneagles
Churchfields
Birkdale Road
Minton Wy
Lunts Heath
101
B5419
Coroner's
Glebe Lane
Lunts Heath Primary School
Wenger Rd
Tuscan Cl
Garrigill Cl
Finsbury Pk
Byland Cl
Eastbury Cl
Wilcote Cl
Bold Industrial Est
Mill La
DERBY ROAD
88
Upton
Tuson Dr
Buckingham Av
BIRCHFIELD ROAD
Clarence Avenue
Holyrood Av
Twyford Cl
Lane
Wedgwood Dr
Ryder Rd
Ganton Cl
Farnworth CE Primary School
St Luke's Crs
Grosvenor
Trent
Claremont Dr
Derby Road
Hampton Ct Wy
Islington Gn
Hmptn Ct Wy
Julian Way
Linden Wy
Ingham
4
Bembridge Cl
Upton Bridle Path
Pit
Lane
Marsh Hall Road
Farnworth Street
Beaconsfield Crs
Beaconsfield Road
Bcn Gv
Mason Av
Widnes CC
Windermere St
Works
A557
Moorfield
Road
Brmndsy Gv
Greenwich Av
Camberwell Pk Rd
Works
Sandringham
Windsor Rd
Balmoral Road
New Barnet
Lessingham Rd
Newbury Cl
Farnworth
Wellfield
Factory La
Derby Road
PO
Whalley Gv
School Wy
Nursery Cl
Higher Ashton
Widnes Crematorium
Borough Cemetery
Cornwall Rd
Gloucester Rd
Rushmore Dr
5
Lancaster Road
Alder Rd
Avenue
Birch Rd
Acacia Av
Peel
Fairfield High School
Bishops Way
Jefferson Gdns
Widnes Station
Victoria Av
387
351
Lockett
Road
Cedar Av
Cypress Av
House
52
125
A
B
C
D
WAY
Wade Deacon High School
BIRCHFIE
Rose View Av
Elm Av
Chestnut Av
Lilac Av
Willow Av
Kirkham Rd
Ansdell Road
Brookslands Pk
Neil St
Barnes Rd
Ireland St
Crow Wood
Bancroft Rd
Crow Wood La
Rossall Rd
Moorfield Road
Brookfields
WA8
1 grid square represents 500 metres
ppleton
Peter

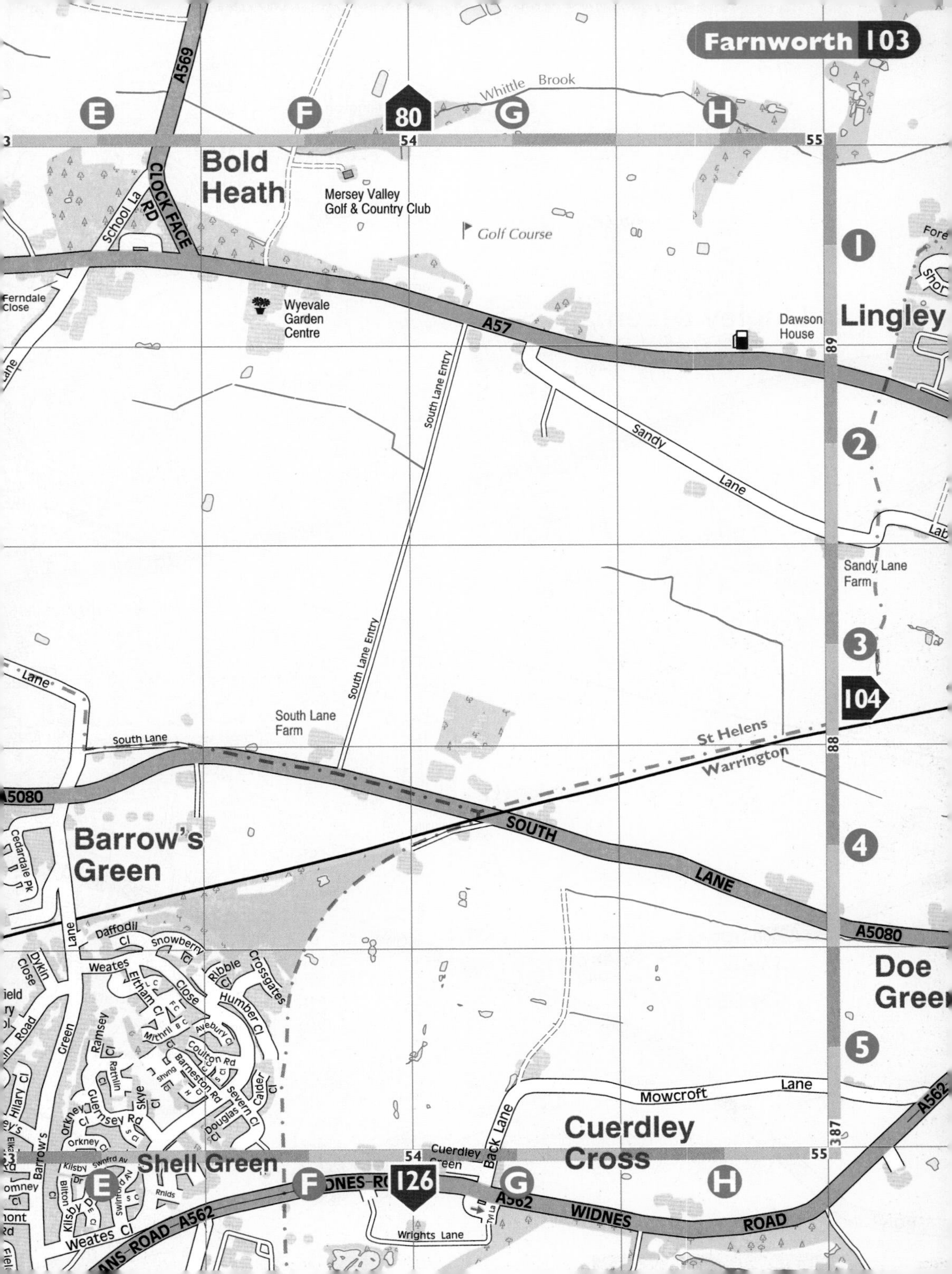
A569
Whittle Brook
80
E
F
G
H
54
55
Bold Heath
School La
CLOCK FACE RD
Mersey Valley Golf & Country Club
Golf Course
Ferndale Close
Wyevale Garden Centre
A57
Dawson House
Lingley
1
2
3
4
5
89
88
387
South Lane Entry
Sandy Lane
Sandy Lane Farm
104
South Lane Farm
South Lane
Lane
St Helens
Warrington
A5080
SOUTH LANE
Barrow's Green
Cedardale Pk
Daffodil Cl
Snowberry Cl
Weates Close
Eltham Cl
Close
Ribble Cl
Crossgates
Humber Cl
Dykin Close
Lane
Green
Ramsey Cl
Mithril
Avebury Cl
Coulton Rd
Barneston Rd
Rathlin Cl
Skye Cl
Severn Cl
Calder Cl
Douglas Cl
Hilary Cl
Orkney Cl
Guernsey Rd
Barrow's
Doe Green
Mowcroft Lane
Back Lane
Cuerdley Cross
Cuerdley Green
Shell Green
126
A562
WIDNES ROAD
Wrights Lane
Kilsby Dr
Weates Cl
Rnlds
A562

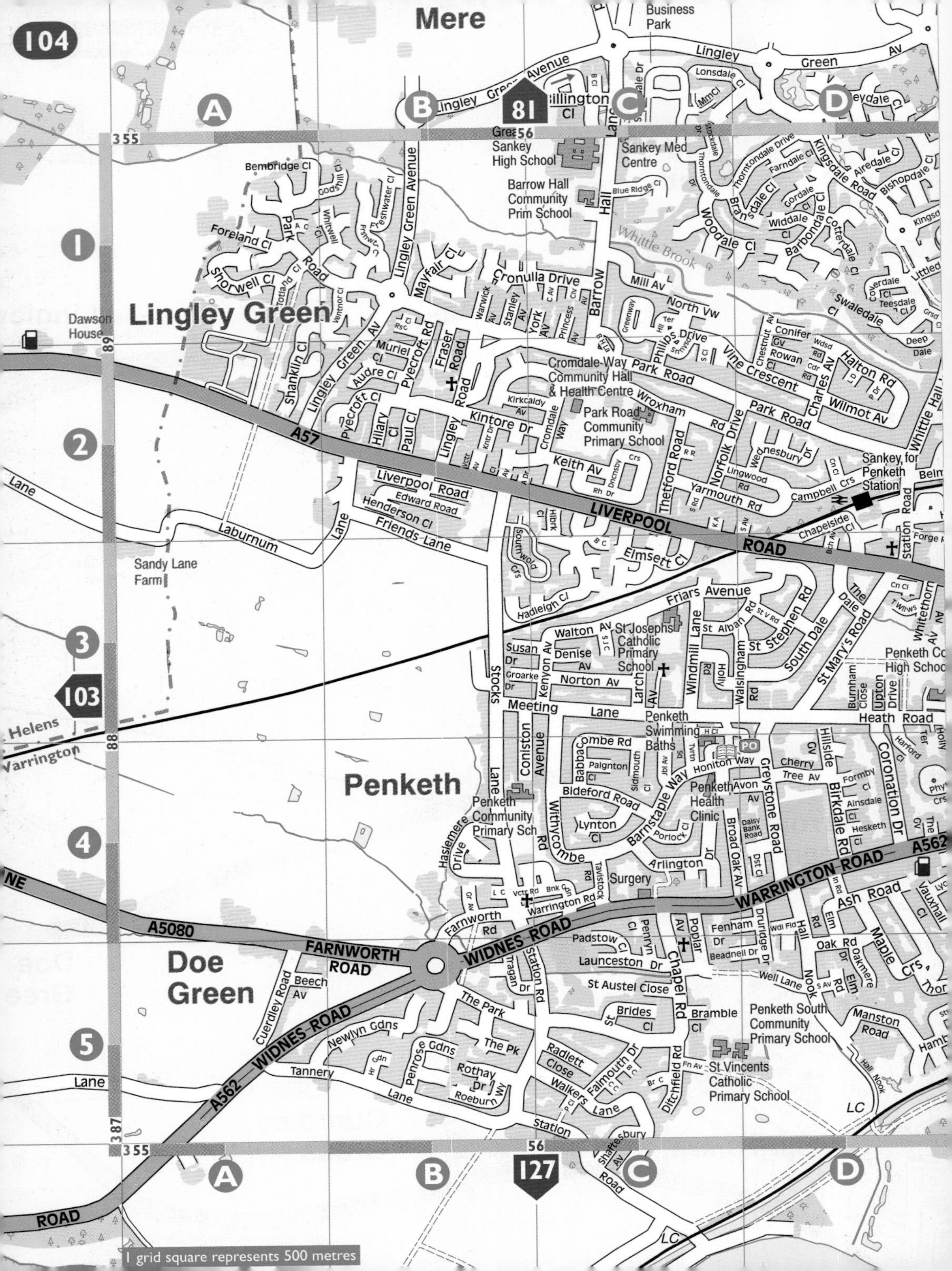
Mere
Business Park
Lingley Green Av
Lingley Green Avenue
Billington Cl
Great Sankey High School
Sankey Med Centre
Barrow Hall Community Prim School
Barrow Hall Lane
Whittle Brook
Lingley Green
Dawson House
Bembridge Cl
Foreland Cl
Shorwell Cl
Park Road
Cronulla Drive
Mill Av
North Vw
Phillips Drive
Vine Crescent
Park Road
Cromdale Way Community Hall & Health Centre
Park Road Community Primary School
Wroxham Rd
Kintore Dr
Keith Av
Thetford Road
Norfolk Drive
Yarmouth Rd
Campbell Crs
Sankey for Penketh Station
A57
LIVERPOOL ROAD
Liverpool Road
Edward Road
Henderson Cl
Friends Lane
Laburnum Lane
Sandy Lane Farm
Elmsett Cl
Hadleigh Cl
Friars Avenue
St Josephs Catholic Primary School
Walton Av
Norton Av
Windmill Lane
Walsingham Rd
St Stephen Rd
South Dale
St Mary's Road
Penketh Co High School
Heath Road
Stocks Lane
Meeting Lane
Coniston Avenue
Penketh
Penketh Swimming Baths
Penketh Community Primary Sch
Penketh Health Clinic
Greystone Road
Birkdale Rd
Coronation Dr
Barnstaple Way
Bideford Road
Withycombe Rd
Surgery
Arlington Dr
Broad Oak Av
WARRINGTON ROAD
A562
Ash Road
Vauxhall Cl
Maple Crs
A5080
FARNWORTH ROAD
WIDNES ROAD
Doe Green
Cuerdley Road
Beech Av
Station Rd
Launceston Dr
Chapel Rd
St Austel Close
Well Lane
Hall Nook
Manston Road
Penketh South Community Primary School
St Vincents Catholic Primary School
Ditchfield Rd
The Park
Newlyn Gdns
Penrose Gdns
Rothay Dr
Radlett Close
Falmouth Dr
Walkers Lane
Tannery Lane
Station Road
Shaftesbury Av
St Helens
Warrington
ROAD
355
56
387
88
89

81
103
127

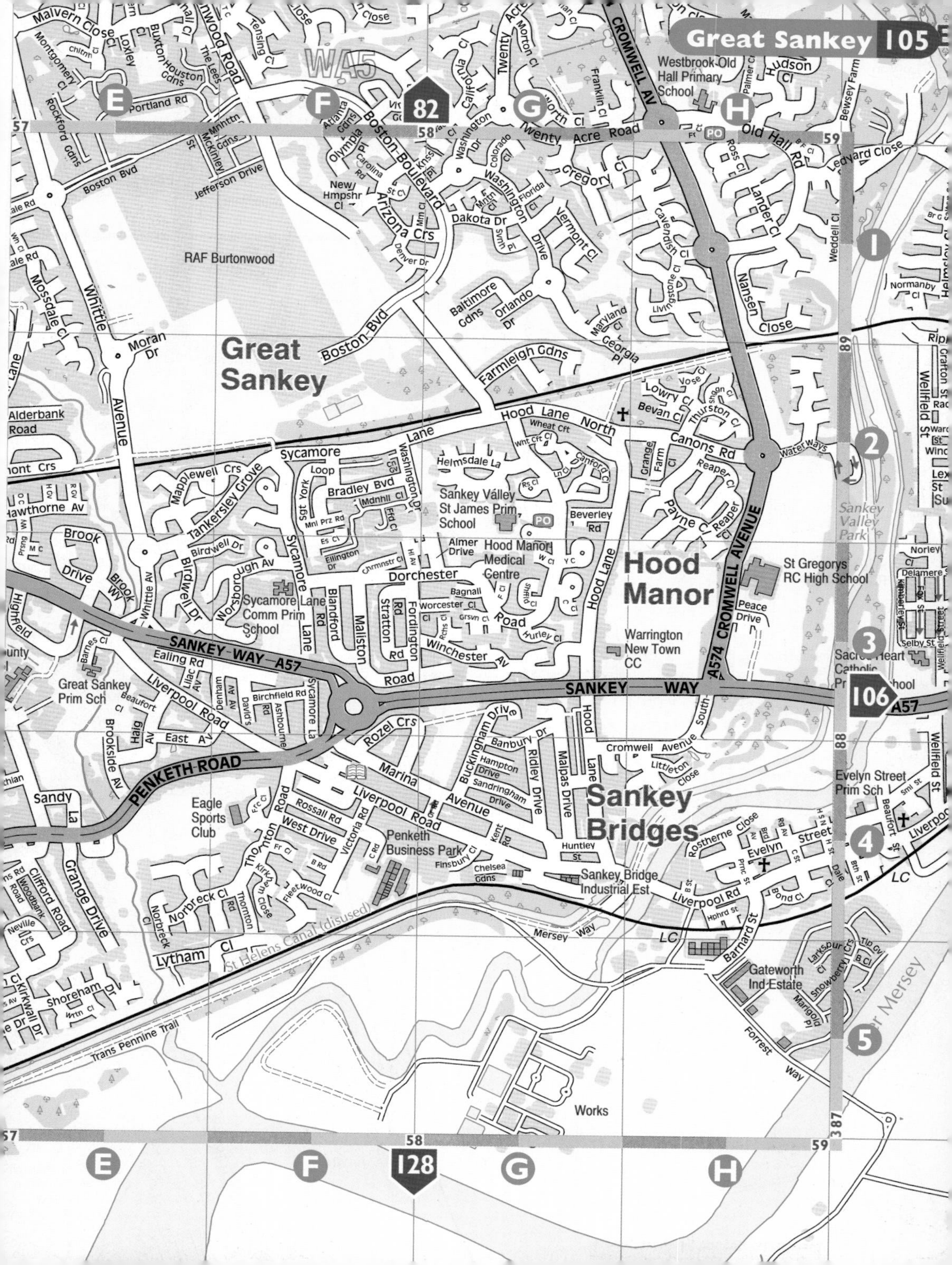

82
WA5
Malvern Close
Montgomery Cl
Loxley
Buxton Houston Gdns
The Lees
Tensing Cl
Portland Rd
Rockford Gdns
Boston Bvd
Jefferson Drive
Boston Boulevard
Atlanta Gdns
Olympia Pl
Carolina Rd
New Hmpshr Cl
Arizona Crs
Denver Dr
California Cl
Twenty Acre Road
Morton Cl
Washington Dr
Colorado Cl
Franklin Cl
Dakota Dr
Florida Cl
Gregory Cl
Vermont Cl
Washington Drive
CROMWELL AV
Westbrook Old Hall Primary School
Hudson Cl
Palmer Cl
Old Hall Rd
Ross Cl
Ledyard Close
Lander Cl
Cavendish Cl
Livingstone Cl
Nansen Close
Weddell Cl
Bewsey Farm
Normanby Cl
RAF Burtonwood
Baltimore Gdns
Orlando Dr
Maryland Cl
Georgia Pl
Great Sankey
Moran Dr
Whittle Avenue
Mossdale Cl
Boston Bvd
Farmleigh Gdns
Lowry Cl
Bevan Cl
Thurston Cl
Hood Lane North
Wheat Cft
Canons Rd
Water Ways
Canford Cl
Grange Farm Cl
Reaper Cl
Payne Cl
Sycamore Lane
Alderbank Road
Mapplewell Crs
Tankersley Grove
Loop
Bradley Bvd
Helmsdale La
Sankey Valley St James Prim School
PO
Beverley Rd
Sankey Valley Park
Hawthorne Av
Brook Drive
Brook Wy
Birdwell Dr
Worsborough Av
Sycamore Lane
Ellington Dr
Almer Drive
Hood Manor Medical Centre
Hood Manor
Hood Lane
St Gregorys RC High School
Dorchester Road
Bagnall
Worcester Cl
Blandford Rd
Maliston Road
Stratton Rd
Fordington Rd
Winchester Av
Hurley Cl
Sycamore Lane Comm Prim School
Peace Drive
Warrington New Town CC
Highfield
SANKEY WAY A57
A574 CROMWELL AVENUE
Norley
Delamere
Selby St
Sacred Heart Catholic Prim School
106
A57
Great Sankey Prim Sch
Ealing Rd
Liverpool Road
Birchfield Rd
Ashbourne
Sycamore La
Rozel Crs
Marina Avenue
Buckingham Drive
Banbury Dr
Hampton Drive
Sandringham Drive
Ridley Drive
Malpas Drive
Cromwell Avenue
Littleton Close
Wellfield St
Evelyn Street Prim Sch
Haig Av
East Av
Brookside Av
PENKETH ROAD
Sandy La
Eagle Sports Club
Thornton Road
Rossall Rd
West Drive
Victoria Rd
Liverpool Road
Penketh Business Park
Kent Rd
Huntley St
Sankey Bridges
Rostherne Close
Evelyn Street
Chelsea Gdns
Sankey Bridge Industrial Est
Liverpool Rd
Bond Cl
Clifford Road
Grange Drive
Norbreck Cl
Kirkham Close
Fleetwood Cl
Neville Crs
Mersey Way
St Helens Canal (disused)
LC
Barnard St
Gateworth Ind Estate
Larkspur Cl
Snowberry Crs
Marigold Pl
Lytham Cl
Shoreham Dr
Kirkwall Dr
Trans Pennine Trail
Forrest Way
Works
128
E
F
G
H
1
2
3
4
5
57
58
59
89
88
387

106
Bewsey
Hawthorne Business Park
Council Building
Kerfoot Business Park
Record Business Park
Hudson Cl
Bewsey Farm Cl
Lilford Avenue
Holford Av
Troutbeck
Bagot Av
83
Hawthorne Business Park
Folly Lane
Kerfoot Street
Jockey St
Surgery
KRFT ST
LONGFORD STREET
North Avenue
Vale Avenue
Ireland Street
Shaw's
West Avenue
A
B
C
D
359
60
Old Hall Rd
Ledyard Close
Lander Cl
Nansen Close
Weddell Cl
Lodge Lane
Trafford Av
Bewsey Park Close
Harrington Av
Gerrard Av
Delves Av
Warwick Av
Saville Av
Wilson St
Dallam Lane
Superstore
Helmsley Cl
Lockton Lane
Bewsey Lodge Primary School
Normanby Cl
High Gates Cl
Clap Gates Rd
Farmside Cl
Lovely La
Bewsey Business Cen
Medical Centre
Ellen St
Hoyle St
Hoyle Street
Lilford St
Catherine St
Pierpoint St
Bewsey Road
Bewsey Bus Cen
Pitt St
Works
12
Owen St
Bewsey Industrial Estate
WINWICK ROAD
Watkin Street
Hale Street
Cyril St
Earl St
Forster St
Clegge St
Bluecoat St
Oliver St
Houghton St
Orford
Cobden St
Warrington Wolves RLFC (Halliwell Jones Stadium)
Warrington Central Trading Estate
Norman Street
Lythgoes Lane
LYTHGOES LANE
Retail Park
Haydock St
John Street
Warrington Central Station
Central Way
A49
1
2
3
4
5
89
88
387
Ripley St
Grafton St
Brighton St
Wellfield St
Radnor St
Wardour St
Windsor St
Lexden St
Surgery
Guardian St
Warrington Hospital
A&E
Levens Cl
Bradgate
St Albans RC Prim Sch
Guardian Street Industrial Estate
Goulden St
Robert St
Guardian Medical Centre
Guardian St
Gladstone St
Walker St
Arthur St
Eustace St
Health Centre
Buckley St
Clinic
FROGHALL LANE
TANNERS LANE
B5210
Dallam Lane
Foundry Street
Rolleston Street
Bewsey Street
Allen St
Sankey Valley Park
CROMWELL AVENUE
St Gregorys RC High School
Peace Drive
Norley Cl
Delamere St
Collin St
Leicester St
Leicester St
St Barnabas CE Prim Sch
FROGHALL LANE
MIDLAND WAY
A57
Cockhedge Centre
Crown St
Warrington Bus Cen
Cncl Bldg
Crosfield Street
Travelodge
Legh Street
Colborne St
Scotland Rd
Law Cts
Town Hall
Bath St
Shopping Centre
Priestley Business Cen
Milner Street
Banksside
Superstore
Whitecross Rd
Hatchmere Cl
Wellfield Street
Selby St
PO
Green St
Sacred Heart Catholic Primary School
105
SANKEY WAY
A5061
A57
Clinic
Regent St
Sankey St
Market Gate
Academy St
Mkt Hall
Palace Theatre
Academy Wy
MERSEY STREET
YMCA
Sankey St
Cncl Bldg
Postal Delivery Office
Factory Lane
Works
Factory Lane
LC
PARKER ST
Dixon St
Arpley St
White St
Henry St
Palmyra Sq N
Palmyra Sq S
Bold Street
Cairo Street
Barbauld St
Bridge St
Thynne Street
Surg
Pyramid
Parr Hall
Austins La
Museum St
Superstore
Med Cen
Pol Stn
Mag Ct
WILSON PATTEN STREET
Arpley Road
Bramhall St
Pickmere St
Thewlis St
Old Liverpool Rd
Wellfield St
Evelyn Street Prim Sch
Beaufort St
Liverpool Rd
Quay Fold
Warrington Bank Quay Station
Slutchers La
Warrington Collegiate
Premier Travel Inn
KNUTSFORD
WILDERSPOOL CAUSEWAY
Old Road
Evelyn Street
Bond Cl
Works
Bank Quay Trading Estate
Park Boulevard
Latchford CE Primary School
Barnard St
Larkspur Crs
Snowberry
Marigold St
Gateworth Ind Estate
River Mersey
Forrest Way
The Village Hotel & Leisure Club
Cygnet Ct
Centre Park
Ibis Ct
Lakeside Drive
Peartree Pl
Firecrest Ct
Slutchers
Mandarin Ct
River Mersey
Fletcher St
A49
Priory St
Central Av
Hillberry Crescent
Manx Road
River Road
Causeway Medical Centre
Wallis St
Sulby Av
Greeba Av
Astley Close
Burgess
CHESTER ROAD
129
Irwell Av
Avenue
Road
Meadow Av
St Weburgh CE Primary School
Boswell
1 grid square represents 500 metres

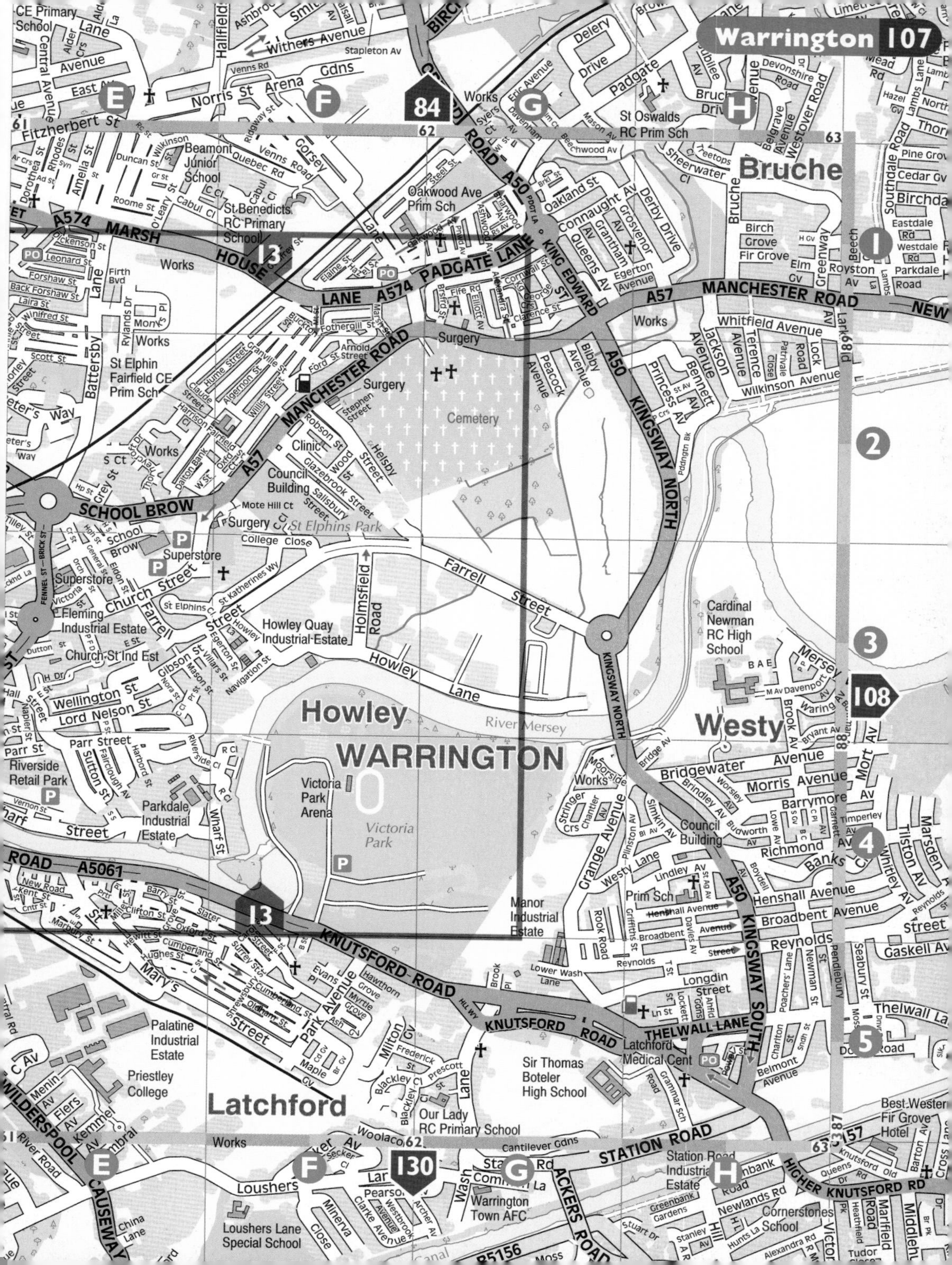

84
62
63
108
13
130
E
F
G
H
1
2
3
4
5
Bruche
Westy
Howley
WARRINGTON
Latchford
River Mersey
Victoria Park
Victoria Park Arena
Cemetery
St Elphins Park
A50 KINGSWAY NORTH
A50 KINGSWAY SOUTH
KING EDWARD ST
A57 MANCHESTER ROAD
A574 MARSH HOUSE LANE
A574 PADGATE LANE
SCHOOL BROW
A5061 KNUTSFORD ROAD
STATION ROAD
HIGHER KNUTSFORD RD
WILDERSPOOL CAUSEWAY
ACKERS ROAD
THELWALL LANE
Farrell Street
Howley Lane
Church Street
Holmsfield Road
Bridgewater Avenue
Morris Avenue
Barrymore Av
Richmond Av
Henshall Avenue
Broadbent Avenue
Reynolds Street
Longdin Street
Grange Avenue
Westy Lane
Padgate
Delery Drive
Norris St
Arena Gdns
Withers Avenue
Fitzherbert St
Gorsey Lane
Venns Road
Quebec Rd
Connaught Av
Derby Drive
Grosvenor Av
Queens Av
Whitfield Avenue
Wilkinson Avenue
Princess Av
Bennett Avenue
Jackson Avenue
Terence Avenue
Peacock Avenue
Bibby Avenue
Beamont Junior School
St Benedicts RC Primary School
Oakwood Ave Prim Sch
St Oswalds RC Prim Sch
St Elphin Fairfield CE Prim Sch
Cardinal Newman RC High School
Sir Thomas Boteler High School
Our Lady RC Primary School
Loushers Lane Special School
Warrington Town AFC
Priestley College
Palatine Industrial Estate
Parkdale Industrial Estate
Riverside Retail Park
Howley Quay Industrial Estate
Church St Ind Est
Fleming Industrial Estate
Manor Industrial Estate
Station Road Industrial Estate
Latchford Medical Cent
Council Building
Best Western Fir Grove Hotel
Cornerstones School
Superstore
Surgery
Clinic
Works
Loushers Lane
Lower Wash Lane
Wharf St
Lord Nelson St
Wellington St
Parr Street
Sutton St
Park Avenue
Manchester Road
Kingsway North
Knutsford Road

108
85
107
131
A
B
C
D
1
2
3
4
5
363
364
388
387
Bruche
Woolston
WA1
River Mersey
The Eyes
Works
Thelwall Heys
Springfield Avenue
Devonshire Road
Belgrave Avenue
Westover Road
Green Lane
Padgate Business Centre
Green Lane Special School
Regent Avenue
Elizabeth Drive
Princess Avenue
Thorn Road
Lambs Lane
Seymour Drive
Pine Grove
Cedar Gv
Holly Gv
Southdale Road
Birchdale Road
Bruche Community Prim Sch
Woolston Community High Sch
Clinic & Welfare Centre
Surgery
Eastdale Rd
Westdale Rd
Paddington House Hotel
Aspen Gv
Rushmore Grove
Parkdale Road
Royston Av
Birch Grove
Fir Grove
Elm Gv
Greenway
Beech Grove
Almond Gv
Wildwood Gv
Heathwood Gv
Manchester Road
NEW MANCHESTER ROAD
MANCHESTER ROAD
A57
Brickhurst Way
Dorset
Wells Close
Yeovil Close
Wareham Cl
Hill Lane
Hayfield Road
Barnfield Road
Hall Road
Woolston Primary School
Austral Avenue
Wentworth Av
Ferndale Cl
Oakdene Av
Rosedale Avenue
Laburnum Av
Ryder Road
Hill Top Rd
Woolston CE Primary School
Epping Drive
Hardwick Gra
Well Farm Cl
Gig Lane
Acacia Av
Alder Road
Warren La
St Peters RC Primary School
Dam Lane
Linden Cl
Vaudrey Dr
Baron Close
Manor Close
Hwthrn Av
Council Offices
New Cut Lane
New Cut La
Cotter Dr
Greymist Avenue
Bridge Road
Bridge Lane
Runnymede
Fitzwalter Road
Parksway
Marshall Rd
Langton Gn
Cliftonville Road
Wiltshire Cl
PO
Whitfield Avenue
Terence Avenue
Patrivale Close
Lock Road
Larkfield Av
Wilkinson Avenue
Cardinal Newman RC High School
Mersey Walk
Westy
Bryant Av
Bowman Av
Mort Av
Morris Avenue
Barrymore Av
Worsley Av
Budworth Av
Timperley Av
Garnett Av
Lowe Av
Banks Crs
Tilston Av
Marsden Av
Whitley Av
Henshall Avenue
Broadbent Avenue
Reynolds Street
Pichael Nook
Moseley Av
Parkfield Av
Gaskell Av
Nook Lane
Brn Av
Richmond St
Newman St
Poachers' Lane
Pendlebury St
Seabury St
Thelwall Lane
Moss Rd
Dover Road
Latchford St
Belmont Avenue
Charlton
A50 KINGSWAY SOUTH
Thelwall New Road Industrial Est
Prestbury Dr
Alderley Road
Wilmslow Crs
Mobberley Cl
Handforth
Woodford Cl
NEW ROAD
THELWALL
Thelwall New Rd
Beech Av
Selworthy Dr
Moore Avenue
Pickering Crs
Thelwall Community Jun Sch
Stanton Road
Pelham Road
Harlow Cl
Walden Cl
Welwyn Cl
Dunmow Rd
Baldock Cl
Watton Cl
Barley Road
Wilson Cl
Thelwall Infant School
Richmond Av
Ashley Cl
Mottram Cl
Ollerton Cl
Surgery
Bradshaw Lane
Poynton Close
Grappenhall Clinic
STOCKPORT
Best Western Fir Grove Hotel
B5157
Springfield Avenue
Knightsbridge Av
Westminster Cl
Windsor Drive
Mayfield Rd
Cawthorne Av
Martham Cl
Barton Av
Bradshaw Community Primary School
A50 KNUTSFORD ROAD
HIGHER KNUTSFORD ROAD
Queens Dr
Knutsford Old Rd
Greenbank Road
Newlands Rd
Cornerstones School
Hunts La
Alexandra Rd
Heathfield Pk
Marlfield Road
Middle
Shirley Dr
Euclid
St Anne
Georges Crs
Nicholls St
Mairesfield Av
East
Ascot
Bridgewater Canal
1 grid square represents 500 metres

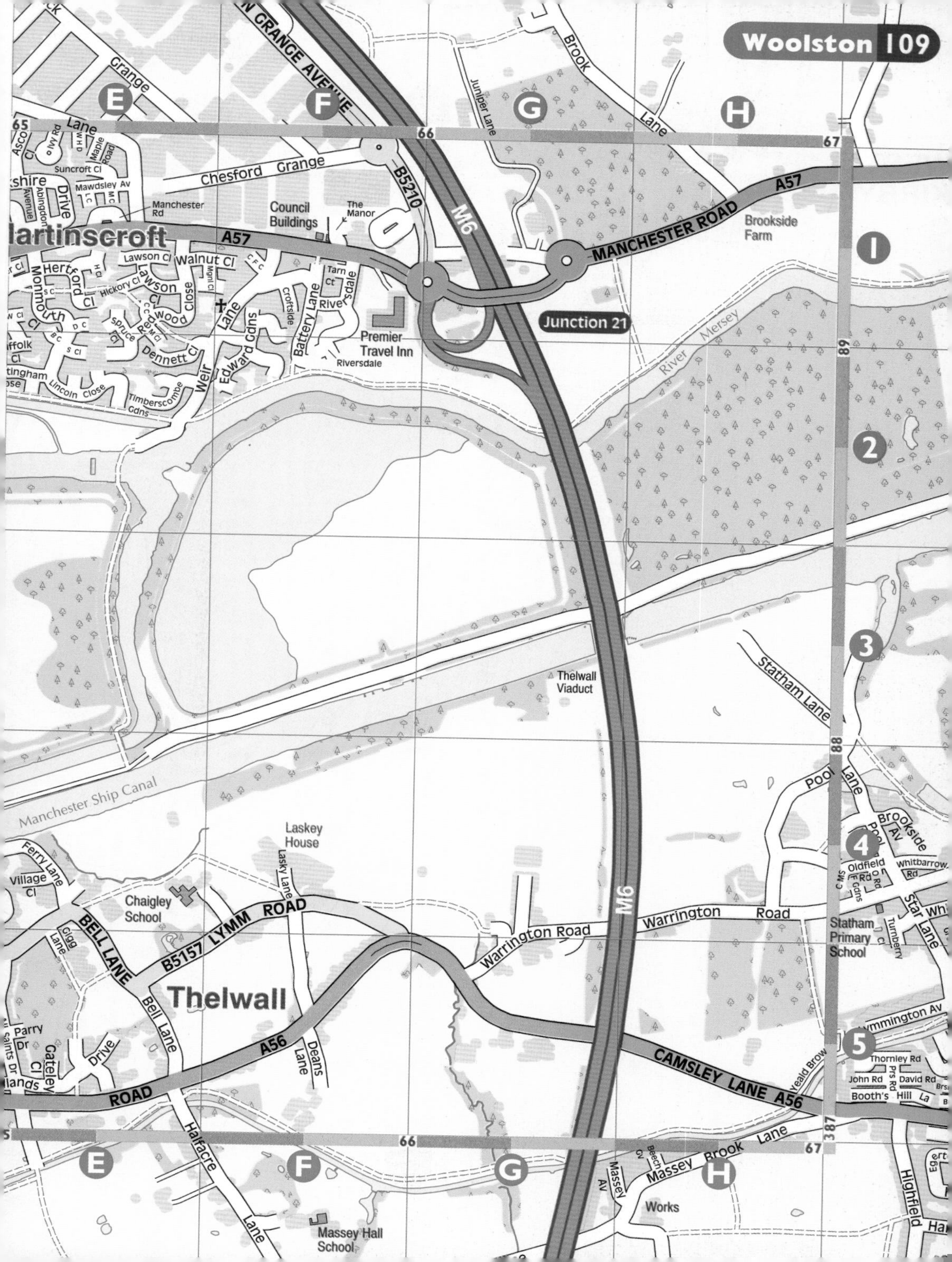
Grange Lane
Grange Avenue
Brook Lane
Juniper Lane
E
F
G
H
65
66
67
Ivy Rd
Maple Road
Suncroft Cl
Mawdsley Av
Abingdon Avenue
Drive
Chesford Grange
B5210
Manchester Rd
Council Buildings
The Manor
Martinscroft
A57
M6
Manchester Road
A57
Brookside Farm
1
Lawson Cl
Walnut Cl
Hertford Cl
Hickory Cl
Lawson Cl
Close
Monmouth Cl
Redwood Cl
Spruce Cl
Dennett Cl
Weir Lane
Edward Gdns
Battery Lane
Croftside
Tarn Ct
Riversdale
Premier Travel Inn
Riversdale
Junction 21
River Mersey
Lincoln Close
Timberscombe Gdns
89
2
3
Thelwall Viaduct
Statham Lane
88
Manchester Ship Canal
Pool Lane
Brookside Av
Pool Lane
4
Oldfield Rd
Whitbarrow Rd
Laskey House
Lasky Lane
Ferry Lane
Village Cl
Chaigley School
Lymm Road
B5157
Bell Lane
Gigg Lane
Warrington Road
Warrington Road
Statham Primary School
Turnberry Cl
Star Lane
Thelwall
Bell Lane
Lymmington Av
5
Thornley Rd
John Rd
David Rd
Booth's Hill La
Parry Dr
Gateley Cl
Drive
A56
Deans Lane
Camsley Lane A56
Yeald Brow
Road
Halfacre Lane
Massey Brook Lane
Massey Av
Beech Gv
387
Works
Highfield
Massey Hall School

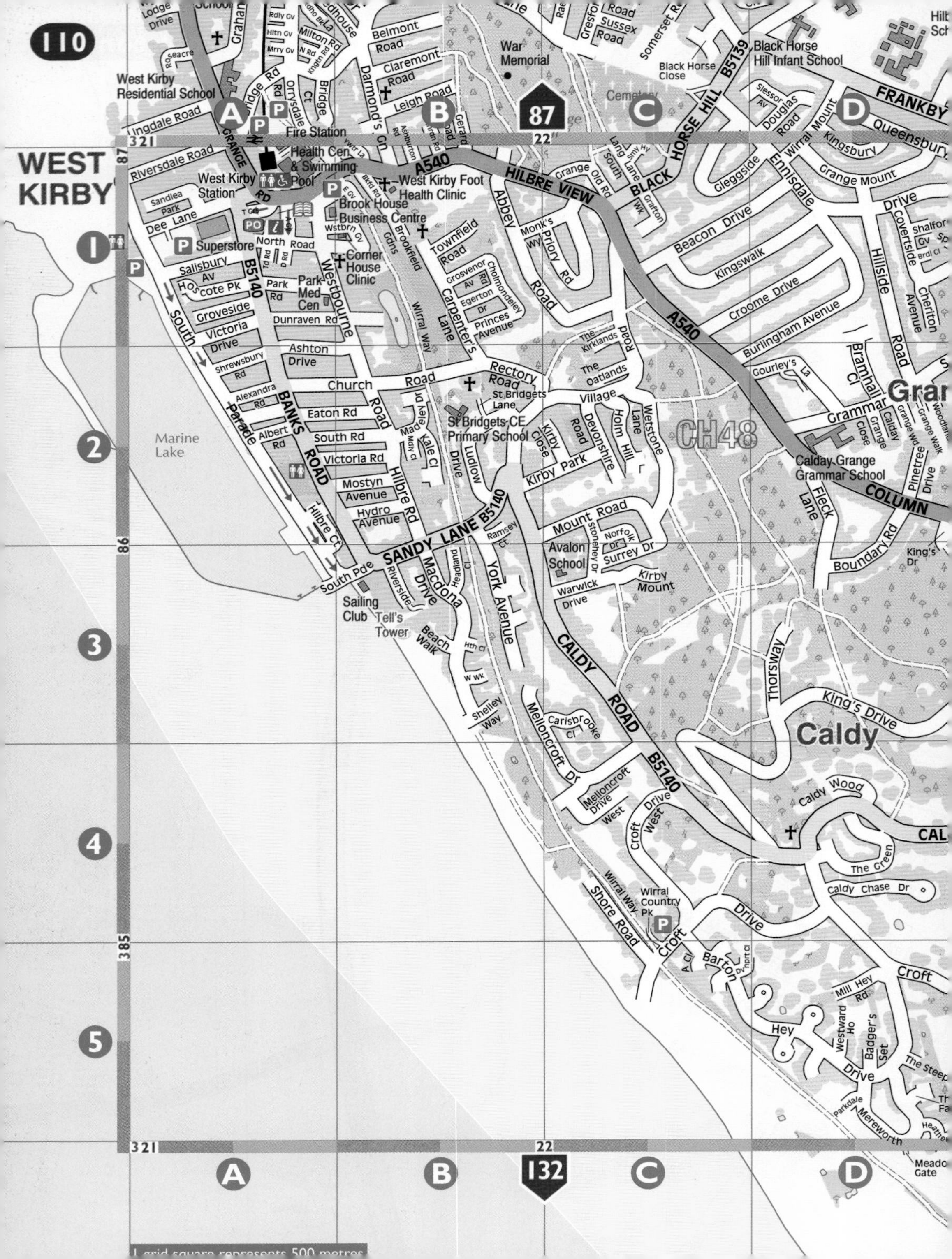
WEST KIRBY
West Kirby Residential School
Lingdale Road
Riversdale Road
Fire Station
Health Cen & Swimming Pool
West Kirby Station
West Kirby Foot Health Clinic
Brook House Business Centre
GRANGE RD
A540
HILBRE VIEW
Belmont Road
Claremont Road
Leigh Road
Darmond's Gn
War Memorial
Cemetery
Black Horse Close
Black Horse Hill Infant School
BLACK HORSE HILL
B5139
FRANKBY
Queensbury
Kingsbury
Grange Mount
Wirral Mount
Slessor Av
Douglas Road
Gleggside
Ennisdale
Beacon Drive
Kingswalk
Croome Drive
Burlingham Avenue
Hillside Road
Covertside Avenue
Cheriton
Sandlea Park
Dee Lane
Superstore
North Road
Salisbury Av
Hoscote Pk
Groveside
Victoria Drive
Shrewsbury Rd
Alexandra Rd
Albert Rd
South Parade
B5140
BANKS ROAD
Park Rd
Park Med Cen
Dunraven Rd
Ashton Drive
Church Road
Eaton Rd
South Rd
Victoria Rd
Mostyn Avenue
Hydro Avenue
Hilbre Rd
Hilbre Ct
Westbourne
Corner House Clinic
Brookfield Gdns
Wirral Way
Carpenter's Lane
Townfield Road
Grosvenor Av
Cholmondeley Rd
Egerton Dr
Princes Avenue
Rectory Road
St Bridgets Lane
St Bridgets CE Primary School
Kale Cl
Ludlow Drive
Abbey Road
Monk's Wy
Priory Rd
Grange Old Rd
Lang Lane South
The Kirklands
The Oatlands
Village Road
Kirby Close
Devonshire Road
Holm Hill
Wetstone Lane
Kirby Park
CH48
Gourley's La
Bramhall Cl
Grammar
Calday Grange Grammar School
COLUMN
Fleck Lane
Boundary Rd
King's Dr
Pinetree Drive
Marine Lake
SANDY LANE
South Pde
Sailing Club
Tell's Tower
Riverside
Macdona Drive
Headland Cl
Ramsey Ct
York Avenue
Beach Walk
Hth Cl
W Wk
Shelley Way
Mount Road
Norfolk Dr
Surrey Dr
Stoneheyy Dr
Avalon School
Warwick Drive
Kirby Mount
CALDY ROAD
Thorsway
King's Drive
Caldy
Carisbrooke Cl
Melloncroft Dr
Melloncroft Drive
West Drive West
Croft
Caldy Wood
The Green
Caldy Chase Dr
Wirral Way
Shore Road
Wirral Country Pk
Croft Drive
Barton
Mill Hey Rd
Hey Drive
Westward Ho
Badger's Set
The Steeple
Parkdale
Mereworth
Meadow Gate
321
22
87
86
385
132
A
B
C
D
1
2
3
4
5
1 grid square represents 500 metres

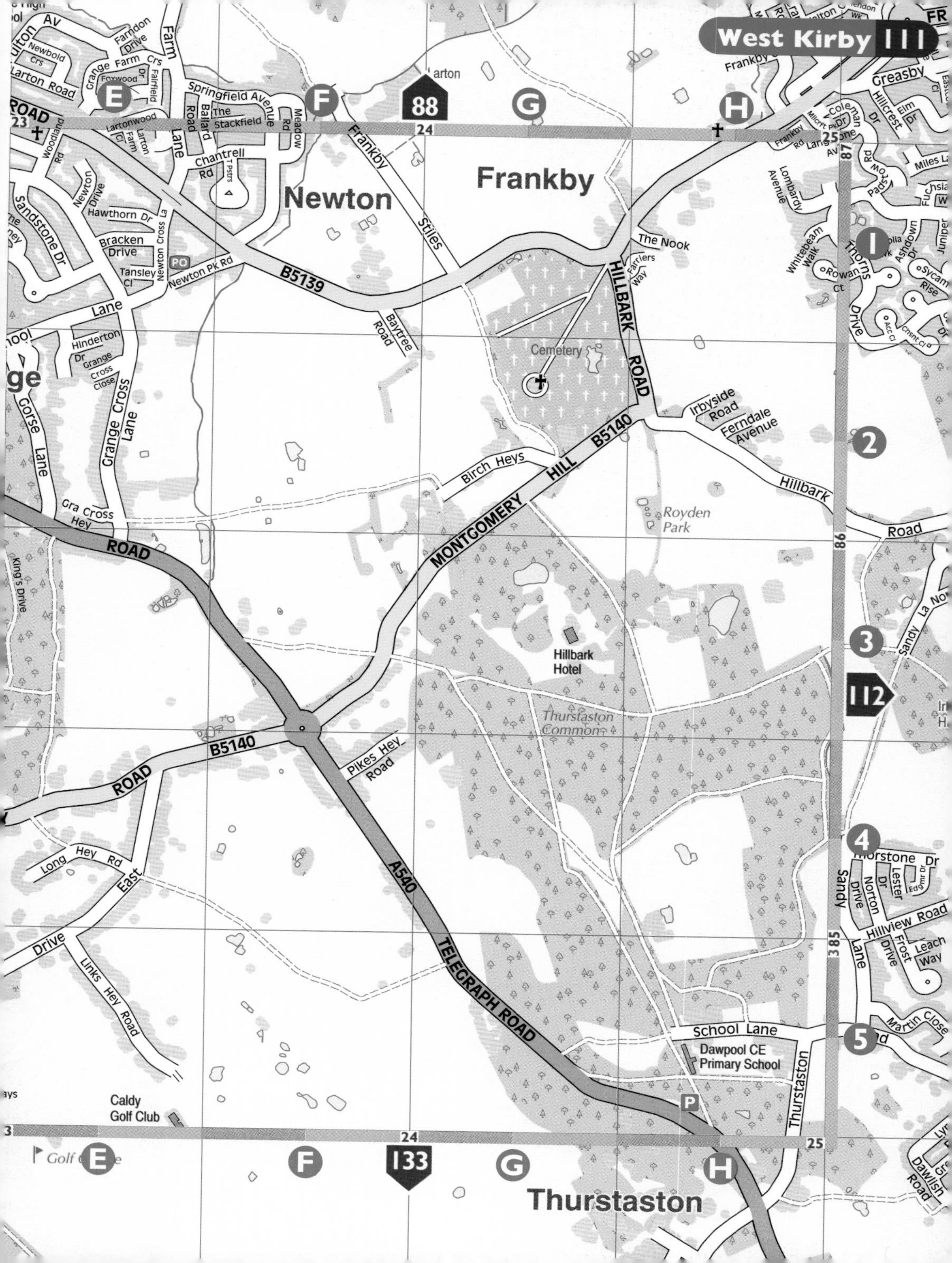
Frankby
Newton
Thurstaston
Larton
Greasby
88
112
133
E
F
G
H
1
2
3
4
5
23
24
25
87
86
385
B5139
B5140
A540
Telegraph Road
Montgomery Hill
Hillbark Road
Road
Frankby Stiles
Baytree Road
The Nook
Farriers Way
Cemetery
Irbyside Road
Ferndale Avenue
Hillbark
Birch Heys
Royden Park
Hillbark Hotel
Thurstaston Common
Pikes Hey Road
Newton Pk Rd
Newton Cross La
PO
Lane
Hinderton Dr
Grange Cross Close
Grange Cross Lane
Gorse Lane
Gra Cross Hey
King's Drive
Sandstone Dr
Bracken Drive
Tansley Cl
Hawthorn Dr
Newton Drive
Woodland Rd
Chantrell Rd
Lartonwood Cl
Larton Farm
Lane
Ballard Road
The Stackfield
Meadow Rd
Springfield Avenue
Grange Farm Crs
Foxwood Dr
Fairfield
Farndon Drive
Newbold Crs
Larton Road
Farm
Av
Long Hey Rd
East
Drive
Links Hey Road
Caldy Golf Club
Golf Course
School Lane
Dawpool CE Primary School
Thurstaston
P
Sandy Lane
Sandy La
Norton Drive
Lester Dr
Hillview Road
Frost Drive
Leach Way
Martin Close
Dawlish Road
Lombardy Avenue
Whitebeam Walk
Rowan Ct
Thorns Drive
Ashdown Dr
Sycam Rise
Hillcrest Dr
Elm Dr
Coleman Dr
Frankby Rd
Miles La
Juniper
Fuchsia
Padstow Rd

112
89
111
134
FRANKBY ROAD
Frankby
Halton Cl
Hendon Wk
Rowan Tr Cl
Circular Drive
The Crs
Windsor Cl
Escolme Drive
Drive
Greasby Road
Well Lane
Old Pump La
PO
Macdonald Dr
Lloyd Drive
Ferguson Avenue
Harvey Av
Hall Dr
Drive
Robert Dr
Gordon Avenue
Caulfield Drive
Neale Drive
Appleton Dr
Brookdale Avenue South
Dingwall Drive
Wirral Business Park
Greasby
East Cl
Hillcrest Dr
Elm Dr
Coleman Dr
Millcroft Pk
Frankby Rd
Langston
A
B
C
D
325
26
87
86
385
Leslie Av
The Cft
Carmichael Av
Rigby Drive
Road
Arrowe Brook Road
CH49
P
Lombardy Avenue
Miles Lane
Miles Cl
Padstow Rd
Fuchsia Wk
Greasby Infant School
Barker Lane
Shaw Lane
Howell Drive
The Close
Magnolia Wk
Ashdown Dr
Juniper Cl
Danefield Rd
Thorns Drive
Rowan Ct
Sycamore Rise
Allangate Close
Our Lady of Pity Primary School
Barker Lane
Arrowe Brook Lane
Oakdale Dr
Chsnt Cl
Acc Cl
Greasby Junior School
1
2
3
4
5
Ferndale Avenue
Road
Hillbark Road
Mill Lane
Arrowe Country Park
Sandy La North
Irby CC
Irby Hill
Mill Hill Road
Thorstone Dr
Sandy Lane
Lester Dr
Norton Drive
Edgmr Dr
Purbeck Drive
Caine Close
Wimborne Wy
Summerwood Cl
Islip
Brook Wk
Cps Gv
Lstn Cl
Brook Meadow
Heathbank Av
Estleigh Dr
Frome Cl
Denning Dr
Devizes Drive
Glenwood Drive
Hillview Road
Frost Drive
Leach Way
Sherwood Avenue
Mrkshm Dr
Vrwd Cl
Hazel Grove
Coombe Road
Irby Primary School
Far Meadow Lane
Seaview Av
Laburnum Grove
Coniston Road
Woodside Rd
Lynwood Dr
Harrock Wd
Close
Thingwall Road
Parkway Close
Dane Close
Loomsway
Irby
Martin Close
School Lane
Dawpool CE Primary School
Thurstaston Road
Sea View Lane
Roslin Rd
The Cl
PO
Surgery
Manor Rd
Thingwall Road
Elm Rd
Menlo Avenue
Oaklea Rd
Whaley Lane
Barker Road
Mayew Rd
Disd Cl
Brian Av
Marlston Av
Lfld Cl
King's Drive
The Crs
Bentley Rd
Lyndhurst Road
Greenheys Rd
South Drive
Drayton Close
Exmoor Cl
Newstr Av
Cornelius Drive
Chatsworth Road
Sandridge Rd
1 grid square represents 500 metres

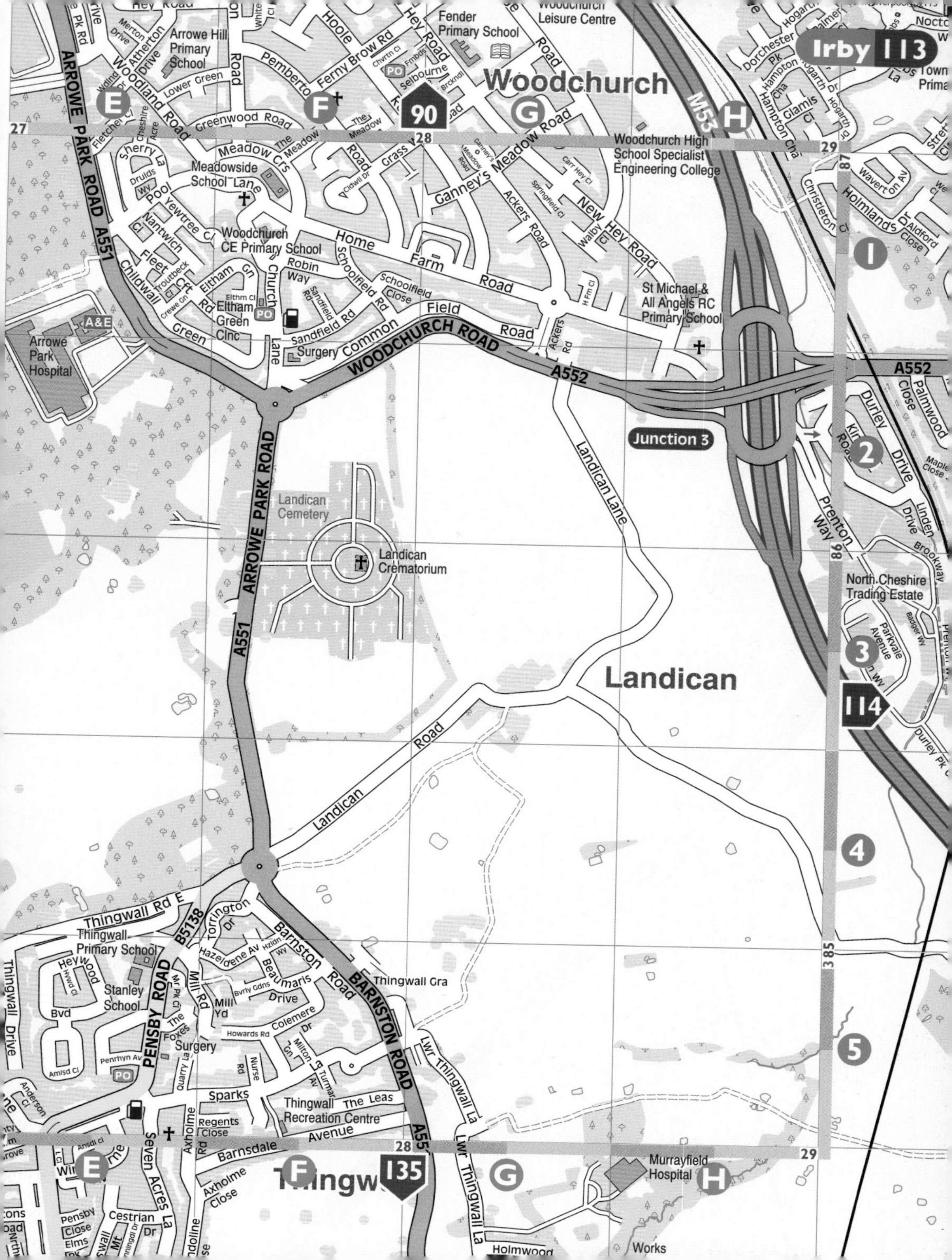

Irby 113
90
114
135
Woodchurch
Landican
Thingw
Woodchurch Leisure Centre
Fender Primary School
Arrowe Hill Primary School
Woodchurch High School Specialist Engineering College
Meadowside School
Woodchurch CE Primary School
St Michael & All Angels RC Primary School
Arrowe Park Hospital
A&E
Landican Cemetery
Landican Crematorium
North Cheshire Trading Estate
Thingwall Primary School
Stanley School
Thingwall Recreation Centre
Murrayfield Hospital
Eltham Green Clnc
Surgery
Works
Junction 3
ARROWE PARK ROAD
A551
WOODCHURCH ROAD
A552
M53
BARNSTON ROAD
PENSBY ROAD
B5138
Woodland Road
Greenwood Road
Lower Green
Ferny Brow Rd
Pemberton
Hoole
Hey Road
Selbourne
Meadow Crs
The Meadow
Sherry La
Druids Wy
Pool
Yewtree Cl
Nantwich Cl
Fleet Cft
Troutbeck
Childwall Green
Crewe Gn
Eltham Gn
Eltham Rd
Church Lane
Robin Way
Schoolfield Rd
Schoolfield Close
Sandfield Rd
Common Field Road
Home Farm Road
Grass Wd
Clwdd Dr
Ganney's Meadow Road
Ackers Road
Ackers Rd
Springfield Cl
Carr Hey Cl
New Hey Road
Walby Cl
H Fm Cl
Dorchester
Hampton Cha
Glamis Cl
Hogarth Dr
Christleton Cl
Holmlands Dr
Waverton Av
Alford Close
Durley Drive
Palmwood Close
Prenton Way
Linden Drive
Brookway
Parkvale Avenue
Badger Wy
Durley Pk
Maple Close
Landican Lane
Landican Road
Thingwall Rd E
Torrington Dr
Hazeldene Av
Beaumaris Drive
Bvrly Gdns
Barnston Road
Thingwall Gra
Heywood Bvd
Thingwall Drive
Mill Rd
Mill Yd
The Foxes
Howards Rd
Colemere Dr
Milton Gn
Nurse Rd
Turmar Av
Quarry La
Penrhyn Av
Anderson Cl
Sparks
Regents Close
Axholme Rd
Axholme Close
Seven Acres La
Barnsdale Avenue
The Leas
Lwr Thingwall La
Pensby Close
Cestrian Dr
Holmwood
27
28
29
87
86
385
E
F
G
H
1
2
3
4
5

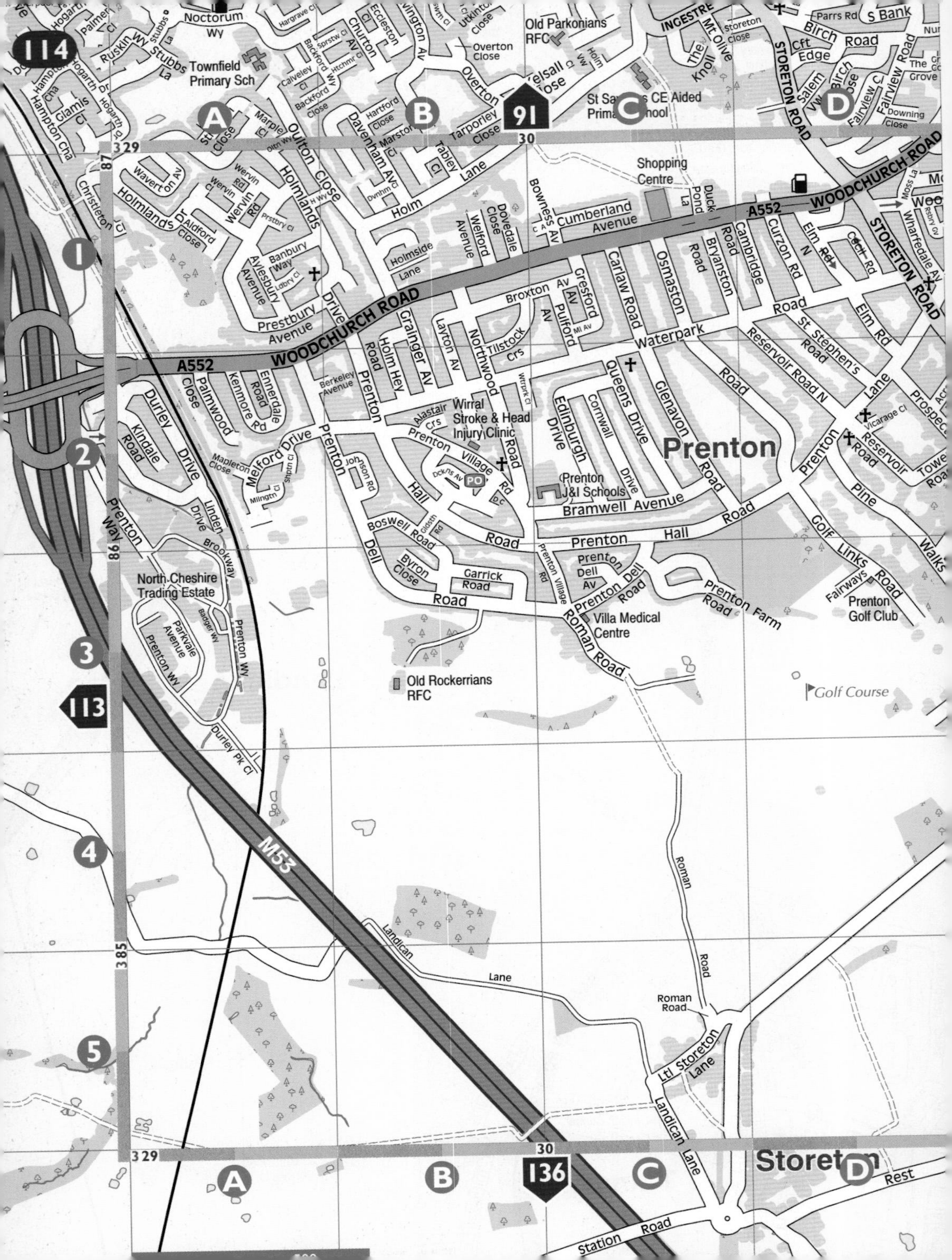
114
91
113
136
A
B
C
D
1
2
3
4
5
329
30
87
86
385
Noctorum Wy
Townfield Primary Sch
Old Parkonians RFC
Overton Close
St Saviours CE Aided Primary School
INGESTRE
Mt Olive
The Knoll
Storeton Close
Parrs Rd
S Bank
Birch Road
Cft Edge
Salem Vw
Birch Close
Fairview Road
Fairview Cl
Downing Close
The Grove
STORETON ROAD
Hampton Cha
Hogarth Dr
Glamis Cl
Ruskin Wy
Stubbs La
Marple Cl
Oulton Close
Davenham Av
Marston Cl
Tarporley Close
Tabley Cl
Holm Lane
Holmlands Dr
Holmlands Close
Waverton Av
Wervin Rd
Aldford Close
Prestbury Cl
Banbury Way
Aylesbury Avenue
Prestbury Avenue
Christleton Cl
Holmside Lane
Welford Avenue
Dovedale Close
Bowness Av
Cumberland Avenue
Shopping Centre
Duck Pond La
A552
WOODCHURCH ROAD
Moss La
Wharfedale Av
Cecil Rd
Elm Rd
Curzon Rd N
Cambridge Road
Bryanston Road
Osmaston Road
Carlaw Road
Cresford Av
Pulford Av
Broxton Av
Tilstock Crs
Waterpark Road
St Stephen's Road
Reservoir Road N
Lane
Prospect
Grainger Av
Holm Hey
Prenton Road
Layton Av
Northwood Road
Berkeley Avenue
Palmwood Close
Kenmore Rd
Ennerdale Road
Durley Drive
Kindale Road
Melford Drive
Mapleton Close
Alastair Crs
Wirral Stroke & Head Injury Clinic
Prenton Village Rd
Dckns Av
PO
Edinburgh Drive
Cornwall Drive
Queens Drive
Glenavon Road
Prenton
Prenton J&I Schools
Bramwell Avenue
Prenton Hall Road
Vicarage Cl
Reservoir Road
Pine Walks
Golf Links Road
Fairways
Prenton Golf Club
Boswell Road
Johnson Rd
Byron Close
Garrick Road
Prenton Dell Road
Prenton Dell Av
Prenton Village Rd
Prenton Farm Road
Villa Medical Centre
Roman Road
Old Rockerrians RFC
Golf Course
Prenton Way
Linden Drive
Brookway
North Cheshire Trading Estate
Parkvale Avenue
Badger Wy
Prenton Wy
Durley Pk Cl
M53
Landican Lane
Ltl Storeton Lane
Storeton
Rest
Station Road

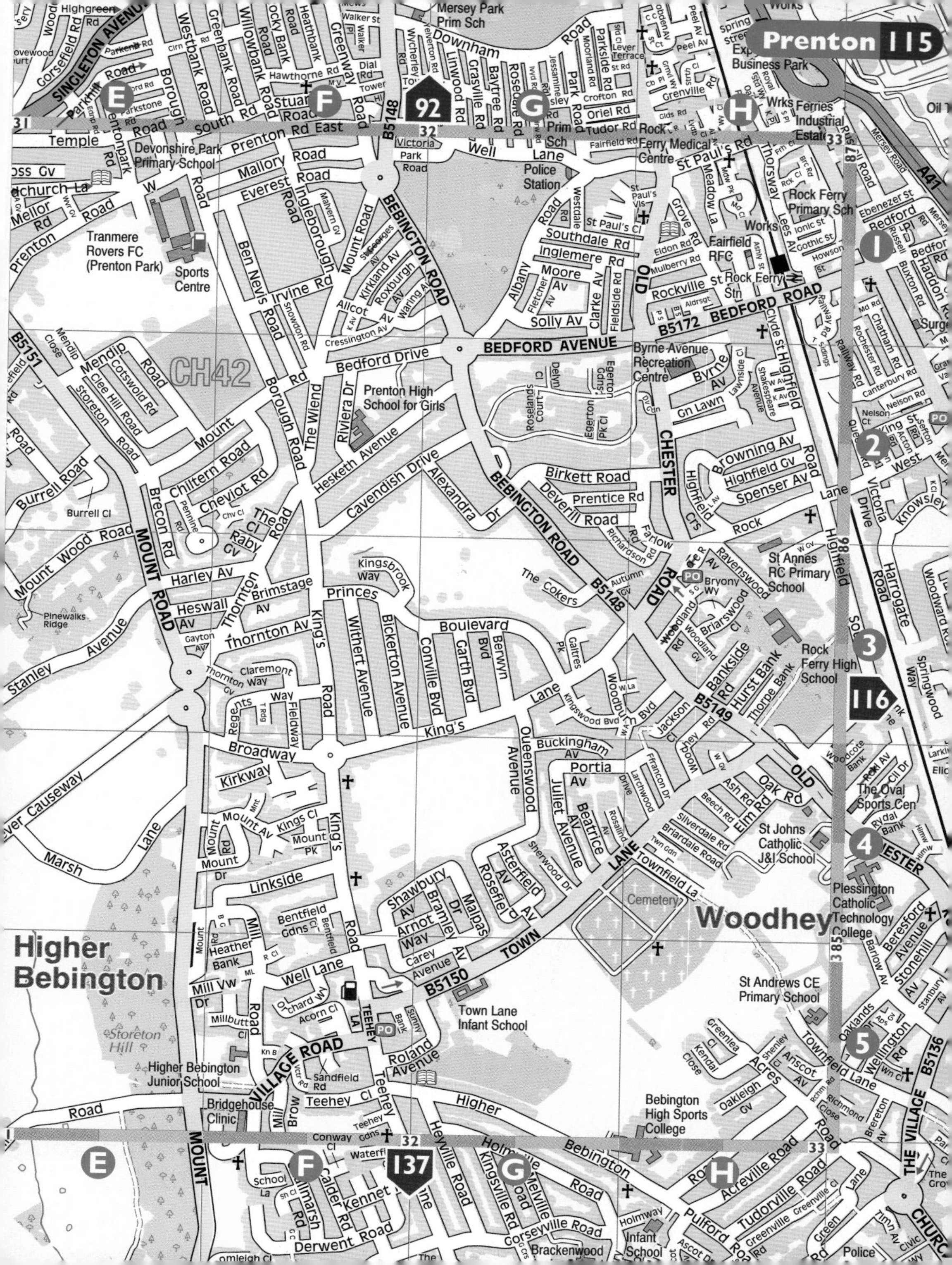
Singleton Avenue
Gorsefield Rd
Highgreen Rd
Parkenhill Rd
Hawthorne Rd
Westbank Road
Greenbank Road
Willowbank Road
Heathbank Road
Greenway Road
Mersey Park Prim Sch
Downham Road
Linwood Rd
Grasville Rd
Baytree Rd
Rosecroft Rd
Park Road
Parkside Rd
Moorland Rd
Lever Terrace
Peel Av
Spring Street
Business Park
Wrks
Ferries Industrial Estate
Crofton Rd
Oriel Rd
Tudor Rd
Grenville Rd
Prim Sch
Temple Road
South Rd
Prenton Rd East
Stuart Road
Borough Road
Devonshire Park Primary School
Mallory Road
Everest Road
Victoria Park Road
Well Lane
Police Station
Rock Ferry Medical Centre
St Paul's Rd
Fairfield Rd
Tranmere Rovers FC (Prenton Park)
Sports Centre
Prenton Road West
Mellor Rd
Ingleborough Road
Ben Nevis Road
Irvine Rd
Mount Road
Bebington Road
B5148
Southdale Rd
Inglemere Rd
Moore Av
Albany Road
Westdale Rd
St Paul's Cl
Grove Rd
Meadow La
Fairfield RFC
Rock Ferry Stn
Rockville St
Mulberry Rd
Eldon Rd
Works
Rock Ferry Primary Sch
Bedford Road
Bedford Av
Ebenezer St
Ionic St
Gothic St
Howson St
Buxton Rd
Haddon Rd
Kirkland Av
Roxburgh Av
Allcot Av
Waring Av
Cressington Av
Solly Av
Clarke Av
Fieldside Rd
Fletcher Av
B5172 Bedford Road
Clyde St
Highfield
Chatham Rd
Rochester Rd
Canterbury Rd
Nelson Rd
King St
Bedford Avenue
Bedford Drive
Byrne Avenue Recreation Centre
Byrne Av
Gn Lawn
Lawnside Cl
Shakespeare Avenue
B5151
Mendip Road
Mendip Close
Cotswold Rd
Clee Hill Road
Storeton Road
CH42
Borough Road
The Wiend
Riviera Dr
Prenton High School for Girls
Hesketh Avenue
Roselands Court
Egerton Pk Cl
Delyn Cl
Chester Road
Browning Av
Highfield Gv
Spenser Av
Highfield Crs
Rock Lane West
Victoria Drive
Knowsley
Burrell Road
Burrell Cl
Chiltern Road
Cheviot Rd
Brecon Rd
Pennine Rd
The Cl
Raby Gv
Cavendish Drive
Alexandra Dr
Birkett Road
Prentice Rd
Deverill Road
Farlow
Richardson Rd
St Annes RC Primary School
Harrogate Road
Woodward Rd
Mount Wood Road
Mount Road
Harley Av
Heswall Av
Thornton Road
Brimstage Av
Princes Boulevard
Kingsbrook Way
The Cokers
Autumn Gv
Ravenswood Av
Bryony Wy
Briarswood Cl
Woodland Rd
Woodland Gv
Pinewalks Ridge
Stanley Avenue
Gayton Av
Thornton Av
King's Road
Withert Avenue
Bickerton Avenue
Conville Bvd
Garth Bvd
Berwyn Bvd
Gatres Pk
Woodburn Bvd
Bankside Rd
Hurst Bank
Thorpe Bank
Rock Ferry High School
Springwood Way
Claremont Way
Thornton Gv
Regents Way
Fieldway
King's Lane
Kingswood Bvd
Jackson Cl
B5149
Old Chester
Woodcote Bank
The Oval Sports Cen
Rydal Bank
Broadway
Buckingham Av
Portia Av
Queenswood Avenue
Ffrancon Dr
Larchwood Drive
Juliet Avenue
Beatrice Av
Rosalind
Ash Rd
Oak Rd
Elm Rd
Beech Rd
Silverdale Rd
Briardale Road
St Johns Catholic J&I School
Kirkway
River Causeway
Marsh Lane
Mount Av
Kings Cl
Mount Pk
Mount Rd
Mount Dr
Linkside
Sherwood Dr
Asterfield Av
Rosefield Av
Town Lane
Townfield La
Cemetery
Woodhey
Plessington Catholic Technology College
Beresford Avenue
Barlow Av
Stonehill Av
Shawbury Av
Bramley Dr
Arnot Way
Malpas Av
Carey Avenue
Bentfield Gdns
Bentfield Cl
Heather Bank
Mill Road
Higher Bebington
Well Lane
Mill Vw Dr
Millbutt Cl
Orchard Wy
Acorn Cl
Teehey La
Sunny Bank
B5150
Town Lane Infant School
St Andrews CE Primary School
Oaklands
Wellington Rd
B5136
Storeton Hill
Higher Bebington Junior School
Village Road
Sandfield Rd
Roland Avenue
Greenlea Cl
Kendal Close
Acres
Anscot Av
Oakleigh Gv
Townfield Lane
Richmond Close
Brereton Av
The Village
Road
Bridgehouse Clinic
Brow
Teehey Cl
Teehey Gdns
Higher Bebington Road
Heyville Road
Bebington High Sports College
Mount Road
Conway Cl
Waterfield
Holmville Road
Acreville Road
Church Road
School La
Calder Rd
Kennet
Kingsville Rd
Melville Road
Road
Tudorville Road
Greenville Cl
Green Lane
Pulford Rd
Holmway
Infant School
Corseyville Road
Brackenwood
Derwent Road
Ascot Dr
Police
Civic
E
F
G
H
1
2
3
4
5
92
116
137
31
32
33
385
387

116
93
115
138
A
B
C
D
1
2
3
4
5
333
34
387
386
385
The Sloyne
Wirral
Liverpool
Rock Ferry
New Ferry
BEBINGTON
Woodhey
Port Sunlight
Bromborough Pool
Express Business Park
Ferries Industrial Estate
Works
A41
ROCK FERRY BY-PASS
NEW FERRY BY-PASS
NEW CHESTER ROAD
BEDFORD ROAD
OLD CHESTER ROAD
BEBINGTON ROAD
BOUNDARY RD
B5136
THE VILLAGE
Rock Ferry Stn
Rock Ferry Primary Sch
Bedford Rd East
Rock Lane East
Rock Lane West
Highfield South
Harrogate Road
Victoria Drive
Knowsley Road
Cammell Laird's Sports Club
The Dell Primary School
Thorburn Road
Tilstock Avenue
Onslow Rd
New Ferry Road
Seafield Road
Henthorne Road
Shore Bank
Shorefields
Stanley Road
Sefton Road
Parkfield Medical Centre
Grove Street Primary School
Springwood Way
Longfellow Drive
Coleridge Dr
Grove Square
Superstore
St Annes RC Primary School
Rock Ferry High School
The Oval Sports Cen
St John's Cath J&I School
Plessington Catholic Technology College
Bebington Station
St Andrews CE Primary School
Lady Lever Art Gallery
Church Drive Primary School
Primrose Hill
Central Road
Pool Bank
Greendale Road
Parkside Road
Queen Mary's Drive
King George's Dr
Church Drive
Corniche Rd
Dock Rd North
Bolton Rd East
Woodhead Road
Shore Drive
Acreville Road
Tudorville Road
Oakleigh Gv
Wellington Rd
Stonehill Av
Beresford Avenue
Mayfields
Alvega Close
Surgery
Bath Street
York Street
Manor Place
1 grid square represents 500 metres

Columbus Quay
Ellerman Road
Badminton St
Garswood St
Dingle Rd
Glendale Cl
Britannia
Shorefield
Matthew Arnold Prim Sch
Shorefields Technology College
Dingle Vale
Westward Vw
Blythswood
Sandhurst
Errol
Rosslyn
Alwyn
Allington
Buckland
Southwood Rd
St Michael's
St Michael In The Hamlet Primary School
Tramway Rd
Burdett St
L17
St Charles RC Primary School
Oxton Cl
Fulwood Dr
Village Ct
Riverside
Promenade
94
Promenade Gdns
Dingle
St Michael's Stn
Beech Av
St Michael's Hamlet
Gardenia
Grove
Floral Wood
Camella Ct
Riverside Drive
Priory Cl
Festival Gardens
Moel Famau View
Penhale Cl
Carleen Cl
Bempton Road
Oylands Cl
Claret Cl
Barchester
Westbury Cl
Riverside Drive
Works
River Mersey
Devil's Bank
86
385
118
139
Dock Rd South
South
E
F
G
H
1
2
3
4
5
35
36
37

118
117
95
A
B
C
D
1
2
3
4
5
337
38
87
86
385
AIGBURTH ROAD
A561
A5058
VICTORIA ROAD
ASHFIELD ROAD
L17
Livingston Drive
Livingston Drive South
Normanton Av
Dalmeny St
Thirlstane Street
St Michael's Rd
Burdett St
Tramway Rd
Southwood Rd
St Michael-In The Hamlet Primary Sch
St Charles RC Primary School
Council Building
Surgery
Aigburth Drive
Aigburth Vale
Mossley Hill
Carnatic Road
Briarwood Rd
Fernwood Rd
Gladeville Rd
Palmerston Close
Elmswood Road
North Sudley Road
Cyril Gv
Latrigg Rd
Elmar Rd
Bundoran Rd
Lisburn Rd
Lucan Rd
Woodlands Road
Lugard Rd
Wingate Road
Lyttelton Rd
Rundle Rd
Cromer Rd
Milner Rd
Brabant Rd
Dundonald Road
Donalds Way
Sudley Infant School
Rosemont Road
Hillview
Sudley House
Mossley Hill Road
Liverpool John Moores University
Aigburth
Sudley Junior School
St Anne's Rd
The Barkhill
St Margarets CE High School
Mersey View Special Sch
Church Lane
Honiton Rd
Minehead Rd
Braunton Rd
Dulverton Rd
Lynmouth Road
Alston Rd
Silverton Rd
Bilston Rd
Hailsham Road
Horringford Rd
Alresford Road
Stratford Road
Desford Rd
Mersey Av
Chequers Gdns
Cheyne Gdns
Ivyhurst Cl
Rookery Dr
Handley Ct
Aigburth Station
Alma Road
Errington Ct
Bentfield
Mines Av
Riversdale Ct
Riversdale Road
Liverpool CC
Mersey Road
Marlcroft Drive
Rimsdale Cl
Hysmr Ct
The Spinnakers
Greenways Special School
Beechwood Rd
Beechwood Gdns
Larch Cl
Stanlowe Vw
Chaloner Grove
Monksferry Wk
Jacksfield Way
Wirral View
Grassendale Esp
North
Fulwood Road
Fulwood Dr
Larkfield Road
Ashbourne Road
Ampthill Road
Ancaster Rd
Amherst Rd
Oxton Cl
Fulwood Park
Fulwood Close
Jericho Cl
Acer Leigh
Silver Leigh
Jericho Farm Cl
Jericho Lane
Osborne Wood
Otterspool Road
Annesley Rd
Fulwood
Bempton Road
Oylands Cl
Claret Cl
Barchester Dr
Riverside Drive
Westbury Cl
Carleen Cl
Moel Famau View
Kerris
Works
Otterspool
Otterspool Drive
Garston Channel
P
PO

1 grid square represents 500 metres

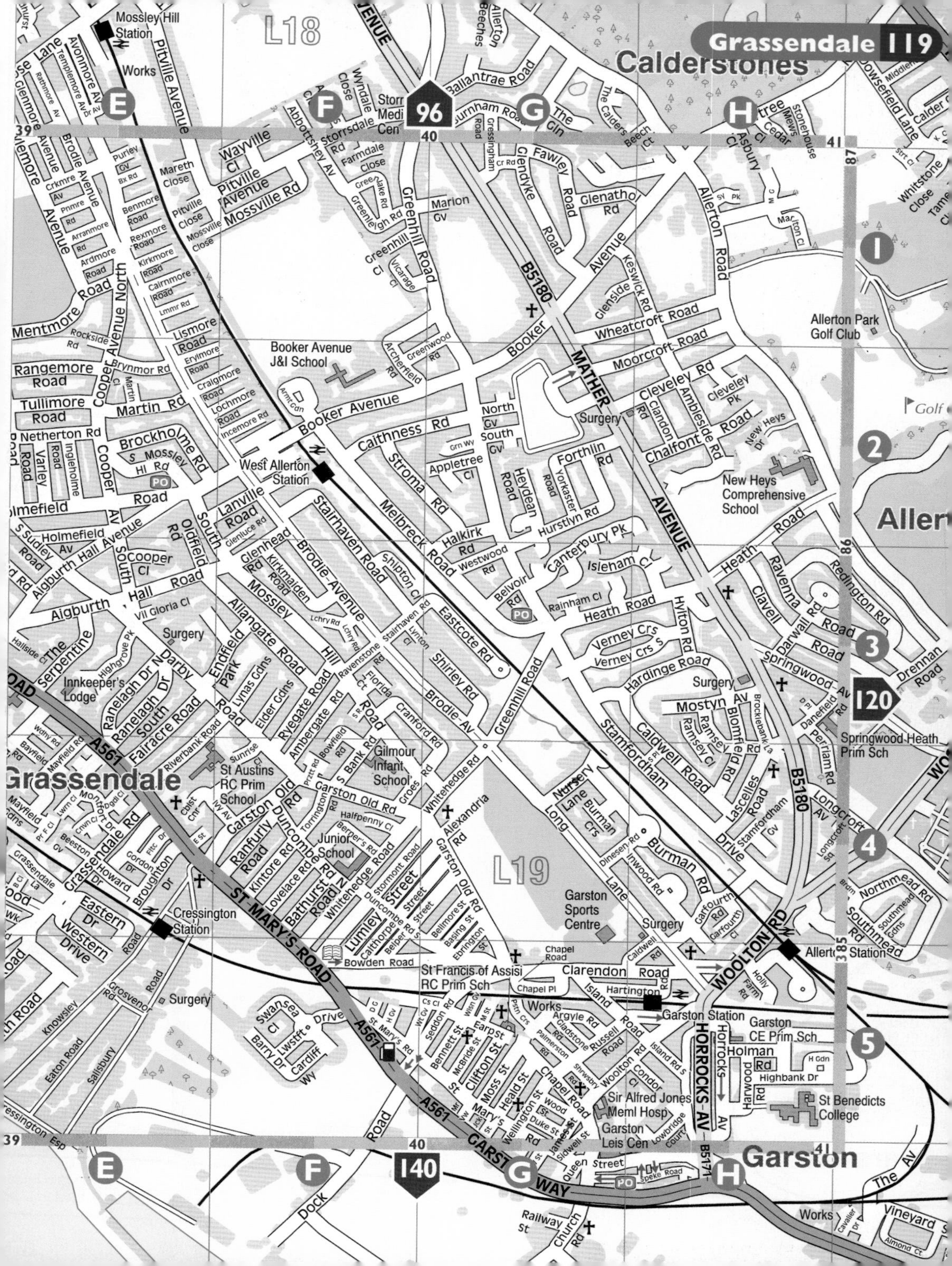
Calderstones
L18
L19
Grassendale
Garston
Allerton Park Golf Club
Mossley Hill Station
West Allerton Station
Cressington Station
Allerton Station
Garston Station
Booker Avenue J&I School
New Heys Comprehensive School
Springwood Heath Prim Sch
St Austins RC Prim School
Gilmour Infant School
Junior School
St Francis of Assisi RC Prim Sch
Garston CE Prim Sch
St Benedicts College
Sir Alfred Jones Meml Hosp
Garston Leis Cen
Garston Sports Centre
Innkeeper's Lodge
Surgery
Works
Pitville Avenue
Mossville Rd
Booker Avenue
Mather Avenue
B5180
Allerton Road
Greenhill Road
Aigburth Hall Road
Mentmore Road
Rangemore Road
Tullimore Road
Martin Rd
Brodie Avenue
Stairhaven Road
Melbreck Road
Caithness Rd
Heath Road
Springwood Av
Woolton Rd
Horrocks Av
St Mary's Road
A561
Garston Way
Grassendale Rd
Garston Old Rd
Long Lane
Burman Rd
Stamfordham Drive
Clarendon Road
Island Road
Bowden Road
Dock Road
Speke Road
Queen Street
Church Rd
Vineyard St
The Av
Holman Rd
Highbank Dr
96
120
140
39
40
41
85
86
87
E
F
G
H
1
2
3
4
5

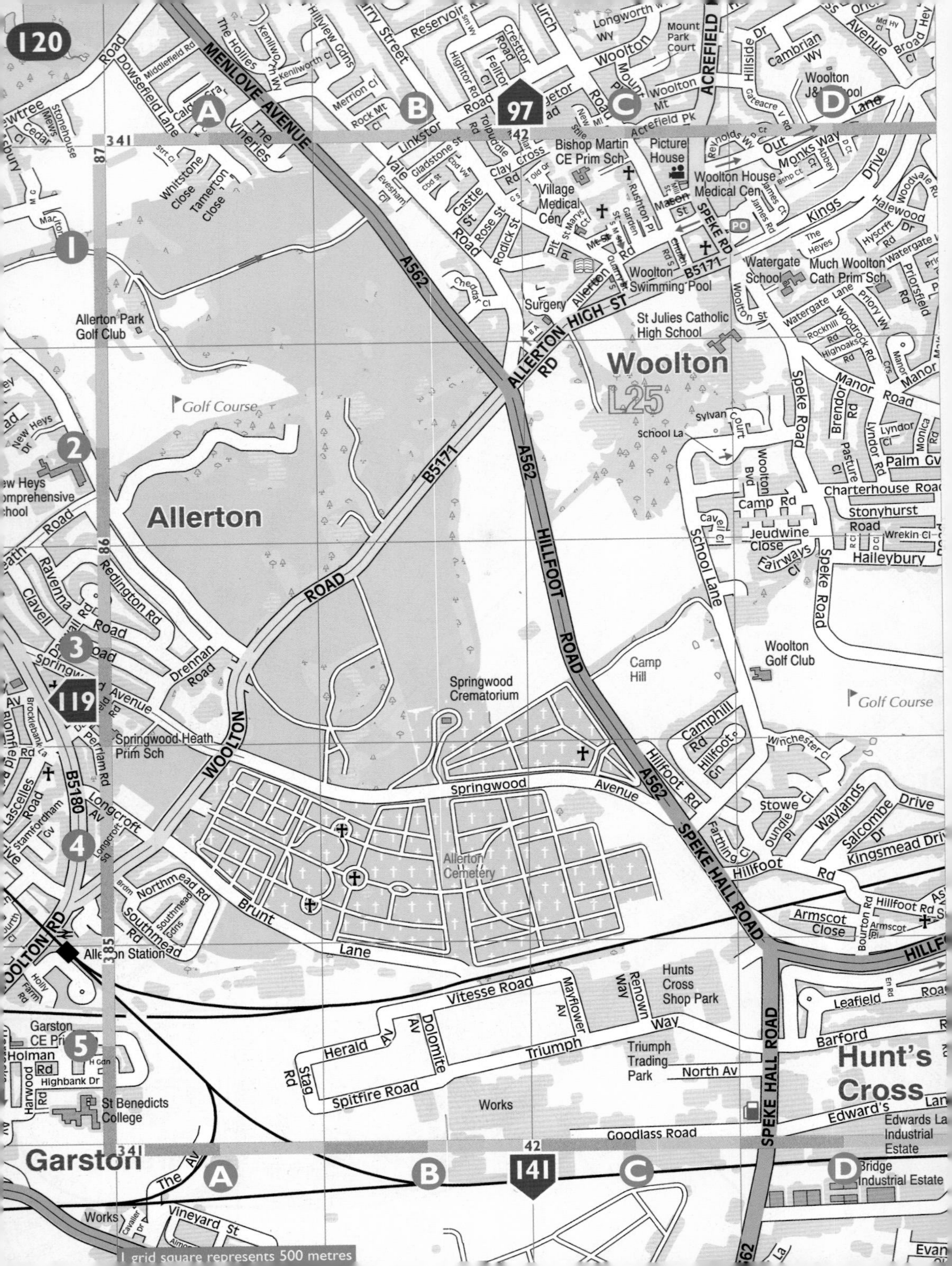
120
97
119
141
A
B
C
D
1
2
3
4
5
341
342
87
86
385
42
Menlove Avenue
A562
Allerton Road
Hillfoot Road
Speke Hall Road
Woolton Road
Springwood Avenue
Brunt Lane
B5171
B5180
Allerton High St
Speke Rd
Acrefield
Woolton
L25
Allerton
Allerton Park Golf Club
Golf Course
Woolton Golf Club
Camp Hill
Springwood Crematorium
Allerton Cemetery
St Julies Catholic High School
Woolton Swimming Pool
Bishop Martin CE Prim Sch
Picture House
Woolton House Medical Cen
Village Medical Cen
Surgery
Watergate School
Much Woolton Cath Prim Sch
Woolton J&I School
New Heys Comprehensive School
Springwood Heath Prim Sch
Allerton Station
Garston CE Prim
St Benedicts College
Garston
Hunts Cross Shop Park
Triumph Trading Park
Works
Hunt's Cross
Edwards La Industrial Estate
Bridge Industrial Estate
Vitesse Road
Mayflower Av
Renown Way
Triumph Way
Herald Av
Dolomite Av
Stag Rd
Spitfire Road
North Av
Goodlass Road
Edward's Lane
Leafield
Barford
Hillfoot Rd
Armscot Close
Bourton Rd
Kingsmead Drive
Salcombe Dr
Waylands Drive
Stowe Cl
Oundle Pl
Farthing Cl
Winchester Cl
Camphill Rd
Hillfoot Gn
School Lane
Speke Road
Fairways Cl
Jeudwine Close
Haileybury
Stonyhurst Road
Charterhouse Road
Camp Rd
Woolton Bvd
Cavell Cl
Palm Gv
Pasture Cl
Lyndor Rd
Brendor Rd
Manor Road
Sylvan Court
School La
Kings Drive
Out Lane
Monks Way
Halewood Dr
Watergate Lane
Priory Wy
Woodrock Rd
Rockhill Rd
Highoaks Rd
Woolton St
Priorsfield
Woodvale Rd
Hyscrft Rd
The Heyes
James Rd
Church Rd
Mason St
Rushton Pl
Garden
Quarry St
Castle St
Rose St
Rodick St
Cheddar Cl
Evesham Cl
Gladstone St
Clay Cross Rd
Linkstor Rd
Vale Rd
Cresttor Road
Felltor Cl
Hightor Rd
Reservoir St
Longworth Wy
Mount Park Court
Woolton Mount
Acrefield Pk
Hillside Dr
Cambrian Wy
Broad Hey Cl
Gateacre V Rd
Woolton Mt
Merrion Cl
Rock Mt Cl
Kenilworth Cl
Hillview Gdns
The Hollies
Dowsefield Lane
Middlefield Rd
The Vineries
Whitstone Close
Tamerton Close
Cedar Cl
Stonehouse Mews
New Heys Dr
Redington Rd
Ravenna Road
Clavell Rd
Drennan Road
Springwood Avenue
Northmead Rd
Southmead Rd
Southmead Gdns
Longcroft Av
Longcroft Sq
Perriam Rd
Lascelles Road
Stamfordham Gv
Brocklebank La
Holly Farm Rd
Holman Rd
Harwood Rd
Highbank Dr
The Av
Vineyard St
Cavalier Dr
1 grid square represents 500 metres

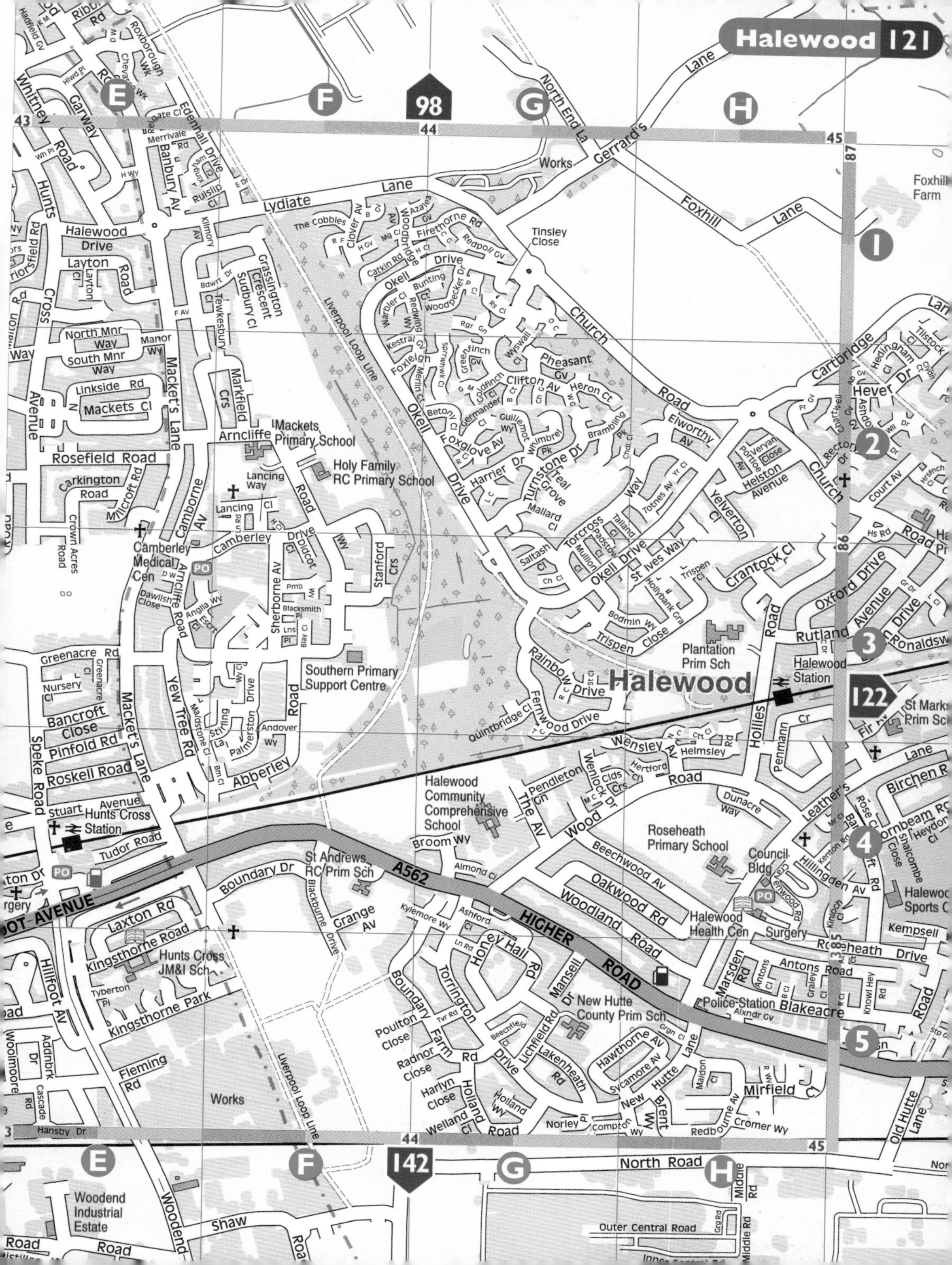
98
E
F
G
H
43
44
45
87
86
385
1
2
3
4
5
122
142
Lane
Gerrard's
North End La
Works
Foxhill Lane
Foxhill Farm
Lydiate Lane
Halewood Drive
Layton Road
Layton Cl
Hunts Cross Avenue
Whitney Road
Garway
Edenhall Drive
Merrivale Rd
Banbury Av
Ruislip Cl
Kilmory Av
Grassington Crescent
Sudbury Cl
Tewkesbury Cl
North Mnr Way
South Mnr Way
Manor Wy
Linkside Rd
Mackets Cl
Mackets Lane
Markfield Crs
Arncliffe
Mackets Primary School
Holy Family RC Primary School
Rosefield Road
Carkington Road
Millcroft Rd
Crown Acres Road
Lancing Way
Lancing Cl
Camberley Drive
Camborne Av
Camberley Medical Cen
PO
Dawlish Close
Arncliffe Road
Anglia Wy
Sherborne Av
Didcot Cl
Pmb
Blacksmith Pl
Stanford Crs
Southern Primary Support Centre
Yew Tree Rd
Maidstone Cl
Stirling La
Palmerston Drive
Andover Wy
Abberley Road
Greenacre Rd
Greenacre Cl
Nursery Cl
Bancroft Close
Pinfold Rd
Roskell Road
Speke Road
Stuart Avenue
Hunts Cross Station
Tudor Road
Mackets Lane
The Cobbles
Clover Av
Woodbridge Av
Azalea Gv
Firethorne Rd
Redpoll Gv
Catkin Rd
Okell Drive
Bunting Ct
Woodpecker Dr
Tinsley Close
Church Road
Warbler Cl
Redwing Wy
Kestrel Gv
Foxleigh
Merlin Ct
Greenfinch Gv
Wyswall Cl
Pheasant Gv
Goldfinch
Clifton Av
Heron Ct
Germander Cl
Guillemot Wy
Foxglove Av
Harrier Dr
Whimbrel Pk
Turnstone Dr
Teal Grove
Mallard Cl
Brambling Pk
Elworthy Av
Liverpool Loop Line
Way
Totnes Av
Torcross Cl
Padstow Cl
Mullion Cl
Saltash Cl
Okell Drive
St Ives Way
Hollybank Gra
Trispen Cl
Crantock Cl
Bodmin Wy
Trispen Close
Rainbow Drive
Fernwood Drive
Quintbridge Cl
Halewood
Plantation Prim Sch
Veryan Close
Portloe Av
Helston Avenue
Yelverton Cl
Cartbridge Lane
Hedingham Cl
Hever Dr
Tilstock
Rectory Dr
Church Road
Court Av
Hs Rd
Oxford Drive
Rutland Avenue
Ronaldsway
Halewood Station
Hollies Road
St Marks Prim Sch
Wensley Av
Helmsley
Hertford Cl
Wenlock Dr
Clds Crs
Pendleton Gn
The Av
Wood Road
Penmann Cr
Lane
Birchen Rd
Leather's Lane
Dunacre Way
Halewood Community Comprehensive School
Broom Wy
Roseheath Primary School
Council Bldg
Hornbeam Rd
Shalcombe Close
Hillingden Av
Kenton Rd
Halewood Sports Cl
St Andrews RC Prim Sch
A562
Almond Cl
Beechwood Av
Oakwood Rd
Woodland Road
Cranwood Rd
Halewood Health Cen
Surgery
Kempsell
Roseheath Drive
HIGHER ROAD
Boundary Dr
Blackburne Drive
Grange Av
Kylemore Wy
Ashford Cl
Honey Hall Rd
Ln Rd
Torrington Drive
Mansell Dr
New Hutte County Prim Sch
Marsden Rd
Antons Cl
Antons Road
Graleve Cl
Knowl Hey Rd
Police Station
Blakeacre Road
Alxndr Gv
Laxton Rd
Kingsthorne Road
Hunts Cross JM&I Sch
Tyberton Pl
Kingsthorne Park
Hillfoot Av
Addnbrk Dr
Woolmoore
Cascade
Fleming Rd
Works
Liverpool Loop Line
Boundary Farm Rd
Poulton Close
Radnor Close
Harlyn Close
Holland Cl
Holland Wy
Beechfield Cl
Lichfield Rd
Lakenheath Rd
Hawthorne Av
Sycamore Av
Hutte Lane
New Hutte Wy
Brent Wy
Maldon Cl
Mirfield Cl
Redbourne Av
Cromer Wy
Norley Pl
Compton Wy
Welland Road
Hansby Dr
Old Hutte Lane
North Road
Midlare Rd
Woodend Industrial Estate
Woodend
Shaw Road
Road
Outer Central Road
Middle Rd

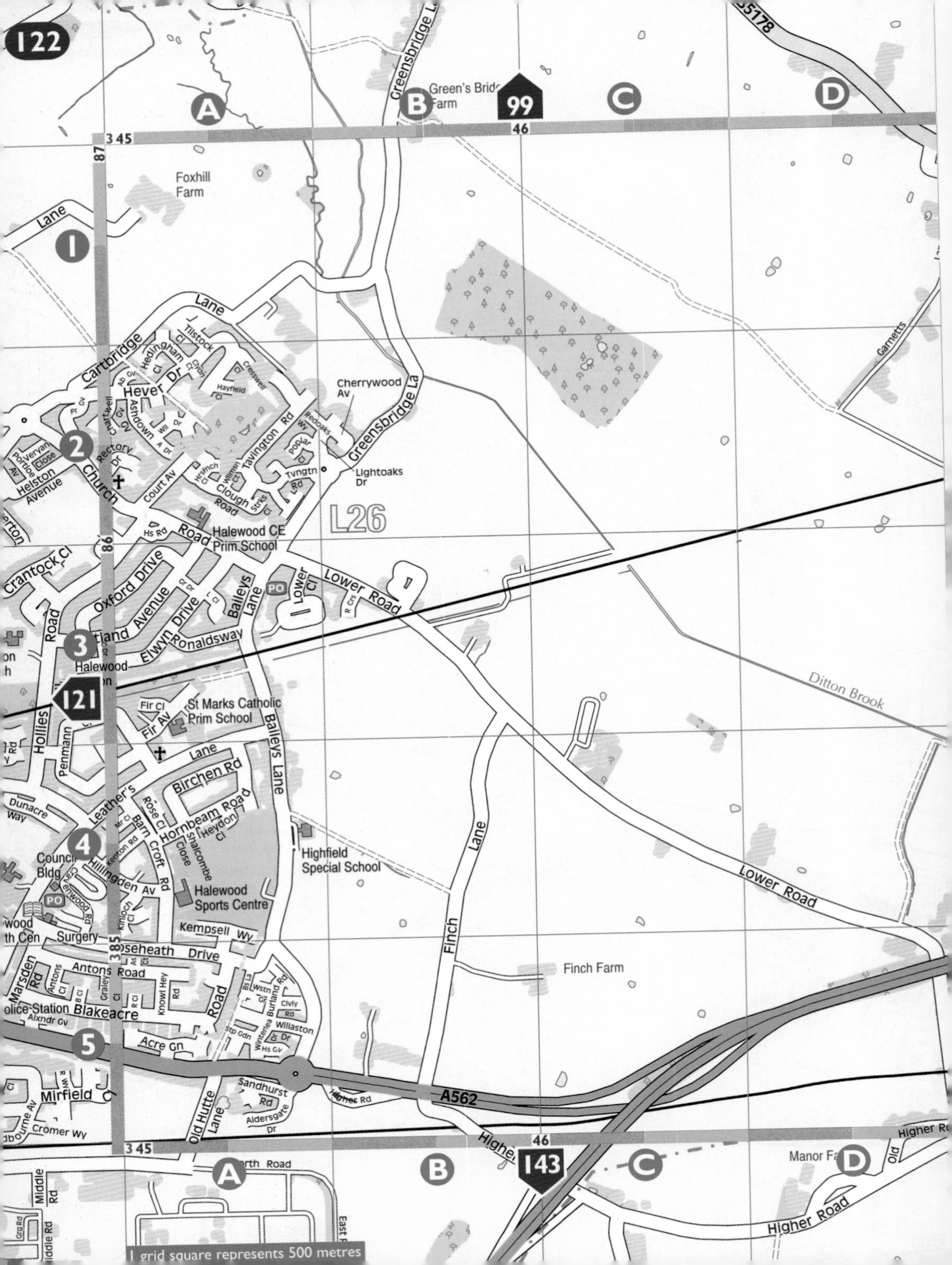
Green's Bridge Farm
Greensbridge La
B5178
99
46
3 45
87
Foxhill Farm
Lane
Cartbridge Lane
Tilstock Cl
Hedingham Cl
Clydon Cl
Cresswell
Hayfield Cl
Hever Dr
Chartwell
Ashdown
Cherrywood Av
Redoaks Wy
Poplar
Tavington Rd
Greensbridge La
Lightoaks Dr
Veryan Close
Helston Avenue
Rectory Dr
Church
Court Av
Clough Road
L26
Halewood CE Prim School
Hs Rd
Road
86
Crantock Cl
Oxford Drive
Avenue
Elwyn Drive
Ronaldsway
Balleys Lane
Lower Cl
Lower Road
PO
R Crs
Halewood
121
Hollies Road
Fir Cl
Fir Av
St Marks Catholic Prim School
Penmann
Lane
Birchen Rd
Leather's
Rose Cl
Barn Croft Rd
Hornbeam Road
Shalcombe Close
Heydon Cl
Dunacre Way
Council Bldg
Hillingden Av
Highfield Special School
Halewood Sports Centre
Baileys Lane
Finch Lane
Lower Road
Ditton Brook
Garnetts
Kempsell Wy
Surgery
Roseheath Drive
385
Marsden Rd
Antons Road
Knowl Hey Rd
Police Station
Blakeacre
Alxndr Gv
Road
Burland Rd
Willaston
Acre Gn
Finch Farm
Mirfield Cl
Cromer Wy
Old Hutte Lane
Sandhurst Rd
Aldersgate Dr
Higher Rd
A562
Higher Road
143
Manor Farm
Old
Higher Road
Middle Rd
East
A
B
C
D
1
2
3
4
5

1 grid square represents 500 metres

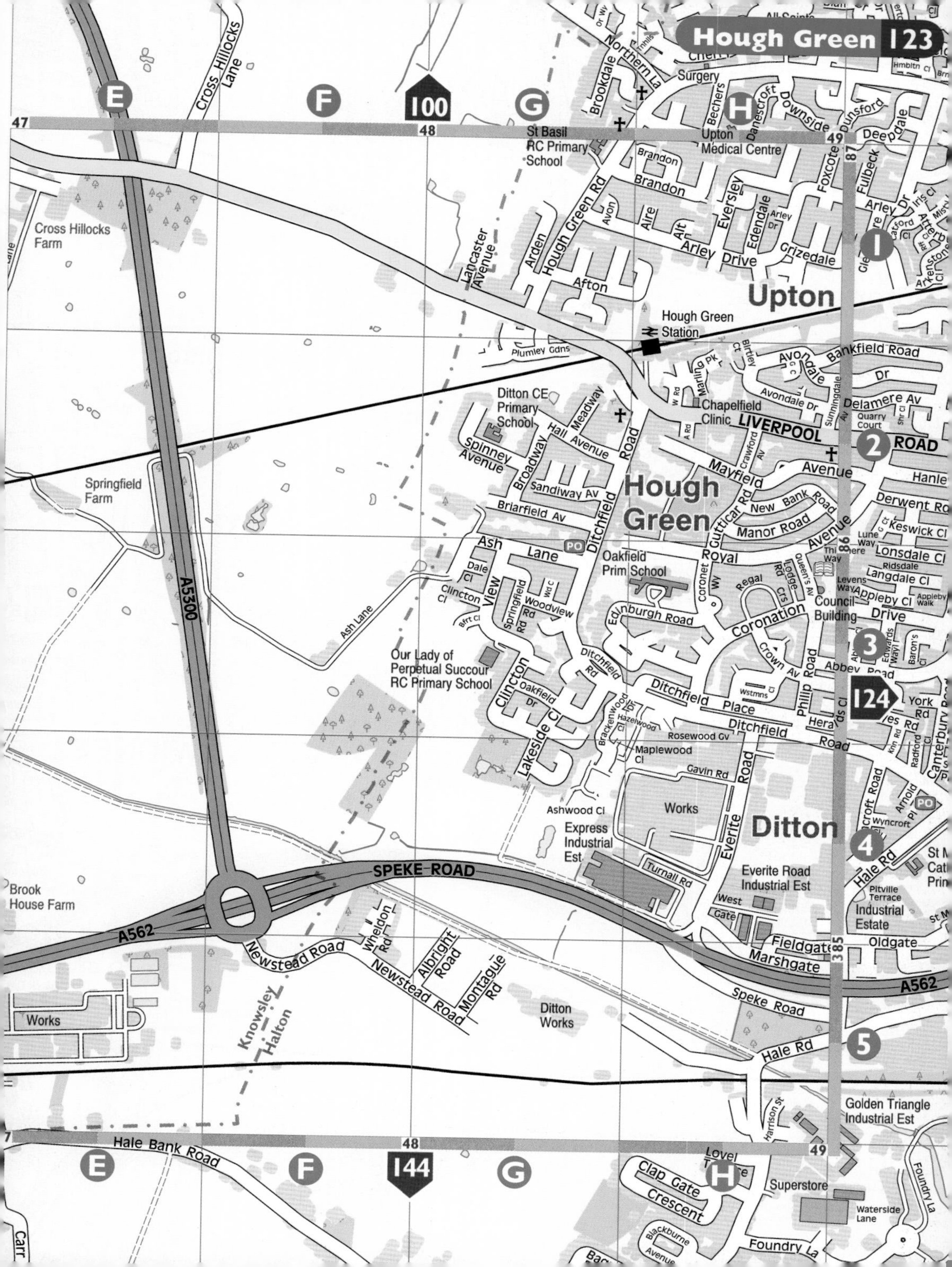
E
F
100
G
H
47
48
49
Cross Hillocks Lane
Northern La
Brookdale
Surgery
Bechers
Danescroft
Downside
Dunsford
Deepdale
St Basil RC Primary School
Upton Medical Centre
Brandon
Foxcote
Fulbeck
Arley Dr
Iris Cl
Cross Hillocks Farm
Hough Green Rd
Avon
Aire
Alt
Eversley
Edendale
Arley Dr
Arley Drive
Grizedale
Lancaster Avenue
Arden
Afton
Upton
Hough Green Station
Plumley Gdns
Birtley Ct
Marling Pk
Avondale Dr
Bankfield Road
Avondale Dr
Delamere Av
Quarry Court
Sunningdale Av
Ditton CE Primary School
Meadway
Hall Avenue
Chapelfield Clinic
LIVERPOOL ROAD
Crawford Av
Springfield Farm
Spinney Avenue
Broadway
Sandiway Av
Briarfield Av
Ditchfield Road
Hough Green
Mayfield Avenue
Gutticar Rd
New Bank Road
Manor Road
Avenue
Hanley
Derwent Rd
Keswick Cl
Lune Way
Lonsdale Cl
Langdale Cl
Appleby Cl
Appleby Walk
Levens Way
Ridsdale
Ash Lane
PO
Dale Cl
Clincton Cl
View
Springfield Rd
Woodview
Oakfield Prim School
Royal
Coronet Wy
Regal Crs
Lodge Rd
Queen's Av
Council Building
Drive
Edinburgh Road
Coronation
A5300
Ash Lane
Our Lady of Perpetual Succour RC Primary School
Ditchfield Rd
Crown Av
Abbey Road
Edwards Way
Baron's Cl
124
Clincton
Oakfield Dr
Lakeside Cl
Ditchfield Place
Wstmns Cl
Philip Road
Heralds Cl
York Rd
Canterbury Road
Hazelwood
Brackenwood
Rosewood Gv
Maplewood Cl
Ditchfield Road
Gavin Rd
Radford Cl
Ashwood Cl
Express Industrial Est
Works
Everite Road
Ditton
Wyncroft
Arnold Pl
PO
Hale Rd
Brook House Farm
SPEKE ROAD
Turnall Rd
Everite Road Industrial Est
West Gate
Pitville Terrace Industrial Estate
A562
Wheldon Rd
Albright Road
Newstead Road
Montague Rd
Fieldgate
Oldgate
Marshgate
385
A562
Works
Ditton Works
Knowsley
Halton
Speke Road
Hale Rd
5
Harrison St
Golden Triangle Industrial Est
Hale Bank Road
144
Clap Gate Crescent
Superstore
Waterside Lane
Foundry La
Blackburne Avenue
Foundry La
Carr
86
87
1
2
3
4

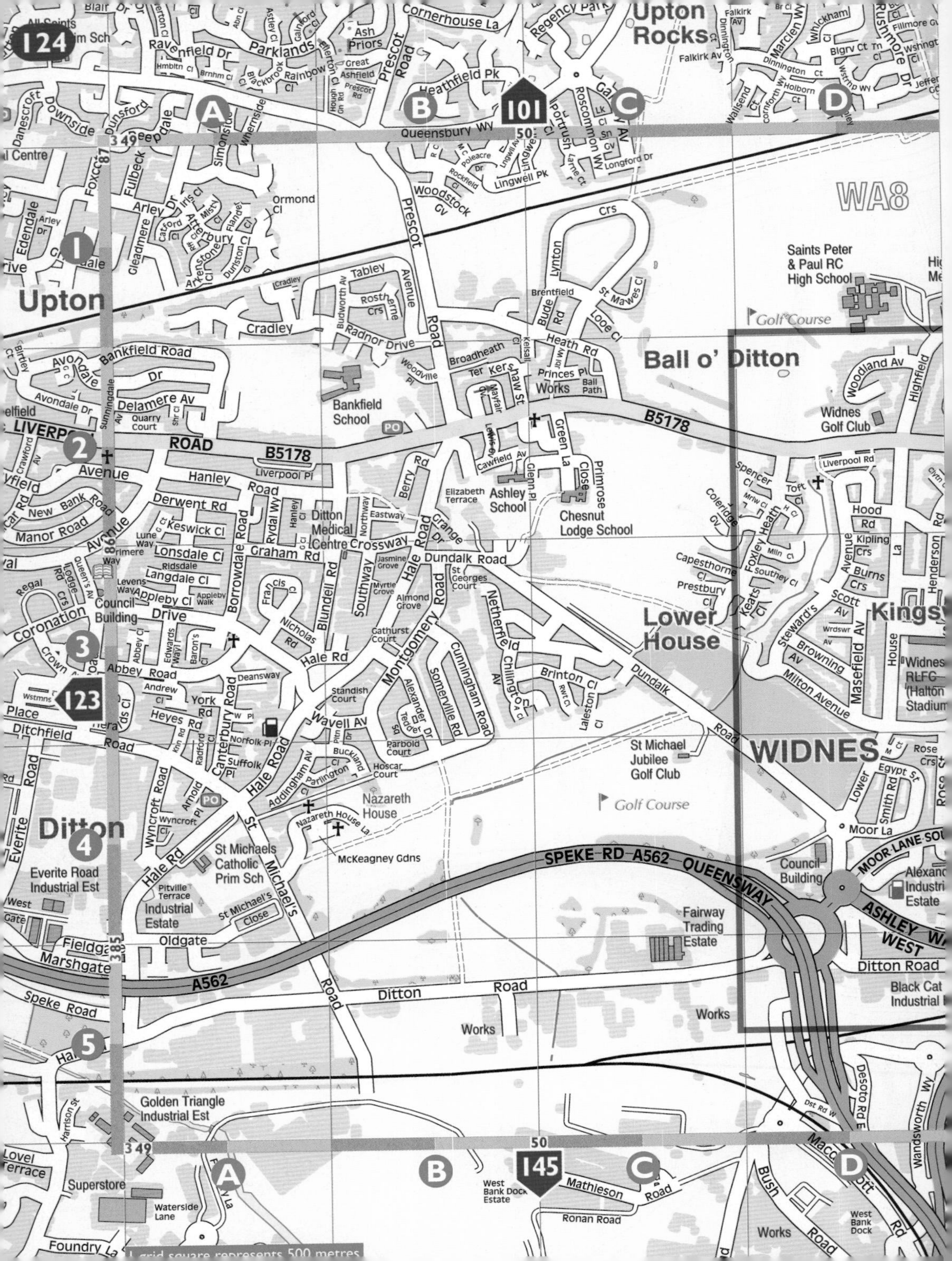
124
101
123
145
A
B
C
D
1
2
3
4
5
3 49
50
WA8
Upton
Upton Rocks
Ball o' Ditton
Lower House
WIDNES
Ditton
Kings
Cornerhouse La
Regency Park
Ravenfield Dr
Parklands
Ash Priors
Great Ashfield
Rainbow
Prescot Road
Heathfield Pk
Queensbury Wy
Downside
Dunsford
Deepdale
Simonside
Whernside
Fulbeck
Danescroft
Foxcote
Arley Dr
Atterbury Cl
Arkenstone Cl
Durlston Cl
Gleadmere
Ormond Cl
Edendale
Chirdale
Roscommon Wy
Portrush Cl
Longford Dr
Lingwell Pk
Woodstock Gv
Lynton Crs
Saints Peter & Paul RC High School
Golf Course
Tabley Avenue
Rosthorne Crs
Budworth Av
Radnor Drive
Cradley
Brentfield
St Mawes Cl
Bude Rd
Looe Cl
Heath Rd
Broadheath
Kershaw St
Princes Pl
Works
Ball Path
Woodland Av
Highfield
Widnes Golf Club
Bankfield Road
Avondale Dr
Delamere Av
Quarry Court
Sunningdale Av
Bankfield School
PO
LIVERPOOL ROAD
B5178
Liverpool Pl
Liverpool Rd
Avenue
Hanley Road
Derwent Rd
New Bank Road
Manor Road
Keswick Cl
Lonsdale Cl
Graham Rd
Rydal Wy
Ditton Medical Centre
Crossway
Northway
Eastway
Berry Rd
Crange Dr
Green La
Glenn Pl
Primrose Close
Elizabeth Terrace
Ashley School
Chesnut Lodge School
Coleridge Gv
Spencer Cl
Toft Cl
Foxley Heath
Hood Rd
Kipling Crs
Burns Crs
Henderson
Capesthorne Cl
Prestbury Cl
Keats Cl
Southey Cl
Scott Av
Steward's Av
Browning Av
Milton Avenue
Masefield Av
Widnes RLFC (Halton Stadium)
Coronation
Regal Crs
Council Building
Appleby Cl
Drive
Langdale Cl
Borrowdale Road
Francis Cl
Nicholas Rd
Blundell Rd
Southway
Jasmine Grove
Myrtle Grove
Almond Grove
Hale Road
Dundalk Road
St Georges Court
Montgomery Road
Netherfield Av
Cathurst Court
Chillington Av
Brinton Cl
Laleston Cl
Dundalk Road
Abbey Road
Crown
Andrew Cl
York Rd
Deansway
Heyes Rd
Canterbury Road
Standish Court
Wavell Av
Alexander Dr
Somerville Rd
Cunningham Road
Parbold Court
Buckland Cl
Hoscar Court
Parlington
Addingham Av
St Michael Jubilee Golf Club
Rose Crs
Egypt St
Lower House La
Smith Rd
Moor La
Ditchfield Road
Norfolk Pl
Suffolk Pl
Wyncroft Road
Arnold Pl
Radford
Nazareth House
Nazareth House La
McKeagney Gdns
St Michaels Catholic Prim Sch
Everite Road
Everite Road Industrial Est
Pitville Terrace
Industrial Estate
St Michael's Close
St Michael's Road
SPEKE RD A562 QUEENSWAY
MOOR LANE SOUTH
Council Building
Alexander Industrial Estate
ASHLEY WAY WEST
Fairway Trading Estate
Oldgate
Fieldgate
Marshgate
A562
Ditton Road
Black Cat Industrial
Speke Road
Works
Golden Triangle Industrial Est
Harrison St
Desoto Rd E
Wandsworth Wy
Macdermott Rd
Lovel Terrace
Superstore
Waterside Lane
West Bank Dock Estate
Mathieson Road
Ronan Road
Bush Road
West Bank Dock
Foundry La
1 grid square represents 500 metres

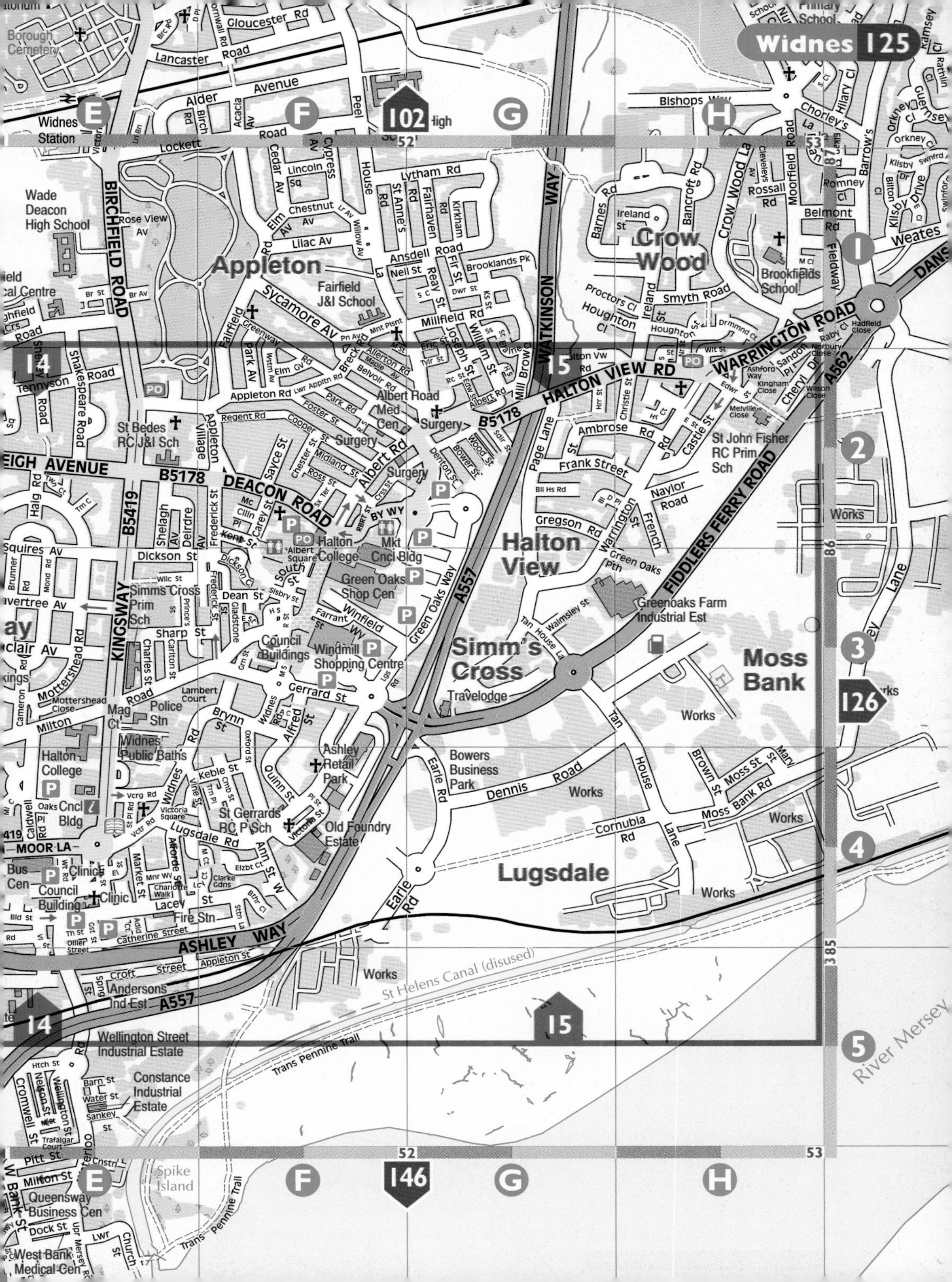
Borough Cemetery
Gloucester Rd
Lancaster Road
Alder Avenue
Widnes Station
Lockett Road
102
E
F
G
H
52
53
Bishops Way
Chorley's
Wade Deacon High School
BIRCHFIELD ROAD
Rose View Av
Lincoln Sq
Cypress Av
Cedar Av
Chestnut Av
Lilac Av
Lytham Rd
St Anne's Rd
Fairhaven Rd
Kirkham Rd
Ansdell Road
Neil St
Brooklands Pk
Appleton
Fairfield J&I School
Sycamore Av
Millfield Rd
WATKINSON WAY
Ireland St
Crow Wood
Crow Wood La
Bancroft Rd
Moorfield Road
Rossall Rd
Belmont
Romney Cl
Weates
Brookfields School
Proctors Cl
Smyth Road
Houghton Cl
Fieldway
Hadfield Close
WARRINGTON ROAD
14
15
Tennyson Road
Shakespeare Road
Park Av
Elm Gv
Belvoir Rd
Appleton Rd
Park Rd
Albert Road Med Cen
Surgery
B5178
HALTON VIEW RD
Ashford Way
Kingham Close
Norbury Close
Wilson Close
Melville Close
Cheryl Dr
A562
St Bedes RC J&I Sch
Regent Rd
Foster St
Cooper St
Appleton Village
Page Lane
Ambrose Rd
Christie St
Castle St
St John Fisher RC Prim Sch
2
Frank Street
FIDDLERS FERRY ROAD
DEACON ROAD
Sayce St
Chester St
Midland St
Ross St
Albert Rd
Denton St
Bower St
Wood St
B5419
Squires Av
Shelagh Av
Deirdre Av
Frederick St
Carey St
Halton College
Albert Square
Mkt Cncl Bldg
Halton View
Gregson Rd
Warrington St
French St
Naylor Road
Works
86
Dickson St
Green Oaks Shop Cen
Green Oaks Pth
Greenoaks Farm Industrial Est
Simms Cross Prim Sch
Dean St
Gladstone St
Winfield Wy
Farrant St
Walmsley St
Tan House La
KINGSWAY
Sharp St
Council Buildings
Windmill Shopping Centre
Simm's Cross
Moss Bank
3
Lane
Mottershead Rd
Charles St
Carlton St
Gerrard St
A557
Green Oaks Way
Travelodge
Lambert Court
Police Stn
Milton Road
Brynn St
Alfred St
Widnes Rd
126
Tan House Lane
Halton College
Widnes Public Baths
Keble St
Quinn St
Ashley Retail Park
Bowers Business Park
Earle Rd
Dennis Road
Brown St
Moss St
Mary St
Moss Bank Rd
Cncl Bldg
Victoria Square
St Gerrards RC P Sch
Lugsdale Rd
Old Foundry Estate
Cornubia Rd
MOOR LA
4
Bus Cen
Clinic
Council Building
Market St
Lacey St
Fire Stn
Lugsdale
Works
Catherine Street
ASHLEY WAY
Appleton St
Croft Street
Andersons Ind Est
St Helens Canal (disused)
385
Wellington Street Industrial Estate
Constance Industrial Estate
Trans Pennine Trail
5
River Mersey
Cromwell St
Wellington St
Nelson St
Trafalgar Court
Pitt St
146
Spike Island
Milton St
Queensway Business Cen
Dock St
West Bank Medical Cen
Church St

126
103
125
147
A
B
C
D
1
2
3
4
5
353
54
78
86
385
Shell Green
Cuerdley Cross
Cuerdley Green
Mowcroft Lane
Back La
WIDNES ROAD
A562
DANS ROAD
WARRINGTON ROAD
FERRY ROAD
Wrights Lane
Bennett's Lane
Johnson's Lane
Gorsey Lane
Warrington
Halton
Works
Brookfields School
St John Fish RC Prim Sch
Moss Bank Rd
Moss St
Mary St
River Mersey
Hempstones Point
Wigg
Primary School
Nursery
Dykin Road
Hilary Cl
Chorley's La
Elk Rd
Barrow's Green
Ramsey Cl
Rathlin
Skye Cl
Orkney Cl
Kilsby Drive
Swinford Av
Weates Cl
Romney Cl
Belmont Rd
Rossall Rd
Moorfield Road
Crow Wood La
Cleveleys Av
Fieldway
Mithril B Cl
Avebury Cl
Coulton Rd
Barnston Rd
Severn Cl
Douglas Cl
Calder Cl
Hadfield Close
Raby Cl
Norbury Close
Sandon Pl
Ashford Way
Kingham Close
Cheryl Dr
Wilson Close
Melville Close
Edwr St
Wlt St
Bilton Cl
Tyl La
1 grid square represents 500 metres

Fiddler's Ferry
WIDNES ROAD
A562
Cuerdley
Newlyn Gdns
Tannery Lane
Penrose Gdns
Rothay Dr
Roeburn Wy
The Pk
Radlett Close
Walkers Lane
Falmouth Dr
St Brides Cl
Bramble Cl
Ditchfield Rd
Penketh South
St Vincents Catholic Primary School
Hall Nook
Trans Pennine Trail
Shaftesbury Av
Road
Station Road
LC
Marsh Lane
PH
Riverside Trading Estate
St Helens Canal (disused)
Trans Pennine Trail
River Mersey
Norton Marsh
Moss Side
Moss Side Lane
Lapwing Lane
Halton Moss
Manchester Ship Canal
Eastgate Road
Lane
Six Acre Lane
E
F
G
H
1
2
3
4
5
56
57
87
86
385
104
128

128
Stris Av
Shoreham
rkwall Dr
Wrtn Cl
Hamble Dr
Trans Pennine Trail
Hall Nook
LC
Forrest Way
A
B
105
C
Works
D
357
58
87
1
2
86
3
Moss Side
127
Lapwing Lane
4
Birch Wood
Moore Lane
Bellhouse Lane
385
Moss Lane
5
Halton Moss
Moore RUFC
Moore
Gigg Lane
Runcorn Road
PO
Hollyhedge Farm
Cheshire Ring Canal Walk
Holly Hedge
Moore Prim Sch
Six Acre Lane
Six Acre Gdns
Lndfld Cl
Canal Side
Hobb
Lane
ROAD
1 grid square represents 500 metres

Higher Walton
Lower Walton
106
130
E
F
G
H
59
60
61
87
86
385
1
2
3
4
5
River
River Mersey
Works
CHESTER ROAD
A5060
Manx
Irwell
Avenue
Rydal
Derwent
Silverdale Road
Meadow Av
Wordsworth Av
Arnside Gv
Road
Copeland Rd
Gainsborough Avenue
Elgin Av
Cranborne Avenue
Landseer
St Weburgh CE Primary School
Boswell Av
Burgess Close
Causeway Medical Centre
Sulby Av
Greeba Av
Wallis St
WILDERSPOOL CAUSEWAY
River Road
Menin Av
Flers Av
Greenall's Av
Superstore
Coopers Pl
Wilderspool Crs
Peartree Pl
Firecrest Ct
Lakeside Drive
Slutchers
Eastford Road
Baronet Ms
Taylor St
Morley Rd
Pool La
ELLESMERE ROAD
B5156
Worsley Road
Stetchworth Rd
Osborne Rd
Walton Heath Rd
Francis Rd
Algernon St
West Avenue
Primary School
Southern St
Bressbrook Road
WALTON NEW ROAD
A56
A56 CHESTER ROAD
Hill Cliffe Road
Rutland Avenue
Grantham Avenue
Belvoir Road
Granby Road
Melton Avenue
Brookwood Cl
Calderfield Cl
Chelford Cl
Old Hall Cl
Whitefield Road
Carlingford Rd
Westbourne Road
Hillfoot Crs
Cranleigh Close
Walton Lea Road
Warrington Sports Club
Walton Lea Crematorium
Birchdale
Kingsley
Red Lane
Lynwood Av
Warren Cliffe Road
Beech
Cawdor
Grange Green Farm
Mill Lane
CHESTER NEW ROAD
Old Chester Road
Walton Lea Rd
Walton Hall Golf Club
Walton Hall
Runcorn Road
Thomasons Br La
Underbridge La
Warrington Road
Hough's Lane
Golf Course
Hillfoot Farm
Rowswood Ctyd
Park Lane
Appleton Reservoir
Firs Lane
Windmill
Field La
Bellcast Cl
Saxon Cl
High Warren Cl
Bellfield Farm

130
107
129
A
B
C
D
1
2
3
4
5
361
62
385
87
98
Latchford
Wilderspool
Stockton Heath
Cobbs
Hillcliffe
Appleton Park
Dudlows Green
Causeway Medical Centre
Palatine Industrial Estate
Priestley College
Sir Thomas Boteler High School
Latchford Medical Cent
Lady RC Primary School
Works
Station Road Industrial Estate
St Weburgh CE Primary School
Loushers Lane Special School
Warrington Town AFC
Cornerstone School
Manchester Ship Canal
Superstore
Medical Centre
St Thomas CE Prim Sch
Grappenhall Sports Club
Primary School
The Forge Shopping Centre
Police Station
Mountain Farm
The Cobbs Infant School
Witherwin Farm
Council Building
Broomfield County Junior School
St Monica's RC Prim School
Bridgewater Upper School
Bridgewater High School
Golf Course
High Warren
Warrington
KNUTSFORD ROAD
THELWALL LANE
STATION ROAD
ACKERS ROAD
WILDERSPOOL CAUSEWAY
FAIRFIELD ROAD B5156
ELLESMERE ROAD
GRAPPENHALL ROAD A56
WALTON ROAD A56
NEW ROAD A56
LONDON ROAD A49
Loushers Lane
Stockton Lane
Lumb Brook Road
Witherwin Avenue
Lyon's Lane
Broomfields Rd
Delphfields Road
Windmill Lane
Dingle Lane
Green Lane
Longwood Road
Pineways
Fairways
Beechways
Hall Drive
Greenfields Avenue
Waverley Av
Dingleway
Bernard Av
Dale Lane
Wood Lane
Ash Lane
Bridge Lane
Cobbs Lane
Waterside Avenue
Sandy Lane
East Av
Victoria Road
Parkgate Rd
Mill Lane
Ackers Lane
Brian Avenue
Denbury Avenue
Top Road
Marlborough Crs
Greenall's Av
Stafford Road
China Lane
Cawdor St
Beech Road
Birchdale Road
Kingsley Drive
Red Lane
Warren Road
Highwood Road
Burfield Drive
Quarry Lane
Field Lane
Firs Lane
Westbourne Road
Chessington Close
Chiswick Gdns
Henley Close
Chalfont Cl
Pangbourne Close
Taplow Cl
Shepperton Close
Broom Av
Cann Lane North
1 grid square represents 500 metres

Dover Road
Latchford
THELWALL
Surgery
Mottram
Thelwall Infant School
Richmond Av
Baldock Rd
Dunmow
Welwyn Cl
Harlow
Walden
Community
Barley
Road
Watton Cl
Wilson Cl
Pickering Crs
Woodlands
Gateley Cl
Poynton Close
Grappenhall Clinic
Oller
Best Western Fir Grove Hotel
108
Springfield Avenue
Bradshaw Lane
Knightsbridge
Westminster Cl
Cross Lane
Barton Av
Cawthorne Av
Mayfield Rd
Windsor Drive
Bradshaw Community Primary School
Knsn Av
Coronation Av
Ascot Cl
Knutsford Old Rd
KNUTSFORD RD
A50
KNUTSFORD ROAD
Heathfield
Marifield Road
Middlehurst Road
Shirley Dr
Kildonan Road
Victoria Av
Albert Road
Clarence Road
St Annes Avenue
Euclid Avenue
Georges Crs
Nicholls St
Malresfield
East Vw
Tudor Close
Hallcroft Pl
Harwood Gdns
York Drive
York Road
Victoria Rd
Grappenhall
St Annes Av E
A56
Shadewood Crs
Lindi Av
PO
Portola Cl
Gilwell Cl
Barnswood Cl
Glebe Av
St Wilfrid's Dr
Mellow Cl
B Cl
Lane
Sharon Pk Cl
Laurel Bank
Beechfield Rd
ROAD
St Wilfrids CE Aided Primary School
Stockton Lane
Church Lane
Bellhouse
Canal Side
Australia Lane
Cliff Lane
Thelwall Heys
Bridgewater Canal
Weaste Lane
Cuerdon Dr
Marie Drive
Stoneleigh Gardens
A50
Parrs Wd View
Grappenhall Hall School
Grappenhall CC
KNUTSFORD ROAD
Knutsford Rd
Tresham Dr
Tresham Drive
Bourchier Wy
Wolfe Cl
Drive
Broad Lane
Hall Lane
Whitehouse Farm
Grappenhall Heys
Chichester Cl
Dashwood Cl
Lichfield Av
Curzon Drive
Strickland Cl
Croft Gdns
Curzon Dr
Yew Tree Farm
Dairy Farm
Witherwin Avenue
Bretland Dr
Stansfield Dr
Keeper's Rd
Grappenhall Heys School
Boddington Dr
Reddish Hall
Cartridge Lane
GRAPPENHALL
B5356
Wright's Green
Dodds Lane
Lumb Brook Road
Lane
GRAPPENHALL LANE
Appleton Thorn Trading Estate
E
F
G
H
1
2
3
4
5
63
64
65
87
86
385

110
A
B
C
D
1
2
3
4
5
321
22
84
83
382
Hey
Badger's Set
Drive
The Steeple
Meadow Gate
1 grid square represents 500 metres

Caldy
Golf Club
Golf Course
Primary School
Thurstaston
H ROAD
Thurstaston
Dawpool
Church
Lane
A540
TELEGRAPH ROAD
Station
Road
Wirral Way
Station Road
Wirral
Country Park
Works
The
Dungeon
Wirral Way
Piper's Lane
Broad Lane
Dee
Side
Target Road
E
F
G
H
111
134
23
24
25
84
83
1
2
3
4
5

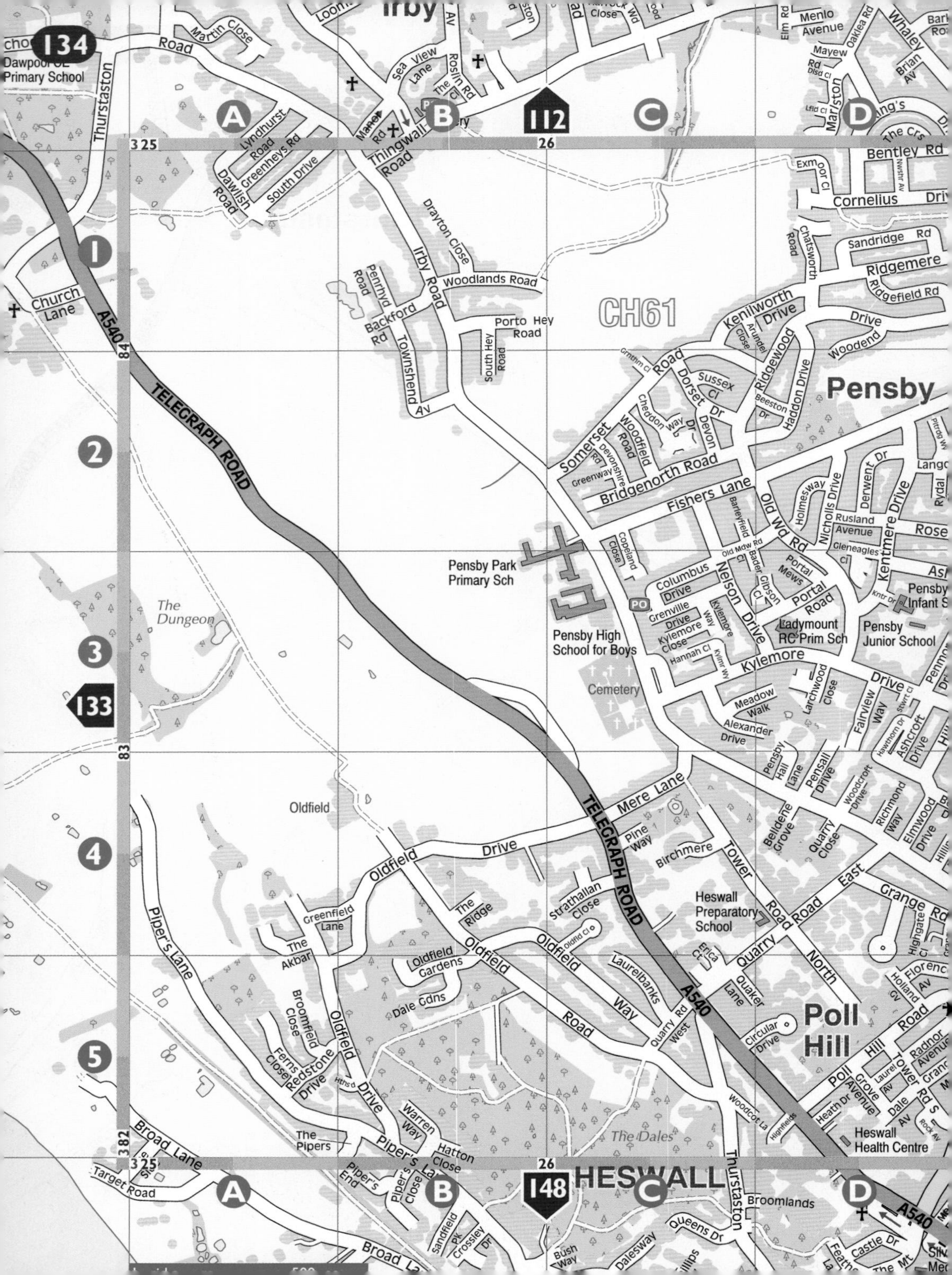

134
112
133
148
Irby
Pensby
Poll Hill
HESWALL
CH61
A
B
C
D
1
2
3
4
5
325
26
84
83
382
Dawpool CE Primary School
Thurstaston Road
Martin Close
Lyndhurst Road
Greenheys Rd
Dawlish Road
South Drive
Sea View Lane
Roslin Rd
The Cl
Manor Rd
Thingwall Road
Menlo Avenue
Mayew Rd
Marlston
Whaley
Oaklea Rd
Brian Av
The Crs
Bentley Rd
Cornelius Dri
Chatsworth Road
Sandridge Rd
Ridgemere
Ridgefield Rd
Drayton Close
Irby Road
Woodlands Road
Penrhyd Road
Backford Rd
Townshend Av
Porto Hey Road
South Hey Road
Church Lane
A540
TELEGRAPH ROAD
Kenilworth Drive
Arundel Close
Ridgewood
Woodend
Haddon Drive
Beeston Dr
Sussex Cl
Dorset Dr
Devon
Cheadon Way
Somerset Road
Woodfield Road
Devonshire Rd
Greenway
Bridgenorth Road
Fishers Lane
Old Wd Rd
Holmesway
Nicholls Drive
Derwent Dr
Kentmere Drive
Rusland Avenue
Gleneagles Cl
Bartleyfield
Copeland Close
Old Mdw Rd
Columbus Drive
Nelson Drive
Bader Cl
Gibson Cl
Portal Mews
Portal Road
Pensby Park Primary Sch
Pensby High School for Boys
Grenville Drive
Kylemore Way
Kylemore Close
Hannah Cl
Kylemore Drive
Ladymount RC Prim Sch
Pensby Infant S
Pensby Junior School
Cemetery
Meadow Walk
Alexander Drive
Larchwood Close
Fairview Way
Ashcroft Drive
Pensby Hall Lane
Pensall Drive
Woodcroft Drive
Richmond Way
Elmwood Drive
The Dungeon
Oldfield
Mere Lane
Pine Way
Birchmere
Belldene Grove
Quarry Close
Oldfield Drive
Tower Road North
Quarry Road East
Grange Rd
Highgate Cl
Heswall Preparatory School
Stratnallan Close
The Ridge
Greenfield Lane
The Akbar
Oldfield Gardens
Oldfield Road
Oldfield Way
Laurelbanks
Erica Ct
Quaker Lane
Dale Gdns
Broomfield Close
Piper's Lane
Ferns Close
Redstone Drive
Oldfield Drive
Quarry Rd West
Circular Drive
Holland Av
Florence Av
Poll Hill Road
Radnor Avenue
Laurel Av
Grove Avenue
Tower Rd S
Dale Av
Heath Dr
Heswall Health Centre
Woodcot La
Highfields
Warren Way
Hatton Close
The Pipers
The Dales
Broad Lane
Target Road
Piper's End
Piper's Close
Sandfield Pk
Crossley Dr
Thurstaston Road
Broomlands
Queens Dr
Bush Way
Dalesway
Castle Dr
The Mt

Thingwall
Barnston
Murrayfield Hospital
Works
Station Road
Private Drive
Overdale Av
Holmwood Avenue
Holmwood Dr
Low Wood Grove
Woodlands Dr
Dale End Road
Lwr Thingwall La
Storeton Lane
Gills Lane
Thorncroft Drive
Marfield Lane
A551
BARNSTON ROAD
PH
Manor House
Carnsdale Farm
Whitehouse Lane
ROAD
Heswall Primary School
Whitfield Lane
Milner Road
Briary Close
Park Road
Fieldway
Brunstath Close
Meadowcroft
Barcombe Rd
Acre Lane
Pear Tree Cl
Brooklet Rd
Brimstage Rd
BRIMSTAGE
Lime Tree Gv
Nigel Road
Carol Dr
Lawford Drive
Pullman Cl
Heswall Sta
Old
PENSBY ROAD
B5138
Pensby Recreation Centre
Pensby Clinic
Belmont Dr
Fender Way
Oaks Lane
Marksway
Laurelhurst Av
Beech Av
Cestrian Dr
Ryland Pk
Heswall Mt
Pensby Close
Elms Pk
Gwendoline Close
Axholme Close
Axholme Rd
Seven Acres La
Wimbourne Av
Barnsdale Avenue
Regents Close
Sparks
Recreation Centre
The Foxes
Surgery
School
Howards Rd
Colemere Dr
Milton Av
Quarry La
Nurse Rd
Penrhyn Av
Mill Yd
PO
Anderson Cl
Kingsley Close
Lyndhurst Avenue
enbank Drive
Napps Wy
Downham Road N
Ravenswood Road
Oaklands Dr
Sandy Lane
Heather Rd
Shrewsbury Rd
Gorsehill Rd
Hesketh Drive
South Road
Milton Crs
Fernlea Road
Forest Road
Downham Dr
Birches Cl
Tengate Buffs Lane
Andrew's Walk
Border
Moorway
Police Station
E
F
G
H
1
2
3
4
5
28
29
84
83
382
113
136
149

136
A
B
114
C
D
329
30
Ltl Storeton
Lane
Storeton
Rest
Station Road
Station Road
Red Hill Road
Keepers Lane
Brimstage
M53
1
84
2
Ley Farm
3
135
83
Brimstage
Green
Bank
Brimstage
4
Fairfield
Lane
5
A5137
Manor Road
Talbot Avenue
ROAD
382
329
30
A
B
150
C
D
Thornton
Manor
1 grid square represents 500 metres

Storeton Hill
Higher Bebington Junior School
Millbutt Cl
Acorn Cl
Orchard
Road
Teehey La
Town Lane Infant School
Village Road
Roland Avenue
Sandfield
Teehey Cl
115
Higher
Bridgehouse Clinic
Road
E
F
G
H
32
33
Bebington High Sports College
Acres
Ascot Av
Richmond Close
Brereton Av
The Village
B5136
Mount
Conway Cl
Teehey Gdns
Waterfield Cl
Heyville Road
Holmville
Road
Bebington
Road
Acreville Road
Tudorville Road
Greenville
Lane
School La
Shallmarsh Rd
Calder Rd
Kennet Rd
Lane
Kingsville Rd
Melville Road
Gorseyville Road
Holmway Infant School
Pulford Road
Green
Heath Rd
Church
1
Station
Derwent Road
Brackenwood Junior School
Ascot Dr
Reedville Road
St Edmunds Rd
The Highcroft
Broomleigh Cl
Elmure Av
The Crescent
Heath Road
Norbury Av
Abbots Dr
Bracken Lane
Ferns Road
Lower Bebington
Highcroft Av
Road
Brackenwood Golf Club
Brackenwood
Heather Road
Hazel Grove
Ivy Av
Plane Rd
Tree
Wirral Grammar School for Girls
Lime Av
Alder Rd
Laurel Av
Cedar Avenue
Yew Tree Road
Wirral Grammar School for Boys
Cross Lane
Heathfield Road
Monks Wy
Kirket Lane
Church Road Medical Centre
Road
Rowan Gv
2
Langdale Road
PO
Mayer Av
Quarry
Fairacre
Avenue
Golf Course
Benty Cl
Peter Price's Lane
Teesdale Rd
Borrowdale Road
Kempson
Corrie Dr
Harding Avenue
Church Road
B5151
Road
Stanton
Patterdale Rd
Beechway
Stanton Road Primary Sch
Priory Cl
Foxcovers Rd
Wirral Cl
Gdns
Firs Av
Pine Av
Lynton Drive
B5136
Holly Av
3
Needwood Dr
Mount Road
Brimstage Road
Delves Av
Stevenson Dr
Mynsule Rd
Royd
Donne Cl
138
Mobberley Wy
Road
Parnell Rd
Thornfield
B5137
Road
Dutton Dr
Poulton
Fulbrook Rd
Winfrith Dr
Gilbert Cl
Buckland
Burdett Av
Inley
Junction 4
Clatterbridge
Harborne Dr
Walford
Road
Inley
Harris
Poulton
Woodkind Hey
Road
4
Brimstage
A5137
Tyburn
Bosworth Cl
M53
Poulton
Bellward Cl
Finstall Road
Old
Mount Road
Royd
CH63
Mount Road
Poulton Gn Cl
Langley
Drive
Warren
Clatterbridge Hospital
Moseley Road
Colmore
Yardley Dr
Woodkind Hey
5
Wirral Hospital
Poulton Road
382
151
Clatterbridge Road
New

138
116
137
152
A
B
C
D
1
2
3
4
5
333
34
84
83
82
Art Gallery
Church Drive Primary School
Bromborough Pool
Port Sunlight
Police Station
Port Sunlight Stn
The Village Hotel & Leisure Club
Works
Lower Bebington
Church Road Medical Centre
Stanton Road Primary Sch
Spital Station
Spital
Surgery
Multibowl
Odeon Cinema
Poulton
Poulton Lancelyn Primary School
Woodslee Primary School
Bromborough
Bromborough Rake Station
NEW CHESTER ROAD
A41
CHURCH ROAD
B5136
B5137
SPITAL ROAD
Bromborough Road
Quarry Road East
Old Ct House Road
Dock Road
Port Causeway
Fairway North
Fairway South
Magazine Road
Mill Road
Heather Dene
Welton Rd
Palatine Road
Dibbins Hey
Woodkind Hey
Poulton Road
Poulton Royd Drive
Colmore Av
Bolton Road East
Wood Street
Park Road
Bath Street
Riverside
The Ginnel
Water St
Wharf St
King George's Dr
Queen Mary's Drive
Greendale Road
Parkside Road
Townfield Lane
Heath Rd
Acreville Road
Tudorville Road
Kirket Lane
Fairacres Road
Harding Avenue
Mayer Avenue
Highcroft Av
Abbots Dr
Priory Cl
Foxcovers Rd
Lynton Drive
Tudor Av
Jocelyn Cl
St Andrews Road
Parkfield Road
Blair Park
Cypress Cft
The Pines
Tanar Cl
The Glen
Arkwood Cl
Oakridge Rd
Birchridge Close
Meadway
Vanderbyl Av
Gotham Road
Elton Dr
Latham Way
Arderne Close
Brome Way
Halsall Gn
Venables Drive
Goostrey Close
Wolfrick Drive
Uplands Rd
Central Av
North Close
Croft Avenue
Hornby Av
Mark Rake
Athelstan Close
Ludlow Gv
Allport Lane
Eccleston Avenue
Hadley Avenue
Alston Cl
Park Vw
The Oaks
The Av
Ashfield
Valley Rd
Dale Avenue
Bradmoor Rd
Gratrix Rd
1 grid square represents 500 metres

E
F
117
G
H
36
37
Dock
South
South
Works
Works
Riverbank
Works
Road
Road
Magazine Works
La
Georgia
Av
Croft
Business
Park
Works
Commercial Road
Croft
Business
Park
Welton
Road
Stadium
Road
Crrck Rd
Dinsdale Rd
Caldbeck
Road
Mosedale
Road
Bassendale
Works
Works
Wirral
International
Business Park
Plantation
Business
Park
Skiddaw Rd
Croft
Business
Park
Thursby
Road
Stdm Ct
Plantation Road
Power Road
Martindale Rd
Road
HW Rd
Old Hall Rd
Works
Premier
Travel Inn
Brunel Rd
Croft
Business
Park
Works
Job's
Ferry
The Rake
Queensbury Av
Riverwood Road
Old Hall Road
Hardknott Road
Village
PO
E
F
153
G
H
CH62
Grisedale Rd
Wrynose Rd
Harrow
Gv
Eastham
Ferry
1
2
3
4
5
84
83
382

South Road
Knowsley Rd
Eaton Road
Salisbury
Surgery
Swansea Cl
Barry Dr
Cardiff Wy
Drive
A561
St Mary's Rd
119
Seddon Rd
Bennett St
McBride St
Earp St
Clifton St
Moss St
Works
Argyle Rd
Gladstone Rd
Palmerston Rd
Russell Road
Wooltton Rd
Chapel Road
Condor Cl
Island Rd S
Garston Station
Garston CE Prim Sch
HORROCKS AV
Horrocks
Holman Rd
Highbank Dr
Sir Alfred Jones Meml Hosp
Wood St
Duke St
James St
Sidwell St
Garston Leis Cen
Lowbridge Court
B5171
Garst
Queen Street
Speke Road
PO
GARSTON WAY
Cressington Esp
Dock Road
Railway St
Church Rd
Works
Dale St
Byron Street
Bank's Road
Holy Trinity RC Primary School
Matchwood Cl
Vesuvian Dr
Logfield
Hughes St
Sinclair St
Lucania St
Otway St
Stanley St
Hardy St
Priory St
Campania St
Saunby St
Window Lane
Canterbury Street
Durham St
Banks Rd Prim Sch
King St
Vulcan St
Lincoln St
Chesterton St
Lyon Street
Brunswick Street
Garston Industrial Estate
York Street
Windfield Road
Bank's La
Monkfield Wy
Blackburne Street
Garston Rocks
Works
Weaver Industrial Estate
Brunswick St
Windfield Cl
York Way
Mersey
A
B
C
D
1
2
3
4
5
339
40
84
83
382

1 grid square represents 500 metres

Vitesse Rd
Mayflower Av
Shop Park
Leafield Rd
Road
Herald Av
Dolomite Av
Stag Rd
Triumph Way
Spitfire Road
Triumph Trading Park
North Av
SPEKE HALL ROAD
Hunt's Cross
Edward's Lane
Cascade Rd
Benedicts College
Work 120
Goodlass Road
Edwards Lane Industrial Estate
Hansby Dr
The Av
Bridge Industrial Estate
Vineyard St
Cavalier Dr
Almond Ct
Mt St
Bk's Rd
Street
Burnsall
Wooden Industrial Estate
Evans Road
Old Distillery Rd
Evans
Chemistry
Pharmacy Road
Botany
SPEKE ROAD
A562
Delf La
New Mersey Retail Park
Works
A561
Bank's Road
Speke Rd
Speke Boulevard
Liverpool Marriott Hotel
Estuary Business Park
Windward Drive
Leeward Drive
Estuary Boulevard
Petworth Cl
Barnham Cl
B Cl
Road
Lydd Cl
Rycot
Tonbridge Cl
Clwrth Rd
Bexhill Cl
Lnhm Wy
Dymchurch
Appledore
Close
Woodend La
Gerneth Cl
Sandgate Cl
Speke Town La
Farm Road
Blacklock Hall Road
PO
Estuary Banks
Works
Speke Hall Av
Colworth Rd
School Way
Gerneth Rd
Speke Church Rd
Greyhound
Blacklock
Stockton
Speke Hall Avenue
Speke Hall Avenue
Stockton Wood Community Primary School
Spindus Road
Speke Hall Industrial Estate
Stirling Rd
Blenheim Wy
All Saints
Sutton Rd
Tewit Rd
Dakota Drive
Bailey's Lane
142
Skypark Industrial Park
Owen Dr
Road
Road
Dunlop Road
The Walk
Bank's Lane
Speke Hall (NT)
Liverpool John Lennon International
Mersey Way
E
F
G
H
1
2
3
4
5
41
42
43
84
83
382

142
Hunt's Cross
121
141
Leafield Rd
Road
Tyberton Pl
Kingsthorne Park
foot Av
Barford Road
Woolmoore Rd
Addnbrk Dr
Cascade Rd
Fleming Rd
Edward's Lane
Edwards Lane Industrial Estate
Hansby Dr
Bridge Industrial Estate
Works
Liverpool Loop Line
Poulton Close
Radnor Close
Farm Rd
Holland Rd
Welland Cl
Tvr Rd
Beechfield Cl
Lichfield Rd
Lakenheath Rd
Drive
New Hutte County Prim Sch
Hawthorne Av
Sycamore Av
New Hutte Lane
Grgn Cl
Police Station
Blakeacre
Alxndr Gv
Maldon Cl
Mirfield Cl
New Brent Wy
Norley Pl
Compton Wy
Redbourn
Cromer Wy
Road
North Road
Middle Rd
Outer Central Road
Grg Rd
Inner Central Rd
Works
Inner West Road
Renaissance Way
Woodend Industrial Estate
Evans Road
Old Distillery Rd
Evans Rd
Shaw Road
Woodend Avenue
Woodend Industrial Estate
Chemistry Rd
Physics Rd
Pharmacy Road
Botany Rd
Speke Bvd
Science Rd
Gaskill Road
Speke Boulevard
SPEKE BOULEVARD
A561
Inner S Road
South Road
Middle Road
Barnham Cl
B Cl
Road
Lydd Cl
Clwrth
Rycot Road
Bray Road
Dymchurch
Appledore
Close
Lnhm Wy
Bd Wy
Gerneth Cl
Speke Town La
PO
Colworth Rd
School Way
Gerneth Rd
Woodend La
Farm Road
Hall Road
Rmsbr Cl
Ramsbrook Rd
Speke Church Rd
Greyhound Farm Road
Blacklock Hall Road
Blackrod Av
Stockton Wd Rd
Goldfinch Farm Road
Western Avenue
Clough Road
Tarbock Road
St Christophers Catholic Primary School
Linner Road
Stapleton Avenue
Road
Hrfld Gn
Conleach Road
Speke
Parklands High School
Clough Road
Surgery
Millwood Road
P Gn
Road
All Hallows Dr
Rd
Heaton Close
Harland Gn
Stockton Wood Community Primary School
All Saints Road
Avenue
Stirling Rd
Blenheim Wy
Hale Road
Sutton Wood Rd
Tewit Hall Rd
Tewit Hall Cl
Lovel Wy
Lovel Road
Harefield
Wltn Gn
Wltn Cl
Austin Rawlinson Sports Centre
Police Stn
Alder Wood Avenue
Canworth Road
Heath
Middlefield Primary School
Oldbridge
Ardwick Rd
Withington Rd
Catford Gn
Skyport Industrial Park
Central Avenue
Fnt Cl
Fntn Gn
Lovel
North Parade
South Parade
M C
PO
Speke Family Health Clinic
Central Way
Para
Holland
Rd
Gnw Cl
Canworth Rd
Brmh Cl
Little
Burnage Cl
Eastern
Alwain
Owen Dr
Dunlop Road
Road
Oglet La
Dam Wood Road
Dam Wood Road
St Rd
Hale Road
Hale Drive
Eas
L24
Liverpool John Lennon International Airport
Liverpool
Halton
Dungeon Lane
Oglet
Oglet Lane
A B C D
1 2 3 4 5
343 44
84 83 382
1 grid square represents 500 metres

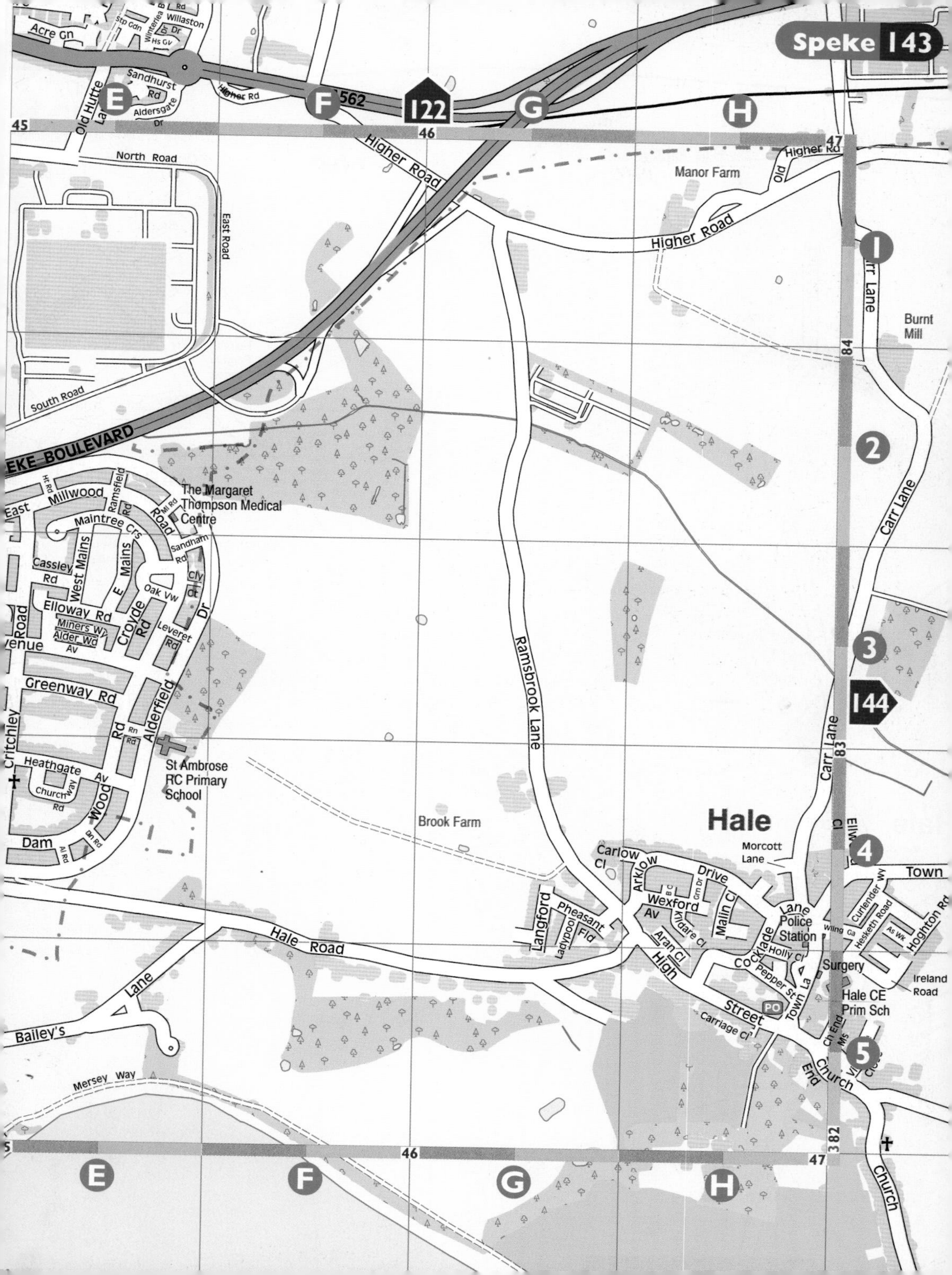

Acre Gn
Willaston
Sandhurst Rd
Aldersgate Dr
Old Hutte La
Higher Rd
A562
122
E
F
G
H
45
46
47
North Road
Higher Road
Manor Farm
Old Higher Rd
East Road
South Road
SPEKE BOULEVARD
I
Carr Lane
Burnt Mill
84
2
3
144
83
382
The Margaret Thompson Medical Centre
Millwood
Ramsfield Rd
Road
Maintree Crs
East
Cassley Rd
West Mains
E Mains
Sandham Rd
Cly Ct
Oak Vw
Elloway Rd
Miners Wy
Alder Wd
Croyde Rd
Leveret Rd
Dr
Avenue
Greenway Rd
Alderfield
Rd
Critchley
Heathgate Av
Church Rd
Wood
Dam
St Ambrose RC Primary School
Ramsbrook Lane
Brook Farm
Hale
Morcott Lane
Carlow Cl
Arklow
Drive
Wexford Av
Kildare Cl
Malin Cl
Aran Cl
Langford
Pheasant Fld
Ladypool
Hale Road
High Street
Cocklade Lane
Police Station
Holly Cl
Pepper St
Town La
Surgery
PO
Carriage Cl
Town
Curlender Wy
Hesketh Road
Hoghton Rd
As Wk
Ireland Road
Hale CE Prim Sch
Ch End Ms
4
5
Church End
Church
Bailey's Lane
Mersey Way

Works
Knowsley
Halton
Road
Ditton Works
Hale Rd
123
Harrison St
Higher Rd
Old
Hale Bank Road
Lovel Terrace
Clap Gate Crescent
Superstore
Blackburne Avenue
Foundry La
Baguley Avenue
Ch M Wk
Pickerings Rd
Broughton Way
Carr Lane
Burnt Mill
Potters La
Heathview Rd
Kenview Cl
Halebank CE Primary School
Mersey View Road
Hale Bank
Garnetts Lane
Pickerings Pasture
Hale Gate Road
Trans Pennine Trail
143
Carr Lane
Halegate Farm
Hale
Morcott Lane
Ellwood Cl
Town Lane
Curlender Wy
Hesketh Road
Hoghton Rd
As Wk
Wling Ga
Malin Cl
Cocklade Lane
Police Station
Holly Cl
Surgery
Ireland Road
Pepper St
Town La
Hale CE Prim Sch
PO
Street
Carriage Cl
Ch End Ms
Vicarage Close
Church End
Within Way
Church
A
B
C
D
1
2
3
4
5
47
48
84
83
82
1 grid square represents 500 metres

Hale Bank 145
Industrial Estate
Works
Works
Golden Triangle Industrial Est
E
F
124
G
H
I
49
50
51
West Bank Dock Estate
Mathieson Road
Ronan Rd
Ronan Road
Waterside Lane
Foundry La
Hale Road Industrial Estate
Works
Works
Desoto Road
Vickers Road
Bush Road
Macdermott Rd
Dock Rd
West Bank Dock
West Bank
Wandsworth Wy
Cromwell St
Nelson St
Wellington St
Trafalgar Court
Pitt St
Milton St
Queensway Business Cen
Dock St
Church St
A533
Trans Pennine Trail
West Bank Prim Sch
8
Runcorn Gap
Runcorn-Widnes Bridge
2
River Mersey
QUEENSWAY
Old Coach Rd
Collier St
Blantyre St
Suffolk St
Cawdor St
Trentham St
Portland St
Bentinck St
Leinster St
Algernon Street
Leinster Gardens
Brindley St
Ashridge St
South Bank Terrace
All Saints Prim Sch
3
Mersey Road
Lord St
Waterloo Rd
Cooper St
146
Church Street
Loch St
HIGH ST
Station Rd
Duke Cl
Lane
Percival
Percival Lane
DARESBURY
4
CHAPEL ST
WESTON POINT EXPRESSWAY A557
Runcorn Station
Shaw St
Cormorant Dr
Road
Adela Rd
Cynthia Rd
Roland Av
Clifton Court
Pimlico Rd
Farm
Penn Lane
Clayton Crs
Works
Westfield Prim Sch
Holloway
Balfour St
Victoria Prim Sch
Picow
Chandlers Ct
Crofton Road
Road
Westfield Crs
Westfield
Queen's Rd
Dale St
5
Higher Runcorn
Morley
Oxford
Norman
War Mem
Manchester Ship Canal
Salt Works Wharf
Weston Point
154
Farm Rd
A557
Russell
Beaconsfield Rd
Weston Road
Hale Vw
Hillside Av
Runcorn Hill Nature Reserve
Royden Av
Coombe
Lawson Ho Htl & Conf Cen
St Clements RC Prim Sch
WA7
Moughland
B5382

Black Cat Industrial Estate
146
Wellington Street Industrial Estate
Constance Industrial Estate
Trans Pennine Trail
A
B
125
C
D
52
351
Spike Island
Pitt St
Milton St
Queensway Business Cen
Dock St
West Bank Dock
West Bank Medical Cen
Catalyst Science Discovery Centre
Church St
Wandsworth Wy
Desoto Rd E
A533
84
West Bank
PO
Works
1
2
West Bank Prim Sch
9
Runcorn-Widnes Bridge
Manchester Ship Canal
All Saints CE Prim Sch
Mersey Road
Mersey St
3
145
Church Street
Mkt
Works
Old Quay St
St Edwards C Prim Sch
Astmoor Rd
Astmoor Road
Astmoor Industrial Estate
Faraday Rd
Hardwick Rd
Lister Road
Jensen Court
Stanley St
Parker St
Pool
B5755
BRIDGE ST
HIGH ST
Surg
Arts Cen
Bridgewater Canal
Linnets Pk
Runcorn AFC
Canal St
Mason St
DARESBURY EXPRESSWAY
A533
HEATH RD
Halton Rd
Dudley Av
Carlton Av
Halton Road
Manor Rd
Castle Rise
Ivychurch Ms
Works
DARESBURY EXPRESSWAY
Campanile Hotel
4
QUEENSWAY
Runcorn Station
Shaw St
Cornwall Av
York St
Victoria Rd
Victoria Road Prim Sch
Cemetery
RUNCORN SPUR ROAD
LATHAM AV
B5155
Union St
Claremont Rd
Picton Avenue
Wicksten Dr
Saxon Road
Stenhills Crs
Stonehills La
The Grange Infant School
Grange Comprehensive School
The Grange Junior School
Latham Avenue
Alexandra Gv
Kent Gv
Boston Av
Halton Brook Av
Hallwood
Ivy Street
Poolside Rd
Harrop Rd
Kingsley Rd
Coronation Rd
Heath Road
Town Hall
RUNCORN
Hinton Rd
Greenway
Oxford
Norman
Balfour St
Holloway
Roland Av
5
Higher Runcorn
War Mem
Southlands Court
382
351
St Clements RC Prim Sch
A
B
Heath Road Medical Cen
RUNCORN
155
52
C
D
Crescent
SPUR ROAD
B5155
Sycamore
Maple Rd
Birch Road
Lilac Crs
Lime
Festival
Avenue
Windsor Grove
Lawson Ho Htl & Conf Cen
Royden Av
Vista Rd
Whitby Rd
Fernhurst
1 grid square represents 500 metres

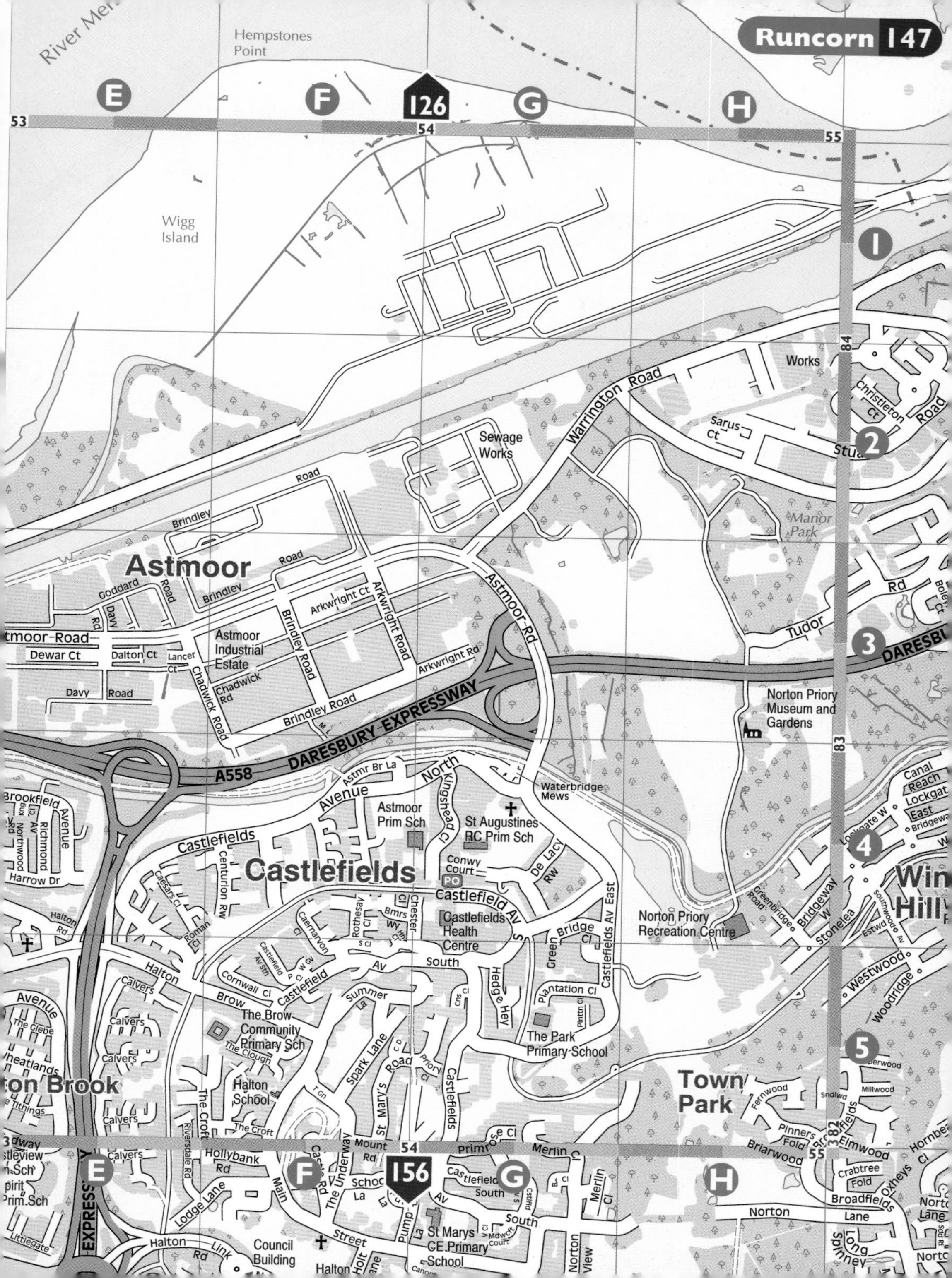
River Mersey
Hempstones Point
Wigg Island
126
156
Works
Christleton Ct
Road
Sarus Ct
Warrington Road
Sewage Works
Manor Park
Brindley Road
Astmoor
Goddard Road
Davy Rd
Arkwright Ct
Arkwright Road
Brindley Road
Astmoor Road
Dewar Ct
Dalton Ct
Lancer Ct
Astmoor Industrial Estate
Chadwick Rd
Chadwick Road
Davy Road
Arkwright Rd
Astmoor Rd
Tudor Rd
Bolton Cl
DARESBURY EXPRESSWAY
A558
Norton Priory Museum and Gardens
Astmr Br La
North Avenue
Kingshead Cl
Waterbridge Mews
Canal Reach
Lockgate East
Bridgewater
Brookfield Avenue
Richmond Av
Northwood Rd
Harrow Dr
Castlefields
Centurion Rw
Astmoor Prim Sch
St Augustines RC Prim Sch
Conwy Court
De Lacy Rw
PO
Castlefield Av
Castlefields Health Centre
Green Bridge Cl
Castlefields Av East
Norton Priory Recreation Centre
Greenbridge Road
Bridgeway
Stonelea
Southwood Av
Westwood
Windmill Hill
Halton Rd
Caesars Cl
Roman Cl
Caernarvon Cl
Rothesay Cl
Chester Cl
Cornwall Cl
Castlefield Av South
Hedge Hey
Plantation Cl
Halton Brow
The Brow Community Primary Sch
The Clough
Summer La
Spark Lane
St Mary's Road
Priory Cl
Castlefields
The Park Primary School
Woodridge
Avenue
The Glebe
Wheatlands
Calvers
Halton Brook
The Tithings
Halton School
The Croft
Riversdale Rd
Town Park
Fernwood
Millwood
Pinners Fold
Briarwood
Elmwood
Hollybank Rd
Mount Rd
Primrose Cl
Merlin Cl
Castle Rd
The Underway
School La
Castlefields South
Crabtree Fold
Broadfields
Oxheys Cl
Hornbeam
Norton Lane
Lodge Lane
Main Street
Pump La
St Marys CE Primary School
Halton Link Rd
Council Building
Norton View
Spinney
Long
Littlegate
EXPRESSWAY
E
F
G
H
53
54
55
84
83
82
1
2
3
4
5

134
HESWALL
Poll Hill
A B C D
1 2 3 4 5
325
26
82
81
80
Broad Lane
Target Road
Dee Side
The Pipers
Piper's Lane
Piper's End
Piper's Close
Hatton Close
Sandfield Pk
Crossley Dr
Croftsway
Mostyn Av
Banks Road
The Moorings
Wittering Lane
Gulls Way
Hawks Way
Teals Way
Rooks Wy
Linnets Wy
Bush Way
Dalesway
Delavor Road
Phillips Way
Queens Dr
Broomlands
Thurstaston Road
Farr Hall Rd
Farr Hall Drive
Church Meadow Lane
Church Farm Court
St Peters CE Primary School
School Hill
Brow Lane
St Peter's Cl
PO
West Cv
Dee View Rd
Rocky Lane
Feather La
Castle Dr
The Mt
A540
Heswall Health Centre
Woodcot La
Highfields
Heath Dr
Grove Avenue
Laurel Av
Dale Av
Tower Rd S
Rock Av
Radnor Avenue
Grange
Circular Drive
Quarry West
The Dales
Redstone Drive
Ferns Close
Warren Way
Park West
Davenport Road
Rectory Lane
Rectory Close
Raby Cl
The Lydiate
Village Road
Wallrake
Hessle Dr
Station Road
Marine Drive
Manners Lane
Seafield Av
Hilbre Av
Seabank Road
Westway
Meadway
Riverbank Cl
Riverbank Road
Hinderton Drive
Lapwing Rl
Gayton
CH60
Long
Lillyfield Lane
Cottage Lane
Cottage Drive West
Cottage Drive East
Gayton Cott
P

1 grid square represents 500 metres

135
150
PENSBY
Shrewsbury Rd
Gorsehill
Hesketh Drive
South Road
Milton Cr
Lane
Milner
Briary Close
Park Road
Pine Rd
Beech Rd
BARNSTON ROAD
Fieldway
Brunstath Close
Acre Lane
Meadowcroft
Barcombe Rd
Brooklet Rd
Brimstage Rd
Whitehouse Lane
ROAD
Heswall Station
Old Lane
Birches Cl
Fernlea Road
Forest Road
Downham Road
Downham Dr
May Road
Pye Rd
Milner Cop
Topgate Cl
Buffs Lane
Andrew's Walk
Border Road
Moorway
Pinewood Drive
Lime Tree Gv
Speedwell Dr
Carol Dr
Lawford Drive
Nigel Road
BRIMSTAGE
Pullman Cl
Police Station
Milner Road
Oban Dr
Boundary Lane
Briar Dr
Mill Lane
Ingleegreen
Tudorway
Hill Top La
Larksway
Rhodesway
Barnston Towers Close
Pond Vw Cl
The Paddock
Redmere Dr
Heythrop Drive
Rocky La S
Beacon Lane
Briarfield Rd
Heathway
Lightfoot La
Dell La
Chalkwell Dr
Brmstg Cl
Bower Rd
Stevens Rd
Aspen Cl
Heswall FC
Broadmead
Wheatland Road
Beacon La
West Drive
North Drive
TELEGRAPH ROAD
The Beacons
South Drive
Ryecroft Road
Sandham Gv
Barnston Primary School
The Ridgeway
Old Ml Cl
Premier Travel Inn
Suncroft Rd
Kestrel Road
Fox Cover Rd
Anthony's Way
Hillside Road
Moorland Pk
Beechfield Cl
The Knap
A540
CHESTER ROAD
Lynton Close
Thornton Crs
Beverley Dr
Parklands Dr
Trent Way
Porlock Close
Chantry Walk
Baskervyle Close
Baskervyle Road
Well Lane
Gayton
Gayton Primary School
Gayton Lane
The Crs
Latchford Road
Oakswa y
Kingsway
Queensway
Dee Park Close
Dee Park Road
Ash Way
Fir Wy
Birchway
St. Stephens Close
Parkway
Gayton Farm Rd
Heswall Golf Club
Cedarway
Gayton
The Spinney
New Hall
Golf Course
Leighton Hall Farm
The Runnell
Backwood Hall
Wirral Way
Leighton Road
B5135
Ashfield Hall
E
F
G
H
1
2
3
4
5
27
28
29
82
81
380

150
Lane
A5137
A
B
Manor Road
Talbot Ave
136
C
D
ROAD
329
30
82
1
Thornton Manor
2
Manor Road
Grange Dr
Works
THORNTON
Thornton Hough
St Grgs Wy
Thornton Hough Primary School
81
Smithy Hill
B5136
PO
Church Road
The Folds
Raby Road
3
New Hall
149
Oxford Drive
Radley Dr
NESTON ROAD
Oxford Drive
Eton Drive
Widgeons Covert
Thornton Hall Hotel
B5136
4
Parkgate Lane
NESTON ROAD
380
The Grange Country Club
Leighton Hall Farm
5
The
Yew Tree Farm
CHESTER HIGH ROAD A540
LIVERPOOL ROAD B5136
Raby Road
329
30
A
B
C
D
Ashfield Hall

E
F
G
H
137
32
33
82
81
380
I
2
3
4
5
152
Poulton Ro
Poulton Hall Road
Raby Mere Road
Blakeley
Raby Hall
B5151 CLATTERBRIDGE ROAD
New Rocklands
Rocklands Lane
COMMON
ROAD
B5136
Thornton Common Road
M53
WILLASTON
ROAD
Raby Vale
Thornton Farm
Four Lanes End
Raby Mere Road
Raby Hall Road
Hargrave Lane
Raby
The Green
B5151
Willowbrow Farm
Hargrave Hall Farm
Willow Lane
Benty Heath
Raby House Farm
Willowbro
OAD

Bromborough
Brookhurst
138
151
A
B
C
D
1
2
3
4
5
333
34
82
81
380
Poulton Road
Poulton Hall Road
Poulton Hall
Nature Reserve
Blakeley Dene
Raby Mere Road
Blakeley Road
Raby Hall
Raby Hall Road
Raby Cl
Blakeley Ct
Blakeley Brow
Ormesby Gv
Drive
Blakeley Dell
Mere Av
Links Cl
Lawns Av
Raby Av
Fairway Cl
Dibbinsdale Road
Dibbins Green
Dell Cl
Barrymore Way
Maelor Cl
Aldford Close
Allport Road
Kent Close
Rickaby Cl
Doe's Meadow Road
Marfords Avenue
Cunningham Drive
Grenville Crs
Greenacre Dr
Blyth Rd
Marten Av
Marline Av
Bromborough Station
Bromborough Rake Station
Bromborough Golf Club
Golf Course
Dibbinsdale Brook
M53
Road
Hargrave Lane
Hargrave Hall Farm
Hargrave House Farm
Raby House Farm
Benty Heath Lane
Brookhurst Road
Brookhurst Avenue
Brookhurst Close
Brookhurst Prim Sch
Somerville Close
Birkdale Av
Angus Rd
Bruce Crs
Alistair Drive
Sunningdale Dr
Sandiway
Malcolm Crs
Ainsdale Cl
Fairhaven Dr
Tavener Cl
Troon Cl
Wentworth Dr
The Chase
Bowness Av
Keswick Av
Keith Dr
Banff Av
Kintore Cl
Rhona Close
Turriff Dr
Duncansby Dr
Cullen
Nairn Close
Greenfields Avenue
Greenfields Crs
Dawpool Drive
Acre Lane
Caldicott Av
At Rd
PO
Westminster Dr
Morland Av
Raeburn Primary School
Limehurst Gv
The Woodcotes
Appleby Grove
Plymyard Avenue
Dale Rd
Crossdale Road
Gorsefield Close
Gorsefield Av
Oakwood Pk
Plymyard Close
Langfield Gv
Oakdene Close
Woodlea Close
Edgewood
Bettisfield Avenue
Brinley Cl
Dearnford Avenue
Dearnford Cl
Springhill Av
Bromington Av
Chesterfield Rd
Harrogate Rd
Harrogate Cl
Redcar Dr
South Wirral High School
Sutherland Avenue
Argyll Avenue
Eastham Rake
Eastham
The Oaks
Park Vw
The Av
Beechwood Road
Maple Gv
Ashfield Road
Ashfield Crs
Oakfield Rd
Valley Rd
Dale Avenue
Oteley Avenue
Mainwaring Rd
Forwood Rd
Bradmoor Rd
Gratrix Rd
Heys Av
Mossley Av
Hawthorn Lane
Meadowside Road
Brancote Gdns
The Allports
Palatine Road
Hadley Avenue
Belmont Av
Alston Cl
Hornby Rd
Hornby Av
Broseley Av
Mark Rake
Athelstan Close
Ludlow Gv
Allport Lane
Church La
Wolfrick Drive
Venables Close
Colmore Av
Mose
1 grid square represents 500 metres

139
CH62
Eastham Ferry
Eastham
Eastham Country Park
Wirral Metropolitan College
Eastham Lodge Golf Club
Golf Course
Eastham Locks
Manchester Ship Canal
Cemetery
Works
Croft Business Park
Premier Travel Inn
Job's Ferry
Mendell Primary School
Christ The King RC Primary School
Heygarth Primary School
The Lyndale School
St Marys CE Primary School
Millfields Primary School
Eastham House
Travelodge
NEW CHESTER ROAD
A41
EASTHAM VILLAGE ROAD
B5132
RIVACRE ROAD
Old Hall Road
Riverwood Road
Hardknott Road
Tebay Road
Neville Road
Woodyear Road
Ferry Road
Wood Heath Wy
Chapel View
Mayfield Dr
Seaview Av
St David Road
St John's Road
Christopher Drive
Ferry Road
Park Road
Bridle Road
Elgar Avenue
Heygarth Road
Kilburn Avenue
Princes Avenue
Eastham Rake
Adaston Av
Athol Drive
Bankfields Drive
Wirral
Cheshire

145
A
B
C
D
349
50
82
81
380
1
2
3
4
5
Weston Point
Salt Works Wharf
Manchester Ship Canal
Works
Weston Point Dock
Post Office La
Clarkes Terrace
Beacon Hill View
Mersey Vw S Rd
Sandy Lane
West Road
Canal Side
Baker Road
South Parade
Leonard St
Sydney St
Lydiate La
Picow Farm Rd
Picow
Chandlers Ct
Westfield Prim Sch
Crofton Road
Westfield Road
Westfield Crs
Cunningham Dr
Beaconsfield Rd
Russell Rd
Hale Vw
Hillside Av
Cameron Av
Hazel Av
Perrin Av
Lncst Av
Minster Ct
Weston Road
Runcorn Hill Nature Reserve
Highlands Road
Southlands Court
Weston Point Primary School
Roscoe Crescent
Castner Av
A557
WESTON POINT EXPRESSWAY
Weston
Collier's Row
Prospect Row
Cheshyres Lane
Cheshyres La
Bankes' La
Heath Dr
Marion
Bankes' La
Road
Halton
Cheshire County
LC

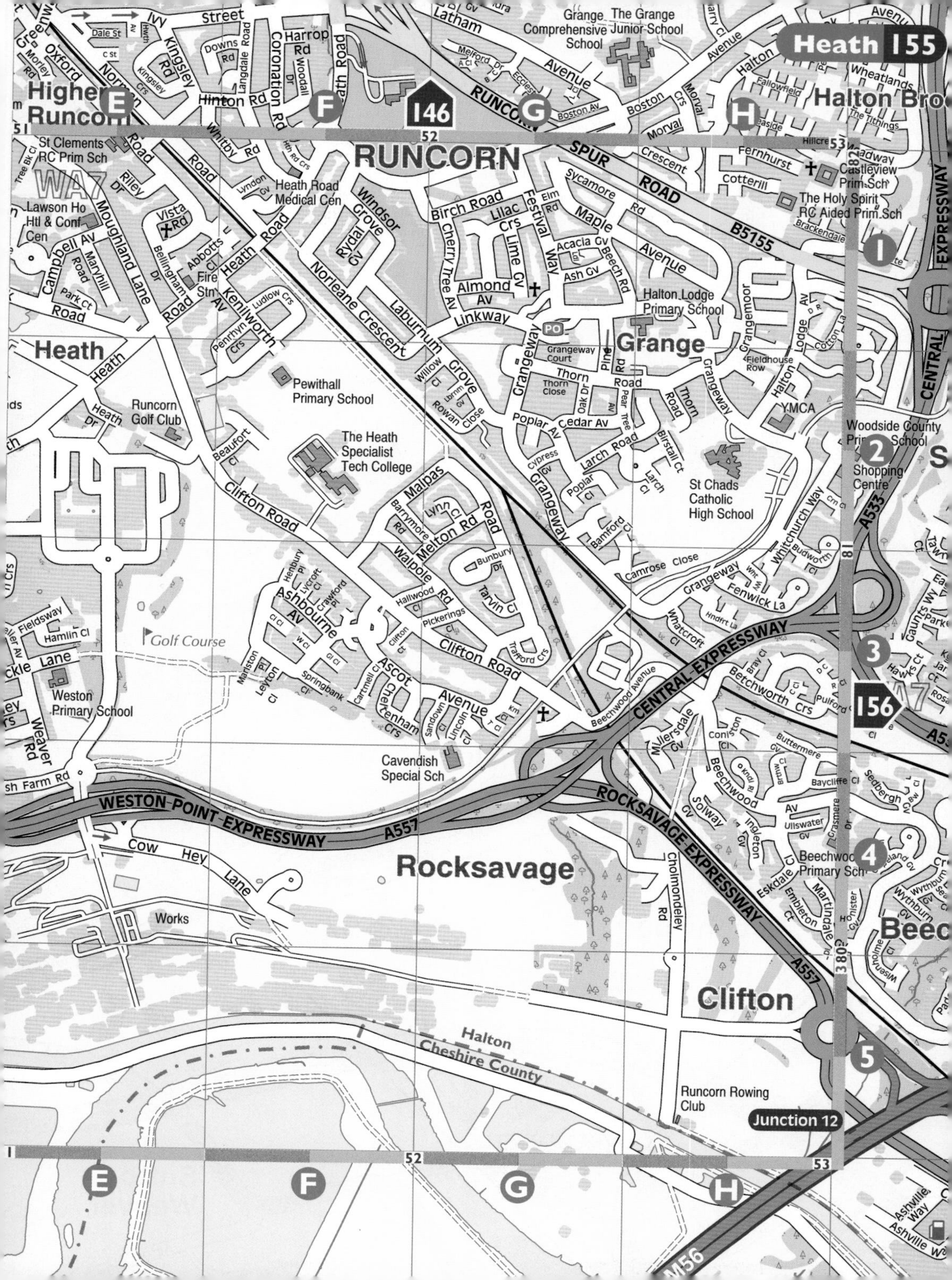
Heath 155
146
156
RUNCORN
Higher Runcorn
Heath
Grange
Rocksavage
Clifton
Halton Brook
WA7
St Clements RC Prim Sch
Lawson Ho Htl & Conf Cen
Heath Road Medical Cen
Grange Comprehensive School
The Grange Junior School
Castleview Prim Sch
The Holy Spirit RC Aided Prim Sch
Halton Lodge Primary School
Pewithall Primary School
Runcorn Golf Club
The Heath Specialist Tech College
St Chads Catholic High School
Woodside County Prim School
Shopping Centre
YMCA
Weston Primary School
Cavendish Special Sch
Beechwood Primary Sch
Runcorn Rowing Club
Junction 12
Golf Course
Works
Halton
Cheshire County
SPUR ROAD
B5155
CENTRAL EXPRESSWAY
A533
WESTON POINT EXPRESSWAY
A557
ROCKSAVAGE EXPRESSWAY
M56
Clifton Road
Heath Road
Moughland Lane
Norleane Crescent
Laburnum Grove
Grangeway
Cow Hey Lane
Cholmondeley Rd
Beechwood Avenue
Beechwood Av
Halton Lodge Av
Whitchurch Way
Camrose Close
Fenwick La
Betchworth Crs
Linkway
Birch Road
Maple Avenue
Thorn Road
Larch Road
Poplar Av
Cedar Av
Malpas Road
Melton Rd
Walpole Rd
Ashbourne Av
Ascot Av
Cheltenham Crs
Kenilworth Av
Windsor Grove
Boston Av
Morval Crescent
Latham Avenue
Coronation Rd
Kingsley Rd
Ivy Street
Weaver Rd
Fieldsway
Hamlin Cl
Runcorn Golf Club
E
F
G
H
1
2
3
4
5
51
52
53
81
82
380

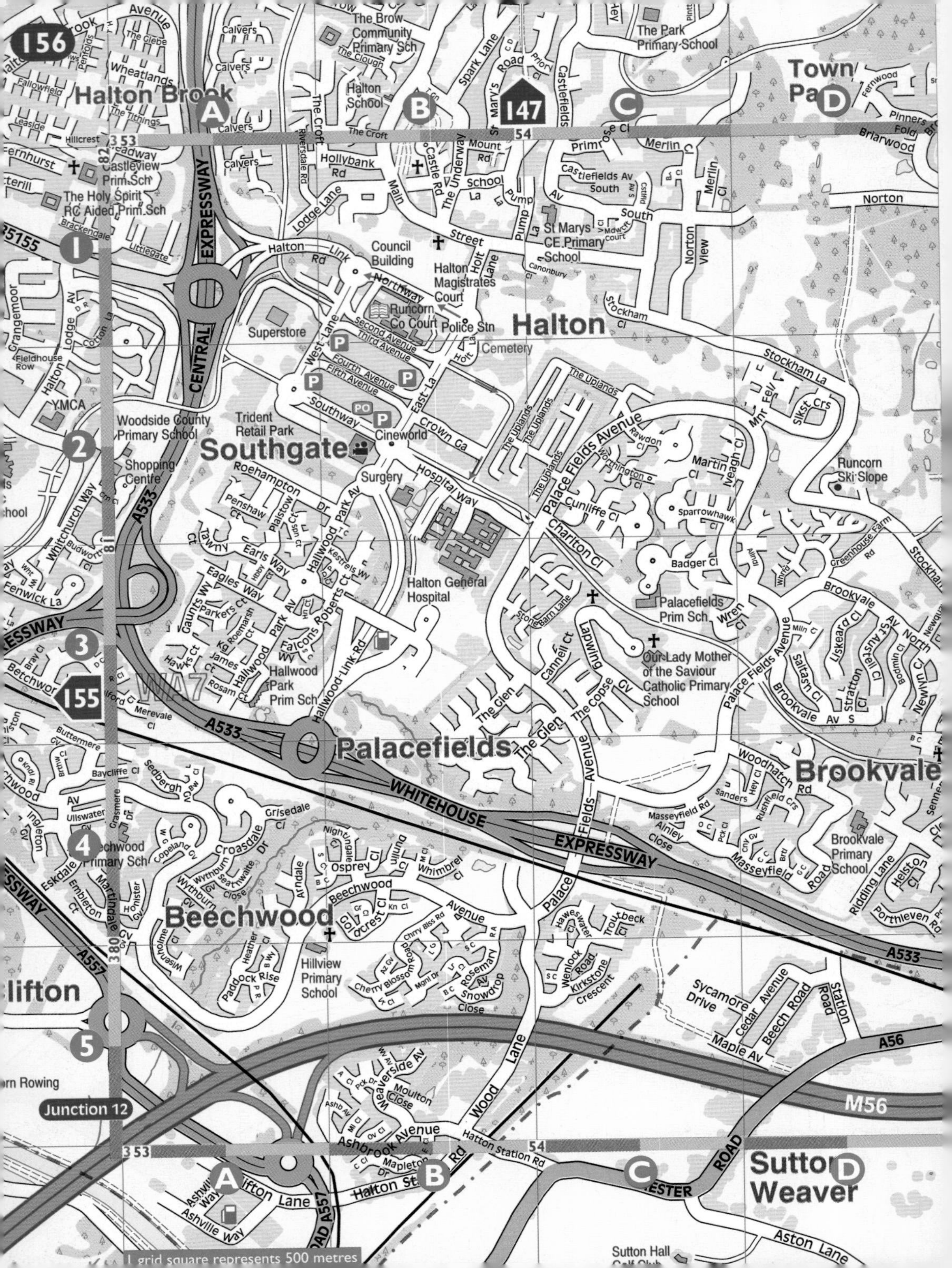
156
147
155
Halton Brook
The Brow Community Primary Sch
The Clough
Halton School
The Park Primary School
Town Park
Castlefields
Calvers
The Glebe
Wheatlands
Fallowfield
The Tithings
Leaside
Hillcrest
Fernhurst
Headway
Castleview Prim Sch
The Holy Spirit RC Aided Prim Sch
Brackendale
Littlegate
A5155
Riversdale Rd
The Croft
Hollybank Rd
Lodge Lane
Main St
Castle Rd
The Underway
Mount Rd
School La
Pump La
Spark Lane
St Mary's Road
Priory Cl
Primrose Cl
Merlin Cl
Castlefields Av South
Norton View
Norton
Fernwood
Pinners Fold
Briarwood
St Marys CE Primary School
Canonbury Cl
Halton Link Rd
Council Building
Halton Magistrates Court
Holt Lane
Northway
Runcorn Co Court
Police Stn
Cemetery
Halton
Stockham Cl
Stockham La
Superstore
Second Avenue
Third Avenue
Fourth Avenue
Fifth Avenue
West Lane
East La
Southway
Crown Ga
Trident Retail Park
Cineworld
Southgate
Woodside County Primary School
Shopping Centre
YMCA
Fieldhouse Row
Grangemoor
Lodge Av
Cotton La
Halton
CENTRAL EXPRESSWAY
A533
Whitchurch Way
Budworth Cl
Fenwick La
EXPRESSWAY
Roehampton Dr
Penshaw Ct
Plaistow Ct
Surgery
Hospital Way
Park Av
Hallwood Park Av
Kestrels Wy
Earls Way
Eagles Way
Gaunts Wy
Parkers Ct
Roemarsh Ct
James Ct
Hawks Ct
Rosam Ct
Falcons Wy
Roberts Ct
Hallwood Park Prim Sch
Hallwood Link Rd
Halton General Hospital
WA7
Bray Cl
Betchworth
Merevale Cl
Buttermere Gv
Baycliffe Cl
Sedbergh
Grasmere Dr
Ullswater Gv
Beechwood Av
Ingleton Gv
Eskdale
Beechwood Primary Sch
Embleton Ct
Martindale Gv
Honister Gv
Copeland Gv
Croasdale Dr
Grisedale Cl
Wythburn Gv
Seathwaite Close
Wisenholme Cl
Heather Cl
Paddock Rise
Beechwood
Nightingale Cl
Dunlin Cl
Osprey Cl
Whimbrel Cl
Arndale
Goldcrest Cl
Beechwood Avenue
Hillview Primary School
Cherry Blossom Road
Rosemary Av
Snowdrop Close
Palacefields
WHITEHOUSE EXPRESSWAY
The Uplands
Palace Fields Avenue
Rawdon Cl
Worthington Cl
Martin Cl
Iveagh Cl
Mnr Fell
Silkst Crs
Cunliffe Cl
Sparrowhawk Cl
Charlton Cl
Badger Cl
Stone Barn Lane
Cannell Ct
Lapwing Gv
The Copse
The Glen
Palacefields Prim Sch
Wren Cl
Our Lady Mother of the Saviour Catholic Primary School
Runcorn Ski Slope
Greenhouse Farm Rd
Brookvale Av North
Brookvale Av S
Liskeard Cl
St Austell Cl
Saltash Cl
Stratton Cl
Bodmin Cl
Newlyn Cl
Brookvale
Woodhatch Rd
Masseyfield Rd
Ainley Close
Rushfield Crs
Sanders Hey Cl
Brookvale Primary School
Riding Lane
Helston Cl
Porthleven Rd
Hawes water Cl
Troutbeck Cl
Wenlock Road
Kirkstone Crescent
Palace Fields Avenue
Sycamore Drive
Cedar Avenue
Beech Road
Station Road
Maple Av
A56
M56
A557
Clifton
Junction 12
Weaverside Av
Moulton Close
Ashbrook Avenue
Mapleton Dr
Wood Lane
Hatton Station Rd
Halton St
Clifton Lane
Ashville Way
CHESTER ROAD
Sutton Weaver
Aston Lane
Sutton Hall Golf Club
353
54
1 grid square represents 500 metres

Norton
Murdishaw
Preston Brook
E
F
G
H
I
2
3
4
5
55
56
57
82
81
380
Copperwood
Millwood
Whitebeam Clos
Nortonwood La
Ledston
Firbank Cl
Elmore Cl
East Avenue
Highgate
Hornbeam
Elmwood
Oxheys Cl
Crabtree Fold
Broadfields
St Berteline CE Prim Sch
Norton Lane
Norton Village
Windmill Hl Av E
Morton Rd
Winslow Cl
Farnhill Cl
Long Spinney
Norton Ga
Norton La
Pochard Rl
Bittern Cl
Plover Dr
Abbey Hey
Meadow
Kings
Gn Coppice
Hillfield
Norton Station Rd
Norgrove Cl
Chatterton Dr
Red Brow Lane
LC
Red Brow Lane
De Ve
Dares
Park
Daresbury Park Business Park
Fox Covert
Eanleywood Lane
Tarnbeck
Holbeck
Barncroft
Tower
Lane
Warren Cft
Delphfield
Runcorn East Station
Barnfield Av
Falstone Dr
Bankside
Quay Pl
Clarendon Cl
Ellerby
Sawley Cl
Chetton Dr
Starling Cl
Robin
Baxter Cl
Petersgate
Moorland Dr
Jays Cl
Barington Drive
Marina La
Folkstone Way
Cleethorpes Road
Fleetwood Walk
Aldersgate Av
St Martins La
Gorsewood Prim Sch
Murdishaw Health Centre
St Martins Catholic Prim Sch
Parkgate Wy
Fltwd Walk
Tynemouth Rd
Cleethorpes Road
Waterford Wy
The Ridgeway
PO
Dukes Whf
Avenue
Mooring Cl
Gorsewood Rd
Plymouth Cl
Bristol Av
Hoylake Cl
Heysham Cl
Barnfield Av
Anchor Cl
Murdishaw
Falmouth Pl
Exmouth Crescent
Tilbury Pl
M56
Wood Lane
The Hove
Brookvale Recreation Centre
Corran Hvn
Redruth Cl
Mariner Cl
Chichester Cl
Sextant Cl
Spinnaker Cl
Rose Cl
Compass Cl
Blyth Cl
Brookvale Av N
Halton High School
Swd Dr
Gillan Cl
Saltwood Dr
Murdishaw Av
Stockham Lane
Pickmere Dr
Fountains Cl
Northwich Rd
Mevagissey Rd
Road
Coronation Rd
Gorsewell La
Sandy Lane
Bridgewater Gra
Council Building
Lockwood Vw
Watermead Dr
CHESTER ROAD
Abbots Pk
Wellfield
Canal Side
Waterfront
Brindley Whf
Hill Top Road
Windmill La
A56
Barker's Hollow
Premier Travel Inn
NORTHWICH RD
Aston La North
CHESTER ROAD
Aston Fields Road
A533
Cheshire Ring Canal Walk
Tunnel Top North
Du
Sutton Fields Farm
Rivington Road
Fairoak Lane
Fairoak Court
Rembury Pl
Redacre Cl

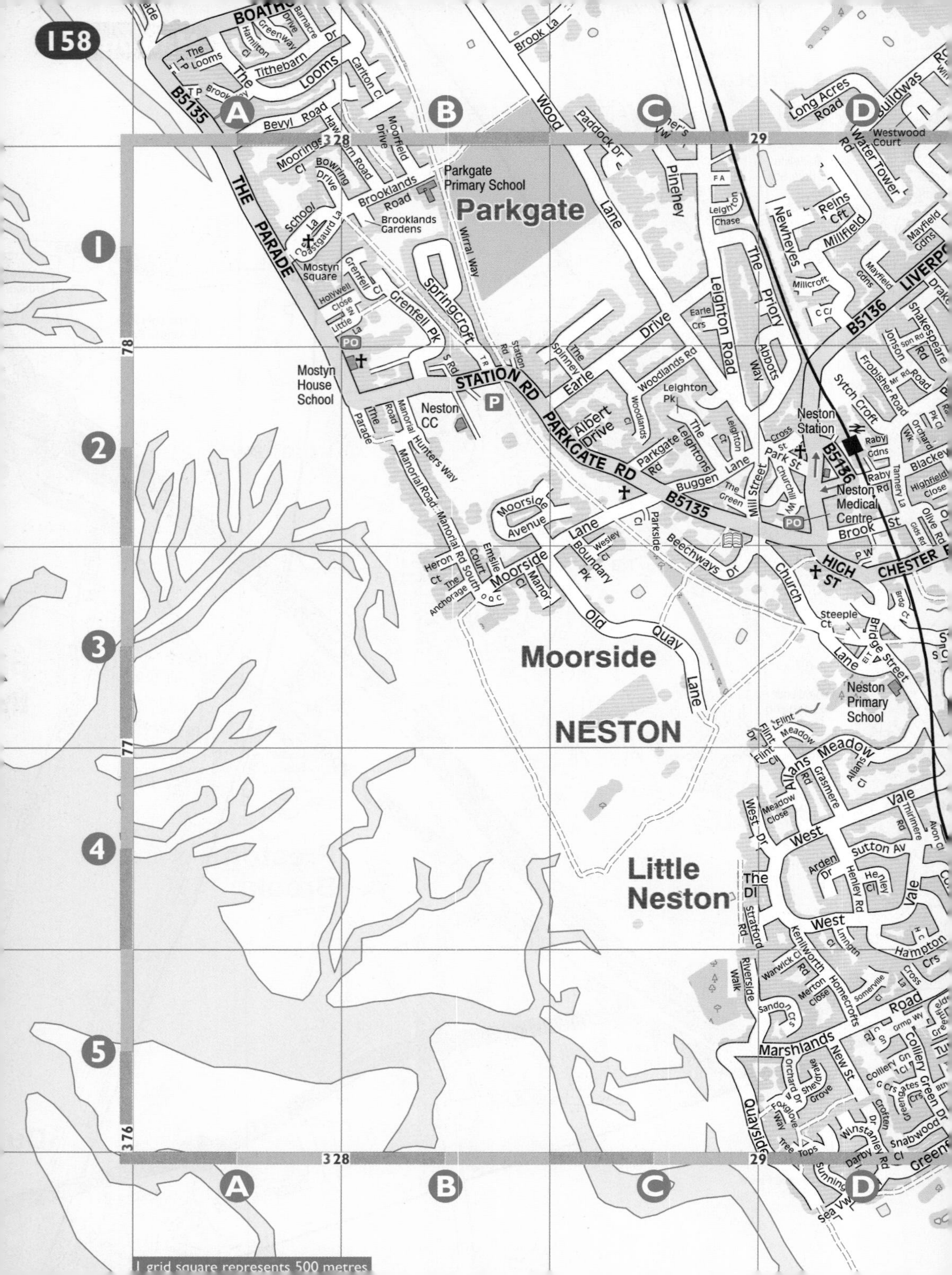
Parkgate
Moorside
NESTON
Little Neston
Parkgate Primary School
Mostyn House School
Neston CC
Neston Station
Neston Medical Centre
Neston Primary School
Brooklands Gardens
Mostyn Square
THE PARADE
STATION RD
PARKGATE RD
HIGH ST
CHESTER RD
B5135
B5136
Boathouse La
Barnacre Drive
Greenway
Hamilton Cl
The Looms
Tithebarn Dr
Brooky Way
Bevyl Road
Hawthorn Road
Moorfield Drive
Carlton Cl
Moorings Cl
Bowring Drive
Brooklands Road
School La
Coastgaurd La
Grenfell Cl
Grenfell Pk
Holywell Close
Springcroft
Wirral Way
Wood Lane
Brook La
Paddock Dr
Pinehey
Leighton Chase
The Priory
Leighton Road
Abbots Way
Earle Drive
Earle Crs
The Spinney
Woodlands Rd
Woodlands Cl
Albert Drive
Leighton Pk
The Leightons
Leighton Ct
Parkgate Rd
Buggen Lane
The Green
Mill Street
Park St
Cross St
Churchill Wy
Brook St
Manorial Road
Hunters Way
Manorial Road South
Emslie Court
Heron Ct
The Anchorage
Moorside
Moorside Avenue
Manor Cl
Moorside Lane
Wesley Cl
Boundary Pk
Parkside
Beechways Dr
Church Lane
Old Quay Lane
Steeple Ct
Bridge Street
Flint Dr
Flint Cl
Flint Meadow
Allans Meadow
Allans Cl
Grasmere Rd
Meadow Close
West Dr
West Vale
Thirlmere Rd
Avon Cl
Sutton Av
Arden Dr
Henley Rd
Henley Cl
The Dl
Stratford Rd
Riverside Walk
Kenilworth Rd
Warwick Cl
Merton Close
Homecrofts
Somerville
Hampton Crs
Cross La
Marshlands Road
New St
Sandon Crs
Orchard Dr
Sheldrake Grove
Foxglove Way
Quayside
Tree Tops
Winstanley Rd
Crofton Dr
Colliery Green Dr
Snabwood Cl
Darby Cl
Sea Vw
Long Acres Road
Buildwas Rd
Westwood Court
Water Tower Rd
Newheyes
Reins Cft
Millfield
Millcroft
Mayfield Gdns
LIVERPOOL RD
Drake Rd
Shakespeare Rd
Jonson Rd
Frobisher Road
Sytch Croft
Raby Gdns
Raby Rd
Tannery La
Orchard Wk
Blackeys La
Highfield Close
Olive Rd
PO
P
328
29
78
77
376
A
B
C
D
1
2
3
4
5
1 grid square represents 500 metres

E
F
G
H
30
31
1
2
3
4
5
78
77
376
Hinderton
Windle Hill
Ness
CH64
Neston High School
Recreation Centre
Westlands Cl
Cemetery
Surgery
St Winefrides RC Prim Sch
Woodfall Primary School
Woodfall Infant School
Weatherstone Business Centre
Leahurst
Haddon Hall Farm
Wirral Way
Cheshire County
Chester High Road
Upper
School Lane
Quarry Road
Hanns Hall Road
Cherry Close
Lees Lane
Cuckoo Lane
Hinderton Road
B5134
Hinderton La
Park Road
Clayhill
Ringway
Breezehill Rd
Breezehill Pk
Gunn Grove
Bushell Road
Bushell Cl
The Quillet
Cedar Gv
Bendee Road
Bendee Av
Raymond Way
Dunraven Rd
Waterford Drive
Ashtree Dr
Ashtree Cl
Mellock Lane
Mellock Cl
Romney Way
Raeburn Av
Landseer Av
Morland Av
Roman Court
Yewtree Cl
Flag La
Newtown
Sandy Lane
Stonebank Dr
Howards Way
Rock Farm Dr
Rock Farm Cl
Rocklee Gdns
Victoria Rd
Gorstons La
Talbot Av
Talbot Cl
Talbot Gdns
Derwent Wy
Rydal Cl
Badger Bait
Badger Park
Rose Gardens
Town La
The Green
Ivy Farm Dr
Woodfall Lane
Woodfall Gv
Woodfall Cl
School Lane
School Av
Old School Cl
Glenton Pk
Hill Road
Bull Hill
The Ct
Cliffe Rd
Riverview Rd
Furrocks La
Furrocks Wy
Furrocks Cl
Dawn Close
Cumbers Dr
Cumbers La
Neston Road
Well Lane
Holt Hey
Mill Lane
Mill Bank
Hill Cl
Hill Ct
Flashes La
Hill Top Lane
Palace Hey
Shones Cft
Bankhey
Drive
Wirral Crs
Well Cl
Hyfi
Neshol

Aigburth 118 D2
Aintree 32 A2
Allerton 120 A2
Anfield 54 C3
Appleton 125 F1
Arrowe Hill 89 H5
Astmoor 147 E3
Ball o' Ditton 124 C2
Barnston 135 G3
Barrow's Green 103 E4
Bebington 116 C4
Beechwood 156 A4
Belle Vale 97 H3
Bewsey 83 E5
Bidston 67 H4
Bidston Hill 67 H5
Birkenhead 2 A4
Blackbrook 84 C3
Blackbrook 49 G2
Blundellsands 20 B5
Bold Heath 103 E1
Bootle 4 A5
Bowring Park 74 D5
Brighton le Sands 28 B1
Brimstage 136 D4
Broad Green 73 H3
Broad Oak 49 F3
Bromborough 138 B5
Bromborough Pool 138 D1
Brookhurst 152 B4
Brookvale 156 D4
Brown Edge 61 E3
Bruche 107 H1
Buckley Hill 22 C5
Calderstones 96 C5
Caldy 110 D4
Callands 82 D3
Castlefields 147 F4
Childwall 97 F2
Cinnamon Brow 85 E1
Claughton 91 E3
Clifton 155 H5
Clinkham Wood 37 E3
Clock Face 79 H2
Clubmoor 55 E3
Cobbs 130 B3
Court Hey 74 B4
Cronton 100 D3
Crosby 28 C3
Crow Wood 125 H1
Croxteth 42 D3
Cuerdley Cross 103 G5
Dallam 83 F4
Denton's Green 10 C1
Derbyshire Hill 49 F5
Dingle 94 C5
Ditton 123 H4
Doe Green 104 A5
Dog & Gun 42 A4
Dovecot 74 B2
Eastham 153 E3
Eastham Ferry 153 G1
Eccleston 47 C1
Eccleston Park 60 C3
Edge Hill 71 H5
Egremont 69 E1
Everton 54 B5
Fairfield 72 B2
Farnworth 102 A5
Fazakerley 41 E2
Fearnhead 85 E3
Fiddler's Ferry 127 E2
Fincham 57 F4
Ford 30 B2
Formby 16 D2
Frankby 111 G1
Freshfield 16 B1
Garston 140 D1
Gateacre 97 H4
Gayton 149 E3
Gemini 82 D2
Gillar's Green 46 A4
Gillmoss 42 C1
Grange 110 D2
Grange 155 G2
Grange Park 60 D2
Grappenhall 131 F1
Grassendale 118 D4
Greasby 89 E4
Great Crosby 21 F5
Great Meols 65 F3
Great Sankey 105 F2
Hale 143 H4
Hale Bank 144 D2
Halewood 121 G3
Halton 156 B1
Halton Brook 146 D5
Halton View 15 H2
Haresfinch 37 E5
Heath 155 E2
Heswall 148 C1
Higher Bebington 115 E5
Higher Runcorn 8 D7
Higher Walton 129 E4
Hillcliffe 130 A4
Hinderton 159 F1
Holt 60 C5
Hood Manor 105 G3
Hough Green 123 G2
Howley 13 H5
Hoylake 87 G1
Hulme 83 H2
Hunt's Cross 120 D5
Huyton 75 H2
Huyton Park 75 E4
Huyton Quarry 76 B3
Huyton-With-Roby 75 E2
Irby 112 B5
Kensington 71 G3
Kingsway 14 C3
Kingswood 82 A3
Kirkby 33 H3
Kirkdale 53 H2
Knotty Ash 73 H2
Knowsley 43 H3
Landican 113 G3
Latchford 107 E5
Lea Green 61 H5
Leasowe 67 E1
Lingley Green 104 A1
Lingley Mere 81 F5
Liscard 51 H5
Litherland 30 B3
Little Altcar 17 F5
Little Crosby 20 D1
Little Neston 158 C4
Liverpool 70 A4
Locking Stumps 85 F1
Longbarn 85 G4
Longford 83 H4
Longview 75 H1
Lower Bebington 137 H1
Lower House 124 C3
Lower Walton 129 G3
Lugsdale 15 G5
Lunt 22 B1
Lunts Heath 102 A3
Lydiate 18 A1
Maghull 24 A1
Marshall's Cross 62 B5
Martinscroft 108 D1
Melling 24 C4
Melling Mount 25 G2
Meols 64 D5
Moore 128 A5
Moorside 158 B3
Moreton 66 C4
Moss Bank 36 D3
Moss Bank 15 K4
Moss Nook 63 F1
Moss Side 35 F5
Moss Side 19 G3
Mossley Hill 95 G4
Murdishaw 157 G2
Ness 159 G5
Neston 158 C3
Netherley 98 B4
Netherton 23 E4
New Brighton 51 G2
New Ferry 116 C3
Newton 111 F1
Newtown 47 E3
Noctorum 90 C3
Norris Green 55 H1
Northwood 34 C1
Nut Grove 61 E4
Old Swan 72 D2
Orford 84 B4
Orrell 39 H1
Otterspool 118 B2
Oxton 91 F5
Paddington 85 F5
Padgate 84 D4
Page Moss 74 D2
Palacefields 156 B4
Parkgate 158 B1
Parr 49 E5
Peasley Cross 62 C1
Penketh 104 B4
Pensby 134 D2
Poll Hill 134 D5
Port Sunlight 138 B1
Portico 60 C2
Poulton 138 B4
Poulton 68 C3
Prenton 114 C2
Prescot 59 F4
Preston Brook 157 H4
Princes Park 94 D2
Raby 151 E5
Rainhill 78 B2
Rainhill Stoops 78 C3
Ravenhead 61 G1
Roby 74 D3
Rock Ferry 116 A1
Rocksavage 155 F4
Runcorn 9 G7
Sandhills 53 G2
Sankey Bridges 105 G4
Saughall Massie 88 D2
Seacombe 69 F4
Seaforth 29 F5
Sefton 23 E2
Sefton Park 95 F4
Shell Green 126 A1
Simm's Cross 15 F4
Southdene 33 H4
Southgate 156 A2
Speke 142 C2
Spital 138 C3
St Helens 11 H2
St Michael's Hamlet 117 H1
Stockbridge Village 57 G2
Stockton Heath 130 B2
Stoneycroft 73 E1
Storeton 136 D1
Sutton 63 E3
Sutton Heath 61 G3
Sutton Leach 63 E5
Sutton Manor 79 E3
Swanside 74 B3
Tarbock Green 99 G4
Thatto Heath 61 F2
Thelwall 109 E5
Thingwall 135 F1
Thornton 22 B3
Thornton Hough 150 C2
Thurstaston 133 G1
Toll Bar 60 D1
Tower Hill 26 A4
Town End 101 E2
Town Park 147 H5
Toxteth 94 A3
Tranmere 92 C5
Tuebrook 55 H5
Upton 123 H1
Upton 89 H3
Upton Rocks 101 G5
Vauxhall 70 B1
Waddicar 24 D5
Wallasey 52 C5
Wallasey Village 50 C4
Walton 40 D5
Warrington 13 J7
Waterloo 29 E2
Waterloo Park 29 G3
Wavertree 95 H1
West Bank 145 H1
West Derby 56 C3
West Park 10 A7
Westbrook 82 A4
Weston 154 D2
Weston Point 154 B1
Westvale 33 G2
Westy 107 H3
Whiston 77 E2
Whiston Cross 76 D2
Whiston Lane Ends 76 C3
Whitefield Lane End 76 B5
Widnes 14 A5
Wilderspool 130 A1
Windle Hill 159 H3
Windy Arbor 76 D5
Winwick Quay 83 H1
Woodchurch 90 C5
Woodhey 115 H4
Woolfall Heath 58 A5
Woolston 108 C1
Woolton 120 C2

USING THE STREET INDEX

Street names are listed alphabetically. Each street name is followed by its postal town or area locality, the Postcode District, the page number, and the reference to the square in which the name is found.

Standard index entries are shown as follows:

Abberton Pk *NTHTN* L30 .... **23** F4

Street names and selected addresses not shown on the map due to scale restrictions are shown in the index with an asterisk:

Abbott Dr *BTL* L20 * **40** A2

GENERAL ABBREVIATIONS

ACC ACCESS
ALY ALLEY
AP APPROACH
AR ARCADE
ASS ASSOCIATION
AV AVENUE
BCH BEACH
BLDS BUILDINGS
BND BEND
BNK BANK
BR BRIDGE
BRK BROOK
BTM BOTTOM
BUS BUSINESS
BVD BOULEVARD
BY BYPASS
CATH CATHEDRAL
CEM CEMETERY
CEN CENTRE
CFT CROFT
CH CHURCH
CHA CHASE
CHYD CHURCHYARD
CIR CIRCLE
CIRC CIRCUS
CL CLOSE
CLFS CLIFFS
CMP CAMP
CNR CORNER
CO COUNTY
COLL COLLEGE
COM COMMON
COMM COMMISSION
CON CONVENT
COT COTTAGE
COTS COTTAGES
CP CAPE
CPS COPSE
CR CREEK
CREM CREMATORIUM
CRS CRESCENT
CSWY CAUSEWAY
CT COURT
CTRL CENTRAL
CTS COURTS
CTYD COURTYARD
CUTT CUTTINGS
CV COVE
CYN CANYON
DEPT DEPARTMENT
DL DALE
DM DAM
DR DRIVE
DRO DROVE
DRY DRIVEWAY
DWGS DWELLINGS
E EAST
EMB EMBANKMENT
EMBY EMBASSY
ESP ESPLANADE
EST ESTATE
EX EXCHANGE
EXPY EXPRESSWAY
EXT EXTENSION
F/O FLYOVER
FC FOOTBALL CLUB
FK FORK
FLD FIELD
FLDS FIELDS
FLS FALLS
FM FARM
FT FORT
FTS FLATS
FWY FREEWAY
FY FERRY
GA GATE
GAL GALLERY
GDN GARDEN
GDNS GARDENS
GLD GLADE
GLN GLEN
GN GREEN
GND GROUND
GRA GRANGE
GRG GARAGE
GT GREAT
GTWY GATEWAY
GV GROVE
HGR HIGHER
HL HILL
HLS HILLS
HO HOUSE
HOL HOLLOW
HOSP HOSPITAL
HRB HARBOUR
HTH HEATH
HTS HEIGHTS
HVN HAVEN
HWY HIGHWAY
IMP IMPERIAL
IN INLET
IND EST INDUSTRIAL ESTATE
INF INFIRMARY
INFO INFORMATION
INT INTERCHANGE
IS ISLAND
JCT JUNCTION
JTY JETTY
KG KING
KNL KNOLL
L LAKE
LA LANE
LDG LODGE
LGT LIGHT
LK LOCK
LKS LAKES
LNDG LANDING
LTL LITTLE
LWR LOWER
MAG MAGISTRATE
MAN MANSIONS
MD MEAD
MDW MEADOWS
MEM MEMORIAL
MI MILL
MKT MARKET
MKTS MARKETS
ML MALL
MNR MANOR
MS MEWS
MSN MISSION
MT MOUNT
MTN MOUNTAIN
MTS MOUNTAINS
MUS MUSEUM
MWY MOTORWAY
N NORTH
NE NORTH EAST
NW NORTH WEST
O/P OVERPASS
OFF OFFICE
ORCH ORCHARD
OV OVAL
PAL PALACE
PAS PASSAGE
PAV PAVILION
PDE PARADE
PH PUBLIC HOUSE
PK PARK
PKWY PARKWAY
PL PLACE
PLN PLAIN
PLNS PLAINS
PLZ PLAZA
POL POLICE STATION
PR PRINCE
PREC PRECINCT
PREP PREPARATORY
PRIM PRIMARY
PROM PROMENADE
PRS PRINCESS
PRT PORT
PT POINT
PTH PATH
PZ PIAZZA
QD QUADRANT
QU QUEEN
QY QUAY
R RIVER
RBT ROUNDABOUT
RD ROAD
RDG RIDGE
REP REPUBLIC
RES RESERVOIR
RFC RUGBY FOOTBALL CLUB
RI RISE
RP RAMP
RW ROW
S SOUTH
SCH SCHOOL
SE SOUTH EAST
SER SERVICE AREA
SH SHORE
SHOP SHOPPING
SKWY SKYWAY
SMT SUMMIT
SOC SOCIETY
SP SPUR
SPR SPRING
SQ SQUARE
ST STREET
STN STATION
STR STREAM
STRD STRAND
SW SOUTH WEST
TDG TRADING
TER TERRACE
THWY THROUGHWAY
TNL TUNNEL
TOLL TOLLWAY
TPK TURNPIKE
TR TRACK
TRL TRAIL
TWR TOWER
U/P UNDERPASS
UNI UNIVERSITY
UPR UPPER
V VALE
VA VALLEY
VIAD VIADUCT
VIL VILLA
VIS VISTA
VLG VILLAGE
VLS VILLAS
VW VIEW
W WEST
WD WOOD
WHF WHARF
WK WALK
WKS WALKS
WLS WELLS
WY WAY
YD YARD
YHA YOUTH HOSTEL

POSTCODE TOWNS AND AREA ABBREVIATIONS

AIG/SPK ....Aigburth/Sefton Park
AIN/FAZ ....Aintree/Fazakerley
ALL/GAR.................. Allerton/Garston
ANF/KKDL................. Anfield/Kirkdale
BEB...Bebington
BIRK.. Birkenhead
BTL .... Bootle
CALD/MH........................Calderstones/ Mossley Hill
CHLDW......................................Childwall
CL/PREN............. Claughton/Prenton
CLB/OSW/ST .... Clubmoor/ Old Swan/Stoneycroft
CLVP.........................Central Liverpool
CLVPS............. Central Liverpool south
CSBY/BLUN...... Crosby/Blundellsands
CSBY/WL.................. Crosby/Waterloo
DV/KA/FCH .... Dovecot/ Knotty Ash/Fincham
ECCL.. Eccleston
EHL/KEN ....Edge Hill/Kensington
EP.......................................Ellesmere Port
EV...Everton
FMBY...Formby
FROD/HEL...............Frodsham/Helsby
GOL/RIS/CUL..............................Golborne/ Risley/Culcheth
GR/UP/WCH.............................Greasby/ Upton/Woodchurch
HES...Heswall
HLWD ....Halewood
HOY ....Hoylake
HTWN.. Hightown
HUY ....Huyton
KKBY.. Kirkby
LITH ....Litherland
LYMM...Lymm
MGHL...Maghull
MOR/LEA...................Moreton/Leasowe
NG/CROX.........Norris Green/Croxteth
NPK/KEN ....Newsham Park/ Kensington
NSTN...Neston
NTHLY..Netherley
NTHTN ....Netherton
NWD/KWIPK........................ Northwood/ Knowsley Industrial Park
ORM ....Ormskirk
PEN/TH.......................Pensby/Thingwall
PR/KW .... Prescot/Knowsley
PS/BROM........................... Port Sunlight/ Bromborough
RAIN/WH ....Rainhill/Whiston
RF/TRAN............ Rock Ferry/Tranmere
RNFD/HAY ....Rainford/Haydock
RUNC ....Runcorn
SFTN... Sefton
SPK/HALE ....Speke/Hale
STBRV ....Stockbridge Village
STHEL..St Helens
TOX...Toxteth
VAUX/LVPD ....Vauxhall/ Liverpool Docks
WAL/EG.................Wallasey/Egremont
WAL/NB .... Wallasey/New Brighton
WARR ....Warrington
WARRN/WOL.......... Warrington north/ Woolston
WARRS ....Warrington south
WARRW/BUR............Warrington west/ Burtonwood
WAV...Wavertree
WD/CROXPK........................West Derby/ Croxteth Park
WDN...Widnes
WGNW/BIL/OR...................Wigan west/ Billinge/Orrell
WKBY .... West Kirby
WLT/FAZ .... Walton/Fazakerley
WLTN...Woolton

Index - streets

A

Abacus Rd CLB/OSW/ST L13 .... 73 E1
Abberley Cl ECCL WA10................. 10 E5
Abberley Rd WLTN L25................. 121 F4
Abberton Pk NTHTN L30.............. 23 F4
Abbey Cl BIRK CH41.......................... 3 H6
FMBY L37.................................... 17 G4
NWD/KWIPK L33 .... 34 A2
WDN WA8.................................... 124 A3
Abbey Ct WLTN L25 .... 120 D1
Abbeyfield Dr WD/CROXPK L12... 42 D5
Abbey Hey RUNC WA7 .... 157 E1
Abbey Rd ECCL WA10..................... 36 C5
WDN WA8 .... 123 H3
WKBY CH48 .... 110 B1
Abbeystead Av NTHTN L30 .... 31 F3
Abbeystead Rd WAV L15 .... 73 F5
Abbey St BIRK CH41 .... 3 H6
Abbeyvale Dr WLTN L25 .... 98 A2
Abbey Vw CHLDW L16 .... 97 E1
Abbeywood Gv RAIN/WH L35........ 77 F3
Abbot Cl CL/PREN CH43.................. 90 C2
Abbotsbury Wy
WD/CROXPK L12........................ 43 E4
Abbots Cl FMBY L37 .... 17 F5
Abbots Dr BEB CH63 .... 137 H1
Abbotsfield Cl WARRS WA4 .... 130 C5
Abbotsfield Rd STHEL WA9 .... 63 E5
Abbotsford Gdns
CSBY/BLUN L23........................... 28 D1
Abbotsford Rd CSBY/BLUN L23... 28 D1
NG/CROX L11 .... 41 G5
Abbotsford St WAL/EG CH44 .... 69 G3
Abbots Hall Av STHEL WA9............ 79 H2
Abbots Pk RUNC WA7 .... 157 G4
Abbots Wy FMBY L37.................... 17 F4
NSTN CH64 .... 158 C1
Abbott Dr BTL L20 * 40 A2
Abbotts Cl CALD/MH L18 .... 96 B5
RUNC WA7 .... 155 E1
Abbottshey Av CALD/MH L18........ 96 B5
Abbotts Wy
WGNW/BIL/OR WN5.................... 37 H1
Abdale Rd NG/CROX L11............... 41 H4
Abercrombie Rd
NWD/KWIPK L33 .... 34 C5
Abercromby Sq EHL/KEN L7 .... 7 K5
Aberdale Rd CLB/OSW/ST L13 ...... 73 F2
Aberdare Cl WARRW/BUR WA5...... 83 E4
Aberdeen St BIRK CH41 .... 2 C3
Aberford Av WAL/NB CH45 .... 51 E5
Abergele Rd CLB/OSW/ST L13 ...... 72 D3
Aber St NPK/KEN L6 .... 71 G2
Abingdon Av WARR WA1 .... 109 E1
Abingdon Gv ANF/KKDL L4............. 41 E5
HLWD L26 .... 122 A2
Abingdon Rd ANF/KKDL L4 .... 41 E5
GR/UP/WCH CH49........................ 88 D5
Abney Cl EHL/KEN L7 .... 71 H5
Aboyne Cl WLT/FAZ L9 .... 40 C3
Abram St EV L5 .... 54 A5
Abratio St BIRK CH41 .... 2 D5
Abstone Cl WARR WA1 .... 108 C1
Abyssinia Cl WAV L15 * 95 G1
Acacia Av HUY L36......................... 75 F4
WARR WA1 .... 85 H5
WDN WA8 .... 102 B5
Acacia Cl GR/UP/WCH CH49....... 112 A1
Acacia Gv ECCL WA10.................... 46 C3
RUNC WA7 .... 155 G1
WAL/EG CH44............................... 69 G3
WKBY CH48 .... 110 A1
WLT/FAZ L9.................................... 40 D1
Academy St WARR WA1 .... 12 E5
Academy Wy WARR WA1 .... 12 D5
Acanthus Rd CLB/OSW/ST L13 ...... 73 E1
Access Rd WD/CROXPK L12 *........ 56 D3
Acer Leigh AIG/SPK L17 .... 118 B2
Acheson Rd CLB/OSW/ST L13 .... 55 G4
Achilles Av WARRN/WOL WA2....... 83 H3
Ackerley Cl WARRN/WOL WA2 ..... 84 D2
Ackers Hall Av DV/KA/FCH L14 ...... 74 B1
Ackers La CSBY/BLUN L23 .... 20 D2
ECCL WA10.................................... 47 E3
WARRS WA4................................ 130 C2
Ackers Rd GR/UP/WCH CH49........ 113 G1
WARRS WA4 .... 130 C1
Acland Rd WAL/EG CH44 * 68 D1
Aconbury Cl NG/CROX L11 .... 41 H4
Aconbury Pl NG/CROX L11 .... 41 H4
Acorn Cl BEB CH63 .... 115 F5
STHEL WA9 * 79 G1
Acorn Ct TOX L8............................. 94 B2
Acornfield Cl NWD/KWIPK L33...... 34 D4
Acornfield Rd NWD/KWIPK L33..... 35 E3
Acorn Wy BTL L20............................. 5 G1
Acrefield Pk WLTN L25 .... 97 G5
Acrefield Rd RF/TRAN CH42 .... 114 D2
WDN WA8 .... 123 H2
WLTN L25 .... 97 G5
Acre Gn HLWD L26 .... 122 A5
Acre La HES CH60 .... 135 G5
PS/BROM CH62.......................... 152 C2
Acres Cl WLTN L25......................... 97 G1
Acresfield CLB/OSW/ST L13 * 73 F3
Acresgate Ct WLTN L25 .... 97 G3
Acres Rd BEB CH63 .... 115 H5
HOY CH47 .... 88 A1
Acreville Rd BEB CH63 .... 137 H1
Acton Gv NPK/KEN L6 .... 55 E4
Acton La MOR/LEA CH46................ 89 E1
Acton Rd KKBY L32......................... 33 F2
RF/TRAN CH42 .... 116 A2
Acton Wy EHL/KEN L7 .... 72 A5
Acuba Gv RF/TRAN CH42 * 92 C4
Acuba Rd WAV L15 .... 73 G4
Adair Pl CLB/OSW/ST L13 .... 55 G3
Adair Rd CLB/OSW/ST L13 .... 55 G3
Adam Cl ALL/GAR L19 .... 140 C1
Adamson Ct WARRS WA4.............. 131 F1
Adamson St EHL/KEN L7 .... 72 B3
WARRS WA4 .... 106 D5
Adam St EV L5 .... 54 B4
WARRN/WOL WA2...................... 107 E1
Adaston Av PS/BROM CH62......... 153 F5
Ada St STHEL WA9.......................... 62 C1
Adcote Cl DV/KA/FCH L14 .... 74 B2
Adcote Rd DV/KA/FCH L14 .... 74 B2
Addenbrook Cl CL/PREN CH43 ...... 90 C2
Addenbrooke Dr
SPK/HALE L24 .... 121 E5
Adderley Cl RUNC WA7 .... 9 H7
Adderley St EHL/KEN L7 .... 71 H3
Addingham Av WDN WA8.......... 124 A4
Addingham Rd CALD/MH L18....... 96 B3
Addington St WAL/EG CH44......... 69 F2
Addison Cl KKBY L32 .... 33 G4
Addison Sq WDN WA8 .... 14 B1
Addison St BTL L20 .... 39 E2
VAUX/LVPD L3 .... 6 E1
Addison Wy VAUX/LVPD L3 .... 6 E1
Adelaide Av STHEL WA9 .... 61 G3
Adelaide Ct WDN WA8 *................ 14 D6
Adelaide Pl EV L5 .... 71 E1
Adelaide Rd EHL/KEN L7 .... 71 H3
LITH L21 .... 29 G5
RF/TRAN CH42 .... 92 A4
Adelaide St WAL/EG CH44 .... 68 D3
Adelaide Ter CSBY/WL L22 .... 28 D3
Adela Rd RUNC WA7 .... 8 B5
Adele Thompson Dr TOX L8........... 94 C1
Adelphi St BIRK CH41 .... 3 F4
Adkins St EV L5 * 54 C4
Adlam Crs WLT/FAZ L9 * 32 B5
Adlam Rd AIN/FAZ L10 .... 32 B4
Adlington St VAUX/LVPD L3 .... 6 E1
Admin Rd NWD/KWIPK L33 .... 34 D4
Admiral Gv TOX L8 .... 94 C3
Admiral St TOX L8 .... 94 B3
Adrian's Wy KKBY L32 .... 33 H2
Adshead Rd CLB/OSW/ST L13........ 55 G3
Adstone Rd WLTN L25.................... 98 A3
Adswood Rd HUY L36..................... 75 G2
Africander Rd RNFD/HAY WA11 .. 37 E4
Afton WDN WA8 .... 123 G1
Agar Rd NG/CROX L11 .... 55 H3
Agate St EV L5 .... 54 C5
Agincourt Rd WD/CROXPK L12...... 56 C5
Agnes Gv WAL/EG CH44................ 52 A5
Agnes Rd CSBY/BLUN L23 .... 28 D1
RF/TRAN CH42 .... 92 C5
Agnes St STHEL WA9 .... 79 G2
Agnes Wy EHL/KEN L7 .... 71 H4
Aiden Long Gv PR/KW L34............ 58 C4
Aigburth Dr AIG/SPK L17 .... 95 E3
Aigburth Hall Av ALL/GAR L19 .... 119 E3
Aigburth Hall Rd ALL/GAR L19.... 119 E3
Aigburth Rd AIG/SPK L17 .... 94 D5
ALL/GAR L19 .... 118 D3
Aigburth St EHL/KEN L7 .... 71 H5
Aigburth V AIG/SPK L17 .... 95 G5
CALD/MH L18 .... 95 G5
Ailsa Rd WAL/NB CH45 .... 51 G5
Ainley Cl RUNC WA7.................... 156 C4
Ainsdale Cl AIN/FAZ L10 .... 32 C4
BEB CH63 .... 152 C4
PEN/TH CH61 .... 135 E1
WARRW/BUR WA5...................... 104 D4
Ainsdale Rd BTL L20 .... 39 H2
Ainsworth Av MOR/LEA CH46........ 89 E2
Ainsworth La PR/KW L34 .... 43 H1
Ainsworth Rd ECCL WA10 .... 10 B2
Ainsworth St VAUX/LVPD L3 .... 7 H4
Aintree Cl MOR/LEA CH46 .... 66 D2
Aintree La AIN/FAZ L10 .... 31 H2
Aintree Rd BTL L20.......................... 5 H2
WLT/FAZ L9.................................. 41 F1
Aintree Wy WLT/FAZ L9 .... 31 H2
Airdale Cl CL/PREN CH43 .... 90 C2
Airdale Rd WAV L15 .... 95 H2
Aire WDN WA8 .... 123 H1
Airedale Cl WARRW/BUR WA5.... 104 D1
Airegate MGHL L31 .... 18 B4
Airlie Gv CLB/OSW/ST L13 .... 55 F4
Airlie Rd HOY CH47 .... 87 F2
Aisthorpe Gv MGHL L31 .... 24 A2
Ajax Av WARRN/WOL WA2 .... 83 H3
The Akbar HES CH60 .... 134 A4
Akenside Ct BTL L20 * 39 E1
Akenside St BTL L20 .... 39 E1
Alabama Wy BIRK CH41 .... 3 J5
Alamein Crs
WARRN/WOL WA2 *................... 106 D1
Alamein Rd HUY L36 .... 75 F1
Alastair Crs CL/PREN CH43 .... 114 B2
Alban Rd CHLDW L16 .... 73 H5
Albany Av PR/KW L34 .... 60 B3
Albany Rd CLB/OSW/ST L13 .... 73 E1
EHL/KEN L7 .... 71 G3
PR/KW L34 .... 60 A4
RF/TRAN CH42 .... 115 G1
WLT/FAZ L9 .... 31 G5
Albany Ter RUNC WA7 .... 8 D5
The Albany VAUX/LVPD L3 * 6 C3
Albemarle Rd WAL/EG CH44 .... 69 F2
Alberta Gv PR/KW L34 .... 58 D5
Albert Dr NSTN CH64 .... 158 C2
WARRW/BUR WA5 .... 104 B2
WLT/FAZ L9 .... 40 B1
Albert Edward Rd EHL/KEN L7 ..... 71 G3
Albert Gv CSBY/BLUN L23 * 21 E5
WAV L15 .... 73 E5
Albert Pk AIG/SPK L17................... 94 D3
Albert Rd CLB/OSW/ST L13 .... 55 F4
CSBY/WL L22 .... 29 E3
HOY CH47 .... 87 F2
RF/TRAN CH42 .... 92 A4
WARRS WA4 .... 131 E1
WDN WA8 .... 15 F2
WKBY CH48 .... 110 A2
Albert Schweitzer Av
NTHTN L30 .... 31 E1
Albert Sq WDN WA8 .... 14 E3
Albert St ECCL WA10..................... 11 G1
EHL/KEN L7 .... 71 G4
RUNC WA7 .... 8 D5
Albion Pl WAL/NB CH45 .... 51 H2
Albion St BIRK CH41 .... 3 H4
ECCL WA10 .... 10 C5
EV L5 .... 54 A4
WAL/NB CH45 .... 51 G2
Albourne Rd KKBY L32 .... 34 B4
Albright Rd WDN WA8 .... 123 G5
Albury Cl WD/CROXPK L12 .... 43 F5
Albury Rd KKBY L32 .... 34 A5
Alcester Rd WD/CROXPK L12 .... 56 C4
Alcock St RUNC WA7 .... 8 E3
Aldams Gv ANF/KKDL L4................ 54 A1
Aldbourne Av WLTN L25 .... 97 E3
Aldbourne Cl WLTN L25 .... 97 E4
Alder Av HUY L36 .... 76 A5
WDN WA8 .... 102 A5
Alderbank Rd
WARRW/BUR WA5 .... 105 E2
Alder Cl PR/KW L34 .... 60 B4
Alder Crs KKBY L32 .... 33 G1
WARRN/WOL WA2........................ 84 A5
Alderfield Dr SPK/HALE L24 .... 143 E4
Alder Gv CSBY/WL L22 .... 29 E2
Alder Hey Rd ECCL WA10 .... 47 E3
Alder La PR/KW L34....................... 43 H4
WARRN/WOL WA2 .... 83 H5
WDN WA8 .... 100 B4
Alderley Av BIRK CH41 .... 91 F1
Alderley Rd HOY CH47 .... 87 F1
WAL/EG CH44 .... 68 D2
WARRS WA4 .... 108 D4
Alderney Rd EV L5 .... 53 H5
Alder Rd BEB CH63 .... 137 F2
PR/KW L34 .... 60 B4
WARR WA1 .... 108 D1
WD/CROXPK L12 .... 56 D5
Aldersey St VAUX/LVPD L3 .... 70 D2
Aldersgate RF/TRAN CH42 .... 115 H1
Aldersgate Av RUNC WA7 .... 157 F2
Aldersgate Dr HLWD L26 .... 122 A5
Alderson Crs FMBY L37 .... 17 E2
Alderson Rd WAV L15 .... 95 F1
Alderville Rd ANF/KKDL L4 .... 41 E5
Alder Wood Av
SPK/HALE L24 .... 142 C3
Alderwood Ct WDN WA8 .... 101 G4
Aldford Cl BEB CH63 .... 152 B3
CL/PREN CH43 .... 114 A1
Aldford Rd KKBY L32 .... 33 H5
Aldridge Cl WD/CROXPK L12 .... 43 E4
Aldrins La NTHTN L30 .... 23 E5
Aldwark Rd DV/KA/FCH L14 .... 74 C1
Aldwych Rd WD/CROXPK L12 .... 56 C4
Aldykes MGHL L31 .... 24 B1
Alexander Dr MGHL L31 .... 18 D3
PEN/TH CH61 .... 134 C3
WDN WA8 .... 124 B3
Alexander Fleming Av
NTHTN L30 .... 23 E5
Alexander Gv RUNC WA7 .... 9 H6
Alexander Wk ANF/KKDL L4........... 54 B2
Alexander Whf MGHL L31 .... 18 C5
Alexandra Cl NPK/KEN L6 .... 71 H2
Alexandra Dr AIG/SPK L17 .... 94 D4
BTL L20 .... 40 A1
ECCL WA10 .... 61 F1
RF/TRAN CH42 .... 115 G2
Alexandra Gn AIG/SPK L17 .... 94 D4
Alexandra Gv HLWD L26 .... 121 H5
Alexandra Mt LITH L21 .... 30 A4
Alexandra Pk AIG/SPK L17 .... 94 D5
Alexandra Rd
CL/PREN CH43 .... 2 B6
CLB/OSW/ST L13 .... 73 E4
CSBY/BLUN L23 .... 21 E5
CSBY/WL L22 .... 29 F4
EHL/KEN L7 .... 72 A5
WAL/NB CH45 .... 51 G2
WARRS WA4 .... 130 B2
WKBY CH48 .... 110 A2
Alexandra St ECCL WA10 .... 61 F1
WARR WA1 .... 13 K1
WDN WA8 .... 14 C6
Alexandra Ter TOX L8 *.................. 94 B1
Alexandria Rd ALL/GAR L19 .... 119 G4
Alex Cl TOX L8 .... 94 B2
Alfonso Rd ANF/KKDL L4 .... 53 H2
Alford Av STHEL WA9 .... 79 F1
Alforde St WDN WA8 .... 14 D6
Alford St EHL/KEN L7 .... 72 C3
Alfred Ms CLVPS L1 .... 94 A1
Alfred Rd CL/PREN CH43 .... 2 B6
WAL/EG CH44 .... 69 G4
Alfred St ECCL WA10 .... 11 J3
WAV L15 .... 72 B5
WDN WA8 .... 14 E4
Alfriston Rd WD/CROXPK L12 ...... 56 C4
Algernon St RUNC WA7 .... 8 B3
WARR WA1 .... 13 H2
WARRS WA4 .... 130 A2
Alice Ct WDN WA8 .... 146 A2
Alice St STHEL WA9 .... 63 E2
Alison Av RF/TRAN CH42 .... 92 D5
Alison Pl CLB/OSW/ST L13 .... 55 G3
Alison Rd CLB/OSW/ST L13 .... 55 G3
Alistair Dr BEB CH63 .... 152 C3
Allangate Cl
GR/UP/WCH CH49 .... 112 A1
Allangate Rd ALL/GAR L19 .... 119 F3
Allan Rd RNFD/HAY WA11 .... 37 G5
Allans Cl NSTN CH64 .... 158 D4
Allans Meadow NSTN CH64......... 158 D4
Allanson St STHEL WA9 .... 48 D5
Allcot Av RF/TRAN CH42 .... 115 F1
Allenby Av CSBY/WL L22 .... 29 G2
Allenby Sq CLB/OSW/ST L13 .... 72 D3
Allendale RUNC WA7 .... 156 D3
Allendale Av RAIN/WH L35 .... 78 B2
WLT/FAZ L9 .... 31 G5
Allengate CSBY/BLUN L23 .... 21 F4
Allen Rd RUNC WA7 .... 154 B2
Allen St WARRN/WOL WA2 .... 12 C3
Allerford Rd WD/CROXPK L12 .... 56 D2
Allerton Beeches CALD/MH L18 .. 96 C5
Allerton Dr CALD/MH L18 .... 96 B4
Allerton Gv RF/TRAN CH42 .... 92 B5
Allerton Rd CALD/MH L18 .... 96 B3
RF/TRAN CH42 .... 92 B5
WAL/NB CH45 .... 51 G4
WAV L15 .... 96 A3
WDN WA8 .... 15 F1
WLTN L25 .... 120 B2
Allesley Rd DV/KA/FCH L14 .... 57 F5
Alleyne Rd ANF/KKDL L4 .... 55 F2
All Hallows Dr SPK/HALE L24 ..... 142 D3
Allington St AIG/SPK L17 .... 94 D5
Allonby Cl CL/PREN CH43 .... 91 E4
Allport La PS/BROM CH62 .... 138 D5
Allport Rd BEB CH63 .... 152 C3
PS/BROM CH62 .... 152 C2
The Allports PS/BROM CH62....... 152 D2
All Saints Cl NTHTN L30 .... 30 D1
All Saints Dr WARRS WA4 .... 109 E5
All Saints Rd SPK/HALE L24 .... 142 A3
Alma Cl AIN/FAZ L10 .... 33 E5
Almacs Cl CSBY/BLUN L23 .... 28 C1
Alma Pl STHEL WA9 .... 48 C5
Alma Rd AIG/SPK L17 .... 118 C3
Alma St BIRK CH41 .... 3 G5
PS/BROM CH62 * 116 A4
STHEL WA9 .... 48 C5
Alma Vale Ter BTL L20 * 4 D5
Almeda Rd SPK/HALE L24 .... 143 E4
Almer Dr WARRW/BUR WA5 .... 105 G3
Almond Av NTHTN L30 .... 30 B1
RUNC WA7 .... 155 G1
Almond Cl HLWD L26 .... 121 G4
RNFD/HAY WA11 .... 49 F2
Almond Ct ALL/GAR L19 .... 141 E1
Almond Gv WARR WA1 .... 108 B1
WDN WA8 .... 124 B3
Almond Pl MOR/LEA CH46 .... 66 D5
Almond's Gn WD/CROXPK L12 ...... 56 A2
Almond's Gv WD/CROXPK L12 ...... 56 A3
Almonds Pk WD/CROXPK L12 .... 56 A2
Almond's Turn NTHTN L30 .... 22 C5
Almond Wy
GR/UP/WCH CH49 * 112 A1
Alness Dr RAIN/WH L35 .... 78 B3
Alnwick Dr MOR/LEA CH46 .... 66 A5
Aloeswood Cl NPK/KEN L6 .... 54 D5
Alpass Rd AIG/SPK L17 * 94 D5
Alpha Dr RF/TRAN CH42 .... 116 A2
Alpha St LITH L21 .... 39 F2
Alpine Cl ECCL WA10 .... 47 E3
Alresford Rd ALL/GAR L19 .... 118 D3
Alroy Rd ANF/KKDL L4 .... 54 C3
Alscot Av AIN/FAZ L10 .... 33 E5
Alscot Cl MGHL L31 .... 24 A1
Alsop Ar VAUX/LVPD L3 * 7 K4
Alsop Ct VAUX/LVPD L3 * 7 K4
Alston Cl PS/BROM CH62 .... 138 C5
Alstonfield Rd DV/KA/FCH L14 ..... 74 C1
Alston Rd AIG/SPK L17 .... 118 C3
Alt WDN WA8 .... 123 H1
Alt Av MGHL L31 .... 23 H2
Altbridge Pk NG/CROX L11 .... 42 B2
Alt Bridge Rd HUY L36 .... 75 F1
Altcar Av EHL/KEN L7 .... 95 F1
Altcar Dr MOR/LEA CH46 .... 89 F1
Altcar La FMBY L37 .... 17 E5
MGHL L31 .... 18 A2
Altcar Rd FMBY L37 .... 17 F4
Altcross Rd NG/CROX L11 .... 42 C3
Altcross Wy NG/CROX L11 .... 42 C3
Altfield Rd DV/KA/FCH L14 .... 57 F3
Altfinch Cl DV/KA/FCH L14 .... 57 G3
Altham Rd NG/CROX L11 .... 55 H3
Althorp St TOX L8 .... 94 B5
Altmoor Rd HUY L36 .... 58 B4
Alton Av LITH L21 .... 29 H3
Alton Rd CL/PREN CH43 .... 91 G3
NPK/KEN L6 .... 55 F5
Alt Rd BTL L20 .... 39 G2
FMBY L37 .... 17 F5
HUY L36 .... 75 G2
Alt Side Ct AIN/FAZ L10 .... 33 E5
Alt St TOX L8 .... 94 D1
Altway AIN/FAZ L10 .... 31 H1
Alundale Rd WD/CROXPK L12 .... 57 E5
Alvanley Pl CL/PREN CH43 .... 2 B5
Alvanley Rd KKBY L32 .... 33 F2
WD/CROXPK L12 .... 56 C5
Alva Rd RAIN/WH L35 .... 78 B3
Alvega Cl PS/BROM CH62 .... 116 C4
Alverstone Av BIRK CH41 .... 91 F1
Alverstone Cl
WARRW/BUR WA5 .... 104 A1
Alverstone Rd CALD/MH L18 .... 95 H3
WAL/EG CH44 .... 69 F2
Alverton Cl WDN WA8 .... 124 B3
Alvina La ANF/KKDL L4 .... 54 A3
NWD/KWIPK L33 .... 26 B4
Alwain Gn SPK/HALE L24 .... 142 D4
Alwen St BIRK CH41 .... 68 B4
Alwyn Av LITH L21 .... 30 A3
Alwyn Gdns MOR/LEA CH46 .... 66 D5
Alwyn St AIG/SPK L17 .... 94 D5
Amanda Rd AIN/FAZ L10 .... 33 E5
RAIN/WH L35 .... 60 D5
Amanda Wy MGHL L31 * 25 E5
Amaury Cl CSBY/BLUN L23 .... 22 A4
Amaury Rd CSBY/BLUN L23 .... 22 A4
Ambassador Dr HLWD L26 .... 122 A2
Ambergate Cl STHEL WA9 * 62 D3
Ambergate Rd ALL/GAR L19 .... 119 F3
Amberley Av MOR/LEA CH46 .... 89 E1
Amberley Cl MOR/LEA CH46 .... 89 E1
NPK/KEN L6 .... 55 F3
Amber Wy DV/KA/FCH L14 .... 57 G3
Ambleside Av MOR/LEA CH46 .... 66 B5
Ambleside Cl PEN/TH CH61 .... 113 E5
PS/BROM CH62 .... 153 E2
Ambleside Crs
WARRN/WOL WA2 .... 84 A2
Ambleside Dr NWD/KWIPK L33 ..... 25 G5
Ambleside Rd CALD/MH L18 .... 119 H2
MGHL L31 .... 18 D4
Amelia Cl NPK/KEN L6 .... 7 K1
WDN WA8 .... 102 B4
Amelia St WARRN/WOL WA2 .... 107 E1
Amersham Rd ANF/KKDL L4 .... 41 E5
Amery Gv RF/TRAN CH42 .... 115 E1
Amethyst Cl NPK/KEN L6 .... 71 H1
Amherst Rd AIG/SPK L17 .... 118 A1
Amity St TOX L8 .... 94 B3
Amos Av LITH L21 .... 30 B4
Ampleforth Cl KKBY L32 .... 33 F3
Ampthill Rd AIG/SPK L17 .... 118 A1
Ampulla Rd NG/CROX L11 .... 42 C4
Ancaster Rd AIG/SPK L17 .... 118 A1

Ancholme Cl RAIN/WH L35 60 C4
Anchorage La CALD/MH L18 95 G5
The Anchorage NSTN CH64 158 B3
VAUX/LVPD L3 93 H2
Anchor Cl RUNC WA7 157 F3
Anchor Ctyd VAUX/LVPD L3 * 6 C7
Ancient Mdw WLT/FAZ L9 31 G5
Ancroft Rd DV/KA/FCH L14 74 C2
Ancrum Rd NWD/KWIPK L33 25 G3
Anders Dr NWD/KWIPK L33 26 B4
Anderson Av BTL L20 4 A2
Anderson Cl PEN/TH CH61 113 E5
RAIN/WH L35 78 B4
WARRN/WOL WA2 85 F3
Anderson Rd LITH L21 30 C3
Anderson St EV L5 54 A4
Anderton Ter HUY L36 75 E3
Andover Cl WARRN/WOL WA2 84 C4
Andover Wy WLTN L25 121 F4
Andrew Av MGHL L31 32 D1
Andrew Cl WDN WA8 124 A3
Andrews Cl FMBY L37 16 D5
Andrews La FMBY L37 16 D5
Andrew St ANF/KKDL L4 54 B1
Andrew's Wk HES CH60 149 F1
Andrews Yort FMBY L37 16 D5
Andromeda Wy STHEL WA9 63 G3
Anemone Wy STHEL WA9 63 G3
Anfield Rd ANF/KKDL L4 54 B3
Angela St EHL/KEN L7 71 H5
Angers La MGHL L31 25 E3
Anglesea Rd WLT/FAZ L9 40 B4
Anglesea Wy TOX L8 94 B4
Anglesey Rd WAL/EG CH44 51 H5
WKBY CH48 87 E5
Anglezark Cl EHL/KEN L7 71 H3
Anglia Wy WLTN L25 121 E3
Anglican Ct TOX L8 94 A1
Anglo Cl WLT/FAZ L9 31 H4
Angus Rd BEB CH63 152 C3
NG/CROX L11 55 H2
Annandale Cl NWD/KWIPK L33 25 G3
Anne Gv STHEL WA9 62 C3
Annerley St EHL/KEN L7 * 72 A5
Annesley Rd AIG/SPK L17 118 A1
WAL/EG CH44 68 D2
Anne St STHEL WA9 79 H2
Annie Rd BTL L20 39 H1
Annie St WARRN/WOL WA2 12 E2
Ann St RUNC WA7 9 F3
Ann St West WDN WA8 14 E6
Anscot Av BEB CH63 115 H5
Ansdell Dr ECCL WA10 46 D2
Ansdell Rd WDN WA8 125 F1
Ansdell Villas' Rd RAIN/WH L35 78 A1
Anson Pl VAUX/LVPD L3 7 J2
Anson St VAUX/LVPD L3 7 J3
Anstey Cl MOR/LEA CH46 65 H4
Anstey Rd CLB/OSW/ST L13 73 F2
Ansty Cl RNFD/HAY WA11 48 D2
Anthony's Wy HES CH60 149 E2
Anthorn Cl CL/PREN CH43 90 D4
Antonio St BTL L20 53 H1
Antons Cl HLWD L26 121 H5
Antons Ct HLWD L26 122 A5
Antons Rd HLWD L26 121 H5
PEN/TH CH61 134 D1
Antony Rd WARRS WA4 129 H1
Antrim Rd WARRN/WOL WA2 83 G3
Antrim St CLB/OSW/ST L13 55 G3
Anvil Cl BTL L20 4 C2
The Anzacs PS/BROM CH62 116 C5
Anzio Rd HUY L36 75 F1
Apex Ct PS/BROM CH62 * 139 E5
Apollo Crs NWD/KWIPK L33 25 H5
Apollo Wy NPK/KEN L6 * 54 D5
NTHTN L30 23 E5
Apostles Wy NWD/KWIPK L33 25 G4
Appin Rd BIRK CH41 3 F7
Appleby Cl WDN WA8 124 A3
Appleby Dr NTHTN L30 30 B1
Appleby Gn WD/CROXPK L12 56 D4
Appleby Gv PS/BROM CH62 152 C3
Appleby Lawn NTHLY L27 99 E4
Appleby Rd NWD/KWIPK L33 25 H5
WARRN/WOL WA2 84 A2
Appleby Wk WDN WA8 124 A3
Applecorn Cl STHEL WA9 62 D4
Apple Ct NPK/KEN L6 71 H2
Appledore Cl SPK/HALE L24 141 H2
Appledore Gv STHEL WA9 79 G1
Appleford Cl WARRS WA4 130 C4
Applegarth MOR/LEA CH46 89 E2
Appleton Dr GR/UP/WCH CH49 89 G5
Appleton Rd ANF/KKDL L4 54 C1
KKBY L32 25 H5
LITH L21 29 H3
STHEL WA9 48 C5
WDN WA8 14 E1
Appleton St WDN WA8 14 E7
Appleton Village WDN WA8 14 D1
Appletree Cl CALD/MH L18 119 G2
Apple Tree Cl STBRV L28 57 H2
Appletree Gv WARRN/WOL WA2 84 D3
April Gv NPK/KEN L6 55 F5
April Ri NTHTN L30 30 D5
Apsley Av WAL/NB CH45 51 H4
Apsley Brow MGHL L31 18 B5
Apsley Gv BEB CH63 116 A5
Apsley Rd PS/BROM CH62 116 B3
WD/CROXPK L12 56 C4
Aquarius Cl DV/KA/FCH L14 74 C1
Aragon Cl MGHL L31 19 E3
Aran Cl SPK/HALE L24 143 H4
Arborn Dr GR/UP/WCH CH49 90 A2
Arbour Ct NWD/KWIPK L33 34 C2
Arbour La NWD/KWIPK L33 34 B3
Arbury Av RNFD/HAY WA11 48 D1
Arcadia Av MGHL L31 18 D3
Archbishop Worlock Ct
VAUX/LVPD L3 70 C1
Archer Av WARRS WA4 130 C1
Archer Cl ANF/KKDL L4 54 A3
Archerfield Rd CALD/MH L18 119 F2
Archer Gv STHEL WA9 49 E3
Archers Cft PS/BROM CH62 * 138 D5
Archers Fold MGHL L31 25 E5
Archers Gn PS/BROM CH62 153 E5
Archers Green Rd
WARRW/BUR WA5 82 A2
Archer St ANF/KKDL L4 * 54 A3
Archers Wy
GR/UP/WCH CH49 * 113 E1
The Arches PR/KW L34 * 59 H4
Arch View Crs CLVPS L1 7 G7
Archway Rd HUY L36 75 G3
Arctic Rd BTL L20 4 B4
Arden WDN WA8 123 G1
Arden Dr NSTN CH64 158 D4
Ardennes Rd HUY L36 75 G2
Arderne Cl BEB CH63 138 B4
Ardleigh Ct CLB/OSW/ST L13 72 D3
Ardleigh Gv CLB/OSW/ST L13 72 D3
Ardleigh Pl CLB/OSW/ST L13 72 D3
Ardleigh Rd CLB/OSW/ST L13 72 C3
Ardmore Rd CALD/MH L18 119 E1
Ardrossan Rd ANF/KKDL L4 55 E2
Ardville Rd NG/CROX L11 41 F4
Ardwick Rd SPK/HALE L24 142 D3
Ardwick St STHEL WA9 11 K5
Arena Gdns WARRN/WOL WA2 84 B5
Argarmeols Gv FMBY L37 16 D1
Argo Rd CSBY/WL L22 29 E3
Argos Pl BTL L20 53 H1
Argos Rd BTL L20 53 H1
Argyle Rd ALL/GAR L19 119 G5
ANF/KKDL L4 54 D4
Argyle St BIRK CH41 3 G4
CLVPS L1 6 E6
ECCL WA10 11 F1
Argyle St South BIRK CH41 2 E7
Argyll Av PS/BROM CH62 152 D5
Aries Cl DV/KA/FCH L14 57 G5
Ariss Gv RAIN/WH L35 * 60 C5
Arizona Crs WARRW/BUR WA5 105 F1
Arkenstone Cl WDN WA8 124 A1
Arkle Rd CL/PREN CH43 68 B5
Arkles La ANF/KKDL L4 54 D3
Arkles Rd ANF/KKDL L4 54 C4
Arklow Dr SPK/HALE L24 143 H4
Ark Royal Wy BIRK CH41 92 D4
Arkwood Cl PS/BROM CH62 138 C3
Arkwright Ct RUNC WA7 147 F3
Arkwright Rd RUNC WA7 147 F3
Arkwright St EV L5 54 A5
Arlescourt Rd WD/CROXPK L12 56 C5
Arley Av WARRS WA4 130 B2
Arley Cl CL/PREN CH43 90 C2
Arley Dr WDN WA8 123 H1
Arley St VAUX/LVPD L3 70 C1
Arlington Av CALD/MH L18 95 H3
Arlington Dr
WARRW/BUR WA5 104 C4
Arlington Rd WAL/NB CH45 51 E4
Armill Rd NG/CROX L11 42 C4
Armitage Gdns CALD/MH L18 119 F2
Armley Rd ANF/KKDL L4 54 D3
Armour Av WARRN/WOL WA2 83 H3
The Armoury WD/CROXPK L12 56 B3
Armscot Cl WLTN L25 120 D4
Armscot Pl WLTN L25 120 D4
Armstrong Cl GOL/RIS/CUL WA3 85 H1
Armstrong Quay VAUX/LVPD L3 94 B5
Arncliffe Rd WLTN L25 121 E3
Arndale RUNC WA7 156 A4
Arnhem Crs WARRN/WOL WA2 107 E1
Arnhem Rd HUY L36 75 F1
Arnold Av ECCL WA10 10 B2
Arnold Cl STHEL WA9 62 C1
TOX L8 94 C2
Arnold Crs TOX L8 94 C2
Arnold Gv WAV L15 73 E5
Arnold Pl WDN WA8 124 A4
Arnold St WAL/NB CH45 * 51 H5
WARR WA1 13 J2
Arno Rd CL/PREN CH43 91 E4
Arnot Cl ECCL WA10 11 F2
Arnot St ANF/KKDL L4 54 B1
Arnot Wy BEB CH63 115 F5
Arnside LITH L21 30 C4
Arnside Av RAIN/WH L35 77 G1
RNFD/HAY WA11 49 G1
Arnside Gv WARRS WA4 129 H1
Arnside Rd CL/PREN CH43 91 G4
EHL/KEN L7 72 A4
HUY L36 74 D3
WAL/NB CH45 51 H5
Aron Ct PR/KW L34 59 H4
Arpley Rd WARR WA1 12 D7
Arpley St WARR WA1 12 B5
Arrad St EHL/KEN L7 7 J6
Arran Cl RNFD/HAY WA11 49 E1
WARRN/WOL WA2 85 E3
Arranmore Rd CALD/MH L18 119 E1
Arrowe Av MOR/LEA CH46 89 F1
Arrowe Brook La
GR/UP/WCH CH49 112 C2
Arrowe Brook Rd
GR/UP/WCH CH49 112 D1
Arrowe Park Rd
GR/UP/WCH CH49 89 H3
Arrowe Rd GR/UP/WCH CH49 89 F5
Arrowe Side GR/UP/WCH CH49 89 G4
Arrowe Vw GR/UP/WCH CH49 * 90 A3
Arthur St ALL/GAR L19 * 140 D1
BIRK CH41 2 B1
RUNC WA7 8 C5
WARRN/WOL WA2 12 B3
WLT/FAZ L9 40 B4
Arundel Av AIG/SPK L17 95 E2
WAL/NB CH45 51 F4
Arundel Cl PEN/TH CH61 134 C1
TOX L8 94 C2
Arundel St ANF/KKDL L4 54 A1
Arvon St BTL L20 39 H1
Asbridge St TOX L8 94 D2
Asbury Cl CALD/MH L18 96 D5
Asbury Rd WAL/NB CH45 50 D4
Ascot Av LITH L21 29 H4
RUNC WA7 155 F3
Ascot Cl WARR WA1 109 E1
WARRS WA4 131 G1
Ascot Dr BEB CH63 137 H1
NWD/KWIPK L33 25 H4
Ascot Gv BEB CH63 137 H1
Ascot Pk CSBY/BLUN L23 21 G5
Ascroft Rd WLT/FAZ L9 31 G4
Ashbank Rd NG/CROX L11 42 A5
Ashbourne Av CSBY/BLUN L23 20 D5
NTHTN L30 30 D2
RUNC WA7 155 F3
Ashbourne Crs HUY L36 74 D3
Ashbourne Rd AIG/SPK L17 118 A1
WARRW/BUR WA5 105 F3
Ashbrook Av RUNC WA7 156 A5
Ashbrook Crs
WARRN/WOL WA2 84 B5
Ashbrook Dr WLT/FAZ L9 41 E1
Ashburn Av NWD/KWIPK L33 25 H5
Ashburton Av CL/PREN CH43 91 F2
Ashburton Rd CL/PREN CH43 91 E2
WAL/EG CH44 68 D1
WKBY CH48 87 F5
Ashbury Rd DV/KA/FCH L14 57 H4
Ashby Cl MOR/LEA CH46 65 H4
Ash Cl WAV L15 72 C5
Ashcombe Rd DV/KA/FCH L14 73 G2
Ash Crs HUY L36 75 G5
Ashcroft Dr PEN/TH CH61 134 D4
Ashcroft Rd FMBY L37 17 E5
NWD/KWIPK L33 34 D1
Ashcroft St BTL L20 4 D5
STHEL WA9 48 C4
Ashdale HUY L36 75 F3
Ashdale Cl FMBY L37 16 B4
Ashdale Pk GR/UP/WCH CH49 88 D5
Ashdale Rd CALD/MH L18 96 A3
CSBY/WL L22 29 E2
WLT/FAZ L9 40 C3
Ashdown Crs STHEL WA9 79 G1
Ashdown Dr
GR/UP/WCH CH49 112 A1
Ashdown Gv HLWD L26 122 A2
Ashfarm Ct DV/KA/FCH L14 74 B2
Ashfield RAIN/WH L35 78 B2
WAV L15 72 B5
Ashfield Crs PS/BROM CH62 152 D1
Ashfield Gdns WARRS WA4 107 H5
Ashfield Rd AIG/SPK L17 118 B1
PS/BROM CH62 152 C1
Ashfield St EV L5 53 G5
Ashford Cl HLWD L26 121 G4
Ashford Rd BIRK CH41 92 A4
HOY CH47 64 C5
Ashford Wy WDN WA8 15 K1
Ash Gv FMBY L37 16 B5
LITH L21 39 E1
RAIN/WH L35 77 E1
RUNC WA7 155 G1
STHEL WA9 79 G1
WAL/NB CH45 52 A3
WARRS WA4 107 F5
WAV L15 72 B5
Ash La WARRS WA4 130 C3
WDN WA8 123 F3
Ashlar Gv AIG/SPK L17 118 C1
Ashlar Rd AIG/SPK L17 118 C1
CSBY/WL L22 29 F2
Ashlea Rd PEN/TH CH61 134 D3
Ashleigh Rd MGHL L31 24 C2
Ashley Av HOY CH47 65 F4
Ashley Cl NWD/KWIPK L33 25 H4
RAIN/WH L35 78 B3
WARRS WA4 108 C5
Ashley Rd RUNC WA7 9 K5
Ashley St RF/TRAN CH42 115 H1
Ashley Wy WDN WA8 14 D7
Ashley Wy West WDN WA8 14 B6
Ashmore Cl WKBY CH48 110 C5
Ashmuir Hey KKBY L32 34 A3
Ashover Av DV/KA/FCH L14 74 C1
Ash Priors WDN WA8 101 F5
Ashridge St RUNC WA7 8 C3
Ash Rd BEB CH63 115 H4
LITH L21 29 H5
RF/TRAN CH42 * 92 B4
WARRW/BUR WA5 104 D4
Ash St BTL L20 5 F3
Ashton Av RAIN/WH L35 78 A3
Ashton Cl RUNC WA7 154 D3
Ashton Dr WKBY CH48 110 A2
WLTN L25 120 D4
Ashtons Green Dr STHEL WA9 49 F5
Ashton St CLB/OSW/ST L13 73 E2
VAUX/LVPD L3 7 K3
WARRN/WOL WA2 12 D3
Ashtree Cl NSTN CH64 159 F3
Ashtree Dr NSTN CH64 159 F4
Ashtree Gv WD/CROXPK L12 43 E3
Ashurst Cl RNFD/HAY WA11 49 E1
WLTN L25 97 H4
Ashurst Ct FMBY L37 16 D4
Ashurst Dr RNFD/HAY WA11 48 D1
Ash V WAV L15 72 C5
Ash Vls WAL/EG CH44 * 69 F3
Ashville Rd BIRK CH41 2 A3
CL/PREN CH43 91 H1
WAL/EG CH44 69 E3
Ashwater Rd WD/CROXPK L12 42 C5
Ash Wy HES CH60 149 F4
Ashwell St TOX L8 94 A1
Ashwood Av WARR WA1 107 G1
Ashwood Cl NWD/KWIPK L33 25 H4
WDN WA8 123 G4
Ashwood Ct CL/PREN CH43 67 G4
Ashwood Dr WD/CROXPK L12 42 D4
Askern Rd KKBY L32 34 A4
Askew Cl WAL/EG CH44 69 F1
Askew St ANF/KKDL L4 54 B1
Askham Cl TOX L8 94 D1
Aspen Cl HES CH60 149 H1
NWD/KWIPK L33 26 A3
Aspendale Rd RF/TRAN CH42 92 B4
Aspen Gv FMBY L37 16 B5
TOX L8 95 E2
WARR WA1 108 A1
Aspes Rd WD/CROXPK L12 57 E3
Aspinall Cl WARRN/WOL WA2 85 E2
Aspinall St BIRK CH41 2 B2
Aspinal St PR/KW L34 59 H4
Aspull Cl GOL/RIS/CUL WA3 85 G1
Asquith Av BIRK CH41 2 A2
Asser Rd NG/CROX L11 55 G2
Assheton Wk SPK/HALE L24 144 A4
Assissian Crs NTHTN L30 22 D5
Aster Crs RUNC WA7 * 156 B5
Aster Dr NWD/KWIPK L33 25 G4
Asterfield Av BEB CH63 115 G4
Astley Cl WARRS WA4 106 D5
WDN WA8 101 E5
Astley Rd HUY L36 58 C4
Astmoor Bridge La
RUNC WA7 147 F4
Astmoor Rd RUNC WA7 9 H3
Aston Cl CL/PREN CH43 91 F5
Aston Ct WARR WA1 85 G4
Aston Fields Rd RUNC WA7 157 F5
Aston Forge RUNC WA7 157 H4
Aston Gn RUNC WA7 * 157 G3
Aston La North RUNC WA7 157 G5
Aston St ALL/GAR L19 140 D2
Astonwood Rd RF/TRAN CH42 92 B5
Astor Dr WARRS WA4 130 D3
Astor St ANF/KKDL L4 40 B5
Atheldene Rd ANF/KKDL L4 41 E5
Athelstan Cl PS/BROM CH62 138 D5
Atherton Cl EV L5 54 B5
Atherton Dr GR/UP/WCH CH49 90 A5
Atherton Rd WLT/FAZ L9 41 E1
Atherton St ECCL WA10 10 E2
PR/KW L34 * 59 H4
WAL/NB CH45 51 G1
Athlone Rd WARRN/WOL WA2 83 G4
Athol Cl PS/BROM CH62 153 E4
Athol Dr PS/BROM CH62 153 E4
Atholl Crs AIN/FAZ L10 32 A2
Athol St BIRK CH41 3 G3
EV L5 53 F5
EV L5 53 H5
Atkinson Gv HUY L36 75 H1
Atlanta Ct NWD/KWIPK L33 25 G3
Atlanta Gdns
WARRW/BUR WA5 82 B5
Atlantic Pavilion
VAUX/LVPD L3 * 6 C7
Atlantic Point Village
VAUX/LVPD L3 70 D2
Atlantic Rd BTL L20 4 C4
Atlantic Wy NTHTN L30 30 D4
VAUX/LVPD L3 93 H4
Atlas Rd BTL L20 4 B4
Atlas St STHEL WA9 11 K4
Atterbury Cl WDN WA8 124 A1
Atterbury St TOX L8 94 A3
Attlee Rd HUY L36 76 A2
Attwood St ANF/KKDL L4 54 B3
Atwell St NPK/KEN L6 71 G1
Aubourn Cl WDN WA8 101 E5
Aubrey Ct NPK/KEN L6 71 G1
Auburn Rd CLB/OSW/ST L13 55 G5
WAL/NB CH45 51 G3
The Aubynes WAL/NB CH45 51 E3
Audlem Av CL/PREN CH43 91 F5
Audlem Cl RUNC WA7 156 B5
Audley St VAUX/LVPD L3 7 H2
Audre Cl WARRW/BUR WA5 104 B2
Aughton Rd BTL L20 39 H2
Augusta Cl CLB/OSW/ST L13 73 E3
August Rd NPK/KEN L6 55 E5
August St BTL L20 5 F1
Aukland Gv STHEL WA9 61 F3
Aukland Rd WAV L15 96 A3
Aurorean Cl NTHLY L27 98 B2
Austell Cl RNFD/HAY WA11 37 H5
Austin Av ECCL WA10 61 E2
Austin Cl KKBY L32 33 G2
Austin St WAL/EG CH44 * 68 C3
Austral Av WARR WA1 108 B1
Australia La WARRS WA4 131 G2
Autumn Gv RF/TRAN CH42 115 G3
Autumn Wy BTL L20 5 F1
Avalon Ter BTL L20 4 B2
Avebury Cl WDN WA8 103 E5
Aveley Cl WARR WA1 108 B1
Avelon Cl CL/PREN CH43 90 D3
MGHL L31 18 B1
The Avenue ALL/GAR L19 141 E1
ECCL WA10 46 D4
HLWD L26 121 G4
HUY L36 75 G2
PR/KW L34 58 C3
PS/BROM CH62 152 C1
Avery Cl WARRN/WOL WA2 84 C3
Aviary Ct WLT/FAZ L9 * 40 B1
Aviemore Dr
WARRN/WOL WA2 85 E2
Aviemore Rd
CLB/OSW/ST L13 72 D2
Avington Cl
WD/CROXPK L12 56 D3
Avocet Cl WARRN/WOL WA2 84 B2
Avolon Rd WD/CROXPK L12 56 D5
Avon WDN WA8 123 G1
Avon Av WARRW/BUR WA5 104 C4
Avon Cl ANF/KKDL L4 54 A2
NSTN CH64 158 D4
NWD/KWIPK L33 26 A3
Avondale Av MGHL L31 23 H1
MOR/LEA CH46 66 D4
PS/BROM CH62 153 E4
Avondale Dr WDN WA8 123 H2
Avondale Rd HOY CH47 87 F1
WAV L15 95 G2
Avonmore Av
CALD/MH L18 96 A5
Avon Rd
WGNW/BIL/OR WN5 37 H1
Avon St BIRK CH41 68 B4
NPK/KEN L6 * 54 D5
Awelon Cl WD/CROXPK L12 56 C4
Axbridge Av STHEL WA9 62 D5
Axholme Cl PEN/TH CH61 135 F1
Axholme Rd PEN/TH CH61 135 E1
Ayala Cl BTL L20 31 E5
Aycliffe Rd STHEL WA9 * 61 F4
Aylesbury Av CL/PREN CH43 114 A1
Aylesbury Rd WAL/NB CH45 52 A3
Aylesford Rd
CLB/OSW/ST L13 73 E2
Aylsham Cl WDN WA8 101 E5
Aylsham Dr
GR/UP/WCH CH49 90 A1
Aylton Rd HUY L36 74 D1
Aylward Pl BTL L20 * 4 D2
Aynsley Ct STHEL WA9 60 D4
Ayres Ct STHEL WA9 61 G3
Ayrshire Gdns ECCL WA10 10 D7
Ayrshire Rd ANF/KKDL L4 55 E2
Aysgarth Av WD/CROXPK L12 56 C4
Aysgarth Rd WAL/NB CH45 51 F4
Azalea Gv HLWD L26 121 F1
RUNC WA7 156 B5

B

Babbacombe Rd CHLDW L16 97 E2
WARRW/BUR WA5 104 C4
Back Beau St VAUX/LVPD L3 * 71 E1
Back Bedford St EHL/KEN L7 7 K6
Back Belmont Rd NPK/KEN L6 54 D5
Back Berry St CLVPS L1 7 G6
Back Blackfield Ter EV L5 53 H3
Back Bold St CLVPS L1 7 F5
Back Boundary St EV L5 53 H4
Back Bridport St VAUX/LVPD L3 7 G3
Back Canning St CLVPS L1 7 J7
Back Catharine St TOX L8 * 7 J7
Back Chadwick Mt EV L5 54 A3
Back Chatham Pl EHL/KEN L7 71 H4
Back Colquitt St CLVPS L1 7 G6
Back Commutation Rw
VAUX/LVPD L3 7 G3
Back Dovecot Pl
DV/KA/FCH L14 74 B1
Back Eastford Rd WARRS WA4 129 G2
Back Egerton St North
TOX L8 * 94 B1
Back Falkner St South TOX L8 7 K7
Backford Cl CL/PREN CH43 91 E5
RUNC WA7 157 E4
Backford Rd PEN/TH CH61 134 B1
Backford Wy CL/PREN CH43 91 E5
Back Forshaw St
WARRN/WOL WA2 12 E1
Back Gillmoss La NG/CROX L11 42 C1
Back Granton Rd EV L5 54 C4
Back Guilford St NPK/KEN L6 71 F1
Back High St RUNC WA7 8 D4
Back Holland Pl EHL/KEN L7 71 H4
Back Hope Pl CLVPS L1 7 J6
Back Huskisson St TOX L8 * 94 B1
Back Kelvin Gv TOX L8 94 C2
Back Knight St CLVPS L1 7 G7
Back La CSBY/BLUN L23 21 G1
WARRW/BUR WA5 126 C1
Back Leeds St VAUX/LVPD L3 6 B1
Back Lime St CLVPS L1 7 F4
Back Little Canning St TOX L8 * 94 B1
Back Luton Gv ANF/KKDL L4 54 A2
Back Maryland St CLVPS L1 * 7 H6
Back Menai St BIRK CH41 2 C5
Back Mount St CSBY/WL L22 * 29 E3
Back Mount Vernon Gn
EHL/KEN L7 * 71 G4
Back Mulberry St EHL/KEN L7 7 K7
Back Oliver St BIRK CH41 3 G5
Back Orford St WAV L15 72 D5
Back Percy St CLVPS L1 94 B1
Back Pickop St VAUX/LVPD L3 6 D2
Back Renshaw St CLVPS L1 7 H6
Back Rockfield Rd
ANF/KKDL L4 54 B3
Back St Bride St EHL/KEN L7 7 K7
Back Sandon St TOX L8 94 B1
Back Sandown La WAV L15 72 D5
Back Sandstone Rd
CLB/OSW/ST L13 72 D1
Back Seaview HOY CH47 87 F1
Back Seel St CLVPS L1 7 F6
Back Sir Howard St EHL/KEN L7 7 K7
Back South Rd CSBY/WL L22 29 F3
Back Stanley Rd BTL L20 5 F4
Back Towerlands St
EHL/KEN L7 71 H4
Back Wellesley Rd TOX L8 94 C4
Back Windsor Vw TOX L8 * 94 D1
Back Winstanley Rd
CSBY/WL L22 29 F2
Back York Ter EV L5 * 54 A4
Badby Wd NWD/KWIPK L33 26 A5
Baddow Cft WLTN L25 97 E5
Baden Rd CLB/OSW/ST L13 73 F2
Bader Cl PEN/TH CH61 134 C3
Badger Bait NSTN CH64 159 E4
Badger Cl RUNC WA7 156 C3
Badgers Pk NSTN CH64 159 E4
Badgers Rake FMBY L37 16 B1
Badger's Set WKBY CH48 110 D5
Badger Wy CL/PREN CH43 114 A3
Badminton St TOX L8 94 B5
Baffin Cl MOR/LEA CH46 67 E1
Bagnall Cl WARRW/BUR WA5 105 G3
Bagnall St ANF/KKDL L4 54 C3
Bagot Av WARRW/BUR WA5 83 F5
Bagot St WAV L15 95 F1
Baguley Av WDN WA8 144 C1
Bailey Dr BTL L20 40 A1
Baileys Cl WDN WA8 102 A3
Baileys La HLWD L26 122 A3
SPK/HALE L24 141 G3
SPK/HALE L24 143 E5
Bailey St CLVPS L1 7 G7
Bailey Wy MGHL L31 23 H2
Bainton Cl KKBY L32 34 B5
Bainton Rd KKBY L32 34 B5
Baird Av BTL L20 4 A2
Baker Rd RUNC WA7 154 B2
Bakers Green Rd HUY L36 75 G1
Bakers St HUY L36 76 A3
Baker St NPK/KEN L6 71 G2
STHEL WA9 48 C4
Baker Wy NPK/KEN L6 71 G2
Bakewell Gv WLT/FAZ L9 31 G5
Bala Cl WARRW/BUR WA5 * 83 E3
Bala Gv WAL/EG CH44 * 68 C2
Bala St ANF/KKDL L4 54 D4
Balcarres Av CALD/MH L18 95 H3
Baldock Cl WARRS WA4 108 C5
Baldwin Av CHLDW L16 74 B5
Baldwin St ECCL WA10 11 G4
The Bales NTHTN L30 23 F5
Balfe St LITH L21 39 E1
Balfour Av BTL L20 * 4 D1
Balfour Rd BTL L20 4 C1
CL/PREN CH43 2 A7
WAL/EG CH44 68 C3
Balfour St ANF/KKDL L4 54 B3

ECCL WA10 10 A6
RUNC WA7 8 C6
Balham Cl WDN WA8 102 A4
Balker Dr ECCL WA10 10 E1
Ballantrae Rd CALD/MH L18 96 C5
Ballantyne Dr CL/PREN CH43 67 G4
Ballantyne Gv BTL L20 40 A1
CLB/OSW/ST L13 55 G3
Ballantyne Pl CLB/OSW/ST L13 55 G3
Ballantyne Rd CLB/OSW/ST L13 55 G4
Ballard Rd WKBY CH48 88 A5
Ballater Dr WARRN/WOL WA2 84 C1
Ball Av WAL/NB CH45 51 G2
Balliol Cl CL/PREN CH43 67 G4
Balliol Gv CSBY/BLUN L23 28 C2
Balliol Rd BTL L20 5 F7
Balliol Rd East BTL L20 5 H6
Ball Pth WDN WA8 124 C2
Ball's Rd CL/PREN CH43 2 B7
Ball's Rd East BIRK CH41 2 B7
Balmer St STHEL WA9 61 F2
Balmoral Av CSBY/BLUN L23 29 F1
STHEL WA9 62 C3
Balmoral Cl NWD/KWIPK L33 25 H4
Balmoral Ct CLB/OSW/ST L13 55 G5
Balmoral Dr FMBY L37 16 D5
Balmoral Gdns
CL/PREN CH43 * 114 B2
Balmoral Gv CL/PREN CH43 90 D5
Balmoral Rd MGHL L31 18 C5
NPK/KEN L6 72 A2
WAL/NB CH45 51 H1
WARRS WA4 130 D1
WDN WA8 102 A4
WLT/FAZ L9 * 40 C1
Balmoral Wy PR/KW L34 58 D5
Balm St EHL/KEN L7 71 H3
Balniel St STHEL WA9 79 H2
Balsham Cl WLTN L25 121 F4
Baltic Rd BTL L20 4 C4
Baltic St ANF/KKDL L4 54 C3
Baltimore Gdns
WARRW/BUR WA5 105 G1
Baltimore St CLVPS L1 7 H6
Bamboo Cl NTHLY L27 98 C2
Bamford Cl RUNC WA7 155 G2
Bampton Av RNFD/HAY WA11 37 F3
Bampton Rd CHLDW L16 73 H5
Banbury Av WLTN L25 121 E1
Banbury Dr WARRW/BUR WA5 105 G4
Banbury Wy CL/PREN CH43 114 A1
Bancroft Cl WLTN L25 121 E4
Bancroft Rd WDN WA8 125 H1
Bandon Cl SPK/HALE L24 143 H4
Banff Av BEB CH63 152 C4
Bangor Rd WAL/NB CH45 50 D4
Bangor St EV L5 53 G5
Bankburn Rd CLB/OSW/ST L13 55 G4
Bank Cl NSTN CH64 159 F4
Bank Dene RF/TRAN CH42 116 A3
Bankes' La RUNC WA7 154 C3
Bankfield Ct CLB/OSW/ST L13 55 H5
Bankfield Rd CLB/OSW/ST L13 55 H5
WDN WA8 123 H2
Bankfields Dr PS/BROM CH62 153 H4
Bankfield St BTL L20 53 F2
Bank Gdns WARRW/BUR WA5 104 C4
Bankhall La BTL L20 53 C3
Bankhall St BTL L20 53 C2
Bankhey NSTN CH64 159 E5
Bankland Rd CLB/OSW/ST L13 55 H5
Bank La MGHL L31 25 F3
NWD/KWIPK L33 25 G5
Bank Rd BTL L20 4 D4
Banks Av HOY CH47 64 D5
Banks Crs WARRS WA4 107 H4
Bankside RUNC WA7 157 G2
WARR WA1 12 A4
Bankside Rd RF/TRAN CH42 115 H3
Bank's La ALL/GAR L19 140 D2
SPK/HALE L24 141 F4
Bank's Rd ALL/GAR L19 140 C1
HES CH60 148 A1
WKBY CH48 110 A2
The Banks WAL/NB CH45 * 51 E3
Bank St BIRK CH41 3 G5
ECCL WA10 10 C6
WARR WA1 12 D5
WDN WA8 146 A2
Bank's Wy ALL/GAR L19 140 D2
Bankville Rd RF/TRAN CH42 92 C5
Banner Hey RAIN/WH L35 76 D4
Bannerman St EHL/KEN L7 72 B5
Banner St ECCL WA10 10 D6
WAV L15 95 G1
Banner Wk ECCL WA10 10 D6
Banning Cl BIRK CH41 2 D3
Banstead Gv WAV L15 96 B1
Barbara Av AIN/FAZ L10 32 D5
Barbara St STHEL WA9 80 A2
Barbauld St WARR WA1 12 D5
Barberry Cl MOR/LEA CH46 65 H5
Barberry Crs NTHTN L30 23 F5
STHEL WA9 48 C3
Barbondale Cl
WARRW/BUR WA5 104 D1
Barbour Dr BTL L20 40 A1
Barbrook Wy WLT/FAZ L9 40 D4
Barchester Dr AIG/SPK L17 118 A2
Barclay St TOX L8 * 94 B4
Barcombe Rd HES CH60 135 H5
Bardley Crs RAIN/WH L35 99 E1
Bardon Cl WLTN L25 98 A3
Bardsay Rd ANF/KKDL L4 54 B1
Bardsley Av WARRW/BUR WA5 83 F3
Barford Cl CL/PREN CH43 90 B2
WARRW/BUR WA5 82 B4
Barford Rd HUY L36 58 D4
WLTN L25 120 D5
Barham Ct GOL/RIS/CUL WA3 85 H1
Barholm CL/PREN CH43 * 91 E4
Barington Dr RUNC WA7 157 G2
Barkbeth Rd HUY L36 58 A5
Barkeley Dr LITH L21 38 D1
Barker Cl HUY L36 75 H5
Barker La GR/UP/WCH CH49 112 A1
Barker Rd PEN/TH CH61 112 D5
Barkerville Cl CLB/OSW/ST L13 55 F3
Barker Wy NPK/KEN L6 54 D5
Barkfield Av FMBY L37 16 D2
Barkfield La FMBY L37 16 C2
FMBY L37 16 D2
Barkhill Ct AIG/SPK L17 * 118 D2
Barkhill Rd AIG/SPK L17 118 D2
Barkiss Cl TOX L8 94 B3
Bark Rd LITH L21 30 B3
Barleyfield PEN/TH CH61 134 C2
Barley Rd WARRS WA4 108 C5
Barlow Av BEB CH63 116 A4
Barlow Gv STHEL WA9 49 G5
Barlow La ANF/KKDL L4 54 A2
Barlows Cl WLT/FAZ L9 32 A4
Barlow's La WLT/FAZ L9 32 A4
Barlow St ANF/KKDL L4 54 A2
Barmouth Cl WARRW/BUR WA5 83 E3
Barmouth Rd WAL/NB CH45 50 D4
Barmouth Wy EV L5 53 G5
Barnack Cl WARR WA1 85 E5
Barnacre La WKBY CH48 88 D2
Barnard Rd CL/PREN CH43 2 A7
Barnard St WARRW/BUR WA5 105 H5
Barn Cl NTHTN L30 23 F5
Barncroft RUNC WA7 157 F2
Barn Croft Rd HLWD L26 122 A4
The Barncroft
GR/UP/WCH CH49 * 89 F4
Barndale Rd CALD/MH L18 95 H4
Barnes Av WARRN/WOL WA2 85 F3
Barnes Cl NWD/KWIPK L33 25 H3
WARRW/BUR WA5 105 E3
WDN WA8 * 125 H1
Barnes Dr MGHL L31 18 C2
Barnes Gn BEB CH63 138 A5
Barnes Rd WDN WA8 125 G1
Barnes St NPK/KEN L6 54 C5
Barneston Rd WDN WA8 103 E5
Barnet Cl EHL/KEN L7 72 A5
Barnfield Av RUNC WA7 157 F3
Barnfield Cl HOY CH47 65 E4
NTHTN L30 30 D2
WD/CROXPK L12 56 B4
Barnfield Dr WD/CROXPK L12 56 B4
Barnfield Rd WARR WA1 108 C1
Barnham Cl SPK/HALE L24 141 H2
Barnham Dr CHLDW L16 97 E1
Barn Hey HOY CH47 87 E3
Barn Hey Crs HOY CH47 65 F5
Barn Hey Gn WD/CROXPK L12 56 B4
Barn Hey Rd NWD/KWIPK L33 34 B2
Barnhill Rd WAV L15 96 A2
Barnhurst Cl CHLDW L16 97 E1
Barnhurst Rd CHLDW L16 97 E1
Barnmeadow Rd WLTN L25 97 G3
Barnsbury Rd ANF/KKDL L4 40 D5
Barnsdale Av PEN/TH CH61 135 F1
Barnside Ct CHLDW L16 97 E1
Barnstaple Wy
WARRW/BUR WA5 104 C4
Barnston La MOR/LEA CH46 66 C4
Barnston Rd HES CH60 149 G1
PEN/TH CH61 113 F4
WLT/FAZ L9 31 F5
Barnston Towers Cl HES CH60 149 G1
Barnstream Cl NTHLY L27 98 A1
Barn St WDN WA8 125 E5
Barnswood Cl WARRS WA4 131 G1
Barnwell Av WAL/EG CH44 51 H5
Barnwood Rd HUY L36 74 D1
Baron Cl WARR WA1 108 D1
Baroncroft Rd WLTN L25 97 F4
Baronet Ms WARRS WA4 129 G2
Baron's Cl WDN WA8 124 A3
Baron's Hey STBRV L28 57 F2
Barren Gv CL/PREN CH43 91 H4
Barrington Rd WAL/EG CH44 69 E2
WAV L15 95 G2
Barrow Av WARRN/WOL WA2 84 C3
Barrow Cl WD/CROXPK L12 56 C1
Barrowfield Rd ECCL WA10 46 C2
Barrow Hall La
WARRW/BUR WA5 104 C1
Barrow's Green La WDN WA8 103 E4
Barrow's Rw WDN WA8 102 B4
Barrow St ECCL WA10 11 G5
Barrule Cl WARRS WA4 130 B4
Barry Dr ALL/GAR L19 119 F5
Barrymore Av WARRS WA4 107 H4
Barrymore Rd CLB/OSW/ST L13 72 D2
RUNC WA7 155 F2
WARRS WA4 131 E2
Barrymore Wy BEB CH63 152 B3
Barry St WARRS WA4 13 G7
Bartholomew Cl RAIN/WH L35 78 C4
Bartlegate RUNC WA7 156 D4
Bartlett St WAV L15 95 G1
Barton Av WARRS WA4 108 A5
Barton Cl ECCL WA10 10 E4
HOY CH47 86 D2
LITH L21 29 H2
RUNC WA7 157 F2
Barton Hey Dr WKBY CH48 110 C5
Barton Heys Rd FMBY L37 16 C5
Barton Rd HOY CH47 87 E2
WLT/FAZ L9 40 B3
Barton St BIRK CH41 2 C5
Barwell Av RNFD/HAY WA11 48 C1
Basil Cl CHLDW L16 74 A5
Basildon Cl STHEL WA9 61 G4
Basil Rd CHLDW L16 73 H5
Basing St ALL/GAR L19 119 G5
Baskervyle Cl HES CH60 149 E3
Baskervyle Rd HES CH60 149 E3
Basnett St CLVPS L1 6 E4
Bassendale Rd
PS/BROM CH62 139 E4
Bassenthwaite Av
CL/PREN CH43 90 D3
NWD/KWIPK L33 25 G5
RNFD/HAY WA11 37 E4
Bates Crs ECCL WA10 61 F2
Batey Av RAIN/WH L35 77 H1
Batherton Cl WDN WA8 14 E6
Bathgate Wy NWD/KWIPK L33 25 G3
Bath St CSBY/WL L22 29 E4
ECCL WA10 10 E6
PS/BROM CH62 138 B1
VAUX/LVPD L3 6 A2
WARR WA1 12 C4
Bathurst Rd ALL/GAR L19 119 F4
Bathwood Dr NSTN CH64 158 D5
Batley St CLB/OSW/ST L13 73 E2
Battenberg St EHL/KEN L7 71 G3
Battersby La WARRN/WOL WA2 13 F2
Battersea Ct WDN WA8 * 101 H5
Battery Cl AIG/SPK L17 118 A1
Battery La WARR WA1 109 F2
Battle Wy FMBY L37 * 17 G4
Baucher Dr BTL L20 30 D5
Baumville Dr BEB CH63 137 H4
Bawtry Ct WARRN/WOL WA2 84 C4
Baxter Cl RUNC WA7 157 F2
Baxters La STHEL WA9 62 D2
Baxter St WARRW/BUR WA5 106 A3
Baycliffe Cl RUNC WA7 155 H4
Baycliff Rd WD/CROXPK L12 57 E2
Bayfield Rd ALL/GAR L19 119 E4
Bayhorse La VAUX/LVPD L3 7 J2
Baysdale Cl TOX L8 94 C4
Bayswater Gdns WAL/NB CH45 50 D3
Bayswater Rd WAL/NB CH45 50 D4
Baythorne Rd ANF/KKDL L4 41 E5
Baytree Gv MGHL L31 32 D1
Bay Tree Gv STHEL WA9 62 C2
Baytree Rd RF/TRAN CH42 92 C5
WKBY CH48 111 F1
Bayview Dr WAL/NB CH45 50 D3
Bayvil Cl RUNC WA7 157 G2
Beach Bank CSBY/WL L22 28 D2
Beachcroft Rd HOY CH47 64 D4
Beach Gv WAL/NB CH45 52 A3
Beach Lawn CSBY/WL L22 28 D3
Beach Rd HOY CH47 86 D2
LITH L21 29 H4
Beach Wk WKBY CH48 110 B3
Beacon Dr WKBY CH48 110 C1
Beacon Gv RNFD/HAY WA11 48 D1
Beacon Hill Vw RUNC WA7 154 B2
Beacon La EV L5 54 B4
HES CH60 149 E1
Beaconsfield Cl RF/TRAN CH42 92 D5
Beaconsfield Crs WDN WA8 102 A4
Beaconsfield Gv WDN WA8 102 B4
Beaconsfield Rd ECCL WA10 47 E2
LITH L21 29 G5
PS/BROM CH62 116 B4
RUNC WA7 154 C1
WDN WA8 102 B5
WLTN L25 97 E5
Beaconsfield St TOX L8 94 C2
Beaconsfield Ter
ALL/GAR L19 * 119 F5
Beacon St EV L5 53 F4
Beadnell Dr WARRW/BUR WA5 104 C5
Beames Cl EHL/KEN L7 72 A4
Beamont St WDN WA8 146 A2
Beatrice Av BEB CH63 115 G4
Beatrice St BTL L20 53 H1
WARRS WA4 107 F5
Beattock Cl NWD/KWIPK L33 25 G3
Beatty Av WARRN/WOL WA2 84 A4
Beatty Cl RAIN/WH L35 76 D3
WKBY CH48 * 110 C5
Beatty Rd CLB/OSW/ST L13 73 E3
Beauclair Dr WAV L15 96 B2
Beaufort FMBY L37 17 F4
Beaufort Cl RUNC WA7 155 F2
WARRW/BUR WA5 105 E3
WDN WA8 123 G3
Beaufort Dr WAL/EG CH44 68 A1
Beaufort Rd BIRK CH41 68 C4
Beaufort St STHEL WA9 62 C1
TOX L8 94 A2
WARRW/BUR WA5 106 A4
Beaumaris Dr PEN/TH CH61 113 F5
Beaumaris Rd WAL/NB CH45 50 D4
Beaumaris St BTL L20 53 F2
Beaumaris Wy RUNC WA7 147 F4
Beaumont Av ECCL WA10 47 E3
Beaumont Dr AIN/FAZ L10 32 B3
Beaumont St TOX L8 94 D1
Beau St VAUX/LVPD L3 71 E2
Beauworth Av
GR/UP/WCH CH49 * 89 E5
Beaver Gv WLT/FAZ L9 40 C1
Bebington Rd PS/BROM CH62 116 A5
RF/TRAN CH42 115 F1
Bechers WDN WA8 100 D5
Bechers Dr WLT/FAZ L9 31 H2
Bechers Rw WLT/FAZ L9 31 E5
Beck Cl AIN/FAZ L10 33 E5
Beckenham Av CALD/MH L18 95 H3
Beckenham Rd WAL/NB CH45 51 H1
Becket St ANF/KKDL L4 53 H3
Beckett Cl NWD/KWIPK L33 34 D4
Beckett Gv BEB CH63 115 F4
Beck Gv RNFD/HAY WA11 37 F4
Beck Rd BTL L20 39 G2
Beckwith St BIRK CH41 2 A1
CLVPS L1 6 E7
Beckwith St East BIRK CH41 2 E3
Becky St NPK/KEN L6 54 D5
Becontree Rd WD/CROXPK L12 73 H1
Bective St EHL/KEN L7 * 72 A5
Bedburn Dr HUY L36 74 C2
Bedford Av MGHL L31 24 B3
RF/TRAN CH42 115 G2
Bedford Cl EHL/KEN L7 7 K7
HUY L36 76 A2
Bedford Dr RF/TRAN CH42 115 F2
Bedford Gdns
RF/TRAN CH42 * 116 A1
Bedford Pl BTL L20 53 F1
LITH L21 * 29 G5
RF/TRAN CH42 116 A1
Bedford Rd ANF/KKDL L4 5 K7
BTL L20 5 H7
RF/TRAN CH42 115 H1
WAL/NB CH45 51 H4
Bedford Rd East
RF/TRAN CH42 116 A1
Bedford St STHEL WA9 48 D5
WARRS WA4 130 A3
Bedford St North EHL/KEN L7 7 K5
Bedford Wk EHL/KEN L7 7 K7
Beecham Cl HUY L36 75 F4
Beech Av AIG/SPK L17 117 H1
CSBY/BLUN L23 21 H3
GR/UP/WCH CH49 89 F2
MGHL L31 33 E1
PEN/TH CH61 135 E2
PR/KW L34 60 B4
STHEL WA9 79 G1
WARRS WA4 108 D5
WARRW/BUR WA5 104 A5
Beechbank Rd CALD/MH L18 95 G3
Beechburn Crs HUY L36 74 D2
Beechburn Rd HUY L36 74 C2
Beech Cl KKBY L32 33 F1
WD/CROXPK L12 42 D4
Beech Ct CALD/MH L18 119 G1
RF/TRAN CH42 92 B4
Beechcroft Rd WAL/EG CH44 69 E3
Beechdale Rd CALD/MH L18 96 A4
Beechdene Rd ANF/KKDL L4 54 D3
Beech Dr FMBY L37 16 C2
The Beeches CALD/MH L18 96 D3
MOR/LEA CH46 66 C2
RF/TRAN CH42 * 116 A2
STHEL WA9 62 D5
Beechfield MGHL L31 19 E5
Beechfield Cl HES CH60 148 D2
HLWD L26 121 G5
Beechfield Rd CALD/MH L18 96 D4
WARRS WA4 131 E2
Beech Gn WD/CROXPK L12 56 A2
Beech Gv LITH L21 38 D1
NTHTN L30 31 F2
WARR WA1 108 A1
WLT/FAZ L9 * 40 D1
Beechill Cl WLTN L25 98 A4
Beech La CALD/MH L18 96 C3
Beech Lawn ALL/GAR L19 118 D4
Beech Mdw PR/KW L34 59 E5
Beech Pk WD/CROXPK L12 56 A4
Beech Rd ANF/KKDL L4 54 C1
BEB CH63 115 H4
HES CH60 149 G1
HUY L36 75 G4
RF/TRAN CH42 92 A4
RUNC WA7 155 G1
WARRS WA4 130 A3
Beech St BTL L20 5 F2
ECCL WA10 * 61 F2
EHL/KEN L7 72 A3
Beech Ter EHL/KEN L7 * 72 A3
Beechtree Rd WAV L15 73 F4
Beechurst Cl WLTN L25 97 H3
Beechurst Rd WLTN L25 97 H3
The Beechwalk
CLB/OSW/ST L13 73 F1
Beechway BEB CH63 137 H3
MGHL L31 19 H4
Beechway Av MGHL L31 19 G4
Beechways Dr NSTN CH64 158 C2
Beechwood Av HLWD L26 121 G4
RUNC WA7 155 G3
WAL/NB CH45 51 E5
WARR WA1 84 C5
WARRW/BUR WA5 104 D3
Beechwood Cl ALL/GAR L19 119 E4
RAIN/WH L35 77 E1
Beechwood Dr CL/PREN CH43 90 B1
FMBY L37 16 B5
Beechwood Gdns
ALL/GAR L19 118 D4
Beechwood Rd ALL/GAR L19 118 D4
LITH L21 39 F1
PS/BROM CH62 152 C1
Beecroft Cl WARRW/BUR WA5 82 D4
Beesands Cl NTHLY L27 98 D4
Beesley Rd PR/KW L34 59 G4
Beeston Cl CL/PREN CH43 90 C2
GOL/RIS/CUL WA3 85 H1
Beeston Dr NTHTN L30 23 G4
PEN/TH CH61 134 C2
Beeston Gv ALL/GAR L19 119 E4
Beeston St ANF/KKDL L4 54 A2
Beetham Wy NWD/KWIPK L33 34 A1
Begonia Gdns STHEL WA9 63 G3
Beldale Pk KKBY L32 25 F5
Beldon Crs HUY L36 74 D2
Belem Cl AIG/SPK L17 95 E3
Belfast Rd CLB/OSW/ST L13 73 F2
Belfield Crs HUY L36 75 G4
Belford Dr CL/PREN CH43 91 H5
Belford Dr MOR/LEA CH46 65 H5
Belfort Rd WLTN L25 97 H4
Belfry Cl MOR/LEA CH46 65 H4
WD/CROXPK L12 57 E4
Belgrave Av WAL/EG CH44 69 E1
WARR WA1 107 H1
Belgrave Cl WDN WA8 103 E5
Belgrave Rd AIG/SPK L17 94 D5
LITH L21 29 G5
Belgrave St WAL/EG CH44 52 A5
Belgravia Ct WDN WA8 101 H5
Belhaven Rd CALD/MH L18 95 H3
Bellair Av CSBY/BLUN L23 21 H5
Bellairs Rd NG/CROX L11 55 G2
Bellamy Rd ANF/KKDL L4 5 K7
Bellcast Cl WARRS WA4 130 A5
Bell Cl HUY L36 75 H5
Belldene Gv HES CH60 134 D4
Bellefield Av WD/CROXPK L12 56 B4
Belle Vale Rd WLTN L25 97 H4
Belle Vue Rd WAL/EG CH44 69 G3
WLTN L25 97 H3
Bellew Rd NG/CROX L11 55 H3
Bellfield Crs WAL/NB CH45 51 G2
Bellflower Cl WDN WA8 101 G4
Bellgreen Rd NG/CROX L11 42 A5
Bellhouse La WARRS WA4 128 D4
WARRS WA4 131 G2
Bell House Rd WDN WA8 15 H2
Bellingham Dr RUNC WA7 155 E1
Bellini Cl LITH L21 38 D2
Bellis Gv NWD/KWIPK L33 * 25 G4
Bell La RAIN/WH L35 79 E3
WARRS WA4 109 E4
Bellmore St ALL/GAR L19 119 G4
Bell Rd WAL/EG CH44 69 F2
Bell's Cl MGHL L31 18 B2
Bell's La MGHL L31 18 A3
Bell St CLB/OSW/ST L13 73 E2
Belltower Rd BTL L20 53 F3
Bellward Cl BEB CH63 137 H4
Belmont BIRK CH41 2 B7
Belmont Av
PS/BROM CH62 138 C5
WARRS WA4 107 H5
Belmont Crs
WARRW/BUR WA5 104 D2
Belmont Dr NPK/KEN L6 55 E5
PEN/TH CH61 135 E3
Belmont Gv CL/PREN CH43 2 B7
NPK/KEN L6 55 E5
Belmont Rd NPK/KEN L6 54 D5
WAL/NB CH45 51 H1
WDN WA8 125 H1
WKBY CH48 87 F5
Belmont St ECCL WA10 10 A6
Beloe St TOX L8 94 B4
Belper St ALL/GAR L19 119 F5
Belsford Wy SPK/HALE L24 141 H2
Belston Rd CHLDW L16 96 D1
Belton Rd HUY L36 58 B4
Belvedere Av STHEL WA9 62 D4
Belvedere Cl PR/KW L34 60 A3
Belvedere Dr FMBY L37 17 E5
Belvidere Pk CSBY/BLUN L23 29 F1
Belvidere Rd CSBY/BLUN L23 29 E1
TOX L8 94 C3
WAL/NB CH45 51 F4
Belvoir Rd CALD/MH L18 119 G3
WARRS WA4 129 H3
WDN WA8 15 F1
Bembridge Cl
WARRW/BUR WA5 104 A1
WDN WA8 101 H4
Bempton Rd AIG/SPK L17 117 H1
Benbow Cl BIRK CH41 68 B5
Benbow St BTL L20 4 C7
Bendee Av NSTN CH64 159 F3
Bendee Rd NSTN CH64 159 E3
Benedict Ct GR/UP/WCH CH49 90 B4
Benedict Ct BTL L20 53 G1
Benedict St BTL L20 53 H1
Bengel St EHL/KEN L7 71 G3
Beniedi St EV L5 53 H5
Benmore Rd CALD/MH L18 119 E1
Bennet's La HOY CH47 65 E3
Bennett Av WARR WA1 107 H2
Bennetts Hl CL/PREN CH43 91 H4
Bennett's La WDN WA8 126 A1
Bennett St ALL/GAR L19 119 G5
WARR WA1 12 E5
Ben Nevis Rd RF/TRAN CH42 115 F1
Bennison Dr ALL/GAR L19 * 119 E4
Ben's Ct PR/KW L34 43 H2
Benson Cl GR/UP/WCH CH49 89 H4
Benson Rd GOL/RIS/CUL WA3 85 H3
Benson St CLVPS L1 7 G5
Bentfield AIG/SPK L17 118 D3
Bentfield Cl BEB CH63 115 F4
Bentfield Gdns BEB CH63 115 F4
Bentham Av WARRN/WOL WA2 84 A2
Bentham Cl CL/PREN CH43 91 E5
Bentham Dr CHLDW L16 73 H5
Bentinck Cl BIRK CH41 2 C4
Bentinck Pl BIRK CH41 2 C5
Bentinck St BIRK CH41 2 C5
EV L5 53 F5
RUNC WA7 8 B3
STHEL WA9 62 D1
Bentley Rd CL/PREN CH43 91 H4
PEN/TH CH61 134 D1
TOX L8 94 D2
Bentley St STHEL WA9 79 G1
Benton Cl EV L5 53 H4
Benty Cl BEB CH63 137 G2
Benty Farm Gv PEN/TH CH61 135 E1
Benwick Rd KKBY L32 33 E3
Berbice Rd WAV L15 96 A2
Beresford Av BEB CH63 116 A5
Beresford Cl CL/PREN CH43 91 G3
Beresford Rd CL/PREN CH43 91 G3
TOX L8 94 B4
WAL/NB CH45 51 F3
Beresford St BTL L20 53 F1
EV L5 71 E1
STHEL WA9 61 G3
WARR WA1 13 K1
Bergen Cl BTL L20 5 J6
Berkeley Av CL/PREN CH43 114 A2
Berkeley Dr WAL/NB CH45 52 A3
Berkeley Rd CSBY/BLUN L23 20 D4
Berkeswell Rd NG/CROX L11 56 A1
Berkley Av WD/CROXPK L12 56 D2
Berkley St TOX L8 94 B1
Berkshire Dr WARR WA1 108 D1
Berkshire Gdns ECCL WA10 47 H5
Bermondsey Gv WDN WA8 102 D4
Bermuda Rd MOR/LEA CH46 66 A4
Bernard Av WAL/NB CH45 * 52 A3
WARRS WA4 130 B3
Berner's Rd ALL/GAR L19 119 F4
Berner St BIRK CH41 2 D1
Berrington Av WLTN L25 120 C1
Berrington's La
RNFD/HAY WA11 36 A2
Berryford Rd DV/KA/FCH L14 57 F4
Berry Hill Av PR/KW L34 44 B4
Berrylands Cl MOR/LEA CH46 66 B4
Berrylands Rd MOR/LEA CH46 66 B3
Berry Rd WDN WA8 124 B2
Berrys La STHEL WA9 63 F1
Berry St BTL L20 4 D5
CLVPS L1 7 G7
Berrywood Dr RAIN/WH L35 77 F3
Bertha Gdns BIRK CH41 68 B5
Bertha St BIRK CH41 68 B5
Bertram Cl HOY CH47 64 D5
Bertram Dr HOY CH47 64 C5
Bertram Dr North HOY CH47 64 D5
Bertram Rd AIG/SPK L17 95 E4
Berwick Av PS/BROM CH62 153 E5
Berwick Cl CL/PREN CH43 * 90 C2
MOR/LEA CH46 65 H5
NPK/KEN L6 71 H1
WARR WA1 109 E2
Berwick Dr CSBY/BLUN L23 20 D4
Berwick St NPK/KEN L6 71 H1
Berwyn Av HOY CH47 * 87 G1
PEN/TH CH61 * 113 E5
Berwyn Bvd BEB CH63 115 G3
Berwyn Dr PEN/TH CH61 134 D4
Berwyn Gv STHEL WA9 49 F4
Berwyn Rd ANF/KKDL L4 55 E2
WAL/EG CH44 52 A5
Beryl Rd CL/PREN CH43 90 C3

Beryl St CLB/OSW/ST L13 73 E4
Besford Rd WLTN L25 97 H3
Bessborough Rd
CL/PREN CH43 91 H4
Bessbrook Rd AIG/SPK L17 118 B1
Bessemer St TOX L8 94 B4
Beta Cl PS/BROM CH62 116 A4
Betchworth Crs RUNC WA7 155 H3
Bethel Gv AIG/SPK L17 95 F2
Betjeman Cl WARRS WA4 107 H4
Betjeman Gv CHLDW L16 74 A5
Betony Cl HLWD L26 121 G2
Bettisfield Av PS/BROM CH62 152 D4
Betula Cl WLT/FAZ L9 41 E3
Bevan Cl STHEL WA9 61 F4
WARRW/BUR WA5 105 H2
Bevan's La WD/CROXPK L12 56 D3
Beverley Av WARRS WA4 130 B3
Beverley Dr HES CH60 149 F2
Beverley Gdns PEN/TH CH61 113 F5
Beverley Rd PS/BROM CH62 116 B3
WAL/NB CH45 51 F4
WARRW/BUR WA5 105 G2
WAV L15 96 A2
Beversbrook Rd NG/CROX L11 42 B5
Bevington Bush VAUX/LVPD L3 70 D2
Bevington St VAUX/LVPD L3 70 D1
Bewey Cl TOX L8 94 A4
Bewley Dr KKBY L32 33 G3
Bewsey Farm Cl
WARRW/BUR WA5 82 D5
Bewsey Park Cl
WARRW/BUR WA5 106 B1
Bewsey Rd WARRW/BUR WA5 106 B1
Bewsey St ECCL WA10 61 F1
WARRN/WOL WA2 12 C3
Bexhill Av WARRN/WOL WA2 83 H1
Bexhill Cl SPK/HALE L24 141 H2
Bexhill Gdns STHEL WA9 61 E4
Bianca St BTL L20 53 G1
Bibby Av WARR WA1 107 G2
Bibby's La BTL L20 4 B1
Bibby St CLB/OSW/ST L13 72 D2
Bickerstaffe St ECCL WA10 11 H5
VAUX/LVPD L3 71 E2
Bickerton Av BEB CH63 115 F3
Bickerton Cl GOL/RIS/CUL WA3 85 H1
Bickerton St AIG/SPK L17 95 E5
Bickley Cl RUNC WA7 9 H7
WARRN/WOL WA2 84 D2
Bicknell Cl WARRW/BUR WA5 82 B5
Bidder St VAUX/LVPD L3 7 H1
Bideford Av STHEL WA9 62 C5
Bideford Rd
WARRW/BUR WA5 104 C4
Bidston Av BIRK CH41 91 F1
RNFD/HAY WA11 48 D2
WAL/NB CH45 51 E4
Bidston Green Ct
CL/PREN CH43 * 67 G5
Bidston Green Dr
CL/PREN CH43 67 G5
Bidston Moss WAL/EG CH44 67 H2
Bidston Rd ANF/KKDL L4 54 D2
CL/PREN CH43 91 F2
Bidston Station Ap
CL/PREN CH43 67 G3
Bidston Village Rd
CL/PREN CH43 67 G4
Bidston Wy RNFD/HAY WA11 48 D2
Bigdale Dr NWD/KWIPK L33 34 B1
Biggin Ct WARRN/WOL WA2 84 C4
Bigham Rd NPK/KEN L6 72 A2
Biglands Dr HUY L36 75 H5
Big Meadow Rd
GR/UP/WCH CH49 90 A4
Billinge Crs RNFD/HAY WA11 48 D1
Billingham Rd STHEL WA9 61 F3
Billings Cl EV L5 53 G4
Billington Cl WARRW/BUR WA5 81 G5
Billington Rd WDN WA8 100 D4
Bilston Rd AIG/SPK L17 118 C3
Bilton Cl WDN WA8 126 A1
Bingley Rd ANF/KKDL L4 54 D3
Binns Rd CLB/OSW/ST L13 72 D3
EHL/KEN L7 72 C3
Binns Wy CLB/OSW/ST L13 72 D4
Binsey Cl GR/UP/WCH CH49 89 F3
Birbeck Rd NWD/KWIPK L33 34 B1
Birchall St BTL L20 53 G3
Birch Av ECCL WA10 47 H1
GR/UP/WCH CH49 89 F2
WARRN/WOL WA2 83 G1
WLT/FAZ L9 40 D1
Birchcliffe Rd RF/TRAN CH42 115 H1
Birch Cl CL/PREN CH43 91 H5
MGHL L31 19 F5
RAIN/WH L35 77 E1
Birchdale Cl GR/UP/WCH CH49 89 F3
Birchdale Ct WARRS WA4 130 A3
Birchdale Crs WARRS WA4 130 A3
Birchdale Rd CSBY/WL L22 29 E2
WARR WA1 108 A1
WARRS WA4 130 A4
WLT/FAZ L9 40 C2
Birchen Rd HLWD L26 122 A4
Birches Cl HES CH60 135 E5
The Birches FMBY L37 16 D1
STBRV L28 57 G3
WAL/EG CH44 69 G3
Birchfield MOR/LEA CH46 89 E1
Birchfield Av WDN WA8 125 E1
Birchfield Cl EHL/KEN L7 72 C3
MOR/LEA CH46 89 E2
Birchfield Rd ANF/KKDL L4 54 C1
EHL/KEN L7 72 C3
WARRW/BUR WA5 105 F3
WDN WA8 102 A5
Birchfield St STHEL WA9 61 F3
VAUX/LVPD L3 7 H1
Birchfield Wy MGHL L31 18 B1
Birch Gdns ECCL WA10 47 H1
Birch Gn FMBY L37 16 C1
Birch Gv HUY L36 75 F3
RAIN/WH L35 77 E1
WAL/NB CH45 52 A3
WARR WA1 107 H1
WARRS WA4 107 F5
WAV L15 73 E4
Birch Heys WKBY CH48 111 G2
Birchill Rd NWD/KWIPK L33 34 D2
Birchley Av
WGNW/BIL/OR WN5 37 G1
Birchley Rd RNFD/HAY WA11 37 F1
WGNW/BIL/OR WN5 37 G1
Birchley St ECCL WA10 11 H3
Birchley Vw RNFD/HAY WA11 37 F2
Birchmere HES CH60 134 C4
Birchmuir Hey KKBY L32 34 A3
Birchridge Cl PS/BROM CH62 138 C4
Birch Rd BEB CH63 138 A2
CL/PREN CH43 91 H5
HOY CH47 65 E5
HUY L36 75 G4
RUNC WA7 155 G1
WDN WA8 102 A5
Birch St EV L5 53 F5
Birch Tree Av RNFD/HAY WA11 36 D4
Birch Tree Ct WD/CROXPK L12 56 A4
Birchtree Dr MGHL L31 32 D1
Birchtree Rd AIG/SPK L17 95 G5
Birchview Wy CL/PREN CH43 90 D3
Birchway HES CH60 149 G3
Birchwood Av BIRK CH41 2 E3
Birchwood Bvd
GOL/RIS/CUL WA3 85 H3
Birchwood Cl BIRK CH41 2 E3
Birchwood Wy
NWD/KWIPK L33 26 B4
WARRN/WOL WA2 85 E4
Bird St EHL/KEN L7 95 E1
Birdwell Dr WARRW/BUR WA5 105 E3
Birdwood Rd NG/CROX L11 55 H2
Birkdale Av BEB CH63 152 C3
Birkdale Cl HUY L36 75 E4
NPK/KEN L6 55 F4
Birkdale Rd WARRW/BUR WA5 104 D4
WDN WA8 102 B3
Birkenhead Rd HOY CH47 64 C5
WAL/EG CH44 69 G4
Birkenshaw Av CSBY/BLUN L23 20 C5
Birket Av MOR/LEA CH46 66 D2
Birket Cl MOR/LEA CH46 67 E2
Birket Sq MOR/LEA CH46 66 D2
Birkett Rd RF/TRAN CH42 115 G2
WKBY CH48 87 F4
Birkett St VAUX/LVPD L3 7 G1
Birkey La FMBY L37 17 E4
Birkin Cl KKBY L32 34 B4
Birkin Rd KKBY L32 34 B4
Birnam Dr RAIN/WH L35 78 B3
Birnam Rd WAL/EG CH44 69 F2
Birstall Av RNFD/HAY WA11 48 C2
Birstall Ct RUNC WA7 155 H2
Birstall Rd NPK/KEN L6 71 H2
Birt Cl TOX L8 94 D1
Birtles Rd WARRN/WOL WA2 84 A4
Bishopdale Cl
WARRW/BUR WA5 104 D1
Bishopdale Dr RAIN/WH L35 78 B3
Bishop Dr RAIN/WH L35 76 D4
Bishopgate St WAV L15 95 G1
Bishop Rd ECCL WA10 10 D2
NPK/KEN L6 55 E3
WAL/EG CH44 68 D3
Bishops Ct WARRN/WOL WA2 83 F1
WLTN L25 120 D1
Bishop Sheppard Ct
VAUX/LVPD L3 70 C1
Bishops Wy WDN WA8 102 D5
Bisley St WAL/NB CH45 51 H5
WAV L15 95 G1
Bispham Dr HOY CH47 88 A1
Bispham Rd
WARRW/BUR WA5 105 F4
Bittern Cl RUNC WA7 157 F1
WARRN/WOL WA2 84 B2
Bixteth St VAUX/LVPD L3 6 C2
Blackberry Gv HLWD L26 121 F1
Blackbrook Av
WARRN/WOL WA2 84 C2
Blackbrook Cl WDN WA8 101 E5
WLT/FAZ L9 40 C4
Blackbrook Rd
RNFD/HAY WA11 49 E2
Blackburne Av WDN WA8 144 D1
Blackburne Cl
WARRN/WOL WA2 85 G3
Blackburne Dr WLTN L25 121 F4
Blackburne Pl TOX L8 7 J7
Blackburne St ALL/GAR L19 140 D3
Blackburne Ter TOX L8 7 J7
Blackburn Ter TOX L8 94 B1
Black Denton's Pl WDN WA8 15 H2
Blackdown Gv STHEL WA9 49 F5
Blackeys La NSTN CH64 158 D2
Blackfield St EV L5 53 H4
Blackheath Dr MOR/LEA CH46 66 D2
Black Horse Cl WKBY CH48 87 G5
Black Horse Hl WKBY CH48 110 C1
Black Horse La
CLB/OSW/ST L13 73 F2
Black Horse Pl CLB/OSW/ST L13 73 F2
Blackhorse St STHEL WA9 48 C3
Blackhurst Rd MGHL L31 18 C1
Blackhurst St WARR WA1 12 E5
Blackledge Cl
WARRN/WOL WA2 85 E2
Blackley Cl WARRS WA4 107 F5
Blackley Gv NWD/KWIPK L33 * 26 B3
Blacklock Hall Rd
SPK/HALE L24 142 A3
Blacklow Brow HUY L36 75 F3
Blackmoor Dr WD/CROXPK L12 56 C4
Blackpool St BIRK CH41 3 G6
Blackrod Av SPK/HALE L24 142 A3
Blackshaw Dr
WARRW/BUR WA5 82 B4
Blacksmith Pl WLTN L25 121 F3
Blackstock St VAUX/LVPD L3 70 C2
Blackstone Av RNFD/HAY WA11 48 D2
Blackstone St EV L5 53 F5
Blackthorn Cl MOR/LEA CH46 89 H1
Blackthorne Crs STBRV L28 57 H2
Blackthorne Rd WLT/FAZ L9 41 E4
Blackwater Rd NG/CROX L11 42 D3
Blackwood Av WLTN L25 97 F4
Blair Dr WDN WA8 100 D5
Blair Pk BEB CH63 138 B3
Blair St TOX L8 94 A1
Blaisdon Cl NG/CROX L11 56 A1
Blakeacre Cl HLWD L26 121 H5
Blakeacre Rd HLWD L26 121 H5
Blakefield Rd CSBY/BLUN L23 22 B3
Blakeley Brow BEB CH63 152 A3
Blakeley Ct BEB CH63 152 A3
Blakeley Dell BEB CH63 152 B3
Blakeley Dene BEB CH63 152 B2
Blakeley Rd BEB CH63 152 A2
Blakeney Cl GR/UP/WCH CH49 90 A1
Blakenhall Wy
GR/UP/WCH CH49 89 F2
Blaking Dr PR/KW L34 44 B3
Blandford Rd
WARRW/BUR WA5 105 F3
Blantyre Rd WAV L15 95 G2
Blantyre St RUNC WA7 8 B2
Blay Cl WLTN L25 121 F3
Blaydon Cl NTHTN L30 31 E3
Blaydon Gv STHEL WA9 61 F3
Blaydon Wk CL/PREN CH43 91 E2
Bleak Hill Cl ECCL WA10 36 A5
Bleak Hill Rd ECCL WA10 46 D1
Bleasdale Av AIN/FAZ L10 32 B2
Bleasdale Cl GR/UP/WCH CH49 89 G2
Bleasdale Rd CALD/MH L18 96 B4
Blenheim Av LITH L21 30 B4
Blenheim Cl WARRN/WOL WA2 84 C3
Blenheim Dr PR/KW L34 58 D5
Blenheim Rd CALD/MH L18 * 95 H3
WAL/EG CH44 52 B5
Blenheim St EV L5 70 C1
Blenheim Wy RNFD/HAY WA11 48 B1
SPK/HALE L24 141 H3
Blessington Rd ANF/KKDL L4 54 B3
Bletchley Av WAL/EG CH44 68 B1
Bligh St WAV L15 95 G1
Blisworth St LITH L21 39 F1
Blomfield Rd ALL/GAR L19 119 H3
Bloomsbury Wy WDN WA8 101 F5
Blossom Gv KKBY L32 34 A5
Blossom St BTL L20 5 F1
Blirtley Ct WDN WA8 123 H1
Blucher St CSBY/WL L22 28 D3
Bluebell Av BIRK CH41 68 B5
Bluebell Cl CSBY/WL L22 29 F3
KKBY L32 25 H5
Bluebell Ct RUNC WA7 156 B5
Blue Bell La HUY L36 75 G1
Blueberry Flds AIN/FAZ L10 41 H1
Bluecoat Chambers CLVPS L1 * 6 E5
Bluecoat St WARRN/WOL WA2 12 D1
Bluefields St TOX L8 94 B1
Blue Jay Cl NTHLY L27 98 C3
Blue Ridge Cl
WARRW/BUR WA5 104 C1
Bluestone La MGHL L31 19 E5
Bluewood Dr BIRK CH41 67 H4
Blundell Av FMBY L37 16 A2
Blundell Rd RAIN/WH L35 60 B5
WDN WA8 124 B3
Blundellsands Rd East
CSBY/BLUN L23 20 D5
Blundellsands Rd West
CSBY/BLUN L23 28 C1
Blundells Dr MOR/LEA CH46 66 C4
Blundell's La RAIN/WH L35 77 G4
Blundell St CLVPS L1 93 H1
Blyth Cl RUNC WA7 157 F4
Blythe Av WDN WA8 102 B4
Blyth Hey NTHTN L30 30 C1
Blyth Rd BEB CH63 152 C2
Blythswood St AIG/SPK L17 94 D5
Boaler St NPK/KEN L6 71 H2
Boardmans La RNFD/HAY WA11 49 E3
Bobbies La ECCL WA10 46 C3
Bodden St STHEL WA9 79 H1
Boddington Dr WARRS WA4 131 E5
Bodley St ANF/KKDL L4 * 54 B3
Bodmin Cl RUNC WA7 156 D3
Bodmin Gv RNFD/HAY WA11 37 H5
Bodmin Rd ANF/KKDL L4 54 B1
Bodmin Wy HLWD L26 121 G3
Bognor Cl SPK/HALE L24 141 H2
Bolan St CLB/OSW/ST L13 73 E2
Bolden Cl NTHTN L30 31 E3
Bolde Wy BEB CH63 138 A5
Bold Pl CLVPS L1 7 G6
Bold Rd STHEL WA9 63 F3
Bold St CLVPS L1 7 F5
ECCL WA10 10 E6
RUNC WA7 9 F3
WARR WA1 12 C5
WDN WA8 14 C6
The Boleyn MGHL L31 19 E3
Bollington Cl CL/PREN CH43 91 F5
Bolton Av KKBY L32 33 F2
WARRS WA4 107 H4
Bolton Cl FMBY L37 17 F4
Bolton Rd PS/BROM CH62 116 C5
Bolton Rd East
PS/BROM CH62 116 C5
Bolton St STHEL WA9 48 C3
VAUX/LVPD L3 7 G4
Bonchurch Dr WAV L15 72 D4
Bond Cl WARRW/BUR WA5 105 H4
Bond St PR/KW L34 59 H4
VAUX/LVPD L3 70 D1
Bonnington Av CSBY/BLUN L23 20 D4
Bonnington Cl ECCL WA10 47 E4
Bonsall Rd WD/CROXPK L12 56 B4
Boode Cft STBRV L28 57 H1
Booker Av CALD/MH L18 119 F2
Booth St CLB/OSW/ST L13 73 E2
STHEL WA9 61 F3
WARRW/BUR WA5 106 A4
Boothwood Cl EHL/KEN L7 * 71 H4
Borax St CLB/OSW/ST L13 73 E3
Bordehill Gdns
WD/CROXPK L12 56 D2
Border Rd HES CH60 149 F1
Border Wy EV L5 54 A4
Borella Rd CLB/OSW/ST L13 55 H4
Borough Pavement BIRK CH41 * 3 F5
Borough Pl BIRK CH41 * 3 G5
Borough Rd BIRK CH41 2 D6
ECCL WA10 10 C7
RF/TRAN CH42 2 C7
WAL/EG CH44 69 F2
Borough Rd East BIRK CH41 3 G5
WAL/EG CH44 * 69 G3
Borough Wy WAL/EG CH44 69 G3
Borrowdale FMBY L37 17 E1
Borrowdale Av
WARRN/WOL WA2 83 H2
Borrowdale Rd BEB CH63 137 G2
ECCL WA10 60 D2
MOR/LEA CH46 66 B5
WAV L15 95 G2
WDN WA8 124 A3
Boscow Crs STHEL WA9 62 D3
Bosnia St TOX L8 94 C5
Bostock St EV L5 53 H5
WARRW/BUR WA5 106 A2
Boston Av RUNC WA7 9 J7
Boston Bvd WARRW/BUR WA5 82 B5
WARRW/BUR WA5 105 E1
WARRW/BUR WA5 105 F2
Boswell Av WARRS WA4 129 H1
Boswell Rd CL/PREN CH43 114 B2
Boswell St BTL L20 4 B1
TOX L8 95 E1
Bosworth Cl BEB CH63 137 H4
Bosworth Rd RNFD/HAY WA11 48 C1
Botanic Gv EHL/KEN L7 72 A3
Botanic Pl EHL/KEN L7 72 A3
Botanic Rd EHL/KEN L7 72 A4
Botany Rd SPK/HALE L24 142 A1
Boteler Av WARRW/BUR WA5 106 B1
Botley Cl GR/UP/WCH CH49 * 89 F3
The Boulevard
WD/CROXPK L12 56 B2
Boulting Av WARRW/BUR WA5 83 F3
Boulton Av PS/BROM CH62 116 B3
WKBY CH48 87 F4
Boundary Dr CSBY/BLUN L23 20 D3
WLTN L25 121 F4
Boundary Farm Rd HLWD L26 121 F5
Boundary La HES CH60 149 E1
NPK/KEN L6 71 H1
NWD/KWIPK L33 35 G2
Boundary Pk NSTN CH64 158 C2
Boundary Rd CL/PREN CH43 67 H5
ECCL WA10 10 C6
HUY L36 75 H5
LITH L21 30 C2
PS/BROM CH62 116 B4
WKBY CH48 110 D3
Boundary St EV L5 53 F4
Boundary St East EV L5 53 H4
Bourchier Wy WARRS WA4 131 E3
Bourne Gdns STHEL WA9 62 B1
Bournemouth Cl RUNC WA7 157 F3
Bourton Rd WLTN L25 120 D5
Bousfield St ANF/KKDL L4 * 54 A3
Bowden Cl ECCL WA10 46 D4
WD/CROXPK L12 43 E5
Bowden Rd ALL/GAR L19 119 F5
Bowden St LITH L21 39 F1
Bowdon Cl WARR WA1 * 84 D5
Bowdon Rd WAL/NB CH45 51 G4
Bowen Cl WDN WA8 101 F4
Bower Gv LITH L21 29 G5
Bower Rd HES CH60 149 G1
HUY L36 75 G1
WLTN L25 97 G4
Bower St WDN WA8 15 G1
Bowfield Rd ALL/GAR L19 119 F4
Bowgreen Cl CL/PREN CH43 90 C1
Bowland Av CHLDW L16 73 H4
STHEL WA9 79 E2
Bowland Cl PS/BROM CH62 138 D5
RUNC WA7 156 A4
Bowland Dr LITH L21 22 B5
Bowles St BTL L20 39 E2
Bowley Rd CLB/OSW/ST L13 55 H5
Bowman Av WARRS WA4 108 A3
Bowness Av BEB CH63 152 C4
CL/PREN CH43 114 C1
RNFD/HAY WA11 37 F4
WARRN/WOL WA2 84 A3
Bowood Ct WARRN/WOL WA2 83 G1
Bowood St TOX L8 94 B5
Bowring Cl TOX L8 * 94 C4
Bowring Dr NSTN CH64 158 A1
Bowring Park Av CHLDW L16 74 C4
Bowring Park Rd
DV/KA/FCH L14 73 G4
Bowring St TOX L8 * 94 C4
Bowscale Cl
GR/UP/WCH CH49 * 89 G3
Bowscale Rd NG/CROX L11 56 A1
Boxdale Rd CALD/MH L18 96 A4
Boxgrove Cl WDN WA8 102 B5
Boxmoor Rd CALD/MH L18 119 E1
Boxtree Cl WD/CROXPK L12 43 F3
Boxwood Cl HUY L36 75 E3
Boycott St EV L5 54 C4
Boyd Cl MOR/LEA CH46 67 F2
Boydell Av WARRS WA4 107 H4
Boydell Cl STBRV L28 57 H3
Boyer Av MGHL L31 24 A2
Boyes Brow NWD/KWIPK L33 25 G5
Boyle Av WARRN/WOL WA2 84 C4
Boyton Ct EHL/KEN L7 72 A5
Brabant Rd AIG/SPK L17 118 C2
Braby Rd LITH L21 39 G1
Bracewell Cl STHEL WA9 62 C4
Bracken Ct STHEL WA9 79 G1
Brackendale GR/UP/WCH CH49 90 C5
RUNC WA7 155 H1
WLT/FAZ L9 * 31 G5
Brackendale Av WLT/FAZ L9 31 G5
Bracken Dr WKBY CH48 111 E1
Brackenhurst Dr WAL/NB CH45 52 A3
Brackenhurst Gn
NWD/KWIPK L33 33 H2
Bracken La BEB CH63 137 F1
Brackenside HES CH60 * 134 D4
Bracken Wd WD/CROXPK L12 43 E3
Brackenwood Dr WDN WA8 123 G1
Brackenwood Gv RAIN/WH L35 77 F2
Brackenwood Rd BEB CH63 137 F1
Brackley Cl WAL/EG CH44 68 C2
Brackley St RUNC WA7 8 B3
WARRS WA4 130 A2
Bracknell Av KKBY L32 33 G4
Bracknell Cl KKBY L32 33 G3
Bradbourne Cl
WD/CROXPK L12 43 E4
Bradda Cl GR/UP/WCH CH49 89 H1
Braddan Av CLB/OSW/ST L13 * 55 G5
Bradden Cl BEB CH63 138 B4
Bradewell Cl ANF/KKDL L4 54 A2
Bradewell St ANF/KKDL L4 54 A2
Bradfield Av AIN/FAZ L10 31 H1
Bradfield St EHL/KEN L7 72 A3
Bradgate Cl MOR/LEA CH46 65 H4
Bradley Bvd
WARRW/BUR WA5 105 F2
Bradley Fold HUY L36 76 A5
Bradley Rd LITH L21 30 A3
Bradley Wy WDN WA8 15 F2
Bradman Rd MOR/LEA CH46 66 A4
NWD/KWIPK L33 34 D1
Bradmoor Rd PS/BROM CH62 152 D1
Bradshaw Cl ECCL WA10 10 A3
Bradshaw La WARRS WA4 108 B5
Bradshaw St WDN WA8 125 E1
Bradstone Cl AIN/FAZ L10 42 B1
Bradville Rd WLT/FAZ L9 31 H5
Bradwell Cl WKBY CH48 110 D1
Braehaven Rd WAL/NB CH45 52 A3
Braemar Cl RAIN/WH L35 77 F2
WARRN/WOL WA2 85 E2
Braemar St BTL L20 * 53 H1
Braemore Rd WAL/EG CH44 68 B1
Braeside Gdns
GR/UP/WCH CH49 89 H3
Brae St EHL/KEN L7 71 H3
Brahms Cl TOX L8 94 D2
Braid St BIRK CH41 2 D1
Brainerd St CLB/OSW/ST L13 55 G5
Braithwaite Cl RAIN/WH L35 78 A2
RUNC WA7 155 H4
Brakenwood Ms
WARRS WA4 * 131 G2
Bramberton Pl ANF/KKDL L4 55 E1
Bramberton Rd ANF/KKDL L4 55 E1
Bramble Av BIRK CH41 68 B5
Bramble Cl WARRW/BUR WA5 104 C5
The Brambles
NWD/KWIPK L33 * 34 C3
Bramble Wy MOR/LEA CH46 66 B3
RUNC WA7 156 A5
Bramblewood Cl
CL/PREN CH43 90 C4
NTHLY L27 98 C3
Brambling Cl RUNC WA7 156 A4
Brambling Pk HLWD L26 121 G2
Bramcote Av RNFD/HAY WA11 48 D1
Bramcote Cl NWD/KWIPK L33 26 B5
Bramcote Rd NWD/KWIPK L33 26 A5
Bramcote Wk NWD/KWIPK L33 26 A5
Bramerton Ct WKBY CH48 86 D5
Bramford Cl GR/UP/WCH CH49 89 G3
Bramhall Cl SPK/HALE L24 142 C4
WKBY CH48 110 D2
Bramhall Rd CSBY/WL L22 29 F4
Bramhall St WARRW/BUR WA5 106 A3
Bramley Av BEB CH63 115 G4
Bramley Cl NTHLY L27 98 C3
Bramley Ms WARRS WA4 130 A3
Bramley Moore Dock
VAUX/LVPD L3 * 53 F4
The Bramleys MGHL L31 23 H2
Brampton Cl KKBY L32 25 H5
Brampton Ct STHEL WA9 49 H4
Brampton Dr TOX L8 71 G5
Bramwell Av CL/PREN CH43 114 C2
Bramwell St STHEL WA9 49 E3
Brancker Av RAIN/WH L35 77 H1
Brancote Gdns
PS/BROM CH62 152 D2
Brancote Mt CL/PREN CH43 * 91 F2
Brancote Rd CL/PREN CH43 91 F2
Brandearth Hey STBRV L28 57 H3
Brandon WDN WA8 123 G1
Brandon St BIRK CH41 3 H4
Brandreth Cl RAIN/WH L35 78 A2
Brandwood Av
WARRN/WOL WA2 83 H3
Branfield Cl WD/CROXPK L12 43 E4
Bransdale Cl
WARRW/BUR WA5 104 C1
Branstree Av NG/CROX L11 41 H5
Brantfield Ct WARRN/WOL WA2 84 C3
Branthwaite Cl NG/CROX L11 56 A1
Branthwaite Crs NG/CROX L11 56 A1
Branthwaite Gv NG/CROX L11 56 A1
Brasenose Rd BTL L20 53 F1
Brassey St BIRK CH41 68 D5
Brathay Cl WARRN/WOL WA2 84 A2
Brattan Rd BIRK CH41 92 A4
Braunton Rd AIG/SPK L17 118 C3
WAL/NB CH45 51 G4
Braybrooke Rd NG/CROX L11 42 A4
Bray Cl RUNC WA7 155 H3
Braydon Cl WLTN L25 * 121 E5
Brayfield Rd ANF/KKDL L4 55 F1
Bray Rd SPK/HALE L24 142 A2
Bray St BIRK CH41 68 D5
Brechin Rd NWD/KWIPK L33 34 A2
Breckfield Pl EV L5 * 54 B5
Breckfield Rd North EV L5 54 B4
Breckfield Rd South EV L5 54 C5
Breck Pl WAL/EG CH44 68 C2
Breck Rd NPK/KEN L6 54 C5
WAL/EG CH44 51 F5
WDN WA8 15 F1
Breckside Av WAL/EG CH44 68 A1
Breckside Pk NPK/KEN L6 55 E4
Brecon Av NTHTN L30 31 E3
Brecon Rd RF/TRAN CH42 115 E2
Brecon Wk NTHTN L30 31 F3
Breeze Hl ANF/KKDL L4 40 B5
BTL L20 5 K6
Breezehill Cl NSTN CH64 158 D2
Breezehill Pk NSTN CH64 159 E2
Breezehill Rd NSTN CH64 159 E2
Breeze La WLT/FAZ L9 40 B4
Brelade Rd CLB/OSW/ST L13 72 D1
Bremhill Rd NG/CROX L11 41 H4
Bremner Cl EHL/KEN L7 72 A4
Brenda Crs CSBY/BLUN L23 21 H2
Brendale Av MGHL L31 23 H1
Brendon Av LITH L21 29 H3
WARRN/WOL WA2 83 G2
Brendon Gv STHEL WA9 * 49 G3
Brendor Rd WLTN L25 120 D2

Brenig St BIRK CH41 68 B4
Brenka Av WLT/FAZ L9 31 G3
Brentfield WDN WA8 124 C1
Brentnall Cl
WARRW/BUR WA5 * 105 G3
Brent Wy HLWD L26 121 H5
Brentwood Av AIG/SPK L17 95 E5
CSBY/BLUN L23 21 G4
Brentwood Cl ECCL WA10 46 D4
Brentwood St WAL/EG CH44 69 E3
Brereton Av BEB CH63 116 A5
WAV L15 96 A1
Brereton Cl RUNC WA7 156 C1
Bretherton Pl RAIN/WH L35 78 A1
Bretherton Rd PR/KW L34 60 A4
Bretland Dr WARRS WA4 131 E4
Bretlands Rd CSBY/BLUN L23 22 A4
Brett St BIRK CH41 68 D5
Brewery La MGHL L31 24 B5
Brewster St ANF/KKDL L4 54 A1
Breydon Gdns STHEL WA9 61 G4
Brian Av PEN/TH CH61 112 D5
WARRN/WOL WA2 84 B5
WARRS WA4 130 C2
Briardale Rd BEB CH63 115 H4
CALD/MH L18 95 H4
RF/TRAN CH42 92 A4
WAL/EG CH44 69 G3
Briar Dr HES CH60 149 E1
HUY L36 75 F3
Briarfield Av WDN WA8 123 G2
Briarfield Rd HES CH60 149 E1
Briars Cl RAIN/WH L35 78 B4
Briars Gn ECCL WA10 10 E2
Briars La MGHL L31 19 E5
Briar St ANF/KKDL L4 53 H3
Briarswood Cl RAIN/WH L35 77 F2
RF/TRAN CH42 115 H3
Briarwood CSBY/BLUN L23 20 C3
Briarwood Av WARR WA1 107 G1
Briarwood Rd AIG/SPK L17 95 G5
Briary Cl HES CH60 135 F5
Brickfields HUY L36 76 A4
Brickhurst Wy WARR WA1 85 F5
Brick St CLVPS L1 93 H1
WARR WA1 13 F4
Brickwall Gn SFTN L29 23 E2
Brickwall La SFTN L29 22 D3
Bride St ANF/KKDL L4 40 B5
Bridge Av WARRS WA4 107 H4
Bridge Av East WARRS WA4 107 H3
Bridge Ct NSTN CH64 158 D3
STHEL WA9 * 79 H2
WKBY CH48 87 E5
Bridge Cft LITH L21 30 B1
Bridgecroft Rd WAL/NB CH45 51 H4
Bridge Farm Cl
GR/UP/WCH CH49 90 B4
Bridge Farm Dr MGHL L31 19 F4
Bridgefield Cl WLTN L25 97 H1
Bridgeford Av WD/CROXPK L12 56 A3
Bridge Gdns WD/CROXPK L12 57 F1
Bridge La NTHTN L30 30 D1
WARR WA1 108 C2
WARRS WA4 130 C4
Bridgeman St ECCL WA10 10 B6
WARRW/BUR WA5 105 H4
Bridgend Cl WDN WA8 101 F5
Bridgenorth Rd PEN/TH CH61 134 C2
Bridge Rd CALD/MH L18 96 A5
CSBY/BLUN L23 28 D1
EHL/KEN L7 72 B5
HUY L36 75 E3
LITH L21 29 H5
MGHL L31 24 A2
PR/KW L34 59 H5
STHEL WA9 79 H3
WARR WA1 108 C1
WKBY CH48 87 E5
Bridges La SFTN L29 23 E2
BIRK CH41 3 H3
Bridge St BIRK CH41 3 F2
BTL L20 4 D7
ECCL WA10 11 F6
NSTN CH64 158 D3
RUNC WA7 9 F4
WARR WA1 12 D5
Bridge View Cl WDN WA8 146 A2
Bridgeview Dr
NWD/KWIPK L33 26 A5
Bridge Wk RUNC WA7 * 156 B2
Bridgewater Av WARRS WA4 107 H4
Bridgewater Cl LITH L21 29 H2
Bridgewater Gra RUNC WA7 157 H3
Bridgewater Ms WARRS WA4 130 A3
Bridgewater St CLVPS L1 93 H1
RUNC WA7 8 D3
Bridgewater Wy HUY L36 76 A5
Bridgeway NG/CROX L11 55 G1
Bridgeway West RUNC WA7 147 H4
Bridle Av WAL/EG CH44 69 G3
Bridle Cl CL/PREN CH43 90 B2
PS/BROM CH62 153 E2
Bridle Ct STHEL WA9 62 C2
Bridlemere Ct WARR WA1 84 C5
Bridle Pk PS/BROM CH62 152 D2
Bridle Rd NTHTN L30 31 F4
PS/BROM CH62 153 E2
WAL/EG CH44 69 G3
Bridle Wy NTHTN L30 31 E4
NWD/KWIPK L33 25 G3
Bridport St VAUX/LVPD L3 7 G3
Brierfield Rd WAV L15 95 H2
Brierley Cl NTHTN L30 23 G5
Brierley St WARRW/BUR WA5 * 12 A3
Briers Cl WARRN/WOL WA2 84 D2
Briery Hey Av NWD/KWIPK L33 34 A2
Brigadier Dr WD/CROXPK L12 57 E3
Brightgate Cl EHL/KEN L7 * 71 H5
Brighton Rd CSBY/WL L22 29 E3
HUY L36 76 B2
Brighton St WAL/EG CH44 69 G2
WARRW/BUR WA5 106 A2
Brighton V CSBY/WL L22 28 D2
Bright St BIRK CH41 2 C5
NPK/KEN L6 71 G2
Brightwell Cl
GR/UP/WCH CH49 * 89 H4
WARRW/BUR WA5 104 C3
Brill St BIRK CH41 68 D5
Brimelow Crs
WARRW/BUR WA5 104 C5
Brimstage Av BEB CH63 115 F3
Brimstage Cl HES CH60 149 G1
Brimstage Gn HES CH60 * 149 H1
Brimstage La BEB CH63 136 D2
Brimstage Rd ANF/KKDL L4 5 K6
BEB CH63 137 E4
BEB CH63 137 H3
HES CH60 149 G1
Brimstage St BIRK CH41 92 A4
Brindley Av WARRS WA4 107 H4
Brindley Cl LITH L21 29 H2
Brindley Rd KKBY L32 33 F2
RUNC WA7 147 E2
STHEL WA9 63 E4
Brindley St RUNC WA7 8 C3
TOX L8 93 H2
Brindley Whf WARRS WA4 157 H3
Brinley Cl PS/BROM CH62 152 D4
Brinton Cl NTHLY L27 98 A2
WDN WA8 124 C3
Brisbane Av WAL/NB CH45 51 G2
Brisbane St STHEL WA9 61 F3
Briscoe Dr MOR/LEA CH46 89 G1
Bristol Av RUNC WA7 157 G3
WAL/EG CH44 69 E1
Bristol Rd WAV L15 96 A2
Bristow Cl WARRW/BUR WA5 82 B5
Britannia Av WAV L15 95 F1
Britannia Crs TOX L8 94 B5
Britannia Pavilion
VAUX/LVPD L3 * 6 C7
Britannia Rd WAL/NB CH45 68 C1
Britonside Av KKBY L32 34 A4
Brittarge Brow NTHLY L27 98 C4
Britten Cl TOX L8 94 D2
Broadbelt St ANF/KKDL L4 40 B5
Broadbent Av WARRS WA4 107 H4
Broadfield Av CL/PREN CH43 67 G5
Broadfield Cl CL/PREN CH43 * 90 B1
Broadfields RUNC WA7 156 D1
Broadgate Av STHEL WA9 62 B1
Broad Green Rd
CLB/OSW/ST L13 73 F3
Broadheath Av CL/PREN CH43 90 C1
Broadheath Ter WDN WA8 124 B2
Broad Hey NTHTN L30 30 C1
Broad Hey Cl WLTN L25 97 H5
Broadhurst Av
WARRW/BUR WA5 105 H4
Broadhurst St AIG/SPK L17 95 E5
Broadlands RAIN/WH L35 60 A5
Broad La ANF/KKDL L4 55 F1
HES CH60 134 A5
KKBY L32 34 A4
NG/CROX L11 55 G1
NG/CROX L11 56 A1
RNFD/HAY WA11 37 F2
WARRS WA4 131 F3
Broad Lane Prec NG/CROX L11 55 G1
Broadmead ALL/GAR L19 120 A4
HES CH60 149 G2
Broad Oak Av RNFD/HAY WA11 49 G1
WARRW/BUR WA5 104 C4
Broadoak Rd DV/KA/FCH L14 74 B2
MGHL L31 19 E5
Broad Oak Rd STHEL WA9 49 E4
Broadoaks GR/UP/WCH CH49 89 G2
Broad Pl NG/CROX L11 55 H2
Broad Sq NG/CROX L11 55 H2
Broadstone Dr BEB CH63 137 H4
Broad Vw NG/CROX L11 55 H2
Broadway BEB CH63 115 F4
ECCL WA10 46 D2
GR/UP/WCH CH49 89 F3
NG/CROX L11 55 G1
WAL/NB CH45 51 F5
WDN WA8 123 G2
WLT/FAZ L9 41 G1
Broadway Av WAL/NB CH45 51 F5
Broadwood Av MGHL L31 23 H2
Broadwood St WAV L15 95 G1
Brockenhurst Rd WLT/FAZ L9 40 C2
Brockhall Cl RAIN/WH L35 60 C4
Brock Hall Cl STHEL WA9 79 G1
Brockholme Rd ALL/GAR L19 119 E2
Brocklebank La ALL/GAR L19 119 H3
Brock Rd GOL/RIS/CUL WA3 85 H2
Brock St ANF/KKDL L4 54 A2
Brodie Av ALL/GAR L19 119 F3
CALD/MH L18 96 A5
Bromborough Rd BEB CH63 138 A1
Bromborough Village Rd
PS/BROM CH62 138 D5
Brome Wy BEB CH63 138 B4
Bromilow Rd STHEL WA9 49 F5
Bromley Av CALD/MH L18 95 H3
Bromley Cl HES CH60 148 C2
WARRN/WOL WA2 84 D2
Bromley Rd WAL/NB CH45 51 G3
Brompton Av AIG/SPK L17 95 E3
CSBY/BLUN L23 28 D1
NWD/KWIPK L33 26 B4
WAL/EG CH44 69 E1
Brompton Gdns
WARRW/BUR WA5 106 A1
Bromsgrove Rd
GR/UP/WCH CH49 89 E4
Bromyard Cl BTL L20 4 C3
Bronington Av
PS/BROM CH62 152 D3
Bronte Cl CSBY/BLUN L23 20 C5
Bronte St ECCL WA10 10 B4
VAUX/LVPD L3 7 H3
Brook Av MGHL L31 19 E4
WARRS WA4 107 H3
Brookbank Cl AIN/FAZ L10 33 E5
Brookbridge Rd
CLB/OSW/ST L13 55 G4
Brook Cl WAL/EG CH44 52 A5
WDN WA8 101 E2
Brookdale WDN WA8 100 C5
Brookdale Av North
GR/UP/WCH CH49 89 G4
Brookdale Av South
GR/UP/WCH CH49 89 G5
Brookdale Cl GR/UP/WCH CH49 89 G4
Brookdale Rd WAV L15 95 G2
Brook Dr WARRW/BUR WA5 105 E3
Brook End STHEL WA9 63 G1
Brooke Rd East CSBY/WL L22 29 E2
Brooke Rd West CSBY/WL L22 28 D2
Brookfield Av CSBY/BLUN L23 29 E1
CSBY/WL L22 29 G4
RAIN/WH L35 61 E5
RUNC WA7 147 E4
Brookfield Dr WLT/FAZ L9 41 E2
Brookfield Gdns WKBY CH48 110 B1
Brookfield La ORM L39 19 G1
Brookfield Pk WARRS WA4 131 E1
Brookfield Rd WKBY CH48 110 B1
Brook Hey Dr NWD/KWIPK L33 26 A5
Brookhill Cl BTL L20 5 G4
Brookhill Rd BTL L20 5 G2
Brook House Gv ECCL WA10 46 C4
Brookhurst Av BEB CH63 152 C3
Brookhurst Cl BEB CH63 152 C4
Brookhurst Rd BEB CH63 152 C3
Brookland La STHEL WA9 49 G5
Brookland Rd BIRK CH41 2 E6
Brookland Rd East
CLB/OSW/ST L13 73 E2
Brookland Rd West
CLB/OSW/ST L13 73 E2
Brooklands BIRK CH41 2 E2
Brooklands Av CSBY/WL L22 29 F4
Brooklands Dr MGHL L31 24 A1
Brooklands Gdns NSTN CH64 158 B1
Brooklands Pk WDN WA8 125 G1
Brooklands Rd ECCL WA10 46 C3
NSTN CH64 158 B1
The Brooklands HUY L36 75 G4
Brookland St WARR WA1 107 G1
Brooklet Rd HES CH60 149 G1
Brook Meadow PEN/TH CH61 112 C4
Brook Pk MGHL L31 23 H2
Brook Pl WARRS WA4 107 G5
Brook Rd BTL L20 4 C4
CSBY/BLUN L23 21 H3
MGHL L31 24 B1
WLT/FAZ L9 40 C3
Brooks Aly CLVPS L1 7 F5
Brookside WD/CROXPK L12 57 F2
Brookside Av CSBY/WL L22 29 G4
DV/KA/FCH L14 73 H2
ECCL WA10 46 D2
WARRS WA4 130 B2
WARRW/BUR WA5 105 E3
Brookside Cl RAIN/WH L35 77 E1
Brookside Crs
GR/UP/WCH CH49 89 F3
Brookside Dr
GR/UP/WCH CH49 * 89 G3
Brookside Rd RAIN/WH L35 77 E1
Brooks Rd FMBY L37 16 C4
The Brooks RNFD/HAY WA11 37 E5
Brook St BIRK CH41 2 C1
ECCL WA10 11 F5
NSTN CH64 158 D2
PS/BROM CH62 116 A5
RAIN/WH L35 60 B5
RUNC WA7 8 D4
VAUX/LVPD L3 6 B2
Brook St East BIRK CH41 3 F3
Brooks Wy FMBY L37 16 C4
Brookthorpe Cl WAL/NB CH45 51 H5
Brook V CSBY/WL L22 29 G4
Brookvale Av North
RUNC WA7 156 D3
Brookvale Av South
RUNC WA7 156 D3
Brook Wk PEN/TH CH61 112 B4
Brookway CL/PREN CH43 114 A2
GR/UP/WCH CH49 89 G3
WAL/NB CH45 51 G5
Brook Wy WARRW/BUR WA5 105 E3
Brookway La STHEL WA9 63 F1
Brook Well NSTN CH64 158 D5
Brookwood Cl WARRS WA4 129 H3
Brookwood Rd HUY L36 75 G1
Broom Av WARRS WA4 130 C5
Broom Cl PR/KW L34 60 B4
Broome Ct RUNC WA7 156 D4
Broomfield Cl HES CH60 134 A5
Broomfield Gdns WLT/FAZ L9 40 B2
Broomfield Rd WLT/FAZ L9 40 B2
Broomfields Rd WARRS WA4 130 B4
Broom Hl CL/PREN CH43 91 F1
Broomhill Cl NTHLY L27 98 A2
Broomlands HES CH60 148 C1
Broomleigh Cl BEB CH63 137 F1
Broom Rd ECCL WA10 60 D2
Broomsgrove AIN/FAZ L10 32 B3
Broom Wy HLWD L26 121 F4
Broseley Av PS/BROM CH62 138 C5
Broster Av MOR/LEA CH46 66 A5
Broster Cl MOR/LEA CH46 66 A5
Brosters La HOY CH47 64 D4
Brotherhood Dr STHEL WA9 62 D3
Brotherton Cl PS/BROM CH62 152 C1
Brougham Av BIRK CH41 92 C4
Brougham Rd WAL/EG CH44 69 F2
Brougham Ter NPK/KEN L6 71 G2
Broughton Av WKBY CH48 87 E5
Broughton Cl WARRS WA4 130 D3
Broughton Dr ALL/GAR L19 119 E4
Broughton Hall Rd
WD/CROXPK L12 57 E5
Broughton Rd WAL/EG CH44 68 D2
Broughton Wy WDN WA8 144 D1
Brow La HES CH60 148 D2
Brownbill Bank NTHLY L27 98 C3
Brown Heath Av
WGNW/BIL/OR WN5 37 H1
Brownhill Dr WARR WA1 84 D5
Browning Av RF/TRAN CH42 115 H2
WDN WA8 14 A4
Browning Cl HUY L36 75 H4
Browning Rd CSBY/WL L22 29 E2
WAL/NB CH45 * 50 D5
Browning St BTL L20 4 B2
Brownlow Ar ECCL WA10 * 11 H6
Brownlow Hl VAUX/LVPD L3 7 G4
Brownlow Rd PS/BROM CH62 116 B4
Brownlow St VAUX/LVPD L3 7 J4
Brownmoor Cl CSBY/BLUN L23 21 H5
Brownmoor La CSBY/BLUN L23 29 G1
Brownmoor Pk CSBY/BLUN L23 29 G1
Brown's La NTHTN L30 31 E1
Brown St WDN WA8 15 J5
Brownville Rd
CLB/OSW/ST L13 * 55 F4
Brow Rd CL/PREN CH43 67 H4
Brows Cl FMBY L37 16 D3
Brow Side NPK/KEN L6 71 F1
Brows La FMBY L37 16 D3
Broxholme Wy MGHL L31 24 A2
Broxton Av CL/PREN CH43 114 B1
WKBY CH48 87 F5
Broxton Cl WDN WA8 101 E5
Broxton St WAV L15 72 C5
Bruce Av WARRN/WOL WA2 84 B4
Bruce Crs BEB CH63 152 C3
Bruce St ECCL WA10 10 D5
TOX L8 94 C4
Bruche Av WARR WA1 107 H1
Bruche Dr WARR WA1 84 D5
Brunel Dr LITH L21 29 H2
Brunel Rd PS/BROM CH62 139 E5
Brunner Rd WDN WA8 14 C3
Brunsborough Cl
PS/BROM CH62 152 C3
Brunsfield Cl MOR/LEA CH46 89 E1
Brunstath Cl HES CH60 135 G5
Brunswick Cl ANF/KKDL L4 * 54 A2
Brunswick Ct BIRK CH41 3 F3
Brunswick Ms BIRK CH41 3 G3
CSBY/WL L22 29 F4
Brunswick Pde CSBY/WL L22 29 E4
Brunswick Pl BTL L20 53 F2
Brunswick Rd NPK/KEN L6 7 K1
Brunswick St ALL/GAR L19 140 C3
CLVP L2 6 C4
STHEL WA9 49 G4
Brunswick Wy VAUX/LVPD L3 93 H3
Brunt La ALL/GAR L19 120 A4
Bruntleigh Av WARRS WA4 108 A5
Bruton Rd HUY L36 58 B4
Bryanston Rd AIG/SPK L17 94 D5
RF/TRAN CH42 114 C1
Bryant Av WARRS WA4 107 H4
Bryant Rd LITH L21 39 F1
The Bryceway WD/CROXPK L12 73 H1
Brydges St EHL/KEN L7 * 71 G4
Bryer Rd RAIN/WH L35 76 D1
Bryn Bank WAL/EG CH44 69 E1
Brynmor Rd CALD/MH L18 119 E2
Brynmoss Av WAL/EG CH44 68 B1
Brynn St ECCL WA10 11 H3
Bryony Wy RF/TRAN CH42 115 H3
Brythen St CLVPS L1 7 F4
Buchanan Cl WDN WA8 101 H5
Buchanan Rd WAL/EG CH44 69 F2
WLT/FAZ L9 40 B4
Buchan Cl WARRW/BUR WA5 82 B5
Buckfast Cl NTHTN L30 23 E5
WARRW/BUR WA5 104 C5
Buckfast Dr FMBY L37 17 G4
Buckingham Av AIG/SPK L17 95 F3
BEB CH63 115 G4
CL/PREN CH43 91 F1
WDN WA8 102 A4
Buckingham Cl ECCL WA10 10 D7
NTHTN L30 30 B1
Buckingham Ct
NWD/KWIPK L33 34 A1
Buckingham Dr
RNFD/HAY WA11 37 E5
WARRW/BUR WA5 105 G4
Buckingham Gv FMBY L37 16 D4
Buckingham Rd
CLB/OSW/ST L13 55 F4
MGHL L31 23 H1
WAL/EG CH44 68 B1
WLT/FAZ L9 40 C1
Buckingham St EV L5 54 A5
Buckland Cl WDN WA8 124 B4
Buckland Dr BEB CH63 137 H4
Buckland St AIG/SPK L17 94 D5
Buckley Hill La NTHTN L30 22 C4
Buckley St WARRN/WOL WA2 12 C2
Buckthorn Cl STBRV L28 57 H3
Buckthorn Gdns STHEL WA9 61 E4
Buckton St WARR WA1 13 H1
Bude Cl CL/PREN CH43 90 C2
Bude Rd WDN WA8 124 C1
Budworth Av STHEL WA9 79 F2
WARRS WA4 107 H4
WDN WA8 124 B1
Budworth Cl CL/PREN CH43 91 E4
RUNC WA7 155 H2
Budworth Dr WLTN L25 121 E1
Budworth Rd CL/PREN CH43 91 E4
Buerton Cl CL/PREN CH43 90 D4
Buffs La HES CH60 149 F1
Buggen La NSTN CH64 158 C2
Bulford Rd WLT/FAZ L9 41 G3
Bulkeley Rd WAL/EG CH44 69 F2
Bull Bridge La AIN/FAZ L10 32 B2
Bull Cop FMBY L37 17 F3
Bullens Rd ANF/KKDL L4 54 B2
KKBY L32 34 A3
Bullfinch Ct HLWD L26 121 G2
Bull Hl NSTN CH64 159 E4
Bull La WLT/FAZ L9 31 G5
Bullrush Dr MOR/LEA CH46 67 E3
The Bulrushes AIG/SPK L17 94 B5
Bulwer St BTL L20 39 E2
EV L5 * 54 C5
RF/TRAN CH42 115 H1
Bunbury Dr RUNC WA7 155 G3
Bundoran Rd AIG/SPK L17 118 C1
Bunter Rd KKBY L32 43 F1
Bunting Ct HLWD L26 121 F1
Buntingford Rd WARRS WA4 108 C5
Burbo Bank Rd CSBY/BLUN L23 20 B5
Burbo Bank Rd North
CSBY/BLUN L23 20 A4
Burbo Bank Rd South
CSBY/BLUN L23 28 C1
Burbo Crs CSBY/BLUN L23 28 C1
Burbo Man CSBY/BLUN L23 * 28 C1
Burbo Wy WAL/NB CH45 51 E2
Burden Rd MOR/LEA CH46 66 A5
Burdett Av BEB CH63 137 H4
Burdett Cl BEB CH63 138 A4
Burdett Rd CSBY/WL L22 29 E3
WAL/NB CH45 50 D5
Burdett St AIG/SPK L17 95 E5
Burfield Dr WARRS WA4 130 A5
Burford Av WAL/EG CH44 68 B2
Burford Rd CHLDW L16 73 G4
Burgess Av WARRS WA4 106 D5
Burgess Gdns MGHL L31 18 C4
Burgess St VAUX/LVPD L3 7 H2
Burghill Rd WD/CROXPK L12 43 F3
Burgundy Cl AIG/SPK L17 118 A1
Burland Cl RUNC WA7 8 C6
Burland Rd HLWD L26 122 A5
Burleigh Ms EV L5 54 B4
Burleigh Rd North EV L5 54 B3
Burleigh Rd South EV L5 54 B4
Burley Cl KKBY L32 34 A3
Burlingham Av WKBY CH48 110 C2
Burlington Av FMBY L37 17 G3
Burlington Rd WAL/NB CH45 51 H1
Burlington St BIRK CH41 3 F4
VAUX/LVPD L3 70 C1
Burman Crs ALL/GAR L19 119 G4
Burman Rd ALL/GAR L19 119 H4
Burnage Av STHEL WA9 79 G1
Burnage Cl SPK/HALE L24 142 D4
Burnand St ANF/KKDL L4 54 B3
Burnard Cl NWD/KWIPK L33 34 A2
Burnard Crs NWD/KWIPK L33 34 A2
Burnard Wk NWD/KWIPK L33 * 34 A2
Burnell Cl ECCL WA10 10 E4
Burnet Cl WARRN/WOL WA2 85 G3
Burnham Cl WARRW/BUR WA5 104 D3
WDN WA8 101 E5
Burnham Rd CALD/MH L18 96 C5
Burnie Av BTL L20 5 J1
Burnley Av MOR/LEA CH46 66 D5
Burnley Cl NPK/KEN L6 71 G1
Burnley Rd MOR/LEA CH46 66 D5
Burnsall Dr WDN WA8 101 E5
Burnsall St ALL/GAR L19 141 E1
Burns Av WAL/NB CH45 51 G5
Burns Cl CHLDW L16 74 B5
RAIN/WH L35 77 E2
Burns Crs WDN WA8 14 B3
Burns Gv HUY L36 76 A4
WARRN/WOL WA2 84 A3
Burnside Av WAL/EG CH44 68 D3
WARRS WA4 130 B2
Burnside Rd WAL/EG CH44 68 D3
Burns Rd STHEL WA9 79 E2
Burns St BTL L20 4 A1
Burnt Ash Cl ALL/GAR L19 118 D4
Burnthwaite Rd
DV/KA/FCH L14 73 G2
Burrell Cl RF/TRAN CH42 115 E2
Burrell Dr MOR/LEA CH46 89 F1
Burrell Rd RF/TRAN CH42 115 E2
Burrell St ANF/KKDL L4 54 B2
Burroughs Gdns
VAUX/LVPD L3 * 70 D1
Burrows Av RNFD/HAY WA11 49 F2
Burrows Ct VAUX/LVPD L3 70 C1
Burrow's La ECCL WA10 46 A5
Burrows St RNFD/HAY WA11 49 G1
Burton Av RAIN/WH L35 77 G1
WAL/NB CH45 51 E5
Burton Cl CLVPS L1 6 E7
RAIN/WH L35 77 G1
WDN WA8 101 H5
Burtonhead Rd STHEL WA9 47 H5
Burton Rd NSTN CH64 158 D4
WARRN/WOL WA2 84 B4
Burton St EV L5 53 G4
Burtons Wy AIN/FAZ L10 33 F5
Burtonwood Rd
WARRW/BUR WA5 81 H1
WARRW/BUR WA5 82 A3
Burtree Rd DV/KA/FCH L14 57 G4
Burwell Av FMBY L37 16 C5
Burwen Dr WLT/FAZ L9 40 B1
Busby's Cottages
WAL/NB CH45 51 H2
Bushby's La FMBY L37 16 B4
Bushby's Pk FMBY L37 16 B4
Bushell Cl NSTN CH64 159 E3
Bushell Rd NSTN CH64 159 E2
Bushel's Dr STHEL WA9 79 H3
Bushey Rd ANF/KKDL L4 41 E5
Bushley Cl BTL L20 4 D3
Bush Rd WDN WA8 145 H1
Bush Wy HES CH60 148 C1
Butchers La ORM L39 19 F1
Bute St EV L5 71 E1
VAUX/LVPD L3 71 E2
Butleigh Rd HUY L36 58 B5
Butler Crs NPK/KEN L6 71 H2
Butler St NPK/KEN L6 71 H1
Buttercup Cl CSBY/WL L22 29 G3
MOR/LEA CH46 67 E3
WARRW/BUR WA5 106 A5
Buttercup Wy WLT/FAZ L9 40 D3
Butterfield St ANF/KKDL L4 54 B3
Buttermarket St WARR WA1 12 E4
Buttermere Av CL/PREN CH43 90 C2
RNFD/HAY WA11 37 E4
WARRN/WOL WA2 84 A2
Buttermere Cl FMBY L37 16 C3
MGHL L31 18 D5
NWD/KWIPK L33 25 G5
Buttermere Gdns
CSBY/BLUN L23 29 G2
Buttermere Gv RUNC WA7 155 H3
Buttermere Rd CHLDW L16 74 C4
Buttermere St TOX L8 94 D1
Butterton Av
GR/UP/WCH CH49 89 F2
Butterwick Dr
WD/CROXPK L12 43 E4
Button St CLVP L2 6 E4
Butts Gn WARRW/BUR WA5 82 A2
Buxted Rd KKBY L32 34 B4
Buxton Cl WARRW/BUR WA5 82 A5
Buxton Rd RF/TRAN CH42 116 A1
Byerley St WAL/EG CH44 69 G2
Byland Cl FMBY L37 17 G4
WDN WA8 102 C3
Byles St TOX L8 94 C4
Byng Pl ANF/KKDL L4 55 F2
Byng Rd ANF/KKDL L4 55 F2
Byng St BTL L20 4 C7
The By-Pass CSBY/BLUN L23 21 F5
Byrne Av RF/TRAN CH42 115 H2

Byrom St CLVP L2 7 F2
VAUX/LVPD L3 7 F2
Byrom Wy VAUX/LVPD L3 7 F1
Byron Av RAIN/WH L35 77 F2
Byron Cl CL/PREN CH43 114 B3
ECCL WA10 11 G2
FMBY L37 17 E2
HUY L36 75 H4
Byron Ct WARRN/WOL WA2 84 A3
Byron Rd CSBY/BLUN L23 20 C5
MGHL L31 18 D3
Byron St ALL/GAR L19 140 C1
BTL L20 4 A1
RUNC WA7 8 C6
The Byway CSBY/BLUN L23 21 F4

C

Cabes Cl DV/KA/FCH L14 57 G4
Cable Rd HOY CH47 87 F1
RAIN/WH L35 60 B5
Cable St CLVP L2 6 D5
FMBY L37 17 F2
Cabot Cl WARRW/BUR WA5 82 C4
Cabot Gn WLTN L25 97 E3
Cabul Cl WARRN/WOL WA2 107 E1
Caddick Rd PR/KW L34 43 H2
Cadet Wy WD/CROXPK L12 57 E3
Cadnam Rd WLTN L25 98 B3
Cadogan St EHL/KEN L7 72 B5
Cadwell Rd MGHL L31 18 B1
Caernarvon Cl
GR/UP/WCH CH49 89 H2
RUNC WA7 147 F4
Caerwys Gv RF/TRAN CH42 92 C4
Caesars Cl RUNC WA7 147 E4
Caird St NPK/KEN L6 71 G2
Cairn Ct STHEL WA9 61 F3
Cairnmore Rd CALD/MH L18 119 E1
Cairns St TOX L8 94 C2
Cairo St ANF/KKDL L4 54 A1
ECCL WA10 61 F1
WARR WA1 12 C5
Caithness Ct RUNC WA7 8 E4
Caithness Dr CSBY/BLUN L23 29 G1
WAL/NB CH45 52 A4
Caithness Gdns
CL/PREN CH43 * 114 B2
Caithness Rd CALD/MH L18 119 F2
Calday Grange Cl WKBY CH48 110 D2
Caldbeck Av WARRN/WOL WA2 84 B3
Caldbeck Gv RNFD/HAY WA11 37 G3
Caldbeck Rd PS/BROM CH62 139 E4
Calder Av CL/PREN CH43 114 C1
Calder Cl NWD/KWIPK L33 26 A3
WDN WA8 103 F5
Calder Dr CALD/MH L18 96 C3
MGHL L31 19 F4
RAIN/WH L35 77 H2
Calderfield Cl WARRS WA4 129 H3
Calderfield Rd CALD/MH L18 96 D3
Calder Gra CALD/MH L18 97 E5
Calderhurst Dr ECCL WA10 46 D1
Calder Rd BEB CH63 137 F1
EV L5 54 B4
The Calders CALD/MH L18 96 C5
Calderstones Av CALD/MH L18 96 C3
Calderstones Rd CALD/MH L18 96 B4
Calderwood Pk NTHLY L27 98 B2
Caldicott Av PS/BROM CH62 152 D2
Caldon Cl LITH L21 29 H3
Caldway Dr NTHLY L27 98 B2
Caldwell Av WARRW/BUR WA5 83 F3
Caldwell Cl NWD/KWIPK L33 * 26 A5
Caldwell Dr GR/UP/WCH CH49 113 F1
Caldwell Rd ALL/GAR L19 119 H3
WDN WA8 14 C5
Caldwell St STHEL WA9 48 D4
Caldy Chase Dr WKBY CH48 110 D4
Caldy Gv RNFD/HAY WA11 48 D2
Caldy Rd WAL/NB CH45 51 H5
WKBY CH48 110 C3
WLT/FAZ L9 31 F5
Caldy Wd WKBY CH48 110 D4
Caldywood Dr RAIN/WH L35 77 E2
Caledonia St CLVPS L1 7 J6
Calgarth Rd HUY L36 58 A5
California Cl WARRW/BUR WA5 82 C5
California Rd CLB/OSW/ST L13 55 F3
Callaghan Cl EV L5 53 H5
Callander Rd NPK/KEN L6 72 B2
Callands Rd WARRW/BUR WA5 82 D3
Callestock Cl NG/CROX L11 42 D2
Callington Cl DV/KA/FCH L14 57 G4
Callon Av RNFD/HAY WA11 49 E2
Callow Rd WAV L15 95 F1
Calmet Cl EV L5 54 A4
Calne Cl PEN/TH CH61 112 B4
Calstock Cl WARRW/BUR WA5 104 C5
Calthorpe St ALL/GAR L19 119 F5
Calthorpe Wy CL/PREN CH43 90 D2
Calton Av CALD/MH L18 * 96 A3
Calvados Cl AIG/SPK L17 118 A2
Calveley Av PS/BROM CH62 153 F5
Calveley Cl CL/PREN CH43 91 E5
Calveley Rd HLWD L26 122 A5
Calverly Cl RUNC WA7 157 E4
Calver Rd WARRN/WOL WA2 83 F1
Calvers RUNC WA7 147 E5
Camarthen Crs TOX L8 93 H2
Camberley Dr WLTN L25 121 F3
Camberwell Park Rd
WDN WA8 102 D4
Camborne Av WLTN L25 121 E3
Camborne Cl RUNC WA7 157 E3
Cambourne Av
RNFD/HAY WA11 37 H5
Cambrai Av WARRS WA4 130 A1
Cambrian Cl MOR/LEA CH46 * 88 D1
Cambrian Rd MOR/LEA CH46 89 E1
Cambrian Wy WLTN L25 97 H5
Cambria St NPK/KEN L6 71 H2
Cambridge Av CSBY/BLUN L23 21 E5
LITH L21 30 A4
Cambridge Cl WARRS WA4 129 H3
Cambridge Dr CSBY/BLUN L23 20 D4
… 121 H3
Cambridge Gdns WARRS WA4 130 A5
Cambridge Rd BTL L20 5 H6
CSBY/BLUN L23 20 D4
CSBY/WL L22 29 F5
ECCL WA10 10 C3
FMBY L37 16 C5
PS/BROM CH62 152 D1
RF/TRAN CH42 114 C1
WAL/NB CH45 51 H3
WLT/FAZ L9 31 G4
Cambridge St EHL/KEN L7 71 G5
PR/KW L34 * 59 H4
RUNC WA7 9 H4
WAV L15 72 B5
WDN WA8 14 E5
Camdale Cl STBRV L28 57 H3
Camden Ms GR/UP/WCH CH49 90 B4
Camden Pl BIRK CH41 3 F4
Camden St VAUX/LVPD L3 7 G2
Camelford Rd NG/CROX L11 42 C2
Camelia Ct AIG/SPK L17 117 G1
Camellia Gdns STHEL WA9 63 H3
Camelot Ter BTL L20 4 C2
Cameo Cl NPK/KEN L6 71 H1
Cameron Av RUNC WA7 154 C1
Cameron Ct WARRN/WOL WA2 83 G1
Cameron Rd MOR/LEA CH46 67 F2
WDN WA8 14 C4
Cameron St EHL/KEN L7 72 A3
Campania St ALL/GAR L19 140 C2
Campbell Av RUNC WA7 155 E1
Campbell Crs NWD/KWIPK L33 25 G3
WARRW/BUR WA5 104 D2
Campbell Dr DV/KA/FCH L14 74 A2
Campbell St BTL L20 4 B5
CLVPS L1 6 E6
ECCL WA10 10 D4
Campbeltown Rd BIRK CH41 92 D4
Camperdown St BIRK CH41 3 H4
Camphill Rd WLTN L25 120 C4
Campion Cl GOL/RIS/CUL WA3 85 G1
RNFD/HAY WA11 37 F5
Campion Wy HUY L36 98 D1
Camp Rd WLTN L25 120 D2
Campsey Ash WDN WA8 101 H5
Camrose Cl RUNC WA7 155 G3
Camsley La LYMM WA13 109 H5
Cam St WLTN L25 * 120 C2
Canada Bvd VAUX/LVPD L3 6 B4
Canada Cl WARRN/WOL WA2 85 E3
Canal Side RUNC WA7 154 B2
RUNC WA7 157 H4
WARRS WA4 131 G2
Canalside Gv EV L5 53 G5
Canal St BTL L20 4 D6
ECCL WA10 11 F7
RUNC WA7 9 G4
Canal Vw MGHL L31 32 D2
Canberra Av STHEL WA9 61 G3
Canberra La NG/CROX L11 42 C2
Canberra Sq WARRN/WOL WA2 84 B3
Candleston Cl
WARRW/BUR WA5 83 E4
Canford Cl WARRW/BUR WA5 105 G2
Cannell Ct RUNC WA7 156 C3
Cannell St WARRW/BUR WA5 105 H4
Canning Pl CLVPS L1 6 D6
Canning St BIRK CH41 3 G2
CSBY/WL L22 29 E3
TOX L8 7 J7
Canniswood Rd
RNFD/HAY WA11 49 G2
Cann La North WARRS WA4 130 C5
Cannock Gn MGHL L31 18 B5
Cannon Hl CL/PREN CH43 91 H2
Cannon St STHEL WA9 79 G2
Canonbury Cl RUNC WA7 156 C1
Canon Rd NPK/KEN L6 55 E3
Canons Rd WARRW/BUR WA5 105 H2
Canon St RUNC WA7 8 C3
Canova Cl NTHLY L27 98 D5
Canrow La PR/KW L34 44 B2
Cansfield St ECCL WA10 11 H4
Canterbury Av CSBY/WL L22 29 E1
Canterbury Cl AIN/FAZ L10 32 B2
FMBY L37 17 E1
PR/KW L34 60 A3
Canterbury Pk CALD/MH L18 119 G3
Canterbury Rd RF/TRAN CH42 116 A2
WAL/EG CH44 69 E2
WDN WA8 124 A4
Canterbury St ALL/GAR L19 140 C2
ECCL WA10 10 D2
VAUX/LVPD L3 7 H1
WARRS WA4 13 F7
Canterbury Wy NTHTN L30 23 E5
VAUX/LVPD L3 * 7 J1
Canter Cl WLT/FAZ L9 32 A4
Cantilever Gdns WARRS WA4 130 C1
Cantley Cl RUNC WA7 155 H3
Cantsfield St EHL/KEN L7 95 E1
Canvey Cl WAV L15 96 B1
Capenhurst Av
WARRN/WOL WA2 85 E3
Cape Rd WLT/FAZ L9 * 41 E1
Capesthorne Cl WDN WA8 124 C3
Capesthorne Rd
WARRN/WOL WA2 84 B4
Caplin Cl NWD/KWIPK L33 25 H3
Capper Gv HUY L36 75 G2
Capricorn Crs DV/KA/FCH L14 57 F5
Capricorn Wy BTL L20 4 D3
Capstick Crs WLTN L25 97 H2
Captain's La NTHTN L30 30 C4
Caradoc Rd LITH L21 38 D1
The Caravan Pk STHEL WA9 62 A2
Caraway Cl CSBY/BLUN L23 22 A4
Caraway Gv ECCL WA10 10 A3
Carbis Cl AIN/FAZ L10 42 A1
Carden Cl ANF/KKDL L4 54 A3
GOL/RIS/CUL WA3 85 G1
Cardiff Wy ALL/GAR L19 119 F5
Cardigan Av BIRK CH41 2 E4
Cardigan Cl ECCL WA10 10 E7
WARRW/BUR WA5 82 D3
Cardigan Rd WAL/NB CH45 51 H3
Cardigan St WAV L15 72 B5
Cardigan Wy NPK/KEN L6 71 H1
NTHTN L30 * 23 G5
Cardus Cl MOR/LEA CH46 65 H5
Cardwell St EHL/KEN L7 71 G5
Carey Av BEB CH63 115 F5
Carey St WDN WA8 14 E2
Carfax Rd NWD/KWIPK L33 26 B5
Cargill Gv RF/TRAN CH42 116 B3
Carham Rd HOY CH47 87 G2
Carina Pk WARRW/BUR WA5 82 B3
Carisbrooke Cl WKBY CH48 110 C3
Carisbrooke Pl ANF/KKDL L4 * 54 B1
Carisbrooke Rd ANF/KKDL L4 54 A1
BTL L20 5 J7
Carkington Rd WLTN L25 121 E2
Carland Cl AIN/FAZ L10 42 B1
Carlaw Rd RF/TRAN CH42 114 C1
Carleen Cl AIG/SPK L17 117 H1
Carlett Bvd PS/BROM CH62 153 F4
Carlile Wy NWD/KWIPK L33 26 A3
Carlingford Cl TOX L8 94 C1
Carlingford Rd WARRS WA4 129 H3
Carlisle Av NTHTN L30 31 E3
Carlisle Cl ANF/KKDL L4 55 F2
Carlisle Ms CL/PREN CH43 2 C6
Carlisle St WARRS WA4 130 A3
Carlis Rd KKBY L32 34 A4
Carlow Cl SPK/HALE L24 143 G4
Carlow St ECCL WA10 61 F1
Carlsruhe Ct TOX L8 * 94 C3
Carl's Wy NWD/KWIPK L33 26 B3
Carlton Av RUNC WA7 146 D4
Carlton La CLB/OSW/ST L13 73 E1
HOY CH47 64 C5
Carlton Mt RF/TRAN CH42 92 C5
Carlton Rd BEB CH63 138 B2
RF/TRAN CH42 92 A4
WAL/NB CH45 51 H2
Carlton St ECCL WA10 10 D6
PR/KW L34 59 H3
VAUX/LVPD L3 70 B1
WARRS WA4 130 A3
WDN WA8 14 D3
Carlton Ter CSBY/BLUN L23 * 21 E5
HOY CH47 * 64 C5
Carlyon Wy HLWD L26 * 121 G3
Carmarthen Cl
WARRW/BUR WA5 82 D3
Carmel Ct WDN WA8 102 B4
Carmelite Crs ECCL WA10 46 C2
Carmichael Av
GR/UP/WCH CH49 112 B1
Carnaby Cl HUY L36 76 A5
Carnarvon Rd WLT/FAZ L9 40 B4
Carnarvon St STHEL WA9 61 F3
Carnatic Rd AIG/SPK L17 95 G5
CALD/MH L18 95 G5
Carnation Rd WLT/FAZ L9 40 D3
Carnegie Av CSBY/BLUN L23 29 E1
Carnegie Crs STHEL WA9 63 E2
Carnegie Rd CLB/OSW/ST L13 72 D1
Carnforth Av KKBY L32 34 A3
Carnforth Cl BIRK CH41 2 C7
WD/CROXPK L12 56 C1
Carnforth Rd CALD/MH L18 119 G1
Carno St WAV L15 * 72 C5
Carnoustie Cl MOR/LEA CH46 65 H4
WD/CROXPK L12 57 F4
Carnoustie Gv RNFD/HAY WA11 49 G2
Carnsdale Rd MOR/LEA CH46 66 D5
Carol Dr HES CH60 149 G1
Carol St WARRS WA4 13 G7
Carole Cl STHEL WA9 63 E4
Carolina Rd WARRW/BUR WA5 105 F1
Carolina St BTL L20 4 E4
Caroline Pl CL/PREN CH43 91 H3
Caroline St WDN WA8 * 14 E6
Carol St WARRS WA4 107 F5
Caronia St ALL/GAR L19 * 140 C2
Carpathia St ALL/GAR L19 140 C2
Carpenter Gv
WARRN/WOL WA2 85 E4
Carpenter's La WKBY CH48 110 B1
Carpenters Rw CLVPS L1 6 D7
Carraway Rd NG/CROX L11 42 B1
Carr Bridge Rd
GR/UP/WCH CH49 90 B4
Carr Cl NG/CROX L11 42 B5
Carr Cft LITH L21 30 A1
Carrfield Av CSBY/BLUN L23 29 H1
Carr Ga MOR/LEA CH46 88 D1
Carr Hey MOR/LEA CH46 65 H5
Carr Hey Cl GR/UP/WCH CH49 113 G1
Carr House La MOR/LEA CH46 65 H5
Carriage Cl SPK/HALE L24 143 H5
Carrickmore Av CALD/MH L18 119 E1
Carrington Cl
GOL/RIS/CUL WA3 85 G1
Carrington Rd WAL/NB CH45 51 H4
Carrington St BIRK CH41 68 C5
Carr La HOY CH47 65 G4
HOY CH47 87 F2
HOY CH47 87 H3
HUY L36 75 E4
MOR/LEA CH46 65 H5
NG/CROX L11 41 H5
PR/KW L34 59 F5
SPK/HALE L24 143 H4
Carr La East NG/CROX L11 42 B5
Carr Meadow Hey NTHTN L30 30 B2
Carr Mill Rd RNFD/HAY WA11 37 G4
Carrock Rd PS/BROM CH62 139 E4
Carrow Cl MOR/LEA CH46 88 D1
Carr Rd BTL L20 30 C5
Carr's Crs FMBY L37 16 C5
Carr's Crs West FMBY L37 16 C5
Carr St ECCL WA10 10 B1
Carruthers St VAUX/LVPD L3 70 C2
Carrville Wy WD/CROXPK L12 43 G5
Carrwood Cl RNFD/HAY WA11 49 G1
Carsdale Rd CALD/MH L18 96 A3
Carsgoe Rd HOY CH47 87 G2
Carsington Rd NG/CROX L11 42 A5
Carstairs Rd NPK/KEN L6 72 A1
Carsthorne Rd HOY CH47 87 G2
Cartbridge La HLWD L26 121 H2
The Carters GR/UP/WCH CH49 89 E4
NTHTN L30 23 F5
Carter St TOX L8 94 B1
Carterton Rd HOY CH47 87 G2
Cartier Cl WARRW/BUR WA5 82 C4
Cartmel Av ECCL WA10 36 C5
MGHL L31 19 E4
WARRN/WOL WA2 84 A2
Cartmel Cl BIRK CH41 * 2 C7
HUY L36 75 F1
WARRW/BUR WA5 83 E3
Cartmel Dr FMBY L37 17 G4
MOR/LEA CH46 89 G1
RAIN/WH L35 77 G1
WD/CROXPK L12 56 C1
Cartmell Cl RUNC WA7 155 F3
Cartmel Rd HUY L36 75 E1
Cartmel Ter NG/CROX L11 42 B4
Cartmel Wy HUY L36 75 E1
Cartridge La WARRS WA4 131 H5
Cartwright St RUNC WA7 9 H5
WARRW/BUR WA5 106 A2
Carver St VAUX/LVPD L3 7 J1
Caryl Gv TOX L8 94 A4
Caryl St TOX L8 93 H2
Cascade Rd SPK/HALE L24 121 E5
Case Gv RAIN/WH L35 60 A5
Cashel Rd BIRK CH41 68 D3
Caspian Pl BTL L20 5 F4
Caspian Rd ANF/KKDL L4 41 E5
Cassia Cl WLT/FAZ L9 40 D3
Cassino Rd HUY L36 75 F2
Cassio St BTL L20 * 5 J7
Cassley Rd SPK/HALE L24 143 E3
Cassville Rd WAV L15 96 A2
Castell Gv ECCL WA10 10 E5
Casterton St EHL/KEN L7 * 72 A5
Castle Av STHEL WA9 49 E4
Castle Cl MOR/LEA CH46 67 E2
Castle Dr FMBY L37 17 E5
HES CH60 148 D1
Castlefield Av South
RUNC WA7 147 F5
Castlefield Cl WD/CROXPK L12 56 A2
Castlefield Rd WD/CROXPK L12 56 A3
Castlefields Av East
RUNC WA7 147 G4
Castlefields Av North
RUNC WA7 147 E4
Castlefields Av South
RUNC WA7 147 F5
Castle Fields Est
MOR/LEA CH46 66 D1
Castleford Ri MOR/LEA CH46 66 C2
Castleford St WAV L15 96 A1
Castlegate Gv WD/CROXPK L12 56 A3
Castlegrange Cl MOR/LEA CH46 66 C1
Castle Gn WARRW/BUR WA5 82 B3
Castleheath Cl MOR/LEA CH46 66 C2
Castle Hl CLVP L2 * 6 C4
Castle Mt HES CH60 * 148 D1
Castle Ri RUNC WA7 9 K5
Castle Rd RUNC WA7 156 B1
WAL/NB CH45 51 G4
Castlesite Rd WD/CROXPK L12 56 B3
Castle St BIRK CH41 3 H4
CLVP L2 6 C4
WDN WA8 15 J2
WLTN L25 120 B1
Castleton Dr NTHTN L30 23 G5
Castletown Cl CHLDW L16 74 A5
Castleview Rd WD/CROXPK L12 56 B3
Castleway North
MOR/LEA CH46 67 E1
Castleway South
MOR/LEA CH46 67 E2
Castlewood Rd NPK/KEN L6 54 D5
Castner Av RUNC WA7 154 C2
Castor St NPK/KEN L6 54 D5
Catchdale Moss La ECCL WA10 46 A2
Catford Cl WDN WA8 124 A1
Catford Gn SPK/HALE L24 142 D3
Catfoss Cl WARRN/WOL WA2 84 C4
Catharine St TOX L8 94 B1
Cathcart Quay BIRK CH41 * 2 E1
Cathcart St BIRK CH41 2 D3
Cathedral Cl CLVPS L1 94 A1
Cathedral Ga CLVPS L1 7 H7
Cathedral Rd NPK/KEN L6 55 E4
Cathedral Wk VAUX/LVPD L3 7 H5
Catherine St BIRK CH41 2 D5
LITH L21 39 F1
WARRW/BUR WA5 12 A1
WDN WA8 14 D7
Catherine Wy
RNFD/HAY WA11 * 49 F1
Catkin Rd HLWD L26 121 F1
Catonfield Rd CALD/MH L18 96 D3
Catterall Av STHEL WA9 62 D4
WARRN/WOL WA2 84 B3
Catterick Cl HLWD L26 121 H3
Caulfield Dr GR/UP/WCH CH49 89 G5
Caunce Av RNFD/HAY WA11 49 H1
Causeway Av WARRS WA4 107 E5
Causeway Cl PS/BROM CH62 138 B1
The Causeway
PS/BROM CH62 138 B1
WD/CROXPK L12 73 H1
Cavalier Dr ALL/GAR L19 141 E1
Cavan Rd NG/CROX L11 55 G2
Cavell Cl WLTN L25 120 C2
Cavendish Cl
WARRW/BUR WA5 105 H1
Cavendish Dr RF/TRAN CH42 115 F2
WLT/FAZ L9 40 C4
Cavendish Farm Rd
RUNC WA7 154 D4
Cavendish Gdns TOX L8 * 94 C3
Cavendish Rd BIRK CH41 91 H1
CSBY/BLUN L23 28 D1
WAL/NB CH45 51 H1
Cavendish St BIRK CH41 2 A1
RUNC WA7 8 C5
Cavendish Whf BIRK CH41 * 69 E4
Cavern Ct NPK/KEN L6 71 H2
Caversham Cl WARRS WA4 130 B4
Cawdor St RUNC WA7 8 B3
TOX L8 94 C2
WARRS WA4 130 A3
Cawfield Av WDN WA8 124 B2
Cawley St RUNC WA7 8 D7
Cawthorne Av KKBY L32 33 H5
WARRS WA4 131 E1
Cawthorne Cl KKBY L32 33 H4
Cawthorne Wk KKBY L32 * 33 H4
Caxton Cl CL/PREN CH43 90 C2
WDN WA8 * 101 E5
Caxton Rd RAIN/WH L35 78 C4
Cazneau St VAUX/LVPD L3 70 D2
Cearns Rd CL/PREN CH43 91 G3
Cecil Dr ECCL WA10 46 C2
Cecil Rd LITH L21 38 D1
PS/BROM CH62 116 B3
RF/TRAN CH42 114 D1
WAL/NB CH45 68 C1
Cecil St STHEL WA9 63 F3
WAV L15 72 B5
Cedar Av BEB CH63 137 G2
RUNC WA7 155 G2
WDN WA8 102 B5
Cedar Cl CALD/MH L18 96 D5
RAIN/WH L35 77 E1
Cedar Crs HUY L36 75 F4
Cedardale Pk WDN WA8 103 E4
Cedardale Rd WLT/FAZ L9 40 C3
Cedar Dr FMBY L37 16 B5
Cedar Gv CSBY/WL L22 29 E2
MGHL L31 24 A3
NSTN CH64 159 E2
TOX L8 95 E2
WARR WA1 108 A1
WARRS WA4 107 F5
Cedar Rd RAIN/WH L35 76 D2
WARRW/BUR WA5 104 D2
WLT/FAZ L9 40 D1
The Cedars MOR/LEA CH46 89 E1
WD/CROXPK L12 43 F4
Cedar St BIRK CH41 2 D6
BTL L20 5 F3
ECCL WA10 10 A7
Cedar Ter TOX L8 94 D2
Cedarway HES CH60 149 F4
Cedarwood Cl
GR/UP/WCH CH49 88 D4
Cedarwood Ct HUY L36 75 G5
Celandine Wy STHEL WA9 63 H3
Celebration Dr NPK/KEN L6 55 E5
Celedine Cl WAV L15 72 C5
Celia St BTL L20 53 H1
Celtic Rd HOY CH47 65 E4
Celtic St TOX L8 94 C2
Celt St NPK/KEN L6 * 72 A1
Cemeas Cl EV L5 53 G5
Centenary Cl ANF/KKDL L4 55 E2
Central Av PR/KW L34 59 G4
PS/BROM CH62 138 C5
SPK/HALE L24 142 B3
WARRN/WOL WA2 84 A5
WARRS WA4 106 D5
Central Dr RNFD/HAY WA11 49 H1
WD/CROXPK L12 56 A5
WD/CROXPK L12 56 B5
Central Expy RUNC WA7 155 H3
Central Park Av WAL/EG CH44 69 E1
Central Rd PS/BROM CH62 116 B4
WARRS WA4 106 D5
Central Sq MGHL L31 18 D4
Central St ECCL WA10 11 G3
Central Wy SPK/HALE L24 142 C4
WARRN/WOL WA2 12 D3
Centre Pk WARR WA1 106 C5
Centre Park Sq WARR WA1 12 C7
WARR WA1 106 C5
Centreville Rd CALD/MH L18 96 A2
Centre Wy HUY L36 75 G3
Centurion Cl GOL/RIS/CUL WA3 85 H1
HOY CH47 65 E4
Centurion Dr HOY CH47 65 E4
Centurion Rw RUNC WA7 147 F4
Ceres St BTL L20 53 G1
Cestrian Dr PEN/TH CH61 135 E1
Chadlow Rd KKBY L32 34 A5
Chadwell Rd NWD/KWIPK L33 26 A5
Chadwick Av WARRS WA4 130 C2
Chadwick Rd RNFD/HAY WA11 37 G5
RUNC WA7 147 E3
Chadwick St MOR/LEA CH46 66 C5
VAUX/LVPD L3 70 B2
Chadwick Wy NWD/KWIPK L33 25 H3
Chaffinch Cl WD/CROXPK L12 57 F1
Chaffinch Gld HLWD L26 121 G2
Chainhurst Cl NTHLY L27 98 B2
Chain La RNFD/HAY WA11 48 D1
Chalfont Cl WARRS WA4 130 C5
Chalfont Rd CALD/MH L18 119 H2
Chalfont Wy STBRV L28 57 H3
Chalgrave Cl WDN WA8 103 E5
Chalkwell Dr HES CH60 149 G2
Challis St BIRK CH41 68 A4
Challoner Cl HUY L36 75 H5
Chaloner Gv ALL/GAR L19 118 D4
Chaloner St CLVPS L1 93 H1
Chalon Wy East ECCL WA10 11 H6
Chalon Wy West ECCL WA10 11 F6
Chamberlain Dr
NWD/KWIPK L33 26 A4
Chamberlain St BIRK CH41 * 92 C4
ECCL WA10 10 A6
WAL/EG CH44 68 C3
Chancellor Ct TOX L8 71 G5
Chancel St ANF/KKDL L4 54 A3
Chancery La STHEL WA9 49 E4
Chandlers Ct RUNC WA7 8 A6
Chandlers Wy STHEL WA9 79 F2
Chandos St EHL/KEN L7 71 H4
Changford Rd
NWD/KWIPK L33 34 B1
Channell Rd NPK/KEN L6 72 A2
Channel Rd CSBY/BLUN L23 28 C1
The Channel WAL/NB CH45 * 51 E2
Chantler Av WARRS WA4 107 G4
Chantrell Rd WKBY CH48 111 E1
Chantry Cl CL/PREN CH43 90 C2
Chantry Wk HES CH60 149 E3
Chapel Av WLT/FAZ L9 40 C2
Chapel Cross Rd
WARRN/WOL WA2 85 E3
Chapel Gdns EV L5 53 H5
Chapelhill Rd MOR/LEA CH46 66 D5
Chapelhouse Wk FMBY L37 17 F3
Chapel La ECCL WA10 46 D3
FMBY L37 17 E3
MGHL L31 24 D5
NTHTN L30 23 F4
RAIN/WH L35 78 D3
WARRS WA4 130 A3
WDN WA8 101 E3

Chapel Pl ALL/GAR L19 119 G5
Chapel Rd ALL/GAR L19 119 G5
HOY CH47 64 B5
NPK/KEN L6 55 E4
WARRW/BUR WA5 104 C5
Chapelside Cl
WARRW/BUR WA5 104 D2
Chapel St CLVP L2 6 B4
ECCL WA10 11 F1
PR/KW L34 * 59 H4
RUNC WA7 8 D4
WDN WA8 14 C6
Chapel Ter BTL L20 4 C6
Chapel Vw PS/BROM CH62 153 G3
Chapel Yd WARRN/WOL WA2 12 C3
WAV L15 96 A1
Chapman Cl TOX L8 * 94 A3
WDN WA8 101 F4
Chapman Gv PR/KW L34 60 A3
Chardstock Dr WLTN L25 * 98 A4
Charing Cross BIRK CH41 2 D5
Charlecombe St RF/TRAN CH42 92 B4
Charlecote St TOX L8 94 B5
Charles Av WARRW/BUR WA5 104 D2
Charles Berrington Rd WAV L15 96 A2
Charles Rd HOY CH47 87 F2
Charles St BIRK CH41 2 D2
ECCL WA10 11 H4
WDN WA8 14 D3
Charleston Gv
WARRW/BUR WA5 105 F2
Charleston Rd TOX L8 94 B4
Charlesville CL/PREN CH43 91 H3
Charles Wk DV/KA/FCH L14 74 B2
Charlesworth Cl MGHL L31 18 B1
Charley Wood Rd
NWD/KWIPK L33 34 C3
Charlock Cl NTHTN L30 23 F5
Charlotte Rd WAL/EG CH44 52 B5
Charlotte's Meadow
BEB CH63 138 A2
Charlotte St CLVPS L1 * 6 E4
Charlotte Wk WDN WA8 14 E6
Charlotte Wy CLVPS L1 * 7 F4
Charlton Cl RUNC WA7 156 C2
Charlton Ct CL/PREN CH43 91 F2
Charlton Pl CLB/OSW/ST L13 73 E4
Charlton Rd CLB/OSW/ST L13 73 E4
Charlton St WARRS WA4 107 H5
Charlwood Av HUY L36 75 G4
Charlwood Cl CL/PREN CH43 90 C2
Charminster Cl
WARRW/BUR WA5 105 F3
Charmouth Cl WD/CROXPK L12 43 E4
Charnley Dr WAV L15 73 G5
Charnock Rd WLT/FAZ L9 41 F4
Charnook Rd WLT/FAZ L9 41 E4
Charnwood Cl WD/CROXPK L12 42 D4
Charnwood Rd HUY L36 74 D2
Charnwood St STHEL WA9 49 E3
Charon Wy WARRW/BUR WA5 82 A2
Charter Av WARRW/BUR WA5 83 G5
Charterhouse Dr AIN/FAZ L10 32 B2
Charterhouse Rd WLTN L25 120 D2
Chartmount Wy WLTN L25 97 H4
Chartwell Gv HLWD L26 122 A2
Chaser Cl WLT/FAZ L9 31 H4
The Chase BEB CH63 152 C4
HUY L36 75 H5
Chase Wy EV L5 71 E1
Chatburn Wk TOX L8 * 94 B4
Chater Cl RAIN/WH L35 60 B5
Chatham Cl LITH L21 29 G5
Chatham Pl EHL/KEN L7 71 H4
Chatham Rd RF/TRAN CH42 116 A1
Chatham St EHL/KEN L7 7 K7
Chatsworth Av WAL/EG CH44 69 E1
WLT/FAZ L9 40 B2
Chatsworth Dr EHL/KEN L7 71 H5
WDN WA8 * 101 E5
Chatsworth Rd PEN/TH CH61 134 D1
RAIN/WH L35 77 H1
RF/TRAN CH42 116 A1
Chatterton Dr RUNC WA7 157 G1
Chatterton Rd DV/KA/FCH L14 73 G1
Chaucer Dr WD/CROXPK L12 43 F5
Chaucer Pl WARRS WA4 107 H4
Chaucer Rd ECCL WA10 47 F1
Chaucer St BTL L20 4 B2
RUNC WA7 8 D6
VAUX/LVPD L3 70 D2
Cheadle Av CLB/OSW/ST L13 72 D2
Cheapside CLVP L2 6 D2
FMBY L37 17 F4
Cheapside Aly CLVP L2 * 6 D3
Cheddar Cl WLTN L25 120 B1
Cheddar Gv KKBY L32 33 H5
Cheddon Wy PEN/TH CH61 134 C2
Chedworth Dr WDN WA8 101 E4
Chedworth Rd DV/KA/FCH L14 74 A1
Cheldon Rd WD/CROXPK L12 42 C5
Chelford Cl CL/PREN CH43 90 C1
WARRS WA4 130 A3
Chellowdene CSBY/BLUN L23 21 H3
Chelmsford Cl EV L5 53 H3
Chelsea Ct WD/CROXPK L12 57 E2
Chelsea Gdns
WARRW/BUR WA5 105 G4
Chelsea Rd LITH L21 39 F1
WLT/FAZ L9 40 C1
Cheltenham Av AIG/SPK L17 95 F2
Cheltenham Cl AIN/FAZ L10 32 B3
WARRW/BUR WA5 82 A5
Cheltenham Crs HUY L36 75 F4
MOR/LEA CH46 66 C2
RUNC WA7 155 F3
Cheltenham Rd WAL/NB CH45 51 E4
Chelwood Av CHLDW L16 74 A4
Chemistry Rd SPK/HALE L24 142 A1
Chenotrie Gdns CL/PREN CH43 90 D3
Chepstow Av WAL/EG CH44 69 E1
Chepstow Cl WARRW/BUR WA5 83 E2
Chepstow St ANF/KKDL L4 54 A1
Chequers Gdns ALL/GAR L19 118 D3
Cheriton Av WKBY CH48 110 D1
Cheriton Cl HLWD L26 121 G3
Chermside Rd AIG/SPK L17 118 C2
Cherry Av ANF/KKDL L4 54 D1
Cherrybank WAL/EG CH44 68 D3
Cherry Blossom Rd
RUNC WA7 156 B4
Cherry Cl ANF/KKDL L4 54 D1
NSTN CH64 159 H2
Cherrydale Rd CALD/MH L18 96 A4
Cherryfield Crs KKBY L32 33 H2
Cherryfield Dr KKBY L32 33 H2
Cherry Gv KKBY L32 34 A5
Cherry La ANF/KKDL L4 54 D1
Cherrysutton WDN WA8 100 D5
Cherrysutton Ms WDN WA8 * 100 D4
Cherry Tree Av RUNC WA7 155 G1
WARRW/BUR WA5 104 D4
Cherry Tree Cl RAIN/WH L35 76 D1
RNFD/HAY WA11 * 49 G2
Cherry Tree Dr STHEL WA9 49 G5
Cherry Tree La
RNFD/HAY WA11 37 E2
Cherry Tree Rd HUY L36 75 G5
MOR/LEA CH46 89 H1
Cherry V WLTN L25 97 H5
Cherry Vw NWD/KWIPK L33 26 A4
Cherrywood Av HLWD L26 122 B2
Cherwell Cl WARRN/WOL WA2 84 B3
Cheryl Dr WDN WA8 15 K1
Chesford Gra WARR WA1 109 E1
Cheshire Acre
GR/UP/WCH CH49 113 E1
Cheshire Av AIN/FAZ L10 33 E5
Cheshire Gdns ECCL WA10 10 D7
Cheshire Gv MOR/LEA CH46 89 G1
Cheshire Ring Canal Wk
WARRS WA4 128 C5
Cheshyre Dr RUNC WA7 147 F5
Cheshyres La RUNC WA7 154 C2
Chesnell Gv NWD/KWIPK L33 26 A4
Chesney Cl TOX L8 94 A2
Chesnut Gv BTL L20 4 D1
RF/TRAN CH42 92 B4
Chessington Cl WARRS WA4 130 C5
Chester Av NTHTN L30 31 E3
Chester Cl CSBY/BLUN L23 22 A5
RUNC WA7 147 F4
Chesterfield Dr
NWD/KWIPK L33 25 H4
Chesterfield Rd
CSBY/BLUN L23 21 H4
PS/BROM CH62 152 D5
Chesterfield St TOX L8 94 A1
Chester High Rd NSTN CH64 150 A5
Chester La STHEL WA9 79 F1
Chester New Rd WARRS WA4 129 F4
Chester Rd HES CH60 149 G3
HUY L36 76 A1
NPK/KEN L6 55 F4
NSTN CH64 158 D3
RUNC WA7 157 E5
WARRS WA4 129 G1
Chester St BIRK CH41 3 H4
PR/KW L34 59 H4
TOX L8 94 A1
WAL/EG CH44 * 68 C2
WDN WA8 14 E2
Chesterton St ALL/GAR L19 140 C2
Chestnut Av CSBY/BLUN L23 21 G3
HUY L36 75 F5
RNFD/HAY WA11 49 F2
WARRW/BUR WA5 104 D1
WDN WA8 125 F1
Chestnut Cl GR/UP/WCH CH49 112 A1
RAIN/WH L35 77 E1
Chestnut Ct BTL L20 4 D2
Chestnut Gv PS/BROM CH62 152 C1
RNFD/HAY WA11 37 H5
WAV L15 72 D5
Chestnut Rd LITH L21 29 G5
WLT/FAZ L9 40 D4
Chestnut St EHL/KEN L7 7 K5
Chestnut Wk MGHL L31 24 D5
Chestnut Wy FMBY L37 16 B5
Cheswood Cl RAIN/WH L35 77 E3
Chetham Ct WARRN/WOL WA2 83 G2
Chetton Dr RUNC WA7 157 G2
Chetwood Av CSBY/BLUN L23 21 G4
Chetwood Dr WDN WA8 101 H4
Chetwynd Cl CL/PREN CH43 91 F4
Chetwynd Rd CL/PREN CH43 * 91 G3
Chetwynd St AIG/SPK L17 94 D5
Chevasse Wk WLTN L25 98 A5
Cheverton Cl
GR/UP/WCH CH49 90 B5
Cheviot Av STHEL WA9 49 F4
WARRN/WOL WA2 83 G2
Cheviot Cl RF/TRAN CH42 115 F2
Cheviot Rd EHL/KEN L7 72 C3
RF/TRAN CH42 115 E2
Cheviot Wy NWD/KWIPK L33 26 A3
Cheyne Cl CSBY/BLUN L23 28 B1
Cheyne Gdns ALL/GAR L19 118 D3
Cheyne Wk STHEL WA9 61 H4
Chichester Cl RUNC WA7 157 F3
WARRS WA4 131 E4
WAV L15 72 B5
Chidden Cl GR/UP/WCH CH49 89 E5
Chidlow Cl WDN WA8 146 A1
Chigwell Cl WD/CROXPK L12 43 E4
Chilcott Rd CLB/OSW/ST L13 73 G2
Childers St CLB/OSW/ST L13 73 E2
Childwall Abbey Rd CHLDW L16 96 D2
Childwall Av EHL/KEN L7 95 F1
MOR/LEA CH46 89 F1
Childwall Bank Rd CHLDW L16 96 D1
Childwall Cl GR/UP/WCH CH49 89 F1
Childwall Crs CHLDW L16 96 D1
Childwall Gn
GR/UP/WCH CH49 113 E1
Childwall Hts WLTN L25 97 F1
Childwall La DV/KA/FCH L14 74 C3
WLTN L25 97 F2
Childwall Mount Rd
CHLDW L16 96 D1
Childwall Park Av CHLDW L16 97 E2
Childwall Priory Rd CHLDW L16 96 D1
Childwall Rd WAV L15 96 A1
Childwall Valley Rd CHLDW L16 74 B5
WLTN L25 74 C5
Chilhem Cl TOX L8 94 B4
Chilington Av WDN WA8 124 B3
Chillerton Rd WD/CROXPK L12 56 D2
Chillingham St TOX L8 94 C4
Chiltern Av WARRN/WOL WA2 83 G2
Chiltern Cl WD/CROXPK L12 43 F5
Chiltern Crs WARRN/WOL WA2 83 G2
Chiltern Dr KKBY L32 25 F5
Chiltern Rd RF/TRAN CH42 115 E2
STHEL WA9 49 G4
WARRN/WOL WA2 83 G2
Chilton Cl MGHL L31 18 D5
Chilton Ms MGHL L31 18 D5
Chilwell Cl WDN WA8 101 F4
China Farm La WKBY CH48 88 A4
China La WARRS WA4 130 A1
Chindit Cl FMBY L37 16 C4
Chippenham Av
GR/UP/WCH CH49 89 E4
Chippingdall Cl
WARRW/BUR WA5 105 G3
Chirkdale St ANF/KKDL L4 54 A1
Chirk Wy MOR/LEA CH46 89 H1
Chisenhale St VAUX/LVPD L3 70 C2
Chislehurst Av WLTN L25 97 H2
Chisnall Av ECCL WA10 47 E3
Chiswell St EHL/KEN L7 72 A3
Chiswick Cl RUNC WA7 * 157 F2
Chiswick Gdns WARRS WA4 130 D5
Cholmondeley Rd RUNC WA7 155 H4
WKBY CH48 110 B1
Cholmondeley St WDN WA8 146 A2
Cholsey Cl GR/UP/WCH CH49 89 H4
Chorley Rd PR/KW L34 59 F4
Chorley's La WDN WA8 102 D5
Chorley St ECCL WA10 10 E3
WARRN/WOL WA2 12 E2
Chorley Wy BEB CH63 138 A5
Chorlton Cl CHLDW L16 74 B5
Chorlton Gv WAL/NB CH45 50 D5
Christchurch Rd CL/PREN CH43 91 H4
Christian St VAUX/LVPD L3 7 F1
Christie St WDN WA8 15 J1
Christleton Cl CL/PREN CH43 113 H1
Christmas St BTL L20 53 H1
Christopher Cl CHLDW L16 73 H5
RAIN/WH L35 77 H3
Christopher Dr
PS/BROM CH62 153 G4
Christophers Cl
PEN/TH CH61 * 135 E2
Christopher St ANF/KKDL L4 54 B2
Christopher Wy CHLDW L16 73 H5
Chris Ward Cl EHL/KEN L7 72 A4
Chudleigh Cl HLWD L26 121 G2
Chudleigh Rd CLB/OSW/ST L13 72 D2
Church Av WLT/FAZ L9 31 G5
Church Cl FMBY L37 17 F3
WAL/EG CH44 69 F1
Church Close Ct FMBY L37 * 17 F3
Church Crs WAL/EG CH44 69 G3
Churchdown Gv
DV/KA/FCH L14 * 74 A1
Churchdown Rd
DV/KA/FCH L14 74 A1
Church Dr PS/BROM CH62 116 B5
WARRN/WOL WA2 85 E4
Church End SPK/HALE L24 143 H5
Church End Ms SPK/HALE L24 143 H5
Church Farm BEB CH63 138 A1
Church Farm Ct HES CH60 148 D2
Churchfield Rd WLTN L25 98 A3
Churchfields STHEL WA9 79 G1
WDN WA8 102 B3
Church Gdns BTL L20 4 C5
WAL/EG CH44 69 F1
Church Gn CHLDW L16 97 F1
FMBY L37 16 B4
KKBY L32 33 H1
Church Gv LITH L21 38 D1
Church Hl WAL/NB CH45 51 F5
Churchhill Av BIRK CH41 2 A2
Churchill Gdns STHEL WA9 61 E4
Churchill Gv WAL/EG CH44 * 52 A5
Churchill Wy CLVPS L1 6 E3
NSTN CH64 158 D2
VAUX/LVPD L3 6 E2
Church La AIG/SPK L17 118 C2
ANF/KKDL L4 40 B5
ECCL WA10 46 C4
GR/UP/WCH CH49 113 F1
NSTN CH64 158 D3
PEN/TH CH61 133 H1
PR/KW L34 44 A3
PS/BROM CH62 138 D5
WAL/EG CH44 69 F1
WARRS WA4 131 F2
Churchmeadow Cl
WAL/EG CH44 69 F1
Church Meadow La HES CH60 148 C2
Church Meadow Wk
WDN WA8 144 D1
Church Ms RF/TRAN CH42 116 A2
Church Mt EHL/KEN L7 71 H4
Church Rd ALL/GAR L19 140 C1
ANF/KKDL L4 40 C5
BEB CH63 138 A1
BEB CH63 150 D3
BTL L20 39 H1
CLB/OSW/ST L13 72 D2
CSBY/BLUN L23 21 F5
CSBY/WL L22 29 F4
FMBY L37 17 F2
GR/UP/WCH CH49 90 A3
HLWD L26 121 G1
HUY L36 75 E2
LITH L21 30 A5
LITH L21 30 B4
LITH L21 38 D1
MGHL L31 24 A2
RF/TRAN CH42 92 B4
WAL/EG CH44 69 G3
WAV L15 96 A2
WKBY CH48 110 A2
WLTN L25 97 G5
Church Rd North WAV L15 96 A1
Church Rd South WLTN L25 120 C1
Church Rd West ANF/KKDL L4 40 B5
Church Sq ECCL WA10 11 G5
Church St BIRK CH41 3 J4
BTL L20 4 B5
CLVPS L1 6 E4
ECCL WA10 11 H6
PR/KW L34 59 G4
RUNC WA7 8 D3
WAL/EG CH44 69 F1
WARR WA1 13 F4
WDN WA8 146 A1
Church Ter RF/TRAN CH42 92 B5
Church Vw BTL L20 4 D5
Churchview Rd BIRK CH41 2 A1
Church Wk BTL L20 4 C5
Church Wy FMBY L37 16 B4
KKBY L32 33 H1
Churchway Rd SPK/HALE L24 143 E4
Churchwood Cl
PS/BROM CH62 138 D5
Churnet St ANF/KKDL L4 54 A2
Churn Wy GR/UP/WCH CH49 89 F4
Churston Rd CHLDW L16 97 E3
Churton Av CL/PREN CH43 91 F5
Churton Ct NPK/KEN L6 * 71 G2
Ciaran Cl WD/CROXPK L12 56 D2
Cicely St EHL/KEN L7 71 H4
Cinder La BTL L20 30 C5
CALD/MH L18 96 C3
Cinnamon La WARRN/WOL WA2 84 D2
Cinnamon La North
WARRN/WOL WA2 84 D1
Cinnamon Pk
WARRN/WOL WA2 * 85 G3
Circular Dr GR/UP/WCH CH49 89 F5
HES CH60 134 C5
PS/BROM CH62 116 B4
Circular Rd BIRK CH41 2 E6
Circular Rd East NG/CROX L11 55 H2
Circular Rd West NG/CROX L11 55 H1
Cirencester Av
GR/UP/WCH CH49 89 E4
Citrine Rd WAL/EG CH44 69 F3
Citron Cl WLT/FAZ L9 40 D3
City Gdns ECCL WA10 47 H1
City Rd ANF/KKDL L4 54 B1
ECCL WA10 47 H1
Civic Wy BEB CH63 138 A1
HUY L36 75 G3
Clairville Cl BTL L20 4 E5
Clairville Wy CLB/OSW/ST L13 55 G5
Clamley Ct SPK/HALE L24 143 E3
Clandon Rd CALD/MH L18 119 H2
Clanfield Av WDN WA8 101 E5
Clanfield Rd NG/CROX L11 56 B1
Clap Gate Crs WDN WA8 144 D1
Clap Gates Rd
WARRW/BUR WA5 106 A1
Clapham Rd ANF/KKDL L4 54 D4
Clare Cl STHEL WA9 61 G3
Clare Crs WAL/EG CH44 68 A1
Claremont Av MGHL L31 23 G1
WDN WA8 102 B4
Claremont Cl LITH L21 29 G5
Claremont Dr WDN WA8 102 B4
Claremont Rd CSBY/BLUN L23 21 E5
LITH L21 29 G5
RUNC WA7 9 G5
WAV L15 95 G2
WKBY CH48 87 F5
Claremont Ter
CSBY/BLUN L23 * 21 E4
Claremont Wy BEB CH63 115 F3
Claremount Dr BEB CH63 137 H2
Claremount Rd WAL/NB CH45 51 F4
Clarence Av WARRW/BUR WA5 104 B2
WDN WA8 102 A4
Clarence Cl STHEL WA9 * 48 C5
Clarence Rd RF/TRAN CH42 92 A5
WAL/EG CH44 69 F3
WARRS WA4 131 F1
Clarence St RUNC WA7 8 C3
VAUX/LVPD L3 7 H4
WARR WA1 13 K1
Clarence Ter RUNC WA7 8 D3
Clarendon Cl CL/PREN CH43 2 B6
RUNC WA7 157 F2
Clarendon Ct WARRN/WOL WA2 83 F1
Clarendon Gv MGHL L31 18 C1
Clarendon Rd ALL/GAR L19 119 G5
LITH L21 38 D1
NPK/KEN L6 55 E4
WAL/EG CH44 69 F2
Clare Rd BTL L20 5 H7
Clares Farm Cl WARR WA1 109 F1
Claret Cl AIG/SPK L17 118 A2
Clare Wy WAL/NB CH45 51 F5
Claribel St TOX L8 94 C2
Clarke Av RF/TRAN CH42 115 G1
WARRS WA4 130 B1
Clarke Gdns WDN WA8 14 E6
Clarke's Crs ECCL WA10 46 D3
Clarkes Ter RUNC WA7 154 B2
Classic Rd CLB/OSW/ST L13 56 A5
Clatterbridge Rd BEB CH63 151 F1
Claude Rd NPK/KEN L6 55 E4
Claude St WARR WA1 13 G2
Claughton Cl EHL/KEN L7 72 A4
Claughton Dr WAL/EG CH44 68 D2
Claughton Firs CL/PREN CH43 91 H4
Claughton Gn CL/PREN CH43 91 H3
Claughton Pl BIRK CH41 2 C5
Claughton Rd BIRK CH41 2 E5
Claughton St ECCL WA10 11 G4
Clavell Rd ALL/GAR L19 119 H3
Claverton Cl RUNC WA7 155 F3
Clay Cross Rd WLTN L25 120 B1
Claydon Ct HLWD L26 122 A2
Clayfield Cl BTL L20 5 H5
Clayford Crs DV/KA/FCH L14 73 F1
Clayford Pl DV/KA/FCH L14 73 F1
Clayford Rd DV/KA/FCH L14 73 G1
Clayford Wy DV/KA/FCH L14 73 G1
Clay La ECCL WA10 46 A4
Claypole Cl EHL/KEN L7 72 A5
Clay St VAUX/LVPD L3 70 B1
Clayton Crs RUNC WA7 8 C6
WDN WA8 14 B2
Clayton La WAL/EG CH44 68 C3
Clayton Pl BIRK CH41 2 C6
Clayton St CL/PREN CH43 2 C6
Cleadon Cl KKBY L32 34 B5
Cleadon Rd KKBY L32 34 A5
Cleadon Wy WDN WA8 101 G4
Clearwater Cl EHL/KEN L7 71 H3
Cleary St BTL L20 4 C2
Clee Hill Rd RF/TRAN CH42 115 E2
Cleethorpes Rd RUNC WA7 157 E2
Cleeves Cl WARR WA1 13 G5
Clegge St WARRN/WOL WA2 12 E1
Clegg St EV L5 71 E1
Clelland St WARRS WA4 107 E5
Clematis Rd NTHLY L27 98 C2
Clement Gdns VAUX/LVPD L3 70 C1
Clementina Rd CSBY/BLUN L23 20 C5
Clements Wy NWD/KWIPK L33 25 G4
Clemmey Dr BTL L20 40 A1
Clent Av MGHL L31 18 C3
Clent Gdns MGHL L31 18 D3
Clent Rd MGHL L31 18 C4
Cleopas St TOX L8 94 B4
Clevedon St TOX L8 94 C4
Cleveland Cl KKBY L32 25 F5
Cleveland Rd WARRN/WOL WA2 83 H2
Cleveland Sq CLVPS L1 6 E6
Cleveland St BIRK CH41 2 E2
STHEL WA9 62 C1
Cleveley Pk CALD/MH L18 119 H2
Cleveley Rd CALD/MH L18 119 H2
HOY CH47 65 E5
Cleveleys Av WDN WA8 102 D5
Cleveleys Rd
WARRW/BUR WA5 105 F4
The Cleves MGHL L31 19 E3
Cleve Wy FMBY L37 17 G4
Clieves Rd KKBY L32 34 A3
Cliff Dr WAL/EG CH44 52 B5
Cliffe Rd NSTN CH64 159 E5
WARRS WA4 130 A4
Cliffe St WDN WA8 15 G1
Cliff La WARRS WA4 131 H1
Clifford Rd WAL/EG CH44 68 D2
WARRW/BUR WA5 105 E4
Clifford St BIRK CH41 68 C5
VAUX/LVPD L3 7 H2
Cliff Rd WAL/EG CH44 68 C2
Cliff St EHL/KEN L7 72 A3
Clifton Av HLWD L26 121 G2
Clifton Cl WARR WA1 108 C1
Clifton Ct RUNC WA7 8 A6
Clifton Crs BIRK CH41 3 F5
Clifton Dr AIN/FAZ L10 32 A2
Clifton Gv EV L5 * 71 E1
WAL/EG CH44 69 F1
Clifton Rd BIRK CH41 2 E7
FMBY L37 17 F1
NPK/KEN L6 55 F5
RUNC WA7 155 F2
Clifton Rd East NPK/KEN L6 55 F5
Clifton St ALL/GAR L19 119 G5
ECCL WA10 11 H3
WARRS WA4 13 G7
Cliftonville Rd PR/KW L34 60 A4
WARR WA1 108 C2
Clincton Cl WDN WA8 123 G3
Clincton Vw WDN WA8 123 G3
Clinton Pl WD/CROXPK L12 55 H3
Clinton Rd WD/CROXPK L12 55 H3
Clint Rd EHL/KEN L7 72 A4
Clint Wy EHL/KEN L7 72 A4
Clipper Vw PS/BROM CH62 116 B3
Clipsley Brook Vw
RNFD/HAY WA11 49 F1
Clipsley La RNFD/HAY WA11 49 H1
Clive Av WARRN/WOL WA2 84 A4
Clive Rd CL/PREN CH43 92 A4
Clock Face Rd STHEL WA9 79 G1
WDN WA8 103 E1
Clock Face Shop Pde
STHEL WA9 * 79 G1
Clock Tower Dr WLT/FAZ L9 40 B4
Clocktower St ECCL WA10 11 F5
The Cloisters CSBY/BLUN L23 29 E1
ECCL WA10 46 D3
FMBY L37 * 17 E3
Clorain Cl PR/KW L34 44 B3
Clorain Rd NWD/KWIPK L33 34 B1
Closeburn Av HES CH60 * 148 C3
Close St STHEL WA9 61 G3
The Close BEB CH63 115 F2
CSBY/BLUN L23 29 E1
ECCL WA10 46 C2
GR/UP/WCH CH49 112 B1
PEN/TH CH61 112 B5
RNFD/HAY WA11 49 F2
STBRV L28 58 A3
WLT/FAZ L9 40 B3
Cloudberry Cl NTHLY L27 98 C2
Clough Av WARRN/WOL WA2 83 H3
Clough Rd HLWD L26 122 A2
SPK/HALE L24 142 B2
The Clough RUNC WA7 147 F5
Cloughton Rd BIRK CH41 2 C5
Clovelly Av STHEL WA9 62 D4
WARRW/BUR WA5 104 C1
Clovelly Gv RUNC WA7 156 D4
Clovelly Rd ANF/KKDL L4 54 D4
Clover Av HLWD L26 121 F1
Clover Ct RUNC WA7 156 D4
Cloverdale Rd WLTN L25 97 H1
Clover Dr BIRK CH41 68 A4
Cloverfield RUNC WA7 * 157 E2
Clover Hey RNFD/HAY WA11 37 F5
Club St RNFD/HAY WA11 37 E3
Clwyd Gv WD/CROXPK L12 56 B2
Clwyd St BIRK CH41 2 E4
WAL/NB CH45 51 G3
Clyde Rd EHL/KEN L7 72 C3
Clydesdale Rd HOY CH47 64 B5
WAL/EG CH44 52 B5
WARRS WA4 130 B3
Clyde St BTL L20 53 G2
RF/TRAN CH42 115 H1
Coachmans Dr
WD/CROXPK L12 57 E1
Coalgate La RAIN/WH L35 76 C3
Coalport Wk STHEL WA9 61 E4
Coal St CLVPS L1 7 G3
Coalville Rd RNFD/HAY WA11 48 D1
Coastal Dr WAL/NB CH45 50 D2
Coastgaurd La NSTN CH64 158 A1
Cobb Av LITH L21 39 F1
The Cobbles HLWD L26 121 F1
Cobblestone Cnr ALL/GAR L19 119 E4
Cobbs La WARRS WA4 130 C3
Cobden Av RF/TRAN CH42 92 D5
Cobden Ct RF/TRAN CH42 92 D5
Cobden Pl RF/TRAN CH42 92 D5

Cobden St NPK/KEN L6 71 F2
WARRN/WOL WA2 12 E1
WLTN L25 120 B1
Cobden Vw WLTN L25 120 B1
Cobham Av WLT/FAZ L9 40 B1
Cobham Rd MOR/LEA CH46 66 B5
Coburg Whf VAUX/LVPD L3 93 G2
Cochrane St EV L5 54 B5
Cockburn St TOX L8 94 B4
Cockerell Cl ANF/KKDL L4 * 54 B3
Cockerham Wy NG/CROX L11 42 B2
Cockhedge La WARR WA1 12 E4
Cockhedge Wy WARR WA1 12 D4
Cocklade La SPK/HALE L24 143 H5
Cock Lane Ends WDN WA8 * 144 D1
Cockshead Rd WLTN L25 97 H3
Cockshead Wy WLTN L25 97 H2
Cockspur St VAUX/LVPD L3 6 D2
Cockspur St West
VAUX/LVPD L3 * 6 C2
Coerton Rd WLT/FAZ L9 31 G5
The Cokers RF/TRAN CH42 115 G3
Colbern Cl MGHL L31 24 B1
Colbrooke Rd AIG/SPK L17 94 D5
Colby Cl CHLDW L16 74 A5
Colden Cl WD/CROXPK L12 57 E3
Coldstream Cl
WARRN/WOL WA2 84 C1
Coleman Dr GR/UP/WCH CH49 88 D5
Colemere Cl WARR WA1 85 E4
Colemere Dr PEN/TH CH61 113 F5
Coleridge Av ECCL WA10 10 B3
Coleridge Ct KKBY L32 33 G4
Coleridge Dr PS/BROM CH62 116 A4
Coleridge Gv WDN WA8 124 C2
Coleridge St BTL L20 4 B3
NPK/KEN L6 71 H2
Colesborne Rd NG/CROX L11 42 A5
Coles Crs CSBY/BLUN L23 22 A3
Coleshill Rd NG/CROX L11 41 G4
Cole St CL/PREN CH43 2 C5
Colette Rd AIN/FAZ L10 33 E5
Coleus Cl WLT/FAZ L9 40 D3
Colin Cl HUY L36 75 E4
Colindale Rd CHLDW L16 97 E1
Colin Dr VAUX/LVPD L3 53 G5
Colinton St WAV L15 72 C5
College Av CSBY/BLUN L23 29 E1
FMBY L37 16 D2
College Cl CL/PREN CH43 90 B2
FMBY L37 16 C2
WAL/NB CH45 51 E4
WARR WA1 13 H3
WARRN/WOL WA2 85 F3
College Ct WD/CROXPK L12 56 A5
College Dr BEB CH63 116 A4
College Flds HUY L36 75 G4
College La CLVPS L1 6 E5
College Pth FMBY L37 16 C1
College Rd CSBY/BLUN L23 20 D5
College Rd North
CSBY/BLUN L23 20 D4
College St ECCL WA10 11 G3
College St North NPK/KEN L6 7 J1
College St South NPK/KEN L6 7 K1
College Vw BTL L20 4 E7
Collier's Rw RUNC WA7 154 C2
Collier St RUNC WA7 8 B2
Colliery Green Cl NSTN CH64 158 D5
Colliery Green Ct NSTN CH64 158 D5
Colliery Green Dr NSTN CH64 158 D5
Collingwood Cl ANF/KKDL L4 53 H2
Collingwood Dock
VAUX/LVPD L3 * 53 F5
Collingwood Rd BEB CH63 138 B2
Collin Rd CL/PREN CH43 68 A5
Collins Cl BTL L20 39 F2
Collin St WARRW/BUR WA5 106 A3
Colmore Av BEB CH63 137 H5
Colmore Rd NG/CROX L11 41 G5
Colne Dr STHEL WA9 62 D3
Colonel Dr WD/CROXPK L12 57 E3
The Colonnades VAUX/LVPD L3 * 6 C7
Colorado Cl WARRW/BUR WA5 105 G1
Colquitt St CLVPS L1 7 G6
Coltart Rd TOX L8 94 D2
Colton Rd WLTN L25 97 F1
Columban Cl NTHTN L30 30 D1
Columbia La CL/PREN CH43 91 H4
Columbia Rd ANF/KKDL L4 40 C5
PR/KW L34 60 A4
Columbine Cl MGHL L31 32 D1
WDN WA8 100 D4
Columbine Wy STHEL WA9 63 H3
Columbus Dr PEN/TH CH61 134 C3
Columbus Quay VAUX/LVPD L3 94 A5
Columbus Wy LITH L21 * 30 A5
Column Rd WKBY CH48 110 D2
Colville Ct WARRN/WOL WA2 83 G2
Colville Rd WAL/EG CH44 68 C1
Colville St WAV L15 72 C5
Colwall Cl NWD/KWIPK L33 34 B2
Colwall Rd NWD/KWIPK L33 34 B2
Colwell Cl DV/KA/FCH L14 57 G3
Colwell Rd DV/KA/FCH L14 57 G4
Colworth Rd SPK/HALE L24 141 H2
Colwyn Cl WARRW/BUR WA5 83 E3
Colwyn Rd CLB/OSW/ST L13 72 D3
Colwyn St BIRK CH41 68 C5
Colyton Av STHEL WA9 62 D5
Combermere St TOX L8 * 94 B2
WAV L15 72 B4
Comely Av WAL/EG CH44 69 E1
Comely Bank Rd WAL/EG CH44 69 F1
Comer Gdns MGHL L31 18 C3
Comfrey Gv HLWD L26 121 G1
Commerce Wy TOX L8 94 D1
Commercial Rd EV L5 53 G4
PS/BROM CH62 139 E3
Common Field Rd
GR/UP/WCH CH49 113 F2
Common La WARRS WA4 130 C1
Common St STHEL WA9 * 63 F3
Commutation Rw VAUX/LVPD L3 7 G3
Company's Cl RUNC WA7 154 D3
Compass Cl RUNC WA7 157 F4
Compton Rd BIRK CH41 67 H4
NPK/KEN L6 71 G1
Compton Wk BTL L20 4 D3
Compton Wy HLWD L26 121 G5
Comus St VAUX/LVPD L3 70 D2
Concert St CLVPS L1 7 F6
Concorde Pl WARRN/WOL WA2 84 B3
Concordia Av
GR/UP/WCH CH49 90 A3
The Concourse WKBY CH48 * 87 E5
Concourse Wy STHEL WA9 49 F5
Condor Cl ALL/GAR L19 119 H5
Condron Rd North LITH L21 30 B3
Condron Rd South LITH L21 30 B3
Coney Crs CSBY/BLUN L23 22 A4
Coney Gv RUNC WA7 156 D4
Coney La HUY L36 98 D1
Coney Wk GR/UP/WCH CH49 89 F2
Conifer Cl NWD/KWIPK L33 25 H4
WLT/FAZ L9 40 D4
Conifer Ct FMBY L37 17 E4
Conifer Gv WARRW/BUR WA5 104 D1
The Conifers MGHL L31 18 C3
Coningsby Dr WAL/EG CH44 68 C1
Coningsby Rd ANF/KKDL L4 54 C3
Coniston Av BEB CH63 152 C4
CL/PREN CH43 90 C3
PR/KW L34 60 B4
WAL/NB CH45 51 E3
WARRW/BUR WA5 104 B4
Coniston Cl NWD/KWIPK L33 25 G5
RUNC WA7 155 H3
WLT/FAZ L9 31 G5
Coniston Gv RNFD/HAY WA11 37 E5
Coniston Rd FMBY L37 16 C4
MGHL L31 19 E2
NSTN CH64 158 D4
PEN/TH CH61 112 B5
Coniston St EV L5 54 C4
Conleach Rd SPK/HALE L24 142 C3
Connaught Av WARR WA1 107 G1
Connaught Rd EHL/KEN L7 71 H3
Connaught Wy BIRK CH41 68 C5
Connolly Av BTL L20 5 K2
Consett Rd STHEL WA9 61 F4
Constables Cl RUNC WA7 147 G5
Constance St ECCL WA10 10 A7
VAUX/LVPD L3 7 J2
Constance Wy WDN WA8 146 A1
Constantine Av HES CH60 135 E5
Convent Cl ALL/GAR L19 119 E4
RF/TRAN CH42 92 B4
Conville Bvd BEB CH63 115 G3
Conway Av WARRW/BUR WA5 83 F3
Conway Cl BEB CH63 137 F1
NWD/KWIPK L33 25 G4
WARRW/BUR WA5 104 D2
Conway Dr BIRK CH41 2 D4
Conway St BIRK CH41 2 C3
EV L5 54 A5
Conwy Ct RUNC WA7 147 G4
Conwy Dr NPK/KEN L6 54 D5
Coogee Av WARRW/BUR WA5 104 C1
Cookes Cl NSTN CH64 158 D1
Cook Glades RAIN/WH L35 76 D4
Cook Rd MOR/LEA CH46 67 F1
Cooks Ct CSBY/BLUN L23 * 20 D4
Cookson Rd LITH L21 39 E1
Cookson St CLVPS L1 94 A1
Cook St BIRK CH41 2 D6
CLVP L2 6 D4
PR/KW L34 59 H4
RAIN/WH L35 60 B5
Coombe Dr RUNC WA7 154 D1
Coombe Rd PEN/TH CH61 112 C4
Cooperage Cl TOX L8 94 A4
Cooper Av WARRN/WOL WA2 83 H3
Cooper Av North
CALD/MH L18 119 E2
Cooper Av South ALL/GAR L19 119 E2
Cooper Cl ALL/GAR L19 119 E3
Cooper's La NWD/KWIPK L33 44 B1
Coopers Pl WARRS WA4 130 A4
Cooper St ECCL WA10 10 E3
RUNC WA7 8 D3
WDN WA8 14 E1
Copeland Cl PEN/TH CH61 134 C2
Copeland Gv RUNC WA7 156 A4
Copeland Rd WARRS WA4 129 H1
Copperas Hl VAUX/LVPD L3 7 G4
Copperas St ECCL WA10 11 F6
Copperfield Cl TOX L8 94 B3
Copperwood Dr RAIN/WH L35 77 E3
Coppice Cl CL/PREN CH43 90 B2
Coppice Crs HUY L36 75 H1
Coppice Gra MOR/LEA CH46 89 E1
Coppice Gn WARRW/BUR WA5 82 A4
Coppice Gv
GR/UP/WCH CH49 * 112 A1
Coppice La HUY L36 99 F1
Coppice Leys FMBY L37 16 D3
The Coppice NPK/KEN L6 55 E4
PR/KW L34 44 B4
WAL/NB CH45 51 G3
The Coppins WARRN/WOL WA2 84 A3
Copple House La AIN/FAZ L10 32 D5
Coppull Rd MGHL L31 18 C2
Copse Gv PEN/TH CH61 112 C4
The Copse CALD/MH L18 96 D3
RUNC WA7 156 C3
Copsmead MOR/LEA CH46 66 D5
Copthorne Rd KKBY L32 33 E2
Copy La NTHTN L30 23 F5
Copy Wy NTHTN L30 23 E4
Coral Av HUY L36 75 F2
STHEL WA9 61 H3
Coral Cl KKBY L32 33 F2
Coral Dr BTL L20 5 F4
Coral Rdg CL/PREN CH43 90 D2
Coral St CLB/OSW/ST L13 73 E4
Corbet Av WARRN/WOL WA2 83 H5
Corbet St WARRN/WOL WA2 * 83 H5
Corbridge Rd CHLDW L16 96 C2
Corbyn St WAL/EG CH44 69 G4
Corfu St BIRK CH41 * 2 C5
Corinthian Av CLB/OSW/ST L13 73 E1
Corinthian St LITH L21 29 G5
RF/TRAN CH42 * 115 H1
Corinto St TOX L8 94 B1
Corkdale Rd WLT/FAZ L9 40 D3
Cormorant Dr RUNC WA7 8 A5
Corncroft Rd PR/KW L34 44 B4
Corndale Rd CALD/MH L18 96 A4
Cornelius Dr PEN/TH CH61 134 D1
Cornel Wy HUY L36 75 H5
Corner Brook STBRV L28 57 F3
Cornerhouse La WDN WA8 101 F5
Cornett Rd WLT/FAZ L9 31 G5
Corney St EHL/KEN L7 95 E1
Cornfields Cl ALL/GAR L19 119 F5
Cornflower Wy MOR/LEA CH46 67 E3
Cornforth Wy WDN WA8 101 H5
Cornhill CLVPS L1 6 E7
Cornice Rd CLB/OSW/ST L13 73 E1
Corniche Rd PS/BROM CH62 116 B5
Corn St TOX L8 94 A3
Cornubia Rd WDN WA8 15 H5
Cornwall Av RUNC WA7 8 D5
Cornwall Cl PS/BROM CH62 116 B3
RUNC WA7 147 F5
Cornwall Dr CL/PREN CH43 114 C2
Cornwall Rd WDN WA8 102 B5
Cornwall St STHEL WA9 48 D5
WARR WA1 13 K1
Cornwood Cl WLTN L25 97 H1
Corona Av MGHL L31 18 C1
Corona Rd CLB/OSW/ST L13 73 E1
CSBY/WL L22 29 E3
PS/BROM CH62 116 C5
Coronation Av DV/KA/FCH L14 74 A2
FMBY L37 17 F4
WAL/NB CH45 51 H3
WARRS WA4 131 F1
Coronation Buildings
WAL/NB CH45 * 51 H5
Coronation Dr CSBY/BLUN L23 29 E1
DV/KA/FCH L14 74 A2
PS/BROM CH62 138 D3
RAIN/WH L35 76 C2
WARRW/BUR WA5 104 D4
WDN WA8 123 H3
Coronation Rd CSBY/BLUN L23 29 E1
ECCL WA10 47 E1
HOY CH47 86 D2
MGHL L31 18 D3
RUNC WA7 9 F6
RUNC WA7 157 H3
Coronation Vls
WD/CROXPK L12 * 56 D3
Coroner's La WDN WA8 102 A3
Coronet Rd NG/CROX L11 42 C4
Coronet Wy WDN WA8 123 H3
Corporal Wy WD/CROXPK L12 57 E3
BIRK CH41 68 C5
Corporation St ECCL WA10 11 G4
ECCL WA10 11 J5
Corrie Dr BEB CH63 137 H2
Corsewall St EHL/KEN L7 72 B5
Corsican Gdns STHEL WA9 61 E4
Cortsway GR/UP/WCH CH49 89 G3
Cortsway West
GR/UP/WCH CH49 89 F3
Corwen Cl CL/PREN CH43 90 B2
MOR/LEA CH46 89 H1
WARRW/BUR WA5 83 E4
Corwen Crs DV/KA/FCH L14 74 B3
Corwen Dr NTHTN L30 23 F5
Corwen Rd ANF/KKDL L4 55 E2
HOY CH47 87 G1
Cosgrove Cl NPK/KEN L6 55 F3
Cossack Av WARRN/WOL WA2 83 H4
Costain St BTL L20 53 G2
Cote Lea Ct RUNC WA7 * 156 B3
Cotham St ECCL WA10 11 G5
Cotsford Cl HUY L36 75 E1
Cotsford Pl HUY L36 75 E1
Cotsford Rd HUY L36 75 E1
Cotsford Wy HUY L36 75 E1
Cotswold Gv STHEL WA9 49 G4
Cotswold Rd RF/TRAN CH42 115 E2
WARRN/WOL WA2 83 H2
Cotswolds Crs HLWD L26 121 G4
Cotswold St EHL/KEN L7 71 H3
Cottage Cl BEB CH63 152 C4
KKBY L32 33 H5
NSTN CH64 158 D3
Cottage Dr East HES CH60 148 D4
Cottage Dr West HES CH60 148 D4
Cottage La HES CH60 148 D4
Cottage Pl STHEL WA9 * 79 G1
Cottage St BIRK CH41 2 D2
Cottam Dr WARRN/WOL WA2 85 E2
Cottenham St NPK/KEN L6 71 H2
Cotterdale Cl STHEL WA9 62 C4
WARRW/BUR WA5 104 D1
Cotterill RUNC WA7 155 H1
Cotterill Dr WARR WA1 108 C1
Cottesbrook Cl NG/CROX L11 42 A4
Cottesbrook Pl NG/CROX L11 42 A4
Cottesbrook Rd NG/CROX L11 42 A4
Cottesmore Dr HES CH60 * 149 H1
Cotton La RUNC WA7 155 H1
Cotton St VAUX/LVPD L3 70 B1
Cotton Ter STHEL WA9 63 F2
Cottonwood AIG/SPK L17 94 B5
Cottrell Cl ALL/GAR L19 140 C2
Coulport Cl DV/KA/FCH L14 74 C1
Coulsdon Pl TOX L8 94 C4
Coulthard Rd RF/TRAN CH42 116 A3
Coulton Rd WDN WA8 103 E5
Council St RAIN/WH L35 60 C5
Countess Pk NG/CROX L11 42 C5
Countisbury Dr CHLDW L16 97 E2
County Dr ECCL WA10 10 D7
County Rd ANF/KKDL L4 40 B5
KKBY L32 25 H5
Court Av HLWD L26 122 A2
Courtenay Av CSBY/WL L22 28 D2
WAL/EG CH44 68 C2
Courtenay Rd CSBY/WL L22 28 D2
HOY CH47 87 E1
WLTN L25 97 F4
Courtfields Cl WD/CROXPK L12 56 B5
Court Hey Av DV/KA/FCH L14 74 C3
Court Hey Dr CHLDW L16 74 B4
Court Hey Rd CHLDW L16 74 B4
Courthope Rd ANF/KKDL L4 54 D1
Courtland Rd CALD/MH L18 96 B3
Courtney Av WAL/EG CH44 68 C2
Courtney Rd RF/TRAN CH42 116 A3
The Court BEB CH63 * 138 A2
NSTN CH64 159 E4
STBRV L28 58 A3
Covent Gdn CLVP L2 6 C4
Coventry Av NTHTN L30 31 E3
Coventry Rd WAV L15 96 A2
Coventry St BIRK CH41 2 D5
Coverdale Av RAIN/WH L35 78 B3
Coverdale Cl
WARRW/BUR WA5 104 D1
Covertside WKBY CH48 110 D1
Cowan Dr NPK/KEN L6 71 G1
Cowanway WDN WA8 101 H3
Cowdell St WARRN/WOL WA2 106 D1
Cowdrey Av CL/PREN CH43 67 G4
Cow Hey La RUNC WA7 155 E4
Cowley Cl GR/UP/WCH CH49 * 89 F3
Cowley Ct ECCL WA10 * 10 E3
Cowley Hill La ECCL WA10 10 D1
Cowley Rd ANF/KKDL L4 54 B1
Cowley St ECCL WA10 11 G2
Cowper Rd CLB/OSW/ST L13 73 F3
Cowper St BTL L20 4 B1
STHEL WA9 * 62 C1
Cowper Wy HUY L36 76 A4
Coylton Av RAIN/WH L35 78 B3
Crab La WARRN/WOL WA2 85 E2
Crab St ECCL WA10 11 F3
Crabtree Cl NTHLY L27 98 B3
Crabtree Fold RUNC WA7 157 E1
Cradley WDN WA8 124 A1
Crag Gv RNFD/HAY WA11 37 F3
Craigburn Rd CLB/OSW/ST L13 55 G4
Craighurst Rd WLTN L25 97 G1
Craigleigh Gv PS/BROM CH62 153 F5
Craigmore Rd CALD/MH L18 119 E2
Craigside Av WD/CROXPK L12 56 A3
Craigs Rd CLB/OSW/ST L13 55 G4
Craigwood Wy HUY L36 74 D2
Craine Cl ANF/KKDL L4 54 D2
Cramond Av CALD/MH L18 96 A3
Cranage Cl RUNC WA7 155 H2
Cranberry Cl ECCL WA10 10 E2
Cranborne Av HOY CH47 65 E4
WARRS WA4 129 H2
Cranborne Rd WAV L15 95 F1
Cranbourne Av BIRK CH41 91 F1
MOR/LEA CH46 89 F1
Crane Av STHEL WA9 62 D4
Cranehurst Rd ANF/KKDL L4 40 D5
Cranfield Rd CSBY/BLUN L23 21 H4
Cranford Cl PS/BROM CH62 153 F5
Cranford Rd ALL/GAR L19 119 F3
Cranford St WAL/EG CH44 69 E3
Crank Rd RNFD/HAY WA11 36 A5
Cranleigh Cl WARRS WA4 129 H4
Cranleigh Pl WLTN L25 97 G2
Cranleigh Rd WLTN L25 97 G3
Cranmer St EV L5 53 G5
Cranmore Av CSBY/BLUN L23 29 F2
Cranshaw Av STHEL WA9 79 H2
Cranshaw La WDN WA8 102 B3
Cranston Cl ECCL WA10 46 D2
Cranston Rd NWD/KWIPK L33 34 D2
Crantock Cl HLWD L26 121 H3
NG/CROX L11 * 42 C3
Crantock Gv ECCL WA10 47 E1
Cranwell Cl AIN/FAZ L10 31 H2
Cranwell Rd GR/UP/WCH CH49 88 D5
WLTN L25 97 G1
Craven Cl BIRK CH41 2 D4
Craven Ct WARRN/WOL WA2 83 F1
Craven Lea WD/CROXPK L12 43 E4
Craven Rd RAIN/WH L35 78 A2
WD/CROXPK L12 56 C4
Craven St BIRK CH41 2 C5
VAUX/LVPD L3 7 H2
Cravenwood Rd HLWD L26 121 H4
Crawford Av CALD/MH L18 95 H3
MGHL L31 18 B3
WDN WA8 123 H2
Crawford Cl STHEL WA9 79 H1
WD/CROXPK L12 56 D3
Crawford Dr WAV L15 73 E4
Crawford Pk CALD/MH L18 95 H5
Crawford Pl RUNC WA7 155 F3
Crawford St STHEL WA9 80 A1
Crawford Wy EHL/KEN L7 72 C3
Crawley Av WARRN/WOL WA2 * 83 G2
Crediton Cl NG/CROX L11 42 C2
The Creek WAL/NB CH45 51 E2
Cremorne Hey STBRV L28 57 H3
Crescent Av FMBY L37 16 D5
Crescent Ct LITH L21 39 E1
Crescent Rd CSBY/BLUN L23 20 C4
LITH L21 39 E1
WAL/EG CH44 69 E1
WLT/FAZ L9 40 D3
The Crescents RAIN/WH L35 77 G1
The Crescent BEB CH63 137 G1
CSBY/BLUN L23 21 H3
CSBY/WL L22 29 F3
GR/UP/WCH CH49 89 F5
HES CH60 149 F3
HUY L36 76 A3
MGHL L31 23 H2
PEN/TH CH61 112 D5
RAIN/WH L35 77 F1
WKBY CH48 110 A1
Cressbrook Rd WARRS WA4 130 A3
Cressingham Rd WAL/NB CH45 51 H2
Cressington Av RF/TRAN CH42 115 F2
Cressington Esp ALL/GAR L19 118 D5
Cresswell Cl HLWD L26 122 A2
WARRW/BUR WA5 82 D3
Cresswell St NPK/KEN L6 71 F1
Cresta Dr RUNC WA7 154 D3
Cresttor Rd WLTN L25 97 F5
Creswell St ECCL WA10 10 C5
Cretan Rd WAV L15 95 F1
Crewe Gn GR/UP/WCH CH49 113 E1
Cricket Pth FMBY L37 17 E1
Cricklade Cl BTL L20 4 C3
Cringles Dr RAIN/WH L35 99 E1
Crispin Rd NTHLY L27 98 B3
Crispin St ECCL WA10 10 D6
Critchley Rd SPK/HALE L24 143 E4
Critchley Wy NWD/KWIPK L33 26 A4
Croasdale Dr RUNC WA7 156 A4
Crockett's Wk ECCL WA10 46 D2
Crocus Av BIRK CH41 68 B5
Crocus Gdns STHEL WA9 63 G3
Crocus St EV L5 53 H3
Croft Av PS/BROM CH62 138 C5
Croft Av East PS/BROM CH62 138 D4
Croft Cl CL/PREN CH43 91 E4
Croft Dr MOR/LEA CH46 89 G1
WKBY CH48 110 C5
Croft Dr East WKBY CH48 111 E4
Croft Dr West WKBY CH48 110 C4
Croft Edge CL/PREN CH43 91 H5
Croft End STHEL WA9 63 F1
Croften Dr NSTN CH64 158 D5
Crofters La NWD/KWIPK L33 26 B4
The Crofters GR/UP/WCH CH49 89 F4
Croft Fld MGHL L31 19 E5
Croft Gdns WARRS WA4 131 E4
Croft Gn PS/BROM CH62 138 D3
Croft La PS/BROM CH62 138 D5
WLT/FAZ L9 32 A5
Crofton Crs CLB/OSW/ST L13 73 F2
Crofton Rd CLB/OSW/ST L13 73 F2
RF/TRAN CH42 92 C5
RUNC WA7 145 G5
Croftside WARR WA1 109 F1
Croft St WDN WA8 14 C7
Croftsway HES CH60 148 B1
The Croft GR/UP/WCH CH49 112 B1
MGHL L31 18 B1
RUNC WA7 147 E5
STBRV L28 * 57 G2
WD/CROXPK L12 56 B3
Croftwood Gv RAIN/WH L35 77 E3
Cromarty Rd CLB/OSW/ST L13 72 D2
WAL/EG CH44 68 B1
Cromdale Gv STHEL WA9 49 E5
Cromdale Wy
WARRW/BUR WA5 104 C2
Cromer Dr WAL/NB CH45 51 G5
Cromer Rd AIG/SPK L17 118 C2
HOY CH47 87 E2
Cromer Wy HLWD L26 121 H5
Cromford Rd HUY L36 58 C5
Crompton Dr WD/CROXPK L12 43 E4
Cromptons La CALD/MH L18 96 D3
Crompton St EV L5 53 H5
Cromwell Av WARRW/BUR WA5 82 C3
Cromwell Av South
WARRW/BUR WA5 105 G4
Cromwell Ct WARR WA1 12 B5
Cromwell Rd ANF/KKDL L4 40 B5
Cromwell St WDN WA8 125 E5
Crondall Gv WAV L15 96 B1
Cronton Av MOR/LEA CH46 66 C2
Cronton La RAIN/WH L35 77 H4
WDN WA8 101 H3
Cronton Park Cl WDN WA8 101 E2
Cronton Rd RAIN/WH L35 99 F1
WAV L15 96 A3
Cronulla Dr WARRW/BUR WA5 104 B1
Croome Dr WKBY CH48 110 C1
Croppers Hl ECCL WA10 10 D6
Croppers Rd WARRN/WOL WA2 84 D2
Cropper St CLVPS L1 7 G5
Cropton Rd FMBY L37 17 E3
Crosby Av WARRW/BUR WA5 83 G5
Crosby Cl GR/UP/WCH CH49 89 H2
Crosby Gn WD/CROXPK L12 56 A3
Crosby Gv ECCL WA10 61 F1
Crosby Rd North CSBY/WL L22 29 F3
Crosby Rd South LITH L21 29 G5
Crosender Rd CSBY/BLUN L23 28 D1
Crosfield Cl EHL/KEN L7 72 A4
Crosfield Rd EHL/KEN L7 72 A4
RAIN/WH L35 77 F1
WAL/EG CH44 69 E2
Crosfield St WARR WA1 12 B4
Crosfield Wk EHL/KEN L7 72 A4
Crosgrove Rd ANF/KKDL L4 55 E1
Crosland Rd KKBY L32 34 B3
Crossacre Rd WLTN L25 97 H1
Crossdale Rd CSBY/BLUN L23 28 D1
PS/BROM CH62 152 D3
Crossdale Wy RNFD/HAY WA11 37 F3
Cross Farm Rd STHEL WA9 62 C1
Crossford Rd DV/KA/FCH L14 57 G4
Crossgates WDN WA8 103 F5
Cross Green Cl FMBY L37 17 F4
Crosshall St CLVPS L1 6 E3
Cross Hey LITH L21 30 A2
MGHL L31 * 24 B2
Cross Hey Av CL/PREN CH43 90 D3
Cross Hillocks La RAIN/WH L35 100 A5
Cross La BEB CH63 137 H2
NSTN CH64 158 D5
RAIN/WH L35 76 D1
WAL/NB CH45 50 D5
WARRS WA4 131 E1
Crossley Dr HES CH60 148 B1
WAV L15 73 E5
Crossley Rd ECCL WA10 61 F2
Crossley St WARR WA1 13 F3
Cross St BIRK CH41 3 H4
CSBY/WL L22 29 E4
ECCL WA10 11 F5
NSTN CH64 158 D2
PR/KW L34 59 H3
PS/BROM CH62 * 138 B1
RUNC WA7 * 8 D3
WARRN/WOL WA2 106 D1
WDN WA8 15 F2
The Cross MOR/LEA CH46 * 66 C5
PS/BROM CH62 138 D5
Crossvale Rd HUY L36 75 G4
Crossway CL/PREN CH43 68 A5
WDN WA8 124 B3
Crossways PS/BROM CH62 138 D3
The Crossway BEB CH63 150 D5
Crosswood Crs HUY L36 75 E2
Crosthwaite Av
PS/BROM CH62 153 F5
Croston Av RAIN/WH L35 60 D5
Croston Cl WDN WA8 101 E4
Crouch St EV L5 54 C4
STHEL WA9 * 62 D2
Crowe Av WARRN/WOL WA2 83 H2
Crowland Wy FMBY L37 17 G4
Crowmarsh Cl
GR/UP/WCH CH49 * 89 H4
Crown Acres Rd WLTN L25 121 E2
Crown Av WDN WA8 123 H3
Crown Cl FMBY L37 17 F4
Crown Ga RUNC WA7 156 B2
Crown Rd WD/CROXPK L12 56 C3

Crown Station Pl EHL/KEN L7 71 G5
Crown St EHL/KEN L7 71 G5
STHEL WA9 61 F3
TOX L8 94 C1
WARR WA1 12 D4
Crownway HUY L36 75 F1
Crow St TOX L8 93 H2
Crowther St ECCL WA10 10 B6
Crow Wood La WDN WA8 125 H1
Crow Wood Pl WDN WA8 * 102 D5
Croxdale Rd DV/KA/FCH L14 57 G3
Croxdale Rd West
DV/KA/FCH L14 57 F3
Croxteth Av LITH L21 29 H5
WAL/EG CH44 68 D1
Croxteth Cl MGHL L31 19 E3
Croxteth Dr AIG/SPK L17 95 E3
Croxteth Gv TOX L8 94 D2
Croxteth Hall La NG/CROX L11 42 C4
WD/CROXPK L12 42 C5
WD/CROXPK L12 56 D2
Croxteth La STBRV L28 57 H1
Croxteth Rd BTL L20 39 F2
TOX L8 94 D3
Croxteth Vw KKBY L32 43 F1
Croyde Pl STHEL WA9 79 G1
Croyde Rd SPK/HALE L24 143 E3
Croydon Av CALD/MH L18 95 H3
Croylands St ANF/KKDL L4 54 A2
Crucian Wy WD/CROXPK L12 42 D4
Crump St CLVPS L1 94 A1
Crutchley Av BIRK CH41 68 D5
Crystal Cl CLB/OSW/ST L13 73 E3
Cubbin Crs EV L5 53 H4
Cubert Rd NG/CROX L11 42 C3
Cuckoo Cl WLTN L25 97 G4
Cuckoo La NSTN CH64 159 G3
WLTN L25 97 G3
Cuerden St VAUX/LVPD L3 7 F2
Cuerdley Gn
WARRW/BUR WA5 126 C1
Cuerdley Rd
WARRW/BUR WA5 104 A5
Cuerdon Dr WARRS WA4 131 H2
Cullen Av BTL L20 39 H2
Cullen Cl BEB CH63 152 C5
Cullen Rd RUNC WA7 154 B2
Cullen St TOX L8 95 E1
Culme Rd WD/CROXPK L12 55 H3
Culzean Cl WD/CROXPK L12 43 E4
Cumberland Av AIG/SPK L17 95 F2
CL/PREN CH43 114 C1
ECCL WA10 60 D2
NTHTN L30 30 B1
Cumberland Cl NPK/KEN L6 55 F4
Cumberland Crs
RNFD/HAY WA11 49 G1
Cumberland Ga NTHTN L30 23 F5
Cumberland Rd WAL/NB CH45 52 A3
Cumberland St CLVP L2 * 6 D3
WARRS WA4 107 E5
Cumber La RAIN/WH L35 77 F2
Cumbers Dr NSTN CH64 159 F5
Cumbers La NSTN CH64 159 F5
Cumbria Wy WD/CROXPK L12 56 C1
Cummings St CLVPS L1 7 G7
Cumpsty Rd LITH L21 30 B3
Cunard Av WAL/EG CH44 52 B5
Cunard Cl CL/PREN CH43 90 C2
Cunard Rd LITH L21 30 A5
Cunliffe Cl RUNC WA7 156 C2
Cunliffe St CLVP L2 6 D2
Cunningham Cl
WARRW/BUR WA5 104 D3
WKBY CH48 * 110 C5
Cunningham Dr BEB CH63 152 C2
RUNC WA7 8 A7
Cunningham Rd
CLB/OSW/ST L13 73 E3
WDN WA8 124 B3
Cuper Crs HUY L36 75 F1
Curate Rd NPK/KEN L6 55 E3
Curlender Cl BIRK CH41 68 A4
Curlender Wy SPK/HALE L24 144 A4
Curlew Av GR/UP/WCH CH49 89 F2
Curlew Cl GR/UP/WCH CH49 89 F2
Curlew Ct MOR/LEA CH46 66 A4
Curlew Wy MOR/LEA CH46 66 A4
Currans Rd WARRN/WOL WA2 83 G3
Curran Wy NWD/KWIPK L33 25 G3
Curtana Crs NG/CROX L11 42 C4
Curtis Rd ANF/KKDL L4 55 E1
Curwell Cl BEB CH63 138 B3
Curzon Av BIRK CH41 2 A2
WAL/NB CH45 51 H2
Curzon Dr WARRS WA4 131 E4
Curzon Rd CSBY/WL L22 29 F3
HOY CH47 87 E1
RF/TRAN CH42 114 D1
Curzon St RUNC WA7 8 C6
Cusson Rd NWD/KWIPK L33 34 C3
Custley Hey STBRV L28 57 H2
Custom House La CLVPS L1 * 6 D5
Cut La NWD/KWIPK L33 35 F5
Cygnet Ct NWD/KWIPK L33 34 B2
WARR WA1 106 C5
Cynthia Av WARR WA1 108 B1
Cynthia Rd RUNC WA7 8 B6
Cypress Av WDN WA8 102 B5
Cypress Cl MGHL L31 32 D1
WARR WA1 109 E1
Cypress Cft BEB CH63 138 B3
Cypress Gdns STHEL WA9 61 E3
Cypress Gv RUNC WA7 155 G2
Cypress Rd HUY L36 75 F5
Cyprus Gv TOX L8 94 C4
Cyprus St PR/KW L34 59 H4
Cyprus Ter WAL/NB CH45 * 51 H3
Cyril Gv AIG/SPK L17 118 C1
Cyril St WARRN/WOL WA2 12 E1

D

Dacre's Bridge La RAIN/WH L35 99 H1
Dacre St BIRK CH41 3 F4
BTL L20 53 F1
Dacy Rd EV L5 54 C5
Daffodil Cl WDN WA8 103 E4
Daffodil Gdns STHEL WA9 63 G3
Daffodil Rd BIRK CH41 91 F1
WAV L15 96 B2
Dagnall Av WARRW/BUR WA5 83 F3
Dagnall Rd KKBY L32 33 F3
Dahlia Cl STHEL WA9 63 G3
WLT/FAZ L9 40 D3
Dairylands Cl CHLDW L16 96 C2
Daisy Bank Rd
WARRW/BUR WA5 104 D4
Daisy Ms LITH L21 39 F1
Daisy Mt MGHL L31 24 B1
Daisy St EV L5 53 H3
Dakota Dr ALL/GAR L19 141 E3
WARRW/BUR WA5 105 G1
Dalby Cl RNFD/HAY WA11 48 C2
Dale Acre Dr NTHTN L30 30 D2
Dale Av HES CH60 134 D5
PS/BROM CH62 152 D1
Dalebrook Cl WLTN L25 97 H1
Dale Cl MGHL L31 18 C4
WARRW/BUR WA5 105 H4
WDN WA8 123 G3
Dale Crs STHEL WA9 62 D4
Dale End Rd PEN/TH CH61 135 G2
Dale Gdns HES CH60 134 B5
Dalegarth Av WD/CROXPK L12 57 F1
Dalehead Pl RNFD/HAY WA11 37 F3
Dale Hey WAL/EG CH44 68 D2
Dalehurst Cl WAL/EG CH44 69 F1
Dale La NWD/KWIPK L33 26 B5
WARRS WA4 130 C3
Dalemeadow Rd
DV/KA/FCH L14 73 H2
Dale Ms WLTN L25 97 H4
Dale Rd PS/BROM CH62 152 D4
Daleside Cl PEN/TH CH61 112 D5
Daleside Rd NWD/KWIPK L33 34 A1
Dales Rw HUY L36 76 B3
Dale St ALL/GAR L19 140 C1
CLVP L2 6 D3
RUNC WA7 8 D7
Dalesway HES CH60 148 C1
The Dale NSTN CH64 158 C4
WARRW/BUR WA5 104 D3
Dale View Cl PEN/TH CH61 135 E1
Dalewood WD/CROXPK L12 43 E4
Dalewood Cl WARRN/WOL WA2 12 A3
Dalewood Gdns RAIN/WH L35 77 F3
Daley Pl BTL L20 30 D5
Daley Rd LITH L21 30 B3
Dallam Ct WARRN/WOL WA2 * 12 C1
Dallam La WARRN/WOL WA2 12 C2
WARRN/WOL WA2 106 C1
WARRW/BUR WA5 12 C1
Dallas Gv WLT/FAZ L9 40 C1
Dalmeny St AIG/SPK L17 94 D5
Dalmorton Rd WAL/NB CH45 52 A2
Dalry Crs KKBY L32 34 A5
Dalrymple St EV L5 53 H5
Dalston Dr RNFD/HAY WA11 37 F3
Dalton Av WARRW/BUR WA5 106 B1
Dalton Bank WARR WA1 13 G3
Dalton Cl WD/CROXPK L12 42 C5
Dalton Ct RUNC WA7 147 E3
Dalton Rd WAL/NB CH45 52 A3
Dalton St RUNC WA7 146 D4
Daltry Cl WD/CROXPK L12 56 A3
Dalwood Cl RUNC WA7 157 G2
Damerham Ms WLTN L25 97 G1
Damfield La MGHL L31 18 C5
Dam La WARR WA1 108 D1
Damson Rd NTHLY L27 98 C3
Dam Wood Rd SPK/HALE L24 142 B4
Danby Cl EV L5 54 B5
RUNC WA7 155 H3
WARRW/BUR WA5 106 A1
Danby Fold RAIN/WH L35 77 H2
Dane Cl PEN/TH CH61 112 D5
Danefield Pl ALL/GAR L19 119 H3
Danefield Rd ALL/GAR L19 119 H3
GR/UP/WCH CH49 112 A1
Danehurst Rd WAL/NB CH45 51 F3
WLT/FAZ L9 31 G5
Danescourt Rd BIRK CH41 68 C5
WD/CROXPK L12 56 C5
Danescroft WDN WA8 100 D5
Dane St ANF/KKDL L4 54 B1
Daneswell Dr MOR/LEA CH46 66 D4
Daneswell Rd SPK/HALE L24 143 E4
Daneville Rd ANF/KKDL L4 41 F5
Danger La MOR/LEA CH46 66 D3
Daniel Cl BTL L20 39 E1
Daniel Davies Dr TOX L8 94 C1
Dannette Hey STBRV L28 58 A4
Dansie St VAUX/LVPD L3 7 J4
Dans Rd WDN WA8 126 A1
Dante Cl WLT/FAZ L9 31 H4
Danube St TOX L8 * 95 E1
Darby Gv ALL/GAR L19 119 F5
Darby Rd ALL/GAR L19 119 E3
Darent Rd RNFD/HAY WA11 49 H1
Daresbury Cl KKBY L32 33 F2
Daresbury Expy RUNC WA7 8 C4
Daresbury Rd ECCL WA10 46 D3
WAL/EG CH44 68 C1
Dark Entry PR/KW L34 58 C1
Dark La MGHL L31 18 D5
Darley Av WARRN/WOL WA2 84 C2
Darley Cl WDN WA8 100 D5
Darleydale Dr PS/BROM CH62 153 F4
Darley Dr WD/CROXPK L12 56 C4
Darlington Cl WAL/EG CH44 69 F1
Darlington St WAL/EG CH44 69 F1
Darmond Rd NWD/KWIPK L33 34 B1
Darmond's Gn WKBY CH48 87 F5
Darmonds Green Av
NPK/KEN L6 55 F4
Darnley St TOX L8 94 A3
Darrel Dr EHL/KEN L7 95 E1
Darsefield Rd CHLDW L16 97 E1
Dartford Cl DV/KA/FCH L14 57 F4
Dartington Rd CHLDW L16 73 H5
Dartmouth Av AIN/FAZ L10 31 H2
Dartmouth Dr ECCL WA10 47 E1
NTHTN L30 22 B5
Darwall Rd ALL/GAR L19 119 H3
Darwen St EV L5 * 53 G5
Darwick Dr HUY L36 76 A5
Darwin Gv STHEL WA9 61 G3
Daryl Rd HES CH60 135 E5
Dashwood Cl WARRS WA4 131 E4
Daulby St VAUX/LVPD L3 7 K3
Dauntsey Brow WLTN L25 97 H1
Dauntsey Ms WLTN L25 97 H1
Davenham Av CL/PREN CH43 91 F5
WARR WA1 84 C5
Davenham Cl CL/PREN CH43 114 B1
Davenham Ct WAV L15 96 B1
Davenham Rd FMBY L37 17 E2
Davenhill Pk AIN/FAZ L10 31 H2
Davenport Av WARRS WA4 107 H3
Davenport Cl WKBY CH48 110 C5
Davenport Gv NWD/KWIPK L33 25 H5
Davenport Rd HES CH60 148 C2
Davenport Rw RUNC WA7 155 H1
Daventree Rd WAL/NB CH45 51 H5
Daventry Rd AIG/SPK L17 118 C1
David's Av WARRW/BUR WA5 105 F3
Davidson Rd CLB/OSW/ST L13 72 D2
David St TOX L8 94 B4
Davids Wk WLTN L25 98 A5
Davies Av WARRS WA4 107 H4
Davies Cl WDN WA8 146 A2
Davies St BTL L20 5 G3
CLVP L2 * 6 D3
STHEL WA9 48 C3
Davis Rd MOR/LEA CH46 67 F2
Davy Cl ECCL WA10 46 D2
Davy Rd RUNC WA7 147 E3
Davy St EV L5 54 C4
Dawber Cl NPK/KEN L6 71 G1
Dawlish Cl WLTN L25 121 E3
Dawlish Rd PEN/TH CH61 134 A1
WAL/EG CH44 68 B1
Dawn Cl NSTN CH64 159 E5
STHEL WA9 61 G3
Dawpool Dr MOR/LEA CH46 66 C5
PS/BROM CH62 152 C2
Dawson Av BIRK CH41 68 D5
STHEL WA9 62 D3
Dawson Gdns MGHL L31 18 C4
Dawson St CLVPS L1 6 E4
Dawson Wy CLVPS L1 * 7 F4
Dawstone Ri HES CH60 148 D2
Dawstone Rd HES CH60 148 D2
Days Meadow
GR/UP/WCH CH49 89 E5
Day St CLB/OSW/ST L13 73 E2
Deacon Cl CSBY/WL L22 29 E4
Deacon Ct CSBY/WL L22 29 E4
WLTN L25 120 D1
Deacon Rd WDN WA8 14 E2
Deakin St BIRK CH41 68 B5
Dean Av WAL/NB CH45 51 E4
Dean Cl WDN WA8 14 E3
WGNW/BIL/OR WN5 37 H1
Dean Crs WARRN/WOL WA2 83 H3
Dean Dillistone Ct CLVPS L1 94 A1
Deane Rd EHL/KEN L7 72 A3
Deansburn Rd CLB/OSW/ST L13 55 G4
Deanscales Rd NG/CROX L11 41 H5
Deans Ct FMBY L37 17 E1
Deansgate La FMBY L37 17 E1
Deans La WARRS WA4 109 F5
Dean St CSBY/WL L22 29 E4
WDN WA8 14 E3
Deans Wy BIRK CH41 68 B5
Deansway WDN WA8 124 A3
Deanwater Cl
GOL/RIS/CUL WA3 85 H1
Dean Wood Cl RAIN/WH L35 77 F3
Dearham Av RNFD/HAY WA11 37 E5
Dearne Cl WD/CROXPK L12 57 E5
Dearnford Av PS/BROM CH62 152 D3
Dearnford Cl PS/BROM CH62 152 D3
Dearnley Av RNFD/HAY WA11 49 E2
Deauville Rd WLT/FAZ L9 31 H5
Debra Cl MGHL L31 25 E5
Dee Cl NWD/KWIPK L33 26 A3
Dee La WKBY CH48 110 A1
Deeley Cl EHL/KEN L7 72 A4
Dee Park Cl HES CH60 149 F3
Dee Park Rd HES CH60 149 F3
Deep Dl WARRW/BUR WA5 104 D2
Deepdale WDN WA8 101 E5
Deepdale Av BTL L20 39 E2
RNFD/HAY WA11 * 37 G3
Deepdale Cl CL/PREN CH43 90 C2
Deepdale Dr RAIN/WH L35 78 B2
Deepdale Rd WLTN L25 97 G1
Deepfield Dr HUY L36 75 H5
Deepfield Rd WAV L15 95 H2
Deepwood Gv RAIN/WH L35 77 E3
Deerbarn Dr NTHTN L30 31 G1
Deerbolt Cl KKBY L32 33 F1
Deerbolt Crs KKBY L32 33 F1
Deerbolt Wy KKBY L32 33 F1
Dee Rd RAIN/WH L35 77 H2
Deer Park Ct RUNC WA7 156 B3
Dee Side HES CH60 148 A1
Deeside Cl CL/PREN CH43 90 B2
Dee View Rd HES CH60 148 D1
De Grouchy St WKBY CH48 * 87 F5
Deirdre Av WDN WA8 14 D2
Dekker Rd NWD/KWIPK L33 25 H3
Delabole Rd NG/CROX L11 42 C2
De Lacy Rw RUNC WA7 147 G4
Delafield Cl WARRN/WOL WA2 84 D2
Delagoa Rd AIN/FAZ L10 41 H1
Delamain Rd CLB/OSW/ST L13 55 G4
Delamere Av PS/BROM CH62 153 E5
STHEL WA9 79 E2
WDN WA8 124 A2
Delamere Cl CL/PREN CH43 90 B2
PS/BROM CH62 153 E5
WD/CROXPK L12 42 D4
Delamere Gv WAL/EG CH44 * 69 G3
Delamere St
WARRW/BUR WA5 106 A3
Delamore Pl ANF/KKDL L4 * 54 A1
Delamore St ANF/KKDL L4 54 A1
Delavor Cl HES CH60 148 C1
Delavor Rd HES CH60 148 C1
Delaware Crs KKBY L32 33 F1
Delaware Rd BTL L20 4 E3
Delenty Dr GOL/RIS/CUL WA3 85 H1
Delery Dr WARR WA1 84 C5
Delfby Crs KKBY L32 34 B3
Delf La ANF/KKDL L4 40 C5
SPK/HALE L24 141 H1
Dell Cl BEB CH63 152 B3
Dell Dr WARRN/WOL WA2 85 E3
Dellfield La MGHL L31 19 E5
Dell Gv RF/TRAN CH42 116 A3
Dell La HES CH60 149 F2
Dellside Gv STHEL WA9 62 C2
Dell St EHL/KEN L7 72 A3
The Dell RF/TRAN CH42 116 B2
WD/CROXPK L12 57 E1
Delphfields Rd WARRS WA4 130 A4
Delph Hollow Wy STHEL WA9 62 B2
Delphfield RUNC WA7 157 F1
Delph La FMBY L37 16 B3
RAIN/WH L35 77 F1
WARRN/WOL WA2 83 F1
Delph Rd CSBY/BLUN L23 21 E1
Delphwood Dr STHEL WA9 62 B1
Delta Crs WARRW/BUR WA5 82 C3
Delta Dr WD/CROXPK L12 57 E2
Delta Rd LITH L21 30 A5
STHEL WA9 49 F3
Delta Rd East RF/TRAN CH42 116 B2
Delta Rd West
RF/TRAN CH42 * 116 B2
Deltic Wy NTHTN L30 31 F4
NWD/KWIPK L33 34 C4
Delves Av BEB CH63 137 H3
WARRW/BUR WA5 106 B1
Delyn Cl RF/TRAN CH42 115 G2
Demesne St WAL/EG CH44 69 G2
Denbigh Av STHEL WA9 62 C3
Denbigh Rd WLT/FAZ L9 40 B4
Denbigh St EV L5 53 F5
Denbury Av WARRS WA4 130 D1
Dencourt Rd NG/CROX L11 56 B1
Denebank Rd ANF/KKDL L4 54 D3
Denehurst Cl
WARRW/BUR WA5 104 D4
Deneshey Rd HOY CH47 64 C5
Denes Wy STBRV L28 57 G3
Denford Rd DV/KA/FCH L14 57 F5
Denham Av WARRW/BUR WA5 105 F3
Denham Cl WD/CROXPK L12 43 F4
Denise Av WARRW/BUR WA5 104 C3
Denise Rd AIN/FAZ L10 33 E5
Denison Gv STHEL WA9 * 61 G3
Denman Dr NPK/KEN L6 71 H2
Denman Gv WAL/EG CH44 * 69 G2
Denman St NPK/KEN L6 71 H2
Denman Wy NPK/KEN L6 72 A1
Denmark St CSBY/WL L22 29 E3
Dennett Cl MGHL L31 24 A2
WARR WA1 109 E2
Dennett Rd RAIN/WH L35 76 C1
Denning Dr PEN/TH CH61 112 B4
Dennis Av ECCL WA10 61 E3
Dennis Rd WDN WA8 15 G5
Denny Cl GR/UP/WCH CH49 89 H4
Densham Av WARRN/WOL WA2 83 H3
Denston Cl CL/PREN CH43 90 B1
Denstone Av AIN/FAZ L10 32 A2
Denstone Cl WLTN L25 120 D3
Dentdale Dr EV L5 71 E1
Denton Dr WAL/NB CH45 52 A4
Denton Gv NPK/KEN L6 55 E5
Dentons Green La ECCL WA10 10 B2
Denton St TOX L8 94 B4
WDN WA8 15 G2
Dentwood St TOX L8 94 C4
Denver Dr WARRW/BUR WA5 105 F1
Denver Rd KKBY L32 33 F3
WARRS WA4 108 A5
Depot Rd NWD/KWIPK L33 26 D5
Derby Dr WARR WA1 107 H1
Derby Gv MGHL L31 24 A3
Derby La CLB/OSW/ST L13 73 E1
Derby Rd BTL L20 4 C6
EV L5 53 F4
FMBY L37 16 D2
HUY L36 75 G3
RF/TRAN CH42 92 B4
WAL/NB CH45 51 G4
WARRS WA4 130 A3
WDN WA8 102 B5
WDN WA8 102 C4
WDN WA8 102 D4
Derbyshire Hill Rd STHEL WA9 49 G4
Derby Sq CLVP L2 6 D5
PR/KW L34 60 A4
Derby St CLB/OSW/ST L13 * 72 D2
HUY L36 76 A3
Dereham Av GR/UP/WCH CH49 90 A1
Dereham Crs AIN/FAZ L10 32 C5
Derek Av WARRN/WOL WA2 84 B4
Derna Rd HUY L36 75 F2
Derringstone Cl ECCL WA10 61 F1
Derwent Av FMBY L37 16 C4
PR/KW L34 60 B4
Derwent Cl BEB CH63 * 137 F1
MGHL L31 19 F4
NWD/KWIPK L33 25 G5
RAIN/WH L35 77 H2
Derwent Dr LITH L21 30 C4
PEN/TH CH61 134 D2
WAL/NB CH45 51 G4
Derwent Rd BEB CH63 137 F1
CL/PREN CH43 91 H4
CSBY/BLUN L23 29 G2
HOY CH47 65 E5
RNFD/HAY WA11 37 F5
WARRS WA4 129 G1
WDN WA8 124 A2
Derwent Rd East
CLB/OSW/ST L13 73 E1
Derwent Rd West
CLB/OSW/ST L13 72 D1
Derwent Sq CLB/OSW/ST L13 73 E1
Derwent Wy NSTN CH64 159 E4
Desborough Crs
WD/CROXPK L12 56 A3
Desford Av RNFD/HAY WA11 48 D1
Desford Cl MOR/LEA CH46 65 H4
Desford Rd AIG/SPK L17 118 C3
Desilva St HUY L36 76 A3
Desmond Cl CL/PREN CH43 90 C1
Desmond Gv CSBY/BLUN L23 29 G1
Desoto Rd WDN WA8 145 G1
Desoto Rd East WDN WA8 124 D5
Desoto Rd West WDN WA8 124 D5
Deva Cl NWD/KWIPK L33 25 H2
Deva Rd WKBY CH48 110 A1
Deveraux Dr WAL/EG CH44 68 D2
Deverell Gv WAV L15 73 F4
Deverell Rd WAV L15 73 F4
Deverill Rd RF/TRAN CH42 115 G2
Devilla Cl DV/KA/FCH L14 57 G5
De Villiers Av CSBY/BLUN L23 21 F4
Devisdale Gv CL/PREN CH43 90 C1
Devizes Dr PEN/TH CH61 112 B4
Devizes Ms WLTN L25 97 H1
Devoke Av RNFD/HAY WA11 37 E3
Devon Av WAL/NB CH45 52 A5
Devon Cl CSBY/BLUN L23 20 B5
Devon Ct EV L5 54 C5
Devondale Rd CALD/MH L18 96 A3
Devon Dr PEN/TH CH61 134 C2
Devon Farm Wy FMBY L37 17 G3
Devonfield Rd WLT/FAZ L9 40 B2
Devon Gdns CHLDW L16 97 E3
RF/TRAN CH42 115 H2
Devon Pl WDN WA8 102 A5
Devonport St TOX L8 94 B3
Devonshire Cl NWD/KWIPK L33 25 H5
Devonshire Pl CL/PREN CH43 91 G3
EV L5 54 A4
RUNC WA7 8 D4
Devonshire Rd CL/PREN CH43 91 H3
CSBY/WL L22 28 D2
ECCL WA10 10 A1
GR/UP/WCH CH49 89 G3
PEN/TH CH61 134 C2
TOX L8 94 C3
WAL/EG CH44 68 D1
WARR WA1 84 D5
WKBY CH48 110 C2
Devonshire Rd West TOX L8 94 C3
Devon St ECCL WA10 10 B4
VAUX/LVPD L3 7 J2
Devonwall Gdns TOX L8 94 D3
Devon Wy CHLDW L16 97 E2
HUY L36 76 A1
Dewar Ct RUNC WA7 147 E3
Dewberry Cl RF/TRAN CH42 92 B4
Dewey Av WLT/FAZ L9 31 G4
Dewhurst Rd GOL/RIS/CUL WA3 85 H2
Dewlands Rd LITH L21 29 G4
Dewsbury Rd ANF/KKDL L4 54 D4
Dexter St TOX L8 94 A2
Deycroft Av NWD/KWIPK L33 26 B5
Deyes End MGHL L31 19 E5
Deyes La MGHL L31 18 D5
MGHL L31 19 E5
MGHL L31 19 F4
Deysbrook La WD/CROXPK L12 56 C4
Deysbrook Side
WD/CROXPK L12 56 C4
Deysbrook Wy
WD/CROXPK L12 56 D2
Dial Rd RF/TRAN CH42 92 B5
Dial St EHL/KEN L7 72 A3
WARR WA1 12 E4
Diamond St EV L5 70 D1
Diana Rd BTL L20 30 C5
Diana St ANF/KKDL L4 54 B2
Dibbinsdale Rd BEB CH63 152 B2
Dibbins Gn BEB CH63 152 B3
Dibbins Hey BEB CH63 138 A4
Dibbinview Gv BEB CH63 138 B4
Dibb La CSBY/BLUN L23 20 D2
Dicconson St ECCL WA10 * 11 G3
Dickens Av CL/PREN CH43 114 B2
Dickens Cl CL/PREN CH43 114 B2
KKBY L32 33 G4
Dickenson St CLVPS L1 * 6 E7
WARRN/WOL WA2 13 F1
Dickens Rd ECCL WA10 61 E2
Dickens St TOX L8 * 94 B2
Dickinson Cl FMBY L37 17 E4
RNFD/HAY WA11 49 G1
Dickinson Rd FMBY L37 17 E4
Dickson Cl WDN WA8 14 E3
Dickson St VAUX/LVPD L3 70 B1
WDN WA8 14 D3
Didcot Cl WLTN L25 121 F3
Didsbury Cl NWD/KWIPK L33 34 A2
Digg La MOR/LEA CH46 66 B4
Dig La WARRN/WOL WA2 85 E1
Digmoor Rd KKBY L32 34 A5
Dignum Md NTHLY L27 98 C2
Dilloway St ECCL WA10 10 C3
Dinaro Cl WLTN L25 98 A4
Dinas La HUY L36 74 C1
Dinesen Rd ALL/GAR L19 119 G4
Dingle Brow TOX L8 94 C5
Dingle Gv TOX L8 94 C4
Dingle La TOX L8 94 C5
WARRS WA4 130 D5
Dingle Mt TOX L8 94 C5
Dingle Rd RF/TRAN CH42 92 A4
TOX L8 94 B5
Dingle V TOX L8 94 C5
Dingleway WARRS WA4 130 B3
Dingley Av WLT/FAZ L9 40 B1
Dingwall Dr GR/UP/WCH CH49 89 G5
Dinmore Rd WAL/EG CH44 68 D1
Dinnington Ct WDN WA8 101 G5
Dinorwic Rd ANF/KKDL L4 54 C4
Dinsdale Rd
PS/BROM CH62 139 E4
Ditchfield FMBY L37 17 F4
Ditchfield Pl WDN WA8 123 H3
Ditchfield Rd
WARRW/BUR WA5 104 C5
WDN WA8 123 G3
Ditton La MOR/LEA CH46 66 C2
Ditton Rd WDN WA8 14 B7
Dixon Rd NWD/KWIPK L33 34 C3
Dixon St WARR WA1 12 B5
Dobbs Dr FMBY L37 17 F2
Dobson St NPK/KEN L6 71 G1
Dock Rd ALL/GAR L19 140 B1
BIRK CH41 68 C3
WDN WA8 145 H1
Dock Rd North
PS/BROM CH62 116 C5
Dock Rd South
PS/BROM CH62 138 D2
Dock St WDN WA8 146 A1

Dodd Av ECCL WA10 47 E3
GR/UP/WCH CH49 89 F5
Doddridge Rd TOX L8 94 A3
Dodd's La MGHL L31 18 D4
Dodleston Cl CL/PREN CH43 90 D4
Dodman Rd NG/CROX L11 42 D2
Doe Park Ctyd WLTN L25 * 120 D3
Doe's Meadow Rd BEB CH63 152 B2
Dolomite Av SPK/HALE L24 120 B5
Domar Cl KKBY L32 33 H4
Dombey St TOX L8 94 B2
Domingo Dr NWD/KWIPK L33 25 G4
Dominic Cl CHLDW L16 74 A5
Dominic Rd CHLDW L16 74 A5
Dominion St NPK/KEN L6 * 55 E5
Domville RAIN/WH L35 77 E3
Domville Rd CLB/OSW/ST L13 73 E4
Donaldson St EV L5 54 C4
Donalds Wy AIG/SPK L17 118 C2
Doncaster Dr
GR/UP/WCH CH49 89 H2
Donegal Rd CLB/OSW/ST L13 73 F2
Donne Av BEB CH63 137 H3
Donne Cl BEB CH63 138 A3
Donnington Cl HUY L36 75 F5
Donsby Rd WLT/FAZ L9 40 D1
Dooley Dr NTHTN L30 23 G5
Doon Cl ANF/KKDL L4 54 A2
Dorbett Dr CSBY/BLUN L23 29 G2
Dorchester Cl
GR/UP/WCH CH49 89 H4
Dorchester Dr NWD/KWIPK L33 26 B4
Dorchester Pk CL/PREN CH43 90 D5
WLTN L25 97 H2
Dorchester Rd
WARRW/BUR WA5 105 F3
WLTN L25 97 H2
Doreen Av MOR/LEA CH46 66 B5
Dorgan Cl RAIN/WH L35 77 H1
Doric Rd CLB/OSW/ST L13 73 E1
Doric St LITH L21 29 G5
RF/TRAN CH42 * 115 H1
Dorien Rd CLB/OSW/ST L13 72 D3
Dorking Gv WAV L15 96 B1
Dorney Cl WARRS WA4 130 C5
Dorney Ct WD/CROXPK L12 56 B2
Dorothea St
WARRN/WOL WA2 107 E1
Dorothy St EHL/KEN L7 71 H4
STHEL WA9 61 G3
Dorrington Cl RUNC WA7 157 F1
Dorrit St TOX L8 94 B2
Dorset Av EHL/KEN L7 95 F1
Dorset Cl BTL L20 5 H2
Dorset Dr PEN/TH CH61 134 C2
Dorset Rd ECCL WA10 61 F1
HUY L36 76 A2
NPK/KEN L6 55 F4
WAL/NB CH45 51 G3
WKBY CH48 87 G5
Dorset Wy WARR WA1 85 F5
Douglas Av STHEL WA9 63 H4
WGNW/BIL/OR WN5 37 H1
Douglas Cl CLB/OSW/ST L13 72 D1
WDN WA8 103 F5
Douglas Dr MGHL L31 19 F4
MOR/LEA CH46 66 A5
Douglas Pl BTL L20 4 D7
Douglas Rd ANF/KKDL L4 54 D4
WKBY CH48 87 H5
Douglas St BIRK CH41 3 G4
ECCL WA10 10 B5
Douglas Wy NWD/KWIPK L33 26 A3
Doulton Cl CL/PREN CH43 90 B1
Doulton Pl RAIN/WH L35 76 C3
Doulton St ECCL WA10 10 A6
Dounrey Cl WARRN/WOL WA2 85 E3
Douro Pl CLB/OSW/ST L13 72 D3
Douro St VAUX/LVPD L3 71 E1
Dovecot Av DV/KA/FCH L14 74 B1
Dovecote Gn WARRW/BUR WA5 82 A4
Dove Ct WLTN L25 120 D1
Dovedale Av MGHL L31 18 C4
PS/BROM CH62 153 E4
Dovedale Cl CL/PREN CH43 114 B1
WARRN/WOL WA2 84 C2
Dovedale Rd CALD/MH L18 95 H3
HOY CH47 64 B5
WAL/NB CH45 51 G3
Dovepoint Rd HOY CH47 65 E4
Dovercliffe Rd
CLB/OSW/ST L13 73 F2
Dover Cl BIRK CH41 2 D3
RUNC WA7 157 G3
Dover Gv CHLDW L16 74 B5
Dove Rd WLT/FAZ L9 40 B1
Dover Rd MGHL L31 23 H3
WARRS WA4 108 A5
Dover St RUNC WA7 9 F3
VAUX/LVPD L3 7 J4
Dovesmead Rd HES CH60 * 149 G2
Dovestone Cl EHL/KEN L7 71 H5
Dove St TOX L8 94 D1
Dovey St TOX L8 94 B3
Doward St WDN WA8 125 G1
Dowhills Dr CSBY/BLUN L23 20 C4
Dowhills Pk CSBY/BLUN L23 20 C3
Dowhills Rd CSBY/BLUN L23 20 C4
Downes Gn BEB CH63 138 A5
Downham Cl WLTN L25 97 F3
Downham Dr HES CH60 149 E1
Downham Gn WLTN L25 97 F3
Downham Rd RF/TRAN CH42 92 C5
Downham Rd North
PEN/TH CH61 135 E4
Downham Rd South
HES CH60 149 E1
Downham Wy WLTN L25 97 F3
Downholland Moss La
FMBY L37 17 H2
Downing Cl CL/PREN CH43 91 H5
Downing Rd BTL L20 5 H7
Downing St EV L5 54 C5
Downlands Rd NTHLY L27 98 D4
Downland Wy STHEL WA9 63 F1
Downside WDN WA8 100 D5
Downside Cl NTHTN L30 22 D5
Downside Dr AIN/FAZ L10 32 C3
Downs Rd ECCL WA10 10 B6
RUNC WA7 8 E7
Downway La STHEL WA9 63 G1
Dowsefield La CALD/MH L18 97 E5
Dragon Cl NG/CROX L11 42 C3
Dragon Crs RAIN/WH L35 77 F1
Dragon La RAIN/WH L35 77 E1
Dragon Yd WDN WA8 102 B4
Drake Cl AIN/FAZ L10 32 D5
RAIN/WH L35 77 E3
WARRW/BUR WA5 82 D4
Drake Crs AIN/FAZ L10 32 D5
Drakefield Rd NG/CROX L11 41 G4
Drake Gdns STHEL WA9 61 G4
Drake Pl AIN/FAZ L10 * 32 C5
Drake Rd AIN/FAZ L10 32 C5
MOR/LEA CH46 67 F1
NSTN CH64 158 D1
Drake St BTL L20 53 F1
ECCL WA10 10 B4
Drake Wy AIN/FAZ L10 32 D5
Draw Well Rd NWD/KWIPK L33 35 E2
Draycott St TOX L8 94 B5
Drayton Cl PEN/TH CH61 134 B1
RUNC WA7 8 B6
Drayton Crs RNFD/HAY WA11 48 D1
Drayton Rd ANF/KKDL L4 * 40 C5
WAL/EG CH44 69 F2
Drennan Rd ALL/GAR L19 120 A3
Drewell Rd CALD/MH L18 95 H5
Driffield Rd PR/KW L34 59 G4
Drinkwater Gdns
VAUX/LVPD L3 71 E2
The Drive WD/CROXPK L12 56 B5
Driveway RAIN/WH L35 77 F2
Droitwich Av
GR/UP/WCH CH49 89 E4
Dromore Av CALD/MH L18 96 A5
Dronfield Wy WLTN L25 97 F1
Druids Cross Gdns
CALD/MH L18 96 D4
Druids Cross Rd CALD/MH L18 96 D4
Druids Pk CALD/MH L18 97 E4
Druidsville Rd CALD/MH L18 97 E4
Druids Wy GR/UP/WCH CH49 113 E1
Drum Cl DV/KA/FCH L14 57 G5
Drummond Ct WDN WA8 125 H1
Drummond Rd ANF/KKDL L4 55 E1
CSBY/BLUN L23 22 A4
HOY CH47 87 E3
Druridge Dr WARRW/BUR WA5 104 D4
Drury La CLVP L2 6 C4
Dryburgh Wy ANF/KKDL L4 54 A2
Dryden Cl CL/PREN CH43 90 C1
RAIN/WH L35 77 E2
Dryden Gv HUY L36 75 H4
Dryden Pl WARRN/WOL WA2 84 A3
Dryden Rd EHL/KEN L7 72 C4
Dryden St BTL L20 4 B1
EV L5 70 D1
Dryebeck Gv STHEL WA9 62 D4
Dryfield Cl GR/UP/WCH CH49 * 89 F4
Drysdale Wk TOX L8 94 C4
Dublin St VAUX/LVPD L3 70 B1
Ducie St TOX L8 94 D2
Duckinfield St VAUX/LVPD L3 7 J4
Duck Pond La RF/TRAN CH42 114 C1
Duckworth Gv
WARRN/WOL WA2 85 E4
Duddingston Av
CALD/MH L18 * 96 A3
CSBY/BLUN L23 29 F2
Duddon Av MGHL L31 19 F4
Duddon Cl CL/PREN CH43 91 F4
Dudley Av RUNC WA7 146 D4
Dudley Cl CL/PREN CH43 91 H4
Dudley Gv CSBY/BLUN L23 29 F2
Dudley Pl STHEL WA9 48 D4
Dudley Rd CALD/MH L18 95 H3
WAL/NB CH45 51 G2
Dudley St WARRN/WOL WA2 106 D1
Dudlow Dr CALD/MH L18 96 C3
Dudlow Gdns CALD/MH L18 96 C2
Dudlow La CALD/MH L18 96 B2
Dudlow Nook Rd CALD/MH L18 96 C2
Dugdale Cl ALL/GAR L19 119 E4
Duke Cl RUNC WA7 8 B4
Dukes Rd EV L5 54 A4
Duke St ALL/GAR L19 119 G5
BIRK CH41 2 A2
CLVPS L1 7 F6
CSBY/WL L22 29 E4
ECCL WA10 10 E3
FMBY L37 16 D4
PR/KW L34 59 H3
WAL/NB CH45 51 H2
Duke Street La CLVPS L1 * 6 E6
Dukes Wy FMBY L37 17 E4
Dukes Whf RUNC WA7 157 G3
Dulas Gn KKBY L32 34 B3
Dulas Rd KKBY L32 34 B3
WAV L15 96 B2
Dulson Wy PR/KW L34 59 E5
Dulverton Rd AIG/SPK L17 118 C3
Dumbarton St ANF/KKDL L4 54 A1
Dumbrees Rd WD/CROXPK L12 57 E2
Dumbreeze Gv PR/KW L34 44 B3
Dumfries Wy NWD/KWIPK L33 25 G3
Dunacre Wy HLWD L26 121 H4
Dunbabin Rd CHLDW L16 96 C2
Dunbar St ANF/KKDL L4 40 B5
Dunbeath Av RAIN/WH L35 78 B4
Dunbeath Cl RAIN/WH L35 78 B4
Duncan Av RUNC WA7 9 H6
Duncan Cl ECCL WA10 10 D7
Duncan Dr GR/UP/WCH CH49 89 F4
Duncansby Crs
WARRW/BUR WA5 104 C2
Duncansby Dr BEB CH63 152 C5
Duncan St BIRK CH41 3 H4
CLVPS L1 94 A1
ECCL WA10 10 D6
WARRN/WOL WA2 107 E1
Dunchurch Rd DV/KA/FCH L14 57 F5
Duncombe Rd North
ALL/GAR L19 119 F4
Duncombe Rd South
ALL/GAR L19 119 F4
Duncote Cl CL/PREN CH43 91 G4
RAIN/WH L35 60 C5
Dundale Rd CLB/OSW/ST L13 73 F2
Dundalk Rd WDN WA8 124 B3
Dundas St BTL L20 53 F1
Dundee Cl WARRN/WOL WA2 84 C1
Dundee Gv WAL/EG CH44 68 C2
Dundonald Av WARRS WA4 130 A2
Dundonald Rd AIG/SPK L17 118 C2
Dundonald St BIRK CH41 68 C5
Dunedin St STHEL WA9 61 G3
Dunes Dr FMBY L37 16 B2
Dunes Wy EV L5 53 G4
Dunfold Cl KKBY L32 34 A3
Dungeon La SPK/HALE L24 142 D5
Dunham Cl PS/BROM CH62 153 F5
Dunham Rd WAV L15 73 E4
Dunkeld Cl NPK/KEN L6 71 G2
Dunkeld St NPK/KEN L6 * 71 G2
Dunkerron Cl NTHLY L27 98 A1
Dunlin Cl NTHLY L27 98 C4
RUNC WA7 156 B4
WARRN/WOL WA2 84 C2
Dunlop Dr MGHL L31 25 E5
Dunlop Rd SPK/HALE L24 141 H4
Dunlop St WARRS WA4 106 D5
Dunluce St ANF/KKDL L4 54 A1
Dunmail Av RNFD/HAY WA11 37 G3
Dunmail Gv RUNC WA7 155 H5
Dunmore Rd CLB/OSW/ST L13 72 C2
Dunmow Rd WARRS WA4 108 C5
Dunmow Wy WLTN L25 121 E3
Dunnerdale Rd NG/CROX L11 42 A5
Dunnett St BTL L20 53 F1
Dunning Cl GR/UP/WCH CH49 89 G3
Dunnings Bridge Rd LITH L21 30 D3
NTHTN L30 23 G4
NTHTN L30 31 E2
Dunnock Cl WARRN/WOL WA2 84 C2
WLTN L25 97 G3
Dunraven Rd NSTN CH64 159 F3
WKBY CH48 110 A1
Dunriding La ECCL WA10 10 A6
Dunscroft STHEL WA9 62 D3
Dunsdon Cl CALD/MH L18 97 E4
Dunsdon Rd WLTN L25 97 E3
Dunsford WDN WA8 101 E5
Dunsop Av STHEL WA9 79 H1
Dunstall Cl MOR/LEA CH46 66 C2
Dunstan La EHL/KEN L7 72 A5
Dunstan St WAV L15 72 C5
Dunster Gv HES CH60 149 F2
STHEL WA9 79 H1
Durban Rd CLB/OSW/ST L13 73 F3
WAL/NB CH45 51 H4
Durden St EHL/KEN L7 95 E1
Durham Av NTHTN L30 31 F3
Durham Cl WARR WA1 109 E1
Durham Ms East NTHTN L30 * 31 F3
Durham Ms West NTHTN L30 * 31 F3
Durham Rd LITH L21 29 F5
WDN WA8 * 102 B5
Durham St ALL/GAR L19 140 D2
Durham Wy NTHTN L30 31 F3
Durley Dr CL/PREN CH43 114 A2
Durley Park Cl CL/PREN CH43 114 A3
Durley Rd WLT/FAZ L9 40 D1
Durlston Cl WDN WA8 124 A1
Durning Rd EHL/KEN L7 72 A4
Durrant Rd NG/CROX L11 55 G2
Dursley RAIN/WH L35 77 F3
Durston Rd CHLDW L16 73 H5
Durweston Wk WLTN L25 98 A2
Dutton Dr BEB CH63 137 H4
Dutton St WARR WA1 13 F5
Duxbury Cl MGHL L31 19 E3
Duxford Ct WARRN/WOL WA2 84 C4
Dwerryhouse La NG/CROX L11 42 B5
Dwerryhouse St TOX L8 93 H2
Dyke St NPK/KEN L6 71 G1
Dykin Cl WDN WA8 103 E5
Dykin Rd WDN WA8 102 D5
Dymchurch Rd SPK/HALE L24 141 H2
Dymoke Rd NG/CROX L11 42 C4
Dyson Hall Dr WLT/FAZ L9 41 F2
Dyson St ANF/KKDL L4 54 B1

E

Eaglehall Rd WLT/FAZ L9 41 H3
Eaglehurst Rd WLTN L25 97 H4
Eagle Park Dr
WARRN/WOL WA2 83 G4
Eagles Ct KKBY L32 33 H2
Eaglesfield Cl STHEL WA9 * 62 C3
Eagles Wy RUNC WA7 156 A3
Ealing Rd WARRW/BUR WA5 105 E3
WLT/FAZ L9 31 G5
Eanleywood La RUNC WA7 157 E2
Eardisley Rd WAV L15 96 A2
Earle Crs NSTN CH64 158 C1
Earle Dr NSTN CH64 158 C2
Earle Rd EHL/KEN L7 72 A5
WDN WA8 15 F6
Earle St VAUX/LVPD L3 6 B2
Earl Rd BTL L20 5 H3
Earl's Cl CSBY/BLUN L23 29 E1
Earlsfield Rd WAV L15 95 H2
Earlston Rd WAL/NB CH45 51 G4
Earl St PS/BROM CH62 116 B4
STHEL WA9 48 C3
WARRN/WOL WA2 106 D1
Earls Wy RUNC WA7 156 A3
Earlswood Cl MOR/LEA CH46 65 H5
Earlwood Gdns RAIN/WH L35 77 E3
Earp St ALL/GAR L19 119 G5
Easby Cl FMBY L37 17 F4
RUNC WA7 9 H5
Easby Rd ANF/KKDL L4 53 H3
Easby Wk ANF/KKDL L4 53 H3
Easedale Wk NWD/KWIPK L33 25 G4
Easenhall Cl WDN WA8 102 B4
Easington Rd STHEL WA9 61 F4
East Albert Rd AIG/SPK L17 94 D4
East Av WARRN/WOL WA2 84 A5
WARRS WA4 130 B2
WARRW/BUR WA5 105 E4
Eastbourne Rd BIRK CH41 2 C5
CSBY/WL L22 28 C2
WLT/FAZ L9 31 G5
Eastbourne Wy NPK/KEN L6 71 F2
Eastbury Cl WDN WA8 102 C3
Eastcliffe Rd CLB/OSW/ST L13 73 F2
East Cl PR/KW L34 60 C3
Eastcote Rd ALL/GAR L19 119 G3
Eastcott Cl GR/UP/WCH CH49 89 E5
Eastcroft NWD/KWIPK L33 26 A4
Eastcroft Rd WAL/EG CH44 69 E2
Eastdale Rd WARR WA1 108 A1
WAV L15 72 D5
East Dam Wood Rd
SPK/HALE L24 142 D4
Easter Ct WARRW/BUR WA5 82 B3
Eastern Av PS/BROM CH62 138 D2
SPK/HALE L24 142 D4
Eastern Dr ALL/GAR L19 119 E4
Eastfield Dr AIG/SPK L17 95 E5
Eastfield Wk KKBY L32 33 E3
East Float BIRK CH41 * 69 F4
Eastford Rd WARRS WA4 129 G2
East Front RAIN/WH L35 77 E4
Eastham Cl CHLDW L16 74 B4
Eastham Crs STHEL WA9 79 G1
Eastham Ms PS/BROM CH62 153 G5
Eastham Rake
PS/BROM CH62 153 E5
Eastham Village Rd
PS/BROM CH62 153 G4
Eastlake Av EV L5 54 B5
East Lancashire Rd ECCL WA10 36 D5
NG/CROX L11 41 H3
PR/KW L34 43 G1
East La RUNC WA7 156 B2
Eastleigh Dr PEN/TH CH61 112 B4
East Mains SPK/HALE L24 143 E3
Eastman Rd CLB/OSW/ST L13 55 G3
East Meade MGHL L31 18 C4
East Millwood Rd
SPK/HALE L24 143 E2
East O' Hills Cl HES CH60 135 E5
Easton Rd HUY L36 74 C2
PS/BROM CH62 116 B3
East Orchard La WLT/FAZ L9 32 A5
East Park Ct WAL/EG CH44 69 G2
East Prescot Rd
DV/KA/FCH L14 74 A1
East Rd CLB/OSW/ST L13 73 G3
DV/KA/FCH L14 73 G3
HLWD L26 143 F1
East Side STHEL WA9 48 C5
East St CSBY/WL L22 29 E3
PR/KW L34 60 A4
VAUX/LVPD L3 6 C2
WAL/EG CH44 69 G3
WDN WA8 15 J1
East Vw WARRS WA4 131 F1
Eastview Cl CL/PREN CH43 90 D4
Eastway GR/UP/WCH CH49 89 G4
MGHL L31 18 D4
East Wy MOR/LEA CH46 66 C4
Eastway WDN WA8 124 B2
Eastwood AIG/SPK L17 94 C5
Eaton Av BTL L20 39 H1
LITH L21 30 A5
WAL/EG CH44 69 E1
Eaton Cl HUY L36 75 E3
WD/CROXPK L12 56 A3
Eaton Gdns WD/CROXPK L12 56 D5
Eaton Pl PR/KW L34 * 59 H4
Eaton Rd ALL/GAR L19 119 E5
CL/PREN CH43 2 A6
ECCL WA10 47 F1
MGHL L31 24 A3
WD/CROXPK L12 56 B3
WKBY CH48 110 A2
Eaton Rd North
WD/CROXPK L12 56 A3
Eaton St PR/KW L34 59 H4
RUNC WA7 8 D5
VAUX/LVPD L3 6 C1
WAL/EG CH44 68 D1
Eaves La STHEL WA9 62 B4
Ebenezer Howard Rd LITH L21 30 B2
Ebenezer St RF/TRAN CH42 116 A1
RNFD/HAY WA11 49 F1
Eberle St CLVP L2 6 D3
Ebony Cl MOR/LEA CH46 * 65 H5
Ebony Wy NWD/KWIPK L33 25 H4
Ebor La EV L5 71 E1
Ebrington St ALL/GAR L19 119 G5
Ecclesall Av LITH L21 30 B4
Eccles Dr WLTN L25 98 A2
Ecclesfield Rd ECCL WA10 46 C2
Eccles Gv STHEL WA9 80 A2
Eccleshall Rd PS/BROM CH62 116 C5
Eccleshill Rd CLB/OSW/ST L13 56 A5
Eccles Rd FMBY L37 16 C5
Eccleston Av PS/BROM CH62 138 C5
Eccleston Cl CL/PREN CH43 91 F5
GOL/RIS/CUL WA3 85 G1
Eccleston Dr RUNC WA7 9 H7
Eccleston Gdns ECCL WA10 60 C1
Eccleston Rd WLT/FAZ L9 40 B1
Eccleston St ECCL WA10 10 C5
PR/KW L34 59 H4
Edale Cl PS/BROM CH62 153 E4
Edale Rd CALD/MH L18 96 A4
Eddarbridge Est WDN WA8 * 145 H1
Eddisbury Rd WAL/EG CH44 52 A5
WKBY CH48 87 E4
Eddisbury Wy WD/CROXPK L12 56 A3
Edelsten St WARRW/BUR WA5 106 B3
Eden Cl NWD/KWIPK L33 26 A3
RAIN/WH L35 77 H3
Edendale WDN WA8 123 H1
Eden Dr North CSBY/BLUN L23 29 H1
Eden Dr South CSBY/BLUN L23 29 H1
Edenfield Crs HUY L36 75 H1
Edenfield Rd WAV L15 95 H2
Edenhall Dr WLTN L25 98 A5
Edenhurst Av CHLDW L16 74 C5
WAL/EG CH44 52 A5
Edenhurst Cl FMBY L37 16 B4
Edenhurst Ct HUY L36 * 74 D1
Edenhurst Dr FMBY L37 16 B4
Edenpark Rd RF/TRAN CH42 92 A5
Eden V NTHTN L30 22 D5
Edgar Ct BIRK CH41 2 D3
LITH L21 30 A3
Edgars Dr WARRN/WOL WA2 85 E3
Edgar St VAUX/LVPD L3 70 D2
Edgbaston Cl HUY L36 75 E4
Edgbaston Wy CL/PREN CH43 67 G5
Edgefield Cl CL/PREN CH43 90 D4
Edgefold Rd KKBY L32 34 A3
Edge Gv EHL/KEN L7 72 C3
Edgehill Rd MOR/LEA CH46 66 A5
Edge La CLB/OSW/ST L13 72 C3
CSBY/BLUN L23 22 B5
EHL/KEN L7 71 H4
Edge Lane Dr CLB/OSW/ST L13 73 E3
Edgeley Gdns WLT/FAZ L9 40 B1
Edgemoor Cl CL/PREN CH43 90 B1
WD/CROXPK L12 56 D5
Edgemoor Dr AIN/FAZ L10 32 D5
CSBY/BLUN L23 21 H4
PEN/TH CH61 112 A4
Edgemoor Rd WD/CROXPK L12 56 D5
Edge St STHEL WA9 61 E4
Edgewell Dr WAV L15 73 E5
Edgewood Dr PS/BROM CH62 152 D4
Edgewood Rd
GR/UP/WCH CH49 89 G2
HOY CH47 64 D4
Edgeworth Cl STHEL WA9 63 E2
Edgeworth St STHEL WA9 63 E3
Edgworth Rd ANF/KKDL L4 54 D4
Edgworth St WARRN/WOL WA2 12 C4
Edinburgh Cl NTHTN L30 31 E4
Edinburgh Dr CL/PREN CH43 114 C2
HUY L36 76 A5
Edinburgh Rd EHL/KEN L7 71 G3
FMBY L37 16 D5
WAL/NB CH45 * 51 H5
WDN WA8 123 G3
Edington St WAV L15 72 C5
Edison Rd RUNC WA7 146 D3
Edith Rd ANF/KKDL L4 54 C4
BTL L20 39 H1
WAL/EG CH44 69 G2
Edith St RUNC WA7 8 C3
STHEL WA9 * 63 F3
Edith Vls BTL L20 * 5 J2
Edmondson St STHEL WA9 * 49 F4
Edmonton Cl EV L5 53 H4
Edmund St VAUX/LVPD L3 6 C3
Edna Av AIN/FAZ L10 32 D5
Edrich Av CL/PREN CH43 * 67 G5
Edward Gdns WARR WA1 109 F2
Edward Jenner Av NTHTN L30 31 E1
Edward Pavilion
VAUX/LVPD L3 * 6 C6
Edward Rd HOY CH47 87 G2
RAIN/WH L35 60 B5
WARRW/BUR WA5 104 B2
Edward's La SPK/HALE L24 120 D5
Edward St RNFD/HAY WA11 49 G1
STHEL WA9 62 D1
VAUX/LVPD L3 7 H4
WDN WA8 15 J1
Edwards Wy WDN WA8 124 A3
Edwin St WDN WA8 15 G1
Effingham St BTL L20 53 F1
Egan Rd BIRK CH41 68 A5
Egbert Rd HOY CH47 64 C5
Egdon Cl WDN WA8 126 A1
Egerton Av WARR WA1 107 G1
Egerton Dr WKBY CH48 110 B1
Egerton Gdns RF/TRAN CH42 115 G2
Egerton Gv WAL/NB CH45 51 H5
Egerton Park Cl
RF/TRAN CH42 115 G2
Egerton Rd CL/PREN CH43 91 G2
PR/KW L34 59 G4
PS/BROM CH62 116 B4
WAV L15 95 F1
Egerton St RUNC WA7 8 C3
STHEL WA9 62 D1
TOX L8 94 B1
WAL/NB CH45 51 H2
WARR WA1 13 G4
WARRS WA4 130 A2
Egerton Whf BIRK CH41 3 G2
Eglington Av RAIN/WH L35 76 D3
Egremont Cl NTHLY L27 99 E4
Egremont Lawn NTHLY L27 99 E4
Egremont Prom WAL/NB CH45 52 B4
Egypt St WARR WA1 12 C5
WDN WA8 14 B5
Eighth Av WLT/FAZ L9 32 A5
Eilian Gv DV/KA/FCH L14 73 H3
Eisenhower Cl
WARRW/BUR WA5 105 F3
Elaine Cl WDN WA8 15 G1
Elaine St TOX L8 94 B2
WARR WA1 13 H1
Elbow La FMBY L37 17 E3
Elderdale Rd ANF/KKDL L4 54 D3
Elderflower Rd ECCL WA10 10 C1
Elder Gdns ALL/GAR L19 119 F3
Elder Gv WKBY CH48 110 B1
Eldersfield Rd NG/CROX L11 42 B5
Elderswood Rd RAIN/WH L35 78 A1
Elderwood Rd RF/TRAN CH42 92 C5
Eldon Cl ECCL WA10 10 C7
Eldonian Wy VAUX/LVPD L3 70 C1
Eldon Pl VAUX/LVPD L3 70 C1
Eldon Rd RF/TRAN CH42 115 H1
WAL/EG CH44 68 D1
Eldon St ECCL WA10 10 C7
VAUX/LVPD L3 70 C1
WARR WA1 13 F4
Eldon Ter NSTN CH64 158 D3
Eldred Rd CHLDW L16 96 C2
Eleanor Pk CL/PREN CH43 67 G5
Eleanor Rd BTL L20 39 H1
CL/PREN CH43 67 G4
MOR/LEA CH46 66 A4
Eleanor St BTL L20 53 F1
WDN WA8 * 14 D6
Elephant La STHEL WA9 61 G4
Elfet St BIRK CH41 68 B5
Elgar Av PS/BROM CH62 153 E4
Elgar Rd DV/KA/FCH L14 57 F5
Elgin Av WARRS WA4 129 G1
Elgin Ct RAIN/WH L35 * 78 B3
Elgin Dr WAL/NB CH45 52 A4
Elgin Wy BIRK CH41 3 G3
Eliot Cl PS/BROM CH62 116 A4
Eliot St BTL L20 39 F2
Elizabeth Ct WDN WA8 14 E6

Elizabeth Dr WARR WA1 85 E5
Elizabeth Rd AIN/FAZ L10 33 E5
BTL L20 39 H1
HUY L36 76 A5
Elizabeth St STHEL WA9 63 E2
STHEL WA9 79 H2
VAUX/LVPD L3 * 7 K3
Elizabeth Ter WDN WA8 124 B2
Eliza St STHEL WA9 63 F3
Elkan Cl WDN WA8 103 E5
Elkan Rd WDN WA8 102 D5
Elkstone Rd NG/CROX L11 56 B1
Ellaby Rd RAIN/WH L35 78 A1
Ellamsbridge Rd STHEL WA9 63 E3
Ellel Gv NPK/KEN L6 55 E5
Ellen Gdn STHEL WA9 63 E3
Ellen's Cl NPK/KEN L6 71 G3
Ellen's La BEB CH63 138 A1
Ellen St STHEL WA9 63 E3
WARRW/BUR WA5 12 A1
Elleray Dr TOX L8 94 B4
Elleray Park Rd WAL/NB CH45 51 G3
Ellerby Cl RUNC WA7 157 G2
Ellergreen Rd NG/CROX L11 41 H5
Ellerman Rd VAUX/LVPD L3 94 B5
Ellerslie Av RAIN/WH L35 61 E5
Ellerslie Rd CLB/OSW/ST L13 55 F4
Ellerton Cl WDN WA8 101 F5
Ellerton Wy WD/CROXPK L12 43 E4
Ellesmere Dr AIN/FAZ L10 31 H2
Ellesmere Gv WAL/NB CH45 51 H4
Ellesmere Rd WARRS WA4 129 H2
Ellesmere St RUNC WA7 9 F4
WARR WA1 13 F5
Ellesworth Cl
WARRW/BUR WA5 82 C5
Ellington Dr
WARRW/BUR WA5 105 F3
Elliot Dr KKBY L32 33 G4
Elliot St CLVPS L1 7 F4
ECCL WA10 10 C5
WDN WA8 14 E3
Elliott Av WARR WA1 13 K1
Ellis Ashton St HUY L36 76 A3
Ellison Dr ECCL WA10 47 E3
Ellison Gv HUY L36 75 F3
Ellison St CLB/OSW/ST L13 72 D1
WARRS WA4 130 B2
Ellis Pl TOX L8 94 B3
Ellis St WDN WA8 14 B6
Ellon Av RAIN/WH L35 78 B3
Elloway Rd SPK/HALE L24 143 E3
Ellwood Cl SPK/HALE L24 144 A4
Elmar Rd AIG/SPK L17 118 C1
Elm Av CSBY/BLUN L23 21 G4
GR/UP/WCH CH49 89 F2
WDN WA8 125 F1
Elm Bank ANF/KKDL L4 54 B3
Elmbank Rd CALD/MH L18 95 G3
PS/BROM CH62 116 B5
Elmbank St WAL/EG CH44 * 69 E2
Elm Cl PEN/TH CH61 134 D2
WD/CROXPK L12 43 F4
Elmcroft Cl WLT/FAZ L9 32 A5
Elmdale Cl FMBY L37 16 C4
Elmdale Rd WLT/FAZ L9 40 C3
Elmdene Ct
GR/UP/WCH CH49 * 112 A1
Elm Dr FMBY L37 16 C5
GR/UP/WCH CH49 89 E5
LITH L21 38 D1
Elmfield Cl STHEL WA9 61 G2
Elmfield Rd WLT/FAZ L9 40 C2
Elm Gdns LITH L21 * 39 E1
Elm Gv EHL/KEN L7 71 G4
HOY CH47 87 F1
PR/KW L34 60 B3
RF/TRAN CH42 92 B4
WARR WA1 107 H1
WDN WA8 14 E1
Elm Hall Dr CALD/MH L18 96 A3
Elmham Crs AIN/FAZ L10 32 C5
Elm House Ms WLTN L25 97 H4
Elmhurst Rd WLTN L25 97 G1
Elmore Cl EV L5 54 B5
Elm Park Rd WAL/NB CH45 51 G3
Elm Rd ANF/KKDL L4 54 C1
BEB CH63 115 H4
ECCL WA10 61 F2
KKBY L32 33 G1
LITH L21 38 D1
PEN/TH CH61 112 D5
RF/TRAN CH42 92 B5
RUNC WA7 155 G1
WARRN/WOL WA2 83 H1
WARRW/BUR WA5 104 D4
Elm Rd North RF/TRAN CH42 114 D1
Elmsdale Rd CALD/MH L18 96 A3
Elmsett Cl WARRW/BUR WA5 104 C3
Elmsfield Cl WLTN L25 97 G3
Elmsfield Rd CSBY/BLUN L23 22 A3
Elms House Rd
CLB/OSW/ST L13 72 D2
Elmsley Rd CALD/MH L18 95 H4
Elms Pk PEN/TH CH61 135 E1
Elms Rd MGHL L31 23 H3
The Elms MGHL L31 18 D3
RUNC WA7 8 C7
TOX L8 94 C4
Elm St BIRK CH41 2 E4
HUY L36 76 A3
Elmswood Av RAIN/WH L35 78 B3
Elmswood Ct CALD/MH L18 * 95 H5
Elmswood Gv HUY L36 74 D2
Elmswood Rd AIG/SPK L17 118 C1
RF/TRAN CH42 92 A4
WAL/EG CH44 69 F1
Elm Ter EHL/KEN L7 * 72 A3
HOY CH47 87 G1
Elm Tree Av WARR WA1 84 D5
Elmtree Cl WD/CROXPK L12 56 C3
Elmtree Gv CL/PREN CH43 68 A5
Elmure Av BEB CH63 137 F1
Elm V NPK/KEN L6 72 B2
Elmway Cl CLB/OSW/ST L13 72 D3
Elmwood Av CSBY/BLUN L23 21 G5
WARR WA1 13 K1
Elmwood Dr PEN/TH CH61 134 D4
Elphin Gv ANF/KKDL L4 54 C1
Elsbeck Gv STHEL WA9 62 D4
Elsie Rd ANF/KKDL L4 54 D4
Elsmere Av AIG/SPK L17 95 E5
Elson Rd FMBY L37 16 C5
Elstead Rd KKBY L32 33 F3
WLT/FAZ L9 41 G3
Elstow St EV L5 53 H3
Elstree Rd NPK/KEN L6 72 B2
Elswick St TOX L8 94 B5
Eltham Av LITH L21 30 A3
Eltham Cl GR/UP/WCH CH49 113 F1
WDN WA8 103 E5
Eltham Gn GR/UP/WCH CH49 113 E1
Eltham St EHL/KEN L7 72 B3
Elton Av CSBY/BLUN L23 20 D5
NTHTN L30 30 D1
Elton Cl GOL/RIS/CUL WA3 85 G1
Elton Dr BEB CH63 138 A4
Elton Head Rd STHEL WA9 61 F5
STHEL WA9 62 A4
Elton St ANF/KKDL L4 40 B5
Elwick Dr NG/CROX L11 42 C5
Elwood Cl NWD/KWIPK L33 25 H3
Elworth Av WDN WA8 102 A3
Elworthy Av HLWD L26 121 H2
Elwyn Dr HLWD L26 122 A3
Elwyn Rd HOY CH47 65 E4
Elwy St TOX L8 94 C3
Ely Av MOR/LEA CH46 66 A5
Ely Cl NTHTN L30 31 E3
Ember Crs NPK/KEN L6 71 F1
Embleton Ct RUNC WA7 155 H4
Emerald Cl NTHTN L30 31 G1
Emerald St TOX L8 94 B5
Emerson St TOX L8 94 B1
Emery St ANF/KKDL L4 54 B1
Emily St STHEL WA9 61 E3
WDN WA8 14 D5
Emlyn St STHEL WA9 62 D1
Emmett St STHEL WA9 62 C1
Empire Rd LITH L21 39 F1
Empress Cl MGHL L31 18 B5
Empress Rd EHL/KEN L7 71 H3
NPK/KEN L6 55 E4
WAL/EG CH44 69 E1
Emslie Ct NSTN CH64 158 B2
Endborne Rd WLT/FAZ L9 40 C1
Endbutt La CSBY/BLUN L23 29 F1
Enderby Av RNFD/HAY WA11 48 C1
Endfield Pk ALL/GAR L19 119 F3
Endmoor Rd HUY L36 58 A5
Endsleigh Rd CLB/OSW/ST L13 72 C2
CSBY/WL L22 28 C2
Enerby Cl CL/PREN CH43 90 C1
Enfield Av CSBY/BLUN L23 21 F5
Enfield Park Rd
WARRN/WOL WA2 84 C1
Enfield Rd CLB/OSW/ST L13 73 F3
Enfield St ECCL WA10 10 C7
Enfield Ter CL/PREN CH43 2 A7
Enford Dr STHEL WA9 62 D3
Enid St TOX L8 94 B2
Ennerdale Av MGHL L31 19 E4
PS/BROM CH62 153 F5
RNFD/HAY WA11 37 F4
WARRN/WOL WA2 83 H2
Ennerdale Cl FMBY L37 16 C3
NWD/KWIPK L33 25 G4
Ennerdale Dr LITH L21 30 C4
Ennerdale Rd CL/PREN CH43 114 A2
FMBY L37 16 C3
WAL/NB CH45 51 F2
WLT/FAZ L9 41 F1
Ennerdale St VAUX/LVPD L3 70 D1
Ennisdale Dr WKBY CH48 110 D1
Ennismore Rd CLB/OSW/ST L13 72 D2
CSBY/BLUN L23 20 D4
Ennis Rd WD/CROXPK L12 57 E4
Ensor St BTL L20 53 F1
Enstone Av LITH L21 29 H3
Enstone Rd WLTN L25 120 D5
Ensworth Rd CALD/MH L18 96 B3
Enterprise Wy CLB/OSW/ST L13 72 C4
Enville St WARRS WA4 13 F7
Epping Av STHEL WA9 79 F2
Epping Cl RAIN/WH L35 78 B3
Epping Ct HES CH60 135 E5
Epping Dr WARR WA1 85 H5
Epping Gv WAV L15 96 B2
Epsom Cl AIN/FAZ L10 32 B3
Epsom Gdns WARRS WA4 130 C4
Epsom Gv NWD/KWIPK L33 26 B3
Epsom Rd MOR/LEA CH46 66 D2
Epsom St STHEL WA9 49 E3
Epsom Wy EV L5 53 H5
Epstein Ct NPK/KEN L6 71 H2
Epworth Cl CL/PREN CH43 91 G2
Epworth Gra CL/PREN CH43 * 91 G2
Epworth St NPK/KEN L6 7 K2
Eremon Cl WLT/FAZ L9 32 A4
Erfurt Av BEB CH63 138 A2
Erica Ct HES CH60 134 C4
Eric Av WARR WA1 84 C5
Eric Gv WAL/EG CH44 68 C1
Eric Rd WAL/EG CH44 68 C1
Eric St WDN WA8 15 G1
Eridge St TOX L8 94 C4
Erin Cl TOX L8 94 A2
Erl St WLT/FAZ L9 40 C1
Ermine Crs EV L5 54 B5
Errington Ct AIG/SPK L17 118 C3
Errington St EV L5 53 F4
Errol St AIG/SPK L17 94 D5
Erskine Cl RNFD/HAY WA11 49 E1
Erskine Rd WAL/EG CH44 69 E2
Erskine St NPK/KEN L6 7 K2
Erwood St WARRN/WOL WA2 12 C2
Erylmore Rd CALD/MH L18 119 E2
Escolme Dr
GR/UP/WCH CH49 89 G5
Escor Rd WLTN L25 97 F2
Escort Cl WLTN L25 121 E3
Eshelby Cl CSBY/WL L22 29 F3
Esher Cl CL/PREN CH43 90 C1
Eshe Rd CSBY/BLUN L23 20 D5
Eshe Rd North CSBY/BLUN L23 20 D5
Esher Rd NPK/KEN L6 72 A2
PS/BROM CH62 116 B3
Eskburn Rd CLB/OSW/ST L13 55 G4
Eskdale Av PS/BROM CH62 153 E4
RNFD/HAY WA11 37 F4
Eskdale Cl FMBY L37 16 C4
RUNC WA7 155 H4
Eskdale Dr FMBY L37 16 C4
MGHL L31 18 D4
Eskdale Rd WLT/FAZ L9 40 C1
Esk St BTL L20 53 F2
Eslington St ALL/GAR L19 119 E4
Esmond St NPK/KEN L6 54 D5
Esonwood Rd RAIN/WH L35 76 D2
Espin St ANF/KKDL L4 54 B1
Esplen Av CSBY/BLUN L23 21 G4
Essex Rd HUY L36 76 A1
WKBY CH48 87 G5
Essex St TOX L8 94 B3
Essex Wy BTL L20 5 G3
Esthwaite Av RNFD/HAY WA11 37 G4
Estuary Banks SPK/HALE L24 141 F2
Estuary Bvd SPK/HALE L24 141 F2
Etal Cl NG/CROX L11 56 B1
Ethelbert Rd HOY CH47 64 C5
Ethel Rd WAL/EG CH44 69 F2
Etna St CLB/OSW/ST L13 72 D2
Eton Ct CALD/MH L18 96 D3
Eton Dr AIN/FAZ L10 31 H2
BEB CH63 150 B3
Eton Hall Dr STHEL WA9 62 C3
Eton St ANF/KKDL L4 54 B1
Etruria St ALL/GAR L19 140 C2
Etruscan Rd CLB/OSW/ST L13 73 E1
Ettington Rd ANF/KKDL L4 54 D3
Ettrick Cl NWD/KWIPK L33 25 G3
Euclid Av WARRS WA4 131 F1
Eurolink STHEL WA9 78 D1
Europa Bvd BIRK CH41 3 F3
WARRW/BUR WA5 82 C2
Eustace St WARRN/WOL WA2 12 A3
Euston Gv CL/PREN CH43 2 B7
Euston St ANF/KKDL L4 40 B5
Evans Pl WARRS WA4 107 F5
Evans Rd HOY CH47 87 F1
SPK/HALE L24 141 H1
Evans St PR/KW L34 59 H3
Evellynne Cl KKBY L32 33 F2
Evelyn Av PR/KW L34 60 A4
STHEL WA9 49 E4
Evelyn Rd WAL/EG CH44 69 E2
Evelyn St EV L5 53 H4
WARRW/BUR WA5 105 H4
Evenson Wy CLB/OSW/ST L13 73 E2
Evenwood STHEL WA9 62 C4
Everdon Wd NWD/KWIPK L33 33 H1
Evered Av WLT/FAZ L9 40 C3
Everest Rd CSBY/BLUN L23 21 E5
RF/TRAN CH42 115 F1
Evergreen Cl GR/UP/WCH CH49 89 F2
NTHLY L27 98 C2
Evergreen Rd STHEL WA9 63 G3
The Evergreens FMBY L37 16 C2
Everite Rd WDN WA8 123 H4
Everleigh Cl CL/PREN CH43 90 B1
Eversleigh Dr BEB CH63 138 A2
Eversley WDN WA8 123 H1
Eversley Pk CL/PREN CH43 * 91 H5
Eversley St TOX L8 94 C2
Everton Brow VAUX/LVPD L3 71 E2
Everton Gv RNFD/HAY WA11 48 D2
Everton Rd NPK/KEN L6 71 F1
Everton Ter EV L5 71 F1
Everton Va EV L5 54 A3
Everton Vw BTL L20 4 C6
Every St NPK/KEN L6 71 H1
Evesham Cl WARRS WA4 130 A3
WLTN L25 120 B1
Evesham Rd ANF/KKDL L4 55 F1
WAL/NB CH45 51 F4
Ewanville HUY L36 75 G4
Ewart Rd CHLDW L16 74 C5
LITH L21 29 G5
RNFD/HAY WA11 48 B1
Ewden Cl CHLDW L16 97 E1
Exchange Pas West CLVP L2 * 6 C3
Exchange Pl RAIN/WH L35 78 A2
Exchange St ECCL WA10 11 G6
Exchange St East CLVP L2 6 C3
Exchange St West CLVP L2 6 C3
Exeley RAIN/WH L35 77 E3
Exeter Cl AIN/FAZ L10 32 B3
Exeter Rd BTL L20 4 E7
WAL/EG CH44 52 A5
Exeter St ECCL WA10 10 B5
Exford Rd WD/CROXPK L12 56 D2
Exmoor Cl PEN/TH CH61 134 D1
Exmouth Cl BIRK CH41 2 D4
Exmouth Crs RUNC WA7 157 G3
Exmouth Gdns BIRK CH41 2 D4
Exmouth St BIRK CH41 2 D4
Exmouth Wy BIRK CH41 2 D4
Extension Vw STHEL WA9 62 D2

F

Factory La WARR WA1 12 A5
WARRW/BUR WA5 12 A5
WDN WA8 102 B5
Factory Rw ECCL WA10 61 G1
Fairacre Rd ALL/GAR L19 119 E4
Fairacres Rd BEB CH63 137 H2
Fairbairn Rd CSBY/WL L22 29 F3
Fairbank St WAV L15 95 G1
Fairbeech Ms CL/PREN CH43 * 90 C1
Fairbourne Cl
WARRW/BUR WA5 83 E2
Fairbrook Dr BIRK CH41 67 H4
Fairbrother Crs
WARRN/WOL WA2 84 B3
Fairburn Cl WDN WA8 103 E5
Fairburn Rd CLB/OSW/ST L13 55 G4
Fairclough Av WARR WA1 13 F6
Fairclough Crs
RNFD/HAY WA11 49 G1
Fairclough La CL/PREN CH43 91 H4
Fairclough Rd ECCL WA10 47 E3
HUY L36 58 A4
RAIN/WH L35 77 H2
Fairclough St CLVPS L1 7 F5
Fairfax Dr RUNC WA7 146 D4
Fairfax Pl NG/CROX L11 41 F5
Fairfax Rd NG/CROX L11 41 G5
RF/TRAN CH42 92 C4
Fairfield CSBY/BLUN L23 21 F5
Fairfield Av HUY L36 74 C3
Fairfield Cl HUY L36 74 C3
Fairfield Crs HUY L36 74 C3
MOR/LEA CH46 66 B5
NPK/KEN L6 72 B2
Fairfield Dr WKBY CH48 88 A5
Fairfield Gdns RNFD/HAY WA11 36 C2
WARRS WA4 130 C1
Fairfield Rd ECCL WA10 47 E2
RF/TRAN CH42 115 G1
WARRS WA4 130 B1
WDN WA8 14 E1
Fairfield St EHL/KEN L7 72 C2
WARR WA1 13 G2
Fairford Cl WARRW/BUR WA5 105 F2
Fairford Crs DV/KA/FCH L14 73 F1
Fairford Rd DV/KA/FCH L14 73 F1
Fairhaven NWD/KWIPK L33 25 H4
Fairhaven Cl RF/TRAN CH42 115 H1
WARRW/BUR WA5 105 F4
Fairhaven Dr BEB CH63 152 C4
Fairhaven Rd WDN WA8 125 G1
Fairholme Av NSTN CH64 158 C1
PR/KW L34 60 C4
Fairholme Cl WD/CROXPK L12 56 A2
Fairholme Rd CSBY/BLUN L23 21 F5
Fairhurst Ter PR/KW L34 * 60 A4
Fairlawn Cl BEB CH63 152 A3
Fairlawne Cl NWD/KWIPK L33 25 H4
Fairlie Crs BTL L20 30 C5
Fairlie Dr RAIN/WH L35 78 B3
Fairmead Rd MOR/LEA CH46 66 C4
NG/CROX L11 41 G5
Fairoak Ms CL/PREN CH43 * 90 C1
Fairview BIRK CH41 92 C4
Fairview Av WAL/NB CH45 51 G5
Fairview Cl CL/PREN CH43 91 H5
Fair View Pl TOX L8 * 94 C4
Fairview Rd CL/PREN CH43 91 H5
Fairview Wy PEN/TH CH61 134 D3
Fair Wy ECCL WA10 47 E2
Fairway HUY L36 76 A1
Fairway Crs PS/BROM CH62 138 D2
Fairway North
PS/BROM CH62 138 D2
Fairways CSBY/BLUN L23 21 E4
RF/TRAN CH42 114 D3
Fairways Cl WLTN L25 120 D3
Fairways Ct FMBY L37 16 B1
Fairway South
PS/BROM CH62 138 D3
The Fairways WKBY CH48 110 D5
The Fairway WD/CROXPK L12 73 H1
Falcon Crs NTHLY L27 98 D4
Falcon Cresent NTHLY L27 98 D4
Falconers Gn
WARRW/BUR WA5 82 B3
Falconer St BTL L20 39 E1
Falconhall Rd WLT/FAZ L9 41 H3
Falcon Hey AIN/FAZ L10 42 A1
Falcon Rd RF/TRAN CH42 92 A4
Falcons Wy RUNC WA7 156 A3
Falkirk Av WDN WA8 101 G5
Falkland Rd WAL/EG CH44 69 F1
Falklands Ap NG/CROX L11 41 G5
Falkland St BIRK CH41 68 C5
VAUX/LVPD L3 7 J2
Falkner Sq TOX L8 71 G5
Falkner St TOX L8 7 J7
Fallbrook Dr WD/CROXPK L12 56 B1
Fallow Cl STHEL WA9 79 G1
Fallowfield NWD/KWIPK L33 25 H4
RUNC WA7 146 D5
Fallowfield Gv
WARRN/WOL WA2 85 F4
Fallowfield Rd WAV L15 95 H2
Fallows Wy HUY L36 76 C4
Falmouth Dr
WARRW/BUR WA5 104 C5
Falmouth Pl RUNC WA7 157 G3
Falmouth Rd NG/CROX L11 42 C2
Falstaff St BTL L20 53 G2
Falstone Dr RUNC WA7 157 G1
Faraday Rd CLB/OSW/ST L13 72 C4
NWD/KWIPK L33 34 C5
RUNC WA7 146 D3
Faraday St EV L5 54 C5
Fareham Cl GR/UP/WCH CH49 89 F2
Fareham Rd EHL/KEN L7 72 B3
Faringdon Cl WLTN L25 * 120 D5
Farley Av PS/BROM CH62 138 C5
Farlow Rd RF/TRAN CH42 115 H2
Farmbrook Rd WLTN L25 97 H1
Farm Cl GR/UP/WCH CH49 89 E4
Farmdale Cl CALD/MH L18 119 F1
Farmdale Dr MGHL L31 19 E5
Far Meadow La PEN/TH CH61 112 A5
Farmer Pl BTL L20 30 D5
Farmfield Dr CL/PREN CH43 90 C1
Farm La WARRS WA4 130 C3
Farmleigh Gdns
WARRW/BUR WA5 105 G2
Far Moss Rd CSBY/BLUN L23 20 C3
Farm Rd STHEL WA9 79 H2
Farmside MOR/LEA CH46 66 D2
Farmside Cl WARRW/BUR WA5 106 A1
Farm Vw LITH L21 30 A2
Farmview Cl NTHLY L27 98 A1
Farnworth St NPK/KEN L6 71 H2
Farnborough Gv HLWD L26 121 H2
Farndale WDN WA8 102 A3
Farndale Cl WARRW/BUR WA5 104 D1
Farndon Av STHEL WA9 79 F1
WAL/NB CH45 51 E4
Farndon Dr WKBY CH48 88 A5
Farndon Wy CL/PREN CH43 91 F4
Farnham Cl KKBY L32 34 A3
WARRS WA4 130 C4
Farnhill Cl RUNC WA7 157 F1
Farnworth Av MOR/LEA CH46 66 C2
Farnworth Cl WDN WA8 102 B4
Farnworth Gv NWD/KWIPK L33 25 H4
Farnworth Rd
WARRW/BUR WA5 104 A5
Farnworth St STHEL WA9 48 C3
WDN WA8 102 B4
Farrant St WDN WA8 15 F3
Farrar St CLB/OSW/ST L13 55 F3
Farrell Cl MGHL L31 25 E5
Farrell Rd WARRS WA4 130 A3
Farrell St WARR WA1 13 G5
Farr Hall Dr HES CH60 148 C2
Farr Hall Rd HES CH60 148 C1
Farrier Rd NWD/KWIPK L33 34 B2
Farriers Wy NTHTN L30 31 E4
WKBY CH48 111 H1
Farrier Wk STHEL WA9 79 G1
Farringdon Cl STHEL WA9 61 H5
Farthing Cl WLTN L25 120 C4
Farthingstone Cl RAIN/WH L35 60 C4
Fatherside Dr NTHTN L30 * 30 B1
Faversham Rd NG/CROX L11 41 G4
Fawcett Rd MGHL L31 18 D3
Fawley Rd CALD/MH L18 119 G1
RAIN/WH L35 78 C4
Fazakerley Cl WLT/FAZ L9 40 C3
Fazakerley Rd RAIN/WH L35 77 E1
WLT/FAZ L9 40 C3
Fazakerley St VAUX/LVPD L3 6 C3
Fearnhead Cross
WARRN/WOL WA2 * 84 C4
Fearnhead La
WARRN/WOL WA2 85 E3
WARRN/WOL WA2 85 G2
Fearnley Rd BIRK CH41 2 E6
Fearnside St EHL/KEN L7 72 A5
Feather La HES CH60 148 D1
Feeny St STHEL WA9 * 79 F3
Feilden Rd BEB CH63 138 A2
Felcroft Wy NWD/KWIPK L33 34 A2
Felicity Gv MOR/LEA CH46 66 B4
Fell Gv RNFD/HAY WA11 37 E4
Fell St EHL/KEN L7 71 H3
WAL/EG CH44 69 G3
Felltor Cl WLTN L25 97 F5
Fellwood Gv RAIN/WH L35 77 E3
Felmersham Av NG/CROX L11 41 H4
Felspar Rd KKBY L32 33 H5
Felsted Av WLTN L25 121 E1
Felsted Dr AIN/FAZ L10 32 B3
Felthorpe Cl GR/UP/WCH CH49 90 B1
Felton Gv CLB/OSW/ST L13 72 D1
Feltwell Rd ANF/KKDL L4 54 D4
Feltwood Cl WD/CROXPK L12 57 F3
Feltwood Rd WD/CROXPK L12 57 F2
Fendale Av MOR/LEA CH46 67 E4
Fender La MOR/LEA CH46 67 E4
Fenderside Rd CL/PREN CH43 67 G5
Fender View Rd
MOR/LEA CH46 67 E5
Fender Wy CL/PREN CH43 67 F5
CL/PREN CH43 90 B1
PEN/TH CH61 135 E2
Fenham Dr WARRW/BUR WA5 104 C4
Fennel St WARR WA1 13 F4
Fenton Cl ECCL WA10 10 E3
NTHTN L30 31 G4
SPK/HALE L24 142 B3
WDN WA8 101 E5
Fenton Gn SPK/HALE L24 142 B4
Fenwick La RUNC WA7 155 H3
Fenwick St CLVP L2 6 C4
Ferguson Av GR/UP/WCH CH49 89 E5
Ferguson Dr WARRN/WOL WA2 84 B4
Ferguson Rd LITH L21 30 B3
NG/CROX L11 55 G2
Fernbank Av HUY L36 75 F3
Fernbank Dr NTHTN L30 23 F5
Fern Cl GOL/RIS/CUL WA3 85 H1
KKBY L32 25 H5
NTHLY L27 98 C4
Ferndale Av WAL/EG CH44 69 E1
WKBY CH48 111 H2
Ferndale Cl WARR WA1 108 C1
WDN WA8 103 E1
WLT/FAZ L9 31 F5
Ferndale Rd CSBY/WL L22 29 E2
HOY CH47 87 F1
WAV L15 95 G2
Fern Gdns PR/KW L34 60 B3
Fern Gv BTL L20 5 F3
CL/PREN CH43 90 D3
TOX L8 95 E2
Fern Hey CSBY/BLUN L23 21 H4
Fern Hl WAL/NB CH45 51 H2
Fernhill Av BTL L20 5 J4
Fernhill Cl BTL L20 5 J5
Fernhill Dr TOX L8 94 C2
Fernhill Gdns BTL L20 5 J5
Fernhill Ms East BTL L20 5 J5
Fernhill Ms West BTL L20 * 5 J5
Fernhill Rd BTL L20 5 J1
Fernhill Wy BTL L20 5 J5
Fernhurst RUNC WA7 155 H1
Fernhurst Rd KKBY L32 33 F3
Fernlea Av STHEL WA9 61 F3
Fernlea Ms CL/PREN CH43 67 G5
Fernlea Rd HES CH60 149 E1
Fernleigh Rd
CLB/OSW/ST L13 * 73 F2
Ferns Cl HES CH60 134 A5
Ferns Rd BEB CH63 137 F1
Fern Vls WAL/EG CH44 * 69 G3
Fernwood RUNC WA7 147 H5
Fernwood Dr HLWD L26 121 G3
Fernwood Rd AIG/SPK L17 118 C1
Ferny Brow Rd
GR/UP/WCH CH49 90 B5
Ferrey Rd AIN/FAZ L10 32 D5
Ferries Cl RF/TRAN CH42 * 116 A3
Ferry La WARRS WA4 109 E4
Ferry Rd PS/BROM CH62 153 G1
Ferryside WAL/EG CH44 69 G3
Ferry View Rd WAL/EG CH44 69 G3
Festival Av WARRN/WOL WA2 84 B3
Festival Ct NG/CROX L11 * 42 B4
Festival Crs WARRN/WOL WA2 84 B3
Festival Wy RUNC WA7 155 G1
Ffrancon Dr BEB CH63 115 H4
Fiddlers Ferry Rd WDN WA8 15 J3
Fidler St ECCL WA10 61 F1
Field Av LITH L21 29 H4
Field Cl PS/BROM CH62 116 B3
Fieldfare Cl WLTN L25 97 G3
Fieldgate WDN WA8 123 H5
Fieldhouse Rw RUNC WA7 155 H2
The Fieldings MGHL L31 18 B2

Fielding St NPK/KEN L6 * 71 G2
Field La AIN/FAZ L10 33 E5
LITH L21 29 H3
WARRS WA4 130 A5
Field Rd STHEL WA9 79 H2
WAL/NB CH45 51 H3
Field's End HUY L36 75 G5
Fieldsend Cl NTHLY L27 98 C4
Fieldside Rd RF/TRAN CH42 115 G1
Field St VAUX/LVPD L3 71 E2
Fieldsway RUNC WA7 155 E3
Fieldton Rd NG/CROX L11 42 B4
Field Vw LITH L21 29 H3
Fieldview Dr WARRN/WOL WA2 84 A4
Fieldway BEB CH63 115 F3
HES CH60 135 G5
HOY CH47 88 B1
HUY L36 75 H5
MGHL L31 24 B2
Field Wy RAIN/WH L35 61 E5
Fieldway WAL/NB CH45 51 G5
WAV L15 73 G5
WDN WA8 126 A1
Fieldway Ct BIRK CH41 2 B1
Fife Rd WARR WA1 13 K1
Fifth Av CL/PREN CH43 90 B1
RUNC WA7 156 B2
WLT/FAZ L9 32 A5
Filbert Cl NWD/KWIPK L33 26 A3
Fildes Cl WARRW/BUR WA5 105 G3
Fillmore Gv WDN WA8 101 H5
Filton Rd DV/KA/FCH L14 57 H5
Finborough Rd ANF/KKDL L4 41 E5
Fincham Cl DV/KA/FCH L14 57 H5
Fincham Gn DV/KA/FCH L14 57 H5
Fincham Rd DV/KA/FCH L14 57 G5
Fincham Sq DV/KA/FCH L14 57 G5
Finch Cl DV/KA/FCH L14 * 57 F4
STHEL WA9 79 H2
Finch Ct BIRK CH41 2 D2
Finchdean Cl GR/UP/WCH CH49 89 E4
Finch Dene DV/KA/FCH L14 57 F4
Finch La DV/KA/FCH L14 57 F4
HLWD L26 122 B5
Finch Lea Dr DV/KA/FCH L14 57 G5
Finchley Dr RNFD/HAY WA11 37 G5
Finchley Rd ANF/KKDL L4 54 D3
Finch Meadow Cl WLT/FAZ L9 41 H3
Finch Pl VAUX/LVPD L3 7 J2
Finch Rd DV/KA/FCH L14 57 G4
Finch Wy DV/KA/FCH L14 57 F5
Findley Dr MOR/LEA CH46 66 D2
Findon Rd KKBY L32 34 A4
Fingall Rd WAV L15 96 B2
Finger House La WDN WA8 79 H4
Fingland Rd WAV L15 95 G1
Finlan Rd WDN WA8 14 B6
Finlay Av WARRW/BUR WA5 104 C5
Finlay St NPK/KEN L6 72 A2
The Finney WKBY CH48 * 110 D5
Finningley Ct WARRN/WOL WA2 84 C4
Finsbury Cl WARRW/BUR WA5 105 G4
Finsbury Pk WDN WA8 102 C3
Finstall Rd BEB CH63 137 H4
Finvoy Rd CLB/OSW/ST L13 55 G3
Fir Avenue HLWD L26 122 A3
Firbrook Ct CL/PREN CH43 67 G4
Fir Cl HLWD L26 122 A3
Firdale Rd WLT/FAZ L9 40 C3
Firdene Crs CL/PREN CH43 91 E4
Firecrest Ct WARR WA1 106 C5
Fire Station Rd RAIN/WH L35 60 B5
Firethorne Rd HLWD L26 121 F1
Fir Gv WARR WA1 107 H1
WLT/FAZ L9 31 H4
Fir La WAV L15 96 A1
Firman Cl WARRW/BUR WA5 82 B5
Fir Rd CSBY/WL L22 29 F2
Firs Av BEB CH63 137 H3
Firs Cl FMBY L37 16 C1
Firs Crs FMBY L37 16 C1
Firshaw Rd HOY CH47 64 C4
Firs La WARRS WA4 129 H5
Firs Link FMBY L37 16 C2
First Av CL/PREN CH43 90 C2
CSBY/BLUN L23 * 21 E5
RAIN/WH L35 77 H1
WLT/FAZ L9 31 H5
WLT/FAZ L9 41 G1
Firstone Gv KKBY L32 33 H4
Fir St ECCL WA10 61 E2
WDN WA8 125 G1
Firth Bvd WARRN/WOL WA2 13 F1
Firthland Wy STHEL WA9 49 F5
Firtree Av WARR WA1 85 E5
Fir Tree Dr North WD/CROXPK L12 42 D4
Fir Tree Dr South WD/CROXPK L12 42 D4
Fir Wy HES CH60 149 F4
Fisher Av RAIN/WH L35 76 D3
WARRN/WOL WA2 83 H4
Fisher Pl RAIN/WH L35 76 D3
Fishers La PEN/TH CH61 134 C2
Fisher St RUNC WA7 9 G3
STHEL WA9 63 E3
TOX L8 93 H2
Fistral Cl AIN/FAZ L10 42 B1
Fistral Dr ECCL WA10 46 D1
Fitzclarence Wy NPK/KEN L6 71 F1
Fitzgerald Rd CLB/OSW/ST L13 73 E2
Fitzherbert St WARRN/WOL WA2 107 E1
Fitzpatrick Ct VAUX/LVPD L3 70 C1
Fitzroy Wy NPK/KEN L6 71 G2
Fitzwalter Rd WARR WA1 108 D1
Fiveways ECCL WA10 46 C3
Flag La NSTN CH64 159 E3
Flail Cl GR/UP/WCH CH49 89 E4
Flambards GR/UP/WCH CH49 90 B5
Flander Cl WDN WA8 124 A1
Flashes La NSTN CH64 159 G5
Flatfield Wy MGHL L31 19 E5
Flatt La CL/PREN CH43 91 F5
Flawn Rd NG/CROX L11 55 G2
Flaxfield Rd FMBY L37 17 F3
Flaxhill MOR/LEA CH46 66 B4
Flaxman St EHL/KEN L7 * 72 A3
Flaybrick Cl CL/PREN CH43 68 A5
Fleck La WKBY CH48 110 D2
Fleet Croft Rd GR/UP/WCH CH49 113 E1
Fleet La STHEL WA9 49 E5
Fleet St CLVPS L1 7 F5
Fleetwood Cl WARRW/BUR WA5 105 F4
Fleetwood Gdns NWD/KWIPK L33 26 A4
Fleetwood's La NTHTN L30 22 C5
Fleetwood Wk RUNC WA7 157 E2
Fleming Ct VAUX/LVPD L3 70 C1
Fleming Rd SPK/HALE L24 121 E5
Flemington Av ANF/KKDL L4 55 F1
Flers Av WARRS WA4 107 E5
Fletcher Av PR/KW L34 60 A3
RF/TRAN CH42 115 G1
Fletcher Cl GR/UP/WCH CH49 113 E1
Fletcher Dr ALL/GAR L19 119 E4
Fletcher St WARRS WA4 106 D5
Flint Cl NSTN CH64 158 C4
Flint Dr NSTN CH64 158 D3
WD/CROXPK L12 56 D1
Flint Meadow NSTN CH64 158 D3
Flintshire Gdns ECCL WA10 10 E7
Flint St CLVPS L1 93 H1
Floral Wd AIG/SPK L17 117 F1
Florence Av HES CH60 134 D5
Florence Cl WLT/FAZ L9 40 B4
Florence Nightingale Cl NTHTN L30 23 E5
Florence Rd WAL/EG CH44 69 G2
Florence St ANF/KKDL L4 54 B2
BIRK CH41 2 E4
STHEL WA9 61 E3
WARRS WA4 107 F5
Florentine Rd CLB/OSW/ST L13 73 E1
Florida Cl WARRW/BUR WA5 105 G1
Florida Ct ALL/GAR L19 119 F3
Florida Wy RAIN/WH L35 76 D1
Flowermead Cl HOY CH47 65 F4
Fluker's Brook La PR/KW L34 43 H5
Fog Cottages STHEL WA9 * 62 A5
Foinavon Cl WLT/FAZ L9 31 E5
Folds La RNFD/HAY WA11 37 E5
Folds Rd RNFD/HAY WA11 49 F1
The Folds BEB CH63 150 C3
Foley St ANF/KKDL L4 54 A3
Folkstone Wy RUNC WA7 157 E2
Folly La WAL/EG CH44 51 E5
WARRW/BUR WA5 106 B1
Fontenoy St CLVP L2 6 E2
Fonthill Cl ANF/KKDL L4 53 H3
Fonthill Rd ANF/KKDL L4 53 H2
Ford Av NWD/KWIPK L33 25 H3
Ford Cl BTL L20 30 D5
GR/UP/WCH CH49 90 B4
LITH L21 30 A2
Fordcombe Rd WLTN L25 98 A4
Ford Dr GR/UP/WCH CH49 90 B3
Fordham St ANF/KKDL L4 54 A2
Fordhill Vw MOR/LEA CH46 67 E5
Fordington Rd WARRW/BUR WA5 105 F3
Ford La GR/UP/WCH CH49 90 B3
LITH L21 30 A1
Fordlea Rd WD/CROXPK L12 56 A2
Fordlea Wy WD/CROXPK L12 56 B2
Ford Rd GR/UP/WCH CH49 90 A3
RAIN/WH L35 60 B4
Ford St VAUX/LVPD L3 70 C2
WARR WA1 13 H2
Ford Vw LITH L21 30 A1
Ford Wy GR/UP/WCH CH49 90 A4
Forefield La CSBY/BLUN L23 21 G5
Foreland Cl WARRW/BUR WA5 104 A1
Forest Cl HOY CH47 64 D4
PR/KW L34 60 B3
Forest Ct CL/PREN CH43 91 F2
Forest Dr HUY L36 75 E2
Forest Gn WD/CROXPK L12 56 B2
Forest Gv PR/KW L34 60 B3
Forest Lawn WD/CROXPK L12 56 B2
Forest Md ECCL WA10 46 C4
Forest Rd CL/PREN CH43 91 G1
HES CH60 149 E1
HOY CH47 64 D4
STHEL WA9 79 E2
Forest Wk RUNC WA7 * 156 B2
Forfar Rd CLB/OSW/ST L13 55 F4
Forge Cl WDN WA8 101 E3
Forge Cottages AIG/SPK L17 * 95 E4
Forge Rd WARRW/BUR WA5 104 D3
Forge St BTL L20 53 G2
Formby Br FMBY L37 16 D4
Formby By-Pass FMBY L37 17 G4
Formby Cl WARRW/BUR WA5 104 D4
Formby Flds FMBY L37 17 F4
Formby Gdns FMBY L37 17 E2
Formby Rd ECCL WA10 61 F1
Formby St FMBY L37 16 D4
Formosa Dr AIN/FAZ L10 32 C5
Formosa Rd AIN/FAZ L10 32 C5
Formosa Wy AIN/FAZ L10 32 C5
Fornalls Green La HOY CH47 88 A1
Forrester Av STHEL WA9 61 E3
Forrest St CLVPS L1 6 E6
Forrest Wy WARRW/BUR WA5 105 H5
Forshaw Av ECCL WA10 61 E2
Forshaw St WARRN/WOL WA2 13 F1
Forster St WARRN/WOL WA2 12 D1
Forsythia Cl WLT/FAZ L9 * 41 E4
Forthlin Rd CALD/MH L18 119 G2
Forth St BTL L20 53 G1
Forton Lodge Flats CSBY/BLUN L23 * 20 D5
Fort St WAL/NB CH45 52 A3
Forwood Rd PS/BROM CH62 152 D1
Foscote Rd NWD/KWIPK L33 26 B5
Foster Cl RAIN/WH L35 60 C5
Foster Rd FMBY L37 16 C4
Fosters Gv RNFD/HAY WA11 49 F1
Fosters Rd RNFD/HAY WA11 49 F1
Foster St BTL L20 53 G3
WDN WA8 15 F1
Fothergill St WARR WA1 13 H1
Foundry La WDN WA8 144 D1
Foundry St ECCL WA10 11 G6
WARRN/WOL WA2 12 D3
Fountain Ct CSBY/BLUN L23 20 B4
Fountain Rd PR/KW L34 44 B4
WAL/NB CH45 51 H3
Fountains Cl ANF/KKDL L4 54 B3
RUNC WA7 157 E4
Fountains Ct EV L5 53 H3
Fountains Rd ANF/KKDL L4 53 H3
Fountain St RF/TRAN CH42 92 A5
STHEL WA9 61 E4
Fountains Wy FMBY L37 17 F4
Four Acre Dr LITH L21 30 A1
Four Acre La STHEL WA9 79 G1
Fouracres MGHL L31 23 G2
Fourth Av CL/PREN CH43 90 B2
RUNC WA7 156 B2
WLT/FAZ L9 32 A5
Fourways Cl NTHLY L27 98 B1
Fowell Rd WAL/NB CH45 51 H2
Fowler Cl EHL/KEN L7 72 A4
Fox Bank Cl WDN WA8 101 H3
Foxcote WDN WA8 123 H1
Fox Cover Rd HES CH60 149 G2
Foxcovers Rd BEB CH63 138 A3
Fox Covert RUNC WA7 157 E2
Foxdale Cl CL/PREN CH43 91 G3
Foxdale Rd WAV L15 95 H2
Foxdell Cl CLB/OSW/ST L13 73 E3
The Foxes PEN/TH CH61 113 E5
Foxfield Cl WARRN/WOL WA2 84 C2
Foxfield Rd HOY CH47 64 D5
Foxglove Av HLWD L26 121 G2
Foxglove Cl WLT/FAZ L9 41 H3
Foxglove Rd BIRK CH41 * 91 F1
Foxglove Wy NSTN CH64 158 D5
Fox Hey Rd WAL/EG CH44 68 B2
Foxhill Cl FMBY L37 16 B3
TOX L8 94 C3
Foxhill La HLWD L26 121 H1
Foxhouse La MGHL L31 24 B1
Foxhunter Dr WLT/FAZ L9 31 H4
Foxleigh HLWD L26 121 F2
Foxley Heath WDN WA8 14 A3
Fox Pl ECCL WA10 11 G2
Fox's Bank La RAIN/WH L35 77 F4
Foxshaw Cl RAIN/WH L35 76 D4
Fox St BIRK CH41 2 C4
RUNC WA7 8 D6
VAUX/LVPD L3 71 E1
WARRW/BUR WA5 106 A3
Foxton Cl MOR/LEA CH46 65 H4
RNFD/HAY WA11 * 48 D2
Foxwood STHEL WA9 61 E3
WD/CROXPK L12 57 E2
Foxwood Cl WKBY CH48 88 A5
Frampton Rd ANF/KKDL L4 41 F5
Franceys St VAUX/LVPD L3 * 7 H4
Francine Cl VAUX/LVPD L3 53 G5
Francis Av CL/PREN CH43 2 A5
MOR/LEA CH46 66 B5
Francis Cl RAIN/WH L35 78 A1
WDN WA8 124 A3
Francis Rd WARRS WA4 129 H2
Francis St STHEL WA9 63 F3
Francis Wy CHLDW L16 74 A5
Frankby Av WAL/EG CH44 68 C1
Frankby Cl GR/UP/WCH CH49 88 D5
Frankby Gv GR/UP/WCH CH49 89 H3
Frankby Rd ANF/KKDL L4 54 D2
GR/UP/WCH CH49 89 E5
HOY CH47 64 D5
WKBY CH48 87 H5
Frankby Stiles WKBY CH48 88 B5
Franklin Cl WARRW/BUR WA5 82 C5
Franklin Gv NWD/KWIPK L33 25 H3
Franklin Pl NPK/KEN L6 * 54 D5
Franklin Rd MOR/LEA CH46 67 E1
Frank St TOX L8 94 A3
WDN WA8 15 H2
Fraser Rd WARRW/BUR WA5 104 B2
Fraser St VAUX/LVPD L3 7 G2
Freckleton Cl WARRW/BUR WA5 105 F4
Freckleton Dr NWD/KWIPK L33 26 B4
Freckleton Rd ECCL WA10 60 D1
Freda Av STHEL WA9 * 62 C4
Frederick Banting Cl NTHTN L30 23 E5
Frederick Gv WAV L15 73 E5
Frederick Lunt Av PR/KW L34 44 A4
Frederick St STHEL WA9 63 F3
WARRS WA4 107 F5
WDN WA8 14 E2
Fredric Pl RUNC WA7 9 F3
Freedom Cl EHL/KEN L7 71 G5
Freehold St EHL/KEN L7 72 B2
Freeland St ANF/KKDL L4 * 54 A3
Freeman St BIRK CH41 3 F2
EHL/KEN L7 72 A5
Freemantle Av STHEL WA9 61 H3
Freemasons Rw VAUX/LVPD L3 6 D1
Freemont Rd WD/CROXPK L12 56 A3
Freeport Gv WLT/FAZ L9 31 G5
Freesia Av WLT/FAZ L9 40 D3
Freme Cl NG/CROX L11 42 B4
French St ECCL WA10 61 F1
WDN WA8 15 J2
Frensham Cl BEB CH63 137 H4
Freshfield Cl HUY L36 75 E2
Freshfield Rd FMBY L37 16 D1
WAV L15 95 H2
Freshfields Dr WARRN/WOL WA2 85 F4
Freshford STHEL WA9 62 D4
Freshwater WARRW/BUR WA5 104 B1
Freshwater Cl WARRW/BUR WA5 104 B1
Friars Av WARRW/BUR WA5 104 C3
Friars Cl BEB CH63 137 H2
Friars Ga WARR WA1 12 D6
Friarsgate Cl CALD/MH L18 96 C3
Friars La WARR WA1 12 D6
Friar St ECCL WA10 36 D5
EV L5 * 54 C5
Friars Wk FMBY L37 17 G4
Friends La WARRW/BUR WA5 104 B2
Frinsted Rd NG/CROX L11 56 A1
Frobisher Ct WARRW/BUR WA5 82 D5
Frobisher Rd MOR/LEA CH46 67 E1
NSTN CH64 158 D2
Frodsham Dr RNFD/HAY WA11 48 D2
Frodsham St ANF/KKDL L4 54 B1
BIRK CH41 92 C4
Froghall La WARR WA1 12 B3
WARRW/BUR WA5 106 B3
Frogmore Rd CLB/OSW/ST L13 72 C2
Frome Cl PEN/TH CH61 112 B4
Frome Wy WLTN L25 121 F3
Frost Dr PEN/TH CH61 112 A4
Frost St EHL/KEN L7 72 A3
Fryer St RUNC WA7 8 D3
Fry St STHEL WA9 49 E4
Fuchsia Wk GR/UP/WCH CH49 112 A1
Fulbeck WDN WA8 124 A1
Fulbrook Cl BEB CH63 137 H4
Fulbrook Rd BEB CH63 137 H4
Fulford Cl WD/CROXPK L12 57 F4
Fulford Pk MOR/LEA CH46 89 G1
Fullerton Gv HUY L36 75 G1
Fulmar Cl NTHLY L27 98 C4
RNFD/HAY WA11 48 B1
Fulmar Gv WD/CROXPK L12 43 E4
Fulshaw Cl NTHLY L27 98 B2
Fulton Av WKBY CH48 87 H5
Fulton St EV L5 53 F4
Fulwood Cl AIG/SPK L17 118 B1
Fulwood Dr AIG/SPK L17 118 A1
Fulwood Pk AIG/SPK L17 118 A2
Fulwood Rd AIG/SPK L17 118 A1
Funchal Av FMBY L37 16 C5
Furlong Cl WLT/FAZ L9 32 A4
Furness Av ECCL WA10 36 C5
FMBY L37 17 E3
WD/CROXPK L12 56 C1
Furness Cl GR/UP/WCH CH49 89 G2
Furness St ANF/KKDL L4 54 A3
Furrocks Cl NSTN CH64 159 E5
Furrocks La NSTN CH64 159 E5
Furrocks Wy NSTN CH64 159 E5

G

Gable Ct NG/CROX L11 * 41 G4
Gables Cl WARRN/WOL WA2 84 D2
The Gables MGHL L31 * 24 B2
Gable Vw NG/CROX L11 * 41 G4
Gabriel Cl MOR/LEA CH46 66 D5
Gainford Cl WDN WA8 101 E5
Gainford Rd DV/KA/FCH L14 57 G4
Gainsborough Av MGHL L31 23 G1
Gainsborough Cl DV/KA/FCH L14 57 E5
Gainsborough Ct WDN WA8 123 H2
Gainsborough Rd GR/UP/WCH CH49 89 G2
WAL/NB CH45 51 E5
WARRS WA4 129 H1
WAV L15 95 G2
Gairloch Cl WARRN/WOL WA2 84 D1
Gaisgill Ct WDN WA8 124 A2
Galbraith Cl AIG/SPK L17 118 A1
Gale Av WARRW/BUR WA5 83 F4
Galemeade NG/CROX L11 * 42 B4
Gale Rd LITH L21 30 B3
NWD/KWIPK L33 34 D4
Galion Wy WDN WA8 101 H4
Galloway Rd CSBY/WL L22 29 F2
Galloway St EHL/KEN L7 72 B5
Galston Av RAIN/WH L35 78 B3
Galston Cl NWD/KWIPK L33 25 G3
Galsworthy Av NTHTN L30 30 C5
Galsworthy Pl NTHTN L30 30 D4
Galton St VAUX/LVPD L3 6 A1
Galtres Pk BEB CH63 115 G3
Galway Av WDN WA8 101 G5
Gambier Ter CLVPS L1 94 A1
Gamble Av ECCL WA10 47 G1
Gamlin St BIRK CH41 68 B5
Gamston Wd KKBY L32 33 F3
Ganney's Meadow Rd GR/UP/WCH CH49 90 C5
Gannock St EHL/KEN L7 72 A3
Ganton Cl WDN WA8 102 B4
Ganworth Cl SPK/HALE L24 142 C4
Ganworth Rd SPK/HALE L24 142 C3
Garage Rd HLWD L26 142 D1
Gardeners Vw NWD/KWIPK L33 26 A3
Gardeners Wy RAIN/WH L35 61 E5
Garden Hey Rd HOY CH47 64 C5
MOR/LEA CH46 88 D1
Gardenia Gv AIG/SPK L17 117 G1
Garden La EV L5 * 71 F1
MOR/LEA CH46 66 C4
WLT/FAZ L9 32 A5
Garden Lodge Gv NTHLY L27 98 B3
Garden Pl BTL L20 * 5 F4
Gardenside MOR/LEA CH46 67 F1
Gardenside St NPK/KEN L6 71 F2
Gardens Rd BEB CH63 138 B1
Garden St WLTN L25 120 C1
Garden Wk PR/KW L34 59 H4
Gardner Av BTL L20 30 C5
Gardner Rd CLB/OSW/ST L13 55 G5
FMBY L37 17 F3
Gardner's Dr NPK/KEN L6 72 A1
Gardner's Rw VAUX/LVPD L3 70 D2
Gareth Av RNFD/HAY WA11 48 B1
Garfield Ter GR/UP/WCH CH49 * 90 A3
Garfourth Cl ALL/GAR L19 119 H4
Garfourth Rd ALL/GAR L19 119 H4
Garmoyle Cl WAV L15 95 G1
Garmoyle Rd WAV L15 95 G2
Garner St WARRN/WOL WA2 107 E1
Garnet St CLB/OSW/ST L13 72 D4
STHEL WA9 62 D3
Garnett Av ANF/KKDL L4 53 H2
WARRS WA4 107 H4
Garnetts La RAIN/WH L35 122 D2
WDN WA8 144 C2
Garrick Av MOR/LEA CH46 66 A5
Garrick Rd CL/PREN CH43 114 B3
Garrick St EHL/KEN L7 95 E1
Garrigill Cl WDN WA8 102 B3
Garrison Cl TOX L8 94 D2
Garrowby Dr HUY L36 75 E2
Garsdale Av RAIN/WH L35 78 B3
Garsdale Cl WARRW/BUR WA5 104 D1
Garsfield Rd ANF/KKDL L4 55 F1
Garston Old Rd ALL/GAR L19 119 F4
Garston Wy ALL/GAR L19 140 C1
Garswood Cl MGHL L31 19 E3
MOR/LEA CH46 66 C1
Garswood St ECCL WA10 11 G3
TOX L8 94 B5
Garter Cl NG/CROX L11 42 C4
Garth Bvd BEB CH63 115 G3
Garthdale Rd CALD/MH L18 96 A4
Garth Dr CALD/MH L18 96 B4
Garthowen Rd EHL/KEN L7 72 B3
Garth Rd KKBY L32 34 B4
The Garth HUY L36 75 G2
Gartons La STHEL WA9 79 G2
Garven Pl WARR WA1 12 C5
Garway WLTN L25 98 A5
Garwood Cl WARRW/BUR WA5 82 B4
Gascoyne St VAUX/LVPD L3 6 C1
Gaskell Av WARRS WA4 108 A5
Gaskell St STHEL WA9 62 D1
WARRS WA4 130 A2
Gaskill Rd SPK/HALE L24 142 B2
Gatclif Rd CLB/OSW/ST L13 55 G2
Gateacre Brow WLTN L25 97 G4
Gateacre Park Dr WLTN L25 97 F2
Gateacre Ri WLTN L25 97 H4
Gateacre Vale Rd WLTN L25 97 H5
Gateley Cl WARRS WA4 109 E5
Gateside Cl NTHLY L27 98 C3
Gate Warth St WARRW/BUR WA5 * 105 H5
Gathurst Ct WDN WA8 124 B3
Gatley Dr MGHL L31 24 B1
Gaunts Wy RUNC WA7 156 A3
Gautby Rd BIRK CH41 68 A4
Gavin Rd WDN WA8 123 H4
Gawsworth Cl CL/PREN CH43 91 F5
ECCL WA10 46 D4
Gaybeech Cl CL/PREN CH43 67 G5
Gayhurst Av WARRN/WOL WA2 84 D3
Gayhurst Crs NG/CROX L11 42 A5
Gayton Av BEB CH63 115 E3
WAL/NB CH45 51 H2
Gayton Farm Rd HES CH60 149 E4
Gayton La HES CH60 149 F3
Gayton Mill Cl HES CH60 * 149 F2
Gayton Pkwy HES CH60 149 F4
Gayton Rd HES CH60 148 D3
Gaywood Av KKBY L32 34 A4
Gaywood Cl CL/PREN CH43 * 90 C1
KKBY L32 34 A4
Gellings La PR/KW L34 43 G2
Gellings Rd PR/KW L34 43 G2
Gelling St TOX L8 94 B3
Gemini Cl BTL L20 4 D3
Gemini Dr DV/KA/FCH L14 74 B1
General St WARR WA1 13 F4
Geneva Rd NPK/KEN L6 72 A2
WAL/EG CH44 69 F3
Genista Cl WLT/FAZ L9 40 C4
Genoa Cl WLTN L25 98 A1
Gentwood Rd HUY L36 75 E1
George Hale Av PR/KW L34 58 C4
George Harrison Cl NPK/KEN L6 71 H2
George Moore Ct CSBY/BLUN L23 * 22 B3
George Rd HOY CH47 87 G2
WARRW/BUR WA5 105 G4
Georges Crs WARRS WA4 131 F1
George's Dock Gates VAUX/LVPD L3 6 B3
Georges Dockway VAUX/LVPD L3 6 B5
Georges Pierhead VAUX/LVPD L3 6 B5
Georges Rd NPK/KEN L6 55 E5
George St BIRK CH41 3 G2
CLVP L2 6 C3
ECCL WA10 11 H5
Georgia Av NWD/KWIPK L33 25 G3
PS/BROM CH62 139 E3
Georgia Cl BTL L20 4 E5
Georgian Cl HLWD L26 121 H5
RAIN/WH L35 60 C4
Georgian Pl FMBY L37 16 D5
Georgia Pl WARRW/BUR WA5 105 G2
Geraint St TOX L8 94 B2
Gerald Rd CL/PREN CH43 91 G4
Gerard Av WAL/NB CH45 51 G3
Gerard Rd WAL/NB CH45 51 G4
WKBY CH48 87 F5
Gerards Ct RNFD/HAY WA11 * 37 G4
Gerards La STHEL WA9 62 D3
Gerard St VAUX/LVPD L3 7 F2
Germander Cl HLWD L26 121 G2
Gerneth Cl SPK/HALE L24 142 A2
Gerneth Rd SPK/HALE L24 141 H3
Gerrard Av WARRW/BUR WA5 106 B1
Gerrard's La HLWD L26 121 G1
Gerrard St WDN WA8 14 E4
Gertrude Rd ANF/KKDL L4 54 C4
Gertrude St BIRK CH41 3 H4
STHEL WA9 61 E4
Geves Gdns CSBY/WL L22 29 F3
Ghyll Gv RNFD/HAY WA11 37 F3
Gibbons Av ECCL WA10 47 E4
Gibraltar Rw VAUX/LVPD L3 6 B2
Gibson Cl NWD/KWIPK L33 25 G4
PEN/TH CH61 134 D3
Gibson Rd TOX L8 94 B1
Gibson St TOX L8 94 B1
WARR WA1 13 G5
Giddygate La MGHL L31 25 E2
Gidlow Rd CLB/OSW/ST L13 72 D2
Gidlow Rd South CLB/OSW/ST L13 72 D2
Gigg La WARRS WA4 109 E4
Gig La WARR WA1 85 H5
Gilbert Cl BEB CH63 137 H4
Gilbert Rd RAIN/WH L35 60 B5
Gilbert St CLVPS L1 6 E6
Gilbrook Sq BIRK CH41 68 B5
Gildarts Gdns VAUX/LVPD L3 * 70 D1
Gildart St VAUX/LVPD L3 7 J2
Gilead St EHL/KEN L7 71 H3
Gillan Cl RUNC WA7 157 E4
Gillars Green Dr ECCL WA10 46 B4
Gillar's La ECCL WA10 46 A4

Gilleney Gv RAIN/WH L35 60 C5
Gillmoss Cl NG/CROX L11 42 C3
Gillmoss La NG/CROX L11 42 C2
Gills La PEN/TH CH61 135 E2
Gill St VAUX/LVPD L3 7 J3
Gilman St ANF/KKDL L4 54 C3
Gilmartin Gv NPK/KEN L6 71 G3
Gilmour Mt CL/PREN CH43 91 H4
Gilpin Av MGHL L31 19 E4
Gilroy Rd NPK/KEN L6 71 H2
WKBY CH48 87 H5
Gilsecroft Av
NWD/KWIPK L33 34 B1
Giltbrook Cl WDN WA8 101 H5
Gilwell Av MOR/LEA CH46 89 G1
Gilwell Cl MOR/LEA CH46 89 G1
WARRS WA4 131 G1
The Ginnel PS/BROM CH62 138 B1
Gipsy Gv CALD/MH L18 97 E3
Gipsy La CALD/MH L18 97 E3
Girton Av BTL L20 5 J6
Girtrell Cl GR/UP/WCH CH49 89 F3
Girtrell Rd GR/UP/WCH CH49 89 F3
Girvin Dr NSTN CH64 158 D4
Givenchy Cl CHLDW L16 74 A5
Glade Rd HUY L36 75 G1
Gladeswood Rd
NWD/KWIPK L33 34 C3
The Glade HOY CH47 64 D4
Gladeville Rd AIG/SPK L17 118 C1
Gladstone Av CHLDW L16 74 C5
LITH L21 29 G5
Gladstone Cl BIRK CH41 2 C4
Gladstone Hall Rd
PS/BROM CH62 * 138 B2
Gladstone Rd ALL/GAR L19 119 G5
EHL/KEN L7 71 H4
LITH L21 29 G5
NSTN CH64 158 D2
RF/TRAN CH42 92 D5
WAL/EG CH44 69 F2
WLT/FAZ L9 40 B4
Gladstone St BIRK CH41 * 2 C4
ECCL WA10 10 A6
VAUX/LVPD L3 6 D1
WARRN/WOL WA2 12 B3
WDN WA8 14 E3
WLTN L25 120 B1
Gladsville Rd NTHLY L27 98 D4
Glaisher St EV L5 54 C4
Glamis Cl CL/PREN CH43 90 D5
Glamis Gv STHEL WA9 62 C3
Glamis Rd CLB/OSW/ST L13 55 F4
Glamorgan Cl ECCL WA10 10 E7
Glan Aber Pk WD/CROXPK L12 57 E2
Glasier Rd MOR/LEA CH46 66 A4
Glaslyn Wy WLT/FAZ L9 40 C4
Glassonby Crs NG/CROX L11 56 A1
Glassonby Wy NG/CROX L11 56 A1
Glastonbury Cl NPK/KEN L6 55 F3
Glasven Rd NWD/KWIPK L33 34 A1
Glazebrook St WARR WA1 13 H3
Gleadmere WDN WA8 124 A1
Gleaston Cl PS/BROM CH62 138 C5
Gleave Crs NPK/KEN L6 71 F1
Gleave St ECCL WA10 11 H3
Glebe Av WARRS WA4 131 G2
Glebe Cl MGHL L31 18 B5
Glebe End SFTN L29 22 D2
Glebe Hey NTHLY L27 98 C3
Glebe Hey Rd
GR/UP/WCH CH49 90 A5
Glebelands Rd MOR/LEA CH46 66 C5
Glebe La WDN WA8 102 A3
Glebe Rd WAL/NB CH45 51 G4
The Glebe RUNC WA7 147 E5
Gleggside WKBY CH48 110 C1
Glegg St VAUX/LVPD L3 70 B1
Glegside Rd NWD/KWIPK L33 34 B2
Glenacres WLTN L25 * 97 G5
Glenalmond Rd WAL/EG CH44 * 69 F1
Glenathol Rd CALD/MH L18 119 G1
Glenavon Rd CHLDW L16 73 G5
CL/PREN CH43 114 C2
Glen Bank CSBY/WL L22 28 D2
Glenbank Cl WLT/FAZ L9 40 C2
Glenburn Av PS/BROM CH62 153 E5
Glenburn Rd WAL/EG CH44 69 F2
Glenby Av CSBY/BLUN L23 29 G2
Glencairn Rd CLB/OSW/ST L13 72 D3
Glencoe Rd WAL/NB CH45 51 H4
Glenconner Rd CHLDW L16 74 A4
Glencourse Rd WDN WA8 102 A3
Glencroft Cl HUY L36 58 A5
Glendale Cl TOX L8 94 B5
Glendale Gv BEB CH63 138 B4
Glendale Wy FMBY L37 17 E4
Glendevon Rd CHLDW L16 73 H4
HUY L36 75 G4
Glendower Rd CSBY/WL L22 29 F3
Glendower St BTL L20 53 G2
Glendyke Rd CALD/MH L18 119 G1
Gleneagles Cl
NWD/KWIPK L33 25 G3
PEN/TH CH61 134 D2
Gleneagles Dr
RNFD/HAY WA11 49 G2
WDN WA8 102 A3
Gleneagles Rd CHLDW L16 74 A4
DV/KA/FCH L14 73 H4
Glenfield Cl CL/PREN CH43 67 G5
MOR/LEA CH46 65 H4
Glenfield Rd WAV L15 96 A2
Glengariff St CLB/OSW/ST L13 55 G3
Glenham Cl HOY CH47 65 E5
Glenhead Rd ALL/GAR L19 119 F3
Glenholm Rd MGHL L31 * 23 H2
Glenluce Rd ALL/GAR L19 119 F3
Glenmarsh Cl BEB CH63 137 F1
WD/CROXPK L12 56 C4
Glenmarsh Wy FMBY L37 17 G3
Glenmaye Cl WD/CROXPK L12 43 E5
Glenmore Av CALD/MH L18 95 H5
Glenmore Rd CL/PREN CH43 91 G4
Glenn Pl WDN WA8 124 B2
Glen Park Rd WAL/NB CH45 51 G3
Glen Rd CLB/OSW/ST L13 73 F3
Glen Ronald Dr
GR/UP/WCH CH49 89 F3
Glenside CALD/MH L18 119 G1
The Glen BEB CH63 138 C3
CALD/MH L18 96 C5
RUNC WA7 156 B3
Glenton Pk NSTN CH64 159 E4
Glentrees Cl GR/UP/WCH CH49 89 F5
Glentrees Rd WD/CROXPK L12 56 B2
Glentworth Cl MGHL L31 24 A1
Glenville Cl RUNC WA7 155 F3
WLTN L25 97 H5
Glen Vine Cl CHLDW L16 * 74 B5
Glenway NWD/KWIPK L33 26 A3
Glenway Cl WD/CROXPK L12 43 F3
Glenwood Cl RAIN/WH L35 77 F3
Glenwood Dr PEN/TH CH61 112 C4
Glenwyllin Rd CSBY/WL L22 29 F2
Globe Rd BTL L20 4 C3
Globe St ANF/KKDL L4 54 A3
Gloucester Cl WARR WA1 108 D1
Gloucester Ct NPK/KEN L6 71 G2
Gloucester Pl NPK/KEN L6 71 G2
Gloucester Rd BTL L20 5 H3
HUY L36 76 A2
NPK/KEN L6 55 F5
WAL/NB CH45 51 E4
WDN WA8 102 B5
Gloucester Rd North
NPK/KEN L6 55 F4
Gloucester St STHEL WA9 48 D4
Gloucestor Ct NPK/KEN L6 71 G2
Glover Pl BTL L20 4 D2
Glover's Brow KKBY L32 25 F5
Glover's La NTHTN L30 22 D5
Glover St ECCL WA10 10 E6
RF/TRAN CH42 92 A4
Glyn Av PS/BROM CH62 153 E2
Glynne Gv CHLDW L16 74 C5
Glynne St BTL L20 39 H1
Glynn St WAV L15 95 H1
Glyn Rd WAL/EG CH44 51 H5
Goddard Rd RUNC WA7 147 E3
Godetia Cl WLT/FAZ L9 * 41 H3
Godfrey St WARRN/WOL WA2 13 H1
Godshill Cl WARRW/BUR WA5 104 B1
Golborne St WARR WA1 12 C4
Goldcliffe Cl WARRW/BUR WA5 82 D3
Goldcrest Cl RUNC WA7 156 B4
WD/CROXPK L12 43 F3
Goldcrest Ms HLWD L26 121 G2
Golden Gv ANF/KKDL L4 54 C1
Goldfinch Cl HLWD L26 121 G2
Goldfinch Farm Rd
SPK/HALE L24 142 A3
Goldie St ANF/KKDL L4 54 B3
Goldsmith Rd CL/PREN CH43 114 B2
Goldsmith St BTL L20 4 B2
NPK/KEN L6 * 71 H2
Goldsmith Wy
CL/PREN CH43 * 114 B2
Goldsworth Fold RAIN/WH L35 77 H2
Golf Links Rd RF/TRAN CH42 114 D2
Golf Rd FMBY L37 16 C1
Gondover Av WLT/FAZ L9 40 B1
Gonville Rd BTL L20 5 H7
Goodacre Rd WLT/FAZ L9 31 G5
Goodaker's Meadow
GR/UP/WCH CH49 * 113 E1
Goodall Pl ANF/KKDL L4 54 A1
Goodall St ANF/KKDL L4 54 A2
Goodban St STHEL WA9 63 E2
Goodison Av ANF/KKDL L4 54 B2
Goodison Pl ANF/KKDL L4 54 B1
Goodison Rd ANF/KKDL L4 54 B1
Goodlass Rd SPK/HALE L24 141 G1
Goodleigh Pl STHEL WA9 62 C5
Good Shepherd Cl
NG/CROX L11 42 B5
Goodwood Cl HUY L36 75 F4
Goodwood Ct STHEL WA9 61 F4
Goodwood Dr MOR/LEA CH46 66 C2
Goodwood St EV L5 54 C4
Goostrey Cl BEB CH63 138 B5
Gordale Cl TOX L8 * 94 C4
WARRW/BUR WA5 104 D1
Gordon Av CSBY/WL L22 28 D2
GR/UP/WCH CH49 89 G5
MGHL L31 18 C3
PS/BROM CH62 153 E2
WARR WA1 108 B1
Gordon Ct GR/UP/WCH CH49 89 G5
Gordon Dr ALL/GAR L19 119 E4
DV/KA/FCH L14 74 A2
Gordon Rd LITH L21 38 D1
WAL/NB CH45 51 H3
Gordon St BIRK CH41 2 C5
WAV L15 95 G1
Goree Piazza CLVP L2 * 6 C4
Gores La FMBY L37 16 D1
Gores Rd NWD/KWIPK L33 34 C3
Gore St TOX L8 94 A2
Gorleston Wy KKBY L32 34 A3
Gorran Hvn RUNC WA7 157 E3
Gorse Av WD/CROXPK L12 56 B1
Gorsebank Rd CALD/MH L18 * 95 G3
Gorsebank St WAL/EG CH44 69 E2
Gorseburn Rd CLB/OSW/ST L13 55 G4
Gorse Crs WAL/EG CH44 69 E3
Gorsedale Pk WAL/EG CH44 * 69 F3
Gorsedale Rd CALD/MH L18 96 A4
WAL/EG CH44 69 E3
Gorsefield STHEL WA9 61 F3
Gorsefield Av CSBY/BLUN L23 21 H4
PS/BROM CH62 152 D4
Gorsefield Cl PS/BROM CH62 152 D4
Gorsefield Rd RF/TRAN CH42 92 A5
Gorse Hey Ct CLB/OSW/ST L13 56 A5
Gorsehill Rd HES CH60 135 E5
WAL/NB CH45 51 G3
Gorse La WKBY CH48 111 E2
Gorse Rd HOY CH47 64 D5
Gorse Wy FMBY L37 16 B2
Gorsewood Gv WLTN L25 97 H3
Gorsewood Rd RUNC WA7 157 F3
WLTN L25 97 H3
Gorsey Av NTHTN L30 30 B1
Gorsey Cop Wy WLTN L25 97 G2
Gorsey Cft PR/KW L34 60 B3
Gorsey La LITH L21 30 A2
NTHTN L30 30 B1
STHEL WA9 80 B1
WAL/EG CH44 69 E3
WARRN/WOL WA2 107 F1
WDN WA8 126 A3
Gorseyville Crs BEB CH63 137 G1
Gorseyville Rd BEB CH63 137 G1
Gorseywell La RUNC WA7 157 H3
Gorstons La NSTN CH64 159 F4
Gorst St ANF/KKDL L4 54 B3
Gorton Rd CLB/OSW/ST L13 73 F3
Gort Rd HUY L36 75 G2
Goschen St CLB/OSW/ST L13 72 D2
EV L5 54 B3
Gosford St TOX L8 94 B4
Gosport Cl WARRN/WOL WA2 84 C4
Goswell St WAV L15 95 G1
Gotham Rd BEB CH63 138 A4
Gothic St RF/TRAN CH42 115 H1
Gough Av WARRN/WOL WA2 83 H3
Gough Rd CLB/OSW/ST L13 55 G3
Goulden St WARRW/BUR WA5 106 A2
Goulders Ct RUNC WA7 156 D4
Gourley Rd CLB/OSW/ST L13 73 F4
Gourley's La WKBY CH48 110 D2
Government Rd HOY CH47 87 F1
Govett Rd STHEL WA9 61 E3
Gower St BTL L20 39 E2
STHEL WA9 62 D1
VAUX/LVPD L3 6 C7
Gowrie Gv LITH L21 29 H5
Graburn Rd FMBY L37 17 E2
Grace Av AIN/FAZ L10 32 D5
WARRN/WOL WA2 83 H5
Grace Cl WAL/NB CH45 51 H5
Grace Rd WLT/FAZ L9 40 C1
Grace St STHEL WA9 62 C2
TOX L8 94 B4
Gradwell St CLVPS L1 6 E5
Grafton Crs TOX L8 94 A2
Grafton Dr GR/UP/WCH CH49 90 A4
Grafton Gv TOX L8 94 A4
Grafton Rd WAL/NB CH45 51 H3
Grafton St CL/PREN CH43 2 A6
ECCL WA10 10 B5
TOX L8 94 A3
WARRW/BUR WA5 106 A2
Grafton Wk WKBY CH48 110 C1
Graham Cl WDN WA8 124 A3
Graham Dr HLWD L26 122 A3
Graham Rd WDN WA8 124 A3
WKBY CH48 87 E5
Graham's Rd HUY L36 75 H3
Graham St STHEL WA9 48 C3
Grainger Av BTL L20 40 A1
CL/PREN CH43 114 B1
WKBY CH48 87 F4
Graley Cl HLWD L26 121 H5
Grammar School Ct
WARRS WA4 * 107 H5
Grammar School La
WKBY CH48 110 D2
Grammar School Rd
WARRS WA4 107 H5
Grampian Av MOR/LEA CH46 66 C5
Grampian Rd EHL/KEN L7 72 C3
Grampian Wy MOR/LEA CH46 66 C5
NSTN CH64 158 D5
PS/BROM CH62 153 E5
Granams Cft NTHTN L30 22 C5
Granard Rd WAV L15 96 A2
Granary Wy VAUX/LVPD L3 93 H2
Granborne Cha KKBY L32 33 E1
Granby Cl RUNC WA7 * 157 E4
Granby Crs BEB CH63 138 A4
Granby Rd WARRS WA4 129 H3
Granby St TOX L8 94 C1
Grandison Rd ANF/KKDL L4 55 E1
Grand National Av WLT/FAZ L9 31 G3
Grange Av WAL/NB CH45 51 H4
WARRS WA4 107 G4
WD/CROXPK L12 57 E5
WLTN L25 121 F4
Grange Av North
WD/CROXPK L12 57 F5
Grange Cross Cl WKBY CH48 111 E2
Grange Cross Hey WKBY CH48 111 E2
Grange Cross La WKBY CH48 111 E2
Grange Dr BEB CH63 150 C2
ECCL WA10 60 D1
HES CH60 134 D5
WARRW/BUR WA5 105 E4
WDN WA8 124 B2
Grange Farm Cl
WARRW/BUR WA5 105 H2
Grange Farm Crs WKBY CH48 88 A5
Grange Green Mnr
WARRS WA4 * 129 E4
Grangehurst Ct WLTN L25 97 H4
Grange La FMBY L37 16 D1
WLTN L25 97 G3
Grangemeadow Rd WLTN L25 97 G3
Grange Ms WLTN L25 * 97 H4
Grangemoor RUNC WA7 155 H2
Grange Mt CL/PREN CH43 2 B6
HES CH60 134 D5
WKBY CH48 110 D1
Grange Old Rd WKBY CH48 110 C1
Grange Pk MGHL L31 24 B2
Grange Park Av RUNC WA7 9 H5
Grange Park Rd ECCL WA10 61 E1
RUNC WA7 9 H5
Grange Pavement BIRK CH41 * 3 F5
Grange Pl BIRK CH41 2 C5
Grange Rd BIRK CH41 2 D5
BIRK CH41 3 F5
HES CH60 134 D4
NTHTN L30 31 G2
RUNC WA7 9 H5
WKBY CH48 87 E5
Grange Rd North RUNC WA7 9 H4
Grange Rd West CL/PREN CH43 2 B5
Grangeside WLTN L25 97 G3
Grange St NPK/KEN L6 55 F5
Grange Ter WAV L15 95 H1
The Grange WAL/EG CH44 69 E1
Grange V RF/TRAN CH42 116 A2
Grange Vw CL/PREN CH43 2 B6
Grange Wk WKBY CH48 110 D2
Grangeway RUNC WA7 155 G2
Grange Wy WLTN L25 97 G3
Grangeway Ct RUNC WA7 155 G2
Grange Weint WLTN L25 97 G4
Grangewood CHLDW L16 74 B4
Grange Wd WKBY CH48 110 D2
Granston Cl WARRW/BUR WA5 83 E3
Grant Av WAV L15 95 H2
Grant Cl DV/KA/FCH L14 74 C2
ECCL WA10 10 D4
WARRW/BUR WA5 82 D4
Grantham Av WARR WA1 107 G1
WARRS WA4 129 H3
Grantham Cl PEN/TH CH61 134 C2
Grantham Crs RNFD/HAY WA11 48 C2
Grantham Rd NWD/KWIPK L33 25 H4
Grantham St NPK/KEN L6 71 H2
Grantham Wy NTHTN L30 23 F5
Grantley Rd WAV L15 96 A2
Granton Cl FMBY L37 16 D3
Granton Rd EV L5 54 B4
Grant Rd DV/KA/FCH L14 74 B2
MOR/LEA CH46 67 F1
Granville Av MGHL L31 18 C4
Granville Cl WAL/NB CH45 51 E4
Granville Rd ALL/GAR L19 * 119 G5
WAV L15 95 F1
Granville St RUNC WA7 8 E3
STHEL WA9 48 D4
WARR WA1 13 H2
Grappenhall La WARRS WA4 131 H5
Grappenhall Rd WARRS WA4 130 B2
Grappenhall Wy CL/PREN CH43 * 90 C1
Grasmere Av CL/PREN CH43 90 C3
PR/KW L34 60 B4
RNFD/HAY WA11 37 F5
WARRN/WOL WA2 84 B2
Grasmere Cl NWD/KWIPK L33 25 G5
RNFD/HAY WA11 * 37 F5
Grasmere Ct RNFD/HAY WA11 37 E5
Grasmere Dr LITH L21 30 D3
RUNC WA7 155 H4
WAL/NB CH45 51 G5
Grasmere Fold
RNFD/HAY WA11 37 F5
Grasmere Gdns CSBY/BLUN L23 29 G1
Grasmere Rd FMBY L37 16 C3
MGHL L31 18 D4
NSTN CH64 158 D4
Grasmere St EV L5 54 C4
Grassendale Esp ALL/GAR L19 118 D5
Grassendale La ALL/GAR L19 119 E4
Grassendale Rd ALL/GAR L19 119 E4
Grassington Crs WLTN L25 121 F1
Grassmoor Cl PS/BROM CH62 153 E1
Grass Wood Rd
GR/UP/WCH CH49 113 F1
Grasville Rd RF/TRAN CH42 92 C5
Gratrix Rd PS/BROM CH62 152 D1
Gray Gv HUY L36 75 H5
Graylag Cl RUNC WA7 156 B4
Graylands Pl ANF/KKDL L4 55 E1
Graylands Rd ANF/KKDL L4 55 E1
PS/BROM CH62 116 C5
Grayling Dr WD/CROXPK L12 42 D4
Grays Av RAIN/WH L35 60 B4
Grayson St CLVPS L1 6 D7
Grayston Av STHEL WA9 62 D4
Gray St BTL L20 39 E2
Greasby Rd GR/UP/WCH CH49 89 E5
WAL/EG CH44 68 C1
Great Ashfield WDN WA8 101 F5
Great Charlotte St CLVPS L1 * 7 F4
Great Crosshall St VAUX/LVPD L3 6 E2
Great George Pl CLVPS L1 94 A1
Great George Sq CLVPS L1 94 A1
Great George's Rd
CSBY/WL L22 29 E4
Great George St CLVPS L1 7 G7
Great Hey NTHTN L30 22 C4
Great Homer St EV L5 54 A5
Great Howard St EV L5 53 F5
VAUX/LVPD L3 6 B1
Great Mersey St EV L5 53 H4
Great Newton St VAUX/LVPD L3 7 J3
Great Orford St VAUX/LVPD L3 7 J5
Great Richmond St
VAUX/LVPD L3 71 E2
Great Riding RUNC WA7 157 E2
Greaves St TOX L8 * 94 B3
Grebe Av ECCL WA10 60 C2
Grecian St LITH L21 29 G4
Grecian Ter EV L5 54 B4
Gredington St TOX L8 94 C5
Greeba Av WARRS WA4 106 D5
Greek St RUNC WA7 8 C3
VAUX/LVPD L3 7 H3
Greenacre Cl WLTN L25 121 E3
Greenacre Dr BEB CH63 152 B2
Greenacre Rd WLTN L25 121 E3
Greenacres Cl CL/PREN CH43 67 G5
Greenall Av
WARRW/BUR WA5 104 B4
Greenall's Av WARRS WA4 130 A2
Greenall St ECCL WA10 10 B3
Green Bank BEB CH63 136 C4
Greenbank CSBY/WL L22 29 F4
Greenbank Av MGHL L31 18 C3
WAL/NB CH45 51 H3
Greenbank Ct AIG/SPK L17 95 G3
Greenbank Crs ECCL WA10 10 E6
Greenbank Dr AIG/SPK L17 95 G3
AIN/FAZ L10 33 E5
PEN/TH CH61 134 D3
Greenbank Gdns WARRS WA4 130 D1
Greenbank La AIG/SPK L17 95 G4
Greenbank Rd CALD/MH L18 95 H3
RF/TRAN CH42 92 A5
WARRS WA4 130 D1
WKBY CH48 87 F4
Greenbank St WARRS WA4 130 A1
Green Bridge Cl RUNC WA7 147 G4
Greenbridge Rd RUNC WA7 147 H4
Greenburn Av RNFD/HAY WA11 37 G3
Green Coppice RUNC WA7 157 E1
Green Cft CSBY/BLUN L23 22 A4
Greencroft Rd WAL/EG CH44 69 E2
Greendale Rd PS/BROM CH62 116 A5
WLTN L25 97 F4
Green End La STHEL WA9 62 B2
Green End Pk WD/CROXPK L12 56 A3
Greene's Rd RAIN/WH L35 76 D3
Greenfield Dr HUY L36 75 H5
Greenfield Gv HUY L36 * 75 H5
Greenfield La HES CH60 134 A4
LITH L21 29 H3
Greenfield Rd CLB/OSW/ST L13 73 E2
ECCL WA10 10 B1
Greenfields Av
PS/BROM CH62 152 C2
WARRS WA4 130 B3
Greenfields Cl NSTN CH64 159 E5
WARR WA1 108 C1
Greenfields Crs
PS/BROM CH62 152 C2
Greenfields Cft NSTN CH64 158 D5
Greenfields Technology Pk
PS/BROM CH62 * 139 E5
Greenfield Wy CALD/MH L18 119 G2
WAL/EG CH44 68 D1
Greenfinch Cl WD/CROXPK L12 43 F4
Greenfinch Gv HLWD L26 121 G2
Greengables Cl TOX L8 94 C3
Green Gates HUY L36 58 C4
Greengates Crs NSTN CH64 158 D5
Greenham Av NWD/KWIPK L33 26 A3
Greenhaven Cl AIN/FAZ L10 32 D5
Greenheath Wy MOR/LEA CH46 66 D2
Green Hey Dr NTHTN L30 30 B2
Green Heys Dr MGHL L31 19 F4
Greenheys Gdns TOX L8 * 94 D2
Greenheys Rd PEN/TH CH61 134 A1
TOX L8 94 D2
WAL/EG CH44 68 D1
Greenhill Av CALD/MH L18 96 C3
Greenhill Cl CALD/MH L18 119 F1
Greenhill Pl HUY L36 75 G4
Greenhill Rd ALL/GAR L19 119 G3
CALD/MH L18 96 B5
Greenholme Cl NG/CROX L11 42 A4
Greenhouse Farm Rd
RUNC WA7 156 D3
Greenhow Av WKBY CH48 87 F5
Greenlake Rd CALD/MH L18 119 F1
Greenlands HUY L36 75 G4
Greenland St TOX L8 93 H1
Green La BEB CH63 137 H1
BIRK CH41 92 C4
CALD/MH L18 96 B4
CLB/OSW/ST L13 72 D1
CSBY/BLUN L23 22 A3
CSBY/WL L22 28 D2
ECCL WA10 46 A1
LITH L21 29 H5
LITH L21 30 A2
MGHL L31 18 A4
MGHL L31 18 C5
MOR/LEA CH46 50 B5
VAUX/LVPD L3 7 H5
WAL/NB CH45 50 D4
WARR WA1 85 E5
WDN WA8 124 C2
Green La North CHLDW L16 96 C2
Green Lawn HUY L36 76 A1
RF/TRAN CH42 115 H2
Green Lawn Gv
RF/TRAN CH42 * 115 H2
Green Leach Av
RNFD/HAY WA11 37 F5
Green Leach Ct
RNFD/HAY WA11 37 G5
Green Leach La
RNFD/HAY WA11 37 F5
Greenlea Cl BEB CH63 115 H5
Greenleaf St TOX L8 95 E1
Greenleas Cl WAL/NB CH45 50 D4
Greenleas Rd WAL/NB CH45 50 D4
Greenleigh Rd CALD/MH L18 119 F1
Green Link MGHL L31 18 B4
Greenloon's Dr FMBY L37 16 B3
Greenloon's Wk FMBY L37 16 B4
Green Mt GR/UP/WCH CH49 90 A3
Green Oaks Pth WDN WA8 15 H3
Green Oaks Wy WDN WA8 15 G3
Greenock Ms WDN WA8 101 G4
Greenock St VAUX/LVPD L3 6 A1
Greenodd Av WD/CROXPK L12 56 C1
Greenore Dr SPK/HALE L24 143 H4
Greenough Av RAIN/WH L35 61 E5
Greenough St WLTN L25 120 B1
Green Pk NTHTN L30 23 E4
Green Park Dr MGHL L31 18 B5
Green Rd PR/KW L34 59 G4
Greensbridge La HLWD L26 122 B2
RAIN/WH L35 99 F5
Greenside NPK/KEN L6 7 K1
Greenside Av AIN/FAZ L10 32 A2
WAV L15 96 A1
Greenside Cl NWD/KWIPK L33 26 B3
Green St EV L5 70 C1
WARRW/BUR WA5 106 B3
The Green BEB CH63 151 E5
CLB/OSW/ST L13 73 G3
NSTN CH64 158 C2
PR/KW L34 60 A3
PS/BROM CH62 139 E1
RUNC WA7 147 F5
WKBY CH48 110 D4
Greenville Cl BEB CH63 137 H1
Greenville Dr MGHL L31 18 C5
Greenville Rd BEB CH63 137 H1
NSTN CH64 159 E1
Greenway CSBY/BLUN L23 21 H4
GR/UP/WCH CH49 89 G4
Green Wy HUY L36 74 D1
Greenway PEN/TH CH61 134 C2
PS/BROM CH62 138 D3
WARR WA1 107 H1
WARRS WA4 130 B4
WARRW/BUR WA5 104 C1
Green Way Cl HUY L36 74 D1
Greenway Rd RF/TRAN CH42 92 B5
RUNC WA7 8 C7
SPK/HALE L24 143 E3
WDN WA8 125 F1
The Greenway
WD/CROXPK L12 74 A1
Greenwich Av WDN WA8 102 D4
Greenwich Ct WLT/FAZ L9 31 G4
Greenwich Rd WLT/FAZ L9 31 G4
Greenwood Cl PR/KW L34 60 A4
Greenwood Ct STHEL WA9 79 G1
Greenwood Crs
WARRN/WOL WA2 84 B3

Greenwood La WAL/EG CH44 52 A5
Greenwood Rd CALD/MH L18 119 F2
GR/UP/WCH CH49 90 A5
HOY CH47 65 E5
Greetham St CLVPS L1 6 E7
Gregory Cl CHLDW L16 73 H5
WARRW/BUR WA5 105 G1
Gregory Wy CHLDW L16 74 A5
Gregson Ct WAL/NB CH45 52 A2
Gregson Rd RAIN/WH L35 59 H5
WDN WA8 15 H2
Gregson's Av FMBY L37 16 D1
Gregson St NPK/KEN L6 71 F2
Grenfell Cl NSTN CH64 158 B1
Grenfell Pk NSTN CH64 158 B1
Grenfell Rd CLB/OSW/ST L13 55 G2
Grenfell St WDN WA8 14 E4
Grennan Ct WAL/NB CH45 * 51 H2
The Grennan WAL/NB CH45 * 51 H2
Grenville Crs BEB CH63 152 C2
Grenville Dr PEN/TH CH61 134 C3
Grenville Rd RF/TRAN CH42 92 D5
Grenville St South CLVPS L1 7 F7
Grenville Wy RF/TRAN CH42 92 D5
Gresford Av AIG/SPK L17 95 F2
CL/PREN CH43 114 C1
WKBY CH48 87 G5
Gresford Cl RAIN/WH L35 77 F2
WARRW/BUR WA5 82 D3
Gresham St EHL/KEN L7 72 B3
Gresley Cl EHL/KEN L7 * 72 A4
Gressingham Rd CALD/MH L18 96 C5
Gretton Rd DV/KA/FCH L14 57 H5
Greyfriars Cl WARRN/WOL WA2 85 F2
Greyhound Farm Rd
SPK/HALE L24 142 A2
Greymist Av WARR WA1 108 C1
Grey Rd WLT/FAZ L9 40 A3
Greys Ct WARR WA1 * 85 G4
Greystoke Cl GR/UP/WCH CH49 89 H4
Greystone Crs DV/KA/FCH L14 74 A2
Greystone Pl AIN/FAZ L10 32 C5
Greystone Rd AIN/FAZ L10 32 B5
DV/KA/FCH L14 74 A3
WARRW/BUR WA5 104 D4
Grey St TOX L8 94 B2
WARR WA1 13 F3
Gribble Rd AIN/FAZ L10 32 D5
Grice St WARRS WA4 130 A2
Grierson St TOX L8 94 D1
Grieve Rd AIN/FAZ L10 32 D5
Griffin Av MOR/LEA CH46 66 C5
Griffin Cl ECCL WA10 46 B3
NG/CROX L11 42 C3
Griffin Ms WDN WA8 102 B5
Griffin St STHEL WA9 63 E3
Griffiths Cl GR/UP/WCH CH49 89 E5
Griffith's Rd HUY L36 75 G3
Griffiths St CLVPS L1 * 7 G7
WARRS WA4 107 H4
Grimley Av BTL L20 4 A2
Grimshaw St BTL L20 4 C6
STHEL WA9 62 C4
Grinfield St EHL/KEN L7 71 G4
Grinshill Cl TOX L8 94 C2
Grinton Crs HUY L36 75 F3
Grisedale Av WARRN/WOL WA2 83 H2
Grisedale Cl FMBY L37 16 D3
RUNC WA7 156 A4
Grisedale Rd PS/BROM CH62 153 E1
Grizedale WDN WA8 123 H1
Grizedale Av RNFD/HAY WA11 37 F4
Grizedale Rd EV L5 54 B4
Groarke Dr WARRW/BUR WA5 104 B3
Groes Rd ALL/GAR L19 119 F4
Grogan Sq BTL L20 39 H1
Gronow Pl BTL L20 * 40 A1
Grosmont Rd KKBY L32 34 A4
Grosvenor Av CSBY/BLUN L23 29 F2
WARR WA1 107 G1
WKBY CH48 110 B1
Grosvenor Cl NTHTN L30 31 E1
WARRW/BUR WA5 105 G3
Grosvenor Ct CL/PREN CH43 91 H3
WAV L15 * 96 C1
Grosvenor Dr WAL/NB CH45 51 H2
Grosvenor Gra WARR WA1 85 F4
Grosvenor Pl CL/PREN CH43 91 G3
Grosvenor Rd ALL/GAR L19 119 E5
CL/PREN CH43 91 G2
ECCL WA10 47 E5
HOY CH47 87 F2
MGHL L31 23 H3
PR/KW L34 59 H4
RNFD/HAY WA11 49 H1
WAL/NB CH45 51 H2
WAV L15 95 F1
WDN WA8 102 B4
Grosvenor St RUNC WA7 9 G3
WAL/EG CH44 51 H5
Grosvenor Ter TOX L8 94 C4
Grounds St WARRN/WOL WA2 12 E1
Grove Av HES CH60 134 D5
Grovedale Dr MOR/LEA CH46 67 E4
Grovedale Rd CALD/MH L18 95 H3
Grovehurst Av DV/KA/FCH L14 74 B1
Groveland Av HOY CH47 87 F1
WAL/NB CH45 50 D4
Groveland Rd WAL/NB CH45 50 D4
Grovelands EHL/KEN L7 * 71 G5
Grove Md MGHL L31 19 F5
Grove Pk TOX L8 93 H3
Grove Park Av WD/CROXPK L12 56 B2
Grove Pl ANF/KKDL L4 54 A3
HOY CH47 87 F1
Grove Rd HOY CH47 87 F1
NPK/KEN L6 72 B2
RF/TRAN CH42 115 H1
WAL/NB CH45 51 E4
Grove Side EHL/KEN L7 71 G5
Groveside WKBY CH48 110 A1
Grove Sq PS/BROM CH62 116 A4
The Groves EHL/KEN L7 * 71 G5
KKBY L32 33 H5
Grove St BTL L20 4 A2
ECCL WA10 11 F6
EHL/KEN L7 71 G5
PS/BROM CH62 116 B4
RUNC WA7 8 C3
TOX L8 94 C1
WARRS WA4 13 G7
WAV L15 72 D5
Grove Ter HOY CH47 87 F1
The Grove BEB CH63 138 A1
CL/PREN CH43 91 H5
CLB/OSW/ST L13 * 55 H5
ECCL WA10 47 E2
STBRV L28 58 A4
WAL/EG CH44 69 E2
WARRW/BUR WA5 104 D4
Grove Wy EHL/KEN L7 71 G5
Grovewood Ct CL/PREN CH43 91 H5
Grovewood Gdns RAIN/WH L35 77 E2
Grundy Cl WDN WA8 101 H5
Grundy St EV L5 53 F4
Guardian St WARRW/BUR WA5 12 A3
WARRW/BUR WA5 106 A2
Guelph St EHL/KEN L7 71 G3
Guernsey Cl WARRS WA4 130 B3
Guernsey Rd CLB/OSW/ST L13 72 D1
WDN WA8 103 E5
Guest St WDN WA8 14 C6
Guffitts Cl HOY CH47 65 E4
Guffitt's Rake HOY CH47 65 E4
Guildford Av NTHTN L30 31 E3
Guildford Cl WARRN/WOL WA2 85 E4
Guildford St WAL/EG CH44 69 F1
Guildhall Rd WLT/FAZ L9 40 C1
Guild Hey PR/KW L34 44 B3
Guillemot Wy HLWD L26 121 G2
Guilsted Rd NG/CROX L11 42 A5
Guion Rd LITH L21 30 A5
Guion St NPK/KEN L6 71 H1
Gulls Wy HES CH60 148 B1
Gunn Gv NSTN CH64 159 E2
Gunning Av ECCL WA10 46 D2
Gunning Cl ECCL WA10 46 D2
Gurnall St ANF/KKDL L4 54 B3
Gutticar Rd WDN WA8 123 H3
Guy Cl BIRK CH41 92 C4
Gwendoline Cl PEN/TH CH61 135 E1
Gwendoline St TOX L8 94 B2
Gwenfron Rd NPK/KEN L6 71 H2
Gwent Cl NPK/KEN L6 54 D5
Gwent St TOX L8 * 94 C2
Gwladys St ANF/KKDL L4 54 B1
Gwydir St TOX L8 94 C3
Gwydrin Rd CALD/MH L18 96 C3

H

Hackett Av BTL L20 39 H1
Hackins Hey CLVP L2 6 C3
Hackthorpe St EV L5 54 A3
Hadassah Gv AIG/SPK L17 95 E4
Hadden Cl RAIN/WH L35 * 77 G1
Haddock St BTL L20 53 F1
Haddon Av WLT/FAZ L9 40 B1
Haddon Dr PEN/TH CH61 134 D2
WDN WA8 101 E5
Haddon Rd RF/TRAN CH42 116 A1
Haddon Wk WD/CROXPK L12 43 E4
Hadfield Av HOY CH47 87 F1
Hadfield Cl WDN WA8 126 A1
Hadfield Gv WLTN L25 98 A5
Hadleigh Cl WARRW/BUR WA5 104 B3
Hadleigh Rd KKBY L32 34 A3
Hadley Av PS/BROM CH62 138 C5
Hadlow Gdns RF/TRAN CH42 92 C5
Hadstock Av FMBY L37 16 C5
Haggerston Rd ANF/KKDL L4 40 C5
Hahnemann Rd ANF/KKDL L4 5 K7
Haig Av MOR/LEA CH46 66 C5
WARRW/BUR WA5 105 E4
Haigh Crs MGHL L31 18 C2
Haigh Rd CSBY/WL L22 29 F3
Haigh St VAUX/LVPD L3 71 F2
Haig Rd WDN WA8 14 C2
Haileybury Av AIN/FAZ L10 32 A2
Haileybury Rd WLTN L25 120 D3
Hailsham Rd ALL/GAR L19 118 C3
Halby Rd WLT/FAZ L9 40 D1
Halcombe Rd WD/CROXPK L12 56 D2
Halcyon Rd BIRK CH41 92 A4
Haldane Av BIRK CH41 91 F1
Haldane Rd ANF/KKDL L4 40 C5
Hale Bank Rd WDN WA8 144 A1
Hale Dr SPK/HALE L24 142 D4
Halefield St ECCL WA10 10 E3
Hale Gate Rd WDN WA8 144 B3
Hale Gv WARRW/BUR WA5 105 E2
Hale Rd ANF/KKDL L4 54 A1
SPK/HALE L24 142 A3
SPK/HALE L24 142 C4
WAL/NB CH45 52 A4
WDN WA8 123 H5
Hale St CLVP L2 6 D3
WARRN/WOL WA2 12 D1
Hale Vw RUNC WA7 154 C1
Hale View Rd HUY L36 76 A3
Halewood Cl WLTN L25 97 H4
Halewood Dr WLTN L25 120 D1
Halewood Pl WLTN L25 98 A5
Halewood Rd WLTN L25 97 H5
Halewood Wy WLTN L25 121 E1
Halfacre La WARRS WA4 109 E5
Half Crown St EV L5 53 G4
Halfpenny Cl ALL/GAR L19 119 F4
Halidon Ct BTL L20 4 B2
Halifax Cl WARRN/WOL WA2 84 B3
Halifax Crs CSBY/BLUN L23 22 A3
Halkirk Rd CALD/MH L18 119 G3
Halkyn Av AIG/SPK L17 95 F2
Halkyn Dr EV L5 54 C5
Hallam Wk EHL/KEN L7 72 A4
Hall Av WDN WA8 123 G2
Halla-way WARRS WA4 107 G5
Hallcroft Pl WARRS WA4 131 E1
Hall Dr GR/UP/WCH CH49 89 E5
KKBY L32 33 H2
WARRS WA4 130 B5
Hallfields Rd WARRN/WOL WA2 84 B5
Hall La EHL/KEN L7 71 G3
HUY L36 76 A3
KKBY L32 33 H2
MGHL L31 24 A1
NWD/KWIPK L33 26 A2
PR/KW L34 59 H5
RAIN/WH L35 78 A4
STHEL WA9 80 B2
WARRS WA4 131 F3
WDN WA8 101 E1
WLT/FAZ L9 31 G5
Hall Nook WARRW/BUR WA5 104 D4
Hallows Av WARRN/WOL WA2 84 B5
Hall Rd WARR WA1 108 C1
Hall Rd East CSBY/BLUN L23 20 C3
Hall Rd West CSBY/BLUN L23 20 B3
Hallsands Rd KKBY L32 33 H4
Hallside Cl ALL/GAR L19 119 E3
Hall St ECCL WA10 11 H5
STHEL WA9 80 A2
WARR WA1 12 E5
Hall Ter WARRW/BUR WA5 104 C1
Halltine Cl CSBY/BLUN L23 20 B4
Hallville Rd CALD/MH L18 96 A3
Hallwood Cl RUNC WA7 155 F3
Hallwood Link Rd RUNC WA7 156 A3
Hallwood Park Av RUNC WA7 156 A3
Halsall Av WARRN/WOL WA2 84 B5
Halsall Cl CSBY/BLUN L23 21 F4
RUNC WA7 157 E4
Halsall Gn BEB CH63 138 B5
Halsall La FMBY L37 17 E2
Halsall Rd BTL L20 39 G2
Halsalls Cottages WDN WA8 * 144 A1
Halsall St PR/KW L34 59 H3
Halsbury Rd NPK/KEN L6 72 A2
WAL/NB CH45 51 H4
Halsey Av WD/CROXPK L12 55 H3
Halsey Crs WD/CROXPK L12 55 H3
Halsnead Av RAIN/WH L35 76 C4
Halstead Rd WAL/EG CH44 69 E2
WLT/FAZ L9 40 B1
Halton Brook Av RUNC WA7 9 K6
Halton Brow RUNC WA7 147 E5
Halton Ct RUNC WA7 9 K5
Halton Crs GR/UP/WCH CH49 88 D5
Halton Hey RAIN/WH L35 76 D4
Halton Link Rd RUNC WA7 156 A1
Halton Lodge Av RUNC WA7 155 H1
Halton Rd MGHL L31 18 D3
RUNC WA7 9 G4
WAL/NB CH45 51 G4
WARRW/BUR WA5 104 D2
Halton View Rd WDN WA8 15 H1
Halton Wd KKBY L32 33 E1
Halville Rd WAL/EG CH44 69 E2
Hambledon Dr
GR/UP/WCH CH49 89 E4
Hamble Dr WARRW/BUR WA5 104 D5
Hambleton Cl NG/CROX L11 42 B3
WDN WA8 101 E5
Hamblett Crs RNFD/HAY WA11 48 B1
Hamer St ECCL WA10 11 F4
Hamil Cl HOY CH47 65 E4
Hamilton La BIRK CH41 3 G3
Hamilton Rd ECCL WA10 46 D1
EV L5 54 B5
WAL/NB CH45 51 G2
Hamilton Sq BIRK CH41 3 G3
Hamilton St BIRK CH41 3 G5
BIRK CH41 3 H3
Hamlet Rd WAL/NB CH45 51 F4
Hamlin Cl RUNC WA7 155 E3
Hammersley Av STHEL WA9 79 G2
Hammersley St STHEL WA9 * 79 G2
Hammill Av ECCL WA10 47 G1
Hammill St ECCL WA10 10 B1
Hammond Rd NWD/KWIPK L33 34 D1
Hammond St STHEL WA9 48 D5
Hamnett Rd PR/KW L34 60 A3
Hampden Gv RF/TRAN CH42 92 C4
Hampden Rd RF/TRAN CH42 92 B4
Hampden St ANF/KKDL L4 40 B5
Hampshire Av NTHTN L30 30 B1
Hampshire Gdns ECCL WA10 47 H5
Hampson St NPK/KEN L6 55 E5
Hampstead Rd NPK/KEN L6 72 B1
WAL/EG CH44 69 E2
Hampton Cha CL/PREN CH43 90 D5
Hampton Cl NSTN CH64 158 D4
WDN WA8 103 E5
Hampton Court Rd
WD/CROXPK L12 56 C5
Hampton Court Wy WDN WA8 102 D4
Hampton Crs NSTN CH64 158 D5
Hampton Dr
WARRW/BUR WA5 105 G4
WDN WA8 101 E3
Hampton Pl RNFD/HAY WA11 48 B1
Hampton Rd FMBY L37 16 D5
Hampton St TOX L8 94 B1
Hanbury Rd ANF/KKDL L4 55 F2
Handel Ct TOX L8 * 94 D2
Handel Rd NTHLY L27 98 A2
Handfield Pl EV L5 54 C5
Handfield Rd CSBY/WL L22 29 E3
Handfield St EV L5 54 C5
Handford Av PS/BROM CH62 153 F4
Handforth Cl WARRS WA4 108 C4
Handforth La RUNC WA7 155 H3
Handley Ct ALL/GAR L19 118 D3
Handley Dr WARRN/WOL WA2 84 C3
Hands St LITH L21 39 F1
Hanford Av WLT/FAZ L9 40 B1
Hankey Dr BTL L20 40 A2
Hankey St RUNC WA7 8 C4
Hankin St EV L5 53 H5
Hanley Cl WDN WA8 124 A2
Hanley Rd WDN WA8 124 A2
Hanlon Av BTL L20 39 H1
Hanmer Rd KKBY L32 33 E2
Hannah Cl PEN/TH CH61 134 C3
Hannan Rd NPK/KEN L6 72 A2
Hanns Hall Rd NSTN CH64 159 H2
Hanover Cl CL/PREN CH43 91 F2
Hanover St CLVPS L1 6 E5
WARR WA1 12 B6
Hansard Ct STHEL WA9 61 F3
Hansby Dr SPK/HALE L24 142 A1
Hanson Pk CL/PREN CH43 91 E3
Hanson Rd WLT/FAZ L9 41 E2
Hans Rd ANF/KKDL L4 54 C1
Hanwell St NPK/KEN L6 54 D4
Hanworth Cl WD/CROXPK L12 42 D4
Hapsford Cl GOL/RIS/CUL WA3 85 G1
Hapsford Rd LITH L21 39 F1
Hapton St EV L5 54 A4
Harbern Cl WD/CROXPK L12 56 D4
Harbord Rd CSBY/WL L22 28 D3
Harbord St EHL/KEN L7 71 H4
WARR WA1 13 G6
Harborne Dr BEB CH63 137 H4
Harcourt Av WAL/EG CH44 69 G2
Harcourt St ANF/KKDL L4 53 H3
BIRK CH41 2 B2
Hardie Av MOR/LEA CH46 66 A4
Hardie Cl STHEL WA9 79 E2
Hardie Rd HUY L36 76 A2
Harding Av BEB CH63 137 H2
WARRN/WOL WA2 84 B4
Harding Cl EV L5 54 C5
Hardinge Rd ALL/GAR L19 119 G3
Harding St TOX L8 71 H5
Hardknott Rd PS/BROM CH62 139 E5
Hard La ECCL WA10 47 F1
Hardman St CLVPS L1 7 H6
Hardshaw St ECCL WA10 11 G5
Hardwick Gra WARR WA1 85 H4
Hardwick Rd RUNC WA7 9 K3
Hardy St ALL/GAR L19 140 D2
CLVPS L1 93 H1
WARRN/WOL WA2 12 E2
Harebell Cl FMBY L37 17 E5
WDN WA8 101 G4
Harebell St EV L5 53 H3
Hare Cft STBRV L28 57 F2
Harefield Gn SPK/HALE L24 142 B3
Harefield Rd SPK/HALE L24 142 B3
Haresfinch Cl HLWD L26 122 A2
Haresfinch Rd RNFD/HAY WA11 11 J1
Haresfinch Vw
RNFD/HAY WA11 48 B1
Harewell Rd NG/CROX L11 56 A1
Harewood Cl HUY L36 75 G2
Harewood Rd WAL/NB CH45 51 G3
Harewood St NPK/KEN L6 * 71 G1
Harford Cl WARRW/BUR WA5 104 D4
Hargate Rd NWD/KWIPK L33 34 A2
Hargrave Av CL/PREN CH43 91 E5
Hargrave Cl CL/PREN CH43 91 E5
Hargrave La BEB CH63 151 H4
Hargreaves Ct WDN WA8 15 J1
Hargreaves Rd AIG/SPK L17 95 E5
Hargreaves St STHEL WA9 49 E3
Harington Cl FMBY L37 16 C3
Harington Gn FMBY L37 16 C3
Harington Rd FMBY L37 16 B2
Harker St VAUX/LVPD L3 7 G1
Harke St EHL/KEN L7 71 H5
Harland Gn SPK/HALE L24 142 D3
Harland Rd RF/TRAN CH42 92 B4
Harlech Cl RUNC WA7 147 F4
WARRW/BUR WA5 83 E3
Harlech Rd CSBY/BLUN L23 28 D1
Harlech St ANF/KKDL L4 54 A1
WAL/EG CH44 69 G4
Harleston Rd NWD/KWIPK L33 34 B1
Harley Av BEB CH63 115 E3
Harley St WLT/FAZ L9 40 C1
Harlian Av MOR/LEA CH46 89 F1
Harlow Cl STHEL WA9 61 H3
WARRS WA4 108 C5
Harlow St TOX L8 94 A4
Harlyn Cl HLWD L26 121 G5
Harlyn Gdns
WARRW/BUR WA5 104 B5
Harmony Wy CLB/OSW/ST L13 73 E4
Haroldene Gv PR/KW L34 58 D5
Harper Rd WLT/FAZ L9 40 C3
Harpers Pond La WAV L15 73 E5
Harpers Rd WARRN/WOL WA2 85 E4
Harp's Cft NTHTN L30 30 B1
Harptree Cl RAIN/WH L35 77 E2
Harradon Rd WLT/FAZ L9 31 G5
Harrier Dr HLWD L26 121 G2
Harrier Rd WARRN/WOL WA2 84 D3
Harringay Av CALD/MH L18 95 H3
Harrington Av HOY CH47 87 G1
Harrington Rd CSBY/BLUN L23 21 E5
LITH L21 30 C3
VAUX/LVPD L3 94 A4
Harrington St CLVP L2 6 D4
Harris Cl BEB CH63 137 H4
Harris Dr BTL L20 30 C5
Harris Gdns STHEL WA9 62 B1
Harrismith Rd AIN/FAZ L10 32 C5
Harrison Cl WARR WA1 13 G2
Harrison Dr BTL L20 5 J4
RNFD/HAY WA11 49 G1
WAL/NB CH45 50 D2
Harrison Hey HUY L36 75 F4
Harrison St WDN WA8 123 H5
Harrisons Yd
PS/BROM CH62 * 153 F3
Harrison Wy VAUX/LVPD L3 94 A4
Harris St ECCL WA10 10 C3
WDN WA8 15 H1
Harrocks Cl NTHTN L30 22 C4
Harrock Wood Cl
PEN/TH CH61 112 C5
Harrogate Cl PS/BROM CH62 152 D5
WARRW/BUR WA5 82 A4
Harrogate Dr EV L5 54 B5
Harrogate Rd PS/BROM CH62 152 D5
RF/TRAN CH42 116 A3
Harron Cl KKBY L32 33 F2
Harrop Rd RUNC WA7 9 F7
Harrops Cft NTHTN L30 22 D4
Harrowby Cl TOX L8 94 C1
Harrowby Rd LITH L21 29 G5
RF/TRAN CH42 92 A4
WAL/EG CH44 69 G1
Harrowby Rd South
RF/TRAN CH42 92 A4
Harrowby St TOX L8 * 94 C1
Harrow Cl NTHTN L30 31 E1
WAL/EG CH44 51 F5
WARRS WA4 130 C5
Harrow Dr AIN/FAZ L10 32 A2
RUNC WA7 147 E4
Harrow Gv PS/BROM CH62 153 E1
Harrow Rd ANF/KKDL L4 54 D4
WAL/EG CH44 51 F5
Hartdale Rd CALD/MH L18 96 A4
CSBY/BLUN L23 21 H3
Hartford Cl CL/PREN CH43 91 F5
Harthill Av CALD/MH L18 96 B4
Harthill Rd CALD/MH L18 96 C5
Hartington Av BIRK CH41 2 A2
Hartington Rd ALL/GAR L19 119 G5
ECCL WA10 47 E2
TOX L8 95 E2
WAL/EG CH44 68 D1
WD/CROXPK L12 56 C4
Hartismere Rd WAL/EG CH44 69 F2
Hartland Cl WDN WA8 102 A3
Hartland Gdns STHEL WA9 61 F4
Hartland Rd NG/CROX L11 41 G5
Hartley Av WLT/FAZ L9 40 D2
Hartley Cl ANF/KKDL L4 54 B3
Hartley Gv ECCL WA10 61 E2
Hartley Quay VAUX/LVPD L3 6 B6
Hartleys Village WLT/FAZ L9 40 D2
Hartnup St EV L5 54 C4
Harton Cl WDN WA8 101 G5
Hartopp Rd WLTN L25 97 G2
Hartsbourne Av WLTN L25 97 F1
Hartsbourne Cl WLTN L25 97 F1
Hartsbourne Wk WLTN L25 97 G1
Hart St VAUX/LVPD L3 7 H3
Hartwell St LITH L21 39 F1
Hartwood Cl KKBY L32 34 A5
Hartwood Rd KKBY L32 34 A5
Hartwood Sq KKBY L32 * 34 A5
Harty Rd RNFD/HAY WA11 49 G2
Harvard Ct WARRN/WOL WA2 83 G2
Harvard Gv PR/KW L34 59 H3
Harvester Wy
GR/UP/WCH CH49 * 89 E4
NTHTN L30 23 F5
Harvest La MOR/LEA CH46 66 B4
Harvest Wy STHEL WA9 79 G1
Harvey Av GR/UP/WCH CH49 89 F5
Harvey Ct WARRN/WOL WA2 83 H2
Harvey Rd WAL/NB CH45 51 G4
Harwich Gv CHLDW L16 74 B5
Harwood Gdns WARRS WA4 131 E1
Harwood Rd ALL/GAR L19 119 H5
Haryngton Av
WARRW/BUR WA5 106 B1
Haselbeech Cl NG/CROX L11 41 H4
Haselbeech Crs NG/CROX L11 41 H4
Hasfield Rd NG/CROX L11 42 B5
Haslemere RAIN/WH L35 77 F2
Haslemere Dr
WARRW/BUR WA5 104 B4
Haslemere Rd WLTN L25 97 G2
Haslemere Wy WLTN L25 97 H2
Haslingden Cl CLB/OSW/ST L13 73 F3
Haslington Gv HLWD L26 122 A5
Hassal Rd RF/TRAN CH42 116 A3
Hastie Cl NTHLY L27 98 C2
Hastings Av WARRN/WOL WA2 83 H1
Hastings Dr HUY L36 76 A5
Hastings Rd CSBY/WL L22 28 C2
Haswell Dr STBRV L28 57 H2
Hatchmere Cl CL/PREN CH43 91 F5
WARRW/BUR WA5 106 A3
Hatfield Cl STHEL WA9 61 H3
WD/CROXPK L12 43 F4
Hatfield Gdns HUY L36 75 H4
Hatfield Rd BTL L20 5 J5
Hathaway MGHL L31 23 G2
Hathaway Cl WLTN L25 97 G2
Hathaway Rd WLTN L25 97 G2
Hatherley Av CSBY/BLUN L23 29 F2
Hatherley Cl TOX L8 94 C1
Hatherley St TOX L8 94 C2
WAL/EG CH44 69 G3
Hathersage Rd HUY L36 58 C5
Hatters Rw WARR WA1 * 12 D4
Hatton Cl HES CH60 134 B5
Hatton Gdn VAUX/LVPD L3 6 D2
Hatton Hill Rd LITH L21 29 H4
Hattons La CHLDW L16 96 C2
Hatton Station Rd RUNC WA7 156 B5
Hauxwell Gv RNFD/HAY WA11 48 C1
Havannah La STHEL WA9 49 H4
Havelock Cl ECCL WA10 10 D5
Haven Rd AIN/FAZ L10 32 C4
Havergal St RUNC WA7 8 C6
Haverstock Rd NPK/KEN L6 72 B2
Haverton Wk WD/CROXPK L12 43 E4
Hawarden Av AIG/SPK L17 95 F2
CL/PREN CH43 2 B5
WAL/EG CH44 69 E1
Hawarden Gv LITH L21 39 E1
Hawdon Ct EHL/KEN L7 72 A5
Hawes Av RNFD/HAY WA11 37 G4
Haweswater Av
RNFD/HAY WA11 49 G1
Haweswater Cl
NWD/KWIPK L33 25 G4
RUNC WA7 156 C4
Haweswater Gv MGHL L31 19 F4
Hawgreen Rd KKBY L32 33 E3
Hawick Cl NWD/KWIPK L33 25 G3
Hawke Gn RAIN/WH L35 99 E1
Hawke St VAUX/LVPD L3 7 G4
Hawkesworth St ANF/KKDL L4 54 C4
Hawkhurst Cl TOX L8 94 B4
Hawkins Rd NSTN CH64 159 E1
Hawkins St NPK/KEN L6 71 H2
Hawks Ct RUNC WA7 156 A3
Hawkshaw Cl
GOL/RIS/CUL WA3 85 G1
Hawkshead Av
WD/CROXPK L12 56 C1
Hawkshead Cl MGHL L31 19 E4
RUNC WA7 * 156 C4
Hawkshead Dr LITH L21 30 C4
Hawkshead Rd
PS/BROM CH62 139 E5
Hawksmoor Cl AIN/FAZ L10 32 D5
Hawksmoor Rd AIN/FAZ L10 42 A1
Hawksmore Cl
GR/UP/WCH CH49 89 F2
Hawkstone St TOX L8 94 C3
Hawkstone Wk TOX L8 * 94 C4
Hawks Wy HES CH60 148 C1
Hawley's La
WARRN/WOL WA2 83 G4
Haworth Dr BTL L20 30 C5
Hawthorn Av RUNC WA7 8 E6
WDN WA8 * 125 F1

Hawthorn Dr ECCL WA10 46 D3
PEN/TH CH61 134 D4
WKBY CH48 111 E1
Hawthorne Av HLWD L26 121 G5
WARR WA1 108 B1
WARRW/BUR WA5 104 D2
Hawthorne Cl RNFD/HAY WA11 49 G2
Hawthorne Crs FMBY L37 17 F4
Hawthorne Gv EHL/KEN L7 71 H4
WAL/EG CH44 69 G3
WARR WA1 107 H1
Hawthorne Rd BTL L20 5 H2
RF/TRAN CH42 92 B5
STHEL WA9 62 D4
WARRS WA4 130 A3
The Hawthornes NTHLY L27 * 98 A2
Hawthorne St
WARRW/BUR WA5 83 G5
Hawthorn Gv EHL/KEN L7 71 H4
WARRS WA4 107 F5
Hawthorn La PS/BROM CH62 152 D1
Hawthorn Rd HUY L36 75 E3
PR/KW L34 60 A4
Hawthorns Gv WD/CROXPK L12 56 B4
Haxted Gdns ALL/GAR L19 119 H5
Haydn Rd DV/KA/FCH L14 57 F5
Haydock Park Rd AIN/FAZ L10 32 B1
Haydock Rd WAL/NB CH45 52 A3
Haydock St ECCL WA10 11 H5
WARRN/WOL WA2 12 D3
Hayes Av RAIN/WH L35 60 A5
Hayes Dr MGHL L31 33 E1
Hayes St ECCL WA10 61 E2
Hayfield Rd WARR WA1 85 G5
Hayfield St ANF/KKDL L4 * 54 B3
Hayfield Cl HLWD L26 122 A2
Hayles Cl WLTN L25 97 G2
Hayles Gn WLTN L25 97 G2
Hayles Gv WLTN L25 97 G2
Haylock Cl TOX L8 94 B4
Hayman's Cl WD/CROXPK L12 * 56 A3
Haymans Gn MGHL L31 19 E5
WD/CROXPK L12 56 A3
Hayman's Gv WD/CROXPK L12 56 A3
Hayscastle Cl
WARRW/BUR WA5 83 E4
Haywood Gdns ECCL WA10 10 A7
Hazel Av KKBY L32 33 F1
RAIN/WH L35 77 E1
RUNC WA7 154 C1
Hazelbank Gdns FMBY L37 * 16 D1
Hazeldale Rd WLT/FAZ L9 40 C3
Hazeldene Av PEN/TH CH61 113 E5
WAL/NB CH45 51 G5
Hazeldene Wy PEN/TH CH61 113 F5
Hazelfield Ct STHEL WA9 * 79 G1
Hazel Gv BEB CH63 137 G2
CSBY/BLUN L23 29 G1
ECCL WA10 47 E4
PEN/TH CH61 112 B4
WARR WA1 85 E5
WLT/FAZ L9 40 D1
Hazelhurst Rd ANF/KKDL L4 54 D3
Hazel Ms MGHL L31 * 33 E1
Hazel Rd BIRK CH41 2 D6
HOY CH47 87 F1
HUY L36 58 D5
Hazelslack Rd NG/CROX L11 42 A5
Hazel St WARR WA1 13 J1
Hazelwood GR/UP/WCH CH49 89 F4
Hazelwood Cl STHEL WA9 79 F2
WDN WA8 123 G3
Hazelwood Gv HLWD L26 121 F1
Hazelwood Ms WARRS WA4 131 G2
Hazlehurst Cl FMBY L37 16 B4
Hazleton Rd DV/KA/FCH L14 73 G2
Headbolt La NWD/KWIPK L33 25 H5
Headbourne Cl WLTN L25 97 F1
Headingley Cl HUY L36 75 E5
STHEL WA9 62 C4
Headington Rd
GR/UP/WCH CH49 89 F3
Headland Cl WKBY CH48 110 B3
Headley Cl ECCL WA10 10 D4
Head St TOX L8 94 A2
Heald St ALL/GAR L19 119 G5
Hearne Rd ECCL WA10 47 E3
Heartwood Cl WLT/FAZ L9 31 F5
Heathbank Av PEN/TH CH61 112 A4
WAL/EG CH44 68 C2
Heathbank Rd RF/TRAN CH42 92 B5
Heath Cl PR/KW L34 60 B3
WKBY CH48 110 B3
WLTN L25 97 F3
Heathcote Cl EHL/KEN L7 * 72 A5
Heathcote Gdns BEB CH63 137 H1
Heathcote Rd ANF/KKDL L4 40 B5
Heath Dl BEB CH63 137 H3
Heath Dr GR/UP/WCH CH49 90 A3
HES CH60 134 D5
RUNC WA7 155 E2
Heather Bank BEB CH63 115 F5
Heather Brow CL/PREN CH43 91 F2
Heather Cl ANF/KKDL L4 * 54 B2
FMBY L37 17 G1
RUNC WA7 156 A5
Heatherdale Cl CL/PREN CH43 91 H5
Heatherdale Rd CALD/MH L18 96 A4
Heather Dene PS/BROM CH62 138 D3
Heatherdene Rd WKBY CH48 87 F5
Heathergreen Ct ANF/KKDL L4 54 D1
Heatherleigh STHEL WA9 61 E4
WKBY CH48 110 D5
Heatherleigh Cl WLT/FAZ L9 31 F5
Heather Rd BEB CH63 137 F2
HES CH60 135 E5
Heathers Cft NTHTN L30 30 D1
Heather Wy CSBY/BLUN L23 22 A3
Heathfield Av STHEL WA9 61 G2
Heathfield Cl LITH L21 39 G1
Heathfield Dr NWD/KWIPK L33 25 H4
Heathfield Pk WARRS WA4 131 E1
WDN WA8 101 F5
Heathfield Rd BEB CH63 137 H2
CL/PREN CH43 92 A4
CSBY/WL L22 28 D2
MGHL L31 24 C2
WAV L15 96 A2
Heathfield St CLVPS L1 7 G5
Heathgate Av SPK/HALE L24 143 E4
Heath Hey WLTN L25 97 F3
Heathland Rd STHEL WA9 79 G1
The Heathlands MOR/LEA CH46 66 C1
Heathmoor Rd MOR/LEA CH46 66 B4
Heath Park Gv RUNC WA7 154 D1
Heath Rd ALL/GAR L19 119 G3
BEB CH63 137 G1
HUY L36 57 H5
RUNC WA7 9 G5
WARRW/BUR WA5 104 D3
WDN WA8 124 C2
Heath Road Crs RUNC WA7 9 F7
Heathside HES CH60 134 A5
Heath St STHEL WA9 61 F3
WARRS WA4 130 A3
The Heath RUNC WA7 * 155 E2
Heath Vw LITH L21 30 A1
Heathview Rd WDN WA8 144 C2
Heathwaite Crs NG/CROX L11 56 A1
Heathway HES CH60 149 F2
Heathwood WD/CROXPK L12 56 B5
Heathwood Gv WARR WA1 108 B1
Heatley Cl CL/PREN CH43 90 C1
Heaton Cl SPK/HALE L24 142 D3
Hebburn Wy WD/CROXPK L12 43 G4
Hebden Pde NG/CROX L11 42 C4
Hebden Rd NG/CROX L11 42 B4
Hector Pl BTL L20 53 H1
Hedgebank Cl WLT/FAZ L9 32 A4
Hedgecroft CSBY/BLUN L23 22 B3
Hedgefield Rd WLTN L25 97 H3
Hedge Hey RUNC WA7 147 G5
Hedges Crs CLB/OSW/ST L13 55 G3
Hedingham Cl HLWD L26 122 A2
Hedworth Gdns STHEL WA9 61 F4
Heigham Gdns STHEL WA9 61 G4
Helena Rd STHEL WA9 63 F3
Helena St BIRK CH41 3 F6
EHL/KEN L7 71 H4
WLT/FAZ L9 40 B4
Helford Cl RAIN/WH L35 60 C4
Helford Rd NG/CROX L11 42 D2
Heliers Rd CLB/OSW/ST L13 73 F3
Helmdon Cl NG/CROX L11 56 A1
Helmingham Gv BIRK CH41 92 C4
Helmsdale La
WARRW/BUR WA5 105 G2
Helmsley Cl WARRW/BUR WA5 106 A1
Helmsley Rd HLWD L26 121 H4
Helsby Rd WLT/FAZ L9 31 G5
Helsby St EHL/KEN L7 71 G4
STHEL WA9 62 D1
WARR WA1 13 J3
Helston Av HLWD L26 121 H2
RNFD/HAY WA11 37 H5
Helston Cl RUNC WA7 156 D4
WARRW/BUR WA5 104 C3
Helston Rd NG/CROX L11 42 D2
Helton Cl CL/PREN CH43 91 E5
Hemans St BTL L20 4 B2
Hemer Ter BTL L20 4 A1
Hemingford St BIRK CH41 2 E4
Hemlock Cl WD/CROXPK L12 42 D4
Hemmingsway RAIN/WH L35 77 G2
Hempstead Cl STHEL WA9 61 H3
Henbury Pl RUNC WA7 155 F3
Henderson Cl
GR/UP/WCH CH49 89 F2
WARRW/BUR WA5 104 B2
Henderson Rd HUY L36 76 A2
WDN WA8 14 B3
Hendon Rd NPK/KEN L6 72 B1
Hendon Wk GR/UP/WCH CH49 89 E5
Henglers Cl NPK/KEN L6 * 71 G2
Henley Av LITH L21 29 H4
Henley Cl BEB CH63 138 A4
NSTN CH64 158 D4
WARRS WA4 130 C5
Henley Ct ECCL WA10 61 F1
RUNC WA7 146 D4
Henley Rd CALD/MH L18 96 B3
NSTN CH64 158 D4
Henllan Gdns STHEL WA9 63 F3
Henlow Av KKBY L32 34 A4
Hennawood Cl NPK/KEN L6 54 D5
Henry Edward St
VAUX/LVPD L3 * 6 E1
Henry Hickman Cl NTHTN L30 23 E5
Henry St BIRK CH41 3 G4
CLB/OSW/ST L13 72 D3
CLVPS L1 6 E6
ECCL WA10 11 F4
WARR WA1 12 B5
WDN WA8 * 15 H1
Henshall Av WARRS WA4 107 H4
Henthorne Rd
PS/BROM CH62 116 B3
Henthorne St CL/PREN CH43 2 B5
Hepherd St WARRW/BUR WA5 105 H4
Herald Av SPK/HALE L24 120 B5
Herald Cl NG/CROX L11 42 C4
Heralds Cl WDN WA8 123 H3
Heralds Gn WARRW/BUR WA5 82 A3
Herbarth Cl WLT/FAZ L9 40 B4
Herbert St STHEL WA9 63 F3
Herbert Taylor Cl NPK/KEN L6 55 E4
Herculaneum Ct TOX L8 94 B5
Herculaneum Rd TOX L8 94 A4
Herdman Cl WLTN L25 97 H3
Hereford Av GR/UP/WCH CH49 89 G2
Hereford Cl WARR WA1 108 D1
Hereford Dr NTHTN L30 31 E3
Hereford Rd LITH L21 29 F5
WAV L15 96 A2
Heriot St EV L5 53 H4
Heriot Wk EV L5 53 H4
Hermes Cl NTHTN L30 30 D4
Hermes Rd NG/CROX L11 42 C1
Hermitage Gv BTL L20 30 C5
Herm Rd EV L5 53 G5
Heron Cl RUNC WA7 * 157 F1
Heron Ct HLWD L26 121 G2
NSTN CH64 158 B3
Herondale Rd CALD/MH L18 95 H4
Heronhall Rd WLT/FAZ L9 41 H3
Heronpark Wy BEB CH63 138 B3
Hero Rd HOY CH47 88 C2
Hero St BTL L20 5 H7
Herrick St CLB/OSW/ST L13 72 D2
Herschell St EV L5 54 B4
Hertford Cl HLWD L26 121 H4
WARR WA1 109 E1
Hertford Dr WAL/NB CH45 52 A4
Hertford Rd BTL L20 4 E7
Hertford St STHEL WA9 48 D5
Hesketh Av RF/TRAN CH42 115 F2
Hesketh Cl WARRW/BUR WA5 104 D4
Hesketh Dr HES CH60 135 E5
MGHL L31 19 F4
Hesketh Rd SPK/HALE L24 144 A4
Hesketh St North
WARRW/BUR WA5 105 H4
Hesketh St AIG/SPK L17 * 95 E4
WARRW/BUR WA5 105 H4
Heskin Cl KKBY L32 33 H5
MGHL L31 18 D2
RAIN/WH L35 77 H2
Heskin Rd KKBY L32 33 H5
Heskin Wk KKBY L32 33 H5
Hessle Dr HES CH60 148 D2
Heswall Av BEB CH63 115 E3
STHEL WA9 79 F1
Heswall Mt PEN/TH CH61 135 E1
Heswall Rd WLT/FAZ L9 31 G5
Hever Dr HLWD L26 122 A2
Heward Av STHEL WA9 * 62 C4
Hewitson Av CLB/OSW/ST L13 55 H4
Hewitson Rd CLB/OSW/ST L13 55 H4
Hewitt Av ECCL WA10 47 E3
Hewitt's La PR/KW L34 35 F5
Hewitts Pl CLVP L2 * 6 D3
Hewitt St WARRS WA4 107 E5
Hexham Cl NTHTN L30 31 F3
STHEL WA9 61 F3
Heyburn Rd CLB/OSW/ST L13 55 G4
Heydale Rd CALD/MH L18 96 A4
Heydean Rd CALD/MH L18 119 G2
Heydon Av KKBY L32 33 F3
Heydon Cl FMBY L37 16 C5
HLWD L26 122 A4
Heyes Dr WAL/NB CH45 67 G1
Heyes La WARRS WA4 130 C3
Heyesmere Ct AIG/SPK L17 118 D4
Heyes Mt RAIN/WH L35 78 A3
Heyes Rd WDN WA8 124 A3
Heyes St EV L5 54 C5
The Heyes WLTN L25 120 D1
Heygarth Dr GR/UP/WCH CH49 89 F4
Heygarth Rd PS/BROM CH62 153 E4
Hey Green Rd WAV L15 72 C5
Hey Rd HUY L36 75 H3
Heys Av PS/BROM CH62 152 D1
Heyscroft Rd WLTN L25 120 D1
Heysham Cl RUNC WA7 157 E3
Heysham Lawn NTHLY L27 99 E4
Heysham Rd NTHTN L30 31 F2
Heysmoor Hts TOX L8 94 D3
The Heys RUNC WA7 147 E5
Heythrop Dr HES CH60 149 G1
Heyville Rd BEB CH63 115 G5
Heywood Bvd PEN/TH CH61 113 E5
Heywood Cl FMBY L37 16 D3
PEN/TH CH61 113 E5
Heywood Ct WAV L15 73 G4
Heywood Gdns RAIN/WH L35 77 E3
Heywood Rd WAV L15 73 G5
Heyworth St EV L5 54 B5
NPK/KEN L6 71 F1
Hibbert St WDN WA8 14 E3
Hickling Gdns STHEL WA9 61 G4
Hickmans Rd BIRK CH41 68 D4
Hickory Cl WARR WA1 109 E1
Hickory Gv MGHL L31 32 D2
Hickson Av MGHL L31 18 C3
Hicks Rd CSBY/WL L22 29 F3
LITH L21 29 H5
Highacre Rd WAL/NB CH45 * 51 G3
Higham Av ECCL WA10 46 B4
WARRW/BUR WA5 83 F4
Higham Sq EV L5 71 E1
High Bank Cl CL/PREN CH43 * 90 D3
Highbank Dr ALL/GAR L19 119 H5
High Banks MGHL L31 18 C3
High Beeches CHLDW L16 74 B4
High Carrs HUY L36 74 D3
High Clere Crs HUY L36 58 C5
Highcroft Av BEB CH63 138 A1
Highcroft Gn BEB CH63 138 A1
The Highcroft BEB CH63 137 H1
Higher Ashton WDN WA8 101 H5
Higher Bebington Rd
BEB CH63 115 G5
Higher End Pk NTHTN L30 22 C4
Higher Knutsford Rd
WARRS WA4 130 D1
Higher La WLT/FAZ L9 31 H5
WLT/FAZ L9 41 F1
WLT/FAZ L9 41 F2
Higher Parr St STHEL WA9 48 C4
Higher Rd HLWD L26 121 G4
Highfield NWD/KWIPK L33 26 A3
Highfield Av
WARRW/BUR WA5 104 D3
Highfield Cl NSTN CH64 158 D2
WAL/EG CH44 68 C2
Highfield Crs RF/TRAN CH42 115 H2
WDN WA8 125 E1
Highfield Dr GR/UP/WCH CH49 89 F4
Highfield Gv CSBY/BLUN L23 21 G4
RF/TRAN CH42 115 H2
Highfield Pk MGHL L31 19 F5
Highfield Pl PR/KW L34 * 59 H4
Highfield Rd CLB/OSW/ST L13 73 E1
LITH L21 29 H4
NSTN CH64 158 D2
RF/TRAN CH42 115 H2
WDN WA8 14 D1
WLT/FAZ L9 40 B3
Highfields HES CH60 134 D5
PR/KW L34 59 G4
Highfield South
RF/TRAN CH42 115 H2
Highfield St STHEL WA9 62 D2
VAUX/LVPD L3 7 G4
Highfield Vw CLB/OSW/ST L13 72 D1
Highgate Cl HES CH60 134 D5
Highgate Ct EHL/KEN L7 71 G4
Highgate Rd MGHL L31 18 D3
High Gates Cl
WARRW/BUR WA5 106 A1
Highgate St EHL/KEN L7 71 G4
Highgreen Rd RF/TRAN CH42 92 A5
Highgrove Pk ALL/GAR L19 119 E3
Highlands Rd RUNC WA7 154 D1
Highoaks Rd WLTN L25 120 D2
Highpark Rd RF/TRAN CH42 * 92 A5
High Park St TOX L8 94 B3
Highsted Gv
NWD/KWIPK L33 25 H4
High St CLVP L2 6 C3
NSTN CH64 158 D3
PR/KW L34 59 H4
PS/BROM CH62 * 139 E5
RUNC WA7 8 C4
SPK/HALE L24 143 H5
WARR WA1 13 F3
WAV L15 95 H1
WLTN L25 120 C1
Highton Rd WLTN L25 97 F5
Highville Rd CHLDW L16 96 D2
Highwood Ct KKBY L32 25 H5
Highwood Rd WARRS WA4 130 A4
Hignett Av STHEL WA9 49 G5
Hilary Av DV/KA/FCH L14 74 A3
Hilary Cl ANF/KKDL L4 55 E2
PR/KW L34 59 G4
WARRW/BUR WA5 104 B2
WDN WA8 103 E5
Hilary Dr GR/UP/WCH CH49 90 A2
Hilary Rd ANF/KKDL L4 55 E2
Hilberry Av CLB/OSW/ST L13 55 G5
Hilbre Av HES CH60 148 C3
WAL/EG CH44 68 C1
Hilbre Ct WKBY CH48 110 A2
Hilbre Rd WKBY CH48 110 B2
Hilbre St BIRK CH41 2 D1
VAUX/LVPD L3 7 G4
Hilbre Vw WKBY CH48 110 B1
Hilcrest Rd ANF/KKDL L4 55 F1
Hilda Rd WD/CROXPK L12 57 E5
Hildebrand Rd ANF/KKDL L4 55 E2
Hilden Rd WARRN/WOL WA2 84 C4
Hillaby Cl TOX L8 * 94 C2
Hillam Rd WAL/NB CH45 50 D4
Hillary Crs MGHL L31* 18 D5
Hillary Dr CSBY/BLUN L23 21 H5
Hillary Rd PS/BROM CH62 153 E4
Hillary Wk CSBY/BLUN L23 * 21 H5
Hillbark Rd WKBY CH48 111 G1
Hillberry Crs WARRS WA4 106 D5
Hillbrae Av RNFD/HAY WA11 37 E4
Hillburn Dr BIRK CH41 68 A4
Hill Cliffe Rd WARRS WA4 129 G2
Hill Cl NSTN CH64 159 F5
Hill Ct NSTN CH64 159 G5
Hill Crest BTL L20 5 K6
Hillcrest MGHL L31 24 C1
RUNC WA7 146 D5
Hillcrest Av HUY L36 76 A3
Hillcrest Dr GR/UP/WCH CH49 89 E5
Hillcrest Rd CSBY/BLUN L23 21 H5
Hillcroft Rd WAL/EG CH44 69 E3
WLTN L25 97 F4
Hillerton Cl WD/CROXPK L12 * 42 C5
Hillfield RUNC WA7 157 F1
Hillfield Dr PEN/TH CH61 134 D3
Hillfoot Av WLTN L25 120 D5
Hillfoot Cl CL/PREN CH43 67 G5
Hillfoot Crs WARRS WA4 129 H4
Hillfoot Gn WLTN L25 120 C4
Hillfoot Rd WLTN L25 120 C2
Hill Gv MOR/LEA CH46 89 G1
Hillhead Rd BTL L20 5 J6
Hillingden Av HLWD L26 121 H4
Hillingdon Av PEN/TH CH61 134 D4
Hillingdon Rd WAV L15 96 B2
Hillock La WARR WA1 85 G5
Hill Rdg CL/PREN CH43 90 D3
Hill Rd CL/PREN CH43 91 E1
Hill School Rd ECCL WA10 60 C2
Hillside Av ECCL WA10 47 G1
HUY L36 58 A4
RUNC WA7 154 C1
Hillside Cl BIRK CH41 92 C4
BTL L20 5 J6
Hillside Ct BIRK CH41 92 C4
Hillside Crs HUY L36 58 A4
Hillside Dr WLTN L25 97 H5
Hillside Gv WARRW/BUR WA5 104 D3
Hillside Rd CALD/MH L18 96 B3
CL/PREN CH43 67 H5
HES CH60 149 E2
HUY L36 58 C5
RF/TRAN CH42 92 C4
WAL/EG CH44 68 A1
WKBY CH48 110 D1
Hillside St NPK/KEN L6 71 F2
Hillside Vw CL/PREN CH43 91 G5
Hills Moss Rd STHEL WA9 63 F3
Hills Pl WAV L15 * 96 A1
Hill St CSBY/BLUN L23 29 G1
ECCL WA10 11 G2
RUNC WA7 8 E5
TOX L8 94 A2
VAUX/LVPD L3 93 H2
WARR WA1 12 D4
Hill Top La HES CH60 149 F1
NSTN CH64 159 G5
Hilltop Rd CHLDW L16 96 D1
Hill Top Rd WARR WA1 85 G5
WARRS WA4 130 D1
WARRS WA4 157 H3
Hillview AIG/SPK L17 118 C1
Hill Vw WDN WA8 101 H3
Hillview Av WKBY CH48 87 F5
Hill View Dr GR/UP/WCH CH49 90 A2
Hillview Gdns WLTN L25 97 E5
Hillview Rd PEN/TH CH61 112 A5
Hillwood Cl BEB CH63 138 A5
Hilton Av WARRW/BUR WA5 105 F3
Hilton Cl BIRK CH41 2 C4
Hilton Gv WKBY CH48 87 E5
Hinchley Gn MGHL L31 18 B5
Hinckley Rd RNFD/HAY WA11 48 C1
Hindburn Av MGHL L31 19 F4
Hinderton Cl BIRK CH41 92 C4
Hinderton Dr HES CH60 148 D3
WKBY CH48 111 E2
Hinderton Gn NSTN CH64 159 E2
Hinderton La NSTN CH64 159 F1
Hinderton Rd BIRK CH41 3 F7
NSTN CH64 159 E3
Hindle Av WARRW/BUR WA5 83 F4
Hindley Beech MGHL L31 18 C4
Hindlip St TOX L8 94 C5
Hind St BIRK CH41 3 G6
Hinson St BIRK CH41 3 G4
Hinton Crs WARRS WA4 130 C3
Hinton Rd RUNC WA7 8 E7
Hinton St LITH L21 39 F1
NPK/KEN L6 72 A2
Hitchen's Cl RUNC WA7 157 F2
Hobart Dr NWD/KWIPK L33 25 H3
Hobart St EV L5 54 A4
STHEL WA9 61 F2
Hobby Ct RUNC WA7 156 A3
Hobhouse Ct CL/PREN CH43 * 2 A5
Hoblyn Rd CL/PREN CH43 68 A5
Hockenhall Aly CLVP L2 6 D3
Hockenhull Cl BEB CH63 * 138 A4
Hodder Av MGHL L31 19 F4
Hodder Cl RNFD/HAY WA11 37 F5
Hodder Pl EV L5 54 B4
Hodder Rd EV L5 54 B4
Hodder St EV L5 54 B4
Hodgkinson Av
WARRW/BUR WA5 83 F4
Hodson Pl NPK/KEN L6 71 F1
Hogarth Dr CL/PREN CH43 90 D5
Hogarth St LITH L21 39 E1
Hogarth Wk ANF/KKDL L4 53 H2
Hoghton Cl STHEL WA9 63 F2
Hoghton Rd SPK/HALE L24 144 A5
STHEL WA9 63 E2
Holbeck RUNC WA7 157 E2
Holbeck St ANF/KKDL L4 54 D4
Holborn Ct WDN WA8 101 H5
Holborn Hl BIRK CH41 92 C4
Holborn Sq BIRK CH41 92 C4
Holbrook Cl STHEL WA9 62 C4
WARRW/BUR WA5 104 C2
Holcombe Cl
GR/UP/WCH CH49 * 89 F4
Holden Gv CSBY/WL L22 28 D2
Holden Rd CSBY/WL L22 28 C2
RAIN/WH L35 76 C1
Holden Rd East CSBY/WL L22 * 28 D2
Holden Ter CSBY/WL L22 28 D2
Holdsworth St EHL/KEN L7 71 H3
Holes La WARR WA1 85 F5
Holford Av WARRW/BUR WA5 83 F5
Holgate CSBY/BLUN L23 22 A2
Holgate Pk CSBY/BLUN L23 22 A2
Holkham Cl WDN WA8 14 A2
Holland Gv HES CH60 134 D5
Holland Pl EHL/KEN L7 71 H4
Holland Rd HLWD L26 121 G5
SPK/HALE L24 142 C4
WAL/NB CH45 52 A3
Holland St EHL/KEN L7 72 B2
Holland Wy HLWD L26 121 G5
Hollies Rd HLWD L26 121 H4
The Hollies RUNC WA7 * 155 H1
WLTN L25 97 E5
Hollingbourne Pl NG/CROX L11 42 A4
Hollingbourne Rd
NG/CROX L11 42 A4
Hollinghurst Rd
NWD/KWIPK L33 26 A4
Hollingworth Cl WLT/FAZ L9 40 D4
Hollinhey Cl NTHTN L30 23 F4
Hollin Hey Cl
WGNW/BIL/OR WN5 37 H1
Hollins Cl WAV L15 73 E5
Hollocombe Rd
WD/CROXPK L12 42 B5
Holloway RUNC WA7 8 C6
Hollow Cft STBRV L28 57 G1
Hollow Dr WARRS WA4 130 C2
Holly Av BEB CH63 137 H3
Hollybank Ct WDN WA8 * 14 B1
Hollybank Gra HLWD L26 121 H3
Hollybank Rd BIRK CH41 2 D6
CALD/MH L18 95 G3
RUNC WA7 156 B1
Holly Bank St STHEL WA9 48 C3
Holly Cl ECCL WA10 46 D3
SPK/HALE L24 143 H5
Hollydale Rd CALD/MH L18 96 A3
Holly Farm Rd ALL/GAR L19 119 H5
Hollyfield Rd WLT/FAZ L9 40 B2
Holly Gv HUY L36 74 D3
LITH L21 38 D1
RF/TRAN CH42 92 C4
WARR WA1 108 A1
Holly Hedge La WARRS WA4 128 D5
Holly Hey RAIN/WH L35 76 D4
Holly Mt WD/CROXPK L12 56 A4
Holly Pl MOR/LEA CH46 89 H1
Holly Rd EHL/KEN L7 72 B3
RNFD/HAY WA11 49 F2
WARRW/BUR WA5 104 C3
Hollyrood PR/KW L34 58 D5
Holly St BTL L20 5 F3
Holly Ter WARRW/BUR WA5 104 D3
Hollytree Rd WLTN L25 97 H5
Hollywood Rd AIG/SPK L17 95 G5
Holman Rd ALL/GAR L19 119 H5
Holme Cl PR/KW L34 60 C3
Holmefield Av ALL/GAR L19 119 E3
Holmefield Gv MGHL L31 18 C5
Holmefield Rd ALL/GAR L19 118 D2
Holme Rd ECCL WA10 46 D5
Holmes Ct GOL/RIS/CUL WA3 85 G1
Holmes La LITH L21 * 29 H5
Holmes St TOX L8 95 E1
Holme St EV L5 53 G4
Holmesway PEN/TH CH61 134 D2
Holmfield CL/PREN CH43 * 114 C1
Holmfield Av RUNC WA7 9 H5
Holmfield Gv HUY L36 75 H5
Holmfield Pk FMBY L37 16 C2
Holm Hey Rd CL/PREN CH43 114 B1
Holm Hl WKBY CH48 110 C2
Holmlands Crs
CL/PREN CH43 * 114 A1
Holmlands Dr CL/PREN CH43 114 A1
Holmlands Wy CL/PREN CH43 114 A1
Holm La CL/PREN CH43 114 B1
Holmleigh Rd WLTN L25 97 G2

Holmrook Rd NG/CROX L11 42 A5
Holmsfield Rd WARR WA1 13 J5
Holmside Cl MOR/LEA CH46 66 D5
Holmside La CL/PREN CH43 114 B1
Holm View Cl CL/PREN CH43 91 G5
Holmville Rd BEB CH63 137 G1
Holmway BEB CH63 137 H1
Holmwood Av PEN/TH CH61 135 G1
Holmwood Cl FMBY L37 16 C3
Holmwood Dr FMBY L37 16 C2
PEN/TH CH61 135 G1
Holmwood Gdns FMBY L37 16 C2
Holt Av MOR/LEA CH46 66 C5
Holt Hey NSTN CH64 159 F5
Holt Hl BIRK CH41 92 C4
Holt Hill Ter RF/TRAN CH42 3 F7
Holt La HUY L36 98 C1
NTHLY L27 98 B2
RAIN/WH L35 77 G1
RUNC WA7 156 B1
Holt Rd BIRK CH41 92 C4
EHL/KEN L7 72 A3
Holycross Cl VAUX/LVPD L3 6 E1
Holyhead Cl WARRW/BUR WA5 82 D2
Holyrood CSBY/BLUN L23 20 B5
Holyrood Av WDN WA8 102 A4
Holywell Cl NSTN CH64 158 A1
STHEL WA9 62 D4
Holywell Dr WARR WA1 13 F5
Homecrofts NSTN CH64 158 D5
Home Farm Cl
GR/UP/WCH CH49 113 G1
Home Farm Rd
GR/UP/WCH CH49 113 F1
PR/KW L34 44 A5
Homer Rd PR/KW L34 44 A4
Homerton Rd NPK/KEN L6 72 B2
Homestall Rd NG/CROX L11 42 A5
Homestead Av NTHTN L30 31 G1
Homestead Cl HUY L36 76 A2
Homestead Ms WKBY CH48 * 110 B1
Honeybourne Dr RAIN/WH L35 60 C4
Honey Hall Rd HLWD L26 121 G5
Honeys Green Cl
WD/CROXPK L12 56 D5
Honey's Green La
WD/CROXPK L12 56 D5
Honey St STHEL WA9 * 61 E3
Honeysuckle Cl HLWD L26 121 F1
WDN WA8 102 B4
Honeysuckle Dr WLT/FAZ L9 40 D4
Honister Av RNFD/HAY WA11 37 G4
WARRN/WOL WA2 84 A3
Honister Cl NTHLY L27 99 E5
Honister Gv RUNC WA7 156 A4
Honiston Av RAIN/WH L35 77 H1
Honiton Rd AIG/SPK L17 118 C3
Honiton Wy
WARRW/BUR WA5 104 C4
Hood La WARRW/BUR WA5 105 G3
Hood La North
WARRW/BUR WA5 105 G2
Hood Rd WDN WA8 14 B2
Hood St BTL L20 4 B1
CLVPS L1 6 E3
WAL/EG CH44 69 F2
Hoole Rd GR/UP/WCH CH49 90 B5
Hooton Rd WLT/FAZ L9 31 G5
Hope Cl ECCL WA10 10 D4
Hope Pk CHLDW L16 96 D3
Hope Pl CLVPS L1 * 7 H6
Hope St BIRK CH41 2 D3
CLVPS L1 94 B1
PR/KW L34 59 H4
WAL/NB CH45 51 H2
Hope Wy TOX L8 7 J7
Hopfield Rd MOR/LEA CH46 66 D5
Hopkins Cl ECCL WA10 10 A4
Hopwood St EV L5 53 G5
WARR WA1 13 F3
Horace St ECCL WA10 10 B3
Hornbeam Cl MOR/LEA CH46 * 65 H5
RNFD/HAY WA11 49 F2
RUNC WA7 157 E1
Hornbeam Rd HLWD L26 122 A4
WLT/FAZ L9 41 E4
Hornby Av BTL L20 4 D1
PS/BROM CH62 138 D5
Hornby Bvd LITH L21 39 F1
Hornby Cha MGHL L31 24 A2
Hornby Cl WLT/FAZ L9 40 B3
Hornby Crs STHEL WA9 79 H1
Hornby Flats LITH L21 * 39 F1
Hornby La CALD/MH L18 96 D3
Hornby Pk CALD/MH L18 96 D3
Hornby Pl WLT/FAZ L9 40 C2
Hornby Rd BTL L20 4 D1
PS/BROM CH62 138 C5
WLT/FAZ L9 40 B3
Hornby St BIRK CH41 3 H4
CSBY/BLUN L23 * 21 F5
LITH L21 39 E1
Hornby Wk EV L5 70 C1
Horne St NPK/KEN L6 71 H1
Hornet Cl NPK/KEN L6 71 G1
Hornhouse La NWD/KWIPK L33 34 C4
Hornsey Rd ANF/KKDL L4 54 D4
Hornspit La WD/CROXPK L12 56 A2
Horringford Rd ALL/GAR L19 118 D3
Horrocks Av ALL/GAR L19 119 H5
Horrocks Cl HUY L36 75 F1
Horrocks La WARR WA1 12 D5
Horrocks Rd HUY L36 75 F2
Horseman Pl WAL/EG CH44 69 G3
Horseshoe Crs
WARRN/WOL WA2 84 C2
Horseshoe Dr AIN/FAZ L10 33 E5
Horseymere Gdns STHEL WA9 61 G4
Horsfall Gv TOX L8 94 A4
Horsfall St TOX L8 94 A4
Horton Cl NWD/KWIPK L33 25 H3
Horwood Av RAIN/WH L35 77 H3
Horwood Cl WD/CROXPK L12 * 42 C5
Hoscar Ct WDN WA8 124 B4
Hoscote Pk WKBY CH48 110 A1
Hose Side Rd WAL/NB CH45 51 G3
Hospital St ECCL WA10 11 H3
Hospital Wy RUNC WA7 156 B2
Hosta Cl NWD/KWIPK L33 25 G4
Hostock Cl RAIN/WH L35 76 D3
Hotham St VAUX/LVPD L3 7 G3
Hothfield Rd WAL/EG CH44 * 69 F2
Hotspur St BTL L20 53 G2
Hough Green Rd WDN WA8 101 F5
Hough's La WARRS WA4 129 G5
Houghton Cl WDN WA8 125 G1
Houghton Cft WDN WA8 101 E3
Houghton La CLVPS L1 * 7 F4
Houghton Rd
GR/UP/WCH CH49 90 B5
Houghton St CLVPS L1 7 F4
PR/KW L34 59 H4
RAIN/WH L35 * 78 A2
WARRN/WOL WA2 12 D2
WDN WA8 125 H1
Houghton Wy CLVPS L1 * 7 F4
Hougoumont Av CSBY/WL L22 29 F3
Hougoumont Gv CSBY/WL L22 29 F3
Houlding St ANF/KKDL L4 * 54 C4
Houlgrave Rd EV L5 53 G5
Houlston Rd KKBY L32 33 E2
Houlton St EHL/KEN L7 72 A3
Houston Gdns
WARRW/BUR WA5 82 A5
The Hove RUNC WA7 157 F3
Howard Av PS/BROM CH62 152 D1
Howard Cl LITH L21 30 B2
MGHL L31 19 F5
Howard Dr ALL/GAR L19 119 E4
Howard Florey Av NTHTN L30 23 E5
Howard's La ECCL WA10 46 A3
Howards Rd PEN/TH CH61 113 F5
Howard St ECCL WA10 61 E2
Howards Wy NSTN CH64 159 F4
Howarth Ct RUNC WA7 9 F4
Howbeck Cl CL/PREN CH43 91 F2
Howbeck Dr CL/PREN CH43 91 F2
Howbeck Rd CL/PREN CH43 91 F3
Howden Dr HUY L36 74 C3
Howell Dr GR/UP/WCH CH49 112 B1
Howell Rd PS/BROM CH62 116 A4
Howells Cl MGHL L31 18 D4
Howe St BTL L20 53 F1
Howley La WARR WA1 13 H5
Howley Quay WARR WA1 * 13 H5
Howson Rd WARRN/WOL WA2 84 A3
Howson St RF/TRAN CH42 115 H1
Hoylake Cl RUNC WA7 157 E3
Hoylake Gv STHEL WA9 79 G1
Hoylake Rd BIRK CH41 67 H4
MOR/LEA CH46 66 D4
Hoyle Rd HOY CH47 64 B5
Hoyle St WARRW/BUR WA5 12 A1
Huddleston Cl
GR/UP/WCH CH49 90 B5
Huddleston Rd WAV L15 73 F4
Hudson Cl WARRW/BUR WA5 82 D5
Hudson Rd MGHL L31 24 A2
MOR/LEA CH46 67 E1
Hudswell Cl NTHTN L30 31 G3
Hughenden Rd
CLB/OSW/ST L13 55 H5
Hughes Av RAIN/WH L35 76 D1
WARRN/WOL WA2 84 B3
Hughes Cl EHL/KEN L7 72 A4
Hughes Dr BTL L20 40 A1
Hughes La CL/PREN CH43 91 H5
Hughes Pl WARRN/WOL WA2 84 B3
Hughes St ALL/GAR L19 140 C1
NPK/KEN L6 71 G1
STHEL WA9 62 D2
WARRS WA4 107 E5
Hughestead Gv ALL/GAR L19 119 F5
Hughson St TOX L8 94 A3
Hulmewood BEB CH63 116 A4
Hulton Av RAIN/WH L35 77 F1
Humber Cl ANF/KKDL L4 54 A2
WDN WA8 103 F5
Humber Crs STHEL WA9 62 C5
Humber Rd WARRN/WOL WA2 84 C3
Hume Ct HOY CH47 64 C5
Hume St WARR WA1 13 G2
Humphrey's Cl RUNC WA7 157 F2
Humphreys Hey
CSBY/BLUN L23 22 A4
Humphrey St BTL L20 39 G1
Huncote Av RNFD/HAY WA11 48 D1
Hunslett Rd WLT/FAZ L9 40 D1
Hunstanton Cl
GR/UP/WCH CH49 90 A1
Hunt Cl WARRW/BUR WA5 * 82 B5
Hunter Av WARRN/WOL WA2 83 H3
Hunter Ct PR/KW L34 60 A4
Hunters Ct RUNC WA7 156 A3
Hunter's La WAV L15 96 A1
Hunter St STHEL WA9 * 48 C5
VAUX/LVPD L3 7 F2
Hunters Wy NSTN CH64 158 B2
Huntingdon Cl MOR/LEA CH46 65 H5
Huntingdon Gv MGHL L31 18 C2
Huntley Gv STHEL WA9 62 C3
Huntley St WARRW/BUR WA5 105 G4
Huntly Rd NPK/KEN L6 72 A2
Hunt Rd MGHL L31 18 D5
Hunts Cross Av WLTN L25 97 H5
WLTN L25 121 E1
Hunts La WARRS WA4 130 D1
Huntsman Cl WLTN L25 121 F2
Huntsman Wd WD/CROXPK L12 57 E2
Hurley Cl WARRW/BUR WA5 105 G3
Hurlingham Rd ANF/KKDL L4 41 E5
Hurrell Rd BIRK CH41 67 H4
Hursley Rd WLT/FAZ L9 41 G3
Hurst Bank RF/TRAN CH42 115 H3
Hurstlyn Rd CALD/MH L18 119 G2
Hurst Park Cl HUY L36 * 76 A1
Hurst Park Dr HUY L36 76 A2
Hurst Rd MGHL L31 24 B2
Hurst St CLVPS L1 6 D7
WDN WA8 8 D1
Huskisson Docks
VAUX/LVPD L3 * 53 F3
Huskisson St TOX L8 94 B1
Hutchinson St NPK/KEN L6 71 G2
WDN WA8 125 E5
Hutchinson Wk NPK/KEN L6 71 G2
Huttfield Rd SPK/HALE L24 143 E2
Huxley Cl MOR/LEA CH46 65 H5
Huxley St CLB/OSW/ST L13 55 F3
Huyton Av ECCL WA10 47 G1
Huyton Brook HUY L36 75 H5
Huyton Church Rd HUY L36 75 G3
Huyton Hall Crs HUY L36 * 75 G3
Huyton Hey Rd HUY L36 75 H3
Huyton House Cl HUY L36 74 D1
Huyton House Rd HUY L36 74 D1
Huyton La HUY L36 75 H1
Hyacinth Gv MOR/LEA CH46 67 E3
Hyde Cl RUNC WA7 * 155 H3
Hyde Rd CSBY/WL L22 29 E3
Hydro Av WKBY CH48 110 B2
Hygeia St NPK/KEN L6 71 G1
Hylton Av WAL/EG CH44 68 C1
Hylton Rd ALL/GAR L19 119 H3
Hyslop St TOX L8 94 A2
Hythe Av LITH L21 30 B4
Hythedale Cl AIG/SPK L17 118 A1

I

Ibbotson's La AIG/SPK L17 95 G4
Iberis Gdns STHEL WA9 63 G3
Ibis Ct WARR WA1 106 C5
Ibstock Rd BTL L20 53 G1
Iffley Cl GR/UP/WCH CH49 89 F3
Ikin Cl CL/PREN CH43 67 G4
Ilchester Rd BIRK CH41 68 B4
CHLDW L16 74 A4
WAL/EG CH44 69 F2
Ilford Av CSBY/BLUN L23 21 E4
WAL/EG CH44 68 D2
Ilford St VAUX/LVPD L3 7 J2
Ilfracombe Rd STHEL WA9 62 C5
Iliad St EV L5 71 E1
Ilsley Cl GR/UP/WCH CH49 89 H4
Imber Rd KKBY L32 34 A4
Imison St WLT/FAZ L9 40 B4
Imison Wy BTL L20 5 K5
Imperial Av WAL/NB CH45 52 A4
Imrie St ANF/KKDL L4 40 B5
Ince Av ANF/KKDL L4 54 D2
CSBY/BLUN L23 20 D4
LITH L21 30 A5
Ince Cl CL/PREN CH43 * 91 F4
Ince Crs FMBY L37 16 C3
Ince Gv CL/PREN CH43 91 F5
Incemore Rd CALD/MH L18 119 F2
Ince Rd CSBY/BLUN L23 21 H2
Inchcape Rd CHLDW L16 74 A4
WAL/NB CH45 * 50 D5
Index St ANF/KKDL L4 54 B1
Ingestre Rd CL/PREN CH43 91 G5
Ingham Rd WDN WA8 101 H4
Ingleborough Rd
RF/TRAN CH42 115 F1
Ingleby Rd PS/BROM CH62 116 B3
WAL/EG CH44 68 C2
Ingledene Rd CALD/MH L18 96 D3
Ingle Gn CSBY/BLUN L23 20 B4
Inglegreen HES CH60 149 E1
Ingleholme Gdns PR/KW L34 60 C3
Ingleholme Rd ALL/GAR L19 119 E2
Inglemere Rd RF/TRAN CH42 115 G1
Inglenook Rd
WARRW/BUR WA5 104 D4
Ingleton Cl GR/UP/WCH CH49 * 89 F4
Ingleton Dr RNFD/HAY WA11 37 F3
Ingleton Gn KKBY L32 34 A4
Ingleton Gv RUNC WA7 155 H4
Ingleton Rd CALD/MH L18 95 H3
KKBY L32 34 A4
Inglewood WD/CROXPK L12 43 G5
Inglewood Av MOR/LEA CH46 89 F1
Inglewood Rd RNFD/HAY WA11 36 A3
Inglis Rd WLT/FAZ L9 31 G5
Ingoe Cl KKBY L32 33 E3
Ingoe La KKBY L32 33 E4
Ingrave Rd ANF/KKDL L4 41 E5
Ingrow Rd NPK/KEN L6 71 H2
Inigo Rd CLB/OSW/ST L13 73 F1
Inley Cl BEB CH63 138 A4
Inley Rd BEB CH63 137 H4
Inman Av STHEL WA9 49 H5
Inman Rd GR/UP/WCH CH49 89 G2
LITH L21 30 A5
Inner Central Rd
SPK/HALE L24 142 D1
Inner Forum NG/CROX L11 41 G4
Inner South Rd SPK/HALE L24 142 D2
Inner West Rd SPK/HALE L24 142 C2
Insall Rd CLB/OSW/ST L13 73 F4
WARRN/WOL WA2 84 D3
Inveresk Ct CL/PREN CH43 91 E2
Invincible Cl NTHTN L30 30 D4
Invincible Wy NG/CROX L11 42 C1
Inwood Rd ALL/GAR L19 119 G4
Iona Cl WD/CROXPK L12 43 G4
Iona Gdns STHEL WA9 62 D3
Ionic Rd CLB/OSW/ST L13 73 E1
Ionic St LITH L21 * 29 G5
RF/TRAN CH42 115 H1
Irby Av WAL/EG CH44 68 C1
Irby Rd ANF/KKDL L4 54 D2
PEN/TH CH61 134 B1
Irbyside Rd WKBY CH48 111 H2
Ireland Rd SPK/HALE L24 144 A5
Ireland St WARRN/WOL WA2 83 H5
WDN WA8 125 H1
Irene Av RNFD/HAY WA11 37 G5
Irene Rd CHLDW L16 96 C2
Ireton St ANF/KKDL L4 40 B5
Iris Av BIRK CH41 68 B5
Iris Cl WDN WA8 124 A1
Iris Park Wk MGHL L31 32 D1
Irlam Dr KKBY L32 33 H2
Irlam Pl BTL L20 4 C3
Irlam Rd BTL L20 4 C3
Ironbridge Vw TOX L8 94 A4
Ironside Rd HUY L36 75 F1
Irvine Rd RF/TRAN CH42 115 F1
Irvine St EHL/KEN L7 71 G4
Irwell Cl AIG/SPK L17 95 G5
Irwell La AIG/SPK L17 95 G5
RUNC WA7 9 G3
Irwell Rd WARRS WA4 129 H1
Irwell St WDN WA8 146 A2
Irwin Rd STHEL WA9 62 C3
Isaac St TOX L8 94 B4
Isabel Gv CLB/OSW/ST L13 55 G3
Isherwood Cl WARRN/WOL WA2 84 D2
Island Pl ALL/GAR L19 * 119 G5
Island Rd ALL/GAR L19 119 G5
Island Rd South ALL/GAR L19 119 H5
Islands Brow RNFD/HAY WA11 48 B1
Isleham Cl CALD/MH L18 119 G3
Islington CSBY/BLUN L23 21 E5
VAUX/LVPD L3 7 G2
Islington Gn WDN WA8 102 D4
Islip Cl PEN/TH CH61 112 B4
Ismay Dr WAL/EG CH44 52 B5
Ismay Rd LITH L21 30 A5
Ismay St ANF/KKDL L4 54 B1
Ivanhoe Rd AIG/SPK L17 95 E4
CSBY/BLUN L23 28 D1
Ivatt Wy EHL/KEN L7 72 A4
Iveagh Cl RUNC WA7 156 C2
Iver Cl WDN WA8 101 E2
Ivernia Rd ANF/KKDL L4 40 D5
Ivor Rd WAL/EG CH44 52 A5
Ivory Dr NWD/KWIPK L33 25 H4
Ivy Av ALL/GAR L19 119 E4
BEB CH63 137 G1
RAIN/WH L35 77 G1
Ivychurch Ms RUNC WA7 9 K5
Ivy Ct STHEL WA9 * 48 C4
Ivydale Rd CALD/MH L18 95 H4
RF/TRAN CH42 92 C5
WLT/FAZ L9 40 D3
Ivy Farm Ct SPK/HALE L24 * 143 H5
Ivy Farm Dr NSTN CH64 159 E4
Ivy Farm Rd RAIN/WH L35 77 H1
Ivyhurst Cl ALL/GAR L19 118 D3
Ivy La MOR/LEA CH46 66 C4
Ivy Leigh CLB/OSW/ST L13 55 G5
Ivy Rd WARR WA1 109 E1
Ivy St BIRK CH41 3 H5
RUNC WA7 8 E6

J

Jack McBain Ct VAUX/LVPD L3 * 70 C1
Jack's Brow PR/KW L34 44 C5
Jacksfield Wy ALL/GAR L19 118 D4
Jackson Av WARR WA1 107 H1
Jackson Cl BEB CH63 115 H3
RAIN/WH L35 78 B4
Jacksons Pond Dr WLTN L25 97 F1
Jackson St ALL/GAR L19 119 G5
BIRK CH41 3 G5
STHEL WA9 48 C4
Jacobs Cl LITH L21 39 F1
Jacob St TOX L8 94 B4
Jacqueline Dr HUY L36 76 A1
Jade Cl NWD/KWIPK L33 34 A1
Jade Rd NPK/KEN L6 71 H1
Jamaica St CLVPS L1 93 H1
Jamesbrook Cl BIRK CH41 68 C5
James Clarke St EV L5 70 C1
James Cl WDN WA8 146 A2
James Ct WLTN L25 120 D1
James Dunne Av EV L5 53 G5
James Gv ECCL WA10 10 C7
James Holt Av KKBY L32 33 F3
James Hopkins Wy
ANF/KKDL L4 53 H3
James Larkin Wy ANF/KKDL L4 53 H3
James Rd WLTN L25 120 D1
James St ALL/GAR L19 140 C1
CL/PREN CH43 2 B7
CL/PREN CH43 92 A4
CLVP L2 6 C5
STHEL WA9 79 H2
WAL/EG CH44 69 G3
WARR WA1 12 E4
Jamieson Av CSBY/BLUN L23 21 H5
Jamieson Rd WAV L15 95 G1
Jane St STHEL WA9 63 F3
Janet St EHL/KEN L7 71 H4
Japonica Gdns STHEL WA9 63 G3
Jarrett Rd NWD/KWIPK L33 26 B5
Jarrow Cl CL/PREN CH43 91 H4
Jasmine Cl EV L5 71 F1
GR/UP/WCH CH49 89 F1
Jasmine Ct HUY L36 58 D5
Jasmine Gdns STHEL WA9 63 G3
Jasmine Gv WDN WA8 124 B3
Jasmine Ms AIG/SPK L17 94 C5
Jason St EV L5 54 A4
Jason Wk EV L5 54 A4
Java Rd ANF/KKDL L4 41 F5
Jays Cl RUNC WA7 157 G2
Jedburgh Dr NWD/KWIPK L33 25 G3
Jeffereys Crs HUY L36 74 D3
Jeffereys Dr HUY L36 74 C2
Jefferson Dr
WARRW/BUR WA5 105 E1
Jefferson Gdns WDN WA8 101 H5
Jeffreys Dr GR/UP/WCH CH49 89 F3
Jellicoe Cl WKBY CH48 * 110 D5
Jenkinson St VAUX/LVPD L3 71 E2
Jensen Ct RUNC WA7 9 K3
Jericho Cl AIG/SPK L17 118 B1
Jericho Ct AIG/SPK L17 * 118 B1
Jericho Farm Cl AIG/SPK L17 118 B2
Jericho La AIG/SPK L17 118 B2
Jermyn St TOX L8 94 C2
Jerningham Rd NG/CROX L11 41 F4
Jersey Av LITH L21 30 A3
Jersey Cl BTL L20 4 E4
Jersey St BTL L20 4 E4
STHEL WA9 79 G2
Jervis Cl WARRN/WOL WA2 85 E2
Jesmond St WAV L15 72 B5
Jessamine Rd RF/TRAN CH42 92 C5
Jet Cl NPK/KEN L6 71 H1
Jeudwine Cl WLTN L25 120 D3
Joan Av GR/UP/WCH CH49 89 G4
MOR/LEA CH46 66 B5
Jocelyn Cl BEB CH63 138 A3
Jockey St WARRN/WOL WA2 106 D1
John Bagot Cl EV L5 54 A5
John F Kennedy Hts
VAUX/LVPD L3 71 E1
John Hunter Wy NTHTN L30 31 E1
John Lennon Dr NPK/KEN L6 71 H2
John Moores Cl EHL/KEN L7 * 71 G5
Johns Av RUNC WA7 8 C7
Johnson Av RAIN/WH L35 76 C1
Johnson Gv WD/CROXPK L12 57 E5
Johnson Rd CL/PREN CH43 114 B2
Johnson's La WDN WA8 126 A3
Johnson St STHEL WA9 48 C3
VAUX/LVPD L3 6 E2
Johnson Wk EHL/KEN L7 72 A4
Johnston Av BTL L20 40 A1
John St BIRK CH41 3 H3
ECCL WA10 * 11 G4
VAUX/LVPD L3 71 E2
WARRN/WOL WA2 12 D3
Jones Farm Rd WLTN L25 98 A4
Jones St VAUX/LVPD L3 7 H4
Jonson Rd NSTN CH64 158 D1
Jonville Rd WLT/FAZ L9 31 H5
Jordan St CLVPS L1 93 H1
Joseph Gardner Wy BTL L20 4 D2
Joseph Lister Cl NTHTN L30 31 E1
Joseph St STHEL WA9 63 E3
WDN WA8 125 G1
Joshua Cl EV L5 54 A4
Joy La WDN WA8 80 A3
Jubilee Av DV/KA/FCH L14 73 H4
WARR WA1 84 D5
WARRW/BUR WA5 104 C4
Jubilee Crs PS/BROM CH62 138 B1
Jubilee Dr EHL/KEN L7 71 H3
NTHTN L30 31 F3
RAIN/WH L35 76 D3
WKBY CH48 87 E4
Jubilee Rd CSBY/BLUN L23 28 D1
FMBY L37 16 C5
LITH L21 30 A5
Jubilee Wy WDN WA8 124 C2
Jubits La WDN WA8 79 E5
Juddfield St RNFD/HAY WA11 49 G1
Judges Dr NPK/KEN L6 72 A1
Judges Wy NPK/KEN L6 72 A1
Julian Wy WDN WA8 101 H4
Julie Gv WD/CROXPK L12 57 E5
Juliet Av BEB CH63 115 G4
Juliet Gdns BEB CH63 * 115 G4
July Rd NPK/KEN L6 55 F5
July St BTL L20 5 F1
Junction La STHEL WA9 63 E3
June Av PS/BROM CH62 153 E1
June Rd NPK/KEN L6 55 F5
June St BTL L20 5 F2
Juniper Cl ECCL WA10 10 A3
GR/UP/WCH CH49 112 A1
STBRV L28 57 H3
Juniper Gdns CSBY/BLUN L23 22 A3
Juniper St BTL L20 53 G3
Jurby Ct WARRN/WOL WA2 84 C4
Justin Wy RAIN/WH L35 60 D5
Juvenal Pl VAUX/LVPD L3 71 E1
Juvenal St VAUX/LVPD L3 70 D2

K

Kaigh Av CSBY/BLUN L23 21 E4
Kale Cl WKBY CH48 110 B2
Kale Gv NWD/KWIPK L33 26 B4
Kansas Pl WARRW/BUR WA5 105 F1
Kara Cl BTL L20 5 F4
Karan Wy MGHL L31 32 D1
Karonga Rd AIN/FAZ L10 32 B5
Karonga Wy AIN/FAZ L10 32 C5
Karslake Rd CALD/MH L18 95 H3
WAL/EG CH44 69 F3
Kearsley Cl ANF/KKDL L4 * 54 A3
Kearsley St ANF/KKDL L4 54 A3
Keates St STHEL WA9 63 F2
Keats Av RAIN/WH L35 77 F2
Keats Cl WDN WA8 14 A3
Keats Gn HUY L36 75 H4
Keats Gv WARRN/WOL WA2 84 A3
Keats St BTL L20 4 C1
Keble Dr AIN/FAZ L10 31 H1
WAL/NB CH45 50 D4
Keble Rd BTL L20 53 G1
Keble St EHL/KEN L7 71 G2
WDN WA8 14 E5
Kedleston St TOX L8 94 C4
Keegan Dr WAL/EG CH44 69 G3
Keele Cl CL/PREN CH43 67 G4
Keenan Dr BTL L20 40 A2
Keepers La BEB CH63 136 D1
Keeper's Rd WARRS WA4 131 E4
Keighley Av WAL/NB CH45 51 E5
Keightley St BIRK CH41 2 D3
Keir Hardie Av BTL L20 5 K1
Keith Av ANF/KKDL L4 54 B1
WARRW/BUR WA5 104 C2
Keith Dr BEB CH63 152 C4
Kelbey Cl TOX L8 94 C4
Kelbrook Cl STHEL WA9 62 D4
Kelburn Gv WD/CROXPK L12 56 D2
Kelby Cl TOX L8 * 94 C4
Kelda Ct WLTN L25 97 G2
Kelday Cl NWD/KWIPK L33 33 H2
Kelkbeck Cl MGHL L31 19 G4
Kellet's Pl RF/TRAN CH42 92 D5
Kellett Rd MOR/LEA CH46 67 F2
Kellitt Rd WAV L15 95 G1
Kelly Dr BTL L20 5 J2
Kelly St PR/KW L34 60 A4
Kelmscott Dr WAL/EG CH44 68 A1
Kelsall Av STHEL WA9 79 F1
Kelsall Cl CL/PREN CH43 91 G5
GOL/RIS/CUL WA3 85 G2
WDN WA8 124 B1
Kelsey Cl ECCL WA10 10 A3
Kelso Cl NWD/KWIPK L33 25 G3
Kelso Rd NPK/KEN L6 72 A2
Kelton Gv AIG/SPK L17 118 C1
Kelvin Gv TOX L8 94 C2
Kelvin Pk BIRK CH41 69 G4
Kelvin Rd BIRK CH41 92 C4
WAL/EG CH44 69 G4
Kelvinside CSBY/BLUN L23 29 G2
WAL/EG CH44 69 F4
Kemberton Dr WDN WA8 102 A3

Kemble St EHL/KEN L7 * 71 H3
PR/KW L34 59 H4
Kemlyn Rd ANF/KKDL L4 54 C4
Kemmel Av WARRS WA4 130 A1
Kempsell Wy HLWD L26 122 A4
Kempsey Gv STHEL WA9 61 G3
Kempson Ter BEB CH63 137 H2
Kempston St VAUX/LVPD L3 7 H2
Kempton Cl HUY L36 75 E4
RUNC WA7 155 G3
Kempton Park Rd AIN/FAZ L10 32 B2
Kempton Rd PS/BROM CH62 116 B3
WAV L15 72 B5
Kemsley Rd DV/KA/FCH L14 74 B2
Kenbury Cl NWD/KWIPK L33 26 B5
Kenbury Rd NWD/KWIPK L33 26 B5
Kendal Av WARRN/WOL WA2 84 A3
Kendal Cl BEB CH63 115 H5
Kendal Dr MGHL L31 18 D4
RAIN/WH L35 77 G2
RNFD/HAY WA11 37 G4
Kendal Pk WD/CROXPK L12 56 D4
Kendal Ri RUNC WA7 155 H4
Kendal Rd CHLDW L16 97 E1
NWD/KWIPK L33 25 G5
WAL/EG CH44 68 C3
WDN WA8 * 124 A2
Kendal St BIRK CH41 * 3 F5
Kendricks Fold RAIN/WH L35 77 H2
Kendrick St WARR WA1 12 B4
Kenilworth Av RUNC WA7 155 E1
Kenilworth Cl WLTN L25 97 E5
Kenilworth Dr PEN/TH CH61 134 C1
WARR WA1 84 D5
Kenilworth Gdns
GR/UP/WCH CH49 89 G2
Kenilworth Rd CHLDW L16 96 D1
CSBY/BLUN L23 28 D1
NSTN CH64 158 D4
WAL/EG CH44 69 F2
Kenilworth St BTL L20 4 D4
Kenilworth Wy WLTN L25 97 E5
Kenley Av WDN WA8 101 F3
Kenley Pde NPK/KEN L6 72 A1
Kenmare Rd WAV L15 95 G2
Kenmore Cottages LITH L21 * 30 B1
Kenmore Rd CL/PREN CH43 114 A2
Kennelwood Av
NWD/KWIPK L33 34 A1
Kennessee Cl MGHL L31 24 B1
Kenneth Cl NTHTN L30 30 D1
Kenneth Rd WDN WA8 124 A4
Kennet Rd BEB CH63 137 F1
Kennford Rd NG/CROX L11 42 C2
Kennington Pk WDN WA8 101 G5
Kensington EHL/KEN L7 71 H3
Kensington Av STHEL WA9 62 C3
WARRS WA4 131 G1
Kensington Cl WDN WA8 102 D4
Kensington Dr PR/KW L34 59 E5
Kensington Gdns
MOR/LEA CH46 66 C5
Kensington Rd FMBY L37 16 D5
Kensington St NPK/KEN L6 71 G2
Kent Av FMBY L37 17 F5
LITH L21 30 B4
Kent Cl BEB CH63 152 B1
BTL L20 5 C3
Kent Gv RUNC WA7 9 C6
Kentmere Av RNFD/HAY WA11 37 G3
Kentmere Dr PEN/TH CH61 134 D3
Kentmere Pl WARRN/WOL WA2 83 G2
Kenton Rd HLWD L26 121 H4
Kent Rd FMBY L37 17 F5
STHEL WA9 62 C2
WAL/EG CH44 68 D2
WARRW/BUR WA5 105 G4
Kents Bank WD/CROXPK L12 56 C1
Kent St CLVPS L1 7 F7
WARRS WA4 13 F7
WDN WA8 14 E2
Kentwell Gv WD/CROXPK L12 56 D3
Kenview Cl WDN WA8 144 C2
Kenwright Crs STHEL WA9 62 C2
Kenwyn Rd WAL/NB CH45 51 H5
Kenyon Av WARRW/BUR WA5 104 C3
Kenyon Cl NWD/KWIPK L33 26 A3
Kenyon Rd WAV L15 96 A3
Kenyons La FMBY L37 17 F3
MGHL L31 18 D2
Kepler St LITH L21 39 E1
Keppel St BTL L20 53 F1
Kerfoot St WARRN/WOL WA2 106 C1
Kerman Cl WD/CROXPK L12 56 B1
Kerr Cl NWD/KWIPK L33 25 H3
Kerr Gv STHEL WA9 49 E4
Kerris Cl AIG/SPK L17 118 A1
Kerrysdale Cl STHEL WA9 62 D3
Kersey Rd KKBY L32 34 A4
Kershaw Av CSBY/BLUN L23 29 G1
Kershaw St WDN WA8 124 B2
Kerswell Cl STHEL WA9 62 D4
Kestral Gv HLWD L26 121 F2
Kestrel Av GR/UP/WCH CH49 89 F2
Kestrel Cl GR/UP/WCH CH49 89 F2
RNFD/HAY WA11 48 B1
Kestrel Rd HES CH60 149 G2
MOR/LEA CH46 66 A5
Kestrels Wy RUNC WA7 156 B3
Keswick Av BEB CH63 152 C4
WARRN/WOL WA2 84 A3
Keswick Cl MGHL L31 19 E4
WDN WA8 124 A2
Keswick Crs WARRN/WOL WA2 84 A3
Keswick Dr LITH L21 30 D4
Keswick Pl CL/PREN CH43 67 H4
Keswick Rd CALD/MH L18 119 G1
ECCL WA10 10 D2
WAL/NB CH45 51 E3
Keswick Vls CHLDW L16 * 74 C5
Keswick Wy CHLDW L16 74 C5
Kevelioc Cl BEB CH63 137 H3
Kew Rd FMBY L37 16 C5
Kew St EV L5 53 H5
Keybank Rd WD/CROXPK L12 56 A2
Kiddman St WLT/FAZ L9 40 B4
Kidstone Cl STHEL WA9 62 D3
Kilburn Av PS/BROM CH62 153 E3
Kilburn Gv STHEL WA9 61 G3
Kilburn St LITH L21 39 F1
Kildale Cl MGHL L31 18 C4
Kildare Cl SPK/HALE L24 143 H4
Kildonan Rd AIG/SPK L17 118 B1
WARRS WA4 131 E1
Kilford Cl WARRW/BUR WA5 83 E3
Kilgraston Gdns AIG/SPK L17 118 D2
Killarney Gv WAL/EG CH44 * 68 C2
Killarney Rd CLB/OSW/ST L13 73 E2
Killester Rd WLTN L25 97 H4
Killington Wy ANF/KKDL L4 54 A2
Kilmalcolm Cl CL/PREN CH43 91 F4
Kilmore Cl WLT/FAZ L9 31 H4
Kilmory Av WLTN L25 121 E1
Kilncroft RUNC WA7 * 156 D4
Kiln Hey WD/CROXPK L12 56 C5
Kiln La ECCL WA10 47 E2
Kiln Rd GR/UP/WCH CH49 90 A5
Kilnyard Rd CSBY/BLUN L23 21 E5
Kilrea Cl NG/CROX L11 55 H2
Kilrea Rd NG/CROX L11 55 G2
NG/CROX L11 55 H2
Kilsail Rd KKBY L32 34 B5
Kilsby Dr WDN WA8 126 A1
Kilshaw St NPK/KEN L6 71 G1
Kilsyth Cl WARRN/WOL WA2 84 D1
Kimberley Av
CSBY/BLUN L23 * 29 E1
STHEL WA9 61 H3
Kimberley Cl TOX L8 94 C1
Kimberley Dr CSBY/BLUN L23 29 E1
WARRS WA4 130 A2
Kimberley Rd WAL/NB CH45 51 H4
Kimberley St
WARRW/BUR WA5 106 A3
Kindale Rd CL/PREN CH43 114 A2
Kinder St NPK/KEN L6 7 K1
King Av BTL L20 40 A1
King Edward Rd ECCL WA10 47 F1
RAIN/WH L35 77 H1
King Edward's Dr
PS/BROM CH62 116 B5
King Edward St VAUX/LVPD L3 6 B2
WARR WA1 107 G1
Kingfield Rd WLT/FAZ L9 40 B2
Kingfisher Cl NTHLY L27 98 D3
NWD/KWIPK L33 25 H3
RUNC WA7 156 B4
Kingfisher Dr RNFD/HAY WA11 48 B1
Kingfisher Gv WD/CROXPK L12 57 F1
Kingfisher Wy
GR/UP/WCH CH49 89 F2
King George Crs WARR WA1 13 K1
King George Dr WAL/EG CH44 52 A5
King George's Dr
PS/BROM CH62 116 B5
Kingham Cl WDN WA8 15 K1
WLTN L25 121 E1
King James Ct RUNC WA7 156 A3
Kinglake Rd WAL/EG CH44 69 F1
Kinglake St EHL/KEN L7 71 H4
Kinglass Rd BEB CH63 138 B3
King's Av HOY CH47 64 D5
Kingsbrook Wy BEB CH63 115 F5
King's Brow BEB CH63 115 F5
Kingsbury WKBY CH48 87 H5
Kings Cl AIG/SPK L17 118 A1
BEB CH63 115 F4
FMBY L37 16 D4
Kings Ct HOY CH47 87 E1
LITH L21 29 G5
Kingscourt Rd WD/CROXPK L12 56 C5
Kingsdale Av RAIN/WH L35 78 B2
RF/TRAN CH42 115 F1
Kingsdale Rd CALD/MH L18 96 A3
WARRW/BUR WA5 104 D1
Kings Dock St CLVPS L1 93 H1
Kingsdown Rd NG/CROX L11 56 A1
Kingsdown St BIRK CH41 92 C4
King's Dr PEN/TH CH61 112 D5
PR/KW L34 59 E5
WKBY CH48 110 D3
WLTN L25 98 A4
Kingsfield Rd MGHL L31 23 H2
The King's Gap HOY CH47 87 E1
Kingshead Cl RUNC WA7 147 G4
Kingsheath Av DV/KA/FCH L14 57 F5
Kingsland Crs NG/CROX L11 41 G4
Kingsland Gra WARR WA1 85 H4
Kingsland Rd NG/CROX L11 41 F4
RF/TRAN CH42 92 A4
King's La BEB CH63 115 G4
Kingsley Cl MGHL L31 18 C1
PEN/TH CH61 135 E3
Kingsley Crs RUNC WA7 8 E7
Kingsley Dr WARRS WA4 130 A4
Kingsley Rd ECCL WA10 47 F1
RUNC WA7 8 E6
TOX L8 94 D1
WAL/EG CH44 69 E2
Kingsley St BIRK CH41 68 C5
Kingsmead Dr WLTN L25 120 D4
Kingsmead Gv CL/PREN CH43 91 F3
Kings Meadow RUNC WA7 157 E1
Kingsmead Rd CL/PREN CH43 91 F3
MOR/LEA CH46 66 D3
Kingsmead Rd North
CL/PREN CH43 91 F3
Kingsmead Rd South
CL/PREN CH43 91 F3
Kings Ms WARRS WA4 * 130 A3
Kings Mt CL/PREN CH43 91 H4
Kingsnorth RAIN/WH L35 77 F3
Kings Pde VAUX/LVPD L3 93 G1
WAL/NB CH45 50 D2
WAL/NB CH45 51 G1
Kings Pk LITH L21 29 G5
King's Rd BEB CH63 115 F3
BTL L20 39 G5
CSBY/BLUN L23 21 E5
ECCL WA10 47 E5
FMBY L37 16 D4
WARRN/WOL WA2 85 E3
King's Sq BIRK CH41 3 H5
Kings Ter BTL L20 4 E7
Kingsthorne Pk WLTN L25 121 E5
Kingsthorne Rd WLTN L25 121 E5
Kingston Av
WARRW/BUR WA5 104 C2
Kingston Cl DV/KA/FCH L14 57 E5
MOR/LEA CH46 66 C5
RUNC WA7 147 E4
King St ALL/GAR L19 140 C2
CSBY/WL L22 29 E3
ECCL WA10 10 E5
RF/TRAN CH42 116 A2
RUNC WA7 8 E3
WAL/EG CH44 52 B5
Kings Vw HOY CH47 * 86 D2
Kingsville Rd BEB CH63 137 G1
Kingswalk WKBY CH48 110 C1
Kingsway CSBY/WL L22 29 F2
HES CH60 149 G3
HUY L36 75 F1
RAIN/WH L35 59 H5
RNFD/HAY WA11 37 E4
WAL/NB CH45 51 G4
WDN WA8 14 D3
Kingsway Ct VAUX/LVPD L3 70 D1
Kingsway North WARR WA1 107 G2
Kingsway Pk VAUX/LVPD L3 * 70 D1
Kingsway South WARRS WA4 107 H4
Kingsway (Tunnel)
VAUX/LVPD L3 70 A2
WAL/EG CH44 69 E3
Kingswell Cl EHL/KEN L7 71 H5
Kings Whf BIRK CH41 69 G4
Kingswood HUY L36 75 F1
Kingswood Av CSBY/WL L22 29 G3
WLT/FAZ L9 31 G5
Kingswood Bvd BEB CH63 115 G3
Kingswood Ct NWD/KWIPK L33 26 A5
Kingswood Dr CSBY/BLUN L23 29 E1
Kingswood Rd WAL/EG CH44 52 A5
WARRW/BUR WA5 82 B3
Kington Rd WKBY CH48 87 E5
Kinley Gdns BTL L20 * 40 A2
Kinloch Cl HLWD L26 122 A4
Kinloss Rd GR/UP/WCH CH49 89 E5
Kinmel Cl ANF/KKDL L4 55 F2
BIRK CH41 2 E3
Kinmel St STHEL WA9 62 C2
TOX L8 94 C3
Kinnaird Rd WAL/NB CH45 51 G4
Kinnaird St TOX L8 94 C5
Kinnerton Cl MOR/LEA CH46 65 H5
Kinross Cl WARRN/WOL WA2 84 D1
Kinross Rd AIN/FAZ L10 32 B5
CSBY/WL L22 29 F4
WAL/NB CH45 50 D4
Kinsale Dr GOL/RIS/CUL WA3 85 G1
Kintore Cl BEB CH63 152 C5
Kintore Dr WARRW/BUR WA5 104 B2
Kintore Rd ALL/GAR L19 119 F4
Kipling Av HUY L36 76 A4
RF/TRAN CH42 115 H2
WARRN/WOL WA2 84 A4
Kipling Crs WDN WA8 14 B3
Kipling Gv STHEL WA9 79 E2
Kipling St BTL L20 39 E2
Kirby Cl WKBY CH48 110 B2
Kirby Mt WKBY CH48 110 C3
Kirby Pk WKBY CH48 110 B2
Kirby Park Man WKBY CH48 * 110 B2
Kirby Rd BTL L20 39 H1
Kirkbride Cl NTHLY L27 99 E4
Kirkburn Cl TOX L8 94 B4
Kirkby Bank Rd
NWD/KWIPK L33 34 C2
Kirkby Rw KKBY L32 33 F1
Kirkcaldy Av
WARRW/BUR WA5 104 B2
Kirkdale Rd EV L5 53 H4
Kirkdale V ANF/KKDL L4 54 A3
Kirket Cl BEB CH63 138 A2
Kirket La BEB CH63 137 H2
Kirkfield Gv RF/TRAN CH42 116 A2
Kirkham Cl WARRW/BUR WA5 105 F4
Kirkham Rd WDN WA8 125 G1
Kirklake Bank FMBY L37 16 B4
Kirklake Rd FMBY L37 16 B4
Kirkland Av RF/TRAN CH42 115 F1
Kirkland Cl WLT/FAZ L9 * 31 E5
Kirkland Rd WAL/NB CH45 52 A2
The Kirklands WKBY CH48 110 C1
Kirkland St ECCL WA10 10 D4
Kirkmaiden Rd ALL/GAR L19 119 F3
Kirkman Fold RAIN/WH L35 77 H2
Kirkmore Rd CALD/MH L18 119 E1
Kirkmount GR/UP/WCH CH49 90 A3
Kirk Rd LITH L21 39 G1
Kirkside Cl WD/CROXPK L12 42 D4
Kirkstall Dr FMBY L37 17 G4
Kirkstead Wk MGHL L31 33 E1
Kirkstone Av RNFD/HAY WA11 37 G4
WARRN/WOL WA2 84 A2
Kirkstone Crs RUNC WA7 156 C5
Kirkstone Rd North LITH L21 30 B3
Kirkstone Rd South LITH L21 30 C4
Kirk Stone Rd West LITH L21 30 A2
Kirk St EV L5 54 A4
Kirkwall Dr WARRW/BUR WA5 105 E5
Kirkway BEB CH63 115 F4
GR/UP/WCH CH49 89 G4
WAL/NB CH45 51 H3
Kitchener Dr WLT/FAZ L9 40 B1
Kitchener St ECCL WA10 10 C4
Kitchen St CLVPS L1 93 H1
Kitling La PR/KW L34 43 H2
Kitling Rd PR/KW L34 44 A2
Kiverley Cl CALD/MH L18 97 E5
The Knap HES CH60 149 E3
Knaresborough Rd
WAL/EG CH44 68 B1
Knighton Rd ANF/KKDL L4 55 F1
Knightsbridge Av
WARRS WA4 108 C5
Knightsbridge Cl WDN WA8 102 D4
Knightsbridge Ct
CL/PREN CH43 90 D4
WARR WA1 * 12 C5
Knightsbridge Wk
NWD/KWIPK L33 25 G3
Knights Gra STHEL WA9 48 C3
Knight St CLVPS L1 7 G7
Knightsway CSBY/WL L22 29 G2
Knoclaid Rd CLB/OSW/ST L13 55 G3
The Knoll CL/PREN CH43 91 G5
Knotty Ms WLTN L25 98 A5
Knowle Cl WD/CROXPK L12 42 C5
Knowles House Av ECCL WA10 46 B4
Knowles St BIRK CH41 2 C3
WDN WA8 125 G1
The Knowle CSBY/BLUN L23 28 C1
Knowl Hey Rd HLWD L26 122 A5
Knowsley Cl RF/TRAN CH42 116 A2
Knowsley Expy RAIN/WH L35 99 H2
Knowsley La PR/KW L34 44 A2
PR/KW L34 58 B3
Knowsley Park La PR/KW L34 59 G3
Knowsley Rd ALL/GAR L19 119 E5
BTL L20 39 E2
ECCL WA10 47 E4
RAIN/WH L35 78 B3
RF/TRAN CH42 116 A2
WAL/NB CH45 51 G4
Knowsley St ANF/KKDL L4 40 B5
Knox Cl PS/BROM CH62 116 B5
Knox St BIRK CH41 3 H5
Knutsford Cl ECCL WA10 46 D5
Knutsford Gn MOR/LEA CH46 66 C4
Knutsford Old Rd
WARRS WA4 131 E1
Knutsford Rd MOR/LEA CH46 66 C4
WARRS WA4 13 F7
WARRS WA4 107 F5
Knutsford Wk MGHL L31 18 D2
Kremlin Dr CLB/OSW/ST L13 55 H5
WD/CROXPK L12 56 A5
Kylemore Av CALD/MH L18 95 H5
Kylemore Cl PEN/TH CH61 134 C3
Kylemore Dr PEN/TH CH61 134 C3
Kylemore Rd CL/PREN CH43 91 G4
Kylemore Wy HLWD L26 121 F4
PEN/TH CH61 134 C3
Kynance Rd NG/CROX L11 42 D2

L

Laburnum Av HUY L36 75 G5
RNFD/HAY WA11 37 H5
WARR WA1 108 C1
Laburnum Crs KKBY L32 33 G1
Laburnum Farm Cl NSTN CH64 159 F5
Laburnum Gv MGHL L31 19 F5
PEN/TH CH61 112 B5
RUNC WA7 155 F1
Laburnum La
WARRW/BUR WA5 104 A2
Laburnum Pl BTL L20 5 G4
Laburnum Rd CL/PREN CH43 92 A4
EHL/KEN L7 72 B2
WAL/NB CH45 51 H3
Laburnum Ter ALL/GAR L19 * 119 G5
Lace St VAUX/LVPD L3 6 E2
Lacey Ct WDN WA8 14 E6
Lacey Rd PR/KW L34 60 A5
Lacey St ECCL WA10 61 F2
WDN WA8 14 D6
Lad La VAUX/LVPD L3 * 6 B2
Ladybower Cl EHL/KEN L7 71 H5
GR/UP/WCH CH49 89 G2
Lady Chapel Cl CLVPS L1 94 A1
Ladycroft Cl WARR WA1 109 E1
Ladyewood Rd WAL/EG CH44 69 E2
Ladyfield CL/PREN CH43 90 C1
Ladyfields WD/CROXPK L12 56 B5
Ladypool SPK/HALE L24 143 G5
Ladysmith Rd AIN/FAZ L10 32 C5
Ladywood Rd
WARRW/BUR WA5 82 C4
Laffak Rd RNFD/HAY WA11 37 H4
Laggan St EHL/KEN L7 * 71 H3
Lagrange Ar ECCL WA10 * 11 G5
Laira Ct WARRN/WOL WA2 * 13 F1
Laira St WARRN/WOL WA2 12 E1
Laird Cl BIRK CH41 68 B5
Lairds Pl VAUX/LVPD L3 70 D1
Laird St BIRK CH41 68 C5
CL/PREN CH43 68 B5
Laithwaite Cl STHEL WA9 79 F2
Lakeland Cl CLVPS L1 6 E6
Lakemoor Cl STHEL WA9 62 D3
Lakenheath Rd HLWD L26 121 G5
Lake Pl HOY CH47 87 F1
Lake Rd HOY CH47 87 F1
WAV L15 96 A1
Lakeside Cl WDN WA8 123 G4
Lakeside Ct WAL/NB CH45 52 A2
Lakeside Dr WARR WA1 106 C5
Lakeside Vw CSBY/WL L22 * 29 E4
Lakes Rd WLT/FAZ L9 32 A5
Lake St ANF/KKDL L4 54 C3
Lake Vw RAIN/WH L35 77 E4
Laleston Cl WDN WA8 124 C3
Lambert Ct WDN WA8 14 E4
Lambert St VAUX/LVPD L3 7 H2
Lambert Wy VAUX/LVPD L3 7 H2
Lambeth Rd EV L5 53 H3
Lambeth Wk ANF/KKDL L4 53 H3
Lambourn Av WDN WA8 101 E3
Lambourne Gv STHEL WA9 49 G4
Lambourne Rd ANF/KKDL L4 55 F1
Lambshear La MGHL L31 18 C2
Lambsickle Cl RUNC WA7 154 D3
Lambsickle La RUNC WA7 154 D3
Lambs La WARR WA1 85 E5
Lambton Rd AIG/SPK L17 94 D5
Lamburn Dr AIG/SPK L17 95 E4
Lamerton Cl
WARRW/BUR WA5 104 B4
Lammermoor Rd
CALD/MH L18 119 E1
Lampeter Cl
WARRW/BUR WA5 * 83 E3
Lampeter Rd NPK/KEN L6 55 E4
Lamport Cl WDN WA8 103 E5
Lamport St TOX L8 94 A2
Lanark Cl ECCL WA10 10 E7
Lanark Gdns WDN WA8 101 G5
Lancashire Gdns
ECCL WA10 10 E7
Lancaster Av AIG/SPK L17 95 F2
CSBY/BLUN L23 29 E1
RAIN/WH L35 76 D2
RUNC WA7 154 C1
WAL/NB CH45 51 H5
WDN WA8 123 G1
Lancaster Cl EV L5 53 H4
MGHL L31 19 F5
PS/BROM CH62 116 B5
WARRN/WOL WA2 * 84 D3
Lancaster Ct WARRS WA4 * 130 C2
Lancaster Rd FMBY L37 16 D5
HUY L36 76 A1
WDN WA8 102 A5
Lancaster St EV L5 53 H4
WARRW/BUR WA5 106 A3
WLT/FAZ L9 40 B4
Lancaster Ter PR/KW L34 * 60 A4
Lancaster Wk EV L5 53 H4
Lance Cl EV L5 71 F1
Lancefield Rd WLT/FAZ L9 * 40 B2
Lance Gv WAV L15 96 A1
Lance La WAV L15 96 A1
Lancelyn Prec BEB CH63 * 138 A3
Lancelyn Ter BEB CH63 137 H2
Lancer Ct RUNC WA7 147 E3
Lancing Av WARRN/WOL WA2 83 G1
Lancing Cl WLTN L25 121 F2
Lancing Dr AIN/FAZ L10 32 A2
Lancing Rd WLTN L25 121 F3
Lancing Wy WLTN L25 121 F2
Lancots La STHEL WA9 62 D2
Land Cut La GOL/RIS/CUL WA3 85 H2
Lander Cl WARRW/BUR WA5 105 H1
Lander Rd LITH L21 39 F1
Landford Av WLT/FAZ L9 41 G3
Landford Pl WLT/FAZ L9 41 G3
Landican La BEB CH63 114 C5
CL/PREN CH43 114 B4
GR/UP/WCH CH49 113 G2
Landican Rd PEN/TH CH61 113 F4
Landor Cl EV L5 53 G5
Landseer Av NSTN CH64 159 E3
WARRS WA4 129 H2
Landseer Rd EV L5 54 B5
Lanfranc Cl CHLDW L16 74 A5
Lanfranc Wy CHLDW L16 74 A5
Langbar RAIN/WH L35 77 E3
Langdale Av FMBY L37 16 C3
PEN/TH CH61 134 D2
Langdale Cl FMBY L37 16 C4
KKBY L32 34 A3
WARRN/WOL WA2 84 C3
WDN WA8 124 A3
Langdale Dr MGHL L31 19 E4
Langdale Gv RNFD/HAY WA11 37 F5
Langdale Rd BEB CH63 137 G2
RUNC WA7 9 F6
WAL/NB CH45 51 G3
WAV L15 95 G2
Langdale St BTL L20 5 G5
Langfield Gv PS/BROM CH62 152 D4
Langford SPK/HALE L24 143 G5
Langford Rd ALL/GAR L19 118 D3
Langham Av AIG/SPK L17 95 E5
Langham St ANF/KKDL L4 54 B2
Langland Cl ANF/KKDL L4 55 F2
WARRW/BUR WA5 83 E3
Lang La WKBY CH48 87 F5
Lang La South WKBY CH48 87 G5
Langley Cl BEB CH63 138 A5
WD/CROXPK L12 43 F4
Langley Rd BEB CH63 138 A4
Langley St TOX L8 94 A2
Langrove St EV L5 54 A5
Langsdale St VAUX/LVPD L3 7 H1
Langshaw Lea NTHLY L27 98 D4
Langstone Av
GR/UP/WCH CH49 111 H1
Langton Cl WDN WA8 100 D5
Langton Gn WARR WA1 108 D1
Langton Rd NWD/KWIPK L33 26 A4
WAV L15 95 F1
Langtree St STHEL WA9 48 C4
Langtry Cl ANF/KKDL L4 53 H2
Langtry Rd ANF/KKDL L4 53 H2
Lansbrook Ct RUNC WA7 * 9 H5
Lansbury Av STHEL WA9 49 E5
Lansbury Rd HUY L36 76 A3
Lansdown WD/CROXPK L12 56 A4
Lansdowne Cl BIRK CH41 68 C5
Lansdowne Ct CL/PREN CH43 68 B5
Lansdowne Pl CL/PREN CH43 68 B5
EV L5 54 B4
Lansdowne Rd BIRK CH41 68 B5
CL/PREN CH43 68 B5
WAL/NB CH45 51 F2
Lanville Rd ALL/GAR L19 119 F2
Lanyork Rd VAUX/LVPD L3 6 B1
Lapford Crs NWD/KWIPK L33 26 B5
Lapwing Cl WD/CROXPK L12 57 E1
Lapwing Ct HLWD L26 121 G2
Lapwing Gv RUNC WA7 156 C3
Lapwing La WARRS WA4 127 H4
Lapwing Ri HES CH60 148 D3
Lapworth Cl MOR/LEA CH46 65 H5
Lapworth St EV L5 53 H4
Larch Av WARRW/BUR WA5 104 C3
WDN WA8 125 F1
Larch Cl ALL/GAR L19 118 D4
RUNC WA7 155 H2
Larchdale Gv WLT/FAZ L9 40 D3
Larchfield Rd CSBY/BLUN L23 21 H4
Larch Gv CL/PREN CH43 68 A5
WAV L15 73 E4
Larch Lea NPK/KEN L6 54 D5
Larch Rd HUY L36 75 E3
RF/TRAN CH42 2 C7
RUNC WA7 155 G2
Larchtree Ms WD/CROXPK L12 57 E2
Larch Wy FMBY L37 16 C2
Larchwood Av MGHL L31 23 H2
Larchwood Cl PEN/TH CH61 134 D3
WLTN L25 97 H3
Larchwood Dr BEB CH63 115 H4
Larcombe Av
GR/UP/WCH CH49 89 H3
Larkfield Av WARR WA1 107 H1
Larkfield Cl AIG/SPK L17 118 A1
Larkfield Gv AIG/SPK L17 118 A1
Larkfield Rd AIG/SPK L17 118 A1
Larkfield Vw WAV L15 72 C5
Larkhill Av GR/UP/WCH CH49 90 A2
Larkhill Cl CLB/OSW/ST L13 55 G3
Larkhill La CLB/OSW/ST L13 55 G3
FMBY L37 16 B2

Larkhill Pl CLB/OSW/ST L13 55 G3
Larkhill Vw CLB/OSW/ST L13 55 H3
Larkhill Wy GR/UP/WCH CH49 90 A1
Larkin Cl PS/BROM CH62 116 A4
Lark La AIG/SPK L17 95 E5
Larkspur Cl RUNC WA7 156 B5
WARRW/BUR WA5 105 H5
Larkstoke Cl WARRS WA4 130 C5
Larksway HES CH60 149 F1
Lark Wy AIG/SPK L17 94 D5
Larne Ct WDN WA8 124 C1
Larton Farm Cl WKBY CH48 88 A5
Larton Rd WKBY CH48 87 H5
Lartonwood WKBY CH48 111 E1
Lascelles Rd ALL/GAR L19 119 H4
Lascelles St STHEL WA9 48 C4
Lasky La WARRS WA4 109 F4
Latchford Rd HES CH60 149 F3
Latchford St WARRS WA4 108 A5
Late Moffatt Rd West
WLT/FAZ L9 * 31 G5
Latham Av RUNC WA7 9 G6
Latham St EV L5 53 H4
Latham Wy BEB CH63 138 B4
Lathbury La AIG/SPK L17 95 G3
Lathom Av LITH L21 38 D1
WAL/EG CH44 68 D1
WARRN/WOL WA2 83 H5
Lathom Dr MGHL L31 19 E3
Lathom Rd BTL L20 39 G2
HUY L36 75 G3
Lathum Cl RAIN/WH L35 60 A5
Latimer St EV L5 53 H5
Latrigg Rd AIG/SPK L17 118 C1
Lauder Cl NWD/KWIPK L33 25 G3
Launceston Cl RUNC WA7 157 E3
Launceston Dr
WARRW/BUR WA5 104 C5
The Laund WAL/NB CH45 51 F5
Laurel Av BEB CH63 137 G2
HES CH60 134 D5
WARR WA1 * 108 D1
Laurel Bank WARRS WA4 131 G2
WDN WA8 102 A5
Laurelbanks HES CH60 134 C5
Laurel Ct RNFD/HAY WA11 37 F5
Laurel Dr ECCL WA10 46 B3
Laurel Gv CSBY/WL L22 29 E2
HUY L36 75 G5
TOX L8 95 E2
Laurelhurst Av PEN/TH CH61 135 E2
Laurel Rd ECCL WA10 10 A7
EHL/KEN L7 72 B3
PR/KW L34 60 A4
RF/TRAN CH42 92 B4
RNFD/HAY WA11 49 F2
Laurel Wy ECCL WA10 * 47 F5
Laurence Deacon Ct
BIRK CH41 * 2 D2
Lauren Cl HUY L36 76 B3
Lauriston Rd ANF/KKDL L4 55 E1
Laurus Cl NTHLY L27 98 D3
Lavan Cl NPK/KEN L6 71 G2
Lavan St NPK/KEN L6 71 G2
Lavender Cl RUNC WA7 9 J7
Lavender Crs PR/KW L34 60 A4
Lavender Gdns STHEL WA9 63 G3
Lavender Wy WLT/FAZ L9 40 D4
Lavrock Bank TOX L8 94 A4
Lawford Dr HES CH60 149 G1
Lawler Gv PR/KW L34 60 A3
Lawler St LITH L21 39 F1
Lawn Av WARR WA1 84 D5
Lawnhurst Gv AIG/SPK L17 118 C3
Lawns Av BEB CH63 152 B3
Lawnside Cl RF/TRAN CH42 115 H2
The Lawns CL/PREN CH43 90 D1
Lawrence Cl ALL/GAR L19 119 E4
Lawrence Gv WAV L15 95 G1
Lawrence Rd ECCL WA10 47 E1
WAV L15 95 F1
Lawrenson St ECCL WA10 10 D6
Lawson Cl WARR WA1 109 E1
Lawson Wk WD/CROXPK L12 42 D4
Lawton Av BTL L20 40 A2
Lawton Rd CSBY/WL L22 29 E2
HUY L36 75 E3
RAIN/WH L35 78 B3
Lawton St CLVPS L1 7 F5
Laxey Av WARR WA1 108 D2
Laxey St TOX L8 94 A2
Laxton Rd WLTN L25 121 E5
Layford Cl HUY L36 58 B4
Layford Rd HUY L36 58 B5
Layton Av CL/PREN CH43 114 B1
Layton Cl WLTN L25 121 E1
Layton Rd WLTN L25 121 E1
Lazonby Cl CL/PREN CH43 67 G5
Leach Cft STBRV L28 57 G3
Leach La STHEL WA9 62 D4
Leach St ECCL WA10 11 F3
Leach Vw RNFD/HAY WA11 * 37 F5
Leach Wy PEN/TH CH61 112 A5
Lea Cl CL/PREN CH43 91 E4
Lea Cross Gv WDN WA8 101 E4
Leadenhall Cl EV L5 54 B4
Leafield Cl PEN/TH CH61 112 D5
Leafield Rd WLTN L25 120 D5
Leagate AIN/FAZ L10 32 C4
Lea Green Rd STHEL WA9 62 A5
Leamington Cl NSTN CH64 158 D4
WARRW/BUR WA5 82 A5
Leamington Rd NG/CROX L11 41 F5
Leander Rd WAL/NB CH45 51 G5
Lea Rd WAL/EG CH44 52 A5
Leaside RUNC WA7 9 K7
Leasowe Av WAL/NB CH45 51 E4
Leasowe Gdns MOR/LEA CH46 66 C2
Leasowe Rd MOR/LEA CH46 67 E1
WLT/FAZ L9 31 G5
Leasoweside MOR/LEA CH46 67 E1
Leas Pk HOY CH47 87 E4
The Leas PEN/TH CH61 113 F5
WAL/NB CH45 51 E3
Leatherbarrows La MGHL L31 24 D2
Leather La CLVP L2 6 D3
Leather's La HLWD L26 121 H4
Leathwood MGHL L31 * 24 B1
Leaway GR/UP/WCH CH49 89 F4
Leawood Gv MOR/LEA CH46 66 D5
Leckwith Rd NTHTN L30 31 G1
Ledbury Cl CL/PREN CH43 114 A1
ECCL WA10 46 D4
WD/CROXPK L12 43 F3
Ledger Rd RNFD/HAY WA11 49 G2
Ledsham Cl CL/PREN CH43 91 E4
GOL/RIS/CUL WA3 85 G2
Ledsham Rd KKBY L32 33 F2
Ledsons Gv MGHL L31 32 D1
Ledyard Cl WARRW/BUR WA5 105 H1
Leece St CLVPS L1 7 G6
Lee Cl RAIN/WH L35 78 B4
Lee Ct WARRN/WOL WA2 84 A3
Leecourt Cl WD/CROXPK L12 56 D5
Leeds St VAUX/LVPD L3 6 C1
Lee Hall Rd WLTN L25 98 A3
Leeming Cl ALL/GAR L19 140 C1
Lee Park Av WLTN L25 98 A3
Lee Rd HOY CH47 87 G1
WARRW/BUR WA5 * 105 F2
Lees Av RF/TRAN CH42 115 H1
Leeside Av KKBY L32 34 A4
Leeside Cl KKBY L32 34 A3
Lees La NSTN CH64 159 G2
WD/CROXPK L12 56 D3
Lees Rd NWD/KWIPK L33 34 C2
The Lees WARRW/BUR WA5 82 A5
Lee St STHEL WA9 63 E2
Leeswood Rd
GR/UP/WCH CH49 90 A5
Lee Vale Rd WLTN L25 98 A4
Leeward Dr SPK/HALE L24 141 G2
Legh Rd PS/BROM CH62 116 B4
RNFD/HAY WA11 49 G1
Legh St WARR WA1 12 C4
Legion La PS/BROM CH62 138 D5
Legion Rd ECCL WA10 61 F2
Leicester Av CSBY/WL L22 29 E2
Leicester Rd BTL L20 5 H2
Leicester St STHEL WA9 61 F2
WARRW/BUR WA5 106 A3
Leigh Av WDN WA8 14 C2
Leigh Pl CLVPS L1 * 7 F4
Leigh Rd WKBY CH48 87 F5
Leighs Hey Crs KKBY L32 34 A3
Leigh St CLVPS L1 7 F4
Leighton Av HOY CH47 65 E5
MGHL L31 18 D4
Leighton Cha NSTN CH64 158 C1
Leighton Ct NSTN CH64 158 C2
Leighton Pk NSTN CH64 158 C2
Leighton Rd BIRK CH41 92 C4
NSTN CH64 158 C1
The Leightons NSTN CH64 158 C2
Leighton St ANF/KKDL L4 54 A1
Leinster Gdns RUNC WA7 8 B3
Leinster Rd CLB/OSW/ST L13 73 F2
Leinster St RUNC WA7 8 B3
Leiria Wy RUNC WA7 9 F4
Leison St ANF/KKDL L4 53 H3
Leiston Cl PEN/TH CH61 112 C4
Lemon Cl EHL/KEN L7 72 A4
Lemon Gv TOX L8 95 E2
Lemon St EV L5 53 H4
Lemon Tree Wk ECCL WA10 61 F1
Lendel Cl FMBY L37 16 D3
Lenfield Dr RNFD/HAY WA11 49 F1
Lenham Wy SPK/HALE L24 141 H2
Lennox Av WAL/NB CH45 * 51 H3
Lennox La CL/PREN CH43 67 G4
Lenthall St ANF/KKDL L4 40 B5
Lenton Av FMBY L37 16 C2
Lenton Rd WLTN L25 98 A3
Leo Cl DV/KA/FCH L14 74 B1
Leominster Rd WAL/EG CH44 68 D1
Leonard Cheshire Dr
NTHTN L30 31 E1
Leonards Cl HUY L36 58 B4
Leonard St RUNC WA7 154 B2
STHEL WA9 63 F3
WARRN/WOL WA2 13 F1
WARRS WA4 130 A2
Leon Cl WARRW/BUR WA5 * 104 B1
Leonora St TOX L8 * 94 C4
Leopold Gv STHEL WA9 62 C5
Leopold Rd CSBY/WL L22 28 D2
EHL/KEN L7 71 H3
Leopold St WAL/EG CH44 * 69 G2
Leslie Av GR/UP/WCH CH49 89 F5
Leslie Rd ECCL WA10 61 E2
Lesseps Rd TOX L8 95 E1
Lessingham Rd WDN WA8 101 H5
Lester Cl ANF/KKDL L4 54 A3
Lester Dr ECCL WA10 46 C2
PEN/TH CH61 112 A4
Lester Gv HUY L36 * 75 H1
Lestock St TOX L8 94 A1
Leta St ANF/KKDL L4 54 B1
Letchworth St NPK/KEN L6 55 E5
Lethbridge Cl EV L5 53 G4
Letitia St TOX L8 94 B3
Levens Cl WARRW/BUR WA5 12 A2
Levens Hey MOR/LEA CH46 66 B5
Leven St ANF/KKDL L4 54 A2
Levens Wy WDN WA8 124 A3
Lever Av WAL/EG CH44 69 G3
Lever Cswy BEB CH63 114 D4
Leveret Rd SPK/HALE L24 143 E3
Lever St STHEL WA9 79 H1
Lever Ter RF/TRAN CH42 92 C5
Leveson Rd CLB/OSW/ST L13 73 F4
Levisham Gdns
WARRW/BUR WA5 106 A1
Lewis Av WARRW/BUR WA5 83 F3
Lewis Crs WDN WA8 14 C5
Lewis Gv WDN WA8 124 B2
Lewisham Rd NG/CROX L11 41 H5
PS/BROM CH62 116 C5
Lewis St ECCL WA10 10 D5
Lewis Wk NWD/KWIPK L33 25 H3
Lexden St WARRW/BUR WA5 106 A2
Lexham Rd DV/KA/FCH L14 73 G2
Lexington Wy NWD/KWIPK L33 25 G3
Leybourne Cl WLTN L25 97 G2
Leybourne Gn WLTN L25 97 G3
Leybourne Gv WLTN L25 97 G3
Leybourne Rd WLTN L25 97 G2
Leyburn Cl KKBY L32 33 H5
Leyburn Rd WAL/NB CH45 51 F5
Ley Cl STHEL WA9 79 G1
Leyfield Cl WD/CROXPK L12 56 D4
Leyfield Rd WD/CROXPK L12 56 C4
Leyland Gv RNFD/HAY WA11 49 H1
Leyland St PR/KW L34 59 H4
Leyton Cl RUNC WA7 155 F3
Liberton Ct EV L5 54 B4
Liberty St WAV L15 95 G1
Libra Cl DV/KA/FCH L14 57 G5
Libson Cl WARRN/WOL WA2 85 E2
Lichfield Av CSBY/WL L22 29 E1
WARRS WA4 131 E4
Lichfield Cl NTHTN L30 31 F3
Lichfield Rd HLWD L26 121 G5
WAV L15 96 A2
Lichfield St WAL/NB CH45 52 A3
Lickers La RAIN/WH L35 77 E3
Liddell Av MGHL L31 24 D5
Liddell Rd WD/CROXPK L12 55 H3
Lidderdale Rd WAV L15 96 A3
Lidgate Cl NWD/KWIPK L33 25 H4
Liffey St TOX L8 94 D1
Lifton Rd NWD/KWIPK L33 34 A2
Lightbody St EV L5 53 F5
Lightburn St RUNC WA7 8 C6
Lightfoot Cl HES CH60 * 149 F2
Lightfoot La HES CH60 149 F2
Lighthouse La FMBY L37 17 F5
Lighthouse Rd HOY CH47 87 E2
Lightoaks Dr HLWD L26 122 B2
Lightwood Dr EHL/KEN L7 72 A5
Lightwood St EHL/KEN L7 72 A5
Lilac Av WARRW/BUR WA5 105 E3
WDN WA8 125 F1
Lilac Crs RUNC WA7 155 G1
Lilac Gv HUY L36 75 F5
RNFD/HAY WA11 49 F2
WARRS WA4 130 C2
Lilford Av WARRW/BUR WA5 83 F5
WLT/FAZ L9 40 B1
Lilford Dr WARRW/BUR WA5 104 D2
Lilford St WARRW/BUR WA5 12 A1
Lilley Rd EHL/KEN L7 72 B2
Lillian Rd ANF/KKDL L4 54 D4
Lillie Cl CL/PREN CH43 67 G5
Lillyfield HES CH60 148 D3
Lilly Gn ANF/KKDL L4 54 D1
Lilly Gv ANF/KKDL L4 54 D1
Lilly V EHL/KEN L7 72 B2
Lily Rd LITH L21 39 F1
Lime Av BEB CH63 137 F2
WDN WA8 * 125 F1
Lime Cl CLB/OSW/ST L13 73 E1
Limedale Rd CALD/MH L18 96 A3
Lime Gv LITH L21 39 E1
RUNC WA7 155 G1
TOX L8 95 E2
Limehurst Gv PS/BROM CH62 152 D3
Limekiln Ct EV L5 70 D1
Limekiln La EV L5 53 H5
VAUX/LVPD L3 70 D1
WAL/EG CH44 68 C3
WARRW/BUR WA5 81 G2
Limerick Cl WDN WA8 101 G5
The Limes GR/UP/WCH CH49 89 H3
Lime St CLVPS L1 7 F3
Limetree Av WARR WA1 84 D5
WARRS WA4 130 C2
Lime Tree Cl WLT/FAZ L9 40 D4
Lime Tree Gv HES CH60 149 G1
Lime Tree Wy FMBY L37 16 B4
Lime Vale Rd
WGNW/BIL/OR WN5 37 G1
Linacre La BTL L20 39 G2
WDN WA8 101 G3
Linacre Rd LITH L21 30 A5
Lincoln Cl HUY L36 76 B2
NPK/KEN L6 71 H1
RUNC WA7 155 G3
WARR WA1 109 E2
Lincoln Crs RNFD/HAY WA11 48 B1
Lincoln Dr AIN/FAZ L10 32 A1
WAL/NB CH45 52 A4
Lincoln Gdns BIRK CH41 * 68 C5
Lincoln Gn MGHL L31 23 G1
Lincoln Rd ECCL WA10 47 F5
Lincoln Sq WDN WA8 125 F1
Lincoln St ALL/GAR L19 140 C2
BIRK CH41 68 C4
Lincoln Wy RAIN/WH L35 78 B4
Lincombe Rd HUY L36 74 D1
Lindale Cl MOR/LEA CH46 67 E4
Lindale Dr STHEL WA9 79 G1
Lindale Rd EHL/KEN L7 72 C2
Lindby Cl KKBY L32 34 B4
Lindby Rd KKBY L32 34 B4
Linden Av CSBY/BLUN L23 20 D5
NTHTN L30 31 E2
Linden Cl WARR WA1 108 D1
Linden Ct WDN WA8 * 101 H4
Linden Dr CL/PREN CH43 114 A2
HUY L36 75 G5
Linden Gv WAL/NB CH45 51 H3
WGNW/BIL/OR WN5 37 G1
Linden Rd NTHLY L27 98 C3
The Lindens CL/PREN CH43 2 B6
MGHL L31 23 H2
Linden Wy ECCL WA10 46 D3
WDN WA8 101 H4
Lindenwood KKBY L32 34 A4
Lindeth Av WAL/EG CH44 68 D3
Lindfield Cl TOX L8 94 A4
Lindi Av WARRS WA4 131 F2
Lindisfarne Ct WDN WA8 101 H2
Lindisfarne Dr WD/CROXPK L12 43 G4
Lindley Av WARRS WA4 107 H4
Lindley Cl EHL/KEN L7 72 A5
Lindley St EHL/KEN L7 72 A5
Lindrick Cl RAIN/WH L35 77 G1
Lindsay Rd ANF/KKDL L4 55 F2
Lindsay St STHEL WA9 80 A2
Lind St ANF/KKDL L4 54 B1
Lindsworth Cl
WARRW/BUR WA5 105 G2
Lindwall Cl CL/PREN CH43 67 G4
Linear Pk MOR/LEA CH46 66 A4
Lineside Cl WLTN L25 97 H3
Linford Gv RNFD/HAY WA11 48 C2
Lingdale Av CL/PREN CH43 91 F2
Lingdale Rd CL/PREN CH43 91 F1
WKBY CH48 87 E5
Lingdale Rd North BIRK CH41 91 F1
Lingfield Cl HUY L36 75 E4
NTHTN L30 31 F3
Lingfield Gv DV/KA/FCH L14 73 H3
Lingfield Rd DV/KA/FCH L14 73 G3
RUNC WA7 154 C1
Lingford Cl NTHLY L27 98 D4
Lingham Cl MOR/LEA CH46 66 B4
Lingham La MOR/LEA CH46 66 A2
Lingholme Rd ECCL WA10 10 D3
Lingley Green Av
WARRW/BUR WA5 81 G5
Lingley Rd WARRW/BUR WA5 104 B2
Lingmell Av RNFD/HAY WA11 37 F3
Lingmell Rd WD/CROXPK L12 56 B2
Ling St EHL/KEN L7 71 H3
Lingtree Rd KKBY L32 33 E2
Lingwell Av WDN WA8 124 B1
Lingwell Pk WDN WA8 124 B1
Lingwood Rd
WARRW/BUR WA5 104 C2
Linhope Wy AIG/SPK L17 95 E5
Link Av CSBY/BLUN L23 21 H4
RNFD/HAY WA11 49 E2
Linkfield Cl NTHLY L27 98 B2
Link Rd HUY L36 76 B4
Links Cl BEB CH63 152 B3
WAL/NB CH45 51 F2
Links Hey Rd WKBY CH48 111 E5
Linkside BEB CH63 115 F4
Links Rd KKBY L32 34 B4
Linkstor Rd WLTN L25 120 B1
Links Vw CL/PREN CH43 91 E3
WAL/NB CH45 51 F2
Linksway WAL/NB CH45 51 F3
Linkway ECCL WA10 46 D1
RUNC WA7 155 G1
Linkway East ECCL WA10 11 J7
Linkway West ECCL WA10 11 F6
Linner Rd SPK/HALE L24 142 B3
Linnet Cl AIG/SPK L17 95 E3
WARRN/WOL WA2 84 B2
Linnet La AIG/SPK L17 94 D3
Linnets Pk RUNC WA7 9 H3
Linnets Wy HES CH60 148 C1
Linnet Wy NWD/KWIPK L33 25 H2
Linslade Cl NWD/KWIPK L33 26 A5
Linslade Crs NWD/KWIPK L33 26 A5
Linton St ANF/KKDL L4 54 B1
Linum Gdns STHEL WA9 63 H3
Linville Av CSBY/BLUN L23 20 C5
Linwood Cl RUNC WA7 157 E4
Linwood Gv RAIN/WH L35 77 E3
Linwood Rd RF/TRAN CH42 92 C5
Lionel St STHEL WA9 63 F3
Lion Hotel Yd WARR WA1 * 12 D5
Lipton Cl BTL L20 4 D7
Lisburn La CLB/OSW/ST L13 55 G3
Lisburn Rd AIG/SPK L17 118 C1
Liscard Crs WAL/NB CH45 51 H5
Liscard Gv WAL/EG CH44 68 C1
Liscard Rd WAL/EG CH44 69 E1
WAV L15 95 F1
Liscard Village WAL/NB CH45 51 H5
Liscard Wy WAL/NB CH45 68 D1
Liskeard Cl RUNC WA7 156 D3
Lisleholme Crs WD/CROXPK L12 56 C4
Lisleholme Rd WD/CROXPK L12 56 C4
Lismore Rd CALD/MH L18 119 E2
Lister Crs EHL/KEN L7 72 A3
Lister Dr CLB/OSW/ST L13 72 C1
Lister Rd EHL/KEN L7 72 A3
RUNC WA7 9 H3
Liston St ANF/KKDL L4 * 40 B5
Litcham Cl GR/UP/WCH CH49 90 A1
Litchborough Gv RAIN/WH L35 60 C4
Litherland Av MOR/LEA CH46 66 B4
Litherland Crs RNFD/HAY WA11 37 G5
Litherland Pk LITH L21 30 A4
Litherland Rd BTL L20 5 F1
Lithou Cl EV L5 53 H5
Little Acre MGHL L31 24 B1
Little Barn Hey NTHTN L30 22 C5
Little Brook La KKBY L32 33 G4
Little Canning St TOX L8 94 B1
Little Catharine St TOX L8 94 B1
Littlecote Cl STHEL WA9 79 G1
Littlecourt VAUX/LVPD L3 70 C1
Little Crosby Rd
CSBY/BLUN L23 21 F2
Little Dl DV/KA/FCH L14 * 73 H2
Littledale DV/KA/FCH L14 73 H2
Littledale Rd WAL/EG CH44 69 F2
WARRW/BUR WA5 104 D1
Littlegate RUNC WA7 156 A1
Little Hardman St CLVPS L1 * 7 H6
Little Heath Rd SPK/HALE L24 142 C3
Little Heyes St EV L5 54 C4
Little Hey La FMBY L37 17 G2
Little Howard St VAUX/LVPD L3 70 B1
Little Huskisson St TOX L8 94 B1
Little La NSTN CH64 158 A1
Littlemore Cl GR/UP/WCH CH49 89 F3
Little Moss Hey STBRV L28 57 H3
Little Parkfield Rd AIG/SPK L17 94 D4
Littler Rd RNFD/HAY WA11 49 G2
Little St Bride St TOX L8 7 J7
Littlestone Cl WDN WA8 102 A4
Little Storeton La BEB CH63 114 C5
Little St STHEL WA9 63 E1
Littleton Cl CL/PREN CH43 * 91 E4
WARRW/BUR WA5 105 H4
Littlewood Cl RAIN/WH L35 77 E3
Little Woolton St
VAUX/LVPD L3 71 G4
Littondale Av RAIN/WH L35 * 78 B3
Liverpool Loop Line HLWD L26 121 F1
WLTN L25 97 F1
Liverpool Pl WDN WA8 124 A2
Liverpool Rd CSBY/BLUN L23 21 F5
FMBY L37 17 F4
HUY L36 58 A5
HUY L36 58 B5
HUY L36 75 E1
MGHL L31 18 D2
NSTN CH64 158 D1
PR/KW L34 59 F4
WARRW/BUR WA5 12 A5
WARRW/BUR WA5 104 B2
WARRW/BUR WA5 104 C2
WARRW/BUR WA5 105 E3
WDN WA8 14 A2
WDN WA8 123 H2
Liverpool Rd North MGHL L31 18 C4
Liverpool Rd South MGHL L31 18 C5
MGHL L31 23 H2
Liverpool St ECCL WA10 10 E6
Liversidge Rd RF/TRAN CH42 92 B4
Liver St CLVPS L1 6 D7
Livingston Av AIG/SPK L17 95 E4
Livingston Dr AIG/SPK L17 95 E5
Livingston Dr North
AIG/SPK L17 95 E5
Livingston Dr South
AIG/SPK L17 95 E5
Livingstone Cl
WARRW/BUR WA5 105 H1
Livingstone Gdns BIRK CH41 2 C2
Livingstone Rd MOR/LEA CH46 67 E1
RF/TRAN CH42 92 D5
Livingstone St BIRK CH41 2 C2
Llanrwst Cl TOX L8 94 A3
Lloyd Av BIRK CH41 2 A2
Lloyd Cl NPK/KEN L6 71 F1
Lloyd Dr GR/UP/WCH CH49 89 F5
Lloyd Rd PR/KW L34 60 A3
Lloyd St RNFD/HAY WA11 49 F1
Lobelia Av WLT/FAZ L9 40 D3
Lobelia Gv RUNC WA7 156 B5
Lochinvar St WLT/FAZ L9 40 B4
Lochmore Rd CALD/MH L18 119 E2
Lochryan Rd ALL/GAR L19 119 F3
Loch St RUNC WA7 8 D3
Locker Av WARRN/WOL WA2 83 H3
Lockerbie Cl WARRN/WOL WA2 84 C1
Lockerby Rd EHL/KEN L7 72 B2
Locker Pk GR/UP/WCH CH49 89 E4
Locke St ALL/GAR L19 140 C2
Lockett Rd WDN WA8 125 E1
Lockett St WARRS WA4 107 H5
Lockfields Vw VAUX/LVPD L3 53 G5
Locking Stumps La
WARRN/WOL WA2 85 F2
Lockington Cl TOX L8 94 C4
Lock Rd PS/BROM CH62 153 H2
WARR WA1 107 H1
Lock St STHEL WA9 48 C2
Lockton La WARRW/BUR WA5 106 A1
Lockton Rd PR/KW L34 43 H2
Lock Vls WARRS WA4 * 108 B5
Lockwood Vw RUNC WA7 157 H4
Loddon Cl GR/UP/WCH CH49 90 A1
Lodge La PS/BROM CH62 116 B5
RUNC WA7 156 A1
TOX L8 94 D1
WARRW/BUR WA5 106 A1
WDN WA8 100 D4
Lodge Rd WDN WA8 123 H3
Lodwick St BTL L20 53 F1
Lofthouse Ga WDN WA8 101 H5
Logan Rd BIRK CH41 68 D4
Logfield Dr ALL/GAR L19 140 D1
Lognor Rd KKBY L32 33 F2
Logwood Rd HUY L36 76 A5
Lombard Rd MOR/LEA CH46 66 D3
Lombardy Av
GR/UP/WCH CH49 111 H1
Lomond Gv MOR/LEA CH46 66 D5
Lomond Rd EHL/KEN L7 72 C3
Londonderry Rd
CLB/OSW/ST L13 55 F3
London Rd VAUX/LVPD L3 7 G3
WARRS WA4 130 B3
Longacre Cl WAL/NB CH45 50 D5
Long Acres GR/UP/WCH CH49 89 F3
Long Av WLT/FAZ L9 40 D1
Longbarn Bvd
WARRN/WOL WA2 85 G3
Long Barn La WARR WA1 85 H5
WARRN/WOL WA2 85 F3
Longborough Rd PR/KW L34 44 A4
Longcroft Av ALL/GAR L19 119 H4
Longcroft Sq ALL/GAR L19 119 H4
Longdale La SFTN L29 22 C2
Longdin St WARRS WA4 107 H5
Longdown Rd AIN/FAZ L10 42 B1
NG/CROX L11 42 B1
Longfellow Cl KKBY L32 33 G4
Longfellow Dr PS/BROM CH62 116 A3
Longfellow St BTL L20 4 B1
TOX L8 95 E1
Longfield FMBY L37 17 G1
Longfield Av CSBY/BLUN L23 21 F3
Longfield Cl GR/UP/WCH CH49 89 E4
Longfield Rd LITH L21 39 F1
WARRN/WOL WA2 84 A4
Longfold MGHL L31 19 E5
Longford Dr WDN WA8 124 C1
Longford St TOX L8 94 C5
WARRN/WOL WA2 106 D1
Long Hey RAIN/WH L35 76 D3
Long Hey Rd WKBY CH48 111 E4
Longland Rd WAL/NB CH45 51 H4
Long La ALL/GAR L19 119 G4
SFTN L29 21 H1
WARRN/WOL WA2 84 A4
WAV L15 72 D5
WLT/FAZ L9 41 E2
WLT/FAZ L9 41 F3
Long Meadow ECCL WA10 46 D3
HES CH60 148 D3
Longmeadow Rd PR/KW L34 44 B3
Longmoor Cl AIN/FAZ L10 32 B5
Longmoor Gv WLT/FAZ L9 31 G5
Longmoor La AIN/FAZ L10 32 D5
WLT/FAZ L9 32 B5
Longreach Rd DV/KA/FCH L14 74 B2
Longridge Av
GR/UP/WCH CH49 89 G2
RNFD/HAY WA11 48 D2
Longridge Wk ANF/KKDL L4 54 A2
Longshaw St WARRW/BUR WA5 83 F3
Long Spinney RUNC WA7 157 E1
Longstone Wk EHL/KEN L7 71 H5
Longton La RAIN/WH L35 60 D5
Longview Av RAIN/WH L35 77 G1
WAL/NB CH45 51 G5
Longview Crs HUY L36 75 H2
Longview Dr HUY L36 76 A2
Longview La HUY L36 58 D5

Longview Rd HUY L36 ... 75 H1
RAIN/WH L35 ... 60 C5
Longville St TOX L8 ... 94 A3
Longwood Rd WARRS WA4 ... 130 C5
Longworth Wy WLTN L25 ... 97 G5
Lonie Gv ECCL WA10 ... 61 E2
Lonsboro Rd WAL/EG CH44 ... 69 E2
Lonsdale Av ECCL WA10 ... 60 D3
WAL/NB CH45 ... 51 G4
Lonsdale Cl LITH L21 ... 30 A2
WARRW/BUR WA5 ... 81 G5
WDN WA8 ... 124 A3
Lonsdale Ms LITH L21 ... 30 A2
Lonsdale Rd FMBY L37 ... 16 D3
HLWD L26 ... 121 G5
LITH L21 ... 30 A2
Lonsdale Vls WAL/NB CH45 * ... 51 G4
Looe Cl WDN WA8 ... 124 C1
Looe Rd NG/CROX L11 ... 42 D2
Loomsway PEN/TH CH61 ... 112 A5
Loraine St EV L5 ... 54 B5
Lordens Cl DV/KA/FCH L14 ... 57 G5
Lordens Rd DV/KA/FCH L14 ... 57 G5
Lord Nelson St CLVPS L1 ... 7 G3
WARR WA1 ... 13 F5
Lords Av CL/PREN CH43 ... 67 G5
Lords La GOL/RIS/CUL WA3 ... 85 G1
Lord St ALL/GAR L19 ... 140 C2
BIRK CH41 ... 3 G3
CLVP L2 ... 6 D4
ECCL WA10 ... 11 F2
RUNC WA7 ... 8 C3
WARRS WA4 ... 12 E7
Loreburn Rd WAV L15 ... 96 A2
Lorenzo Dr NG/CROX L11 ... 55 H1
Loretto Dr GR/UP/WCH CH49 ... 90 A2
Loretto Rd WAL/EG CH44 ... 51 F5
Lorn Ct BIRK CH41 * ... 3 G4
Lorne Ct CL/PREN CH43 * ... 91 H3
Lorne Rd CL/PREN CH43 ... 91 G4
CSBY/WL L22 ... 29 E3
Lorne St EHL/KEN L7 ... 72 C2
Lorn St BIRK CH41 ... 3 G4
Lorton Av RNFD/HAY WA11 ... 37 E4
Lorton St TOX L8 ... 94 D1
Lostock Av WARRW/BUR WA5 ... 83 F5
Lothair Rd ANF/KKDL L4 ... 54 C3
Lothian St TOX L8 ... 94 C2
Lotus Gdns STHEL WA9 ... 63 G3
Loudon Gv TOX L8 ... 94 C2
Lough Gn BEB CH63 ... 138 A4
Loughlin Dr NWD/KWIPK L33 ... 26 A4
Loughrigg Av RNFD/HAY WA11 ... 37 F3
Louis Braille Cl NTHTN L30 ... 23 E5
Louis Pasteur Av NTHTN L30 ... 23 E5
Loushers La WARRS WA4 ... 130 B1
Lovage Cl WARRN/WOL WA2 ... 85 G3
Lovelace Rd ALL/GAR L19 ... 119 F4
Love La VAUX/LVPD L3 ... 70 C1
WAL/EG CH44 ... 68 D2
Lovel Rd SPK/HALE L24 ... 142 B4
Lovel Ter WDN WA8 ... 144 D1
Lovel Wy SPK/HALE L24 ... 142 B3
Lovely La WARRW/BUR WA5 ... 106 A2
Lovett Dr RAIN/WH L35 ... 60 A5
Lowbridge Ct ALL/GAR L19 ... 140 D1
Lowden Av LITH L21 ... 30 A2
Lowe Av WARRS WA4 ... 107 H4
Lowell St ANF/KKDL L4 ... 54 B1
Lower Appleton Rd WDN WA8 ... 15 F1
Lower Bank Vw BTL L20 ... 53 F1
Lower Breck Rd NPK/KEN L6 ... 55 E4
Lower Castle St CLVP L2 ... 6 C4
Lower Church St WDN WA8 ... 146 A1
Lower Cl HLWD L26 ... 122 A3
Lower Farm Rd WLTN L25 ... 97 F1
Lower Flaybrick Rd
CL/PREN CH43 ... 68 A5
Lower Gn GR/UP/WCH CH49 ... 90 A5
Lower Hey CSBY/BLUN L23 ... 22 A4
Lower House La NG/CROX L11 ... 42 A4
WDN WA8 ... 14 B3
Lower La WLT/FAZ L9 ... 32 B5
Lower Mersey Vw BTL L20 ... 53 F1
Lower Milk St VAUX/LVPD L3 ... 6 D2
Lower Rd HLWD L26 ... 122 B3
PS/BROM CH62 ... 116 B5
Lowerson Crs NG/CROX L11 ... 55 G2
Lowerson Rd NG/CROX L11 ... 55 G2
Lower Thingwall La
PEN/TH CH61 ... 113 G5
Lower Wash La WARRS WA4 ... 107 G5
Lowes Gn FMBY L37 ... 17 G3
Lowestoft Dr ALL/GAR L19 ... 119 F5
Lowe St ECCL WA10 ... 10 E4
Lowe St South ECCL WA10 ... 11 F5
Loweswater Cl
WARRN/WOL WA2 ... 83 H2
Loweswater Crs
RNFD/HAY WA11 ... 49 G1
Loweswater Wy
NWD/KWIPK L33 ... 25 G5
Lowfield La STHEL WA9 ... 61 H5
Lowfield Rd DV/KA/FCH L14 ... 73 G2
Lowlands Rd RUNC WA7 ... 8 C4
Lowndes Rd NPK/KEN L6 ... 55 F4
Lowry Bank WAL/EG CH44 ... 69 G2
Lowry Cl NWD/KWIPK L33 ... 25 H3
WARRW/BUR WA5 ... 105 H2
Lowther Av AIN/FAZ L10 ... 32 A2
MGHL L31 ... 19 E4
Lowther Crs ECCL WA10 ... 60 D2
Lowther Dr RAIN/WH L35 ... 77 H2
Lowther St TOX L8 ... 94 C1
Lowwood Gv BIRK CH41 ... 2 E6
Low Wood Gv PEN/TH CH61 ... 135 G2
Lowwood Rd BIRK CH41 ... 2 E6
Low Wood St NPK/KEN L6 ... 71 G3
Loxdale Cl TOX L8 ... 94 C5
Loxley Cl WARRW/BUR WA5 ... 82 A5
Loyola Hey RAIN/WH L35 ... 78 C5
Lucania St ALL/GAR L19 ... 140 C2
Lucan Rd AIG/SPK L17 ... 118 C1
Lucerne Rd WAL/EG CH44 ... 69 F3
Lucerne St AIG/SPK L17 ... 95 E5
Lucius Cl WLT/FAZ L9 ... 31 E5
Lucknow St AIG/SPK L17 * ... 95 E4
Ludlow Cl WARR WA1 ... 85 F4
Ludlow Crs RUNC WA7 ... 155 F1
Ludlow Dr WKBY CH48 ... 110 B2
Ludlow Gv PS/BROM CH62 ... 138 D5
Ludlow St ANF/KKDL L4 ... 54 B1
Ludwig Rd ANF/KKDL L4 ... 54 D5
Lugard Rd AIG/SPK L17 ... 118 C1
Lugsdale Rd WDN WA8 ... 14 D5
WDN WA8 ... 15 F4
Lugsmore La ECCL WA10 ... 61 E1
Luke St TOX L8 ... 94 B2
WAL/EG CH44 ... 69 G3
Lulworth Av CSBY/WL L22 ... 28 D3
Lulworth Rd WLTN L25 ... 98 A3
Lumb Brook Ms WARRS WA4 ... 130 C2
Lumb Brook Rd WARRS WA4 ... 130 C3
WARRS WA4 ... 130 D5
Lumley Rd WAL/EG CH44 ... 69 F2
Lumley St ALL/GAR L19 ... 119 F5
Lunar Dr NTHTN L30 ... 23 E4
Lunar Rd WLT/FAZ L9 ... 40 D1
Lune Av MGHL L31 ... 19 E4
Lunesdale Av WLT/FAZ L9 ... 31 G5
Lune St CSBY/BLUN L23 ... 21 F5
Lune Wy WDN WA8 ... 124 A2
Lunsford Rd DV/KA/FCH L14 ... 74 B1
Lunt Av NTHTN L30 ... 31 F2
RAIN/WH L35 ... 77 E2
Lunt Rd BTL L20 ... 39 G1
SFTN L29 ... 22 D2
Lunts Heath Rd WDN WA8 ... 102 A3
Lupton Dr CSBY/BLUN L23 ... 21 H5
Luscombe Cl HLWD L26 ... 122 A3
Lusitania Rd ANF/KKDL L4 ... 40 C5
Luther Gv STHEL WA9 ... 49 H5
Luton Gv ANF/KKDL L4 ... 54 B2
Luton St EV L5 ... 53 G4
WDN WA8 * ... 14 D6
Lutyens Cl ANF/KKDL L4 ... 54 B3
Luxmore Rd ANF/KKDL L4 ... 54 B1
Lycett Rd ANF/KKDL L4 ... 55 E3
WAL/EG CH44 ... 51 E5
Lychgate WARRS WA4 ... 129 F4
Lycroft Cl RUNC WA7 ... 155 F3
Lydbrook Cl RF/TRAN CH42 ... 92 D5
Lydbury Cl WARRW/BUR WA5 ... 82 D3
Lydbury Crs KKBY L32 ... 34 A4
Lydd Cl SPK/HALE L24 ... 141 H2
Lydford Rd WD/CROXPK L12 ... 56 B2
Lydia Ann St CLVPS L1 ... 7 F6
Lydiate La CSBY/BLUN L23 ... 22 A3
RUNC WA7 ... 154 C2
WLTN L25 ... 121 F1
Lydiate Pk CSBY/BLUN L23 ... 22 A3
Lydiate Rd BTL L20 ... 39 G2
The Lydiate HES CH60 ... 148 D2
Lydieth Lea NTHLY L27 ... 98 C2
Lydney Rd HUY L36 ... 74 D1
Lydstep Ct WARRW/BUR WA5 * ... 83 E3
Lyelake Cl KKBY L32 ... 34 A3
Lyelake Rd KKBY L32 ... 34 A3
Lyle St EV L5 ... 53 H5
Lyme Cl HUY L36 ... 59 E4
Lyme Cross Rd HUY L36 ... 58 D4
Lyme Gv HUY L36 ... 58 D5
Lymington Gv NTHTN L30 ... 31 E1
Lymington Rd WAL/EG CH44 ... 68 B1
Lymm Rd CL/PREN CH43 ... 90 C1
WARRS WA4 ... 109 F5
Lynas Gdns ALL/GAR L19 ... 119 F3
Lynas St BIRK CH41 ... 2 D1
Lyncot Rd WLT/FAZ L9 ... 31 G4
Lyncroft Rd WAL/EG CH44 ... 69 E3
Lyndale RUNC WA7 ... 155 G1
Lyndale Av PS/BROM CH62 ... 153 E5
WARRN/WOL WA2 ... 84 B5
Lyndene Rd WLTN L25 ... 97 G1
Lyndhurst Av CALD/MH L18 ... 95 H5
PEN/TH CH61 ... 135 E3
Lyndhurst Cl PEN/TH CH61 ... 135 E1
Lyndhurst Rd CALD/MH L18 ... 95 H4
CSBY/BLUN L23 ... 21 H5
HOY CH47 ... 65 E4
PEN/TH CH61 ... 134 A1
WAL/NB CH45 ... 51 F4
Lyndhurst Wy HUY L36 ... 75 G3
Lyndon Dr CALD/MH L18 ... 96 B4
Lyndon Gv RUNC WA7 ... 155 F1
Lyndor Cl WLTN L25 ... 120 D2
Lyndor Rd WLTN L25 ... 120 D2
Lyneham RAIN/WH L35 ... 77 F3
Lynham Av
WARRW/BUR WA5 * ... 105 F3
Lynholme Rd ANF/KKDL L4 ... 54 D3
Lynmouth Rd AIG/SPK L17 ... 118 C3
Lynnbank CL/PREN CH43 ... 91 H4
Lynnbank Rd CALD/MH L18 ... 96 D3
Lynn Cl ECCL WA10 ... 47 E3
RUNC WA7 ... 155 G2
Lynscott Pl CHLDW L16 ... 73 H5
Lynsted Rd DV/KA/FCH L14 ... 74 B2
Lynton Cl ALL/GAR L19 ... 119 F3
HES CH60 ... 149 F3
WARRW/BUR WA5 ... 104 C4
Lynton Crs WDN WA8 ... 124 C1
Lynton Dr BEB CH63 ... 138 A3
Lynton Gn WLTN L25 ... 97 F4
Lynton Gv STHEL WA9 ... 62 C5
Lynton Rd HUY L36 ... 76 B2
WAL/NB CH45 ... 51 E4
Lynton Wy ECCL WA10 ... 46 D1
Lynwood Av WAL/EG CH44 ... 68 C2
WARRS WA4 ... 130 A4
Lynwood Dr PEN/TH CH61 ... 112 C5
Lynwood Gdns WLT/FAZ L9 ... 40 B2
Lynwood Rd WLT/FAZ L9 ... 40 B2
The Lynxway WD/CROXPK L12 ... 56 D5
Lyon Cl ECCL WA10 ... 10 E5
Lyon Rd ANF/KKDL L4 ... 54 D4
Lyons Cl MOR/LEA CH46 ... 66 C4
Lyon's La WARRS WA4 ... 130 B5
Lyons Pl WLTN L25 ... 121 F3
Lyons Rd MOR/LEA CH46 ... 66 C4
WARRW/BUR WA5 ... 104 D4
Lyon St ALL/GAR L19 ... 140 C2
ECCL WA10 ... 10 D5
WARRS WA4 ... 107 H5
Lyra Rd CSBY/WL L22 ... 29 E3
Lyster Rd BTL L20 ... 4 B4
Lytham Cl AIN/FAZ L10 ... 32 C3
WARRW/BUR WA5 ... 105 E5
Lytham Ct KKBY L32 ... 25 F5
Lytham Rd WDN WA8 ... 125 F1
Lytham Wy WD/CROXPK L12 ... 57 E4
Lythgoes La WARRN/WOL WA2 ... 12 D2
Lytles Cl FMBY L37 ... 17 F4
Lyttelton Rd AIG/SPK L17 ... 118 C1
Lytton Av RF/TRAN CH42 ... 115 H2
Lytton Gv LITH L21 ... 39 E1
Lytton St NPK/KEN L6 ... 71 F2

M

Mab La WD/CROXPK L12 ... 57 F2
Macalpine Cl GR/UP/WCH CH49 ... 90 A2
Macarthur Rd
WARRW/BUR WA5 * ... 105 F2
Macbeth St BTL L20 ... 53 G1
Macdermott Rd WDN WA8 ... 145 H1
Macdona Dr WKBY CH48 ... 110 B3
Macdonald Av
RNFD/HAY WA11 * ... 49 E2
Macdonald Dr
GR/UP/WCH CH49 ... 89 F5
Macdonald Rd
MOR/LEA CH46 ... 66 A5
Macdonald St WAV L15 ... 72 C5
Mace Rd NG/CROX L11 ... 42 C4
Macfarren St CLB/OSW/ST L13 ... 73 E2
Mackenzie Rd MOR/LEA CH46 ... 67 F2
Mackenzie St NPK/KEN L6 ... 54 C5
Mackets Cl WLTN L25 ... 121 E2
Macket's La WLTN L25 ... 121 E2
Mack Gv NTHTN L30 ... 30 C2
Macqueen St CLB/OSW/ST L13 ... 73 E3
Maddock Rd WAL/EG CH44 ... 52 B5
Maddocks St CLB/OSW/ST L13 ... 73 E3
Maddock St BIRK CH41 ... 2 C1
Maddrell St VAUX/LVPD L3 ... 70 B1
Madelaine St TOX L8 ... 94 C2
Madeley Cl WKBY CH48 ... 110 B2
Madeley Dr WKBY CH48 ... 110 B2
Madeley St NPK/KEN L6 ... 72 A1
Madeline McKenna Ct
WDN WA8 * ... 101 E5
Madiera Dr WLTN L25 ... 97 H2
Madryn Av NWD/KWIPK L33 ... 34 B2
Madryn St TOX L8 ... 94 C3
Maelor Cl BEB CH63 ... 152 B3
Mafeking Cl WAV L15 ... 72 D5
Magazine Av WAL/NB CH45 ... 51 H3
Magazine Brow WAL/NB CH45 ... 52 A3
Magazine La PS/BROM CH62 ... 139 E3
WAL/NB CH45 ... 51 H3
Magazine Rd PS/BROM CH62 ... 138 D3
Magazines Prom WAL/NB CH45 ... 52 A3
Magazine Wk
PS/BROM CH62 * ... 138 D3
Magdala St TOX L8 ... 95 E1
Magdalene Sq NTHTN L30 * ... 23 E5
Maghull La MGHL L31 ... 19 H5
Maghull St CLVPS L1 ... 6 D7
Magnolia Cl HLWD L26 ... 121 F1
RNFD/HAY WA11 ... 49 F2
WARR WA1 ... 109 E1
Magnolia Dr RUNC WA7 ... 156 B5
Magnolia Wk
GR/UP/WCH CH49 ... 112 A1
Magnus Cl CLB/OSW/ST L13 ... 55 H5
Maguire Av BTL L20 ... 5 K3
Mahon Av BTL L20 ... 39 H1
Mahon Ct TOX L8 * ... 94 B1
Maiden La CLB/OSW/ST L13 ... 55 F3
Maidford Rd DV/KA/FCH L14 ... 57 F5
Maidstone Cl WLTN L25 ... 121 E3
Maidstone Dr WD/CROXPK L12 ... 57 F5
Main Av ECCL WA10 ... 61 E2
Main Cl RNFD/HAY WA11 ... 49 G1
Main Dr RAIN/WH L35 ... 77 E4
Main Front RAIN/WH L35 ... 77 E4
Main Hall BIRK CH41 * ... 3 F5
Main Rd BEB CH63 ... 138 B2
Mainside Rd KKBY L32 ... 34 A3
Main St RUNC WA7 ... 156 B1
Maintree Crs SPK/HALE L24 ... 143 E2
Mainwaring Rd
PS/BROM CH62 ... 152 D1
WAL/EG CH44 ... 69 F2
Mairesfield Av WARRS WA4 ... 131 F1
Maitland Cl TOX L8 ... 94 D1
Maitland Rd WAL/NB CH45 ... 52 A2
Maitland St TOX L8 * ... 94 D1
Major Cross St WDN WA8 ... 14 E5
Major St EV L5 ... 53 H4
Makin St ANF/KKDL L4 ... 40 B5
Malcolm Av WARRN/WOL WA2 ... 84 B4
Malcolm Crs BEB CH63 ... 152 C3
Malcolm Gv BTL L20 ... 53 H1
Malcolm Pl WAV L15 ... 72 D4
Malcolm St RUNC WA7 ... 9 G5
Malden Rd NPK/KEN L6 ... 72 A2
Maldon Cl HLWD L26 ... 121 H5
Maldwyn Rd WAL/EG CH44 ... 51 H5
Maley Cl TOX L8 ... 94 C4
Malham Cl WARRW/BUR WA5 ... 81 G5
Malhamdale Av RAIN/WH L35 ... 78 B3
Malin Cl SPK/HALE L24 ... 143 H4
Maliston Rd
WARRW/BUR WA5 ... 105 F3
Mallaby St BIRK CH41 ... 68 C5
Mallard Cl HLWD L26 ... 121 G2
RUNC WA7 ... 156 B4
WARRN/WOL WA2 ... 84 B2
WD/CROXPK L12 ... 43 F4
Mallard Gdns STHEL WA9 ... 61 G4
Mallard Wy MOR/LEA CH46 ... 66 A4
RNFD/HAY WA11 ... 48 B1
Malleson Rd CLB/OSW/ST L13 ... 55 G3
Mallins Cl TOX L8 ... 94 C4
Mallory Av MGHL L31 ... 18 B2
Mallory Gv RNFD/HAY WA11 ... 48 D1
Mallory Rd RF/TRAN CH42 ... 115 F1
Mallowdale Cl PS/BROM CH62 ... 153 E4
Mallow Rd NPK/KEN L6 ... 72 A2
Mallow Wy HUY L36 ... 75 H5
The Mall EV L5 * ... 54 C5
Malmesbury Cl
GR/UP/WCH CH49 ... 89 E4
Malmesbury Rd NG/CROX L11 ... 41 G5
Malpas Av CL/PREN CH43 ... 114 C1
Malpas Dr BEB CH63 ... 115 G4
WARRW/BUR WA5 ... 105 G4
Malpas Gv WAL/NB CH45 ... 51 G4
Malpas Rd NG/CROX L11 ... 42 D2
RUNC WA7 ... 155 F2
WAL/NB CH45 ... 51 F4
Malpas Wy
WARRW/BUR WA5 * ... 105 G4
Malta Cl HUY L36 ... 75 F2
Malta St TOX L8 ... 94 B3
Malta Wk TOX L8 ... 94 B3
Malt House Ct ECCL WA10 ... 47 E1
Malton Cl WDN WA8 ... 101 E3
Malton Rd WLTN L25 ... 121 E2
Malt St EHL/KEN L7 ... 71 H5
Malvern Av DV/KA/FCH L14 ... 74 B3
Malvern Cl KKBY L32 ... 25 F5
WARRW/BUR WA5 ... 82 A5
Malvern Crs DV/KA/FCH L14 ... 74 B3
Malvern Gv AIN/FAZ L10 ... 31 H2
RF/TRAN CH42 ... 115 F1
Malvern Rd BTL L20 ... 39 G2
NPK/KEN L6 ... 72 A2
STHEL WA9 ... 49 F4
WAL/NB CH45 ... 50 D5
The Malverns CL/PREN CH43 * ... 91 G5
Malwood St TOX L8 ... 94 B5
Manchester Rd
GOL/RIS/CUL WA3 ... 109 G1
PR/KW L34 ... 59 G4
WARR WA1 ... 13 G3
WARR WA1 ... 108 A1
WARR WA1 ... 108 C1
WARR WA1 ... 109 E1
WARR WA1 * ... 109 F1
Mancroft Cl WARR WA1 ... 109 E1
Mandarin Ct WARR WA1 ... 106 C5
Manderston Dr
WD/CROXPK L12 ... 56 D3
Mandeville St ANF/KKDL L4 ... 40 B5
Manesty's La CLVPS L1 ... 6 E5
Manhattan Gdns
WARRW/BUR WA5 ... 105 E1
Manica Crs AIN/FAZ L10 ... 41 H1
Manion Av MGHL L31 ... 18 B1
Manion Cl MGHL L31 ... 18 B1
Manley Cl CL/PREN CH43 ... 91 F5
Manley Gdns
WARRW/BUR WA5 ... 106 B3
Manley Pl STHEL WA9 ... 61 G3
Manley Rd CSBY/WL L22 ... 28 D2
HUY L36 ... 76 A5
Mannering Rd AIG/SPK L17 ... 94 D4
Manners La HES CH60 ... 148 C3
Manningham Rd ANF/KKDL L4 ... 54 D4
Manning St ECCL WA10 ... 10 E6
Mannington Cl HOY CH47 ... 65 E5
Mann Island VAUX/LVPD L3 ... 6 B5
Mann St TOX L8 ... 94 A2
Manor Av CSBY/BLUN L23 ... 21 E4
RAIN/WH L35 ... 78 A3
Manorbier Crs WLT/FAZ L9 ... 40 C4
Manor Cl BTL L20 ... 5 K6
NSTN CH64 ... 158 B3
WARR WA1 ... 108 D1
Manor Crs WLTN L25 ... 120 D2
Manor Dr CSBY/BLUN L23 ... 21 E4
GR/UP/WCH CH49 ... 89 H1
NTHTN L30 ... 31 G1
Manor Farm Rd HUY L36 ... 75 H4
Manor Fell RUNC WA7 ... 156 D2
Manor Gv KKBY L32 ... 33 E2
Manor Hl CL/PREN CH43 ... 91 G2
Manor House Cl MGHL L31 ... 18 C5
RNFD/HAY WA11 ... 37 E2
Manorial Rd NSTN CH64 ... 158 B2
Manorial Rd South NSTN CH64 ... 158 B2
Manor La RF/TRAN CH42 ... 116 A1
WAL/NB CH45 ... 52 A5
Manor Ldg FMBY L37 ... 16 D2
Manor Ms WAL/NB CH45 * ... 52 A5
Manor Park Cl PEN/TH CH61 ... 113 E5
Manor Pl PS/BROM CH62 ... 138 D1
Manor Rd BEB CH63 ... 136 B5
CSBY/BLUN L23 ... 20 D3
HOY CH47 ... 64 C5
PEN/TH CH61 ... 112 B5
PS/BROM CH62 ... 153 E3
RUNC WA7 ... 146 D4
WAL/EG CH44 ... 51 H5
WDN WA8 ... 123 H2
WLTN L25 ... 120 D2
Manorside Cl
GR/UP/WCH CH49 ... 89 H2
Manor St STHEL WA9 ... 48 C5
The Manor WARR WA1 ... 109 F1
Manor Vw WD/CROXPK L12 ... 57 F1
Manor Wy WLTN L25 ... 120 D2
Manorwood Dr RAIN/WH L35 ... 77 E3
Mansell Cl WDN WA8 ... 102 C3
Mansell Dr HLWD L26 ... 121 G5
Mansell Rd NPK/KEN L6 ... 71 H2
Mansfield St VAUX/LVPD L3 ... 7 G1
Mansion Dr NG/CROX L11 ... 42 B3
Manston Rd
WARRW/BUR WA5 ... 104 D5
Manton Rd NPK/KEN L6 ... 72 A2
Manuel Perez Rd
WARRW/BUR WA5 ... 105 F2
Manvers Rd CHLDW L16 ... 74 A4
Manville Rd WAL/NB CH45 ... 51 H3
Manville St STHEL WA9 ... 62 C1
Manx Rd WARRS WA4 ... 106 D5
Maple Av RUNC WA7 ... 155 G1
WDN WA8 * ... 15 F1
Maple Cl FMBY L37 ... 16 B5
LITH L21 ... 39 E1
RAIN/WH L35 ... 77 E2
WD/CROXPK L12 ... 42 D4
Maple Crs HUY L36 ... 75 F3
WARRW/BUR WA5 ... 104 D4
Mapledale Rd
CALD/MH L18 ... 96 A3
Maple Gv ECCL WA10 ... 47 E4
PS/BROM CH62 ... 152 C1
RAIN/WH L35 ... 60 A5
TOX L8 ... 95 E2
WARRS WA4 ... 107 F5
Maple Rd WARR WA1 ... 109 E1
Maple St BIRK CH41 ... 2 D7
Mapleton Cl CL/PREN CH43 ... 114 A2
Maple Tree Gv HES CH60 ... 135 G5
Maplewood KKBY L32 ... 34 A4
Maplewood Cl NTHLY L27 ... 98 C3
WDN WA8 ... 123 H4
Maplewood Gv CL/PREN CH43 ... 68 A5
Mapplewell Crs
WARRW/BUR WA5 ... 105 E2
Maranatha Bungalows
HES CH60 * ... 135 E5
Marathon Cl NPK/KEN L6 ... 71 F1
Marble Cl BTL L20 ... 4 E7
Marbury Rd KKBY L32 ... 33 F2
Marbury St WARRS WA4 ... 13 F7
Marc Av MGHL L31 ... 25 E5
Marcham Wy NG/CROX L11 ... 56 B1
Marchant Cl NTHTN L30 ... 31 F4
Marchfield Rd WLT/FAZ L9 ... 40 B2
March Rd NPK/KEN L6 ... 55 F5
Marchwood Wy WLTN L25 ... 97 G1
Marcien Wy WDN WA8 ... 101 H5
Marcot Rd NPK/KEN L6 ... 72 B1
Marcross Cl WARRW/BUR WA5 ... 83 E4
Marcus St BIRK CH41 ... 2 E1
Mardale Av RNFD/HAY WA11 ... 37 F4
WARRN/WOL WA2 ... 84 A2
Mardale Cl NTHLY L27 ... 99 E5
Mardale Lawn NTHLY L27 ... 99 E5
Mardale Rd HUY L36 ... 58 A5
Mareth Cl CALD/MH L18 ... 119 E1
Marford Rd WD/CROXPK L12 ... 56 B3
Marfords Av BEB CH63 ... 152 C2
Margaret Av BTL L20 ... 30 B5
STHEL WA9 ... 62 C3
WARR WA1 ... 108 B1
Margaret Ct WDN WA8 * ... 14 E6
Margaret Rd ANF/KKDL L4 ... 5 K7
CSBY/BLUN L23 ... 20 B4
Margaret St NPK/KEN L6 ... 71 G1
STHEL WA9 * ... 80 A2
Margery Rd ECCL WA10 ... 61 E1
Marian Cl RAIN/WH L35 ... 78 A3
The Marian Cl NTHTN L30 ... 22 D5
Marian Dr MOR/LEA CH46 ... 66 C5
RAIN/WH L35 ... 77 H3
The Marian Sq NTHTN L30 ... 22 D5
The Marian Wy NTHTN L30 ... 30 D1
Maria Rd WLT/FAZ L9 ... 40 B4
Marie Curie Av NTHTN L30 ... 23 E5
Marie Dr WARRS WA4 ... 131 H1
Marigold Pl WARRW/BUR WA5 ... 105 H5
Marigold Wy STHEL WA9 ... 63 G3
Marina Av LITH L21 ... 30 A4
STHEL WA9 ... 62 C3
WARRW/BUR WA5 ... 105 F4
Marina Crs HUY L36 ... 75 F4
NTHTN L30 ... 31 F3
Marina Dr WARRN/WOL WA2 ... 84 A4
Marina Gv RUNC WA7 ... 9 G5
Marina La RUNC WA7 ... 157 G2
Marina Rd FMBY L37 ... 17 E5
The Marina CSBY/WL L22 * ... 28 D2
Marina Village RUNC WA7 ... 157 G2
Marine Crs CSBY/WL L22 ... 29 E3
Marine Dr HES CH60 ... 148 B2
Marine House VAUX/LVPD L3 * ... 93 H2
Marine Pk WKBY CH48 ... 87 F4
Marine Prom WAL/NB CH45 ... 51 H1
Mariner Cl RUNC WA7 ... 157 F3
Marine Rd HOY CH47 ... 87 E1
Mariners Rd CSBY/BLUN L23 ... 28 C2
WAL/NB CH45 ... 52 A3
Mariners Whf VAUX/LVPD L3 ... 93 G2
Marine Ter CSBY/WL L22 ... 29 E4
Marion Dr RUNC WA7 ... 154 D3
Marion Gv CALD/MH L18 ... 119 G1
Marion Rd BTL L20 ... 39 H1
Marion St BIRK CH41 ... 3 F4
Maritime Ct NTHTN L30 ... 23 E4
Maritime Enterprise Pk
BTL L20 * ... 4 C3
Maritime Pk BIRK CH41 * ... 2 C6
Maritime Pl VAUX/LVPD L3 * ... 7 H1
Maritime Vw RF/TRAN CH42 ... 92 B5
Mariton Cl CALD/MH L18 ... 119 H1
Marius Cl ANF/KKDL L4 ... 54 B2
Market Ga WARR WA1 ... 12 D5
Market Pl BIRK CH41 ... 3 G5
PR/KW L34 ... 59 H4
Market Sq CLVPS L1 * ... 7 F4
Market St BIRK CH41 ... 3 G4
ECCL WA10 ... 11 G6
HOY CH47 ... 87 F1
WDN WA8 ... 14 D5
Market Wy CLVPS L1 * ... 7 F4
Markfield Crs RNFD/HAY WA11 ... 48 C2
WLTN L25 ... 121 F2
Markfield Rd BTL L20 ... 39 F2
Markham Gv CL/PREN CH43 ... 68 B5
Mark Rake PS/BROM CH62 ... 138 D5
Mark St EV L5 ... 54 A4
Marksway PEN/TH CH61 ... 135 E2
Marlborough Av MGHL L31 ... 18 D3
NTHTN L30 ... 31 F2
Marlborough Crs WARRS WA4 ... 130 D1
WDN WA8 ... 102 A3
Marlborough Gv
CL/PREN CH43 ... 91 H4
Marlborough Pl VAUX/LVPD L3 * ... 6 D1
Marlborough Rd
CLB/OSW/ST L13 ... 55 F4
CSBY/BLUN L23 ... 29 E1
CSBY/WL L22 ... 29 F4
PR/KW L34 ... 60 A3
Marlborough St
VAUX/LVPD L3 ... 6 D1
Marlbrook Rd WLTN L25 ... 97 H2
Marlcroft Dr AIG/SPK L17 ... 118 C4
Marldon Av CSBY/BLUN L23 ... 29 F2
Marldon Rd WD/CROXPK L12 ... 56 B2
Marled Hey STBRV L28 ... 57 G2
Marley Cl RAIN/WH L35 ... 78 C4
Marlfield La PEN/TH CH61 ... 135 E2
Marlfield Rd WARRS WA4 ... 131 E1
WD/CROXPK L12 ... 56 B4
Marline Av BEB CH63 ... 152 C3
Marling Pk WDN WA8 ... 123 H2
Marlowe Cl ALL/GAR L19 ... 140 C1
WDN WA8 ... 14 A2
Marlowe Dr WD/CROXPK L12 ... 56 A4

Marlowe Rd NSTN CH64 158 D2
WAL/EG CH44 68 C1
Marl Rd NTHTN L30 31 G1
NWD/KWIPK L33 34 D1
Marlsford St NPK/KEN L6 72 A2
Marlston Av PEN/TH CH61 112 D5
Marlston Pl RUNC WA7 155 F3
Marlwood Av WAL/NB CH45 51 E5
Marmaduke St EHL/KEN L7 71 H4
Marmion Av BTL L20 30 D5
Marmion Rd AIG/SPK L17 94 D4
HOY CH47 87 F1
Marmonde St ANF/KKDL L4 54 A2
Marnwood Rd KKBY L32 33 G3
Marple Cl CL/PREN CH43 91 E5
Marquis St BIRK CH41 92 C4
PS/BROM CH62 116 B4
VAUX/LVPD L3 7 H3
Marram Cl MOR/LEA CH46 67 E4
Marron Av WARRN/WOL WA2 83 H3
Marsden Av ECCL WA10 10 A3
WARRS WA4 108 A4
Marsden Cl WAL/EG CH44 52 B5
Marsden Ct WDN WA8 101 G4
Marsden Rd HLWD L26 121 H5
Marsden St NPK/KEN L6 71 G2
Marsden Wy NPK/KEN L6 * 71 G2
Marshall Av STHEL WA9 * 62 C2
WARRW/BUR WA5 83 F3
Marshall Pl VAUX/LVPD L3 * 70 C1
Marshall Rd WARR WA1 108 D1
Marshallsay FMBY L37 17 F4
Marshall's Cl MGHL L31 18 C2
Marshalls Cross Rd STHEL WA9 62 B3
Marshall St BIRK CH41 2 C1
Marsham Cl
GR/UP/WCH CH49 * 90 A1
Marsham Rd WLTN L25 98 A3
Marsh Av BTL L20 40 A1
Marsh Brows FMBY L37 16 D4
Marshfield Cl HUY L36 75 H2
Marshfield Ct MOR/LEA CH46 66 C2
Marshfield Rd NG/CROX L11 56 B1
Marshgate WDN WA8 123 H5
Marsh Hall Rd WDN WA8 102 B4
Marsh House La
WARRN/WOL WA2 107 E1
Marshlands Rd NSTN CH64 158 D5
WAL/NB CH45 51 E4
Marsh La BEB CH63 115 E4
BTL L20 4 C2
RUNC WA7 147 F3
WARRW/BUR WA5 127 E1
Marshside Cl TOX L8 94 B3
Marsh St BTL L20 53 H1
STHEL WA9 48 C3
WARR WA1 13 J1
WDN WA8 125 E5
Marsland Gv STHEL WA9 63 E2
Marson St WARRN/WOL WA2 12 C3
Marston Cl CL/PREN CH43 114 B1
Marsworth Dr NPK/KEN L6 71 F1
Marten Av BEB CH63 152 C2
Martensen St EHL/KEN L7 71 H4
Martham Cl WARRS WA4 108 A5
Martham Gdns STHEL WA9 61 G4
Martin Av ECCL WA10 47 H1
WARRN/WOL WA2 84 B4
Martin Cl CALD/MH L18 119 E2
PEN/TH CH61 112 A5
RAIN/WH L35 77 G1
RUNC WA7 156 C2
Martindale Gv RUNC WA7 155 H4
Martindale Rd CHLDW L16 96 D3
PS/BROM CH62 139 E5
RNFD/HAY WA11 37 F2
Martine Cl MGHL L31 25 E5
Martin Gv RAIN/WH L35 60 A5
Martinhall Rd WLT/FAZ L9 41 H3
Martin Rd CALD/MH L18 119 E2
Martin's La WAL/EG CH44 69 E1
Martland Av AIN/FAZ L10 32 B1
Martland Rd WLTN L25 98 A4
Martlesham Crs
GR/UP/WCH CH49 88 D5
Martlett Rd WD/CROXPK L12 56 D5
Martock RAIN/WH L35 77 F3
Marton Cl SPK/HALE L24 142 B4
Marton Gn SPK/HALE L24 * 142 B4
Marton Rd HUY L36 58 C4
Marvin St EHL/KEN L7 71 G2
NPK/KEN L6 71 G2
Marybone VAUX/LVPD L3 6 E2
Maryhill Rd RUNC WA7 155 E1
Maryland Cl
WARRW/BUR WA5 105 G1
Maryland La MOR/LEA CH46 66 B4
Maryland St CLVPS L1 7 H6
Marylebone Av STHEL WA9 61 H4
Maryport Cl EV L5 54 B4
Mary Rd BTL L20 39 H1
Mary Stockton Ct LITH L21 * 39 E1
Mary St STHEL WA9 80 A2
WDN WA8 15 K5
Maryton Gra CALD/MH L18 119 H1
Maryville Rd PR/KW L34 60 A4
Marywell Cl STHEL WA9 62 D3
Masefield Av WDN WA8 14 B4
Masefield Cl PS/BROM CH62 116 A4
Masefield Crs NTHTN L30 30 C4
Masefield Gv CHLDW L16 74 B5
ECCL WA10 10 A1
Masefield Pl NTHTN L30 30 D4
Masefield Rd CSBY/BLUN L23 22 D3
Maskell Rd CLB/OSW/ST L13 72 D2
Mason Av WARR WA1 84 C5
WDN WA8 102 A4
Mason St CSBY/WL L22 29 E3
EHL/KEN L7 71 G4
RUNC WA7 9 H3
WAL/NB CH45 51 H2
WARR WA1 13 G5
WLTN L25 120 C1
Massey Av WARRW/BUR WA5 83 F3
Masseyfield Rd RUNC WA7 156 C4
Massey Pk WAL/NB CH45 51 G5
Massey St BIRK CH41 2 D1
STHEL WA9 62 C2
Masters Wy ALL/GAR L19 140 D2
Matchwood Cl ALL/GAR L19 140 D1
Mather Av CALD/MH L18 96 B4
STHEL WA9 49 E4
Mather Rd CL/PREN CH43 91 H3
Mathers Cl WARRN/WOL WA2 85 E1
Mathew St CLVP L2 6 D4
Mathieson Rd WDN WA8 145 G1
Matlock Av WLT/FAZ L9 40 C1
Matlock Cl WARRW/BUR WA5 82 A4
Matthew Cl WAL/EG CH44 69 G3
Matthews St WARR WA1 13 H1
Matthew St WAL/EG CH44 69 G3
Maud St TOX L8 94 C2
Maunders Ct CSBY/BLUN L23 21 G4
Mauretania Rd ANF/KKDL L4 40 C5
Mavis Dr GR/UP/WCH CH49 90 A5
Mawdsley Av WARR WA1 109 E1
Mawdsley Cl FMBY L37 17 G3
Mawson Cl WARRW/BUR WA5 82 D5
Max Rd DV/KA/FCH L14 57 F5
Maxton Rd NPK/KEN L6 72 A2
Maxwell Cl GR/UP/WCH CH49 90 A2
Maxwell Pl CLB/OSW/ST L13 55 H4
Maxwell Rd CLB/OSW/ST L13 55 H4
Maxwell St ECCL WA10 10 D6
May Av WAL/EG CH44 69 F3
Maybank Gv AIG/SPK L17 118 D2
Maybank Rd RF/TRAN CH42 92 B4
Mayberry Gv WARRN/WOL WA2 85 E4
Maybury Wy AIG/SPK L17 118 A1
May Cl LITH L21 39 F1
Mayer Av BEB CH63 137 H2
Mayew Rd PEN/TH CH61 112 D5
Mayfair Av CSBY/BLUN L23 21 F4
DV/KA/FCH L14 74 B2
Mayfair Cl NPK/KEN L6 71 H1
WARRW/BUR WA5 104 B1
Mayfair Gv WDN WA8 124 B2
Mayfayre Av MGHL L31 18 B1
Mayfield ANF/KKDL L4 54 A2
Mayfield Av FMBY L37 16 B5
STHEL WA9 61 G2
WDN WA8 123 H2
Mayfield Cl WD/CROXPK L12 56 C4
Mayfield Ct FMBY L37 16 D1
Mayfield Dr PS/BROM CH62 153 H3
Mayfield Gdns ALL/GAR L19 119 E4
NSTN CH64 158 D1
Mayfield Rd ALL/GAR L19 119 E4
BEB CH63 138 A3
WAL/NB CH45 51 E5
WARRS WA4 108 B5
Mayfields North
PS/BROM CH62 116 B4
Mayfields South
PS/BROM CH62 116 B4
Mayflower Av SPK/HALE L24 120 C5
May Pl VAUX/LVPD L3 7 H5
Maypole Ct NTHTN L30 22 C4
PR/KW L34 44 A3
May Rd HES CH60 149 E1
May St BTL L20 5 F2
VAUX/LVPD L3 7 H5
Maytree Cl NTHLY L27 98 A2
Mayville Rd CALD/MH L18 96 B3
Mazenod Ct VAUX/LVPD L3 6 E1
Mazzini Cl EV L5 54 A5
McBride St ALL/GAR L19 119 G5
Mc Clellan Pl WDN WA8 14 E2
McCormack Av STHEL WA9 49 E3
McCulloch St STHEL WA9 11 K5
McFarlane Av ECCL WA10 47 E3
McGough Cl STHEL WA9 79 E2
McKeagney Gdns WDN WA8 124 B4
McKee Av WARRN/WOL WA2 83 H3
McKeown Cl EV L5 53 H5
McKinley St WARRW/BUR WA5 105 E1
McKinley Wy WDN WA8 101 H5
McMinnis Av STHEL WA9 49 G5
McVinnie Rd RAIN/WH L35 60 B4
Mead Av LITH L21 30 B4
Meade Cl RAIN/WH L35 78 B4
Meade Rd CLB/OSW/ST L13 55 G4
Meadfoot Rd MOR/LEA CH46 66 B4
Meadow Av STHEL WA9 79 H2
WARRS WA4 129 G1
Meadow Bank MGHL L31 18 B4
Meadowbank Cl
DV/KA/FCH L14 57 E5
Meadowbarn Cl KKBY L32 33 H3
Meadow Brook Cl AIN/FAZ L10 33 E5
Meadowbrook Rd
MOR/LEA CH46 89 F1
Meadow Cl NSTN CH64 158 D4
WDN WA8 101 F5
Meadow Crs
GR/UP/WCH CH49 113 F1
Meadowcroft FMBY L37 17 E4
HES CH60 135 G5
STHEL WA9 62 C4
Meadowcroft Ct RUNC WA7 156 C1
Meadowcroft Pk
WD/CROXPK L12 73 H1
Meadowcroft Rd HOY CH47 65 E4
Meadow Dr HUY L36 75 H5
Meadowfield Cl
RF/TRAN CH42 115 H1
WLT/FAZ L9 31 F5
Meadow Ga WKBY CH48 132 D1
Meadow Hey BTL L20 39 E2
Meadow Hey Cl WLTN L25 97 H5
Meadow La MGHL L31 19 E5
RF/TRAN CH42 115 H1
STHEL WA9 63 F1
WARRN/WOL WA2 85 E3
WD/CROXPK L12 56 B3
Meadow Oak Dr WLTN L25 97 G3
Meadow Pk RF/TRAN CH42 115 H1
Meadow Rd WKBY CH48 88 B5
Meadowside MOR/LEA CH46 67 F1
Meadowside Dr
NWD/KWIPK L33 26 A3
Meadowside Rd
PS/BROM CH62 152 D2
The Meadows MGHL L31 18 D5
NSTN CH64 159 E4
RAIN/WH L35 78 A3
Meadow St WAL/NB CH45 51 G2
The Meadow
GR/UP/WCH CH49 90 B5
Meadow Vw LITH L21 30 A1
Meadow Wk PEN/TH CH61 134 C3
RUNC WA7 * 156 B2
Meadow Wy NG/CROX L11 56 B1
Mead Rd WARR WA1 85 E5
Meadway GR/UP/WCH CH49 90 B2
HES CH60 148 D3
MGHL L31 23 G2
NTHTN L30 31 E2
PS/BROM CH62 138 C4
RAIN/WH L35 77 F1
RUNC WA7 146 D5
WAL/NB CH45 51 G5
WAV L15 73 G5
WDN WA8 123 G2
The Meander WD/CROXPK L12 57 E1
Measham Cl RNFD/HAY WA11 48 C2
Measham Wy WD/CROXPK L12 43 E4
Medbourne Crs KKBY L32 34 A4
Medea St EV L5 54 A4
Medlock St ANF/KKDL L4 54 A2
Medway Cl WARRN/WOL WA2 84 C3
Medway Ct STHEL WA9 49 F4
Medway Rd RF/TRAN CH42 116 A1
Meeting La WARRW/BUR WA5 104 B3
Melbreck Rd CALD/MH L18 119 F2
Melbury Rd DV/KA/FCH L14 57 H4
Melda Cl NPK/KEN L6 7 K1
Meldon Cl WD/CROXPK L12 42 C5
Meldreth Cl FMBY L37 16 B5
Meldrum Rd WAV L15 96 B2
Melford Ct WARR WA1 * 85 H5
Melford Dr CL/PREN CH43 114 A2
RUNC WA7 9 H7
Melford Gv NPK/KEN L6 55 F4
Meliden Gdns STHEL WA9 63 F3
Melksham Dr PEN/TH CH61 112 B4
Melling Av WLT/FAZ L9 31 G5
Melling Dr KKBY L32 33 H1
Melling La MGHL L31 24 B2
Melling Rd BTL L20 5 F1
WAL/NB CH45 52 A3
WLT/FAZ L9 31 G4
Melling Wy KKBY L32 33 H1
Mellock Cl NSTN CH64 159 E4
Mellock La NSTN CH64 159 E3
Melloncroft Dr WKBY CH48 110 B3
Melloncroft Dr West
WKBY CH48 110 C4
Mellor Cl RAIN/WH L35 99 E1
RUNC WA7 157 F1
Mellor Rd RF/TRAN CH42 115 E1
Melly Rd AIG/SPK L17 94 D5
Melrose Av CSBY/BLUN L23 29 F1
ECCL WA10 46 D2
HOY CH47 87 F1
WARRS WA4 130 B3
Melrose Gdns CL/PREN CH43 * 114 B2
Melrose Rd ANF/KKDL L4 53 H2
CSBY/WL L22 29 F4
NWD/KWIPK L33 25 G3
Melton Av WARRS WA4 129 H3
Melton Cl GR/UP/WCH CH49 89 G3
Melton Rd RUNC WA7 155 F3
Melverley Rd KKBY L32 33 E2
Melville Av RF/TRAN CH42 116 A2
Melville Cl WARRN/WOL WA2 12 D1
WDN WA8 15 K1
Melville Pl EHL/KEN L7 71 G5
Melville Rd BEB CH63 137 G1
BTL L20 30 B5
Melville St TOX L8 94 B3
Melwood Dr WD/CROXPK L12 56 C3
Menai Ms PR/KW L34 * 60 A4
Menai Rd BTL L20 39 H1
Menai St BIRK CH41 2 C5
Mendell Cl PS/BROM CH62 153 E1
Mendip Av WARRN/WOL WA2 83 H2
Mendip Cl HLWD L26 121 G4
RF/TRAN CH42 115 E2
Mendip Gv STHEL WA9 49 F4
Mendip Rd RF/TRAN CH42 115 E2
WAV L15 96 A2
Menin Av WARRS WA4 107 E5
Menlo Av PEN/TH CH61 112 D5
Menlo Cl CL/PREN CH43 91 E4
Menlove Av CALD/MH L18 96 A3
Menlove Gdns North
CALD/MH L18 96 B3
Menlove Gdns South
CALD/MH L18 96 B3
Menlove Gdns West
CALD/MH L18 96 B3
Menlove Man CALD/MH L18 96 C2
Menlow Cl WARRS WA4 131 G2
Menstone Rd CLB/OSW/ST L13 72 D1
Mentmore Crs NG/CROX L11 56 B1
Mentmore Rd CALD/MH L18 119 E2
Menzies St TOX L8 94 C4
Meols Cl FMBY L37 16 D4
Meols Dr WKBY CH48 87 E4
Meols Pde HOY CH47 64 B5
Mercer Av KKBY L32 33 F3
Mercer Ct WD/CROXPK L12 57 E5
Mercer Dr ANF/KKDL L4 54 A2
Mercer Rd CL/PREN CH43 68 A5
Mercer St ALL/GAR L19 * 140 C1
Mere Av BEB CH63 152 B3
Merebank CL/PREN CH43 91 E4
Merebrook Gv NWD/KWIPK L33 26 A4
Merecroft Av WAL/EG CH44 69 E3
Meredale Rd CALD/MH L18 96 A4
Meredith Av WARRS WA4 131 F1
Meredith St ALL/GAR L19 141 E1
Mere Farm Gv CL/PREN CH43 91 F4
Mere Farm Rd CL/PREN CH43 91 E4
Mere Fld CL/PREN CH43 * 91 F4
Mere Gn ANF/KKDL L4 54 C1
Mere Gv RNFD/HAY WA11 37 F3
Mereheath MOR/LEA CH46 66 C2
Mere Hey ECCL WA10 46 C4
Mereland Wy STHEL WA9 49 F5
Mere La EV L5 54 B5
HES CH60 134 C4
WAL/NB CH45 51 E3
Mere Park Rd
GR/UP/WCH CH49 89 E5
Mere Rd FMBY L37 16 C4
WARRN/WOL WA2 85 E3
Meres Rd WLT/FAZ L9 32 B5
Merevale Cl RUNC WA7 156 A3
Mereview Crs WD/CROXPK L12 42 D4
Merewood KKBY L32 34 A4
Merewood Cl
WARRN/WOL WA2 84 B2
Mereworth WKBY CH48 110 D5
Meribel Cl CSBY/BLUN L23 21 H4
Meriden Av BEB CH63 138 A5
Meriden Cl RNFD/HAY WA11 48 D1
Meriden Rd WLTN L25 97 H2
Merlin Av GR/UP/WCH CH49 89 F2
Merlin Cl GR/UP/WCH CH49 89 E2
RNFD/HAY WA11 48 B1
RUNC WA7 156 C1
Merlin Ct HLWD L26 121 F2
Merlin Rd RF/TRAN CH42 92 A5
Merlin St TOX L8 94 B2
Merrick Cl WARRN/WOL WA2 84 C3
Merrills La GR/UP/WCH CH49 90 A3
Merrilocks Rd CSBY/BLUN L23 20 B4
Merrilox Av MGHL L31 18 D4
Merrion Cl WLTN L25 97 F5
Merritt Av BIRK CH41 68 D5
Merrivale Rd WLTN L25 121 E1
Merrydale Dr NG/CROX L11 42 C4
Merryford Gn ANF/KKDL L4 54 D1
Mersey Av ALL/GAR L19 118 D3
MGHL L31 19 F4
Mersey Bank Rd
PS/BROM CH62 116 B3
Mersey La South
RF/TRAN CH42 116 A1
Mersey Rd AIG/SPK L17 118 C3
CSBY/BLUN L23 28 D1
RF/TRAN CH42 93 E5
RUNC WA7 8 C2
WDN WA8 146 A2
Mersey St STHEL WA9 49 G4
WAL/EG CH44 69 G3
WARR WA1 12 E6
Mersey Vw ALL/GAR L19 119 G5
CSBY/WL L22 28 D2
RUNC WA7 154 B1
Mersey View Rd WDN WA8 144 D2
Mersey View South Rd
RUNC WA7 154 B2
Mersey Wk WARRS WA4 107 H3
Mersey Wy ALL/GAR L19 140 D4
WARRW/BUR WA5 105 G4
Mersham Ct WDN WA8 101 H4
Merstone Cl HLWD L26 121 H4
Merthyr Gv CHLDW L16 74 A4
Merton Bank Rd STHEL WA9 48 C2
Merton Cl NSTN CH64 158 D5
Merton Crs HUY L36 74 D3
Merton Dr GR/UP/WCH CH49 90 A5
HUY L36 74 C3
Merton Gv BTL L20 4 E5
CSBY/BLUN L23 28 D1
Merton Pl CL/PREN CH43 2 B5
Merton Rd BTL L20 4 D5
WAL/NB CH45 51 G5
Merton St STHEL WA9 48 C2
Mertoun Rd WARRS WA4 129 H2
Mesham Cl GR/UP/WCH CH49 89 G3
Metcalf Cl NWD/KWIPK L33 25 G3
Meteor Crs WARRN/WOL WA2 84 B3
Methuen St BIRK CH41 68 C5
WAV L15 95 G1
Mevagissey Rd RUNC WA7 157 E4
The Mews AIG/SPK L17 118 D2
STBRV L28 58 A3
Meyrick Rd NG/CROX L11 41 G5
Miami Cl WARRW/BUR WA5 105 F1
Micawber Cl TOX L8 94 B3
Michael Dragonette Ct
VAUX/LVPD L3 70 C1
Michaels Cl FMBY L37 16 D3
Michigan Cl NTHLY L27 98 C3
Micklefield Rd WAV L15 * 95 H2
Micklegate RUNC WA7 157 F2
Middlefield Rd CALD/MH L18 97 E5
Middleham Cl KKBY L32 33 F3
Middlehey Rd PR/KW L34 44 B3
Middlehurst Av ECCL WA10 11 F3
Middlehurst Cl PR/KW L34 60 C3
Middlehurst Rd WARRS WA4 131 E1
Middlemass Hey NTHLY L27 98 C3
Middle Rd HLWD L26 142 D1
SPK/HALE L24 142 D1
Middlesex Rd BTL L20 5 H2
Middleton Rd CSBY/WL L22 29 G2
EHL/KEN L7 72 C3
Middle Wy NG/CROX L11 42 D2
Middlewood KKBY L32 34 A4
Midghall St VAUX/LVPD L3 6 D1
Midhurst Rd WD/CROXPK L12 43 F4
Midland St BIRK CH41 * 2 C6
WDN WA8 15 F2
Midland Ter CSBY/WL L22 29 E3
Midland Wy WARR WA1 12 B4
WARRN/WOL WA2 12 E3
Midlothian Dr CSBY/BLUN L23 28 D1
Midway Rd HUY L36 75 G1
Midwood St WDN WA8 14 E4
Milbrook Crs KKBY L32 33 H1
Milbrook Dr KKBY L32 33 H1
Mildenhall Cl
WARRW/BUR WA5 105 F2
Mildenhall Rd WLTN L25 97 G2
Mildmay Rd BTL L20 39 F2
NG/CROX L11 * 41 G5
Mile End EV L5 70 D1
Miles Cl GR/UP/WCH CH49 112 A1
Miles La GR/UP/WCH CH49 112 A1
Miles St TOX L8 94 C4
Milestone Hey STBRV L28 57 H2
Milford Cl FMBY L37 16 B5
Milford Dr WD/CROXPK L12 43 E4
Milford St EV L5 53 F4
Milland Cl NG/CROX L11 42 C4
Millar Crs WDN WA8 14 C5
Mill Av WARRW/BUR WA5 104 C1
Mill Bank CLB/OSW/ST L13 55 H4
NSTN CH64 159 F5
Millbank La MGHL L31 19 F3
Millbank Rd WAL/EG CH44 * 68 C2
Millbeck Cl KKBY L32 25 H5
Millbeck Gv RNFD/HAY WA11 37 F2
Millbrook Ct PR/KW L34 44 A2
Millbrook La ECCL WA10 46 D3
Millbrook Rd BIRK CH41 68 D3
Mill Brow BEB CH63 115 F5
ECCL WA10 46 D3
STHEL WA9 62 D5
WDN WA8 15 H1
Mill Brow Cl STHEL WA9 62 D5
Millbutt Cl BEB CH63 115 F5
Mill Cl CSBY/BLUN L23 21 F3
WARRN/WOL WA2 84 C1
Mill Ct NTHTN L30 22 C4
Millcroft CSBY/BLUN L23 21 H4
NSTN CH64 158 D1
Millcroft Pk GR/UP/WCH CH49 88 D5
Millcroft Rd WLTN L25 121 E2
Millenium Rd TOX L8 94 C2
Millennium Rd TOX L8 94 C2
Miller Av CSBY/BLUN L23 21 E4
Miller Cl TOX L8 94 B4
Miller's Br BTL L20 4 C7
Millers Cl MOR/LEA CH46 88 D1
Millerscroft KKBY L32 33 F1
Millersdale STHEL WA9 79 G1
Millersdale Av WLT/FAZ L9 31 G5
Millersdale Cl PS/BROM CH62 153 F4
Millersdale Gv RUNC WA7 155 H4
Millersdale Rd CALD/MH L18 96 A4
Millers Fold ECCL WA10 46 D3
Miller St WARRS WA4 13 G7
Millers Wy MOR/LEA CH46 * 66 A5
Mill Farm Cl WARRN/WOL WA2 84 C2
Millfield NSTN CH64 158 D1
Millfield Cl CLB/OSW/ST L13 56 A4
Millfield Rd WDN WA8 125 G1
Millfields ECCL WA10 46 C4
Millgreen Cl WD/CROXPK L12 43 E4
Mill Green La WDN WA8 102 D3
Mill Hey RAIN/WH L35 78 C4
Mill Hey Rd WKBY CH48 110 D5
Mill Hl CL/PREN CH43 91 G5
Mill Hill Rd PEN/TH CH61 112 A4
Millhouse Av WARRS WA4 130 B2
Millhouse Cl MOR/LEA CH46 65 H4
Millhouse La MOR/LEA CH46 65 H4
Millington Cl CL/PREN CH43 114 A2
RUNC WA7 156 B5
WDN WA8 14 A3
Mill La BTL L20 5 G4
CLB/OSW/ST L13 73 E3
GR/UP/WCH CH49 112 A2
HES CH60 149 F1
KKBY L32 25 F5
NSTN CH64 159 H5
PR/KW L34 44 B2
RAIN/WH L35 78 A4
STHEL WA9 62 C5
VAUX/LVPD L3 7 G2
WAL/EG CH44 68 C2
WARRN/WOL WA2 83 G2
WARRS WA4 129 E4
WAV L15 73 E5
WD/CROXPK L12 56 A4
WDN WA8 101 F3
Millom Av RAIN/WH L35 77 H1
Millom Gv ECCL WA10 61 E2
WD/CROXPK L12 56 C1
Millport Cl WARRN/WOL WA2 85 E3
Mill Rd BEB CH63 115 F4
NPK/KEN L6 71 G2
PEN/TH CH61 113 E5
PS/BROM CH62 138 D3
Mill Sq AIN/FAZ L10 32 B2
Millstead Rd WAV L15 73 E5
Mill St ECCL WA10 11 F3
NSTN CH64 158 D2
PR/KW L34 59 H4
RF/TRAN CH42 92 B4
TOX L8 94 A2
WLTN L25 120 C1
Mill Ter BEB CH63 * 137 F1
Millthwaite Rd WAL/EG CH44 68 B1
Millvale St NPK/KEN L6 72 A2
Mill Vw TOX L8 94 A3
Mill View Dr BEB CH63 115 E5
Millway Rd SPK/HALE L24 143 E2
Millwood BEB CH63 115 F5
Mill Wood Av ECCL WA10 46 B4
Millwood Ct SPK/HALE L24 * 143 E2
Millwood Gdns RAIN/WH L35 77 F3
Millwood Rd SPK/HALE L24 142 C3
Mill Yd PEN/TH CH61 113 F5
Milman Cl GR/UP/WCH CH49 89 H4
Milman Rd ANF/KKDL L4 54 B1
Milner Cop HES CH60 149 E1
Milne Rd CLB/OSW/ST L13 55 G2
Milner Rd AIG/SPK L17 118 C2
HES CH60 135 F5
Milner St BIRK CH41 68 C5
WARRW/BUR WA5 12 A5
Milnthorpe Cl ANF/KKDL L4 54 A2
Milnthorpe St ALL/GAR L19 119 G5
Milroy St EHL/KEN L7 71 H4
Milton Av DV/KA/FCH L14 74 B3
RAIN/WH L35 77 E2
WDN WA8 14 A4
Milton Cl RAIN/WH L35 77 E2
Milton Crs HES CH60 135 E5
Milton Gn PEN/TH CH61 113 F5
Milton Gv WARRS WA4 107 F5
Milton Pavement BIRK CH41 * 2 E5
Milton Rd ANF/KKDL L4 5 K6
CSBY/WL L22 29 F2
EHL/KEN L7 72 C3
RF/TRAN CH42 92 A4
WAL/EG CH44 69 F3
WDN WA8 14 C4
WKBY CH48 87 E5
Milton Rd East RF/TRAN CH42 92 B4
Milton St BTL L20 4 C2
STHEL WA9 79 E3
WDN WA8 146 A1
Milton Wy MGHL L31 18 B5
Milvain Dr WARRN/WOL WA2 84 A4
Milverny Wy STHEL WA9 48 A5
Milverton St NPK/KEN L6 72 A1
Mimosa Rd WAV L15 96 B1
Minehead Gv STHEL WA9 62 D5
Minehead Rd AIG/SPK L17 118 C2
Miners Wy SPK/HALE L24 143 E3
WDN WA8 14 D6
Minerva Cl WARRS WA4 130 B1

Mines Av AIG/SPK L17 118 D3
PR/KW L34 60 A4
Minshull St EHL/KEN L7 71 G4
Minstead Av NWD/KWIPK L33 34 B2
Minster Ct EHL/KEN L7 71 G5
RUNC WA7 154 C1
Minto Cl EHL/KEN L7 72 A3
Minton Cl WD/CROXPK L12 43 F4
Minton Wy WDN WA8 102 B3
Mintor Rd NWD/KWIPK L33 34 B2
Minto St EHL/KEN L7 71 H3
Minver Rd WD/CROXPK L12 56 D3
Miranda Pl BTL L20 53 H1
Miranda Rd BTL L20 5 G7
Mirfield Cl HLWD L26 121 H5
Mirfield St NPK/KEN L6 71 H2
Miriam Rd ANF/KKDL L4 54 C4
Miskelly St BTL L20 53 G2
Mission Wk NPK/KEN L6 71 H2
Missouri Rd CLB/OSW/ST L13 55 F3
Mistlethrush Wy
WD/CROXPK L12 43 F4
Misty Cl WDN WA8 124 A1
Mitchell Crs LITH L21 30 A3
Mitchell Pl CLVPS L1 7 G4
Mitchell Rd ECCL WA10 61 E1
PR/KW L34 59 G4
Mitchell St WARRS WA4 130 A3
Mithril Cl WDN WA8 103 E5
Mitre Cl RAIN/WH L35 76 D4
Mitylene St EV L5 * 54 A4
Mobberley Cl WARRS WA4 108 D5
Mobberley Wy BEB CH63 138 A3
Mockbeggar Dr WAL/NB CH45 50 D3
Mockbeggar Whf
WAL/NB CH45 50 D3
Modred St TOX L8 94 B3
Moel Famau Vw AIG/SPK L17 117 H1
Moffatdale Rd ANF/KKDL L4 55 E2
Moffat Rd WLT/FAZ L9 * 31 H5
Moffatt Rd WLT/FAZ L9 31 G5
Molesworth Gv CHLDW L16 74 B4
Molineux Av DV/KA/FCH L14 73 H4
Molland Cl WD/CROXPK L12 56 D2
Mollington Av NG/CROX L11 41 H5
Mollington Link BIRK CH41 3 G7
Mollington Rd KKBY L32 33 F2
WAL/EG CH44 69 E2
Mollington St BIRK CH41 3 F6
Molly's La NWD/KWIPK L33 35 E5
Molton Rd WAV L15 73 G5
Molyneux Av
WARRW/BUR WA5 83 F5
Molyneux Cl GR/UP/WCH CH49 89 H3
HUY L36 75 H3
RAIN/WH L35 76 D1
Molyneux Ct NG/CROX L11 * 42 B4
Molyneux Dr RAIN/WH L35 76 D1
WAL/NB CH45 51 H2
Molyneux Rd CALD/MH L18 95 H4
CSBY/WL L22 29 F2
MGHL L31 24 C2
NPK/KEN L6 71 H2
Molyneux Wy AIN/FAZ L10 31 H1
Monaghan Cl WLT/FAZ L9 31 E5
Monash Rd NG/CROX L11 55 H2
Monastery La STHEL WA9 62 D3
Monastery Rd NPK/KEN L6 55 E4
STHEL WA9 63 E3
Mona St BIRK CH41 91 F1
BTL L20 39 H1
ECCL WA10 10 A6
Mond Rd AIN/FAZ L10 32 C5
WDN WA8 14 C4
Monfa Rd BTL L20 39 G1
Monica Dr WDN WA8 102 A3
Monica Rd WLTN L25 120 D2
Monkfield Wy ALL/GAR L19 140 D2
Monk Rd WAL/EG CH44 68 D1
Monks Cl FMBY L37 17 F5
Monksdown Rd NG/CROX L11 56 A1
Monks Dr FMBY L37 17 F5
Monks Ferry BIRK CH41 3 J5
Monksferry Wk ALL/GAR L19 118 D4
Monks Pl WARRN/WOL WA2 13 G1
Monks St WARRW/BUR WA5 * 106 A2
Monk St BIRK CH41 3 H5
EV L5 * 54 B4
Monks Wy BEB CH63 137 H2
WKBY CH48 110 B1
WLTN L25 120 D1
Monkswell Dr WAV L15 73 E5
Monkswell St TOX L8 94 C5
Monkswood Cl
WARRW/BUR WA5 83 E3
Monmouth Cl WARR WA1 109 E1
Monmouth Dr AIN/FAZ L10 32 C3
Monmouth Gv STHEL WA9 48 D5
Monmouth Rd WAL/EG CH44 68 B1
Monro Cl TOX L8 * 94 B4
Monroe Cl WARR WA1 108 B1
Monro St TOX L8 94 B4
Montague Rd CLB/OSW/ST L13 73 E3
WDN WA8 123 G5
Montagu Rd FMBY L37 16 D1
Montana Cl WARRW/BUR WA5 105 G1
Montclair Dr CALD/MH L18 96 B3
Montclare Crs WARRS WA4 130 C2
Monterey Rd CLB/OSW/ST L13 73 F3
Montfort Dr ALL/GAR L19 119 E4
Montgomery Cl RAIN/WH L35 76 D3
WARRW/BUR WA5 82 A5
Montgomery Hl WKBY CH48 111 G3
Montgomery Rd HUY L36 75 F1
WDN WA8 124 B3
WLT/FAZ L9 31 F5
Montgomery Wy NPK/KEN L6 71 H1
Montpelier Av RUNC WA7 154 D3
Montpelier Dr TOX L8 94 B4
Montpellier Crs WAL/NB CH45 51 G2
Montreal Rd NTHLY L27 98 C3
Montrose Av WAL/EG CH44 69 G4
Montrose Cl WARRN/WOL WA2 84 D1
Montrose Rd CLB/OSW/ST L13 55 G4
Montrose Wy CLB/OSW/ST L13 72 D3
Montrovia Crs AIN/FAZ L10 32 C5
Monville Rd WLT/FAZ L9 31 H5
Moorbridge Cl NTHTN L30 23 F5
Moor Cl CSBY/BLUN L23 21 G4
Moor Coppice CSBY/BLUN L23 21 G4
Moorcroft Rd CALD/MH L18 119 G2
HUY L36 58 C5
WAL/NB CH45 50 D5
Moor Dr CSBY/BLUN L23 21 F4
Moore Av RF/TRAN CH42 115 G1
STHEL WA9 49 G4
WARRS WA4 108 D5
Moore Cl WDN WA8 125 H1
Moore La WARRS WA4 128 B4
Moore St BTL L20 4 C1
Mooreway RAIN/WH L35 78 C4
Moorfield NWD/KWIPK L33 26 A4
Moorfield Rd CSBY/BLUN L23 21 H4
ECCL WA10 47 E2
WDN WA8 102 D4
Moorfields CLVP L2 6 D3
Moorfields Av CL/PREN CH43 90 D4
Moorfoot Rd STHEL WA9 49 F4
Moorfoot Wy NWD/KWIPK L33 25 G3
Moorgate Av CSBY/BLUN L23 29 F1
Moorgate Rd KKBY L32 43 F1
Moorgate St EHL/KEN L7 71 H4
Moorhey Rd MGHL L31 * 24 A2
Mooring Cl RUNC WA7 157 F3
Moorings Cl NSTN CH64 158 A1
The Moorings BIRK CH41 * 2 E6
HES CH60 148 A1
MGHL L31 18 B2
Moorland Av CSBY/BLUN L23 21 F4
Moorland Cl HES CH60 149 E2
Moorland Dr RUNC WA7 157 G2
Moorland Pk HES CH60 149 E2
Moorland Rd MGHL L31 23 H3
RF/TRAN CH42 92 C5
Moorlands Rd CSBY/BLUN L23 22 A3
Moor La AIN/FAZ L10 32 D5
ANF/KKDL L4 40 C5
CSBY/BLUN L23 21 F4
CSBY/BLUN L23 21 G4
HES CH60 148 D1
KKBY L32 33 E4
WDN WA8 14 B6
Moor La South WDN WA8 14 B6
Moor Pl VAUX/LVPD L3 7 H3
Moorside WARRS WA4 107 G4
Moorside Av NSTN CH64 158 B2
Moorside Cl CSBY/BLUN L23 21 G5
Moorside Ct WDN WA8 14 B5
Moorside La NSTN CH64 158 B3
Moorside Rd CSBY/BLUN L23 21 G5
Moor St CLVP L2 6 C5
Moorway HES CH60 149 F1
Moorwood Crs STHEL WA9 79 G1
Moran Dr WARRW/BUR WA5 105 E2
Moray Cl ECCL WA10 10 D1
Morcott La SPK/HALE L24 143 H4
Morden St NPK/KEN L6 72 A2
Morecambe St NPK/KEN L6 * 55 E5
Morecroft Rd RF/TRAN CH42 116 A1
Morella Rd ANF/KKDL L4 55 E2
Morello Cl ECCL WA10 11 F2
Morello Dr BEB CH63 138 B4
Moresby Cl RUNC WA7 157 G2
Moret Cl CSBY/BLUN L23 21 H4
Moreton Av STHEL WA9 79 G1
Moreton Gv WAL/NB CH45 51 E4
Moreton Rd GR/UP/WCH CH49 89 H2
Morgan Av WARRN/WOL WA2 84 A3
Morgan Ms NTHTN L30 30 C1
Morgan St STHEL WA9 48 D5
Morland Av NSTN CH64 159 E3
PS/BROM CH62 152 D2
Morley Av BIRK CH41 91 H1
Morley Rd RUNC WA7 8 D7
WAL/EG CH44 68 C2
WARRS WA4 129 G2
Morley St ANF/KKDL L4 * 54 A3
ECCL WA10 10 E1
WARR WA1 13 G3
Morley Wy ECCL WA10 10 E3
Morningside CSBY/BLUN L23 29 G1
Morningside Pl NG/CROX L11 55 H1
Morningside Rd NG/CROX L11 55 H2
Morningside Wy NG/CROX L11 55 H2
Mornington Av CSBY/BLUN L23 29 F2
Mornington Rd WAL/NB CH45 51 H4
Mornington St TOX L8 94 A3
Morpeth Cl MOR/LEA CH46 65 H5
Morpeth Dock BIRK CH41 * 3 H2
Morpeth Rd HOY CH47 87 E3
Morpeth St TOX L8 94 B1
Morpeth Whf BIRK CH41 3 G1
Morris Av WARRS WA4 107 H4
Morris Cl RNFD/HAY WA11 49 G2
Morrison Cl WARRW/BUR WA5 105 E3
Morrissey Cl ECCL WA10 10 A3
Morris St STHEL WA9 63 E1
Morston Av KKBY L32 33 H4
Morston Crs KKBY L32 33 H4
Mort Av WARRS WA4 108 A4
Mortimer Av WARRN/WOL WA2 83 H5
Mortimer St BIRK CH41 3 H4
Mortlake Cl WDN WA8 101 E5
Morton Cl WARRW/BUR WA5 82 C5
Morton Rd RUNC WA7 157 F1
Morton St TOX L8 94 B3
Morvah Cl WD/CROXPK L12 42 C5
Morval Crs ANF/KKDL L4 5 K6
RUNC WA7 9 J7
Morven Cl WARRN/WOL WA2 84 C2
Moscow Dr CLB/OSW/ST L13 55 H5
Mosedale Av RNFD/HAY WA11 37 F3
Mosedale Gv RUNC WA7 * 156 A4
Mosedale Rd PS/BROM CH62 139 E4
WLT/FAZ L9 40 C2
Moseley Av WAL/NB CH45 68 C1
WARRS WA4 108 A4
Moseley Rd BEB CH63 138 A5
Moses St TOX L8 94 B4
Moss Bank Pk LITH L21 29 H4
Moss Bank Rd RNFD/HAY WA11 37 E3
WDN WA8 15 J5
Mossbrow Rd HUY L36 75 G1
Moss Cl WARRS WA4 130 C1
Mosscroft Cl HUY L36 76 A1
Mossdale Cl WARRW/BUR WA5 105 E1
Mossdale Dr RAIN/WH L35 78 B2
Mossdale Rd NWD/KWIPK L33 26 A4
Mossdene Rd WAL/EG CH44 68 B1
Moss End Wy NWD/KWIPK L33 35 E1
Mossfield Rd WLT/FAZ L9 40 B1
Moss Gate Gv DV/KA/FCH L14 74 C2
Moss Gate Rd DV/KA/FCH L14 74 C2
Moss Green Wy STHEL WA9 63 G1
Moss Gv RF/TRAN CH42 114 D1
TOX L8 95 E2
Mosshill Cl MGHL L31 18 C3
Mosslands ECCL WA10 46 C3
Mosslands Dr WAL/NB CH45 68 A1
Moss La BTL L20 40 A1
LITH L21 30 B4
MGHL L31 18 D1
MGHL L31 19 E4
NWD/KWIPK L33 26 A1
NWD/KWIPK L33 34 C1
RF/TRAN CH42 114 D1
STHEL WA9 63 G1
WARRS WA4 128 A5
WLT/FAZ L9 40 B1
Mosslawn Rd KKBY L32 34 A3
Mosslea Pk CALD/MH L18 95 H4
Mossley Av CALD/MH L18 95 H3
PS/BROM CH62 152 D1
Mossley Hill Dr AIG/SPK L17 95 F3
Mossley Hill Rd CALD/MH L18 118 D1
Mossley Rd RF/TRAN CH42 92 C5
Moss Nook La MGHL L31 25 E1
Moss Pits Cl AIN/FAZ L10 32 B5
Moss Pits La AIN/FAZ L10 32 B5
WAV L15 96 B1
Moss Rd WARRS WA4 108 A5
Moss Side DV/KA/FCH L14 74 C2
FMBY L37 17 G2
Moss Side La WARRS WA4 127 G4
Moss St ALL/GAR L19 119 G5
NPK/KEN L6 7 J2
PR/KW L34 59 H3
WDN WA8 15 K5
Moss Vw LITH L21 30 B4
MGHL L31 19 F5
Mossville Cl CALD/MH L18 119 E1
Mossville Rd CALD/MH L18 119 F1
Moss Wy NG/CROX L11 42 C3
Mossy Bank Rd WAL/EG CH44 69 F1
Mostyn Av AIN/FAZ L10 31 H2
ALL/GAR L19 119 H3
HES CH60 148 A1
WKBY CH48 110 B2
Mostyn Cl ANF/KKDL L4 * 54 A3
Mostyn Sq NSTN CH64 158 A1
Mostyn St WAL/EG CH44 68 D2
Mote Hill Ct WARR WA1 13 H3
Motherwell Cl WDN WA8 101 G4
Mottershead Cl WDN WA8 14 C4
Mottershead Rd WDN WA8 14 C4
Mottram Cl NWD/KWIPK L33 34 A2
WARRS WA4 108 B5
Moughland La RUNC WA7 155 E1
Moulders La WARR WA1 12 E6
Mould St EV L5 53 H5
Moulton Cl RUNC WA7 156 B5
Mounsey Rd RF/TRAN CH42 2 D7
Mount Av BEB CH63 115 F4
BTL L20 39 H1
HES CH60 * 148 D1
Mount Cl KKBY L32 25 F5
Mount Ct HES CH60 * 148 D1
Mount Crs KKBY L32 25 F5
Mount Dr BEB CH63 115 E4
Mount Gv BIRK CH41 2 C7
Mount Grove Pl BIRK CH41 2 B7
Mount Haven Cl
GR/UP/WCH CH49 90 A3
Mount House Cl FMBY L37 17 G1
Mount House Rd FMBY L37 17 G1
Mount Ms HES CH60 * 148 D1
Mount Olive CL/PREN CH43 91 G5
Mount Pk BEB CH63 115 F4
WLTN L25 97 G5
Mount Park Ct WLTN L25 97 G5
Mount Pleasant CL/PREN CH43 91 H5
CLVPS L1 7 H5
CSBY/WL L22 29 E3
EHL/KEN L7 7 K5
WDN WA8 125 F1
Mount Pleasant Av STHEL WA9 49 G4
Mount Pleasant Cl
WAL/NB CH45 51 H3
Mount Pleasant Rd
WAL/NB CH45 51 G3
Mount Rd BEB CH63 115 E5
BEB CH63 137 E1
BEB CH63 137 F5
GR/UP/WCH CH49 90 A3
KKBY L32 25 E5
RF/TRAN CH42 115 E2
RUNC WA7 156 B1
WAL/NB CH45 51 G2
WKBY CH48 110 C2
Mount St CLVPS L1 7 H7
CSBY/WL L22 29 E3
WDN WA8 125 F1
WLTN L25 120 C1
The Mount HES CH60 148 D1
WAL/EG CH44 69 E1
Mount Vernon EHL/KEN L7 71 G3
Mount Vernon St EHL/KEN L7 71 G3
Mount Vernon Vw EHL/KEN L7 71 G3
Mountview Cl TOX L8 94 C3
Mountway BEB CH63 115 F4
Mount Wood Rd
RF/TRAN CH42 115 E3
Mowbray Av RNFD/HAY WA11 48 C2
Mowbray Gv CLB/OSW/ST L13 73 E4
Mowcroft La
WARRW/BUR WA5 103 H5
Moxon Av WARRS WA4 107 H3
Moxon St ECCL WA10 10 A7
Moyles Cl WDN WA8 124 B4
Mozart Cl TOX L8 94 D2
Muirfield Cl WARRN/WOL WA2 85 E2
WD/CROXPK L12 57 E4
Muirfield Rd HUY L36 75 E4
Muirhead Av CLB/OSW/ST L13 55 G4
Muirhead Av East
NG/CROX L11 56 A2
Mulberry Av ECCL WA10 47 E4
Mulberry Cl NWD/KWIPK L33 26 A3
WARR WA1 109 E1
Mulberry Ct WARRS WA4 * 130 B2
Mulberry Gv WAL/EG CH44 69 F2
Mulberry Pl EHL/KEN L7 * 7 K6
Mulberry Rd RF/TRAN CH42 115 H1
Mulberry St EHL/KEN L7 7 K5
Mulcrow Cl STHEL WA9 48 D3
Mulgrave St TOX L8 94 C1
Mullen Cl WARRW/BUR WA5 * 106 B2
Mulliner St EHL/KEN L7 95 E1
Mullion Cl HLWD L26 121 G3
RUNC WA7 156 D3
Mullion Gv WARRN/WOL WA2 85 E4
Mullion Rd NG/CROX L11 42 C3
Mullion Wk NG/CROX L11 * 42 C2
Mullwood Cl WD/CROXPK L12 43 F4
Mulveton Rd BEB CH63 137 H3
Mumfords La HOY CH47 64 D4
Muncaster Cl PS/BROM CH62 138 D5
Munster Rd CLB/OSW/ST L13 73 F2
Murat Gv CSBY/WL L22 28 D3
Murat St CSBY/WL L22 28 D3
Murcote Rd DV/KA/FCH L14 57 F5
Murdishaw Av RUNC WA7 157 E4
Muriel Cl WARRW/BUR WA5 104 B2
Muriel St ANF/KKDL L4 54 C1
Murphy Gv STHEL WA9 49 E3
Murrayfield Dr MOR/LEA CH46 66 D1
Murrayfield Rd WLTN L25 97 G2
Murray Gv WKBY CH48 87 E5
Museum St WARR WA1 12 B6
Musker Dr NTHTN L30 30 B1
Musker St CSBY/BLUN L23 29 G1
Muspratt Rd LITH L21 39 E2
Myers Av RAIN/WH L35 60 C5
Myerscough Av BTL L20 5 K1
Myers Rd East CSBY/BLUN L23 29 F1
Myers Rd West CSBY/BLUN L23 29 E1
Mynsule Rd BEB CH63 137 H3
Myrtle Gv CSBY/WL L22 29 E2
WAL/EG CH44 69 F2
WARRS WA4 107 F5
WDN WA8 124 B3
Myrtle Pde EHL/KEN L7 7 K7
Myrtle St CLVPS L1 7 J6
EHL/KEN L7 71 G5
Myrtle Wy GR/UP/WCH CH49 90 B4

N

Naburn Gv MOR/LEA CH46 89 G1
Nairn Cl BEB CH63 152 D5
WARRN/WOL WA2 85 E2
Nansen Cl WARRW/BUR WA5 105 H1
Nansen Gv ANF/KKDL L4 54 C1
Nant Park Ct WAL/NB CH45 52 A2
Nantwich Cl
GR/UP/WCH CH49 113 E1
Napier Cl ECCL WA10 10 D5
Napier Dr MOR/LEA CH46 66 D5
Napier Rd PS/BROM CH62 116 B3
Napier St BTL L20 53 F1
ECCL WA10 10 D5
WARR WA1 13 F5
Naples Rd WAL/EG CH44 69 F2
Napps Cl WLTN L25 97 F1
Napps Wy PEN/TH CH61 135 E4
WLTN L25 74 B5
Nares Cl WARRW/BUR WA5 82 C4
Naseby Cl CL/PREN CH43 90 C4
Naseby St ANF/KKDL L4 40 B5
Natal Rd WLT/FAZ L9 40 D1
Nathan Gv NWD/KWIPK L33 26 A5
Naughton Lea WDN WA8 101 F5
Navigation Cl NTHTN L30 23 F5
RUNC WA7 157 F3
Navigation St WARR WA1 13 H5
Navigation Whf VAUX/LVPD L3 93 H2
Naylor Rd CL/PREN CH43 68 A5
WDN WA8 15 J2
Naylorsfield Dr NTHLY L27 98 A2
Naylor's Rd NTHLY L27 98 B1
Naylor St VAUX/LVPD L3 6 D1
WARR WA1 12 E4
Nazareth House La WDN WA8 124 A4
Nazeby Av CSBY/BLUN L23 29 G1
Neale Dr GR/UP/WCH CH49 89 G5
Neasham Cl HLWD L26 121 H4
Nedens Gv MGHL L31 18 C3
Nedens La MGHL L31 18 C3
Needham Cl RUNC WA7 9 K4
Needham Rd EHL/KEN L7 72 A3
Needwood Dr BEB CH63 137 H3
Neills Rd STHEL WA9 63 H4
Neilson Rd AIG/SPK L17 94 D5
Neil St WDN WA8 125 F1
Nell's La ORM L39 19 F1
Nelson Av RAIN/WH L35 77 E3
Nelson Ct RF/TRAN CH42 116 A2
Nelson Dr PEN/TH CH61 134 C3
Nelson Pl RAIN/WH L35 77 E3
Nelson Rd EHL/KEN L7 71 H4
GOL/RIS/CUL WA3 85 H1
LITH L21 * 30 A5
RF/TRAN CH42 116 A2
Nelson's Cft BEB CH63 138 A3
Nelson St BTL L20 4 C7
CLVPS L1 93 H1
WAL/NB CH45 52 A3
WAV L15 95 G1
WDN WA8 125 E5
Nelville Rd WLT/FAZ L9 31 H5
Neptune Cl RUNC WA7 157 F2
Neptune St BIRK CH41 2 E2
Ness Gv KKBY L32 33 F2
Neston Av STHEL WA9 79 F1
Neston Gdns BIRK CH41 2 A1
Neston Rd BEB CH63 150 C3
NSTN CH64 150 B4
NSTN CH64 159 E5
Neston St ANF/KKDL L4 54 B1
Netherby St TOX L8 94 B5
Netherfield WDN WA8 124 B3
Netherfield Cl CL/PREN CH43 90 C4
Netherfield Rd North EV L5 54 A4
Netherfield Rd South EV L5 71 E1
Netherley Rd NTHLY L27 98 D3
RAIN/WH L35 99 G4
Netherton Gra NTHTN L30 31 G1
Netherton Gn NTHTN L30 23 E4
Netherton La NTHTN L30 22 D4
Netherton Park Rd LITH L21 30 C4
Netherton Rd ALL/GAR L19 119 E2
BTL L20 39 H1
MOR/LEA CH46 66 C5
Netherton Wy LITH L21 30 D4
Netherwood Rd NG/CROX L11 41 G5
Netley St ANF/KKDL L4 54 A2
Nettlestead Rd NG/CROX L11 56 A2
Neva Av MOR/LEA CH46 66 B5
Nevada Cl WARRW/BUR WA5 82 C5
Neville Av STHEL WA9 49 H5
WARRN/WOL WA2 84 B4
Neville Cl CL/PREN CH43 90 C4
Neville Crs WARRW/BUR WA5 105 E5
Neville Rd CSBY/WL L22 29 F3
PS/BROM CH62 153 E2
WAL/EG CH44 68 C1
Nevin St NPK/KEN L6 71 G2
Nevison St EHL/KEN L7 71 H4
Nevitte Cl STBRV L28 57 G2
New Acres Cl CL/PREN CH43 67 G5
Newark Cl CL/PREN CH43 90 C4
HUY L36 58 B4
NTHTN L30 23 G4
Newark St ANF/KKDL L4 54 A1
New Bank Rd WDN WA8 123 H2
New Barnet WDN WA8 101 H5
New Bird St CLVPS L1 93 H1
Newbold Crs WKBY CH48 88 A5
Newbold Gv WD/CROXPK L12 43 H5
Newborough Av CALD/MH L18 95 H3
CSBY/BLUN L23 21 H5
Newborough Cl
WARRW/BUR WA5 82 D3
Newbridge Cl
GR/UP/WCH CH49 90 B4
RUNC WA7 157 E3
WARRW/BUR WA5 82 C3
Newburns La CL/PREN CH43 91 H5
Newburn St ANF/KKDL L4 54 B1
Newbury Cl HUY L36 75 F4
WDN WA8 101 H5
Newbury Wy MOR/LEA CH46 66 C2
WD/CROXPK L12 57 E5
Newby Av RAIN/WH L35 77 G1
Newby Dr HUY L36 75 E2
Newby Gv WD/CROXPK L12 42 C5
Newby St ANF/KKDL L4 54 B2
Newcastle Rd WAV L15 96 A2
New Chester Rd BIRK CH41 3 H6
PS/BROM CH62 138 C1
RF/TRAN CH42 116 A2
Newchurch Rd NTHLY L27 98 D4
Newcombe Av
WARRN/WOL WA2 84 B5
Newcombe St NPK/KEN L6 54 D5
Newcroft Rd WLTN L25 97 F4
New Cross St ECCL WA10 11 F4
PR/KW L34 * 59 H3
New Cut La NWD/KWIPK L33 35 H4
WARR WA1 108 B1
Newdales Cl CL/PREN CH43 90 C1
Newdown Rd NG/CROX L11 42 D2
Newell Rd WAL/EG CH44 68 D1
Newenham Crs DV/KA/FCH L14 74 A1
New Ferry By-Pass
PS/BROM CH62 116 B4
New Ferry Rd PS/BROM CH62 116 B3
Newfield Cl CSBY/BLUN L23 22 B3
Newfields ECCL WA10 47 E3
New Fort Wy BTL L20 39 E1
New Glade Hl RNFD/HAY WA11 48 D1
New Grey Rock Cl NPK/KEN L6 71 H1
Newhall La HOY CH47 87 F2
New Hall La NG/CROX L11 55 G1
Newhall St CLVPS L1 * 94 A1
New Hampshire Cl
WARRW/BUR WA5 105 F1
Newhaven Rd WAL/NB CH45 52 A3
WARRN/WOL WA2 83 H1
New Hedley Gv EV L5 53 G5
New Henderson St TOX L8 94 A2
New Hey CLB/OSW/ST L13 56 A5
Newheyes NSTN CH64 158 D1
New Hey Rd GR/UP/WCH CH49 90 B4
New Heys Dr CALD/MH L18 119 H2
Newholme Cl WD/CROXPK L12 43 E4
Newhope Rd BIRK CH41 2 B2
Newhouse Rd WAV L15 * 95 F1
New Hutte La HLWD L26 121 H5
Newick Pk KKBY L32 33 F3
Newick Rd KKBY L32 33 F3
Newington CLVPS L1 7 G5
New Islington VAUX/LVPD L3 7 H2
Newland Cl WDN WA8 101 E5
Newland Ct AIG/SPK L17 95 E5
Newland Dr WAL/EG CH44 68 C1
Newlands Rd BEB CH63 * 138 A2
RNFD/HAY WA11 37 G5
WARRS WA4 130 D1
Newling St BIRK CH41 2 B2
Newlyn Av LITH L21 29 H3
MGHL L31 19 E5
Newlyn Cl HOY CH47 65 E3
RUNC WA7 156 D3
Newlyn Gdns
WARRW/BUR WA5 104 B5
Newlyn Gv RNFD/HAY WA11 37 H5
Newlyn Rd HOY CH47 65 E4
NG/CROX L11 42 D2
Newlyn Wk NG/CROX L11 * 42 D2
New Manchester Rd
WARR WA1 108 A1
Newman St ANF/KKDL L4 53 H2
WARRS WA4 107 H5
New Market Rd LITH L21 30 A5
New Mill Stile WLTN L25 97 G5
Newmorn Ct AIG/SPK L17 118 A1
Newport Av WAL/NB CH45 50 D3
Newport Cl CL/PREN CH43 90 C4
Newport Ct EV L5 53 G5
New Quay VAUX/LVPD L3 6 B3
Newquay Cl RUNC WA7 156 D3
New Red Rock Cl NPK/KEN L6 71 H1
New Rd CLB/OSW/ST L13 55 G5
FMBY L37 17 F1
PR/KW L34 60 A3
WARRS WA4 12 E7

Newsham Cl WDN WA8 100 D4
Newsham Dr NPK/KEN L6 55 E5
Newsham Rd HUY L36 76 A5
Newsham St EV L5 53 H5
Newstead Av CSBY/BLUN L23 28 C1
Newstead Rd HLWD L26 123 F5
TOX L8 * 95 E1
WDN WA8 123 F5
Newstet Rd NWD/KWIPK L33 34 C2
New St NSTN CH64 158 D5
RUNC WA7 8 D5
STHEL WA9 62 C4
WAL/EG CH44 69 G3
Newton Cl WD/CROXPK L12 56 B2
Newton Ct CLB/OSW/ST L13 72 C4
Newton Cross La WKBY CH48 111 E1
Newton Dr WKBY CH48 111 E1
Newton Gv WARRN/WOL WA2 84 D2
Newton Park Rd WKBY CH48 111 E1
Newton Rd CLB/OSW/ST L13 72 C1
HOY CH47 87 G1
STHEL WA9 49 G4
WAL/EG CH44 68 C1
WARRN/WOL WA2 83 G2
Newton St BIRK CH41 2 C3
Newton Wk BTL L20 4 D3
Newton Wy GR/UP/WCH CH49 89 H3
VAUX/LVPD L3 7 J4
New Tower Ct WAL/NB CH45 52 A2
Newtown NSTN CH64 159 E4
Newway DV/KA/FCH L14 57 G5
Nicander Rd CALD/MH L18 95 H3
Nicholas Rd CSBY/BLUN L23 20 C5
WDN WA8 124 A3
Nicholas St VAUX/LVPD L3 * 70 D2
Nicholl Rd ECCL WA10 46 C1
Nicholls Dr PEN/TH CH61 134 D2
Nicholls St WARRS WA4 131 F1
Nicholson St STHEL WA9 49 E3
WARR WA1 12 A4
Nickleby Cl TOX L8 94 B3
Nickleford Hall Dr WDN WA8 101 H2
Nidderdale Av RAIN/WH L35 78 B2
Nigel Rd HES CH60 149 G1
Nightingale Cl KKBY L32 33 E1
NTHLY L27 98 D3
RUNC WA7 156 A4
Nightingale Rd
WD/CROXPK L12 43 F4
Nimrod St ANF/KKDL L4 54 B1
Ninth Av WLT/FAZ L9 32 A5
Nithsdale Rd WAV L15 95 G2
Nixon St ANF/KKDL L4 40 B5
Noctorum Av CL/PREN CH43 90 C3
Noctorum Dell CL/PREN CH43 90 D4
Noctorum La CL/PREN CH43 91 E2
Noctorum Rd CL/PREN CH43 90 D3
Noctorum Wy CL/PREN CH43 90 D4
Noel St TOX L8 94 D1
Nook La STHEL WA9 63 F1
WARRN/WOL WA2 85 F3
WARRS WA4 108 A5
Nook Ri WAV L15 73 F5
The Nook CL/PREN CH43 2 A6
ECCL WA10 46 D1
WKBY CH48 111 H1
WLTN L25 97 H5
Noonan Cl WLT/FAZ L9 40 B3
Nora St WARR WA1 13 G5
Norbreck Av DV/KA/FCH L14 74 A3
Norbreck Cl WARRW/BUR WA5 105 E4
Norbreck Crs
WARRW/BUR WA5 105 E4
Norburn Crs FMBY L37 17 E4
Norbury Av BEB CH63 137 G1
CALD/MH L18 95 H3
WARRN/WOL WA2 84 B5
Norbury Cl BEB CH63 137 H1
WDN WA8 15 K1
Norbury Fold RAIN/WH L35 78 C4
Norbury Rd KKBY L32 33 G2
Norcliffe Rd RAIN/WH L35 77 H1
Norcott Av WARRS WA4 130 B1
Norfolk Cl BTL L20 5 G3
CL/PREN CH43 90 C3
Norfolk Dr WARRW/BUR WA5 104 C2
WKBY CH48 110 C2
Norfolk Pl LITH L21 * 29 H5
WDN WA8 124 A3
Norfolk Rd ECCL WA10 61 F1
MGHL L31 23 H2
Norfolk St CLVPS L1 93 H1
RUNC WA7 9 G3
Norgate St ANF/KKDL L4 54 B3
Norgrove Cl RUNC WA7 157 F1
Norland's La RAIN/WH L35 78 C5
WDN WA8 101 H1
Norlands Pk WDN WA8 101 H2
Norland St WDN WA8 15 J1
Norleane Crs RUNC WA7 155 F1
Norley Cl WARRW/BUR WA5 106 A3
Norley Dr ECCL WA10 46 C4
Norley Pl HLWD L26 121 G5
Normanby Cl
WARRW/BUR WA5 106 A1
Normandale Rd ANF/KKDL L4 55 F1
Normandy Rd HUY L36 75 F2
Norman Rd BTL L20 30 B5
CSBY/BLUN L23 29 E1
RUNC WA7 8 D7
WAL/EG CH44 69 G3
Norman Salisbury Ct
ECCL WA10 11 F3
Normans Rd STHEL WA9 63 F3
Normanston Rd CL/PREN CH43 91 H4
Norman St BIRK CH41 68 B5
WARRN/WOL WA2 12 E2
Normanton Av AIG/SPK L17 95 E5
Normanton Cl CL/PREN CH43 91 G4
Norma Rd CSBY/WL L22 29 F3
Norreys Av WARRW/BUR WA5 83 F5
Norric Ct SPK/HALE L24 * 141 H1
Norris Cl CL/PREN CH43 90 C4
Norris Green Crs NG/CROX L11 56 A1
Norris Green Rd
WD/CROXPK L12 56 B4
Norris Green Wy NG/CROX L11 56 A1
Norris Rd PR/KW L34 59 G4
Norris St WARRN/WOL WA2 84 A5
Norris Wy FMBY L37 17 G3
Norseman Cl WD/CROXPK L12 56 B2
North Alfred Dock BIRK CH41 * 69 H4
North Av AIN/FAZ L10 32 B2
SPK/HALE L24 120 C5
WARRN/WOL WA2 83 H5
North Barcombe Rd
CHLDW L16 96 D1
Northbrook Cl TOX L8 94 C1
Northbrook Rd WAL/EG CH44 69 F2
Northbrook St TOX L8 94 C1
North Cantril Av
WD/CROXPK L12 57 E2
North Cl PS/BROM CH62 138 C4
Northcote Cl EV L5 71 F1
Northcote Rd WAL/NB CH45 50 D4
WLT/FAZ L9 * 40 B4
Northdale Rd WARR WA1 85 E5
WAV L15 72 D5
North Dingle ANF/KKDL L4 53 H2
North Dr HES CH60 149 E2
WAV L15 72 D5
WD/CROXPK L12 56 B5
North End La HLWD L26 98 C5
Northern La WDN WA8 100 C5
Northern Perimeter Rd
NTHTN L30 22 D4
The Northern Rd
CSBY/BLUN L23 21 F5
Northfield Cl NWD/KWIPK L33 26 B5
STHEL WA9 79 H2
Northfield Rd BTL L20 40 A1
North Front RAIN/WH L35 77 E4
Northgate Rd CLB/OSW/ST L13 55 H5
North Gv CALD/MH L18 119 G2
North Hill St TOX L8 94 B3
North John St CLVP L2 6 D3
ECCL WA10 11 F4
North Linkside Rd WLTN L25 121 E2
North Manor Wy WLTN L25 121 E2
North Meade MGHL L31 18 B4
Northmead Rd ALL/GAR L19 120 A4
North Mossley Hill Rd
CALD/MH L18 95 H4
North Mount Rd KKBY L32 25 E5
Northolt Ct WARRN/WOL WA2 84 C4
North Pde HOY CH47 87 E1
KKBY L32 33 H2
SPK/HALE L24 142 C3
North Park Brook Rd
WARRW/BUR WA5 83 E4
North Park Ct WAL/EG CH44 69 G2
North Park Rd KKBY L32 25 F5
North Perimeter Rd
NWD/KWIPK L33 27 E5
Northridge Rd PEN/TH CH61 135 E1
North Rd ALL/GAR L19 118 D5
DV/KA/FCH L14 73 G3
ECCL WA10 11 F1
HLWD L26 142 D1
RF/TRAN CH42 92 A5
WKBY CH48 110 A1
North St VAUX/LVPD L3 6 E2
North Sudley Rd AIG/SPK L17 118 C1
Northumberland Gv TOX L8 93 H3
Northumberland St TOX L8 94 A3
Northumberland Ter EV L5 54 A4
Northumberland Wy
NTHTN L30 30 B1
North Vw EHL/KEN L7 71 G4
HUY L36 76 A3
WARRW/BUR WA5 104 C1
Northway HES CH60 * 135 H5
MGHL L31 18 D4
RUNC WA7 156 B1
WARRN/WOL WA2 83 H3
WAV L15 73 F5
WDN WA8 124 B2
Northways PS/BROM CH62 138 D3
Northwich Cl CSBY/BLUN L23 22 A3
Northwich Rd RUNC WA7 157 E4
North William St
WAL/EG CH44 * 69 G3
Northwood Rd CL/PREN CH43 114 B1
HUY L36 75 H1
RUNC WA7 147 E4
Norton Av WARRW/BUR WA5 104 C3
Norton Dr PEN/TH CH61 112 A4
Norton Ga RUNC WA7 157 E1
Norton Gv MGHL L31 23 H3
STHEL WA9 61 F3
Norton La RUNC WA7 156 D1
Norton Rd WKBY CH48 87 E5
Norton Station Rd RUNC WA7 157 F1
Norton St BTL L20 4 C1
VAUX/LVPD L3 7 G2
Norton Vw RUNC WA7 156 C1
Norton Village RUNC WA7 157 F1
Norville Rd DV/KA/FCH L14 73 G3
Norwich Dr GR/UP/WCH CH49 90 A1
Norwich Rd WAV L15 96 A2
Norwich Wy KKBY L32 33 H2
Norwood Av LITH L21 30 A3
Norwood Ct GR/UP/WCH CH49 89 F5
Norwood Gv NPK/KEN L6 71 H1
Norwood Rd GR/UP/WCH CH49 89 F4
WAL/EG CH44 68 D3
Norwyn Rd NG/CROX L11 41 G5
Nottingham Cl RAIN/WH L35 61 E5
WARR WA1 108 D2
Nottingham Rd HUY L36 75 E4
Nowshera Av PEN/TH CH61 134 D1
Nuffield Cl GR/UP/WCH CH49 89 H4
Nun Cl CL/PREN CH43 91 H4
Nunn St STHEL WA9 48 D4
Nunsford Cl LITH L21 30 C2
Nunthorpe Rd PR/KW L34 43 H2
The Nurseries FMBY L37 17 F4
Nurse Rd PEN/TH CH61 113 F5
Nursery Cl CL/PREN CH43 91 H5
WDN WA8 102 D5
WLTN L25 121 E3
Nursery Dr FMBY L37 17 E4
Nursery La ALL/GAR L19 119 G4
Nursery Rd MGHL L31 18 C2
STHEL WA9 61 F3
Nutgrove Av STHEL WA9 * 61 F3
Nutgrove Hall Dr STHEL WA9 61 F3
Nutgrove Rd STHEL WA9 61 E4
Nut St STHEL WA9 61 F3
Nuttall Ct GOL/RIS/CUL WA3 85 G1
Nuttall St EHL/KEN L7 72 A4
Nyland Rd HUY L36 58 B5

O

Oak Av GR/UP/WCH CH49 89 F2
WLT/FAZ L9 40 D1
Oak Bank BIRK CH41 2 C6
Oakbank Rd CALD/MH L18 95 G3
Oakbank St WAL/EG CH44 69 E2
Oakbourne Cl AIG/SPK L17 118 A1
Oak Cl MOR/LEA CH46 89 F1
RAIN/WH L35 77 E2
WD/CROXPK L12 57 F1
Oakdale Av WAL/EG CH44 69 F3
WARRS WA4 130 B2
Oakdale Cl KKBY L32 33 E3
Oakdale Dr GR/UP/WCH CH49 112 A1
Oakdale Rd BIRK CH41 69 F4
CALD/MH L18 96 A3
CSBY/WL L22 29 E2
WAL/EG CH44 69 F3
Oakdene Av WARR WA1 108 C1
Oakdene Cl PS/BROM CH62 152 D4
Oakdene Rd ANF/KKDL L4 54 D3
RF/TRAN CH42 92 A5
Oak Dr RUNC WA7 155 G2
Oakenholt Rd MOR/LEA CH46 66 C4
Oakes St VAUX/LVPD L3 7 J3
Oakfield ANF/KKDL L4 54 D4
Oakfield Av WLTN L25 97 G4
Oakfield Cl STHEL WA9 61 F3
Oakfield Dr FMBY L37 16 C2
HUY L36 75 H5
WDN WA8 123 G3
Oakfield Gv HUY L36 75 H5
Oakfield Rd ANF/KKDL L4 54 C4
PS/BROM CH62 152 C1
Oakgate Cl NG/CROX L11 42 B4
Oakham Dr AIN/FAZ L10 32 C3
MOR/LEA CH46 65 H4
Oakham St TOX L8 93 H2
Oakhill Cl MGHL L31 18 D4
WD/CROXPK L12 42 D4
Oakhill Cottage La MGHL L31 18 D2
Oakhill Dr MGHL L31 18 C2
Oakhill Pk CLB/OSW/ST L13 73 F3
Oakhill Rd CLB/OSW/ST L13 73 F3
MGHL L31 18 D4
Oakhurst Cl WLTN L25 97 H4
Oakland Cl LITH L21 39 G1
Oakland Dr GR/UP/WCH CH49 90 A2
Oakland Rd ALL/GAR L19 118 D3
Oaklands RAIN/WH L35 78 A3
Oaklands Av CSBY/BLUN L23 21 F4
Oaklands Ct STHEL WA9 79 G1
Oaklands Dr BEB CH63 116 A5
PEN/TH CH61 135 E5
Oaklands Ter PEN/TH CH61 * 135 E4
Oakland St WARR WA1 107 G1
WDN WA8 146 A2
Oak La NG/CROX L11 56 B1
Oak La North NG/CROX L11 42 C5
Oakleaf Ms CL/PREN CH43 90 D3
Oaklea Rd PEN/TH CH61 112 D5
Oaklee Gv NWD/KWIPK L33 26 B5
Oak Leigh CLB/OSW/ST L13 55 G5
Oakleigh Gv BEB CH63 115 H5
Oakley Cl WD/CROXPK L12 43 E4
Oak Meadows Ct RAIN/WH L35 78 C4
Oakmere Cl MOR/LEA CH46 66 C1
WLT/FAZ L9 31 F5
Oakmere Dr GR/UP/WCH CH49 89 E4
WARRW/BUR WA5 104 D5
Oakmere St RUNC WA7 8 D5
Oakridge Cl PS/BROM CH62 138 C4
Oakridge Rd PS/BROM CH62 138 C4
Oak Rd BEB CH63 115 H4
HUY L36 75 F5
RAIN/WH L35 77 E2
WARRW/BUR WA5 104 D5
Oaks Cl STHEL WA9 79 H2
Oaks La PEN/TH CH61 135 E2
Oaksmeade Cl WD/CROXPK L12 43 F4
Oaks Pl WDN WA8 14 C5
The Oaks PS/BROM CH62 152 C1
STHEL WA9 * 79 H1
WD/CROXPK L12 43 F4
WKBY CH48 * 110 C2
Oakston Av RAIN/WH L35 78 B3
Oak St BTL L20 5 F2
STHEL WA9 63 E2
Oakway HES CH60 149 F3
Oak Ter EHL/KEN L7 * 72 A3
Oaktree Pl RF/TRAN CH42 92 D5
Oaktree Rd ECCL WA10 46 C2
Oak Vw CLB/OSW/ST L13 73 F3
Oak Vw SPK/HALE L24 143 E3
Oak Wharf Ms WARRS WA4 * 130 A3
Oakwood Av WARR WA1 13 J1
Oakwood Cl WLTN L25 97 H3
Oakwood Dr CL/PREN CH43 68 A5
HUY L36 75 H4
Oakwood Ga GOL/RIS/CUL WA3 85 H1
Oakwood Pk PS/BROM CH62 152 D4
Oakwood Rd HLWD L26 121 G4
Oakworth Cl NWD/KWIPK L33 25 H5
Oakworth Dr PS/BROM CH62 116 C4
RAIN/WH L35 99 E1
Oarside Dr WAL/NB CH45 51 G4
Oatfield La LITH L21 30 A2
Oatlands Rd KKBY L32 * 33 F2
The Oatlands WKBY CH48 110 C2
Oban Dr HES CH60 149 E1
Oban Gv WARRN/WOL WA2 85 E2
Oban Rd ANF/KKDL L4 54 D4
Oberon St BTL L20 53 G1
O'Brien Gv STHEL WA9 49 E3
Observatory Rd CL/PREN CH43 67 H5
Oceanic Rd CLB/OSW/ST L13 72 D3
Ocean Rd LITH L21 30 A5
O'Connell Rd VAUX/LVPD L3 70 D1
O'Connor Dr NWD/KWIPK L33 25 H3
Octavia Ct HUY L36 * 76 A4
Octavia Hill Rd LITH L21 30 B3
October Dr NPK/KEN L6 55 F4
Odsey St EHL/KEN L7 72 A3
Ogle Cl RAIN/WH L35 60 A5
Oglet La SPK/HALE L24 142 A4
Oil St VAUX/LVPD L3 70 B1
O'Keeffe Rd STHEL WA9 48 C3
Okehampton Rd CHLDW L16 73 H5
Okell Dr HLWD L26 121 F1
Okell St RUNC WA7 8 D5
Old Barn Rd ANF/KKDL L4 54 D4
WAL/EG CH44 68 C2
Old Bidston Rd BIRK CH41 2 A1
Oldbridge Rd SPK/HALE L24 142 D3
Old Chester Rd BEB CH63 115 H4
RF/TRAN CH42 115 H1
WARRS WA4 129 F4
Old Church Cl WLT/FAZ L9 31 G5
Old Church Yd CLVP L2 6 B4
Old Clatterbridge Rd
BEB CH63 137 G4
Old Coach Rd RUNC WA7 8 A3
Old College Pl EHL/KEN L7 72 A4
Old Colliery Rd RAIN/WH L35 76 D2
Old Court House Rd
PS/BROM CH62 138 D1
Old Distillery Rd
SPK/HALE L24 141 H1
Old Dover Rd HUY L36 75 E5
Old Eccleston La ECCL WA10 47 E4
Old Farm Rd CSBY/BLUN L23 21 G5
KKBY L32 43 F1
Oldfield Cl HES CH60 134 C4
Oldfield Dr HES CH60 134 A5
Oldfield Gdns HES CH60 134 B5
Oldfield La WKBY CH48 88 C3
Oldfield Rd ALL/GAR L19 119 E2
HES CH60 134 B4
Oldfield St ECCL WA10 11 F1
Oldfield Wy HES CH60 134 B4
Oldgate WDN WA8 124 A5
Old Gorsey La WAL/EG CH44 68 D3
Old Greasby Rd
GR/UP/WCH CH49 89 H3
Old Hall RAIN/WH L35 77 E5
Old Hall Cl MGHL L31 24 A2
WARRS WA4 129 G3
Old Hall La KKBY L32 33 G2
Old Hall Rd MGHL L31 24 A2
PS/BROM CH62 139 E5
WARRW/BUR WA5 82 D5
Old Hall St VAUX/LVPD L3 6 B2
Oldham Pl CLVPS L1 7 G5
Oldham St CLVPS L1 7 G6
WARRS WA4 107 F5
Old Haymarket CLVPS L1 6 E3
Old Higher Rd WDN WA8 143 H1
Old Hutte La HLWD L26 122 A5
Old Kennel Cl WD/CROXPK L12 57 F2
Old La HES CH60 149 H1
MGHL L31 19 E2
PR/KW L34 60 B4
RAIN/WH L35 77 H3
Old Leeds St VAUX/LVPD L3 6 B2
Old Liverpool Rd
WARRW/BUR WA5 106 A4
Old Lodge Cl WD/CROXPK L12 56 B2
Old Market Pl WARR WA1 12 C4
Old Maryland La
MOR/LEA CH46 66 C4
Old Meadow PR/KW L34 44 B2
Old Meadow Rd PEN/TH CH61 134 C3
Old Mill Av STHEL WA9 62 D5
Old Mill Cl HES CH60 149 F2
Old Mill La FMBY L37 17 E2
PR/KW L34 44 C2
WAV L15 73 E5
Old Nook La RNFD/HAY WA11 49 E1
Old Orch RAIN/WH L35 77 E4
Old Post Office Pl CLVPS L1 * 6 E5
Old Pump La GR/UP/WCH CH49 89 E5
The Old Quarry WLTN L25 120 C1
Old Quay Cl NSTN CH64 158 B3
Old Quay La NSTN CH64 158 C3
Old Quay St RUNC WA7 9 G3
Old Racecourse Rd MGHL L31 23 G1
Old Rectory Gn SFTN L29 22 D2
Old Riding DV/KA/FCH L14 57 F5
Old Rd WARRS WA4 12 E7
Old Ropery CLVP L2 * 6 C4
Old Rough La NWD/KWIPK L33 33 H4
Old School Cl NSTN CH64 159 E5
Old School Wy CL/PREN CH43 * 91 E1
The Old Tennis Club
RF/TRAN CH42 * 114 D1
Old Thomas La DV/KA/FCH L14 73 H4
Old Town La FMBY L37 16 D2
Old Upton La WDN WA8 101 G4
Old Whint Rd RNFD/HAY WA11 49 G1
Old Wood Rd PEN/TH CH61 134 D2
Oleander Dr ECCL WA10 47 E3
O'Leary St WARRN/WOL WA2 107 E1
Olga Rd STHEL WA9 62 C3
Olinda St PS/BROM CH62 116 B4
Olive Cl MGHL L31 * 32 D2
Olive Crs BIRK CH41 92 C4
Olivedale Rd CALD/MH L18 95 H4
Olive Dr NSTN CH64 158 D2
Olive Gv HUY L36 75 F3
NTHTN L30 31 F3
WAV L15 73 E4
Olive La WAV L15 73 E4
Olive Mt BIRK CH41 92 C4
Olive Mount Rd WAV L15 73 E5
Oliver La BIRK CH41 3 F5
Oliver Lyme Rd PR/KW L34 60 A4
Olive Rd CSBY/WL L22 29 F4
NSTN CH64 158 D2
Oliver Rd ECCL WA10 61 E1
Oliver St BIRK CH41 2 D5
WARRN/WOL WA2 12 D2
Oliver St East BIRK CH41 3 F5
Olivetree Rd WAV L15 73 F5
Olive Vw WAV L15 72 D5
Olivia Cl CL/PREN CH43 90 C4
Olivia St BTL L20 53 H1
Olivia Wy HUY L36 76 B3
Ollerton Cl CL/PREN CH43 90 C4
WARRS WA4 108 B5
Ollery Gn NTHTN L30 23 G5
Ollier St WDN WA8 14 C6
Olney St ANF/KKDL L4 40 B5
Olton St WAV L15 72 C5
Olympia Pl WARRW/BUR WA5 105 F1
Olympia St NPK/KEN L6 71 G2
Olympic Wy NTHTN L30 31 F4
Omega Bvd WARRW/BUR WA5 81 F4
O'Neill St BTL L20 4 C2
Onslow Rd NPK/KEN L6 72 A2
PS/BROM CH62 116 B3
WAL/NB CH45 51 H2
Opal Cl LITH L21 30 B4
NPK/KEN L6 71 H1
Openfields Cl HLWD L26 121 G1
Oppenheim Av ECCL WA10 61 E2
Orange Gv TOX L8 95 E2
WARRN/WOL WA2 84 C3
Orange Tree Cl STBRV L28 * 57 H2
Oran Wy HUY L36 75 F2
Orb Cl NG/CROX L11 42 C4
Orchard Av DV/KA/FCH L14 73 H4
Orchard Cl PR/KW L34 60 C3
RAIN/WH L35 77 E4
RNFD/HAY WA11 37 H5
Orchard Ct BIRK CH41 92 D5
Orchard Dl CSBY/BLUN L23 21 G5
Orchard Dr NSTN CH64 158 D5
Orchard Gdns RAIN/WH L35 77 E5
Orchard Gra MOR/LEA CH46 89 E1
Orchard Hey ECCL WA10 46 C4
MGHL L31 24 B1
NTHTN L30 31 G1
Orchard Rd MOR/LEA CH46 66 C4
Orchard St WARR WA1 13 F4
WARRN/WOL WA2 85 E3
WARRS WA4 130 A3
The Orchard AIG/SPK L17 118 D2
HUY L36 75 G4
WAL/NB CH45 51 G3
Orchard Wk NSTN CH64 158 D2
RUNC WA7 * 156 B2
Orchard Wy BEB CH63 115 F5
WDN WA8 100 C5
Orchid Gv AIG/SPK L17 94 B5
Orchid Wy STHEL WA9 63 H3
O'Reilly Ct VAUX/LVPD L3 70 C1
Orford Gn WARRN/WOL WA2 84 B4
Orford La WARRN/WOL WA2 12 E1
Orford Rd WARRN/WOL WA2 84 B5
Orford St WARR WA1 12 E4
WAV L15 72 D5
Oriel Cl AIN/FAZ L10 32 A1
Oriel Crs BTL L20 53 G1
Oriel Dr AIN/FAZ L10 32 A1
Oriel Rd BTL L20 4 D6
RF/TRAN CH42 92 C5
Oriel St VAUX/LVPD L3 70 C2
Orient Dr WLTN L25 97 H5
Origen Rd CHLDW L16 73 H4
Oriole Cl ECCL WA10 60 D3
Orion Bvd WARRW/BUR WA5 81 G4
Orith Av ECCL WA10 46 B4
Orkney Cl RNFD/HAY WA11 37 H5
WDN WA8 103 E5
Orlando Cl CL/PREN CH43 90 C4
Orlando Dr WARRW/BUR WA5 105 G1
Orlando St BTL L20 53 G1
Orleans Rd CLB/OSW/ST L13 73 E2
Ormande St STHEL WA9 62 B1
Ormesby Gv BEB CH63 152 A3
Ormiston Rd WAL/NB CH45 51 H3
Ormond Cl WDN WA8 124 A1
Ormonde Av MGHL L31 23 H2
Ormonde Crs NWD/KWIPK L33 34 B2
Ormonde Dr MGHL L31 23 H1
Ormond St VAUX/LVPD L3 6 C3
WAL/NB CH45 51 H5
Ormond Wy CL/PREN CH43 90 C4
Ormsby St WAV L15 95 G1
Ormside Gv STHEL WA9 62 D3
Ormskirk Rd PR/KW L34 44 B1
WLT/FAZ L9 31 G2
WLT/FAZ L9 31 G4
Ormskirk St ECCL WA10 11 F4
Orms Wy FMBY L37 16 D3
Orphan Dr NPK/KEN L6 55 F5
Orphan St EHL/KEN L7 71 G5
Orrell Cl WARRW/BUR WA5 105 E2
Orrell Hey BTL L20 30 C5
Orrell La BTL L20 31 E5
WLT/FAZ L9 40 C1
Orrell Mt BTL L20 30 B5
Orrell Rd BTL L20 30 B5
WAL/NB CH45 52 A3
Orrell St STHEL WA9 48 C4
Orret's Meadow Rd
GR/UP/WCH CH49 90 B5
Orrysdale Rd WKBY CH48 87 E5
Orry St EV L5 53 H5
Orsett Rd KKBY L32 34 A4
Orston Crs BEB CH63 138 A4
Ortega Cl PS/BROM CH62 116 C4
Orthes St VAUX/LVPD L3 7 J5
Orton Rd CHLDW L16 73 G5
Orville St STHEL WA9 63 F3
Orwell Cl FMBY L37 16 C5
STHEL WA9 79 E2
Orwell Rd ANF/KKDL L4 53 H2
Osbert Rd CSBY/BLUN L23 20 C5
Osborne Av WAL/NB CH45 51 H3
WARRN/WOL WA2 84 B4
Osborne Ct PS/BROM CH62 116 B4
Osborne Gv PR/KW L34 59 E5
WAL/NB CH45 51 H4
Osborne Rd CL/PREN CH43 2 A6
CLB/OSW/ST L13 55 G4
ECCL WA10 46 C2
FMBY L37 16 D5
LITH L21 30 B3
WAL/NB CH45 52 A3
WARRS WA4 129 H2
Osborne Wd AIG/SPK L17 118 B2
Osbourne Cl PS/BROM CH62 153 E2
Osmaston Rd RF/TRAN CH42 114 C1
Osprey Cl NTHLY L27 98 D3
RUNC WA7 156 B4
WARRN/WOL WA2 84 C2
Ossett Cl CL/PREN CH43 90 C4
RUNC WA7 157 F1
Osterley Gdns WLT/FAZ L9 40 B1
O'Sullivan Crs RNFD/HAY WA11 49 E2
Oteley Av PS/BROM CH62 152 D1
Othello Cl BTL L20 53 G1

Otterburn Cl MOR/LEA CH46 65 H5
Otterspool Dr AIG/SPK L17 118 B3
Otterspool Rd AIG/SPK L17 118 B2
Otterton Rd NG/CROX L11 42 C2
Ottley St NPK/KEN L6 72 A2
Otway St ALL/GAR L19 140 C1
Oueenswood Av BEB CH63 115 G3
Oulton Cl CL/PREN CH43 91 E5
MGHL L31 18 B2
Oulton La HUY L36 75 E5
Oulton Rd CHLDW L16 96 D2
Oulton Wy CL/PREN CH43 114 A1
Oundle Dr AIN/FAZ L10 31 H1
Oundle Pl WLTN L25 120 D4
Oundle Rd MOR/LEA CH46 66 C4
Outer Central Rd HLWD L26 142 C1
Outer Forum NG/CROX L11 41 G5
Out La WLTN L25 120 D1
The Oval WAL/NB CH45 51 F4
Overbrook La PR/KW L34 44 A2
Overbury St EHL/KEN L7 71 H4
Overchurch Rd
GR/UP/WCH CH49 89 G2
Overdale Av PEN/TH CH61 135 H1
Overdene Wk KKBY L32 34 A3
Overgreen Gv MOR/LEA CH46 66 B4
Overton Av LITH L21 30 A3
Overton Cl CL/PREN CH43 91 F5
KKBY L32 33 G3
Overton Rd WAL/EG CH44 68 D1
Overton St EHL/KEN L7 71 H4
Overton Wy CL/PREN CH43 91 F5
Ovington Cl RUNC WA7 156 B5
Ovolo Rd CLB/OSW/ST L13 73 E1
Owen Cl ECCL WA10 61 E1
Owen Dr SPK/HALE L24 141 H4
Owen Rd ANF/KKDL L4 53 H2
NWD/KWIPK L33 34 D5
RAIN/WH L35 78 A3
Owen St ECCL WA10 61 E1
WARRN/WOL WA2 12 C1
WARRN/WOL WA2 106 C1
Oxborough Cl WDN WA8 101 H5
Oxbow Rd WD/CROXPK L12 57 E2
Oxendale Cl TOX L8 94 D1
Oxenham Rd WARRN/WOL WA2 83 G2
Oxenholme Crs NG/CROX L11 56 A1
Oxford Av BTL L20 5 J5
LITH L21 30 A4
Oxford Cl AIG/SPK L17 118 A1
Oxford Ct WARR WA1 13 G3
Oxford Dr BEB CH63 150 B3
CSBY/WL L22 28 D3
HLWD L26 121 H3
Oxford Rd BTL L20 5 H5
CSBY/WL L22 28 D2
HUY L36 76 A1
RUNC WA7 8 D7
WAL/EG CH44 69 E1
WLT/FAZ L9 31 G4
Oxford St ECCL WA10 10 E2
WARRS WA4 13 G7
WDN WA8 14 E4
Oxheys RUNC WA7 157 E1
Ox La RAIN/WH L35 99 G2
Oxley Av MOR/LEA CH46 67 F2
Oxley St STHEL WA9 62 D3
Oxmead Cl WARRN/WOL WA2 85 F4
Oxmoor Cl RUNC WA7 156 C4
Oxton Cl AIG/SPK L17 118 A1
KKBY L32 33 E4
WDN WA8 101 E4
Oxton Rd BIRK CH41 2 C7
WAL/EG CH44 68 D2
Oxton St ANF/KKDL L4 54 B2

P

Pacific Rd BIRK CH41 3 H2
BTL L20 4 C3
Packenham Rd
CLB/OSW/ST L13 55 H4
Padbury St TOX L8 94 C3
Paddington EHL/KEN L7 71 G4
Paddington Bank WARR WA1 107 H2
Paddock Cl CSBY/BLUN L23 20 C3
Paddock Gv STHEL WA9 79 H2
Paddock Ri RUNC WA7 156 A5
The Paddock FMBY L37 17 F1
GR/UP/WCH CH49 90 B3
HES CH60 149 G1
KKBY L32 33 G5
MOR/LEA CH46 89 E1
PR/KW L34 60 B3
WLTN L25 97 H4
Padeswood Cl STHEL WA9 62 C4
Padgate La WARR WA1 13 K1
Padstow Cl HLWD L26 121 H2
WARRW/BUR WA5 104 C5
Padstow Dr ECCL WA10 46 D1
Padstow Rd CHLDW L16 73 H5
GR/UP/WCH CH49 112 A1
Pagebank Rd DV/KA/FCH L14 74 C2
Page Ct FMBY L37 17 E3
Pagefield Rd WAV L15 96 A2
Page La WDN WA8 15 H2
Page Moss Av HUY L36 74 D1
Page Moss La DV/KA/FCH L14 74 C2
HUY L36 74 D1
Page Wk VAUX/LVPD L3 7 H1
Pagewood Cl CL/PREN CH43 90 D4
Paignton Cl HUY L36 76 B3
WARRW/BUR WA5 104 C4
Paignton Rd CHLDW L16 73 H5
WAL/NB CH45 51 E4
Paisley Av PS/BROM CH62 153 E5
RNFD/HAY WA11 37 H5
Paisley St VAUX/LVPD L3 6 B1
Palace Fields Av RUNC WA7 156 C2
Palace Hey NSTN CH64 159 F5
Palace Rd WLT/FAZ L9 40 C3
Palatine Ar ECCL WA10 * 11 G5
Palatine Rd PS/BROM CH62 138 C5
WAL/EG CH44 69 F3
Palermo Cl WAL/EG CH44 69 F3
Paley Cl ANF/KKDL L4 54 A3
Palin Dr WARRW/BUR WA5 104 D2
Palladio Rd CLB/OSW/ST L13 73 F1
Pall Ml VAUX/LVPD L3 70 B2
Palm Cl WLT/FAZ L9 41 E4
Palmer Cl CL/PREN CH43 90 D5
ECCL WA10 10 E4
Palmer Crs WARRW/BUR WA5 82 D5
Palmerston Av LITH L21 29 H5
Palmerston Cl CALD/MH L18 95 H5
Palmerston Crs ALL/GAR L19 119 G5
Palmerston Dr LITH L21 39 F1
WLTN L25 121 F3
Palmerston Rd ALL/GAR L19 119 G5
CALD/MH L18 95 H5
WAL/EG CH44 68 B1
Palmerston St RF/TRAN CH42 115 H1
Palm Gv CL/PREN CH43 91 H3
WLTN L25 120 D2
Palm Hl CL/PREN CH43 91 H4
Palmwood Av RAIN/WH L35 78 B3
Palmwood Cl CL/PREN CH43 114 A2
Palmyra Sq North WARR WA1 12 C5
Palmyra Sq South WARR WA1 12 C5
Paltridge Wy PEN/TH CH61 134 D2
Pamela Cl AIN/FAZ L10 33 E5
Pampas Gv WLT/FAZ L9 40 D3
Pangbourne Cl WARRS WA4 130 C3
Pankhurst Rd LITH L21 30 B2
Pansy St EV L5 53 H3
Papillon Dr WLT/FAZ L9 32 A4
Parade Crs SPK/HALE L24 142 C4
Parade St ECCL WA10 11 G4
The Parade NSTN CH64 158 A1
Paradise La FMBY L37 17 F1
RAIN/WH L35 76 D3
Paradise Rw WLTN L25 * 97 H4
Paradise St CLVPS L1 6 E4
Paragon Cl WDN WA8 102 B3
Parbold Av RNFD/HAY WA11 48 D2
Parbold Ct WDN WA8 124 B4
Parbrook Cl HUY L36 58 B4
Parbrook Rd HUY L36 58 B5
Park Av CALD/MH L18 95 G5
CSBY/BLUN L23 21 F4
FMBY L37 17 E5
MGHL L31 18 D3
PR/KW L34 60 B3
RAIN/WH L35 78 A1
RNFD/HAY WA11 49 G1
WAL/EG CH44 69 F2
WARRS WA4 107 F5
WDN WA8 14 E1
WLT/FAZ L9 32 A5
Park Bvd WARR WA1 12 C7
Parkbourn MGHL L31 19 G4
Parkbourn Dr MGHL L31 19 G4
Parkbourn North MGHL L31 19 G4
Parkbourn Sq MGHL L31 19 G4
Parkbridge Rd RF/TRAN CH42 92 A5
Park Brow Dr KKBY L32 34 A4
Parkbury Ct CL/PREN CH43 91 G5
Park Cl BIRK CH41 2 C4
KKBY L32 33 E1
Park Ct CSBY/WL L22 29 F3
RUNC WA7 155 E1
Park Crs WARRS WA4 130 B5
Parkdale WKBY CH48 110 D5
Parkdale Av WLT/FAZ L9 31 F5
Parkdale Rd WARR WA1 108 A1
Park Dr BIRK CH41 2 B3
CL/PREN CH43 2 A4
CL/PREN CH43 91 G1
CSBY/BLUN L23 20 B5
CSBY/BLUN L23 21 H2
Parkend Rd RF/TRAN CH42 92 A5
Parker Av LITH L21 29 G5
Parker Cl NTHTN L30 31 G3
Parkers Ct RUNC WA7 156 A3
Parker St CLVPS L1 7 F4
RUNC WA7 9 F3
WARR WA1 12 B6
Parkfield Av BIRK CH41 2 E4
NTHTN L30 31 F3
WARRS WA4 108 A4
Parkfield Dr WAL/EG CH44 68 D1
Parkfield Gv MGHL L31 18 C5
Parkfield Pl BIRK CH41 2 D4
Parkfield Rd AIG/SPK L17 94 D4
BEB CH63 138 A3
CSBY/WL L22 29 F2
Parkfields La WARRN/WOL WA2 84 D3
Parkgate Cl AIG/SPK L17 118 C2
Parkgate La NSTN CH64 150 A4
Parkgate Rd NSTN CH64 158 B2
WARRS WA4 130 B2
Parkgate Wy RUNC WA7 157 E2
Park Gv BIRK CH41 2 D7
Parkhill Ct TOX L8 94 B4
Parkhill Rd RF/TRAN CH42 92 A5
Park Hill Rd TOX L8 94 B4
Parkhurst Rd NG/CROX L11 55 H1
RF/TRAN CH42 * 115 E1
Parkinson Rd WLT/FAZ L9 40 C3
Parkland Cl TOX L8 94 C3
Parkland Ct CL/PREN CH43 67 G5
Parklands PR/KW L34 44 B4
WDN WA8 101 E5
Parklands Dr HES CH60 149 F3
Parklands Wy CSBY/WL L22 29 G3
Park La BTL L20 30 D5
CLVPS L1 6 E6
HOY CH47 65 G3
MGHL L31 19 E3
NTHTN L30 31 E2
Park Lane Dr MGHL L31 19 H4
Park La West NTHTN L30 31 E1
Park Pl BTL L20 5 F5
TOX L8 94 A2
Park Rd CSBY/WL L22 29 F3
FMBY L37 16 D5
HES CH60 135 F5
HOY CH47 65 E4
KKBY L32 33 E1
PR/KW L34 59 G3
PS/BROM CH62 138 B1
PS/BROM CH62 153 F3
RF/TRAN CH42 92 C5
RUNC WA7 154 D1
STHEL WA9 48 C3
TOX L8 94 B3
WAL/EG CH44 69 E2
WARRN/WOL WA2 84 B4
WARRW/BUR WA5 104 A1
WDN WA8 15 F1
WKBY CH48 110 A1
Park Rd East BIRK CH41 2 C4
Park Rd North BIRK CH41 2 A2
Park Rd South CL/PREN CH43 2 B5
Park Rd West CL/PREN CH43 91 G1
Parkside WAL/EG CH44 69 E2
Parkside Av STHEL WA9 79 F2
Parkside Cl BEB CH63 116 A5
NSTN CH64 158 C2
NTHLY L27 98 C4
Parkside Dr WD/CROXPK L12 56 A2
Parkside Rd BEB CH63 116 A5
RF/TRAN CH42 92 C5
Parkside St NPK/KEN L6 71 F2
Parkstile La NG/CROX L11 42 C3
Parkstone Rd RF/TRAN CH42 92 A5
Park St BIRK CH41 2 E3
BTL L20 5 H4
NSTN CH64 158 D2
RNFD/HAY WA11 49 F1
STHEL WA9 48 C3
TOX L8 94 A3
WAL/EG CH44 69 E1
Parksway WARR WA1 108 D1
Park Ter CSBY/WL L22 29 F4
The Park HUY L36 75 G4
WARRW/BUR WA5 104 B5
Parkvale Av CL/PREN CH43 114 A3
Park Vale Rd WLT/FAZ L9 40 C1
Park Vw CSBY/WL L22 29 E2
HUY L36 75 E1
NPK/KEN L6 55 F5
PS/BROM CH62 152 C1
WARRN/WOL WA2 * 84 C2
Parkview Cl BIRK CH41 2 B2
Parkview Dr NTHLY L27 98 C4
Park View Flats LITH L21 * 29 H4
Parkview Rd NG/CROX L11 42 D3
Parkway CSBY/BLUN L23 29 G2
Park Wy FMBY L37 17 E5
HOY CH47 65 E5
HUY L36 58 B3
Parkway NTHTN L30 23 E4
Park Wy TOX L8 94 B1
Parkway WAL/NB CH45 51 E3
Parkway Cl PEN/TH CH61 112 D4
Park Wy West KKBY L32 * 33 E1
Park West HES CH60 148 B2
Parkwood Cl PS/BROM CH62 153 E1
Parkwood Rd RAIN/WH L35 77 E3
WLTN L25 97 G4
Park Works SPK/HALE L24 * 120 D5
Parlane St STHEL WA9 48 C3
Parliament Cl CLVPS L1 94 A1
Parliament Pl TOX L8 94 B1
Parliament St STHEL WA9 61 F3
TOX L8 93 H1
Parlington Cl WDN WA8 124 A4
Parlow Rd NG/CROX L11 55 G2
Parnell Rd BEB CH63 138 A4
Parren Av RAIN/WH L35 76 C4
Parr Gv GR/UP/WCH CH49 89 E4
RNFD/HAY WA11 49 G1
Parr Mount Ct STHEL WA9 48 C4
Parr Mount St STHEL WA9 48 C4
Parrs Rd CL/PREN CH43 91 H5
Parr Stocks Rd STHEL WA9 48 D4
Parr St CLVPS L1 7 F6
LITH L21 30 A3
STHEL WA9 11 J6
STHEL WA9 48 C4
WARR WA1 12 E6
WDN WA8 * 15 G1
Parrs Wood View WARRS WA4 131 E2
Parry Dr WARRS WA4 109 E5
Parry St WAL/EG CH44 69 F3
Parsonage Rd WDN WA8 8 D1
Parsonage Wy
WARRW/BUR WA5 105 E3
Parthenon Dr NG/CROX L11 41 F4
Partington Av BTL L20 5 J2
Parton St NPK/KEN L6 72 A2
Partridge Cl WD/CROXPK L12 43 F4
Partridge Rd CSBY/BLUN L23 20 C5
KKBY L32 33 E1
Pasture Av MOR/LEA CH46 66 C3
Pasture Cl STHEL WA9 79 G1
WLTN L25 120 D2
Pasture Crs MOR/LEA CH46 66 C4
Pasture La WARRN/WOL WA2 85 F4
Pasture Rd MOR/LEA CH46 66 B2
The Pastures STHEL WA9 63 G3
WKBY CH48 111 F1
Pateley Cl KKBY L32 33 F3
Paterson St BIRK CH41 2 C5
Patmos Cl EV L5 54 A4
Paton Cl WKBY CH48 87 G5
Patricia Av BIRK CH41 68 A4
Patricia Gv BTL L20 39 H1
Patrick Av BTL L20 30 C5
Patrivale Cl WARR WA1 107 H1
Patten La WARR WA1 * 12 D5
Patten's Cl NTHTN L30 22 C5
Patten St BIRK CH41 68 D5
Patten's Wk PR/KW L34 44 C2
Patterdale Av
WARRN/WOL WA2 84 A3
Patterdale Crs MGHL L31 19 E4
Patterdale Dr ECCL WA10 60 D2
Patterdale Rd BEB CH63 137 H3
WAV L15 95 G2
Paul Cl WARRW/BUR WA5 104 B2
Paul McCartney Wy
NPK/KEN L6 71 H2
Paul Orr Ct VAUX/LVPD L3 70 C1
Paulsfield Dr MOR/LEA CH46 89 G1
Paul St VAUX/LVPD L3 70 C2
WARRN/WOL WA2 12 B3
Paulton Cl TOX L8 94 B4
Paveley Bank NTHLY L27 98 B3
Pavilion Cl TOX L8 94 D1
Paxton Rd HUY L36 75 G1
Payne Cl WARRW/BUR WA5 105 H2
Peace Dr WARRW/BUR WA5 105 H3
Peacehaven Cl CHLDW L16 74 B5
Peach Gv MGHL L31 25 E5
Peach St EHL/KEN L7 7 K5
Peacock Av WARR WA1 107 G2
Pearce Cl WLTN L25 97 F2
Pear Gv NPK/KEN L6 71 H2
Pearson Av WARRS WA4 130 B1
Pearson Ct WAV L15 * 96 A2
Pearson Dr BTL L20 30 D5
Pearson Rd BIRK CH41 3 F7
Pearson St WAV L15 95 H1
Pear Tree Av RUNC WA7 155 G2
Peartree Av WD/CROXPK L12 57 F1
Pear Tree Cl HES CH60 135 G5
Peartree Pl WARR WA1 106 C5
WARRS WA4 13 F7
Pear Tree Rd HUY L36 75 G5
Peasefield Rd DV/KA/FCH L14 74 C1
Peasley Cl WARRN/WOL WA2 85 F4
Peasley Cross La STHEL WA9 11 K6
Peatwood Av KKBY L32 34 A5
Peckers Hill Rd STHEL WA9 63 E3
Peckfield Cl RUNC WA7 156 C4
Peckforton Cl CLB/OSW/ST L13 55 G4
Peckforton Dr RUNC WA7 156 B5
Peckmill Gn NTHLY L27 98 D4
Pecksniff Cl TOX L8 94 B3
Peebles Av RNFD/HAY WA11 48 D1
Peebles Cl NWD/KWIPK L33 25 G3
Peel Av RF/TRAN CH42 92 D5
Peel Cl RAIN/WH L35 77 E2
WARR WA1 108 D2
Peel House La WDN WA8 102 B5
Peel Pl ECCL WA10 11 G2
TOX L8 94 B1
Peel Rd BTL L20 4 A1
Peel St RUNC WA7 8 C3
TOX L8 94 C4
Peerswood Ct NSTN CH64 158 D5
Peet Av ECCL WA10 47 E3
Peet St EHL/KEN L7 71 H4
Pelham Gv AIG/SPK L17 95 E4
Pelham Rd WAL/EG CH44 68 C2
WARRS WA4 108 C5
Pemberton Rd
CLB/OSW/ST L13 73 E2
GR/UP/WCH CH49 90 B5
Pembertons Ct PR/KW L34 60 A4
Pemberton St ECCL WA10 * 10 D6
Pembrey Wy WLTN L25 121 F3
Pembroke Av MOR/LEA CH46 89 G1
Pembroke Ct BIRK CH41 92 C4
Pembroke Gdns VAUX/LVPD L3 7 J3
Pembroke Pl VAUX/LVPD L3 7 H3
Pembroke Rd BTL L20 4 E5
Pembroke St VAUX/LVPD L3 7 J3
Pembury Cl WD/CROXPK L12 43 E4
Penarth Cl EHL/KEN L7 71 H5
Pencombe Rd HUY L36 74 D1
Penda Dr NWD/KWIPK L33 25 H3
Pendennis Rd WAL/EG CH44 68 D2
Pendennis St ANF/KKDL L4 54 D5
Pendine Cl NPK/KEN L6 72 A1
WARRW/BUR WA5 82 C3
Pendle Av RNFD/HAY WA11 48 D2
Pendlebury St STHEL WA9 79 G1
WARRS WA4 107 H5
Pendle Cl GR/UP/WCH CH49 * 89 G2
Pendle Dr LITH L21 22 B5
Pendleton Gn HLWD L26 121 G4
Pendleton Rd ANF/KKDL L4 40 C5
Penfold MGHL L31 19 E5
Penfold Cl CALD/MH L18 96 D3
Penfolds RUNC WA7 146 D5
Pengallo Hey NTHLY L27 98 D3
Pengwern Gv WAV L15 72 B5
Pengwern St TOX L8 94 C3
Penhale Cl AIG/SPK L17 117 H1
Peninsula Cl WAL/NB CH45 51 E2
Penketh Av WARRW/BUR WA5 83 F5
Penketh Ct RUNC WA7 8 E4
Penketh Rd WARRW/BUR WA5 105 E4
Penkeths La RUNC WA7 8 E3
Penkett Gv WAL/NB CH45 52 A4
Penkett Rd WAL/NB CH45 51 H4
Penlake La STHEL WA9 63 E3
Penley Crs KKBY L32 33 E2
Penlinken Dr NPK/KEN L6 * 71 H1
Penmann Cl HLWD L26 * 121 H4
Penmann Crs HLWD L26 121 H4
Penmark Cl WARRW/BUR WA5 82 C3
Penmon Dr PEN/TH CH61 134 D3
Pennant Av WD/CROXPK L12 56 C1
Pennard Av HUY L36 58 B5
Pennine Cl STHEL WA9 49 E4
Pennine Dr STHEL WA9 49 F4
Pennine Rd RF/TRAN CH42 115 E2
WAL/EG CH44 68 B1
WARRN/WOL WA2 84 C3
Pennine Wy KKBY L32 25 F5
Pennington Av BTL L20 30 D5
Pennington Rd LITH L21 39 G1
Pennington St ANF/KKDL L4 40 B5
Pennington's Went
NSTN CH64 158 D3
Penn La RUNC WA7 8 B6
Pennsylvania Rd NPK/KEN L6 55 F3
Pennyford Dr CALD/MH L18 95 G5
Penny La CALD/MH L18 95 H3
RAIN/WH L35 100 B1
WDN WA8 100 C1
Pennystone Cl
GR/UP/WCH CH49 89 F2
Pennywood Dr RAIN/WH L35 77 E3
Penrhos Rd HOY CH47 86 D2
Penrhyd Rd PEN/TH CH61 134 B1
Penrhyn Av LITH L21 30 A5
PEN/TH CH61 113 E5
Penrhyn Crs RUNC WA7 155 E2
Penrhyn Rd PR/KW L34 43 H2
Penrhyn St EV L5 53 H5
Penrith Av WARRN/WOL WA2 84 A2
Penrith Crs MGHL L31 19 E4
Penrith Rd ECCL WA10 60 D2
Penrith St BIRK CH41 2 C7
Penrose Av East
DV/KA/FCH L14 74 A3
Penrose Av West
DV/KA/FCH L14 74 A3
Penrose Gdns
WARRW/BUR WA5 104 B5
Penrose St EV L5 54 B4
Penryn Av RNFD/HAY WA11 37 H5
Penryn Cl WARRW/BUR WA5 104 C4
Pensall Dr PEN/TH CH61 134 D4
Pensarn Gdns
WARRW/BUR WA5 * 82 D3
Pensarn Rd CLB/OSW/ST L13 72 D3
Pensby Cl PEN/TH CH61 135 E1
Pensby Hall La PEN/TH CH61 134 D4
Pensby Rd HES CH60 135 E5
PEN/TH CH61 113 E5
Penshaw Ct RUNC WA7 156 A2
Pentire Av ECCL WA10 46 D1
Pentire Cl AIN/FAZ L10 42 B1
Pentland Av ANF/KKDL L4 54 C1
STHEL WA9 49 F4
WARRN/WOL WA2 83 H2
Pentland Pl WARRN/WOL WA2 83 H2
Pentland Rd NWD/KWIPK L33 26 B5
Penuel Rd ANF/KKDL L4 40 B5
Penvalley Crs NPK/KEN L6 72 A1
Peony Gdns STHEL WA9 63 H3
Peover St VAUX/LVPD L3 70 D2
Peploe Rd ANF/KKDL L4 41 F5
Peplow Rd KKBY L32 33 E2
Pepper St SPK/HALE L24 143 H5
Pera Cl NPK/KEN L6 71 G2
Percival La RUNC WA7 8 A4
Percival St WARR WA1 13 F5
Percival Wy ECCL WA10 47 E2
Percy Rd WAL/EG CH44 69 G3
Percy St BTL L20 4 C1
STHEL WA9 63 F3
TOX L8 94 B1
WARRW/BUR WA5 * 106 A3
Percy Vls WLT/FAZ L9 * 40 C3
Perimeter Rd NWD/KWIPK L33 35 E4
Perimeter Stalls BIRK CH41 * 3 F5
Perrey St RUNC WA7 9 G4
Perriam Rd ALL/GAR L19 119 H3
Perrin Av RUNC WA7 154 C1
Perrin Rd WAL/EG CH44 51 E5
Perrygate Cl EHL/KEN L7 71 H5
Perry St TOX L8 93 H2
Pershore Rd KKBY L32 33 H4
Perth Av STHEL WA9 61 G3
Perth Cl NWD/KWIPK L33 25 G3
WARRN/WOL WA2 84 D1
Perth St NPK/KEN L6 71 G2
Peterborough Dr NTHTN L30 22 D5
Peterborough Rd WAV L15 96 A2
Peterlee Cl STHEL WA9 61 H3
Peter Mahon Wy BTL L20 4 C3
Peter Price's La BEB CH63 137 G2
Peter Rd ANF/KKDL L4 40 B5
Petersfield Cl NTHTN L30 31 E3
Petersgate RUNC WA7 157 F2
Peter's La CLVPS L1 6 E5
Peterstone Cl
WARRW/BUR WA5 82 D3
Peter St CLVPS L1 6 E3
ECCL WA10 10 D4
WAL/EG CH44 69 G3
Peterwood RF/TRAN CH42 116 A2
Petherick Rd NG/CROX L11 42 C2
Petton St EV L5 54 B4
Petunia Cl DV/KA/FCH L14 * 74 C1
STHEL WA9 63 G3
Petworth Av WARRN/WOL WA2 83 H2
Petworth Cl SPK/HALE L24 141 H2
Peveril Cl WARRS WA4 130 B4
Peveril St WLT/FAZ L9 40 B4
Pex Hill Ct WDN WA8 101 G3
Pharmacy Rd SPK/HALE L24 142 A2
Pheasant Fld SPK/HALE L24 143 G4
Pheasant Gv HLWD L26 121 G2
Philbeach Rd ANF/KKDL L4 41 F5
Philip Gv STHEL WA9 62 C3
Philip Rd WDN WA8 123 H3
Philips Dr WARRW/BUR WA5 104 C2
Phillimore Rd NPK/KEN L6 * 72 A2
Phillip Gv WD/CROXPK L12 57 F5
Phillips Cl CSBY/BLUN L23 22 A3
FMBY L37 17 E4
Phillips La FMBY L37 17 E4
Phillips St VAUX/LVPD L3 6 D1
Phillips Wy HES CH60 148 C1
Phoenix Av WARRW/BUR WA5 83 F3
Phoenix Brow STHEL WA9 11 K5
Phoenix Dr DV/KA/FCH L14 74 C1
Physics Rd SPK/HALE L24 142 A1
Phythian Cl NPK/KEN L6 71 H2
Phythian Crs
WARRW/BUR WA5 104 D4
Phythian St NPK/KEN L6 71 G2
RNFD/HAY WA11 49 F1
Pichael Nook WARRS WA4 108 A4
Pickerill Rd GR/UP/WCH CH49 89 F5
Pickering Crs WARRS WA4 108 D5
Pickering Rd WAL/NB CH45 51 H2
Pickerings Cl RUNC WA7 155 G3
Pickerings Rd WDN WA8 144 D1
Pickering St NPK/KEN L6 54 C5
Pickmere Dr PS/BROM CH62 153 F5
RUNC WA7 157 E4
Pickmere St
WARRW/BUR WA5 106 A3
Pickop St VAUX/LVPD L3 6 D2
Pickwick St TOX L8 94 B2
Pickworth Wy MGHL L31 33 E2
Picow Farm Rd RUNC WA7 8 B5
Picow St RUNC WA7 8 C6
Picton Av RUNC WA7 9 G6
Picton Cl CL/PREN CH43 91 F5
GOL/RIS/CUL WA3 85 G1
Picton Crs WAV L15 72 C5
Picton Gv WAV L15 72 B5
Picton Rd CSBY/WL L22 29 E3
WAV L15 72 C5
Piercefield Rd FMBY L37 17 E2
Pier Head VAUX/LVPD L3 6 B5
Pier Head Houses BIRK CH41 * 69 H4
Pierpoint St WARRW/BUR WA5 12 A1
Pighue La CLB/OSW/ST L13 72 C4
CLB/OSW/ST L13 73 E4
Pigot Pl WARRS WA4 107 H3
Pigot St ECCL WA10 10 D5
Pike House Rd ECCL WA10 46 C2
Pike Pl ECCL WA10 46 D3
Pikes Bridge Fold ECCL WA10 46 C3
Pikes Hey Rd WKBY CH48 111 F4
Pike St WARRS WA4 130 A2

Pilchbank Rd DV/KA/FCH L14 74 A1
Pilch La DV/KA/FCH L14 74 A2
Pilch La East HUY L36 74 C3
Pilgrim St BIRK CH41 3 H4
CLVPS L1 7 H7
Pilling La MGHL L31 18 A1
Pilot Gv WAV L15 72 B5
Pimbley Gv East MGHL L31 23 H3
Pimbley Gv West MGHL L31 23 H3
Pimhill Cl TOX L8 94 C2
Pimlico Rd RUNC WA7 8 A5
Pincroft Wy ANF/KKDL L4 53 H3
Pinders Farm Dr WARR WA1 13 F4
Pine Av BEB CH63 137 H3
ECCL WA10 47 H1
WDN WA8 125 F1
Pine Cl HUY L36 75 F1
KKBY L32 33 F1
RAIN/WH L35 77 E2
Pine Ct BIRK CH41 2 E4
Pinedale Cl CL/PREN CH43 90 D4
Pine Gv BTL L20 5 G3
CSBY/WL L22 29 E2
WARR WA1 108 A1
Pinehey NSTN CH64 158 C1
Pinehurst Av ANF/KKDL L4 54 D3
CSBY/WL L22 28 D1
Pinehurst Rd ANF/KKDL L4 54 D3
Pinellas RUNC WA7 9 G3
Pine Ms CLVPS L1 94 A1
Pinemore Rd CALD/MH L18 119 E1
Pineridge Cl PS/BROM CH62 138 C3
Pine Rd HES CH60 135 G5
RUNC WA7 155 G2
The Pines BEB CH63 138 B3
WD/CROXPK L12 43 F3
Pinetop Cl NPK/KEN L6 71 H1
Pine Tree Av CL/PREN CH43 90 C4
Pine Tree Cl MOR/LEA CH46 66 D5
Pinetree Cl NTHTN L30 31 E1
Pinetree Ct WAL/NB CH45 51 F5
Pinetree Dr WKBY CH48 110 D2
Pine Tree Gv MOR/LEA CH46 66 D5
Pine Tree Rd HUY L36 75 F5
Pine View Dr PEN/TH CH61 134 D4
Pine Wks RF/TRAN CH42 114 D2
Pinewalks Rdg RF/TRAN CH42 115 E3
Pine Wy HES CH60 134 C4
Pinewood Av FMBY L37 16 C5
WARR WA1 107 G1
WD/CROXPK L12 42 D4
Pinewood Cl FMBY L37 16 C4
NTHLY L27 98 C2
Pinewood Dr HES CH60 149 F1
Pinewood Gdns
NWD/KWIPK L33 25 H4
Pinfold Cl NTHTN L30 22 C4
Pinfold Crs KKBY L32 34 B4
Pinfold Dr ECCL WA10 46 C4
Pinfold La PR/KW L34 43 H4
WKBY CH48 87 E4
Pinfold Rd WLTN L25 121 E4
Pingwood La NWD/KWIPK L33 26 B3
Pinners Brow
WARRN/WOL WA2 12 D2
Pinners Fold RUNC WA7 147 H5
Pinnington Pl HUY L36 75 F3
Pinnington Rd RAIN/WH L35 77 E2
Pintail Cl RNFD/HAY WA11 48 B1
Piper's Cl HES CH60 148 B1
Piper's End HES CH60 148 B1
Piper's La HES CH60 134 A4
The Pipers HES CH60 134 A5
Pipit Cl HLWD L26 121 G1
Pippits Rw RUNC WA7 156 A5
Pirrie Rd WLT/FAZ L9 41 F4
Pitch Cl GR/UP/WCH CH49 * 89 F4
Pit La WDN WA8 102 A4
Pit Pl WLTN L25 120 C1
Pitsmead Rd KKBY L32 33 H3
Pitt St CLVPS L1 7 F7
STHEL WA9 48 C3
WARRW/BUR WA5 12 A2
WDN WA8 146 A1
Pitville Av CALD/MH L18 96 A5
Pitville Cl CALD/MH L18 119 E1
Pitville Gv CALD/MH L18 96 A5
Pitville Rd CALD/MH L18 96 A5
Pitville Ter WDN WA8 124 A4
Plaistow Ct RUNC WA7 156 A2
Plane Cl WLT/FAZ L9 41 E4
Plane Tree Rd BEB CH63 137 G2
Planetree Rd WD/CROXPK L12 57 F3
Plantation Cl RUNC WA7 147 G5
Plantation Rd PS/BROM CH62 139 F5
The Planters GR/UP/WCH CH49 89 E4
NTHTN L30 23 F5
Platt Gv RF/TRAN CH42 116 A3
Platts St RNFD/HAY WA11 49 G1
Plattsville Rd CALD/MH L18 96 A3
Playfield Rd WD/CROXPK L12 57 F3
Pleasant Hill St TOX L8 93 H2
Pleasant St BTL L20 4 C6
VAUX/LVPD L3 7 H5
WAL/NB CH45 51 H3
Pleasant Vw BTL L20 4 C6
Pleasington Cl CL/PREN CH43 91 E4
Pleasington Dr CL/PREN CH43 91 E4
Plemont Rd CLB/OSW/ST L13 56 A5
Plimsoll St EHL/KEN L7 71 H4
Plinston Av WARRS WA4 107 H4
Plover Dr RUNC WA7 157 F1
Pluckington Rd HUY L36 76 B3
Plumbers Wy HUY L36 75 H3
Plumer St BIRK CH41 68 C5
WAV L15 95 G1
Plumley Gdns WDN WA8 123 G2
Plumpton St NPK/KEN L6 71 F1
Plumtre Av WARRW/BUR WA5 83 F5
Plum Tree Cl RAIN/WH L35 60 B4
STBRV L28 57 H2
Plymouth Cl RUNC WA7 157 G3
Plymyard Av PS/BROM CH62 152 D3
Plymyard Cl PS/BROM CH62 152 D4
Poachers' La WARRS WA4 107 H5
Pochard Ri RUNC WA7 157 F1
Pocket Nook St STHEL WA9 11 K4
Pocklington Ct
WARRN/WOL WA2 84 D4
Podium Rd CLB/OSW/ST L13 73 E1
Poets Cnr PS/BROM CH62 * 138 B1
Poleacre Dr WDN WA8 124 B1
Pollard Rd WAV L15 73 E4
Poll Hill Rd HES CH60 134 D5
Pollitt Crs STHEL WA9 79 G2
Pollitt Sq PS/BROM CH62 116 C3
Polperro Cl NG/CROX L11 42 D2
WARRW/BUR WA5 104 C5
Pomfret St TOX L8 94 B2
Pomona St VAUX/LVPD L3 7 H5
Pond Cl NPK/KEN L6 72 A1
Pond Green Wy STHEL WA9 63 F1
Pond View Cl HES CH60 149 G1
Pond Wk STHEL WA9 63 G1
Pondwater Cl KKBY L32 33 H3
Ponsonby Rd WAL/NB CH45 51 E5
Ponsonby St TOX L8 94 C2
Pool Bank PS/BROM CH62 116 B4
Poolbank Rd PS/BROM CH62 116 B4
Poole Av WARRN/WOL WA2 83 H3
Poole Crs WARRN/WOL WA2 83 H3
Pool End STHEL WA9 49 F5
Poole Rd WAL/EG CH44 52 B5
Poole Wk TOX L8 94 C4
Pool Hey STBRV L28 57 H2
Pool La GR/UP/WCH CH49 113 E1
LYMM WA13 109 H4
PS/BROM CH62 138 C2
RUNC WA7 9 F3
WARRS WA4 129 G2
Poolside Rd RUNC WA7 9 F6
Pool St BIRK CH41 2 E2
WDN WA8 15 F5
Poolwood Rd
GR/UP/WCH CH49 90 B4
Pope St BTL L20 39 F2
Poplar Av CSBY/BLUN L23 21 G4
ECCL WA10 46 C3
GR/UP/WCH CH49 89 H3
RUNC WA7 155 G2
WARRW/BUR WA5 104 C4
Poplar Bank HUY L36 75 G3
Poplar Cl HLWD L26 122 A2
RUNC WA7 155 G2
Poplar Dr BEB CH63 138 A2
EV L5 54 C5
KKBY L32 33 G1
Poplar Farm Cl MOR/LEA CH46 89 E2
Poplar Gv ECCL WA10 47 E4
LITH L21 38 D1
RAIN/WH L35 60 A5
Poplar Rd CL/PREN CH43 91 H4
WLTN L25 97 F5
Poplars Av WARRN/WOL WA2 83 G1
Poplar Ter WAL/NB CH45 51 H3
Poplar Vw WARRS WA4 * 128 A4
Poplar Wy ANF/KKDL L4 53 H2
HUY L36 76 A3
Poppleford Cl WLTN L25 98 A4
Poppy Cl MOR/LEA CH46 66 D3
Porchester Rd NG/CROX L11 55 H1
Porchfield Cl NG/CROX L11 42 B4
Porlock Av CHLDW L16 97 E3
STHEL WA9 62 C5
Porlock Cl HES CH60 149 F3
WARRW/BUR WA5 104 C4
Portal Ms PEN/TH CH61 134 D3
Portal Rd PEN/TH CH61 134 D3
Portal Wy AIN/FAZ L10 33 F5
Portbury Cl PS/BROM CH62 116 B5
Portbury Wy PS/BROM CH62 116 B5
Port Cswy PS/BROM CH62 138 D2
Portelet Rd CLB/OSW/ST L13 72 D1
Porter Cl RAIN/WH L35 78 B4
Porter St RUNC WA7 9 J4
VAUX/LVPD L3 70 B1
Portgate Cl WD/CROXPK L12 42 C5
Porthcawl Cl WDN WA8 101 E5
Porthleven Rd RUNC WA7 156 D4
Portia Av BEB CH63 115 G4
Portia Gdns BEB CH63 * 115 G4
Portia St BTL L20 53 G2
Portico Av RAIN/WH L35 60 C4
Portico La RAIN/WH L35 60 B5
Portland Av CSBY/WL L22 28 D2
Portland Gdns VAUX/LVPD L3 70 C1
Portland Pl EV L5 71 E1
Portland Rd WARRW/BUR WA5 82 A5
Portland St BIRK CH41 68 C5
EV L5 70 C1
RUNC WA7 8 B3
WAL/NB CH45 51 G1
Portland Wy STHEL WA9 63 F1
Portlemouth Rd NG/CROX L11 42 C2
Portloe Av HLWD L26 121 H2
Portman Rd WAV L15 95 F1
Porto Hey Rd PEN/TH CH61 134 B1
Portola Cl WARRS WA4 131 G1
Porton Rd KKBY L32 33 F3
Portreath Wy ECCL WA10 46 D1
Portree Av BEB CH63 152 D4
Portree Cl WLT/FAZ L9 40 C2
Portrush Cl WDN WA8 101 G5
Portrush St CLB/OSW/ST L13 55 G4
Portsmouth Pl RUNC WA7 157 G3
Portwood Cl EHL/KEN L7 * 71 H5
Post Office La RUNC WA7 154 B2
Potters La WDN WA8 144 B2
Pottery Flds PR/KW L34 60 A4
Pottery La RAIN/WH L35 76 C2
Poulsom Dr NTHTN L30 30 B2
Poulter Rd WLT/FAZ L9 31 G5
Poulton Cl HLWD L26 121 F5
Poulton Crs WARR WA1 85 G5
Poulton Dr WDN WA8 124 B3
Poulton Green Cl BEB CH63 137 H5
Poulton Hall Rd BEB CH63 152 A2
WAL/EG CH44 68 C2
Poulton Rd BEB CH63 138 A4
WAL/EG CH44 68 C2
Poulton Royd Dr BEB CH63 137 H4
Poverty La MGHL L31 24 C1
Povey Rd WARRN/WOL WA2 84 A4
Powell Dr WGNW/BIL/OR WN5 37 H1
Powell St STHEL WA9 63 E3
WARRS WA4 107 H5
Power Rd PS/BROM CH62 139 F5
RF/TRAN CH42 116 A3
Powis St TOX L8 94 C3
Pownall St CLVPS L1 6 D6
Powys St WARRW/BUR WA5 106 B3
Poynter St STHEL WA9 61 G3
Poynton Cl WARRS WA4 108 B5
Pratt Rd PR/KW L34 59 G4
The Precincts CSBY/BLUN L23 21 F5
Preece Cl WDN WA8 101 F5
Preesall Wy NG/CROX L11 42 C2
Premier St EV L5 54 B5
Prentice Rd RF/TRAN CH42 115 G2
Prenton Av STHEL WA9 79 F1
Prenton Dell Av
CL/PREN CH43 114 C3
Prenton Dell Rd
CL/PREN CH43 114 A2
Prenton Farm Rd
CL/PREN CH43 114 C3
Prenton Gn SPK/HALE L24 142 C3
Prenton Hall Rd
CL/PREN CH43 114 B2
Prenton La RF/TRAN CH42 114 D2
Prentonpark Rd RF/TRAN CH42 92 A5
Prenton Rd East
RF/TRAN CH42 115 F1
Prenton Rd West
RF/TRAN CH42 115 E1
Prenton Village Rd
CL/PREN CH43 114 B2
Prenton Wy CL/PREN CH43 113 H2
Prescot Centre PR/KW L34 * 59 H4
Prescot Dr EHL/KEN L7 72 B2
Prescot Rd CLB/OSW/ST L13 73 F2
ECCL WA10 60 D2
KKBY L32 25 F5
MGHL L31 25 F3
NPK/KEN L6 72 C2
RAIN/WH L35 60 B5
WDN WA8 100 B3
Prescot St EHL/KEN L7 7 K2
WAL/NB CH45 51 G2
Prescott St WARRS WA4 107 G5
Preseland Rd CSBY/BLUN L23 29 F1
Prestbury Av CL/PREN CH43 114 A1
Prestbury Cl CL/PREN CH43 114 A1
WDN WA8 124 C3
Prestbury Dr ECCL WA10 46 D5
WARRS WA4 108 D5
Prestbury Rd NG/CROX L11 41 H3
Preston Av PR/KW L34 59 G5
Preston Gv NPK/KEN L6 55 E5
Preston St CLVPS L1 6 E3
STHEL WA9 79 F3
Preston Wy CSBY/BLUN L23 21 H5
Prestwick Dr CSBY/BLUN L23 20 D3
Prestwood Rd DV/KA/FCH L14 74 B4
Pretoria Rd WLT/FAZ L9 40 D1
Price Gv STHEL WA9 49 G5
Price's La CL/PREN CH43 91 H4
Price St BIRK CH41 2 A1
CLVPS L1 * 6 E6
Priesthouse Cl FMBY L37 17 F3
Priesthouse La FMBY L37 17 F3
Primary Av NTHTN L30 23 G5
Primrose Cl FMBY L37 17 G1
RUNC WA7 156 C1
WARRN/WOL WA2 84 A4
WDN WA8 124 C2
Primrose Ct HUY L36 58 C5
Primrose Dr HUY L36 58 C5
Primrose Gv WAL/EG CH44 * 69 G3
Primrose Hl PS/BROM CH62 116 B5
VAUX/LVPD L3 6 E2
Primrose Rd BIRK CH41 91 F1
CALD/MH L18 96 C3
Primrose St EV L5 53 H3
Primula Cl STHEL WA9 63 G3
Primula Dr WLT/FAZ L9 40 D3
Prince Albert Ct STHEL WA9 63 F1
Prince Albert Ms CLVPS L1 94 A1
Prince Alfred Rd WAV L15 96 A1
Prince Andrew's Gv ECCL WA10 47 E1
Prince Edward St BIRK CH41 2 C2
Prince Edwin St EV L5 71 E1
Prince Henry Sq WARR WA1 12 D4
Princes Av CSBY/BLUN L23 21 E5
PS/BROM CH62 153 E3
TOX L8 94 B1
WKBY CH48 110 B1
Princes Bvd BEB CH63 115 F3
Princes Cl RUNC WA7 147 F5
Princes Gdns VAUX/LVPD L3 6 D2
Princes Ga West TOX L8 94 D2
Princes Pde VAUX/LVPD L3 6 A2
Princes Pavement BIRK CH41 * 3 F5
Princes Pl WDN WA8 124 C2
Princes Rd ECCL WA10 61 E1
TOX L8 94 B1
Princess Av ECCL WA10 47 G1
WARR WA1 85 E5
WARRW/BUR WA5 104 C2
Princess Crs WARR WA1 107 H2
Princess Dr DV/KA/FCH L14 57 F4
WD/CROXPK L12 57 E3
Princess Rd WAL/NB CH45 51 H3
Princess St CLVP L2 6 D4
RUNC WA7 8 D3
WARRW/BUR WA5 105 H4
Princess Ter CL/PREN CH43 2 B7
Princes St BTL L20 53 F1
CLVP L2 6 D3
WDN WA8 14 D3
Princess Wy LITH L21 29 H5
Prince St CSBY/WL L22 29 E4
Princes Wy
RNFD/HAY WA11 37 E4
Princesway WAL/NB CH45 51 G4
Prince William St TOX L8 94 A2
Prior Farm Cl ALL/GAR L19 119 E4
Priors Cl WLTN L25 120 D1
Priorsfield MOR/LEA CH46 66 C5
Priorsfield Rd WLTN L25 120 D1
Prior St BTL L20 39 E1
Priory Cl AIG/SPK L17 117 H1
BEB CH63 138 A3
FMBY L37 17 G4
RAIN/WH L35 76 C4
RUNC WA7 147 G5
Priory Ct HUY L36 * 75 G3
RUNC WA7 * 157 G4
Priory Gdns ECCL WA10 36 D5
Priory Ms BIRK CH41 3 J5
Priory Rd ANF/KKDL L4 54 C2
WAL/EG CH44 69 G2
WKBY CH48 110 B1
Priory St ALL/GAR L19 140 D2
BIRK CH41 3 J5
WARRS WA4 106 D5
The Priory NSTN CH64 158 C1
RAIN/WH L35 78 A2
Priory Wy WLTN L25 120 D1
Priory Whf BIRK CH41 3 J4
Pritchard Av LITH L21 29 G5
Pritt St VAUX/LVPD L3 71 E2
Private Dr PEN/TH CH61 135 H1
Prizett Rd ALL/GAR L19 119 F4
Probyn Rd WAL/NB CH45 51 E5
Procter Rd RF/TRAN CH42 116 A2
Proctor Rd FMBY L37 16 B2
HOY CH47 87 G2
Proctors Cl WDN WA8 125 G1
Progress La CLVPS L1 6 D3
Promenade Gdns AIG/SPK L17 94 C5
The Promenade WARRS WA4 * 128 A4
Prospect Ct NPK/KEN L6 * 72 B2
Prospect Rd RF/TRAN CH42 114 D2
STHEL WA9 48 D3
Prospect Rw RUNC WA7 154 D2
Prospect V NPK/KEN L6 72 B1
WAL/NB CH45 51 F5
Prospect Wy NTHTN L30 31 G1
Providence Crs TOX L8 94 A2
Provident St STHEL WA9 49 G4
Province Rd BTL L20 39 H1
Prussia St VAUX/LVPD L3 6 C2
Public Hall St RUNC WA7 8 E3
Pudsey St CLVPS L1 7 G3
Pugin St ANF/KKDL L4 54 A3
Pulford Av CL/PREN CH43 114 C1
Pulford Cl RUNC WA7 155 H3
Pulford Rd BEB CH63 137 H1
Pulford St ANF/KKDL L4 54 B3
Pullman Cl HES CH60 149 H1
Pumpfields Rd VAUX/LVPD L3 70 C2
Pump La GR/UP/WCH CH49 88 D4
RUNC WA7 156 B1
Purbeck Dr PEN/TH CH61 112 B4
Purdy Cl WARRW/BUR WA5 82 D4
Purley Gv CALD/MH L18 119 E1
Purley Rd CSBY/WL L22 * 28 D2
Purser Gv WAV L15 72 B5
Putney Ct RUNC WA7 * 156 A2
Pyecroft Cl WARRW/BUR WA5 104 B2
Pyecroft Rd
WARRW/BUR WA5 104 B2
Pye Rd HES CH60 149 E1
Pyes Gdns RNFD/HAY WA11 37 F5
Pyes La HUY L36 58 A3
Pye St WAV L15 96 A1
Pym St ANF/KKDL L4 40 B5
The Pyramids BIRK CH41 * 2 E5

Q

Quadrangle VAUX/LVPD L3 * 7 K4
The Quadrangle
CALD/MH L18 * 96 B4
Quadrant Cl RUNC WA7 157 F3
Quail Cl WARRN/WOL WA2 84 B2
Quaker La HES CH60 134 C5
Quakers Meadow PR/KW L34 44 B3
Quarry Av BEB CH63 137 H2
Quarry Bank BIRK CH41 2 D6
NWD/KWIPK L33 34 A1
WAL/NB CH45 51 H4
Quarrybank St BIRK CH41 2 C6
Quarry Cl CLB/OSW/ST L13 55 H5
NWD/KWIPK L33 34 A1
PEN/TH CH61 134 D4
RUNC WA7 9 K6
Quarry Ct HES CH60 * 134 C5
WDN WA8 124 A2
Quarry Dl NWD/KWIPK L33 34 A1
Quarry Gn NWD/KWIPK L33 34 A1
Quarry Hey NWD/KWIPK L33 34 A1
Quarry La PEN/TH CH61 113 E5
WARRS WA4 130 B5
Quarry Rd BTL L20 5 H6
CLB/OSW/ST L13 56 A5
CSBY/BLUN L23 21 H3
NSTN CH64 159 G1
Quarry Rd East BEB CH63 138 A2
HES CH60 134 C5
Quarry Rd West HES CH60 134 C5
Quarryside Dr NWD/KWIPK L33 34 B2
Quarry St WLTN L25 97 F5
Quarry St South WLTN L25 120 C1
Quartz Wy LITH L21 30 B4
The Quay Centre
WARRN/WOL WA2 * 83 F2
Quay Fold WARRW/BUR WA5 106 A4
Quay Pl RUNC WA7 157 G2
Quayside NSTN CH64 158 C5
Quebec Quay VAUX/LVPD L3 93 G2
Quebec Rd WARRN/WOL WA2 107 F1
Queen Anne St VAUX/LVPD L3 7 G1
Queen Av CLVP L2 * 6 D4
Queen Mary's Dr
PS/BROM CH62 116 B5
Queens Av FMBY L37 16 D1
HOY CH47 64 D5
WARR WA1 107 G1
WDN WA8 123 H3
Queensberry St TOX L8 94 B3
Queensbury WKBY CH48 87 H5
Queensbury Av
PS/BROM CH62 139 E5
Queensbury Wy WDN WA8 101 F5
Queen's Cl RUNC WA7 8 C7
Queens Ct NPK/KEN L6 54 C5
Queenscourt Rd
WD/CROXPK L12 56 C5
Queens Crs WARR WA1 * 85 E5
Queens Cft FMBY L37 16 C4
Queensdale Rd
CALD/MH L18 96 A3
Queens Dr CL/PREN CH43 114 C2
ECCL WA10 47 E1
HES CH60 148 C1
WARRS WA4 130 D1
Queens Drive Mossley Hl
CALD/MH L18 95 G4
Queens Drive Stoneycroft
CLB/OSW/ST L13 73 F1
Queens Drive Walton
ANF/KKDL L4 40 C5
Queens Drive (Wavertree)
WAV L15 73 G5
Queens Drive West Derby
CLB/OSW/ST L13 55 G2
Queensland Av STHEL WA9 61 G3
Queensland Pl STHEL WA9 61 G3
Queensland St EHL/KEN L7 71 H4
Queens Ms NPK/KEN L6 54 C5
Queen Sq CLVPS L1 7 F3
Queen's Rd BTL L20 4 E7
CSBY/BLUN L23 21 F5
ECCL WA10 61 E1
FMBY L37 16 C4
HOY CH47 87 E1
NPK/KEN L6 71 G1
PR/KW L34 60 A4
RF/TRAN CH42 116 A2
RUNC WA7 8 C6
WAL/EG CH44 69 G2
Queen St ALL/GAR L19 140 C1
BIRK CH41 92 C4
CSBY/WL L22 29 E4
ECCL WA10 11 F2
RUNC WA7 8 D3
WAL/NB CH45 51 H5
Queensway CSBY/WL L22 29 G2
HES CH60 149 G3
RNFD/HAY WA11 37 E4
RUNC WA7 8 C3
WAL/NB CH45 51 G4
WDN WA8 124 C4
Queensway Entrance
(Mersey Tunnel) CLVPS L1 * 6 E3
Queensway (Mersey Tunnel)
BIRK CH41 3 F2
VAUX/LVPD L3 6 B3
Queens Whf VAUX/LVPD L3 93 G1
Quernmore Rd
NWD/KWIPK L33 34 B1
Quernmore Wk
NWD/KWIPK L33 34 B1
Quickswood Cl WLTN L25 97 F3
Quickswood Dr WLTN L25 97 F3
Quickswood Gn WLTN L25 97 F3
Quickthorn Crs STBRV L28 57 H3
Quigley Av NTHTN L30 31 F3
Quigley St BIRK CH41 92 C4
The Quillet NSTN CH64 159 E3
Quinesway GR/UP/WCH CH49 90 A3
Quinn St WDN WA8 14 E5
Quintbridge Cl HLWD L26 121 G3
Quorn St EHL/KEN L7 71 H3

R

Raby Av BEB CH63 152 B3
Raby Cl BEB CH63 152 A2
HES CH60 148 D2
WDN WA8 125 H1
Raby Dr BEB CH63 152 A2
MOR/LEA CH46 89 F1
Raby Gdns NSTN CH64 158 D2
Raby Gv BEB CH63 115 F3
Raby Hall Rd BEB CH63 151 G4
Raby Mere Rd BEB CH63 151 E4
Raby Park Cl NSTN CH64 158 D2
Raby Park Rd NSTN CH64 158 D2
Raby Rd BEB CH63 150 D3
NSTN CH64 150 D5
Rachel St EV L5 70 D1
Radburn Cl CSBY/BLUN L23 22 A4
Raddon Pl WARRS WA4 * 107 G5
Radford Av BEB CH63 138 B4
Radford Cl WDN WA8 124 A3
Radlett Cl WARRW/BUR WA5 104 C5
Radley Dr AIN/FAZ L10 31 H1
BEB CH63 150 B3
Radley La WARRN/WOL WA2 84 B2
Radley Rd WAL/EG CH44 51 F5
Radleys Ct TOX L8 * 94 B2
Radley St STHEL WA9 61 G3
Radmore Rd DV/KA/FCH L14 73 H2
Radnor Av HES CH60 134 D5
Radnor Cl HLWD L26 121 F5
Radnor Dr BTL L20 5 J3
WAL/NB CH45 52 A4
WDN WA8 124 B1
Radnor Pl CL/PREN CH43 2 B5
NPK/KEN L6 55 F5
Radnor St WARRW/BUR WA5 106 A2
Radstock Gv STHEL WA9 62 D5
Radstock Rd NPK/KEN L6 72 A2
WAL/EG CH44 51 E5
Radway Rd HUY L36 58 D4
Raeburn Av NSTN CH64 159 E3
PS/BROM CH62 152 D3
WKBY CH48 87 G5
Raffles Rd RF/TRAN CH42 2 D7
Raffles St CLVPS L1 94 A1
Rafter Av BTL L20 40 A1
Raglan St ALL/GAR L19 140 C1
Railbrook Hey CLB/OSW/ST L13 72 D4
Railside Ct EV L5 * 53 G5
Railton Av RAIN/WH L35 78 B3
Railton Cl RAIN/WH L35 78 B4
Railton Rd NG/CROX L11 41 G5
Railway Rd RF/TRAN CH42 115 H1
Railway St ALL/GAR L19 140 C1
ECCL WA10 11 J3
Rainbow Cl WDN WA8 101 E5
Rainbow Dr HLWD L26 121 G3
MGHL L31 25 E5
Raines Cl GR/UP/WCH CH49 89 G4
Rainford Av BTL L20 40 A2
Rainford Rd ECCL WA10 47 E1
RNFD/HAY WA11 36 A5
Rainham Cl CALD/MH L18 119 G3
Rainhill Rd RAIN/WH L35 61 E5
Rake Hey MOR/LEA CH46 65 H5
Rake Hey Cl MOR/LEA CH46 66 A5

Rake La GR/UP/WCH CH49 90 A4
WAL/NB CH45 51 H4
Rakersfield Ct WAL/NB CH45 52 A2
Rakersfield Rd WAL/NB CH45 52 A2
The Rake PS/BROM CH62 139 E5
Raleigh Av RAIN/WH L35 76 D3
Raleigh Cl WARRW/BUR WA5 82 D4
Raleigh Rd MOR/LEA CH46 67 F1
NSTN CH64 158 D1
Raleigh St BTL L20 53 F1
Rame Cl AIN/FAZ L10 42 B1
Ramford St STHEL WA9 48 D5
Ramilies Rd CALD/MH L18 95 H3
Ramleh Cl CSBY/BLUN L23 28 C1
Ramleh Pk CSBY/BLUN L23 28 B1
Ramsbrook Cl SPK/HALE L24 142 A2
Ramsbrook La SPK/HALE L24 143 G3
Ramsbrook Rd SPK/HALE L24 142 A2
Ramsey Cl ALL/GAR L19 119 H3
RAIN/WH L35 77 E2
WDN WA8 103 E5
Ramsey Ct WKBY CH48 110 B2
Ramsey Rd ALL/GAR L19 119 H3
Ramsfield Rd SPK/HALE L24 143 E2
Ramsons Cl HLWD L26 121 G2
Randall Dr NTHTN L30 30 B1
Randle Cl BEB CH63 138 A4
Randles Rd PR/KW L34 43 G2
Randolph St ANF/KKDL L4 54 B3
Randon Gv ECCL WA10 10 E4
Ranelagh Av LITH L21 29 H4
Ranelagh Dr North
ALL/GAR L19 119 E3
Ranelagh Dr South
ALL/GAR L19 119 E4
Ranelagh St CLVPS L1 7 F5
Ranfurly Rd ALL/GAR L19 119 F4
Rangemore Rd CALD/MH L18 119 E2
Rankin St WAL/EG CH44 68 C3
Ranworth Cl NG/CROX L11 41 G4
Ranworth Pl NG/CROX L11 41 H4
Ranworth Rd
WARRW/BUR WA5 104 C2
Ranworth Sq NG/CROX L11 41 H4
Ranworth Wy NG/CROX L11 41 H4
Rappart Rd WAL/EG CH44 69 F2
Ratcliff Pl RAIN/WH L35 77 H1
Rathbone Rd WAV L15 72 D4
Rathlin Cl WDN WA8 103 E5
Rathmore Av CALD/MH L18 96 A5
Rathmore Cl CL/PREN CH43 91 G5
Rathmore Dr CL/PREN CH43 91 G4
Rathmore Rd CL/PREN CH43 91 G4
Raven Cl NPK/KEN L6 * 71 G2
Ravendale Cl CL/PREN CH43 90 D4
Ravenfield Cl HLWD L26 121 G3
Ravenfield Dr WDN WA8 101 E5
Ravenglass Av MGHL L31 18 D4
Ravenhead Av KKBY L32 33 H5
Ravenhead Rd ECCL WA10 61 G1
Ravenhead Rw ECCL WA10 * 61 G1
Ravenhill Crs MOR/LEA CH46 66 D2
Ravenhurst Wy RAIN/WH L35 76 C4
Raven Meols La FMBY L37 16 D4
Ravenna Rd ALL/GAR L19 119 H3
Ravenscourt HLWD L26 * 121 H4
Ravenscroft FMBY L37 17 E4
Ravenscroft Rd CL/PREN CH43 2 B6
Ravensdale Cl
WARRN/WOL WA2 84 B2
The Ravens FMBY L37 17 E4
Ravensthorpe Gn NG/CROX L11 41 H4
Ravenstone Cl
GR/UP/WCH CH49 89 G1
Ravenstone Dr STHEL WA9 62 D3
Ravenstone Rd ALL/GAR L19 119 F3
Ravenswood Av
RF/TRAN CH42 115 H3
Ravenswood Rd
CLB/OSW/ST L13 73 E2
PEN/TH CH61 135 E4
Rawcliffe Cl WDN WA8 101 H4
Rawcliffe Rd RF/TRAN CH42 2 D7
WLT/FAZ L9 40 B3
Rawdon Cl RUNC WA7 156 C2
Rawlinson Crs HLWD L26 122 B3
Rawlinson Rd CLB/OSW/ST L13 72 D2
Rawlins St EHL/KEN L7 72 B2
Rawson Cl LITH L21 29 G5
Rawson Rd LITH L21 29 G5
Raydale Cl WLT/FAZ L9 40 C4
Raymond Av NTHTN L30 31 F3
WARRS WA4 130 B1
Raymond Pl EV L5 70 D1
Raymond Rd WAL/EG CH44 69 E2
Raymond Wy NSTN CH64 159 F3
Raynham Rd CLB/OSW/ST L13 72 D3
Reade Cl BEB CH63 138 A5
Reading Cl EV L5 53 H3
Reads Ct WLT/FAZ L9 40 B1
Reaper Cl WARRW/BUR WA5 105 H2
Reapers Wy NTHTN L30 23 F5
Reay St WDN WA8 125 G1
Rebecca Gdns STHEL WA9 62 C3
Recreation St STHEL WA9 48 C4
Rector Rd NPK/KEN L6 55 E3
Rectory Cl HES CH60 148 D2
RF/TRAN CH42 92 B4
Rectory Dr HLWD L26 121 H2
Rectory Gdns STHEL WA9 62 C4
Rectory La HES CH60 148 C2
Rectory Rd WKBY CH48 110 B2
Redbourne Av HLWD L26 121 H5
Redbourne Dr WDN WA8 100 D4
Redbourn St NPK/KEN L6 55 E4
Redbrook Cl PS/BROM CH62 152 D3
Redbrook St NPK/KEN L6 55 E4
Red Brow La RUNC WA7 157 G1
Redbrow Wy NWD/KWIPK L33 25 H5
Redburn Cl TOX L8 94 C4
Redcap Cl WAL/NB CH45 51 E2
Redcar Dr PS/BROM CH62 152 D4
Redcar Ms NPK/KEN L6 54 D4
Redcar Rd WAL/NB CH45 50 D4
Redcar St NPK/KEN L6 55 E4
Redcroft GR/UP/WCH CH49 * 89 E5
Red Cross St VAUX/LVPD L3 6 C5
Red Cut La NWD/KWIPK L33 35 G4
Redditch Cl GR/UP/WCH CH49 89 E4
Redesdale Cl WARRN/WOL WA2 84 C3
Redfern St BTL L20 53 G2
Redfield Cl WAL/EG CH44 69 F1
Redford Cl GR/UP/WCH CH49 89 E4
Redford St NPK/KEN L6 55 E5
Redgate FMBY L37 17 F4
Redgate Av CSBY/BLUN L23 21 H5
Redgate Dr FMBY L37 17 G4
STHEL WA9 48 D4
Redgrave St EHL/KEN L7 72 A3
Redhill Av KKBY L32 34 A4
Red Hill Rd BEB CH63 136 D1
Redhouse Bank WKBY CH48 87 E5
Redhouse La WKBY CH48 87 E5
Redington Rd ALL/GAR L19 119 H3
Redland Rd WLT/FAZ L9 31 G4
Red La WARRS WA4 130 A4
Red Lion Cl MGHL L31 18 C5
Red Lomes NTHTN L30 22 C4
Redmain Wy WD/CROXPK L12 43 F5
Redmere Dr HES CH60 149 G1
Redmires Cl EHL/KEN L7 * 71 H5
Redmond St BIRK CH41 92 C4
Redmoor Crs NWD/KWIPK L33 25 H5
Redoaks Wy HLWD L26 122 A2
Redpoll Gv HLWD L26 121 G1
Red Rock Ct NPK/KEN L6 71 H1
Red Rum Cl WLT/FAZ L9 32 A4
Redruth Av RNFD/HAY WA11 37 H5
Redruth Cl RUNC WA7 157 E3
Redruth Rd NG/CROX L11 42 D2
Redstone Cl HOY CH47 64 D5
Redstone Dr HES CH60 134 A5
Redstone Pk WAL/NB CH45 * 51 G2
Redstone Ri CL/PREN CH43 90 D2
Redvales Ct GOL/RIS/CUL WA3 85 G1
Redvers Dr WLT/FAZ L9 40 B1
Redwald Cl NWD/KWIPK L33 26 A3
Redwing La WLTN L25 97 G4
Redwing Wy HLWD L26 121 F1
Redwood Av MGHL L31 18 C3
Redwood Cl CL/PREN CH43 * 114 B1
WARR WA1 109 E2
Redwood Dr RNFD/HAY WA11 49 F2
Redwood Gv BTL L20 * 5 F3
Redwood Rd WLTN L25 97 H3
Redwood Wy NWD/KWIPK L33 25 H3
Reedale Cl CALD/MH L18 96 A4
Reedale Rd CALD/MH L18 96 A4
Reeds Av East MOR/LEA CH46 66 D2
Reeds Av West MOR/LEA CH46 66 D2
Reeds La MOR/LEA CH46 66 D2
Reedsmere Cl WARRS WA4 130 C1
Reeds Rd HUY L36 75 G1
Reedville CL/PREN CH43 2 A7
Reedville Gv MOR/LEA CH46 66 D3
Reedville Rd BEB CH63 137 H1
Reeves Av BTL L20 5 J1
Reeves St STHEL WA9 49 E3
Regal Crs WDN WA8 123 H3
Regal Dr ECCL WA10 47 E2
Regal Rd NG/CROX L11 42 C4
Regal Wk ANF/KKDL L4 54 B3
Regency Pk WDN WA8 101 G5
Regency Sq WARRW/BUR WA5 12 A1
Regent Av DV/KA/FCH L14 74 A3
NTHTN L30 31 E1
WARR WA1 85 E5
Regent Rd BTL L20 4 A4
BTL L20 53 F1
CSBY/BLUN L23 21 E5
EV L5 53 F4
VAUX/LVPD L3 53 F5
WAL/NB CH45 50 D4
WDN WA8 14 E1
Regents Cl PEN/TH CH61 113 F5
Regents Fld FMBY L37 * 16 C1
Regents Rd ECCL WA10 61 E1
Regent St RUNC WA7 8 D3
VAUX/LVPD L3 70 B1
WARR WA1 12 C5
Regents Wy BEB CH63 115 F4
Regina Av CSBY/WL L22 28 D2
Reginald Rd STHEL WA9 63 E4
Regina Rd WLT/FAZ L9 40 C1
Reid Av WARRW/BUR WA5 83 F5
Reigate Cl WLTN L25 121 E1
Reins Cft NSTN CH64 158 D1
Renaissance Wy
SPK/HALE L24 142 B2
Rendal Cl EV L5 54 C5
Rendcombe Gn NG/CROX L11 41 H4
Rendelsham Cl
GR/UP/WCH CH49 89 G3
Rendel St BIRK CH41 2 E2
Renfrew Av PS/BROM CH62 153 E4
Renfrew St EHL/KEN L7 71 G4
Rennell Rd DV/KA/FCH L14 73 G2
Rennie Av ECCL WA10 47 E3
Renown Cl GOL/RIS/CUL WA3 85 H1
Renown Wy SPK/HALE L24 120 C5
Renshaw St CLVPS L1 7 G5
Renton Av RUNC WA7 146 D4
Renville Rd DV/KA/FCH L14 73 G4
Renwick Av RAIN/WH L35 77 G1
Renwick Rd WLT/FAZ L9 40 C2
Repton Gv AIN/FAZ L10 31 H2
Repton Rd CHLDW L16 73 H5
Reservoir Rd RF/TRAN CH42 114 D2
WLTN L25 97 F5
Reservoir Rd North
RF/TRAN CH42 114 D1
Reservoir St NPK/KEN L6 71 G1
STHEL WA9 61 E3
Rest Hill Rd BEB CH63 115 E5
Retford Rd NWD/KWIPK L33 34 A2
Reva Rd DV/KA/FCH L14 74 B2
Revesby Cl WDN WA8 124 B1
Rexmore Rd CALD/MH L18 119 E1
Rexmore Wy WAV L15 95 G1
Reynolds Av STHEL WA9 49 H5
Reynolds Cl NPK/KEN L6 71 G1
Reynolds St WARRS WA4 107 G5
Reynolds Wy WLTN L25 120 C1
Rhiwlas St TOX L8 94 C3
Rhodesia Rd WLT/FAZ L9 40 D1
Rhodes St WARRN/WOL WA2 107 E1
Rhodesway HES CH60 149 F2
Rhona Cl BEB CH63 152 C5
Rhona Dr WARRW/BUR WA5 104 C2
Rhosesmor Cl KKBY L32 43 F1
Rhosesmor Rd KKBY L32 43 F1
Rhuddlan Cl CLB/OSW/ST L13 72 D3
Rhyl St TOX L8 94 B3
WDN WA8 * 14 B6
Rialto Cl TOX L8 94 B1
Ribble Av MGHL L31 19 E4
RAIN/WH L35 78 A2
Ribble Cl WDN WA8 103 F5
Ribble Crs WGNW/BIL/OR WN5 37 G1
Ribbledale Rd CALD/MH L18 96 A4
Ribble Rd WLTN L25 98 A5
Ribbler's La KKBY L32 33 G5
PR/KW L34 43 F1
Ribblesdale Av WLT/FAZ L9 31 G5
Ribblesdale Cl PS/BROM CH62 153 F4
Ribble St BIRK CH41 68 B4
Ribchester Wy RAIN/WH L35 99 E1
Rice Hey Rd WAL/EG CH44 52 A5
Rice La WAL/EG CH44 52 A5
WLT/FAZ L9 40 B4
Rice St CLVPS L1 7 H7
Richard Allen Wy EV L5 71 E1
Richard Chubb Dr
WAL/NB CH45 52 B4
Richard Gv WD/CROXPK L12 57 E5
Richard Hesketh Dr KKBY L32 33 F2
Richard Kelly Cl ANF/KKDL L4 * 55 F2
Richard Kelly Dr ANF/KKDL L4 41 F5
Richard Kelly Pl ANF/KKDL L4 * 55 F2
Richard Martin Rd LITH L21 * 30 B3
Richard Rd CSBY/BLUN L23 20 B3
Richards Gv STHEL WA9 49 E3
Richardson Rd RF/TRAN CH42 115 G2
Richardson St EHL/KEN L7 95 E1
WARRN/WOL WA2 84 C5
Richland Rd CLB/OSW/ST L13 55 H5
Richmond Av LITH L21 29 H4
RUNC WA7 147 E4
WARRS WA4 107 H4
Richmond Cl BEB CH63 115 H5
ECCL WA10 46 B3
Richmond Ct LITH L21 * 29 H4
Richmond Cresent NTHTN L30 31 E1
Richmond Gv MGHL L31 19 E3
Richmond Pk NPK/KEN L6 54 D4
Richmond Rd BEB CH63 115 H5
CSBY/BLUN L23 21 F4
Richmond Rw VAUX/LVPD L3 71 E2
Richmond St CLVPS L1 * 6 E4
WAL/NB CH45 51 H1
WARRS WA4 108 A5
WDN WA8 15 G1
Richmond Ter NPK/KEN L6 54 C5
Richmond Wy PEN/TH CH61 * 113 E5
RAIN/WH L35 99 E1
Rich Vw CL/PREN CH43 91 H5
Rickaby Cl BEB CH63 152 C1
Rickman St ANF/KKDL L4 53 H2
Rickman Wy HUY L36 75 H5
Ridding La RUNC WA7 156 D4
Riddock Rd LITH L21 39 F2
Ridgeborne Cl
WARRW/BUR WA5 82 D3
Ridgefield Rd PEN/TH CH61 134 D1
Ridgemere Rd PEN/TH CH61 134 D1
The Ridge HES CH60 134 B4
Ridgetor Rd WLTN L25 97 G5
Ridgeview Rd CL/PREN CH43 90 D3
Ridgeway Dr MGHL L31 18 D3
The Ridgeway BEB CH63 115 F3
HES CH60 149 F2
HOY CH47 88 A1
RUNC WA7 157 F3
WDN WA8 101 E2
WLTN L25 97 G5
Ridgewood Dr PEN/TH CH61 134 D2
STHEL WA9 62 D4
Ridgewood Wy WLT/FAZ L9 31 F5
Ridgmont Av NG/CROX L11 41 H5
Ridgway St WARRN/WOL WA2 84 B5
Riding Cl STHEL WA9 * 79 G1
Riding Fold HLWD L26 121 F1
Riding Hill Rd PR/KW L34 44 B5
Ridings Hey CL/PREN CH43 90 D4
The Ridings CL/PREN CH43 90 D3
Riding St VAUX/LVPD L3 7 J3
Ridley Dr WARRW/BUR WA5 105 G4
Ridley Gv WKBY CH48 87 E5
Ridley La MGHL L31 18 D5
Ridley Rd NPK/KEN L6 72 A2
Ridley St CL/PREN CH43 2 B6
Ridsdale WDN WA8 124 A3
Riesling Dr NWD/KWIPK L33 25 H4
Rigby Dr GR/UP/WCH CH49 112 B1
Rigby Rd MGHL L31 18 B3
Rigby St ECCL WA10 11 F4
VAUX/LVPD L3 6 B2
Riley Av BTL L20 5 H1
Riley Dr RUNC WA7 155 E1
Rimmer Av CHLDW L16 74 C4
Rimmer Cl LITH L21 30 A5
Rimmer Gv STHEL WA9 49 E4
Rimmers Ct BIRK CH41 * 91 F1
Rimmer St VAUX/LVPD L3 7 H2
Rimmington Rd AIG/SPK L17 118 C1
Rimrose Rd BTL L20 4 B2
BTL L20 4 B4
Rimrose Valley Rd
CSBY/BLUN L23 22 A5
Rimsdale Cl AIG/SPK L17 118 C4
Ringcroft Rd CLB/OSW/ST L13 73 F2
Ringo Starr Dr NPK/KEN L6 * 71 H2
Ringsfield Rd SPK/HALE L24 143 E3
Ringway NSTN CH64 158 D1
Ringway Rd RUNC WA7 9 K5
WLTN L25 98 A4
Ringways PS/BROM CH62 138 D3
Ringwood CL/PREN CH43 91 G5
Ringwood Av DV/KA/FCH L14 74 B3
Ringwood Ct CL/PREN CH43 * 91 G5
Rio Ct PR/KW L34 59 H3
Ripley Av LITH L21 30 A3
Ripley Cl MGHL L31 19 E5
Ripley St WARRW/BUR WA5 106 A1
Ripon Cl HUY L36 76 A2
NTHTN L30 31 E3
Ripon Rd WAL/NB CH45 51 E4
Ripon St ANF/KKDL L4 54 B1
BIRK CH41 * 92 C4
Risbury Cl NG/CROX L11 41 H5
Rishton Cl EV L5 54 C5
Ritchie Av WLT/FAZ L9 31 H5
Ritherup La RAIN/WH L35 78 A1
Ritson St TOX L8 94 D2
Rivacre Rd PS/BROM CH62 153 G5
River Avon St TOX L8 * 95 E1
Riverbank Cl HES CH60 148 D3
Riverbank Rd ALL/GAR L19 119 E4
HES CH60 148 C3
PS/BROM CH62 139 E2
River Cl FMBY L37 17 G5
River Gv PS/BROM CH62 116 B3
River Rd WARRS WA4 106 D5
Riversdale WARR WA1 109 F1
Riversdale Cl NWD/KWIPK L33 25 H5
Riversdale Ct AIG/SPK L17 118 D3
Riversdale Ms ALL/GAR L19 118 D3
Riversdale Rd ALL/GAR L19 118 D4
LITH L21 29 G5
RUNC WA7 147 E5
WAL/EG CH44 69 F1
WKBY CH48 110 A1
Riverside PS/BROM CH62 138 B1
WD/CROXPK L12 57 E1
WKBY CH48 110 B3
Riverside Cl BTL L20 39 E2
WARR WA1 13 G5
Riverside Dr AIG/SPK L17 117 G1
VAUX/LVPD L3 94 B5
Riverside Gv STHEL WA9 62 D3
Riverside Wk NSTN CH64 158 C5
Riverslea Rd CSBY/BLUN L23 28 C2
River St BIRK CH41 2 D5
River Vw CSBY/WL L22 28 C2
Riverview Rd NSTN CH64 159 E5
WAL/EG CH44 69 G2
Riverview Wk TOX L8 94 B4
River Wk RUNC WA7 * 156 B2
Riverwood Rd PS/BROM CH62 139 F5
Riviera Dr NG/CROX L11 42 C3
RF/TRAN CH42 115 F2
Rivington Av CL/PREN CH43 91 E4
ECCL WA10 47 G1
Rivington Rd ECCL WA10 10 B4
WAL/EG CH44 69 F2
Rivington St ECCL WA10 10 A7
Rixton Av WARRW/BUR WA5 83 F5
Roadwater Cl WLTN L25 98 A1
Robarts Rd ANF/KKDL L4 54 C4
Robeck Rd CLB/OSW/ST L13 73 F4
Robert Dr GR/UP/WCH CH49 89 G5
Robert Gv WD/CROXPK L12 57 E5
Roberts Av RNFD/HAY WA11 49 G2
Roberts Ct RUNC WA7 156 A3
Roberts Dr BTL L20 30 D5
Robertson St TOX L8 94 A3
Roberts St VAUX/LVPD L3 6 A1
Robert St BIRK CH41 2 E3
RUNC WA7 9 H4
WARRW/BUR WA5 106 B2
WDN WA8 15 F2
Robina Rd STHEL WA9 62 D2
Robin Cl RUNC WA7 157 F2
Robins La STHEL WA9 62 C2
Robinson Ms BIRK CH41 * 3 H4
Robinson Pl STHEL WA9 48 D4
Robinson Rd LITH L21 30 B3
Robin Wy GR/UP/WCH CH49 113 F1
Robsart St EV L5 54 A5
Robson St CLB/OSW/ST L13 72 D4
EV L5 54 B4
WARR WA1 13 H2
Roby Cl RAIN/WH L35 78 A1
Roby Gv WARRW/BUR WA5 105 E2
Roby Mount Av HUY L36 75 F3
Roby Rd HUY L36 74 C3
HUY L36 75 E3
Roby St BTL L20 5 F2
ECCL WA10 61 F1
WAV L15 95 G1
Rocastle Cl NPK/KEN L6 71 G2
Rochester Av NTHTN L30 31 E3
Rochester Cl
WARRW/BUR WA5 105 G3
Rochester Gdns ECCL WA10 61 F1
Rochester Rd RF/TRAN CH42 116 A1
Rock Av HES CH60 134 D5
Rockbank Rd CLB/OSW/ST L13 55 H5
Rockbourne Av WLTN L25 97 F3
Rockbourne Gn WLTN L25 97 F3
Rockbourne Wy WLTN L25 97 F3
Rock Cl RF/TRAN CH42 115 H1
Rock Farm Cl NSTN CH64 159 F4
Rock Farm Dr NSTN CH64 159 F4
Rock Farm Gv NSTN CH64 * 159 F4
Rock Ferry By-Pass
RF/TRAN CH42 116 A1
Rockfield Cl WDN WA8 124 B1
Rockfield Ms WARRS WA4 130 D1
Rockfield Rd ANF/KKDL L4 54 B3
Rockford Av KKBY L32 33 H5
Rockford Cl KKBY L32 33 H5
Rockford Gdns
WARRW/BUR WA5 82 A5
Rockford Wk KKBY L32 33 H5
Rock Gv CLB/OSW/ST L13 73 E2
Rockhill Rd WLTN L25 120 D2
Rockhouse St NPK/KEN L6 55 E5
Rockingham Ct
NWD/KWIPK L33 * 26 A5
Rockland Rd CSBY/WL L22 29 E2
Rocklands Av BEB CH63 116 A4
Rocklands La BEB CH63 151 E2
Rock La MGHL L31 24 C3
WDN WA8 101 G5
Rock La East RF/TRAN CH42 116 A2
Rock La West RF/TRAN CH42 115 H2
Rocklee Gdns NSTN CH64 159 F4
Rockley St ANF/KKDL L4 54 A2
Rock Mount Cl WLTN L25 97 F5
Rockmount Rd AIG/SPK L17 118 D2
Rock Park Rd RF/TRAN CH42 116 B2
Rockpoint Av WAL/NB CH45 52 A3
Rocksavage Expy RUNC WA7 155 G4
Rockside Rd CALD/MH L18 119 E1
Rock St CLB/OSW/ST L13 73 E2
ECCL WA10 61 E2
Rock Vw EV L5 54 A4
MGHL L31 24 D5
Rockville Rd DV/KA/FCH L14 73 G4
Rockville St RF/TRAN CH42 115 H1
Rockwell Rd WD/CROXPK L12 56 D2
Rocky Bank Rd RF/TRAN CH42 92 B5
Rocky La CHLDW L16 73 G5
HES CH60 148 D1
NPK/KEN L6 55 E5
Rocky La South HES CH60 149 E1
Roderick Rd ANF/KKDL L4 40 C5
Roderick St VAUX/LVPD L3 * 7 H1
Rodick St WLTN L25 120 B1
Rodmell Rd WLT/FAZ L9 40 D1
Rodney St BIRK CH41 2 E7
CLVPS L1 7 H6
ECCL WA10 10 C5
WARRN/WOL WA2 12 D2
Rodwater Cl WLTN L25 97 H1
Roe Aly CLVPS L1 7 F5
Roeburn Wy
WARRW/BUR WA5 104 B5
Roedean Cl MGHL L31 18 D4
WLTN L25 120 D3
Roehampton Dr
CSBY/BLUN L23 20 D3
RUNC WA7 156 A2
Roemarsh Ct RUNC WA7 156 A3
Roe St CLVPS L1 7 F4
Rogers Av BTL L20 5 K1
Rogerson's Gn HLWD L26 121 G1
Rokeby Cl VAUX/LVPD L3 71 E2
Rokeby St VAUX/LVPD L3 71 E2
Roker Av WAL/EG CH44 68 C2
Rokesmith Av EHL/KEN L7 72 A5
Roland Av BEB CH63 115 F5
RNFD/HAY WA11 37 G5
RUNC WA7 8 B6
Roleton Cl NTHTN L30 23 G5
Rolleston Dr BEB CH63 138 A2
WAL/NB CH45 51 F3
Rolleston St WARRN/WOL WA2 12 B3
Rolling Mill La STHEL WA9 63 F2
Rollo St ANF/KKDL L4 53 H3
Roman Cl RUNC WA7 147 E5
Roman Ct NSTN CH64 159 E3
Roman Rd BEB CH63 114 C4
CL/PREN CH43 114 C3
HOY CH47 64 D4
WARRS WA4 130 A2
Rome Cl HUY L36 75 F2
Romer Rd NPK/KEN L6 72 A2
Romford Wy HLWD L26 121 H5
Romilly St NPK/KEN L6 71 G2
Romley St ANF/KKDL L4 54 B1
Romney Cl WDN WA8 125 H1
Romney Wy NSTN CH64 159 E3
Romsey Av FMBY L37 17 G4
Romulus St EHL/KEN L7 72 B3
Ronald Cl CSBY/WL L22 29 G3
Ronald Dr WARRN/WOL WA2 85 F3
Ronald Rd CSBY/WL L22 29 G3
Ronald Ross Av NTHTN L30 31 E1
Ronaldshay WDN WA8 126 A1
Ronald St CLB/OSW/ST L13 72 D2
Ronaldsway AIN/FAZ L10 32 D5
CSBY/BLUN L23 21 H3
GR/UP/WCH CH49 89 H2
HES CH60 148 D3
HLWD L26 122 A3
Ronan Cl BTL L20 4 B2
Ronan Rd WDN WA8 145 G1
Rone Cl MOR/LEA CH46 66 B5
Roofers Wy HUY L36 76 A3
Rookery Dr ALL/GAR L19 118 D3
Rookley Cl NTHLY L27 98 D4
Rook Rd WARRS WA4 107 G4
Rooks Wy HES CH60 148 C1
The Rooley HUY L36 75 F4
Roome St WARRN/WOL WA2 107 E1
Roosevelt Dr WLT/FAZ L9 31 G4
Ropers Bridge Cl RAIN/WH L35 76 D3
Roper St STHEL WA9 48 C3
TOX L8 94 B3
The Ropewalk NSTN CH64 158 B2
Rosalind Av BEB CH63 115 G4
Rosalind Wy BTL L20 53 H1
Rosam Ct RUNC WA7 156 A3
Rosclare Dr WAL/NB CH45 51 F4
Roscoe Av WARRN/WOL WA2 84 B5
Roscoe Cl RAIN/WH L35 99 E1
Roscoe Crs RUNC WA7 * 154 C2
Roscoe La CLVPS L1 7 G6
Roscoe Pl CLVPS L1 7 G6
Roscoe St CLVPS L1 7 H7
ECCL WA10 10 B6
Roscommon St EV L5 71 E1
Roscommon Wy WDN WA8 101 G5
Roscote Cl HES CH60 * 148 D2
The Roscote HES CH60 148 D2
Roseacre WKBY CH48 87 E5
Rose Av BTL L20 30 B5
STHEL WA9 62 C3
Rose Bank Rd CHLDW L16 96 D1
Rosebank Rd HUY L36 58 A4
Rosebank Wy HUY L36 58 A5
Rosebay Cl FMBY L37 17 F3
Rosebery Av CSBY/WL L22 28 D2
WAL/EG CH44 69 E1
Rosebery Gv RF/TRAN CH42 114 D1
Rosebery Rd ECCL WA10 47 F1
Rosebery St TOX L8 94 C1
Rosebourne Cl AIG/SPK L17 118 A1
Rose Brae CALD/MH L18 96 B4
Rose Brow WLTN L25 97 G4
Rose Cl HLWD L26 122 A4
RUNC WA7 157 F4
Rose Ct WAV L15 95 G1
Rose Crs WDN WA8 14 B5
Rosecroft PS/BROM CH62 152 C3
Rosecroft Ct HOY CH47 * 87 E2
Rosedale Av CSBY/BLUN L23 21 F5
WARR WA1 108 C1
Rosedale Cl WLT/FAZ L9 40 D3
Rosedale Rd CALD/MH L18 96 A4
RF/TRAN CH42 92 C5
Rosefield Av BEB CH63 115 G4
Rosefield Rd WLTN L25 121 E2
Rose Gdns NSTN CH64 159 E4
Roseheath Dr HLWD L26 121 H5
Rose Hl VAUX/LVPD L3 70 D2
Rosehill Av STHEL WA9 63 H5
Rosehill Ct WLTN L25 97 G4

Roseland Cl MGHL L31 18 B2
Roselands Ct RF/TRAN CH42 115 G2
Rose La CALD/MH L18 95 H5
Rose Lea Cl WDN WA8 102 A4
Rosemary Av RUNC WA7 156 B4
WARRS WA4 130 C1
Rosemary Cl CL/PREN CH43 68 A5
EHL/KEN L7 71 G5
WARRW/BUR WA5 105 G2
Rosemary La FMBY L37 16 D3
Rosemead Av PEN/TH CH61 134 D2
Rosemont Rd AIG/SPK L17 118 D1
Rosemoor Dr CSBY/BLUN L23 21 H4
Rose Mt CL/PREN CH43 91 H5
CSBY/WL L22 * 28 D3
RUNC WA7 * 157 H3
Rose Mount Cl CL/PREN CH43 91 G5
Rose Mount Dr WAL/NB CH45 51 G4
Rose Pth FMBY L37 17 F4
Rose Pl BIRK CH41 92 D5
RF/TRAN CH42 92 B4
VAUX/LVPD L3 70 D2
Roseside Dr NTHLY L27 98 D2
Rose St CLVPS L1 * 7 F3
WDN WA8 14 B5
WLTN L25 120 B1
Rose V EV L5 54 A5
Rose View Av WDN WA8 125 E1
Rose Vls WAV L15 95 H1
Rosewarne Cl AIG/SPK L17 117 H1
Rosewell Ct STBRV L28 57 H4
Rosewood Av WARR WA1 107 G1
Rosewood Cl NTHLY L27 98 C3
STBRV L28 57 H3
Rosewood Dr MOR/LEA CH46 65 H5
Rosewood Gdns NG/CROX L11 56 B1
Rosewood Gv WDN WA8 123 H3
Roseworth Av WLT/FAZ L9 31 F5
Roskell Rd WLTN L25 121 E4
Roslin Rd CL/PREN CH43 91 H4
PEN/TH CH61 112 B5
Roslyn St BIRK CH41 92 D5
Rossall Av AIN/FAZ L10 32 A1
Rossall Cl MOR/LEA CH46 66 D3
Rossall Rd CLB/OSW/ST L13 73 F3
MOR/LEA CH46 66 D4
WARRW/BUR WA5 105 F4
WDN WA8 125 H1
Ross Av MOR/LEA CH46 67 G1
Ross Cl PR/KW L34 44 B4
WARRW/BUR WA5 82 D5
Rossendale Cl CL/PREN CH43 90 D4
Rossett Av AIG/SPK L17 95 F2
Rossett Cl WARRW/BUR WA5 83 E3
Rossett Rd CSBY/BLUN L23 28 D1
Rossett St NPK/KEN L6 55 E5
Rossini St LITH L21 39 E1
Rosslyn Av MGHL L31 23 G1
Rosslyn Crs MOR/LEA CH46 66 C5
Rosslyn Dr MOR/LEA CH46 66 C5
Rosslyn Pk MOR/LEA CH46 89 G1
Rosslyn St AIG/SPK L17 94 D5
Rossmore Gdns ANF/KKDL L4 54 D3
Ross St STHEL WA9 48 C3
WDN WA8 15 F2
Ross Tower Ct WAL/NB CH45 52 A2
Rostherne Av WAL/EG CH44 68 C2
Rostherne Cl
WARRW/BUR WA5 105 H4
Rostherne Crs WDN WA8 124 B1
Rosthwaite Gv
RNFD/HAY WA11 37 F3
Rosthwaite Rd
WD/CROXPK L12 56 C4
Rostron Crs FMBY L37 16 D5
Rosyth Cl WARRN/WOL WA2 84 D2
Rothay Dr WARRW/BUR WA5 104 B5
Rothbury Cl MOR/LEA CH46 66 A5
RUNC WA7 155 H3
Rothbury Ct STHEL WA9 79 F3
Rothbury Rd DV/KA/FCH L14 57 F4
Rotherham Cl HUY L36 75 G1
Rotherwood Cl BEB CH63 115 F5
Rothesay Cl RUNC WA7 147 F4
Rothesay Dr CSBY/BLUN L23 29 F1
PS/BROM CH62 152 D5
Rothesay Gdns
CL/PREN CH43 * 114 B2
Rothsay Cl RNFD/HAY WA11 49 E1
Rothwells La CSBY/BLUN L23 22 A3
Rothwell St NPK/KEN L6 71 G1
Rotunda St EV L5 53 H5
Roughdale Av KKBY L32 34 A5
STHEL WA9 * 79 F1
Roughdale Cl KKBY L32 34 A5
Roughley Av
WARRW/BUR WA5 105 H4
Roughwood Dr
NWD/KWIPK L33 34 A1
The Roundabout WDN WA8 101 F2
Round Hey STBRV L28 57 G2
The Round Meade MGHL L31 18 B4
Roundwood Dr STHEL WA9 62 B1
Routledge St WDN WA8 15 F1
Rowan Av WD/CROXPK L12 57 E1
Rowan Cl RNFD/HAY WA11 37 H5
RNFD/HAY WA11 49 F2
RUNC WA7 155 G2
WARRW/BUR WA5 104 D2
Rowan Ct AIG/SPK L17 118 C1
GR/UP/WCH CH49 111 H1
Rowan Dr KKBY L32 33 G1
Rowan Gv BEB CH63 137 G2
HUY L36 75 F5
Rowan Tree Cl
GR/UP/WCH CH49 88 D5
Rowena Cl CSBY/BLUN L23 21 G5
Rowland Cl WARRN/WOL WA2 85 E2
Rowlings Wy KKBY L32 * 34 A4
Rowsley Gv WLT/FAZ L9 31 G5
Rowson St PR/KW L34 59 H3
WAL/NB CH45 51 H1
Rowthorn Cl WDN WA8 124 C3
Rowton Cl CL/PREN CH43 91 F5
Roxborough Wk WLTN L25 98 A5
Roxburgh Av AIG/SPK L17 95 E5
RF/TRAN CH42 115 F1
Roxburgh St ANF/KKDL L4 54 A1
BTL L20 5 J7
Royal Av WDN WA8 123 H3
Royal Cl FMBY L37 17 F5
Royal Crs FMBY L37 17 F4
Royal Cft WD/CROXPK L12 73 F1
Royal Gv ECCL WA10 61 F1
Royal Mail St VAUX/LVPD L3 7 G4
Royal Standard Wy
RF/TRAN CH42 92 D5
Royal St ANF/KKDL L4 54 A3
The Royal HOY CH47 86 D2
Royden Av RUNC WA7 154 D1
WAL/EG CH44 52 B5
Royden Rd GR/UP/WCH CH49 89 G2
Royden Wy VAUX/LVPD L3 94 A5
Royhsay Cl EV L5 71 E1
Roysten Gdns STHEL WA9 48 D5
Royston Av WAL/EG CH44 69 F1
WARR WA1 107 H1
Royston St EHL/KEN L7 71 H4
Royton Rd CSBY/WL L22 29 G2
Rozel Crs WARRW/BUR WA5 105 F4
Rubbing Stone WKBY CH48 * 110 D5
Ruby Cl LITH L21 30 B4
Ruby St TOX L8 94 B5
Rudd Av STHEL WA9 49 G5
Rudd St HOY CH47 87 F1
Rudgate RAIN/WH L35 77 E3
Rudgrave Ms WAL/EG CH44 52 B5
Rudgrave Pl WAL/EG CH44 52 B5
Rudgrave Sq WAL/EG CH44 52 B5
Rudloe Ct WARRN/WOL WA2 84 D4
Rudston Rd CHLDW L16 73 G5
Rudyard Cl DV/KA/FCH L14 73 G2
Rudyard Rd DV/KA/FCH L14 73 G2
Rufford Av MGHL L31 19 E3
Rufford Cl AIN/FAZ L10 32 C3
RAIN/WH L35 60 B5
WDN WA8 124 A1
Rufford Rd BTL L20 39 G2
NPK/KEN L6 72 A2
WAL/EG CH44 69 E2
Rugby Dr AIN/FAZ L10 32 B3
Rugby Rd WAL/EG CH44 51 F5
WLT/FAZ L9 31 G4
Ruislip Cl WLTN L25 121 E1
Ruislip Ct WARRN/WOL WA2 84 D4
Rullerton Rd WAL/EG CH44 68 C1
Rumford Pl VAUX/LVPD L3 6 B3
Rumford St CLVP L2 6 C3
Rumney Pl ANF/KKDL L4 53 H2
Rumney Rd ANF/KKDL L4 54 A2
Rumney Rd West ANF/KKDL L4 53 H2
Runcorn Docks Rd RUNC WA7 8 A5
Runcorn Spur Rd RUNC WA7 9 G6
Runcorn-Widnes Br WDN WA8 8 D1
Rundle Rd AIG/SPK L17 118 C1
Rundle St BIRK CH41 68 C5
Runic St CLB/OSW/ST L13 72 D3
Runnells La CSBY/BLUN L23 22 B4
The Runnell NSTN CH64 149 H5
Runnymede WARR WA1 108 C1
Runnymede Cl WLTN L25 97 G4
Runnymede Dr
RNFD/HAY WA11 * 49 G1
Runnymede Wk WDN WA8 * 125 G1
Runton Rd WLTN L25 98 A3
Rupert Dr NPK/KEN L6 71 G2
Rupert Rd HUY L36 75 E2
Ruscar Cl HLWD L26 121 G1
Ruscolm Cl WARRW/BUR WA5 104 B1
Ruscombe Rd DV/KA/FCH L14 57 F4
Rushden Rd KKBY L32 34 B3
Rushey Hey Rd KKBY L32 33 H3
Rushfield Crs RUNC WA7 156 D4
Rushgreen Cl CL/PREN CH43 90 C1
Rushlake Dr NTHLY L27 98 B3
Rushmere Rd NG/CROX L11 41 H5
Rushmore Dr WDN WA8 101 H5
Rushmore Gv WARR WA1 108 A1
Rusholme Cl HLWD L26 122 A5
Rushton Cl WDN WA8 101 H5
Rushton Pl WLTN L25 120 C1
Ruskin Av RF/TRAN CH42 * 115 H2
WAL/EG CH44 68 C2
WARRN/WOL WA2 84 A3
Ruskin Cl BTL L20 4 E5
Ruskin Dr ECCL WA10 10 B3
Ruskin Wy CL/PREN CH43 90 D5
HUY L36 75 F4
Rusland Av PEN/TH CH61 134 D2
Rusland Rd KKBY L32 34 A4
Russell Rd ALL/GAR L19 119 G5
CALD/MH L18 95 H3
HUY L36 76 B3
RF/TRAN CH42 92 D5
RUNC WA7 154 C1
WAL/EG CH44 51 E5
Russell St BIRK CH41 3 F3
VAUX/LVPD L3 7 H4
Russet Cl ECCL WA10 10 E2
NTHLY L27 98 C3
Russian Dr CLB/OSW/ST L13 55 H5
Rutherford Cl CLB/OSW/ST L13 72 C4
Rutherford Rd CALD/MH L18 96 B2
ECCL WA10 47 E1
MGHL L31 24 B2
Rutherglen Av CSBY/BLUN L23 29 G2
Ruth Evans Ct RAIN/WH L35 77 G1
Ruthin Cl WARRW/BUR WA5 * 83 E2
Ruthven Rd CLB/OSW/ST L13 73 F4
LITH L21 29 H5
Rutland Av AIG/SPK L17 95 F2
HLWD L26 121 H3
WARRS WA4 129 H3
Rutland Cl EV L5 54 C5
Rutland St BTL L20 5 G2
ECCL WA10 10 E2
RUNC WA7 8 C4
Rutter Av WARRW/BUR WA5 83 F3
Rutter St TOX L8 94 A3
Rycot Rd SPK/HALE L24 142 A2
Rycroft Rd AIN/FAZ L10 32 B4
HOY CH47 65 E5
WAL/EG CH44 69 E3
Rydal Av CL/PREN CH43 90 C3
CSBY/BLUN L23 29 G2
FMBY L37 16 C4
PR/KW L34 60 B4
WARRS WA4 129 G1
Rydal Bank BEB CH63 116 A4
WAL/EG CH44 69 E1
Rydal Cl AIN/FAZ L10 32 C2
NSTN CH64 159 E4
NWD/KWIPK L33 25 G5
PEN/TH CH61 134 D2
Rydal Gv RNFD/HAY WA11 37 E5
RUNC WA7 155 F1
Rydal Rd HUY L36 75 G4
Rydal St EV L5 54 C4
Rydal Wy WDN WA8 124 A3
Ryder Cl RAIN/WH L35 77 G1
Ryder Rd WARR WA1 85 G5
WDN WA8 102 B4
Rye Cl STHEL WA9 79 G1
Ryecote KKBY L32 33 H5
Rye Cft LITH L21 30 A1
Ryecroft Rd HES CH60 149 G2
Ryedale Cl TOX L8 94 D1
Ryefield La LITH L21 30 A1
Ryegate Rd ALL/GAR L19 119 F4
Ryeground La FMBY L37 17 F1
Rye Gv WD/CROXPK L12 57 E4
Rye Hey Rd KKBY L32 33 H2
Ryland Pk PEN/TH CH61 135 E1
Rylands Dr WARRN/WOL WA2 13 G2
Rylands Hey GR/UP/WCH CH49 89 F4
Rylands St WARR WA1 12 D5
WDN WA8 14 E3
Ryleys Gdns CLVP L2 6 D3
Rymer Gv ANF/KKDL L4 54 C1
Rymers Gn FMBY L37 16 D2

S

Sabre Cl RUNC WA7 * 157 F2
Sackville Rd ECCL WA10 47 E1
Saddle Cl WLT/FAZ L9 32 A4
Saddlers Ri RUNC WA7 157 E1
Saddlestone Gv TOX L8 94 A3
Sadler St WDN WA8 15 G1
Saffron Cl WARRN/WOL WA2 85 F4
Saffron Gdns STHEL WA9 48 D5
Saffron Ms CSBY/BLUN L23 22 A3
Sage Cl WARRN/WOL WA2 85 G3
St Agnes Rd ANF/KKDL L4 53 H2
HUY L36 75 H3
St Aidans Ct CL/PREN CH43 91 F2
St Aidan's Gv HUY L36 58 A3
St Aidan's Ter CL/PREN CH43 91 F2
EV L5 53 H4
St Aidan's Wy NTHTN L30 22 D5
St Alban Rd WARRW/BUR WA5 104 C3
St Albans NPK/KEN L6 55 G4
St Albans Ct EV L5 53 G5
St Alban's Rd BTL L20 5 F5
CL/PREN CH43 91 G1
WAL/NB CH45 68 D1
St Alban's Sq BTL L20 5 F6
St Alexander Cl BTL L20 53 H1
St Ambrose Cft NTHTN L30 22 D5
St Ambrose Gv ANF/KKDL L4 54 D4
St Ambrose Rd WDN WA8 15 H1
St Ambrose Wy EV L5 71 E1
St Andrew Rd ANF/KKDL L4 54 D4
St Andrews Av
WD/CROXPK L12 57 E4
St Andrews Cl
WARRN/WOL WA2 85 E1
St Andrews Ct CL/PREN CH43 90 D2
St Andrew's Dr CSBY/BLUN L23 20 C3
HUY L36 58 A3
St Andrew's Gv NTHTN L30 * 30 B1
RNFD/HAY WA11 48 B1
St Andrews Rd BEB CH63 138 A3
CL/PREN CH43 91 H2
CSBY/BLUN L23 20 C2
LITH L21 39 G2
St Andrew St VAUX/LVPD L3 7 H4
St Andrew's Vw
NWD/KWIPK L33 25 H4
St Annes Av WARRS WA4 131 F1
St Annes Av East WARRS WA4 131 F1
St Anne's Cl BIRK CH41 2 E3
St Annes Ct VAUX/LVPD L3 * 71 E2
St Anne's Gdns AIG/SPK L17 118 D2
St Anne's Gv AIG/SPK L17 118 C2
BIRK CH41 2 B1
St Anne's Pl BIRK CH41 2 B1
St Anne's Rd AIG/SPK L17 118 C2
HUY L36 75 G4
WDN WA8 125 F1
St Annes Ter BIRK CH41 2 B2
St Anne St BIRK CH41 2 B1
BIRK CH41 2 D2
VAUX/LVPD L3 71 E2
St Anne Wy BIRK CH41 2 E3
St Ann Pl RAIN/WH L35 78 A1
St Anns Rd ECCL WA10 47 E4
St Anthonys Centre EV L5 * 53 H5
St Anthony's Cl HUY L36 58 A3
St Anthony's Gv NTHTN L30 30 C1
St Anthony's Rd
CSBY/BLUN L23 20 C5
St Asaph Dr WARRW/BUR WA5 82 D3
St Asaph Gv NTHTN L30 31 E3
St Augustine's Av WARRS WA4 107 H4
St Augustine St EV L5 * 53 H5
St Augustine's Wy NTHTN L30 22 C5
St Austell Cl WARRW/BUR WA5 104 C5
St Austell Cl MOR/LEA CH46 65 H4
RUNC WA7 156 D3
St Austells Rd ANF/KKDL L4 5 K7
St Austins La WARR WA1 12 C6
St Barnabas Pl
WARRW/BUR WA5 106 A2
St Benard's Cl TOX L8 94 D1
St Benedicts Cl
WARRN/WOL WA2 12 E1
St Benedict's Gv HUY L36 58 A3
St Benet's Wy NTHTN L30 30 D1
St Bernard's Cl NTHTN L30 30 C1
St Bernard's Dr NTHTN L30 30 C1
St Brendan's Cl HUY L36 58 A3
St Brides Cl WARRW/BUR WA5 104 C5
St Bride's Rd WAL/EG CH44 52 B5
St Bride St TOX L8 7 K7
St Bridget's Cl
WARRN/WOL WA2 84 D2
WDN WA8 146 A1
St Bridget's Gv NTHTN L30 * 30 C1
St Bridgets La WKBY CH48 110 B2
St Brigids Crs VAUX/LVPD L3 53 G5
St Catherine's RF/TRAN CH42 92 B4
St Catherines Cl HUY L36 75 G4
St Catherines Gdns
RF/TRAN CH42 92 B4
St Catherine's Rd BTL L20 4 E5
St Chad's Dr KKBY L32 33 H2
St Christopher's Av NTHTN L30 22 C5
Stchristopher's Dr HUY L36 58 A3
St Columba's Cl WAL/EG CH44 * 52 B5
St Cuthbert's Cl
WD/CROXPK L12 * 43 E4
St Cyrils Cl NTHLY L27 98 A1
St Damian's Cft NTHTN L30 30 D1
St David Rd CL/PREN CH43 91 G2
PS/BROM CH62 153 G3
St Davids Cl RAIN/WH L35 78 A1
St Davids Dr WARRW/BUR WA5 83 E3
St Davids Gv NTHTN L30 30 C2
St Davids La CL/PREN CH43 90 D3
St David's Rd ANF/KKDL L4 54 D4
DV/KA/FCH L14 57 H5
St Domingo Gv EV L5 54 C4
St Domingo Rd EV L5 54 A4
St Domingo V EV L5 54 C4
St Dunstan's Gv NTHTN L30 30 C2
St Edmond's Rd BTL L20 4 E6
St Edmunds Rd BEB CH63 137 H1
St Edwards Cl BIRK CH41 2 A1
St Edwards Ms BIRK CH41 * 2 A1
St Elmo Rd WAL/EG CH44 52 B5
St Elphins Cl WARR WA1 13 G4
St Gabriel's Av HUY L36 76 A3
St George's Av ECCL WA10 47 E2
RF/TRAN CH42 115 F1
St Georges Ct WDN WA8 124 B3
St Georges Gv NTHTN L30 30 C2
St George's Hl EV L5 54 B5
St George's Mt WAL/NB CH45 51 H2
St George's Pk WAL/NB CH45 51 H2
St George's Pl CLVPS L1 7 F3
St Georges Rd ECCL WA10 10 A7
FMBY L37 16 D2
HUY L36 58 C5
WAL/NB CH45 51 E4
St George's Wy BEB CH63 150 C2
CLVPS L1 * 7 F4
St Gerard's Cl EV L5 53 H4
St Gregory's Cft NTHTN L30 22 D5
St Helen's Cl CL/PREN CH43 2 A5
St Helens Linkway
RAIN/WH L35 78 D3
STHEL WA9 61 H3
St Helens Rd PR/KW L34 59 H4
Saint Helens Rd PR/KW L34 60 B3
RNFD/HAY WA11 36 A4
St Hilary Brow WAL/NB CH45 68 B1
St Hilary Dr WAL/NB CH45 51 F5
St Hilda St ANF/KKDL L4 * 54 A2
St Hugh's Cl CL/PREN CH43 2 A5
St Ives Gv CLB/OSW/ST L13 72 D2
St Ives Rd CL/PREN CH43 91 G2
St Ives Wy HLWD L26 121 H3
St James Cl GR/UP/WCH CH49 89 F4
WD/CROXPK L12 56 A4
St James Ct BTL L20 4 C3
St James Dr BTL L20 4 C3
St James Mt RAIN/WH L35 78 A3
St James Pl TOX L8 94 A1
St James Rd BIRK CH41 68 B5
CLVPS L1 94 A1
HUY L36 75 G4
PR/KW L34 60 A3
Saint James Rd RAIN/WH L35 78 A3
St James Rd WAL/NB CH45 51 H2
St James St CLVPS L1 93 H1
St Jerome's Wy NTHTN L30 22 D5
St John Av WARRS WA4 129 H1
St John's Av WLT/FAZ L9 40 C2
St John's Brow RUNC WA7 * 9 F3
St John's Cl HOY CH47 64 D5
St John's La CLVPS L1 7 F3
St Johns Pavement BIRK CH41 * 2 E5
St John's Pl CSBY/WL L22 29 E3
St John's Rd BTL L20 53 F1
CSBY/WL L22 29 E3
HUY L36 75 H4
PS/BROM CH62 153 G4
WAL/NB CH45 51 E5
St Johns Sq BIRK CH41 * 2 E5
CLVPS L1 * 7 F4
St John's St RUNC WA7 9 F3
St John's Ter BTL L20 * 53 F1
St John St BIRK CH41 2 E5
ECCL WA10 61 F1
St Johns Wy CLVPS L1 * 7 F4
St Josephs Cl HUY L36 58 A3
WARRW/BUR WA5 104 C3
St Josephs Crs VAUX/LVPD L3 7 G1
St Jude's Cl HUY L36 * 58 A3
St Katherines Wy WARR WA1 13 H4
St Kevin's Dr KKBY L32 25 H5
St Kilda's Rd MOR/LEA CH46 89 F1
St Laurence Cl BIRK CH41 2 E3
St Laurence Dr BIRK CH41 2 E4
St Laurence Gv KKBY L32 * 34 A4
St Lawrence Cl TOX L8 94 C4
St Leonard's Cl NTHTN L30 22 C5
St Lucia Rd WAL/EG CH44 52 B5
St Luke's Church Rd FMBY L37 16 B4
St Lukes Cl DV/KA/FCH L14 57 F4
St Lukes Ct ANF/KKDL L4 40 C5
St Luke's Crs WDN WA8 102 B4
St Luke's Dr FMBY L37 16 B4
St Luke's Gv NTHTN L30 22 C5
St Luke's Rd CSBY/BLUN L23 21 E5
ECCL WA10 10 A5
St Luke's Wy HUY L36 58 A3
St Margaret's Av
WARRN/WOL WA2 84 B4
St Margaret's Gv NTHTN L30 30 B2
St Margaret's Rd HOY CH47 87 E1
St Mark's Gv NTHTN L30 22 B5
St Mark's Rd HUY L36 75 H4
St Mark's St RNFD/HAY WA11 49 G1
St Martins Gv KKBY L32 34 A4
St Martins La RUNC WA7 157 F2
St Martin's Ms EV L5 71 E1
St Marys Ar ECCL WA10 * 11 H6
St Mary's Av ANF/KKDL L4 * 40 C5
St Marys Cl BTL L20 4 C4
WARRS WA4 130 A5
St Marys Ct WLTN L25 120 C1
St Mary's Ga BIRK CH41 3 H5
St Mary's Gv ANF/KKDL L4 * 40 C5
NTHTN L30 30 B2
St Mary's La ANF/KKDL L4 40 C5
St Mary's Pl ANF/KKDL L4 * 40 C5
St Mary's Rd ALL/GAR L19 119 F4
CSBY/WL L22 29 G4
HUY L36 75 G3
RUNC WA7 147 F5
WARRW/BUR WA5 104 D3
WDN WA8 8 D1
St Mary's St WAL/EG CH44 68 D1
WLTN L25 120 C1
St Mathews Cl ANF/KKDL L4 41 F5
HUY L36 75 H2
St Matthews Av LITH L21 30 B4
St Matthew's Cl HUY L36 * 75 H2
WARRS WA4 130 B4
St Matthews Gv ECCL WA10 61 E2
St Mawes Cl WDN WA8 124 C1
St Mawes Wy ECCL WA10 46 D1
St Mawgan Ct
WARRN/WOL WA2 84 D3
St Michael's Church Rd
AIG/SPK L17 117 H1
St Michael's Cl AIG/SPK L17 118 A1
WDN WA8 124 A4
St Michaels Ct HUY L36 75 G2
St Michael's Gv NPK/KEN L6 71 H1
NTHTN L30 30 B1
St Michael's Pk
PS/BROM CH62 116 B5
St Michael's Rd AIG/SPK L17 94 D5
CSBY/BLUN L23 20 C4
STHEL WA9 79 E2
WDN WA8 124 A4
St Monica's Cl WARRS WA4 130 B4
St Monica's Dr NTHTN L30 22 C5
St Nicholas' Dr NTHTN L30 30 C1
St Nicholas Gv STHEL WA9 * 62 D3
St Nicholas Pl VAUX/LVPD L3 6 A4
St Nicholas Rd RAIN/WH L35 76 C4
WAL/NB CH45 50 D5
St Oswald's Av CL/PREN CH43 67 G4
St Oswalds Ct NTHTN L30 * 31 E1
St Oswald's La NTHTN L30 23 E5
St Oswald's Ms CL/PREN CH43 67 G4
St Oswald's St CLB/OSW/ST L13 73 E3
St Paschal Baylon Bvd
CHLDW L16 74 B5
St Patrick's Cl
NWD/KWIPK L33 * 25 H4
WDN WA8 146 A1
St Patrick's Dr NTHTN L30 * 22 C5
St Pauls Av WAL/EG CH44 69 G3
St Pauls Cl NWD/KWIPK L33 25 G4
RF/TRAN CH42 115 G1
St Pauls Ms RUNC WA7 * 8 E4
St Paul's Rd RF/TRAN CH42 115 H1
WAL/EG CH44 69 F3
WDN WA8 14 D5
St Paul's Sq VAUX/LVPD L3 6 C2
St Paul St ECCL WA10 10 D5
St Paul's Vls RF/TRAN CH42 115 G1
St Peter's Av FMBY L37 16 C2
St Peter's Cl FMBY L37 16 C2
HES CH60 148 D2
NWD/KWIPK L33 25 G4
St Peters Ct AIG/SPK L17 * 94 D4
St Peter's Ms RF/TRAN CH42 116 B2
St Peter's Rd RF/TRAN CH42 116 A2
WLT/FAZ L9 31 H5
St Peter's Wy CL/PREN CH43 90 C4
WARRN/WOL WA2 12 E2
St Philip's Av LITH L21 30 B4
St Richards Cl BTL L20 53 H1
St Seiriol Gv CL/PREN CH43 91 G2
St Stephen Rd
WARRW/BUR WA5 104 D3
St Stephen's Av
WARRN/WOL WA2 83 H2
St Stephens Cl HES CH60 149 G3
WLTN L25 98 A3
St Stephen's Gv NTHTN L30 30 C1
St Stephens Pl VAUX/LVPD L3 6 E1
St Stephen's Rd
RF/TRAN CH42 114 D1
St Teresa's Rd ECCL WA10 10 A4
St Thomas Ct WDN WA8 * 124 C2
St Thomas's Dr NTHTN L30 30 C1
St Vincent Rd CL/PREN CH43 91 G2
WAL/EG CH44 52 B5
WARRW/BUR WA5 104 D3
St Vincent's Cl WD/CROXPK L12 57 E4
St Vincent St VAUX/LVPD L3 7 H3
St Werburgh's Sq BIRK CH41 3 F5
St Wilfrid's Dr WARRS WA4 131 G2
St William Rd CSBY/BLUN L23 22 A5
St Winifred Rd RAIN/WH L35 60 D5
WAL/NB CH45 51 H3
Saker St ANF/KKDL L4 54 B3
Salacre Cl GR/UP/WCH CH49 90 A4
Salacre Crs GR/UP/WCH CH49 90 A4
Salacre La GR/UP/WCH CH49 90 A3
Salacre Ter GR/UP/WCH CH49 * 90 A3
Salcombe Dr WLTN L25 120 D4
Salem Vw CL/PREN CH43 91 H5
Salerno Dr HUY L36 75 F2
Saleswood Av ECCL WA10 46 C4
Saline Cl DV/KA/FCH L14 57 G4
Salisbury Av NTHTN L30 31 F3
WKBY CH48 110 A1
Salisbury Dr PS/BROM CH62 116 B4
Salisbury Pk CHLDW L16 96 D2
Salisbury Rd ALL/GAR L19 119 E5
BTL L20 4 C2
EV L5 54 C4
WAL/NB CH45 51 G2
WAV L15 95 F1
Salisbury St BIRK CH41 2 D6
PR/KW L34 59 H3
RUNC WA7 8 D6
VAUX/LVPD L3 71 F2
WARR WA1 13 H3
WDN WA8 14 E3

Salisbury Ter *WAV* L15 72 D5
Salop St *ANF/KKDL* L4 54 B2
Saltash Cl *HLWD* L26 121 G3
RUNC WA7 156 D3
Saltburn Rd *WAL/NB* CH45 50 D5
Saltergate Rd *TOX* L8 94 C4
Salthouse Quay *VAUX/LVPD* L3 6 C6
Saltney St *VAUX/LVPD* L3 70 B1
Salton Gdns
WARRW/BUR WA5 106 A1
Saltpit La *MGHL* L31 19 E5
Saltwood Dr *RUNC* WA7 157 E4
Salvia Wy *NWD/KWIPK* L33 25 G4
Samaria Av *PS/BROM* CH62 116 C4
Samphire Gdns *STHEL* WA9 63 H3
Samuel St *STHEL* WA9 61 F3
WARRW/BUR WA5 106 A4
Sanbec Gdns *WDN* WA8 101 F3
Sandalwood *RUNC* WA7 147 H5
Sandalwood Cl *NPK/KEN* L6 54 D5
WARRN/WOL WA2 84 B3
Sandalwood Dr *CL/PREN* CH43 90 D4
Sandalwood Gdns *STHEL* WA9 62 C3
Sandbeck St *TOX* L8 94 B5
Sandbrook La *MOR/LEA* CH46 66 C5
Sandbrook Rd *WLTN* L25 74 C5
Sandcliffe Rd *WAL/NB* CH45 51 E2
Sandeman Rd *ANF/KKDL* L4 55 F1
Sanderling Rd *NWD/KWIPK* L33 34 B1
Sanders Hey Cl *RUNC* WA7 156 C4
Sanderson Cl
WARRW/BUR WA5 * 104 B2
Sandfield *HUY* L36 75 F3
Sandfield Av *HOY* CH47 64 D4
Sandfield Cl *BEB* CH63 * 115 F5
WD/CROXPK L12 56 C5
Sandfield Crs *ECCL* WA10 10 E6
Sandfield Pk *HES* CH60 148 B1
Sandfield Pk East
WD/CROXPK L12 56 C4
Sandfield Pl *BTL* L20 4 C2
Sandfield Rd *BEB* CH63 115 F5
BTL L20 5 H6
ECCL WA10 46 C2
GR/UP/WCH CH49 113 F1
WAL/NB CH45 51 H3
WLTN L25 97 H4
Sandfield Ter *WAL/NB* CH45 51 H3
Sandfield Wk *CLB/OSW/ST* L13 73 F1
Sandford Dr *MGHL* L31 18 D4
Sandford St *BIRK* CH41 3 G3
Sandforth Cl *WD/CROXPK* L12 56 A5
Sandforth Ct
CLB/OSW/ST L13 * 56 A5
Sandforth Rd *WD/CROXPK* L12 56 A5
Sandgate Cl *SPK/HALE* L24 141 H2
Sandham Gv *HES* CH60 149 G2
Sandham Rd *SPK/HALE* L24 143 E3
Sandhead St *EHL/KEN* L7 72 B5
Sandhey Rd *HOY* CH47 64 C5
Sandheys *NSTN* CH64 158 B1
Sandheys Av *CSBY/WL* L22 28 D3
Sandheys Cl *ANF/KKDL* L4 54 A3
Sandheys Gv *CSBY/WL* L22 28 D2
Sandheys Rd *WAL/NB* CH45 51 H3
Sandheys Ter *CSBY/WL* L22 28 D3
Sandhills La *EV* L5 53 G3
The Sandhills *MOR/LEA* CH46 66 C2
Sandhills Vw *WAL/NB* CH45 50 D5
Sandhurst Cl *FMBY* L37 16 B5
LITH L21 29 G5
Sandhurst Dr *AIN/FAZ* L10 32 B2
Sandhurst Rd *HLWD* L26 122 A5
RAIN/WH L35 60 C5
Sandhurst St *AIG/SPK* L17 94 B5
WARRS WA4 107 H5
Sandhurst Wy *MGHL* L31 18 B1
Sandicroft Rd *WD/CROXPK* L12 43 F5
Sandino St *TOX* L8 94 A2
Sandirngham Dr *AIG/SPK* L17 94 D4
Sandiway *BEB* CH63 152 C3
HOY CH47 64 D4
HUY L36 75 H4
RAIN/WH L35 76 D3
Sandiway Av *WDN* WA8 123 G2
Sandiways Av *NTHTN* L30 31 E2
Sandiways Rd *WAL/NB* CH45 51 E4
Sandlea Pk *WKBY* CH48 110 A1
Sandlewood Gv
NWD/KWIPK L33 26 A5
Sandon Cl *RAIN/WH* L35 77 H1
Sandon Crs *NSTN* CH64 158 D5
Sandon Pl *WDN* WA8 15 K1
Sandon Rd *WAL/EG* CH44 69 F1
Sandon St *CSBY/WL* L22 29 E3
TOX L8 94 C1
Sandon Wy *EV* L5 53 F4
Sandown Cl *RUNC* WA7 155 G3
Sandown La *WAV* L15 72 D5
Sandown Park Rd *AIN/FAZ* L10 32 B1
Sandown Rd *WAV* L15 72 D5
Sandpiper Cl *GR/UP/WCH* CH49 89 F2
Sandpiper Gv *HLWD* L26 * 121 G2
Sandpipers Ct *CSBY/BLUN* L23 28 D2
Sandridge Rd *PEN/TH* CH61 134 D1
WAL/NB CH45 51 H3
Sandringham Av *CSBY/WL* L22 29 F4
HOY CH47 64 C5
Sandringham Cl *HOY* CH47 * 87 G1
NWD/KWIPK L33 25 H4
PS/BROM CH62 * 116 A4
Sandringham Dr *STHEL* WA9 62 C4
WAL/NB CH45 51 G2
WARRW/BUR WA5 105 G4
Sandringham Ms *HOY* CH47 * 64 C5
Sandringham Rd
CLB/OSW/ST L13 55 G4
CSBY/WL L22 29 F4
FMBY L37 16 D5
MGHL L31 * 23 H1
WDN WA8 101 H4
Sandrock Cl *WAL/NB* CH45 51 H3
Sandrock Rd *WAL/NB* CH45 51 H3
Sands Rd *CALD/MH* L18 95 H4
Sandstone Cl *RAIN/WH* L35 78 A4
Sandstone Dr *RAIN/WH* L35 60 B5
WKBY CH48 111 E1
Sandstone Ms *WDN* WA8 101 G4
Sandstone Rd East
CLB/OSW/ST L13 73 E1
Sandstone Rd West
CLB/OSW/ST L13 72 D1
Sandstone Wk *HES* CH60 149 E2
Sandway Crs *NG/CROX* L11 42 A5
Sandy Brow La
NWD/KWIPK L33 35 F5
Sandy Gn *WLT/FAZ* L9 41 E1
Sandy Gv *CLB/OSW/ST* L13 55 H4
Sandy Knowe *WAV* L15 * 73 E5
Sandy La *CLB/OSW/ST* L13 55 H4
HES CH60 135 E5
LITH L21 29 G5
MGHL L31 18 C1
MGHL L31 24 D4
NSTN CH64 159 F4
PEN/TH CH61 112 A4
RNFD/HAY WA11 36 B4
RNFD/HAY WA11 36 D3
RUNC WA7 154 B2
RUNC WA7 157 G3
WAL/NB CH45 51 E4
WARRN/WOL WA2 83 H2
WARRS WA4 130 B3
WARRW/BUR WA5 105 E4
WDN WA8 101 G4
WDN WA8 103 H2
WKBY CH48 110 B3
WLT/FAZ L9 40 D1
Sandy La North *PEN/TH* CH61 112 A3
Sandy La West
WARRN/WOL WA2 83 G2
Sandymount Dr *BEB* CH63 * 137 H2
WAL/NB CH45 51 G3
Sandy Rd *LITH* L21 29 G4
Sandyville Gv *ANF/KKDL* L4 55 G2
Sandyville Rd *ANF/KKDL* L4 55 F2
Sandy Wy *CL/PREN* CH43 91 G3
Sankey Mnr
WARRW/BUR WA5 * 104 C2
Sankey Rd *MGHL* L31 24 A2
RNFD/HAY WA11 49 F2
Sankey St *CLVPS* L1 7 G7
STHEL WA9 48 D5
WARR WA1 12 B5
WDN WA8 125 E5
Sankey Wy *WARRW/BUR* WA5 105 G3
Santon Av *CLB/OSW/ST* L13 55 G5
Sapphire Dr *NWD/KWIPK* L33 25 H4
Sapphire St *CLB/OSW/ST* L13 72 D4
Sarah's Cft *NTHTN* L30 30 D1
Sark Rd *CLB/OSW/ST* L13 72 D1
Sartfield Cl *CHLDW* L16 74 A5
Sarum Rd *WLTN* L25 97 G1
Sarus Ct *RUNC* WA7 147 H2
Satinwood Crs *MGHL* L31 32 D1
Saughall Massie La
GR/UP/WCH CH49 89 G3
Saughall Massie Rd *WKBY* CH48 87 H5
Saughall Rd *MOR/LEA* CH46 89 E1
Saunby St *ALL/GAR* L19 140 C2
Saunders Av *RAIN/WH* L35 76 D1
Saundersfoot Cl
WARRW/BUR WA5 83 E3
Saunders Rd *RAIN/WH* L35 76 D1
Savannah Pl
WARRW/BUR WA5 105 G1
Saville Av *WARRW/BUR* WA5 106 B1
Saville Rd *CLB/OSW/ST* L13 73 F3
MGHL L31 18 C3
Savon Hook *FMBY* L37 17 G5
Savoylands Cl *AIG/SPK* L17 118 A1
Sawley Cl *RUNC* WA7 157 G2
Sawpit La *HUY* L36 75 H3
Saxby Rd *DV/KA/FCH* L14 57 G4
Saxon Cl *NPK/KEN* L6 54 D5
Saxonia Rd *ANF/KKDL* L4 40 D5
Saxon Rd *CSBY/BLUN* L23 29 E1
HOY CH47 64 C5
MOR/LEA CH46 66 D4
RUNC WA7 9 H5
Saxon Ter *WDN* WA8 15 F2
Saxon Wy *NWD/KWIPK* L33 25 H3
Saxony Rd *EHL/KEN* L7 71 G3
Sayce St *WDN* WA8 14 E2
Scafell Av *WARRN/WOL* WA2 84 A2
Scafell Lawn *NTHLY* L27 99 E5
Scafell Rd *RNFD/HAY* WA11 37 E5
Scape La *CSBY/BLUN* L23 21 F4
Scargreen Av *NG/CROX* L11 41 H4
Scarisbrick Av *LITH* L21 30 A5
Scarisbrick Cl *MGHL* L31 19 E3
Scarisbrick Crs *NG/CROX* L11 41 F4
Scarisbrick Dr *NG/CROX* L11 41 F4
Scarisbrick Pl *NG/CROX* L11 41 F5
Scarisbrick Rd *NG/CROX* L11 41 F5
Scarsdale Rd *NG/CROX* L11 55 H1
Sceptre Rd *NG/CROX* L11 42 C4
Sceptre Wk *NG/CROX* L11 * 42 C4
Scholar St *EHL/KEN* L7 95 E1
Scholes La *ECCL* WA10 60 C3
Scholes Pk *ECCL* WA10 60 D3
Schomberg St *NPK/KEN* L6 71 G2
School Av *FMBY* L37 17 E3
NSTN CH64 159 E4
School Brow *WARR* WA1 13 F3
School Cl *MOR/LEA* CH46 66 D3
NTHLY L27 98 A1
The Schooles *ECCL* WA10 60 D3
Schoolfield Cl
GR/UP/WCH CH49 113 F1
Schoolfield Rd
GR/UP/WCH CH49 113 F1
School Hl *HES* CH60 148 D2
School La *AIN/FAZ* L10 32 A3
BEB CH63 137 F1
CL/PREN CH43 67 G4
CLVPS L1 6 E5
FMBY L37 17 E3
HOY CH47 64 D4
HOY CH47 87 F1
HUY L36 76 A3
LITH L21 29 H5
LITH L21 30 A4
MGHL L31 19 G5
MGHL L31 24 D4
NSTN CH64 158 A1
NSTN CH64 159 E4
PEN/TH CH61 111 H5
PR/KW L34 43 G1
PR/KW L34 44 A2
PS/BROM CH62 116 B4
RAIN/WH L35 78 D4
RUNC WA7 156 B1
WAL/EG CH44 68 A1
WDN WA8 103 E1
WLTN L25 120 C2
School Rd *WARRN/WOL* WA2 84 A4
School St *RNFD/HAY* WA11 49 F1
WARRS WA4 12 E7
School Wy *SPK/HALE* L24 141 H3
WDN WA8 102 D5
Schooner Cl *RUNC* WA7 157 F3
Science Rd *SPK/HALE* L24 142 A2
Scone Cl *NG/CROX* L11 42 C4
Scorecross *STHEL* WA9 62 B2
Score La *CHLDW* L16 73 G4
Scoresby Rd *MOR/LEA* CH46 67 F2
The Score *STHEL* WA9 62 A4
Scorpio Cl *DV/KA/FCH* L14 57 G5
Scorton St *NPK/KEN* L6 55 E5
Scotchbarn La *PR/KW* L34 60 A4
Scoter Rd *NWD/KWIPK* L33 34 A2
Scotia Av *PS/BROM* CH62 116 C4
Scotia Rd *CLB/OSW/ST* L13 73 E1
Scotland Pl *VAUX/LVPD* L3 7 F1
Scotland Rd *EV* L5 53 H5
VAUX/LVPD L3 70 D2
WARR WA1 12 D4
Scott Av *HUY* L36 76 A5
RAIN/WH L35 77 F2
WDN WA8 14 A3
Scott Cl *ANF/KKDL* L4 54 B3
MGHL L31 18 D5
Scotts Av *STHEL* WA9 79 E2
Scotts Pl *BIRK* CH41 91 F1
Scotts Quays *BIRK* CH41 69 G4
Scott St *BTL* L20 4 C1
WAL/NB CH45 51 H5
WARRN/WOL WA2 12 E2
The Scythes *GR/UP/WCH* CH49 89 E4
NTHTN L30 23 G5
Scythia Cl *PS/BROM* CH62 116 C3
Seabank Av *WAL/EG* CH44 52 A5
Seabank Rd *HES* CH60 148 C3
WAL/NB CH45 52 A3
Seabury St *WARRS* WA4 108 A5
Seacole Cl *TOX* L8 94 D2
Seacombe Prom *WAL/EG* CH44 69 G1
Seacombe Vw *WAL/EG* CH44 69 G3
Seacroft Cl *DV/KA/FCH* L14 57 G4
Seacroft Rd *DV/KA/FCH* L14 57 G4
Seafield *FMBY* L37 17 F4
Seafield Av *CSBY/BLUN* L23 21 G5
HES CH60 148 C3
Seafield Cottages
ALL/GAR L19 * 119 G5
Seafield Rd *BTL* L20 * 4 C2
PS/BROM CH62 116 B3
Seaford Pl *WARRN/WOL* WA2 83 G1
Seafore Cl *MGHL* L31 18 B2
Seaforth Dr *MOR/LEA* CH46 89 G1
Seaforth Rd *LITH* L21 39 E1
Seaforth V North *LITH* L21 29 H5
Seaforth V West *LITH* L21 39 E1
Seagram Cl *WLT/FAZ* L9 31 H4
Sealand Av *FMBY* L37 16 C4
Sealand Cl *FMBY* L37 16 C4
WARRN/WOL WA2 84 C5
Sea La *RUNC* WA7 146 D4
Sealy Cl *BEB* CH63 138 A5
Seaman Rd *WAV* L15 95 G1
Seaport St *TOX* L8 94 C2
Sea Rd *WAL/NB* CH45 51 F2
Seascale Av *ECCL* WA10 60 D2
Seath Av *STHEL* WA9 49 E3
Seathwaite Cl *CSBY/BLUN* L23 28 C1
RUNC WA7 156 A4
Seathwaite Crs
NWD/KWIPK L33 25 G5
Seaton Cl *WD/CROXPK* L12 43 G4
Seaton Gv *STHEL* WA9 61 F4
Seaton Rd *RF/TRAN* CH42 92 A4
WAL/NB CH45 51 G4
Seattle Cl *WARRW/BUR* WA5 105 F1
Sea Vw *HOY* CH47 87 F1
Seaview Av *PEN/TH* CH61 112 B5
PS/BROM CH62 153 H3
WAL/NB CH45 51 G5
Sea View La *PEN/TH* CH61 112 B5
Sea View Rd *BTL* L20 4 B3
Seaview Rd *WAL/NB* CH45 51 G4
Seawood Gv *MOR/LEA* CH46 89 F1
Secker Av *WARRS* WA4 130 B1
Secker Cl *WARRS* WA4 130 B1
Second Av *CL/PREN* CH43 90 B2
CSBY/BLUN L23 * 21 E5
RAIN/WH L35 77 H1
RUNC WA7 156 B1
WLT/FAZ L9 31 H5
WLT/FAZ L9 41 G1
Sedbergh Av *AIN/FAZ* L10 31 H1
Sedbergh Gv *RUNC* WA7 156 A4
Sedbergh Rd *WAL/EG* CH44 51 F5
Sedburgh Gv *HUY* L36 74 D2
Sedburn Rd *KKBY* L32 34 B5
Seddon Cl *ECCL* WA10 46 B4
Seddon Rd *ALL/GAR* L19 119 G5
ECCL WA10 60 D1
Seddons Ct *PR/KW* L34 59 H2
Seddon St *CLVPS* L1 6 E6
ECCL WA10 36 D5
Sedgefield Rd *MOR/LEA* CH46 67 E5
Sedgemoor Rd *NG/CROX* L11 41 G4
Sedley St *ANF/KKDL* L4 54 D4
Sedum Gv *NWD/KWIPK* L33 25 G4
Seeds La *WLT/FAZ* L9 31 H5
Seeley Av *BIRK* CH41 91 G1
Seel Rd *HUY* L36 75 H3
Seel St *CLVPS* L1 7 F6
Sefton Av *LITH* L21 30 A5
WDN WA8 102 A5
Sefton Cl *KKBY* L32 33 F1
Sefton Coastal Footpath
CSBY/BLUN L23 20 A3
CSBY/WL L22 28 C2
Sefton Dr *AIN/FAZ* L10 32 B2
CSBY/BLUN L23 21 H2
KKBY L32 33 F1
MGHL L31 23 F1
TOX L8 95 E3
Sefton Gv *AIG/SPK* L17 95 E4
Sefton La *MGHL* L31 23 G1
Sefton Mill Ct *SFTN* L29 * 23 E2
Sefton Mill La *SFTN* L29 23 E2
Sefton Moss La *NTHTN* L30 30 C1
Sefton Moss Vls *LITH* L21 30 A4
Sefton Park Rd *TOX* L8 94 D2
Sefton Rd *BTL* L20 39 H2
FMBY L37 16 D4
LITH L21 30 A4
PS/BROM CH62 116 A3
RF/TRAN CH42 116 A2
WAL/NB CH45 51 H3
WLT/FAZ L9 32 A5
WLT/FAZ L9 40 C3
Sefton St *LITH* L21 30 A5
TOX L8 94 A4
VAUX/LVPD L3 93 H2
Sefton Vw *CSBY/BLUN* L23 21 G5
Sefton Vls *BTL* L20 * 5 J2
Selborne *RAIN/WH* L35 77 F3
Selborne Cl *TOX* L8 94 C1
Selborne St *TOX* L8 94 C1
Selbourne Cl *GR/UP/WCH* CH49 90 B5
Selby Cl *ECCL* WA10 10 B7
Selby Dr *FMBY* L37 17 G4
Selby Gv *HUY* L36 76 B1
Selby Rd *WLT/FAZ* L9 40 C1
Selby St *WAL/NB* CH45 51 H5
WARRW/BUR WA5 106 A3
Seldon St *EHL/KEN* L7 * 71 H3
Selina Rd *ANF/KKDL* L4 5 K6
Selkirk Av *PS/BROM* CH62 153 E4
WARRS WA4 108 A5
Selkirk Dr *ECCL* WA10 46 D2
Selkirk Rd *CLB/OSW/ST* L13 72 D3
Sellar St *ANF/KKDL* L4 54 A3
Selsdon Rd *CSBY/WL* L22 28 D2
Selsey Cl *EHL/KEN* L7 71 H5
Selside Wk *NTHLY* L27 99 E5
Selston Cl *BEB* CH63 138 A4
Selworthy Dr *WARRS* WA4 108 D5
Selworthy Gn *CHLDW* L16 97 E2
Selwyn Cl *WDN* WA8 102 D5
Selwyn St *ANF/KKDL* L4 54 A1
Senator Point
NWD/KWIPK L33 * 34 C4
Seneschal Ct *RUNC* WA7 156 A3
Sennen Cl *RUNC* WA7 156 D4
Sennen Rd *KKBY* L32 34 A4
Sentinel Wy *NTHTN* L30 31 G4
September Rd *NPK/KEN* L6 55 E5
Serenade Rd *NWD/KWIPK* L33 26 A3
Sergeant Rd *WD/CROXPK* L12 57 E3
Sergeant York Loop
WARRW/BUR WA5 105 F2
Sergrim Rd *HUY* L36 75 F2
Serpentine Rd *WAL/EG* CH44 52 A5
The Serpentine South
CSBY/BLUN L23 20 B5
The Serpentine *ALL/GAR* L19 119 E3
CSBY/BLUN L23 20 B5
Servia Rd *LITH* L21 30 A5
Servite Cl *CSBY/WL* L22 28 D2
Sessions Rd *ANF/KKDL* L4 54 A2
Seth Powell Wy *HUY* L36 58 A4
Settrington Rd *NG/CROX* L11 55 H1
Seven Acre Rd *CSBY/BLUN* L23 22 A4
Seven Acres La *PEN/TH* CH61 113 E5
Sevenoak Gv *RAIN/WH* L35 99 F1
Sevenoaks Cl *EV* L5 54 A5
Seventh Av *WLT/FAZ* L9 * 32 A5
Severn Cl *STHEL* WA9 62 C4
WARRN/WOL WA2 84 C3
WDN WA8 103 F5
Severn Rd *NWD/KWIPK* L33 26 A3
RAIN/WH L35 77 H2
Severn St *BIRK* CH41 68 C4
EV L5 54 B4
Severs St *NPK/KEN* L6 71 G1
Sewell St *PR/KW* L34 59 H4
RUNC WA7 9 G4
Sextant Cl *RUNC* WA7 157 F3
Sexton Av *STHEL* WA9 49 H5
Sexton Wy *DV/KA/FCH* L14 74 A3
Seymour Dr *MGHL* L31 19 E3
WARR WA1 108 A1
Seymour Pl West
WAL/NB CH45 51 H2
Seymour Rd *DV/KA/FCH* L14 73 H4
LITH L21 30 A5
Seymour St *BTL* L20 4 C7
RF/TRAN CH42 92 B4
VAUX/LVPD L3 7 H3
WAL/NB CH45 51 H2
Shacklady Rd *NWD/KWIPK* L33 26 B5
Shackleton Cl
WARRW/BUR WA5 82 D5
Shackleton Rd *MOR/LEA* CH46 67 F1
Shadewood Crs *WARRS* WA4 131 F1
Shadwell Cl *EV* L5 53 F5
Shadwell St *EV* L5 53 F5
Shaftesbury Av
WARRW/BUR WA5 127 G1
Shaftesbury Rd
CSBY/BLUN L23 21 E5
Shaftesbury St *TOX* L8 94 A2
Shaftesbury Ter
CLB/OSW/ST L13 * 73 E2
Shaftsbury Av *NWD/KWIPK* L33 25 G4
Shakespeare Av *KKBY* L32 33 G3
RF/TRAN CH42 115 H2
Shakespeare Cl *NPK/KEN* L6 71 G1
Shakespeare Gv
WARRN/WOL WA2 83 H3
Shakespeare Rd *NSTN* CH64 158 D1
STHEL WA9 79 E2
WAL/EG CH44 69 F3
WDN WA8 14 C1
Shakespeare St *ALL/GAR* L19 140 C1
BTL L20 4 B1
Shakspeare Cl *NPK/KEN* L6 71 G1
Shalcombe Cl *HLWD* L26 122 A4
Shaldon Cl *KKBY* L32 34 B4
Shaldon Gv *KKBY* L32 34 B4
Shaldon Rd *KKBY* L32 34 B5
Shalford Gv *WKBY* CH48 110 D1
Shallcross Ct *NPK/KEN* L6 71 G1
Shallcross Pl *NPK/KEN* L6 71 G1
Shallmarsh Cl *BEB* CH63 137 F1
Shallmarsh Rd *BEB* CH63 137 F1
Shalom Ct *AIG/SPK* L17 95 G3
Shamrock Rd *BIRK* CH41 91 F1
Shand St *ALL/GAR* L19 140 C2
Shanklin Cl *WARRW/BUR* WA5 104 A2
Shanklin Rd *WAV* L15 72 D4
Shannon Gv *WDN* WA8 124 C1
Shannons La *PR/KW* L34 58 A1
Shannon St *BIRK* CH41 68 B4
Shard Cl *NG/CROX* L11 42 B2
Shard St *STHEL* WA9 63 E3
Sharon Park Cl *WARRS* WA4 131 G2
Sharpeville Cl *ANF/KKDL* L4 53 H3
Sharples Crs *CSBY/BLUN* L23 29 G1
Sharp St *WARRN/WOL* WA2 12 E1
WDN WA8 14 D3
Sharwood Rd *NTHLY* L27 98 D4
Shavington Av *CL/PREN* CH43 91 F5
Shawbury Av *BEB* CH63 115 F4
Shawbury Gv *WARR* WA1 85 E4
Shaw Crs *FMBY* L37 17 G2
Shawell Ct *WDN* WA8 126 A1
Shaw Entry *RAIN/WH* L35 100 C1
Shaw Hill St *CLVPS* L1 * 6 E3
Shaw La *GR/UP/WCH* CH49 112 A1
RAIN/WH L35 77 E1
Shaw Rd *SPK/HALE* L24 142 B1
Shaws Aly *CLVPS* L1 6 E7
Shaw's Av *WARRN/WOL* WA2 83 H5
Shaws Dr *HOY* CH47 64 D5
Shaw St *BIRK* CH41 2 D7
ECCL WA10 11 J4
HOY CH47 87 F1
NPK/KEN L6 71 F2
RUNC WA7 8 C5
STHEL WA9 11 J6
Shawton Rd *CHLDW* L16 73 H5
Shearman Cl *PEN/TH* CH61 135 E2
Shearman Rd *PEN/TH* CH61 134 D2
Sheen Rd *WAL/NB* CH45 52 A3
Sheerwater Cl *WARR* WA1 107 H1
Sheffield Cl *WARRW/BUR* WA5 105 G3
Sheil Rd *NPK/KEN* L6 72 A1
Shelagh Av *WDN* WA8 14 D2
Sheldon Cl *BEB* CH63 138 A5
Sheldon Rd *WD/CROXPK* L12 56 D2
Sheldrake Gv *NSTN* CH64 158 D5
Shelley Cl *HUY* L36 75 H4
Shelley Ct *KKBY* L32 33 G4
Shelley Gv *ALL/GAR* L19 140 C1
WARRS WA4 107 H4
Shelley Pl *RAIN/WH* L35 77 F2
Shelley Rd *WDN* WA8 14 C1
Shelley St *BTL* L20 4 C1
STHEL WA9 79 F3
Shelley Wy *WKBY* CH48 110 B3
Shellingford Rd *DV/KA/FCH* L14 74 C1
Shelmore Dr *TOX* L8 94 A4
Shelton Cl *CLB/OSW/ST* L13 73 E3
WDN WA8 103 F5
Shelton Rd *WAL/NB* CH45 51 G4
Shenley Cl *BEB* CH63 115 H5
Shenley Rd *WAV* L15 * 73 G5
Shenstone St *EHL/KEN* L7 71 H4
Shenton Av *RNFD/HAY* WA11 48 D1
Shepherd Cl *GR/UP/WCH* CH49 89 E4
Shepherds Fold Cl *TOX* L8 94 C2
Shepherd St *NPK/KEN* L6 7 K2
Sheppard Av *CHLDW* L16 74 C5
Shepperton Cl *WARRS* WA4 130 B5
Shepston Av *ANF/KKDL* L4 54 C1
Shepton Rd *HUY* L36 58 B4
Sherborne Av *WLTN* L25 121 F3
Sherbrooke Cl *DV/KA/FCH* L14 57 E5
WD/CROXPK L12 74 A1
Sherburn Cl *WLT/FAZ* L9 32 A4
Sherdley Park Dr *STHEL* WA9 62 B4
Sherdley Rd *STHEL* WA9 61 H3
STHEL WA9 62 A2
STHEL WA9 62 B1
Sherford Cl *NTHLY* L27 98 D4
Sheriff Cl *EV* L5 71 E1
Sheringham Cl
GR/UP/WCH CH49 90 A1
STHEL WA9 48 D4
Sheringham Rd
WARRW/BUR WA5 104 C2
Sherlock La *WAL/EG* CH44 68 C3
Sherman Dr *RAIN/WH* L35 78 B4
Sherry Ct *AIG/SPK* L17 * 95 G3
Sherry La *GR/UP/WCH* CH49 113 E1
Sherwell Cl *WAV* L15 73 E4
Sherwood Av *CSBY/BLUN* L23 21 E4
PEN/TH CH61 112 A4
Sherwood Cl *RAIN/WH* L35 60 D5
WDN WA8 124 A2
Sherwood Ct *HUY* L36 75 H3
WD/CROXPK L12 43 F4
Sherwood Dr *BEB* CH63 115 G4
RAIN/WH L35 77 F3
Sherwood Gv *HOY* CH47 88 B1
Sherwood Rd *CSBY/BLUN* L23 20 D4
HOY CH47 65 F5
WAL/EG CH44 69 E2
Sherwood's La *AIN/FAZ* L10 32 C4
Sherwood St *VAUX/LVPD* L3 70 B1
Sherwyn Rd *ANF/KKDL* L4 55 E3
Shetland Cl *WARRN/WOL* WA2 84 C1
WDN WA8 103 E5
Shetland Dr *PS/BROM* CH62 153 E1
Shevington Cl *STHEL* WA9 62 C3
WDN WA8 103 E5
Shevington's La
NWD/KWIPK L33 25 H4
Shewell Cl *RF/TRAN* CH42 92 B4
Shiel Rd *WAL/NB* CH45 51 G3
Shiggins Cl *WARRW/BUR* WA5 105 H2
Shimmin St *EHL/KEN* L7 71 G4
Shipton Cl *ALL/GAR* L19 119 F3
CL/PREN CH43 114 A2
WARRW/BUR WA5 82 B5
WDN WA8 101 F5
Shirdley Av *KKBY* L32 34 A5
Shirdley Wk *KKBY* L32 34 A5
Shirebourne Av
RNFD/HAY WA11 37 F5
Shireburn Rd *FMBY* L37 16 B1
Shire Gn *STHEL* WA9 62 C4
The Shires *ECCL* WA10 10 D7
Shirley Dr *WARRS* WA4 131 E1

Shirley Rd ALL/GAR L19 119 G3
Shirley St WAL/EG CH44 69 G2
Shirwell Gv STHEL WA9 79 G1
Shobdon Cl WD/CROXPK L12 43 F3
Shones Cft NSTN CH64 159 F5
Shop La MGHL L31 18 C5
Shop Rd PR/KW L34 44 A3
Shore Bank PS/BROM CH62 116 C3
Shore Dr PS/BROM CH62 116 C5
Shorefields PS/BROM CH62 116 B3
Shorefields Village TOX L8 94 B5
Shoreham Dr
WARRW/BUR WA5 105 E5
Shore Rd BIRK CH41 3 G2
LITH L21 38 D2
WKBY CH48 110 C4
Shortfield Rd
GR/UP/WCH CH49 90 A4
Shortfield Wy
GR/UP/WCH CH49 * 90 A4
Short St WDN WA8 146 A1
Shortwood Rd DV/KA/FCH L14 74 B2
Shorwell Cl WARRW/BUR WA5 104 A1
Shrewsbury Av AIN/FAZ L10 31 H1
CSBY/WL L22 29 E1
Shrewsbury Cl CL/PREN CH43 91 F2
Shrewsbury Dr
GR/UP/WCH CH49 90 A2
Shrewsbury Rd ALL/GAR L19 119 G5
CL/PREN CH43 91 F1
HES CH60 135 E5
WAL/NB CH45 51 F5
WKBY CH48 110 A2
Shrewsbury St WARRS WA4 107 F5
Shrewton Rd WLTN L25 97 G1
Shropshire Cl NTHTN L30 23 F5
WARR WA1 109 E2
Shropshire Gdns ECCL WA10 10 E7
Sibford Rd WD/CROXPK L12 56 D5
Siddall St ECCL WA10 36 D5
Siddeley St AIG/SPK L17 95 E5
Sidgreave St ECCL WA10 10 D6
Sidings Ct WARR WA1 13 F3
The Sidings RF/TRAN CH42 115 H1
Sidlaw Av STHEL WA9 49 F4
Sidmouth Cl ECCL WA10 47 E1
WARRW/BUR WA5 104 C4
Sidney Av WAL/NB CH45 51 G2
Sidney Gdns RF/TRAN CH42 92 C4
Sidney Pl EHL/KEN L7 71 G4
Sidney Powell Av KKBY L32 33 F2
Sidney Rd BTL L20 5 H6
NSTN CH64 159 E1
RF/TRAN CH42 92 C4
Sidney St BIRK CH41 3 G3
ECCL WA10 10 B4
Sidney Ter RF/TRAN CH42 92 C5
Sidwell St ALL/GAR L19 140 C1
Signal Works Rd WLT/FAZ L9 32 B4
Silcroft Rd KKBY L32 33 H4
Silkstone Cl ECCL WA10 10 B6
EHL/KEN L7 71 H5
Silkstone Crs RUNC WA7 156 D2
Silkstone St ECCL WA10 10 B6
Silver Av RNFD/HAY WA11 49 G2
Silverbeech Av CALD/MH L18 96 B4
Silverbeech Rd WAL/EG CH44 69 E2
Silver Birch Wy MGHL L31 18 B1
Silverbrook Rd NTHLY L27 98 A1
Silverburn Av MOR/LEA CH46 66 C4
Silverdale Av CLB/OSW/ST L13 55 G5
Silverdale Cl HUY L36 75 G5
Silverdale Dr LITH L21 30 C4
Silverdale Gv RNFD/HAY WA11 37 E4
Silverdale Rd BEB CH63 115 H4
CL/PREN CH43 91 G4
WARRS WA4 129 H1
Silverlake Cl WLT/FAZ L9 40 C4
Silverlea Av WAL/NB CH45 51 H5
Silver Leigh AIG/SPK L17 118 B2
Silverlime Gdns STHEL WA9 60 D3
Silverstone Dr HUY L36 75 F5
Silverstone Gv MGHL L31 18 B1
Silver St WARRN/WOL WA2 12 D2
Silverton Rd AIG/SPK L17 118 C3
Silverwell Rd NG/CROX L11 42 D2
Silvester St EV L5 53 G5
Simkin Av WARRS WA4 107 H4
Simms Av STHEL WA9 49 E4
Simm's Rd NPK/KEN L6 55 F4
Simnel Cl WLTN L25 97 H2
Simonsbridge WKBY CH48 * 110 D5
Simons Cl RAIN/WH L35 76 C5
Simon's Cft NTHTN L30 30 B1
Simonside WDN WA8 124 A1
Simonstone Gv STHEL WA9 62 D3
Simonswood La
NWD/KWIPK L33 34 B2
Simpson St BIRK CH41 2 E4
CLVPS L1 * 93 H1
Sim St VAUX/LVPD L3 7 H1
Sinclair Av RAIN/WH L35 60 B5
WARRN/WOL WA2 83 H3
WDN WA8 14 B3
Sinclair Cl RAIN/WH L35 60 B4
Sinclair Dr CALD/MH L18 96 B2
Sinclair St ALL/GAR L19 140 C1
Singleton Av RF/TRAN CH42 92 A5
RNFD/HAY WA11 48 D2
Singleton Dr PR/KW L34 44 B4
Sirdar Cl EHL/KEN L7 71 H5
Sir Howard St EHL/KEN L7 * 7 K7
Sir Howard Wy TOX L8 * 7 K7
Sir Thomas St CLVP L2 6 D3
CLVPS L1 * 6 E3
Siskin Gn WLTN L25 97 G4
Sisters Wy BIRK CH41 2 D4
Sixth Av WLT/FAZ L9 32 B5
Skeffington RAIN/WH L35 77 E3
Skelhorne St VAUX/LVPD L3 7 G4
Skelton Cl RNFD/HAY WA11 37 E5
Skerries Rd ANF/KKDL L4 54 C4
Skiddaw Cl RUNC WA7 156 C5
Skiddaw Rd PS/BROM CH62 139 E4
Skipton Cl RUNC WA7 147 F5
Skipton Rd ANF/KKDL L4 54 D3
HUY L36 76 B2
Skirving Pl EV L5 53 H4
Skirving St EV L5 53 H4
Skye Cl WDN WA8 103 E5
Sky Lark Ri STHEL WA9 49 G4
Slater Pl CLVPS L1 7 F6
Slater St CLVPS L1 7 F6
WARRS WA4 13 G7
Slatey Rd CL/PREN CH43 2 A7
Sleaford Rd DV/KA/FCH L14 57 H5
Sleepers Hl ANF/KKDL L4 54 B3
Sienna Cl NTHLY L27 98 A2
Slessor Av WKBY CH48 87 H5
Slim Rd HUY L36 75 G1
Slingsby Dr GR/UP/WCH CH49 90 A4
Slutchers La WARR WA1 12 B6
Small Av WARRN/WOL WA2 84 A3
Small Crs WARRN/WOL WA2 84 A3
The Smallholdings MGHL L31 * 19 G3
Smallridge Cl PEN/TH CH61 * 134 C2
Smallwoods Ms HES CH60 * 134 C5
Smeaton St ANF/KKDL L4 54 A1
Smilie Av MOR/LEA CH46 66 A4
Smith Av BIRK CH41 68 D5
Smith Crs WARRN/WOL WA2 84 B5
Smithdown Gv EHL/KEN L7 71 G5
Smithdown La EHL/KEN L7 71 G4
Smithdown Pl WAV L15 96 A3
Smithdown Rd EHL/KEN L7 95 E1
WAV L15 95 G2
Smith Dr BTL L20 40 A2
WARRN/WOL WA2 84 B5
Smithfield St CLVP L2 6 D2
STHEL WA9 48 C5
Smithford Wk RAIN/WH L35 99 F1
Smith Pl EV L5 53 H4
Smith Rd WDN WA8 14 B5
Smith St EV L5 54 A3
PR/KW L34 * 60 A4
STHEL WA9 63 E3
WARR WA1 12 E4
Smithy Cl FMBY L37 17 G2
WDN WA8 101 E2
Smithy Gn FMBY L37 17 F2
Smithy Hey WKBY CH48 110 C1
Smithy Hl BEB CH63 150 C3
Smithy La WDN WA8 101 E3
Smithystone Cl WAV L15 96 A1
Smollett St BTL L20 38 D4
EHL/KEN L7 * 71 H3
Smugglers Wy WAL/NB CH45 51 E2
Smyth Rd WDN WA8 125 H1
Snabwood Cl NSTN CH64 158 D5
Snaefell Av CLB/OSW/ST L13 55 G5
Snaefell Gv CLB/OSW/ST L13 55 G5
Snaefell Ri WARRS WA4 130 A4
Snave Cl LITH L21 39 F2
Snottesbrook Gn NG/CROX L11 41 H4
Snowberry Cl WDN WA8 103 E4
Snowberry Cresent
WARRW/BUR WA5 105 H5
Snowberry Rd DV/KA/FCH L14 57 F4
Snowden Rd MOR/LEA CH46 66 A5
Snowdon Cl
WARRW/BUR WA5 104 C2
Snowdon Gv STHEL WA9 62 C3
Snowdon La EV L5 53 G5
Snowdon Rd RF/TRAN CH42 115 F1
Snowdrop Av BIRK CH41 68 B5
Snowdrop Cl RUNC WA7 156 B5
Snowdrop Ms LITH L21 39 F1
Snowdrop St EV L5 53 H3
Soho Pl VAUX/LVPD L3 71 E2
Soho St VAUX/LVPD L3 71 E2
Solar Rd WLT/FAZ L9 40 D1
Solly Av RF/TRAN CH42 115 G1
Solomon St EHL/KEN L7 71 H3
Solway Cl WARRN/WOL WA2 84 D1
Solway Gv RUNC WA7 155 H4
Solway St East TOX L8 94 D1
Solway St West TOX L8 94 D1
Soma Av LITH L21 30 B4
Somerford Rd DV/KA/FCH L14 74 B1
Somerset Pl NPK/KEN L6 55 F5
Somerset Rd BTL L20 5 H2
CSBY/WL L22 28 D2
PEN/TH CH61 134 C2
WAL/NB CH45 51 E5
WKBY CH48 87 G5
Somerset St STHEL WA9 48 D5
Somerset Wy WARR WA1 85 F5
Somerton St WAV L15 72 C5
Somerville Cl BEB CH63 152 B3
NSTN CH64 158 D5
Somerville Gv CSBY/WL L22 29 E2
Somerville Rd CSBY/WL L22 29 E2
WDN WA8 124 B3
Sommer Av WD/CROXPK L12 * 56 A3
Sonning Av LITH L21 29 H3
Sonning Rd ANF/KKDL L4 41 F5
Sorany Cl CSBY/BLUN L23 22 A3
Sorogold St STHEL WA9 48 C4
Sorrel Cl CL/PREN CH43 90 D3
WARRN/WOL WA2 85 G3
South Albert Rd AIG/SPK L17 94 D4
Southampton Wy RUNC WA7 157 G3
South Av PR/KW L34 59 G5
WARRN/WOL WA2 83 H5
WARRS WA4 130 A2
South Bank CL/PREN CH43 91 H5
South Bank Rd ALL/GAR L19 119 F4
EHL/KEN L7 72 B3
South Bank Ter RUNC WA7 8 C3
South Barcombe Rd
CHLDW L16 97 E1
South Boundary Rd
NWD/KWIPK L33 34 C4
Southbourne Rd WAL/NB CH45 50 D5
Southbrook Rd NTHLY L27 98 A1
South Cantril Av
WD/CROXPK L12 57 F3
South Chester St TOX L8 94 A2
South Cloughton Rd BIRK CH41 2 D5
Southcroft Rd WAL/NB CH45 50 D5
South Dl WARRW/BUR WA5 104 D3
Southdale Rd RF/TRAN CH42 115 G1
WARR WA1 108 A1
WAV L15 72 D5
Southdean Rd DV/KA/FCH L14 57 H4
South Dr GR/UP/WCH CH49 90 A3
HES CH60 149 E2
PEN/TH CH61 134 A1
WAV L15 72 D5
WD/CROXPK L12 56 B5
Southern Crs TOX L8 94 A3
Southern Rd SPK/HALE L24 142 C4
Southern St WARRS WA4 130 A2
Southey Cl WDN WA8 14 A3
Southey Gv MGHL L31 24 A3
Southey Rd ECCL WA10 61 E2
Southey St BTL L20 4 C1
WAV L15 95 G1
South Ferry Quay
VAUX/LVPD L3 93 H2
Southfield Rd WLT/FAZ L9 40 B1
Southfields Av
WARRW/BUR WA5 104 D2
South Front RAIN/WH L35 77 E5
Southgate Cl WD/CROXPK L12 43 E4
Southgate Rd CLB/OSW/ST L13 73 F2
South Gv CALD/MH L18 119 G2
TOX L8 94 C4
South Heath Rd RUNC WA7 154 D2
South Hey Rd PEN/TH CH61 134 B2
South Highville Rd CHLDW L16 96 D2
South Hill Gv CL/PREN CH43 91 H5
TOX L8 94 C4
South Hill Rd CL/PREN CH43 91 H4
TOX L8 94 B5
South Hunter St CLVPS L1 7 J6
South John St CLVP L2 6 D4
STHEL WA9 * 48 C4
Southlands Av
WARRW/BUR WA5 104 D5
Southlands Ct RUNC WA7 * 8 C7
Southlands Ms RUNC WA7 145 H5
South La WDN WA8 103 E3
South Lane Entry WDN WA8 103 F3
South Manor Wy WLTN L25 121 E2
South Meade MGHL L31 18 B5
Southmead Gdns ALL/GAR L19 120 A4
Southmead Rd ALL/GAR L19 120 A4
South Mossley Hill Rd
ALL/GAR L19 119 E2
Southney Cl MGHL L31 33 E2
South Pde KKBY L32 33 H2
RUNC WA7 154 B2
SPK/HALE L24 142 C4
WKBY CH48 110 A1
South Park Ct WAL/EG CH44 69 G2
South Park Rd KKBY L32 33 F1
South Parkside Dr
WD/CROXPK L12 56 C3
South Park Wy BTL L20 5 G6
Southport Rd BTL L20 5 J5
BTL L20 5 K1
CSBY/BLUN L23 21 H2
FMBY L37 17 F1
MGHL L31 18 B2
Southport St STHEL WA9 49 G4
Southridge Rd PEN/TH CH61 135 E1
South Rd ALL/GAR L19 118 D5
CSBY/WL L22 29 E4
DV/KA/FCH L14 73 H2
RF/TRAN CH42 115 E1
SPK/HALE L24 142 D2
WKBY CH48 110 A2
WLT/FAZ L9 41 F1
South Station Rd WLTN L25 97 H3
South St STHEL WA9 61 F3
TOX L8 94 C3
South Sudley Rd ALL/GAR L19 119 E2
South Vw CSBY/WL L22 * 29 F4
HUY L36 76 B3
PS/BROM CH62 138 D1
TOX L8 * 94 C4
South Vls WAL/NB CH45 51 H3
Southway RUNC WA7 156 A2
South Wy WAV L15 73 F5
Southway WDN WA8 124 B3
Southway Av WARRS WA4 130 B4
Southwell Pl TOX L8 94 A3
Southwick Rd RF/TRAN CH42 92 C5
Southwold Crs
WARRW/BUR WA5 104 B2
Southwood Cl KKBY L32 34 B5
Southwood Rd AIG/SPK L17 117 H1
Southworth Av
WARRW/BUR WA5 83 F5
Sovereign Cl RUNC WA7 157 F1
Sovereign Ct GOL/RIS/CUL WA3 85 G1
Sovereign Rd NG/CROX L11 42 C4
Sovereign Wy BIRK CH41 69 F4
NG/CROX L11 42 C4
Spark La RUNC WA7 147 F5
Sparks La PEN/TH CH61 113 F5
Sparling St CLVPS L1 93 H1
Sparrow Hall Cl WLT/FAZ L9 * 41 H3
Sparrow Hall Rd NG/CROX L11 41 H3
Sparrowhawk Cl HLWD L26 121 G2
RUNC WA7 156 C2
Speakman Rd ECCL WA10 47 F1
Speakman St RUNC WA7 8 C3
Speedwell Cl HES CH60 * 149 G1
Speedwell Dr HES CH60 149 G1
Speedwell Rd BIRK CH41 91 F1
Speke Bvd SPK/HALE L24 141 H2
SPK/HALE L24 142 B2
Speke Church Rd
SPK/HALE L24 141 H3
Speke Hall Av SPK/HALE L24 141 G2
Speke Hall Rd SPK/HALE L24 141 H1
WLTN L25 120 C4
Spekeland Rd EHL/KEN L7 72 A5
Speke Rd ALL/GAR L19 140 D1
WDN WA8 123 F4
WLTN L25 120 C1
Speke Town La SPK/HALE L24 141 H2
Spellow La ANF/KKDL L4 54 B2
Spence Av BTL L20 39 H2
Spencer Av MOR/LEA CH46 67 E4
Spencer Cl HUY L36 * 75 H5
WDN WA8 * 14 A2
Spencer Gdns STHEL WA9 62 D2
Spencer Pl BTL L20 30 C5
Spencer's La MGHL L31 32 C1
Spencer St NPK/KEN L6 71 F1
Spennymoor Ct RUNC WA7 156 A2
Spenser Av RF/TRAN CH42 115 H2
Spenser Rd NSTN CH64 158 D2
Spenser St BTL L20 4 C2
Spicer Gv KKBY L32 33 H2
Spice St WLT/FAZ L9 40 D2
Spindle Cl NPK/KEN L6 71 F1
Spindus Rd SPK/HALE L24 141 G3
Spinnaker Cl RUNC WA7 157 F3
The Spinnakers ALL/GAR L19 118 D4
Spinners Dr STHEL WA9 63 F2
Spinners Pl WARR WA1 13 G2
Spinney Av WDN WA8 123 G2
Spinney Cl NWD/KWIPK L33 34 D4
STHEL WA9 79 G1
Spinney Crs CSBY/BLUN L23 20 C3
Spinney Gn ECCL WA10 46 C4
Spinney Houses CLVPS L1 * 6 E5
Spinney Rd NWD/KWIPK L33 34 D4
The Spinney BEB CH63 138 B3
FMBY L37 17 F1
HES CH60 149 G4
NSTN CH64 158 C2
PR/KW L34 59 G3
STBRV L28 57 G3
WKBY CH48 110 D1
Spinney Vw NWD/KWIPK L33 35 E4
Spire Gn WLT/FAZ L9 40 C1
The Spires ECCL WA10 46 C3
Spital Heyes BEB CH63 138 B3
Spital Rd BEB CH63 138 B3
PS/BROM CH62 138 D4
Spitfire Rd SPK/HALE L24 120 B5
Spofforth Rd EHL/KEN L7 72 B5
Spooner Av LITH L21 30 B5
Sprainger St VAUX/LVPD L3 70 B1
Sprakeling Pl BTL L20 30 D5
Spray St ECCL WA10 10 D3
Spreyton Cl WD/CROXPK L12 42 C5
Sprig Cl WLT/FAZ L9 32 A4
Springbank Cl RUNC WA7 155 F3
Spring Bank Rd ANF/KKDL L4 54 D5
Springbourne Rd AIG/SPK L17 117 H1
Springbrook Cl ECCL WA10 46 C3
Spring Cl NWD/KWIPK L33 * 26 B4
Spring Ct RUNC WA7 8 E4
Springcroft NSTN CH64 158 B1
Springdale Cl MOR/LEA CH46 67 E4
WD/CROXPK L12 56 C3
Springfield VAUX/LVPD L3 7 G1
Springfield Av LITH L21 30 B4
WARR WA1 84 D5
WARRS WA4 108 B5
WKBY CH48 88 A5
Springfield Cl FMBY L37 16 B4
GR/UP/WCH CH49 113 G1
Springfield La ECCL WA10 46 C2
Springfield Rd ECCL WA10 61 E2
ORM L39 19 F1
WDN WA8 123 G3
Springfield Sq ANF/KKDL L4 54 B2
Springfield St WARR WA1 12 B5
Springfield Wy
WD/CROXPK L12 57 E2
Spring Gdns MGHL L31 24 B1
Spring Gv WD/CROXPK L12 56 C4
Springhill Av PS/BROM CH62 152 D3
Springhill Ct WAV L15 96 A2
Springmeadow Rd WLTN L25 97 G3
Springpool STHEL WA9 62 D3
Springs Cl BTL L20 * 5 G3
Springside Cl HUY L36 58 A4
Spring St RF/TRAN CH42 92 D5
WDN WA8 14 D7
Spring V WAL/NB CH45 51 E3
Spring Vls CL/PREN CH43 * 91 H4
Springville Rd WLT/FAZ L9 * 31 H5
Springwell Rd BTL L20 30 B5
Springwood Av ALL/GAR L19 119 H3
WLTN L25 120 B4
Springwood Gv KKBY L32 34 A5
Springwood Wy
PS/BROM CH62 116 A3
Spruce Cl RF/TRAN CH42 92 B4
WARR WA1 109 E1
Spruce Gv STBRV L28 57 H3
Spruce Wy FMBY L37 16 B3
Sprucewood Cl NPK/KEN L6 54 D5
Spur Cl NG/CROX L11 42 C4
Spurgeon Cl EV L5 54 B5
Spurrier's La MGHL L31 25 G1
Spurstow Cl CL/PREN CH43 91 F5
The Spur CSBY/BLUN L23 29 E1
Squires Av WDN WA8 14 C3
Squires Cl RNFD/HAY WA11 49 H1
Squires St EHL/KEN L7 71 G4
Squirrel Gn FMBY L37 16 B1
Stable Cl GR/UP/WCH CH49 89 E4
The Stables CSBY/BLUN L23 * 21 H4
The Stackfield WKBY CH48 88 A5
Stadium Ct PS/BROM CH62 139 F4
Stadium Rd PS/BROM CH62 139 E3
Stafford Cl HUY L36 76 A1
Stafford Moreton Wy
MGHL L31 * 18 C5
Stafford Rd ECCL WA10 61 F1
WARRS WA4 130 A1
Staffordshire Cl EV L5 54 A4
Stafford St VAUX/LVPD L3 7 H2
Stag Rd SPK/HALE L24 120 A5
Stainburn Av NG/CROX L11 41 H4
Stainer Cl WD/CROXPK L12 57 F5
Stainton Cl HLWD L26 121 G3
RNFD/HAY WA11 37 F4
Stairhaven Rd ALL/GAR L19 119 F2
The Stakes MOR/LEA CH46 66 C2
Stalbridge Av CALD/MH L18 95 H3
Staley Av CSBY/BLUN L23 29 G1
Staley St BTL L20 39 G1
Stalisfield Av NG/CROX L11 42 A5
Stalisfield Gv NG/CROX L11 42 A5
Stalisfield Pl NG/CROX L11 42 A5
Stalmine Rd WLT/FAZ L9 40 C3
Stamfordham Dr ALL/GAR L19 119 G3
Stamfordham Gv
ALL/GAR L19 119 H4
Stamfordham Pl ALL/GAR L19 119 H4
Stamford St EHL/KEN L7 72 A3
Stanbury Av BEB CH63 116 A5
Standale Rd WAV L15 72 D5
Standard Pl RF/TRAN CH42 92 D5
Standard Rd NG/CROX L11 42 C3
Standedge Wy DV/KA/FCH L14 57 G4
Standen Cl ECCL WA10 10 D4
Stand Farm Rd
WD/CROXPK L12 43 F4
Standish Ct WDN WA8 124 B3
Standish St ECCL WA10 11 J3
VAUX/LVPD L3 6 E2
Stand Park Av NTHTN L30 31 E2
Stand Park Cl NTHTN L30 * 31 E2
Stand Park Rd CHLDW L16 96 D2
Stand Pkwy NTHTN L30 30 D2
Standring Gdn ECCL WA10 60 D2
Stanfield Av EV L5 54 B5
Stanfield Dr BEB CH63 137 H3
Stanford Av WAL/NB CH45 51 H3
Stanford Crs WLTN L25 121 F3
Stangate MGHL L31 18 B4
Stanhope Dr HUY L36 75 E2
PS/BROM CH62 138 D5
Stanhope St ECCL WA10 10 E1
TOX L8 93 H2
Stanier Wy EHL/KEN L7 72 A4
Staniforth Pl CHLDW L16 73 H4
Stanlawe Rd FMBY L37 16 D1
Stanley Av BEB CH63 115 E3
WAL/NB CH45 50 D4
WARRS WA4 130 D1
WARRW/BUR WA5 104 B1
Stanley Bank Wy
RNFD/HAY WA11 49 F1
Stanley Bungalows
PR/KW L34 * 44 A3
Stanley Cl ANF/KKDL L4 53 H3
WAL/EG CH44 69 G3
WDN WA8 125 G1
Stanley Ct RF/TRAN CH42 92 D5
Stanley Crs PR/KW L34 59 G4
Stanley Dock EV L5 * 53 F5
Stanley Gdns WLT/FAZ L9 40 B2
Stanley La PS/BROM CH62 153 F4
Stanley Pk LITH L21 30 A3
Stanley Park Av North
ANF/KKDL L4 54 D1
Stanley Park Av South
ANF/KKDL L4 54 D2
Stanley Pl WARRS WA4 * 130 D1
Stanley Prec BTL L20 5 F6
Stanley Rd BIRK CH41 68 B4
BTL L20 4 E1
CSBY/WL L22 29 F4
EV L5 53 H3
HOY CH47 87 E2
HUY L36 75 G3
LITH L21 39 F1
MGHL L31 23 H3
PS/BROM CH62 116 A3
Stanley St ALL/GAR L19 140 C2
CLVP L2 6 D4
CLVPS L1 6 D3
EHL/KEN L7 72 C2
RUNC WA7 9 F3
WAL/EG CH44 69 G3
WARR WA1 12 D6
Stanley Vls RUNC WA7 * 8 C7
Stanlowe Vw ALL/GAR L19 118 D5
Stanmore Pk
GR/UP/WCH CH49 88 D5
Stanmore Rd WAV L15 96 B2
Stanner Cl WARRW/BUR WA5 82 D3
Stanney Cl NSTN CH64 158 D3
Stannyfield Cl CSBY/BLUN L23 22 A3
Stanny Field Dr CSBY/BLUN L23 22 A3
Stansfield Av MGHL L31 19 F5
WARR WA1 107 H2
Stansfield Dr WARRS WA4 131 E4
Stanstead Av
WARRW/BUR WA5 104 D5
Stanton Av LITH L21 29 H3
Stanton Cl NTHTN L30 22 C4
Stanton Ct NSTN CH64 158 D2
Stanton Crs KKBY L32 33 F2
Stanton Rd BEB CH63 137 G3
CALD/MH L18 * 95 H3
WARRS WA4 108 D5
Stanwood Cl ECCL WA10 46 B4
Stanwood Gdns RAIN/WH L35 77 E2
Stapehill Cl CLB/OSW/ST L13 73 F3
Stapeley Gdns HLWD L26 122 A5
Staplands Rd DV/KA/FCH L14 73 H3
Stapleford Rd WLTN L25 98 A2
Staplehurst Cl WD/CROXPK L12 43 E4
Stapleton Av GR/UP/WCH CH49 89 F4
RAIN/WH L35 78 A1
SPK/HALE L24 142 B3
WARRN/WOL WA2 84 B5
Stapleton Cl RAIN/WH L35 78 A1
WLTN L25 97 H1
Stapleton Rd RAIN/WH L35 60 D5
Stapley Cl RUNC WA7 8 B6
Starkey Gv WARRS WA4 * 107 H4
Starling Cl RUNC WA7 157 F2
Starling Gv WD/CROXPK L12 57 F1
Star St TOX L8 94 A2
Startham Av
WGNW/BIL/OR WN5 37 H1
Starworth Dr PS/BROM CH62 116 C4
Statham Av
WARRN/WOL WA2 84 A3
Statham La LYMM WA13 109 H3
Statham Rd CL/PREN CH43 67 G5
Station Ap HOY CH47 65 E5
MOR/LEA CH46 66 C3
Station Cl NSTN CH64 159 E3
Station Ms KKBY L32 * 33 F1
Station Rd BEB CH63 136 C1
BIRK CH41 68 B4
HES CH60 148 D3
HOY CH47 87 F2
HUY L36 75 E3
MGHL L31 24 B1
MGHL L31 33 E1
NSTN CH64 158 B1
NSTN CH64 158 D3
PEN/TH CH61 133 F2
PEN/TH CH61 136 A1
PR/KW L34 59 H5
RAIN/WH L35 78 A2
RUNC WA7 8 C4
RUNC WA7 156 D5
STHEL WA9 63 E3
WAL/EG CH44 68 C1
WARRS WA4 130 C1
WARRW/BUR WA5 104 B5
WARRW/BUR WA5 104 D2
WLTN L25 97 H3

Station Rd North
WARRN/WOL WA2 85 E3
Station Rd South
WARRN/WOL WA2 85 E4
Station St RAIN/WH L35 * 78 A2
Station Wy HUY L36 76 A3
Station Yd WARR WA1 * 85 E5
Statton Rd CLB/OSW/ST L13 73 F4
Staveley Rd ALL/GAR L19 119 F3
Stavert Cl NG/CROX L11 42 B4
Staverton Pk KKBY L32 33 F3
Stavordale Rd MOR/LEA CH46 67 E5
Steble St TOX L8 94 B3
Steel Av WAL/NB CH45 52 A4
Steel Ct EV L5 53 G5
Steel St WARR WA1 107 G1
Steeplechase Cl WLT/FAZ L9 31 H4
Steeple Ct NSTN CH64 158 D3
The Steeple WKBY CH48 110 D5
Steeple Vw NWD/KWIPK L33 25 H4
Steers Cft STBRV L28 57 F2
Steinberg Ct VAUX/LVPD L3 70 C1
Steley Wy PR/KW L34 59 H5
Stella Prec LITH L21 * 39 E1
Stenhills Crs RUNC WA7 9 G5
RUNC WA7 9 H5
Stephens La CLVP L2 * 6 D3
Stephenson Ct EHL/KEN L7 * 72 A4
Stephenson Rd
CLB/OSW/ST L13 * 73 E3
Stephenson Wy FMBY L37 17 G3
WAV L15 72 C4
Stephen St WARR WA1 13 J2
Stephen Wy RAIN/WH L35 * 60 D5
Stepney Gv ANF/KKDL L4 54 C1
Sterling Wy EV L5 53 H4
Sterndale Cl EHL/KEN L7 71 H5
Sterrix Av LITH L21 30 B2
Sterrix Gn LITH L21 30 B2
Sterrix La NTHTN L30 30 B2
Stetchworth Rd WARRS WA4 129 H2
Steve Biko Cl TOX L8 94 D1
Stevenage Cl STHEL WA9 61 H3
Steven Dr BEB CH63 137 H3
Stevenson Crs ECCL WA10 10 B4
Stevenson Dr BEB CH63 137 H3
Stevenson St WAV L15 72 D5
Stevens Rd HES CH60 149 G2
Stevens St STHEL WA9 61 F2
Steward Ct RAIN/WH L35 60 B5
Steward's Av WDN WA8 14 A3
Stewart Av BTL L20 5 J3
Stewart Cl PEN/TH CH61 134 D3
Stile Hey CSBY/BLUN L23 22 A4
Stiles Rd NWD/KWIPK L33 26 A3
Stillington Rd TOX L8 94 C4
Stirling Av CSBY/BLUN L23 29 F1
Stirling Cl WARR WA1 109 E1
Stirling Crs STHEL WA9 62 B4
Stirling La WLTN L25 121 F4
Stirling Rd SPK/HALE L24 141 H3
Stirling St WAL/EG CH44 68 D3
Stirrup Cl WARRN/WOL WA2 85 E2
Stockbridge La HUY L36 58 A4
Stockbridge Pl EV L5 54 C4
Stockbridge St EV L5 54 C5
Stockdale Cl VAUX/LVPD L3 * 6 D1
Stockdale Dr
WARRW/BUR WA5 81 G5
Stockham Cl RUNC WA7 156 C1
Stockham La RUNC WA7 156 D2
Stockmoor Rd NG/CROX L11 41 H4
Stockpit Rd NWD/KWIPK L33 35 E2
Stockport Rd WARRS WA4 108 D5
Stocks Av STHEL WA9 49 E4
Stocks La WARRW/BUR WA5 104 B3
Stockswell Rd WDN WA8 100 B4
Stockton Crs NWD/KWIPK L33 25 G3
Stockton Gv STHEL WA9 61 F4
Stockton La WARRS WA4 130 C2
Stockton Wood Rd
SPK/HALE L24 142 A3
Stockville Rd CALD/MH L18 97 E4
Stoddart Rd ANF/KKDL L4 40 C5
Stoker Wy WLT/FAZ L9 40 C2
Stokesay CL/PREN CH43 90 D2
Stokesley Av KKBY L32 33 F2
Stoke St BIRK CH41 * 2 B1
Stonebank Dr NSTN CH64 159 F4
Stonebarn Dr MGHL L31 18 C3
Stone Barn La RUNC WA7 156 B3
Stonebridge La AIN/FAZ L10 42 A1
NG/CROX L11 42 B2
Stoneby Dr WAL/NB CH45 51 G3
Stonechat Cl NTHLY L27 98 C4
RUNC WA7 156 A4
Stonecrop CALD/MH L18 97 E3
Stonecrop Cl
GOL/RIS/CUL WA3 85 G1
RUNC WA7 156 B5
Stonecross Dr RAIN/WH L35 78 B4
Stone Cross Dr WDN WA8 101 G3
Stonedale Crs NG/CROX L11 42 B3
Stonedale Pk NG/CROX L11 * 42 A3
Stonefield Rd DV/KA/FCH L14 74 B1
Stonefont Cl WLT/FAZ L9 40 C4
Stonegate Dr TOX L8 94 B4
Stonehaven Cl CHLDW L16 74 B5
Stonehaven Dr
WARRN/WOL WA2 85 E2
Stone Hay RAIN/WH L35 76 D4
Stonehey Dr WKBY CH48 110 C2
Stonehey Rd KKBY L32 33 H4
Stonehill Av ANF/KKDL L4 54 D4
BEB CH63 116 A5
Stonehills Ct RUNC WA7 9 J4
Stonehills La RUNC WA7 9 J5
Stonehill St ANF/KKDL L4 54 D4
Stonehouse Ms CALD/MH L18 96 D5
Stonehouse Rd WAL/NB CH45 51 E5
Stonelea RUNC WA7 147 H4
Stoneleigh Gdns WARRS WA4 131 H2
Stoneleigh Gv RF/TRAN CH42 115 H3
Stoneridge Ct CL/PREN CH43 * 67 G5
Stone Sq BTL L20 40 A2
Stone St VAUX/LVPD L3 70 B1
Stoneville Rd CLB/OSW/ST L13 73 E1
Stoneycroft CLB/OSW/ST L13 73 F1
Stoneycroft Cl
CLB/OSW/ST L13 56 A5
Stoneycroft Crs
CLB/OSW/ST L13 56 A5
Stoney Hey Rd WAL/NB CH45 51 G3
Stoney Holt RUNC WA7 157 E1
Stoneyhurst Av AIN/FAZ L10 31 H1
Stoney La RAIN/WH L35 77 F1
Stonham Cl GR/UP/WCH CH49 89 G3
Stonyfield NTHTN L30 22 D4
Stonyhurst Cl RNFD/HAY WA11 37 F5
Stonyhurst Rd WLTN L25 120 D2
Stopford St TOX L8 94 B4
Stopgate La NG/CROX L11 41 F4
NWD/KWIPK L33 26 B3
WLT/FAZ L9 41 F3
Store St BTL L20 53 H1
Storeton Cl CL/PREN CH43 91 G5
Storeton La PEN/TH CH61 135 G2
Storeton Rd CL/PREN CH43 91 H5
RF/TRAN CH42 114 D1
Stormont Rd ALL/GAR L19 119 F4
Storrington Av NG/CROX L11 42 A4
Storrington Heys NG/CROX L11 42 B3
Storrsdale Rd CALD/MH L18 119 F1
Stour Av RAIN/WH L35 78 A2
Stourcliffe Rd WAL/EG CH44 68 C2
Stourport Cl
GR/UP/WCH CH49 * 89 E4
Stourton Rd KKBY L32 33 H4
Stourton St WAL/EG CH44 69 E3
Stourvale Rd HLWD L26 * 121 H4
Stowe Av AIN/FAZ L10 32 B2
Stowe Cl WLTN L25 120 D4
Stowell St EHL/KEN L7 7 J6
Stowford Cl WD/CROXPK L12 42 C5
Strada Wy VAUX/LVPD L3 7 J1
Strafford Dr BTL L20 5 J3
Strand Rd BTL L20 4 B5
BTL L20 5 F3
HOY CH47 87 F1
Strand St VAUX/LVPD L3 6 C5
The Strand CLVP L2 6 B4
Stratford Rd ALL/GAR L19 118 D3
NSTN CH64 158 C4
Strathallan Cl HES CH60 134 C4
Strathcona Rd WAL/NB CH45 51 H4
WAV L15 95 G1
Strathearn Rd HES CH60 148 D3
Strathlorne Cl RF/TRAN CH42 92 D5
Strathmore Dr CSBY/BLUN L23 29 F1
Strathmore Gv STHEL WA9 62 C4
Strathmore Rd NPK/KEN L6 72 A1
Stratton Cl CALD/MH L18 120 A1
RUNC WA7 156 D3
WAL/NB CH45 52 A4
Stratton Dr STHEL WA9 61 F4
Stratton Pk WDN WA8 101 H3
Stratton Rd KKBY L32 33 F3
WARRW/BUR WA5 105 F3
Strauss Cl TOX L8 94 D2
Strawberry Cl
GOL/RIS/CUL WA3 85 G1
Strawberry Rd NG/CROX L11 41 G5
Streatham Av CALD/MH L18 95 H3
The Street BIRK CH41 68 B4
Stretford Cl NWD/KWIPK L33 25 H4
Stretton Av STHEL WA9 49 F4
WAL/EG CH44 68 C1
Stretton Cl CL/PREN CH43 91 E5
WD/CROXPK L12 43 G4
Stretton Wy HUY L36 76 B4
Strickland Cl WARRS WA4 131 E4
Strickland St ECCL WA10 11 J2
Stringer Crs WARRS WA4 107 G4
Stringhey Rd WAL/EG CH44 52 A5
Strokes Cl HLWD L26 122 A2
Stroma Rd CALD/MH L18 119 F2
Stromness Cl
WARRN/WOL WA2 85 F2
Stroud Cl GR/UP/WCH CH49 89 E5
Stuart Av MOR/LEA CH46 66 D4
WLTN L25 121 E4
Stuart Cl MOR/LEA CH46 67 E5
Stuart Dr DV/KA/FCH L14 74 A2
WARRS WA4 130 D1
Stuart Gv BTL L20 53 H1
Stuart Rd ANF/KKDL L4 5 K6
BTL L20 5 K5
CSBY/WL L22 29 F2
ECCL WA10 47 E1
MGHL L31 33 E1
RF/TRAN CH42 92 B5
RUNC WA7 147 H2
Stuart Rd North BTL L20 5 K4
Stubbs La CL/PREN CH43 91 E5
Studholme St BTL L20 53 G3
Studland Rd WLT/FAZ L9 41 G3
Studley Rd WAL/NB CH45 51 E4
Sturdee Rd CLB/OSW/ST L13 73 F4
Suburban Rd NPK/KEN L6 55 E4
Sudbury Cl WLTN L25 121 F1
Sudbury Rd CSBY/WL L22 28 C2
Sudell Av MGHL L31 19 F4
Sudley Gra AIG/SPK L17 118 C2
Sudworth Rd WAL/NB CH45 51 G3
Suez St WARR WA1 12 C5
Suffield Rd ANF/KKDL L4 53 H2
Suffolk Cl WARR WA1 108 D2
Suffolk Pl WDN WA8 124 A4
Suffolk St BTL L20 5 G2
CLVPS L1 7 F6
RUNC WA7 8 B3
Suffton Pk KKBY L32 33 F3
Sugar La PR/KW L34 44 B4
Sugnall St EHL/KEN L7 7 J6
Sulby Av CLB/OSW/ST L13 55 G5
WARRS WA4 106 D5
Sulgrave Cl CHLDW L16 73 G4
Sullington Dr NTHLY L27 98 C2
Sullivan Av GR/UP/WCH CH49 89 H4
Sullivan's Wy STHEL WA9 62 B2
Sumley Cl RNFD/HAY WA11 48 D2
Summerfield
PS/BROM CH62 138 D4
Summerfield Av ECCL WA10 46 B4
WARRW/BUR WA5 83 F3
Summerford Cl
RF/TRAN CH42 92 C5
Summerhill Dr MGHL L31 24 C2
Summer La RUNC WA7 147 F5
Summers Av BTL L20 5 J2
Summer Seat BTL L20 4 B5
VAUX/LVPD L3 70 C1
Summers Rd VAUX/LVPD L3 93 H3
Summertrees Av
GR/UP/WCH CH49 89 F4
Summertrees Cl
GR/UP/WCH CH49 89 F4
Summerville Gdns
WARRS WA4 130 D2
Summer Wy BTL L20 5 F1
Summerwood PEN/TH CH61 112 B4
The Summit WAL/EG CH44 52 A5
Summit Wy WLTN L25 97 F5
Sumner Cl EV L5 53 G5
RAIN/WH L35 78 B4
Sumner Gv NWD/KWIPK L33 26 A4
Sumner Rd CL/PREN CH43 68 B5
FMBY L37 17 E3
Sumner St RNFD/HAY WA11 49 G1
Sunbeam Rd CLB/OSW/ST L13 73 E2
Sunbourne Rd AIG/SPK L17 117 H1
Sunbury Gdns WARRS WA4 130 C4
Sunbury Rd ANF/KKDL L4 54 D3
WAL/EG CH44 69 E2
Sunbury St ECCL WA10 * 61 E2
Suncroft Cl WARR WA1 109 E1
Suncroft Rd HES CH60 149 G2
Sundale Av RAIN/WH L35 60 B5
Sundew Cl WLT/FAZ L9 31 E5
Sundridge St TOX L8 * 94 C4
Sunfield Rd MOR/LEA CH46 66 D3
Sunflower Cl STHEL WA9 63 G3
Sunlight St NPK/KEN L6 55 E5
Sunloch Cl WLT/FAZ L9 32 A4
Sunningdale MOR/LEA CH46 67 E5
Sunningdale Av WDN WA8 123 H2
Sunningdale Cl HUY L36 75 E4
Sunningdale Dr BEB CH63 152 B3
CSBY/BLUN L23 20 D3
PEN/TH CH61 135 E1
Sunningdale Gdns FMBY L37 16 D3
Sunningdale Rd WAL/NB CH45 51 F2
WAV L15 72 D5
Sunny Bank BEB CH63 115 F5
GR/UP/WCH CH49 89 H2
Sunnybank Av CL/PREN CH43 90 D4
Sunny Bank Rd CHLDW L16 96 D1
Sunnydale RAIN/WH L35 78 B2
Sunnygate Rd ALL/GAR L19 * 119 E3
Sunnymede Dr MGHL L31 18 D3
Sunnyside TOX L8 94 C3
WARRW/BUR WA5 104 C2
Sunnyside Rd CSBY/BLUN L23 28 D1
Sunrise Cl ALL/GAR L19 119 F4
Sunsdale Rd CALD/MH L18 * 96 A3
Sunset Cl NWD/KWIPK L33 26 B4
Superior Cl NTHLY L27 98 C3
Surby Cl CHLDW L16 74 A5
Surlingham Gdns STHEL WA9 61 G4
Surrey Av GR/UP/WCH CH49 89 G3
Surrey Dr WKBY CH48 110 C3
Surrey St BTL L20 5 G2
CLVPS L1 6 E7
RUNC WA7 8 D5
WAL/EG CH44 68 C2
WARRS WA4 107 F5
Susan Dr WARRW/BUR WA5 104 B3
Susan Gv MOR/LEA CH46 66 B5
Susan St WDN WA8 125 G1
Sussex Cl BTL L20 5 G2
PEN/TH CH61 134 C2
Sussex Gv STHEL WA9 48 C5
Sussex Rd MGHL L31 24 A2
WKBY CH48 87 G5
Sussex St BTL L20 5 H3
CSBY/WL L22 * 28 D2
WDN WA8 15 J1
Sutcliffe St NPK/KEN L6 71 H2
Sutherland Ct RUNC WA7 9 F4
Sutherland Dr
PS/BROM CH62 152 D5
Sutherland Rd PR/KW L34 60 A4
Sutton Av NSTN CH64 158 D4
Sutton Fold STHEL WA9 62 D2
Sutton Heath Rd STHEL WA9 61 G4
STHEL WA9 61 H1
Sutton Moss Rd STHEL WA9 63 F1
Sutton Oak Dr STHEL WA9 62 C1
Sutton Park Dr STHEL WA9 62 C3
Sutton Rd FMBY L37 16 D5
STHEL WA9 62 D1
WAL/NB CH45 51 H3
Sutton's La WDN WA8 14 E6
Sutton St CLB/OSW/ST L13 55 G5
RUNC WA7 9 G5
WARR WA1 13 F6
Sutton Wood Rd
SPK/HALE L24 142 A3
Swainson Rd AIN/FAZ L10 32 B5
Swale Av RAIN/WH L35 78 A2
Swaledale Av RAIN/WH L35 78 B2
Swaledale Cl PS/BROM CH62 153 E4
WARRW/BUR WA5 104 D1
Swalegate MGHL L31 18 C4
Swallow Cl NTHLY L27 98 D3
NWD/KWIPK L33 25 H2
WD/CROXPK L12 43 F4
Swallow Ct ECCL WA10 10 A5
Swallow Flds WLT/FAZ L9 41 H3
Swallowhurst Crs
NG/CROX L11 42 A5
Swanage Cl WARRS WA4 130 C1
Swan Av STHEL WA9 49 G5
Swan Crs WAV L15 73 F5
Swan Gdns STHEL WA9 61 G4
Swan Hey MGHL L31 * 24 B2
Swansea Cl ALL/GAR L19 119 F5
Swanside Av DV/KA/FCH L14 74 A2
Swanside Rd DV/KA/FCH L14 74 A2
Swanston Av ANF/KKDL L4 54 C1
Swan St CLB/OSW/ST L13 72 D2
Swan Wk MGHL L31 24 B2
Sweden Gv CSBY/WL L22 * 29 E3
Sweet Briar Ct STHEL WA9 * 79 H2
Sweet Brier Ct STHEL WA9 79 H3
Sweeting St CLVP L2 6 C4
Swift Cl WARRN/WOL WA2 84 C2
Swift Gv WD/CROXPK L12 43 F3
Swift's Cl NTHTN L30 22 C5
Swift's La NTHTN L30 22 C5
Swift St ECCL WA10 11 H2
Swinbrook Gn NG/CROX L11 41 H5
Swinburne Cl CHLDW L16 74 B5
Swinburne Rd ECCL WA10 10 A2
Swindale Av WARRN/WOL WA2 83 H2
Swindale Cl TOX L8 94 D1
Swinderby Dr MGHL L31 33 E1
Swindon Cl EV L5 53 H3
GR/UP/WCH CH49 89 E4
Swindon St EV L5 53 H3
Swinford Av WDN WA8 126 A1
Swisspine Gdns STHEL WA9 61 E3
Swiss Rd NPK/KEN L6 72 A2
Sword Wk NG/CROX L11 42 C4
Swynnerton Wy WDN WA8 102 B3
Sybil Rd ANF/KKDL L4 54 C3
Sycamore Av CSBY/BLUN L23 21 G3
GR/UP/WCH CH49 89 F2
HLWD L26 121 G5
RNFD/HAY WA11 49 G2
WDN WA8 125 F1
Sycamore Cl ECCL WA10 46 D3
GR/UP/WCH CH49 89 F1
WLT/FAZ L9 41 E4
Sycamore Dr RUNC WA7 156 C5
Sycamore Gdns ECCL WA10 47 G1
Sycamore Gv FMBY L37 16 B5
Sycamore La
WARRW/BUR WA5 105 F2
Sycamore Pk CALD/MH L18 119 H1
Sycamore Ri
GR/UP/WCH CH49 112 A1
Sycamore Rd CSBY/WL L22 29 F2
HUY L36 75 G4
RF/TRAN CH42 92 B4
RUNC WA7 155 G1
Sydenham Av AIG/SPK L17 95 E3
Sydney St RUNC WA7 154 B2
WLT/FAZ L9 40 C1
Syers Ct WARR WA1 84 C5
Sylvan Ct WLTN L25 120 C2
Sylvandale Gv PS/BROM CH62 138 D4
Sylvania Rd ANF/KKDL L4 40 C5
Sylvia Cl AIN/FAZ L10 42 B1
Sylvia Crs WARRN/WOL WA2 84 B4
Synge St WARRN/WOL WA2 107 E1
Syren St BTL L20 53 G2
Syston Av RNFD/HAY WA11 48 C1
Sytch Cft NSTN CH64 158 D2

T

Tabley Av WDN WA8 124 B1
Tabley Cl CL/PREN CH43 91 F5
Tabley Gdns STHEL WA9 61 F4
Tabley Rd WAV L15 95 F1
Tabley St CLVPS L1 6 E7
Tace Cl TOX L8 94 B1
Tadlow Cl FMBY L37 16 B5
Taggart Av CHLDW L16 96 D2
Tagus Cl TOX L8 94 D2
Tagus St TOX L8 94 D2
Tailor's La MGHL L31 24 B1
Talbot Av BEB CH63 136 C5
NSTN CH64 159 E4
Talbot Cl ECCL WA10 10 E4
NSTN CH64 159 E4
Talbot Ct CL/PREN CH43 91 G4
HUY L36 75 F4
Talbot Gdns NSTN CH64 159 E4
Talbot Rd CL/PREN CH43 91 G4
Talbotville Rd CLB/OSW/ST L13 73 G4
Talgarth Wy WLTN L25 97 G1
Taliesin St EV L5 53 H5
Talisman Cl RUNC WA7 157 F2
Talisman Wy BTL L20 4 B2
Talland Cl HLWD L26 121 G2
Tallarn Rd KKBY L32 33 E2
Tall Trees STHEL WA9 62 B2
Talton Rd WAV L15 95 F1
Tamar Cl NPK/KEN L6 71 G1
Tamar Gv MOR/LEA CH46 89 F1
Tamarisk Gdns STHEL WA9 61 E3
Tamerton Cl CALD/MH L18 120 A1
Tamworth St ECCL WA10 10 C4
Tanar Cl BEB CH63 138 B3
Tanat Dr CALD/MH L18 96 B4
Tancred Rd ANF/KKDL L4 54 C3
WAL/NB CH45 51 G5
Tan House La
WARRW/BUR WA5 82 A1
WDN WA8 15 H3
Tanhouse Rd CSBY/BLUN L23 22 A4
Tankersley Gv
WARRW/BUR WA5 105 E3
Tanners La WARRN/WOL WA2 12 C3
Tannery La NSTN CH64 158 D2
WARRW/BUR WA5 104 A5
Tanning Ct WARR WA1 12 E5
Tansley Cl WKBY CH48 111 E1
Tanworth Gv MOR/LEA CH46 65 H4
Tapley Pl CLB/OSW/ST L13 72 D3
Taplow Cl WARRS WA4 130 C5
Taplow St ANF/KKDL L4 54 D4
Tapton Wy CLB/OSW/ST L13 72 C4
Tarbock Rd HUY L36 75 F4
SPK/HALE L24 142 B2
Tarbot Hey MOR/LEA CH46 66 A5
Tariff St EV L5 53 H5
Tarleton Cl HLWD L26 121 G3
Tarleton St CLVPS L1 6 E4
Tarlton Cl RAIN/WH L35 60 C5
Tarnbeck RUNC WA7 157 E2
Tarn Ct WARR WA1 109 F1
Tarn Gv RNFD/HAY WA11 37 F4
Tarn Rd FMBY L37 16 C3
Tarporley Cl CL/PREN CH43 91 F5
Tarran Dr MOR/LEA CH46 66 B3
Tarran Rd MOR/LEA CH46 66 B3
Tarran Wy East MOR/LEA CH46 66 B3
Tarran Wy North
MOR/LEA CH46 66 B3
Tarran Wy South
MOR/LEA CH46 66 B3
Tarran Wy West
MOR/LEA CH46 66 B2
Tarvin Cl RUNC WA7 155 G3
STHEL WA9 79 F1
Tarvin Rd PS/BROM CH62 153 F5
Tasker Ter RAIN/WH L35 78 A1
Tasman Cl WARRW/BUR WA5 82 C5
Tasman Gv STHEL WA9 61 G3
Tate Cl WDN WA8 * 124 B1
Tate St ANF/KKDL L4 54 B2
Tatlock St EV L5 70 C1
Tattersall Rd LITH L21 29 H5
Tattersall Wy EHL/KEN L7 72 C3
Tatton Ct WARR WA1 * 85 H5
Tatton Rd RF/TRAN CH42 2 D7
WLT/FAZ L9 40 C1
Taunton Av STHEL WA9 62 D5
Taunton Dr AIN/FAZ L10 32 B2
Taunton Rd HUY L36 76 B3
WAL/NB CH45 51 E4
Taunton St WAV L15 72 C5
Taurus Pk WARRW/BUR WA5 82 D1
Taurus Rd DV/KA/FCH L14 74 C1
Tavener Cl BEB CH63 152 C4
Tavington Rd HLWD L26 122 A2
Tavistock Rd WAL/NB CH45 51 E4
WARRW/BUR WA5 104 C4
Tavlin Av WARRW/BUR WA5 83 F4
Tavy Rd NPK/KEN L6 71 G1
Tawd St ANF/KKDL L4 54 A2
Tawny Ct RUNC WA7 156 A2
Taylor Cl STHEL WA9 63 E2
Taylors Cl WLT/FAZ L9 40 B4
Taylor's La WARRW/BUR WA5 126 C1
Taylors La WLT/FAZ L9 40 A4
Taylors Rw RUNC WA7 9 J5
Taylor St BIRK CH41 3 G2
EV L5 53 H5
STHEL WA9 63 E2
WARRS WA4 129 G2
WDN WA8 15 G1
Teakwood Cl NPK/KEN L6 54 D5
Teal Cl RNFD/HAY WA11 48 B1
WARRN/WOL WA2 84 C2
Teal Gv HLWD L26 121 G2
Teals Wy HES CH60 148 B1
Teasville Rd CALD/MH L18 97 E4
Tebay Cl MGHL L31 19 F4
Tebay Rd PS/BROM CH62 153 E1
Teck St EHL/KEN L7 71 G3
Tedburn Cl WLTN L25 98 A4
Tedbury Wk KKBY L32 33 H5
Tedder Sq WDN WA8 124 B3
Teehey Cl BEB CH63 115 F5
Teehey Gdns BEB CH63 115 F5
Teehey La BEB CH63 115 F5
Tees Cl ANF/KKDL L4 53 H1
Teesdale Cl WARRW/BUR WA5 104 D1
Teesdale Rd BEB CH63 137 G2
Tees Pl ANF/KKDL L4 53 H1
Tees St ANF/KKDL L4 53 H1
Teilo St TOX L8 94 C3
Telary Cl EV L5 53 G5
Telegraph Rd HES CH60 134 C4
PEN/TH CH61 134 A2
WKBY CH48 111 G5
Telford Cl CL/PREN CH43 91 H4
WDN WA8 101 F4
Telford Dr STHEL WA9 63 F3
Tempest Hey CLVP L2 6 C3
Temple Ct CLVP L2 6 D4
Temple La CLVP L2 6 D3
Templemore Av CALD/MH L18 96 A5
Templemore Rd CL/PREN CH43 91 G4
Temple Rd RF/TRAN CH42 115 E1
Temple St CLVP L2 6 D4
Templeton Crs WD/CROXPK L12 56 B1
Templeton Dr
WARRN/WOL WA2 85 E2
Tenbury Cl WARRW/BUR WA5 82 A4
Tenby Av LITH L21 29 H3
Tenby Cl WARRW/BUR WA5 83 F3
Tenby Dr MOR/LEA CH46 89 H1
RUNC WA7 146 D4
Tenby St EV L5 54 C4
Tennis St ECCL WA10 10 B2
Tennis St North ECCL WA10 10 C1
Tennyson Av RF/TRAN CH42 * 115 H2
Tennyson Dr WARRN/WOL WA2 84 A3
Tennyson Rd HUY L36 76 A5
WDN WA8 14 C1
Tennyson St BTL L20 4 C1
STHEL WA9 79 E3
Tennyson Wy KKBY L32 33 G3
Tensing Cl WARRW/BUR WA5 82 B5
Tensing Rd MGHL L31 18 D5
Tenterden St EV L5 * 70 D1
Tenth Av WLT/FAZ L9 32 A5
Terence Av WARR WA1 107 H1
Terence Rd CHLDW L16 96 D2
Terminus Rd HUY L36 57 H5
PS/BROM CH62 138 D3
Tern Cl NWD/KWIPK L33 25 H2
WDN WA8 102 B4
Ternhall Rd WLT/FAZ L9 41 H3
Tern Wy ECCL WA10 60 C3
MOR/LEA CH46 65 H4
Terrace Rd WDN WA8 146 A1
Terret Cft STBRV L28 57 H3
Tetbury St BIRK CH41 2 C6
Tetchill Cl RUNC WA7 157 F1
Tetlow St ANF/KKDL L4 54 B2
Tetlow Wy ANF/KKDL L4 54 B2
Tewit Hall Cl SPK/HALE L24 142 A3
Tewit Hall Rd SPK/HALE L24 142 A3
Tewkesbury Cl
WD/CROXPK L12 43 F3
WLTN L25 121 E1
Teynham Crs NG/CROX L11 41 H5
Thackeray Cl TOX L8 * 94 B2
Thackeray Gdns NTHTN L30 30 C4
Thackeray Pl TOX L8 94 B2
Thackeray Sq TOX L8 94 B2
Thackeray St TOX L8 94 B2
Thackray Rd ECCL WA10 61 E2
Thames Cl WARRN/WOL WA2 84 B3
Thames Rd STHEL WA9 62 C4
Thames St TOX L8 94 D2
Thatto Heath Rd ECCL WA10 61 F2
STHEL WA9 61 F3
Thelwall La WARRS WA4 107 H5
Thelwall New Rd WARRS WA4 108 B5
WARRS WA4 108 D5
Thelwall Viad LYMM WA13 109 G3

Thermal Rd PS/BROM CH62 138 D2
Thetford Rd
WARRW/BUR WA5 104 C2
Thewlis St WARRW/BUR WA5 106 A3
Thingwall Av DV/KA/FCH L14 73 H3
Thingwall Dr PEN/TH CH61 113 E5
Thingwall Gra PEN/TH CH61 113 F5
Thingwall Hall Dr
DV/KA/FCH L14 73 H3
Thingwall La DV/KA/FCH L14 73 H2
Thingwall Rd PEN/TH CH61 112 D5
WAV L15 73 F5
Thingwall Rd East
PEN/TH CH61 113 E4
Third Av AIN/FAZ L10 32 B5
CL/PREN CH43 90 B2
CSBY/BLUN L23 * 21 E5
RUNC WA7 156 B1
WLT/FAZ L9 32 A5
Thirlmere Av CL/PREN CH43 90 C2
FMBY L37 17 F4
LITH L21 30 C4
RNFD/HAY WA11 37 F4
WARRN/WOL WA2 84 A2
Thirlmere Cl MGHL L31 19 E4
Thirlmere Dr LITH L21 30 C4
WAL/NB CH45 51 H5
Thirlmere Gn EV L5 54 C5
Thirlmere Rd EV L5 54 C5
NSTN CH64 158 D4
Thirlmere Wk NWD/KWIPK L33 25 C5
Thirlmere Wy WDN WA8 123 H3
Thirlstane St AIG/SPK L17 94 D5
Thirsk Cl RUNC WA7 155 G3
Thistledown Cl AIG/SPK L17 94 C5
Thistleton Av BIRK CH41 68 B5
Thistlewood Rd EHL/KEN L7 72 C3
Thistley Hey Rd KKBY L32 34 A2
Thomas Cl ALL/GAR L19 140 C1
Thomas Ct RUNC WA7 156 B2
Thomas Dr DV/KA/FCH L14 73 G3
RAIN/WH L35 76 C1
Thomas La DV/KA/FCH L14 73 H2
Thomasons Bridge La
WARRS WA4 129 E5
Thomas St BIRK CH41 3 G6
RUNC WA7 9 F3
WDN WA8 14 C6
Thomaston St EV L5 54 A4
Thomas Winder Ct EV L5 * 53 H4
Thompson St BIRK CH41 92 C4
ECCL WA10 61 F1
Thomson Rd LITH L21 29 H5
Thomson St NPK/KEN L6 71 H1
Thorburn Cl PS/BROM CH62 116 B3
Thorburn Crs PS/BROM CH62 116 B3
Thorburn Rd PS/BROM CH62 116 B3
Thorburn St EHL/KEN L7 71 H4
Thorley Cl WAV L15 73 E4
Thornaby Gv STHEL WA9 61 F4
Thornbeck Cl WD/CROXPK L12 43 F4
Thornbridge Av LITH L21 30 C4
Thornbrook Cl WD/CROXPK L12 56 D3
Thornbury Rd ANF/KKDL L4 55 E3
Thorncliffe Rd WAL/EG CH44 68 C2
Thorn Cl RUNC WA7 155 G2
WARRW/BUR WA5 104 D5
Thorncroft Dr PEN/TH CH61 135 F2
Thorndale Rd CSBY/WL L22 29 E2
Thorndyke Cl RAIN/WH L35 78 C4
Thornes Rd NPK/KEN L6 71 H2
Thorness Cl
GR/UP/WCH CH49 * 112 A1
Thorneycroft Dr WARR WA1 13 G3
Thorneycroft St BIRK CH41 68 C5
Thornfield Hey BEB CH63 138 A4
Thornfield Rd CSBY/BLUN L23 21 H3
WLT/FAZ L9 40 B2
Thornham Av STHEL WA9 62 C2
Thornham Cl GR/UP/WCH CH49 90 A1
Thornhead La WD/CROXPK L12 56 D4
Thornhill Rd WAV L15 96 A1
Thornhills WDN WA8 100 D5
Thornholme Crs NG/CROX L11 56 A1
Thornhurst KKBY L32 33 H5
Thornley Rd MOR/LEA CH46 88 D1
Thorn Rd ECCL WA10 47 E4
RUNC WA7 155 G2
WARR WA1 85 E5
Thorns Dr GR/UP/WCH CH49 112 A1
The Thorns MGHL L31 18 B4
Thornton WDN WA8 * 124 C3
Thornton Av BEB CH63 115 F3
BTL L20 39 H1
Thornton Common Rd
BEB CH63 150 D2
Thornton Crs HES CH60 149 F3
Thorntondale Dr
WARRW/BUR WA5 104 C1
Thornton Gv BEB CH63 115 E3
Thornton Rd BEB CH63 115 F3
BTL L20 5 F1
BTL L20 39 G2
CHLDW L16 74 A4
WAL/NB CH45 51 G4
WARRW/BUR WA5 105 F4
Thornton St BIRK CH41 68 C5
LITH L21 39 F1
Thorntree Cl AIG/SPK L17 94 C5
Thornwood Cl NPK/KEN L6 54 D5
Thornycroft Rd WAV L15 95 F2
Thorpe Bank RF/TRAN CH42 115 H3
Thorstone Dr PEN/TH CH61 112 A4
Thorsway RF/TRAN CH42 115 H1
WKBY CH48 110 D3
Threadneedle Ct STHEL WA9 63 F2
Three Butt La WD/CROXPK L12 55 H4
Three Tuns La FMBY L37 17 E3
Threlfall St TOX L8 94 C4
Thresher Av GR/UP/WCH CH49 * 89 E4
The Threshers NTHTN L30 * 23 G5
Throne Rd NG/CROX L11 42 C4
Thurne Wy WLTN L25 97 G2
Thurnham St NPK/KEN L6 55 E5
Thursby Cl KKBY L32 34 A4
Thursby Crs KKBY L32 34 A4
Thursby Rd PS/BROM CH62 139 E4
Thursby Wk KKBY L32 34 A4
Thurstaston Rd HES CH60 134 C5
PEN/TH CH61 111 H5
Thurston Cl WARRW/BUR WA5 105 H2
Thurston Rd ANF/KKDL L4 54 D4
Thynne St WARR WA1 12 B6
Tibbs Cross La WDN WA8 79 H4
Tichbourne Wy NPK/KEN L6 7 K1
Tickle Av STHEL WA9 48 D4
Tidal La WARR WA1 84 D5
Tideswell Cl EHL/KEN L7 71 H5
Tide Wy WAL/NB CH45 51 E2
Tilbrook Dr STHEL WA9 62 D4
Tilbury Pl RUNC WA7 157 F3
Tildsley Crs RUNC WA7 154 D3
Tilley St WARR WA1 12 E3
Tillotson Cl TOX L8 94 A3
Tilman Cl WARRW/BUR WA5 82 B5
Tilney St WLT/FAZ L9 40 C1
Tilstock Av PS/BROM CH62 116 B3
Tilstock Cl HLWD L26 122 A1
Tilstock Crs CL/PREN CH43 114 B2
Tilston Av WARRS WA4 108 A4
Tilston Cl NG/CROX L11 41 F4
Tilston Rd KKBY L32 33 F2
WAL/NB CH45 51 G4
WLT/FAZ L9 41 F3
Timberscombe Gdns
WARR WA1 109 E2
Time Pk RAIN/WH L35 60 B5
Timmis Cl WARRN/WOL WA2 85 E2
Timmis Crs WDN WA8 14 C2
Timms Cl FMBY L37 17 E1
Timms La FMBY L37 17 E1
Timon Av BTL L20 5 J2
Timor Av STHEL WA9 61 G2
Timperley Av WARRS WA4 108 A4
Timperley St WDN WA8 * 14 E4
Timpron St EHL/KEN L7 72 A5
Timway Dr WD/CROXPK L12 57 E2
Tinas Wy GR/UP/WCH CH49 90 A3
Tinling Cl PR/KW L34 60 A4
Tinsley Cl HLWD L26 121 G1
Tinsley St ANF/KKDL L4 54 C3
WARRS WA4 107 H5
Tintagel Cl RUNC WA7 157 E3
Tintagel Rd NG/CROX L11 42 D2
Tintern Cl WARRW/BUR WA5 * 83 E3
Tintern Dr FMBY L37 17 G4
MOR/LEA CH46 66 C5
Tiptree Cl WD/CROXPK L12 43 F3
Titchfield St EV L5 70 C1
Tithebarn Cl HES CH60 * 148 D2
Tithebarn Gv WAV L15 96 A1
Tithe Barn La KKBY L32 33 G3
Tithebarn La MGHL L31 24 D4
Tithebarn Rd CSBY/BLUN L23 21 G4
PR/KW L34 44 B3
Tithebarn St CLVP L2 6 C3
Titherington Wy AIG/SPK L17 95 F2
The Tithings RUNC WA7 147 E5
Tiverton Av WAL/EG CH44 68 D1
Tiverton Cl HUY L36 76 B3
WDN WA8 101 E5
Tiverton Rd HLWD L26 121 G5
Tiverton Sq WARRW/BUR WA5 104 C4
Tiverton St WAV L15 72 C5
Tobermory Cl RNFD/HAY WA11 49 G2
Tobin Cl EV L5 70 C1
Tobin St WAL/EG CH44 69 F1
Tobruk Rd HUY L36 75 F1
Todd Rd STHEL WA9 11 J6
Toft Cl WDN WA8 14 D3
Toft St EHL/KEN L7 72 A3
Toftwood Av RAIN/WH L35 78 B4
Tokenspire Pk
NWD/KWIPK L33 * 34 C5
Toleman Av BEB CH63 138 A1
Toll Bar Rd WARRN/WOL WA2 83 G2
Tollemache Rd BIRK CH41 68 A5
CL/PREN CH43 91 F1
Tollemache St WAL/NB CH45 52 A1
Tollerton Rd WD/CROXPK L12 55 H4
Tolpuddle Rd WLTN L25 97 F5
Tolpuddle Wy ANF/KKDL L4 53 H2
Tolver St ECCL WA10 11 H4
Tomlinson Av
WARRN/WOL WA2 84 B5
Tom Mann Cl VAUX/LVPD L3 7 F2
Tonbridge Cl SPK/HALE L24 141 H2
Tonbridge Dr AIN/FAZ L10 32 A1
Topaz Cl ANF/KKDL L4 5 K6
Topcliffe Gv WD/CROXPK L12 43 G4
Topgate Cl HES CH60 149 F1
Topham Dr WLT/FAZ L9 31 G2
Topping Ct GOL/RIS/CUL WA3 85 F1
Topsham Cl WLTN L25 98 A4
Torcross Wy HLWD L26 121 G3
WLTN L25 98 A4
Tordelow Cl NPK/KEN L6 71 G1
Toronto Cl HUY L36 58 B4
Toronto St WAL/EG CH44 69 G2
Torr Dr PS/BROM CH62 153 G2
Torrington Dr HLWD L26 121 G5
PEN/TH CH61 113 F5
Torrington Rd ALL/GAR L19 119 F4
WAL/EG CH44 68 C1
Torrisholme Rd WLT/FAZ L9 41 F4
Torr St EV L5 54 A4
Torus Rd CLB/OSW/ST L13 73 E1
Tor View Rd WAV L15 96 A2
Torwood CL/PREN CH43 90 D1
Tothale Turn NTHLY L27 98 D4
Totland Cl WARRW/BUR WA5 104 A1
Totnes Av HLWD L26 121 H2
Totnes Rd NG/CROX L11 42 C2
Tourney Gn WARRW/BUR WA5 82 A3
Towcester St LITH L21 39 F1
Tower End FMBY L37 16 B1
Tower Gdns VAUX/LVPD L3 6 B4
Tower Hl RF/TRAN CH42 92 B5
Tower La RUNC WA7 157 E2
Tower Prom WAL/NB CH45 52 A1
Tower Quays BIRK CH41 * 3 F1
Tower Rd BIRK CH41 3 F1
RF/TRAN CH42 * 92 B5
Tower Rd North HES CH60 134 C4
Tower Rd South HES CH60 134 D5
Towers Av MGHL L31 18 C4
Towers Rd CHLDW L16 96 C2
The Towers RF/TRAN CH42 * 115 F1
Tower St VAUX/LVPD L3 93 H3
Tower Wy WLTN L25 97 G5
Tower Whf BIRK CH41 3 F1
Towneley Ct WDN WA8 14 C2
Townfield Cl CL/PREN CH43 91 E5
Townfield Gdns BEB CH63 115 H4
Townfield La BEB CH63 115 H4
CL/PREN CH43 91 F5
Townfield Rd WKBY CH48 110 B1
Town Hl WARR WA1 12 D4
Town La BEB CH63 115 G5
NSTN CH64 159 E4
SPK/HALE L24 143 H5
Town Meadow La
MOR/LEA CH46 65 H4
Town Rd RF/TRAN CH42 92 B5
Town Rw WD/CROXPK L12 56 B3
Townsend Av NG/CROX L11 41 G4
Townsend La CLB/OSW/ST L13 55 F3
NPK/KEN L6 55 E4
Townsend St BIRK CH41 68 A4
EV L5 53 F4
Townsend Vw LITH L21 30 A2
NG/CROX L11 41 G4
Townshend Av PEN/TH CH61 134 B1
Town Sq RUNC WA7 * 156 B2
Town Vw CL/PREN CH43 2 B6
Town Wk RUNC WA7 * 156 B2
Towson St EV L5 54 B4
Toxteth Gv TOX L8 94 C4
Toxteth St TOX L8 94 B3
Trafalgar Av WAL/EG CH44 52 B5
Trafalgar Ct WDN WA8 125 E5
Trafalgar Dr BEB CH63 138 A2
Trafalgar Rd WAL/EG CH44 52 A5
Trafalgar St ECCL WA10 10 B3
Trafalgar Wy NPK/KEN L6 * 7 K1
Trafford Av WARRW/BUR WA5 83 E5
Trafford Crs RUNC WA7 155 G3
Tragan Dr WARRW/BUR WA5 104 B5
Tramway Rd AIG/SPK L17 95 E5
Trans Pennine Trail
AIG/SPK L17 95 E3
CLVP L2 6 D5
MGHL L31 23 G3
NG/CROX L11 41 F5
NTHTN L30 31 G1
TOX L8 94 D3
WARRW/BUR WA5 127 F2
WD/CROXPK L12 56 B5
WD/CROXPK L12 73 G1
WDN WA8 144 C3
WDN WA8 146 A1
WLT/FAZ L9 40 D2
WLTN L25 97 F1
Trap Hl FMBY L37 16 B4
Trapwood Cl ECCL WA10 46 D4
Travandon Cl AIN/FAZ L10 * 42 B1
Travanson Cl AIN/FAZ L10 42 B1
Travers' Entry STHEL WA9 63 G4
Traverse St STHEL WA9 48 C4
Travis St WDN WA8 14 E3
Treborth St TOX L8 94 C3
Trecastle Rd NWD/KWIPK L33 26 B5
Tree Bank Cl RUNC WA7 155 E1
Tree Tops NSTN CH64 158 D5
Treetops Cl WARR WA1 107 H1
Treetops Dr BIRK CH41 67 H4
Treforris Rd WAL/NB CH45 51 F3
Trefula Pk WD/CROXPK L12 56 A4
Trelawney Cl WLTN L25 97 H2
Tremore Cl WD/CROXPK L12 56 C1
Trenance Cl RUNC WA7 156 D4
Trendeal Rd NG/CROX L11 42 D2
Trent Av DV/KA/FCH L14 74 B3
MGHL L31 19 F4
Trent Cl RAIN/WH L35 77 H2
STHEL WA9 62 C5
WD/CROXPK L12 42 D4
WDN WA8 102 B4
Trentham Av CALD/MH L18 95 H3
Trentham Cl WDN WA8 102 B4
Trentham Rd KKBY L32 33 F3
WAL/EG CH44 69 E2
Trentham St RUNC WA7 8 B2
Trent Rd RAIN/WH L35 77 H2
Trent St EV L5 53 G4
Trent Wy HES CH60 149 F3
LITH L21 29 H3
Tresham Dr WARRS WA4 131 E3
Tressel Dr STHEL WA9 79 E2
Tressell St WLT/FAZ L9 40 B4
Trevelyan St WLT/FAZ L9 40 B4
Treviot Cl NWD/KWIPK L33 25 G3
Trevor Dr CSBY/BLUN L23 29 G1
Trevor Rd WLT/FAZ L9 40 C1
The Triad BTL L20 4 E3
Trident Pk RUNC WA7 * 156 A2
Trimley Cl GR/UP/WCH CH49 89 G3
Tring Cl GR/UP/WCH CH49 90 A1
Trinity Gv CSBY/BLUN L23 28 C2
Trinity La BIRK CH41 3 F3
Trinity Pl BTL L20 5 G5
WDN WA8 14 E5
Trinity Rd BTL L20 4 E6
HOY CH47 87 F1
WAL/EG CH44 51 H5
Trinity St BIRK CH41 2 C3
STHEL WA9 48 C3
Trinity Wk VAUX/LVPD L3 7 H1
Trispen Cl HLWD L26 121 G3
Trispen Rd NG/CROX L11 42 D3
Trispen Wk NG/CROX L11 * 42 D3
Triumph Wy SPK/HALE L24 120 B5
Triam Rd BTL L20 4 C3
Troon Cl BEB CH63 152 C4
RNFD/HAY WA11 49 G2
WD/CROXPK L12 57 E4
Trossach Cl WARRN/WOL WA2 84 C3
Trotwood Cl WLT/FAZ L9 32 A4
Troutbeck Av MGHL L31 19 E4
WARRW/BUR WA5 83 F5
Troutbeck Cl
GR/UP/WCH CH49 113 E1
RUNC WA7 156 C4
Troutbeck Gv RNFD/HAY WA11 37 F2
Troutbeck Rd CALD/MH L18 96 D3
Trouville Rd ANF/KKDL L4 55 E3
Trowbridge St VAUX/LVPD L3 7 H4
Trueman Cl CL/PREN CH43 67 G5
Trueman St VAUX/LVPD L3 6 E2
Truman Cl WDN WA8 101 H5
Truro Av NTHTN L30 23 E5
Truro Cl RNFD/HAY WA11 37 H5
RUNC WA7 157 E3
WARR WA1 85 F5
Truro Rd WAV L15 96 A2
Tudor Av BEB CH63 138 A3
WAL/EG CH44 69 G3
Tudor Cl EHL/KEN L7 7 K5
WARRS WA4 131 E1
Tudor Ct WARRS WA4 * 130 C2
Tudor Gra GR/UP/WCH CH49 89 F5
Tudor Rd CSBY/BLUN L23 29 E1
RF/TRAN CH42 92 C5
RUNC WA7 147 H3
WLTN L25 121 E4
Tudor St NPK/KEN L6 71 H2
Tudor Vw NWD/KWIPK L33 25 H4
Tudorville Rd BEB CH63 137 H1
Tudorway HES CH60 149 F1
Tue La WDN WA8 100 D2
Tuffins Cnr NTHLY L27 98 B3
Tulip Av BIRK CH41 68 B5
Tulip Gv WARRW/BUR WA5 106 A5
Tulip Rd WAV L15 96 A1
Tullimore Rd CALD/MH L18 119 E2
Tullis St ECCL WA10 10 C7
Tulloch St NPK/KEN L6 71 H2
Tumilty Av BTL L20 5 J2
Tunbridge Cl WARRW/BUR WA5 82 A5
Tunnel Rd BIRK CH41 3 H5
EHL/KEN L7 71 H5
Tunstall Cl GR/UP/WCH CH49 89 G3
Tunstall St EHL/KEN L7 95 E1
Tunstall's Wy STHEL WA9 79 H1
Tupelo Cl WD/CROXPK L12 43 F3
Tupman St TOX L8 94 B3
Turmar Av PEN/TH CH61 113 F5
Turnacre DV/KA/FCH L14 74 A2
Turnall Rd WDN WA8 123 H4
Turnberry Cl HUY L36 75 E4
MOR/LEA CH46 65 H4
WD/CROXPK L12 57 F4
Turnbridge Rd MGHL L31 18 C3
Turner Av BTL L20 40 A1
Turner Cl TOX L8 94 C5
WDN WA8 101 F5
Turner Gv NWD/KWIPK L33 25 H3
Turner St BIRK CH41 2 C7
Turney Rd WAL/EG CH44 68 C1
Turnstone Cl WD/CROXPK L12 43 E4
Turnstone Dr HLWD L26 121 G2
Turret Rd WAL/NB CH45 51 G4
Turriff Dr BEB CH63 152 C5
Turriff Rd DV/KA/FCH L14 57 G5
Turrocks Cl NSTN CH64 158 D5
Turrocks Cft NSTN CH64 158 D5
Turton St EV L5 * 53 H4
Tuscan Cl WDN WA8 102 B3
Tuson Dr WDN WA8 101 H4
Tweed Cl NPK/KEN L6 72 A1
Tweedsmuir Cl
WARRN/WOL WA2 85 E1
Tweed St BIRK CH41 68 C4
Twenty Acre Rd
WARRW/BUR WA5 82 C5
Twickenham Dr HUY L36 75 E4
MOR/LEA CH46 67 E2
Twigden Cl AIN/FAZ L10 32 C4
Twig La HUY L36 75 E1
MGHL L31 18 D5
Two Butt La RAIN/WH L35 60 C5
Twomey Cl EV L5 70 C1
Twyford Av LITH L21 30 A3
Twyford Cl MGHL L31 * 19 E5
WDN WA8 102 B3
Twyford La WDN WA8 102 D2
Twyford St NPK/KEN L6 54 D4
Tyberton Pl WLTN L25 121 E5
Tyburn Cl BEB CH63 137 H4
Tyburn Rd BEB CH63 137 H4
Tyndall Av CSBY/WL L22 29 G4
Tyne Cl ANF/KKDL L4 54 A2
STHEL WA9 61 F4
WARRN/WOL WA2 84 C3
Tynemouth Cl EV L5 54 C5
Tynemouth Rd RUNC WA7 157 E3
Tynron Gv CL/PREN CH43 90 D3
Tynville Rd WLT/FAZ L9 31 H5
Tynwald Cl CLB/OSW/ST L13 55 H5
Tynwald Crs WDN WA8 101 H3
Tynwald Dr WARRS WA4 130 A4
Tynwald Hl CLB/OSW/ST L13 72 D1
Tynwald Pl CLB/OSW/ST L13 72 D1
Tynwald Rd WKBY CH48 110 A1
Tyrer Gv PR/KW L34 60 A3
Tyrer's Av MGHL L31 18 C1
Tyrers Cl FMBY L37 17 E4
Tyrer St BIRK CH41 68 B4
CLVPS L1 * 7 F4

U

Uldale Cl NG/CROX L11 42 A5
Uldale Wy NG/CROX L11 42 A5
Ullet Rd AIG/SPK L17 95 F3
TOX L8 94 C4
Ullswater Av CL/PREN CH43 90 C2
RNFD/HAY WA11 37 E4
WARRN/WOL WA2 84 A2
Ullswater Cl NWD/KWIPK L33 25 G5
Ullswater Gv RUNC WA7 155 H4
Ullswater St EV L5 54 C4
Ulster Rd CLB/OSW/ST L13 73 F2
Ultonia St ALL/GAR L19 140 C2
Ulverscroft CL/PREN CH43 91 F4
Ulverston Av WARRN/WOL WA2 83 H2
Ulverston Cl MGHL L31 19 E4
RNFD/HAY WA11 49 G1
Ulverston Lawn NTHLY L27 98 D4
Umbria St ALL/GAR L19 140 C2
Underbridge La WARRS WA4 129 E5
Undercliffe Rd
CLB/OSW/ST L13 73 E1
Underhill Rd ECCL WA10 10 B7
Underley St EHL/KEN L7 95 E1
The Underway RUNC WA7 156 B1
Unicorn Rd NG/CROX L11 42 C3
Unicorn Wy BIRK CH41 3 H7
Union Bank La WDN WA8 79 F4
Union Ct CLVP L2 6 D4
Union St ECCL WA10 11 G2
RF/TRAN CH42 92 D5
RUNC WA7 9 G5
VAUX/LVPD L3 6 B3
WAL/EG CH44 69 F1
Unity Gv PR/KW L34 43 G2
University Rd BTL L20 5 G5
Unsworth Ct
WARRN/WOL WA2 * 84 D4
Upavon Av GR/UP/WCH CH49 * 88 D5
Upchurch Cl TOX L8 94 B4
Upland Cl ECCL WA10 61 E2
Upland Rd ECCL WA10 60 D2
GR/UP/WCH CH49 89 H2
Uplands Cl ECCL WA10 60 D2
Uplands Rd PS/BROM CH62 138 C5
The Uplands RUNC WA7 156 B2
Upper Baker St NPK/KEN L6 71 G2
Upper Beau St VAUX/LVPD L3 71 E1
Upper Beckwith St BIRK CH41 68 D5
Upper Brassey St BIRK CH41 68 C5
Upper Bute St EV L5 71 E1
Upper Duke St CLVPS L1 7 G7
Upper Essex St TOX L8 94 B3
Upper Flaybrick Rd
CL/PREN CH43 91 E1
Upper Frederick St CLVPS L1 93 H1
Upper Hampton St TOX L8 94 B1
Upper Harrington St TOX L8 94 A2
Upper Hill St TOX L8 94 A2
Upper Hope Pl EHL/KEN L7 * 7 J6
Upper Huskisson St TOX L8 94 C1
Upper Main St TOX L8 94 A3
Upper Mann St TOX L8 94 A2
Upper Mersey Rd WDN WA8 146 A1
Upper Newington CLVPS L1 7 G5
Upper Park St TOX L8 94 B3
Upper Parliament St TOX L8 94 A1
Upper Pitt St CLVPS L1 94 A1
Upper Pownall St CLVPS L1 6 E7
Upper Rice La WAL/EG CH44 52 A5
Upper Stanhope St TOX L8 94 A1
Upper Warwick St TOX L8 94 B2
Upper William St VAUX/LVPD L3 70 B1
Uppingham Av AIN/FAZ L10 32 B2
Uppingham Rd
CLB/OSW/ST L13 55 H5
WAL/EG CH44 51 F5
Upton Barn MGHL L31 18 C4
Upton Bridle Pth WDN WA8 101 H4
Upton By-Pass
GR/UP/WCH CH49 89 G3
Upton Cl GR/UP/WCH CH49 89 H3
SPK/HALE L24 * 142 C3
Upton Ct GR/UP/WCH CH49 89 H2
Upton Dr WARRW/BUR WA5 104 D3
Upton Gra WDN WA8 101 F4
Upton Gn SPK/HALE L24 * 142 C3
Upton La WDN WA8 101 G4
Upton Park Dr
GR/UP/WCH CH49 90 A2
Upton Rd GR/UP/WCH CH49 90 A4
MOR/LEA CH46 66 C5
Upton Rocks Av WDN WA8 101 G4
Urmson Rd WAL/NB CH45 51 H5
Ursula St BTL L20 53 H1
Utkinton Cl CL/PREN CH43 91 F5
Utting Av ANF/KKDL L4 54 D2
Utting Av East NG/CROX L11 42 A5
NG/CROX L11 55 G1
Uxbridge St EHL/KEN L7 71 H5

V

Vahler Ter RUNC WA7 9 H4
Vale Av WARRN/WOL WA2 83 H5
Vale Dr WAL/NB CH45 52 A3
Vale Gv KKBY L32 34 B3
Vale Ldg WLT/FAZ L9 * 40 C4
Valencia Gv PR/KW L34 60 C3
Valencia Rd WAV L15 73 E5
Valentia Rd HOY CH47 87 E2
Valentine Gv AIN/FAZ L10 32 B3
Valentines Wy WLT/FAZ L9 31 H3
Vale Owen Rd
WARRN/WOL WA2 84 B4
Valerian Rd BIRK CH41 91 F1
Valerie Cl AIN/FAZ L10 42 B1
Vale Rd CSBY/BLUN L23 21 E5
WLTN L25 120 B1
Valescourt Rd WD/CROXPK L12 56 C5
Valiant Cl WARRN/WOL WA2 84 D3
WD/CROXPK L12 43 G5
Valiant Wy BIRK CH41 92 D4
Valkyrie Rd WAL/NB CH45 51 G5
Vallance Rd ANF/KKDL L4 55 E3
Valleybrook Gv BEB CH63 138 B4
Valley Cl AIN/FAZ L10 32 C3
CSBY/BLUN L23 22 A5
Valley Ct WARRN/WOL WA2 84 D4
Valley Rd AIN/FAZ L10 32 D5
ANF/KKDL L4 54 C4
BIRK CH41 67 H3
KKBY L32 33 G3
PS/BROM CH62 152 D1
Vanbrugh Crs ANF/KKDL L4 55 E3
Vanbrugh Rd ANF/KKDL L4 55 E2
Vancouver Rd NTHLY L27 98 C3
Vanderbilt Av WLT/FAZ L9 31 G4
Vanderbyl Av PS/BROM CH62 138 B4
Vandries St VAUX/LVPD L3 70 B1
Vandyke St TOX L8 95 E1
Vanguard Ct GOL/RIS/CUL WA3 85 H1
Vanguard St EV L5 54 B4
Vanguard Wy BIRK CH41 92 D5
Vardon St BIRK CH41 2 D1
Varley Rd ALL/GAR L19 119 E2
STHEL WA9 48 C3
Varthen St EV L5 54 C4
Vaudrey Dr WARR WA1 108 D1
Vaughan Cl FMBY L37 16 C2
Vaughan Rd WAL/NB CH45 52 A2
Vaughan St BIRK CH41 68 B5
Vaux Crs BTL L20 39 H2

Vauxhall Cl WARRW/BUR WA5 104 D4
Vauxhall Rd EV L5 53 G5
VAUX/LVPD L3 70 C2
Vaux Pl BTL L20 5 H1
Venables Cl BEB CH63 138 B5
Venables Dr BEB CH63 138 A4
Venice St EV L5 54 B4
Venmore St EV L5 54 B4
Venns Rd WARRN/WOL WA2 84 B5
Ventnor Cl WARRW/BUR WA5 104 B1
Ventnor Rd WAV L15 72 D5
Verbena Cl RUNC WA7 156 B5
Verdala Pk CALD/MH L18 * 119 H1
Verdi Av LITH L21 39 E1
Verdi St LITH L21 38 D2
Verdi Ter LITH L21 38 D2
Vere St TOX L8 * 94 A3
Vermont Av CSBY/BLUN L23 21 E5
Vermont Cl NWD/KWIPK L33 25 G2
WARRW/BUR WA5 105 G1
Vermont Rd CSBY/BLUN L23 21 E5
Vermont Wy BTL L20 4 E3
Verney Crs ALL/GAR L19 119 G3
Verney Crs South
ALL/GAR L19 119 G3
Vernon Av WAL/EG CH44 69 F3
Vernon St CLVP L2 6 D2
STHEL WA9 48 C3
WARR WA1 12 E6
WARRS WA4 12 E6
Verona St EV L5 54 B4
Verulam Cl TOX L8 94 C1
Verwood Cl PEN/TH CH61 112 B4
Verwood Dr WD/CROXPK L12 43 G4
Veryan Cl HLWD L26 121 H2
Vescock St EV L5 70 D1
Vesta Rd ALL/GAR L19 140 D2
Vesuvian Dr ALL/GAR L19 140 D1
Vesuvius Pl EV L5 53 H4
Vicarage Cl CALD/MH L18 119 F1
FMBY L37 16 C2
RF/TRAN CH42 114 D2
SPK/HALE L24 144 A5
Vicarage Gv WAL/EG CH44 52 A5
Vicarage Lawn WLTN L25 98 A3
Vicarage Pl PR/KW L34 59 G4
Vicarage Rd FMBY L37 16 C2
WDN WA8 14 D5
Vicar Rd NPK/KEN L6 55 E3
Viceroy St EV L5 54 B4
Vickers Rd WDN WA8 145 G2
Victoria Av CSBY/BLUN L23 20 D5
DV/KA/FCH L14 73 H3
HES CH60 148 D3
RNFD/HAY WA11 37 E4
WARRS WA4 131 E1
WARRW/BUR WA5 104 B2
WAV L15 72 D5
WDN WA8 125 E1
Victoria Cl AIG/SPK L17 95 G5
Victoria Ct WAV L15 73 E5
Victoria Dr RF/TRAN CH42 116 A2
WKBY CH48 110 A1
WLT/FAZ L9 40 B1
Victoria Falls Rd NTHLY L27 98 D4
Victoria Flds RF/TRAN CH42 92 A4
Victoria Gdns CL/PREN CH43 91 H4
Victoria Gv WDN WA8 102 A5
Victoria La CL/PREN CH43 91 H4
Victoria Mt CL/PREN CH43 91 H4
Victoria Pde WAL/NB CH45 52 A1
Victoria Park Rd
RF/TRAN CH42 115 F1
Victoria Pl RAIN/WH L35 78 A2
WAL/EG CH44 69 G3
WARRS WA4 130 A2
Victoria Rd AIG/SPK L17 118 C1
BEB CH63 115 F5
CLB/OSW/ST L13 55 G4
CSBY/WL L22 29 F4
FMBY L37 16 A1
HUY L36 75 H3
NSTN CH64 159 F4
RF/TRAN CH42 92 A4
RUNC WA7 8 E5
RUNC WA7 9 F4
WAL/NB CH45 51 G2
WARRS WA4 130 B2
WARRS WA4 130 D1
WARRW/BUR WA5 104 B4
WDN WA8 14 C6
WKBY CH48 110 A2
Victoria Rd West
CSBY/BLUN L23 21 E5
Victoria Sq ECCL WA10 11 G4
WDN WA8 14 D5
Victoria St CLVP L2 6 D4
ECCL WA10 11 G2
PS/BROM CH62 138 B1
RAIN/WH L35 78 A2
WARR WA1 13 F4
WDN WA8 14 E5
Victoria Ter RAIN/WH L35 78 A2
WAV L15 96 A2
Victoria Wy FMBY L37 16 C1
Victor St WAV L15 72 B5
Victory Cl NTHTN L30 30 D4
Vienna St EV L5 54 B4
Viennese Rd WLTN L25 * 97 H1
Viewpark Cl CHLDW L16 97 F1
View Rd RAIN/WH L35 78 A3
Viking Cl LITH L21 29 H5
Village Cl RUNC WA7 156 C1
WAL/NB CH45 51 E4
WARRS WA4 109 E4
Village Ct AIG/SPK L17 118 A1
Village Green Ct
CL/PREN CH43 * 67 G5
Village Moor AIN/FAZ L10 32 B2
Village Nook AIN/FAZ L10 * 32 B2
Village Rd BEB CH63 115 F5
CL/PREN CH43 91 G4
HES CH60 148 D2
WKBY CH48 110 C2
Village St NPK/KEN L6 71 F1
The Village BEB CH63 138 A1
Village Wy WAL/NB CH45 51 E5
Villa Gloria Cl ALL/GAR L19 119 E3
Villars St WARR WA1 13 G5
Villas Rd MGHL L31 19 H4
Villiers Crs ECCL WA10 46 B2
Villiers Rd PR/KW L34 43 H1
Vincent Cl WARRW/BUR WA5 82 B5
Vincent Ct CLVPS L1 7 F7
Vincent Rd LITH L21 30 B3
RAIN/WH L35 77 H1
Vincent St CLB/OSW/ST L13 72 D4
ECCL WA10 11 H4
Vine Crs WARRW/BUR WA5 104 C2
The Vineries WLTN L25 97 E5
Vineside Rd WD/CROXPK L12 56 B2
Vine St EHL/KEN L7 71 G5
RUNC WA7 8 D5
WDN WA8 14 D5
Vine Ter WDN WA8 * 123 G1
Vineyard St ALL/GAR L19 141 E1
Vining Rd RAIN/WH L35 60 B4
Vining St TOX L8 * 94 B2
Viola St BTL L20 53 G1
Violet Cl GOL/RIS/CUL WA3 85 G1
Violet Rd BIRK CH41 91 F1
LITH L21 39 F1
Violet St WDN WA8 14 C6
Virgil St ECCL WA10 10 C4
EV L5 70 D1
Virginia Av MGHL L31 18 C3
Virginia Gdns
WARRW/BUR WA5 82 B5
Virginia Gv MGHL L31 18 D3
Virginia Rd WAL/NB CH45 51 H1
Virginia St VAUX/LVPD L3 * 6 B2
Virgin's La CSBY/BLUN L23 21 G2
Viscount Rd WARRN/WOL WA2 84 C3
Vista Rd RUNC WA7 155 E1
Vitesse Rd SPK/HALE L24 120 B5
Vittoria Cl BIRK CH41 2 D3
Vittoria Dock BIRK CH41 * 69 F5
Vittoria St BIRK CH41 2 D3
Vivian Av WAL/EG CH44 69 G3
Vixen Gv WDN WA8 101 H4
Voelas St TOX L8 94 C2
Vogan Av CSBY/BLUN L23 29 H1
Volunteer St ECCL WA10 11 F3
Vose Cl WARRW/BUR WA5 105 H2
Vronhill Cl TOX L8 94 C2
Vulcan Cl CL/PREN CH43 68 B5
WARRN/WOL WA2 84 D2
Vulcan St ALL/GAR L19 140 C2
BTL L20 4 B3
VAUX/LVPD L3 70 B1
Vyner Cl CL/PREN CH43 91 E2
Vyner Pk CL/PREN CH43 91 E2
Vyner Rd WAL/NB CH45 51 F5
Vyner Rd North CL/PREN CH43 90 D1
WLTN L25 97 G3
Vyner Rd South CL/PREN CH43 90 D2
WLTN L25 97 G3
Vyrnwy St EV L5 54 B3

W

Waddicar La MGHL L31 24 D5
Waddington Cl
WARRN/WOL WA2 84 D4
Wadebridge Rd AIN/FAZ L10 42 A1
Wadeson Rd ANF/KKDL L4 41 F5
Wadham Pk BTL L20 53 G1
Wadham Rd BTL L20 53 G1
Wagon La RNFD/HAY WA11 49 H1
Waine Gv RAIN/WH L35 60 C5
Waine St RNFD/HAY WA11 49 F1
STHEL WA9 48 D3
Wainwright Cl EHL/KEN L7 * 71 H5
Wainwright Gv ALL/GAR L19 119 G5
Wakefield Dr MOR/LEA CH46 66 D1
Wakefield Rd NTHTN L30 31 F2
Wakefield St VAUX/LVPD L3 7 G1
Walby Cl GR/UP/WCH CH49 113 G1
Walden Cl WARRS WA4 108 D5
Walden Rd DV/KA/FCH L14 73 G2
Waldgrave Pl WAV L15 73 F4
Waldgrave Rd WAV L15 73 E4
Waldron Cl VAUX/LVPD L3 6 D1
Walford Cl BEB CH63 137 H4
Walker Av STHEL WA9 79 F2
Walker Cl FMBY L37 17 E4
Walker Dr BTL L20 30 B5
Walker Ms RF/TRAN CH42 92 B5
Walker Pl RF/TRAN CH42 92 B5
Walker Rd LITH L21 29 H5
Walker's Cft WAL/NB CH45 51 F5
Walkers La STHEL WA9 79 E2
WARRW/BUR WA5 104 C5
Walker St HOY CH47 87 F1
NPK/KEN L6 71 G2
PS/BROM CH62 * 116 B5
RF/TRAN CH42 92 B5
WARRN/WOL WA2 12 B3
Walker Wy WLT/FAZ L9 40 B1
The Walk SPK/HALE L24 141 G4
STBRV L28 * 58 A3
Wallace Av HUY L36 75 H1
Wallace Dr HUY L36 75 H1
Wallace St WDN WA8 14 D3
WLT/FAZ L9 40 C1
Wallacre Rd WAL/EG CH44 68 A1
Wallasey Bridge Rd BIRK CH41 68 B4
Wallasey Rd WAL/EG CH44 68 B1
Wallasey Village WAL/EG CH44 51 E5
WAL/NB CH45 51 E4
Waller Cl ANF/KKDL L4 54 A3
Waller St BTL L20 39 E1
Wallgate Rd WLTN L25 97 F2
Wallgate Wy WLTN L25 97 F2
Wallingford Rd
GR/UP/WCH CH49 89 H3
Wallis St WARRS WA4 106 D5
Wallrake HES CH60 148 D2
Wallsend Ct WDN WA8 101 G5
Walmer Rd CSBY/WL L22 29 F4
Walmesley Rd ECCL WA10 46 C2
Walmsley St EV L5 53 G5
WAL/EG CH44 52 A5
WDN WA8 15 H3
Walney Rd WD/CROXPK L12 56 A2
Walnut Av WLT/FAZ L9 41 E4
Walnut Cl WARR WA1 109 E1
Walnut Gv MGHL L31 32 D1
STHEL WA9 62 B2
Walpole Av RAIN/WH L35 77 F2
Walpole Gv WARRN/WOL WA2 84 A3
Walpole Rd RUNC WA7 155 F3
Walsham Gdns STHEL WA9 61 G4
Walsh Cl EV L5 70 C1
Walsh Rd DV/KA/FCH L14 73 G3
Walsingham Ct WAL/EG CH44 69 F2
Walsingham Rd CHLDW L16 74 A4
WAL/EG CH44 69 F2
WARRW/BUR WA5 104 D3
Walter Beilin Ct AIG/SPK L17 * 95 G3
Walter Gv STHEL WA9 63 F3
Walter St EV L5 53 F5
WARR WA1 107 G1
WDN WA8 15 J1
Waltham Rd NPK/KEN L6 55 E4
Waltho Av MGHL L31 19 E5
Walton Av WARRW/BUR WA5 104 C3
Walton Breck Rd ANF/KKDL L4 54 B3
Walton Gra WLT/FAZ L9 41 F4
Walton Hall Av ANF/KKDL L4 40 D5
NG/CROX L11 41 F4
Walton Heath Rd WARRS WA4 129 H2
Walton La ANF/KKDL L4 54 B3
Walton Lea Rd WARRS WA4 129 F4
Walton New Rd WARRS WA4 129 H3
Walton Pk WLT/FAZ L9 40 C5
Walton Park Gdns
ANF/KKDL L4 40 C5
Walton Rd ANF/KKDL L4 54 A2
ECCL WA10 47 F1
WARRS WA4 130 A3
Walton St BIRK CH41 * 3 F5
RUNC WA7 8 E5
Walton V WLT/FAZ L9 40 C1
Walton Village ANF/KKDL L4 40 B5
Wambo La WLTN L25 98 A3
Wandsworth Rd NG/CROX L11 55 H1
Wandsworth Wy WDN WA8 145 H1
Wango La AIN/FAZ L10 32 B3
Wansfell Pl WARRN/WOL WA2 83 G2
Wantage Vw HUY L36 75 E5
Wapping CLVPS L1 6 D7
Wapping Quay VAUX/LVPD L3 93 G1
Wapshare Rd NG/CROX L11 55 G1
Warbler Cl HLWD L26 121 F1
Warbreck Av WLT/FAZ L9 31 F5
Warbreck Moor WLT/FAZ L9 31 G5
Warbreck Rd WLT/FAZ L9 40 C1
Warburton Hey RAIN/WH L35 77 H1
Warburton St WARRS WA4 130 B2
Ward Av FMBY L37 16 C4
Ward Cl WARRW/BUR WA5 82 B4
Warden St ANF/KKDL L4 54 A2
Wardgate Av WD/CROXPK L12 43 E4
Ward Gv RF/TRAN CH42 115 H3
Wardour St WARRW/BUR WA5 106 A2
Ward Rd CSBY/BLUN L23 20 B3
Ward St ECCL WA10 11 G3
PR/KW L34 59 H3
VAUX/LVPD L3 7 G3
Wareham Cl WARR WA1 85 G5
Wareing Rd WLT/FAZ L9 41 E1
Waresley Crs WLT/FAZ L9 41 G3
Warham Rd ANF/KKDL L4 55 E3
Waring Av RF/TRAN CH42 115 F1
STHEL WA9 49 H5
WARRS WA4 107 H3
Warkworth Cl WDN WA8 101 E5
Warmington Rd
DV/KA/FCH L14 73 G2
Warner Dr ANF/KKDL L4 55 E2
Warnerville Rd
CLB/OSW/ST L13 73 F4
Warnley Cl WDN WA8 101 F5
Warren Cft RUNC WA7 157 E2
Warrender Dr CL/PREN CH43 68 B5
Warren Dr CL/PREN CH43 90 C2
WAL/NB CH45 51 F2
WARRS WA4 130 A3
Warren Gn FMBY L37 16 C2
Warren Hey BEB CH63 138 A5
Warren House Rd
CSBY/WL L22 28 C2
Warrenhouse Rd
NWD/KWIPK L33 26 B5
Warren La WARR WA1 85 H5
Warren Rd CSBY/BLUN L23 20 B4
HOY CH47 87 E1
WARRN/WOL WA2 84 B4
WARRS WA4 130 A4
Warren St VAUX/LVPD L3 7 H4
The Warren GR/UP/WCH CH49 90 B3
Warren Wy HES CH60 134 B5
Warrington New Rd
STHEL WA9 11 K6
Warrington Old Rd STHEL WA9 11 J6
Warrington Rd
GOL/RIS/CUL WA3 85 G2
LYMM WA13 109 G5
RAIN/WH L35 60 A5
RAIN/WH L35 78 B2
RAIN/WH L35 78 D5
RUNC WA7 * 147 E5
RUNC WA7 147 G2
WARRS WA4 129 F5
WARRW/BUR WA5 104 B4
WDN WA8 15 G4
WDN WA8 15 J1
WDN WA8 102 D1
Warrington St BIRK CH41 92 C4
Warton Cl WARRW/BUR WA5 105 E5
Warton St BTL L20 39 E1
Warton Ter BTL L20 39 E1
Warwick Av CSBY/BLUN L23 29 E1
WARRW/BUR WA5 104 B1
WARRW/BUR WA5 106 B1
Warwick Cl CL/PREN CH43 2 C6
HUY L36 76 A2
NSTN CH64 158 D5
Warwick Dr WAL/NB CH45 52 A4
WKBY CH48 110 C3
Warwick Gv RUNC WA7 147 F5
Warwick Rd BTL L20 5 H3
GR/UP/WCH CH49 89 H2
HUY L36 76 A2
Warwick St ECCL WA10 10 A6
TOX L8 94 A2
Wasdale Av MGHL L31 19 F4
RNFD/HAY WA11 37 F4
Wasdale Rd WLT/FAZ L9 40 C2
Washbrook Av CL/PREN CH43 * 67 G5
Washbrook Cl ECCL WA10 46 D3
Washington Cl WDN WA8 101 H5
Washington Dr
NWD/KWIPK L33 25 G3
WARRW/BUR WA5 105 F2
Washington Pde BTL L20 4 E3
Washington Rd NTHLY L27 98 D4
Wash La WARRS WA4 130 C1
Washway La ECCL WA10 37 E5
Wasley Cl WARRN/WOL WA2 84 D2
Wastdale Ct MOR/LEA CH46 66 A4
Wastdale Dr MOR/LEA CH46 66 A4
Wastdale Ms MOR/LEA CH46 66 A4
Wastle Bridge Rd HUY L36 58 C5
Watchyard La FMBY L37 17 F3
Waterbridge Ct WARRS WA4 130 B3
Waterbridge Ms RUNC WA7 147 G4
Waterdale Crs STHEL WA9 62 D3
Waterdale Pl STHEL WA9 62 D3
Waterfall Dr ANF/KKDL L4 40 C4
Waterfield Cl BEB CH63 137 F1
Waterford Dr NSTN CH64 159 F3
Waterford Rd
CL/PREN CH43 91 E3
NTHLY L27 98 A2
Waterford Wy RUNC WA7 157 E3
Waterfront WARRS WA4 157 H3
Watergate La WLTN L25 120 D1
Watergate Wy WLTN L25 120 D1
Waterhouse Cl NPK/KEN L6 54 D5
Waterhouse St EV L5 * 71 F1
Waterland La STHEL WA9 49 F5
Water La RAIN/WH L35 99 H4
Waterloo Centre WDN WA8 * 125 E5
Waterloo Cl CSBY/WL L22 29 E4
Waterloo Pl BIRK CH41 3 G6
Waterloo Rd CSBY/WL L22 29 F4
RUNC WA7 8 C3
WAL/NB CH45 51 H1
WDN WA8 125 E5
Waterloo St ECCL WA10 11 F5
WAV L15 96 A1
Watermead Dr RUNC WA7 157 H4
Waterpark Cl CL/PREN CH43 114 B2
Waterpark Dr STBRV L28 57 F2
STBRV L28 57 H3
Waterpark Rd CL/PREN CH43 114 C2
Watersedge Apartments
WAL/NB CH45 * 52 A1
Waterside NTHTN L30 22 D4
STHEL WA9 11 K3
WARRS WA4 130 B3
Waterside Ct STHEL WA9 11 K3
Waterside La WDN WA8 145 E1
Waterside Pk HUY L36 75 F4
Waterstone Cl NG/CROX L11 42 B4
Water St BIRK CH41 3 H4
CLVP L2 6 C4
CSBY/BLUN L23 22 A3
CSBY/WL L22 * 29 E4
ECCL WA10 11 F5
PS/BROM CH62 116 B5
RUNC WA7 8 E3
VAUX/LVPD L3 6 B4
WAL/EG CH44 69 E1
WDN WA8 125 E5
Waterway Av NTHTN L30 31 G1
Waterways WARRW/BUR WA5 105 H2
Waterworks St BTL L20 5 G4
Watery La STHEL WA9 63 E2
Watford Rd ANF/KKDL L4 54 D3
Watkin Cl NTHTN L30 31 G3
Watkinson St CLVPS L1 93 H1
Watkinson Wy WDN WA8 15 G3
Watkin St WARRN/WOL WA2 12 D1
WARRN/WOL WA2 106 D1
Watling Av LITH L21 29 H3
Watling Wy RAIN/WH L35 60 C5
Watmough St EV L5 71 E1
Watson St BIRK CH41 2 E2
Watton Beck Cl MGHL L31 19 F4
Watton Cl WARRS WA4 108 C5
WD/CROXPK L12 43 G5
Watts Clift Wy STHEL WA9 11 J6
Watts Cl NWD/KWIPK L33 26 B5
Watts La BTL L20 40 A1
Wauchope St WAV L15 72 C5
Wavell Av WDN WA8 124 A3
Wavell Rd HUY L36 75 G1
Waverley Av WARRS WA4 130 B3
Waverley Dr PR/KW L34 58 D5
Waverley Gv RF/TRAN CH42 115 E1
Waverley Rd AIG/SPK L17 95 E4
CSBY/BLUN L23 28 D1
HOY CH47 87 G1
Waverley St BTL L20 4 D4
Waverton Av CL/PREN CH43 114 A1
Wavertree Av CLB/OSW/ST L13 72 C4
WDN WA8 14 C3
Wavertree Bvd EHL/KEN L7 72 B4
Wavertree Bvd South
EHL/KEN L7 72 C4
Wavertree Gn WAV L15 96 A1
Wavertree Nook Rd WAV L15 73 G4
Wavertree Rd EHL/KEN L7 71 H4
Wavertree V WAV L15 95 F1
Waylands Dr WLTN L25 120 D4
Wayville Cl CALD/MH L18 119 F1
Waywell Cl WARRN/WOL WA2 84 D2
Weardale Rd WAV L15 95 G2
Weasdale Cl STHEL WA9 62 D3
Weaste La WARRS WA4 131 H1
Weates Cl WDN WA8 103 E5
Weaver Av NWD/KWIPK L33 26 A3
RAIN/WH L35 77 H2
Weaver Gv STHEL WA9 49 G4
Weaver Rd RUNC WA7 155 E3
Weaverside Av RUNC WA7 156 B5
Weavers La MGHL L31 24 C3
Weaver St WLT/FAZ L9 40 B4
Webb Cl EHL/KEN L7 72 A4
Webber Rd NWD/KWIPK L33 34 C3
Webb St EHL/KEN L7 95 E1
STHEL WA9 62 D1
The Web Complex
NWD/KWIPK L33 * 34 D4
Webster Av BTL L20 5 J2
WAL/EG CH44 52 B5
Webster Ct WARRW/BUR WA5 82 B3
Webster Dr KKBY L32 33 H2
Webster Rd EHL/KEN L7 95 F1
Webster St LITH L21 39 F1
VAUX/LVPD L3 6 E2
Weddell Cl WARRW/BUR WA5 105 H1
Wedge Av RNFD/HAY WA11 49 G2
Wedgewood Gdns STHEL WA9 60 D4
Wedgewood St EHL/KEN L7 72 A3
Wedgwood Dr WDN WA8 102 B4
Wednesbury Dr
WARRW/BUR WA5 104 D2
Weightman Gv WLT/FAZ L9 40 C1
Weir La WARR WA1 109 E2
Weir St WARRS WA4 129 G2
Welbeck Av CALD/MH L18 95 H3
Welbeck Ct CSBY/WL L22 * 29 E3
Welbourne Rd CHLDW L16 73 G4
Weld Blundell Av MGHL L31 18 B2
Weld Dr FMBY L37 16 C2
Weldon St ANF/KKDL L4 40 B5
Weld Rd CSBY/BLUN L23 28 D1
Welfield Pl TOX L8 94 C4
Welford Av CL/PREN CH43 114 B1
Welland Cl HLWD L26 142 C1
Welland Rd BEB CH63 * 137 F1
Wellbank Dr HLWD L26 122 A2
Wellbrae Cl GR/UP/WCH CH49 89 F3
Wellbrook Cl RUNC WA7 157 E4
SPK/HALE L24 * 142 B2
Wellbrook Gn SPK/HALE L24 * 142 B3
Well Brow Rd ANF/KKDL L4 40 C5
Wellcroft Rd HUY L36 75 G1
Weller St TOX L8 94 B3
Weller Wy TOX L8 94 C4
Wellesbourne Pl NG/CROX L11 42 A5
Wellesbourne Rd NG/CROX L11 42 A4
Wellesley Gv BEB CH63 116 A5
Wellesley Rd TOX L8 94 C4
WAL/EG CH44 68 D1
Well Farm Cl WARR WA1 85 H5
Wellfarm Cl WLT/FAZ L9 41 F4
Wellfield RUNC WA7 157 G4
WDN WA8 102 A4
Wellfield Av KKBY L32 33 H3
Wellfield Rd WLT/FAZ L9 40 C3
Wellfield St WARRW/BUR WA5 106 A2
Wellgreen Rd WLTN L25 97 F1
Wellington Av WAV L15 95 F1
Wellington Cl AIN/FAZ L10 31 H1
BEB CH63 116 A5
WARRN/WOL WA2 84 D3
Wellington Flds WAV L15 95 F2
Wellington Ga SPK/HALE L24 143 H4
Wellington Gv WAV L15 * 72 C5
Wellington Rd BEB CH63 116 A5
CL/PREN CH43 91 G4
LITH L21 29 H5
TOX L8 94 B4
WAL/NB CH45 51 G2
WAV L15 95 G1
Wellington St ALL/GAR L19 140 C1
CSBY/WL L22 29 E3
RUNC WA7 8 D3
WARR WA1 13 F5
WDN WA8 125 E5
Wellington Ter ECCL WA10 11 F2
RF/TRAN CH42 2 E7
TOX L8 94 C3
Well La BEB CH63 115 F5
BTL L20 5 G4
CHLDW L16 97 F1
GR/UP/WCH CH49 89 E5
HES CH60 149 E3
NSTN CH64 159 E5
RF/TRAN CH42 115 G1
WARRW/BUR WA5 104 D5
WLTN L25 97 F1
Well Lane Gdns BTL L20 5 G4
Wells Cl WARR WA1 85 F5
Wells St WAV L15 95 H1
Wellstead Cl WAV L15 73 E5
Wellstead Rd WAV L15 96 A1
Welsby Cl WARRN/WOL WA2 84 D2
Welshpool Cl WARRW/BUR WA5 82 D2
Welton Av GR/UP/WCH CH49 89 H3
Welton Cl SPK/HALE L24 142 B3
Welton Gn SPK/HALE L24 142 B3
Welton Rd PS/BROM CH62 138 D4
Welwyn Cl STHEL WA9 61 G4
WARRS WA4 108 C5
Wembley Gdns WLT/FAZ L9 40 B1
Wembley Rd CALD/MH L18 96 B3
CSBY/BLUN L23 * 29 G1
Wendell St TOX L8 95 E1
Wendover Av AIG/SPK L17 95 E5
Wendover Cl CL/PREN CH43 90 D4
Wendron Rd NG/CROX L11 * 42 D2
Wenger Rd WDN WA8 102 B3
Wenlock Cl WARR WA1 85 E5
Wenlock Dr HLWD L26 121 G4
Wenlock Rd ANF/KKDL L4 54 D3
RUNC WA7 156 C5
Wenning Av MGHL L31 19 E4
Wensley Av HLWD L26 121 G4
Wensleydale WLT/FAZ L9 31 F5
Wensleydale Av
PS/BROM CH62 153 E4
RAIN/WH L35 78 B2
Wensleydale Cl MGHL L31 18 B4
WARRW/BUR WA5 81 H5
Wensley Rd WLT/FAZ L9 31 F5
Wentworth Av WAL/NB CH45 51 H3
WARR WA1 108 B1
Wentworth Cl CL/PREN CH43 90 D4
WDN WA8 102 A3
Wentworth Dr BEB CH63 152 B4
EV L5 71 F1
Wentworth Gv HUY L36 74 D3
Wernbrook Cl CL/PREN CH43 90 D4
Wernbrook Rd ANF/KKDL L4 55 E3
Wervin Cl CL/PREN CH43 114 A1
Wervin Rd CL/PREN CH43 114 A1
KKBY L32 33 G3
Wesley Av WAL/NB CH45 52 A5
Wesley Cl NSTN CH64 158 C3
Wesley Gv WAL/EG CH44 69 G2
Wesley Hall Gdns STHEL WA9 61 F4

Wesley St CSBY/WL L22 29 E4
Wessex Cl WARR WA1 108 D1
West Albert Rd AIG/SPK L17 94 D4
West Av WARRN/WOL WA2 83 H5
WARRS WA4 130 A2
Westbank Av WAL/NB CH45 52 A3
West Bank Dock WDN WA8 145 H1
West Bank Dock Est
WDN WA8 145 F1
West Bank Rd EHL/KEN L7 72 C3
Westbank Rd RF/TRAN CH42 92 A5
West Bank St WDN WA8 146 A1
Westbourne Av CSBY/BLUN L23 22 A3
Westbourne Gv WKBY CH48 110 A1
Westbourne Rd CL/PREN CH43 2 B6
WAL/EG CH44 68 B1
WARRS WA4 129 H4
WKBY CH48 110 A1
Westbrook Av PR/KW L34 59 F4
WARRS WA4 130 B1
Westbrook Centre
WARRW/BUR WA5 82 C4
Westbrook Crs
WARRW/BUR WA5 82 B3
Westbrook Rd MOR/LEA CH46 89 E1
WLTN L25 98 A3
Westbrook Wy
WARRW/BUR WA5 82 A4
West Brow Gdns
CL/PREN CH43 67 G5
Westbury Cl AIG/SPK L17 118 A2
WARR WA1 85 E5
WLTN L25 121 F3
Westbury St BIRK CH41 92 C4
Westcliffe Ct WDN WA8 102 B4
Westcliffe Rd WD/CROXPK L12 56 A3
West Cl CL/PREN CH43 90 D3
PR/KW L34 60 C3
Westcombe Rd ANF/KKDL L4 55 E3
Westcott Rd ANF/KKDL L4 54 D4
Westcott Wy CL/PREN CH43 90 D4
Westdale Rd RF/TRAN CH42 115 G1
WARR WA1 108 A1
WAV L15 72 D5
Westdale Vw WAV L15 72 D5
West Derby Rd
CLB/OSW/ST L13 55 G4
NPK/KEN L6 71 H1
West Derby St VAUX/LVPD L3 7 K3
West Derby Village
WD/CROXPK L12 56 B3
West Dr GR/UP/WCH CH49 90 A3
HES CH60 149 E2
NSTN CH64 158 C4
WARRW/BUR WA5 105 F4
West End Gv RNFD/HAY WA11 49 F1
West End Rd RNFD/HAY WA11 49 F1
Westerhope Wy WDN WA8 101 H5
Western Av HUY L36 74 D2
PS/BROM CH62 138 D2
SPK/HALE L24 142 A3
Western Dr ALL/GAR L19 119 E4
Westerton Rd WD/CROXPK L12 57 E4
Westfield Av DV/KA/FCH L14 74 A3
Westfield Crs RUNC WA7 8 B7
Westfield Dr WD/CROXPK L12 43 E4
Westfield Ms RUNC WA7 8 B6
Westfield Rd BIRK CH41 69 F4
RUNC WA7 8 A7
WLT/FAZ L9 40 A1
Westfield St ECCL WA10 10 E6
Westfield Wk KKBY L32 33 E2
West Float BIRK CH41 * 68 D4
Westford Rd WARRS WA4 129 G2
West Ga WDN WA8 123 H4
Westgate Rd BEB CH63 138 B2
WAV L15 * 96 A3
West Gv HES CH60 148 D1
Westhead Av NWD/KWIPK L33 34 A2
Westhead Cl NWD/KWIPK L33 34 B3
Westhead Wk NWD/KWIPK L33 34 A2
Westhouse Cl BEB CH63 152 C4
West Huskisson Dock BTL L20 * 53 F1
West Kirby Rd MOR/LEA CH46 89 E3
West Knowe CL/PREN CH43 * 91 F4
Westland Dr WARRN/WOL WA2 84 C3
Westlands Cl NSTN CH64 159 E1
West La RUNC WA7 156 A2
Westleigh Pl STHEL WA9 62 C5
West Lodge Dr WKBY CH48 87 E5
West Mains SPK/HALE L24 143 E3
West Meade MGHL L31 18 B4
Westminster Av NTHTN L30 22 D5
Westminster Cl WARRS WA4 131 G1
WDN WA8 123 H3
Westminster Dr
PS/BROM CH62 152 D3
Westminster Gv PR/KW L34 59 E5
Westminster Pl WARR WA1 12 D4
Westminster Rd ANF/KKDL L4 54 A3
BTL L20 53 H1
WAL/EG CH44 68 D1
Westmoreland Pl EV L5 53 H5
Westmoreland Rd
WAL/NB CH45 52 A3
Westmorland Av NTHTN L30 30 B1
WDN WA8 14 E1
Westmorland Dr VAUX/LVPD L3 6 D1
Westmorland Pl EV L5 * 53 H5
Westmorland Rd HUY L36 75 G3
West Oakhill Pk
CLB/OSW/ST L13 73 E3
Weston Crs RUNC WA7 154 D3
Weston Gv HLWD L26 122 A5
MGHL L31 24 A3
Weston Point Dock
RUNC WA7 154 A2
Weston Point Expy
RUNC WA7 145 G5
Weston Rd RUNC WA7 154 C2
West Orchard La WLT/FAZ L9 32 A4
Westover Rd MGHL L31 18 C5
WARR WA1 107 H1
West Park Rd ECCL WA10 10 B7
West Quay Rd
WARRN/WOL WA2 83 F2
West Rd BTL L20 40 B3
CL/PREN CH43 90 D3
DV/KA/FCH L14 73 G3
RUNC WA7 154 B2
Westry Cl MOR/LEA CH46 65 H5
West Side STHEL WA9 48 C5
West Side Av RNFD/HAY WA11 49 G1
West St ECCL WA10 61 F1
PR/KW L34 59 G4
WAL/NB CH45 * 51 H5
WARRN/WOL WA2 106 D1
West V NSTN CH64 158 D4
West Vw HUY L36 76 B3
WARRN/WOL WA2 85 E4
West View Av HUY L36 76 B3
Westview Cl CL/PREN CH43 90 D4
West View Cl HUY L36 76 A3
West View St BIRK CH41 92 D4
Westward Ho WKBY CH48 110 D5
Westward Vw AIG/SPK L17 94 C5
CSBY/WL L22 28 C2
Westway CL/PREN CH43 90 D4
GR/UP/WCH CH49 89 F4
HES CH60 148 D3
MGHL L31 18 C4
West Wy MOR/LEA CH46 66 C4
RUNC WA7 * 156 A1
Westway WAV L15 73 F5
Westwick Pl HUY L36 74 D2
Westwood Gv WAL/EG CH44 68 C1
Westwood Rd CALD/MH L18 119 G3
CL/PREN CH43 90 C2
Westy La WARRS WA4 107 G4
Wetherby Av WAL/NB CH45 51 E5
Wetherby Ct HUY L36 58 A5
Wethersfield Rd CL/PREN CH43 91 E4
Wetstone La WKBY CH48 110 C2
Wexford Av SPK/HALE L24 143 H4
Wexford Cl CL/PREN CH43 91 E4
Wexford Rd CL/PREN CH43 91 F4
Wexwood Gv RAIN/WH L35 77 E3
Weybourne Cl
GR/UP/WCH CH49 90 A1
Weybridge Cl WARRS WA4 130 C4
Weyman Av RAIN/WH L35 77 E2
Weymoor Cl BEB CH63 137 H4
Weymouth Av STHEL WA9 63 F1
Weymouth Cl CHLDW L16 74 B5
RUNC WA7 157 G3
Whaley La PEN/TH CH61 112 D5
Whalley Av ECCL WA10 36 C5
Whalley Ct NTHTN L30 22 C5
Whalley Dr FMBY L37 17 F4
Whalley Gv WDN WA8 102 D5
Whalley Rd RF/TRAN CH42 2 D7
Whalley St TOX L8 * 94 B4
WARR WA1 13 G3
Wharfdale Cl
WARRW/BUR WA5 105 E1
Wharfedale RUNC WA7 156 D3
Wharfedale Av RF/TRAN CH42 114 D1
Wharfedale Dr
PS/BROM CH62 153 F4
RAIN/WH L35 78 B2
Wharfedale Rd WAL/NB CH45 51 F4
Wharfside Ct WARRS WA4 130 C3
Wharf St PS/BROM CH62 138 B1
WARR WA1 13 G6
WARRS WA4 12 E6
Wharncliffe Rd
CLB/OSW/ST L13 73 E2
Wharton Cl GR/UP/WCH CH49 89 F2
Wharton St STHEL WA9 62 B1
Whatcroft Cl RUNC WA7 155 H3
Wheat Cft WARRW/BUR WA5 105 G2
Wheat Croft Cl
WARRW/BUR WA5 105 G2
Wheatcroft Rd CALD/MH L18 119 G1
Wheatear Cl NTHLY L27 98 C4
Wheatfield Cl MOR/LEA CH46 89 H1
NTHTN L30 31 G1
Wheatfield Rd WDN WA8 101 E3
Wheatfield Vw LITH L21 30 A2
Wheat Hill Rd HUY L36 98 C1
Wheatland Cl STHEL WA9 79 G1
Wheatland La WAL/EG CH44 69 F2
Wheatland Rd HES CH60 149 G2
Wheatlands RUNC WA7 147 E5
Wheatley Av BTL L20 40 A2
Wheatsheaf Av STHEL WA9 62 D4
Wheeler Dr MGHL L31 33 E1
Whelan Gdns STHEL WA9 61 G4
Wheldon Rd WDN WA8 123 F5
Whernside WDN WA8 124 A1
Whetstone La BIRK CH41 2 D5
Whickham Cl WDN WA8 101 H5
Whimbrel Cl RUNC WA7 156 B4
Whimbrel Pk HLWD L26 121 G2
Whinbury Ct STHEL WA9 79 G1
Whinfell Gv RUNC WA7 156 A4
Whinfell Rd WD/CROXPK L12 56 B5
Whinfield Rd CSBY/BLUN L23 21 H3
WLT/FAZ L9 40 B1
Whinhowe Rd NG/CROX L11 42 B5
Whinmoor Cl CL/PREN CH43 90 D2
Whinmoor Rd AIN/FAZ L10 32 D5
WD/CROXPK L12 56 C5
Whinney Gv East MGHL L31 23 H3
Whinney Gv West MGHL L31 23 H3
Whiston La HUY L36 76 A1
Whitburn Rd
NWD/KWIPK L33 26 B5
Whitby Av WAL/NB CH45 51 E5
WARRN/WOL WA2 84 B3
Whitby Rd RUNC WA7 8 E7
Whitby St NPK/KEN L6 55 F4
Whitchurch Cl WARR WA1 85 E5
Whitchurch Wy RUNC WA7 155 H3
Whitcroft Rd NPK/KEN L6 72 B2
Whitebeam Cl NWD/KWIPK L33 26 A3
Whitebeam Dr
WD/CROXPK L12 42 D4
Whitebeam Gdns STHEL WA9 61 E4
Whitebeam Wk
GR/UP/WCH CH49 111 H1
Whitechapel CLVPS L1 6 E3
Whitecross Rd
WARRW/BUR WA5 106 A3
Whiteeside Cl
GR/UP/WCH CH49 90 A4
Whitefield Av ANF/KKDL L4 54 A2
Whitefield Cl GR/UP/WCH CH49 90 B5
Whitefield Dr KKBY L32 33 E2
Whitefield La RAIN/WH L35 99 E2
Whitefield Rd ECCL WA10 10 A1
NPK/KEN L6 71 H1
WARRS WA4 129 H3
WLT/FAZ L9 40 C2
Whitefield Wy NPK/KEN L6 71 G1
Whitefriars ECCL WA10 46 C4
Whitegate Cl PR/KW L34 44 B3
Whitehall Cl ANF/KKDL L4 53 H1
Whitehart Cl ANF/KKDL L4 54 D1
Whitehaven Rd EV L5 54 B4
Whitehedge Rd ALL/GAR L19 119 F4
Whitehorn Dr STBRV L28 57 H2
Whitehouse Av FMBY L37 17 F3
White House Cl
RNFD/HAY WA11 49 H1
White House Dr WARR WA1 109 E1
Whitehouse Expy RUNC WA7 156 B4
Whitehouse La FMBY L37 17 F3
HES CH60 135 H5
Whitehouse Rd
CLB/OSW/ST L13 73 F3
Whitehouse V RUNC WA7 * 157 H4
Whitelands Meadow
GR/UP/WCH CH49 89 G3
White Lodge Av HUY L36 75 F2
White Lodge Cl
PS/BROM CH62 153 E4
Whitely Gv NWD/KWIPK L33 26 B3
White Meadow Dr
CSBY/BLUN L23 21 H3
White Rock St NPK/KEN L6 71 H1
Whiteside Av RNFD/HAY WA11 49 E2
Whiteside Cl EV L5 53 H5
Whiteside Rd RNFD/HAY WA11 49 H1
Whitestone Cl PR/KW L34 44 A5
White St CLVPS L1 7 F7
WARR WA1 12 B5
WARRS WA4 130 A2
WDN WA8 146 A2
Whitethorn Av
WARRW/BUR WA5 104 D3
Whitewell Dr
GR/UP/WCH CH49 89 H2
Whitewood Pk WLT/FAZ L9 41 F1
Whitfield Av WARR WA1 107 H1
Whitfield Ct RF/TRAN CH42 92 B4
Whitfield Gv RNFD/HAY WA11 49 G1
Whitfield La HES CH60 135 E5
Whitfield St RF/TRAN CH42 92 B4
Whitford Rd RF/TRAN CH42 92 A4
Whitham Av CSBY/BLUN L23 29 G2
Whithorn St EHL/KEN L7 72 B5
Whitland Rd NPK/KEN L6 72 B2
Whitley Av WARRS WA4 108 A4
Whitley Cl RUNC WA7 154 D1
Whitley St VAUX/LVPD L3 70 B1
Whitman St WAV L15 95 G1
Whitmoor Cl RAIN/WH L35 78 C4
Whitney Pl WLTN L25 121 E1
Whitney Rd WLTN L25 98 A5
Whitstable Pk WDN WA8 101 G4
Whitstone Cl CALD/MH L18 120 A1
Whittaker Av
WARRN/WOL WA2 84 B3
Whittaker Cl CLB/OSW/ST L13 * 72 D4
Whittier St TOX L8 95 E1
Whittle Av RNFD/HAY WA11 49 G2
WARRW/BUR WA5 82 A4
WARRW/BUR WA5 105 E1
Whittle Cl EV L5 54 A4
Whittle Hall La
WARRW/BUR WA5 104 D2
Whittle St ECCL WA10 61 F1
EV L5 54 A4
Whittlewood Ct
NWD/KWIPK L33 26 A5
Whitwell Cl WARRW/BUR WA5 104 A1
Wicket Cl NG/CROX L11 42 D2
Wickham Cl WAL/EG CH44 69 F3
Wicks Crs FMBY L37 16 B2
Wicks Gdns FMBY L37 16 D3
Wicks Gn FMBY L37 16 B3
Wicks Green Cl FMBY L37 16 B2
Wicks La FMBY L37 16 B3
Wicksten Dr RUNC WA7 9 H5
Widdale Av RAIN/WH L35 * 78 B2
Widdale Cl WARRW/BUR WA5 104 D1
Widgeons Covert BEB CH63 150 B4
Widmore Rd WLTN L25 98 A4
Widnes Rd WARRW/BUR WA5 104 A5
WDN WA8 14 D4
The Wiend BEB CH63 138 A1
RF/TRAN CH42 115 F2
Wightman St NPK/KEN L6 71 H2
Wignall Cl KKBY L32 * 33 H5
Wilberforce Rd ANF/KKDL L4 54 D1
Wilbraham Pl EV L5 53 H5
Wilbraham St BIRK CH41 3 G5
EV L5 53 H5
STHEL WA9 80 A2
Wilburn St ANF/KKDL L4 54 B1
Wilbur St STHEL WA9 63 E3
Wilcock Cl EV L5 53 H5
Wilcote Cl WDN WA8 102 C4
Wildbrook Dr BIRK CH41 67 H3
Wildcherry Gdns STHEL WA9 60 D3
Wilderspool Cswy WARRS WA4 12 D7
Wilderspool Crs WARRS WA4 129 H2
Wilde St VAUX/LVPD L3 * 7 G3
Wilding Av RUNC WA7 9 G4
Wild Pl BTL L20 30 D5
Wildwood Gv WARR WA1 108 B1
Wilfer Cl EHL/KEN L7 72 A5
Wilfred Owen Dr BIRK CH41 91 E1
Wilkes Av MOR/LEA CH46 67 F2
Wilkie St WAV L15 95 G1
Wilkinson Av WARR WA1 107 H2
Wilkinson Cl WDN WA8 146 A1
Wilkinson St BIRK CH41 2 C6
WARRN/WOL WA2 107 E1
Wilkin St ANF/KKDL L4 * 54 A3
Willan St CL/PREN CH43 91 H4
Willard St BTL L20 39 H1
Willaston Dr HLWD L26 122 A5
Willaston Rd ANF/KKDL L4 54 D1
BEB CH63 151 F3
MOR/LEA CH46 66 B4
Willedstan Av CSBY/BLUN L23 29 F1
William Brown St VAUX/LVPD L3 7 F2
William Harvey Cl NTHTN L30 31 E1
William Henry St BTL L20 4 D7
VAUX/LVPD L3 71 E2
William Jessop Wy
VAUX/LVPD L3 6 A2
William Morris Av BTL L20 40 A2
William Moult St EV L5 53 H5
William Penn Cl
WARRW/BUR WA5 * 104 C4
William Rd RNFD/HAY WA11 49 F2
William Roberts Av KKBY L32 33 F2
Williams Av BTL L20 5 K1
Williamson Ct HLWD L26 122 A2
WLTN L25 * 121 E2
Williamson Sq CLVPS L1 6 E4
Williamson St CLVPS L1 6 E4
Williams St PR/KW L34 59 H4
William St BIRK CH41 3 G4
ECCL WA10 * 11 G4
WAL/EG CH44 69 G3
WDN WA8 125 G1
William Wall Rd LITH L21 30 A2
Willingdon Rd CHLDW L16 74 A4
Willink Rd RNFD/HAY WA11 37 G5
Willis Cl RAIN/WH L35 76 D3
Willis La RAIN/WH L35 76 D3
Willis St WARR WA1 13 H2
Williton Rd CHLDW L16 97 E3
Willmer Rd ANF/KKDL L4 54 D3
RF/TRAN CH42 2 C7
Willoughby Cl
WARRW/BUR WA5 82 C4
Willoughby Dr ECCL WA10 60 D2
Willoughby Rd CSBY/WL L22 29 F3
DV/KA/FCH L14 74 A3
WAL/EG CH44 68 B1
Willow Av HUY L36 75 G5
KKBY L32 33 F1
RAIN/WH L35 76 D2
WDN WA8 125 F1
Willowbank Cl HUY L36 58 A5
Willowbank Rd
PS/BROM CH62 116 B5
RF/TRAN CH42 92 B5
Willow Cl RUNC WA7 155 F2
Willow Ct TOX L8 * 94 C4
Willow Crs WARR WA1 85 F5
WARRS WA4 * 128 A4
Willowcroft Rd WAL/EG CH44 * 69 E3
Willowdale Rd CALD/MH L18 95 H3
WLT/FAZ L9 40 C3
Willow Dr WARRS WA4 130 B2
Willow Gn WLTN L25 97 F4
Willow Gv FMBY L37 17 E2
MOR/LEA CH46 89 F1
RAIN/WH L35 60 A5
WAV L15 73 E5
Willow Hey MGHL L31 24 B2
Willow Lea CL/PREN CH43 91 F4
Willow Moss Cl MOR/LEA CH46 67 E3
Willow Pk GR/UP/WCH CH49 89 E4
Willow Rd ECCL WA10 47 E4
WAV L15 72 C5
The Willows STHEL WA9 * 79 G1
WAL/NB CH45 51 E3
WARRW/BUR WA5 104 D3
Willow Tree Av STHEL WA9 79 H1
Willow Wy CSBY/BLUN L23 21 F4
NG/CROX L11 42 D1
Wills Av MGHL L31 18 C4
Willsford Av MGHL L31 33 E1
Wilmere La WDN WA8 102 A2
Wilmot Av WARRW/BUR WA5 104 D2
Wilmslow Crs WARRS WA4 108 D4
Wilne Rd WAL/NB CH45 * 51 G4
Wilsden Rd WDN WA8 123 H2
Wilson Av WAL/EG CH44 69 G1
Wilson Cl ECCL WA10 10 D5
WARRS WA4 108 D5
WDN WA8 15 K1
Wilson Gv ALL/GAR L19 119 G5
Wilson Patten St WARR WA1 12 B6
Wilson Rd HUY L36 75 H3
RAIN/WH L35 76 D1
WAL/EG CH44 * 69 G1
Wilsons La LITH L21 30 A4
Wilson St WARRW/BUR WA5 106 C1
Wilstan Av BEB CH63 137 F1
Wilstone Cl NPK/KEN L6 71 F1
Wilton Gv CLB/OSW/ST L13 73 E3
Wilton Rd HUY L36 75 F3
RF/TRAN CH42 116 A2
Wiltons Dr PR/KW L34 44 A4
Wilton St WAL/EG CH44 68 D1
Wiltshire Cl WARR WA1 108 D2
Wiltshire Gdns ECCL WA10 47 H5
Wimbald Cl WLTN L25 98 A3
Wimbledon St WAL/NB CH45 51 H5
WAV L15 95 G1
Wimborne Cl DV/KA/FCH L14 57 H4
Wimborne Pl DV/KA/FCH L14 57 H5
Wimborne Rd DV/KA/FCH L14 57 H5
Wimborne Wy PEN/TH CH61 112 B4
Wimbourne Av PEN/TH CH61 135 E1
Wimbrick Cl MOR/LEA CH46 66 D5
Wimbrick Ct MOR/LEA CH46 * 66 D5
Wimbrick Hey MOR/LEA CH46 66 D5
Wimpole St EHL/KEN L7 71 H3
Winchester Av AIN/FAZ L10 32 A1
CSBY/WL L22 28 D2
WARRW/BUR WA5 105 G3
Winchester Cl WLTN L25 120 D4
Winchester Dr WAL/EG CH44 51 G5
Winchester Pl WDN WA8 124 A3
Winchester Rd NPK/KEN L6 55 E4
Winchfield Rd WAV L15 95 H2
Windbourne Rd AIG/SPK L17 117 H1
Windermere Av
RNFD/HAY WA11 37 E4
WARRN/WOL WA2 84 A2
WDN WA8 102 B5
Windermere Cl NSTN CH64 159 E3
Windermere Dr MGHL L31 19 E4
NWD/KWIPK L33 25 G5
WD/CROXPK L12 56 C1
Windermere Rd CL/PREN CH43 90 C2
RNFD/HAY WA11 49 H1
Windermere St EV L5 54 C4
WDN WA8 102 B4
Windermere Ter TOX L8 * 94 D3
Windfield Cl NWD/KWIPK L33 26 B3
Windfield Gn ALL/GAR L19 140 D3
Windfield Rd ALL/GAR L19 140 D2
Windle Ash MGHL L31 18 C4
Windle Av CSBY/BLUN L23 21 H5
Windlebrook Crs ECCL WA10 46 D1
Windle City ECCL WA10 47 H1
Windle Ct GOL/RIS/CUL WA3 * 85 G1
Windle Gv ECCL WA10 47 E1
Windle Hall Dr ECCL WA10 36 C5
Windlehurst Av ECCL WA10 47 G1
Windlehurst Cottages
ECCL WA10 * 47 G1
Windleshaw Rd ECCL WA10 10 B1
Windle St ECCL WA10 10 E2
Windle V ECCL WA10 10 C2
Windmill Av CSBY/BLUN L23 21 G4
Windmill Cl NWD/KWIPK L33 * 25 H4
WARRS WA4 130 A5
Windmill Gdns STHEL WA9 48 D3
Windmill Hill Av East
RUNC WA7 157 F1
Windmill La WARRS WA4 130 A5
WARRW/BUR WA5 104 C3
Windmill St RUNC WA7 9 G4
Window La ALL/GAR L19 140 C2
Windscale Rd
WARRN/WOL WA2 85 E3
Windsor Av LITH L21 29 H4
Windsor Cl GR/UP/WCH CH49 89 F5
NTHTN L30 23 E4
PS/BROM CH62 116 A4
Windsor Ct BTL L20 40 A2
WARRS WA4 * 130 C2
Windsor Dr WARRS WA4 108 B5
Windsor Gv RUNC WA7 155 F1
Windsor Ms PS/BROM CH62 * 116 B4
Windsor Park Rd AIN/FAZ L10 32 B1
Windsor Rd BTL L20 40 A2
CLB/OSW/ST L13 55 F4
ECCL WA10 10 A5
FMBY L37 16 D5
HUY L36 74 D2
MGHL L31 23 H1
RAIN/WH L35 77 E1
WDN WA8 102 A4
WLT/FAZ L9 40 C1
Windsor St BIRK CH41 2 C6
TOX L8 94 B1
WAL/NB CH45 51 H1
WARRW/BUR WA5 106 A2
Windsor Vw TOX L8 94 D1
Windus St ECCL WA10 10 D5
Windward Dr SPK/HALE L24 141 F2
Windy Arbor Cl RAIN/WH L35 76 D4
Windy Arbor Rd RAIN/WH L35 76 C5
Windy Bank PS/BROM CH62 116 A5
Wineva Gdns CSBY/BLUN L23 29 G1
Winfield Wy WDN WA8 15 F3
Winford St WAL/EG CH44 69 F2
Winfrith Cl BEB CH63 137 H4
Winfrith Dr BEB CH63 137 H4
Winfrith Rd WARRN/WOL WA2 85 E4
WLTN L25 98 A4
Wingate Av STHEL WA9 61 F4
Wingate Cl CL/PREN CH43 * 91 E4
Wingate Rd AIG/SPK L17 118 C1
NWD/KWIPK L33 26 A5
PS/BROM CH62 153 E4
Wingfield Cl SFTN L29 22 C1
Wingrave Wy NG/CROX L11 56 B1
Winhill WLTN L25 97 G4
Winifred Rd AIN/FAZ L10 33 E5
Winifred St EHL/KEN L7 71 H4
WARRN/WOL WA2 12 D1
Winkle St TOX L8 * 94 B3
Winmarleigh St WARR WA1 12 B5
Winmoss Dr NWD/KWIPK L33 26 A4
Winnington Rd HOY CH47 87 E4
Winnipeg Dr NTHLY L27 98 C3
The Winnows RUNC WA7 146 D5
Winsford Rd CLB/OSW/ST L13 55 H4
Winsham Cl KKBY L32 33 H4
Winsham Rd KKBY L32 33 H4
Winskill Rd NG/CROX L11 56 A1
Winslade Ct ANF/KKDL L4 40 D5
Winslade Rd ANF/KKDL L4 54 D1
Winslow Cl RUNC WA7 157 F1
Winslow St ANF/KKDL L4 54 B2
Winstanley Cl
WARRW/BUR WA5 105 G3
Winstanley Rd CSBY/WL L22 29 F2
NSTN CH64 158 D5
PS/BROM CH62 116 B4
Winster Dr NTHLY L27 99 E5
Winston Av STHEL WA9 49 H5
Winston Dr CL/PREN CH43 90 C3
Winstone Rd DV/KA/FCH L14 74 C1
Winston Gv MOR/LEA CH46 66 C5
Winterburn Crs
WD/CROXPK L12 56 D3
Winter Gv STHEL WA9 49 H4
Winterhey Av WAL/EG CH44 68 D3
Winterlea Dr HLWD L26 122 A5
Winter St NPK/KEN L6 71 G2
Winthrop Pk CL/PREN CH43 91 E3
Winton Cl WAL/NB CH45 51 G2
Winwick Quay
WARRN/WOL WA2 83 G2
Winwick Rd WARRN/WOL WA2 12 D1
Winwick St WARR WA1 12 D4
WARRN/WOL WA2 12 D3
Wirral Cl BEB CH63 137 H3
Wirral Country Pk WKBY CH48 110 C4
Wirral Crs NSTN CH64 159 E5
Wirral Gdns BEB CH63 137 H3
Wirral Mt WAL/NB CH45 51 F5
WKBY CH48 110 D1
Wirral Vw ALL/GAR L19 118 D5
Wirral Vls WAL/NB CH45 51 E4
Wirral Wy CL/PREN CH43 90 C3
HES CH60 133 H4
NSTN CH64 158 B1
PEN/TH CH61 133 F2
WKBY CH48 110 B1
Wisenholme Cl RUNC WA7 156 A5
Wisteria Wy STHEL WA9 63 G3
Witham Cl NTHTN L30 23 F5
Withburn Cl GR/UP/WCH CH49 89 G3
Withensfield WAL/NB CH45 51 H4
Withen's La WAL/NB CH45 51 H5

Withens Rd *MGHL* L31 18 D3
The Withens *STBRV* L28 57 H3
Withers Av *WARRN/WOL* WA2 84 B5
Withert Av *BEB* CH63 115 F3
Witherwin Av *WARRS* WA4 130 C4
Withington Rd *SPK/HALE* L24 142 D3
WAL/EG CH44 69 E2
Within Wy *SPK/HALE* L24 144 A5
Withnell Cl *CLB/OSW/ST* L13 73 F3
Withnell Rd *CLB/OSW/ST* L13 73 F3
Withycombe Rd
WARRW/BUR WA5 104 C4
Witley Av *MOR/LEA* CH46 66 C4
Witley Cl *MOR/LEA* CH46 66 C4
Witney Cl *GR/UP/WCH* CH49 89 E5
Witney Gdns *WARRS* WA4 130 D5
Wittenham Cl
GR/UP/WCH CH49 * 89 H4
Wittering La *HES* CH60 148 B2
Wittom Rd *CLB/OSW/ST* L13 55 F4
Witt Rd *WDN* WA8 14 C6
Wivern Pl *RUNC* WA7 9 G3
Woburn Cl *CLB/OSW/ST* L13 72 D1
Woburn Dr *WDN* WA8 101 F3
Woburn Hl *CLB/OSW/ST* L13 72 D1
Woburn Pl *RF/TRAN* CH42 * 115 H1
Woburn Rd *WAL/NB* CH45 51 H4
WARRN/WOL WA2 83 G1
Wokefield Wy *ECCL* WA10 46 D3
Wokingham Gv *HUY* L36 75 G5
Wolfe Cl *WARRS* WA4 131 E3
Wolfenden Av *BTL* L20 40 A2
Wolferton Cl *GR/UP/WCH* CH49 90 B1
Wolfe St *TOX* L8 94 A3
Wolfrick Dr *BEB* CH63 138 B5
Wolseley Rd *ECCL* WA10 10 D2
Wolsey St *BTL* L20 53 G1
Wolstenholme Sq *CLVPS* L1 7 F6
Wolverton St *NPK/KEN* L6 55 E4
Woodale Cl *WARRW/BUR* WA5 104 C1
Woodall Dr *RUNC* WA7 9 F7
Wood Av *BTL* L20 5 K1
Woodbank Cl *CHLDW* L16 74 B5
Woodbank Pk *CL/PREN* CH43 91 E4
Woodbank Rd
WARRW/BUR WA5 105 E4
Woodberry Cl *CL/PREN* CH43 90 D4
NWD/KWIPK L33 26 A3
Woodbine St *EV* L5 53 H3
Woodbourne Rd
DV/KA/FCH L14 73 H1
Woodbridge Av *HLWD* L26 121 F1
Woodbrook Av *WLT/FAZ* L9 40 B1
Woodburn Bvd *BEB* CH63 115 G3
Woodburn Dr *HES* CH60 148 D3
Woodchurch Ct
CL/PREN CH43 92 A5
Woodchurch La
RF/TRAN CH42 114 D1
Woodchurch Rd
CL/PREN CH43 114 A2
CLB/OSW/ST L13 73 E1
GR/UP/WCH CH49 113 F2
RF/TRAN CH42 92 A4
RF/TRAN CH42 114 D1
Wood Cl *BIRK* CH41 2 E2
KKBY L32 33 G2
Woodcote Bank
RF/TRAN CH42 115 H4
Woodcote Cl *NWD/KWIPK* L33 26 B5
WARRN/WOL WA2 84 B4
The Woodcotes
PS/BROM CH62 152 D3
Woodcot La *HES* CH60 134 C5
Woodcroft Dr *PEN/TH* CH61 134 D4
Woodcroft Gdns *WARRS* WA4 130 C5
Woodcroft La *BEB* CH63 115 G3
Woodcroft Rd *WAV* L15 95 F1
Woodcroft Wy *STHEL* WA9 * 79 G1
Woodend *PEN/TH* CH61 134 D2
Woodend Av *CSBY/BLUN* L23 21 F3
MGHL L31 23 H2
SPK/HALE L24 142 A1
Woodend La *SPK/HALE* L24 142 A2
Woodene Cl *KKBY* L32 34 B5
Woodfall Cl *NSTN* CH64 159 F4
Woodfall Gv *NSTN* CH64 159 F4
Woodfall La *NSTN* CH64 159 E4
Woodfarm Hey *STBRV* L28 57 G2
Woodfield Av *BEB* CH63 115 G3
Woodfield Rd *BEB* CH63 138 A3
PEN/TH CH61 134 C2
WLT/FAZ L9 40 B2
Woodford Cl *RUNC* WA7 155 F3
WARRS WA4 108 C5
Woodford Rd *DV/KA/FCH* L14 74 A1
ECCL WA10 47 E1
PS/BROM CH62 116 B3
Woodgate *NTHLY* L27 98 A2
Woodger St *ALL/GAR* L19 140 C1
Wood Gn *CL/PREN* CH43 * 67 G5
PR/KW L34 59 G4
Woodgreen Rd
CLB/OSW/ST L13 73 E1
Wood Gv *CLB/OSW/ST* L13 72 D3
Woodhall Av *WAL/EG* CH44 69 F1
Woodhall Cl *WARRW/BUR* WA5 82 A5
Woodhall Rd *CLB/OSW/ST* L13 73 E2
Woodham Gv *NSTN* CH64 159 E5
Woodhatch Rd *RUNC* WA7 156 C4
Woodhead Rd *PS/BROM* CH62 116 C5
Woodhead St *PS/BROM* CH62 116 B4
Wood Heath Wy
PS/BROM CH62 153 G2
Woodhey Gv *BEB* CH63 115 H4
Woodhey Rd *ALL/GAR* L19 119 E3
BEB CH63 115 H4
Woodhouse Cl *ANF/KKDL* L4 54 A3
Woodin Rd *RF/TRAN* CH42 116 A3
Woodkind Hey *BEB* CH63 138 A4
Woodland Av *HOY* CH47 64 D4
WDN WA8 14 B1
Woodland Dr
GR/UP/WCH CH49 90 A5
WAL/NB CH45 52 A3
Woodland Gv *RF/TRAN* CH42 115 H3
Woodland Rd *ANF/KKDL* L4 55 F2
GR/UP/WCH CH49 90 A5
HLWD L26 121 G4
LITH L21 29 F5
MGHL L31 24 D5
RF/TRAN CH42 115 H3
WKBY CH48 111 E1
Woodlands Cl *FMBY* L37 16 C4
NSTN CH64 158 C2
Woodlands Dr *PEN/TH* CH61 135 G2
WARRS WA4 108 D5
Woodlands La *WKBY* CH48 110 D2
Woodlands Pk *WD/CROXPK* L12 56 A5
Woodlands Rd *AIG/SPK* L17 118 C1
FMBY L37 16 C4
HUY L36 74 D3
NSTN CH64 158 C2
PEN/TH CH61 134 B1
RNFD/HAY WA11 37 G5
WLT/FAZ L9 41 F1
The Woodlands *BIRK* CH41 2 D6
GR/UP/WCH CH49 89 H2
PR/KW L34 60 B3
Woodland Vw *CSBY/BLUN* L23 21 H2
Wood La *GR/UP/WCH* CH49 89 F3
HUY L36 76 B3
NTHLY L27 98 D3
PR/KW L34 59 F4
RUNC WA7 156 B5
WAL/NB CH45 51 E4
WARRS WA4 130 C3
Wood Lea *WD/CROXPK* L12 43 E4
Woodlea Cl *PS/BROM* CH62 152 D4
Woodlee Rd *WLTN* L25 98 A4
Woodleigh Cl *MGHL* L31 18 B1
Woodley Fold
WARRW/BUR WA5 104 D4
Woodley Rd *MGHL* L31 23 H3
Woodpecker Cl
GR/UP/WCH CH49 89 F3
WD/CROXPK L12 57 F1
Woodpecker Dr *HLWD* L26 121 G1
Wood Rd *HLWD* L26 121 G4
Woodrock Rd *WLTN* L25 120 D1
Woodruff St *TOX* L8 94 B4
Woodside Av *MOR/LEA* CH46 89 F1
RNFD/HAY WA11 36 D4
Woodside Cl *WD/CROXPK* L12 56 B2
Woodside Ferry Ap *BIRK* CH41 3 J3
Woodside Rd *PEN/TH* CH61 112 C5
WARRW/BUR WA5 104 D2
Woodside St *EHL/KEN* L7 71 H4
Woodside Wy *NWD/KWIPK* L33 26 A4
Woodsorrel Rd *BIRK* CH41 91 F1
WAV L15 96 B1
Woodstock Gdns *WARRS* WA4 130 D5
Woodstock Gv *WDN* WA8 124 B1
Woodstock Rd *WAL/EG* CH44 68 C2
Woodstock St *EV* L5 53 H5
Wood St *ALL/GAR* L19 119 G5
BIRK CH41 3 F2
CLVPS L1 7 F5
HOY CH47 * 87 F1
LITH L21 30 A5
PR/KW L34 59 H4
PS/BROM CH62 138 B1
STHEL WA9 48 C3
WARR WA1 13 J3
WDN WA8 15 G1
Wood V *STHEL* WA9 61 G4
Woodvale Cl *CL/PREN* CH43 67 G5
WARRN/WOL WA2 84 C4
Woodvale Rd *WD/CROXPK* L12 43 F4
WLTN L25 120 D1
Woodview *PR/KW* L34 44 B4
Woodview Av *WAL/EG* CH44 69 F3
Woodview Crs *WDN* WA8 123 G3
Woodview Rd *WDN* WA8 123 G3
Wood View Rd *WLTN* L25 97 F3
Woodville Av *CSBY/BLUN* L23 29 E1
Woodville Pl *WDN* WA8 124 B2
Woodville Rd *RF/TRAN* CH42 92 A4
Woodville St *ECCL* WA10 11 J3
Woodville Ter *NPK/KEN* L6 54 D5
Woodward Rd *NWD/KWIPK* L33 26 D5
RF/TRAN CH42 116 A3
Woodway *GR/UP/WCH* CH49 89 F4
Woodyear Rd *PS/BROM* CH62 153 E2
Woolacombe Av *STHEL* WA9 62 C5
Woolacombe Cl *WARRS* WA4 107 F5
Woolacombe Rd *CHLDW* L16 97 E2
Wooler Cl *MOR/LEA* CH46 66 A5
Woolfall Cl *HUY* L36 74 D1
Woolfall Crs *HUY* L36 74 D1
Woolfall Heath Av *HUY* L36 58 A5
Woolfall Ter *LITH* L21 39 E1
Woolhope Rd *ANF/KKDL* L4 40 D5
Woolmoore Rd *SPK/HALE* L24 121 E5
Woolston Grange Av
WARRN/WOL WA2 85 G3
Woolton Bvd *WLTN* L25 120 D2
Woolton Hill Rd *WLTN* L25 97 E4
Woolton Mt *WLTN* L25 97 G5
Woolton Pk *WLTN* L25 97 G5
Woolton Park Cl *WLTN* L25 97 G5
Woolton Rd *ALL/GAR* L19 119 G5
CALD/MH L18 96 D3
WAV L15 96 A1
WLTN L25 97 F3
Woolton St *WLTN* L25 120 D1
Worcester Av
CLB/OSW/ST L13 * 55 F3
CSBY/WL L22 28 D2
Worcester Cl *ECCL* WA10 10 E7
WARRW/BUR WA5 105 F3
Worcester Dr *CLB/OSW/ST* L13 55 F3
Worcester Dr North
CLB/OSW/ST L13 55 F3
Worcester Rd *BTL* L20 5 H2
CL/PREN CH43 67 H5
Wordsworth Av
RF/TRAN CH42 115 H2
STHEL WA9 79 E2
WARRS WA4 106 D5
WDN WA8 14 A3
Wordsworth Ct *KKBY* L32 33 F4
Wordsworth St *BTL* L20 4 B1
TOX L8 95 E1
Wordsworth Wk *WKBY* CH48 110 B3
Wordsworth Wy *HUY* L36 75 H4
Worrow Cl *NG/CROX* L11 42 B4
Worrow Rd *NG/CROX* L11 42 B4
Worsborough Av
WARRW/BUR WA5 105 F3
Worsley Av *WARRS* WA4 107 H4
Worsley Brow *STHEL* WA9 63 E2
Worsley Rd *WARRS* WA4 129 H2
Worsley St *RNFD/HAY* WA11 49 F1
WARRW/BUR WA5 106 B1
Worthing St *CSBY/WL* L22 28 C2
Worthington Cl *RUNC* WA7 156 C2
Worthington St *TOX* L8 93 H2
Wortley Rd *AIN/FAZ* L10 32 B4
Wray Av *STHEL* WA9 79 H1
Wrayburn Cl *EHL/KEN* L7 72 A5
Wrekin Cl *WLTN* L25 120 D3
Wrekin Dr *AIN/FAZ* L10 32 B2
Wrenbury Cl *CL/PREN* CH43 * 114 B1
Wrenbury St *EHL/KEN* L7 72 A3
Wren Cl *RUNC* WA7 156 C3
Wrenfield Gv *AIG/SPK* L17 118 A1
Wren Gv *HLWD* L26 121 G2
Wrexham Cl *WARRW/BUR* WA5 83 E3
Wright Crs *WDN* WA8 146 A2
Wrights Gn *WARRS* WA4 * 131 E5
WARRW/BUR WA5 81 G2
Wrights La *WARRW/BUR* WA5 126 B1
Wrights Ter *WAV* L15 96 A1
Wright St *EV* L5 53 H5
WAL/EG CH44 69 F1
Wrigleys Cl *FMBY* L37 17 E1
Wrigleys La *FMBY* L37 17 E1
Wroxham Cl *GR/UP/WCH* CH49 90 A3
Wroxham Dr *GR/UP/WCH* CH49 90 A4
Wroxham Rd
WARRW/BUR WA5 104 C2
Wroxham Wy
GR/UP/WCH CH49 * 90 A3
Wryneck Cl *ECCL* WA10 60 D3
Wrynose Rd *PS/BROM* CH62 153 E1
Wulstan St *EV* L5 53 H3
Wycherley Rd *RF/TRAN* CH42 92 B5
Wycherley St *PR/KW* L34 * 59 H4
Wychwood *GR/UP/WCH* CH49 89 H3
Wycliffe Rd *ANF/KKDL* L4 55 E3
Wycliffe St *RF/TRAN* CH42 * 115 H1
Wye Cl *RF/TRAN* CH42 92 D5
Wye St *EV* L5 54 B4
Wykeham St *ANF/KKDL* L4 53 H3
Wykeham Wy *ANF/KKDL* L4 53 H3
Wyken Gv *RNFD/HAY* WA11 48 C2
Wyke Rd *RAIN/WH* L35 60 A5
Wyllin Rd *NWD/KWIPK* L33 34 B2
Wylva Av *CSBY/BLUN* L23 29 H1
Wylva Rd *ANF/KKDL* L4 54 C4
Wyncroft Cl *WDN* WA8 124 A4
Wyncroft Rd *WDN* WA8 124 A4
Wyncroft St *TOX* L8 94 C4
Wyndale Cl *CALD/MH* L18 96 B5
Wyndcote Rd *CALD/MH* L18 96 B3
Wyndham Av *DV/KA/FCH* L14 74 C3
Wyndham Rd *WAL/NB* CH45 50 D5
Wyndham St *ANF/KKDL* L4 40 B5
Wynne Rd *ECCL* WA10 10 D2
Wynnstay Av *MGHL* L31 18 D3
Wynnstay St *TOX* L8 94 C2
Wynstay Rd *HOY* CH47 64 C5
Wynwood Pk *HUY* L36 75 E4
Wyre Rd *EV* L5 54 B3
Wyrescourt Rd
WD/CROXPK L12 56 D5
Wyresdale Av *ECCL* WA10 36 C5
Wyresdale Rd *WLT/FAZ* L9 31 G5
Wysall Cl *RNFD/HAY* WA11 48 D2
Wyswall Cl *HLWD* L26 121 G2
Wythburn Crs *RNFD/HAY* WA11 37 F4
Wythburn Gv *RUNC* WA7 156 A4
Wyvern Rd *MOR/LEA* CH46 66 C5

Y

Yanwath St *TOX* L8 94 D1
Yarcombe Cl *HLWD* L26 121 H2
Yardley Av *WARRW/BUR* WA5 83 F5
Yardley Dr *BEB* CH63 138 A5
Yardley Rd *NWD/KWIPK* L33 34 D3
Yarmouth Rd
WARRW/BUR WA5 104 C2
Yarrow Av *MGHL* L31 19 F4
Yates Cl *WARRW/BUR* WA5 105 G3
Yates' Ct *PR/KW* L34 59 H5
Yates St *TOX* L8 94 A3
Yeald Brow *LYMM* WA13 109 H5
Yelverton Cl *HLWD* L26 121 H2
Yelverton Rd *ANF/KKDL* L4 55 E3
RF/TRAN CH42 92 B5
Yeoman Cottages *HOY* CH47 87 G2
Yeovil Cl *WARR* WA1 85 G5
Yew Bank Rd *CHLDW* L16 96 D1
Yewdale Av *RNFD/HAY* WA11 37 F3
Yewdale Pk *CL/PREN* CH43 91 H4
Yewdale Rd *WLT/FAZ* L9 40 D3
Yew Tree Av *STHEL* WA9 62 C4
Yewtree Cl *GR/UP/WCH* CH49 113 E1
NSTN CH64 159 E3
Yew Tree Cl *WD/CROXPK* L12 57 E4
Yew Tree Gn *MGHL* L31 25 E5
Yew Tree La *WD/CROXPK* L12 57 E4
Yewtree La *WKBY* CH48 87 F5
Yew Tree Rd *BEB* CH63 137 G2
Yewtree Rd *CALD/MH* L18 96 D5
Yew Tree Rd *HUY* L36 75 F5
MOR/LEA CH46 66 D3
WLT/FAZ L9 40 B3
WLTN L25 121 E3
Yew Wy *MOR/LEA* CH46 66 D4
Yorkaster Rd *CALD/MH* L18 119 G2
York Av *AIG/SPK* L17 95 F2
CSBY/BLUN L23 21 E5
WAL/EG CH44 69 F2
WARRW/BUR WA5 104 C1
WKBY CH48 110 B3
York Cl *ECCL* WA10 10 E3
NTHTN L30 23 E4
York Cottages *WLTN* L25 97 H4
York Ct *WARRS* WA4 * 130 C2
York Dr *WARRS* WA4 131 E1
York Mnr *FMBY* L37 * 17 E3
York Pl *RUNC* WA7 8 E5
York Rd *CSBY/BLUN* L23 21 F5
FMBY L37 17 E3
HUY L36 76 A2
MGHL L31 24 A3
WAL/EG CH44 69 F3
WARRS WA4 131 E1
WDN WA8 124 A3
Yorkshire Gdns *ECCL* WA10 10 E7
York St *ALL/GAR* L19 140 C2
CLVPS L1 6 E6
CSBY/WL L22 29 E4
PS/BROM CH62 138 D1
RUNC WA7 8 D5
WARRS WA4 12 E7
WLT/FAZ L9 40 B4
York Ter *EV* L5 54 A4
York Vls *ANF/KKDL* L4 * 54 B3
York Wy *ALL/GAR* L19 140 D3
Youatt Av *RAIN/WH* L35 77 E1
Youens Wy *DV/KA/FCH* L14 74 A1
Yoxall Dr *NWD/KWIPK* L33 25 G3

Z

Zander Gv *WD/CROXPK* L12 43 G4
Zante Cl *EV* L5 54 A4
Zenith Wk *WLTN* L25 97 G1
Zetland Rd *BIRK* CH41 2 D6
CALD/MH L18 * 95 H3
WAL/NB CH45 51 F3
Zig Zag Rd *WAL/NB* CH45 51 H4
WD/CROXPK L12 56 D5
Zircon Cl *LITH* L21 30 B4

Index - featured places

59 Rodney Street (NT)
CLVPS L1 7 H7
Abbey Sefton Hospitals
CSBY/WL L22 29 F3
Abbeystead Medical Centre
WAV L15 96 B1
Abbotsfield Road Industrial Park
STHEL WA9 63 E5
Abbots Lea Special School
CALD/MH L18 97 E4
Abercromby Health Centre
EHL/KEN L7 71 G5
Abingdon Medical Centre
ANF/KKDL L4 55 E1
The Academy of St Francis of Assisi
NPK/KEN L6 72 A1
Acorn Business Centre
NWD/KWIPK L33 34 C3
Aintree Davenhill Primary School *AIN/FAZ* L10 32 A2
Aintree Industrial Estate
WLT/FAZ L9 40 D2
Aintree Osteopathic Clinic
WLT/FAZ L9 31 H5
Aintree Racecourse Retail & Business Park
WLT/FAZ L9 31 H3
Alban Retail Park
WARRN/WOL WA2 83 G3
Albert Dock Village
VAUX/LVPD L3 6 B7
Albert Road Medical Centre
WDN WA8 15 F1
Alexandria Industrial Estate
WDN WA8 14 B6
Alicia Hotel *AIG/SPK* L17 95 E4
Allanson Street CP School
STHEL WA9 48 D5
Allerton Cemetery
WLTN L25 120 B4
Allerton Health Centre
WAV L15 96 A3
Allerton Park Golf Club
CALD/MH L18 119 H1
Allerton Remedial Clinic
AIG/SPK L17 95 G3
All Saints Catholic Primary School *ANF/KKDL* L4 54 D4
All Saints CE Primary School
RUNC WA7 8 D3
All Saints High School
KKBY L32 33 H3
All Saints Upton Primary School *WDN* WA8 100 D5
Alsop High School
ANF/KKDL L4 40 C5
Alt Bridge Secondary Support Centre
HUY L36 75 H1
Alternative Medical Centre
ECCL WA10 11 F4
Andersons Industrial Estate
WDN WA8 14 D7
The Andrew Collinge Academy
VAUX/LVPD L3 7 H3
Anfield Cemetery
ANF/KKDL L4 54 C2
Anfield Community Comprehensive School
ANF/KKDL L4 54 D2
Anfield Crematorium
ANF/KKDL L4 54 C2
Anfield J & I School
ANF/KKDL L4 54 D4
Anfield Medical Centre
ANF/KKDL L4 54 D3
Archbishop Beck Catholic High School Sports College
WLT/FAZ L9 40 C1
Archbishop Blanch CE High School *EHL/KEN* L7 71 G4
Argyle Health Centre
BIRK CH41 3 F5
Arncot CP School
ANF/KKDL L4 54 B1
Arrowe Country Park
GR/UP/WCH CH49 112 D2
Arrowe Hill Primary School
GR/UP/WCH CH49 90 A5
Arrowe Park Hospital
GR/UP/WCH CH49 113 E2
Ashfield Special School
CHLDW L16 97 E2
Ashley Business Centre
PR/KW L34 59 H4
Ashley Retail Park
WDN WA8 15 F5
Ashley School *WDN* WA8 124 B2
Ashurst Primary School
RNFD/HAY WA11 48 D1
Ashville FC *WAL/NB* CH45 67 H1
Ashworth Hospital *MGHL* L31 19 G4
Astmoor Industrial Estate
RUNC WA7 147 F3
Astmoor Primary School
RUNC WA7 147 F4
Atherton House School
CSBY/BLUN L23 21 E5
Auckland College *AIG/SPK* L17 94 D5
Austin Rawlinson Sports Centre
SPK/HALE L24 142 C3
Avalon School *WKBY* CH48 110 C3
Bankfield School *WDN* WA8 124 B2
Bank Quay Trading Estate
WARR WA1 106 B4
Banks Road Primary School
ALL/GAR L19 140 D2
Barlows Primary School
WLT/FAZ L9 32 A5
Barnston Primary School
HES CH60 149 G2
Barrow Hall Community Primary School
WARRW/BUR WA5 104 B1
Baycliff Road Health Centre
WD/CROXPK L12 57 E3
BBC North & BBC Radio Merseyside *CLVPS* L1 6 D5
Beach Road Primary School
LITH L21 29 H5
The Beacon CE Primary School
EV L5 54 A5
Beamont Junior School
WARRN/WOL WA2 107 E1
The Beatles Story
VAUX/LVPD L3 6 B7
Beaufort Park CP School
TOX L8 94 B3
Beaufort Park School *TOX* L8 94 B4
Bebington High Sports College
BEB CH63 115 H5
Bechers Business Centre
NTHTN L30 31 F2
Bedford Primary School
BTL L20 5 H6
Beechenhurst School
CALD/MH L18 96 D3
Beechwood CP School
HUY L36 58 A4
Beechwood Primary School
RUNC WA7 155 H4
Belair Industrial Estate
CSBY/BLUN L23 29 G1
Bellerive High School *TOX* L8 94 D3
Belle Vale Health Centre
WLTN L25 97 H2
Belle Vale Shopping Centre
WLTN L25 97 H2

Belle Vale Swimming Pool WLTN L25 98 A2
The Belvedere School TOX L8 94 D4
Best Western Fir Grove Hotel WARRS WA4 108 A5
Bewsey Business Centre WARRW/BUR WA5 12 A2
Bewsey Lodge Primary School WARRW/BUR WA5 106 A1
BICC Athletic Club RAIN/WH L35 60 B5
Bidston Avenue Primary School CL/PREN CH43 91 E1
Bidston Golf Club WAL/EG CH44 67 G2
Bidston Industrial Estate WAL/EG CH44 67 H2
Bigdale Medical Centre NWD/KWIPK L33 34 B1
Bigham Road Medical Centre NPK/KEN L6 72 A2
Binns Road Industrial Estate EHL/KEN L7 72 C3
Birchwood Community High School GOL/RIS/CUL WA3 85 H2
Birkenhead County Court BIRK CH41 3 G5
Birkenhead High School CL/PREN CH43 91 G3
Birkenhead High School for Girls CL/PREN CH43 91 G3
Birkenhead Park CC CL/PREN CH43 91 H2
Birkenhead Park RUFC BIRK CH41 91 G1
Birkenhead Preparatory School CL/PREN CH43 91 G3
Birkenhead Priory & Museum BIRK CH41 3 J5
Birkenhead School CL/PREN CH43 91 F3
Birkenhead Sixth Form College BIRK CH41 91 F1
Bishop Martin CE Primary School WLTN L25 120 C1
Blackbrook St Marys Catholic Primary School RNFD/HAY WA11 49 E1
Black Cat Industrial Estate WDN WA8 14 B7
Black Horse Hill Infant School WKBY CH48 87 H5
Black Horse Hill Junior School WKBY CH48 87 H5
Blacklow Brow Primary School HUY L36 75 F4
Blackmoor Park Infant School WD/CROXPK L12 56 D4
Blackmoor Park Junior School WD/CROXPK L12 56 D5
Bleak Hill Primary School ECCL WA10 46 D1
Blessed Sacrament RC Infant School WLT/FAZ L9 40 D1
Blessed Sacrament RC Junior School WLT/FAZ L9 40 D1
Blueberry Park CP School DV/KA/FCH L14 57 G4
Blueberry Park Primary School DV/KA/FCH L14 57 E5
The Blue Coat School WAV L15 96 A2
Blundells Hill Golf Club RAIN/WH L35 77 H4
Boaler Street Industrial Estate NPK/KEN L6 71 G2
Bold Business Centre STHEL WA9 63 H3
Bold Industrial Estate WDN WA8 102 C3
Bold Industrial Park STHEL WA9 63 H4
Bold Street Medical Centre WARR WA1 12 C6
Booker Avenue J & I School CALD/MH L18 119 F2
Bootle Cricket Club BTL L20 5 G7
Bootle Golf Club LITH L21 30 D3
Bootle High School NTHTN L30 23 F5
Bootle Leisure Centre BTL L20 4 E1
Bootle Stadium Sports Centre BTL L20 5 K3
Borough Cemetery ECCL WA10 36 B5
WDN WA8 102 A5
Botanic Estate EHL/KEN L7 72 B4
Bousfield Health Centre ANF/KKDL L4 54 A3
Bowers Business Park WDN WA8 15 G5
Bowring Community Sports College HUY L36 74 D2
Bowring Park Golf Club HUY L36 74 D4
The Bowry Health Centre STHEL WA9 61 F2
Brackenwood Golf Club BEB CH63 137 F2
Brackenwood Infant School BEB CH63 137 H1
Brackenwood Junior School BEB CH63 137 G1
Bradshaw Community Primary School WARRS WA4 131 F1
Breckfield Community Comprehensive School EV L5 54 B5
Breckfield Primary School EV L5 54 C4
Bridgehouse Clinic BEB CH63 115 F5
Bridge Industrial Estate SPK/HALE L24 141 H1
Bridgewater High School WARRS WA4 130 B5
Bridgewater Upper School WARRS WA4 130 B4
Brindley Arts Centre RUNC WA7 8 E4
Britonwood Trading Estate NWD/KWIPK L33 34 C5
Broadgreen Community Comprehensive School CLB/OSW/ST L13 73 F3
Broadgreen High School CLB/OSW/ST L13 73 F3
Broadgreen Hospital DV/KA/FCH L14 73 H3
Broad Green JMI School CLB/OSW/ST L13 73 F3
Broad Oak Primary School STHEL WA9 49 G4
Broad Square Community Primary School NG/CROX L11 55 H2
Broadway Community High School ECCL WA10 61 E2
Bromborough Golf Club BEB CH63 152 B3
Bromborough Pool Primary School PS/BROM CH62 138 D1
Brook Acre Primary School WARRN/WOL WA2 84 C4
Brookdale Primary School GR/UP/WCH CH49 89 G5
Brookfield High School KKBY L32 33 G4
Brookfields School WDN WA8 125 H1
Brook House Business Centre WKBY CH48 110 B1
Brookhurst Primary School BEB CH63 152 C3
Brookside Primary School STBRV L28 57 H3
Brookvale Primary School RUNC WA7 156 D4
Brookvale Recreation Centre RUNC WA7 157 E3
Broomfield County Junior School WARRS WA4 130 C4
Broughton Hall High School Technology College WD/CROXPK L12 57 E5
The Brow Community Primary School RUNC WA7 147 F5
Bruche Community Primary School WARR WA1 108 A1
Brunswick Business Park VAUX/LVPD L3 93 H4
Business Development Centre STHEL WA9 11 K3
Business Resource Centre NWD/KWIPK L33 34 D4
Byrne Avenue Recreation Centre RF/TRAN CH42 115 H2
Cabinet War Rooms CLVP L2 6 C3
Cables Retail Park PR/KW L34 59 H4
Calday Grange Grammar School WKBY CH48 110 D2
Calderstones School CALD/MH L18 96 C4
Caldy Golf Club WKBY CH48 111 E5
Camberley Medical Centre WLTN L25 121 E3
Cammell Laird's Sports Club RF/TRAN CH42 116 A2
Campanile Hotel RUNC WA7 8 D4
VAUX/LVPD L3 93 H1
Campion Catholic High School EV L5 71 E1
Capitol Trading Estate NWD/KWIPK L33 35 E2
Cardinal Heenan Catholic High School WD/CROXPK L12 56 D5
Cardinal Newman RC High School WARR WA1 107 H3
Carleton House Preparatory School CALD/MH L18 95 H5
Carmel College ECCL WA10 60 D1
Carr Lane Industrial Estate HOY CH47 87 G1
Carr Mill Primary School RNFD/HAY WA11 37 G3
Castlefields Health Centre RUNC WA7 147 G4
Castleview Primary School RUNC WA7 155 H1
Castleway Primary School MOR/LEA CH46 67 E1
Catalyst Science Discovery Centre WDN WA8 146 A1
Cathcart Street Primary School BIRK CH41 2 D2
Causeway Medical Centre WARRS WA4 106 D5
Cavendish Medical Centre BIRK CH41 91 H1
Cavendish Special School RUNC WA7 155 F4
Cavern Club CLVP L2 6 D4
Cedar Cross Medical Centre RAIN/WH L35 76 D2
Centec Business Centre AIN/FAZ L10 42 B2
Central Library VAUX/LVPD L3 7 F2
Chadwick Court Industrial Centre VAUX/LVPD L3 70 B2
Chaigley School WARRS WA4 109 E4
Chalon Way Industrial Estate ECCL WA10 11 H7
Chapelfield Clinic WDN WA8 123 H2
Chapel Street Clinic WDN WA8 14 D6
Charles Wooton Centre of Futher Education TOX L8 94 D1
Cherryfield Primary School KKBY L32 33 H5
Chesnut Lodge School WDN WA8 124 C2
Chesterfield High School Sports College CSBY/BLUN L23 21 H5
Childwall CE Primary School CHLDW L16 96 D3
The Childwall Golf Club NTHLY L27 98 C1
Childwall School WAV L15 73 G5
Childwall Valley Primary School WLTN L25 97 G1
Chinese Arch CLVPS L1 7 G7
Christ Church CE Primary School BTL L20 5 G3
MOR/LEA CH46 66 C5
WARRN/WOL WA2 85 E4
Christchurch CE Primary School BIRK CH41 2 C7
Christian Fellowship School EHL/KEN L7 71 H5
Christ the King RC Primary School PS/BROM CH62 153 E2
Church Drive Primary School PS/BROM CH62 116 B5
Churchill Industrial Estate WLT/FAZ L9 31 H4
Church Road Medical Centre BEB CH63 138 A2
Church Square Shopping Centre ECCL WA10 11 G5
Church Street Industrial Estate WARR WA1 13 F5
Cineworld ECCL WA10 11 F5
RUNC WA7 156 B2
Cineworld Liverpool CLB/OSW/ST L13 72 D3
Cinnamon Brow CE Primary School WARRN/WOL WA2 84 D2
The Citadel ECCL WA10 11 G5
Claremont Medical Centre MGHL L31 23 G1
Claremont Special School WAL/NB CH45 51 F4
Claremount School MOR/LEA CH46 67 E4
Clatterbridge Hospital BEB CH63 137 F5
Claughton Medical Centre CL/PREN CH43 91 G1
Clayton Square Shopping Centre CLVPS L1 7 F4
Cleveland Business Park BIRK CH41 2 C1
Clifford Holroyde Centre of Expertise DV/KA/FCH L14 73 H2
Clinic for the Handicapped WARRN/WOL WA2 12 C3
Clock Face Country Park STHEL WA9 80 B2
The Cobbs Infant School WARRS WA4 130 C3
Cockhedge Centre WARR WA1 12 E4
Cole Street Primary School BIRK CH41 2 B5
Collins Industrial Estate STHEL WA9 48 C2
Commercial Business Centre RAIN/WH L35 78 A2
Common Ground Sign Dance Theatre CLVPS L1 6 E5
Community Care for Health WDN WA8 14 D5
Constance Industrial Estate WDN WA8 125 E5
Copplehouse Medical Centre AIN/FAZ L10 32 D5
Corinthian Community Primary School CLB/OSW/ST L13 73 F1
Corner House Clinic WKBY CH48 110 B1
Cornerstones School WARRS WA4 130 D1
Cornerways Medical Centre HUY L36 58 A5
County Fire HQ VAUX/LVPD L3 6 D2
County Sessions House VAUX/LVPD L3 7 G2
Cowley Language College ECCL WA10 47 F1
Craighurst JMI School WLTN L25 97 G1
Craven Business Centre BIRK CH41 2 D4
Croft Business Park PS/BROM CH62 138 D4
Cromdale Way Community Hall & Health Centre WARRW/BUR WA5 104 C2
Cronton CE Primary School WDN WA8 101 E2
Crosby Baths CSBY/BLUN L23 28 C2
Crosby High School CSBY/BLUN L23 21 F3
Cross Farm Primary School NTHLY L27 98 D4
Crowne Plaza Hotel VAUX/LVPD L3 6 A3
Croxteth Community Comprehensive School NG/CROX L11 42 C2
Croxteth Community Primary School NG/CROX L11 42 D3
Croxteth Country Park WD/CROXPK L12 42 D5
Croxteth Family Health Centre NG/CROX L11 42 C3
Croxteth Hall WD/CROXPK L12 56 D1
Croxteth Sports Centre NG/CROX L11 42 C3
Cunard Building VAUX/LVPD L3 6 B4
Dallam Community Primary School WARRW/BUR WA5 83 F4
Daresbury Park Business Park WARRS WA4 157 H1
Dawpool CE Primary School PEN/TH CH61 111 H5
De La Salle RC High School NG/CROX L11 42 B5
De La Salle School ECCL WA10 47 E3
The Dell Primary School RF/TRAN CH42 116 B2
Derby Lane Medical Centre CLB/OSW/ST L13 73 E2
Devaney Medical Centre CL/PREN CH43 2 A7
Devonshire Park Primary School RF/TRAN CH42 115 E1
Deyes High School MGHL L31 18 D5
Deysbrook Medical Centre WD/CROXPK L12 56 C3
Dibbinsdale Local Nature Reserve BEB CH63 152 B2
Dinas Lane Medical Centre HUY L36 75 E1
Ditton CE Primary School WDN WA8 123 G2
Ditton Medical Centre WDN WA8 124 A2
Dovecot Health Clinic DV/KA/FCH L14 74 B1
Dovecot JMI School DV/KA/FCH L14 74 C2
Dovedale County Infant School CALD/MH L18 96 A3
Dovedale Junior School CALD/MH L18 96 A3
Drug Dependency Clinic CLVPS L1 7 H5
Drug Dependency Clinic Widnes WDN WA8 14 D6
Dunnys Sports Club WLT/FAZ L9 40 C3
Eagle Sports Club WARRW/BUR WA5 105 E4
Earle Road Medical Centre EHL/KEN L7 72 A5
Eastcroft Park CP School NWD/KWIPK L33 26 A4
Eastham Country Park PS/BROM CH62 153 G2
Eastham Lodge Golf Club PS/BROM CH62 153 G3
Eastside Industrial Estate STHEL WA9 48 C5
Eastway Primary School MOR/LEA CH46 66 C4
Eaton Road Medical Centre WD/CROXPK L12 56 C5
Eaves Primary School STHEL WA9 62 C4
Eccleston Lane Ends Primary School PR/KW L34 60 B3
Eccleston Medical Centre ECCL WA10 46 D2
Eccleston Mere Primary School ECCL WA10 46 C4
Eccleston Park Golf Club RAIN/WH L35 60 D4
Edge Hill Enterprises WLT/FAZ L9 41 F1
Edge Hill Enterprise Training Centre WLT/FAZ L9 41 G1
Edge Hill Health Centre EHL/KEN L7 72 A4
Edge Lane Medical Centre EHL/KEN L7 71 H4
Edge Lane Retail Park CLB/OSW/ST L13 72 D3
Edwards Lane Industrial Estate SPK/HALE L24 120 D5
Egremont Medical Centre WAL/EG CH44 69 F1
Egremont Primary School WAL/EG CH44 69 F1
Elaine Norris Sports Centre VAUX/LVPD L3 70 C1
Elimu Academy TOX L8 94 D1
Elleray Park School WAL/NB CH45 51 G3
Ellergreen Medical Centre NG/CROX L11 41 H5
The Elms Special School STBRV L28 57 H2
Eltham Green Clinic GR/UP/WCH CH49 113 F1
Emmaus Primary School WD/CROXPK L12 43 F4
English Martyrs Catholic Primary School LITH L21 30 A4
Eric Moore Health Centre WARRN/WOL WA2 12 C3
Ernest Cookson Special School WD/CROXPK L12 56 B4
Erskine Street Industrial Estate NPK/KEN L6 7 K2
Estuary Business Park SPK/HALE L24 141 G2
Europa Pool BIRK CH41 2 E4
Evelyn Primary School PR/KW L34 60 A3
Evelyn Street Primary School WARRW/BUR WA5 106 A4
Everite Road Industrial Estate WDN WA8 123 H4
Everton FC (Goodison Park) ANF/KKDL L4 54 B2
Everton Park Sports Centre EV L5 54 A5
Everton Road Health Clinic NPK/KEN L6 71 F1
Everyman Theatre VAUX/LVPD L3 7 J5
Express Industrial Estate WDN WA8 123 G4
Expressway Business Park RF/TRAN CH42 92 D5
FACT-Foundation for Art & Creative Technology CLVPS L1 7 G6
Fairfield High School WDN WA8 102 B5
Fairfield Hospital RNFD/HAY WA11 36 C2
Fairfield J & I School WDN WA8 125 F1
Fairfield Medical Centre NPK/KEN L6 72 A2
Fairfield RFC RF/TRAN CH42 115 H1
Fairway Trading Estate WDN WA8 124 C4
Faith House Yoga & Natural Health Centre WAL/NB CH45 51 H2
Faith Primary School VAUX/LVPD L3 71 E2
Falcongate Industrial Estate BIRK CH41 68 D4
Family Health Centre KKBY L32 33 F2
Farnworth CE Primary School WDN WA8 102 A4
Fazakerley High School AIN/FAZ L10 32 C5
Fazakerley Primary School AIN/FAZ L10 32 C5
Fazakerley Sports Centre AIN/FAZ L10 32 C4
Fearnhead Cross Medical Centre WARRN/WOL WA2 84 D3
Fender Primary School GR/UP/WCH CH49 90 C5
Fernhill Sports Centre BTL L20 39 H1
Ferries Industrial Estate RF/TRAN CH42 92 D5
Fingerprints of Elvis VAUX/LVPD L3 6 B6
Fir Tree Drive South Medical Centre WD/CROXPK L12 43 F4
Fishwicks Industrial Estate STHEL WA9 62 D2
Fleet Lane Industrial Estate STHEL WA9 49 E5
Fleming Industrial Estate WARR WA1 13 F4
Floral Pavilion Theatre WAL/NB CH45 52 A1
Florence Melly Community Primary School ANF/KKDL L4 41 E5
Fordton Leisure Centre WARRN/WOL WA2 83 G2
Forefield Infant School CSBY/BLUN L23 21 H5
Forefield Junior School CSBY/BLUN L23 21 G5
The Forge Shopping Centre WARRS WA4 130 A2
Formby Clinic FMBY L37 17 E4
Formby AFC FMBY L37 17 E3
Formby Business Park FMBY L37 17 H3
Formby CC FMBY L37 17 E1
Formby Golf Club FMBY L37 16 C1
Formby High School FMBY L37 16 D2
Formby Junior Sports Club FMBY L37 17 F1
Formby Ladies Golf Club FMBY L37 16 C1
Formby Lawn Tennis Club FMBY L37 17 E1
Four Acre Lane Shopping Centre STHEL WA9 79 F1
Foxfield School MOR/LEA CH46 66 B5
Freight Terminal Buildings (Euro-Rail) LITH L21 38 C1
Freshfield Primary School FMBY L37 17 F2
Freshlea Private Clinic FMBY L37 16 C5
Gallagher Industrial Estate BIRK CH41 68 D3
Garston CE Primary School ALL/GAR L19 119 H5
Garston Industrial Estate ALL/GAR L19 140 C2
Garston Leisure Centre ALL/GAR L19 119 G5
Garston Sports Centre ALL/GAR L19 119 G4
Garven Place Clinic WARR WA1 12 B5
Gateacre Community Comprehensive School WLTN L25 97 G3
Gateworth Industrial Estate WARRW/BUR WA5 105 H5
Gayton Primary School HES CH60 149 E3
Gemini Business Park WARRW/BUR WA5 83 F2
Gillmoss Industrial Estate NG/CROX L11 42 B1
Gillmoss Medical Centre NG/CROX L11 42 C2
Gilmour Infant School ALL/GAR L19 119 F4
Gilmour Junior School ALL/GAR L19 119 F4
Golden Square Shopping Centre WARR WA1 12 C5
Golden Triangle Industrial Estate WDN WA8 124 A5
Gorsewood Primary School RUNC WA7 157 G2
Grain Industrial Estate TOX L8 94 A4
Granada Television VAUX/LVPD L3 6 C6
The Grand National Experience WLT/FAZ L9 31 G3
The Grange Comprehensive School RUNC WA7 9 J7
The Grange Country Club NSTN CH64 150 B5
The Grange Infant School RUNC WA7 9 J6
The Grange Junior School RUNC WA7 9 J6
Grange Park Golf Club ECCL WA10 61 E1
Grange Primary School NTHTN L30 22 D4
The Grange Shopping Precinct BIRK CH41 2 E5
Grappenhall CC WARRS WA4 131 E2
Grappenhall Clinic WARRS WA4 108 B5
Grappenhall Hall School WARRS WA4 131 F2
Grappenhall Heys Primary School WARRS WA4 130 D4
Grappenhall Sports Club WARRS WA4 130 D2
Greasby Health Centre GR/UP/WCH CH49 89 F5
Greasby Infant School GR/UP/WCH CH49 112 A1
Greasby Junior School GR/UP/WCH CH49 112 B2

Great Crosby RC Primary School *CSBY/BLUN* L23 .... 21 G5
Great Homer Street Medical Centre *EV* L5 .... 54 A5
Great Meols Primary School *HOY* CH47 .... 65 E4
Great Sankey High School *WARRW/BUR* WA5 .... 81 F5
Great Sankey Primary School *WARRW/BUR* WA5 .... 105 E3
Greenbank Primary School *CALD/MH* L18 .... 95 H3
Green Lane Medical Centre *CLB/OSW/ST* L13 .... 55 G5
Green Lane Special School *WARR* WA1 .... 85 F5
Greenleas School *WAL/NB* CH45 .... 50 C4
Greenoaks Farm Industrial Estate *WDN* WA8 .... 15 H3
Green Oaks Shopping Centre *WDN* WA8 .... 15 F3
Green Park Primary School *MGHL* L31 .... 18 B4
Greenways Special School *ALL/GAR* L19 .... 118 D4
Gresford Medical Centre *DV/KA/FCH* L14 .... 74 B2
Grove House Hotel *WAL/NB* CH45 .... 51 E3
Grove Street Primary School *PS/BROM* CH62 .... 116 A4
Guardian Medical Centre *WARRW/BUR* WA5 .... 106 B2
Guardian Street Industrial Estate *WARRW/BUR* WA5 .... 12 A3
Guinea Gap Baths & Recreation Centre *WAL/EG* CH44 .... 69 G2
Gulliver's World Theme Park *WARRW/BUR* WA5 .... 83 E4
Gwladys Street Community Primary School *ANF/KKDL* L4 .... 54 C2
Halebank CE Primary School *WDN* WA8 .... 144 C2
Hale CE Primary School *SPK/HALE* L24 .... 144 A5
Hale Road Industrial Estate *WDN* WA8 .... 145 E1
Halewood CE Primary School *HLWD* L26 .... 122 A2
Halewood Community Comprehensive School *HLWD* L26 .... 121 G4
Halewood Health Centre *HLWD* L26 .... 121 H4
Halewood Sports Centre *HLWD* L26 .... 122 A4
Hall Street Medical Centre *ECCL* WA10 .... 11 H5
Hallwood Park Primary School *RUNC* WA7 .... 156 A3
Halsnead Community Primary School *RAIN/WH* L35 .... 76 D3
Halton General Hospital *RUNC* WA7 .... 156 B3
Halton College *WDN* WA8 .... 14 C4
WDN WA8 .... 14 E2
Halton High School *RUNC* WA7 .... 157 E4
Halton Lodge Primary School *RUNC* WA7 .... 155 H1
Halton Magistrates Court *RUNC* WA7 .... 156 B1
Halton School *RUNC* WA7 .... 147 F5
Hanson Road Business Park *WLT/FAZ* L9 .... 41 E2
The Hardshaw Shopping Centre *ECCL* WA10 .... 11 G5
Harold Magnay Special School *WLTN* L25 .... 97 F4
Hartley Trading Estate *WLT/FAZ* L9 .... 40 D2
Hatton Garden Industrial Estate *CLVP* L2 .... 6 D2
Hatton Hill Primary School *LITH* L21 .... 30 A2
Hawthorne Business Park *WARRW/BUR* WA5 .... 83 F5
Hayfield School *GR/UP/WCH* CH49 .... 90 A2
Heath Road Medical Centre *RUNC* WA7 .... 155 F1
The Heath Specialist Technology College *RUNC* WA7 .... 155 F2
Heatwaves Leisure Centre *STBRV* L28 .... 57 H2
Hebrew Cemetery *CLB/OSW/ST* L13 .... 55 G5
DV/KA/FCH L14 .... 73 G3
EHL/KEN L7 .... 72 A3
WLT/FAZ L9 .... 40 C4
Heswall FC *HES* CH60 .... 149 G2
Heswall Golf Club *HES* CH60 .... 149 E4
Heswall Health Centre *HES* CH60 .... 134 D5
Heswall Preparatory School *HES* CH60 .... 134 C4
Heswall Primary School *PEN/TH* CH61 .... 135 E5
Heygarth Primary School *PS/BROM* CH62 .... 153 E4
Heygreen Community Primary School *WAV* L15 .... 72 C5
Higher Bebington Junior School *BEB* CH63 .... 115 E5
Higher Side Community Comprehensive School *RAIN/WH* L35 .... 77 F2
Highfield Medical Centre *WDN* WA8 .... 124 D1
Highfield School *CL/PREN* CH43 .... 91 E2
Highfield Special School *HLWD* L26 .... 122 A4
Hilbre High School *WKBY* CH48 .... 87 H5
Hillbark Hotel *WKBY* CH48 .... 111 G3
The Hillcrest Hotel *WDN* WA8 .... 101 H3
Hillside High School *BTL* L20 .... 5 K5
Hillside Primary School *CL/PREN* CH43 .... 90 D3
Hill Street Business Centre *TOX* L8 .... 93 H2
Hillview Primary School *RUNC* WA7 .... 156 A5
Historic Warships Museum *BIRK* CH41 .... 69 F4
HM Customs & Excise National Museum *VAUX/LVPD* L3 .... 6 A6
HM Prison *BTL* L20 .... 40 B2
WLT/FAZ L9 .... 41 F1
Holly Lodge Girls College *CLB/OSW/ST* L13 .... 56 A4
Hollywood Superbowl *CLB/OSW/ST* L13 .... 72 D4
Holy Angels Catholic Primary School *KKBY* L32 .... 33 F2
Holy Cross Catholic Primary School *VAUX/LVPD* L3 .... 6 E1
Holy Cross RC Primary School *BIRK* CH41 .... 68 A4
ECCL WA10 .... 11 J4
Holy Family Catholic High School *CSBY/BLUN* L23 .... 21 H3
Holy Family RC Primary School *WDN* WA8 .... 101 F2
WLTN L25 .... 121 F2
Holy Name RC Primary School *WLT/FAZ* L9 .... 32 B5
Holy Rosary RC Junior School *AIN/FAZ* L10 .... 32 A1
Holy Rosary RC Primary School *AIN/FAZ* L10 .... 31 H1
Holy Spirit Primary School *STHEL* WA9 .... 49 G4
The Holy Spirit RC Aided Primary School *RUNC* WA7 .... 155 H1
Holy Spirit RC Primary School *NTHTN* L30 .... 30 C1
Holy Trinity CE Primary School *HOY* CH47 .... 87 G1
Holy Trinity RC Primary School *ALL/GAR* L19 .... 140 D1
Homoeopathic Medical Centre *CLB/OSW/ST* L13 .... 73 E2
Hood Manor Medical Centre *WARRW/BUR* WA5 .... 105 G3
Hope School *NTHLY* L27 .... 98 B1
Hope Street Natural Health Centre *CLVPS* L1 .... 7 J7
Hope Valley Community Primary School *EV* L5 .... 54 B3
Hornspit Medical Centre *NG/CROX* L11 .... 56 A2
Hotel Ibis *CLVPS* L1 .... 6 D7
Howley Quay Industrial Estate *WARR* WA1 .... 13 H4
Hoylake Business Centre *HOY* CH47 .... 64 C5
Hoylake Cottage Hospital *HOY* CH47 .... 64 C5
Hoylake Golf Club *HOY* CH47 .... 87 F2
Hoylake RFC *HOY* CH47 .... 87 F1
Hudson Primary School *MGHL* L31 .... 24 A2
Hugh Baird College of Further Education *BTL* L20 .... 5 F7
Hugh Baird College of Technology *BTL* L20 .... 5 F7
Hunts Cross JMI School *WLTN* L25 .... 121 E5
Hunts Cross Shopping Park *SPK/HALE* L24 .... 120 C5
Huyton Leisure Centre *HUY* L36 .... 75 E4
Huyton & Prescot Golf Club *HUY* L36 .... 59 E5
Huyton with Roby CE Primary School *HUY* L36 .... 75 F2
IKEA Store Warrington *WARRW/BUR* WA5 .... 82 C2
Innkeeper's Lodge *ALL/GAR* L19 .... 119 E3
CLB/OSW/ST L13 .... 73 F1
Interactive College *CLVP* L2 .... 6 D3
Interchange Motorway Industrial Estate *HUY* L36 .... 76 A4
International Business Centre *WARRW/BUR* WA5 .... 82 C3
Irby CC *PEN/TH* CH61 .... 112 B3
Irby Primary School *PEN/TH* CH61 .... 112 C4
Irwin Road Health Centre *STHEL* WA9 .... 62 D3
Isle of Man Ferry Terminal *VAUX/LVPD* L3 .... 6 A3
Islington House Medical Centre *VAUX/LVPD* L3 .... 7 K1
Job's Ferry *PS/BROM* CH62 .... 139 G5
Jubilee Medical Centre *NG/CROX* L11 .... 42 C5
Junction 1 Retail Park *WAL/EG* CH44 .... 67 H2
Kensington CP Infant School *EHL/KEN* L7 .... 71 H3
Kensington CP Junior School *EHL/KEN* L7 .... 71 H3
Kensington Medical Centre *NPK/KEN* L6 .... 71 G2
Kerfoot Business Park *WARRN/WOL* WA2 .... 83 G5
The King David High School *WAV* L15 .... 96 C1
King David Primary School *WAV* L15 .... 96 C1
King Edward Industrial Estate *VAUX/LVPD* L3 .... 6 A1
Kingfisher Business Park *BTL* L20 .... 39 G1
LITH L21 .... 30 A5
Kings Business Park *PR/KW* L34 .... 59 E5
Kings Gap Court Hotel *HOY* CH47 .... 87 E2
Kingsley Community School *TOX* L8 .... 94 C1
Kingsmead School *HOY* CH47 .... 64 C5
Kingsway Industrial Park *VAUX/LVPD* L3 .... 70 D1
Kingsway Primary School *WAL/EG* CH44 .... 69 E3
Kingsway Surgery *CSBY/WL* L22 .... 29 F2
Kirby-Liverpool Municipal Golf Club *KKBY* L32 .... 33 E4
Kirkby CE Primary School *KKBY* L32 .... 33 G1
Kirkby Sports Centre *KKBY* L32 .... 33 F4
Kirkdale St Lawrence CE Primary School *ANF/KKDL* L4 .... 53 H2
Knotty Ash Primary School *DV/KA/FCH* L14 .... 73 H1
Knowsley Business Park *PR/KW* L34 .... 43 H2
Knowsley Central Primary Support Centre *HUY* L36 .... 75 H1
Knowsley Community College *HUY* L36 .... 75 G3
KKBY L32 .... 33 G2
Knowsley Community College (Roby Campus) *HUY* L36 .... 75 E3
Knowsley Hey School *HUY* L36 .... 75 H2
Knowsley Industrial Park *NWD/KWIPK* L33 .... 34 D2
NWD/KWIPK L33 .... 43 G1
Knowsley Magistrates Court *HUY* L36 .... 75 G3
Knowsley Medical Centre *PR/KW* L34 .... 44 B4
Knowsley Northern Primary Support Centre *NWD/KWIPK* L33 .... 26 A5
Knowsley Village Primary School *PR/KW* L34 .... 44 A5
Lady Lever Art Gallery *PS/BROM* CH62 .... 116 B5
Ladymount RC Primary School *PEN/TH* CH61 .... 134 D3
Lairdside Technology Park *BIRK* CH41 .... 92 D4
Lakeside School *NTHLY* L27 .... 98 B1
Lancaster House Medical Centre *ECCL* WA10 .... 11 F3
Lance Lane Medical Centre *WAV* L15 .... 96 A1
Lander Road Primary School *LITH* L21 .... 39 G1
Landican Cemetery *GR/UP/WCH* CH49 .... 113 F2
Landican Crematorium *GR/UP/WCH* CH49 .... 113 F3
Langbank Medical Centre *NG/CROX* L11 .... 55 H1
Langham Street Industrial Estate *ANF/KKDL* L4 .... 54 B2
Lansbury Bridge School *STHEL* WA9 .... 49 E4
Latchford CE Primary School *WARRS* WA4 .... 12 E7
Latchford Medical Centre *WARRS* WA4 .... 107 G5
Lathom Road Health Centre *HUY* L36 .... 75 G2
Laurel Business Centre *EHL/KEN* L7 .... 72 B3
Lawson House Hotel & Conference Centre *RUNC* WA7 .... 155 E1
Lea Green Business Park *STHEL* WA9 .... 78 D1
Leamington Community School *NG/CROX* L11 .... 41 F5
Leasowe Castle Hotel *MOR/LEA* CH46 .... 66 C1
Leasowe Golf Club *MOR/LEA* CH46 .... 66 D1
Leasowe Millennium Centre *MOR/LEA* CH46 .... 67 E2
Leasowe Primary School *MOR/LEA* CH46 .... 67 F1
Leasowe Recreation Centre *MOR/LEA* CH46 .... 67 E2
Lee Park Golf Club *WLTN* L25 .... 98 B4
Legh Vale Primary School *RNFD/HAY* WA11 .... 49 H1
Lifeboat House *HOY* CH47 .... 87 E1
Linacre Primary School *BTL* L20 .... 39 G2
Lingham Primary School *MOR/LEA* CH46 .... 66 B4
Lingholme Health Centre *ECCL* WA10 .... 11 F4
Lingley Mere Business Park *WARRW/BUR* WA5 .... 81 G5
Liscard Primary School *WAL/NB* CH45 .... 52 A5
Lister Drive Infant School *CLB/OSW/ST* L13 .... 72 C1
Lister Drive Junior School *CLB/OSW/ST* L13 .... 72 C1
Litherland High School *LITH* L21 .... 30 C2
Litherland Moss Primary School *LITH* L21 .... 30 C3
Little Theatre *BIRK* CH41 .... 2 C5
Liver Industrial Estate *WLT/FAZ* L9 .... 41 E3
Liverpool Anglican Cathedral *CLVPS* L1 .... 94 A1
Liverpool College *CALD/MH* L18 .... 95 H4
Liverpool Community College *CLB/OSW/ST* L13 .... 55 H4
CLB/OSW/ST L13 .... 73 E2
CLVPS L1 .... 7 G7
EHL/KEN L7 .... 71 G5
EV L5 .... 53 H4
VAUX/LVPD L3 .... 7 H5
VAUX/LVPD L3 .... 70 C2
Liverpool CC *ALL/GAR* L19 .... 118 D3
Liverpool Empire Theatre *CLVPS* L1 .... 7 F3
Liverpool FC (Anfield) *ANF/KKDL* L4 .... 54 C3
Liverpool FC Museum *ANF/KKDL* L4 .... 54 C3
Liverpool Hope University *VAUX/LVPD* L3 .... 7 J1
Liverpool Hope University College *CHLDW* L16 .... 96 D2
Liverpool Hope University Education Deanery *CHLDW* L16 .... 96 D2
Liverpool Institute for Performing Arts *CLVPS* L1 .... 7 H7
Liverpool Institute of Higher Education *CHLDW* L16 .... 96 D2
Liverpool Intermodal Freeport Terminal *BTL* L20 .... 4 A4
Liverpool John Lennon International Airport *SPK/HALE* L24 .... 142 A4
Liverpool John Moores University *AIG/SPK* L17 .... 118 D2
CLVP L2 .... 6 D2
CLVP L1 .... 7 G3
CLVP L1 .... 7 J5
CLVP L1 .... 7 H7
EHL/KEN L7 .... 72 B3
VAUX/LVP L3 .... 7 F1
Liverpool Magistrates Court *CLVP* L2 .... 6 D3
Liverpool Museum *VAUX/LVPD* L3 .... 7 F2
Liverpool Playhouse Theatre *CLVPS* L1 .... 7 F4
Liverpool University Dental Hospital *VAUX/LVPD* L3 .... 7 K3
Liverpool Womens Hospital *TOX* L8 .... 71 G5
Longbarn CP School *WARRN/WOL* WA2 .... 85 F4
Long Lane CP School *WARRN/WOL* WA2 .... 83 H4
Long Lane Medical Centre *WLT/FAZ* L9 .... 41 H3
Longmoor Community Primary School *WLT/FAZ* L9 .... 40 D1
Longton Lane Community Primary School *RAIN/WH* L35 .... 60 D5
Longton Medical Centre *RAIN/WH* L35 .... 77 H2
Longview Community Primary School *HUY* L36 .... 58 C4
Lourdes Hospital *CALD/MH* L18 .... 95 H4
Loushers Lane Special School *WARRS* WA4 .... 130 B1
Lower Lee Special School *WLTN* L25 .... 97 E4
Lowfield Industrial Estate *STHEL* WA9 .... 61 H5
Lunts Heath Primary School *WDN* WA8 .... 102 B3
Lydiate Primary School *MGHL* L31 .... 18 C2
The Lyndale School *PS/BROM* CH62 .... 153 F4
Lyon Industrial Estate *STHEL* WA9 .... 79 H1
Mab Lane Junior Mixed & Infants School *STBRV* L28 .... 57 F3
Mackets Primary School *WLTN* L25 .... 121 F2
Maghull Health Centre *MGHL* L31 .... 18 C5
Maghull High School *MGHL* L31 .... 23 H2
Malvern Primary School *DV/KA/FCH* L14 .... 74 B3
Manor Farm Medical Centre *HUY* L36 .... 75 H4
Manor Industrial Estate *WARRS* WA4 .... 13 K7
Manor Primary School *CL/PREN* CH43 .... 90 C1
The Margaret Thompson Medical Centre *SPK/HALE* L24 .... 143 E2
Maricourt Catholic High School *MGHL* L31 .... 24 B1
Marine FC *CSBY/BLUN* L23 .... 28 D1
Marriott Hotel *CLVPS* L1 .... 7 F3
SPK/HALE L24 .... 141 F2
Martlew Day Hospital *RAIN/WH* L35 .... 61 E5
Maryland Health Centre *CLVPS* L1 .... 7 J6
Maternity & Child Welfare Clinic *STHEL* WA9 .... 49 F4
Matthew Arnold Primary School *TOX* L8 .... 94 C5
Mayflower Industrial Estate *FMBY* L37 .... 17 F5
Meadow Bank Special School *AIN/FAZ* L10 .... 32 C4
Meadowside School *GR/UP/WCH* CH49 .... 113 E1
Megabowl *NTHTN* L30 .... 31 F1
Melling Primary School *MGHL* L31 .... 25 E5
Mendell Primary School *PS/BROM* CH62 .... 153 E1
Merchant Taylors Junior School for Girls *CSBY/BLUN* L23 .... 29 F1
Merchant Taylors School *CSBY/BLUN* L23 .... 29 F1
Merchant Taylors School for Girls *CSBY/BLUN* L23 .... 21 E5
Mersey Ferries Terminal *VAUX/LVPD* L3 .... 6 B5
Mersey Park Primary School *RF/TRAN* CH42 .... 92 C5
Merseyside Maritime Museum & International Slavery Museum *VAUX/LVPD* L3 .... 6 A6
Merseyside Police Headquarters *CLVPS* L1 .... 6 D6
Mersey Valley Golf & Country Club *WDN* WA8 .... 103 F1
Mersey View Special School *AIG/SPK* L17 .... 118 C2
Merton Bank Primary School *STHEL* WA9 .... 48 C3
Met Quarter (under development) *CLVPS* L1 .... 6 E4
Metropolitan Cathedral of Christ the King *VAUX/LVPD* L3 .... 7 J4
Middlefield Primary School *SPK/HALE* L24 .... 142 C3
Millbrook Business Centre *RNFD/HAY* WA11 .... 36 A1
Millbrook Primary School *KKBY* L32 .... 33 G1
Millfields Primary School *PS/BROM* CH62 .... 153 E5
Millstead Special School *WAV* L15 .... 73 E5
Mill Street Medical Centre *ECCL* WA10 .... 11 F3
Miriam Health Centre *BIRK* CH41 .... 68 B5
Monksdown Primary School *NG/CROX* L11 .... 56 A1
Moore RUFC *WARRS* WA4 .... 128 B5
Moorfield Primary School *WDN* WA8 .... 102 D5
Moorfoot Road Industrial Estate *STHEL* WA9 .... 49 F3
Moor Lane Business Centre *WDN* WA8 .... 14 C6
Moreton Medical Centre *MOR/LEA* CH46 .... 66 C5
Mornington Business Centre *CLVPS* L1 .... 7 H7
Mosscroft Primary School *HUY* L36 .... 76 A2
Mosslands School *WAL/NB* CH45 .... 68 A1
Moss Lane Sports Centre *LITH* L21 .... 30 C3
Mossley Hill Hospital *AIG/SPK* L17 .... 95 G4
Mosspits J & I School *WAV* L15 .... 96 B2
Mostyn House School *NSTN* CH64 .... 158 A2
Mount Primary School *WAL/NB* CH45 .... 51 G2
The Mount-St Marys Preparatory School *CSBY/BLUN* L23 .... 28 C1
Much Woolton Catholic Primary School *WLTN* L25 .... 120 D1
Multibowl *PS/BROM* CH62 .... 138 D3
Murdishaw Health Centre *RUNC* WA7 .... 157 F2
Murrayfield Hospital *PEN/TH* CH61 .... 135 H1
Museum of Liverpool *VAUX/LVPD* L3 .... 6 B5
National Conservation Centre *CLVPS* L1 .... 6 E3
National Discovery Park *VAUX/LVPD* L3 .... 6 D5
National Museums & Galleries Merseyside *CLVPS* L1 .... 7 F3
National Wildflower Centre *CHLDW* L16 .... 74 B4
Natural Health Clinic *PR/KW* L34 .... 59 H4
Neptune Theatre *CLVPS* L1 .... 6 E5
Neston CC *NSTN* CH64 .... 158 B2
Neston High School *NSTN* CH64 .... 159 E1
Neston Medical Centre *NSTN* CH64 .... 158 D2
Neston Primary School *NSTN* CH64 .... 158 D3
Neston Recreation Centre *NSTN* CH64 .... 159 E1
Netherfield Family Health Clinic *EV* L5 .... 54 A5
Netherley Health Centre *NTHLY* L27 .... 98 C3
Netherley Sports Centre *NTHLY* L27 .... 98 B3
Netherton Industrial Estate *NTHTN* L30 .... 31 E4
Netherton Moss Primary School *NTHTN* L30 .... 30 D1
New Brighton Primary School *WAL/NB* CH45 .... 52 A2
New Brighton RUFC *MOR/LEA* CH46 .... 66 D1
Newfield Special School *CSBY/BLUN* L23 .... 22 A4
New Heys Comprehensive School *CALD/MH* L18 .... 119 H2
New Hutte CP School *HLWD* L26 .... 121 G5
New Lodge Industrial Estate *NWD/KWIPK* L33 .... 34 C4
New Market Hall *RUNC* WA7 .... 8 E3
New Mersey Retail Park *SPK/HALE* L24 .... 141 F1
New Park Primary School *NPK/KEN* L6 .... 71 H2
New Solar School *WAL/NB* CH45 .... 50 C5
Newstead Abbey *TOX* L8 .... 95 E1
Newstead Vocational Education Centre *KKBY* L32 .... 33 H4
New Way Business Centre *BIRK* CH41 .... 69 F3
Nine Tree Primary School *STBRV* L28 .... 57 G1
The Norman Pannell School *NTHLY* L27 .... 98 C3
Norris Green Family Health Clinic *NG/CROX* L11 .... 55 G1

North Cheshire Trading Estate *CL/PREN* CH43 114 A3
North Clinic *CL/PREN* CH43 91 G1
Northcote Primary School *WLT/FAZ* L9 40 C4
Northern CC *CSBY/BLUN* L23 21 G3
North Mersey Business Centre *NWD/KWIPK* L33 26 D5
North Mersey Community Hospital *WLT/FAZ* L9 41 F1
North Park Health Centre *BTL* L20 4 D1
Northway Community Primary School *MGHL* L31 19 E3
Northway Primary School *WAV* L15 73 F4
North Western Hall *CLVPS* L1 7 G3
North Wirral Coastal Park *MOR/LEA* CH46 66 B1
Norton Priory Museum & Gardens *RUNC* WA7 147 H3
Norton Priory Recreation Centre *RUNC* WA7 147 H4
Notre Dame Catholic College *ANF/KKDL* L4 54 A3
Nutgrove Methodist Primary School *STHEL* WA9 61 F3
Oak Cottage Medical Centre *HUY* L36 75 G4
Oakdene Primary School *RAIN/WH* L35 78 A3
Oakfield Primary School *WDN* WA8 123 G3
Oak Remedial Clinic *WD/CROXPK* L12 43 E3
Oakwood Avenue Primary School *WARR* WA1 107 F1
Odeon Cinema *CALD/MH* L18 96 B4
CLVPS L1 7 F3
NTHTN L30 31 F1
PS/BROM CH62 138 D4
Oldershaw School *WAL/NB* CH45 51 G5
Old Foundry Estate *WDN* WA8 14 E6
Old Parkonians RFC *CL/PREN* CH43 91 G5
Old Rockerrians RFC *CL/PREN* CH43 114 B3
Old Swan Health Centre *CLB/OSW/ST* L13 73 E3
Orrets Meadow School *MOR/LEA* CH46 66 D5
Our Lady Immaculate RC Primary School *EV* L5 54 A4
Our Lady Mother of the Saviour Catholic Primary School *RUNC* WA7 156 C3
Our Lady of Compassion RC Primary *FMBY* L37 17 F3
Our Lady of Good Help RC Primary School *WAV* L15 73 E5
Our Lady of Lourdes RC Primary School *MOR/LEA* CH46 67 F1
Our Lady of Mount Carmel RC Primary School *TOX* L8 94 B3
Our Lady of Perpetual Succour RC Primary School *WDN* WA8 123 F3
Our Lady of Pity Primary School *GR/UP/WCH* CH49 112 B1
Our Lady of the Assumption Primary School *WLTN* L25 97 H2
Our Lady of Walsingham RC Infant School *NTHTN* L30 30 D2
Our Lady of Walsingham RC Junior School *NTHTN* L30 30 D2
Our Lady Queen of Peace RC Primary School *LITH* L21 29 H2
Our Lady RC Primary School *WARRS* WA4 107 G5
Our Lady & St Edwards RC Primary School *BIRK* CH41 68 D5
Our Lady & St Philomenas Catholic Primary School *WLT/FAZ* L9 41 G3
Our Lady & St Swithins Catholic Primary School *NG/CROX* L11 42 C2
Our Ladys Bishop Eton RC Primary School *CALD/MH* L18 96 C3
Our Ladys RC Primary School *PR/KW* L34 59 H3
Our Lady Star of the Sea RC Primary School *LITH* L21 39 E1
The Oval Sports Centre *BEB* CH63 116 A4
Overchurch J & I School *GR/UP/WCH* CH49 89 H2
Overdale Primary School *KKBY* L32 26 A5
Oxton CC *CL/PREN* CH43 91 F4
Paddington House Hotel *WARR* WA1 108 A1
Padgate Business Centre *WARR* WA1 85 E5
Padgate Community High School *WARRN/WOL* WA2 84 D3
Padgate Medical Centre *WARRN/WOL* WA2 85 E4
Paerr Hall *WARR* WA1 12 C6
Palacefields Primary School *RUNC* WA7 156 C3
Palace Theatre *WARR* WA1 12 D5
Palatine Industrial Estate *WARRS* WA4 107 E5
Palmerston Special School *WLTN* L25 97 E5
Paradise Street Bus Station *CLVP* L2 6 D5
Parish CE Primary School *ECCL* WA10 11 H3
Park Brow Primary School *KKBY* L32 34 B4
Parkdale Industrial Estate *WARR* WA1 13 G6
Parkfield Medical Centre *PS/BROM* CH62 116 A3
Parkgate Primary School *NSTN* CH64 158 B1
Park High Lower School *BIRK* CH41 91 G1
Park High School Sports College *CL/PREN* CH43 91 H2
Park House Medical Centre *PR/KW* L34 59 H4
Parklands High School *SPK/HALE* L24 142 C3
Park Medical Centre *WKBY* CH48 110 A1
Park Primary School *WAL/EG* CH44 68 D2
The Park Primary School *RUNC* WA7 147 G5
Park Road Community Primary School *WARRW/BUR* WA5 104 C2
Park Road Sports Centre *TOX* L8 94 B3
Park View Primary School *HUY* L36 75 E1
Parliament Street North Waterfront Business Area *VAUX/LVPD* L3 93 G1
Parliament Street South Waterfront Business Area *TOX* L8 94 A1
Parr Industrial Estate *STHEL* WA9 49 E5
Parr Swimming Baths *STHEL* WA9 48 C4
Parrs Corner Trading Estate *BTL* L20 4 E1
Pasture Road Health Centre *MOR/LEA* CH46 66 C4
Peatwood Medical Centre *KKBY* L32 34 A5
Peninsula Business Park *MOR/LEA* CH46 67 E3
Penketh Business Park *WARRW/BUR* WA5 105 F4
Penketh Community Primary School *WARRW/BUR* WA5 104 B4
Penketh County High School *WARRW/BUR* WA5 104 D3
Penketh Health Clinic *WARRW/BUR* WA5 104 C4
Penketh South Community Primary School *WARRW/BUR* WA5 104 D5
Penketh Swimming Baths *WARRW/BUR* WA5 104 C3
Penlake Industrial Estate *STHEL* WA9 63 E4
Penpoll Industrial Estate *BTL* L20 39 G1
Penpoll Trading Estate *BTL* L20 39 G1
Pensby Clinic *PEN/TH* CH61 135 E3
Pensby High School for Boys *PEN/TH* CH61 134 C3
Pensby Infant School *PEN/TH* CH61 134 D3
Pensby Junior School *PEN/TH* CH61 134 D3
Pensby Park Primary School *PEN/TH* CH61 134 B3
Pensby Recreation Centre *PEN/TH* CH61 135 E1
Peter Lloyd Leisure Centre *CLB/OSW/ST* L13 55 H5
Pewithall Primary School *RUNC* WA7 155 F2
Philharmonic Hall *CLVPS* L1 7 J6
Phoenix Medical Centre *ECCL* WA10 11 F4
Phoenix Primary School *EHL/KEN* L7 72 C3
Picture House Cinema *WLTN* L25 120 C1
Pinehurst Primary School Infant Department *ANF/KKDL* L4 55 E3
Pinehurst Primary School Junior Department *ANF/KKDL* L4 55 E3
Pinners Brow Retail Park *WARRN/WOL* WA2 12 D2
Plantation Business Park *PS/BROM* CH62 139 F4
Plantation Primary School *HLWD* L26 121 H3
Plaza Cinema *CSBY/WL* L22 29 E3
Pleasant Street Primary School *VAUX/LVPD* L3 7 H5
Plessington Catholic Technology College *BEB* CH63 116 A4
Portland Primary School *BIRK* CH41 68 C5
Port of Liverpool Building *VAUX/LVPD* L3 6 C5
Poulter Road Medical Centre *WLT/FAZ* L9 31 G5
Poulton Lancelyn Primary School *BEB* CH63 138 A4
Poulton Park Golf Club *WARRN/WOL* WA2 85 E1
Poulton Primary School *WAL/EG* CH44 68 C2
Premier Travel Inn *CLB/OSW/ST* L13 56 A4
CLVP L2 6 D3
GR/UP/WCH CH49 89 G4
HES CH60 149 F2
HUY L36 74 D3
HUY L36 76 B5
NTHTN L30 23 G5
PS/BROM CH62 139 E5
RAIN/WH L35 78 C4
RNFD/HAY WA11 37 G4
RUNC WA7 157 F5
STHEL WA9 78 D2
VAUX/LVPD L3 6 C7
WARR WA1 12 C7
WARR WA1 109 F2
WARRN/WOL WA2 83 G1
WLT/FAZ L9 31 G3
Prenton Golf Club *RF/TRAN* CH42 114 D3
Prenton High School for Girls *RF/TRAN* CH42 115 F2
Prenton J & I Schools *CL/PREN* CH43 114 C2
Prenton Preparatory School *CL/PREN* CH43 91 H5
Prescot AFC *PR/KW* L34 59 H3
Prescot Leisure Centre *PR/KW* L34 60 A5
Prescot Medical Centre *PR/KW* L34 59 H4
Prescot Museum *PR/KW* L34 59 G4
Prescot Primary School *PR/KW* L34 60 B4
Prescot School *PR/KW* L34 59 G3
Price Street Business Centre *BIRK* CH41 2 B1
Priestley Business Centre *WARRW/BUR* WA5 106 B3
Priestley College *WARRS* WA4 107 E5
Prince Edwin Adult Centre *EV* L5 71 E1
Princes Park Health Centre *TOX* L8 94 D2
Princess Drive Medical Centre *DV/KA/FCH* L14 57 G4
Princes Special School *TOX* L8 94 C1
The Priory CE Primary School *BIRK* CH41 2 C2
The Priory Medical Centre *NPK/KEN* L6 55 E5
Pump House Museum *BIRK* CH41 3 H3
Pyramid *WARR* WA1 12 B6
Pyramids Shopping Centre *BIRK* CH41 2 E5
Quay Business Centre *WARRN/WOL* WA2 83 G2
Queen Elizabeth II Law Courts *VAUX/LVPD* L3 6 C5
Queens Dock Business Centre *VAUX/LVPD* L3 93 H1
Queens Drive Family Health Clinic *ANF/KKDL* L4 40 C4
Queens Park CE/URC Primary School *ECCL* WA10 10 B3
Queens Park Community Leisure Centre *ECCL* WA10 10 D4
Queen Square Bus Station *CLVPS* L1 6 E3
Queensway Business Centre *WDN* WA8 146 A1
Racecourse Retail Park *WLT/FAZ* L9 31 H2
Radio City *CLVPS* L1 7 F4
Radisson SAS Hotel *VAUX/LVPD* L3 6 B2
Radnor Medical Centre *NPK/KEN* L6 55 F5
Raeburn Primary School *PS/BROM* CH62 152 D3
RAF Burtonwood *WARRW/BUR* WA5 105 E1
Rainbow Medical Centre *STHEL* WA9 63 E3
Rainhill Clinic *RAIN/WH* L35 78 A2
Rainhill High School *RAIN/WH* L35 78 C3
Ravenhead Retail Park *STHEL* WA9 62 A1
Ravenscroft Primary School *NWD/KWIPK* L33 25 H4
Record Business Park *WARRN/WOL* WA2 83 G5
Redbridge High School *AIN/FAZ* L10 32 C4
Redcourt St Anselms School *CL/PREN* CH43 91 G3
Redgate Primary School *FMBY* L37 17 F4
Red Lion Shopping Centre *MGHL* L31 18 D5
Reginald Road Industrial Park *STHEL* WA9 63 F4
Rice Lane J & I Schools *WLT/FAZ* L9 40 C2
Richard Evans Community Primary School *RNFD/HAY* WA11 49 F1
Ridgeway High School *CL/PREN* CH43 90 D4
Rimrose Business Park *BTL* L20 4 A2
Rimrose Valley Country Park *CSBY/BLUN* L23 29 H2
Riverhill Hotel *CL/PREN* CH43 91 G5
Riverside Bowl *WAL/NB* CH45 51 H1
Riverside Primary School *WAL/EG* CH44 69 G2
Riverside Retail Park *WARR* WA1 13 F6
Riverside Trading Estate *WARRW/BUR* WA5 127 F2
Rivington Primary School *ECCL* WA10 10 C1
Robins Lane Community Primary School *STHEL* WA9 62 C2
Robson Street Clinic *WARR* WA1 13 H3
Roby Medical Centre *HUY* L36 74 C3
Roby Park Primary School *HUY* L36 74 D2
Rocket Trading Centre *DV/KA/FCH* L14 73 G4
Rock Ferry High School *RF/TRAN* CH42 115 H3
Rock Ferry Medical Centre *RF/TRAN* CH42 92 D5
Rock Ferry Primary School *RF/TRAN* CH42 115 H1
Rock Retail Park *BIRK* CH41 3 H7
Rodney Fertility Clinic *CLVPS* L1 7 H6
Roscoe Junior School *CLB/OSW/ST* L13 55 H3
Rosebank *BIRK* CH41 2 D3
Roseheath Primary School *HLWD* L26 121 H4
Rowan Park Special School *LITH* L21 30 C2
Royal College of Nursing *CLVP* L2 6 C4
Royal Court Theatre *CLVPS* L1 7 F3
The Royal Hotel *CSBY/WL* L22 29 E4
Royal Liver Building *VAUX/LVPD* L3 6 B4
Royal Liverpool Childrens Hospital (Alder Hey) *DV/KA/FCH* L14 73 G1
Royal Liverpool Golf Club *HOY* CH47 87 E2
Royal Liverpool University Hospital *EHL/KEN* L7 7 K3
Royal School for the Blind *WAV* L15 95 H1
Roy Castle International Centre for Lung Research *VAUX/LVPD* L3 7 K2
Rudston J & I School *CHLDW* L16 73 H5
Ruffwood School *NWD/KWIPK* L33 33 H1
Runcorn AFC *RUNC* WA7 9 G4
Runcorn County Court *RUNC* WA7 156 B1
Runcorn Golf Club *RUNC* WA7 155 E2
Runcorn Rowing Club *RUNC* WA7 155 H5
Runcorn Ski Slope *RUNC* WA7 156 D2
Runcorn Swimming Pool *RUNC* WA7 9 F3
Runnymede St Edwards School *WD/CROXPK* L12 56 B5
Rutherford Medical Centre *WAV* L15 96 B2
Sacred Heart Catholic College *CSBY/BLUN* L23 21 F5
CSBY/BLUN L23 29 F1
Sacred Heart Catholic Primary School *WARRW/BUR* WA5 106 A3
Sacred Heart RC Primary School *EHL/KEN* L7 71 G3
MOR/LEA CH46 66 D4
SAE Institute *CLVP* L2 6 C4
St Agnes RC Primary School *HUY* L36 75 H4
St Aidans RC Primary School *HUY* L36 75 H2
St Albans RC Primary School *WAL/EG* CH44 68 C1
WARRW/BUR WA5 12 A2
St Alberts RC Primary School *STBRV* L28 57 G1
St Aloysius RC Primary School *HUY* L36 75 E1
St Ambrose Barlow Catholic College *NTHTN* L30 23 F4
St Ambrose RC Primary School *SPK/HALE* L24 143 E4
St Andrews CE Primary School *BEB* CH63 115 H5
WARRN/WOL WA2 84 A2
St Andrews Maghull CE Primary School *MGHL* L31 18 D5
St Andrews RC Primary School *WLTN* L25 121 F4
St Annes CE Primary School *CLB/OSW/ST* L13 72 D2
St Annes RC Primary School *EHL/KEN* L7 71 H5
HUY L36 75 F4
RF/TRAN CH42 115 H3
STHEL WA9 62 D3
St Anns CE Primary School *RAIN/WH* L35 78 A2
WARRN/WOL WA2 84 A5
St Anselms College *CL/PREN* CH43 91 G2
St Anthony of Padua RC Primary School *CALD/MH* L18 95 H4
St Anthony's Shopping Centre *EV* L5 54 A5
St Augustine of Canterbury RC High School *RNFD/HAY* WA11 49 E2
St Augustines Catholic Primary School *WARRS* WA4 107 H4
St Augustines RC Primary School *RUNC* WA7 147 G4
St Austins RC Primary School *ALL/GAR* L19 119 F4
STHEL WA9 61 E3
St Barnabas CE Primary School *WARRW/BUR* WA5 106 B3
St Bartholomews RC Primary School *RAIN/WH* L35 78 C4
St Basil RC Primary School *WDN* WA8 100 C5
St Bedes RC J & I School *WDN* WA8 14 D1
St Benedicts College *ALL/GAR* L19 119 H5
St Benedicts RC Primary School *NTHTN* L30 23 E4
WARRN/WOL WA2 107 F1
St Berteline CE Primary School *RUNC* WA7 157 E1
St Bridgets Catholic Primary School *WARRN/WOL* WA2 84 D2
St Bridgets CE Primary School *WKBY* CH48 110 B2
St Brigids RC Primary School *DV/KA/FCH* L14 57 G3
St Catherines Centre for Girls *RNFD/HAY* WA11 49 E1
St Catherine's Hospital *RF/TRAN* CH42 92 B5
St Cecilias RC Infant School *CLB/OSW/ST* L13 55 G5
St Chads Catholic High School *RUNC* WA7 155 H2
St Charles RC Primary School *AIG/SPK* L17 118 A1
St Christophers Catholic Primary School *SPK/HALE* L24 142 B2
St Clares RC Primary School *WAV* L15 95 F1
St Clements RC Primary School *RUNC* WA7 8 D7
St Cleopas CE Primary School *TOX* L8 94 B4
St Columbas RC Primary School *HUY* L36 58 C5
St Cuthberts Catholic High School *STHEL* WA9 63 F1
St Cuthberts RC Primary School *CLB/OSW/ST* L13 72 D2
St Dominics RC J & I School *DV/KA/FCH* L14 57 H4
St Edmund Arrowsmith Catholic High School *RAIN/WH* L35 60 B5
St Edmund of Canterbury Catholic High School *DV/KA/FCH* L14 57 H4
St Edmund's & St Thomas Catholic Primary School *CSBY/WL* L22 29 E3
St Edwards RC Primary School *RUNC* WA7 9 G3
St Elizabeths Catholic Primary School *LITH* L21 39 G1
St Elphin Fairfield CE Primary School *WARR* WA1 13 G2
St Finbars Catholic Primary School *TOX* L8 94 C5
St Francis De Sales Catholic Junior Mixed School *ANF/KKDL* L4 54 A1
St Francis de Sales RC Infant School *ANF/KKDL* L4 5 K7
St Francis of Assisi RC Primary School *ALL/GAR* L19 119 G5
St Francis Xaviers College *WLTN* L25 97 E4
St George of England High School *BTL* L20 39 H1
St George's Hall *CLVPS* L1 7 F3
St Georges Medical Centre *WAL/NB* CH45 51 H3
St Georges Primary School *WAL/NB* CH45 51 E5
St Georges RC Primary School *MGHL* L31 24 A2
St Gerrards RC Primary School *WDN* WA8 14 E5
St Gregorys Catholic Primary School *MGHL* L31 18 C2
St Gregorys RC High School *WARRW/BUR* WA5 105 H3
St Gregorys RC JMI School *NTHLY* L27 98 C3
St Helens AFC *STHEL* WA9 63 F3
St Helens Bus Station *ECCL* WA10 11 H5
St Helens College *ECCL* WA10 11 F5
St Helens Crematorium *ECCL* WA10 36 A5
St Helens Cricket Club *ECCL* WA10 10 C1
St Helens Hospital *STHEL* WA9 62 C1
St Helens Retail Park *STHEL* WA9 11 K6
St Helens RLFC (Knowsley Road Stadium) *ECCL* WA10 47 E4
St Helens Theatre Royal *ECCL* WA10 11 H5
St Hildas CE High School *AIG/SPK* L17 95 F3
St Hughs JMI School *WAV* L15 95 F1
St James RC Primary School *BTL* L20 4 C2
St Joan of Arc RC Primary School *BTL* L20 4 B1
St John Bosco High School *NG/CROX* L11 42 A4
St John Bosco RC Primary School *MGHL* L31 18 B4
St John Fisher J & I School *WDN* WA8 15 K1
St John Fisher RC Primary School *PR/KW* L34 44 A3
St John's Beacon *CLVPS* L1 7 F4
St Johns Catholic J & I School *BEB* CH63 115 H4
St Johns CE Primary School *CSBY/WL* L22 29 E3
St Johns Primary School *ANF/KKDL* L4 54 A2
St John's Shopping Centre *CLVPS* L1 7 F4
St John Vianney RC Primary School *STHEL* WA9 61 G4
St Josephs Catholic Primary *WARRW/BUR* WA5 104 C3
St Josephs RC Primary School *GR/UP/WCH* CH49 90 A3
HUY L36 75 H2
KKBY L32 33 H3
WAL/EG CH44 69 F3
St Julie RC Primary School *ECCL* WA10 46 C3
St Julies Catholic High School *WLTN* L25 120 C1
St Laurence Medical Centre *KKBY* L32 34 A3
St Laurences RC Primary School *BIRK* CH41 2 E3
KKBY L32 34 A3
St Lawrence CE Primary School *ANF/KKDL* L4 54 A1
St Leos RC Primary School *RAIN/WH* L35 77 E3
St Lukes CE Primary School *FMBY* L37 16 C5
St Lukes Halsall CE Primary School *CSBY/BLUN* L23 21 E4
St Lukes RC Primary School *RAIN/WH* L35 77 F1
St Malachys RC Primary School *TOX* L8 94 A3

St Margaret Marys RC J & I School DV/KA/FCH L14 74 B2
St Margarets Anfield CE Primary School NPK/KEN L6 55 E5
St Margarets CE High School AIG/SPK L17 118 B2
St Margarets CE Primary School TOX L8 94 B1
St Margarets CE Primary School (Infant Department) WARRN/WOL WA2 84 A3
St Margarets CE Primary School (Junior Department) WARRN/WOL WA2 84 A4
St Marie RC Primary School NWD/KWIPK L33 34 B1
St Marks Catholic Primary School HLWD L26 122 A3
St Martins Catholic Primary School RUNC WA7 157 G3
St Mary & St Paul's CE Primary School RAIN/WH L35 76 D1
St Marys Catholic College WAL/NB CH45 51 E4
St Marys CE Primary School PS/BROM CH62 153 F4
RUNC WA7 156 C1
WD/CROXPK L12 56 B3
St Marys' Market ECCL WA10 11 H6
St Marys RC Primary School CSBY/BLUN L23 21 F1
St Mary & Thomas CE Primary School ECCL WA10 10 E4
St Matthews Catholic Primary School ANF/KKDL L4 55 F2
St Michael & All Angels RC Primary School GR/UP/WCH CH49 113 H1
St Michael in the Hamlet Primary School AIG/SPK L17 94 D5
St Michael Jubilee Golf Club WDN WA8 124 C4
St Michaels Catholic Primary School NPK/KEN L6 71 H1
WDN WA8 124 A4
St Michaels Church of England High School CSBY/BLUN L23 20 D3
St Monicas RC Primary School BTL L20 5 J1
St Monica's RC Primary School WARRS WA4 130 B4
St Nicholas Catholic Primary School VAUX/LVPD L3 7 J5
St Nicholas CE Primary School CSBY/BLUN L23 28 C1
St Oswalds Catholic Junior School CLB/OSW/ST L13 73 E3
St Oswald's CE Primary School CL/PREN CH43 67 G4
St Oswalds CE Primary School NTHTN L30 31 E1
St Oswalds C Infant School CLB/OSW/ST L13 73 E2
St Oswalds RC Primary School WARR WA1 84 C5
St Paschal Baylon RC Primary School CHLDW L16 74 B5
St Patricks Catholic Primary School TOX L8 94 B2
St Pauls RC Primary School CL/PREN CH43 90 B1
St Peter & St Pauls Catholic Primary School RNFD/HAY WA11 37 F5
St Peter & Paul RC Primary School WAL/NB CH45 51 G2
St Peters CE Primary School FMBY L37 17 F1
HES CH60 148 D2
St Peters RC Primary School CL/PREN CH43 90 C4
WARR WA1 108 C1
St Philips CE Primary School LITH L21 30 B4
St Philip Westbrook CE Primary School WARRW/BUR WA5 82 B4
St Robert Bellarmine RC Primary School LITH L21 30 C5
St Saviours CE Aided Primary School CL/PREN CH43 91 G5
St Sebastians Primary School EHL/KEN L7 72 B3
St Silas CE Primary School TOX L8 94 C3
SS Pauls & Timothys RC Infant School WD/CROXPK L12 56 C3
SS Peter & Paul Catholic School NWD/KWIPK L33 26 A4
SS Peter & Paul RC High School WDN WA8 124 D1
St Stephens Catholic Primary School WARRN/WOL WA2 83 H2
St Teresa of Lisieux Catholic Infant School NG/CROX L11 41 H5
St Teresas Catholic Primary School ECCL WA10 10 B4
St Theresas Primary School STHEL WA9 79 G2
St Thomas Becket School HUY L36 76 A2
St Thomas CE Primary School MGHL L31 18 D2
WARRS WA4 130 B2
St Thomas of Canterbury Catholic Primary School ECCL WA10 47 F1
St Thomas of Canterbury RC School CSBY/WL L22 29 F4
St Vincent de Paul Catholic Primary School CLVPS L1 7 F7
St Vincents Catholic Primary School WARRW/BUR WA5 104 C5
St Vincents School for the Blind & Partially Sighted WD/CROXPK L12 57 E4
St Weburgh CE Primary School WARRS WA4 129 H1
St Werburghs RC Primary School BIRK CH41 2 D7
St Wilfrids CE Aided Primary School WARRS WA4 131 F2
St Wilfrids RC High School LITH L21 30 B5
St William of York RC Primary School CSBY/BLUN L23 22 A4
St Winefrides RC Primary School NSTN CH64 159 E3
Salt Works Wharf RUNC WA7 154 A1
Sandbrook Primary School MOR/LEA CH46 66 D5
Sandfield Medical Centre ECCL WA10 10 E6
Sandfield Park Special School WD/CROXPK L12 56 B5
Sandhills Business Park EV L5 53 G4
Sandon Industrial Estate VAUX/LVPD L3 53 F4
Sandringham Medical Centre TOX L8 94 D4
Sankey Bridge Industrial Estate WARRW/BUR WA5 105 G4
Sankey Medical Centre WARRW/BUR WA5 104 C1
Sankey Valley Country Park WARRW/BUR WA5 82 D4
Sankey Valley St James Primary School WARRW/BUR WA5 105 G2
Savio High School NTHTN L30 30 D4
School of Good Shepherd ANF/KKDL L4 54 B1
Seabank Medical Centre WAL/NB CH45 51 H3
Seaforth Health Clinic LITH L21 29 H5
Sefton Business Park NTHTN L30 31 F4
Sefton CC AIG/SPK L17 95 E4
Sefton Lane Industrial Estate MGHL L31 23 F1
Sefton Park Medical Centre WAV L15 95 F2
Sefton Road Health Clinic LITH L21 30 A4
Senate Business Park NTHTN L30 31 E4
Sherdley Business Park STHEL WA9 62 B2
Sherdley Park Golf Club STHEL WA9 62 A3
Sherdley Primary School STHEL WA9 62 C4
Shorefields Community Comprehensive School AIG/SPK L17 94 D4
Shorefields Technology College AIG/SPK L17 94 C5
Shorrocks Hill Country Club FMBY L37 16 A5
Showcase Cinemas NG/CROX L11 42 A3
Silverdale Medical Centre HES CH60 148 D1
Simms Cross CP School WDN WA8 14 C4
Simonswood Industrial Park NWD/KWIPK L33 26 C3
Simonswood Primary School NWD/KWIPK L33 34 A2
Sir Alfred Jones Memorial Hospital ALL/GAR L19 119 G5
Sir Thomas Boteler High School WARRS WA4 107 G5
Skypark Industrial Park SPK/HALE L24 141 H3
Small Business Centre VAUX/LVPD L3 93 H3
Smithdown CP School EHL/KEN L7 71 H5
Smithy Heritage Centre ECCL WA10 47 E2
SMM Business Park BIRK CH41 69 E4
Somerville Primary School WAL/EG CH44 69 E2
Southdene Medical Centre KKBY L32 34 B4
Southern Primary Support Centre WLTN L25 121 F3
Southmead Community Primary School RAIN/WH L35 77 E3
South Sefton Business Centre BTL L20 4 D6
South Wallasey Neighbourhood College WAL/EG CH44 68 D3
South Wirral High School PS/BROM CH62 152 D5
Speke Family Health Clinic SPK/HALE L24 142 C3
Speke Hall Industrial Estate SPK/HALE L24 141 H3
Speke Hall (NT) SPK/HALE L24 141 F4
Springfield Special School KKBY L32 33 H5
Springwell Park Primary School BTL L20 39 H2
Springwood Crematorium WLTN L25 120 B3
Springwood Heath Primary School ALL/GAR L19 120 A3
The Stables Business Centre CLB/OSW/ST L13 55 G3
Stadt Moers Country Park RAIN/WH L35 76 C3
Stanley Medical Centre EV L5 53 H4
Stanley School PEN/TH CH61 113 E5
Stanton Road Primary School BEB CH63 137 H3
Station Road Industrial Estate WARRS WA4 130 D1
St Helens & Knowsley Magistrates & County Courts ECCL WA10 11 G4
Stockbridge Village Health Centre STBRV L28 57 G2
Stockton Heath Community Primary School WARRS WA4 130 A2
Stockton Heath Medical Centre WARRS WA4 130 A2
Stockton Wood Community Primary School SPK/HALE L24 142 A3
Stonebridge Business Park (Under Development) NG/CROX L11 42 A2
Stonedale Park Retail Park NG/CROX L11 42 A3
Stopgate Medical Centre WLT/FAZ L9 41 F4
Storrsdale Medical Centre CALD/MH L18 96 B5
The Strand Medical Centre BTL L20 4 E2
Strand Shopping Centre BTL L20 4 E3
Streatham House School CSBY/BLUN L23 20 D5
Sudley House CALD/MH L18 118 D1
Sudley Infant School AIG/SPK L17 118 C1
Sudley Junior School AIG/SPK L17 118 C2
Summerhill Primary School MGHL L31 24 B1
Sutton CC STHEL WA9 62 C4
Sutton Community Leisure Centre Track STHEL WA9 62 A4
Sutton High Sports College STHEL WA9 62 B4
Sutton Manor Community Primary School STHEL WA9 79 E3
Sutton Oak CE Primary School STHEL WA9 63 E2
Sycamore Lane Community Primary School WARRW/BUR WA5 105 F3
Sylvester Primary School HUY L36 75 H4
Tanhouse Industrial Estate WDN WA8 15 H5
Tanning Court Industrial Estate WARR WA1 12 E6
Tate Gallery VAUX/LVPD L3 6 B7
Taylor Street Industrial Estate EV L5 53 H5
Temple of Praise EV L5 54 C4
Thatto Heath Community Primary School STHEL WA9 61 G2
Thelwall Community Junior School WARRS WA4 108 D5
Thelwall Infant School WARRS WA4 108 C5
Thelwall New Road Industrial Estate WARRS WA4 108 C4
Thelwall New Road Surgery WARRS WA4 108 B5
Thingwall Primary School PEN/TH CH61 113 E5
Thingwall Recreation Centre PEN/TH CH61 113 F5
Thistle Hotel VAUX/LVPD L3 6 B3
Thomas Gray Infant School BTL L20 4 C2
Thomas Gray Primary School BTL L20 4 D1
Thornton Crematorium CSBY/BLUN L23 22 B2
Thornton Hall Hotel NSTN CH64 150 B4
Thornton Hough Primary School BEB CH63 150 D2
Thornton Primary School CSBY/BLUN L23 22 A3
Titanic Memorial VAUX/LVPD L3 6 A4
Tower College RAIN/WH L35 78 B4
Tower Hill Health Centre NWD/KWIPK L33 26 A4
Townfield Primary School CL/PREN CH43 91 E5
Town Lane Infant School BEB CH63 115 G5
Toxteth Community College TOX L8 7 K7
Toxteth Park Cemetery TOX L8 95 F2
Toxteth Sports Centre TOX L8 94 B2
Tranmere Oil Terminal RF/TRAN CH42 93 E5
Tranmere Rovers FC (Prenton Park) RF/TRAN CH42 115 E1
Transport Museum BIRK CH41 3 H2
Travelodge CLVPS L1 6 E3
VAUX/LVPD L3 93 H3
WARR WA1 12 B4
WDN WA8 15 G4
Trentham Road Medical Centre KKBY L32 33 E3
Trident Retail Park RUNC WA7 156 A2
The Trinity RC Primary School VAUX/LVPD L3 70 C1
Triumph Trading Park SPK/HALE L24 120 C5
Twelve Quays Ferry Terminal BIRK CH41 69 H4
Twig Lane Clinic HUY L36 75 E1
Unity Theatre CLVPS L1 7 H6
University Hospital Aintree WLT/FAZ L9 32 A5
WLT/FAZ L9 41 G1
University of Liverpool Sports Centre EHL/KEN L7 7 K5
University of Liverpool EHL/KEN L7 7 K6
VAUX/LVP L3 7 J3
Upper Parliament Medical Centre EHL/KEN L7 71 H5
Upton CC GR/UP/WCH CH49 89 H3
Upton Hall School FCJ GR/UP/WCH CH49 89 H3
Upton Medical Centre WDN WA8 100 D5
Ursuline RC Primary School CSBY/BLUN L23 28 C1
Uveco Business Centre BIRK CH41 68 D4
Valewood Primary School CSBY/BLUN L23 21 E4
Valley Medical Centre ANF/KKDL L4 54 A3
CHLDW L16 97 E1
Valley Road Business Park WAV L15 73 F5
VAT House & HM Customs & Excise VAUX/LVPD L3 93 G2
Vauxhall Business Centre VAUX/LVPD L3 70 C2
Vauxhall Health Centre EV L5 70 D1
Vernon Sangster Sports Centre ANF/KKDL L4 54 C3
Victoria Central Hospital WAL/EG CH44 68 D2
Victoria Park Arena WARRS WA4 13 J6
Victoria Road Primary School RUNC WA7 8 D6
Victoria Trading Estate RAIN/WH L35 78 A2
The Village Hotel & Leisure Club PS/BROM CH62 138 C2
RAIN/WH L35 76 C5
WARR WA1 106 C5
Village Medical Centre WLTN L25 120 C1
Villa Medical Centre CL/PREN CH43 114 C3
Virgin Cinemas EHL/KEN L7 72 D4
Vittoria Medical Centre BIRK CH41 2 D2
Vue Cinema BIRK CH41 3 F4
Vyner Primary School CL/PREN CH43 67 H4
Wade Deacon High School WDN WA8 125 E1
Wakefield Industrial Estate NTHTN L30 31 F1
Walker Art Gallery VAUX/LVPD L3 7 F2
Wallasey Golf Club WAL/NB CH45 50 D3
Wallasey RFC WAL/NB CH45 50 D5
Wallasey School MOR/LEA CH46 67 E2
Walton Hall WARRS WA4 129 G5
Walton Hall Golf Club WARRS WA4 129 F4
Walton Hall Medical Centre ANF/KKDL L4 54 C1
Walton Hospital WLT/FAZ L9 40 B4
Walton Lea Crematorium WARRS WA4 129 G4
Walton Medical Centre ANF/KKDL L4 40 B5
Walton Progressive School WLT/FAZ L9 40 B4
Walton St Mary CE Primary School ANF/KKDL L4 40 B5
Walton Sports Centre ANF/KKDL L4 40 D5
Walton Village Medical Centre ANF/KKDL L4 54 C1
Warren Golf Club WAL/NB CH45 51 F3
Warrington Business Centre WARR WA1 12 D4
Warrington Business Park WARRN/WOL WA2 84 A4
Warrington Bus Interchange WARR WA1 12 C4
Warrington Central Trading Estate WARRN/WOL WA2 12 B2
Warrington Collegiate WARR WA1 12 C6
Warrington Hospital WARRW/BUR WA5 106 B2
Warrington Museum & Library WARR WA1 12 C6
Warrington New Town CC WARRW/BUR WA5 105 G3
Warrington Sports Club WARRS WA4 129 G4
Warrington Town AFC WARRS WA4 130 C1
Warrington Wolves RLFC (Halliwell Jones Stadium) WARRN/WOL WA2 12 C2
Waterfront Business Area VAUX/LVPD L3 93 G1
Watergate North Primary School AIN/FAZ L10 32 C4
Watergate School WLTN L25 120 D1
Waterloo FC CSBY/BLUN L23 20 C4
Waterloo Primary School CSBY/WL L22 29 F3
Wavertree Athletics Centre WAV L15 95 H1
Wavertree CE Primary School WAV L15 95 H1
Wavertree CC WAV L15 72 D5
Wavertree Health Clinic WAV L15 96 A2
Wavertree Retail Park EHL/KEN L7 72 A4
Wavertree Technology Park EHL/KEN L7 72 C4
Wavertree Town Hall WAV L15 96 A1
Wavertree Trading Estate WAV L15 95 G1
Weatherhead High School & Media Arts College WAL/EG CH44 68 B2
Weatherstone Business Centre NSTN CH64 159 H2
Weaver Industrial Estate ALL/GAR L19 140 C3
Wellesbourne Primary School NG/CROX L11 41 H5
Wellington Employment Park (Under Development) EV L5 53 G4
Wellington Street Industrial Estate WDN WA8 14 C7
Well Lane Primary School RF/TRAN CH42 92 C5
Wesley House ECCL WA10 11 H4
West Bank Medical Centre WDN WA8 146 A1
West Bank Primary School WDN WA8 145 H2
Westbourne School WAL/NB CH45 52 A4
Westbrook Medical Centre WARRW/BUR WA5 82 C4
Westbrook Old Hall Primary School WARRW/BUR WA5 82 D5
West Derby Cemetery NG/CROX L11 42 A3
West Derby Comprehensive School CLB/OSW/ST L13 56 A5
West Derby Golf Club WD/CROXPK L12 57 E4
Westfield Primary School RUNC WA7 8 B6
West Kirby Foot Health Clinic WKBY CH48 110 B1
West Kirby Grammar School WKBY CH48 87 E5
West Kirby Health Centre & Swimming Pool WKBY CH48 110 A1
West Kirby Primary School WKBY CH48 87 E4
West Kirby Residential School WKBY CH48 86 D5
West Kirby Sailing Club WKBY CH48 110 B3
West Lancashire Golf Club CSBY/BLUN L23 20 B3
Westminster Medical Centre ANF/KKDL L4 54 A1
Westminster Road Swimming Pool ANF/KKDL L4 54 A3
Weston Point Primary School RUNC WA7 154 C2
Weston Primary School RUNC WA7 155 E3
West Park RFC ECCL WA10 60 D1
Westside Industrial Estate STHEL WA9 48 C5
Westvale Health Centre KKBY L32 33 F2
Westvale Primary School KKBY L32 33 E2
Wheathill Industrial Estate NTHLY L27 98 B2
Wheatland Business Park WAL/EG CH44 69 F3
Whetstone Lane Health Centre BIRK CH41 2 D6
Whiston Health Centre RAIN/WH L35 76 D2
Whiston Hospital RAIN/WH L35 77 F1
Whiston Willis Primary School RAIN/WH L35 77 F2
Whitefield CC CHLDW L16 74 B4
Whitefield Primary School NPK/KEN L6 71 G1
White Thorn Special School WLT/FAZ L9 31 H4

Widnes Crematorium
WDN WA8 ... 101 H5
Widnes CC
WDN WA8 ... 102 B4
Widnes Golf Club
WDN WA8 ... 14 B1
Widnes Public Baths
WDN WA8 ... 14 D4
Widnes & Runcorn Sixth Form College
WDN WA8 ... 101 G3
Widnes Vikings RLFC (Halton Stadium)
WDN WA8 ... 14 B4
William Beamont Community High School & Specialist Sports College
WARRN/WOL WA2 ... 83 H4
William Gladstone CE Primary School
LITH L21 ... 29 H5
Willow Tree Primary School
STHEL WA9 ... 79 H1
Wilson Business Centre
HUY L36 ... 76 A4
Windlehurst Community Primary School
ECCL WA10 ... 47 G1
Windmill Shopping Centre
WDN WA8 ... 15 F3
Windsor Community Primary School TOX L8 ... 94 B2
Wingate Medical Centre
NWD/KWIPK L33 ... 34 B1
Winstanley Industrial Estate
WARRN/WOL WA2 ... 83 H4
Wirral Borough Magistrates Court BIRK CH41 ... 3 J4
Wirral Business Centre
BIRK CH41 ... 69 E4
Wirral Business Park
GR/UP/WCH CH49 ... 89 H5
Wirral Country Park
PEN/TH CH61 ... 133 F3
Wirral Grammar School for Boys BEB CH63 ... 137 G2
Wirral Grammar School for Girls
BEB CH63 ... 137 G2
Wirral Hospital
BEB CH63 ... 137 F5
Wirral International Business Park
PS/BROM CH62 ... 139 F4
Wirral Ladies Golf Club
CL/PREN CH43 ... 91 E2
Wirral Metropolitan College
BIRK CH41 ... 7 K6
BIRK CH41 ... 7 J3
PS/BROM CH62 ... 153 G2
Wirral Museum
BIRK CH41 ... 3 H4
Wirral Stroke & Head Injury Clinic CL/PREN CH43 ... 114 B2
Wirral Tennis & Sports Centre
CL/PREN CH43 ... 67 H3
Woodchurch CE Primary School
GR/UP/WCH CH49 ... 113 F1
Woodchurch High School Specialist Engineering College
GR/UP/WCH CH49 ... 90 C5
Woodchurch Leisure Centre
GR/UP/WCH CH49 ... 90 C5
Woodchurch Road Primary School
RF/TRAN CH42 ... 92 A4
Woodend Industrial Estate
SPK/HALE L24 ... 142 A1
Woodfall Infant School
NSTN CH64 ... 159 F4
Woodfall Primary School
NSTN CH64 ... 159 F4
Woodlands Primary School
BIRK CH41 ... 2 E7
FMBY L37 ... 16 C3
Woodside Business Park
BIRK CH41 ... 3 J2
Woodside CP School
RUNC WA7 ... 156 A2
Woodside Ferry Landing Stage
BIRK CH41 ... 3 K2
Woodslee Primary School
PS/BROM CH62 ... 138 D4
Woolston CE Primary School
WARR WA1 ... 85 G5
Woolston Community High School
WARR WA1 ... 108 B1
Woolston Community Primary School
WARR WA1 ... 108 C1
Woolton Golf Club
WLTN L25 ... 120 D3
Woolton House Medical Centre
WLTN L25 ... 120 C1
Woolton J & I School
WLTN L25 ... 97 H5
Woolton Swimming Pool
WLTN L25 ... 120 C1
World of Glass
ECCL WA10 ... 11 G6

Acknowledgements

Schools address data provided by Education Direct

Petrol station information supplied by Johnsons

Garden centre information provided by:

Garden Centre Association Britains best garden centres

Wyevale Garden Centres

The statement on the front cover of this atlas is sourced, selected and quoted from a reader comment and feedback form received in 2004

Notes

Notes

Notes

Notes

AA Street by Street QUESTIONNAIRE

Dear Atlas User
Your comments, opinions and recommendations are very important to us. So please help us to improve our street atlases by taking a few minutes to complete this simple questionnaire.

You do not need a stamp (unless posted outside the UK). If you do not want to remove this page from your street atlas, then photocopy it or write your answers on a plain sheet of paper.

Send to: Marketing Assistant, AA Publishing, 14th Floor Fanum House, Freepost SCE 4598, Basingstoke RG21 4GY

ABOUT THE ATLAS...

Please state which city / town / county you bought:

____

Where did you buy the atlas? (City, Town, County)

____

For what purpose? (please tick all applicable)

To use in your local area ☐ **To use on business or at work** ☐

Visiting a strange place ☐ **In the car** ☐ **On foot** ☐

Other (please state)

____

Have you ever used any street atlases other than AA Street by Street?

Yes ☐ **No** ☐

If so, which ones?

____

Is there any aspect of our street atlases that could be improved?
(Please continue on a separate sheet if necessary)

____

____

____

ML47y

continued overleaf

Please list the features you found most useful:

Please list the features you found least useful:

LOCAL KNOWLEDGE...

Local knowledge is invaluable. Whilst every attempt has been made to make the information contained in this atlas as accurate as possible, should you notice any inaccuracies, please detail them below (if necessary, use a blank piece of paper) or e-mail us at *streetbystreet@theAA.com*

ABOUT YOU...

Name (Mr/Mrs/Ms)

Address

Postcode

Daytime tel no

E-mail address

Which age group are you in?

Under 25 ☐ **25-34** ☐ **35-44** ☐ **45-54** ☐ **55-64** ☐ **65+** ☐

Are you an AA member? **YES** ☐ **NO** ☐

Do you have Internet access? **YES** ☐ **NO** ☐

Thank you for taking the time to complete this questionnaire. Please send it to us as soon as possible, and remember, you do not need a stamp (unless posted outside the UK).

We may use information we hold about you to, telephone or email you about other products and services offered by the AA, we do NOT disclose this information to third parties.

Please tick here if you do not wish to hear about products and services from the AA. ☐